36th International System Safety Conference 2018

Phoenix, Arizona, USA
13 - 17 August 2018

ISBN: 978-1-5108-8039-9

Printed from e-media with permission by:

Curran Associates, Inc.
57 Morehouse Lane
Red Hook, NY 12571

Some format issues inherent in the e-media version may also appear in this print version.

Printed by Curran Associates, Inc. (2019)

International System Safety Society
P.O. Box 70
Unionville, Virginia 22567-0070
USA

Phone: 540-854-8630

systemsafety@system-safety.org

Additional copies of this publication are available from:

Curran Associates, Inc.
57 Morehouse Lane
Red Hook, NY 12571 USA
Phone: 845-758-0400
Fax: 845-758-2633
Email: curran@proceedings.com
Web: www.proceedings.com

TABLE OF CONTENTS

Learning by Playing: Serious Games for Safety Education

Zia Ud Din, Ph.D.; School of Sustainable Engineering and the Built Environment, Arizona State University, Tempe, Arizona 85281, USA

G. Edward Gibson, Jr., Ph.D., P.E.; School of Sustainable Engineering and the Built Environment, Arizona State University, Tempe, Arizona 85281, USA

Keywords: Prevention through Design, serious game, teaching effectiveness

Abstract

Many accidents occur during construction and maintenance of facilities. Both research and practice have established that choices made during the design and planning phases can affect worker safety. The prevention through design (PtD) concept is the consideration of construction site safety into the design of a project. Unfortunately, fresh engineering and design graduates do not possess the knowledge of construction worker safety and construction methods essential to successfully eliminate construction hazards through design. In most curricula, there is no room for an entire course focused on PtD. So, there is an opportunity to teach PtD to students using simulation games, as digital games are routinely considered as the most important and influential medium by college students. This research measures the effectiveness of the serious game developed to teach PtD to undergraduate construction engineering and management students. The results show that the game was more effective as compared to the traditional teaching method of lecturing.

INTRODUCTION

The construction industry employs 4.5 percent of the entire nonfarm workforce (BLS, 2017) and has 19 percent of the fatalities (BLS, 2016). These statistics indicate the seriousness of the safety problem in the construction industry. Over the past decades, concerns about the consequences of poor safety have increased, resulting in a decline in the incidence rate of fatal and disabling injuries. Despite all the development in safety science and engineering, construction is prominent for its poor safety performance. Mostly, the efforts to address safety concerns have been focused mainly on the construction phase, while the safety consideration in the pre-construction phase of a project is often overlooked. Consistently researchers find a strong link between workplace fatalities and the absence of a safety consideration in designs. Hence it is vital to identify potential risks and develop solutions to prevent work-related injuries, illnesses, and fatalities through design—this approach is called prevention through design (PtD) (Manuele, 2008).

In one research study, more than 200 fatal accident investigation reports were reviewed, and the results showed that 42 percent of the fatalities examined were connected to the absence of the safety in design approach (Behm, 2005). The underlying reasons for unsafe designs are the absence formal safety training of new engineering and design graduates, inadequate learning resources, and a shortage of the trained faculty to teach the prevention through design topics (Popov et al., 2013; Toole, 2005). The situation in construction management programs is somewhat better than engineering and design programs. Nearly all construction management programs teach construction safety, but there is no uniformity or consistency in the course syllabi, textbooks, or reference materials used in the various institutions in the United States (Z. Din, Rahman, & Gibson, 2017). Also, these construction programs focus on teaching a passive approach of safety management during construction rather than the active approach of prevention through design. Hence a practical approach is to improve the safety environment is training engineers, construction managers, and designers to address safety hazards in design and pre-construction.

However, in most curricula, there is no room for an entire course focused on PtD. Therefore, several efforts are underway to find alternative ways to teach PtD. Under the NIOSH's PtD initiative, textbooks' updates to provide PtD content and PtD teaching modules' development are being encouraged. One researcher implemented a 70-minute-long lecture-based intervention in the project management class of the civil engineering discipline, but this approach did not prove effective (Behm, Culvenor, & Dixon, 2014). Similarly, updating all the textbooks for every engineering program may take a significant amount of time and resources.

Hence, there is an opportunity to teach PtD to students using simulation games, as digital games are routinely considered as the most important and influential medium by college students. In digital game-based training systems, serious games are a predominant application type. Serious games are video games that allow the player to learn content in game-like environments (Michael & Chen, 2006). In particular, today's "millennial" college students enjoy playing video games more so than past generations (Prensky, 2003), and this is evident from the increasing popularity of gaming over the past quarter-century. Therefore, by incorporating characteristics of games with the instructional material of PtD, the potential for motivating students to learn the new concepts in less time may increase. Students may also improve retention of knowledge through experiential learning using the game environment.

In this study, the researchers will explore how the prevention through design education of construction engineering and management students can be delivered effectively through the implementation of serious game activity. The study will also try to understand the relationship, if any, between variables (gender, relevant work experience, engagement, computers use frequency, and game-play frequency) and student test performance among different instructional techniques such as serious game, paper-based game, and lecture-based teaching. This work is part of dissertation research presented in partial fulfillment of the requirements for the Ph.D. degree in Civil, Environmental and Sustainable Engineering at Arizona State University (Zia Din, 2017).

RESEARCH METHODOLOGY

The research methodology selected for this research is quasi-experimental design. In educational interventions, the random assignment of participants to experimental (a game playing group for this study) or control groups (non-gamer in this study) is not always possible. Therefore, a quasi-experimental design would have to be used (Field & Hole, 2003). The intervention evaluation studies have used a pretest and posttest approach. The analysis techniques for the data collected are descriptive statistical analysis and inferential statistical analysis.

To find the effectiveness of different teaching methods, an in-class lecture, a paper-based game, and a serious game were developed and implemented to teach Prevention through Design to undergraduate construction engineering and management students. These pedagogies were used to study the impact of a teaching approach on learning performance. A total number of 118 students from three classes at Arizona State University took part in the research study. Out of 118 students, 88 participants finished all the required phases of the data collection.

The proposed game "SafeDesign" was a computer-based application asked students to identify hazards and suggest solutions for a given scenario. The scenarios for the paper-based games and serious game were developed based on the PtD research carried out by Jimme Hinze and colleagues who provided a checklist to ensure safety consideration in the design, redesign and pre-construction processes (Gambatese, Hinze, & Haas, 1997). The lecture contents were adapted from NIOSH's educational modules for teaching the PtD concepts (CDC, 2013).

The authors developed the game for this research and documented the process of the game development, which can serve as a guideline for other teachers and learners interested in the game development for their classes (Zia Din & Gibson Jr., 2018). Students were tasked with identifying hazards, such as falls, electrocution, and structural design-related hazards. A typical scenario is shown in Figure 1. After identifying hazards, students were asked to rectify the hazardous situation. The developed prototype allowed students to perform the following functions: to explore several scenarios such as working at the height or in a confined space; to visualize the design hazards that were present in the given scenario; to eliminate hazards and receive feedback about their hazard identification and elimination. A typical feedback screenshot is shown in Figure 2. With the incorporation of feedback in the game interface, users were challenged to think critically, to identify hazards correctly and to determine how to modify a particular design to improve safety. To complete this hazard identification and elimination activity, students were required to utilize higher-level thinking skills, beyond simple knowledge-based understanding. To suggest corrective measures, students needed to understand safety based on common sense.

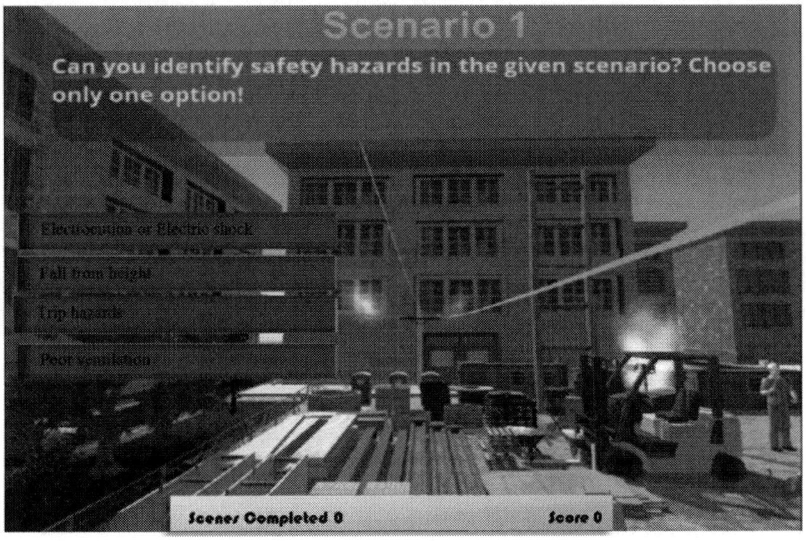

Figure 1— A Typical Scenario of the Safedesign Game

Based on the educational pedagogical research theory students were divided among three groups. One group was only delivered a lecture; the second group was given instructions and the SafeDesign game to play, and the third group was given a paper-based game. The data collected through the different treatment activities were compared to assess specific aspects of the learning that varied based upon the format of the activity. This process of implementing the serious game, paper-based games, and lecture-based versions of the Prevention through Design activity as well as the analysis of results helped to answer specific research questions.

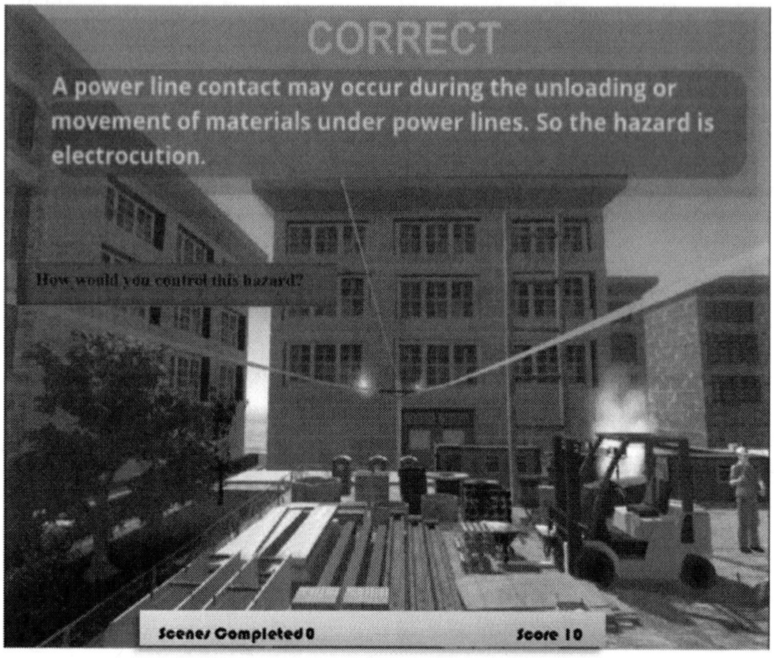

Figure 2— A Typical Safedesign Game Scenario Providing Feedback

Learning score from three pedagogies was identified as the main effect to be studied during this research. The pedagogical approaches were considered as independent variables. While gender, game-playing frequency, relevant work experience, and computer use frequency was considered as confounding independent variables and covariates. Learning score was measured as the difference between the posttest score and the pretest score and was considered as the dependent variable.

RESULTS

The results showed that the SafeDesign game had a positive impact on learning; similarly, in-class lecture intervention also has the positive effect on learning. However, the overall performance of the serious game group was higher than the other intervention groups as shown in Figure 3. The paper-based game intervention did not work, and the students who used it earned the lowest score. The possible reason for better performance within the lecture intervention group was that the lecture was delivered during the class of a construction safety course. The students in the class were already familiar with terminologies and concepts of safe construction; this probably helped them to understand the prevention through design lecture, and this might have benefited them in the tests. The paper-based game and the serious game groups were truly comparable because the students in those groups had not taken any safety course previously. In those two groups, the students in the serious game group performed better on their post-test results. In order to determine whether gender, the learning game-playing experience, computer use, and the relevant work experience contributed to any of the pedagogical interventions, individual factorial design analysis was carried out to identify the main effects and the interaction effects of these covariates. It was found that none of the factors had a statically significant impact on learning. Factors such as gender, the learning game playing experience, previous computer use experience

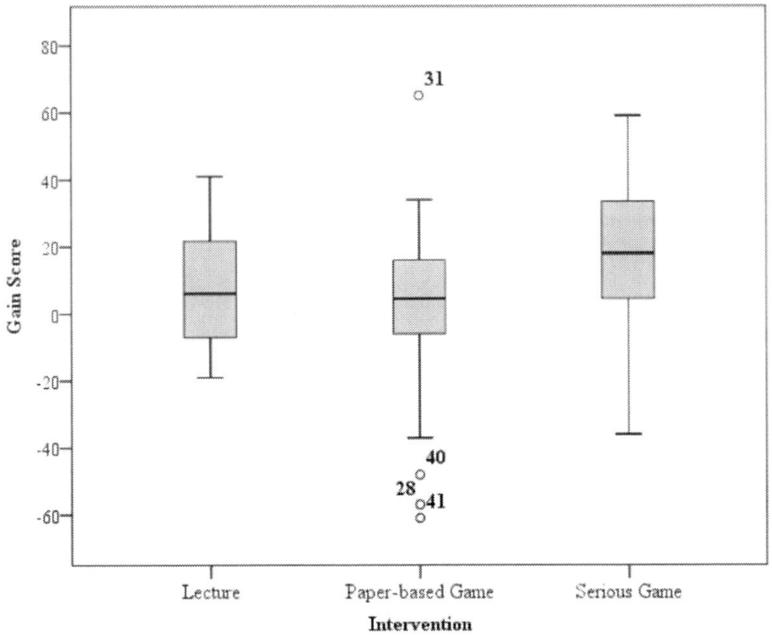

Figure 3—Gain Score Range for Three Pedagogical Interventions

and the relevant work experience did have a positive impact on the serious game performance, but the effect was not statistically significant. Figure 3 presents the ranges of average gain scores achieved by the participants in the three pedagogies. The box plot shows that the students in the paper-based game intervention performed differently as compared to the other two interventions. The paper-based game results contain four mild outliers marked by a circle (o).

CONCLUSIONS

Well-designed serious games have the potential to turn learning into a challenge through the right blend of instructive and entertaining elements. Furthermore, lecture-based teaching and learning can also help a student when teaching is based on the adult education principles of relevance, meet student's needs, interactive education and connecting student's background knowledge and experience. Among the various factors studied, no one proved to be an essential element of the study, which positively augmenting learning. For example, gender, previous knowledge, previous work experience and game playing experience did not seem to help toward learning for this relatively small sample. The illustrations on the paper-based game distracted students from the educational feature of the game in this study. Also, more work needs to be done concerning whether the SafeDesign game will have a positive effect to retain that knowledge in the long-term. Furthermore, future studies may be able to explore what features of a serious game are necessary for a positive impact on learning such as, improved visuals, audio, and 3D navigation functions. We should never consider serious games as a "magic wand" to improve learning performance, but serious games have the potential to be a great instrument for effective learning.

REFERENCES

Behm, M. (2005). Linking construction fatalities to the design for construction safety concept. *Safety Science*, *43*(8), 589–611. https://doi.org/10.1016/j.ssci.2005.04.002

Behm, M., Culvenor, J., & Dixon, G. (2014). Development of safe design thinking among engineering students. *Safety Science*, *63*, 1–7. https://doi.org/10.1016/j.ssci.2013.10.018

BLS. (2016). *U.S. Bureau of Labor Statistics, Current Population Survey, Census of Fatal Occupational Injuries*. Retrieved from https://www.bls.gov/iif/oshwc/cfoi/cfch0014.pdf

BLS. (2017). Employment by industry, 1910 and 2015: The Economics Daily: U.S. Bureau of Labor Statistics. Retrieved July 10, 2017, from https://www.bls.gov/opub/ted/2016/employment-by-industry-1910-and-2015.htm

CDC. (2013). CDC - Engineering Education in Occupational Safety and Health - NIOSH Workplace Safety and Health Topic. Retrieved June 2, 2017, from https://www.cdc.gov/niosh/topics/SHAPE/

Din, Z. (2017). *Teaching Prevention through Design (PtD) Principles Using A Nontraditional Pedagogical Strategy*. Arizona State University.

Din, Z., & Gibson Jr., G. E. (2018). Leveraging Pedagogical Innovation for Prevention through Design Education: Lessons Learned from Serious Game Development. In *Construction Research Congress*. New Orleans.

Din, Z., Rahman, R. A., & Gibson, G. E. (2017). Comparative Study of University Courses On Construction Safety at Undergraduate Level. In F. Sadeghpour & T. Froese (Eds.), *6th CSCECRC International Construction Specialty Conference* (pp. 165-1-165–169). Vancouver. Retrieved from https://www.xcdsystem.com/csce/proceedings2017/CONSPEC.cfm

Field, A. P., & Hole, G. (2003). *How to design and report experiments*. Sage. Retrieved from https://books.google.com/books?id=awtu_c7NofwC

Gambatese, J. a., Hinze, J. W., & Haas, C. T. (1997). Tool to Design for Construction Worker Safety. *Journal of Architectural Engineering*, *3*(1), 32–41. https://doi.org/10.1061/(ASCE)1076-0431(1997)3:1(32)

Manuele, F. A. (2008). Prevention Through Design: Addressing Occupational Risks In the Design And Redesign Processes. *Professional Safety*, *53*(10).

Michael, D. R., & Chen, S. (2006). *Serious Games: Games that Educate, Train and Inform*. Thomson Course Technology. Retrieved from https://books.google.com/books?id=49kTAQAAIAAJ

Popov, G., Blunt, L. A., Mcglothlin, J., Young-Corbett, D., Zey, J. N., Heckel, P., Heckel, P. (2013). Integrating PTD Into Undergraduate Curricula. *Professional Safety*, *58*(03), 44–49.

Prensky, M. (2003). Digital game-based learning. *Computers in Entertainment*, *1*(1), 21. https://doi.org/10.1145/950566.950596

Toole, T. M. (2005). Increasing Engineers' Role in Construction Safety: Opportunities and Barriers. *Professional Issues in Engineering Education and Practice*, *131*(3), 199–207. https://doi.org/https://doi.org/10.1061/(ASCE)1052-3928(2005)131:3(199)

The Processes and Requirements for Developing and Maintaining a Certification Program for Safety Professionals

David B. West, CSP, ASP, PE, CHMM; Board of Certified Safety Professionals; Indianapolis, Indiana, U.S.A.

Keywords: certification, credentialing, competency, CSP, ASP

Abstract

Certification is one of various types of formal recognition programs, which are often collectively referred to as "credentialing." Certification is a voluntary process through which an organization confers recognition to qualified individuals after determining that they meet pre-established minimum standards of competency, including but not limited to passing a rigorous examination. While many practitioners in the Safety field may be familiar with programs of professional certification, most may not understand all that is involved in establishing and maintaining a reputable and sustainable program. Certification programs are operated as businesses. As such, they must be developed following a well-thought-out business plan. A worthwhile certification program must be run according to a governance plan by an organization with a clearly defined structure, a certification scheme, key staff and operations, and established policies and procedures. Examinations that are administered as part of a certification program are developed by subject matter experts, and examination results are subjected to statistical analysis. To be recognized as a high-quality certification, the program should be accredited on a recurring basis by a qualified third-party organization. Earning a high-quality certification offers value to certificants in many areas, including compensation, recognition, and personal satisfaction.

Introduction

Many professions have formal means of either ensuring or recognizing the level of competency for practitioners of the profession expected by peers, mandated by government or standards-setting organizations, and/or required for the protection of the general public. These formal recognition programs are often collectively referred to as “credentialing” programs. Credentials held by members of a profession can include certification, licenses, or certificates. Earning and maintaining a credential can prove or enhance one’s value as a qualified practitioner within the profession.

This paper will focus on the form of credentialing known as “certification.” To give some context for the whole concept of certification, the paper will summarize the similarities and differences between certification and other types of credentials. It will also briefly discuss generally understood aspects of the value of certification. A brief explanation will be given of accreditation, which, for the purposes of this paper, means a rigorous process involving third-party review of the certification program to ensure it meets recognized and documented standards of excellence and fairness.

The primary objective of the paper, however, is to explain how extensive the efforts must be to establish and run a certification program, and to develop and maintain quality examinations, which are at the heart of assessing the knowledge and skills of certification candidates to determine if they have the requisite level of competency to be granted the certification in question.

Overview of Professional Certification

Certification vs. Licensure or Certificate Programs

There are significant distinctions between certification and licensure, and between the earning of a certification and the earning of a certificate. Professional certification is defined by the Institute for Credentialing Excellence (ICE) as a "voluntary process by which a non-governmental entity grants a time-limited recognition and use of a credential to an individual after verifying that he or she has met predetermined and standardized criteria" (Knapp et al., 2006). By contrast, a license to practice in a regulated field is granted by a government agency or its designated agent. As such, the licensing process is controlled by law, and holding it is mandatory. Licensed individuals are granted permission to use a designation and its associated acronym, such as "Professional Engineer" (PE), or "Registered Nurse" (RN).

Like certifications, certificate programs are voluntary. However, unlike certification, which focuses on verifying experience and education/training obtained elsewhere and assessing current knowledge and skills, a certificate focuses on a specific course of education or training, and then a determination as to whether the trainee attained the intended learning outcomes (Rops, 2011).

Certification – which, again, is the focus of this paper – is voluntary. Certification programs evaluate professionals against an established industry standard set through a defensible process resulting in the establishment of appropriate benchmarks of required knowledge and skills (Wright et al., 2015). The certification is awarded for a specified duration with required continuing professional development reported on a set cycle (Ibid.). If a certificant does not fulfill the required certification maintenance activities, the certification award expires.

The Value of Certification

A professional certification represents something of value – not only to the certificant, but also to the individual's employer. According to research by the International Data Corporation (IDC), and one hiring manager that was interviewed as part of that research, "Hiring is faster because the screening process is simplified with certification as a criterion, and the weeding out of candidates happens more quickly" (Anderson et al., 2015). In addition to hiring efficiency, higher productivity (after hiring) is also a benefit. An IT manager at a transportation company stated that "Certification improves productivity right out of the chute. It also, I think, strengthens their commitment to the job." (Anderson et al., 2015)

A research study on the perceived value of certification among occupational safety and health (OSH) professionals conducted for the Board of Canadian Registered Safety Professionals (BCRSP) identified that certification:

- is an indication of professional growth,
- enhances professional credibility,
- provides evidence of professional commitment,
- enhances employability and mobility, and
- increases earning potential (Assessment Strategies Inc., 2011; Wright et al., 2015).

The increased earning potential of certified professionals is also supported through salary survey data collected by the Board of Certified Safety Professionals (BCSP), the American Board of Industrial Hygiene (ABIH), the American Society of Safety Engineers (ASSE), the American Industrial Hygiene Association (AIHA), the Alliance of Hazardous Materials Professionals (AHMP), and the Institute of Hazardous Materials Management (IHMM) (BCSP, 2015). The survey confirmed that employers recognize the value of certification and reflect this value through increased salaries and/or promotions (Wright et al., 2015).

In addition to the tangible aspects of value, an individual who earns a certification is rewarded by the feeling of accomplishment that results from setting a goal, dedicating oneself to achieving it, and then being recognized by the profession for the hard work and perseverance it took to meet the challenge.

As with anything of value, certifications need to be protected. Organizations that administer programs for evaluating candidates and awarding certifications will also implement measures for guarding against any fraudulent or unauthorized use of the certification mark. These measures often include tools, such as online certificant directories to facilitate verifying the current certification status of someone claiming to hold the certification, or convenient methods for reporting unauthorized use to the certification organization. When an unauthorized user of the certification mark is identified, the organization will generally have policies for penalizing the offender. These policies may include disciplinary action, such as publishing a list of offenders or preventing offenders from applying for the certification for several years.

Accreditation

Accreditation is, itself, a type of credential. In this case, an organization that administers a certification program can earn accreditation for their program by demonstrating compliance with established performance standards. A third party accrediting organization will interview key staff members and will review policies, procedures, and other documentation provided by the certification organization. The main objective of the accreditor's review is to verify that the certification program meets the requirements of the standard(s) to which the program is assessed. Following their assessment, the accrediting body will report any findings, highlighting any non-compliances, deficiencies, areas for improvement, or similar concerns. To maintain their accreditation, the certification organization generally needs to respond to the accreditor's findings and explain what they have done or will do to address and correct any problems identified. Compliance with standard requirements gives assurance to prospective certificants that they are pursuing and earning a quality certification that is administered fairly and securely.

A widely used standard for the certification of individuals is the international standard ISO/IEC 17024, "Conformity Assessment – General Requirements for Bodies Operating Certification of Persons." Certification programs of both the BCSP and BCRSP are accredited to this standard through the American National Standards Institute (ANSI) and the Standards Council of Canada (SCC), respectively. ANSI and SCC conduct annual surveillance audits and a full reaccreditation audit at regular intervals. For ANSI, the reaccreditation audit is conducted every five years. SCC conducts its reaccreditation audit every four years.

Developing and Running a Certification Program

Business Planning

Certification programs must be run as businesses. It costs money to maintain the staff and infrastructure and do the work required to develop and administer the certification. Revenues brought in by the certification organization must at least equal the expenses of the program, for it to remain viable. Before launching a certification program, the organization must develop a business plan. The business plan should identify the need for the certification program and the strengths of the organization in meeting that need. It should clearly state the purpose and goals of the certification program. The business plan should also summarize the results of research that has been performed to understand the target market, gage stakeholder interest, and quantify the perceived value of the certification. (Rops, 2011)

There are a number of areas common to many types of businesses that should be covered by the business plan and represented in the eventual structure of the organization. These include governance, payroll and finance, human resources, marketing and communications, customer service, information technology, and legal support. While these areas are all essential to the success of the organization, they will not be covered in any more detail here.

Developing and Maintaining Examinations

A certification scheme spells out what eligibility requirements, such as educational background and applicable experience, must be satisfied by candidates for the certification. The certification scheme also describes the mechanism or instrument for determining whether candidates have the requisite knowledge and skills to be considered as qualified to hold the certification. And finally, the certification scheme specifies what must be accomplished by the certificant, on a regular basis, to maintain certification. It is the second of these components – the assessment mechanism, or examination – that is discussed in this section and its subsections.

Rigorous examinations, which must be successfully passed by certification candidates, are at the heart of most certification programs. Certifications in the Safety field are no exception. There is a great deal more to developing and maintaining quality examinations, that fairly and reliably measure what they need to measure, than most people realize!

Standard Setting & Examination Development. When developing certification examinations, a quality credentialing program must follow logically sound and legally defensible procedures (Wright et al., 2015). ISO/IEC 17024, mentioned above under "Accreditation," provides "a globally accepted process of assessment and periodic reassessments of the competence of certified persons" (ISO/IEC, 2012). In the United States, the certification of OSH professionals through the use of a standardized assessment tool, such as a multiple-choice examination, has been the industry standard for more than 40 years (Wright et al., 2015). Standardized tests ensure a consistent method of scoring and facilitates legal defensibility (Wright et al., 2015).

Developing and administering a standardized test is done through what is called a psychometric process. Psychometrics literally means "mental measurement." The psychometric process consists of a systematic method of establishing and delivering a quality certification examination that will objectively measure the knowledge and skills of the individuals being evaluated. The psychrometric examination development process includes the following steps:

- Job Task Analysis/Role Delineation
- Validation Survey
- Item Development
- Cut Score Determination
- Statistical Analysis
- Continuous Improvement (Wright et al., 2015)

These steps are discussed in more detail in the subsections that follow.

Job Task Analysis/Role Delineation. The Job Task Analysis (JTA), or Role Delineation, is often considered the starting point of the periodic examination revalidation cycle. The purpose of the JTA is to identify the various tasks that must be performed as part of the certificant's job and develop a list of the knowledge and skills that the individual must possess to be able to execute each task successfully. This list of required knowledge and skills is what the exam content is eventually based on.

The JTA is performed by a panel of subject matter experts (SMEs) representing a diversity of the certificant population, in terms of geography, experience, and other demographics. To ensure that the competencies identified as critical to practice within the certification are reflective of current practices, the JTA is repeated after a set interval by a newly selected panel of SMEs. For the BCSP and BCRSP, this interval is five years (Wright et al., 2015). This periodic reprise of the JTA allows the exam content to be refreshed so that it reflects knowledge of scientific and technological advances in the profession.

Validation Survey. The next step in the examination development process is a validation survey taken by another representative sample of SMEs to review and validate the results of the JTA. In this survey, the SMEs are instructed to rate the importance, criticality, and frequency of use of each task, knowledge, or skill identified in the JTA. The results of this validation survey are used to provide the framework for the examination structure (Wright et al., 2015). For example, if the compiled survey results reveal that a particular task scored relatively high on the importance, criticality, and/or frequency scales, this would indicate a necessity for the certification candidate to have the associated knowledge or skills, meaning they should definitely be included on the examination.

The results of the JTA and validation survey are compiled into what is called an examination blueprint, which provides information on domains and competencies that may be tested (Wright et al., 2015), as well as the number of examination items (or questions) that should come from each domain and knowledge/skills area. The final blueprint is then approved by the appropriate Board or committee authorized to do so (Wright et al., 2015). The examination blueprint is published as reference for potential candidates to use when preparing for the examination.

Item Development. Once the examination blueprint has been finalized, the certification examination can be developed. Examination "questions" are more correctly referred to as "items," because in addition to the question, which may be preceded by an optional scenario (the scenario and question together make up what is called the "stem"), the item also includes the answer options (in a multiple-choice format examination). The correct answer is called the "key," while incorrect answers are called "distractors." Items are developed to evaluate whether a candidate has a particular knowledge or skill requirement identified on the blueprint.

The item development process is designed to develop examination items that are fair and that represent current and relevant industry practice for the profession (Wright et al., 2015). Another group of SMEs who hold the certification for which the items are being developed are gathered together and trained on the process of item writing and review. Items are written by these SMEs utilizing applicable globally-recognized resources and references, and the reference source of the information in the test question is documented for each item (Wright et al., 2015). Items undergo multiple levels of review to confirm that the item is relevant to the profession and certification, grammatically correct, applicable to a global audience, and linked to the examination blueprint (Wright et al., 2015). The answer options must all be of similar length and grammatically parallel. One answer option must be the correct or best alternative, and the distractors must be plausible, but specious.

Before the item is used to contribute to a candidate's score on an exam, it must go through a beta testing process to be sure it meets certain criteria to appropriately evaluate the candidate's knowledge or skills. During this beta testing phase, items that are too easy (e.g., more than 80% of the candidates answer it correctly), and items that are too hard (e.g., less than 40% of the candidates answer correctly) are tagged for revision or removal. By eliminating both the very easy and the very difficult items, the items that remain are those that will truly differentiate between candidates that meet the minimum qualification standard and those that do not. This is important in understanding why the cut score (or passing score), discussed next, appears to the general public to be relatively low (usually below 70%). When all the easy items that the vast majority of candidates would answer correctly are removed, the overall score will be lower than a typical academic-style examination. It is appropriate for academic-style examinations to evaluate the test takers over a broader achievement scale (e.g., A, B, C, D, or F), but certification examinations are only intended to evaluate which side of a very narrow pass/fail dividing line the candidates fall.

Cut Score Determination. The goal of a certification examination is to determine whether a candidate has the minimum knowledge and skills to be considered competent. This determination is made based on whether the candidate's score on the exam meets or exceeds what is called the cut score, or passing score, for the examination. A common and generally accepted best practice for setting the cut score for certification examinations is to use the Angoff Method or Modified Angoff Method (Wright et al., 2015). These methods begin with a panel of representative SMEs that are provided information on the process to be used, the purpose of a cut score, and the definitions of "not acceptable," "minimally acceptable," and "superior" candidate profiles for the exam (Young, 2015). A common understanding of the experience level and expectations of the minimally acceptable candidate, which is the target audience for the examination, is critical because the process involves the SME's evaluation of what percentage of these minimally qualified candidates would be expected to know the answer.

SMEs are trained in the Angoff or modified Angoff rating process by first using individual examination items. Participants are asked to read the test item, identify the correct answer, review the distractors, and provide an estimate of the percentage of minimally acceptable candidates that would correctly answer the item. The SME ratings are evaluated, and if ratings among the SMEs show too much variation (e.g., the ratings exceeded a 30-point spread or standard deviation of 0.10), the SMEs with high and low Angoff ratings are asked to share the rationales for their ratings so that the group may discuss the differences in opinions. Then, the SMEs are given an opportunity to adjust their initial Angoff ratings and this process is repeated until SMEs are consistently making Angoff ratings with little variation (e.g., a 30-point spread or less or standard deviation of 0.10 or less). Finally, the SMEs provide an Angoff rating for all the scored items on the examination being evaluated and an Angoff cut score (i.e., a tentative cut score) is calculated from these values by a qualified psychometrician (Young, 2015). Based on the calculated cut score and item performance statistics from previously administered exams, an appropriate cut score is set, and this final passing score for the examination is then approved by the Board or a committee authorized to do so (Wright et al., 2015). This complicated method results in a passing score that reflects current, relevant, and applicable knowledge and skills established through a peer review process.

Statistical Analysis. Statistical analysis of the exam as a whole, and each individual test item, provides a benchmark of the overall performance of a certification examination (Wright, et al., 2015). An annual statistical report is developed by a psychometrician to provide information on the reliability and validity of the examination forms, item bank statistics, program activities/initiatives undertaken towards process improvement, recommendations based on industry best practices, etc. (Wright et al., 2015). The methodology for reliability and validity of assessment is a key component within the ISO/IEC 17024 Standard, which states in Paragraph 9.3.5 that, "appropriate methodology and procedures shall be documented and implemented in order to reaffirm, at justified defined intervals, the fairness, validity, reliability and general performance of each examination, and that all identified deficiencies are corrected" (ISO/IEC, 2012). The ISO/IEC 17024 Standard defines reliability as an "indicator of the extent to which examination scores are consistent across different examination times and locations." Validity is defined as "evidence that the assessment measures what it is intended to measure, as defined by the certification scheme" (Ibid.).

Continuous Improvement. Certification organizations work in a continuous improvement mode to regularly monitor, measure, and analyze each step, including established standardized review periods for the examination blueprint, ongoing item bank development and maintenance, and policy review (Wright et al., 2015). For example, the BCSP and BCRSP review and update the Associate Safety Professional (ASP), Certified Safety Professional (CSP), and Canadian Registered Safety Professional (CRSP) blueprints at least every five years to ensure that the certifications reflect current professional requirements and practices (Wright et al., 2015). Certification organizations may also benchmark their policies and procedures to other similar organizations and/or certification industry best practices, as published by organizations such as ICE or the Association of Test Publishers (ATP) (Wright et al., 2015). The certification programs as a whole may also be evaluated and accredited by third-party agencies such as the National Commission for Certifying Agencies (NCCA), ANSI, or SCC to evaluate whether the process meets the ISO/IEC 17024 standard or other national or international standard for certification. These continuous improvement and external review processes ensure that the certification is relevant, reliable, valid, and defensible.

Conclusion

Certification is often used by employers, recruiters, and clients as a minimum qualification for safety professional positions. Some research suggests that up to 70% of job postings for safety professionals require or prefer a certified professional (Wright et al., 2015). The certification management process is often not understood by the employer or even those holding the certification. As detailed in this paper, the processes for developing and maintaining a certification program – particularly the processes for developing and periodically revalidating the certification examination – can be complicated and somewhat daunting. But knowing and understanding that the process is methodical, reliable, statistical, and validated is an important component of the value of the certification and its representation as the mark of excellence in the Safety field.

Acknowledgements

The author wishes to thank Treasa Turnbeaugh, PhD, MBA, CSP, and Ann Chacko, PhD for their support, encouragement, and valuable reference material used in preparing this paper, and for providing review comments on the initial draft.

References

Knapp, J., Fabrey, L., Rops, M. & McCurray, N. (2006). Basic guide to credentialing terminology. Washington, DC: Institute for Credentialing Excellence.

Rops, M. (2011). Certification Simplified, A Primer for Staff and Volunteer Leaders. Washington, DC: ASAE: The Center for Association Leadership.

Wright, N., Turnbeaugh, T., Weldon, C. & Lyons, D. (2015). Certification of OSH professionals through an accredited competency assessment model. *Proceedings Book of the WOS 8th International Conference* (pp. 1-9). Porto Portugal: WOS2015 Scientific Committee.

Anderson, C., Marden, M, & Perry, R. (2015). IT Certifications: Shorter Road to Valuable Positions. Retrieved July 16, 2018, from http://download.microsoft.com/download/E/4/1/E4101D56-EBEE-49C1-806E-2A22A5CCF79D/BVW_Microsoft_US40548215.pdf?cid=20346

Assessment Strategies Inc. (2011). Report on the perceived value of certification survey. Mississauga, Ontario.

Board of Certified Safety Professionals. (2018). The 2018 SH&E Industry Salary Survey and Calculator. Retrieved July 16, 2018 from http://www.bcsp.org/SH-E-Practice/Salary-Survey

International Organization for Standardization and International Electrotechnical Commission. (2012). ISO/IEC 17024, "Conformity Assessment – General Requirements for Bodies Operating Certification of Persons." Geneva, Switzerland.

Young, P. (2015). Safety Trained Supervisor Construction (STSC) Exam Standard Setting Report. Phoenix, AZ: Kryterion, Inc.

Delivering System Safety Through Design Tutorial

Galen Ressler
GM Technical Fellow
Principal System Safety Engineer – High Voltage Systems

Mark A Vernacchia
GM Technical Fellow
Principal System Safety Engineer – Propulsion Systems

Tutorial Goals

- Provide an understanding of the following topics:
  - What is "Safety"?
  - What is "System Safety"? - Compare and contrast between various perspectives
  - What is "Risk"? - Compare and contrast between various perspectives
  - Risk Assessment - Compare and contrast between various perspectives
  - Risk Management - Compare and contrast between various perspectives
  - Being Part of the Engineering Process
  - Systems Engineering – Balance and Optimization
  - System Safety Analyses
  - Requirements and Validation
- Apply principles to real world automotive examples in real time
  - High Voltage Propulsion System
  - Compressed Natural Gas Propulsion System

Tutorial Introduction

- Convey the critical concepts and approaches to accommodate safety as an integral part of the design process itself using a high-voltage automotive propulsion system and a compressed natural gas system propulsion system as the examples to convey these concepts and approaches
- Safety team needs to be an integral part of the actual design team, not an ancillary group volunteering opinions from afar. Aspects of management structure and decision making approaches for accepting responsibility for acceptable risk are discussed. In addition, communication techniques to convey safety requirements to the engineering release responsible groups will be illustrated.

What is Safety?

- GM Safety Process
  - Freedom from unacceptable risk
- MIL-STD-882E [1]
  - Freedom from conditions that can cause death, injury, occupational illness, damage to or loss of equipment or property, or damage to the environment
- NASA Systems Engineering [2]
  - Freedom from those conditions that can cause death, injury, occupational illness, damage to or loss of equipment or property, or damage to the environment
- Leveson (MIT – STPA) [3]
  - Freedom from accidents (loss events)
- ISO-26262 [4]
  - Absence of unacceptable risk

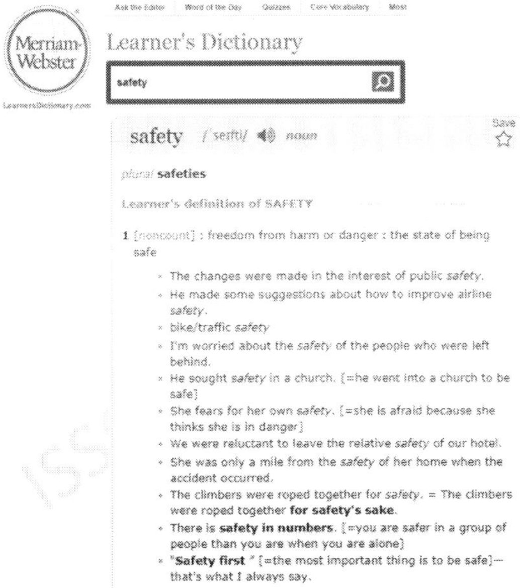

Ask the Editor | Word of the Day | Quizzes | Core Vocabulary | Most

Merriam-Webster
LearnersDictionary.com

Learner's Dictionary

safety

safety /ˈseɪfti/ *noun*

Save

plural **safeties**

Learner's definition of SAFETY

1 [noncount] : freedom from harm or danger : the state of being safe

- The changes were made in the interest of public *safety*.
- He made some suggestions about how to improve airline *safety*.
- bike/traffic *safety*
- I'm worried about the *safety* of the people who were left behind.
- He sought *safety* in a church. [=he went into a church to be safe]
- She fears for her own *safety*. [=she is afraid because she thinks she is in danger]
- We were reluctant to leave the relative *safety* of our hotel.
- She was only a mile from the *safety* of her home when the accident occurred.
- The climbers were roped together for *safety*. = The climbers were roped together **for safety's sake**.
- There is **safety in numbers**. [=you are safer in a group of people than you are when you are alone]
- "**Safety first**." [=the most important thing is to be safe]—that's what I always say.

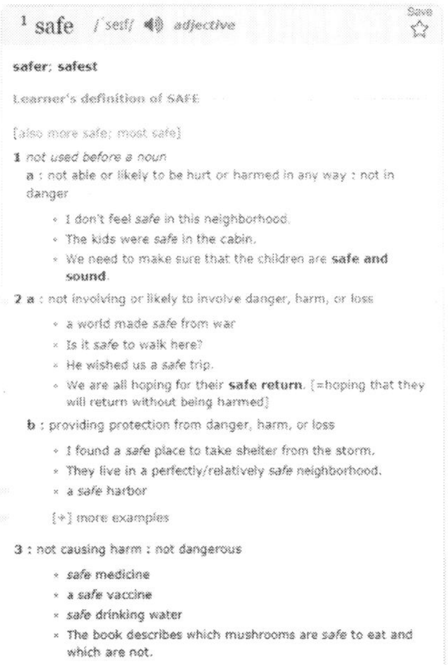

[1] **safe** /ˈseɪf/ *adjective*

Save

safer; safest

Learner's definition of SAFE

[also more safe; most safe]

1 *not used before a noun*

a : not able or likely to be hurt or harmed in any way : not in danger

- I don't feel *safe* in this neighborhood.
- The kids were *safe* in the cabin.
- We need to make sure that the children are **safe and sound**.

2 a : not involving or likely to involve danger, harm, or loss

- a world made *safe* from war
- Is it *safe* to walk here?
- He wished us a *safe* trip.
- We are all hoping for their **safe return**. [=hoping that they will return without being harmed]

b : providing protection from danger, harm, or loss

- I found a *safe* place to take shelter from the storm.
- They live in a perfectly/relatively *safe* neighborhood.
- a *safe* harbor

[+] more examples

3 : not causing harm : not dangerous

- *safe* medicine
- a *safe* vaccine
- *safe* drinking water
- The book describes which mushrooms are *safe* to eat and which are not.

Safety Summary – Things in Common and Differences

- What do all these viewpoints have in common?
  - Highlight the absence of any danger
  - Discuss safety in terms of "risk"
- Safety has multiple meanings depending on industry but all are concerned with providing end solutions that have an appropriate level of acceptable risk
- What is different?
  - Harm extending past just humans
  - Use of specific risk type – "unacceptable"

36th International System Safety Conference, Aug 13-17, 2018
Reproduction or Reuse of this Material is Prohibited without Express Permission from GM

What is System Safety?

- GM Safety Process
  - System safety is a specialty within systems engineering that supports program risk management. It is the application of engineering and management principles to optimize safety
- MIL-STD-882E [1]
  - The application of engineering and management principles, criteria, and techniques to achieve acceptable risk within the constraints of operational effectiveness and suitability, time, and cost throughout all phases of the system life-cycle
- FAA Systems Safety Handbook [5]
  - The application of engineering and management principles, criteria, and techniques to optimize safety within the constraints of operational effectiveness, time, and cost throughout all phases of system life cycle

System Safety – Common Things and Differences

- What do all these things have in common?
  - Apply engineering and management approaches
  - Work to achieve a level of acceptable risk
- What is different?
  - "Optimize" or "achieve" safety
  - Extent to which safety is balanced with other program initiatives (cost, timing, etc.)

System Safety Summary

- System Safety is a disciplined and comprehensive engineering effort to identify safety related risks to be either eliminated or controlled
  - Involves the identification of potential hazards, assessment of the risk, and mitigation of the risk to acceptable levels through design requirements
  - Analyzes the overall effect at the vehicle level including the operator and the environment as part of the system
  - Considers entire life cycle requirements including operation, maintenance and disposal phases where appropriate
- System can be comprised of software and hardware components. Each software and hardware component by itself can be safe, but **interactions** must also be analyzed

What is Risk?

- ARP-4754A [6]
  - The combination of the frequency (probability) of an occurrence and its associated level of severity
- ARP-4761 [7]
  - The frequency (probability) of occurrence and associated level of hazard
- NASA Systems Engineering [2]
  - In the context of mission execution, risk is the potential for performance shortfalls that may be realized in the future with respect to achieving explicitly established and stated performance requirements.
- GM Safety Process
  - Combination of likelihood of occurrence of a hazard, controllability and severity of that hazard that could potentially lead to harm

Risk – NASA System Safety Handbook [8]

- **Risk –** The potential for shortfalls, which may be realized in the future, with respect to achieving explicitly stated performance requirements. Risk is characterized by a set of triplets:
  1. the scenario(s) leading to degraded performance in one or more performance measures
  2. the likelihood(s) of those scenarios, and
  3. the consequence(s) of impact on performance that would result if those scenarios occur.

- **Risk Driver –** A significant source of performance risk. Operationally, a risk driver can be a single performance parameter, a single event, a set of performance parameters collectively, or a set of events collectively that, when varied over their range of uncertainty, causes the performance risk to change from tolerable to intolerable (or marginal).

Risk – NASA Systems Engineering Handbook [2]

- **RISK** - In the context of mission execution, risk is the potential for performance shortfalls that may be realized in the future with respect to achieving explicitly established and stated performance requirements. The performance shortfalls may be related to any one or more of the following mission execution domains:
  1. Safety
  2. Technical
  3. Cost
  4. Schedule

Risk – FAA System Safety Handbook [5]

- **Risk** is an expression of possible loss over a specific period of time or number of operational cycles. It may be indicated by the probability of an accident times the damage in dollars, lives, and / or operating units. Hazard Probability and Severity are measurable and, when combined, give us risk. **Total risk** is the sum of **identified** and **unidentified** risks.
- **Identified risk** is that risk which has been determined through various analysis techniques. The first task of system safety is to identify, within practical limitations, all possible risks. This step precedes determining the significance of the risk (severity) and the likelihood of its occurrence (hazard probability). The time and costs of analysis efforts, the quality of the safety program, and the state of technology impact the number of risks identified.
- **Unidentified risk** is the risk not yet identified. Some unidentified risks are subsequently identified when a mishap occurs. Some risk is never known.

Perhaps Most Useful Risk Summary – FAA System Safety Handbook [5]

- **Unacceptable risk** is that risk which cannot be tolerated by the managing activity. It is a subset of identified risk that must be eliminated or controlled.
- **Acceptable risk** is the part of identified risk that is allowed to persist without further engineering or management action. Making this decision is a difficult yet necessary responsibility of the managing activity. This decision is made with full knowledge that it is the user who is exposed to this risk.
- **Residual risk** is the risk left over after system safety efforts have been fully employed. It is not necessarily the same as acceptable risk. **Residual risk** is the sum of **acceptable risk** and **unidentified risk**. This is the total risk passed on to the user.

Risk Summary – FAA System Safety Handbook [5]

RISK TYPE	MEANING
Identified Risk	Risk which has been determined through various analysis techniques (Identified Risk = Eliminated + Controlled + Acceptable)
Residual Risk	Risk left over after system safety efforts have been fully employed (Residual Risk = Acceptable + Unidentified)
Acceptable Risk	Part of identified risk that is allowed to persist without further engineering or management action
Unidentified Risk	Risk not yet identified
Unacceptable Risk	Risk which cannot be tolerated by the managing activity (Unacceptable Risk = Eliminated + Controlled)

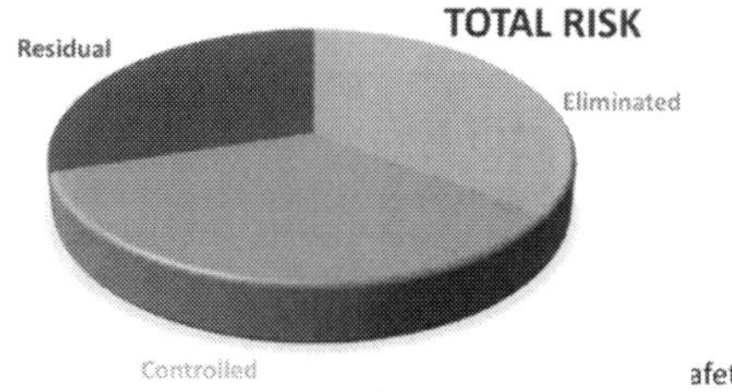

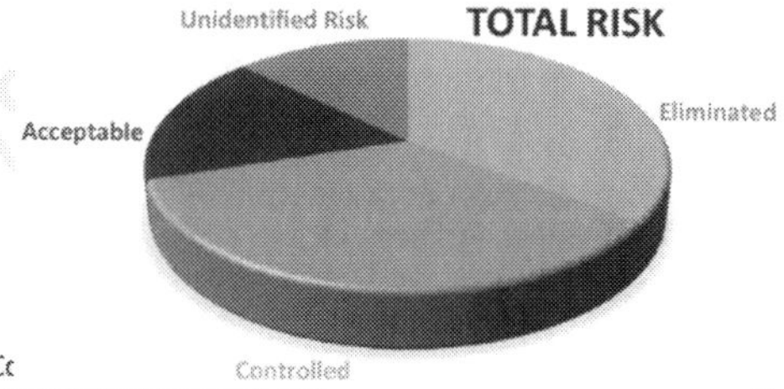

RISK Summary

- What do all these things have in common?
  - Consider "likelihood" (occurrence) and "severity"
  - Apply risk within the confines of the program context
- What is different?
  - Identification of specific types of risk (FAA)
  - "Probability" vs "Likelihood" of occurrence
    - "Probability" implies quantitative
    - "Likelihood" implies qualitative
  - Controllability inclusion in ISO and GM SS Process
  - Cost and timing exclusion in GM SS process

Risk Assessment – NASA Systems Engineering Handbook [2]

➢ **RISK Assessment** - An evaluation of a risk item that determines

1. what can go wrong,
2. how likely it is to occur,
3. what the consequences are,
4. what the uncertainties associated with the likelihood and consequences are, and
5. what the mitigation plans are

Risk Assessment – NASA Systems Engineering Handbook [2]

6.4.1.2.3 Conduct Technical Risk Assessment

Until recently, NASA's Risk Management (RM) approach was based almost exclusively on Continuous Risk Management (CRM), which stresses the management of individual risk issues during implementation. In December of 2008, NASA revised its RM approach in order to more effectively foster proactive risk management.

The new approach, which is outlined in NPR 8000.4, Agency Risk Management Procedural Requirements and further developed in *NASA/SP-2011-3422, NASA Risk Management Handbook*, evolves NASA's risk management to entail two complementary processes: Risk-Informed Decision Making (RIDM) and CRM. RIDM is intended to inform direction-setting systems engineering (SE) decisions (e.g., design decisions) through better use of risk and uncertainty information in selecting alternatives and establishing baseline performance requirements (for additional RIDM technical information, guidance, and process description, see *NASA/SP-2010-576 Version 1, NASA Risk-Informed Decision Making Handbook*).

36th International System Safety Conference, Aug 13-17, 2018

Risk Assessment – ISO26262 [4]

- Risk is expressed in terms of an **A**utomotive **S**afety **I**ntegrity **L**evel (**ASIL**)
- **ASIL** = function of (S, E, C)
  - S = Severity of the Hazard
  - E = Likelihood of Exposure to the operating scenario
  - C = Controllability of the operator and/or involved people
- Each of the factors have to be applied based on available data/statistics, experience and best engineering judgment
- ASIL specifies the developmental process rigor, the required hardware and software integrity requirements for the safety-critical system

Severity Definition (based on ISO 26262/DIS)

Risk = function of (S, E, C) = (**Severity**, Exposure, Controllability)

Definition for Hazard Severity

Hazard Severity	Title	Description
S0*	Low	No injuries
S1	Moderate	Light or moderate non life-threatening injuries to the driver or passengers or people around the vehicle
S2	Serious	Severe and life-threatening (Survival possible) to the driver or passengers or people around the vehicle or in other surrounding vehicles
S3	Severe	Life-threatening injuries (Survival uncertain, fatal injuries) to the driver or passengers or people around the vehicle or in other surrounding vehicles

Note: *No ASIL is assigned for S0

- In evaluating the severity component of risk for a hazard, always work with the **WORST CREDIBLE** consequence.

Exposure Definition (based on ISO 26262/DIS)

Risk = function of (S, E, C) = (Severity, **Exposure**, Controllability)

Definition for Likelihood of Exposure to Vehicle Operating Scenarios

Exposure	Title	Definition
E0*	Incredible	Situations that are extremely unusual.
E1	Rare	Very low probability. Situations that occur less often than once a year for the great majority of drivers
E2	Sometimes	Low probability. Situations that occur a few times a year for the great majority of drivers. < 1% of average operating time
E3	Quite often	Medium probability. Situations that occur once a month or more often for an average driver. 1% - 10% of average operating time.
E4	Often-Always	High probability. All situations that occur during almost every drive on average. > 10% of average operating time

Note: *No ASIL is assigned for E0

Note:

1. Exposure is the exposure to vehicle operating scenarios
2. Its usage in the risk assessment process should be generally conservative in consultation with safety experts.

Controllability Definition (based on ISO 26262/DIS)

Risk = function of (S, E, C) = (Severity, Exposure, **Controllability**)

Definition for Controllability

Note: *No ASIL is assigned for C0

Vehicle Controllability	Title	Definition
C0*	Controllable in general	Generally Controllable by all drivers;
C1	Simply Controllable	Less than 1% of average drivers or other traffic participants are usually unable to control the damage. In this kind of a hazard scenario, it is likely that the vehicle will be controllable by most drivers. Again controllable is used in the sense that most drivers will be able to prevent a mishap by applying corrective counter steering/ or corrective braking.
C2	Normally Controllable	Less than 10% of average drivers or other traffic participants are usually unable to control the damage. In this kind of a hazard scenario, it is possible that the vehicle will be controllable by some drivers. Again controllable is used in the sense that some drivers will be able to prevent a mishap by applying corrective counter steering/ or corrective braking..
C3	Difficult to Control	The average driver or other traffic participant is usually unable, or barely able, to control the damage. In this kind of a hazard scenario, it is unlikely that the vehicle will be controllable by average driver. Again uncontrollable is used in the sense that the average driver will be unable to prevent a mishap by applying corrective counter steering/ or corrective braking

Reproduction or Reuse of this Material is Prohibited without Express Permission from GM

Risk Matrix with ASIL (based on ISO 26262/DIS)

				Controllability		
				C1	C2	C3
Severity	S1	Exposure	E1	QM	QM	QM
			E2	QM	QM	QM
			E3	QM	QM	ASIL A
			E4	QM	ASIL A	ASIL B
	S2		E1	QM	QM	QM
			E2	QM	QM	ASIL A
			E3	QM	ASIL A	ASIL B
			E4	ASIL A	ASIL B	ASIL C
	S3		E1	QM	QM	ASIL A
			E2	QM	ASIL A	ASIL B
			E3	ASIL A	ASIL B	ASIL C
			E4	ASIL B	ASIL C	ASIL D

QM= Quality Managed; Not a safety risk; ASIL = Automotive Safety Integrity Level
No ASIL is assigned for S0, C0 or E0

Risk Assessment – DOD MIL-STD-882E [1] – Risk Assessment

- 4.3.3 Assess and document risk. The severity category and probability level of the potential mishap(s) for each hazard across all system modes are assessed using the definitions in Tables I and II.
- To determine the appropriate severity category as defined in Table I for a given hazard at a given point in time, identify the potential for death or injury, environmental impact, or monetary loss. A given hazard may have the potential to affect one or all of these three areas

TABLE I. Severity categories

SEVERITY CATEGORIES		
Description	**Severity Category**	**Mishap Result Criteria**
Catastrophic	1	Could result in one or more of the following: death, permanent total disability, irreversible significant environmental impact, or monetary loss equal to or exceeding $10M.
Critical	2	Could result in one or more of the following: permanent partial disability,injuries or occupational illness that may result in hospitalization of at least three personnel, reversible significant environmental impact, or monetary loss equal to or exceeding $1M but less than $10M.
Marginal	3	Could result in one or more of the following: injury or occupational illness resulting in one or more lost work day(s), reversible moderate environmental impact, or monetary loss equal to or exceeding $100K but less than $1M.
Negligible	4	Could result in one or more of the following: injury or occupational illness not resulting in a lost work day, minimal environmental impact, or monetary loss less than $100K.

Risk Assessment – DOD MIL-STD-882E [1] – Risk Assessment

- To determine the appropriate probability level as defined in Table II for a given hazard at a given point in time, assess the likelihood of occurrence of a mishap. Probability level F is used to document cases where the hazard is no longer present. No amount of doctrine, training, warning, caution, or Personal Protective Equipment (PPE) can move a mishap probability to level F.

TABLE II. Probability levels

PROBABILITY LEVELS			
Description	Level	Specific Individual Item	Fleet or Inventory
Frequent	A	Likely to occur often in the life of an item.	Continuously experienced.
Probable	B	Will occur several times in the life of an item.	Will occur frequently.
Occasional	C	Likely to occur sometime in the life of an item.	Will occur several times.
Remote	D	Unlikely, but possible to occur in the life of an item.	Unlikely, but can reasonably be expected to occur.
Improbable	E	So unlikely, it can be assumed occurrence may not be experienced in the life of an item.	Unlikely to occur, but possible.
Eliminated	F	Incapable of occurence. This level is used when potential hazards are identified and later eliminated.	Incapable of occurence. This level is used when potential hazards are identified and later eliminated.

Risk Assessment – DOD MIL-STD-882E [1] – Risk Assessment

- Assessed risks are expressed as a Risk Assessment Code (RAC) which is a combination of one severity category and one probability level. For example, a RAC of 1A is the combination of a Catastrophic severity category and a Frequent probability level. Table III assigns a risk level of High, Serious, Medium, or Low for each RAC.

TABLE III. Risk assessment matrix

RISK ASSESSMENT MATRIX				
SEVERITY / PROBABILITY	Catastrophic (1)	Critical (2)	Marginal (3)	Negligible (4)
Frequent (A)	High	High	Serious	Medium
Probable (B)	High	High	Serious	Medium
Occasional (C)	High	Serious	Medium	Low
Remote (D)	Serious	Medium	Medium	Low
Improbable (E)	Medium	Medium	Medium	Low
Eliminated (F)	Eliminated			

Risk Assessment – DOD MIL-STD-882E [1] – SOFTWARE Risk Assessment

- The degree of software control is defined using the Software Control Categories (SCC) in Table IV (or approved tailored alternative).

TABLE IV. Software control categories

SOFTWARE CONTROL CATEGORIES		
Level	Name	Description
1	Autonomous (AT)	• Software functionality that exercises autonomous control authority over potentially safety-significant hardware systems, subsystems, or components without the possibility of predetermined safe detection and intervention by a control entity to preclude the occurrence of a mishap or hazard. *(This definition includes complex system/software functionality with multiple subsystems, interacting parallel processors, multiple interfaces, and safety-critical functions that are time critical.)*
2	Semi-Autonomous (SAT)	• Software functionality that exercises control authority over potentially safety-significant hardware systems, subsystems, or components, allowing time for predetermined safe detection and intervention by independent safety mechanisms to mitigate or control the mishap or hazard. *(This definition includes the control of moderately complex system/software functionality, no parallel processing, or few interfaces, but other safety systems/mechanisms can partially mitigate. System and software fault detection and annunciation notifies the control entity of the need for required safety actions.)* • Software item that displays safety-significant information requiring immediate operator entity to execute a predetermined action for mitigation or control over a mishap or hazard. Software exception, failure, fault, or delay will allow, or fail to prevent, mishap occurrence. *(This definition assumes that the safety-critical display information may be time-critical, but the time available does not exceed the time required for adequate control entity response and hazard control.)*
3	Redundant Fault Tolerant (RFT)	• Software functionality that issues commands over safety-significant hardware systems, subsystems, or components requiring a control entity to complete the command function. The system detection and functional reaction includes redundant, independent fault tolerant mechanisms for each defined hazardous condition. *(This definition assumes that there is adequate fault detection, annunciation, tolerance, and system recovery to prevent the hazard occurrence if software fails, malfunctions, or degrades. There are redundant sources of safety-significant information, and mitigating functionality can respond within any time-critical period.)* • Software that generates information of a safety-critical nature used to make critical decisions. The system includes several redundant, independent fault tolerant mechanisms for each hazardous condition, detection and display.
4	Influential	• Software generates information of a safety-related nature used to make decisions by the operator, but does not require operator action to avoid a mishap.
5	No Safety Impact (NSI)	• Software functionality that does not possess command or control authority over safety-significant hardware systems, subsystems, or components and does not provide safety-significant information. Software does not provide safety-significant or time sensitive data or information that requires control entity interaction. Software does not transport or resolve communication of safety-significant or time sensitive data.

Risk Assessment – DOD MIL-STD-882E [1] – SOFTWARE Risk Assessment

- Software assessments
- Table V provides the Software Safety Criticality Matrix (SSCM) based on Table I severity categories (or approved tailored severity categories) and Table IV SCCs.
- The SSCM establishes the Software Criticality Indices (SwCIs) used to define the required LOR tasks.

TABLE V. Software safety criticality matrix

SOFTWARE SAFETY CRITICALITY MATRIX				
	SEVERITY CATEGORY			
SOFTWARE CONTROL CATEGORY	Catastrophic (1)	Critical (2)	Marginal (3)	Negligible (4)
1	SwCI 1	SwCI 1	SwCI 3	SwCI 4
2	SwCI 1	SwCI 2	SwCI 3	SwCI 4
3	SwCI 2	SwCI 3	SwCI 4	SwCI 4
4	SwCI 3	SwCI 4	SwCI 4	SwCI 4
5	SwCI 5	SwCI 5	SwCI 5	SwCI 5

SwCI	Level of Rigor Tasks
SwCI 1	Program shall perform analysis of requirements, architecture, design, and code; and conduct in-depth safety-specific testing.
SwCI 2	Program shall perform analysis of requirements, architecture, and design; and conduct in-depth safety-specific testing.
SwCI 3	Program shall perform analysis of requirements and architecture; and conduct in-depth safety-specific testing.
SwCI 4	Program shall conduct safety-specific testing.
SwCI 5	Once assessed by safety engineering as Not Safety, then no safety specific analysis or verification is required.

NOTE: Consult the Joint Software Systems Safety Engineering Handbook and AOP 52 for additional guidance on how to conduct required software analyses.

Risk Assessment – DOD MIL-STD-882E [1] – SOFTWARE Risk Assessment

- Table VI provides the relationship between the SwCI, the LOR tasks, and how not meeting the LOR task requirements affects software's contribution to risk

TABLE VI. Relationship between SwCI, risk level, LOR tasks, and risk

RELATIONSHIP BETWEEN SwCI, RISK LEVEL, LOR Tasks, AND RISK		
Software Criticality Index (SwCI)	Risk Level	Software LOR Tasks and Risk Assessment/Acceptance
SwCI 1	High	• If SwCI 1 LOR tasks are unspecified or incomplete, the contributions to system risk will be documented as HIGH and provided to the PM for decision. The PM shall document the decision of whether to expend the resources required to implement SwCI 1 LOR tasks or prepare a formal risk assessment for acceptance of a HIGH risk.
SwCI 2	Serious	• If SwCI 2 LOR tasks are unspecified or incomplete, the contributions to system risk will be documented as SERIOUS and provided to the PM for decision. The PM shall document the decision of whether to expend the resources required to implement SwCI 2 LOR tasks or prepare a formal risk assessment for acceptance of a SERIOUS risk.
SwCI 3	Medium	• If SwCI 3 LOR tasks are unspecified or incomplete, the contributions to system risk will be documented as MEDIUM and provided to the PM for decision. The PM shall document the decision of whether to expend the resources required to implement SwCI 3 LOR tasks or prepare a formal risk assessment for acceptance of a MEDIUM risk.
SwCI 4	Low	• If SwCI 4 LOR tasks are unspecified or incomplete, the contributions to system risk will be documented as LOW and provided to the PM for decision. The PM shall document the decision of whether to expend the resources required to implement SwCI 4 LOR tasks or prepare a formal risk assessment for acceptance of a LOW risk.
SwCI 5	Not Safety	• No safety-specific analyses or testing is required.

RISK ASSESSMENT Summary – COMMON Attributes and Differences

- What do all these things have in common?
  - Separate assessments of severity and likelihood
  - Discrete scale for risk level, not a continuous function
- What is different?
  - How varying levels of severity and likelihood translate to risk level
  - NASA: No formal assessment – intended to influence decision making in a general sense (specifics left to responsible authorities)

Risk Management – NASA Systems Engineering Handbook [2]

6.4 Technical Risk Management

The Technical Risk Management Process is one of the crosscutting technical management processes. Risk is the potential for performance shortfalls, which may be realized in the future, with respect to achieving explicitly established and stated performance requirements. The performance shortfalls may be related to institutional support for mission execution or related to any one or more of the following mission execution domains:

- Safety
- Technical
- Cost
- Schedule

Risk is characterized by three basic components:

1. The scenario(s) leading to degraded performance with respect to one or more performance measures (e.g., scenarios leading to injury, fatality, destruction of key assets; scenarios leading to exceedance of mass limits; scenarios leading to cost overruns; scenarios leading to schedule slippage);
2. The likelihood(s) (qualitative or quantitative) of those scenario(s); and
3. The consequence(s) (qualitative or quantitative severity of the performance degradation) that would result if the scenario(s) was (were) to occur.

Uncertainties are included in the evaluation of likelihoods and consequences.

Risk Management – NASA Systems Engineering Handbook [2]

6.4.1 Risk Management Process Description

Figure 6.4-3 provides a typical flow diagram for the Risk Management Process and identifies typical inputs, activities, and outputs to consider in addressing risk management.

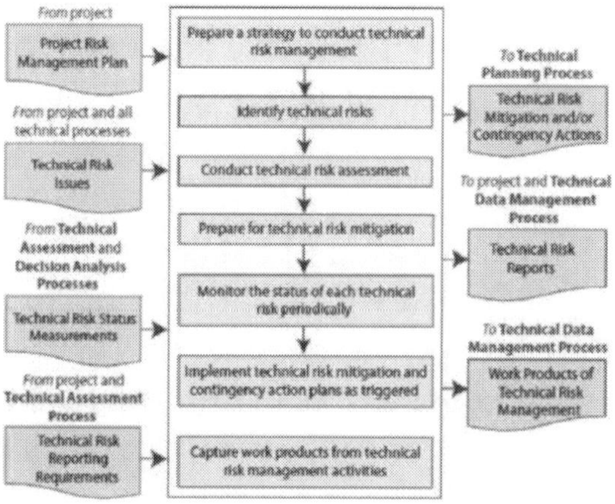

Figure 6.4-3 Risk Management Process

Risk Management – NASA Systems Engineering Handbook [2]

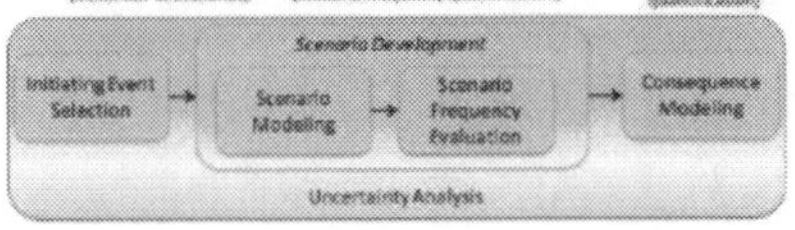

Figure 6.4-1 Risk Scenario Development *(Source: NASA/SP-2011-3421)*

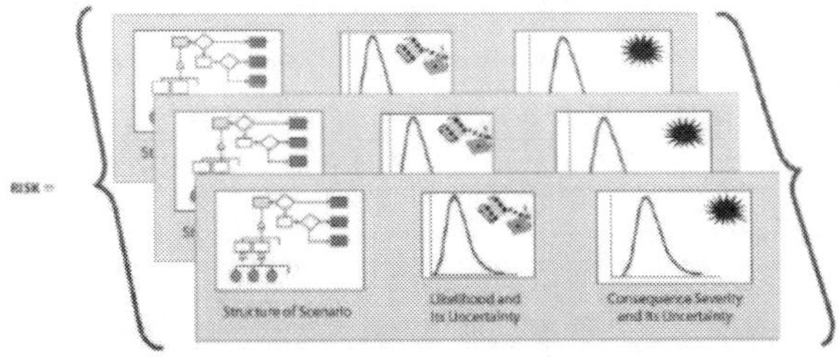

Figure 6.4-2 Risk as an Aggregate Set of Risk Triplets

Undesired scenario(s) might come from technical or programmatic sources (e.g., a cost overrun, schedule slippage, safety mishap, health problem, malicious activities, environmental impact, or failure to achieve a needed scientific or technological objective or success criterion). Both the likelihood and consequences may have associated uncertainties.

Risk Management – NASA System Safety Engineering Handbook [8]

2. Key Concepts

2.1 System Safety, Risk, and Safety Performance

System safety is defined within NASA as the application of engineering and management principles,[1] criteria, and techniques to optimize safety[2] and reduce safety risk within the constraints of operational effectiveness, time, and cost throughout all phases of the system life cycle [6]. System safety is more than just the pursuit of safety performance; it also entails making the case to relevant decision makers that the pursuit of safety performance is on track to be successful throughout the system life cycle.

TERMS PERTAINING TO THE DEFINITION OF SYSTEM SAFETY

- **Safety** – Safety is defined as freedom from those hazards that can result in failure to meet one or more safety objectives by causing death, injury, or illness in humans, adversely affecting the environment, and/or causing damage to or loss of equipment or property.
- **Safety Performance** – In this handbook, safety performance is the complement of the probability of harm, i.e., one minus the probability of adverse safety consequences. Thus, a system need not have perfect safety performance in order to eliminate safety risk; it need only achieve the safety performance specified in the levied safety performance requirements.
- **Safety Performance Requirement** – A safety performance requirement is the specification of a minimum acceptable level of safety performance (i.e., a maximum acceptable value for the probability of harm).
- **Risk** – The use of the term risk in this handbook is consistent with its use in NPR 8000.4A [4], namely that risk is the potential for performance shortfalls, which may be realized in the future, with respect to achieving explicitly established and stated performance requirements in any one or more of the mission execution domains of safety, technical, cost, and schedule.
- **Safety Risk** – Safety risk (sometimes referred to as "safety performance risk") is the potential for shortfalls with respect to safety performance requirements. This differs from the common use of the term risk in a safety context as being the probability of some form of harm (e.g., as expressed by measures such as the probability of loss of crew (LOC), the probability of planetary contamination, or the public casualty expectation). Safety risk only arises to the extent that there is uncertainty as to whether the system's safety performance meets requirements.
- **Risk Burndown** – Risk burndown refers to the expectation that as a program/project evolves over time, mitigations are implemented; and as risk concerns are retired and the state of knowledge about the performance measures improves, uncertainty should decrease, with an attendant lowering of risk.

Risk Management – NASA System Safety Engineering Handbook [8]

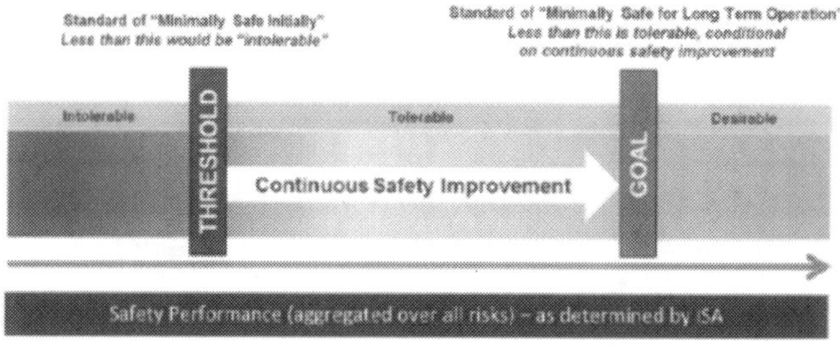

Figure 2-3. Safety Threshold and Safety Goal for a Generic Safety Performance Measure

SAFETY THRESHOLDS AND SAFETY GOALS

Safety Threshold – The level of safety performance against which initial system performance is assessed (i.e., the maximum tolerable probability of harm or loss from all sources of risk when the system is first put into operation)

Safety Goal – A target level of safety performance that is expected from continuous safety upgrades and improvements to the system (i.e., the maximum tolerable probability of harm or loss from all sources of risk when the system has been operational long enough to uncover and correct significant unknown and underappreciated risks)

Risk Management – NASA System Safety Engineering Handbook [8]

2.3.2 Being As Safe As Reasonably Practicable

An adequately safe system is as safe as reasonably practicable (ASARP).[4] A determination that a system is ASARP entails weighing its safety performance against the commitments and tradeoffs needed to further improve it. The system is ASARP if an incremental improvement in safety would require an intolerable or disproportionate deterioration of system performance in other areas. Thus, a system that is ASARP is one where safety is given the highest priority within the constraints of operational effectiveness, time, and cost, throughout all phases of the system life cycle. Figure 2-4, a close adaptation of Figure 3-4 in Volume 1, illustrates the ASARP region for a generic set of alternatives.

Being ASARP is a separate and distinct consideration from meeting a minimum tolerable level of safety. ASARP makes no explicit reference to the absolute value of a system's safety performance or the tolerability of that performance. It is strictly concerned with the system's safety performance relative to a comprehensively identified set of other alternatives. ASARP reflects a mindset that values safety improvement regardless of the current level of safety. It is an integral aspect of a good systems engineering process that guides risk-informed decision making throughout the system life cycle. Correspondingly, the condition of ASARP is demonstrated to some extent through process considerations.

Risk Management – NASA System Safety Engineering Handbook [8]

(A) Large increases in safety can be achieved by addressing low hanging fruit. Little cost/schedule/technical impact for doing so.

(B) Low hanging fruit has been addressed, but significant increases in safety can still be "bought" without failing to meet cost/schedule/technical performance requirements

(C) Limit of ASARP regime has been reached. Increased safety cannot be "bought" without exceeding tolerable limits of cost/schedule/technical performance

(D) Limit of achievable safety has been reached. Increased safety cannot be "bought" at any cost.

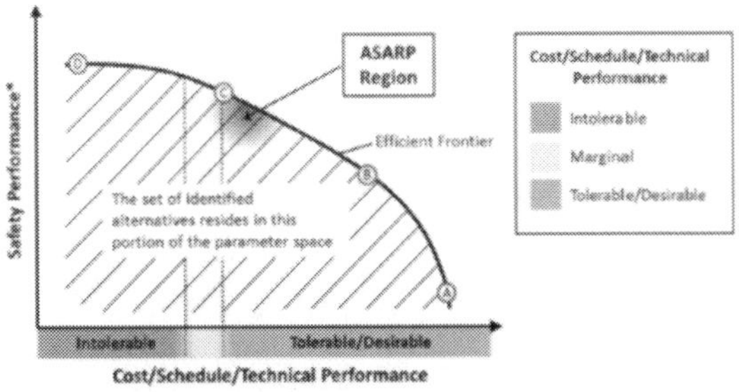

Figure 2-4. As Safe As Reasonably Practicable (ASARP)

[4] The ASARP concept is closely related to the "as low as reasonably achievable" (ALARA) and "as low as reasonably practicable" (ALARP) concepts that are common in U.S. nuclear applications and U.K. Health and Safety law, respectively [9, 10].

Risk Management – NASA System Safety Engineering Handbook [8]

2.3.3 State of the System with Respect to Adequate Safety

Table 2-1 illustrates the four possible states of a system with respect to adequate safety, based on whether or not it meets the minimum tolerable level of safety and whether or not it is ASARP.

Table 2-1. Possible Combinations of Meeting the Minimum Tolerable Level of Safety and Being ASARP

System is ASARP?	System meets minimum tolerable level of safety? Yes	System meets minimum tolerable level of safety? No
Yes	System is adequately safe	System is inherently unsafe
No	System is sub-optimally safe as designed	System is unsafe as designed

Risk Management – NASA System Safety Engineering Handbook [8]

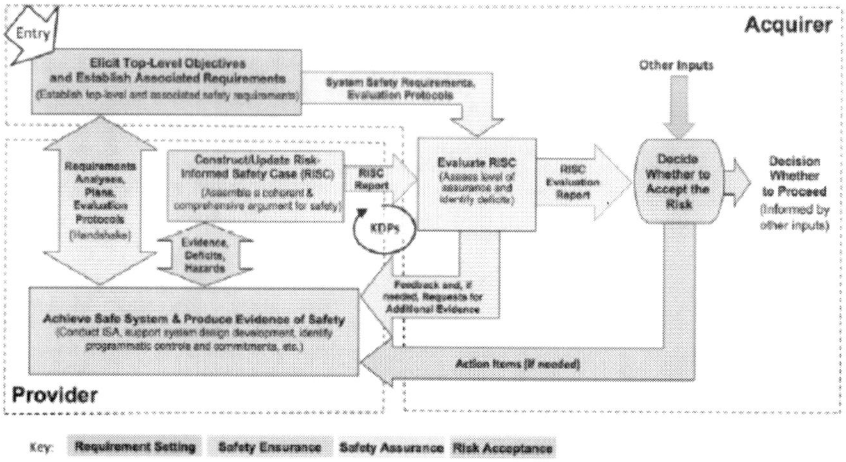

Figure 3-1. The NASA System Safety Framework

Risk Management – INCOSE Systems Engineering Handbook [9]

- States the purpose of a Risk Management process is to identify, analyze, treat, and monitor the risks continually
- Should be applied with understanding of risk management approaches sufficient, consistent, and appropriate to specific context, scope, and objectives of the targeted application
- Defines Risk Management as a disciplined approach for dealing with the uncertainty present throughout entire life cycle
- List of Risk Management activities
  - Plan risk management
  - Manage the risk profile
  - Analyze risk
  - Treat risks
  - Monitor risks

Risk Management – FAA System Safety Handbook [5]

➢ **15.6 Acceptability of Risk**

Risk management requires a clear understanding of what constitutes unnecessary risk, i.e., when benefits actually outweigh costs. Accepting risk is a function of both risk assessment and risk management, and is not as simple a matter as it may first appear. Several principles apply:

- Some degree of risk is a fundamental reality
- Risk management is a process of tradeoffs
- Quantifying risk does not in itself ensure safety
- Risk is often a matter of perspective
- Realistically, some risk must be accepted. How much is accepted, or not accepted, is the prerogative of the defined decision authority. That decision is affected by many inputs. As tradeoffs are considered and operation planning progresses, it may become evident that some of the safety parameters are forcing higher risk to successful operation completion. When a manager decides to accept risk, the decision should be coordinated whenever practical with the affected personnel and organizations, and then documented so that in the future everyone will know and understand the elements of the decision and why it was made.

Risk Management – FAA System Safety Handbook [5]

15.7 General Risk Management Guidelines

- All human activity involving technical devices or complex processes entails some element of risk.
- Hazards can be controlled; they are not a cause for panic.
- Problems should be kept in perspective.
- Judgments should be based upon knowledge, experience and mission requirements.
- Encouraging all participants in an operation to adopt risk management principles both reduces risk and makes the task of reducing it easier.
- Good analysis tilts the odds in favor of safe and successful operation.
- Hazard analysis and risk assessment do not replace good judgment: they improve it.
- Establishing clear objectives and parameters in risk management works better than using cookbook approach
- No one best solution may exist. Normally, there are a variety of alternatives, each of which may produce a different degree of risk reduction.
- Tact is essential. It is more productive to show a mission planner how he can better manage risk than to condemn his approach as unworkable, risky, unsafe or unsound.
- Seldom can complete safety be achieved.
- There are no "safety problems" in planning or design, only management problems that may cause accidents, if left unresolved.

Risk Management – FAA System Safety Handbook [5]

15.8 Risk Management Responsibilities

15.8.1 Managers

- Are responsible for effective management of risk.
- Select from risk reduction options recommended by staff.
- Accept or reject risk based upon the benefit to be derived.
- Train and motivate personnel to use risk management techniques.
- Elevate decisions to a higher level when it is appropriate.

15.8.2 Staff

- Assess risks and develop risk reduction alternatives.
- Integrate risk controls into plans and orders.
- Identify unnecessary risk controls.

15.8.3 Supervisors

- Apply the risk management process
- Consistently apply effective risk management concepts and methods to operations and tasks.
- Elevate risk issues beyond their control or authority to superiors for resolution.

15.8.4 Individuals

- Understand, accept and implement risk management processes.
- Maintain a constant awareness of the changing risks associated with the operation or task.
- Make supervisors immediately aware of any unrealistic risk reduction measures or high-risk procedures.

Food & Drug Administration (FDA) – Safety Perspective [10]

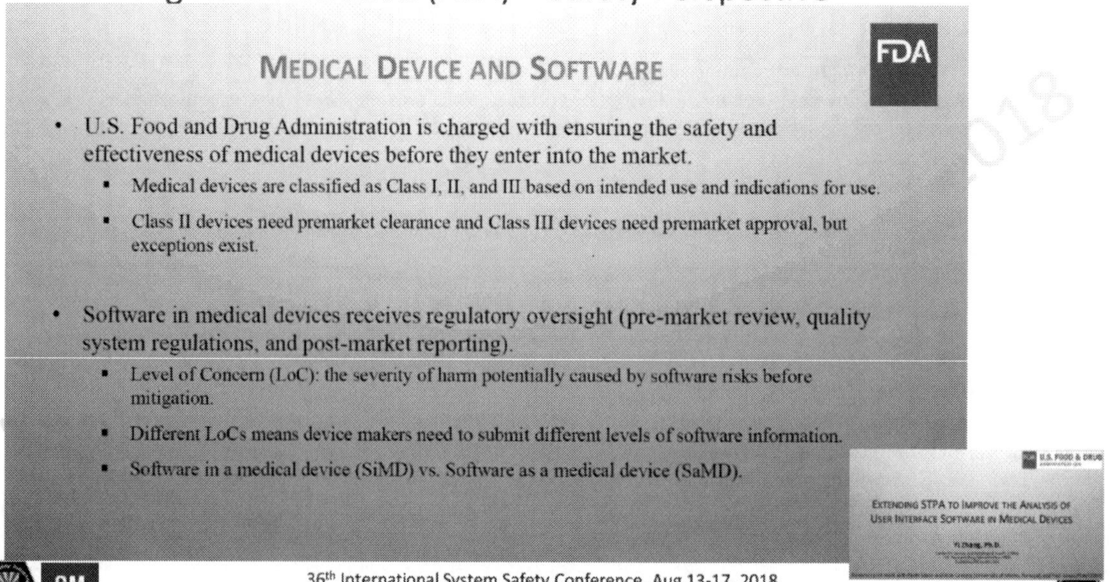

Food & Drug Administration (FDA) – Safety Perspective [10]

FDA

Medical Device Use Errors

- **Use Error:**
  User action or lack of user action while using the medical device that leads to a different result than that intended by the manufacturer or expected by the user. (IEC 62366)
- **Use Error or User Error?**
  [Use Error] was chosen over ... "human error" because not all errors associated with the use of medical device are the result of oversight or carelessness of the part of the user of the medical device. Much more commonly, <u>use errors are the direct result of poor user interface design.</u>" (IEC 62366)

Food & Drug Administration (FDA) – Safety Perspective [10]

FDA

Risk Management Process for Medical Devices

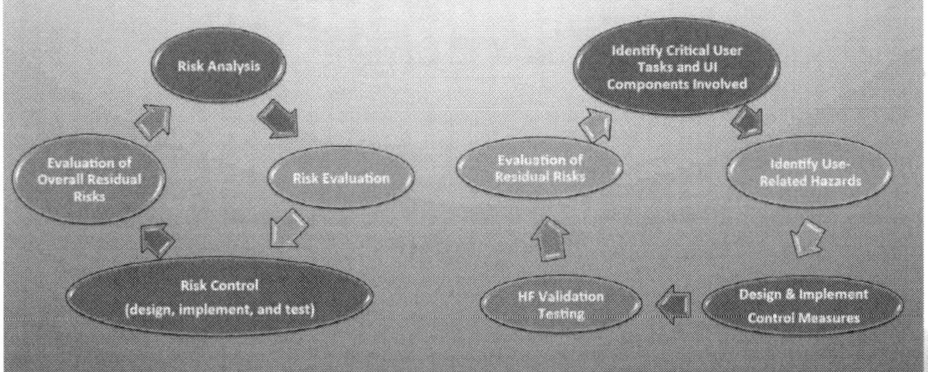

Risk Management Process Defined in ISO 14971

Risk Management Process for Use-Related Hazards Recommended by FDA's HF Guidance

Risk Management – ISO-26262 [4] Risk Management

- ISO-26262 outlines risk management as part of the larger safety management umbrella.
- Presents two safety management objectives:
  - Define the safety management roles and responsibilities
  - Define requirements for safety management during all safety phases of program
- Performance of:
  - confirmation reviews to check compliance of selected work products to corresponding requirements
  - functional safety audits to evaluate the implementation of supporting processes of safety activities
  - functional safety assessments to evaluate the achieved safety level
- Verification that work products required by the safety process have been satisfactorily completed

Risk Management Summary – COMMON Attributes and Differences

- What do all these things have in common?
  - Risk management is part of the engineering process
  - Occurs concurrently with product design
- What is different?
  - How final risk level is determined to be acceptable or not (e.g., responsible authority sign-off)

Being Part of the Engineering Process – Helpful Aspects / Attributes

- Understand and employ "Systems Thinking"
- Utilize Systems Engineering methods and techniques for system balance and optimization
- Be an integrated part of engineering teams
- Understand Stakeholder Expectations and initial Program Requirements
- Look for emergent behaviors at the system level due to interactions
- Don't confuse interactions with interfaces
- Educate program design team members in regards to system safety
- Execute safety risk assessment and risk management evaluations with program engineers as task members

Integrated Process Approach to System Design

- Use of an integrated design and development process that considers all elements of the system lifecycle needs to be recognized
- Items to consider would include performance requirements, safety impact, quality, cost, timing, requirements, manufacturing capabilities, support services, and long term disposal to name a few
- For example, INCOSE recognizes that risks in concurrent product development are reduced by using an integrated product team approach rather than traditional top down management structures
- Other methodologies prioritize this approach such as the graphics shown on the next slide from the NASA Systems Engineering Handbook

Systems Engineering – Architecture Development Methodology

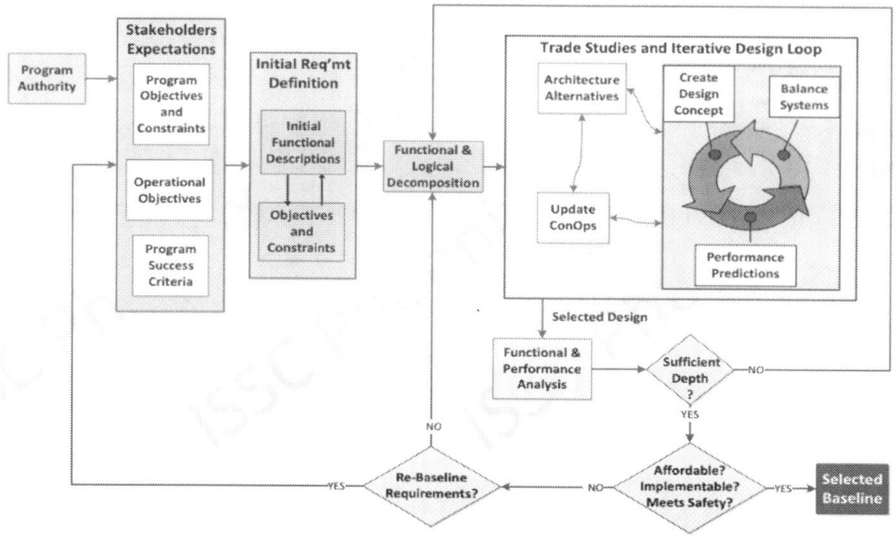

Figure 4.0-1 Interrelationships among the system design processes
Modified – Mark V
NASA Systems Engineering Handbook • 31

System, Architecture, and Concept Definitions For "Balance"

System: *a set of elements which, working together, produce a desired result not achievable by the elements alone.* Systems are evaluate from multiple perspectives (e.g., Functional, Performance, QRD, Safety, etc.). Systems may be developed (modeled) at different levels with one group's "system" being an "element" within another group's system.

Architecture: *the overall structure and interactions of the elements of a system.* Architectures may represent various perspectives of the system including functional and physical, or a combination of the two. The architecture represents how the system elements are arranged relative to each other and provides the structure within which they interact to provide desired results.

Concept: *an idea of what something is or how it works.* Concepts are used to lay out how different elements and their functions need to interact and how physical arrangements need to be constructed to achieve desired results.

System Engineering – Architecture Development Methodology

- Stakeholder Expectation Determination
- Initial Requirements Identification
- *Architecture Development and Modifications* ***Iterative Activities***
- *Balance, Trade Studies, Optimization Activities Between Functional Domain Elements and then Up-Level System(s)*
- *Analysis Verification (Functional, Performance, and Safety)*
- *Program Validation Against Stakeholder Expectations with Balanced System Architecture (May include expectation modifications)*
- System Architecture Selection

Systems Engineering – Architecture Development Methodology

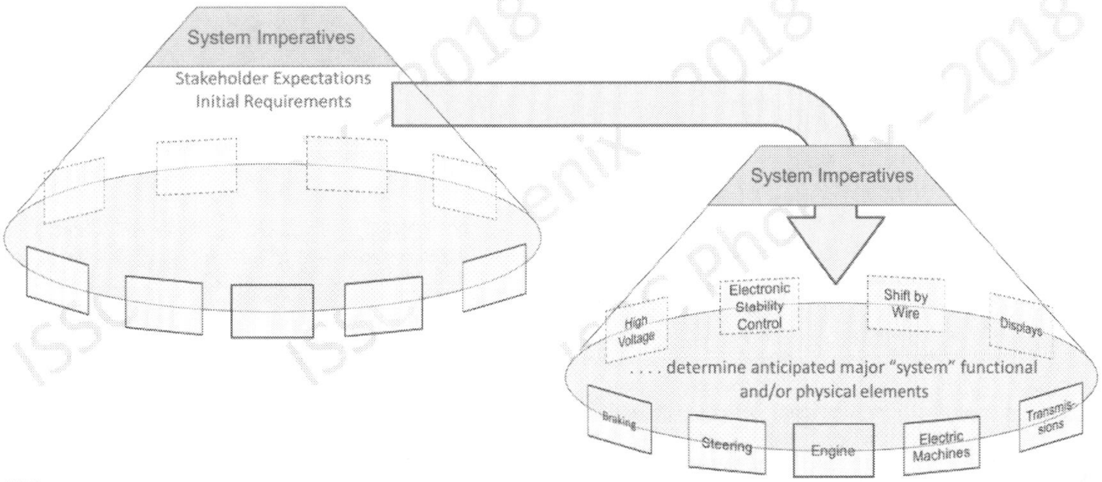

Systems Engineering – Architecture Development Methodology

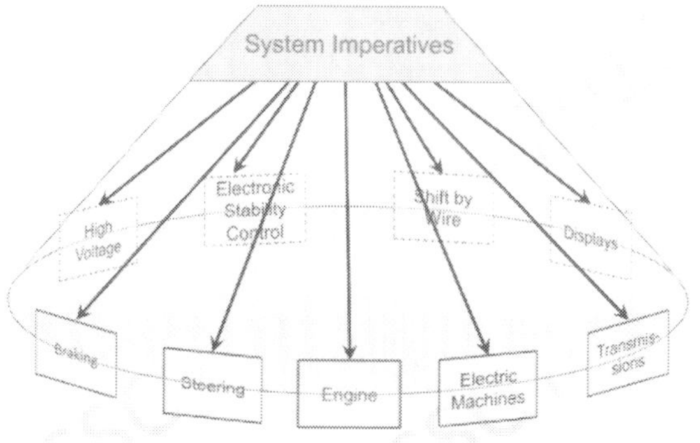

- Stakeholder Expectation Determination
- Initial Requirements Identification

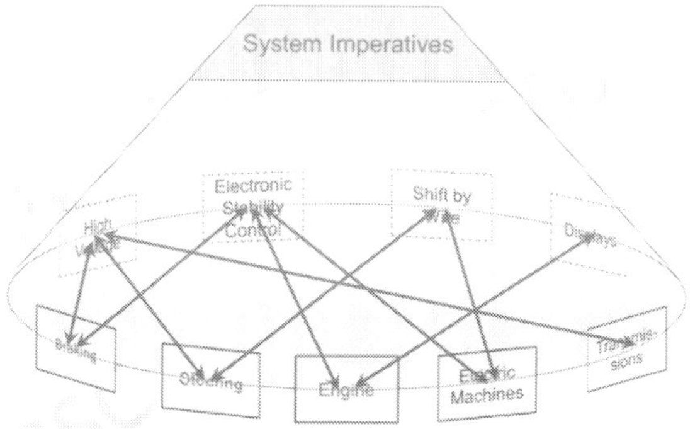

- Architecture Development and Modifications
- Balance, Trade Studies, Optimization Activities Between Functional Domain Elements

Systems Engineering – Architecture Development Methodology

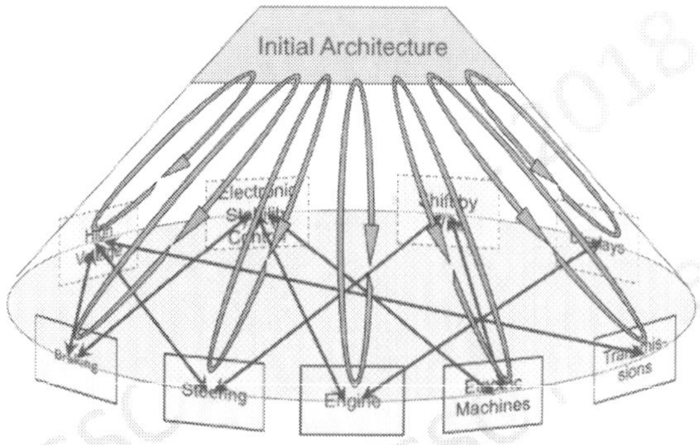

- Architecture Development and Modifications
- Balance, Trade Studies, Optimization Activities Between Functional Domain Elements and Up-Level System
- System Verification (Functional, Performance, and Safety)

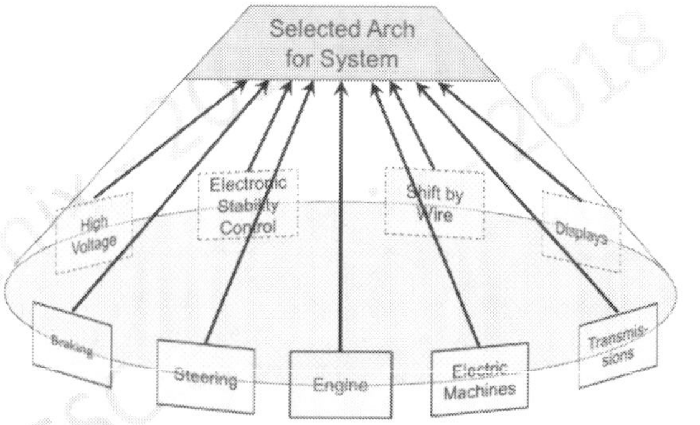

- Program Validation Against Stakeholder Expectations with Balanced System Architecture (May include expectation modifications)
- System Architecture Selection (Behavioral Perspective)

Systems Engineering – Architecture Development Methodology

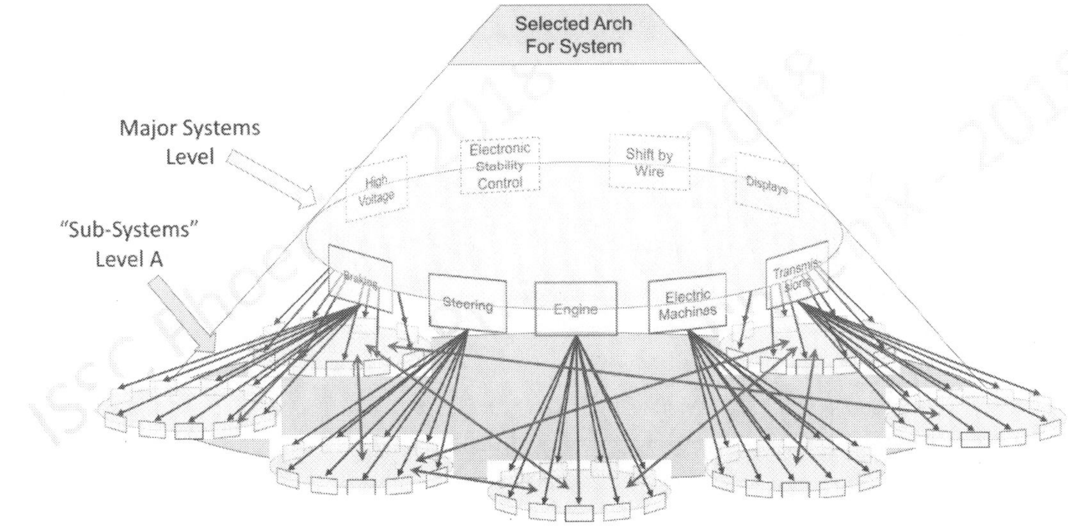

36th International System Safety Conference, Aug 13-17, 2018

57

Systems Engineering – Architecture Development Methodology

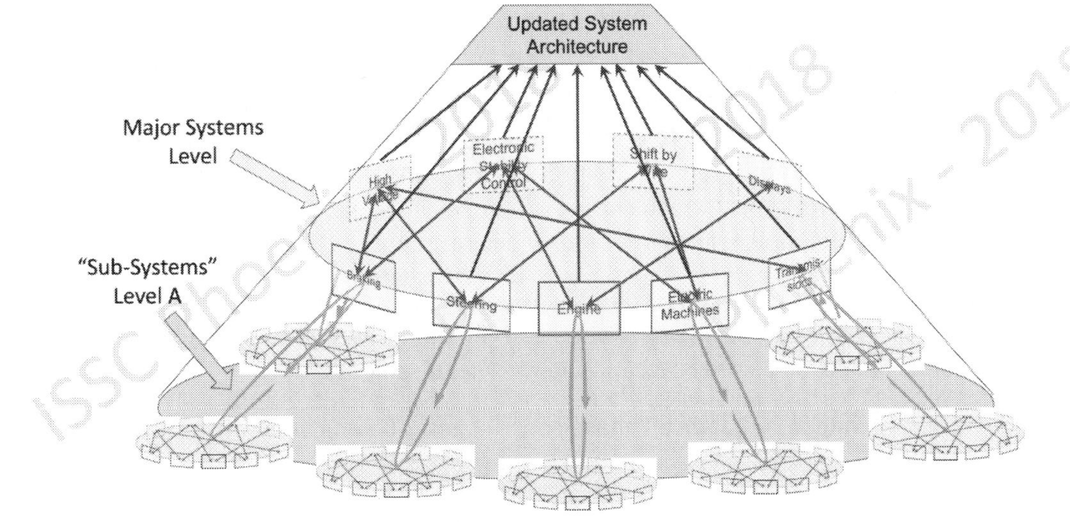

36th International System Safety Conference, Aug 13-17, 2018

58

Systems Engineering – Architecture Development Methodology

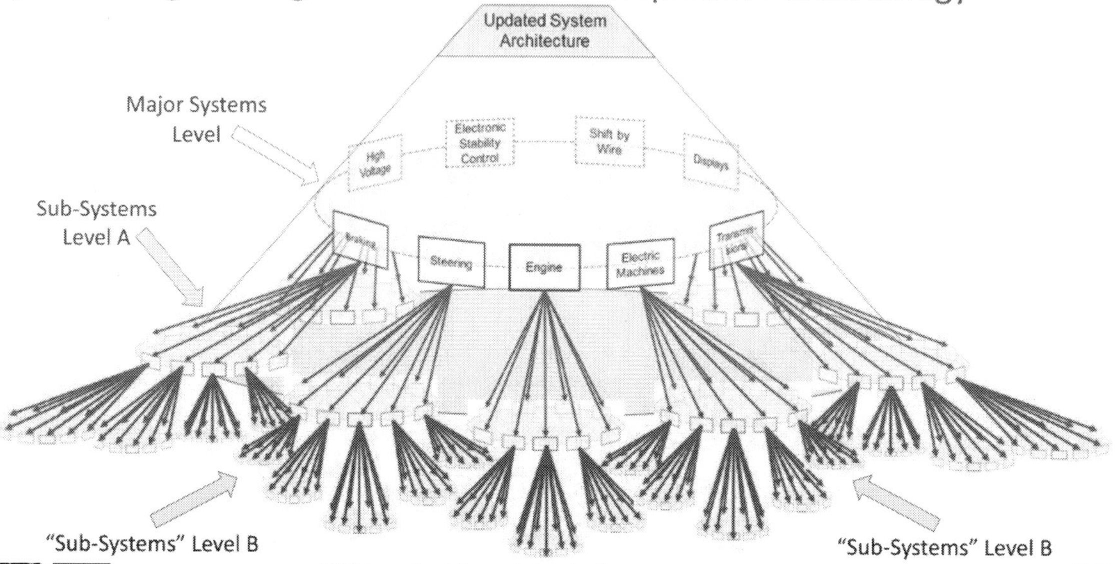

System Balance and Optimization - Systems Engineering Summary

- Effective safety analysis methods provide value through the entire engineering design, development, testing and manufacturing phases of a system's implementation process.
- These analysis methods have a significant impact on system content in early phases of a program as major expenditures for critical component procurements and manufacturing tooling have yet to be committed. There is much less cost associated with design changes at this point in the process than there are with changes that occur later in the process (e.g., it is much cheaper to move lines on paper than it is to move/change actual tooling lines in a factory environment).
- Early in the design process, exploration of various design concepts is conducted to determine the optimized balance between system imperatives such as cost, timing, mass, performance, and safety "acceptable risk" requirements.
- This "system architecture balance" phase contains tasks having an iterative nature between them

System Balance and Optimization - Systems Engineering Summary

- Incorporating safety evaluations this early in the process enables changes to be made to system architecture and to functional interactions within minimal cost and timing impact
- Balance and optimization tasks are iterative where a system element may be "sub-optimized" to enable a more effective system design. Optimizing all system elements tends to drive unnecessary cost and timing into the overall solution.
- Safety risk assessment is integrated directly into the initial system design
- Decision for "level of acceptable risk" (risk management) becomes part of this early system architecture development

System Safety Analysis – Initial Topics

- System Level Analysis Advantages
  - Systems thinking focuses on how system interacts with other constituents in system instead of viewing the system/elements in isolation
  - Allows comprehension of interactions between systems
    - A safe state for one system does not necessarily mean it is a safe state for the other
  - Allows risk assessment to consider dependencies between systems
    - Risk can be different when viewed from a top level considering the various interactions and dependencies between systems
- Systems approach treats safety as an <u>emergent</u> property that arises when system components interact within an environment *

* Nancy. Leveson- System Safety Engineering: Back To The Future, 2008

System Engineering "V" Model

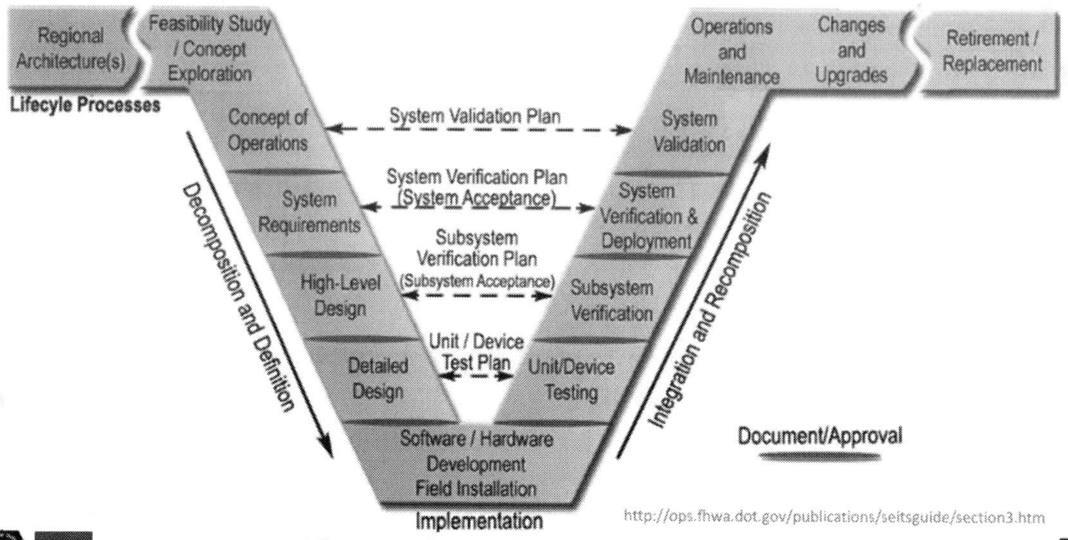

http://ops.fhwa.dot.gov/publications/seitsguide/section3.htm

36th International System Safety Conference, Aug 13-17, 2018

System Engineering "V" Model with Safety Phases

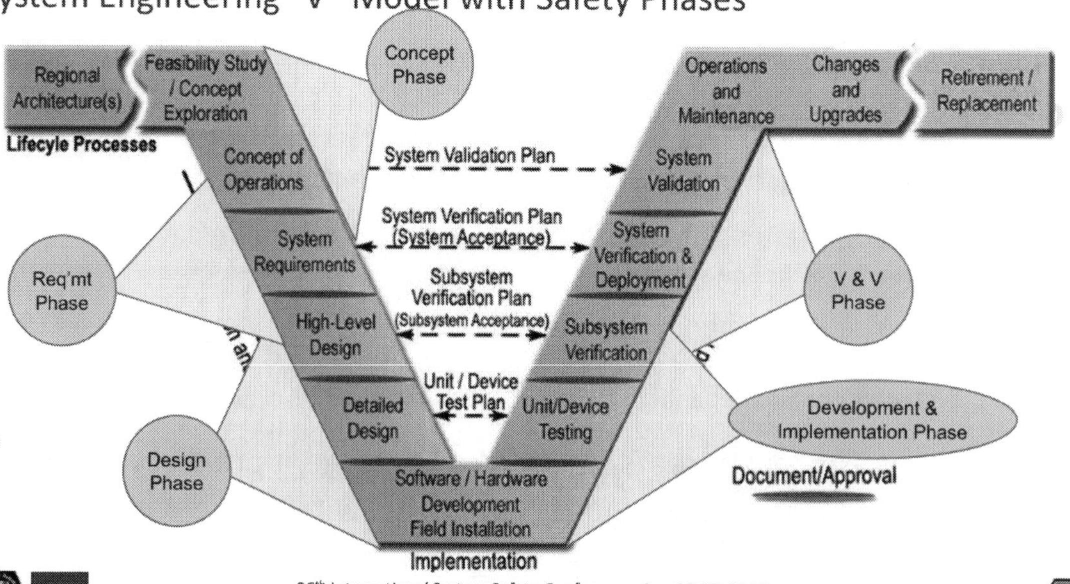

36th International System Safety Conference, Aug 13-17, 2018

Typical "Waterfall" Model Safety Tasks by Phases

Preliminary Hazard Analysis
System Safety Program Planning
System Element Fault Analysis
Systems-Theoretic Process Analysis
System Safety Concept
Safety Concept Review
Safety Functional Interface Analysis
Hazard Translation Metric
Safety Requirements (RTM)
Safety V&V Planning
Safety Requirements Review
System / Component DFMEA
System Level Fault Tree Analysis
Common Cause Failure Analysis
Refine / Update Safety Requirements
Safety V&V Plan Update
System Technical Safety Concept Update
Safety Design Solution Review
Software Fault Tree Analysis
Software Detailed FMEA
Software Code Reviews
Closure of FTA / FMEA Issues
Safety Verification / Validation
Component, Sub-system, System, Vehicle
FTA & DFMEA Verification
System Safety Report & Assessment
Production Safety Design & Test Review

Safety Phases Activities According to Program Timing

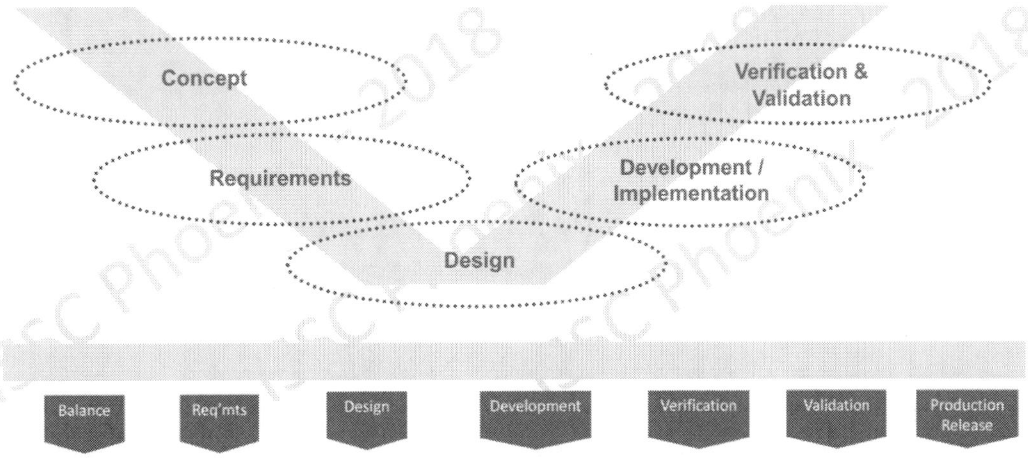

Realistic Iterative Model Safety Tasks by Phases

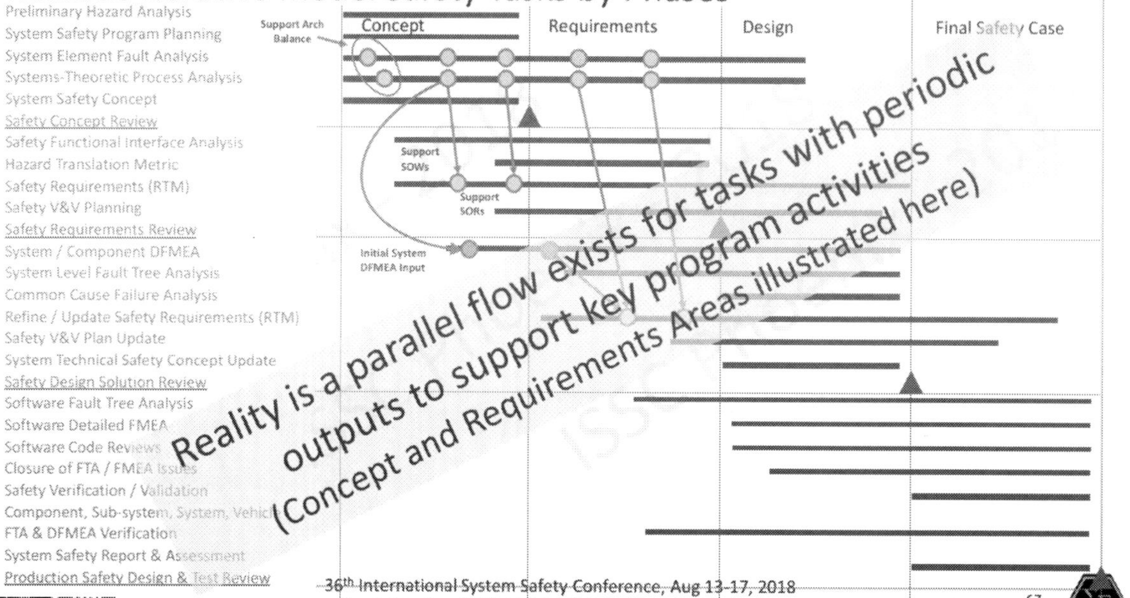

Initial Activity - Define System Scope and Content

- ➢ Identify major systems and the interfaces between these systems
- ➢ Identify the safety-critical systems
- ➢ Determine scope boundary for desired safety evaluation

GM

System Safety Engineer Questions

- What is the goal or mission of the system?
- What does the system look like from architecture or controls structure perspective?
- Is there an operational description of the system's expected functions, capabilities and interactions with other systems, users, and human operators?
- What are the required and expected functions for each of the system elements?
- What happens to the system when a system element fails or misbehaves?
- Does the resulting system behavior create potentially hazardous situations?
- What are the risks and risk assessment associated with these potential hazards?
- Which part of the system assumes the failed/misbehaving element's functions?

System Safety Engineer Questions

- What are the resulting system capabilities after the failure/misbehavior?
- Do these resulting system capabilities create any potentially hazardous situations?
- Are these resulting system capabilities sufficient to achieving system goals/missions?
- What are required diagnostic strategies & rigor level necessary to detect failures and/or system/element misbehaviors?
- What are the mitigation strategies and actions necessary to transition the system from a detected failed/misbehaving state to a known acceptable safe state?
- Based on the severity and exposure factors of the risk assessment (and potential operator controllability where applicable), is residual risk acceptable?

System Analysis Methodologies

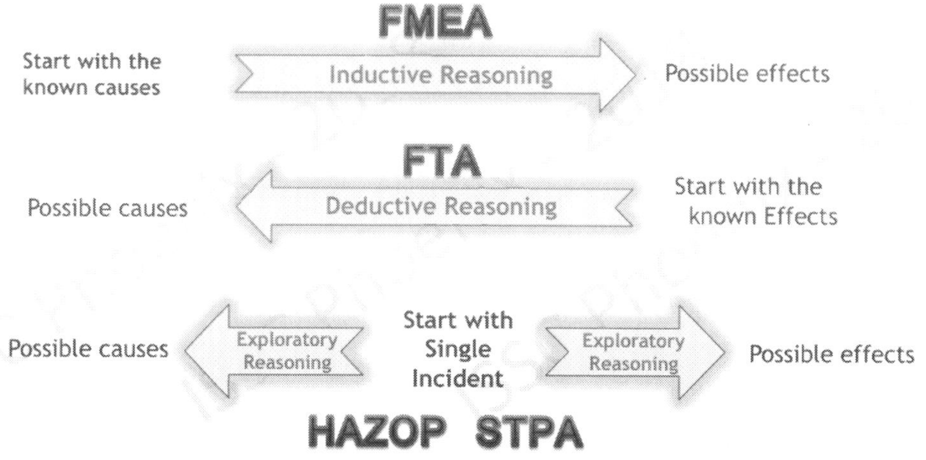

System Analysis Methodologies

		Causes: Unknown	Causes: Known
Effects	Unknown	*Exploratory Analysis*	*Inductive Analysis*
	Known	*Deductive Analysis*	*Descriptive Analysis*

- Deductive Analysis (e.g., FTA)
- Inductive Analysis (e.g., FMEA, Interface Analysis, Sneak Circuit Analysis)
- Exploratory Analysis (e.g., HAZOP, what-if, STPA)
- Descriptive Analysis (relatively straight forward observations)

Interface vs Interaction

- Interface
  - When there is some kind of direct data/info transfer and/or communication between two systems or system elements within a system
- Interaction
  - When a system state affects or influences one or more vehicle systems, or system elements, even if they may not be connected or communicating with each other
    - Impact may be due to physics, vehicle design/configuration, and/or architectural design dependencies

Activities Associated with System Analysis

- System level fault analysis of the subsystems, controllers and modules can support identification of critical components of the system
- Determine how system will behave when different portions of the system fail under different operating scenarios
  - Performed at a high level (system vs. component)
  - Fail one entity at a time and determine effect on system
- Determine how system will behave under different operating scenarios
  - Engine provided vs. electric machine provided propulsion modes
  - Park vs. Reverse vs. Neutral vs. Drive
- Define safety hazards that may appear when fault(s) occur
- Outline the initial diagnostic and mitigation strategies
- Define the resulting "safe" system state
- Identify the need for additional sensors, diagnostic SW, or required changes to system safety strategy so that critical component faults do not lead to potential safety hazards

System Thinking and SEFA - Overview

System Element Fault Analysis (SEFA)

- Utilizes System Thinking - Focus on system taken as a whole, not on parts taken separately
- SEFA is a technique used to identify the impact of individual system element failures upon the system as a whole
- SEFA can be conducted on system elements such as actuators, motors, sensors and clutches, as well as functional elements
- Controllers can be included in the SEFA and treated as one element
- SEFA's are not very useful for software analysis as Software analysis conducted with Functional Interface Analysis & SW DFMEA's

SEFA Overview

- SEFA is a methodical review of the potential errors and/or faults of system elements
- SEFA analysis is based on a system architecture design and assists in understanding flaws within the design
- SEFA typically used at "system" level versus "feature" level but may be useful if the "feature" has a number of interactions between other "features" or "systems"

SEFA Overview

- SEFA results are used to:
  - Develop diagnostic and mitigation strategies
  - Identify initial system requirements necessary to mitigate system behavior caused by system element faults
  - Assess recovered states after system element fault
  - Identify changes to system architecture to ensure adequate diagnostic capability prior to the system design freeze

System SEFA – Hybrid Propulsion System Example

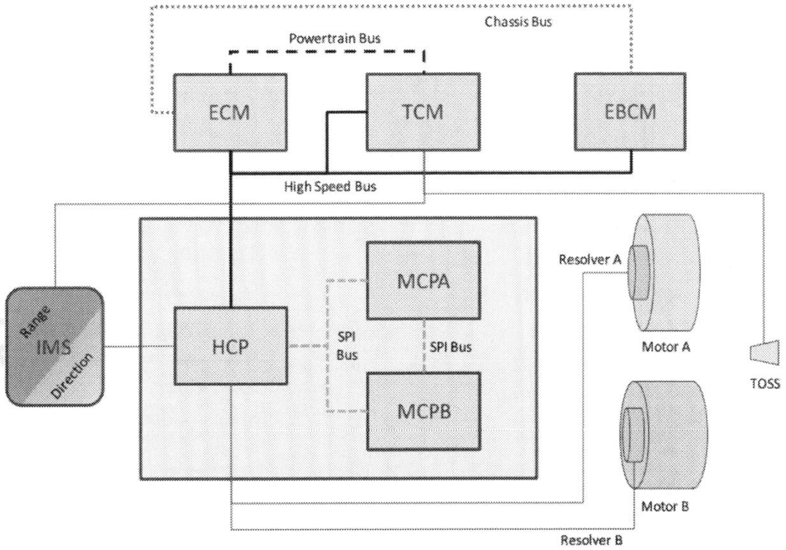

System SEFA – Hybrid Propulsion System Example

Item Number	Multiple Ranges (P,R,N,D)	Function(s) (Responsibilities)	ECM	HCP	MCP1	MCP2	TCM	EBCM	Direction IMS	Range IMS	TOSS	Motor A Resolver	Motor B Resolver	Impact of Element Fault (Impact prior to any remedial or mitigation actions)	Immediate Resulting State (State of the system prior to any remedial or mitigation actions)
			PRIMARY Fault						RESULTING Fault						
	Normal Operation	Provide Propulsion in an Electric Vehicle	1	1	1	1	1	1	1	1	1	1	1	NORMAL OPERATION	Selected Range
1	ECM	* Read accelerator pedal inputs * Determine req'd torque based on driving condition and accel pedal input * Provide EBCM with Regen Braking Capacity * Performs plausiblity check btw HCP and TCM IMS inputs	0	1	1	1	1	1	0	1	1	1	1	Engine not available or shuts <OFF>	Park - Park Reverse - Reverse Neutral - Neutral Drive - Possible Acceleration
2	HCP	* Determines torque and commands MCPs * Reads Motor Resolver inputs * Reads IMS Direction input * Provides IMS Direction to ECM	1	0	1	1	1	1	1	1	1	0	0	IMS info to HCP not evaluated Loss of Motor Resolver info	Park - Park Reverse - Reverse Neutral - Neutral Drive - Possible Acceleration
3	MCP1	* Commands torque to Motor A * Provides MPM function to HCP	1	1	0	1	1	1	1	1	1	0	1	Motor 1 shuts down	Park - Park Reverse - Possible Decel Neutral - No Issue Drive - Possible Acceleration
4	MCP2	* Commands torque to Motor B * Provides MPM function to HCP	1	1	1	0	1	1	1	1	1	1	0	Motor 2 shuts down	Park - Park Reverse - Possible Accel Neutral - No Issue Drive - Possible Deceleration

System SEFA – Hybrid Propulsion System Example

Item Number	Multiple Ranges (P,R,N,D)	Potential Safety Hazard(s)	Diagnostic Method(s)	Mitigation Action(s)	System State After Mitigation	SAFETY Requirements
	Normal Operation	NONE	NONE	NONE	NONE	NONE
1	ECM	**Loss of Propulsion**	Lack of ECM communication detected by HCP and TCM	Set MIL light and go to reduced power	Reduced Propulsion	* System shall move to reduced propulsion when ECM fails * TCM and HCP shall detect ECM loss using CAN diagnostics
2	HCP	**Unintended Propulsion <OR> Unintended Direction**	TCM and ECM detect loss of HCP. IMS info from TCM used for Driver intent MCPs detect HCL loss.	Set MIL light and go to reduced power	Reduced Propulsion	* ECM shall set DTC and instruct BCM to display driver message * ECM shall default to TCM IMS info * MCPs shall limit mtr torques to RP * The system shall transition to RP without violating the Unintended Direction & Unintended Prop Engagement metric * The system shall provide ASIL D hardware design integrity
3	MCP1	**Unintended Accel <OR> Unintended Deceleration**	HCP and MCP2 detect loss of MCP1	Command TCM to go to Mode 2	Mode 2 (High Speed) Acceleration may be affected at low speeds or launch	* System shall allow Motor A to free-wheel when MCP1 is lost * System shall tranistion to Mode 2 when MCP1 is lost without violating the Unintended Direction & Unintended Prop Engagement metric * HCP shall inform ECM of Mode 2 * ECM shall command BCM to display RP message * The system shall provide ASIL D hardware design integrity
4	MCP2	**Unintended Accel <OR> Unintended Deceleration**	HCP and MCP1 detect loss of MCP2	Command TCM to go to Mode 1	Mode 1 (Low Speed) Top speed may be loss than normal operation	* System shall allow Motor B to free-wheel when MCP2 is lost * System shall tranistion to Mode 1 when MCP2 is lost without violating the Unintended Direction & Unintended Prop Engagement metric * HCP shall inform ECM of Mode 1 * ECM shall command BCM to display limited speed message * The system shall provide ASIL D hardware design integrity

Systems-Theoretic Process Analysis (STPA) Overview

- Identify accidents (potential losses)
- Identify hazards (unsafe system states)
- Generate safety constraints (safety requirements)
- Build model of control structure. Identify:
  - Responsibilities for each component
  - Control actions which can be provided
  - Process model variables (for controlled process)

"Engineering a Safer and More Secure World" Prof. Nancy Leveson - MIT

STPA Methodology Review

STPA
(System-Theoretic Process Analysis)

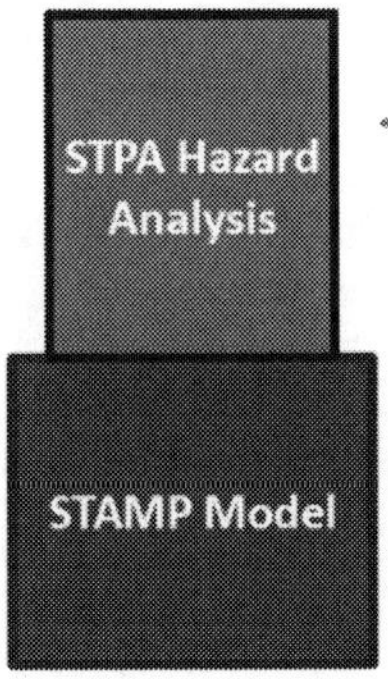

- System engineering foundation
  - Define accidents, hazards, constraints
  - Control structure
- Step 1: Identify unsafe control actions
- Step 2: Identify accident causal scenarios

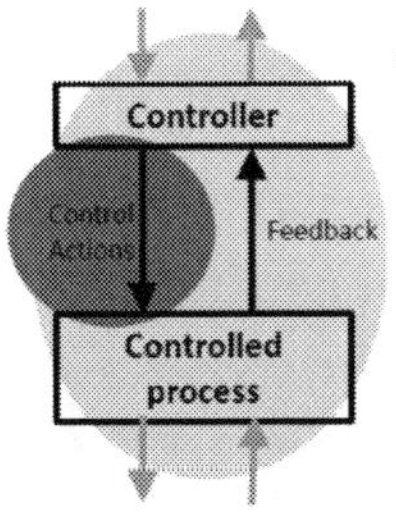

(Leveson, 2012) © Copyright John Thomas 2014

Generic Control Structure

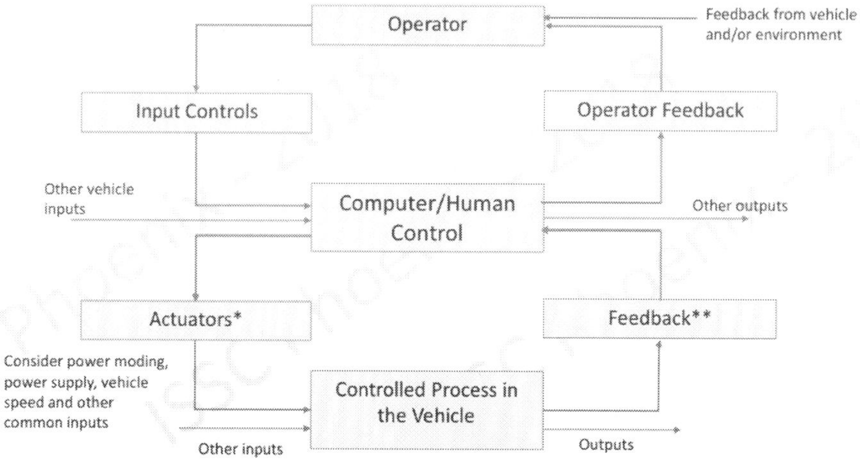

*** Actuator control can be manual and/or electrical/electronic based**
**** Feedback can be tactile/perceptible and/or electrical/electronic based**

STPA Step 1

- Define Unsafe Control Actions (UCA) by using guidewords such as:
  - Not Provided
  - Provided but Leads to Hazardous State
  - Too Early, Too Late, Wrong Time, Wrong Sequence
  - Stopped Too Soon, Applied Too Long
- Identify potential causal scenarios for each UCA
- Define design constraints (requirements) to prevent and/or minimize potential causes

	"NOT Providing" Cause Hazard	"Providing" Cause Hazard	Incorrect Timing Incorrect Order	Stopped Too Soon Applied Too Long
Suggested Helpful Words	Missing Not Followed	Provided More/Less than Required Provided Content Results in Contol Conflict	Provided Too Early/Late When Required Provided Before/After When Required Provided Content in Wrong Order Provided Opposite of What Expected	Providing Instable or Osscilating Content Providing Truncated Content Providing Stuck Content

STPA Step 2

Solution: Start with high-level abstract scenarios and refine them!

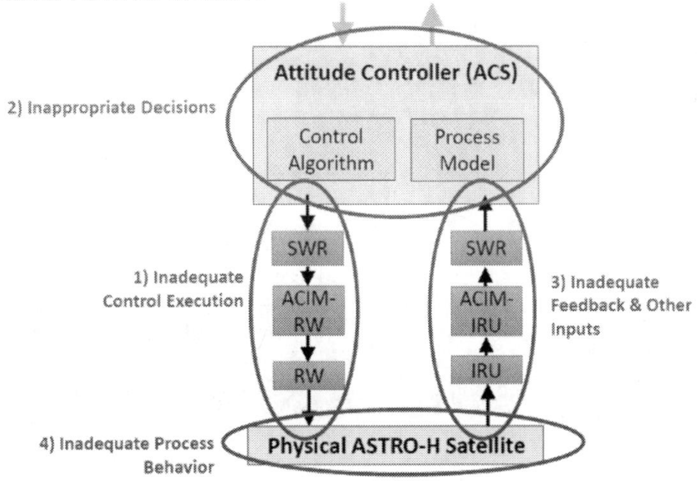

Summary STPA Analysis

- Develop Controls Structure and select detail level
- Identify functions of system elements
- Define Unsafe Control Actions (UCA) by using guidewords such as:
  - Not Provided
  - Provided but Incorrect
  - Too Early, Too Late, Wrong Time, Wrong Sequence
  - Stopped Too Soon, Applied Too Long
- Develop potential causal scenarios for each UCA
- Define design requirements to prevent and/or minimize potential hazards due to causal scenarios

System Safety Strategy Determination Contributors

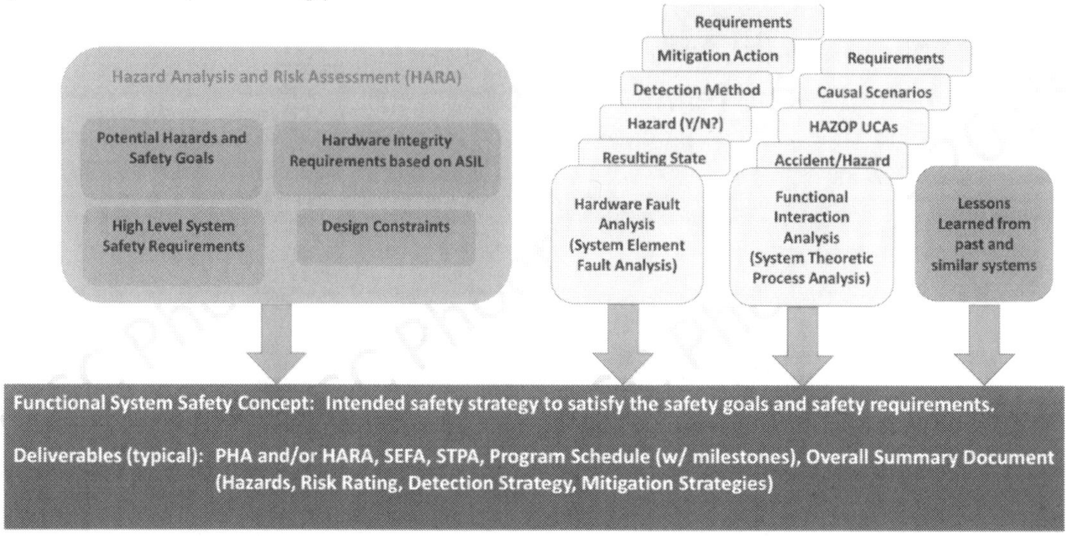

Allocate Safety Requirements to Engineering and Sourcing Documents

- Determine which engineering groups need to know about these requirements
- Communicate the requirements to these groups
- Confirm requirements have been accommodated in external sourcing documents and internal engineering specifications

Requirement Summary and Allocation

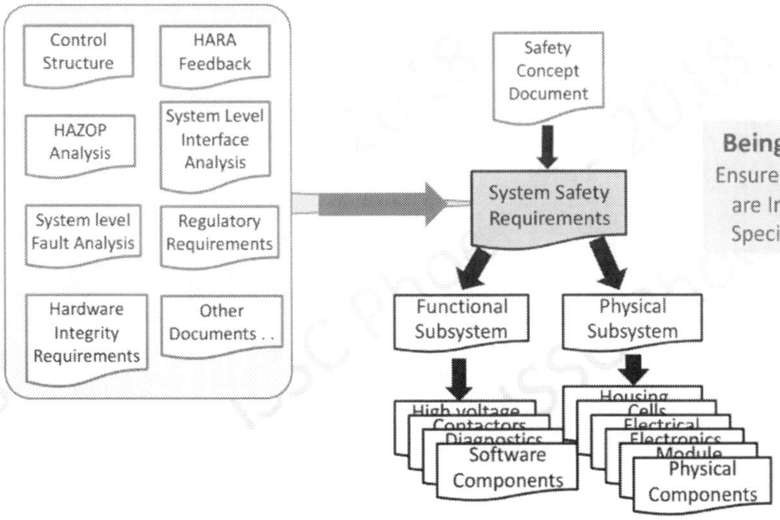

Being Part of Process:
Ensure Safety Requirements are Included in Technical Specification Documents

Perform Final Vehicle Safety Testing

- Verification confirms that work products properly reflect the requirements specified for them ("you built it right")
  - Methods used for Verification are: Analysis (e.g. FTA, FMEA), Demonstration, Inspection and Testing
- Validation confirms that the product fulfills its intended use in all of the environments that the product will be used in ("you built the right thing")
  - During Safety validation, e.g. hazard testing is performed to confirm that the hazard metrics are satisfied
- Complete Vehicle Level Safety Conformance Eva

Being Part of Process:
Ensure Safety Requirements are Included in V&V Plans

Document Safety Validation Results

- Traceability to Requirements
  - Source of Requirement
  - HW and SW Content Technical Specifications
  - V&V Test Procedures
- Objective Evidence
  - Safety Reviews
  - V&V Test Result Summaries
- Final Safety Assessment
  - Approvals
  - Documentation
  - Archive and Retention

Being Part of Process:
Provide Clear Traceability for Safety Requirements throughout Engineering Process

- Questions Before We Take a Break ???

System Content Example Illustration

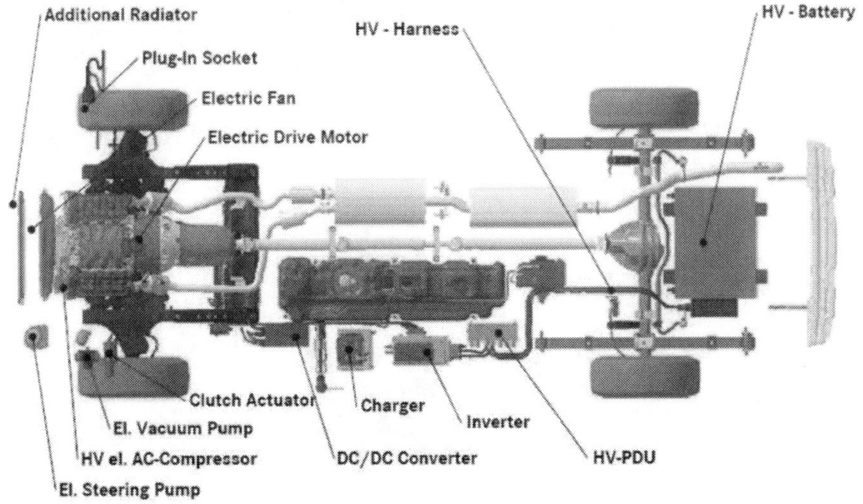

System Content – Safety Critical Areas

System Content – Power and Communication

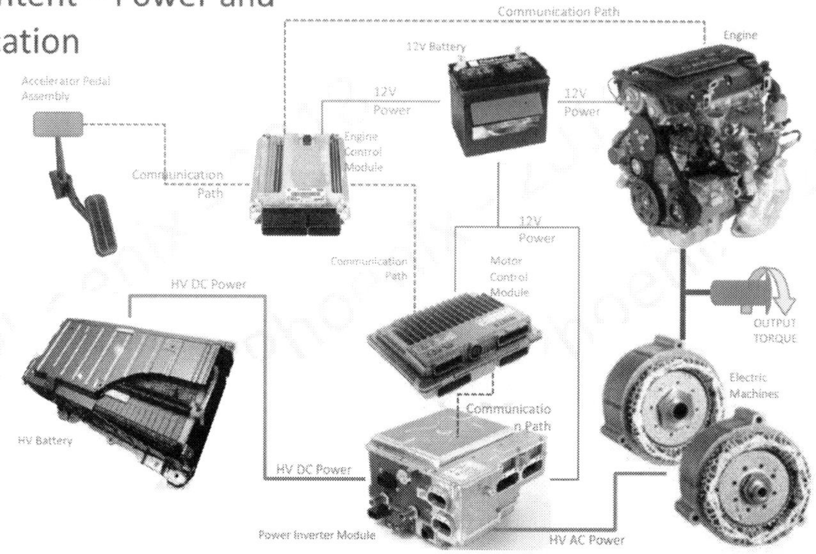

System Control Structure View

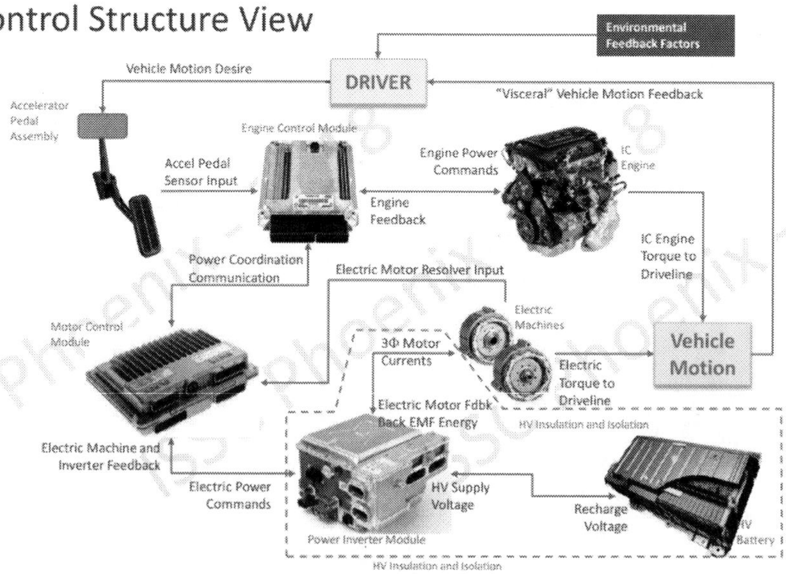

Assessing Risk - Exercise

- How do you start to assess "risk"?
- Do you have established risk assessment criteria?
- How will you decide "when you are done" applying risk management?

Workshop Example Possible Answers

- Assess Potential Hazards

High Voltage Hazards	Vehicle Motion Hazards

- Different Operating Scenarios
  - ???
  - ????
  - ?????
  - ??????
  - Etc.?

Workshop Example Possible Answers

- Assess Potential Hazards

High Voltage Hazards	Vehicle Motion Hazards
Electrical Shock	Unintended/Unwanted Acceleration
Physical Burns from HV Arcing	Unintended/Unwanted Deceleration
Excessive Heat Leading to Fires	Unintended/Unwanted Change of Direction

- Different Operating Scenarios
  - Driving
  - Charging
  - Service
  - Crash
  - Towing

Workshop Example Possible Answers

- Rating Potential Hazards (Scale - High, Medium, or Low ??)

High Voltage Hazards	Vehicle Motion Hazards
Electrical Shock	Unintended/Unwanted Acceleration
Physical Burns from HV Arcing	Unintended/Unwanted Deceleration
Excessive Heat Leading to Fires	Unintended/Unwanted Change of Direction

- Result of Severity, Exposure, and Controllability

- High => ASIL ???
- Medium => ASIL ???
- Low => ASIL ???

Example ASIL Determination

Hazard	Operating Scenario	Severity	Controllability	Exposure	ASIL
Shock	Driving	S3	C3	E4	D
	Crash	S3	C3	E2	B
	Service	S3	C2	E3	B

Severity

S0	S1	S2	S3
No injuries	Light and moderate injuries	Severe and life-threatening injuries (survival probable)	Life-threatening injuries (survival uncertain), fatal injuries

Exposure

E0	E1	E2	E3	E4
Incredible	Very low probability	Low probability	Medium probability	High probability

Controllability

C0	C1	C2	C3
Controllable in general	Simply controllable	Normally controllable	Difficult to control or uncontrollable

Workshop Example Possible Answers

- Rating Potential Hazards (High, Medium, or Low)

HV Hazards	Vehicle Motion Hazards
Electrical Shock - High	Acceleration - High
Physical Burns from HV Arcing - Medium	Deceleration - Medium
Excessive Heat Leading to Fires - High	Direction - Medium

- Result of Severity, Exposure, and Controllability (S, E, C)
  - High => ASIL C and D
  - Medium => ASIL B
  - Low => ASIL A

Managing Risk - Exercise

- Do more "serious risks" require additional attention?
- Do you have a standard approach for determining "how good" it must be?
- Can you summarize the impact on the organization to implement the required management strategy??

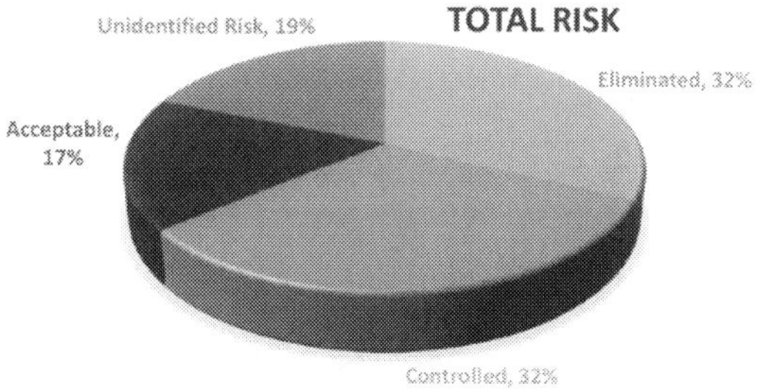

?????

NOTE: Percentages shown in this and any subsequent pie charts are provided for illustration purposes only.

Workshop Example Possible Answers

- Diagnostic Integrity Requirements **

HV and Motion Hazards	Single Point	Dual Point	Safety Metric
Shock - High	High	High	HV Metric
Burn - Medium	High	Medium	Burn Metric
Heat - High	High	High	Thermal Metric
Acceleration - High	High	High	Accel Metric
Deceleration - Medium	High	Medium	Decel Metric
Direction - Medium	High	Medium	Direction Metric

** Consult ISO-26262 Part 5 for Diagnostic Integrity Details

Workshop Example Possible Answers

- Diagnostic Integrity Requirements **

HV and Motion Hazards	Safety Metric
Shock - High	Metric
Burn - Med	Metric
Heat - High	al Metric
Acceleration	Metric
Deceleratior	l Metric
Direction -	on Metric

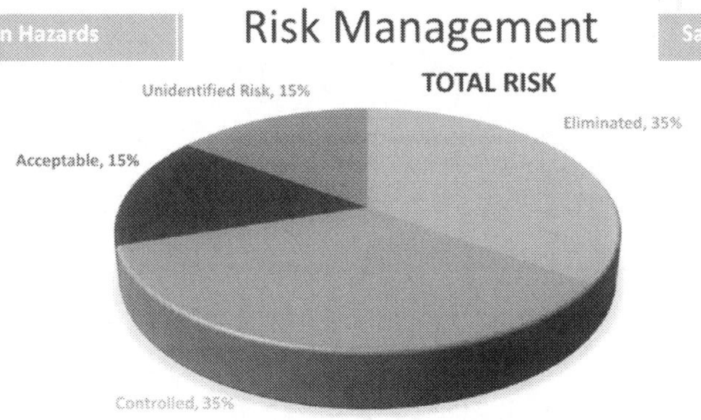

** Consult ISO-26262 Part 5 for Diagnostic Integrity Details

System Control Structure View

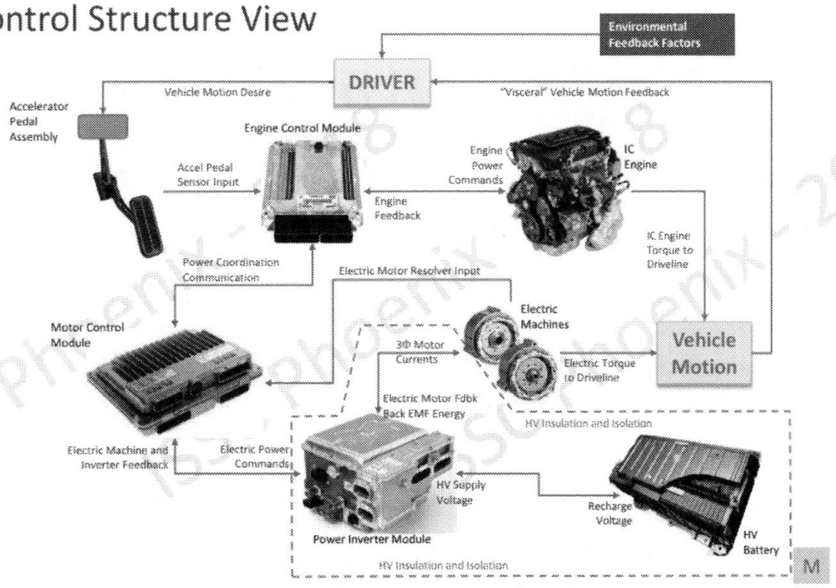

Workshop Example Possible Answers

- Fault Analysis Results

HV / Motion Hazards	Detection	Mitigation
Shock - High		
Burn - Medium		
Heat - High		
Acceleration - High		
Deceleration - Medium		
Direction - Medium		

Workshop Example Possible Answers

- Fault Analysis Results

HV / Motion Hazards	Detection	Mitigation
Shock - High	Current Sensors	
Burn - Medium	None	
Heat - High	Temp Sensors	
Acceleration - High	Vehicle Speed, Clutch Speeds, Current Sensors, Torque Command Monitors	
Deceleration - Medium	Vehicle Speed, Clutch Speeds, Current Sensors	
Direction - Medium	Directional Speed Sensors, Torque Command Monitors	

Workshop Example Possible Answers

- Fault Analysis Results

HV / Motion Hazards	Detection	Mitigation
Shock - High	Current Sensors	Insulation, Physical Barriers, Protective Covers, Cable Routing, Driver Notification, Disconnect HV Battery
Burn - Medium	None	Prevention used to eliminate "hot spots" in design: Thermal Insulation / Isolation; Heat capacity of devices
Heat - High	Temp Sensors	Heat Shields, Protective Covers Disconnect HV Battery
Acceleration - High	Vehicle Speed, Clutch Speeds, Current Sensors, Torque Command Monitors	Disconnect HV Battery, Shutdown Motor Controller, Depower Motors
Deceleration - Medium	Vehicle Speed, Clutch Speeds, Current Sensors	Open Clutches, Shutdown Motor Controller, Depower Motors
Direction - Medium	Directional Speed Sensors, Torque Command Monitors	Override Torque Command, Open Clutches, Shutdown Motor Controller, Depower Motors

36th International System Safety Conference, Aug 13-17, 2018

109

Workshop Example Possible Answers

- Fault Analysis Results

HV / Motion Hazards	Detection	Mitigation
Shock - High	Current Sensors	Insulation, Physical Barriers, Protective Covers, Cable Routing, Driver Notification, Disconnect HV Battery
Burn - Medium	None	Prevention used to eliminate "hot spots" in design: Thermal Insulation / Isolation; Heat capacity of devices
Heat - High	Temp Sensors	Heat Shields, Protective Covers Disconnect HV Battery
Acceleration - High	Vehicle Speed, Clutch Speeds, Current Sensors, Torque Command Monitors	Disconnect HV Battery, Shutdown Motor Controller, Depower Motors
Deceleration - Medium	Vehicle Speed, Clutch Speeds, Current Sensors	Open Clutches, Shutdown Motor Controller, Depower Motors
Direction - Medium	Directional Speed Sensors, Torque Command Monitors	Override Torque Command, Open Clutches, Shutdown Motor Controller, Depower Motors

36th International System Safety Conference, Aug 13-17, 2018

Reproduction or Reuse of this Material is Prohibited without Express Permission from GM

110

System Control Structure View

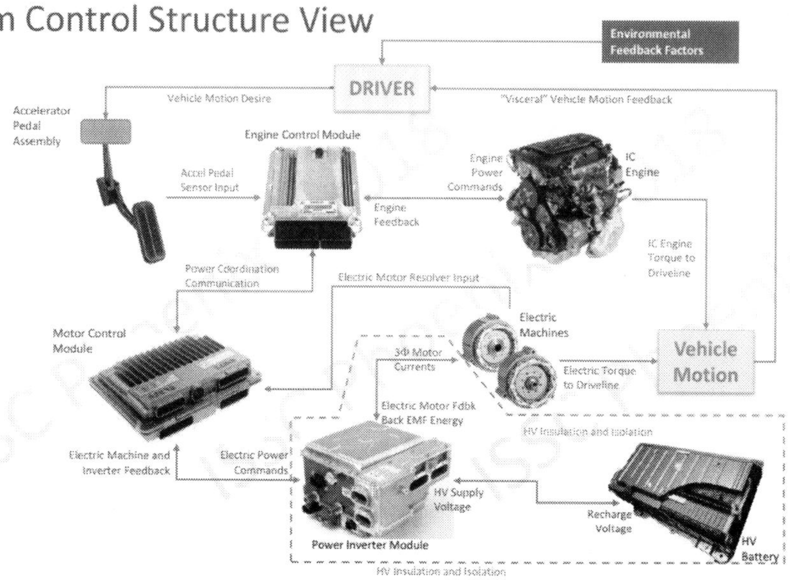

36th International System Safety Conference, Aug 13-17, 2018

111

System Control Structure View

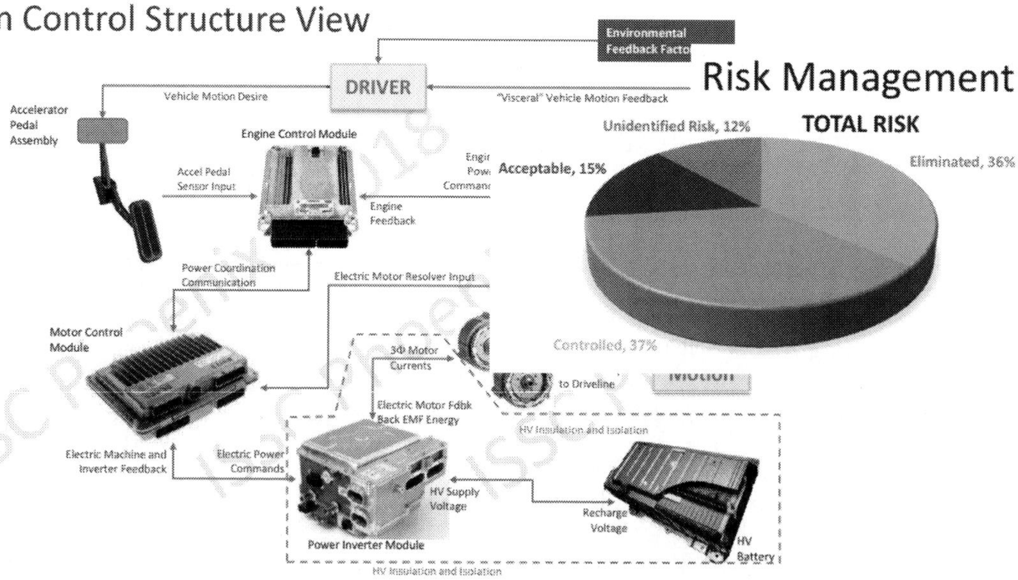

36th International System Safety Conference, Aug 13-17, 2018

112

System Control Structure View

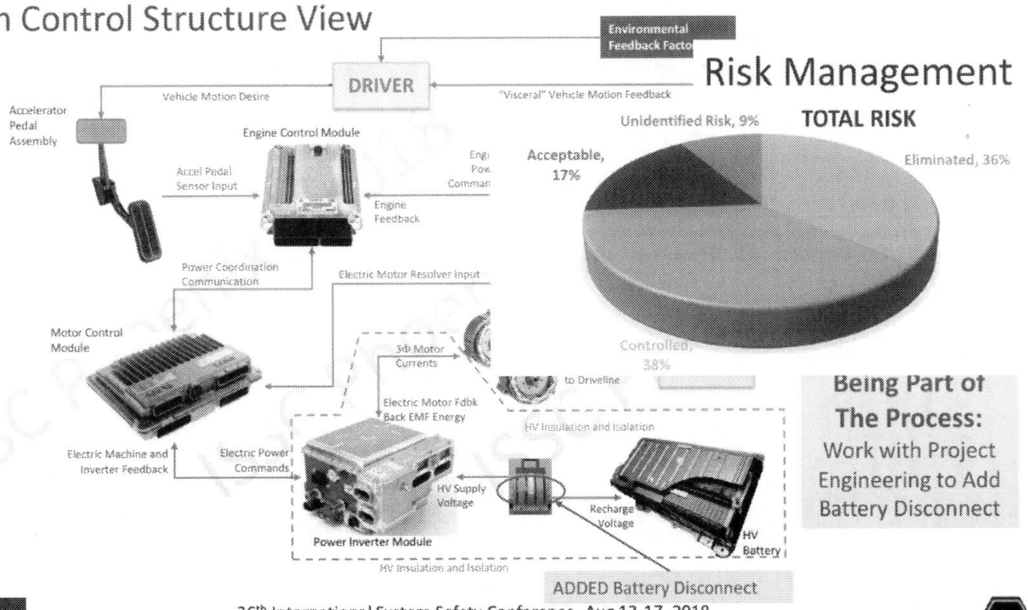

Define System Requirements

- HV Requirements May Apply to Components
  - Electrical Isolation
  - Cable Routing Clearances and Radii
  - Protective Covers
  - Finger Proof Connectors
  - Heat Shields
  - Battery Voltage/Current Sensors
- Propulsion Requirements May Apply to Components
  - Electric Machine Speed Sensors
  - Electric Machine Current Sensors
  - Vehicle Speed Sensors
  - Controller Microprocessor Architecture

Identify and Inform Groups Needing System Requirements

Functional Group	Requirements
Propulsion Systems	Output Shaft Speed Sensors, SW monitors
Chassis Systems	Electrical isolation
Power Inverters	Protective covers
High Voltage Systems	Finger proof connectors, electrical isolation, HV Battery Disconnect
Wire Harnesses	Cable routing clearances and bend radii
Sensors and Actuators	Sensing rates, resolution, response times
Software	Safety requirements integrity level (ASIL) Safety strategy and mitigation actions

Identify and Inform Groups Needing System Requirements

Functional Group	Requirements
Propulsion Systems	ensors, SW monitors
Chassis Sy	
Power Inv	
High Volt	lation, HV
Wire Har	dii
Sensors a	mes
Software	SIL) Safety strategy and mitigation actions

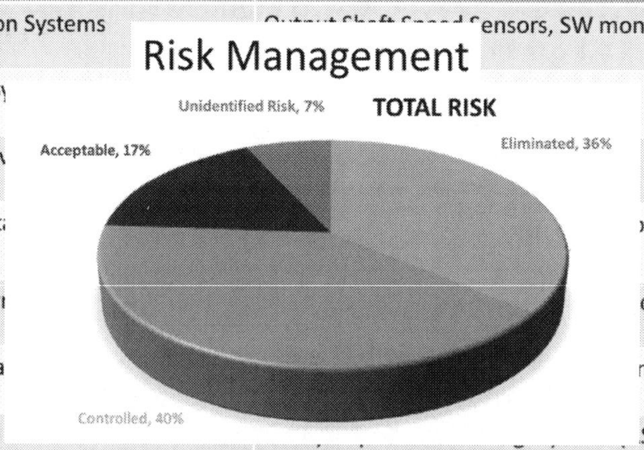

CNG System Overview

- The scope of the CNG fuel system is from the fill valve/fuel filter to the fuel injectors and includes all sensors, actuators, an Electronic Control Module (ECM) and a Fuel Injection Control Module (FICM) that controls the CNG fuel containment, handling and delivery.
- Vehicles are bi-fuel vehicles with discrete gasoline and CNG fuel systems
- Fuel Injection Control Module (FICM) controls CNG fuel storage, and fuel handling and delivery, and the CNG Engine fuel injector system
- CNG fuel system will have a tank where the high pressure CNG is stored. The high pressure CNG from the tank is regulated to a low pressure by means of an electronic pressure regulator (EPR) and then is delivered to the fuel rail and injectors.

CNG Overview

Engine Control Module

Pressure Regulator Assembly

Fuel Fill Nozzle Assembly

Electric Tank Shutoff Valve

High Pressure CNG Tank

Fuel Injection Control Module

Manual Service Shutoff Valve

CNG Engine

CNG Planned Physical Architecture

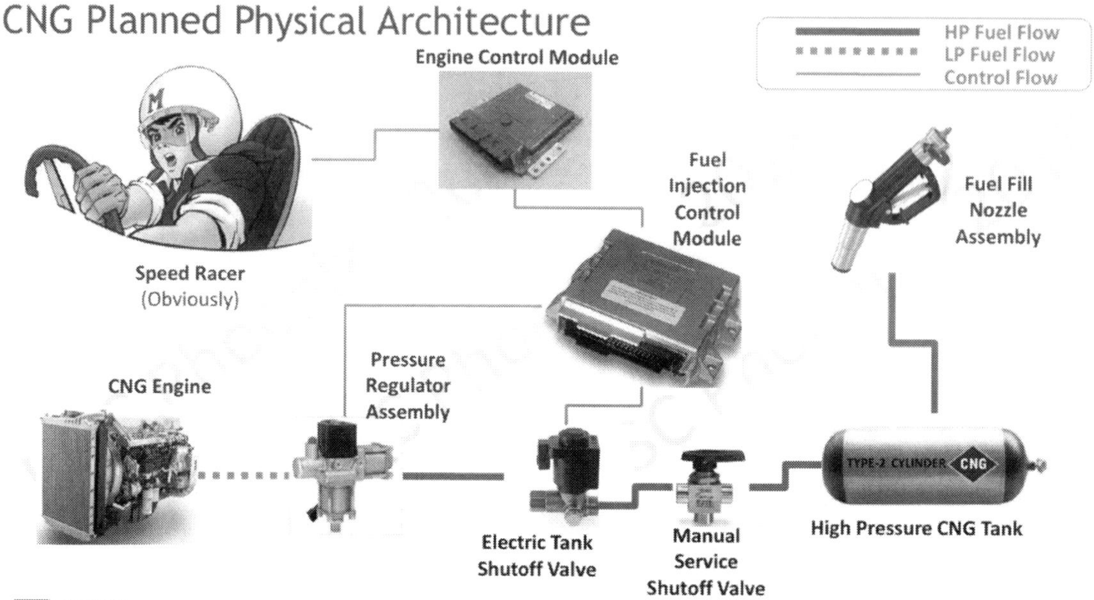

CNG Hazards from PHA

Engine PHA Hazard ID	Potential Vehicle Level Hazard
HAZARDS DEEMED APPLICABLE TO ALTERNATE FUEL SYSTEMS:	
Fuel_Haz_01-a	Unintended Loss of Vehicle Acceleration
Fuel_Haz_02-a	Vehicle fire or fire damage to surrounding area
Fuel_Haz_02-b	Vehicle fire or fire damage to surrounding area due to system over temperature
Fuel_Haz_02-c	Unintended Release of Chemical Energy during refueling
Fuel_Haz_02-d	Vehicle fire or fire damage to surrounding area due to excess fuel delivery
Fuel_Haz_02-f	Vehicle fire or fire damage to surrounding area due to collision
Fuel_Haz_02-g	Vehicle fire or fire damage to surrounding area due to overfilling
Fuel_Haz_03-d	Injury or illness due to Asphyxiation in a confined space.
Fuel_Haz_03-e	Injury or illness due to Asphyxiation inside the passenger compartment.

Draw the High Level 3 Tiered Controls Structure

Draw the High Level 3 Tiered Controls Structure

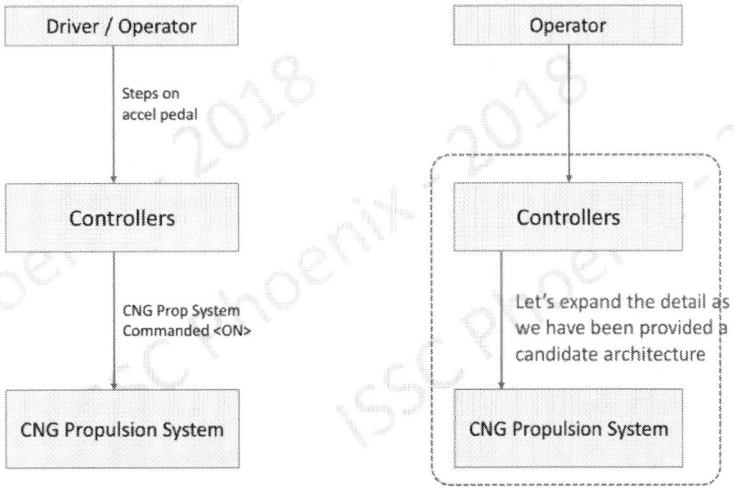

Draw More Detailed Controls Structure

Draw More Detailed Controls Structure

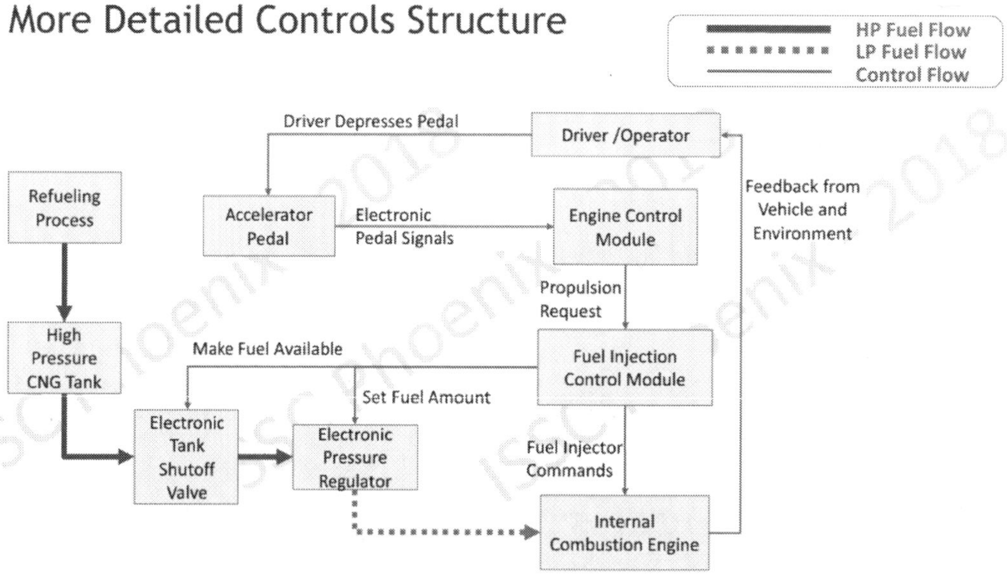

Define Functions (Responsibilities) for System Elements

- FICM
  - Provide Control to Shut-Off Valves- For Engine Running in CNG mode, shut-off valves are OPEN
  - Provide control to Fuel Injectors
  - Provide control to Electronic Pressure Regulator (EPR)
- Electronic Pressure Regulator
  - Receives fuel delivery control commands from FICM
  - Controls fuel delivery from HP side to fuel rail and injectors
  - Acts as a mechanical pressure relief device - will vent CNG when pressure in LP side > 10 bar

Define Functions (Responsibilities) for System Elements

FICM Functions	Control Action NOT Provided	Control Action Provided But Causes Hazard	Control Action Provided Too Early, Too Late, at Wrong Time, or in Wrong Sequence	Control Action Stopped Too Soon or Applied Too Long

Elect. Pressure Regulator Functions	Control Action NOT Provided	Control Action Provided But Causes Hazard	Control Action Provided Too Early, Too Late, at Wrong Time, or in Wrong Sequence	Control Action Stopped Too Soon or Applied Too Long

STPA Step 1:

FICM Functions	Control Action NOT Provided	Control Action Provided But Causes Hazard	Control Action Provided Too Early, Too Late, at Wrong Time, or in Wrong Sequence	Control Action Stopped Too Soon or Applied Too Long
Provide Control to Shut Off Valves- For Engine Running in CNG mode, shut-off valves are OPEN	UCA1: Controller does not open the shut-off valve during Engine Running mode	None	None	None
Provide control to Fuel Injectors	UCA2: Controller does not activate fuel injectors		UCA3: Controller actuated fuel injectors sooner than intended injection event	UCA5: Controller actuated fuel injectors in such a way that they are open over elapsed period of time (few minutes)
Provide control to Electronic Pressure Regulator (EPR)	UCA6: Controller does not control Electronic Pressure Regulator (EPR)	UCA7: Controller commands EPR in such a way that it over pressurizes fuel rail and injectors (LP side)	UCA8: Controller commands EPR in such a way that low fuel quantity is delivered to fuel injectors.	
			UCA9: Controller commands EPR in such a way that high fuel quantity is delivered to fuel injectors.	

36th International System Safety Conference, Aug 13-17, 2018

127

STPA Step 1:

Electric Pressure Regulator Functions	Control Action NOT Provided	Control Action Provided But Causes Hazard	Control Action Provided Too Early, Too Late, at Wrong Time, or in Wrong Sequence	Control Action Stopped Too Soon or Applied Too Long
Receives fuel delivery control commands from FICM	UCA35: EPR does not receive control from FICM	UCA36: EPR receives command from FICM in such a way that it over pressurizes fuel rail and injectors (LP side)	UCA37: EPR receives command from FICM in such a way that low fuel quantity is delivered to fuel injectors.	
Controls fuel delivery from HP side to fuel rail and injectors	UCA39: EPR does not delivers fuel from HP side to fuel rail and injectors	UCA40: EPR delivers fuel from HP side to fuel rails in such a way that it over pressurizes fuel rail and injectors	UCA41: EPR delivers low quantity of fuel from HP side to fuel rail	
Acts as a mechanical pressure relief device - will vent CNG when pressure in LP side > 10 bar		UCA43: EPR does not vent CNG even when pressure in LP side >10 bar		

36th International System Safety Conference, Aug 13-17, 2018

Reproduction or Reuse of this Material is Prohibited without Express Permission from GM

128

More Detailed Controls Structure

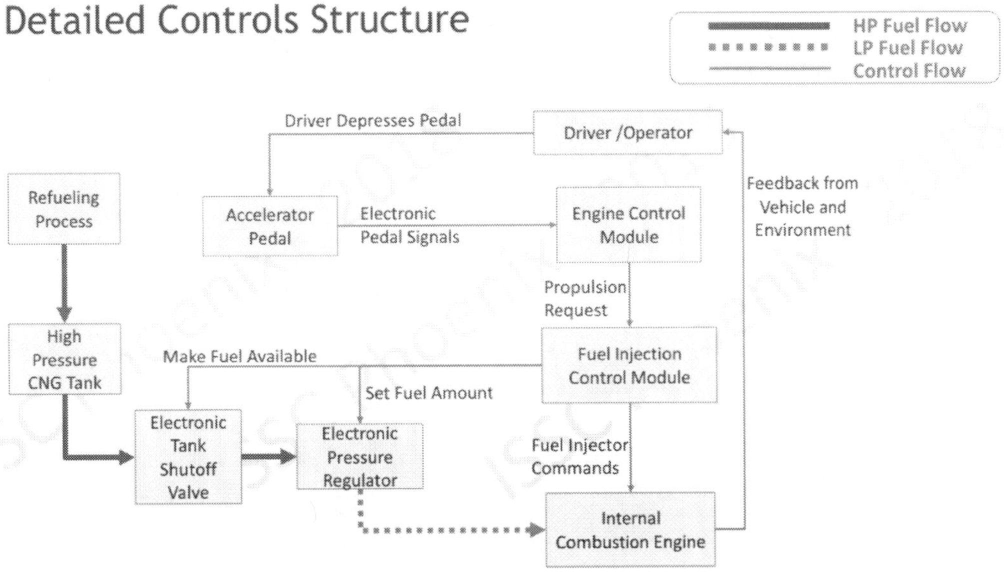

36th International System Safety Conference, Aug 13-17, 2018

129

Update Controls Structure to Add Feedback

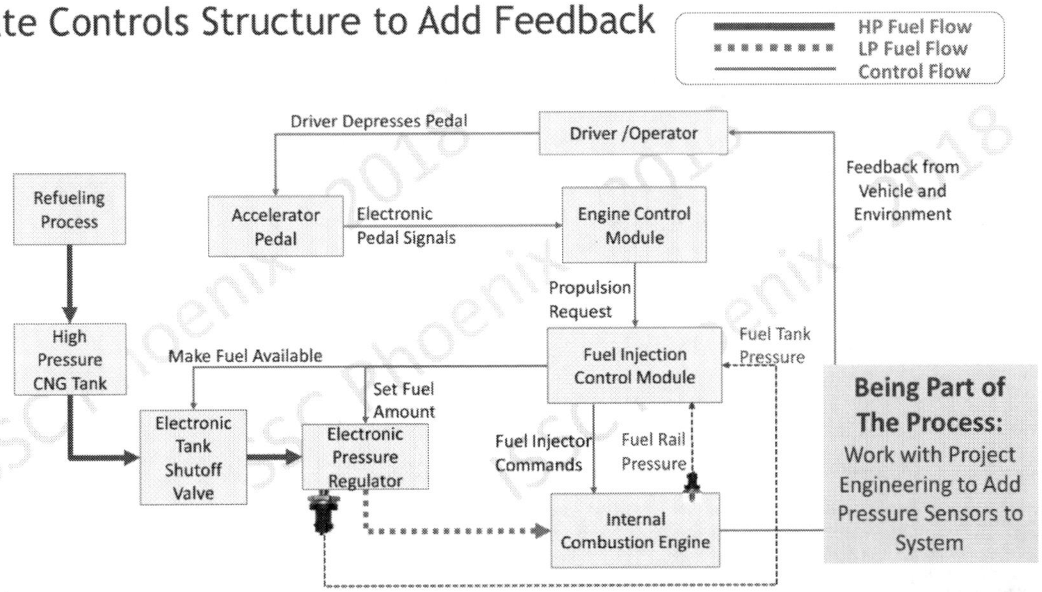

36th International System Safety Conference, Aug 13-17, 2018

130

STPA Step 2:

- High-level Causal Scenarios *(Keep asking "Why?")*
  - Inadequate Control Execution
  - Inappropriate Decisions
  - Inadequate Feedback & Other Inputs
  - Inadequate Process Behavior

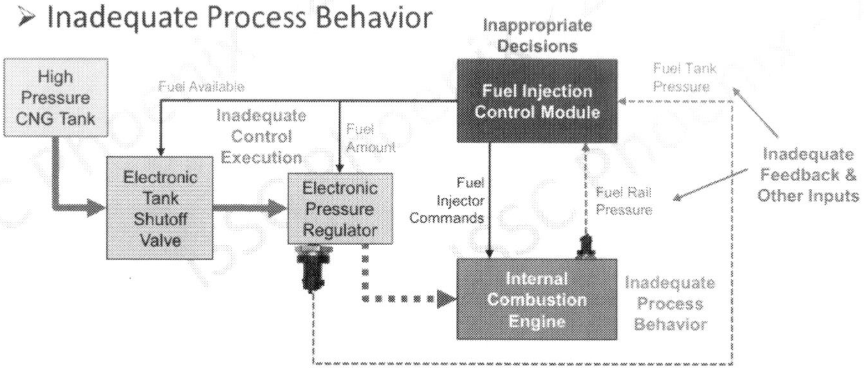

STPA Step 2:

- High-level Causal Scenarios *(Keep asking "Why?")*
  - Inadequate Control Execution (Actuators)
  - Inappropriate Decisions (FICM)
  - Inadequate Feedback & Other Inputs (Sensors)
  - Inadequate Process Behavior (CNG Engine)

STPA Step 2:

- High-level Causal Scenarios *(Keep asking "Why?")*
  - Inadequate Control Execution (Actuators)
    - Over pressurizes fuel rail and injectors
    - Pressure regulator response time too slow
    - Shutoff valve does not close completely
  - Inappropriate Decisions (FICM)
    - Commands too high of pressure for situation
    - Commands CNG <ON> when in Gasoline mode
  - Inadequate Feedback & Other Inputs (Sensors)
    - Low voltage to Fuel Tank Pressure Sensor
    - Fuel Tank Pressure Sensor resolution inadequate
  - Inadequate Process Behavior (CNG Engine)
    - Fuel Injectors do not provide appropriate pressure
    - Fuel Injectors provide CNG when in gasoline mode

STPA Step 2: Proposed Requirements to Causal Scenarios

- Inadequate Control Execution (Actuators)

- Inappropriate Decisions (FICM)

- Inadequate Feedback & Other Inputs (Sensors)

- Inadequate Process Behavior (CNG Engine)

STPA Step 2: Proposed Requirements to Causal Scenarios

- Inadequate Control Execution (Actuators)
  - Fuel rail pressure shall be monitored by the FICM during CNG operation
  - Pressure regulator response time shall be a maximum of 25 msec
  - Fuel tank pressure shall be monitored by the FICM after shutoff valve is commanded <OFF>
- Inappropriate Decisions (FICM)
  - ECM shall send a secured torque request to FICM based on accel pedal position
  - FICM shall monitor fuel rail pressure to rationalize requested torque anticipated pressure with actual pressure during CNG operation
  - Who/What commands CNG <ON>??
- Inadequate Feedback & Other Inputs (Sensors)
  - Fuel Tank Pressure (FTP) Sensor voltage supply shall be monitored by FICM
  - FICM shall disable CNG operation during if FTP sensor not available
  - FTP Sensor resolution shall be 3 psi over full operating range
- Inadequate Process Behavior (CNG Engine)
  - Fuel rail pressure shall be monitored by the FICM during CNG operation
  - Fuel rail pressure shall be monitored by the FICM during gasoline mode

Being Part of The Process:
Work with Project Engineering to Include Safety Requirements in Specification and Technical Documents

STPA Step 2: Proposed Requirements to Causal Scenarios

- Inadequate Control Execution (Actuators)
  - Fuel rail pressure shall be monitored by the FICM during CNG operation
  - Pressure regulator response time shall be a maximum of 25 msec
  - Fuel tank pressure shall be monitored by the FICM after shutoff valve is commanded <OFF>
- Inappropriate Dec
  - ECM shall send a s ... sed on accel pedal position
  - FICM ... anticipated pressure with actua
  - Who/
- Inadeq
  - Fuel ... FICM
  - FICM
  - FTP S
- Inadeq
  - Fuel ... ion
  - Fuel ... de

Risk Management

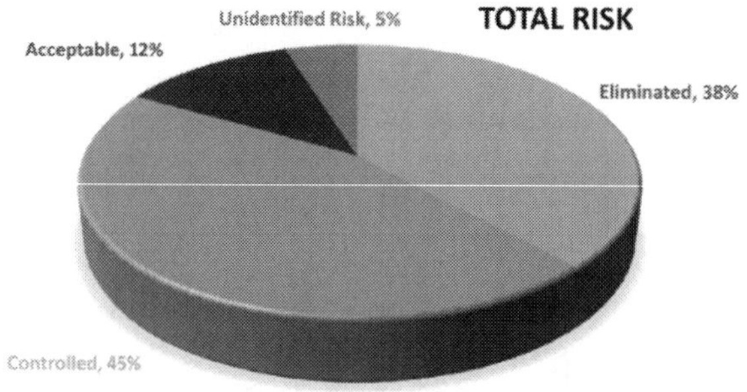

Being Part of The Process:
Work with Project Engineering to Include Safety Requirements in Specification and Technical Documents

Tutorial Conclusion

- Understand what "Safety", "System Safety" and "Risk" mean to your organization
- Risk Assessment and Risk Management are critical to successful system safety execution
- Utilizing a system level approach in early program evaluations allows appropriate architecture structure and content decisions to be made with minimal program impact
- Safety needs to be an integrated part of the engineering process, not an add-on entity
- All of these create a means for a traceable linkage from Accidents to Requirements

- Be brave and be prepared to "speak boldly to power". Have your objective data well laid out to illustrate why requirements will prevent or effectively manage the risk associated with potential accidents. Objective data helps remove emotion from challenging decisions

References

[1] MIL-STD-882E - Department of Defense Standard Practice System Safety

[2] NASA System Engineering Handbook - NASA/SP-2016-6105 Rev2

[3] Leveson, Nancy, MIT, STPA Handbook 2018

[4] ISO-26262 – Version 1 2011

[5] FAA Systems Safety Handbook - December 30, 2000

[6] ARP-4754A - Guidelines for Development of Civil Aircraft And Systems

[7] ARP-4761 - Guidelines and Methods for Conducting the Safety Assessment Process on Civil Airborne Systems and Equipment

[8] NASA System Safety Handbook - NASA/SP-2014-612 Version 1.0, November 2014

[9] INCOSE Systems Engineering Handbook – Fourth Edition, INCOSE-TP-2003-002-04 2015

[10] Food and Drug Administration (FDA) - EXTENDING STPA TO IMPROVE THE ANALYSIS OF USER INTERFACE SOFTWARE IN MEDICAL DEVICES, Yi Zhang, Ph.D., Center for Devices and Radiological Health (CDRH), U.S. Food and Drug Administration (FDA), YI.ZHANG2@FDA.HHS.GOV

Thank You
Questions ?????

Galen Ressler
GM Technical Fellow
Principal System Safety Engineer - High Voltage Systems
galen.ressler@gm.com

Mark A Vernacchia
GM Technical Fellow
Principal System Safety Engineer - Propulsion Systems
mark.a.vernacchia@gm.com

Delivering Safety Through Design Using Early Analysis Methods

Mark A. Vernacchia, MSES, PE
General Motors Company; Milford, Michigan, USA

Keywords: systems engineering, SEFA, STPA, interactions, safety, emergent behavior

Abstract

This paper describes two system analysis methods used in the GM Systems Safety Process to initiate the process of delivering safety directly through the design process. These analyses facilitate the safety team as an integrated part of design teams early in the design process, a key factor in successful hazard identification, risk assessment, and determination of appropriate content to eliminate or manage potential risk to an acceptable level.

Analyses results are used to identify possible revisions to the system content necessary to ensure adequate diagnostic capability and mitigation management prior to design freeze. In addition, these methods determine initial system requirements necessary to support management/mitigation of resulting unintended or unwanted system behavior caused by system element failures.

The paper first summarizes how results from a SEFA/STPA analysis are used to identify content revisions to the system architecture necessary to ensure adequate diagnostic capability for mitigation management prior to design freeze. Second, the paper reviews how SEFA/STPA processes identify initial system requirements necessary to support the management/mitigation of unintended or unwanted system behavior caused by system element functional failures. Finally, the paper summarizes how STPA requirements were integrated into the production-released button-based design of the 2018 GMC Terrain shift-by-wire shifter.

Introduction

Effective safety analysis methods provide value through the entire engineering design, development, testing and manufacturing phases of a system's implementation process. These analysis methods have a significant impact on system content in early phases of a program as major expenditures for critical component procurements and manufacturing tooling have yet to be committed. There is much less cost associated with design changes at this point in the process than there are with changes that occur later in the process (e.g., it is much cheaper to move lines on paper than it is to move/change actual physical tooling lines in a manufacturing environment).

Early in the design process, exploration of various design concepts is conducted to determine the optimized balance between system imperatives such as cost, timing, mass, performance, and safety "acceptable risk" requirements. This "system architecture balance" phase typically contains tasks such as the ones shown here in Table 1, with some tasks having an iterative nature between them. Of course, if an optimal balance cannot be achieved the iterative nature would be extended to early tasks for modification of Stakeholder Expectations and Initial Requirements.

Table 1 – System Concept / Architecture Tasks Involving Early Safety Analysis Methods

System Concept / Architecture Tasks	Safety Analysis Methods Areas
Stakeholder Expectation Determination	
Initial Requirements Identification	
Architecture Development / Modification	Iterative Loops Between these Tasks Until Optimum Balance Achieved
Balance, Trade Studies, Optimization Activities Leading to Design Selection within Functional Domain(s)	
Analysis Verification (Functional, Performance, and Safety)	
Program Validation Against Stakeholder Expectations	
Concept / Architecture Selection	

An underlying assumption in Table 1 is that system safety is an integrated part of the system engineering process to be optimally effective. The iterative loop shown in Table 1 above may be further illustrated by a systems engineering "cascading conic" depiction shown in Figures 1, 2, 3, 4 and 5 below. Figure 1 shows the initial allocation of system imperatives to major systems. Figure 2 shows the interactions between these major systems during the balance, tradeoff and optimizations steps. Figure 3 shows the rebalance and optimization at the top system level leading to an initial concept / architecture and Figure 4 depicts the concept / architecture selection.

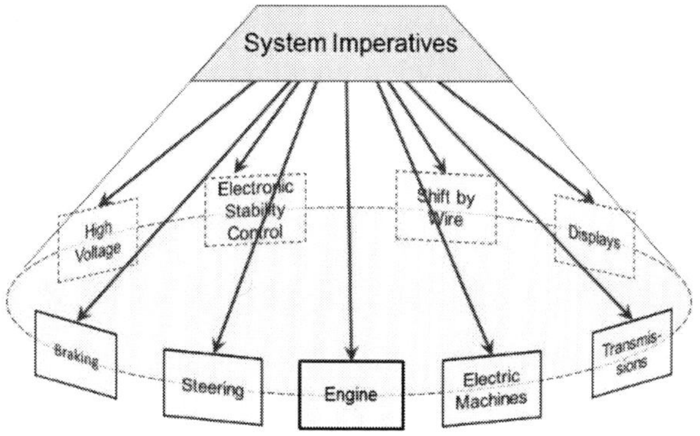

Figure 1 – Initial Allocation to Major Systems

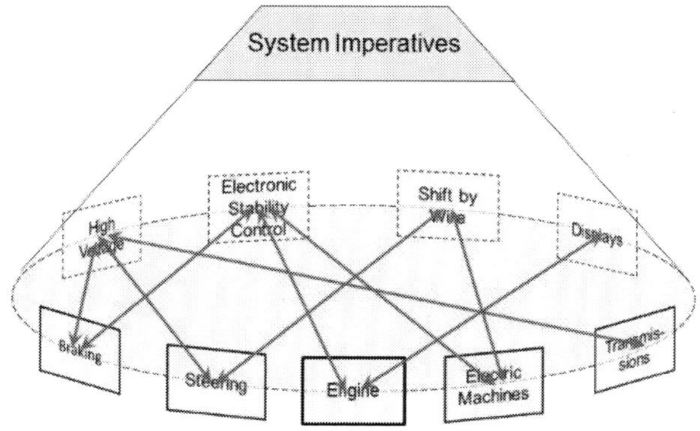

Figure 2 – Interactions between Major Systems

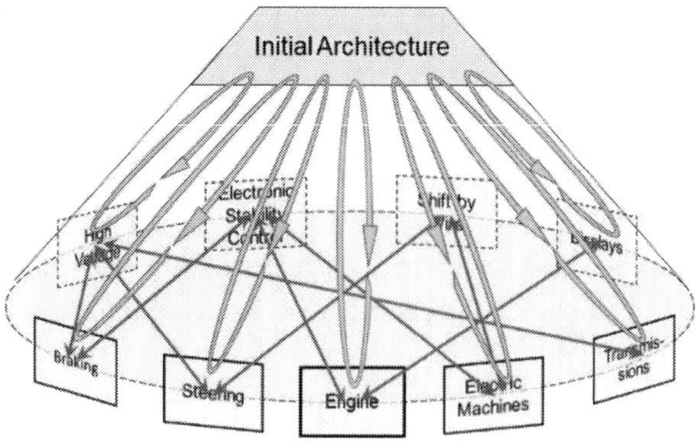

Figure 3 – Rebalance and Optimize Initial Concept

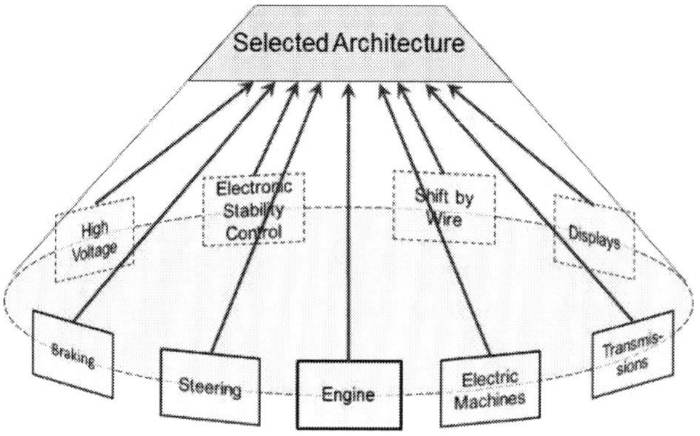

Figure 4 – Selected Concept / Architecture

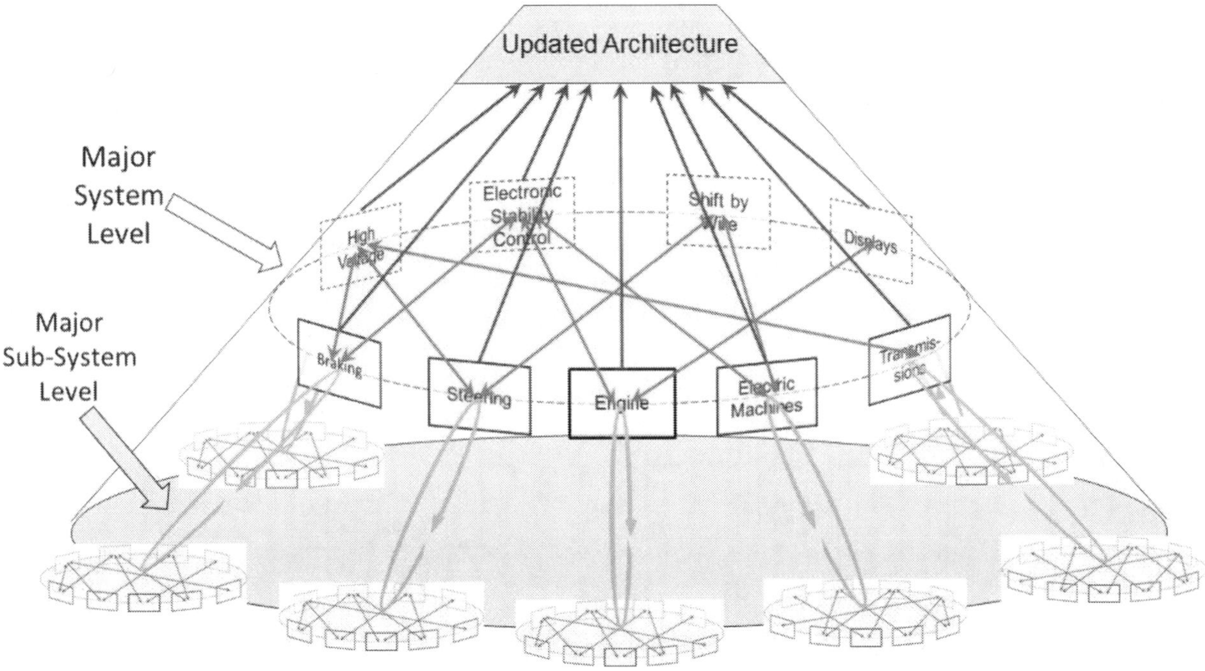

Figure 5 – Multiple Level Balancing and Optimization for Continued Concept / Architecture Improvement

Figure 5 illustrates the allocation to the major subsystems of each major system where the balance, tradeoff and optimization process repeats at this lower level and updates are transposed back up to the top level. Two levels of evaluation tend to be sufficient for initial safety task activities. Deeper levels of the engineering process are very well served by familiar evaluations methodologies such as DFMEAs, FTAs, and FIAs.

Within this systems engineering process framework, safety tasks performed early in the design process support the balance and optimization tasks by identifying what hazardous conditions potentially could arise due to system element misbehavior and assessing the risk associated with such hazards. This effort defines the required system content and the detection and mitigation strategies necessary to eliminate or manage the assigned risk to acceptable levels. Within the GM System Safety Process safety tasks such as Preliminary Hazard Analysis (PHA), Hazard Analysis and Risk Assessment (HARA), SEFA (System Element Fault Analysis) and STPA (Systems-Theoretic Process Analysis) are utilized at this time. It is the latter two tasks that the remainder of this paper describes.

This paper focused on two early analysis methodologies used within this system engineering context. The first method is the SEFA technique. The second method is the STPA approach, developed at MIT by Professor Nancy Leveson, which is used to evaluate failures associated with "functions" assigned to system elements and the impact of these failures on system behaviors during expected operating scenarios. (Leveson & Thomas, 2018)

GM System Safety Process with SEFA and STPA

The SEFA and STPA are two analysis tasks within the Concept Phase of the GM System Safety Process, leveraging the output of the Preliminary Hazard Analysis (PHA) (e.g., list of system-level hazards), the HARA, and the physical or functional architecture of the system.

There may be times where the system design is not fully mature or that allocation documents are not in their final form. Under this condition, the SEFA and STPA evaluations can still be started and then subsequently refined and updated as the system design matures. Once the system concept / architecture is determined, final versions of the SEFA and STPA analyses would be completed for the Safety Concept, shown at the end of Figure 6.

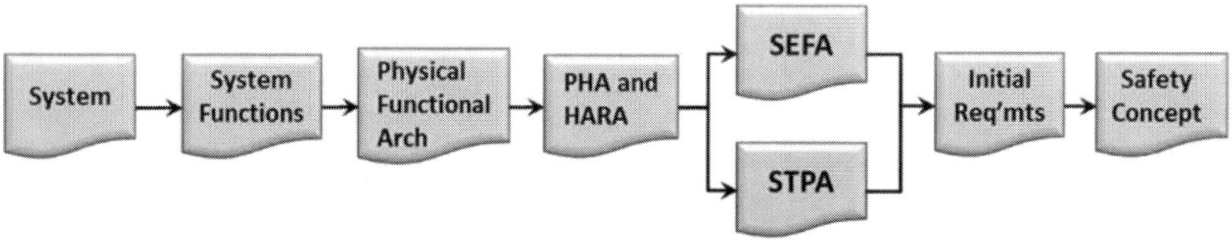

Figure 6 - Location of SEFA and STPA in Concept Phase of GM System Safety Process

SEFA and STPA evaluations are performed by one or more subject matter experts for the given system, function or component, with subsequent review by a cross-section of engineers with expertise pertinent to the scope of the system under study. The number of subject matter experts performing the SEFA or its subsequent review is dependent on the maturity and complexity of the system, e.g., high-risk designs or those involving significant invention will require additional participants. In addition, inclusion of a cross-section of experienced individuals aids in ensuring that any questions about the system can be resolved efficiently, thus reducing the tendency for making inaccurate assumptions, generating significant action items resulting from inadequate information, etc.

Depending on the system content, the list of engineers participating in the analyses may include:

- System Engineer(s) (SE)**
- System Safety Engineer(s) (SSE)**
- Controls Architecture Engineer(s)**
- Control Algorithm Engineer(s)**
- Control Diagnostic Engineer(s)**
- Driver Performance Specialist(s)**
- Design Release Engineer(s) (DRE)
- Controls Product Design Team (PDT) Leader
- Component Supplier Engineer(s)

** These engineers are key participants for SEFA and STPA development.

System Element Fault Analysis (SEFA)

The first method to discuss is the System Element Fault Analysis (SEFA) technique. It is system-level, top-down, exploratory analysis technique to evaluate the impact of system element faults upon the system as a whole and to determine if the system has sufficient content to detect and mitigate potential hazardous states created due to the fault. In the SEFA, a methodical review of the faults of system elements is conducted from which the consequences of each fault are identified. The analysis is performed based on a system's physical architecture design and assists in understanding flaws within the design or inadequacies in the design's ability to prevent, detect or respond appropriately to the impact of the faults of system elements.

The SEFA uses a "binary" assessment approach where system elements are either <ON> or <OFF>; <WORKING> or <NOT WORKING>; <"0" POSITION> or < "1" POSITION>; etc. and takes into account the scenarios in which the system is expected to operate. The "NORMAL" state of all system elements is defined first for each scenario. The analysis proceeds to have each element (one by one) enter a state where that element experiences an abnormal behavior or attains a defective state versus its "normal" state. System elements may be items such as actuators, motors, sensors, etc. Controllers are included in a SEFA and typically are treated as one system element.

SEFA Electric Vehicle Propulsion Example

A "System Block Diagram" propulsion system for an electric vehicle is provided in Figure 7 below. This system contains two electric machines (EMs) that function either as a motor or a generator depending on driving conditions. These EMs are controlled by dedicated control processors (MCPA and MCPB) that use feedback from EM mounted resolvers. EM torque commands are determined by a hybrid control processor (HCP) that receives accelerator and brake pedal information from an engine control module (ECM) and an electric brake control module (EBCM) respectively. A transmission control module (TCM) selects different gear ratios based on ECM and transmission output speed sensor (TOSS) input. An internal mode switch (IMS) tells the system what range (Park, Reverse, Neutral, or Drive) the driver has selected. All of these entities constitute the system's elements.

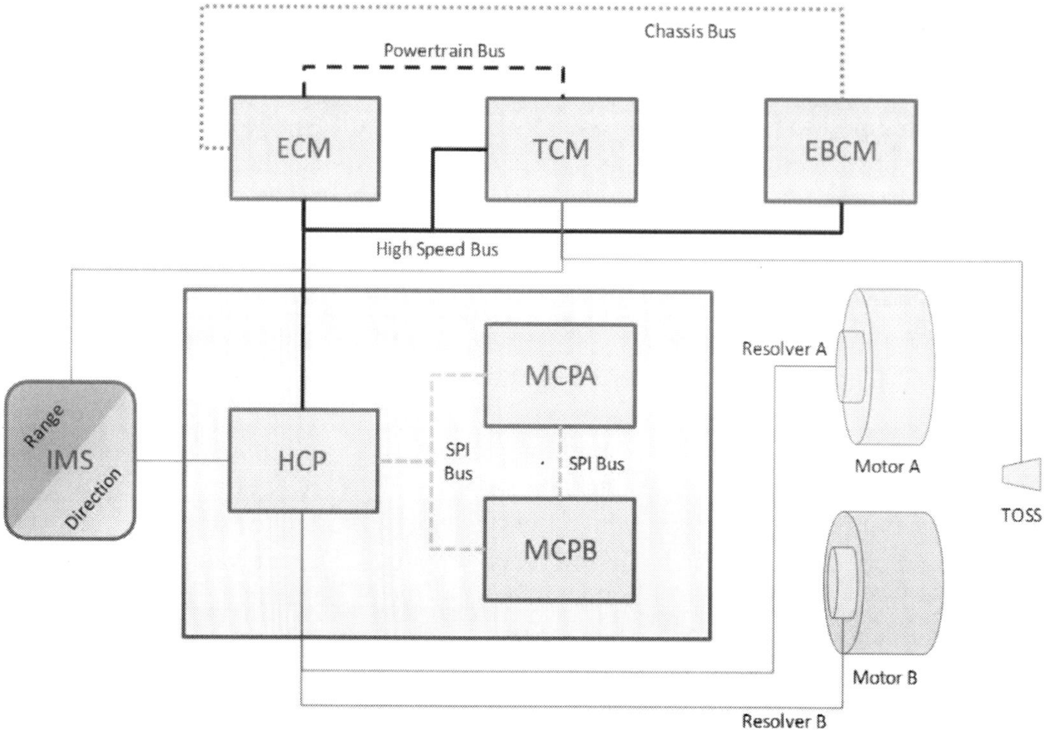

Figure 7 - Hybrid Propulsion System Concept / Architecture "System Block Diagram"

The SEFA utilizes a standard template within the GM Safety Process that contains cells for each system element's assigned or expected "responsibilities". The template provides an area to "fail" each element, one at a time, and then record the resulting system behavior. These resulting system behaviors are then evaluated for potential safety hazards. If a hazard is possible, detection and mitigation strategies are recorded. The final system state after any mitigation action is evaluated to be sure new/different hazardous states are not created. At the end of the template is a column to record initial safety requirements to ensure the system is capable of performing the specified diagnostics and executing the defined mitigation strategies. Table 2 below shows the template.

Table 2 - SEFA Template

			Element Operating States																
Item Number	***"Operating Scenario"***	**Function(s) (Responsibilities)**	Element name 1	Element name 2	Element name 3	Element name 4	Element name 5	Element name 6	Element name 7	Element name 8	Element name 9	Element name 10	**Impact of Element Fault** (Impact prior to any remedial or mitigation actions)	**Immediate Resulting State** (State of the system prior to any remedial or mitigation actions)	**Potential Safety Hazard(s)**	**Diagnostic Method(s)**	**Mitigation Action(s)**	**System State After Mitigation**	**SAFETY Requirements**
	Normal Operation	*System Functions to be Delivered*											NORMAL OPERATION		NONE	NONE	NONE	NONE	NONE
1	Element name 1	*Element Functions*																	
2	Element name 2																		
3	Element name 3																		

Table 3 shows the SEFA filled out for ECM and HCP element faults. Notice there is a way to record "primary" (yellow filled cell) and "resulting" (magenta filled cell) faults. One will see that when the HCP has failed (yellow cell with "0"), Directional IMS information (magenta cell with "0") is not available any more. The Directional IMS itself has not failed, but the ability to read its output is gone. Table 3 goes on to illustrate where potential safety hazards are present due to the resulting system state.

Table 3 - SEFA Evaluating ECM and HCP Faults for Hazards

Item Number	Multiple Ranges (P,R,N,D)	Function(s) (Responsibilities)	ECM	HCP	MCP1	MCP2	TCM	EBCM	Direction IMS	Range IMS	TOSS	MotorA Resolver	MotorB Resolver	Impact of Element Fault (Impact prior to any remedial or mitigation actions)	Immediate Resulting State (State of the system prior to any remedial or mitigation actions)	Potential Safety Hazard(s)
			PRIMARY Fault	RESULTING Fault												
	Normal Operation	Provide Propulsion in an Electric Vehicle	1	1	1	1	1	1	1	1	1	1	1	NORMAL OPERATION	Selected Range	NONE
1	ECM	* Read accelerator pedal inputs * Determine req'd torque based on driving condition and accel pedal input * Provide EBCM with Regen Braking Capacity * Performs plausiblity check btw HCP and TCM IMS inputs	0	1	1	1	1	1	1	1	1	1	1	Engine not available or shuts <OFF>	Park - Park Reverse - Reverse Neutral - Neutral Drive - Possible Acceleration	Loss of Propulsion
2	HCP	* Determines torque and commands MCPs * Reads Motor Resolver inputs * Reads IMS Direction input * Provides IMS Direction to ECM	1	0	1	1	1	1	0	1	1	0	0	IMS info to HCP not evaluated Loss of Motor Resolver Info	Park - Park Reverse - Reverse Neutral - Neutral Drive - Possible Acceleration	Unintended Propulsion <OR> Unintended Direction

Table 4 is an extension of the SEFA rows from Table 3 and shows information in columns "Potential Safety Hazard(s)", "Diagnostic Method(s)" and "Mitigation Action(s)" that is critical for downstream Safety Process documents and activities. The information in the "Diagnostic Method(s)" and Mitigation Action(s) columns will be the starting point for detection and mitigation strategy discussions and the resulting safety requirements.

Table 4 - SEFA Template Extension with Safety Requirements

Item Number	Multiple Ranges (P,R,N,D)	Function(s) (Responsibilities)	Potential Safety Hazard(s)	Diagnostic Method(s)	Mitigation Action(s)	System State After Mitigation	SAFETY Requirements
	Normal Operation	Provide Propulsion in an Electric Vehicle	NONE	NONE	NONE	NONE	NONE
1	ECM	* Read accelerator pedal inputs * Determine req'd torque based on driving condition and accel pedal input * Provide EBCM with Regen Braking Capacity * Performs plausiblity check btw HCP and TCM IMS inputs	Loss of Propulsion	Lack of ECM communication detected by HCP and TCM	Set MIL light and go to reduced power	Reduced Propulsion	* System shall move to reduced propulsion when ECM fails * TCM and HCP shall detect ECM loss using CAN diagnostics
2	HCP	* Determines torque and commands MCPs * Reads Motor Resolver inputs * Reads IMS Direction input * Provides IMS Direction to ECM	Unintended Propulsion <OR> Unintended Direction	TCM and ECM detect loss of HCP. IMS info from TCM used for Driver intent MCPs detect HCL loss.	Set MIL light and go to reduced power	Reduced Propulsion	* ECM shall set DTC and instruct BCM to display driver message * ECM shall default to TCM IMS info * MCPs shall limit mtr torques to RP * The system shall transition to RP without violating the Unintended Direction & Unintended Prop Engagement metric * The system shall provide ASIL D hardware design integrity

The requirements are written at this high level with the expectation that they will be expanded upon and rolled-down to sub-system and component levels as part of the Requirements Phase and Design Phase safety process activities.

Systems-Theoretic Process Analysis (STPA)

The second method is the Systems-Theoretic Process Analysis (STPA) technique that represents the system content from a controls perspective, not a reliability point of view, and treats the system failures as control problems. It is used to evaluate failures associated with "functions" assigned to system elements and the impact of these failures on system behaviors during the defined operating scenarios. STPA determines unsafe controls actions created when each system element's functions fail according to a list of "misbehavior" guidewords; the possible causes that could lead to these unsafe control actions; and, finally, the constraints and/or requirements necessary to prevent or manage these causes to an acceptable risk level.

The STPA analysis is used to evaluate the impact when system element functions experience failures. This approach enables an evaluation to be done on either physical or functional architectures of a system and allows a system with complex and multiple interactions to be evaluated methodically in a clear and concise manner.

STPA is useful when evaluating systems that contain expected driver and machine interactions. The evaluation would focus on accidental and inadvertent interactions between the driver and particular system elements that could lead to potential safety hazards, including hazards associated with purposeful activation. STPA is a vital addition to the GM Safety Process as ISO26262 does not address the evaluation of human behavior as part of its process to the desired level of detail GM desires.

STPA should also be used to evaluate the safety impact of "emergent behaviors" not seen at the system's element level. Emergent behavior is behavior of a system that does not depend on its individual elements, but on their interactive relationships to one another. Thus, emergent behavior is "unplanned" or "unexpected" and cannot be predicted by examination of a system's individual elements. It can only be predicted, managed, or controlled by understanding the elements and their interactive relationships. The impact of emergent behavior may be "positive" or "negative" (leading to a potential hazard) in nature and it is the negative impacts that are of interest from a safety perspective.

STPA Human Machine Interaction Example

The control structure for an ETRS shift-by-wire driver interaction system is presented in this example. The control structure shows the control flow of information, commands, actions, and feedback for a system comprising the driver, shifter interface device and the vehicle. The arrows illustrate the main control activities for this system.

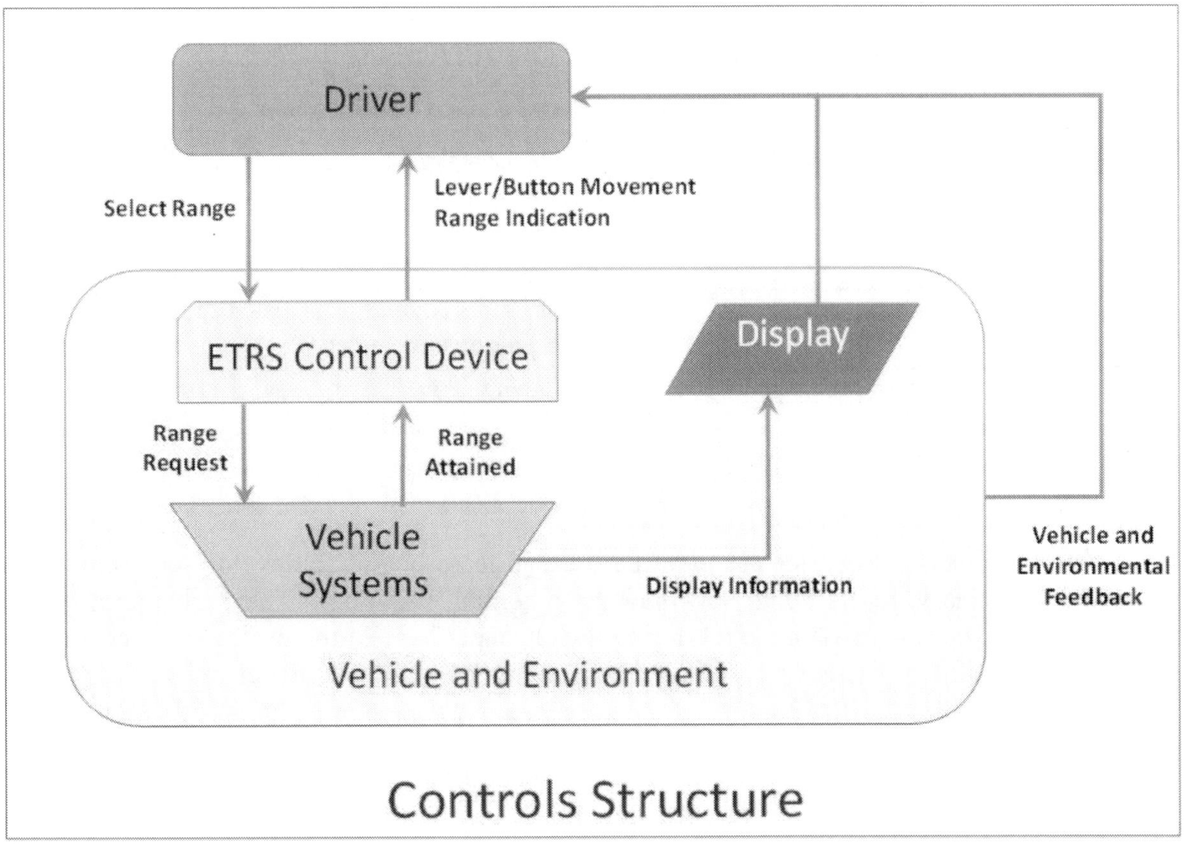

Figure 8 - Human Machine Interaction Control Structure Example

The next step, once the control structure has been created, is to evaluate each system element's "functions" against a series of "misbehavior" guidewords. Doing this results in a listing of unsafe (undesired/unexpected) control actions (UCAs). Table 5 shows one of the functions of the "Driver" system element and the resulting UCAs. The guidewords are shown to the right of the "Driver Control Functions".

Table 5 - Functions and Unsafe Control Actions

Identify Unsafe Control Actions (UCAs)				
Driver Control Functions (Actions or Responsibilities)	"NOT Providing" Cause Hazard	"Providing" Cause Hazard	Incorrect Timing Incorrect Order	Stopped Too Soon Applied Too Long
Decide when to shift	UCA0.5: Driver does not put car in Park prior to exiting vehicle	UCA5: Driver puts car in a Non-Park range when intending to go to Park	UCA9: Driver selects Reverse at speed	UCA11: Driver quickly taps desried range
	UCA0.7: Driver does not put car in Park remaining in vehicle	UCA6: Driver decides to select Drive when Reverse is needed	UCA10: Driver selects Park at speed	UCA12: Driver holds desired range I/F for prolonged time

With the control actions identified (or once any of the unsafe control actions are identified, i.e., the process does not have to be completely serial), the STPA progresses to identify the potential causes of scenarios leading to unsafe control. In this step, information is generated to assist designers in eliminating or mitigating the potential causes of the hazard. This step involves examining the control loop and its parts, and identifying how they could lead to an undesired control action. Table 6 illustrates potential causal scenarios for this example.

Table 6 - Unsafe Control Actions and Potential Causal Scenarios

Identify Causes for Unsafe Control Actions (UCAs)	
UCA	Potential Causal Scenarios
UCA0.5: Driver does not put car in park prior to exiting vehicle	Driver is distracted, or in a panic mode, or is rushing to decide to get into Park
UCA0.5: Driver does not put car in park prior to exiting vehicle	Driver already thinks the car is in Park because of a previous action
UCA0.5: Driver does not put car in park prior to exiting vehicle	Driver thinks it is already in Park because belief the vehicle will do it automatically
UCA0.5: Driver does not put car in park prior to exiting vehicle	Driver cannot find Park
UCA0.5: Driver does not put car in park prior to exiting vehicle	Driver performs prior habitual actions leads to not selecting Park in this vehicle (Prior Learned Behavior)

Once the causal scenarios are identified, the process begins to develop requirements and constraints necessary to eliminate or manage potential hazards. These requirements and constraints may start out at a high level during the concept phase of the project and become more detailed as the STPA methodology continues to evaluate more detailed levels of the design.

Both requirements and constraints need to be accommodated in Human-Machine Interaction (HMI) design. Requirements provide component design teams with specific parameters, such as depression forces, toggle angles, and button-to-bezel interface dimensions. Constraints inform design studio teams that they need to design buttons or toggle levers in a manner that accommodates certain types of activation sequences, but not specify the exact look or feel of the interaction. Where necessary, requirements parameter values should be obtained from user clinics employing both static (bench) and dynamic (in vehicle) testing conducted by both GM and independent test groups. Table 7 shows requirements conveyed to the design studio to manage the HMI risk.

Table 7 - Requirements to Prevent or Manage Causal Scenarios

Identify Requirements to Prevent or Manage Causal Scenarios		
UCA	Potential Causal Scenarios	Requirements
UCA0.5: Driver does not put car in park prior to exiting vehicle	Driver is distracted, or in a panic mode, or is rushing to decide to get into Park	Controls are clearly identified and obvious, easily accessable
UCA0.5: Driver does not put car in park prior to exiting vehicle	Driver already thinks the car is in Park because of a previous action	Display P in large font
UCA0.5: Driver does not put car in park prior to exiting vehicle	Driver thinks it is already in Park because belief the vehicle will do it automatically	Chime/Warning/Message when exit
UCA0.5: Driver does not put car in park prior to exiting vehicle	Driver thinks it is already in Park because belief the vehicle will do it automatically	Audible feedback for Park and Reverse achievement
UCA0.5: Driver does not put car in park prior to exiting vehicle	Driver cannot find Park	Controls are clearly identified and obvious, easily accessable
UCA0.5: Driver does not put car in park prior to exiting vehicle	Driver performs prior habitual actions leads to not selecting Park in this vehicle (Prior Learned Behavior)	Park located at end of PRNDL pattern

Understanding the generated requirements' and constraints' linkage to potential hazardous states allows "Design Center" teams to accommodate safety requirements (data driven) directly into the system design components.

Figure 9 – Logic Flow for STPA Generated Requirements

Resulting requirements are transposed to a System Safety Concept document (used during the Concept review) and/or to production specific collateral documenting requirements and constraints. Figure 10 illustrates the overall STPA process from control structure to requirement and constraints incorporation into appropriate production specifications.

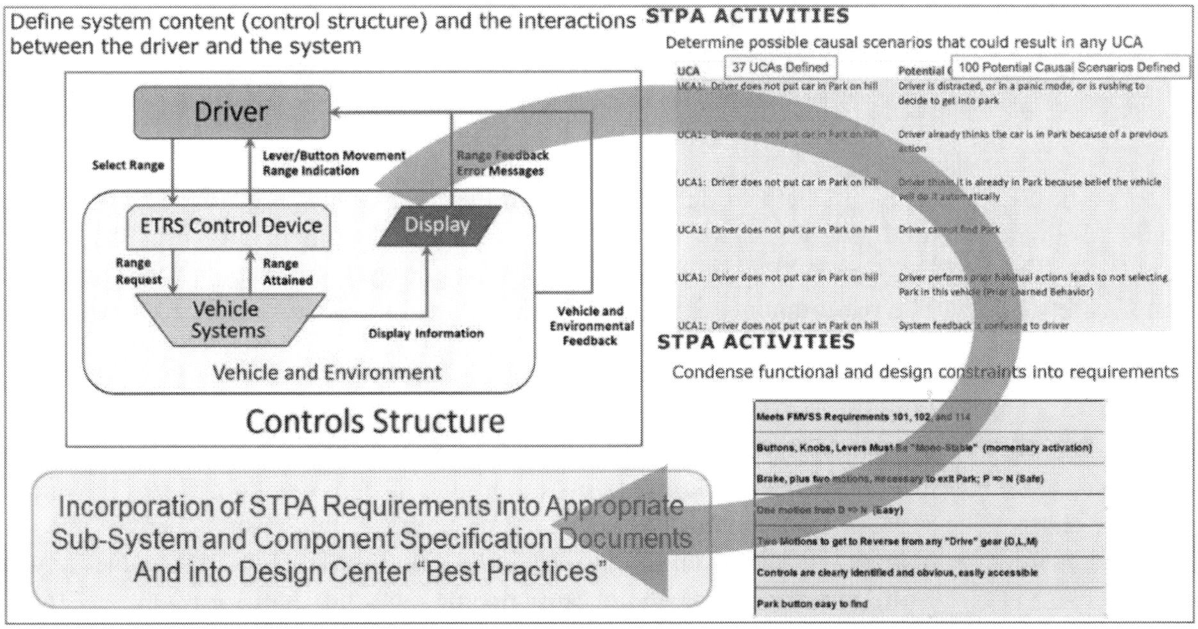

Figure 10 – STPA Requirements Allocated to Requirements Documents

A successful example where STPA generated requirements were incorporated into a production design is shown in Figure 11 where these requirements were captured for, and implemented on, the 2018 GMC Terrain.

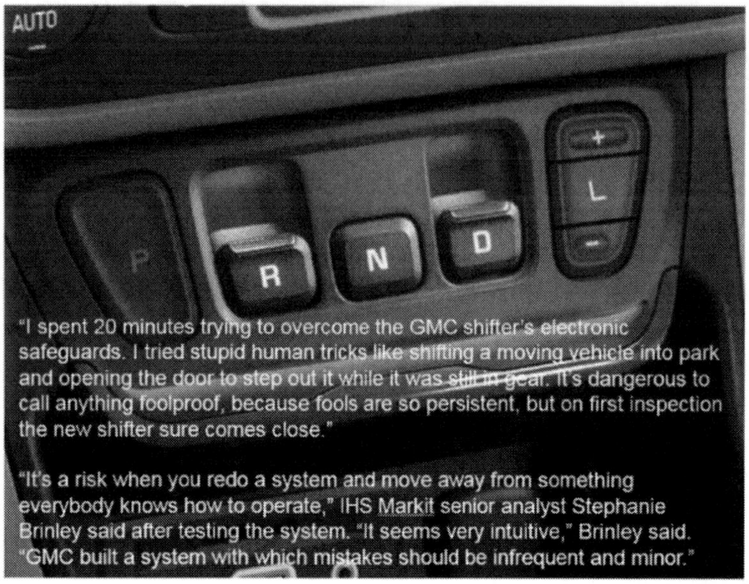

Mark Phelan ,
Detroit Free Press
Auto Critic
Published 10:38 p.m. ET July 1, 2017 **Updated 4:24 p.m. ET July 2, 2017**

http://www.freep.com/story/money/cars/mark-phelan/2017/07/02/gmc-2018-terrain-suv/441807001/
for video and full article

Figure 11 – 2018 GMS Terrain Shift by Wire Example

Safety Concept Requirements

The SEFA and STPA help to determine the faults, failures and user interface issues that could result in potential safety hazards. The Safety Concept document will use SEFA/STPA results (as well as PHA and HARA information) to assess the system's capability to satisfy the stated safety goals. The requirements defined in the SEFA and the STPA are transposed into the Safety Concept document and appropriate system requirements documents where they will represent the initial set of safety critical system-level requirements.

Feedback from the SEFA/STPA evaluations may drive changes to the system design necessary to satisfy the safety metric requirements before the system design matures beyond the concept phase. The SEFA/STPA content provides the rationale for such design changes in a clear and understandable manner. In addition, diagnostic and algorithm development teams may use the SEFA/STPA results as a starting point for diagnostic and fault mitigation strategy development. These teams can consult the requirements section of the SEFA/STPA and/or the Safety Concept to begin the diagnostic architecture and the mitigation action implementations.

Summary

The SEFA is a system-level, top-down, exploratory analysis technique to evaluate the impact of system element faults upon the system as a whole and to determine if the system has sufficient content to detect and mitigate potential hazardous states created due to the failure. The result of this evaluation provides constraints and requirements necessary to achieve the stated safety goals of the system.

Application of STPA analysis should be used on systems that have complex, or numerous system element, functional interactions as well as any system that includes driver interactions as part of the system where accidental and inadvertent interactions between driver and system could lead to potential safety hazards.

An example of when both a SEFA and STPA evaluation should be conducted would be a hybrid system that has been specified to use ETRS. The various controllers of a system (e.g., ECM, TCM, HCP, MCP, etc.), CAN and LIN communications, door switches, seat belt switches, display devices, and internal transmission parts like Park-inhibit solenoids, and Park attainment switches, etc., would be included in the SEFA "working, not-working" evaluation. However, driver interactions with shifter devices and the driver recognition and internalization of feedback messages or system status messages are not easily covered by a SEFA approach. This is where the STPA approach may be linked to the system's SEFA effort, as it would take the next step to look at causal scenarios where inadvertent or accidental activation of shift-by-wire devices may lead to undesired system behaviors. Appropriate message content and presentation criteria for driver action and intervention requests or system status feedback then could be developed. The STPA methodology is extremely effective in these types of evaluations.

For systems like shift-by-wire, the STPA process could evaluate specific portions of this complex system, or the whole system as the STPA process is hierarchical in nature. Engineers could perform a detailed evaluation of the potential causes of unsafe control actions based on the functions of those elements being assessed by the STPA guideword interaction testing. Therefore, a detailed set of requirements based on the STPA effort could be provided without first doing a SEFA. GM is in the process of evaluating potential overlap between SEFA and STPA evaluations.

Results from SEFA/STPA analyses are useful for identifying possible content revisions to the system architecture necessary to ensure adequate diagnostic capability and mitigation management. This enables safety to be "built into the design" right from initial engineering efforts prior to freeze of the concept/architecture content. These methodologies identify initial system requirements necessary to eliminate, and/or manage and mitigate resulting unintended or unwanted system behavior caused by system element faults eliminating cost and timing impacts later.

References

Leveson, N., & Thomas, J. (2018). *STPA Handbook.* Cambridge MA: MIT.

Biography

Mark A. Vernacchia, BSME, MSES, P.E. - GM Technical Fellow, Principal System Safety Engineer – Propulsion Systems (Worldwide)

Mark is a GM Technical Fellow and the Principal Systems Safety Engineer for all propulsion systems at General Motors. Mark has extensive experience in systems engineering and systems safety processes.

He is a registered Professional Engineer in the State of Michigan

Mark holds a Master's Degree in Engineering Sciences from Rensselaer Polytechnic Institute and a Bachelor's of Science in Mechanical Engineering from Purdue University.

Automated Human Performance Monitoring for Air Traffic Control Safety through Bayesian Network Modeling and Video Surveillance

Zhe Sun, MS; Arizona State University; Tempe, AZ, USA

Jiawei Chen, BS; Arizona State University; Tempe, AZ, USA

Rui Li, MS; Arizona State University; Tempe, AZ, USA

Shuai Li, MS; Arizona State University; Tempe, AZ, USA

Pingbo Tang, Ph.D.; Arizona State University; Tempe, AZ, USA

Yongming Liu, Ph.D.; Arizona State University; Tempe, AZ, USA

Keywords: human behavior monitoring, Bayesian Network modeling, video surveillance

Abstract

Human behaviors, such as facial and motion behaviors indicate the physiological condition of air traffic controllers (ATCs) and could affect aviation safety. Excessive eye-blinks and looking away from the surveillance screen are anomalous behaviors of ATCs, which frequently occurred while coordinating air traffic. These behaviors are indicators of fatigue and distraction of ATCs, which induces human errors that have contributed to more than 75% of aviation accidents in the United States (U.S.). Human behavior monitoring of ATCs is thus necessary to not only recognize anomalous behaviors but also predict how human errors occur and propagate during air traffic control. Few existing studies have investigated spatiotemporal details about how human errors occurred due to anomalous human behaviors. Limited studies have quantified the dependence relationship between anomalous human behaviors and human errors that might lead to accidents during ground and near-ground movement (e.g. taxi, take-off, and landing) of aircraft. The goal of the presented research is to evaluate how automatic video analysis algorithms could help detect anomalous behaviors of ATCs and spatiotemporal details about how errors due to fatigue and distractions eventually lead to incidents/accidents. This study uses a Bayesian Network (BN) model derived from historical records of air traffic control to quantitatively assess how fatigue and distraction cause human errors and lead to accidents eventually. The authors integrated this BN model with a video-based tracking algorithm for automatically alarming potentially problematic ATCs in videos.

Introduction

Air traffic control is a complex process, which involves maintaining a minimum separation between aircraft in order to prevent collisions and maintaining an orderly and expeditious air traffic flow (Shafique & Author, 2014; Wu, Mu, & Feng, 2015). Air traffic controllers (ATCs) need to continuously monitor the movements of all aircraft and communicate with pilots to provide instructions (Loft, Sanderson, Neal, & Mooij, 2007). However, human errors of ATCs have been claimed as the major threat to aviation safety and contributed to more than 75% of aviation accidents (Wu et al., 2015). The Federal Aviation Administration (FAA) stated that human errors remain the major threat to aviation safety (FAA, 2005). Due to the increasing volume of air traffic, the complexity and workload of air traffic controllers increase significantly, which induce the risks of human errors. Pape claimed that as the number of aircraft and demands on air traffic control services has increased over the decades, the number of accidents and incidents increase as well (Pape, Wiegmann, & Shappell, 2001). At most of the airports in the United States (U.S.), several ATCs have to work in shifts and ensure 24 hours monitoring and control of the ground operation of an airport (Wu et al., 2015). During air traffic control processes, ATCs need to be multi-tasking, such as passing the weather information to the pilots, give necessary instruction to ground workers and pilots, handling aircrafts experiencing emergencies (Shafique & Author, 2014). Due to high workloads during air traffic control, the physical and mental condition of ATCs is critical to ensure the safety of air traffic control.

Facial and motion behaviors of air traffic controllers (ATCs) indirectly indicate the underlying physical and mental condition of ATCs during air traffic control (Tobaruela et al., 2014). Since most tasks of ATCs are cognitive tasks that have a high reliance on mental processes (Isaac, Shorrock, & Kirwan, 2002), distraction and fatigue of ATCs can be harmful and has been identified as the major threats to aviation safety. Anomalous behaviors (e.g. abnormal eye-blinks, distracted from the surveillance screen while controlling aircraft, etc.) of ATCs could occur due to high workload, which indicates the poor conditions of ATCs and increases the probabilities of human errors and causes air traffic control failures. Few studies have determined that abnormal eye-blink rates of human are indicators of fatigue and could be detected through surveillance monitoring (Ahmad & Borole, 2015; Pimplaskar, Nagmode, & Borkar, 2013). Wu stated that among all human-error-related aviation accidents, fatigue of ATCs has contributed to more than 21% of the accidents (Wu et al., 2015). Ameen claimed that most incidents involved lapses (i.e., failures to perform a required action) or mistakes and fatigue has been identified as one of the major factors that directly affect human behavior in term of accuracy and reaction time (Ameen, 2014). In addition, distractions of ATCs could also seriously increase the probabilities of human errors during air traffic control and cause accidents. It is thus necessary to monitor the behavior of ATCs detect anomalous behavior during air traffic control and avoid ATC-related accidents.

The current practice of human behavior monitoring in air traffic control heavily relies on the judgment of air traffic manager to determine whether an ATC need to be replaced. However, tedious manual monitoring through human observations might prone to supervisory errors. It is thus important to have an automated monitoring system to not only monitor human behaviors and also assess the physical and mental conditions of ATCs. Automated anomalous human behavior detection through video surveillance could help to identify ATCs' anomalous behaviors during air traffic control. Facial expression analysis could be used as the source of information for analyzing the fatigue and distraction of ATCs (Ameen, 2014). A human face is a complex three-dimensional object, with overlying surface pigmentation that specifies the reflectance properties of the skin, eyes, mouth and other features (O'Toole, Roark, Jiang, & Abdi, 2005). Analyzing human behaviors through automated video surveillance-based facial expression analysis is crucial to identify anomalous human behaviors (Tian, Kanade, & Cohn, 2005). Kulkarni has claimed that facial expressions could help better understand the emotion and mood of human and a classification of facial expressions could be used as an effective tool in the behavioral analysis (Kulkarni, Reddy, & Hariharan, 2009). Considering the fact that an effective tool to recognize and measure the behaviors of ATCs is a lack in the real practice of air traffic control. It is thus important to have an effective automated video surveillance system, which could automatically recognize anomalous ATCs' behaviors through facial expression analysis.

Previous studies have investigated how video surveillance could help to monitor human behavior through facial expression analysis (Ameen, 2014; Shan, Gong, & McOwan, 2009). Rhodes has developed an algorithm to assess anxiety of human through facial expression analysis (Palermo et al., 2017). The potential for using this technology has already been demonstrated in previous studies. Limited studies have examined how detected anomalous behaviors could cause human errors and then lead to accidents. Some studies have used data-driven BN modeling approach to provide a quantitative risk prediction of human error and accident occurrences by analyzing accident reports (Yang, 2009). However, few studies have examined to use video surveillance to monitor ATCs' behaviors and interpret the detected anomalies (e.g. abnormal eye-blinks), which can be used as inputs to a Bayesian Network to predict the likelihood of potential human errors and correlated accidents. This study proposes to integrate a Bayesian Network model derived from air traffic control records with a video-based tracking algorithm for automatically identifying problematic facial expression and motions of ATCs in videos to predict the likelihood of human errors and related accidents during air traffic control.

Methodology

The overall goal of this study is to evaluate how automatic video analysis algorithms could help detect distraction and fatigue of ATCs and spatiotemporal details about how errors due to fatigue and distractions eventually lead to ground and near-ground (the point between ramp and airborne during take-off/departing processes) incidents/accidents. The proposed research consists of two parts (see Figure 1): 1) *Real-time Video Surveillance*: the authors have developed an algorithm by integrating state-of-the-art video analysis algorithms and facial expression analysis to help detect distraction and fatigue in real-time. The developed algorithms will use the Eye Aspect Ratio (EAR) as an observable feature to feed into the Hidden Markov Model (HMM) to identify distraction and fatigue of ATCs; 2) *Knowledge Elicitation*: the authors collected air traffic control-related accident/incident reports from the Aviation Safety Reporting System (ASRS) and extract information about how distraction and fatigue of ATCs cause human errors in air traffic control and result in accidents/incidents. The authors then construct a Bayesian Network (BN) model to quantitatively assess the relationship between anomalous human behaviors (distraction and fatigue), human errors and ATC-related accidents using the extracted information. The proposed approach will use the detected anomalies based on the HH-based human behavior monitoring algorithm to feed into the developed BN for real-time risk assessment.

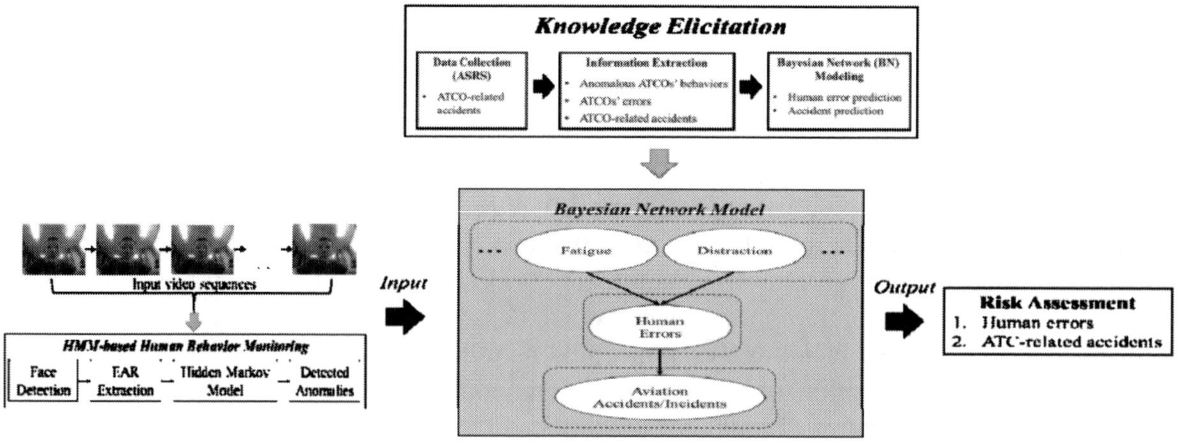

Figure 1— Overall Framework

Real-time Video Surveillance Monitoring for Distraction and Fatigue Detection

The authors developed a sensor-based human behavior-monitoring algorithm through a state-of-the-art automatic facial expression analysis. This algorithm uses a standard camera of a laptop and uses the laptop screen as the information display in the air traffic control room. The authors ask one volunteer to sit in front of the laptop and performing air traffic control duties by playing the video game *Airport Madness 3D* (an air traffic control video game, the user need to act as an ATC to control multiple aircraft at the selected airport) to simulate the air traffic control process. In the meantime, the authors use the front camera of the laptop to examine how the distraction and fatigue detection algorithms could help recognize the behaviors of the volunteer within the certain time frame. The developed algorithm aims at helping identify ATCs' poor physical/mental conditions by recognizing anomalous behaviors and use the detected anomalies as input to the BN. This algorithm could help identify anomalous ATC behaviors during air traffic control in the control room in real-time.

Distraction detection. The control room is a complex work environment where ATCs need to conduct multi-tasks by monitoring certain information displays (e.g. radar, weather displays, etc.) to ensure safe operations of air traffic control. Distraction could be harmful and induce risks of human errors (e.g. communication errors). While controlling the aircraft during take-off or landing processes, ATC needs to continuously monitor the surveillance screen or the aircraft to ensure a minimum separation between aircraft for safe takeoff and landing. Distracted from the screen or aircraft could be critical and induce risks of having accidents. The authors established a simulated environment with one participant sitting in front of a laptop act as an ATC to control aircraft by playing video game *Airport Madness 3D*. During the simulation game, the participant (ATC) need to give directions to aircraft for take-off or landing and ensuring minimum separation between several aircraft with his face facing to the screen. The participant can also take breaks and does not have to stare at the screen while the air traffic volume is low. During the game, the participant will receive messages while controlling aircraft and taking breaks. The authors then developed a real-time distraction detection algorithm using the video camera of a laptop to detect whether the "ATC" playing the video game has been distracted. This algorithm uses the face detection to determine whether the person using the laptop is facing the screen. In this experiment, only if the "ATC" check and reply messages with his head facing down to his cell phone while controlling aircraft will be considered as a distracted.

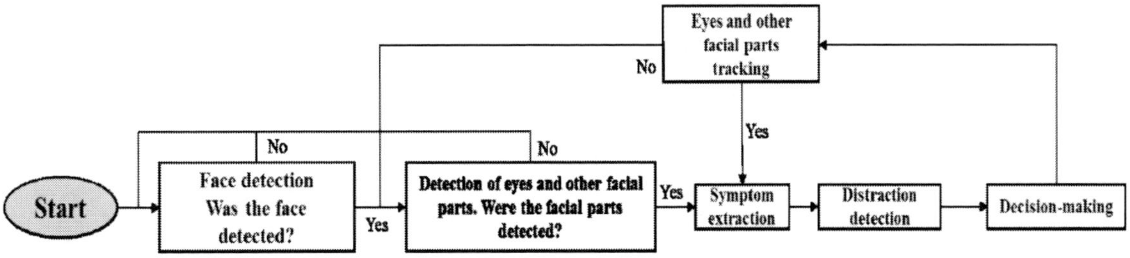

Figure 2— Distraction Detection Flowchart

Figure 2 shows the major steps of image processing for distraction monitoring. The proposed method includes preprocessing, detection and tracking of face, eyes and other facial components (Sigari, Fathy, & Soryani, 2013). The first step is to locate the face in the image. After the algorithm locates where the face is, the algorithm detects facial parts such as the eyes, nose, and mouth. The algorithm extracts the symptoms of human (e.g. face pose direction), which indicate whether the ATC in front of a computer screen is looking away from the screen or not. Continuous tracking of eyes and other facial parts is important to ensure that the algorithm can obtain the symptoms continuously.

Fatigue detection. Air traffic control involves a large number of complex tasks and requires extended periods of high concentration. ATC fatigue can compromise aviation safety. Frequent eye blinks are important indicators of ATCs' fatigue. Soukupová has developed a real-time eye blink detection algorithm using facial landmarks in a video sequence from a standard camera (Soukupová, 2016). The proposed research uses facial landmark detection and Hidden Markov Model (HMM) to recognize human fatigue in real time (see Figure 3). Hidden Markov Models (HMM) are a set of statistical models used to characterize the statistical properties of a signal (Nefian et al. 1998). Since human's facial states are dependent and different at each frame but are closely related with each other. HMM could effectively characterize the statistical properties of each frame and recognize whether a human is being concentrated or fatigue.

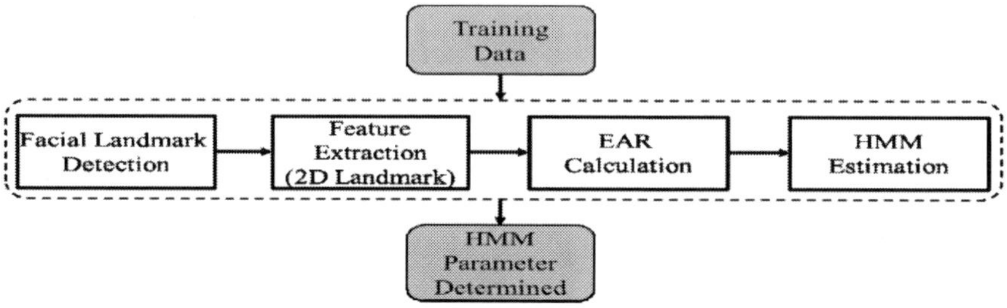

Figure 3— Fatigue Detection Algorithm Flowchart

The researchers first collected the training data, which is a series of video clips with the labeled facial expressions in the video frame while the volunteer is playing the video game in front of the laptop. In the training stage, the authors first feed the videos into the face detection model to get the detected face. Then we compute the 68 facial landmarks at the detected face region and extract the Eye Aspect Ratio (EAR) as our observable feature to feed into the HMM (Bailenson et al., 2008) (see Figure 4). The authors then use the Expectation Maximization algorithm to learn the HMM's parameters until the model converge. In the end, this algorithm could use the learned model to recognize the hidden states of the HMM which in our case is the human's behaviors (e.g. fatigue or concentrate).

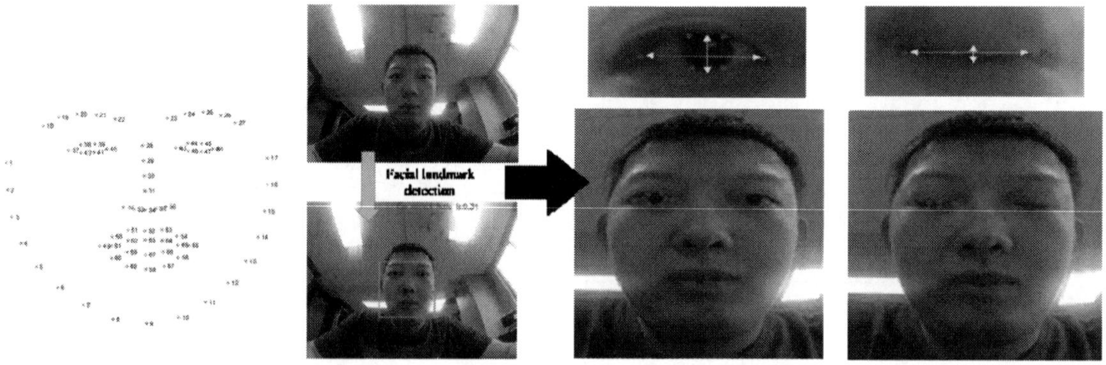

Figure 4— Facial Landmark Extraction for EAR Calculation (Soukupová, 2016)

$$EAR = \frac{\|p_2 - p_6\| + \|p_3 - p_5\|}{2\|p_1 - p_4\|}$$

(1)

where P_1, …, P_6 is the 2D landmark locations, depicted in Figure 4.

Bayesian Network (BN) Modeling

The authors constructed a Bayesian Network (BN) model (see Figure 5) using a large number of accident reports retrieved from the Aviation Safety Reporting System (ASRS), which captures the relationships between poor conditions of ATCs (fatigue and distraction), human errors, and ATC-related accidents. This BN model can provide useful information to assist aviation managers to understand how human errors occur while ATCs are in poor physical and mental conditions. The model can take detected anomalies of ATCs during aircraft take-offs and land as inputs and estimate the probabilities of human errors and then accidents thereafter.

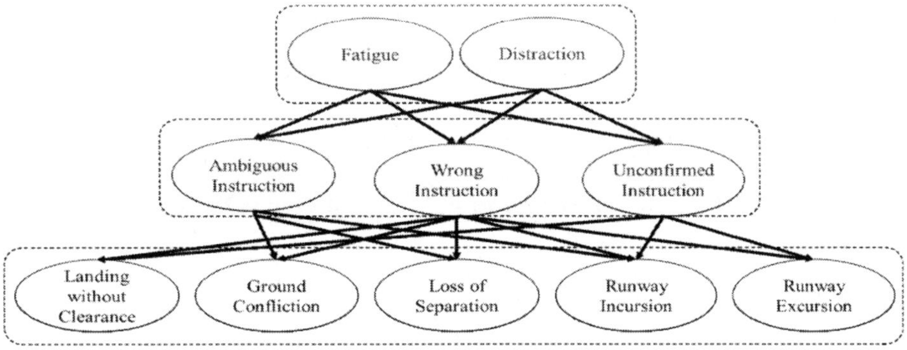

Figure 5—Bayesian Network Model

The authors first collect accident/incident reports of accidents/incidents caused by ATCs' distraction and fatigue during air traffic control from the Aviation Safety Report System (ASRS). The authors then extract the corresponding human errors due to fatigue and distraction. Three major types of human errors have been found in the accident/incident report: ambiguous instruction, wrong instruction, and unconfirmed instruction. During normal air traffic control operations, ATCs have to give clear instructions with "call sign" (flight number, e.g. AA888) to the specific pilot to resolve conflictions. When ATCs forget the call sign while issuing the instructions, there can be confusion among all pilots on the frequency as to whom the instructions were intended. Additionally, pilots are required to readback instructions over the radio so ATCs can confirm the instructions were heard and understood correctly. Errors in instructions call signs and readback confirmation can all occur during periods of ATC distraction and fatigue.

The authors then classify the accident/incident types and correlated with the human errors. Five major accidents/incidents occur frequently in the historical records including landing without clearance, ground confliction, loss of separation, runway incursion and runway excursion. The classification of anomalies are based on following principles, 1) Landing without clearance describes the scenarios that the aircraft landing at the wrong runway due to the unclear instruction is given by the ATCs; 2) Ground Confliction indicate the confliction between multiple aircraft or vehicle during the ground movement; 3) Loss of Separation describes the separation of aircrafts was under the minim separation requirement; 4) Runway Incursion describes any occurrence at an aerodrome involving the incorrect presence of an aircraft vehicle or person on the protected area of a surface designated for the landing and take-off of aircraft; 5) Runway Excursion describes when the situation when the wheels of an aircraft on the runway surface depart the end or the side of the runway surface.

Discussion

Distraction and Fatigue Detection

The research team set up an experiment at an indoor workspace to examine the proposed real-time distraction and fatigue detection algorithms. The research team complete one set of experiment with one participant act as an ATC to sit in front of a laptop play the video game (*Airport Madness 3D*) to simulate the air traffic control process. In the game, participants need to control multiple aircraft and give instructions to guide the pilots to take-off or landing. In addition, in cases of wrong or inappropriate instructions given to the pilots, collisions might happen between aircraft and the game will be over. While the volunteer is playing the video game, the authors will create some random noise (e.g. loud music, phone ringing, etc.) around the volunteer to create a distraction for the volunteer. The authors then used the front camera of the laptop to collect the video data of the volunteer for real-time distraction and fatigue detection while the volunteer is playing the game. Results showing in Table 1 indicate that within 5 minutes, 2,930 frames have been collected and 525 frames have been identified as "user being distracted" and 1,460 frames has been recognized as "fatigue".

Table 1— Distraction and Fatigue Detection Results

Time period/Total Frames	5 minutes/2930 frames
Times of being Distracted Recognized	525
Times of being Concentrate Recognized	2405
Times of fatigue recognized (True Positive)	1460
Times of fatigue recognized (False Positive)	35

Bayesian Network Modeling

In this section, the authors are showing the results indicate the probabilistic relationship according to the risk knowledge captured in the developed BN. In the BN model, the first layer includes fatigue and distraction, which are the causal conditions that frequently occur in the historical records. The corresponding human errors are described in the second layer of the BN. The third layer of the BN indicates the most common accident/incident types that occur due to human errors illustrated in the second layer. This BN provides useful information on how distraction and fatigue will cause certain human errors during air traffic control and eventually result in different kinds of accidents/incidents. Results in Table 2 indicate that ATCs are more likely to give wrong and ambiguous instructions when he/she is distracted. In addition, when ATCs are fatigued, it is more likely he/she will give wrong instructions to pilots.

Table 2—Conditional Probability of Human Errors on Distraction and Fatigue

Poor Conditions of ATCs	Human Errors	Conditional Probability
Distraction	Ambiguous Instruction	0.4
	Wrong Instruction	0.4
	Unconfirmed Instruction	0.2
Fatigue	Ambiguous Instruction	0.3
	Wrong Instruction	0.5
	Unconfirmed Instruction	0.2

Results in Table 3 indicate that ambiguous instructions given by ATCs will usually cause loss of separation between aircraft and runway incursions. Wrong instructions will cause more loss of separation and ground conflicts between multiple aircraft and ground vehicles. In addition, when ATCs forget to confirm the read-back from pilots, runway incursions are more likely to occur.

Table 3—Conditional Probability of Most Frequent Accidents/Incidents on Human Errors

Human Errors	Accidents/Incidents	Conditional Probability
Ambiguous Instruction	Loss of Separation	0.47
	Runway Incursion	0.17
Wrong Instruction	Loss of Separation	0.45
	Ground Confliction	0.16
Unconfirmed Instruction	Runway Incursion	0.51

Conclusion

This research proposed a real-time fatigue and distraction monitoring of ATCs to ensure aviation safety through real-time video surveillance and BN modeling. BN offers the capability of modeling the process of how fatigue and distractions of ATCs cause human errors that eventually result in accidents/incidents. The developed BN also help quantify the correlation between anomalous human behaviors (distraction and fatigue), human errors and accidents/incidents. The real-time human behavior monitoring algorithm uses facial expression detection techniques to capture abnormal eye-blinks and whether an ATC is looking away from surveillance screen. These anomalous behaviors are indicators of fatigue and distraction of ATCs, which then used as input to feed into the developed BN to get real-time risk assessment during air traffic control.

However, since the proposed research uses video game and student volunteer to examine the capability of using a video analysis algorithm to detect fatigue and distraction, the results might not be reliable and representative. In addition, due to the limited amount of incident reports being analyzed in this study, the probabilistic relationship captured by the developed BN could only apply to the selected dataset and might not be representative for all cases. The research team will establish a more compelling experiment design that includes baseline (undistracted and rested) and differentiate "types" of distraction (e.g. looking away from the screen, looking at wrong part of the screen, looking away at critical times) to better link these anomalies to ATCs' performance.

Acknowledgment

The research reported in this paper was supported by funds from NASA University Leadership Initiative program (Contract No. NNX17AJ86A, Project Officer: Dr. Kai Goebel, Principal Investigator: Dr. Yongming Liu). The support is gratefully acknowledged. The authors would also like to express our very great appreciation to Dr. Yezhou Yang for his valuable and constructive suggestions during the planning and development of this research work. His willingness to give his time so generously has been very much appreciated.

Copyrights

References

Ahmad, R., & Borole, P. J. N. (2015). Drowsy Driver Identification Using Eye Blink detection, *6*(1), 270–274.

Ameen, S. (2014). Review of Fatigue Systems and Implementation of Face Components Segregation, 5–8.

Bailenson, J. N., Pontikakis, E. D., Mauss, I. B., Gross, J. J., Jabon, M. E., Hutcherson, C. A. C., … John, O. (2008). Real-time classification of evoked emotions using facial feature tracking and physiological responses. *International Journal of Human-Computer Studies*, *66*(5), 303–317. https://doi.org/10.1016/j.ijhcs.2007.10.011

FAA. (2005). Runway Incursion Trends and Initiatives at Towered Airports in the United States, FY 2001 through FY 2004, (August).

Isaac, A., Shorrock, S. T., & Kirwan, B. (2002). Human error in European air traffic management: The HERA project. *Reliability Engineering and System Safety*, *75*(2), 257–272. https://doi.org/10.1016/S0951-8320(01)00099-0

Kulkarni, S. S., Reddy, N. P., & Hariharan, S. I. (2009). Facial expression (mood) recognition from facial images using committee neural networks. *BioMedical Engineering Online*, *8*, 1–12. https://doi.org/10.1186/1475-925X-8-16

Loft, S., Sanderson, P. M., Neal, A., & Mooij, M. (2007). Modeling and Predicting Mental Workload in En Route Air Traffic Control□: Critical Review and Broader Implications. *Human Factors*, *49*(3), 376–399. https://doi.org/10.1518/001872007X197017.

O'Toole, A. J., Roark, D. A., Jiang, F., & Abdi, H. (2005). Predicting Human Performance for Face Recognition. *Face Processing: Advanced Modeling and Methods*, (2006), 293–319.

Palermo, R., Jeffery, L., Lewandowsky, J., Fiorentini, C., Irons, J. L., Dawel, A., … Rhodes, G. (2017).

Adaptive Face Coding Contributes to Individual Differences in Facial Expression Recognition Independently of Affective Factors. *Journal of Experimental Psychology: Human Perception and Performance*, *44*(4), 503–517. https://doi.org/10.1037/xhp0000463

Pape, A. M., Wiegmann, D. A., & Shappell, S. (2001). Air traffic control (ATC) related accidents and incidents: A human factors analysis, 1–4.

Pimplaskar, D., Nagmode, M. S., & Borkar, A. (2013). Real-Time Eye Blinking Detection and Tracking Using OpenCV, *3*(5), 1780–1787.

Shafique, Y., & Author, C. (2014). Managing the Performance of Air Traffic Controllers□: Developing and Proposing a Conceptual Perspective, *6*(7), 267–277.

Shan, C., Gong, S., & McOwan, P. W. (2009). Facial expression recognition based on Local Binary Patterns: A comprehensive study. *Image and Vision Computing*, *27*(6), 803–816. https://doi.org/10.1016/j.imavis.2008.08.005

Sigari, M. H., Fathy, M., & Soryani, M. (2013). A driver face monitoring system for fatigue and distraction detection. *International Journal of Vehicular Technology*, *2013*. https://doi.org/10.1155/2013/263983

Soukupová, T. (2016). Real-Time Eye Blink Detection using Facial Landmarks. *Rimske Toplice*.

Tian, Y. L., Kanade, T., & Cohn, J. F. (2005). Facial expression analysis. *Handbook of Face Recognition*, 247–275. https://doi.org/10.1007/0-387-27257-7_12

Tobaruela, G., Schuster, W., Majumdar, A., Ochieng, W. Y., Martinez, L., & Hendrickx, P. (2014). A method to estimate air traffic controller mental workload based on traffic clearances. *Journal of Air Transport Management*, *39*, 59–71. https://doi.org/10.1016/j.jairtraman.2014.04.002

Wu, F., Mu, H., & Feng, S. (2015). Analysis of the Risk of Air Traffic Controllers' Fatigue Based on the SHEL Model. *ASCE ICTE*, 2951–2958.

Yang, G. (2009). Analysis of Runway Incursion in Civil Airport Based on Bayesian Network, 927–933.

Mathematical Techniques to Improve the Utility of a Hazard Risk Matrix

Don Swallom
U.S. Army Aviation and Missile Command
Redstone Arsenal, Alabama

August 2018

1

Caveat

Opinions expressed are those of the author and not the coordinated position of AMCOM, Army Materiel Command, the US Army or the Department of Defense.

But they should be...

Topics for this Tutorial

- Purpose of a Hazard Risk Matrix
- Understanding the Attributes of a well-designed risk assessment matrix
- How to Assign a Risk Assessment Code
- Understanding Probability
- Building an Expanded Matrix
- Plotting Accidents on a Matrix
- Using Relative Risk Values
- Building Hazard Risk Profiles

3

Source of the DOD Hazard Risk Matrix

4

Purpose of a Hazard Risk Matrix

- Determine who accepts the risk of a particular hazard

"...The Program Manager will use the methodology in MIL-STD-882E...Prior to exposing people, equipment, or the environment to known system-related ESOH hazards, the Program Manager will document that the associated risks have been accepted by the following acceptance authorities: the CAE for high risks, Program Executive Officer-level for serious risks, and the Program Manager for medium and low risks..." - Department of Defense Instruction 5000.02, January 7, 2015.

5

Purpose of a Hazard Risk Matrix

- Inform the risk acceptor of the nature of the risk.
- "It's a 1D, Serious" does not really do that.

"The standard for risk management is leadership at the appropriate level of authority making **informed** decisions to control hazards or accept risks."

Army Regulation 385-10
The Army Safety Program
29 February 2000

6

Topics for this Tutorial

- Purpose of a Hazard Risk Matrix
- **Understanding the Attributes of a well-designed risk assessment matrix**
- How to Assign a Risk Assessment Code
- Understanding Probability
- Building an Expanded Matrix
- Plotting Accidents on a Matrix
- Using Relative Risk Values
- Building Hazard Risk Profiles

7

Attributes of a well-designed risk assessment matrix

① Severity scale covers full range of possible outcomes

Severity		1	2	3	4	5	6	7	8
		≥$2k	≥$20k	≥$200k	≥$2M	≥$20M	≥$200M	≥$2B	≥$20B
Frequency		Injury, no lost work day	Lost Work Day	Permanent partial disability	≥1 Fatality	≥10 Fatalities	≥100 Fatalities	≥1,000 Fatalities	≥10,000 Fatalities
A	>100								
B	>10								
C	>1							Prohibitive SECDEF	
D	>0.1						High - CAE		
E	>0.01					Serious - PEO			
F	>0.001			Medium - PM			Proposed		
G	>0.0001	Low – SSWG/Principal for Safety					DOD		
H	>0.00001						Matrix		
I	> 0.000001								
J	≤ 0.000001								

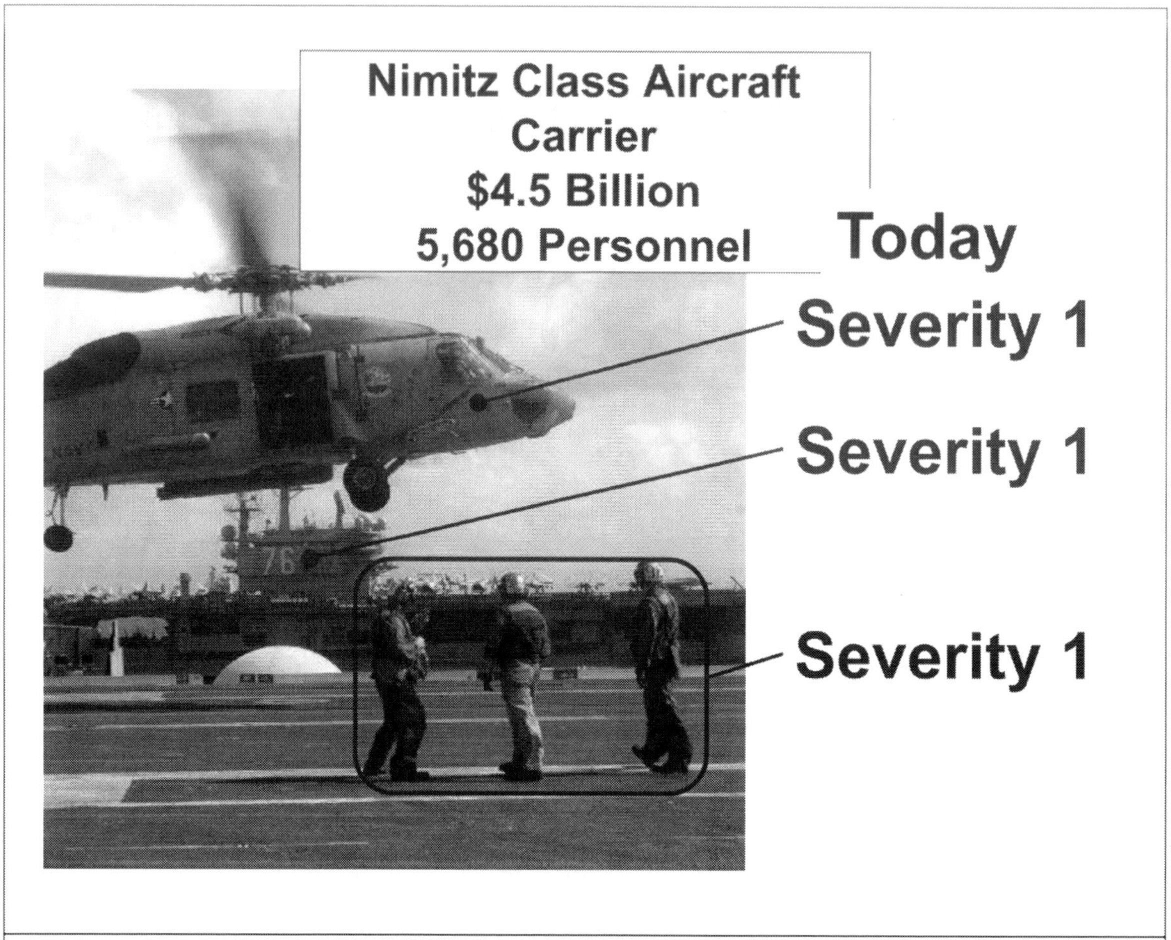
Nimitz Class Aircraft
Carrier
$4.5 Billion
5,680 Personnel
Today
Severity 1
Severity 1
Severity 1

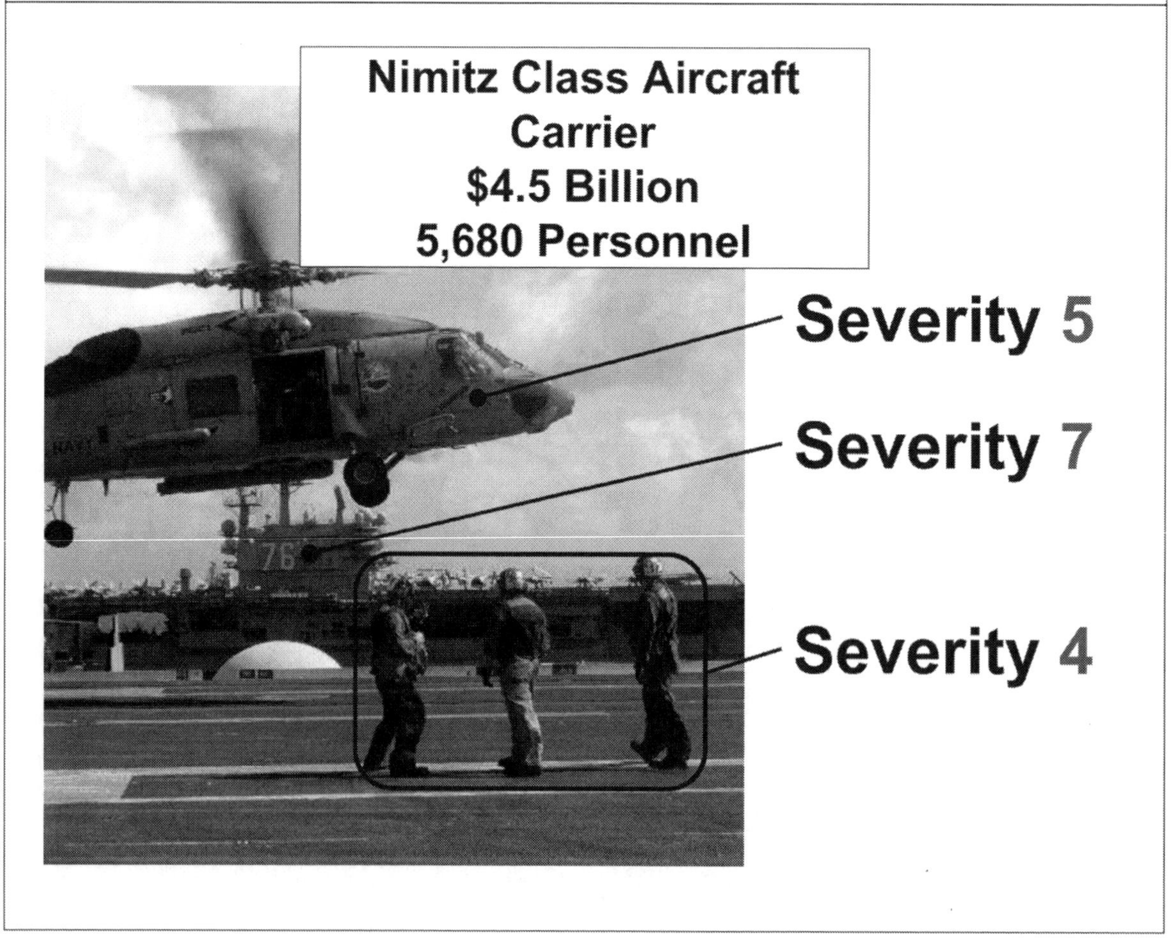
Nimitz Class Aircraft
Carrier
$4.5 Billion
5,680 Personnel
Severity 5
Severity 7
Severity 4

Politics

Navy Seeks $30 Million to Fix Gear That Hobbled Its New Carrier

By Anthony Capaccio
July 25, 2018, 10:04 AM CDT

- Congress asked to shift funds to repair Ford aircraft carrier
- Huntington Ingalls continues talks with General Electric

LIVE ON BLOOMBERG
Watch Live TV
Listen to Live Radio

LISTEN TO ARTICLE
▶ 1:25

SHARE THIS ARTICLE
Facebook
Twitter
LinkedIn
Email

The Navy is asking Congress to shift $30 million from other accounts to start repairing a damaged gear on the service's costliest warship, the Gerald R. Ford aircraft carrier.

The request for funds to repair the $13 billion carrier is part of a Pentagon package asking congressional approval to shift $4.7 billion in previously approved Army, Air Force and Navy funding into new programs or higher-priority projects. The package must be approved by all four congressional defense committees, where it's pending.

11

Attributes of a well-designed risk assessment matrix

② Severity / Frequency

Probability calibrated with reference to an exposure interval (accidents per 1,000 troops per year, accidents per 100,000 FH, accidents per 1,000,000 missile firings, etc.)

Severity		1	2	3	4	5	6	7	8
Frequency		≥$2k	≥$20k	≥$200k	≥$2M	≥$20M	≥$200M	≥$2B	≥$20B
A	>100								
B	>10								
C	>1							Prohibitive SECDEF	
D	>0.1						High - CAE		
E	>0.01					Serious - PEO			
F	>0.001				Medium - PM				
G	>0.0001	Low – SSWG/Principal for Safety							
H	>0.00001								
I	> 0.000001								
J	≤ 0.000001								

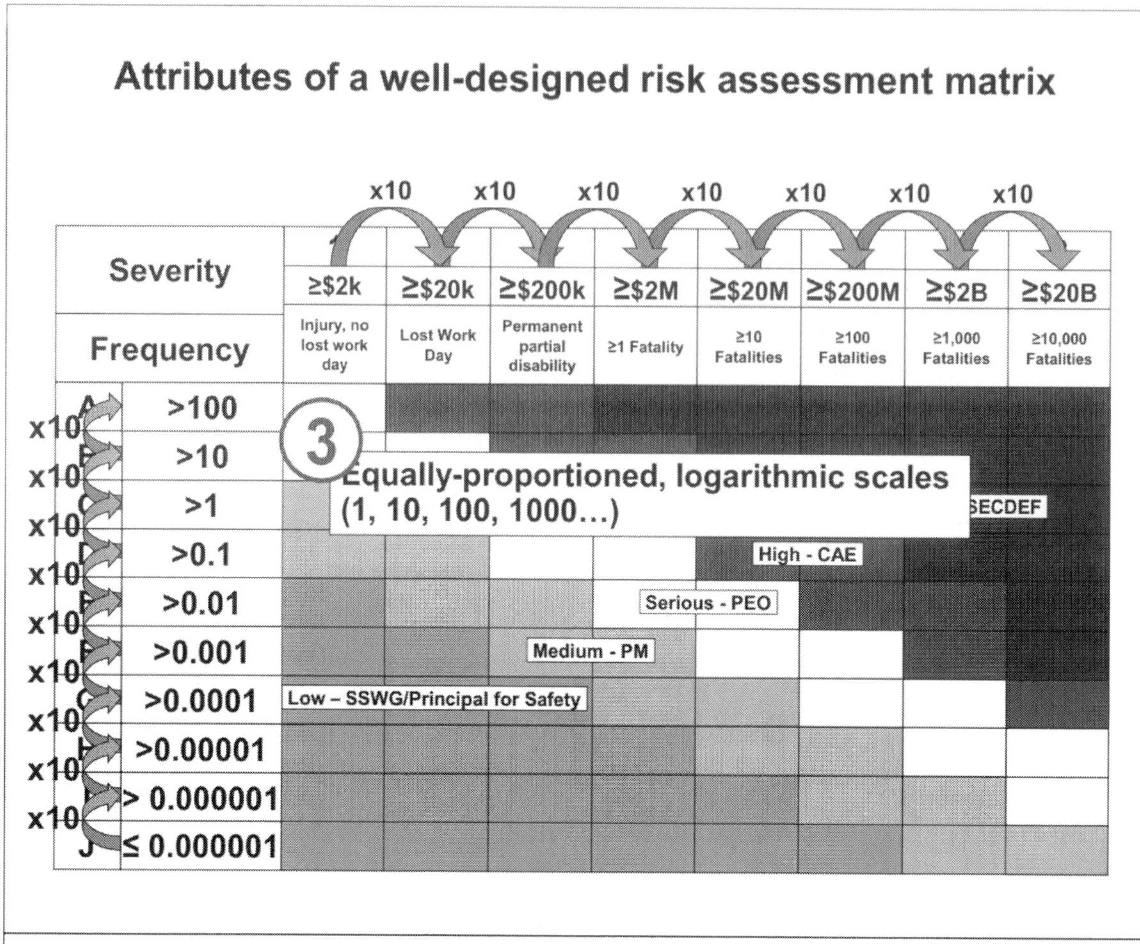
Attributes of a well-designed risk assessment matrix
x10 x10 x10 x10 x10 x10 x10
Severity
≥$2k ≥$20k ≥$200k ≥$2M ≥$20M ≥$200M ≥$2B ≥$20B
Injury, no lost work day
Lost Work Day
Permanent partial disability
≥1 Fatality
≥10 Fatalities
≥100 Fatalities
≥1,000 Fatalities
≥10,000 Fatalities
Frequency
>100
>10
>1
>0.1
>0.01
>0.001
>0.0001
>0.00001
> 0.000001
J ≤ 0.000001
x10
3
Equally-proportioned, logarithmic scales (1, 10, 100, 1000…)
High - CAE
Serious - PEO
Medium - PM
Low – SSWG/Principal for Safety

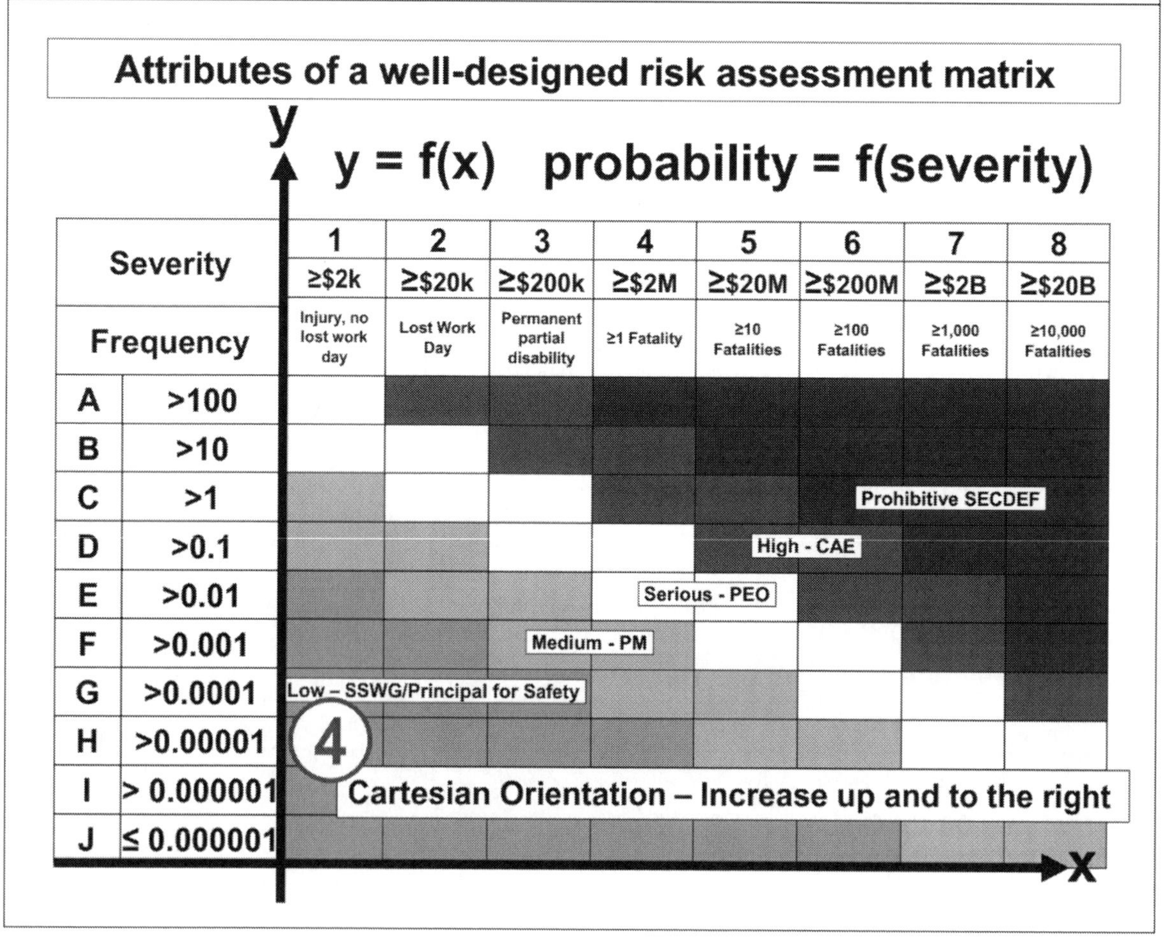
Attributes of a well-designed risk assessment matrix
y
y = f(x) probability = f(severity)
Severity
1 2 3 4 5 6 7 8
≥$2k ≥$20k ≥$200k ≥$2M ≥$20M ≥$200M ≥$2B ≥$20B
Injury, no lost work day
Lost Work Day
Permanent partial disability
≥1 Fatality
≥10 Fatalities
≥100 Fatalities
≥1,000 Fatalities
≥10,000 Fatalities
Frequency
A >100
B >10
C >1
D >0.1
E >0.01
F >0.001
G >0.0001
H >0.00001
I > 0.000001
J ≤ 0.000001
Prohibitive SECDEF
High - CAE
Serious - PEO
Medium - PM
Low – SSWG/Principal for Safety
4
Cartesian Orientation – Increase up and to the right
X

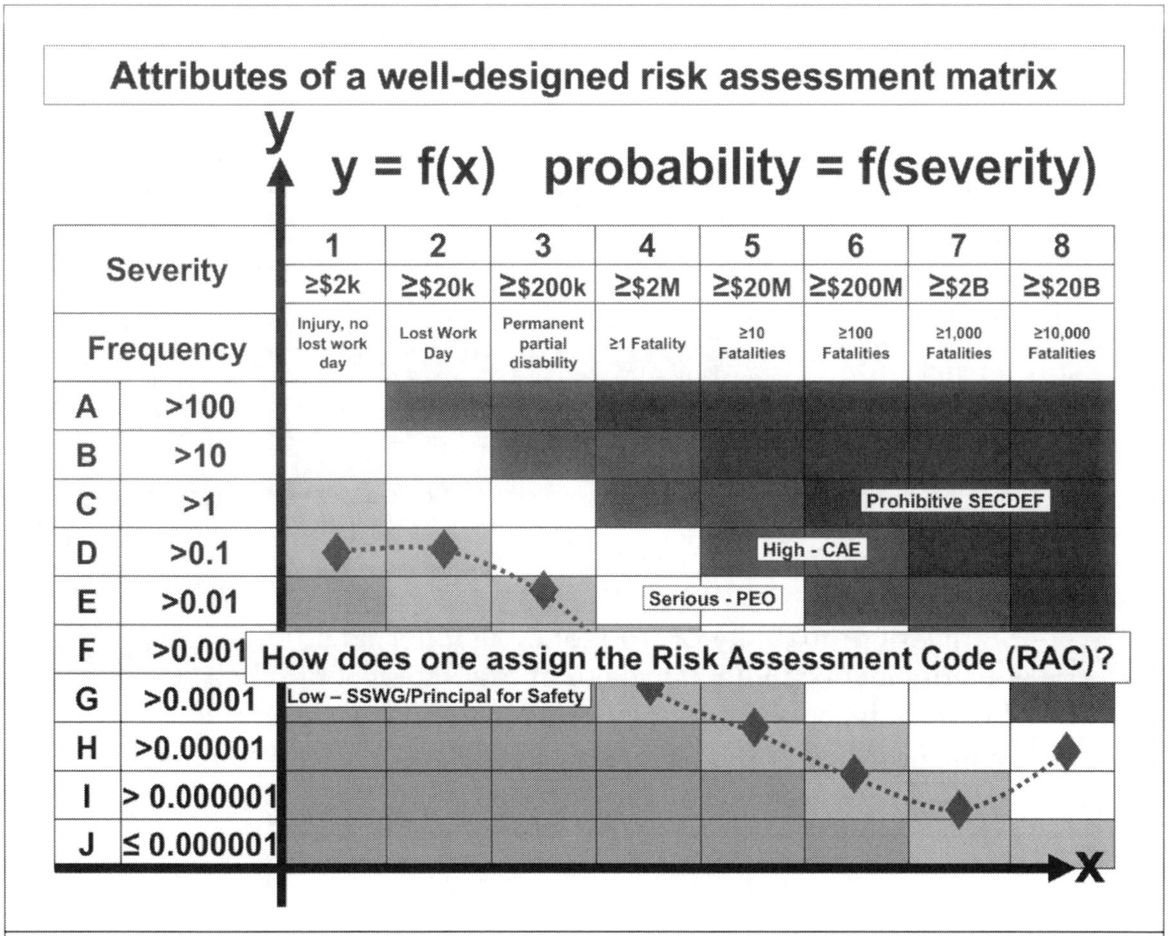
Attributes of a well-designed risk assessment matrix
y
y = f(x) probability = f(severity)
Severity
Frequency
1 ≥$2k Injury, no lost work day
2 ≥$20k Lost Work Day
3 ≥$200k Permanent partial disability
4 ≥$2M ≥1 Fatality
5 ≥$20M ≥10 Fatalities
6 ≥$200M ≥100 Fatalities
7 ≥$2B ≥1,000 Fatalities
8 ≥$20B ≥10,000 Fatalities
A >100
B >10
C >1
D >0.1
E >0.01
F >0.001
G >0.0001
H >0.00001
I > 0.000001
J ≤ 0.000001
Prohibitive SECDEF
High - CAE
Serious - PEO
How does one assign the Risk Assessment Code (RAC)?
Low – SSWG/Principal for Safety
X

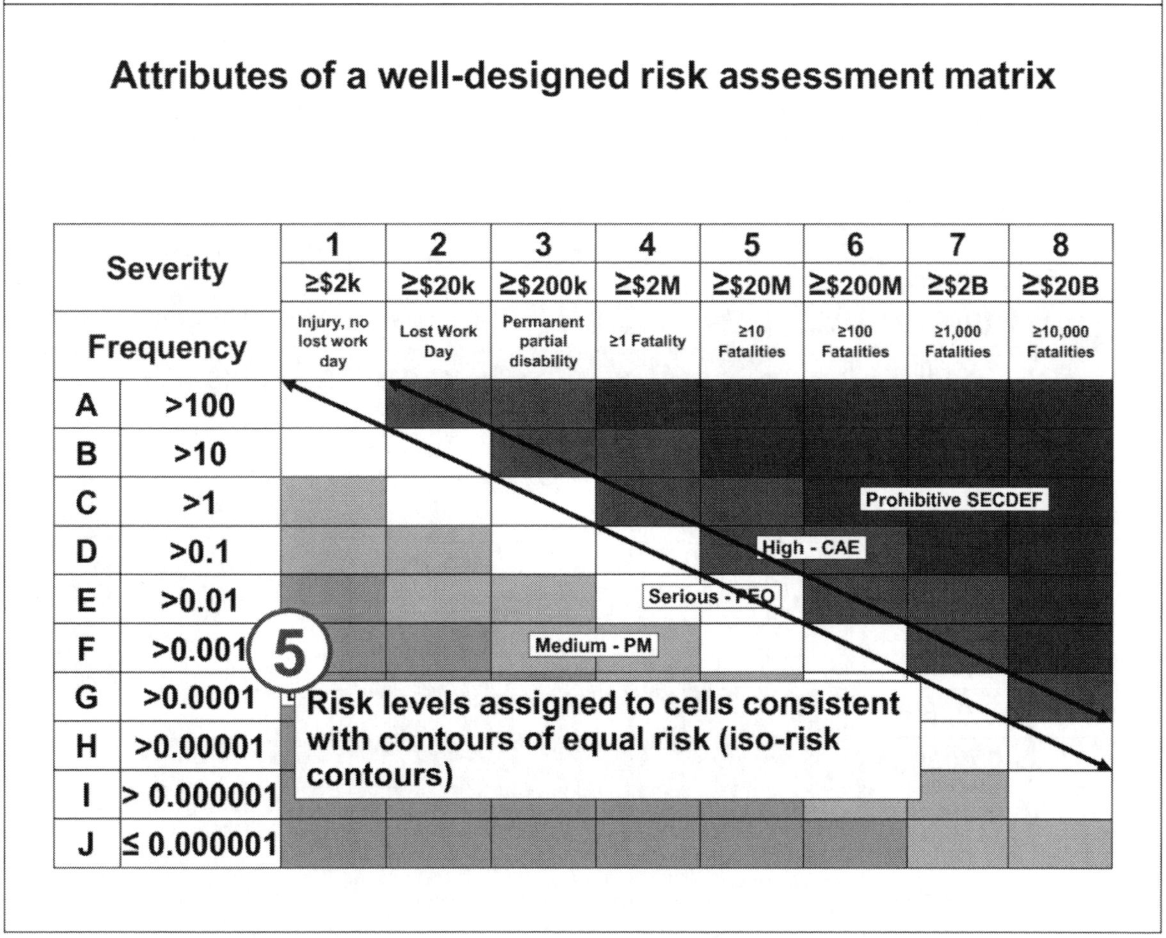
Attributes of a well-designed risk assessment matrix
Severity
Frequency
1 ≥$2k Injury, no lost work day
2 ≥$20k Lost Work Day
3 ≥$200k Permanent partial disability
4 ≥$2M ≥1 Fatality
5 ≥$20M ≥10 Fatalities
6 ≥$200M ≥100 Fatalities
7 ≥$2B ≥1,000 Fatalities
8 ≥$20B ≥10,000 Fatalities
A >100
B >10
C >1
D >0.1
E >0.01
F >0.001
G >0.0001
H >0.00001
I > 0.000001
J ≤ 0.000001
Prohibitive SECDEF
High - CAE
Serious - PEO
Medium - PM
5
Risk levels assigned to cells consistent with contours of equal risk (iso-risk contours)

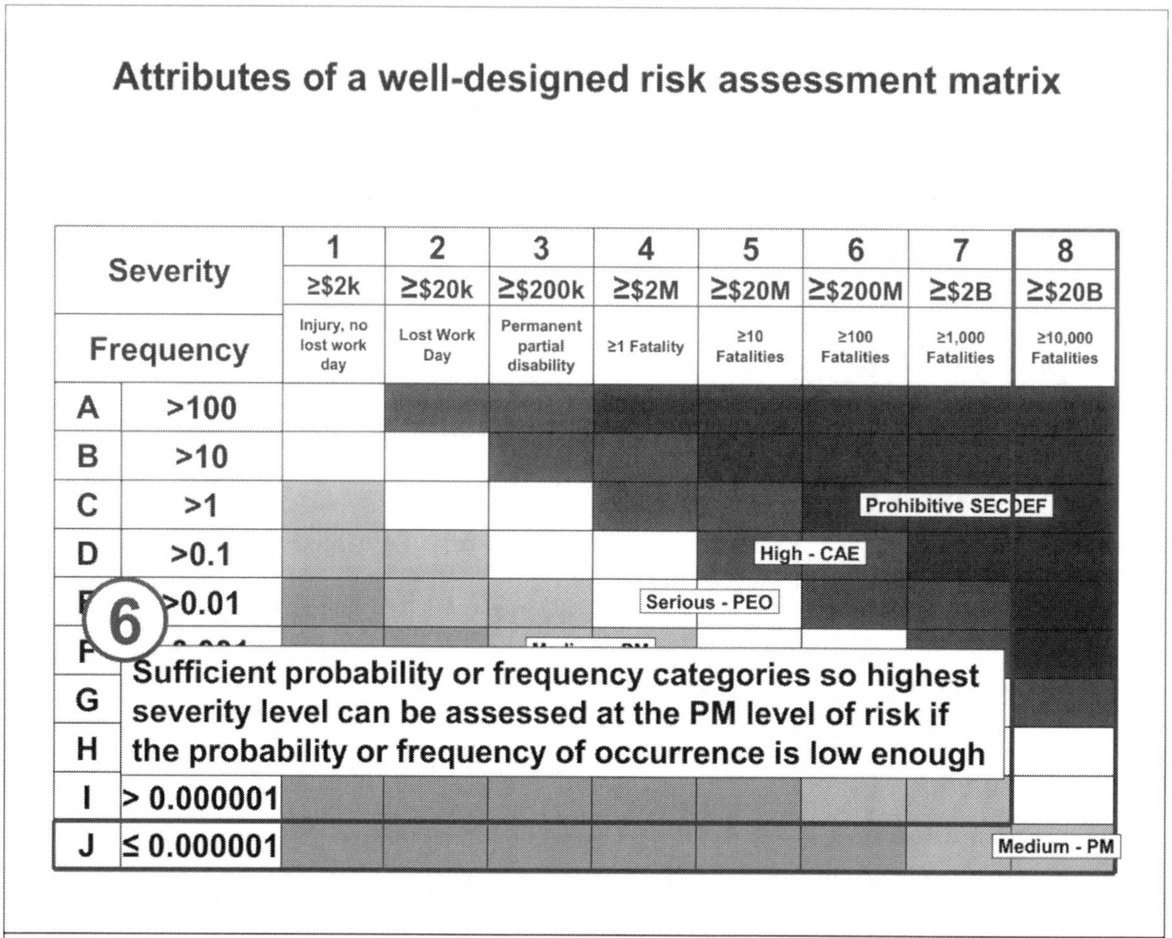
Attributes of a well-designed risk assessment matrix
Severity
Frequency
1 ≥$2k Injury, no lost work day
2 ≥$20k Lost Work Day
3 ≥$200k Permanent partial disability
4 ≥$2M ≥1 Fatality
5 ≥$20M ≥10 Fatalities
6 ≥$200M ≥100 Fatalities
7 ≥$2B ≥1,000 Fatalities
8 ≥$20B ≥10,000 Fatalities
A >100
B >10
C >1
D >0.1
>0.01
G
H
I > 0.000001
J ≤ 0.000001
Prohibitive SECDEF
High - CAE
Serious - PEO
Medium - PM
6
Sufficient probability or frequency categories so highest severity level can be assessed at the PM level of risk if the probability or frequency of occurrence is low enough

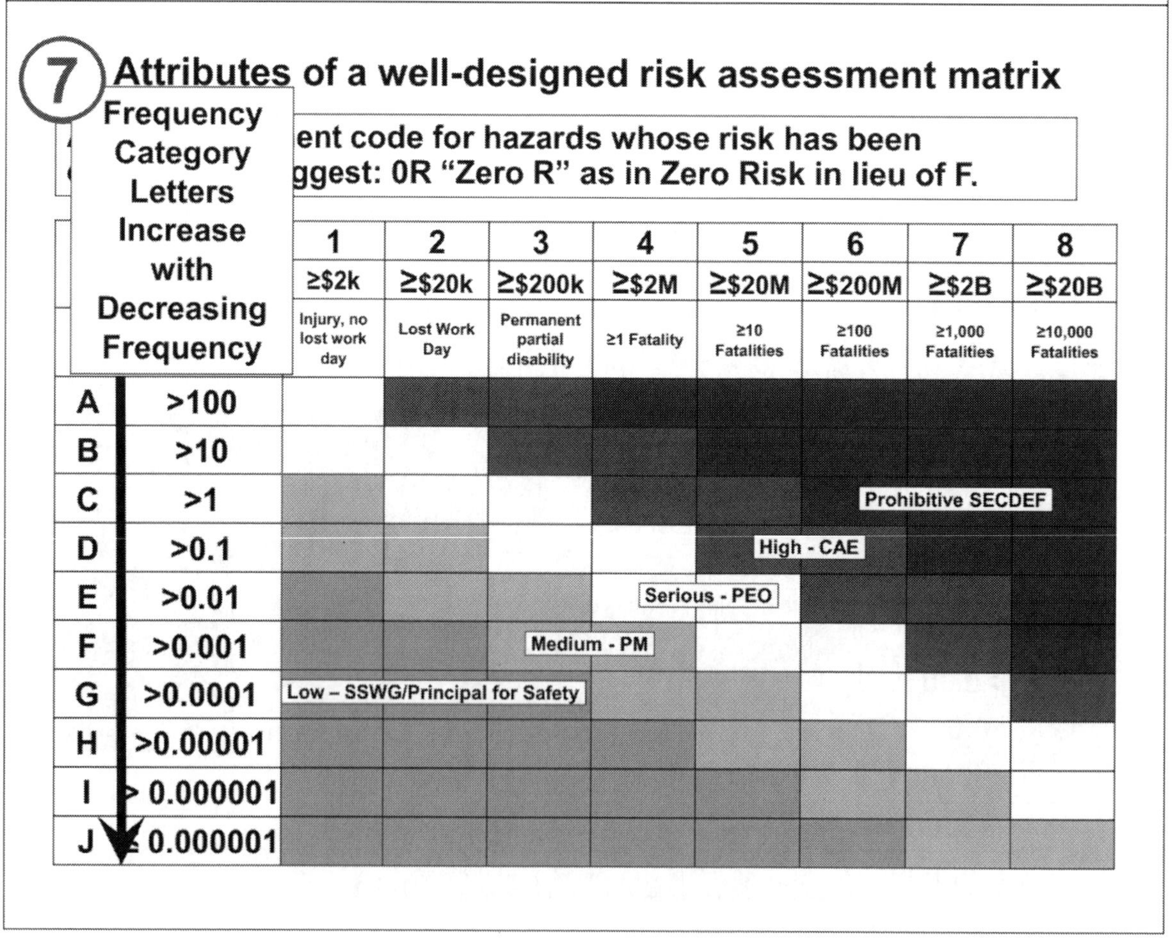
7
Attributes of a well-designed risk assessment matrix
Frequency Category Letters Increase with Decreasing Frequency
ent code for hazards whose risk has been
ggest: 0R “Zero R” as in Zero Risk in lieu of F.
1 ≥$2k Injury, no lost work day
2 ≥$20k Lost Work Day
3 ≥$200k Permanent partial disability
4 ≥$2M ≥1 Fatality
5 ≥$20M ≥10 Fatalities
6 ≥$200M ≥100 Fatalities
7 ≥$2B ≥1,000 Fatalities
8 ≥$20B ≥10,000 Fatalities
A >100
B >10
C >1
D >0.1
E >0.01
F >0.001
G >0.0001
H >0.00001
I > 0.000001
J 0.000001
Prohibitive SECDEF
High - CAE
Serious - PEO
Medium - PM
Low – SSWG/Principal for Safety

7 Attributes of a well-designed risk assessment matrix

Frequency Category Letters Increase with Decreasing Frequency

...ent code for hazards whose risk has been ...ggest: 0R "Zero R" as in Zero Risk in lieu of F.

		1	2	3	4	5	6	7	8
		≥$2k	≥$20k	≥$200k	≥$2M	≥$20M	≥$200M	≥$2B	≥$20B
		Injury, no lost work day	Lost Work Day	Permanent partial disability	≥1 Fatality	≥10 Fatalities	≥100 Fatalities	≥1,000 Fatalities	≥10,000 Fatalities
A	>100								
B	>10								
C	>1						Prohibitive SECDEF		
D	>0.1					High - CAE			
E	>0.01				Serious - PEO				
F		MIL-STD-882E Eliminated							

8 Attributes of a well-designed risk assessment matrix

A risk assessment code for hazards whose risk has been eliminated. Suggest: 0R "Zero R" as in Zero Risk in lieu of F.

Severity		1	2	3	4	5	6	7	8
		≥$2k	≥$20k	≥$200k	≥$2M	≥$20M	≥$200M	≥$2B	≥$20B
Frequency		Injury, no lost work day	Lost Work Day	Permanent partial disability	≥1 Fatality	≥10 Fatalities	≥100 Fatalities	≥1,000 Fatalities	≥10,000 Fatalities
A	>100								
B	>10								
C	>1						Prohibitive SECDEF		
D	>0.1					High - CAE			
E	>0.01				Serious - PEO				
F	>0.001			Medium - PM					
G	>0.0001	Low – SSWG/Principal for Safety							
H	>0.00001								
I	> 0.000001								
J	≤ 0.000001								

Attributes of a well-designed risk assessment matrix

Severity		1	2	3	4	5	6	7	8
		≥$2k	≥$20k	≥$200k	≥$2M	≥$20M	≥$200M	≥$2B	≥$20B
Frequency		Injury, no lost work day	Lost Work Day	Permanent partial disability	≥1 Fatality	≥10 Fatalities	≥100 Fatalities	≥1,000 Fatalities	≥10,000 Fatalities
A	>100								
B	>10								
C	>1							Prohibitive SECDEF	
D	>0.1					High - CAE			
E	>0.01				Serio	5E			
F	>0.001			Medium - PM					
G	>0.0001	Low – SSWG/Principal for Safety							
	>0.00001								
J	≤ 0.000001								

9 Easily tailored with reporting of risk consistent with other systems within the family of systems.

Attributes of a well-designed risk assessment matrix

10 Severity Category numbers increase with increasing Severity

Severity		1	2	3	4	5	6	7
		≥$2k	≥$20k	≥$200k	≥$2M	≥$20M		
Frequency		Injury, no lost work day	Lost Work Day	Permanent partial disability	≥1 Fatality	≥10 Fatalities		
A	>100				Prohibitive SECDEF			
B	>10							
C	>1							
D	>0.1					High - CAE		
E	>0.01				Serio	5E		
F	>0.001			Medium - PM				
G	>0.0001	Low – SSWG/Principal for Safety						

Mother of All Risk Assessment Matrices (Spaceship Earth)

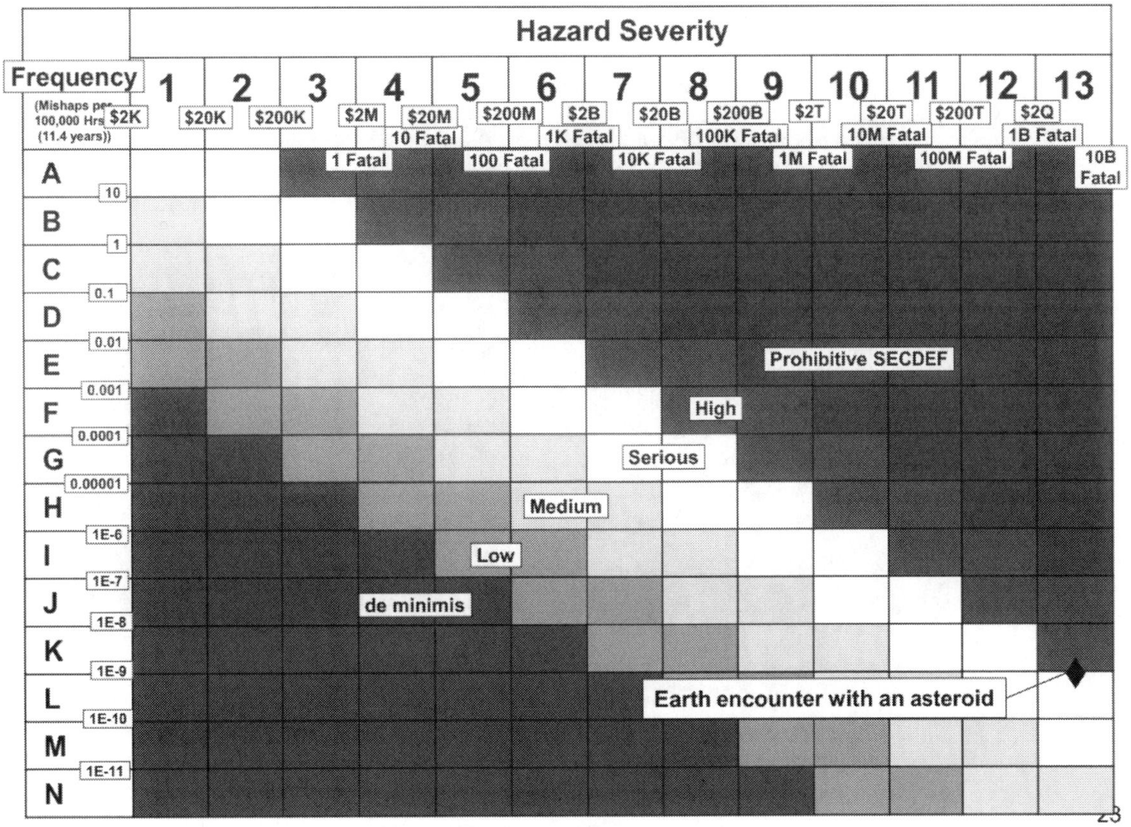

Mother of All Risk Assessment Matrices (Spaceship Earth)

Even the Mother of All Risk Assessment Matrices can be tailored to the area most useful for the user.

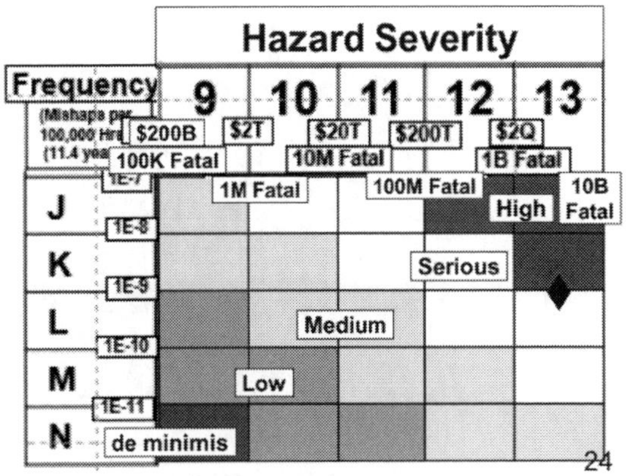

Additional Recommendation

- Eliminate one-word labels for Severity (Catastrophic, Critical, Marginal, Negligible) and Probability (Frequent, Probable, Occasional, Remote, Improbable)

Additional Recommendation

- Just use Severity 1, Severity 2, Probability C, etc.

MIL-STD-882D Matrix

RISK ASSESSMENT MATRIX				
SEVERITY / PROBABILITY	Catastrophic (1) $1M	Critical (2) $200K	Marginal (3) $10K	Negligible (4) $2K
Frequent (A)	High	High	Serious	Medium
Probable (B)	High	High	Serious	Medium
Occasional (C)	High	Serious	Medium	Low
Remote (D)	Serious	Medium	Medium	Low
Improbable (E)	Medium	Medium	Medium	Low

10^{-1}

10^{-2}

10^{-3}

10^{-6}

MIL-STD-882D Matrix

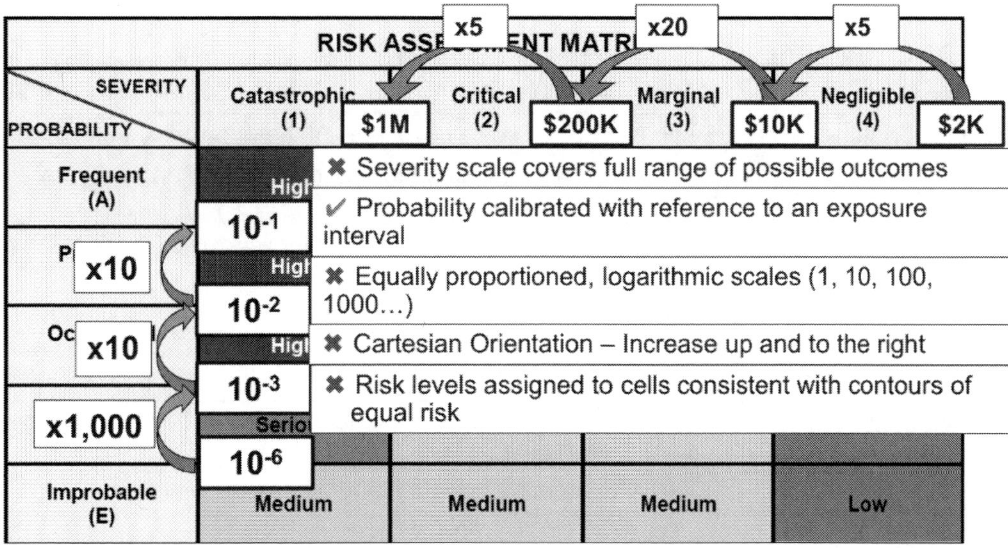

MIL-STD-882D Matrix

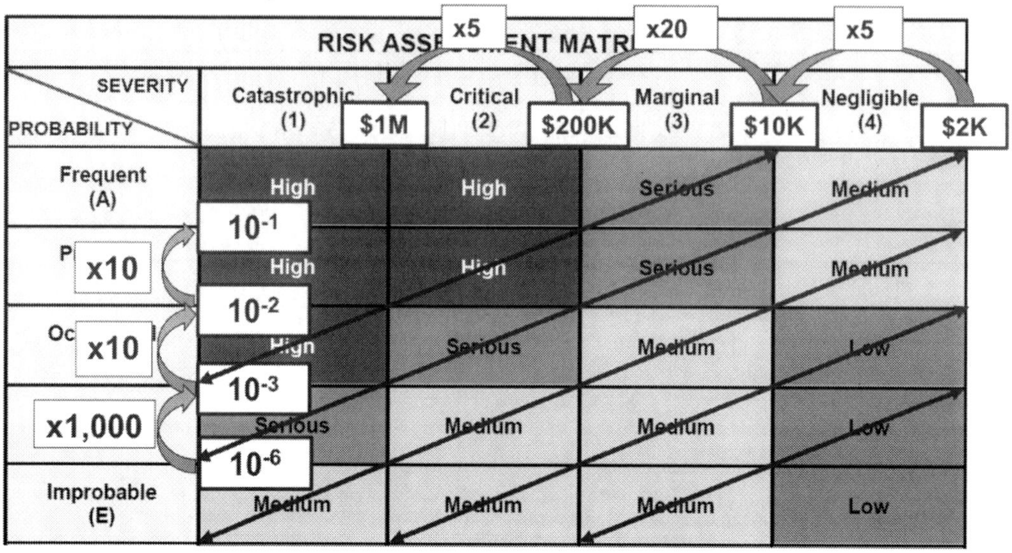

MIL-STD-882D Matrix

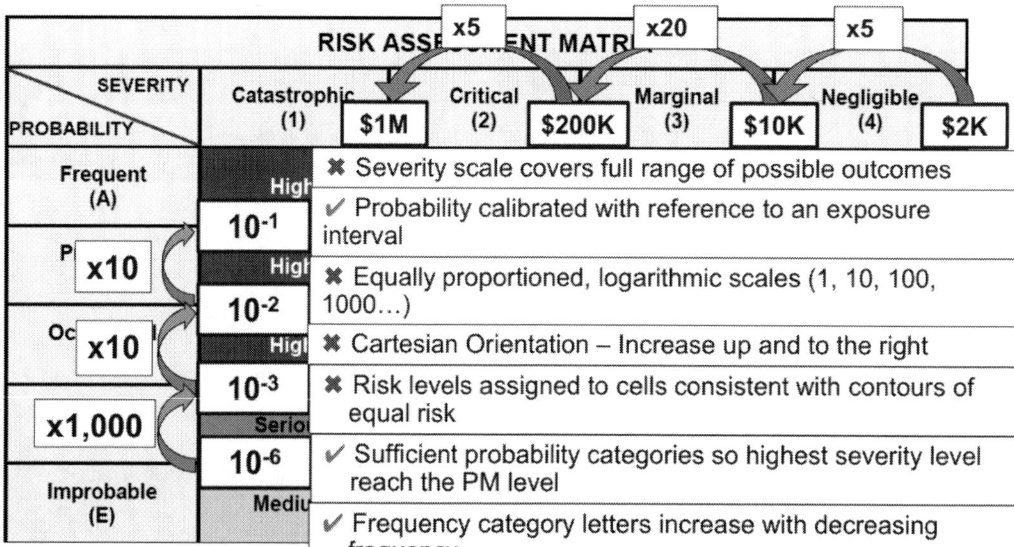

- ✖ Severity scale covers full range of possible outcomes
- ✔ Probability calibrated with reference to an exposure interval
- ✖ Equally proportioned, logarithmic scales (1, 10, 100, 1000…)
- ✖ Cartesian Orientation – Increase up and to the right
- ✖ Risk levels assigned to cells consistent with contours of equal risk
- ✔ Sufficient probability categories so highest severity level reach the PM level
- ✔ Frequency category letters increase with decreasing frequency
- ✖ A RAC for hazards whose risk has been eliminated
- ✖ Easily tailored & consistent with other systems within its family of systems
- ✖ Severity Category numbers increase with increasing Severity

0

MIL-STD-882E Matrix

RISK ASSESSMENT MATRIX				
SEVERITY / PROBABILITY	Catastrophic (1)	Critical (2)	Marginal (3)	Negligible (4)
Frequent (A)	High	High	Serious	Medium
Probable (B)	High	High	Serious	Medium
Occasional (C)	High	Serious	Medium	Low
Remote (D)	Serious	Medium	Medium	Low
Improbable (E)	Medium	Medium	Medium	Low
Eliminated (F)	Eliminated			

$10M | $1M | $100K

10^{-1} | 10^{-2} | 10^{-3} | 10^{-6}

31

MIL-STD-882E Matrix

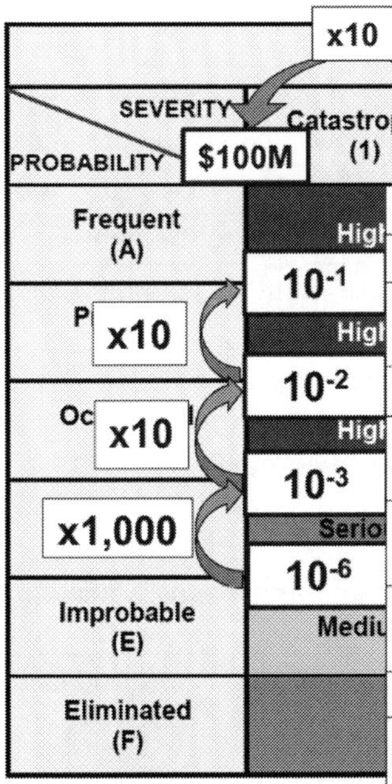

- ? Severity scale covers full range of possible outcomes
- ✔ Probability calibrated with reference to an exposure interval
- ✔ ✖ Equally proportioned, logarithmic scales (1, 10, 100, 1000…)
- ✖ Cartesian Orientation – Increase up and to the right
- ✖ Risk levels assigned to cells consistent with contours of equal risk
- ✔ Sufficient probability categories so highest severity level reach the PM level
- ✔ ✖ Frequency category letters increase with decreasing frequency but only to E as F = Eliminated
- ✔ A RAC for hazards whose risk has been eliminated
- ✖ Easily tailored & consistent with other systems within its family of systems
- ✖ Severity Category numbers increase with increasing Severity

32

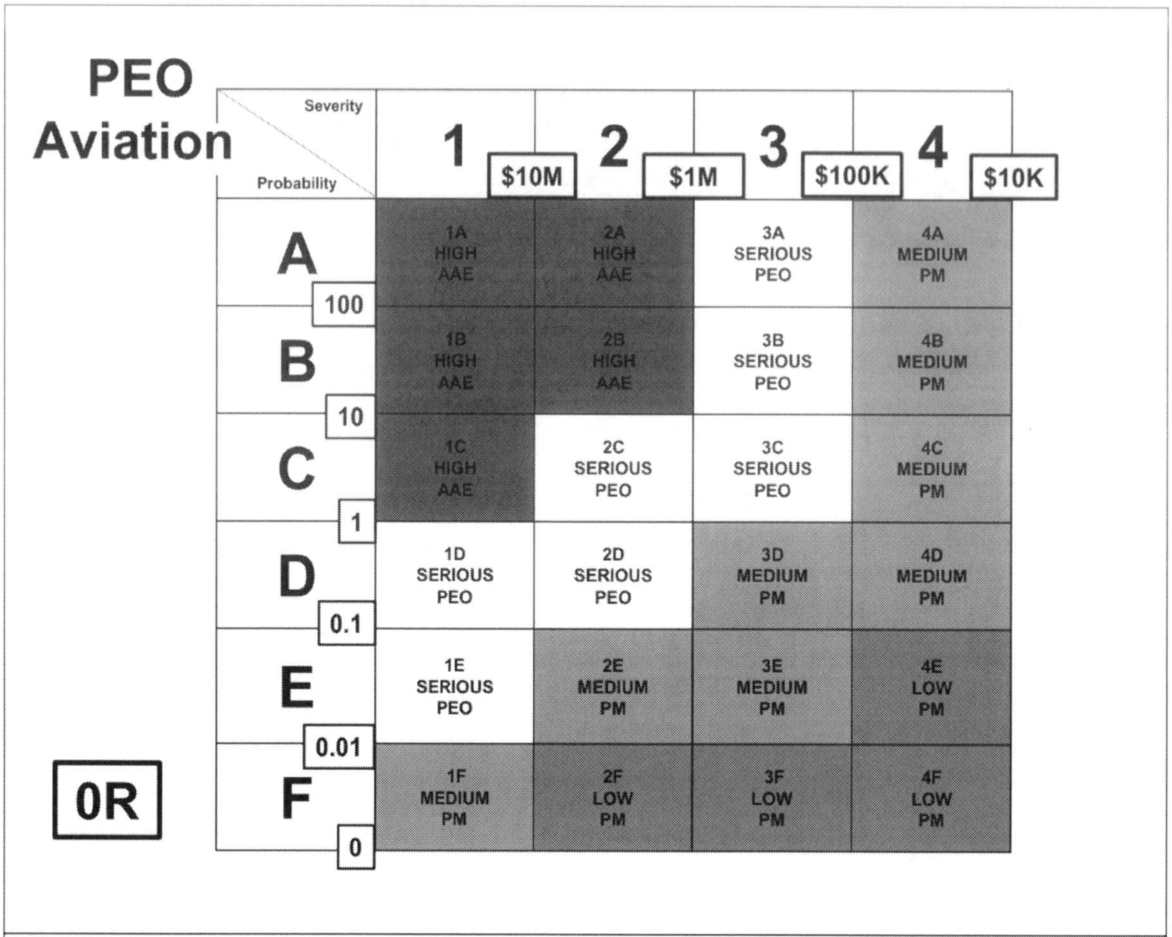
PEO
Aviation
Severity
Probability
1 $10M
2 $1M
3 $100K
4 $10K
A 100
B 10
C 1
D 0.1
E 0.01
F 0
1A HIGH AAE
2A HIGH AAE
3A SERIOUS PEO
4A MEDIUM PM
1B HIGH AAE
2B HIGH AAE
3B SERIOUS PEO
4B MEDIUM PM
1C HIGH AAE
2C SERIOUS PEO
3C SERIOUS PEO
4C MEDIUM PM
1D SERIOUS PEO
2D SERIOUS PEO
3D MEDIUM PM
4D MEDIUM PM
1E SERIOUS PEO
2E MEDIUM PM
3E MEDIUM PM
4E LOW PM
1F MEDIUM PM
2F LOW PM
3F LOW PM
4F LOW PM
0R

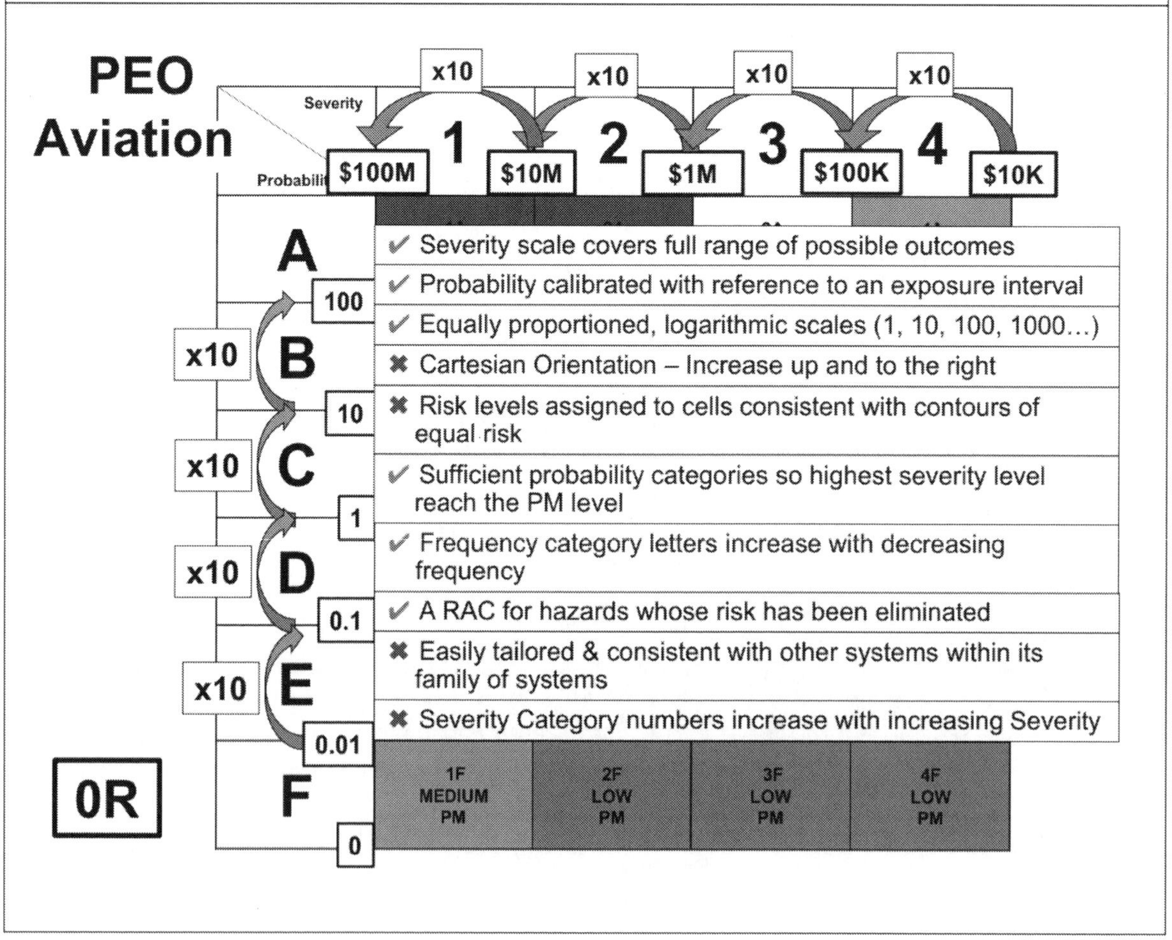
PEO
Aviation
Severity
x10
x10
x10
x10
$100M
1 $10M
2 $1M
3 $100K
4 $10K
A 100
x10 B 10
x10 C 1
x10 D 0.1
x10 E 0.01
F 0
✔ Severity scale covers full range of possible outcomes
✔ Probability calibrated with reference to an exposure interval
✔ Equally proportioned, logarithmic scales (1, 10, 100, 1000…)
✖ Cartesian Orientation – Increase up and to the right
✖ Risk levels assigned to cells consistent with contours of equal risk
✔ Sufficient probability categories so highest severity level reach the PM level
✔ Frequency category letters increase with decreasing frequency
✔ A RAC for hazards whose risk has been eliminated
✖ Easily tailored & consistent with other systems within its family of systems
✖ Severity Category numbers increase with increasing Severity
1F MEDIUM PM
2F LOW PM
3F LOW PM
4F LOW PM
0R

Topics for this Tutorial

- Purpose of a Hazard Risk Matrix
- Understanding the Attributes of a well-designed risk assessment matrix
- **How to Assign a Risk Assessment Code**
- Understanding Probability
- Building an Expanded Matrix
- Plotting Accidents on a Matrix
- Using Relative Risk Values
- Building Hazard Risk Profiles

35

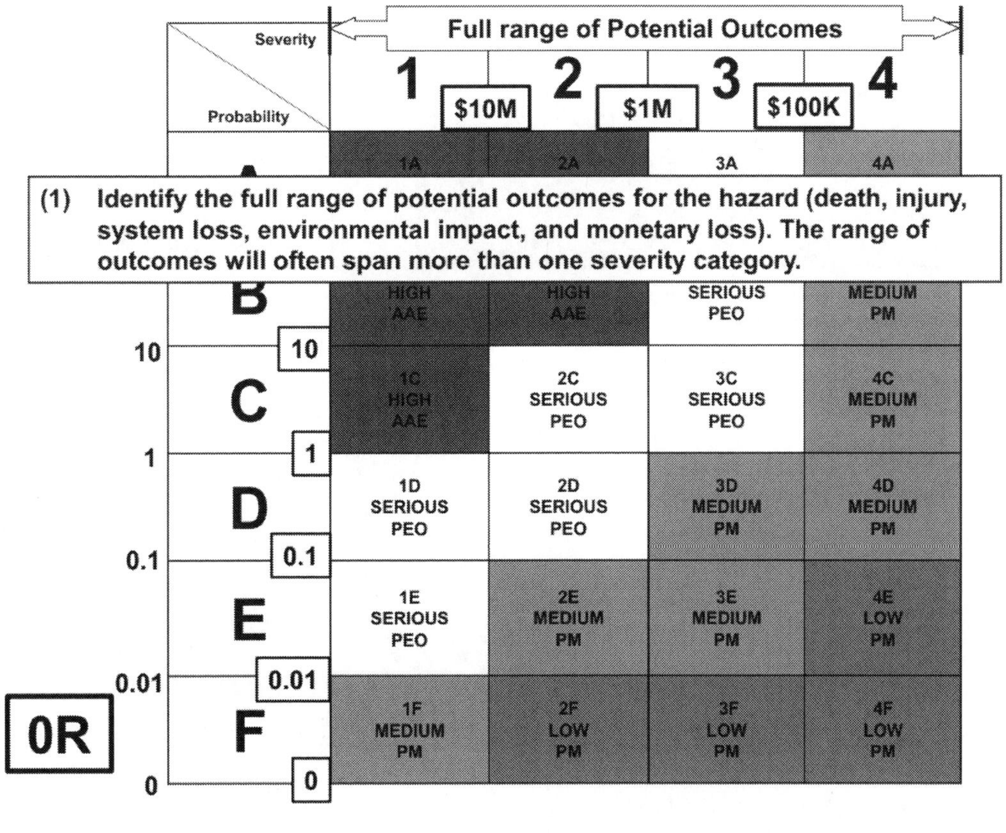

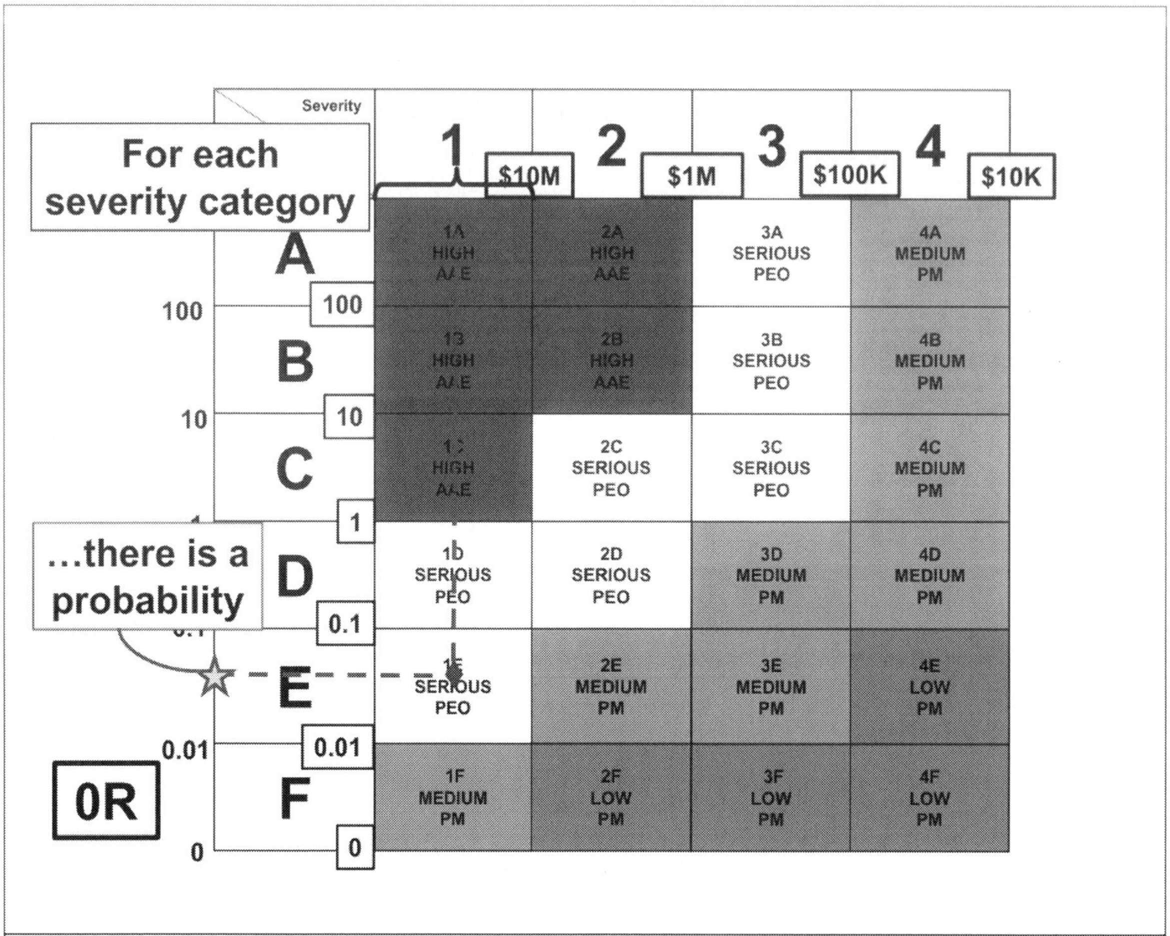
For each severity category
...there is a probability
Severity
1
2
3
4
$10M
$1M
$100K
$10K
A
B
C
D
E
F
100
10
1
0.1
0.01
0
1A HIGH AAE
2A HIGH AAE
3A SERIOUS PEO
4A MEDIUM PM
1B HIGH AAE
2B HIGH AAE
3B SERIOUS PEO
4B MEDIUM PM
1C HIGH AAE
2C SERIOUS PEO
3C SERIOUS PEO
4C MEDIUM PM
1D SERIOUS PEO
2D SERIOUS PEO
3D MEDIUM PM
4D MEDIUM PM
1E SERIOUS PEO
2E MEDIUM PM
3E MEDIUM PM
4E LOW PM
1F MEDIUM PM
2F LOW PM
3F LOW PM
4F LOW PM
0R

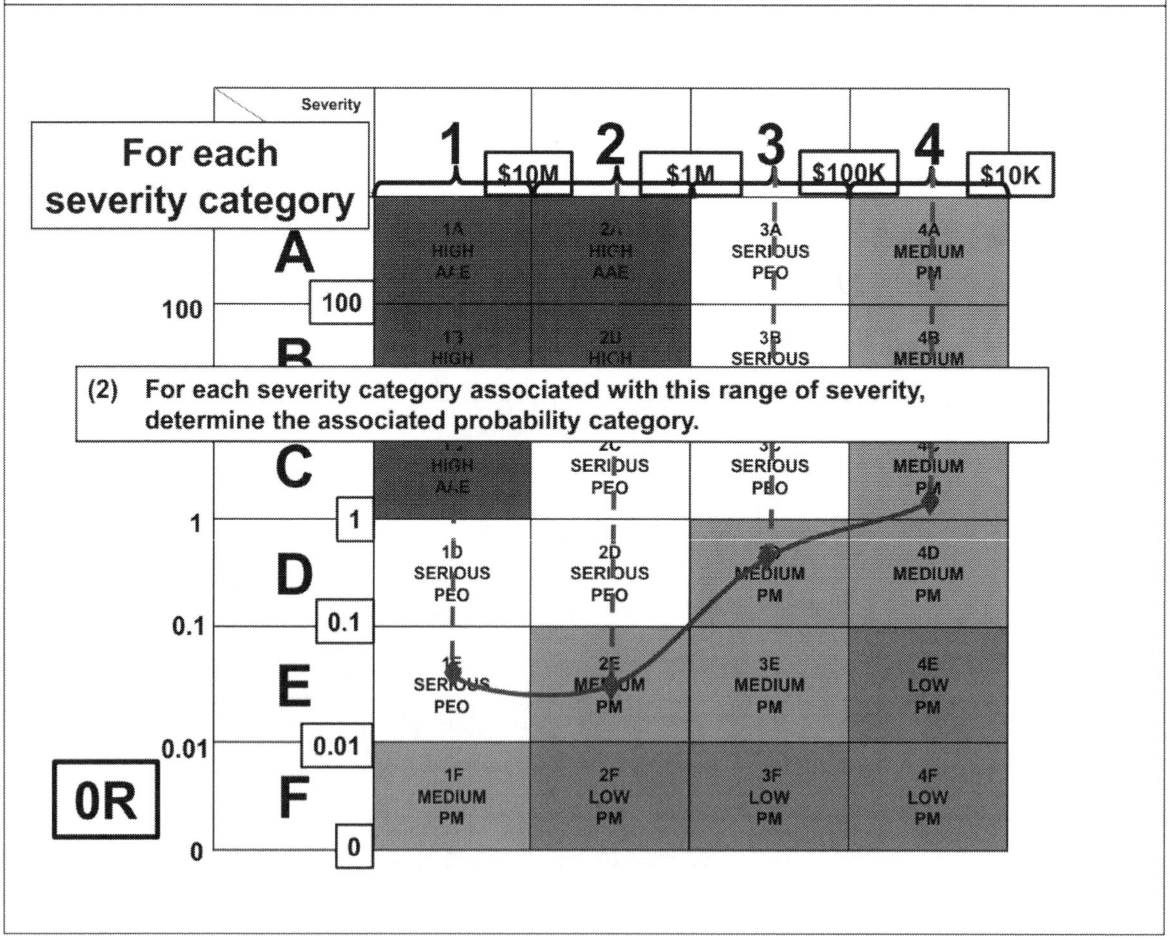
For each severity category
(2) For each severity category associated with this range of severity, determine the associated probability category.
Severity
1
2
3
4
$10M
$1M
$100K
$10K
A
B
C
D
E
F
100
1
0.1
0.01
0
0R

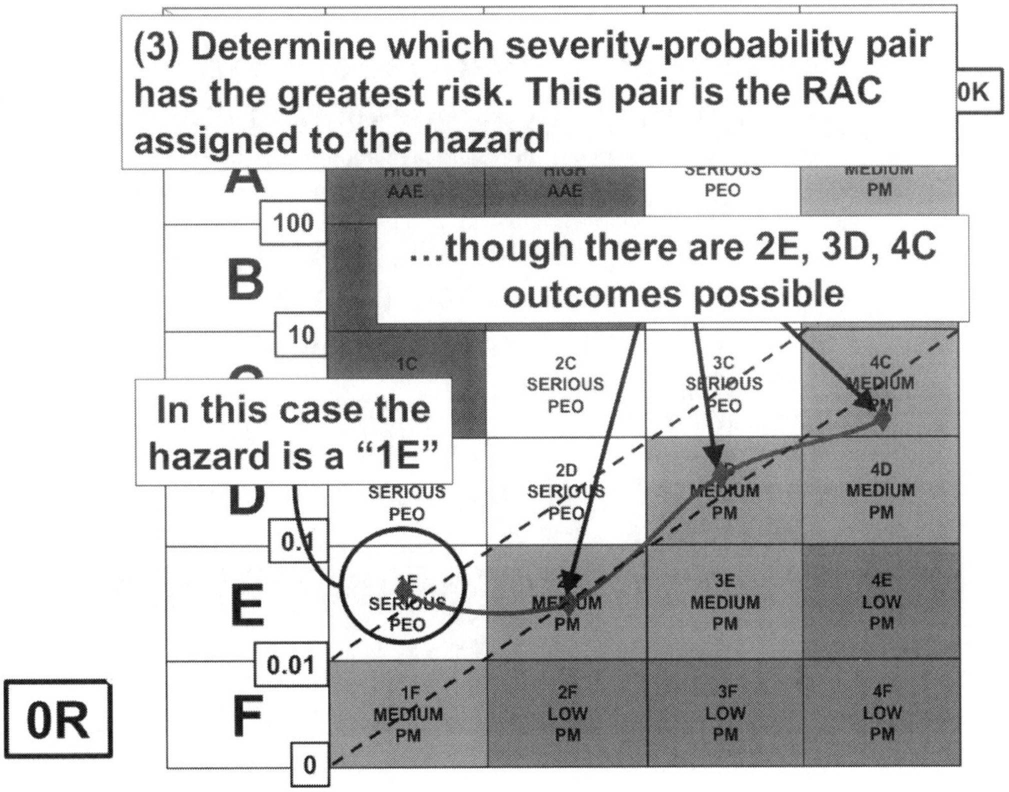
(3) Determine which severity-probability pair has the greatest risk. This pair is the RAC assigned to the hazard
...though there are 2E, 3D, 4C outcomes possible
In this case the hazard is a "1E"
0R
A
B
C
D
E
F
100
10
0.1
0.01
0
HIGH AAE
SERIOUS PEO
MEDIUM PM
1C
2C SERIOUS PEO
3C SERIOUS PEO
4C MEDIUM PM
SERIOUS PEO
2D SERIOUS PEO
3D MEDIUM PM
4D MEDIUM PM
1E SERIOUS PEO
2E MEDIUM PM
3E MEDIUM PM
4E LOW PM
1F MEDIUM PM
2F LOW PM
3F LOW PM
4F LOW PM

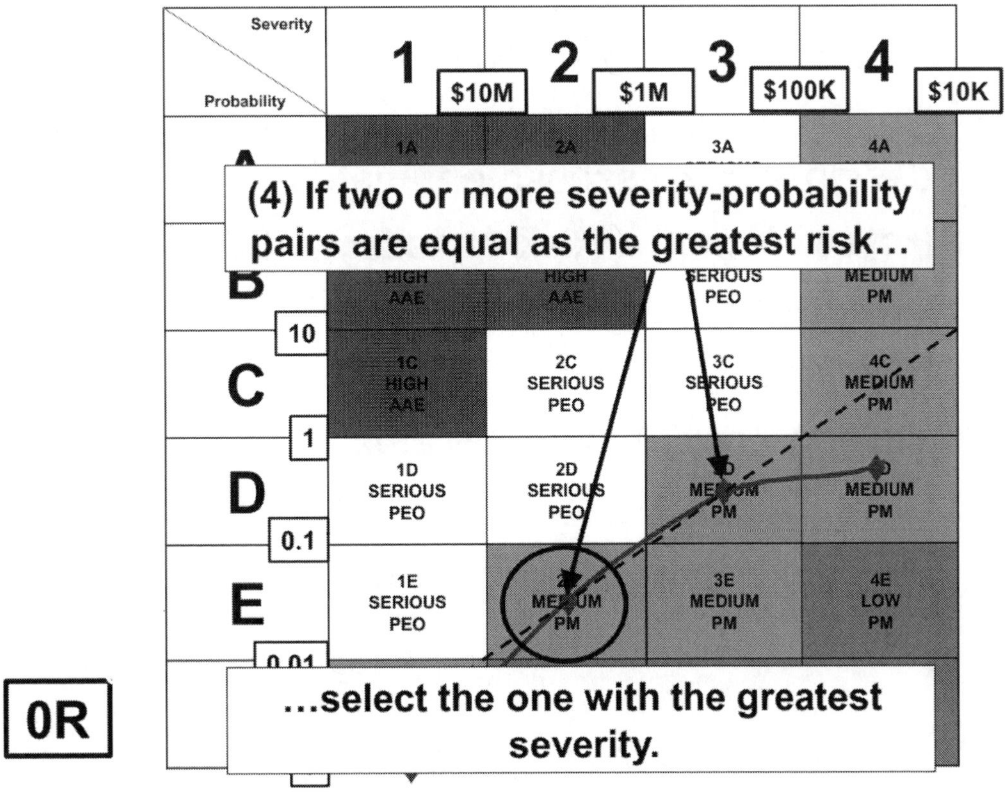
Severity
Probability
1
2
3
4
$10M
$1M
$100K
$10K
(4) If two or more severity-probability pairs are equal as the greatest risk...
...select the one with the greatest severity.
0R
C
D
E
10
1
0.1
1A
2A
3A
4A
HIGH AAE
SERIOUS PEO
MEDIUM PM
1C HIGH AAE
2C SERIOUS PEO
3C SERIOUS PEO
4C MEDIUM PM
1D SERIOUS PEO
2D SERIOUS PEO
3D MEDIUM PM
4D MEDIUM PM
1E SERIOUS PEO
2E MEDIUM PM
3E MEDIUM PM
4E LOW PM

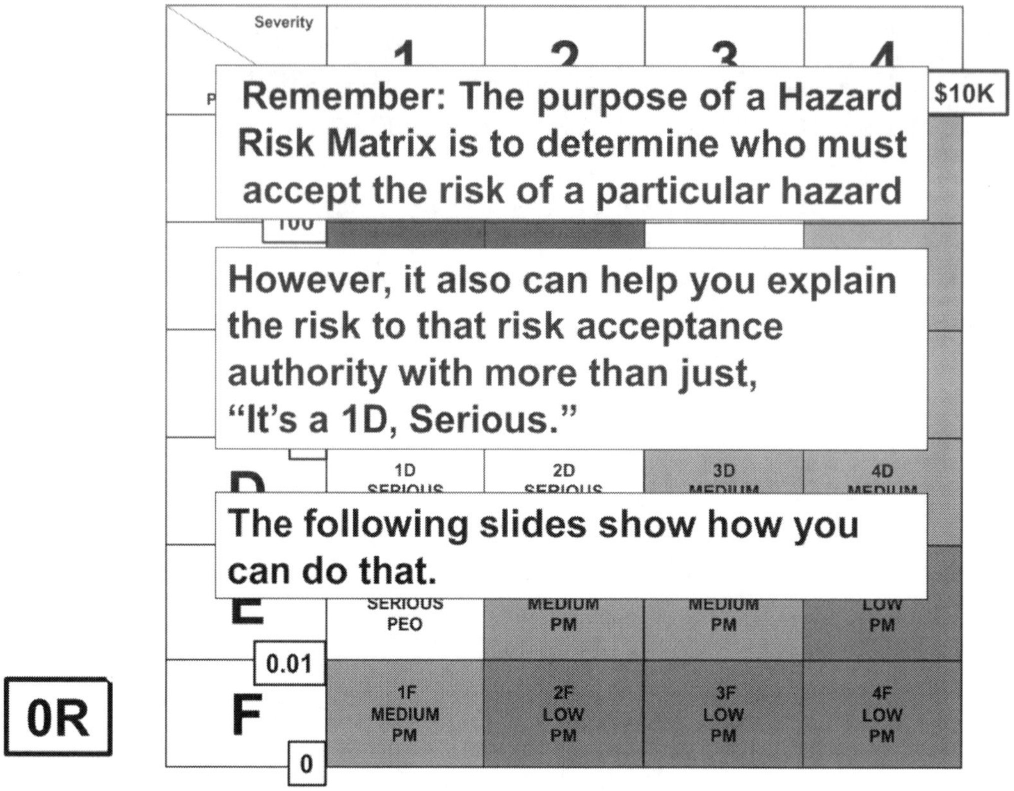

Topics for this Tutorial

- Purpose of a Hazard Risk Matrix
- Understanding the Attributes of a well-designed risk assessment matrix
- How to Assign a Risk Assessment Code
- **Understanding Probability**
- Building an Expanded Matrix
- Plotting Accidents on a Matrix
- Using Relative Risk Values
- Building Hazard Risk Profiles

42

Understanding Probability

Probability:

"A number expressing the likelihood that a specific event will occur, expressed as the ratio of the number of actual occurrences to the number of possible occurrences."

- The American Heritage® Dictionary of the English Language, Fourth Edition

43

Understanding Probability

Math Definition:

- **Repeat a random experiment "n" number of times.**
- **If a specific outcome has occurred "f" times in these n trials, the number "f" is the frequency of the outcome.**
- **The ratio f/n is the relative frequency of the outcome.**
- **A relative frequency is usually very unstable for small values of "n," but it tends to stabilize about some number "p" as "n" increases.**
- **The number "p" is the probability of the outcome.**

$$p = f / n$$

for very large values of n

44

Understanding Probability

Simple example:

Probability of rolling a “3” with one die.

- **Roll #1 - “5”, f/n = 0/1 = 0**
- **Roll #2 - “2”, f/n = 0/2 = 0**
- **Roll #3 - “3”, f/n = 1/3 = .333…**
- **Roll #4 - “4”, f/n = 1/4 = .25**
- **Roll #1,000: 163 “3”s, f/n = 163/1000 = .163**
- **Rolls approach infinity f/n = .166666….**

45

Rolling Dice

Roll a single die 30 times. The expected value of each roll is 3.5. What you actually get is somewhat different.

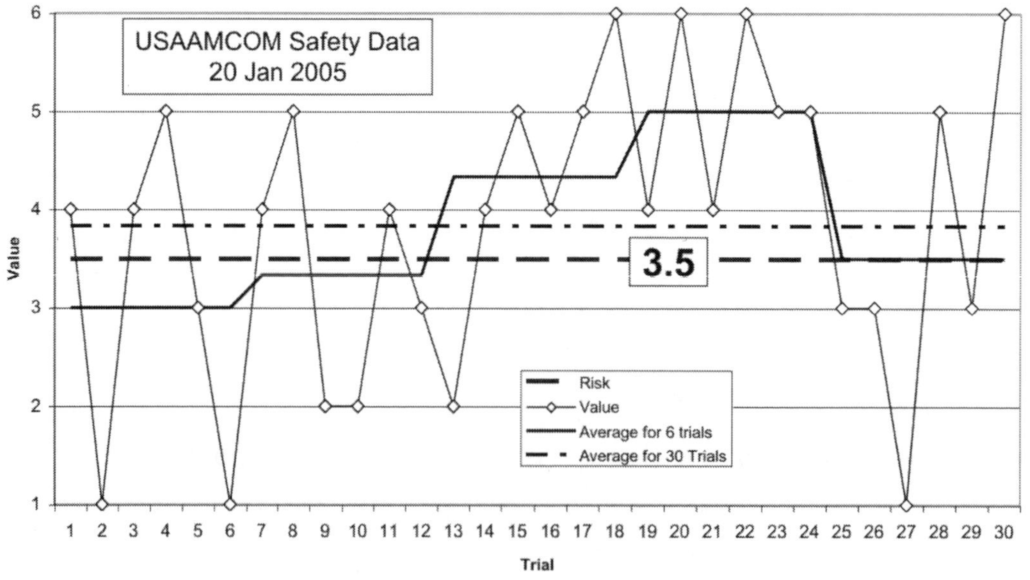

46

Understanding Probability

Hazard: Helicopter strikes wire; results in Class A mishap

Probability: 4.406E-06 occurrences per flight hour

1 Flight Hr, no mishap, rate = 0

1,000 Flight Hrs, no mishap, rate = 0

176,182 Flight Hrs, 1st mishap, rate = 5.676E-06 /flt hr

274,539 Flight Hrs, 2nd mishap, rate = 7.285E-06 /flt hr

700,462 Flt Hrs, 3rd mishap, rate = 4.283E-06 /flt hr

10,000,000 Flt Hrs, 46 mishaps, rate = 4.600E-06 /flt hr

1,000,000,000 Hrs, 4407 mishaps, rate = 4.407E-06 /flt hr

Flight hours approach infinity, rate = 4.406E-06 /flt hr

47

Topics for this Tutorial

- Purpose of a Hazard Risk Matrix
- Understanding the Attributes of a well-designed risk assessment matrix
- How to Assign a Risk Assessment Code
- Understanding Probability
- **Building an Expanded Matrix**
- Plotting Accidents on a Matrix
- Using Relative Risk Values
- Building Hazard Risk Profiles

48

PEO Aviation Risk Decision Authority Matrix

Probability \ Severity	1 ($10M)	2 ($1M)	3 ($100K)	4 ($10K)
A (100)	1A HIGH AAE	2A HIGH AAE	3A SERIOUS PEO	4A MEDIUM PM
B (10)	1B HIGH AAE	2B HIGH AAE	3B SERIOUS PEO	4B MEDIUM PM
C (1)	1C HIGH AAE	2C SERIOUS PEO	3C SERIOUS PEO	4C MEDIUM PM
D (0.1)	1D SERIOUS PEO	2D SERIOUS PEO	3D MEDIUM PM	4D MEDIUM PM
E (0.01)	1E SERIOUS PEO	2E MEDIUM PM	3E MEDIUM PM	4E LOW PM
F (0)	1F MEDIUM PM	2F LOW PM	3F LOW PM	4F LOW PM

0R

Applying Probability Classifications to a military helicopter

Fleet Size = 368 aircraft

Utilization = 240 hours/year

Life = 12 years/aircraft

Aircraft Life = 240 x 12
= 2,880 hours

Fleet Exposure Hours = 368 x 240 x 12
= 1,059,840 hours

Fleet Hours per Year = 368 x 240
= 88,320 hours

50

US Army PEO Aviation Enhanced Matrix

	Events per Flight Hour	Flight Hours per Event	Events per 100,000 Flt Hrs	Events per Year	Years per Event
Frequent **A**	10^{-3}	1,000	100	88.32	0.0113
Probable **B**	10^{-4}	10,000	10	8.832	0.113
Occasional **C**	10^{-5}	100,000	1	0.8832	1.13
Remote **D**	10^{-6}	1,000,000	0.1	0.0883	11.3
Improbable **E**	10^{-7}	10,000,000	0.01	0.00883	113
Very Improbable **F**	0		0	0	
Zero Risk **0R**					

51

US Army PEO Aviation Enhanced Matrix

$$\frac{88{,}320 \text{ flt hrs}}{\text{Year}} \times \frac{10 \text{ Events}}{100{,}000 \text{ flt hrs}} = \frac{8.832 \text{ Events}}{\text{Year}}$$

	Events per Flight Hour	Flight Hours per Event	Events per 100,000 Flt Hrs	Events per Year	Years per Event
Probable **B**	10^{-4}	10,000	10	8.832	0.113
Occasional **C**	10^{-5}	100,000	1	0.8832	1.13
Remote **D**	10^{-6}	1,000,000	0.1	0.0883	11.3
Improbable **E**	10^{-7}	10,000,000	0.01	0.00883	113
Very Improbable **F**	0		0	0	
Zero Risk **0R**					

52

US Army PEO Aviation Enhanced Matrix

	Events per Flight Hour	Flight Hours per Event	Events per 100,000 Flt Hrs	Events per Year	Years per Event	Event per Fleet Life	Fleet Life per Event
Frequent **A**	10^{-3}	1,000	100	88.32	0.0113	1,060	0.000944
Probable **B**	10^{-4}	10,000	10	8.832	0.113	105.98	0.00944
Occasional **C**	10^{-5}	100,000	1	0.8832	1.13	10.598	0.0944
Remote **D**	10^{-6}	1,000,000	0.1	0.0883	11.3	1.0598	0.944
Improbable **E**	10^{-7}	10,000,000	0.01	0.00883	113	0.106	9.44
Very Improbable **F**	0		0	0		0	
Zero Risk **0R**							

53

US Army PEO Aviation Enhanced Matrix

$$\frac{1{,}059{,}840\ \cancel{\text{flt hrs}}}{1\ \text{fleet life}} \times \frac{10\ \text{Events}}{100{,}000\ \cancel{\text{flt hrs}}} = \frac{105.98\ \text{Events}}{1\ \text{Fleet Life}}$$

	Events per Flight	Flight Hours per	Events per 100,000	Events per	Years per	Event per Fleet	Fleet Life per
Probable	10^{-4}	10,000	10	8.832	0.113	105.98	0.00944
Occasional **C**	10^{-5}	100,000	1	0.8832	1.13	10.598	0.0944
Remote **D**	10^{-6}	1,000,000	0.1	0.0883	11.3	1.0598	0.944
Improbable **E**	10^{-7}	10,000,000	0.01	0.00883	113	0.106	9.44
Very Improbable **F**	0		0	0		0	
Zero Risk **0R**							

54

US Army PEO Aviation Enhanced Matrix

	Events per Flight Hour	Flight Hours per Event	Events per 100,000 Flt Hrs	Events per Year	Years per Event	Event per Fleet Life	Fleet Life per Event
Frequent **A**	10^{-3}	1,000	100	88.32	0.0113	1,060	0.000944
Probable **B**	10^{-4}	10,000	10	8.832	0.113	105.98	0.00944
Occasional **C**	10^{-5}	100,000	1	0.8832	1.13	10.598	0.0944
Remote **D**	10^{-6}	1,000,000	0.1	0.0883	11.3	1.0598	0.944
Improbable **E**	10^{-7}	10,000,000	0.01	0.00883	113	0.106	9.44
Very Improbable **F**	0		0	0		0	
Zero Risk **0R**							

Numbers greater than 1 are easier to comprehend

55

US Army PEO Aviation Enhanced Matrix

- Input
- Calculated

Assumptions	
Fleet Size:	368 aircraft
Utilization:	240.0 hours/yr
Aircraft Life:	12 years
Calculations	
Aircraft Exposure Hours:	2,880 hours
Fleet Exposure Hours:	1,059,840 hours
Fleet Hours per Year:	88,320 hours

	Events per Flight Hour	Flight Hours per Event	Events per 100,000 Flt Hrs	1	2	3	4	Fleet-wide Events per Year	Years per Event	Event per Fleet Life	Fleet Life per Event
				$10M	$1M	$100K					
A	10^{-3}	1,000	100	1A	2A	3A	4A	88.32	0.0113	1,060	0.000944
B	10^{-4}	10,000	10	1B (High AAE)	2B	3B	4B	8.832	0.113	105.98	0.00944
C	10^{-5}	100,000	1	1C	2C (Serious PEO)	3C	4C	0.8832	1.13	10.598	0.0944
D	10^{-6}	1,000,000	0.1	1D	2D	3D	4D	0.0883	11.3	1.0598	0.944
E	10^{-7}	10,000,000	0.01	1E	2E (Medium PM)	3E	4E	0.00883	113	0.106	9.44
F	0		0	1F	2F (Low PM)	3F	4F	0		0	
0R											

56

Consequences of Risk Acceptance

Consequences of Risk Acceptance:
On the order of 2 to 10 Class A accidents due to this hazard over the remaining life cycle of the aircraft.

Aircraft Exposure Hours:	2,880 hours
Fleet Exposure Hours:	1,059,840 hours
Fleet Hours per Year:	88,320 hours

	Events per Flight Hour	Flight Hours per Event	Events per 100,000 Flt Hrs	1 ($10M)	2 ($1M)	3 ($100K)	4	Fleet-wide: Events per Year	Fleet-wide: Years per Event	Fleet-wide: Event per Fleet Life	Fleet-wide: Fleet Life per Event
A	10^{-3}	1,000	100	1A	2A (High AAE)	3A	4A	88.32	0.0113	1,060	0.000944
B	10^{-4}	10,000	10	1B	2B	3B	4B	8.832	0.113	10[illegible].98	0.00944
C	10^{-5}	100,000	1	1C	2C (Serious PEO)	3C	4C	0.8832	1.13	10.598	0.0944
D	10^{-6}	1,000,000	0.1	1D	2D	3D	4D	0.0883	11.3	1.0598	0.944
E	10^{-7}	10,000,000	0.01	1E	2E (Medium PM)	3E	4E	0.00883	113	0.106	9.44
F	0		0	1F	2F (Low PM)	3F	4F	0		0	
0R											

2 - 10

57

Consequences of Risk Acceptance

Consequences of Risk Acceptance:
On the order of 2 to 10 Class A accidents due to this hazard over the remaining life cycle of the aircraft.

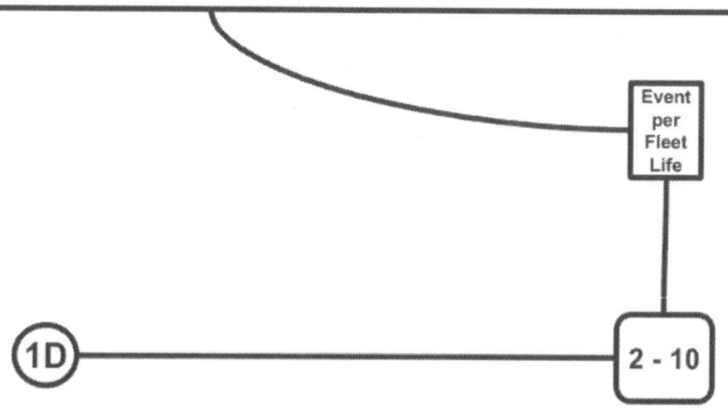

58

Topics for this Tutorial

- Purpose of a Hazard Risk Matrix
- Understanding the Attributes of a well-designed risk assessment matrix
- How to Assign a Risk Assessment Code
- Understanding Probability
- Building an Expanded Matrix
- **Plotting Accidents on a Matrix**
- Using Relative Risk Values
- Building Hazard Risk Profiles

59

Mishap Risk & Mishap Loss

Mishap Risk over Time results in Mishap Loss

Operate the system

Risk (Predicted Loss) ($/Flt Hour) (Fatalities/Flt Hour) → **Time (Flight Hours)** → **Mishap Rate (Actual Loss) ($/Flt Hour) (Fatalities/Flt Hour)**

60

Mishap History

Based on this relationship between mishap risk and mishap loss, we can plot mishap histories on a risk matrix as follows:

$$\text{Severity} = \frac{\text{Total Cost from Class A mishaps}}{\text{Total Number of Class A mishaps}}$$

$$= \frac{\$361{,}671{,}038}{59} = \$\ 6{,}130{,}018$$

$$\text{Probability} = \frac{\text{Total Number of Class A mishaps}}{\text{Total Hours Flown}}$$

$$= \frac{59}{1{,}588{,}597} = 3.714 \text{ mishaps / 100,000 Flt Hrs}$$

61

Mishap History

Class	No	Total Cost	Cost/Mishap	Mishaps per 100,000 Flt Hrs
A	59	$361,671,038	$6,130,018	3.714
B	39	$18,854,121	$483,439	2.455
C	245	$17,114,206	$69,854	15.422
D	112	$970,148	$8,662	7.050
Total	455	$398,609,513		

62

Mishaps

The numbers plot on a chart like this.

Class	No	Total Cost	Cost/Mishap	Mishaps per 100,000 Flt Hrs
A	59	$361,671,038	$6,130,018	3.714
B	39	$18,854,121	$483,439	2.455
C	245	$17,114,206	$69,854	15.422
D	112	$970,148	$8,662	7.050
Total	455	$398,609,513		

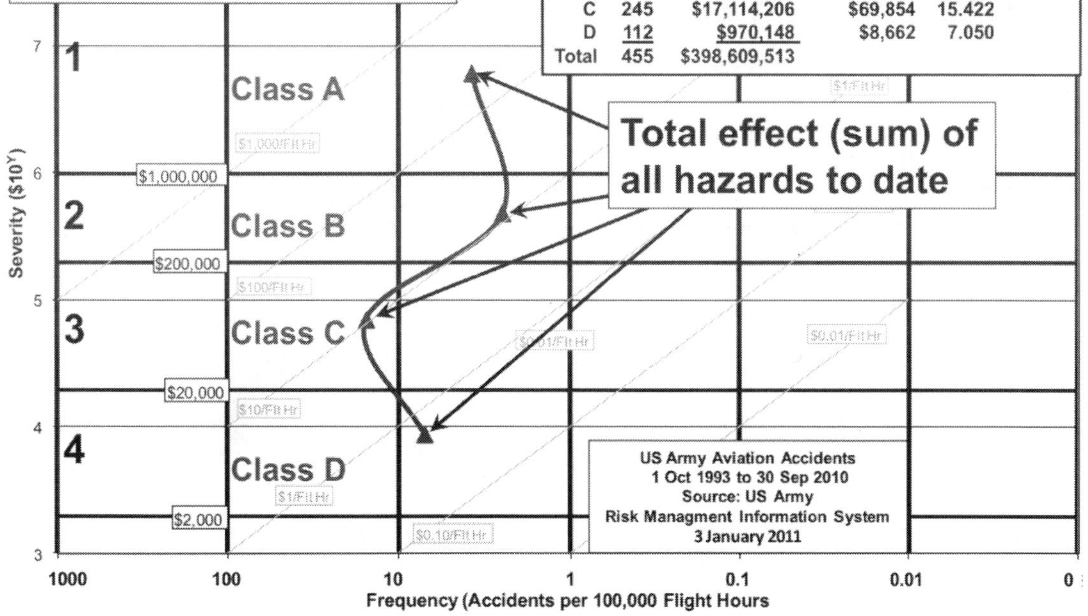

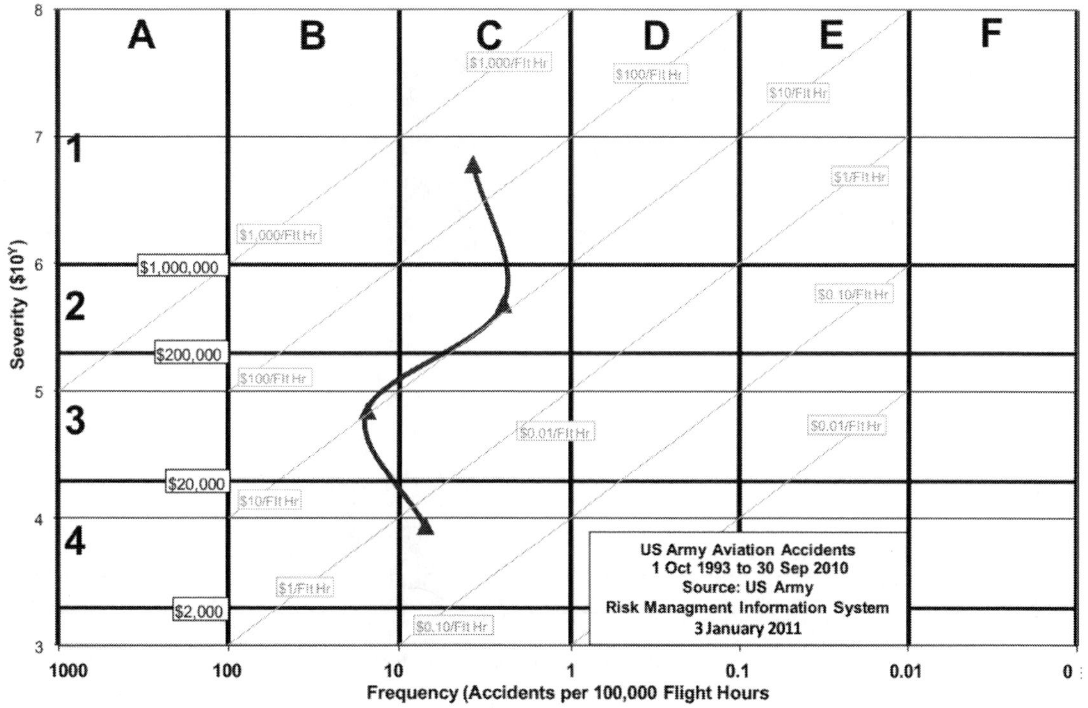

64

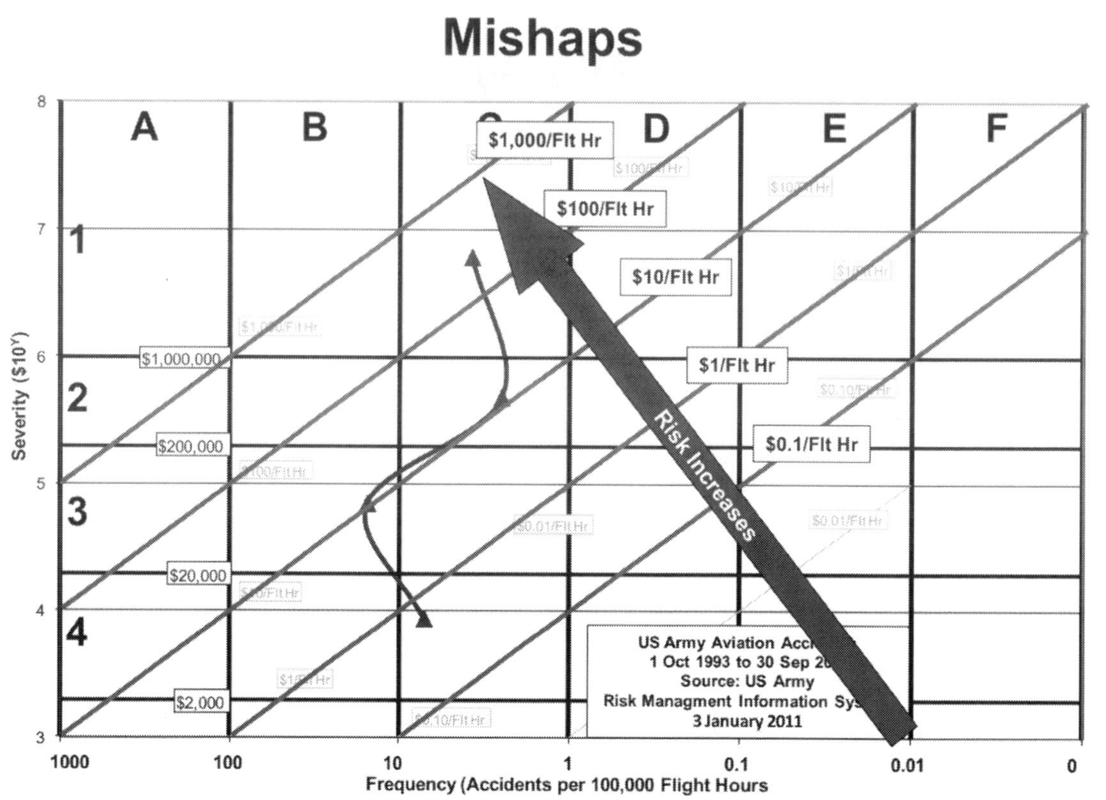
Mishaps
A
B
D
E
F
$1,000/Flt Hr
$100/Flt Hr
$10/Flt Hr
$1/Flt Hr
$0.1/Flt Hr
Risk Increases
1
2
3
4
$1,000,000
$200,000
$20,000
$2,000
Severity ($10^Y)
US Army Aviation Acci
1 Oct 1993 to 30 Sep 2
Source: US Army
Risk Managment Information Sy
3 January 2011
1000
100
10
1
0.1
0.01
0
Frequency (Accidents per 100,000 Flight Hours

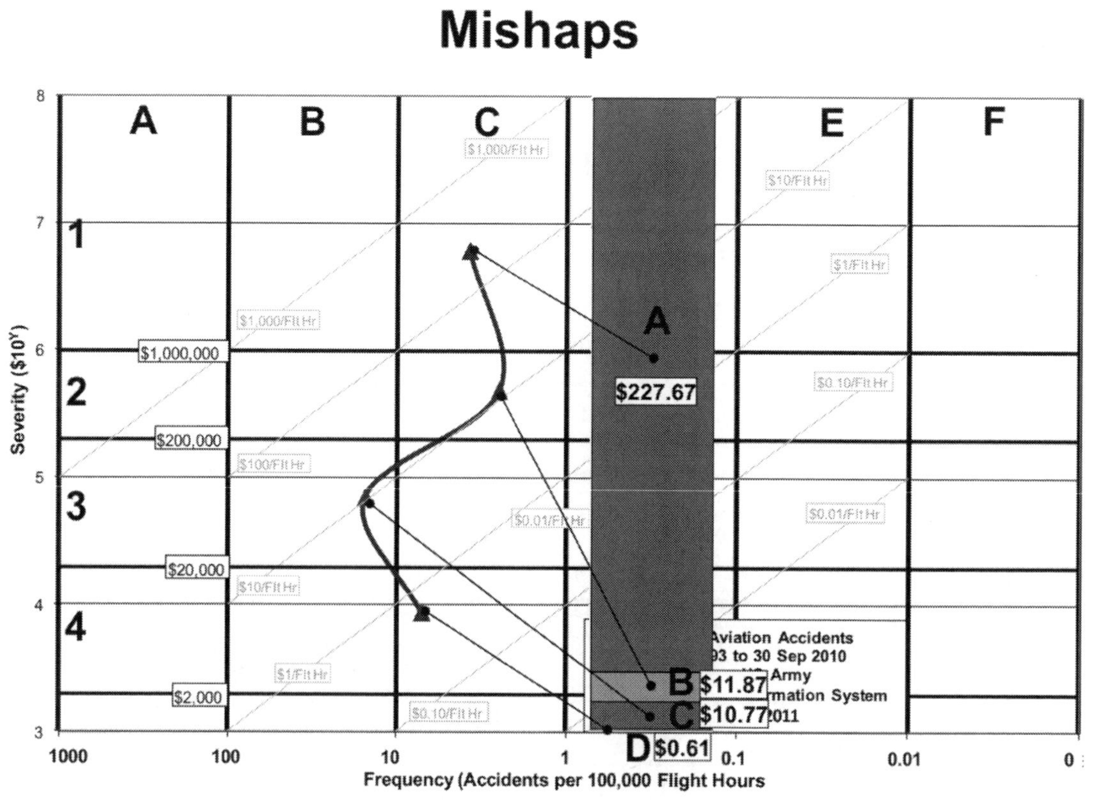
Mishaps
A
B
C
E
F
1
2
3
4
$1,000,000
$200,000
$20,000
$2,000
Severity ($10^Y)
A
$227.67
B $11.87
C $10.77
D $0.61
Aviation Accidents
93 to 30 Sep 2010
Army
rmation System
1000
100
10
1
0.1
0.01
0
Frequency (Accidents per 100,000 Flight Hours

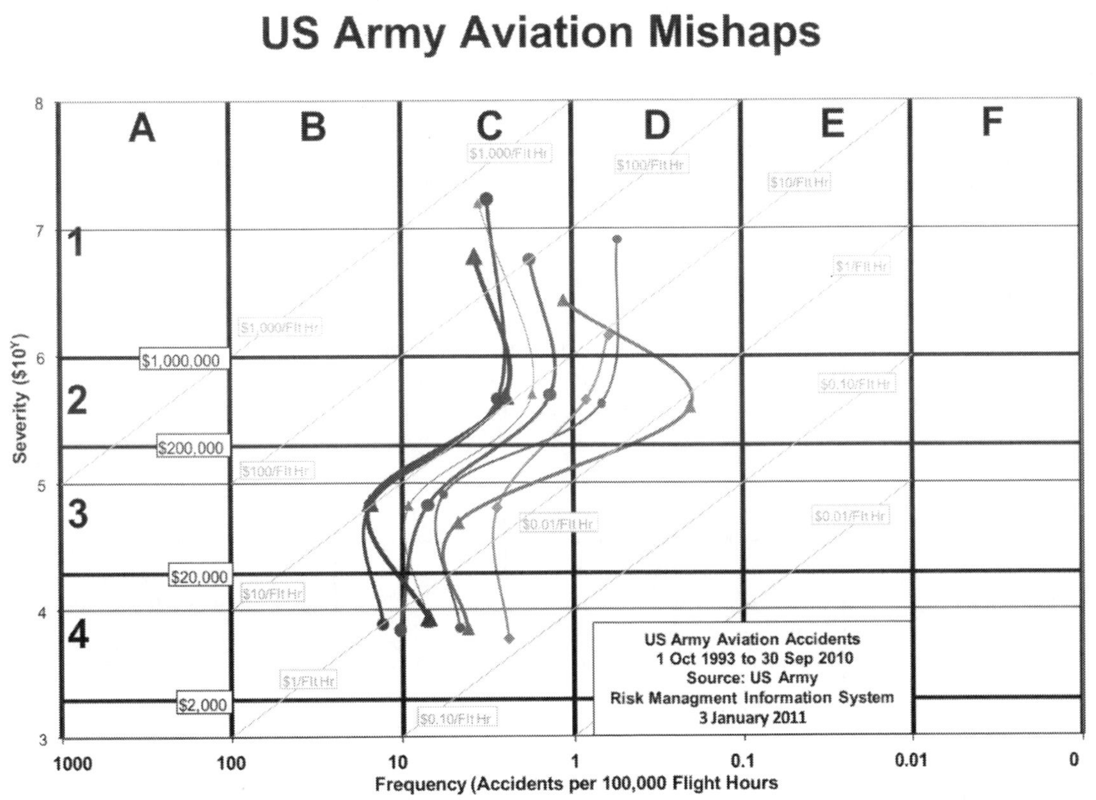
US Army Aviation Mishaps
A
B
C
D
E
F
1
2
3
4
$1,000,000
$200,000
$20,000
$2,000
Severity ($10^Y)
1000
100
10
1
0.1
0.01
0
Frequency (Accidents per 100,000 Flight Hours
US Army Aviation Accidents
1 Oct 1993 to 30 Sep 2010
Source: US Army
Risk Managment Information System
3 January 2011

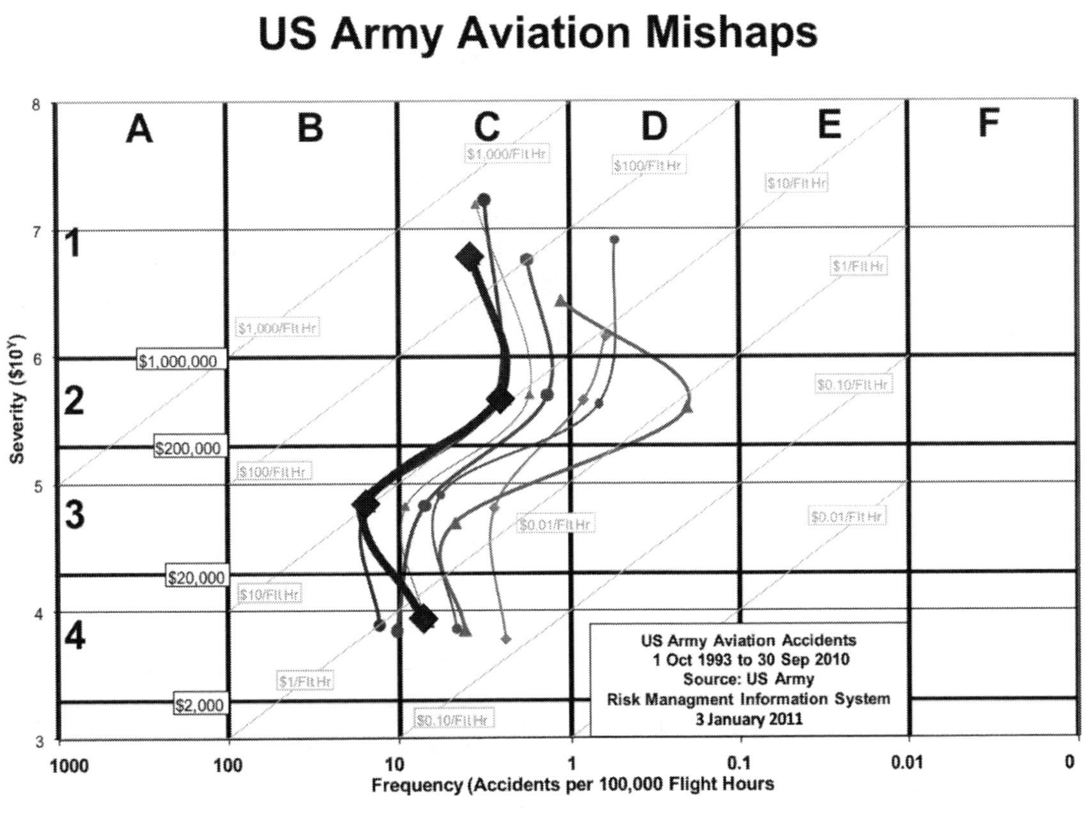
US Army Aviation Mishaps
A
B
C
D
E
F
1
2
3
4
$1,000,000
$200,000
$20,000
$2,000
Severity ($10^Y)
1000
100
10
1
0.1
0.01
0
Frequency (Accidents per 100,000 Flight Hours
US Army Aviation Accidents
1 Oct 1993 to 30 Sep 2010
Source: US Army
Risk Managment Information System
3 January 2011

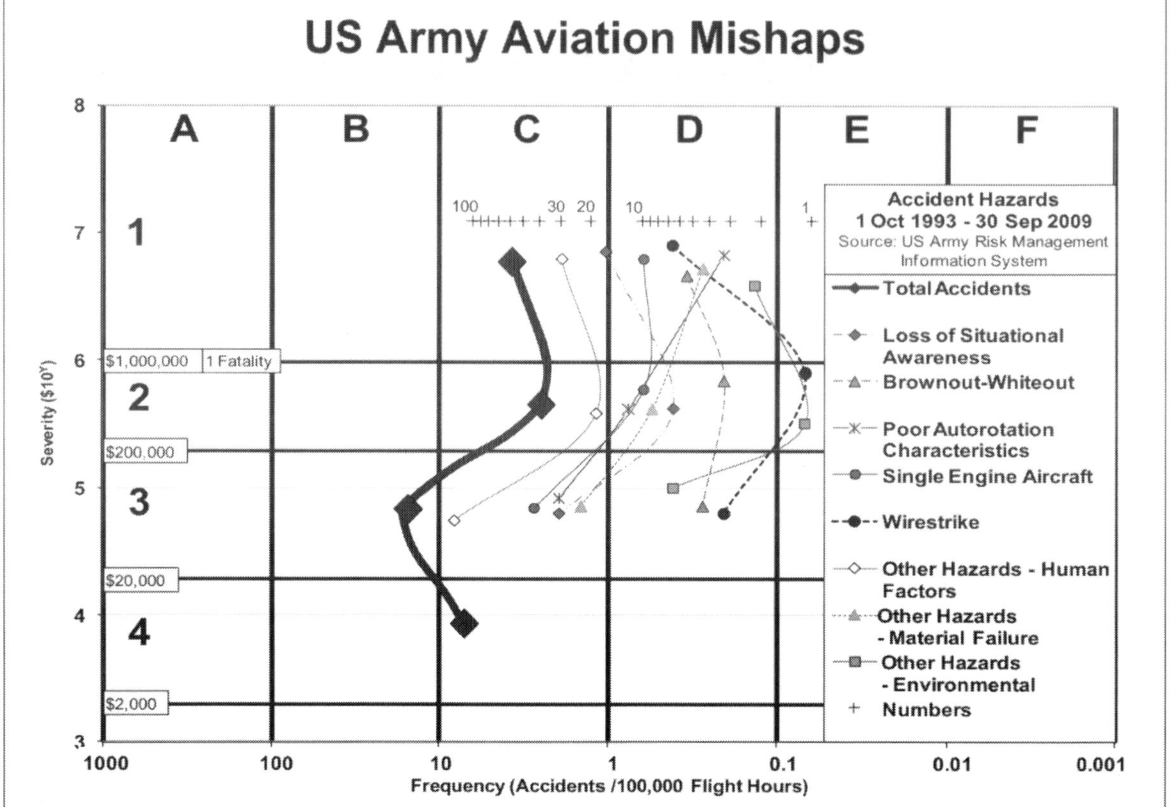
US Army Aviation Mishaps
A
B
C
D
E
F
1
2
3
4
Accident Hazards
1 Oct 1993 - 30 Sep 2009
Source: US Army Risk Management Information System
Total Accidents
Loss of Situational Awareness
Brownout-Whiteout
Poor Autorotation Characteristics
Single Engine Aircraft
Wirestrike
Other Hazards - Human Factors
Other Hazards - Material Failure
Other Hazards - Environmental
Numbers
$1,000,000
1 Fatality
$200,000
$20,000
$2,000
Severity ($10^x)
Frequency (Accidents /100,000 Flight Hours)

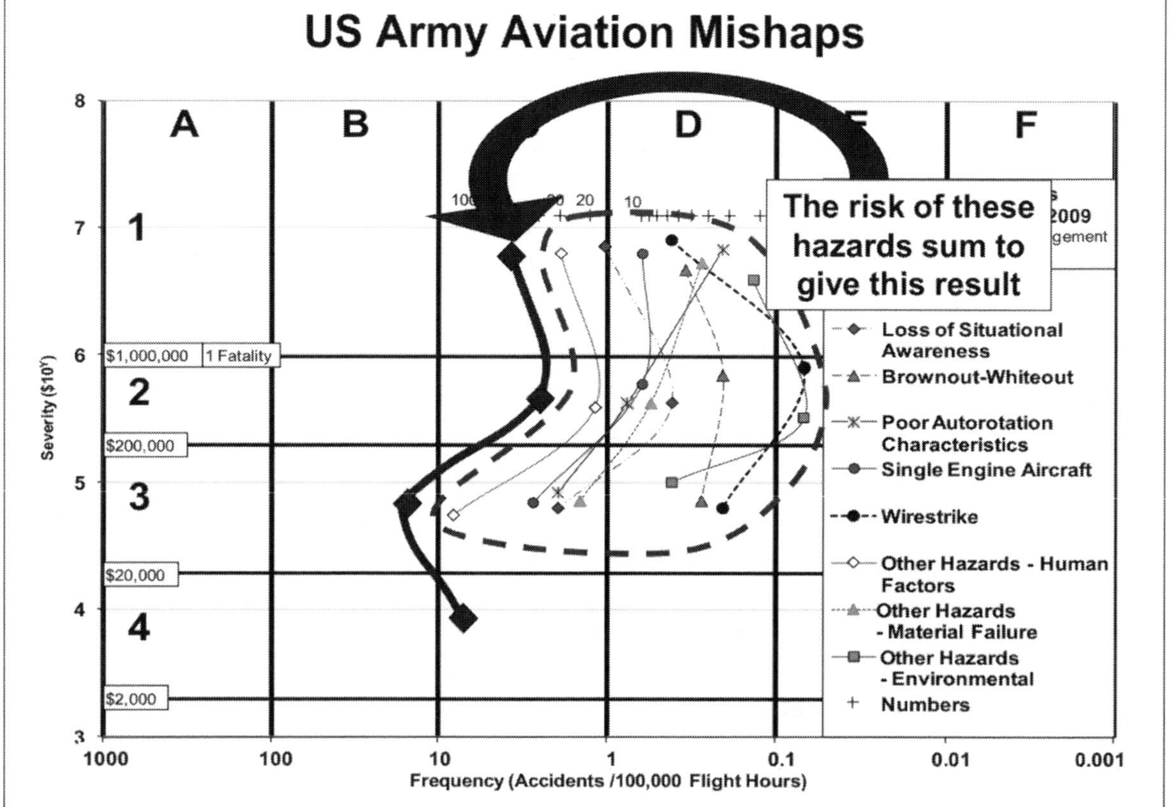
US Army Aviation Mishaps
A
B
D
F
1
2
3
4
The risk of these hazards sum to give this result
Loss of Situational Awareness
Brownout-Whiteout
Poor Autorotation Characteristics
Single Engine Aircraft
Wirestrike
Other Hazards - Human Factors
Other Hazards - Material Failure
Other Hazards - Environmental
Numbers
$1,000,000
1 Fatality
$200,000
$20,000
$2,000
Severity ($10^x)
Frequency (Accidents /100,000 Flight Hours)

Topics for this Tutorial

- Purpose of a Hazard Risk Matrix
- Understanding the Attributes of a well-designed risk assessment matrix
- How to Assign a Risk Assessment Code
- Understanding Probability
- Building an Expanded Matrix
- Plotting Accidents on a Matrix
- **Using Relative Risk Values**
- Building Hazard Risk Profiles

71

Matrix Relative Risk Values (Risk Units)(Clemens)

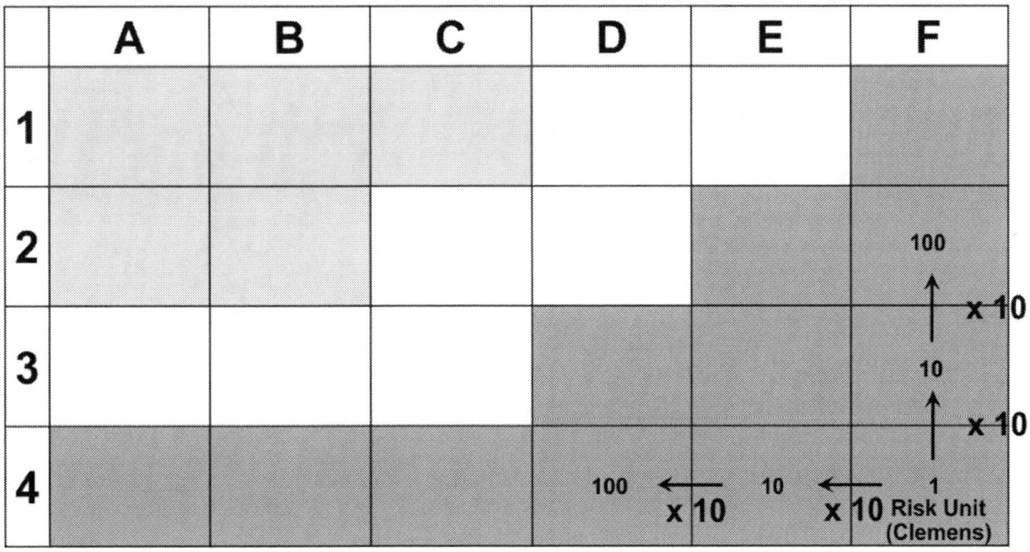

Matrix Relative Risk Values (Clemens)

	A	B	C	D	E	F
1	100,000,000	10,000,000	1,000,000	100,000	10,000	1,000
2	10,000,000	1,000,000	100,000	10,000	1,000	100
3	1,000,000	100,000	10,000	1,000	100	10
4	100,000	10,000	1,000	100	10	1

Helo A Hazard Distribution

	A	B	C	D	E	F
1				5	14	65
2				4	6	2
3			1	7	5	4
4				2	1	

Helo A Matrix
Relative Values (Clemens)

	A	B	C	D	E	F
1				5 x 100,000 = 500,000	14 x 10,000 = 140,000	65 x 1,000 = 65,000
2				4 x 10,000 = 40,000	6 x 1,000 = 6,000	2 x 100 = 200
3			1 x 10,000 = 10,000	7 x 1,000 = 7,000	5 x 100 = 500	4 x 10 = 40
4				2 x 100 = 200	1 x 10 = 10	

Helo A Matrix
Relative Values (Clemens)

	A	B	C	D	E	F
1				500,000	140,000	65,000
2				40,000	6,000	200
3			10,000	7,000	500	40
4				200	10	

Helicopter A

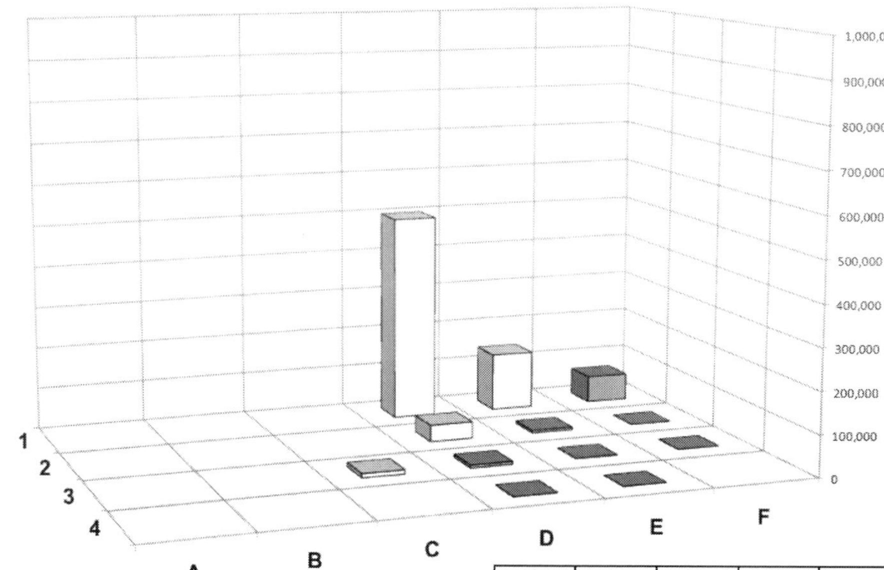

	A	B	C	D	E	F
1				5	14	65
2				4	6	2
3			1	7	5	4
4				2	1	

Helicopter B

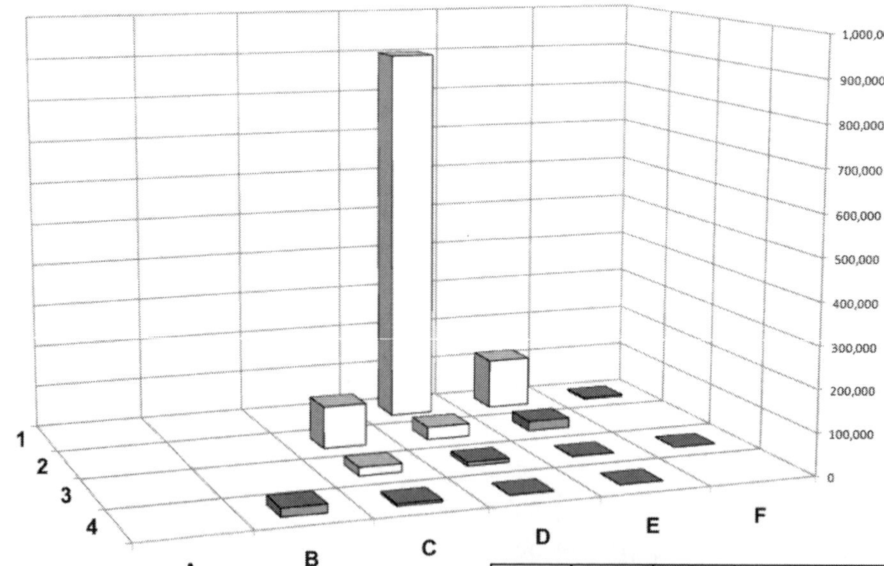

	A	B	C	D	E	F
1				9	12	4
2			1	3	23	
3			2	9	6	1
4		2	5	5	2	

Helicopter C

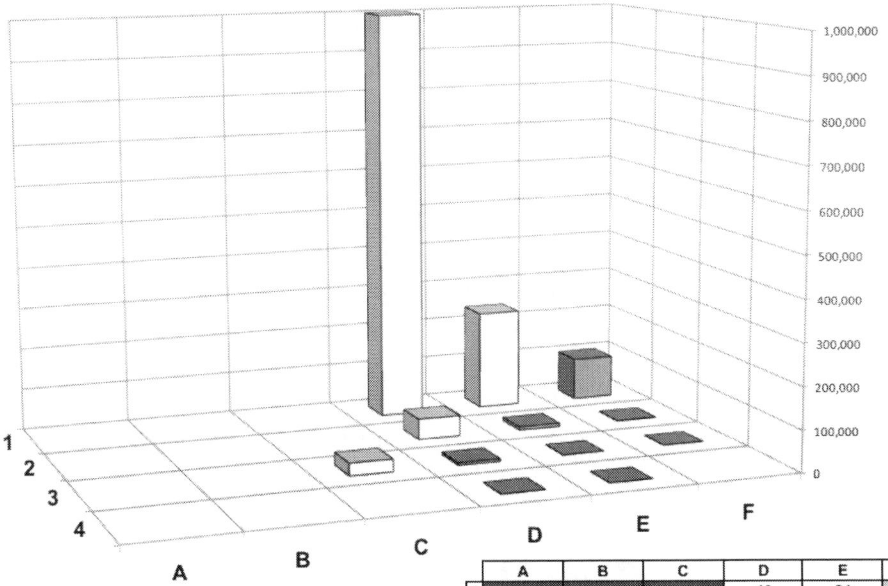

	A	B	C	D	E	F
1				10	24	102
2				5	8	8
3			3	6	3	2
4				1	1	

Side by Side Relative Risk by RAC

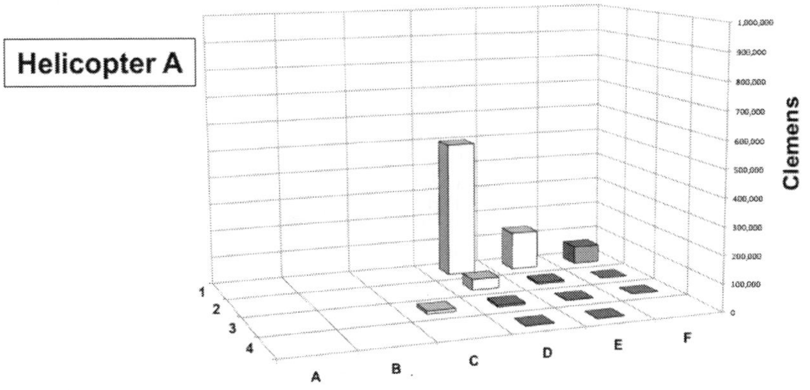

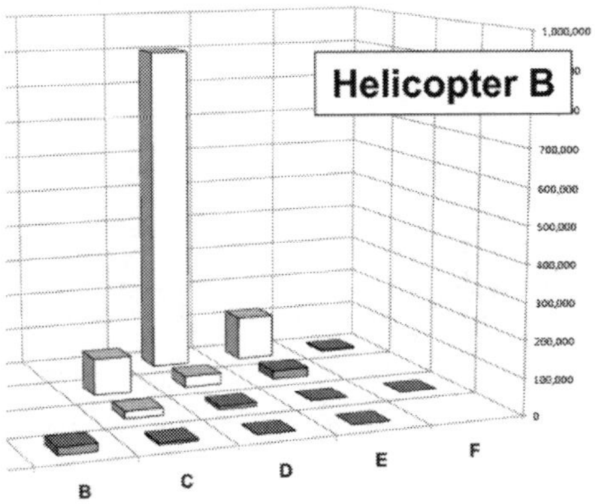

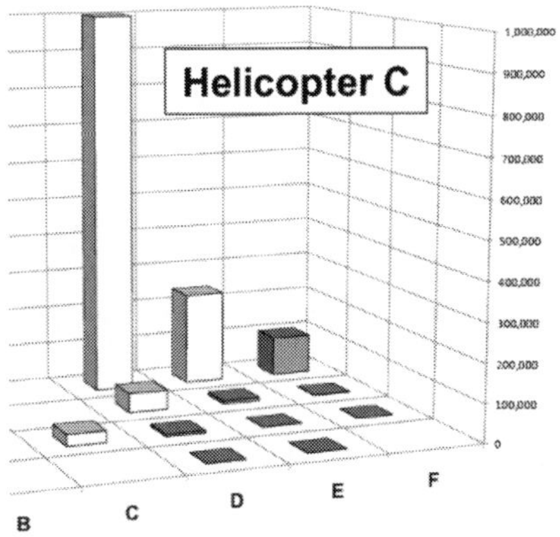

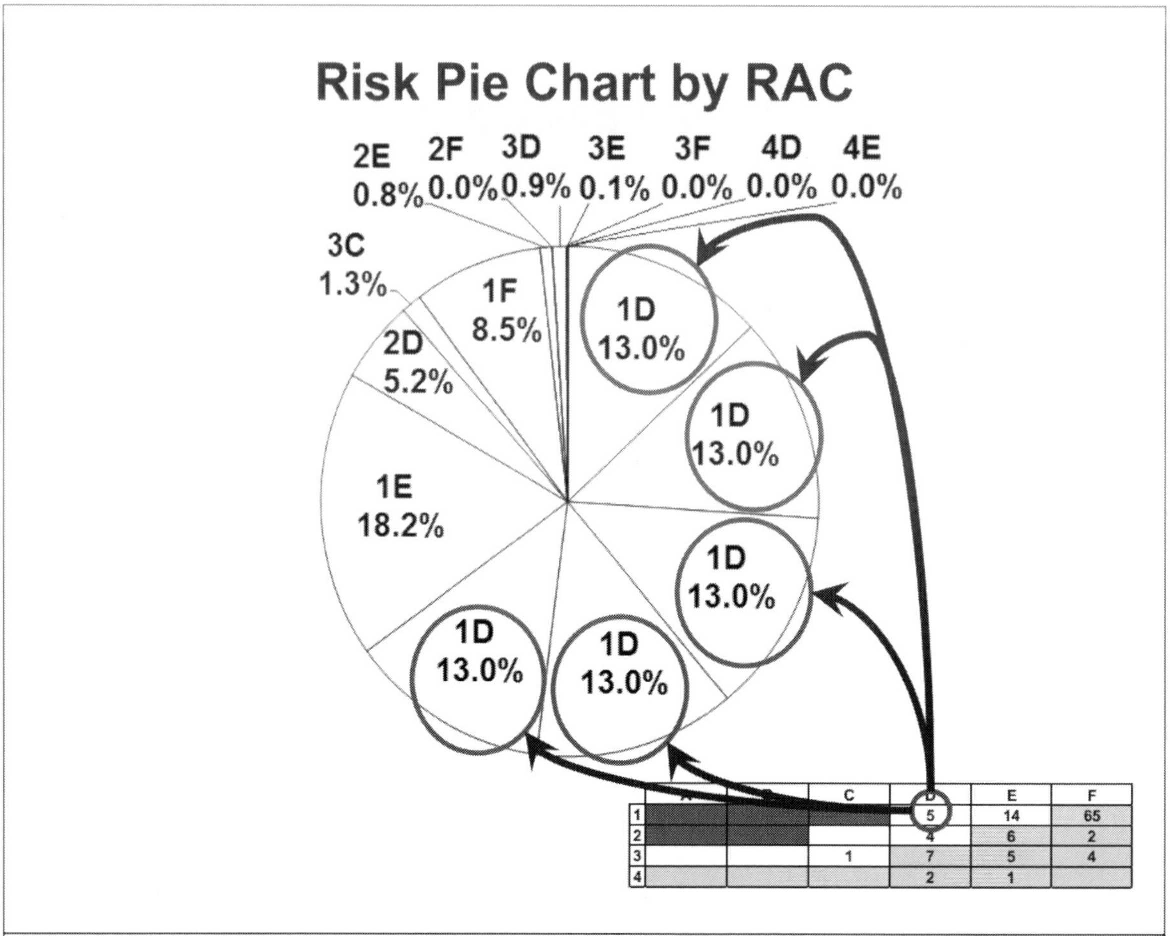
Risk Pie Chart by RAC
2E 0.8%
2F 0.0%
3D 0.9%
3E 0.1%
3F 0.0%
4D 0.0%
4E 0.0%
3C 1.3%
1F 8.5%
2D 5.2%
1E 18.2%
1D 13.0%
1D 13.0%
1D 13.0%
1D 13.0%
1D 13.0%
C E F
1 5 14 65
2 4 6 2
3 1 7 5 4
4 2 1

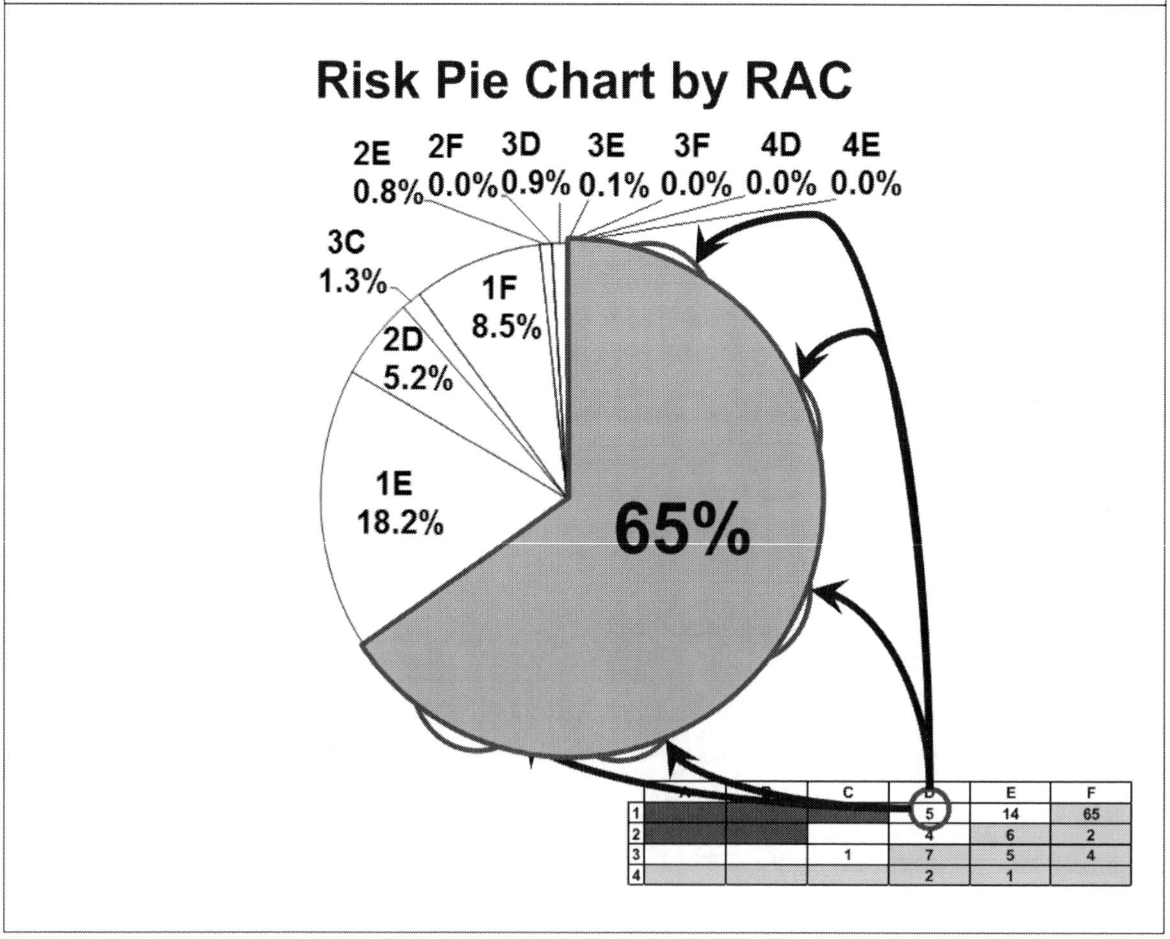
Risk Pie Chart by RAC
2E 0.8%
2F 0.0%
3D 0.9%
3E 0.1%
3F 0.0%
4D 0.0%
4E 0.0%
3C 1.3%
1F 8.5%
2D 5.2%
1E 18.2%
65%
C E F
1 5 14 65
2 4 6 2
3 1 7 5 4
4 2 1

Risk Pie Chart by RAC

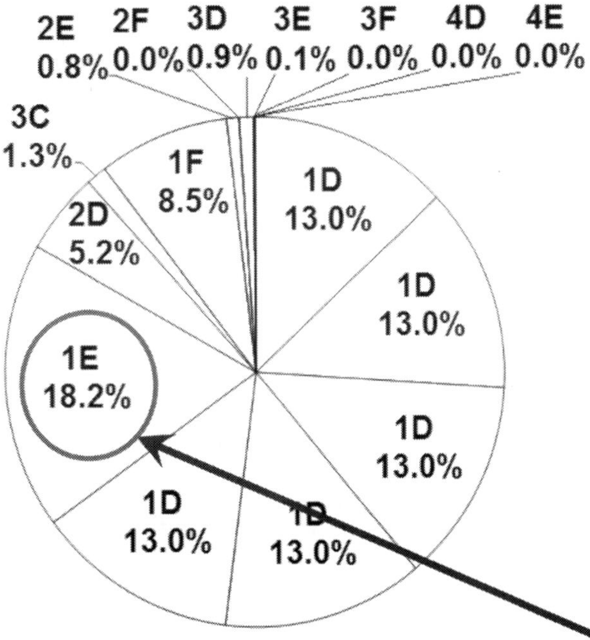

	A	B	C	D	E	F
1				5	14	65
2				4	6	2
3			1	7	5	4
4				2	1	

Risk Pie Chart by RAC

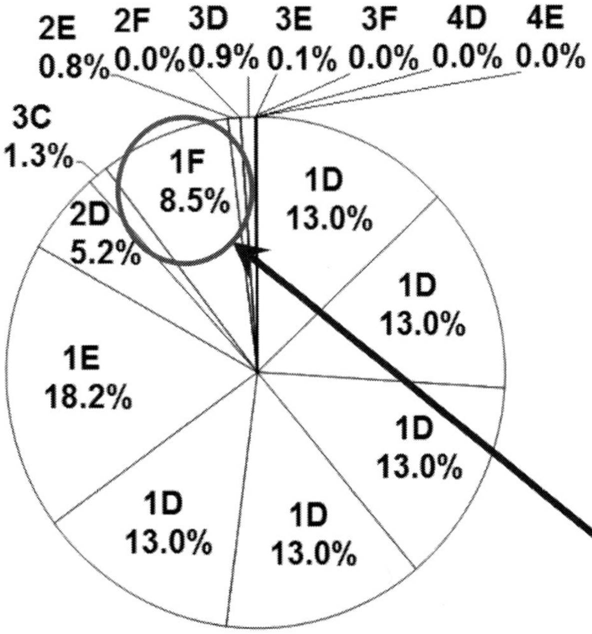

	A	B	C	D	E	F
1				5	14	65
2				4	6	2
3			1	7	5	4
4				2	1	

Topics for this Tutorial

- Purpose of a Hazard Risk Matrix
- Understanding the Attributes of a well-designed risk assessment matrix
- How to Assign a Risk Assessment Code
- Understanding Probability
- Building an Expanded Matrix
- Plotting Accidents on a Matrix
- Using Relative Risk Values
- **Building Hazard Risk Profiles**

85

Hazard Risk Profile

	A	B	C	D	E	F
1				5	14	65
2				4	6	2
3			1	7	5	4
4				2	1	

Hazard Risk Profile

	A	B	C	D	E	F
	3.16E-04	3.16E-05	3.16E-06	3.16E-07	3.16E-08	
1					14	65
2					6	2
3			1		5	4
4					1	

Hazard Risk Profile

	A	B	C	D	E	F
	3.16E-04	3.16E-05	3.16E-06	3.16E-07	3.16E-08	
1	2.23E-05	Sum		5 x 3.16E-06 = 1.58E-05	14 x 3.16E-07 = 4.43E-06	65 x 3.16E-08 = 2.06E-06
2	1.46E-05	Sum		4 x 3.16E-06 = 1.26E-05	6 x 3.16E-07 = 1.90E-06	2 x 3.16E-08 = 6.32E-08
3	5.55E-05	Sum	1 x 3.16E-05 = 3.16E-05	7 x 3.16E-06 = 2.21E-05	5 x 3.16E-07 = 1.58E-06	4 x 3.16E-08 = 1.26E-07
4	6.64E-06	Sum		2 x 3.16E-06 = 6.32E-06	1 x 3.16E-07 = 3.16E-07	

Hazard Risk Profile

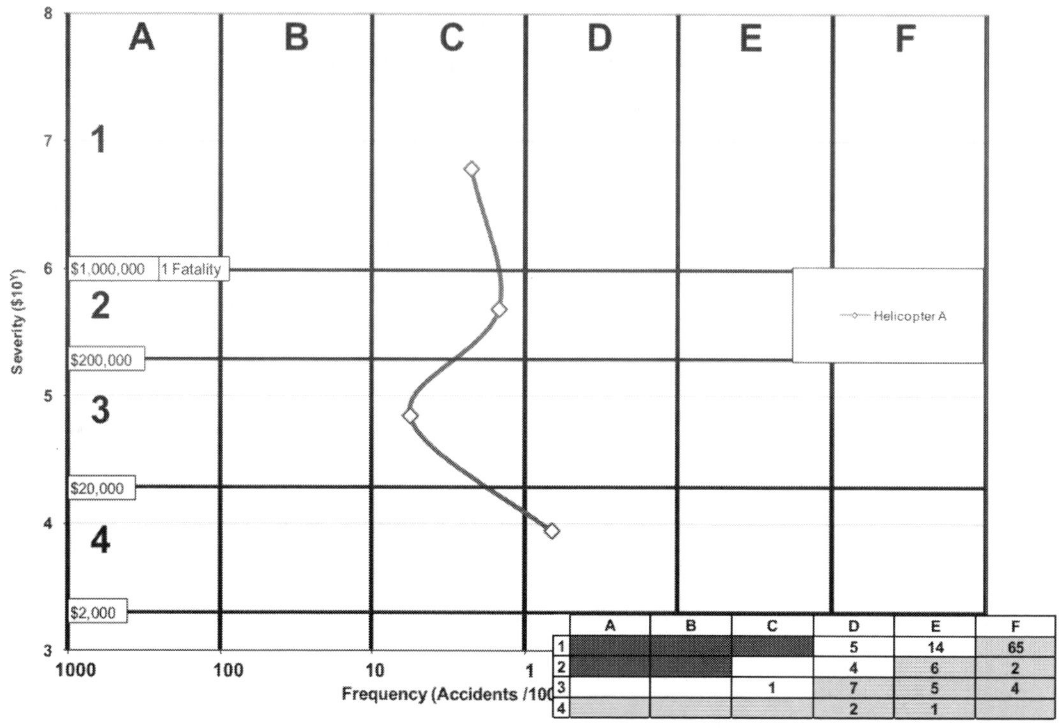

	A	B	C	D	E	F
1				5	14	65
2				4	6	2
3			1	7	5	4
4				2	1	

Comparing Hazard Profile to Accident History

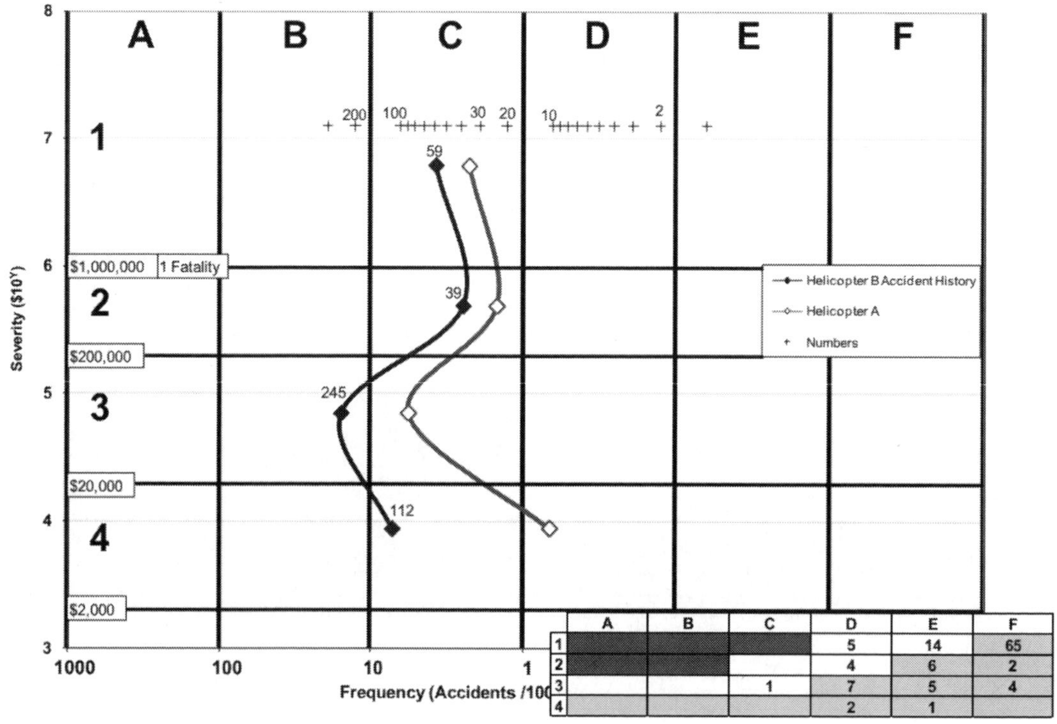

	A	B	C	D	E	F
1				5	14	65
2				4	6	2
3			1	7	5	4
4				2	1	

Comparing Hazard Profile to Accident History

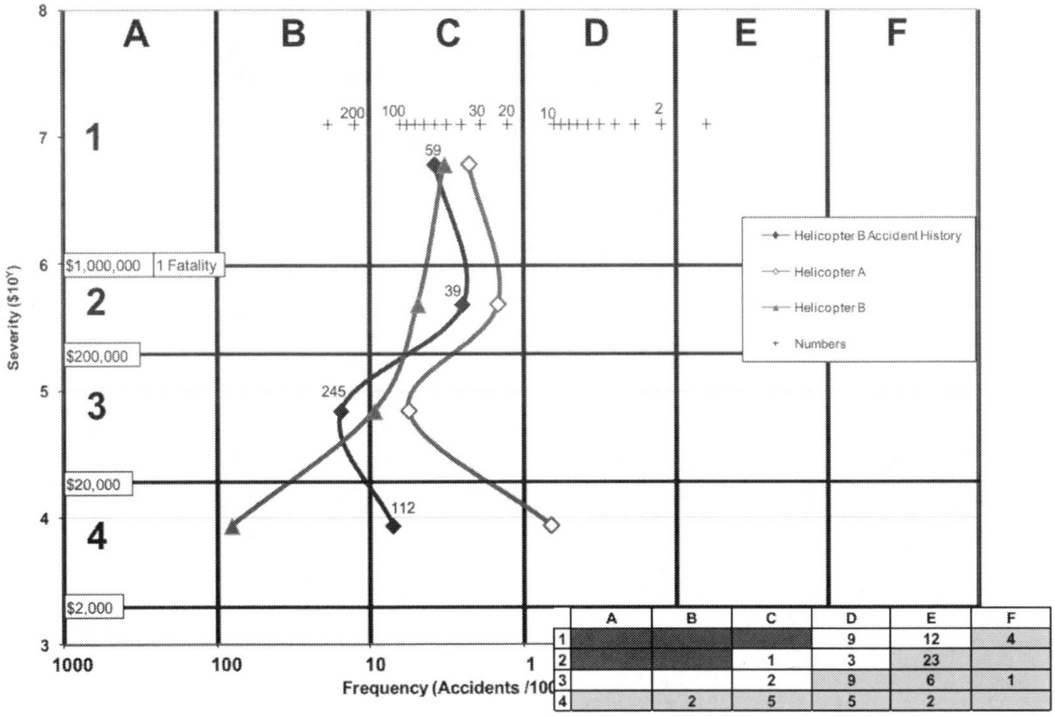

	A	B	C	D	E	F
1				9	12	4
2			1	3	23	
3			2	9	6	1
4		2	5	5	2	

Comparing Hazard Profile to Accident History

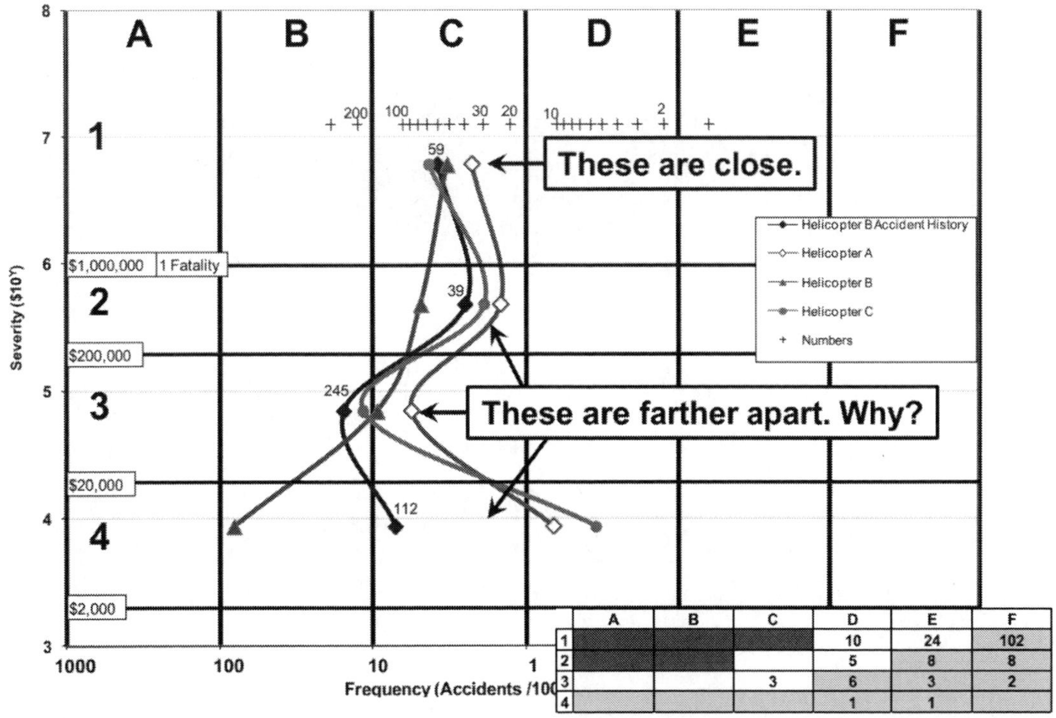

	A	B	C	D	E	F
1				10	24	102
2				5	8	8
3			3	6	3	2
4				1	1	

US Army Aviation Mishaps

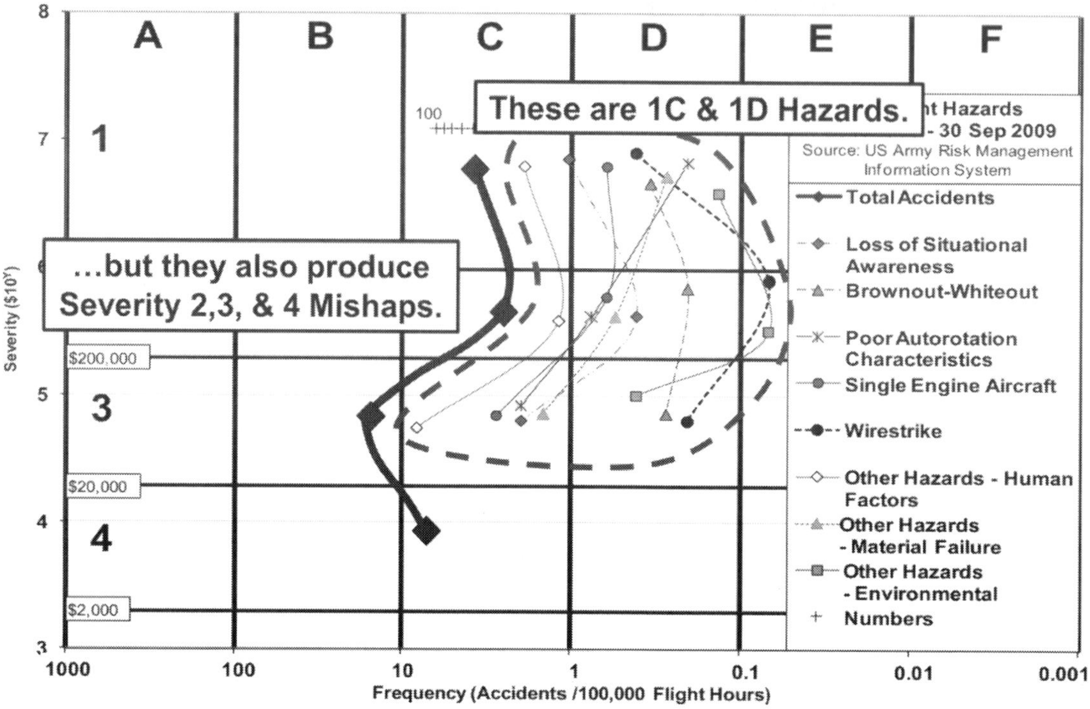

Missile Risk Matrix

RISK ASSESSMENT MATRIX				
SEVERITY / PROBABILITY *	Catastrophic (1) [1 Fatal, $10M]	Critical (2) [$1M]	Marginal (3) [$100K]	Negligible (4)
Frequent (A) [10^{-1}]	High	High	Serious	Medium
Probable (B) [10^{-2}]	High	High	Serious	Medium
Occasional (C) [10^{-3}]	High	Serious	Medium	Low
Remote (D) [10^{-6}]	Serious	Medium	Medium	Low
Improbable (E)	Medium	Medium	Medium	Low
Eliminated (F)	Eliminated			

Missile Hazard Risk Matrix

RISK ASSESSMENT MATRIX				
SEVERITY / PROBABILITY *	Catastrophic (1) 1 Fatal $10M	Critical (2) $1M	Marginal (3) $100K	Negligible (4)
Frequent (A) 1/10	High	High	Serious	Medium
Probable (B) 1/100	High	High	Serious	Medium
Occasional (C) 1/1,000	High	Serious	Medium	Low
Remote (D) 1/1,000,000	Serious	Medium	Medium	Low
Improbable (E)	Medium	Medium	Medium	Low
Eliminated (F)	Eliminated			

Back of the Envelope Calculation

40,000 Shishkebab Missiles

Delivered over 20 years

Assume all fired

1 accident in 1,000,000 firings

$$\frac{\text{1 accident}}{\text{1,000,000 } \cancel{\text{firings}}} \times \frac{\text{40,000 } \cancel{\text{firings}}}{\text{20 years}} = \frac{\text{1 accident}}{\text{500 years}}$$

Missile Hazard Risk Matrix

RISK ASSESSMENT MATRIX				
SEVERITY / PROBABILITY *	Catastrophic (1)	1 Fatal / $10M — Critical (2)	$1M — Marginal (3)	$100K — Negligible (4)
Frequent (A)	High	High	Serious	Medium
1 in < 2 days				
Probable (B)	High	High	Serious	Medium
1 in 18.5 days				
Occasional (C)	High	Serious	Medium	Low
1 in 6 months				
Remote (D)	Serious	Medium	Medium	Low
1 in 500 years				
Improbable (E)	Medium	Medium	Medium	Low
Eliminated (F)	Eliminated			

Matrix Relative Risk Values

	1	2	3	4
A	1,000,000,000	100,000,000	10,000,000	1,000,000
10^{-1}				
B	100,000,000	10,000,000	1,000,000	100,000
10^{-2}				
C	10,000,000	1,000,000	100,000	10,000
10^{-3}				
D	1,000,000	100,000	10,000	1,000
10^{-4}				
D	100,000	10,000	1,000	100
10^{-5}				
D	10,000	1,000	100	10
10^{-6}				
E	1,000	100	10	1

Matrix Relative Risk Values

	1	2	3	4
A	1,000,000,000	100,000,000	10,000,000	1,000,000
10^{-1}				
B	100,000,000	10,000,000	1,000,000	100,000
10^{-2}				
C	10,000,000	1,000,000	100,000	10,000
10^{-3}				
D	1,110,000	111,000	11,100	1,110
10^{-6}				
E	1,000	100	10	1

Matrix Relative Risk Values

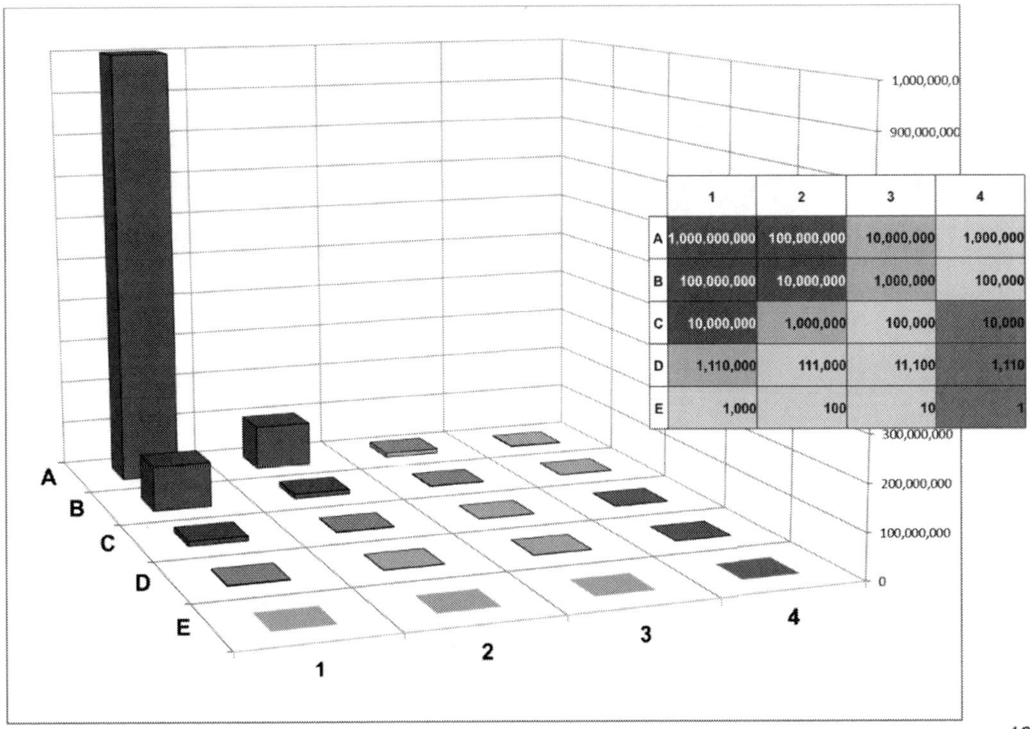

100

Matrix Relative Risk Values

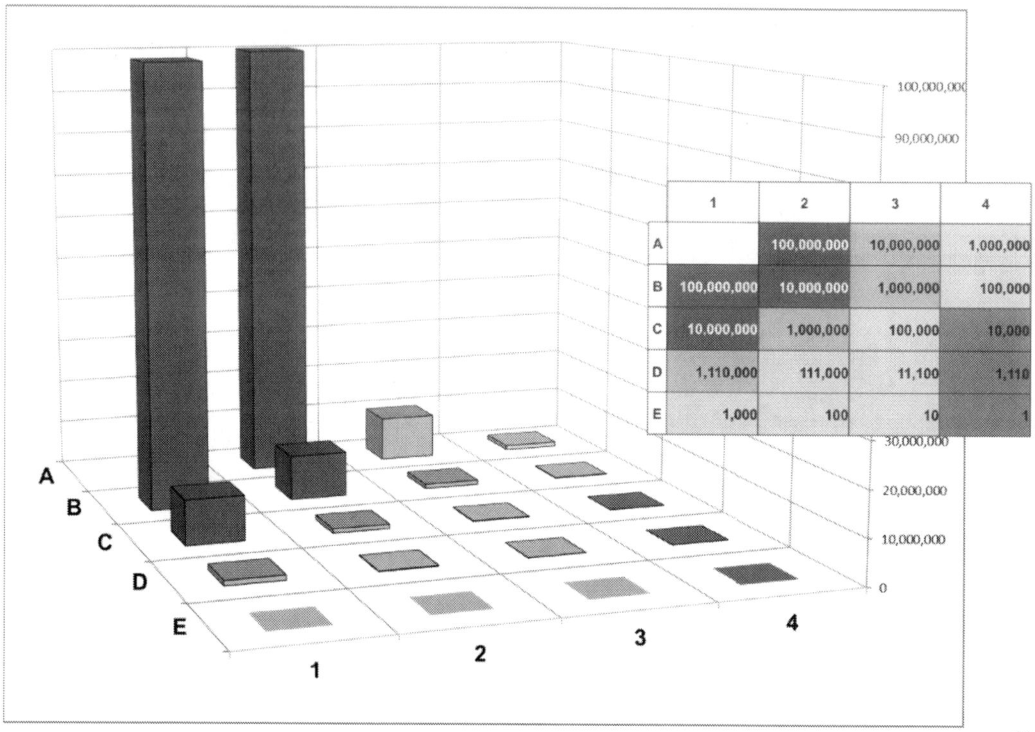

	1	2	3	4
A		100,000,000	10,000,000	1,000,000
B	100,000,000	10,000,000	1,000,000	100,000
C	10,000,000	1,000,000	100,000	10,000
D	1,110,000	111,000	11,100	1,110
E	1,000	100	10	1

101

Matrix Relative Risk Values

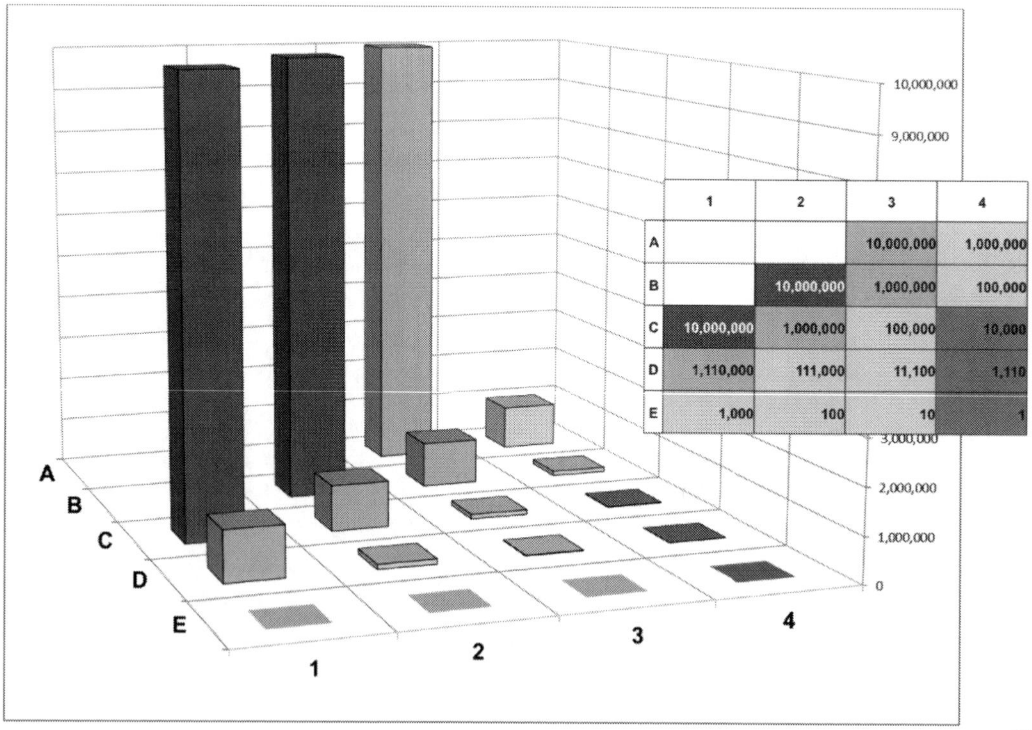

	1	2	3	4
A			10,000,000	1,000,000
B		10,000,000	1,000,000	100,000
C	10,000,000	1,000,000	100,000	10,000
D	1,110,000	111,000	11,100	1,110
E	1,000	100	10	1

102

Matrix Relative Risk Values

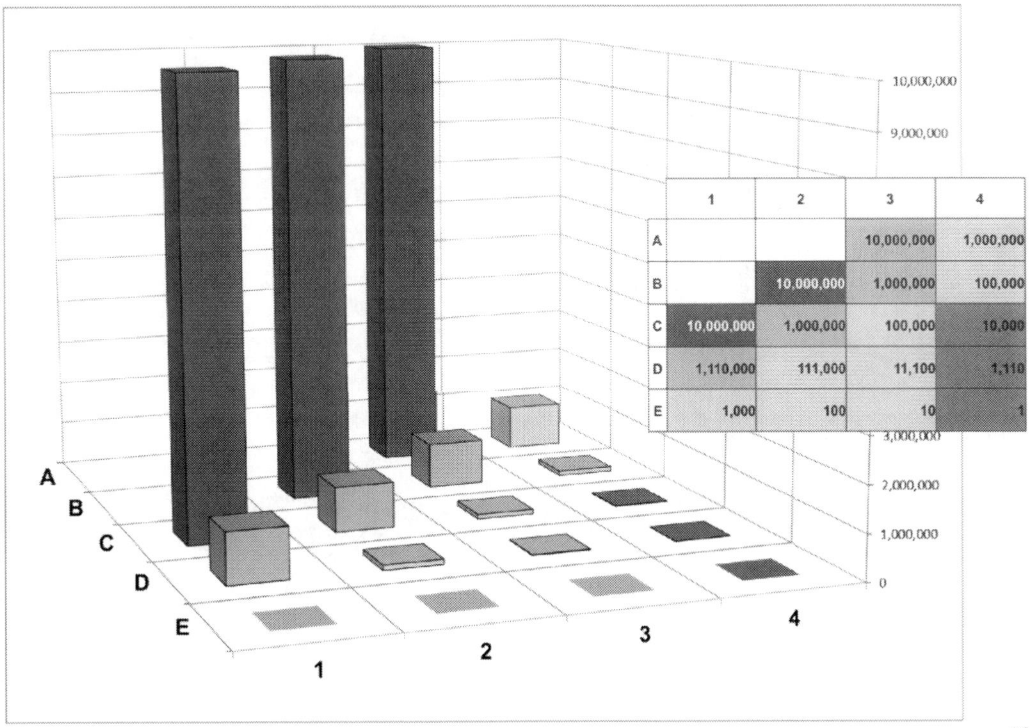

	1	2	3	4
A			10,000,000	1,000,000
B		10,000,000	1,000,000	100,000
C	10,000,000	1,000,000	100,000	10,000
D	1,110,000	111,000	11,100	1,110
E	1,000	100	10	1

103

Matrix Relative Risk Values

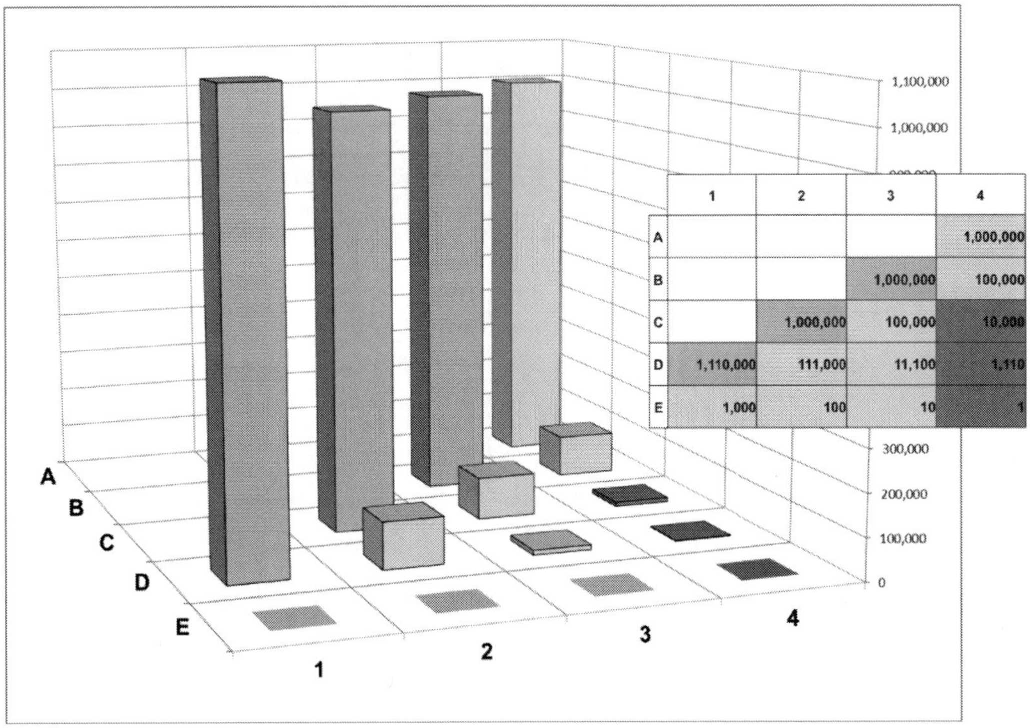

	1	2	3	4
A				1,000,000
B			1,000,000	100,000
C		1,000,000	100,000	10,000
D	1,110,000	111,000	11,100	1,110
E	1,000	100	10	1

Matrix Relative Risk Values

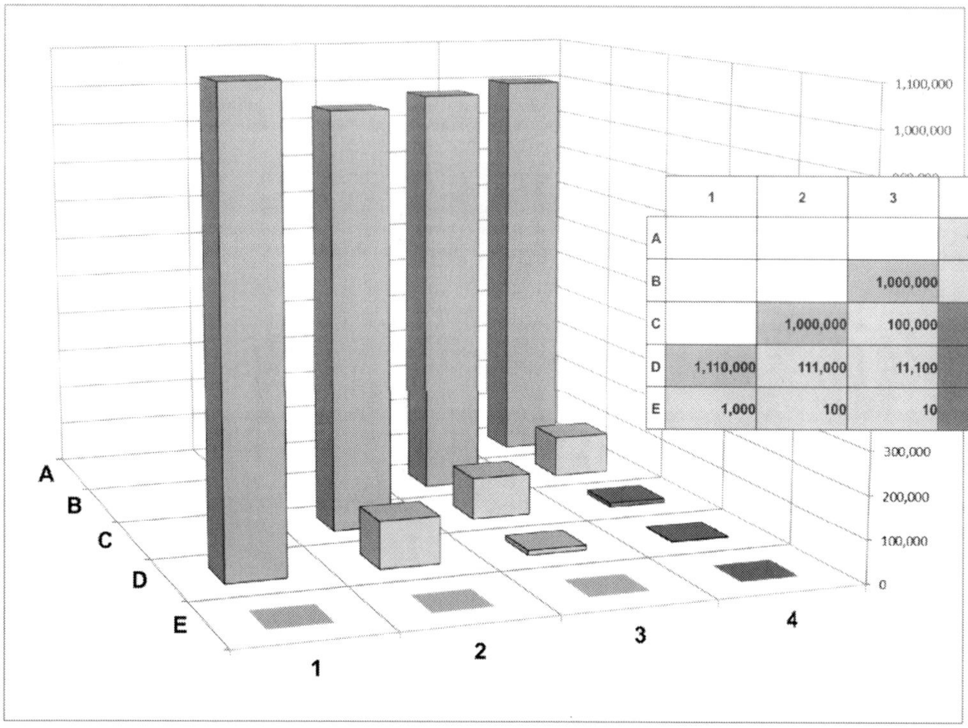

	1	2	3	4
A				1,000,000
B			1,000,000	100,000
C		1,000,000	100,000	10,000
D	1,110,000	111,000	11,100	1,110
E	1,000	100	10	1

Matrix Relative Risk Values

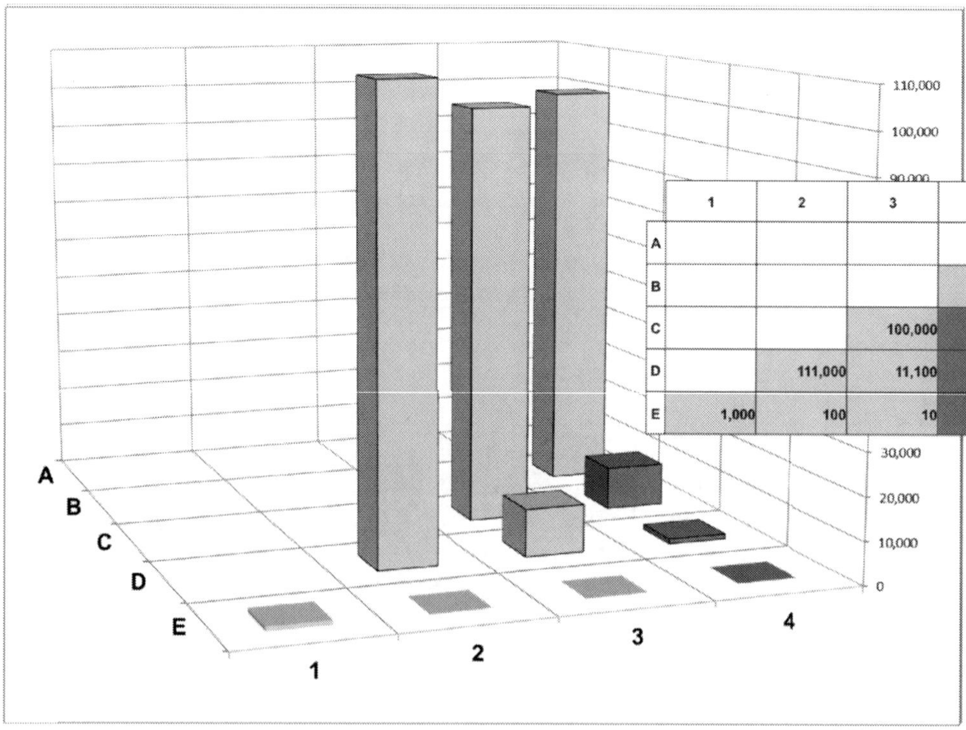

	1	2	3	4
A				
B				100,000
C			100,000	10,000
D		111,000	11,100	1,110
E	1,000	100	10	1

Matrix Relative Risk Values

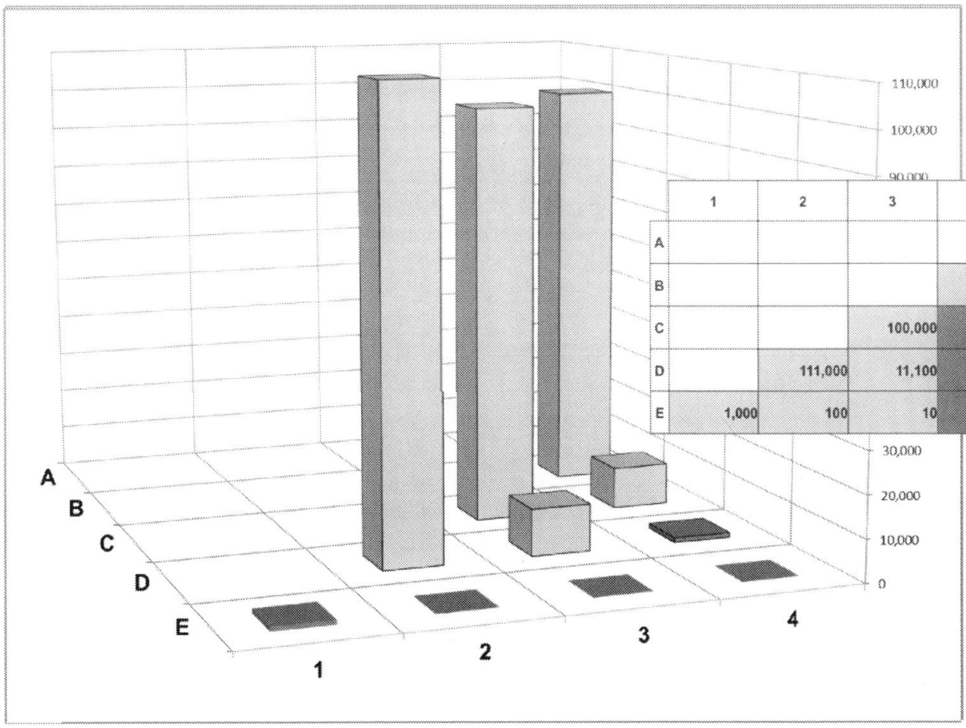

Matrix Relative Risk Values

	1	2	3	4
A	1,000,000,000	100,000,000	10,000,000	1,000,000
10^{-1} B	100,000,000	10,000,000	1,000,000	100,000
10^{-2} C	10,000,000	1,000,000	100,000	10,000
10^{-3} D	1,110,000	111,000	11,100	1,110
10^{-6} E	1,000	100	10	1

Matrix Relative Risk Values

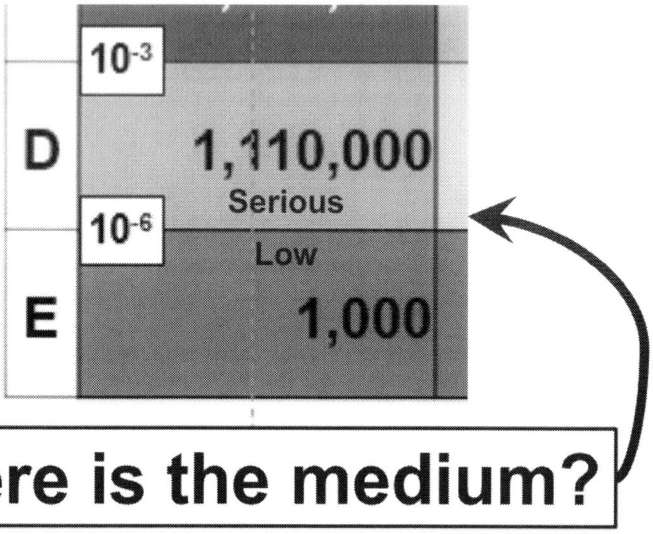

Matrix Relative Risk Values

	1	2	3	4
A	10,000,000	1,000,000	100,000	10,000
10^{-3} B	1,000,000	100,000	10,000	1,000
10^{-4} C	100,000	10,000	1,000	100
10^{-5} D	10,000	1,000	100	10
10^{-6} E	1,000	100	10	1

Matrix Relative Risk Values

	1	2	3	4
A	10,000,000	1,000,000	100,000	10,000
B	1,000,000	100,000	10,000	1,000
C	100,000	10,000	1,000	100
D	10,000	1,000	100	10
E	1,000	100	10	1

1 in 6 months
1 in 5 years
1 in 50 years
1 in 500 years

Matrix Relative Risk Values

	1	2	3	4
A	10,000	100,000	1,000,000	10,000,000
B	1,000	10,000	100,000	1,000,000
C	100	1,000	10,000	100,000
D	10	100	1,000	10,000
E	1	10	100	1,000

1 in 6 months
1 in 5 years
1 in 50 years
1 in 500 years

Summary

113

Summary
Attributes of a well-designed risk assessment matrix

- ✔ Severity scale covers full range of possible outcomes
- ✔ Probability calibrated with reference to an exposure interval
- ✔ Equally proportioned, logarithmic scales (1, 10, 100, 1000…)
- ✔ Cartesian Orientation – Increase up and to the right
- ✔ Risk levels assigned to cells consistent with contours of equal risk

Severity		1	2	3	4	5	6	7	8
		≥$2k	≥$20k	≥$200k	≥$2M	≥$20M	≥$200M	≥$2B	≥$20B
Frequency		Injury, no lost work day	Lost Work Day	Permanent partial disability	≥1 Fatality	≥10 Fatalities	≥100 Fatalities	≥1,000 Fatalities	≥10,000 Fatalities
A	>100								
B	>10								
C	>1						Prohibitive SECDEF		
D	>0.1					High - CAE			
E	>0.01				Serious - PEO				
F	>0.001			Medium - PM					
G	>0.0001	Low – SSWG/Principal for Safety							
H	>0.00001								
I	> 0.000001								
J	≤ 0.000001								

Summary
Attributes of a well-designed risk assessment matrix

- ✓ Sufficient probability categories so highest severity level reach the PM level
- ✓ Frequency category letters increase with decreasing frequency
- ✓ A RAC for hazards whose risk has been eliminated
- ✓ Easily tailored & consistent with other systems within its family of systems
- ✓ Severity Category numbers increase with increasing Severity

Severity		1	2	3	4	5	6	7	8
		≥$2k	≥$20k	≥$200k	≥$2M	≥$20M	≥$200M	≥$2B	≥$20B
Frequency		Injury, no lost work day	Lost Work Day	Permanent partial disability	≥1 Fatality	≥10 Fatalities	≥100 Fatalities	≥1,000 Fatalities	≥10,000 Fatalities
A	>100								
B	>10								
C	>1							Prohibitive SECDEF	
D	>0.1					High - CAE			
E	>0.01				Serious - PEO				
F	>0.001			Medium - PM					
G	>0.0001	Low – SSWG/Principal for Safety							
H	>0.00001								
I	> 0.000001								
J	≤ 0.000001								

How to Determine the Risk Assessment Code (RAC)

To determine the appropriate RAC for a given hazard:

(1) Identify the full range of potential outcomes for the hazard (death, injury, system loss, environmental impact, and monetary loss). The range of outcomes will often span more than one severity category.

(2) For each severity category associated with this range of severity, determine the associated probability category.

(3) Determine which severity-probability pair has the greatest risk. This pair is the RAC assigned to the hazard.

(4) If two or more severity-probability pairs are equal as the greatest risk, select the one with the greatest severity.

116

Summary Understanding Probability

Math Definition:

- Repeat a random experiment "n" number of times.
- If a specific outcome has occurred "f" times in these n trials, the number "f" is the frequency of the outcome.
- The ratio f/n is the relative frequency of the outcome.
- A relative frequency is usually very unstable for small values of "n," but it tends to stabilize about some number "p" as "n" increases.
- The number "p" is the probability of the outcome.

$$p = f / n$$

for very large values of n

Simple example:

Probability of rolling a "3" with one die.

Roll #1 - "5", f/n = 0

Roll #2 - "2", f/n = 0

Roll #3 - "3", f/n = 1/3 = .333...

Roll #4 - "4", f/n = 1/4 = .25

Roll #1,000: 163 "3"s, f/n = 163/1000 = .163

Rolls approach infinity f/n = .166666....

Roll a single die 30 times. The expected value of each roll is 3.5. What you actually get is somewhat different.

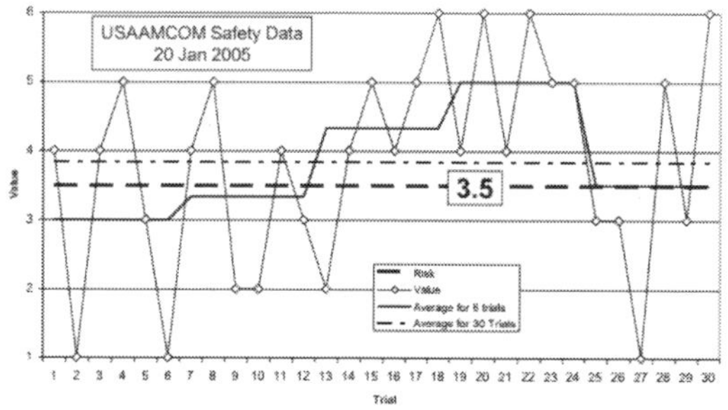

12

Hazard: AH-64 strikes wire results in Class A mishap

Probability: 4.406E-06 occurrences per flight hour

1 Flight Hr, no mishap, rate = 0

1,000 Flight Hrs, no mishap, rate = 0

176,182 Flight Hrs, 1 mishap, rate = 5.676E-06 /flt hr

274,539 Flight Hrs, 2 mishaps, rate = 7.285E-06 /flt hr

700,462 Flt Hrs, 3 mishaps, rate = 4.283E-06 /flt hr

10,000,000 Flt Hrs, 46 mishaps, rate = 4.600E-06 /flt hr

1,000,000,000 Hrs, 4407 mishaps, rate = 4.407E-06 /flt hr

Flight hours approach infinity, rate = 4.406E-06 /flt hr

117 13

Summary Expanded Matrix

Applying Probability Classifications to a military helicopter

Fleet Size = 368 aircraft

Utilization = 240 hours/year

Life = 20 years/aircraft

Aircraft Life = 240 x 20
= 4,800 hours

Fleet Exposure Hours = 368 x 240 x 20
= 1,776,400 hours

Fleet Hours per Year = 368 x 240
= 88,320 hours

US Army PEO Aviation Expanded Matrix

	Events per Flight Hour	Flight Hours per Event	Events per 100,000 Flt Hrs	Events per Year	Years per Event	Event per Fleet Life	Fleet Life per Event
Frequent A	10^{-3}	1,000	100	88.32	0.0113	1,060	0.000944
Probable B	10^{-4}	10,000	10	8.832	0.113	105.98	0.00944
Occasional C	10^{-5}	100,000	1	0.8832	1.13	10.598	0.0944
Remote D	10^{-6}	1,000,000	0.1	0.0883	11.3	1.0598	0.944
Improbable E	10^{-7}	10,000,000	0.01	0.00883	113	0.106	9.44
Very Improbable F	0		0	0		0	
Zero Risk 0R							

Numbers greater than 1 are easier to comprehend

29

16

☐ Input
☐ Calculated

Assumptions	
Fleet Size:	368 aircraft
Utilization:	240.0 hours/yr
Aircraft Life:	12 years
Calculations	
Aircraft Exposure Hours:	2,880 hours
Fleet Exposure Hours:	1,059,840 hours
Fleet Hours per Year:	88,320 hours

	Events per Flight Hour	Flight Hours per Event	Events per 100,000 Flt Hrs	1 Catastrophic	2 Critical	3 Marginal	4 Negligible	Fleet-wide: Events per Year	Fleet-wide: Years per Event	Fleet-wide: Event per Fleet Life	Fleet-wide: Fleet Life per Event
Frequent A	10^{-3}	1,000	100	1A	2A	3A	4A	88.32	0.0113	1,060	0.000944
Probable B	10^{-4}	10,000	10	1B	2B	3B	4B	8.832	0.113	105.98	0.00944
Occasional C	10^{-5}	100,000	1	1C	2C	3C	4C	0.8832	1.13	10.598	0.0944
Remote D	10^{-6}	1,000,000	0.1	1D	2D	3D	4D	0.0883	11.3	1.0598	0.944
Improbable E	10^{-7}	10,000,000	0.01	1E	2E	3E	4E	0.00883	113	0.106	9.44
Very Improbable F	0		0	1F	2F	3F	4F	0		0	
Zero Risk 0R											

Labels within the matrix: $10M (between 1 and 2), $1M (between 2 and 3), $100K (between 3 and 4); High AAE (1A/1B–2A/2B); Serious PEO (2C–3C); Medium PM (2E–3E); Low PM (2F–3F).

118

Summary Accidents on a Matrix

Based on this relationship between mishap risk and mishap loss, we can plot mishap histories on a risk matrix as follows:

$$\text{Severity} = \frac{\text{Total Cost from Class A mishaps}}{\text{Total Number of Class A mishaps}}$$

$$= \frac{\$1,305,079,886}{83} = \$\ 15,723,854$$

$$\text{Probability} = \frac{\text{Total Number of Class A mishaps}}{\text{Total Hours Flown}}$$

$$= \frac{83}{2,351,860} = 3.529 \text{ mishaps / 100,000 Flt Hrs}$$

21

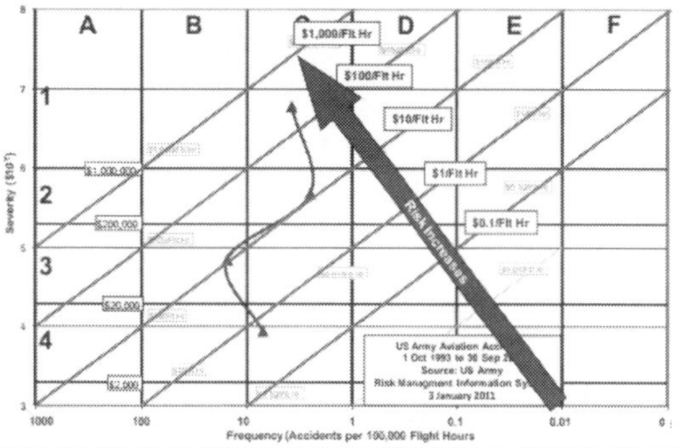

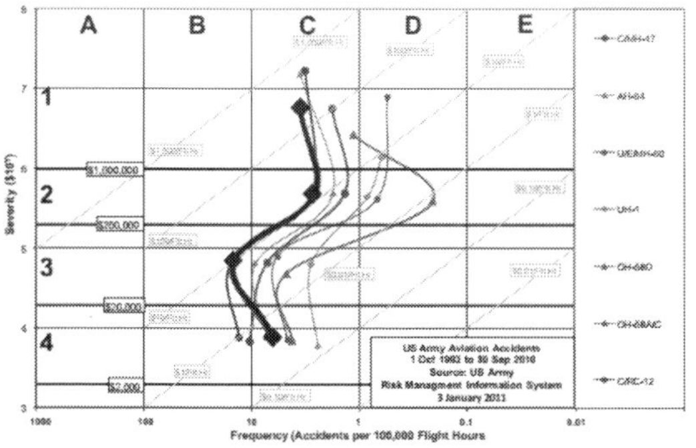

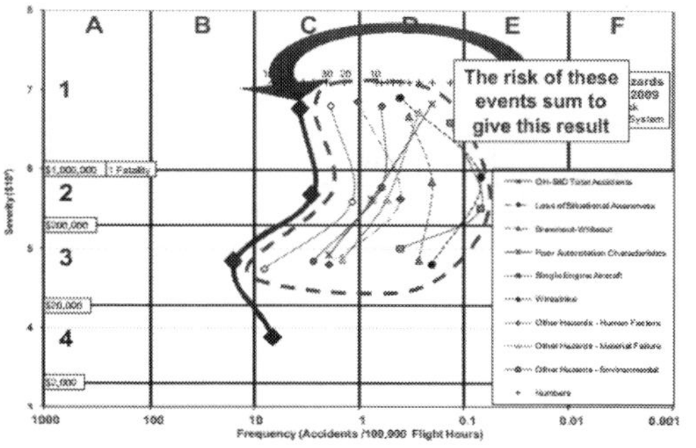

119

Summary Relative Risk Values (Clemens)

	A	B	C	D	E	F
1	100,000,000	10,000,000	1,000,000	100,000	10,000	1,000
2	10,000,000	1,000,000	100,000	10,000	1,000	100
3	1,000,000	100,000	10,000	1,000	100	10
4	100,000	10,000	1,000	100	10	1

	A	B	C	D	E	F
1				500,000	140,000	65,000
2				40,000	6,000	200
3			10,000	7,000	500	40
4				200	10	

Helicopter A

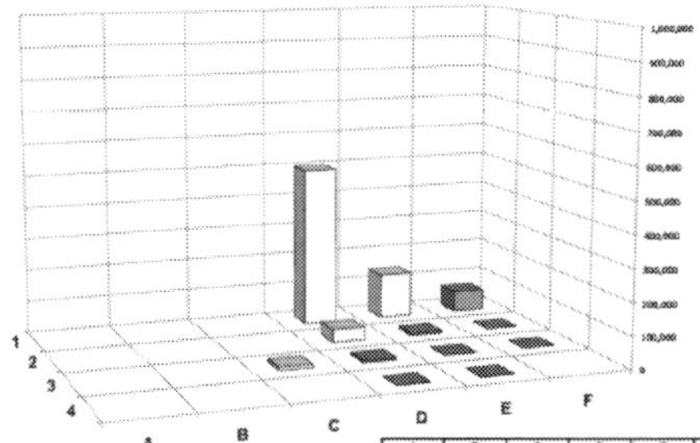

	A	B	C	D	E	F
1				5	14	65
2				4	6	2
3			1	7	5	4
4				2	1	

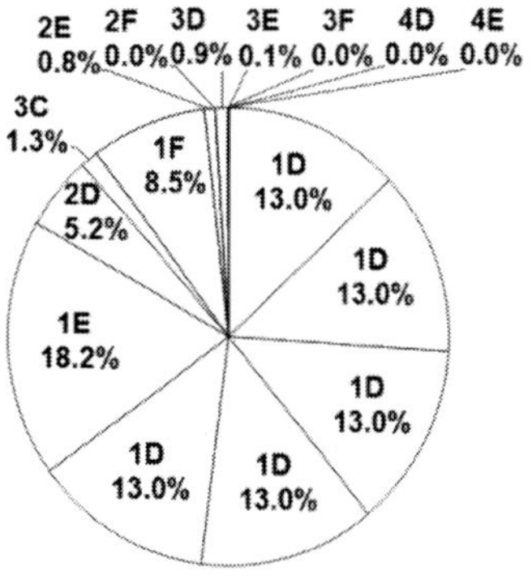

	A	B	C	D	E	F
1				5	14	65
2				4	6	2
3			1	7	5	4
4				2	1	

120

Summary Hazard Risk Profile

	A	B (3.16E-04)	C (3.16E-05)	D (3.16E-06)	E (3.16E-07)	F (3.16E-08)
1					14	65
2					6	2
3			1		5	4
4					1	

	A	B (3.16E-04)	C (3.16E-05)	D (3.16E-06)	E (3.16E-07)	F (3.16E-08)
1	2.23E-05	Sum		5 x 3.16E-06 = 1.58E-05	14 x 3.16E-07 = 4.43E-06	65 x 3.16E-08 = 2.06E-06
2	1.46E-05	Sum		4 x 3.16E-06 = 1.26E-05	6 x 3.16E-07 = 1.90E-06	2 x 3.16E-08 = 6.32E-08
3	5.55E-05	Sum	1 x 3.16E-05 = 3.16E-05	7 x 3.16E-06 = 2.21E-05	5 x 3.16E-07 = 1.58E-06	4 x 3.16E-08 = 1.26E-07
4	6.64E-06	Sum		2 x 3.16E-06 = 6.32E-06	1 x 3.16E-07 = 3.16E-07	

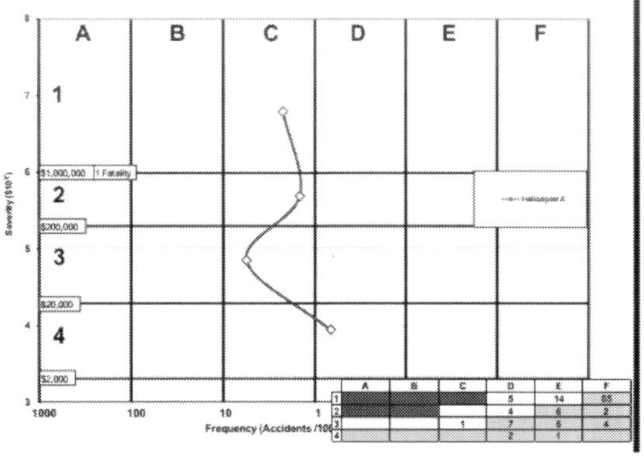

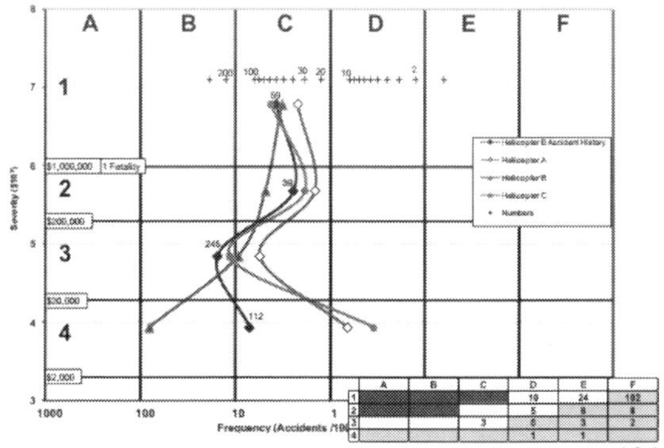

121

Summary Missile Risk Matrix

RISK ASSESSMENT MATRIX

SEVERITY / PROBABILITY	Catastrophic (1)	Critical (2)	Marginal (3)	Negligible (4)
	1 Fatal / $10M	$1M	$100K	
Frequent (A)	High	High	Serious	Medium
10^{-1}				
Probable (B)	High	High	Serious	Medium
10^{-2}				
Occasional (C)	High	Serious	Medium	Low
10^{-3}				
Remote (D)	Serious	Medium	Medium	Low
10^{-4}				
Improbable (E)	Medium	Medium	Medium	Low
Eliminated (F)	Eliminated			

Back of the Envelope Calculation

40,000 Shishkebab Missiles

Delivered over 20 years

Assume all fired

1 accident in 1,000,000 firings

$$\frac{\text{1 accident}}{\text{1,000,000 firings}} \times \frac{\text{40,000 firings}}{\text{20 years}} = \frac{\text{1 accident}}{\text{500 years}}$$

	1	2	3	4
A	1,000,000,000	100,000,000	10,000,000	1,000,000
10^{-1}				
B	100,000,000	10,000,000	1,000,000	100,000
10^{-2}				
C	10,000,000	1,000,000	100,000	10,000
10^{-3}				
D	1,000,000	100,000	10,000	1,000
10^{-4}				
D	100,000	10,000	1,000	100
10^{-5}				
D	10,000	1,000	100	10
10^{-6}				
E	1,000	100	10	1

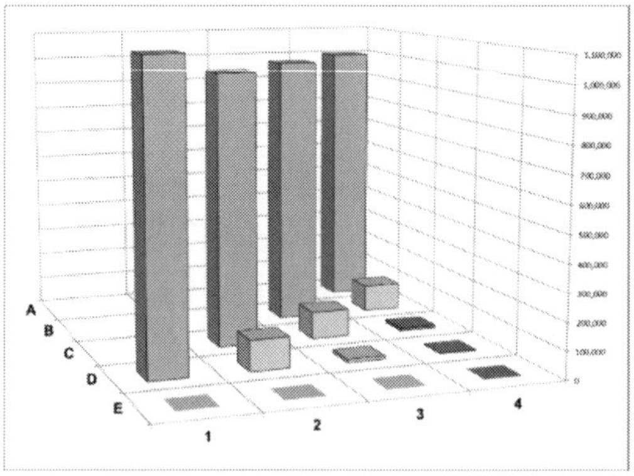

122

Take-aways

- High degree of precision? – No
- Gets hazards to the correct cell of the matrix
- Confidence that overall assessment ≈ reality
- Helps communicate risk to the risk acceptor
- Very useful for programs with:
  - Reasonably good accident data for analysis
  - A well-designed matrix
- Just one of many tools for managing system safety risk

123

End of Presentation

Don Swallom
Safety Engineer
AMCOM Safety Office
(256) 842-8641
donald.w.swallom.civ@mail.mil

124

Why You Should Care About the "-ilities"!

- **Alan Southwick,**
  CSP, CRE & CQE
  (Retired)
- *Senior Systems Engineer*

AUGUST 2018

What are the "-ilities"?

Most grew out of Quality Control Support Activities

The "*-ilities*" are typically <u>Support</u> Engineering roles.

***<u>Specialty Engineering</u>* is the management of specialty requirements and products.**

- **QUALITY**
- **RELIABILITY**
- **MAINTAINABILITY**
- **SUPPORTABILITY**
- **HUMAN FACTORS**
- **SAFETY**
- **SECURITY (IA)**

Why You Should Care About the "-ilities"!

- Quality, Quality Control, and Quality Engineering
- Specialty Engineering Definition
- Specialty Engineering Roles and Relationships
- Reliability
- Maintainability
- Supportability
- Human Factors
- Safety
- Information Assurance (IA) / Cyber Security-Safety

 Slide 3 of 156

Quality and Quality Control
(Where most of the "-ilities" started)

- **Classic Definitions of Quality (Juran):**
  - "*Degree to which an inherent characteristic fulfills **requirements**.*"
  - "*The Quality Function is the entire collection of activities through which we achieve **fitness for use**, no matter where these activities are performed.*"

➢ *Reference*: Juran's Quality Handbook, The Complete Guide to Performance Excellence, Sixth Edition

Publisher: McGraw Hill International

 Slide 4 of 156

Quality and Quality Control (Where most of the "-ilities" started)

- **Classic Definition of Quality Control (Juran):**
  - ✓ *"Quality control is a universal managerial process for conducting operations so as to provide stability over time, and to prevent adverse change and to maintain the status quo.*
  - ✓ *Quality control takes place by use of the feedback loop(s).*
  - ✓ *Quality control entails the maintenance or restoration of the operating status quo and as measured by (meeting) the acceptable level of defects and provision of customer needs.*

➢ *Reference*: Juran's Quality Handbook, The Complete Guide to Performance Excellence, Sixth Edition

Publisher: McGraw Hill International

Quality Engineering

Interrelation Among Specialty Engineering Disciplines

- Early Quality Control successes starting in the 1930's spawned a series of new disciplines designed to improve product quality and customer satisfaction, which can collectively be called *Specialty Engineering*.
- Specialty Engineering disciplines can be sketched out in the form of a "tree" which helps bring out the interrelationships with Quality Control, Quality Engineering, and Quality Assurance.

Quality Engineering (again, from Juran)

All these activities typically require some form of Proprietary Controls (Security) to protect and track the design, manufacture, and sometimes the customer.

All "-ilities!"

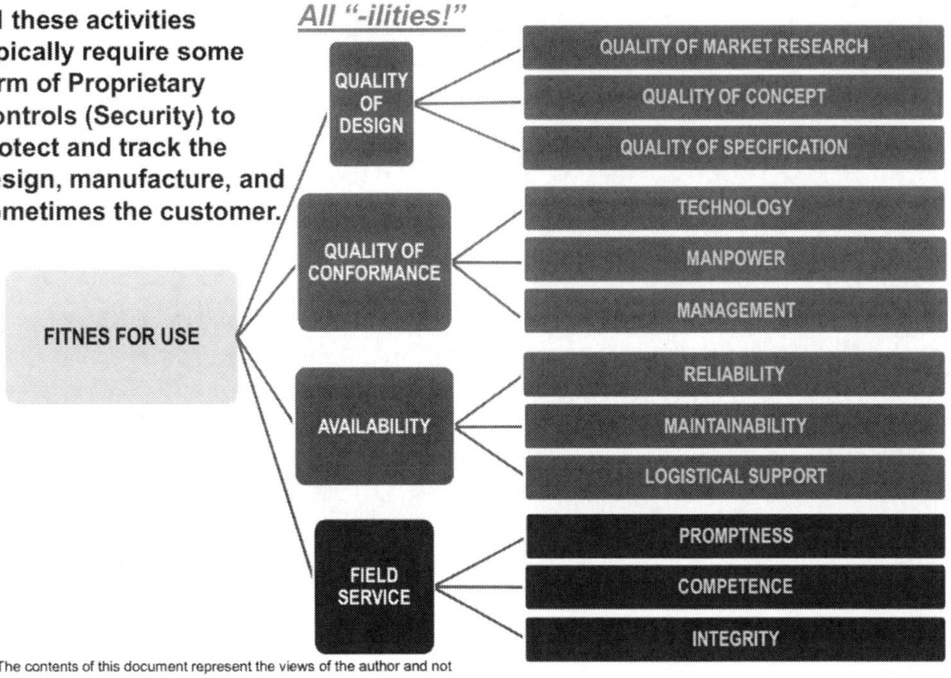

 Slide 7 of 156

Ways That Quality Can Improve Things

TO ASSURE FITNESS FOR USE!

TRY TO FOCUS UPON

Application of Juran's "Pareto Principle"

or,

80 / 20 RULE [after Vilfredo Pareto (15 July 1848 – 19 August 1923)]

80% of your problems occur with 20% of your "sources".

THE VITAL FEW AND TRIVIAL MANY

 Slide 8 of 156

Quality Engineering

- **Myron Tribus' Perversity Principle:**
  - "If you try to improve the performance of a system of people, procedures, practices and machines by setting goals and targets (and incentives) for the individual parts of the system, *the system will defeat you every time, and you will pay a price where you least expected it.*"

The contents of this document represent the views of the author and not necessarily those of former employers or associated employee personnel.

 Slide 9 of 156

CRITICAL FACTORS FOR ANY SYSTEM

- **SYSTEM REQUIREMENTS must provide comprehensive, verifiable attributes for every step in a system life cycle, including but not limited to:**
  - **Concept**
  - **Design**
  - **Development**
  - **Parts Selection & Procurement**
  - **Manufacture**
  - **Operation**
  - **Operational Environments**
  - **Deployment**
  - **Field Maintenance**
  - **Logistics Support**
  - **Upgrades & Updates**
  - **End-Of-Life and Disposal**

CLEAR, TRACEABLE & VERIFIABLE REQUIREMENTS ARE CRITICAL FOR HIGH PERFORMANCE SYSTEMS

The contents of this document represent the views of the author and not necessarily those of former employers or associated employee personnel.

 Slide 10 of 156

Ways That Quality Can Improve Things

1. Maintain Continuous Communication with the *everyone* on the project, including the "customers".
2. Institute Formalized, "living" Processes and Procedures that are understandable, straightforward and easy to implement.
3. Design Quality and Producibility into the Front End First by leveraging the "-ilities" through Specialty Engineering and thoroughly assessed Requirements.
4. Introduce Quality Techniques into the Product Design, Development, Manufacturing, Distribution and User Processes.
5. Focus on Efficiencies in Designs and Materials.
6. Work on Current, Prioritized tasking.
7. Provide Necessary Tools, Training, and Supplies to perform tasks efficiently to Quality Standards.
8. Use Appropriate Materials, Tools, Equipment, and Training.
9. Do Not Reward Predatory Behavior for "getting it done"!
10. Eliminate Bottlenecks ["Alligators" that'll eat your productivity]!
11. Implement Statistical Process Controls (SPC) to track Quality.
12. Use Technology Wisely, not because it's the "latest 'n greatest"!

- Quality, Quality Control, and Quality Engineering
- **Specialty Engineering Definition**
- Specialty Engineering Roles and Relationships
- Reliability
- Maintainability
- Supportability
- Human Factors
- Safety
- Information Assurance (IA) / Cyber Security-Safety

Specialty Engineering Benefits

The Specialty Engineer:

- Helps the Systems Engineers with in-depth knowledge and experience in a *narrow specialty*.
- Coordinates with Systems Engineers to address specific technical aspects of the program and review work products.
- Coordinates with customers to appraise the specialty requirements and review the work products.
- Works with both Systems Engineers and Customers to reduce **risks** and **control costs** over the **whole life** of the system.

Why? Consider these Headlines

- "LED Lamps Last Over 50,000 Hours!" [MTTF]
- "Automaker offers 10 Year or 100,000 Mile Power Train Warranty"
- "Microwave Oven Returned for 3rd Replacement in Two Months"
- "Company Files Bankruptcy Over Faulty Airbags"
- "$30 Timing Belt Takes a Week to Replace and Costs $800" [MTTR]
- "FAA Investigates Why Jet Nearly Landed on Taxi Way, Potentially Colliding with Other Planes" [HSI / HFE, and Safety]
- "OPM Announces More Than 21 Million Affected by Second Data Breach" [Cyber Security-Safety / Information Assurance]
- "Iranian Forces Hack and Capture a U.S. UAV, Landing It Near Kashmar, Iran" [Cyber Security-Safety / Information Assurance]
- "Hackers Remotely Kill a Jeep on the Highway – With me in it!" [Cyber Security-Safety / Information Assurance]
- "Massive "*Wanna Cry*" ransomware campaign infects millions of computers across the world"

- **Do some of these sound familiar?**
- **How do these issues relate to the "-ilities"?**
- **And, what do they have to do with "Quality"?**

Percent of Life Cycle Cost Incurred During Each Phase of a Program

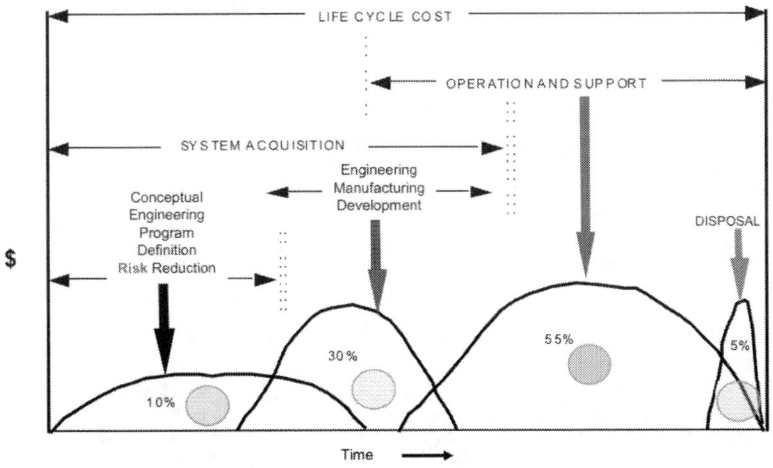

Non-recurring (NR) costs (Mostly) | **Recurring costs (Mostly)** | **NR costs for disposal**

The contents of this document represent the views of the author and not necessarily those of former employers or associated employee personnel.

Roles of "Specialty" Engineers

- Provide skills in special area(s)
- Support concurrent engineering and account for cross product and design dependencies:
  - Reliability and maintainability / life cycle costs and logistics
  - Producibility and supportability / performance
  - System Safety and Human factors / liability and costs
  - Quality / Assures product design and manufacture integrity
  - Design and Development Proprietary Issues (Security)
- Specialty Engineers have roles in **ALL** phases of the system's lifecycle (Whole System Life):
  - Program Conceptualization and "Capture"
  - System **Requirements**
  - Design, Development and Manufacture and Test
  - Deployment, Operation and Maintenance
  - End of Life Equipment Disposal

The contents of this document represent the views of the author and not necessarily those of former employers or associated employee personnel.

Design Influence and Interfaces

Objectives:

Through the system engineering process, identify items / processes that

1) Impact the design from inception throughout the life cycle;
2) Facilitate supportability to maximize usage availability of a system; and,
3) Enhance system effectiveness and capability at the lowest life cycle cost

Reliability, Availability, Maintainability (RAM)	Standardization and Interoperability
Survivability	Testability
Environmental (e.g., air, waste, noise)	Transportability
Corrosion & Non-Destructive Inspection	Energy Management
System Safety	Hazardous Material (HAZMAT) Management
Human Factors, Human System Interface & Usability	Affordability
Quality	Security

The contents of this document represent the views of the author and not necessarily those of former employers or associated employee personnel.

 Slide 17 of 156

Specialty Engineering Relationship with Systems Engineering

- Systems Engineers must plan and develop a timely and effective process to establish and coordinate specialty disciplines.
- Systems Engineering integrates the technical specialties into the program.
  - Defining and integrating technical **requirements** for specialty engineering, with Specialty Engineering assistance.
  - Ensuring each Specialty and the overall design team understands the system **requirements**.
  - Include necessary Specialties in program plans.
  - Include Specialty Engineers in product development.
  - Monitor, assess, and report status of technical specialty areas.
- Where applicable, Specialty Engineers should be consulted for design concept support, proposal inputs, program planning, **requirements definition**, development support, manufacturing support, deployment support, security issue management, and end-of-life disposal.
- Failure to do so may have repercussions across the system and / or product life cycle creating risks affecting both **schedule** and **costs**.

The contents of this document represent the views of the author and not necessarily those of former employers or associated employee personnel.

 Slide 18 of 156

ASSESSING RISK –
One Type of Risk Assessment Chart

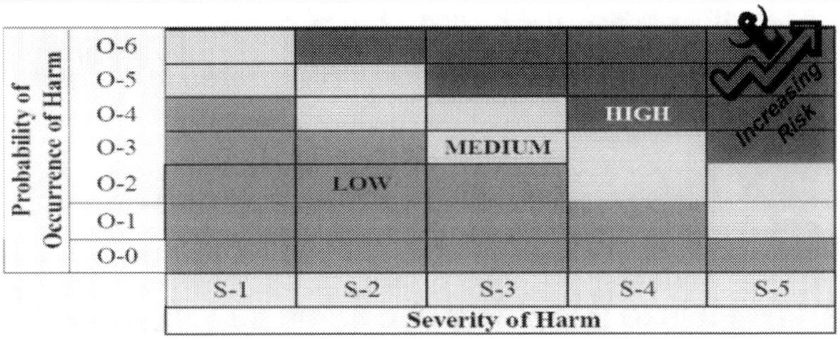

Legend

Severity of Harm		Probability of Occurrence of Harm	
S-5	Catastrophic	**O-6**	Always
S-4	Critical	**O-5**	Frequent
S-3	Serious	**O-4**	Probable
S-2	Minor	**O-3**	Occasional
S-1	Negligible	**O-2**	Remote
		O-1	Improbable
		O-0	None Observed

- **Quality, Quality Control, and Quality Engineering**
- **Specialty Engineering Definition**
- **Specialty Engineering Roles and Relationships**
- **Reliability**
- **Maintainability**
- **Supportability**
- **Human Factors**
- **Safety**
- **Information Assurance (IA) / Cyber Security-Safety**

Definition of Reliability

- **Reliability** is the _probability_ that an item will perform its _specified or intended function_ under _specified conditions_ for a _specified interval_.

  4 parts ***NECESSARY*** **to defining reliability**:

  - It must be quantifiable (*probability*)
  - It has to do with getting some specific work done (*intended function*)
  - It assumes a specific operating environment (*under specified, stated conditions*)
  - It depends on duration (*specified interval*)

➢ ***References***: **ANSI / GEIA-STD-0009, IEEE 1633**

The contents of this document represent the views of the author and not necessarily those of former employers or associated employee personnel.

 Slide 21 of 156

Reliability Engineering

Reliability represents the percent or probability of items that would survive a predetermined time with the specified (or applied) stresses.

A more understandable application of *reliability* applies to **Warranty Periods** as they include intended operating environments.

Reliability is a cradle to grave discipline designed to characterize and define a system's life cycle performance.

The contents of this document represent the views of the author and not necessarily those of former employers or associated employee personnel.

 Slide 22 of 156

Reliability Engineering

Why is Reliability Measured?

The risk of a failure and cause needs to be evaluated to decide on mitigation by

- eliminating failure modes by re-design, or
- reducing *probability of occurrences* by managing the cause(s).
  - Reduction is possible only when those causes and probabilities are known or estimated.

The contents of this document represent the views of the author and not necessarily those of former employers or associated employee personnel.

Reliability Engineering

Reliability information must come from:

- Reliability calculations with the Physics of Failure (PoF, stress information).
- The part's manufacturer… recalculated for the correct use conditions, if necessary.
- Testing
- The field… but this data also must be re-calculated based on the use condition of the fielded product to the use conditions of the product under analysis.

The contents of this document represent the views of the author and not necessarily those of former employers or associated employee personnel.

Reliability Engineering

- **Measures of Reliability**

  Reliability: Probability of survival *after* the end of a predetermined period.

  Unreliability: Probability of failure *before* the end of the period.

  - Probabilities
  - Failure Distributions
    - In Reliability
    - In Quality Assurance
  - Hazard rate, failure rate, failure frequency
  - MTTF, MTBF

 Slide 25 of 156

Reliability Engineering

- **Reliability analysis methods –**

  Designing for reliability

  - Reliability prediction with modeling, HW and SW
  - Failure Mode and Effects [Criticality] Analysis (FME[C]A)

    HW and SW
  - Fault tree analysis (FTA) –

    Dynamic modeling basics
  - Planning and monitoring of reliability growth in design and Development
- **Reliability Tests and Verification –**

  Demonstration, Growth, Accelerated

The contents of this document represent the views of the author and not necessarily those of former employers or associated employee personnel.

Copyright © 2018 Alan E. Southwick, All rights reserved. Slide 26 of 156

Hardware Reliability Engineering

Reliability may be applied to many systems, but is most commonly applied to hardware equipment and software.

The more familiar application is for ***hardware***, modeled through the conceptual "Bathtub Curve" model, which though insightful, is **a really poor approximation** for the "real world".

Hardware model "Bathtub Curve" -

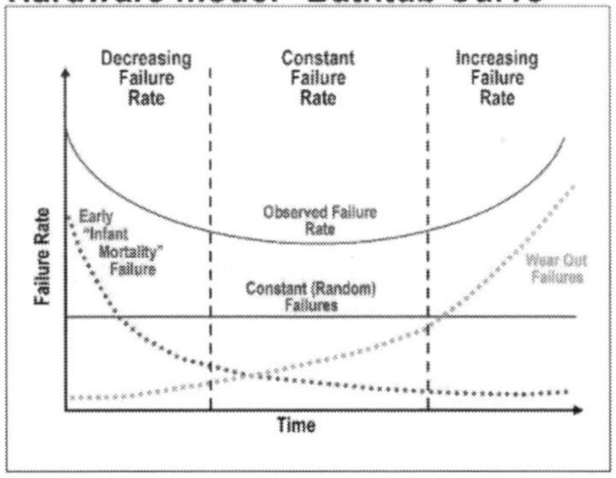

Availability for Service (Reliability is typically high, e.g. 99.9%)

Software Reliability Engineering

Unlike hardware, where improvements typically stop with the termination of a test, software improvements continue in the field if not continuously, then in batches with regular software updates / upgrades (most folks should be quite familiar with software updates these days!).

This means that software reliability can be projected in the field as the software continues to improve in deployment. Field data is also analyzed to further project the software reliability growth.

Software Reliability Engineering

Software / Firmware Reliability may require very different approaches based on a number of factors:

- Stepwise life cycle
- Cyclical Test Analyze And Fix (**TAAF**). Usually a one-shot fix / repair for one software issue, but can cause other faults in software functionality
- Program Branching which typically leads to Software Errors / Faults
- Creation of "Protected Memory" to prevent critical data overwrites in memory systems
- Adequate memory resources / space for program resources
- Software / Firmware Obsolescence – Often driven by Hardware Obsolescence

Hardware versus Software Modeling

- **Reliability Block Diagrams (RBD's)**
  - Applicable only if the blocks representing entities that compose the system physically are independent and can fail by themselves, can be physically separated from the rest of the system and repaired or replaced (for repairable systems),

    or,
  - to the systems where their failure does not affect any other blocks in the system or is not affected by any other blocks but not repaired (again, independent blocks)
  - Mostly useful for hardware – seldom or never for software where the trigger event is a usual precursor of a failure or sequence of events is a factor to reliability
  - Standby redundancy may be represented by blocks, but does *NOT* represent an RBD
  - Software and the hardware where the software is physically located must not to be represented as separate blocks of series:
    - Software cannot work without the hardware it is on, OS, or an additional platform or utility SW (Like "Love & Marriage", you usually can't have one without the other!)
  - When multiple SW located on one server it should not be in an independent box and assumed all In series configuration

    (e.g. MS Word works even if Excel on the same hardware failed)

Software Reliability Definitions

- The American Institute of Aeronautics and Astronautics (AIAA)
  - **"the application of statistical techniques to data collected during system development and operation to specify, predict, estimate, and assess the reliability of software-based systems."**
- **IEEE 1633 – *Recommended Practice on Software Reliability*:**
  - **(A)** The probability that software will not cause the failure of a system for a specified time under specified conditions.
  - **(B)** The ability of a program to perform a required function under stated conditions for a stated period of time (*Classic Reliability Definition*).

Software Reliability – One Approach: The Capability Maturity Model

- **Model Assumptions**
  - The defect rate observed during the development process is positively correlated with the defect rate in the field (The more area under the curve, the higher the field defect rate).
  - Given the same error injection rate, if more defects are discovered and removed earlier, fewer will remain in later stages.
- Reference Reading: *Metrics and Models in Software Quality Engineering*, by Stephen Kan, Addison Wesley Publishing

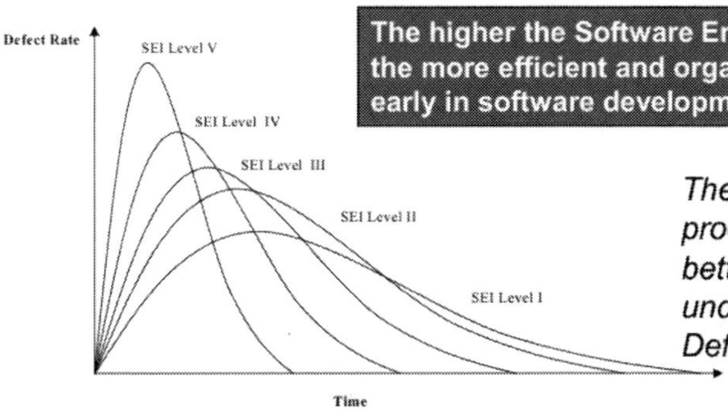

The higher the Software Engineering Institute's (SEI) Level the more efficient and organization is in detecting defects early in software development

The better the process, the better the process capability ratings and the better the delivered code, developed under that process, will perform… Defects will be lower.

➢ ***Compare to Hardware Reliability "Bathtub" Curve.***

Another Combined Hardware and Software Reliability Assessment Process

A Power Law (Krasich-Peterson) Model has been developed utilizing an adaptation of the Weibull Intensity Function (an instantaneous discrete rate, NOT to be confused with the continuous Weibull Reliability Distribution Function) to characterize the early life cycles of both hardware AND software.

Actual assessments appear to closely agree with real world performance based on research into developmental and fielded systems.

The contents of this document represent the views of the author and not necessarily those of former employers or associated employee personnel.

The Combined Hardware and Software Reliability Assessment Process

The authors presented a paper entitled: ***"Modeling of Software Reliability in Early Design with Planning and Measurement of its Reliability Growth"*** at the 2015 RAMS conference.

What's interesting about this model is by using the Power Law, **BOTH Hardware and Software Reliability can be simultaneously modeled as a SYSTEM**. The software reliability model is compatible with the hardware reliability growth mathematical model so that the estimate of the system level reliability growth for combining both Hardware and Software is achievable.

The contents of this document represent the views of the author and not necessarily those of former employers or associated employee personnel.

Hardware and Software Faults and Failures

A comparison between SW and HW failures and failure modes

- **Both SW and HW failure modes that allow mitigation and reliability growth are systematic – design related**
- **HW has "random" failure modes (stress related, but undetermined causes) usually originating within the components – faults in the components [which based on Physics of Failure analysis are really NOT "random"]**
- **Frequency of both failure modes in HW and in SW may be considered constant and dependent on conditions and profile of use**

The contents of this document represent the views of the author and not necessarily those of former employers or associated employee personnel.

Hardware and Software Faults and Failures

A comparison between SW and HW failures and failure modes (continued)

- **Changes (reduction in magnitude) in HW and SW systematic failure modes frequency of appearance are achieved by design improvements**
- **Reduction in failure rate can be represented by a step function which can then be fitted with a power law model, with different parameters, but the same mathematical rationale**
- **Power law fittings for HW & SW represent failure frequency where the Mean Time Between Failures (MTBF) is applicable to most of the systems in use.**

The contents of this document represent the views of the author and not necessarily those of former employers or associated employee personnel.

Software Reliability Value Added Benefits

- Reduce cost of failures later in the development process (similar to Hardware Reliability)
- Track failure trends of probabilistic conditions (e.g. race conditions) and systemic process-related issues
- Drive software design corrective actions to improve reliability results in a lower customer Total Cost of Ownership (TCO)

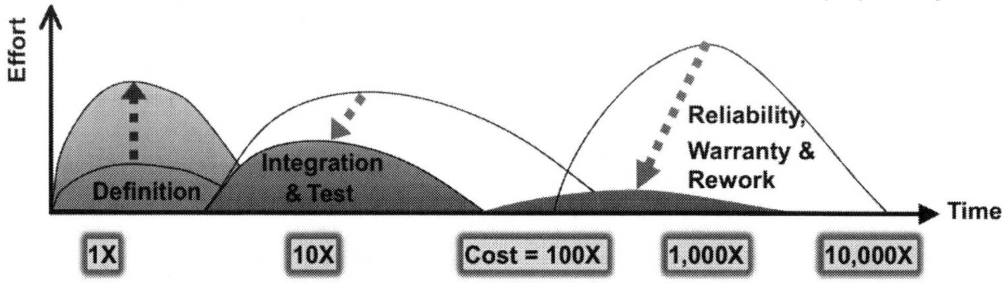

➢ *Note curve similarities to previous life cycle costs [slide 15].*

The contents of this document represent the views of the author and not necessarily those of former employers or associated employee personnel.

Reliability Design and Evaluation

Reliability design and evaluation covers:

- Single Point of Failure
- Failure Mode, Effects and Criticality Analysis (**FMECA**, or, **FMEA** – No Quantification of Criticalities incorporated)
- Fault Tree Analysis (**FTA**)
- Electronic Parts/Circuit Tolerance worst case analysis (**WCA**)
- Component Stress Analysis (Life Tests, HALT, HASS, etc.)
- Reliability Modeling – MIL, IEEE, NASA Handbooks, etc.
- Physics of Failure (**PoF**)
- Reliability Assessment and **FRACAS**

The contents of this document represent the views of the author and not necessarily those of former employers or associated employee personnel.

Reliability Design and Evaluation (Continued)

Reliability design and evaluation covers:

- Failure Mode, Effects and Criticality Analysis (**FMECA**),
  or,
  FMEA – No Quantification of Criticalities incorporated)
  (***a "Bottom Up" Analysis***)
  - FMEA is a continuing process in a system life cycle – it is not done when delivered to the customer
  - It is a tool for making the system better – higher reliability, safer, more cost effective, better performance…
  - FMEA is a living document "subpoenable to the Court of Law"
  - FMEA is adaptable to the project needs
  - It is applicable to various levels of the system: function loss and causes
  - Investigates system function loss or degradation, the effect of that loss, potential causes of the undesirable effect and mitigation.

FME(C)A Criticality

- Criticality is a two-dimensional measure which provides the degree of effect severity with the likelihood of occurrence of the failure mode which initiates the effect
- For the repaired items where availability is the reliability (dependability) measure, likelihood of failure occurrence is substituted by unavailability of component to operate which then results in the undesirable event.
- When criticality measure is considered the analysis is becomes a Failure Mode Effects and Criticality Analysis (FMECA).
- For simplicity, whether quantitative or qualitative, the analysis is often typically referred to as an "FMEA".

Reliability Design and Evaluation

Reliability design and evaluation covers:

- **Fault Tree Analysis (FTA) [a "Top Down" Analysis, utilizing Boolean Logic for Systems]**
  - identification of the causes or combinations of causes leading to the top event);
  - determination of whether a particular system reliability measure meets a stated requirement;
  - determination which potential failure mode(s) or factor(s) would be the highest contributor to the system probability of failure (unreliability) or unavailability for possible system reliability improvements;
  - analysis and comparison of various design alternatives to improve system reliability;

Reliability Design and Evaluation (Continued)

Reliability design and evaluation covers:

- **Fault Tree Analysis (FTA) [a "Top Down" Analysis, utilizing Boolean Logic for Systems]**
  - the demonstration that assumptions made in other analyses (such as Markov and FMEA) are not violated;
  - identification of common events
  - search for an event or combinations of events which are the most likely to cause the top event to occur;
  - assessment of the impact of the occurrence of a primary event on the probability of the top event; calculation of system failure probability or unavailability
  - Limitation: used for independent events like Reliability Block Diagrams (RBD's) unless it is a dynamic FTA

Reliability Design and Evaluation

Combined "Top Down and Bottom Up" Approach

- Start the Top Down analysis (FTA) from the system functions
  - ➢ Follow the thread wherever it takes to
    - Hardware through SW (SW failure due to server or power supply or optical switches or other systemic failures)
    - SW through HW Software functions through HW path down to the requests – placed using SW
    - Only HW
    - Only SW
    - Down to CRITICAL causes
  - ➢ Failure mode is mitigated by failure cause mitigation.
- Then apply the Bottom Up FME(C)A approach to form the final product – an analysis easy to follow line by line – through the incremental, tabular reporting with an FME(C)A format

Examples of Potential Reliability Terms and Requirements

- Mean Time Between Failure (**MTBF**) <u>or</u> Mean Time To Failure (**MTTF**)
  - **MTBF is the Reciprocal of an item's Failure Rate (FR)**
    - ***Provides a false idea of a Reliability attribute <u>without the inclusion of the applied Stresses</u> when FR is developed.***
    - **Usually based on measured failure data**
    - **Physics of Failure (PoF) analysis (e.g. durability, accelerated life tests, environmental extremes, etc.)**
    - **Calculated per industry methods (e.g. MIL-HDBK-217, BELCORE, etc.)**
- Mean Time Between Critical Failure (**MTBCF**)
  - **Inherent reliability of the system taking into account redundancies and allowable degradation,** ***but its not real helpful as a metric because it's "after the fact"!***

Example Reliability Requirements

- Mean Time Between Demand (**MTBD**)
  - **Fielded reliability of units / modules taking into account inherent failures, performance failures, FD/FI, BIT false alarms, etc.**
  - **Example:** ***Flight hours divided by Unit Removals***
- Mean Time Between Maintenance Action (**MTBMA**)
  - **Fielded reliability of the system taking into account inherent failures, performance failures, FD/FI, BIT false alarms, pilot observations, S/W false alarms, maintenance practices, etc.**
  - **Example:** ***Flight hours divided by Maintenance Actions***
- A ***Warranty Period*** provides a much more understandable representation for reliability performance and system availability. **WHY?**

The Lifecycle of Reliability Growth

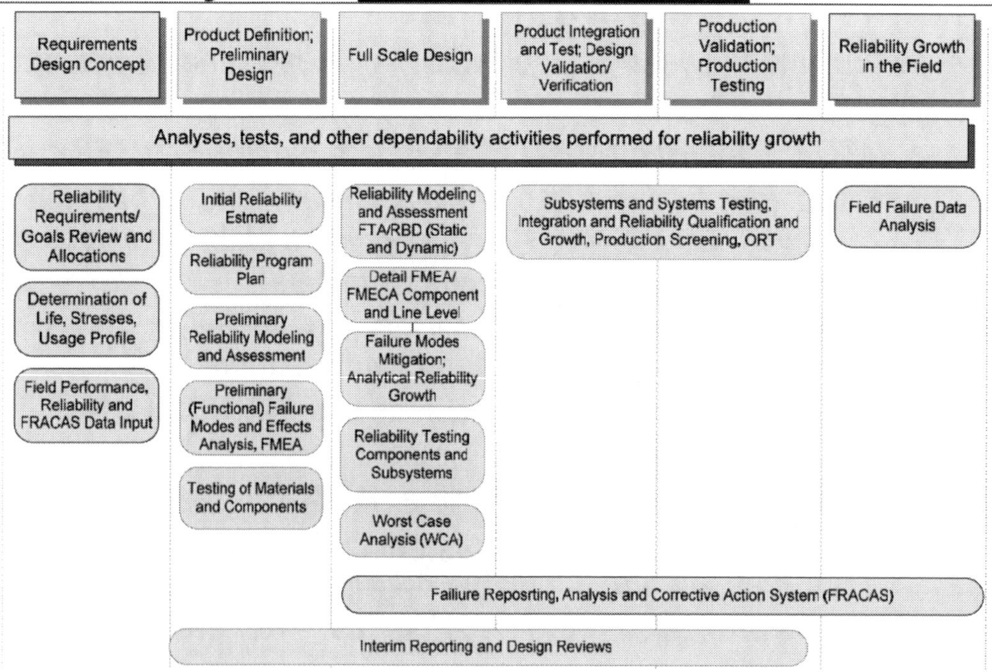

Reliability versus Availability

FOR SPECIFIED STRESSES AND ENVIRONMENT -

- **Reliability** defines how often, on average, failures can occur for a particular system, subsystem or component. Intrinsic Reliability is typically specified as Mean Time Between Failures (MTBF) for repairable items.
- **Availability** typically defines the average percentage of time a system, subsystem or component is OPERATIONALLY available for use.

$$A_o = \frac{\text{Uptime}}{\text{Total Time}} = \frac{\text{MTBF}}{\text{MTBF} + \text{MTTR} + \text{MLDT}}$$

MTBF = Mean Time Between Failure (Reliability)

MTTR = Mean Time to Repair (Maintainability)

MLDT = Mean Logistics Delay Time

➢ **NOTE: *Total Time* may include Storage, Standby, and Multiple Intervals (e.g. Missile Test, Launch, Powered Flight, Free Flight, Detonation, etc.); and thus, may also be broken into separate, individual intervals.**

The contents of this document represent the views of the author and not necessarily those of former employers or associated employee personnel.

How to Model System Availability

- Availability modeling of a complex system follows all of the rules of the reliability modeling:
  - The expressions valid for reliability modeling all apply for availability
    - Series systems
    - Parallel systems
    - Mixed systems
  - The same rules apply: the blocks must be INDEPENDENT, capable of being maintained simultaneously by two different maintenance technicians.

The contents of this document represent the views of the author and not necessarily those of former employers or associated employee personnel.

Criticality and Risk

- Criticality is a two-dimensional measure which provides the degree of effect severity with the likelihood of occurrence of the failure mode which initiates the effect
- For the repaired items where availability is the reliability (dependability) measure, likelihood of failure occurrence is substituted by unavailability of component to operate which then results in the undesirable event. Risk is measured in association with mission loss or degradation, comparison with the allocated maximum criticality requirements as allocated to the system and its subsystems, increased maintenance costs for pares and maintenance operations, liability, etc.
- The risk may be measured monetarily or might have some other quantitative or qualitative measure and the proportionality factor varies from one industry to another or on a case by case basis.
- When criticality measure is considered the analysis becomes a Failure Mode Effects and Criticality Analysis (FMECA). For simplicity, in this discussion whether quantitative or qualitative, the analysis is typically referred to as FMEA.

The contents of this document represent the views of the author and not necessarily those of former employers or associated employee personnel.

 Slide 49 of 156

What is FRACAS?

Failure Reporting and Corrective Action System **(FRACAS) is a closed-loop coordinated system that identifies failures, implements and verifies corrective actions to help preclude recurrence of the failure.**

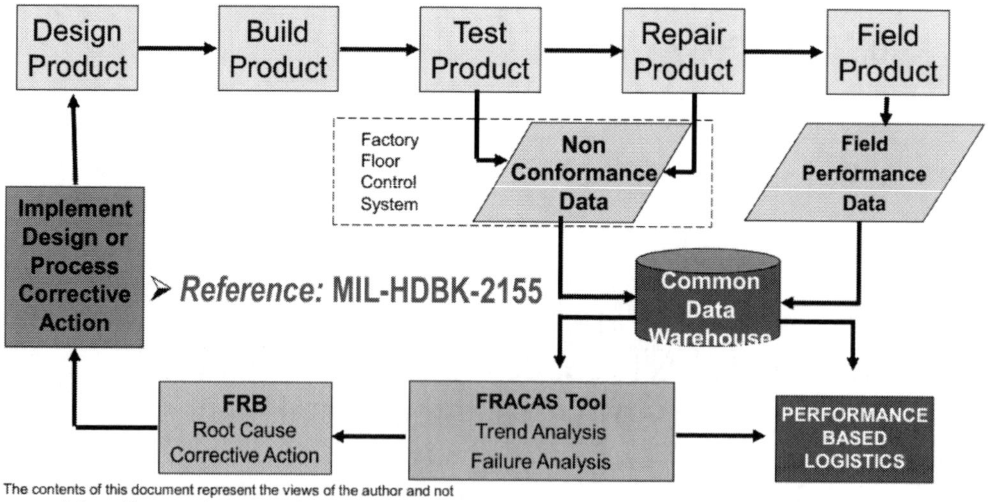

The contents of this document represent the views of the author and not necessarily those of former employers or associated employee personnel.

 Slide 50 of 156

Reliability Tasks and Tools

- Requirements Analysis
- Allocation to system elements/components
- Reliability design guidelines
- Reliability Modeling (Block Diagrams)
- Reliability Prediction
- Reliability critical items and risks
- Hazard tracking
- Failure Reporting, Analysis and Corrective Action System (**FRACAS**)
- Failure *Mode*, Effects, and Criticality Analysis (**FMECA,** 'bottom up" analysis)
  - *ref: MIL-STD-1629 (cancelled in 1998, but still available and useful);*
  - *DI-SESS-81495A, DATA ITEM DESCRIPTION (DID): Failure Modes, Effects, and Criticality Analysis Report;*
  - *Also numerous documentation is available via a Google search*
- Fault Tree Analysis (**FTA**, "top down" analysis)
- Reliability Growth through Analysis, Test, and Operations
- Reliability Stress Testing (**HALT**, **HASS**, **Quantitative Accelerated Testing**, etc.)
- Subcontractor guidelines/control

The contents of this document represent the views of the author and not necessarily those of former employers or associated employee personnel.

Reliability Engineering

➤ Additional References:

- ANSI-GEIA-STD-0009, Reliability Program Standard for System Design, Development, and Manufacturing
- IEC 61710 Power law model – goodness of fit tests and estimation methods.
- IEC 61014 Programmes for reliability growth
- IEC 61164 Statistical methods for reliability growth
- MIL-HDBK-189, Reliability Growth Management
- IEC 62506 Methods for products accelerated reliability testing
- IEC 61124 tests for constant failure rate and failure intensity
- M. Krasich; Accelerated Reliability Growth and Data Analysis, Journal of the IEST; V. 50, No.2© 2007
- M. Krasich; Reliability Growth Testing, What is the Real Final Result? Accelerated Test Methodology for Reliability Growth, RAMS 2014
- M. Krasich; Modeling of SW Reliability in Early Design with Planning and Measurement of Reliability Growth, RAMS 2015

The contents of this document represent the views of the author and not necessarily those of former employers or associated employee personnel.

Why Reliability Matters

- Reliability analyses and assessments help identify Critical Failures & Failure Modes leading to potentially imminent hazards
- In conjunction with Maintainability and Supportability, helps determine system Availability for mission success
- Clarifies equipment and system Life Cycles (e.g. Missiles spend most of their life cycle in storage)
- Defines System Warranty periods
- The higher the reliability…the greater the availability…less time for corrective maintenance…and less spares required
- Assists with Design to Failure and Environmental Performance
- Stress Testing and Accelerated Life Testing help determine overall system performance limitations and lifetimes
- Helps Manage System Performance, planning, **Costs** and **Risks**

- **Quality, Quality Control, and Quality Engineering**
- **Specialty Engineering Definition**
- **Specialty Engineering Roles and Relationships**
- **Reliability**
- **Maintainability**
- **Supportability**
- **Human Factors**
- **Safety**
- **Information Assurance (IA) / Cyber Security-Safety**

The contents of this document represent the views of the author and not necessarily those of former employers or associated employee personnel.

Copyright © 2018 Alan E. Southwick, All rights reserved.

BREAK TIME?

ENOUGH OF THE "-ILITIES"

FOR NOW?!?

PLEASE BE BACK IN 10 MINUTES

Maintainability Engineering

Maintainability is the ability to quickly, economically, and safely maintain readiness or restore a failed system to its operational state.

(Maintenance is the activity necessary to prevent failure or restore an item to serviceability.)

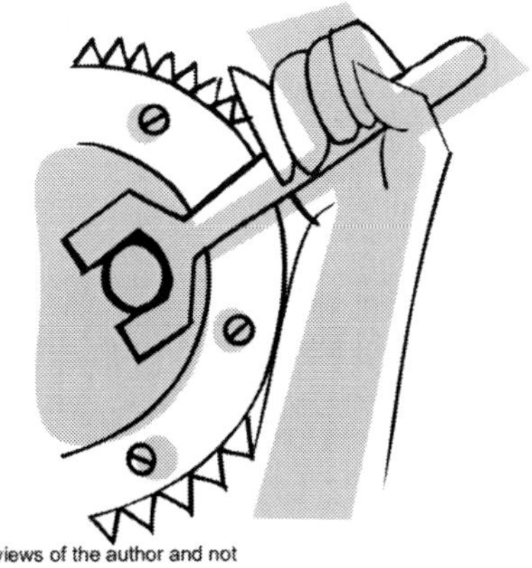

Maintainability Tasks

- **Flow-down maintainability REQUIREMENTS**
- **Develop design criteria**
- **Assess maturity**
- **Perform Trade Studies**
- **Identify potential design improvements**
- **Manage Maintenance Costs and Risks**

The contents of this document represent the views of the author and not necessarily those of former employers or associated employee personnel.

Maintainability REQUIREMENTS

Example maintainability requirements are:

- Mean Time To Repair (**MTTR**)
- Maximum Time to Repair (**MMAX**)
- Maintenance Manhours to Repair (**MMH/repair**)
- Maintenance Manhours to Overhaul (**MMH/OH**)
- Maintenance Manhours per Flight Hour (**MMH/FH**)

NOTE: DETAILED INTEGRATED REQUIREMENTS ASSIST IN DESIGNING A SYSTEM FOR FACILE MAINTENANCE!

The contents of this document represent the views of the author and not necessarily those of former employers or associated employee personnel.

Maintainability Design and Evaluation

Maintainability design and evaluation regards issues such as:

- Modeling
- Predictions
- Data Collection
- Data Analysis
- Maintainability Testing
- Testability Assessment and Analyses
- Maintainer Skillset(s)
- Failure Reporting, Analysis and Corrective Action System (**FRACAS**)
- Maintainability Growth through Analysis, Test, Operations, and Design Updates
- Failure Review Board (**FRB**)

➢ ***References*: MIL-HDBK-470, MIL-HDBK-2165**

Reliability Centered Maintenance

- **Reliability Centered Maintenance is a process merging Reliability and Maintainability Analyses (along with practical user / maintainer / customer focus) to determine what must be done to ensure that any asset continues to do what its users want or need it to do in its present operating context.**

Reliability Centered Maintenance

- The technical standard SAE JA1011, *Evaluation Criteria for RCM Processes*, sets out the minimum criteria that any process should meet before it can be called RCM. This starts with the 7 questions below, worked through in the order that they are listed:
  1. What is the item supposed to do and its associated performance standards? (**Requirements**)
  2. In what ways can it fail to provide the required functions? (**FTA**)
  3. What are the events that cause each failure? (**FMEA**)
  4. What happens when each failure occurs? (**FMECA and / or FTA**)
  5. In what way does each failure matter? (the "**C**" of **FMECA**)
  6. What systematic task can be performed proactively to prevent, or to diminish to a satisfactory degree, the consequences of the failure? (**Logistics Support and Preventive Maintenance or "PM"**)
  7. What must be done if a suitable preventive task cannot be found? (**Risk Assessment**)

Reliability Centered Maintenance

- Among some of the paradigm shifts inspired by RCM are:
  - Failures are not necessarily linked to the age of the asset (this is often modeled by the "memoryless" exponential probability distribution)
  - Changing from efforts to predict life expectancies to trying to manage the process of failure, through analysis processes such as **Physics of Failure** (**POF**) and **FRACAS**
  - Understanding of the difference between the requirements of assets from a user perspective, and the design reliability of the asset (**User / Customer Focused**)
  - Acknowledging the importance of managing assets on condition (often referred to as **condition monitoring**, **condition based maintenance**, and **predictive maintenance**)
  - Implementing the four basic routine maintenance tasks:
    1. Inspect to Detect a Potential Failure
    2. Rework Prior to Failure
    3. Discard Prior to Failure
    4. Ascertain or Find Failures that have Already Occurred
  - Link levels of tolerable **risk** to maintenance strategy development

Reliability Centered Maintenance

- **References:**

  As mentioned, RCM is defined in:

  SAE JA1011, *Evaluation Criteria for Reliability-Centered Maintenance (RCM) Processes.*

  More recent references are:

  MIL-STD-3034, DEPARTMENT OF DEFENSE STANDARD PRACTICE, Reliability-Centered Maintenance (RCM) Process

  NAVSEA S9081-AB-GIB-010, *Reliability-Centered Maintenance (RCM) Handbook.*

Why Maintainability Matters

- Helps identify specific maintenance tasks to support deployed equipment and system(s).
- Defines maintenance times for both individual tasks and system wide maintenance: scheduled and un-scheduled.
- Identifies times, equipment, and maintenance "talents" required to accomplish specifically defined maintenance tasks.
- In conjunction with Supportability, defines levels of maintainer training required to accomplish specific maintenance tasks.
- The higher the reliability…the greater the availability…less time for corrective maintenance…and less spares required
- Thorough Requirements Assessment helps define individual and overall system maintenance periods, management planning, **costs** and **risks**.

- Quality, Quality Control, and Quality Engineering
- Specialty Engineering Definition
- Specialty Engineering Roles and Relationships
- Reliability
- Maintainability
- **Supportability**
- Human Factors
- Safety
- Information Assurance (IA) / Cyber Security-Safety

The contents of this document represent the views of the author and not necessarily those of former employers or associated employee personnel.

 Slide 65 of 156

Supportability Engineering (alias: LOGISTICS)

Supportability ensures that the appropriate structure is in place to supply and maintain a system throughout its life cycle, from cradle to grave; also referred to as "Logistics".

Supportability = Logistics = Integrated Logistics Support (ILS)

- ***Reference: MIL-HDBK-2097***

The contents of this document represent the views of the author and not necessarily those of former employers or associated employee personnel.

 Slide 66 of 156

Supportability Engineering (alias: LOGISTICS)

TO PARAPHRASE AN ADVERTISING CAMPAIGN SEVERAL YEARS AGO BY A WORLDWIDE SHIPPING CORPORATION:

Logistics makes the world work better

When it's planes in the sky
For a chain of supply

That's logistics

When the needed parts
come precisely on time

That's logistics

The contents of this document represent the views of the author and not necessarily those of former employers or associated employee personnel.

 Slide 67 of 156

Supportability Engineering (alias: LOGISTICS)

When technology knows
right where everything goes

That's logistics

The contents of this document represent the views of the author and not necessarily those of former employers or associated employee personnel.

 Slide 68 of 156

Supportability Engineering (alias: LOGISTICS)

Yup! That's LOGISTICS!

The contents of this document represent the views of the author and not necessarily those of former employers or associated employee personnel.

 Slide 69 of 156

Trivia Questions

1. **Any idea what the name of the shipping company is? [Hint: their corporate catch phrase was once: "We Love Logistics"]**

2. **And, what was the name of the original song?**

3. **Who was the well known media star who used the original song for this company's "*Logistics*" advertisement campaign as a signature "theme" song?**

The contents of this document represent the views of the author and not necessarily those of former employers or associated employee personnel.

 Slide 70 of 156

Supportability, Integrated Logistics Support

Elements integrated in Supportability:

- Maintenance Planning and Scheduling (including identification of critical parts through various analyses)
- Support and Field Test Equipment
- Supply Support
- Manpower, Personnel, and Training
- Facilities
- Packaging, Handling, Storage, and Transportation (PHS&T)
- Post Production Support Costs
- Computer Resources
- Technical Data, including maintenance and repair documents
- Design Influence (e.g., Repair Level Analysis: Local, Intermediate, Depot / Manufacturer)

Supportability Tasks

- Requirements Allocation
- Guidelines Flow-down
- Software Supportability (Type, Versions, Revision Level Tracking)
- Support Equipment Identification
- Testability Design and Evaluation
- Supportability Design and Evaluation
- Supportability Management

Why Supportability Matters

- The higher the reliability…the greater the availability…less time for corrective maintenance…and less spares required
- The greater the availability…less assets required to perform a mission and higher state of readiness
- More time spent performing scheduled and unscheduled maintenance reduces system availability and may increase required manpower, tools, and costs
- For Testability, a careful balance of the right amount of alerts, minimizing false alarms and high level of confidence in quickly locating the fault
- FRACAS and FRB's provide data to focus on critical issues related to Supportability in the field.

- Quality, Quality Control, and Quality Engineering
- Specialty Engineering Definition
- Specialty Engineering Roles and Relationships
- Reliability
- Maintainability
- Supportability
- **Human Factors**
- Safety
- Information Assurance (IA) / Cyber Security-Safety

The contents of this document represent the views of the author and not necessarily those of former employers or associated employee personnel.

Copyright © 2018 Alan E. Southwick, All rights reserved.

Human Systems Integration (HSI) or, Human Factors Engineering (HFE)

Human factors is the discipline involved with ensuring that the human operator and / or maintainer's physiological, psychological and anthropometric factors are an integral part of the system design for operation and maintenance.

CAN THIS SOLDIER, OPERATOR, USER, MAINTAINER
WITH THIS TRAINING
PERFORM THESE TASKS
TO THESE STANDARDS
UNDER THESE CONDITIONS?

The contents of this document represent the views of the author and not necessarily those of former employers or associated employee personnel.

 Slide 75 of 156

Human Systems Integration (HSI) is One Discipline with Many Parts

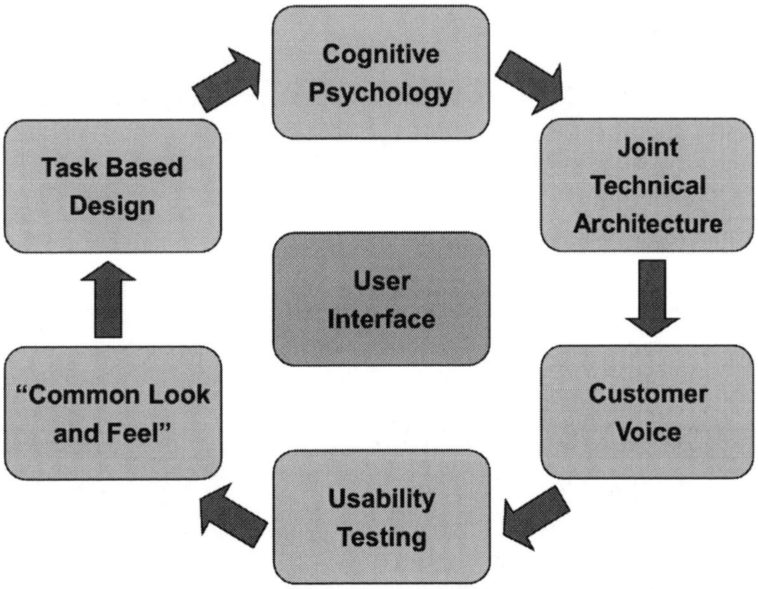

The contents of this document represent the views of the author and not necessarily those of former employers or associated employee personnel.

 Slide 76 of 156

Human Factors Tasks

- **Improve human and overall system performance**
- **Make effective use of manpower and personnel**
- **Optimize the human-machine interface**
- **Minimize training needs and cost**
- **Minimize equipment losses**
- **Maximize equipment effectiveness**
- **Increase safety**
- **Increase acceptance by the user**
- **Ensure system fits the user population**

Human Factors Design and Evaluation

Human factors affect design and evaluation by:

- Designing for human limitations
- Designing for environmental conditions (i.e. Temperature, Noise Levels, Communications, Vibration, Shock, Fatigue, etc.)
- Completing Human Factors Analyses Review of Design and Final Equipment for Effective System Implementation
- **NOTE: Most of these issues must be addressed up front by integration into system *REQUIREMENTS*!**

➢ ***Reference*: MIL-STD-1472** (*a lengthy but really interesting read regarding many aspects present in Human Engineering*)

Why Human Factors Matters

- **Standardization:** The process of developing and agreeing upon technical standards.
  - Goal is to help with the independence of suppliers, compatibility, interoperability, safety, repeatability, quality, and/or commonality of function across platforms
  - Unique standards drive up cost with some doubt of their effectiveness and longevity for supportability
- **Interoperability:** Product/system properties with understood common interfaces which facilitates usage with other present/future systems without restricted access or implementation.
  - Note that the definition does not discuss backward capability which is also very significant

 Slide 79 of 156

Why Human Factors Matters

- Ease of use and "learn-ability" of a human-made object Includes a software application, website, book, tool, machine, process, or just about anything with which a human interacts.
- **Design and Requirement goals**:
  - How easy is it to learn?
  - Once a user is trained, how quickly can they perform tasks?
  - How quickly can proficiency be re-gained after not using it for a while?
  - How many user errors? How severe? How recoverable?
  - How pleasant is it to use the human interactive design?
  - Is there a usage "Fatigue Factor" making it prone to errors?
- When the market is densely populated with competing brands… usability can become a distinguishing characteristic

➢ ***Item should be designed with the human user in mind, sometimes referred to "user-friendly"***

 Slide 80 of 156

Human Factors May Include Operations While Wearing Personal Protective Equipment (PPE)

- **MOPP** (**M**ission **O**riented **P**rotective **P**osture) (acronym pronounced as "mop") is a military term used to describe protective gear to be used in a toxic environment, i.e., during a chemical, biological, radiological, or nuclear (CBRN) attack. [This is similar to what's known as Hazmat apparel or PPE.]
- There are 5 levels ranging from no protection ("0") to:
  - **MOPP4.** Personnel completely encapsulate themselves by closing their overgarments, adjusting all drawstrings to minimize the likelihood of any openings, and putting on their protective gloves. MOPP4 is used when the highest degree of protection is required, or if CB agents are present but the actual hazard is not determined. As with every other MOPP level, flexibility is built into the system to provide relief to the individual. Once the hazard is identified and risk assessment measures are employed, the overgarment may be left open.

A Simple Example

CONSIDER TRYING TO USE YOUR CELLPHONE WEARING *LEVEL 4 MOPP GEAR*

(ALMOST like being in a space suit)!

NOTE:

- **It's much more difficult than wearing a snowsuit and thick gloves!**

The contents of this document represent the views of the author and not necessarily those of former employers or associated employee personnel.

Sample HSI / HFE Assessment

- ***What are some HSI (and Safety) Issues with this Control Station?***

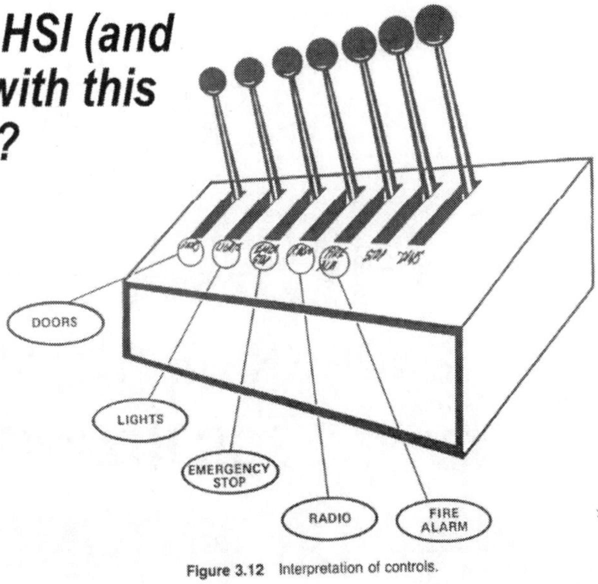

Figure 3.12 Interpretation of controls.

- ➢ **Quality, Quality Control, and Quality Engineering**
- ➢ **Specialty Engineering Definition**
- ➢ **Specialty Engineering Roles and Relationships**
- ➢ **Reliability**
- ➢ **Maintainability**
- ➢ **Supportability**
- ➢ **Human Factors**
- ➢ **Safety**
- ➢ **Information Assurance (IA) / Cyber Security-Safety**

BREAK TIME?

ENOUGH OF THE "-ILITIES" FOR NOW?!?

PLEASE BE BACK IN 10 MINUTES

The contents of this document represent the views of the author and not necessarily those of former employers or associated employee personnel.

 Slide 85 of 156

Safety Engineering

SYSTEM SAFETY is the application of engineering and management principles, requirements criteria, and techniques to optimize all aspects of safety within the constraints of operational effectiveness, time, cost, and risks throughout all phases of the system life cycle.

The contents of this document represent the views of the author and not necessarily those of former employers or associated employee personnel.

 Slide 86 of 156

Safety Tasks

- Requirements Analysis
- Program Tailoring
- Program Plan
  - System Safety Program Plan (SSPP)
  - Hazardous Material Management Plan (HMMP)
  - Checklists, Hazard Tracking & Mitigations
- Design Requirements and Guidelines
  (including COTS)
- Test and Evaluation Safety (Plans)
- (Material) Safety Data Sheets (MSDS or **SDS**) for Hazmats
- Environmental Health & Safety (EHS, Facilities and Environment)
- E^3 (Electromagnetic Environmental Effects, including Lasers)

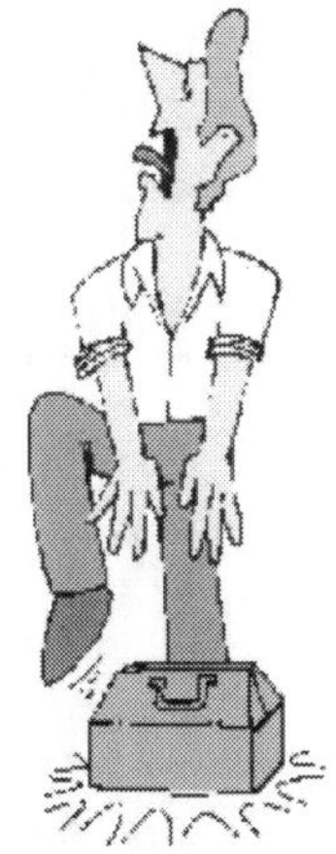

The contents of this document represent the views of the author and not necessarily those of former employers or associated employee personnel.

Safety Design and Evaluation

Safety Design and Evaluation may Include:

- Hazard Analyses, Identification and Tracking
- Safety Verification and Validation
  - **VERIFICATION ANSWERS THE QUESTION, "DID YOU BUILD IT RIGHT?"**
  - **WHILE VALIDATION ANSWERS THE QUESTION, "DID YOU BUILD THE RIGHT THING?"**
- Identification of Safety Procedures
- Identify Safety Critical Functions in both H/W and S/W
- Hazard Mitigation(s) and Safety Testing
- Commercial Off The Shelf (COTS) and Nationally Recognized Test Laboratory (NRTL) Listings for Products & Components
- Safety Assessment
- Hazardous Material (Hazmat) Identification and Traceability (generally for Maintenance, Demilitarization / Teardown, and Disposal)
- ***References*: MIL-STD-882, ANSI / GEIA-Std-0010, DO-178, UL / EN Standards (i.e. UL/EN 60950 for IT Equipment)**

The contents of this document represent the views of the author and not necessarily those of former employers or associated employee personnel.

Simple Safety Evaluation

Have a look around this presentation room.

- **What do you see that might be either a hazard or a mitigation for a hazard?**

The contents of this document represent the views of the author and not necessarily those of former employers or associated employee personnel.

Hardware Mishap Severity Categories

MIL-STD-882E

TABLE I. Severity categories

SEVERITY CATEGORIES		
Description	**Severity Category**	**Mishap Result Criteria**
Catastrophic	1	Could result in one or more of the following: death, permanent total disability, irreversible significant environmental impact, or monetary loss equal to or exceeding $10M.
Critical	2	Could result in one or more of the following: permanent partial disability,injuries or occupational illness that may result in hospitalization of at least three personnel, reversible significant environmental impact, or monetary loss equal to or exceeding $1M but less than $10M.
Marginal	3	Could result in one or more of the following: injury or occupational illness resulting in one or more lost work day(s), reversible moderate environmental impact, or monetary loss equal to or exceeding $100K but less than $1M.
Negligible	4	Could result in one or more of the following: injury or occupational illness not resulting in a lost work day, minimal environmental impact, or monetary loss less than $100K.

NOTE: *These are guidelines which can be tailored.*

The contents of this document represent the views of the author and not necessarily those of former employers or associated employee personnel.

Hardware Mishap Probability of Occurrence

MIL-STD-882E

TABLE II. Probability levels

PROBABILITY LEVELS			
Description	Level	Specific Individual Item	Fleet or Inventory
Frequent	A	Likely to occur often in the life of an item.	Continuously experienced.
Probable	B	Will occur several times in the life of an item.	Will occur frequently.
Occasional	C	Likely to occur sometime in the life of an item.	Will occur several times.
Remote	D	Unlikely, but possible to occur in the life of an item.	Unlikely, but can reasonably be expected to occur.
Improbable	E	So unlikely, it can be assumed occurrence may not be experienced in the life of an item.	Unlikely to occur, but possible.
Eliminated	F	Incapable of occurence. This level is used when potential hazards are identified and later eliminated.	Incapable of occurence. This level is used when potential hazards are identified and later eliminated.

NOTE: *These are guidelines which can also be tailored.*

The contents of this document represent the views of the author and not necessarily those of former employers or associated employee personnel.

Typical Hardware Safety Mishap Risk Index Matrix

MIL-STD-882E

TABLE III. Risk assessment matrix

RISK ASSESSMENT MATRIX				
SEVERITY / PROBABILITY	Catastrophic (1)	Critical (2)	Marginal (3)	Negligible (4)
Frequent (A)	High	High	Serious	Medium
Probable (B)	High	High	Serious	Medium
Occasional (C)	High	Serious	Medium	Low
Remote (D)	Serious	Medium	Medium	Low
Improbable (E)	Medium	Medium	Medium	Low
Eliminated (F)	Eliminated			

The contents of this document represent the views of the author and not necessarily those of former employers or associated employee personnel.

Another Hardware Safety Mishap Risk Index Matrix

This MIL-STD-882E Eyechart Mishap Risk Index was developed by U.S. Army's Aviation and Missile Command (AMCOM) to detail ALL the information related to a Mishap Risk Index Matrix in ONE CHART.

RISK Acceptance Levels per DODI 5000.02, 8 Dec 2008
Risk Assessment Leves and Definitions per
Tables I through III of MIL-STD-882E, 11 May 2012

HAZARD PROBABILITY	Specific Individual Item	Fleet or Inventory		HAZARD SEVERITY: Catastrophic	Critical	Marginal	Negligible
				Could result in one of more of the following: death, peramnent total disability, irreversible significant environmental impact, or monetary loss equal to or exceeding $10M.	Could result in one or more of the following: permanent partial disability, injuries or occupational illness that may result in hospitalization of at least three personnel, reversible significant environmental impact, or monetary loss equal to or exceeding $1M but less than $10M.	could result in one or more of the following: injury or occupational illness resulting in one or more lost work day(s), reversible moderate environmental impact, or monetary loss equal to or exceeding $100K but less than $1M.	Could result in one or more of the following: injury or occupational illness not resulting in a lost work day, minimal environmental impact, or monetary loss less than $100K.
				1	2	3	4
Frequent	Likely to occur often in the life of an item.	Continuously experienced.	A	1-A HIGH MRI = 1 CAE	2-A HIGH MRI = 3 CAE	3-A SERIOUS MRI = 7 PEO	4-A MEDIUM MRI = 13 PEO
Probable	Will occur several times in the life of an item.	Will occur frequently.	B	1-B HIGH MRI = 2 CAE	2-B HIGH MRI = 5 CAE	3-B SERIOUS MRI = 9 PEO	4-B MEDIUM MRI = 16 PM
Occasional	Likely to occur sometime in the life of an item	Will occur several times.	C	1-C HIGH MRI = 4 CAE	2-C SERIOUS MRI = 6 PEO	3-C MEDIUM RHI = 11 PM	4-C LOW MRI = 18 PM
Remote	Unlikely, but possible to occur in the life of an item.	Unlikely, but can reasonably be expected to occur.	D	1-D SERIOUS MRI = 8 PEO	2-D MEDIUM MRI = 10 PM	3-D MEDIUM MRI = 14 PM	4-D LOW MRI = 19 PM
Improbable	So unlikely, it can be assumed occurrence may not be experienced in the life of an item.	Unlikely to occur, but possible.	E	1-E MEDIUM MRI = 12 PM	2-E MEDIUM MRI = 15 PM	3-E MEDIUM MRI = 17 PM	4-E LOW MRI = 20 PM
Eliminated	Incapable of occurrence. This level is used when potential hazards are identified and later eliminated.	Incapable of occurrence. This level is used when potential hazards are identified and later eliminated.	F	ELIMINATED			

*** NOTE: FOLLOWING RISK ACCEPTANCE AUTHORITIES ***
CAE: COMPONENT ACQUISITION EXECUTIVE
[illegible]
PEO: PROGRAM EXECUTIVE OFFICER
PM: PROGRAM MANAGER
PM: PROGRAM MANAGER

MRI: MISHAP RISK INDEX FOR HAZARD PRIORITIZATION

The contents of this document represent the views of the author and not necessarily those of former employers or associated employee personnel.

Another Hardware Safety Mishap Risk Index Matrix

NAVSEA 5100.12-M, System Safety Engineering (SSE) Manual
Table 10-3. NAVSEA ESOH Risk Matrix

Frequency and Probability	Severity: CVN Loss 2 (1)	Ship Loss 2 (2)	Catastrophic (3)	Critical (4)	Significant (5)	Margina l (6)	Negligible (7)	N/A
Frequent (A)	High	High	High	High	High	Serious	Medium	
Probable (B)	High	High	High	High	Serious	Serious	Medium	
Occasional (C)	High	High	High	Serious	Serious	Medium	Medium	
Infrequent (D)	High	High	Serious	Serious	Medium	Medium	Low	
Rare (E)	High	Serious	Serious	Medium	Medium	Low	Low	
Remote (F)	Serious	Serious	Medium	Medium	Low	Low	Low	
Improbable (G)	Serious 3	Serious 4	Medium	Low	Low	Low	Low	
Eliminated 5 (H)								

Footnotes:
1 - Retired risks may be removed, at program's discretion, from the ESOH Risk Index.
2 - Requires COMNAVSEA concurrence prior to serious risk acceptance.
3 - Considered Medium Risk if $<1x10^{-11}$ and may be accepted as a medium risk without COMNAVSEA concurrence.
4 - Considered Medium Risk if $<1x10^{-9}$ and may be accepted as a medium risk without COMNAVSEA concurrence.
5 - Administrative controls cannot move risk to Eliminated (e.g., Training, Warnings, Procedures, etc.). Risk can be moved to Eliminated only by design or engineering changes that remove the hazard or engineer it out.

The contents of this document represent the views of the author and not necessarily those of former employers or associated employee personnel.

And What About SOFTWARE and SAFETY?

[YOIKS!!!]

MIL-STD-882E **TABLE IV. Software control categories**

SOFTWARE CONTROL CATEGORIES		
Level	**Name**	**Description**
1	**Autonomous (AT)**	• Software functionality that exercises autonomous control authority over potentially safety-significant hardware systems, subsystems, or components without the possibility of predetermined safe detection and intervention by a control entity to preclude the occurrence of a mishap or hazard. *(This definition includes complex system/software functionality with multiple subsystems, interacting parallel processors, multiple interfaces, and safety-critical functions that are time critical.)*
2	**Semi-Autonomous (SAT)**	• Software functionality that exercises control authority over potentially safety-significant hardware systems, subsystems, or components, allowing time for predetermined safe detection and intervention by independent safety mechanisms to mitigate or control the mishap or hazard. *(This definition includes the control of moderately complex system/software functionality, no parallel processing, or few interfaces, but other safety systems/mechanisms can partially mitigate. System and software fault detection and annunciation notifies the control entity of the need for required safety actions.)* • Software item that displays safety-significant information requiring immediate operator entity to execute a predetermined action for mitigation or control over a mishap or hazard. Software exception, failure, fault, or delay will allow, or fail to prevent, mishap occurrence. *(This definition assumes that the safety-critical display information may be time-critical, but the time available does not exceed the time required for adequate control entity response and hazard control.)*
3	**Redundant Fault Tolerant (RFT)**	• Software functionality that issues commands over safety-significant hardware systems, subsystems, or components requiring a control entity to complete the command function. The system detection and functional reaction includes redundant, independent fault tolerant mechanisms for each defined hazardous condition. *(This definition assumes that there is adequate fault detection, annunciation, tolerance, and system recovery to prevent the hazard occurrence if software fails, malfunctions, or degrades. There are redundant sources of safety-significant information, and mitigating functionality can respond within any time-critical period.)* • Software that generates information of a safety-critical nature used to make critical decisions. The system includes several redundant, independent fault tolerant mechanisms for each hazardous condition, detection and display.
4	**Influential**	• Software generates information of a safety-related nature used to make decisions by the operator, but does not require operator action to avoid a mishap.
5	**No Safety Impact (NSI)**	• Software functionality that does not possess command or control authority over safety-significant hardware systems, subsystems, or components and does not provide safety-significant information. Software does not provide safety-significant or time sensitive data or information that requires control entity interaction. Software does not transport or resolve communication of safety-significant or time sensitive data.

Typical Software Safety Criticality Indices

MIL-STD-882E

TABLE V. Software safety criticality matrix

Software Criticality Indices

SwCI	Level of Rigor Tasks
SwCI 1	Program shall perform analysis of requirements, architecture, design, and code; and conduct in-depth safety-specific testing.
SwCI 2	Program shall perform analysis of requirements, architecture, and design; and conduct in-depth safety-specific testing.
SwCI 3	Program shall perform analysis of requirements and architecture; and conduct in-depth safety-specific testing.
SwCI 4	Program shall conduct safety-specific testing.
SwCI 5	Once assessed by safety engineering as Not Safety, then no safety specific analysis or verification is required.

NOTE: Consult the Joint Software Systems Safety Engineering Handbook and AOP 52 for additional guidance on how to conduct required software analyses.

Typical Software Safety Criticality Matrix

MIL-STD-882E **TABLE V. Software safety criticality matrix, Continued**

SOFTWARE SAFETY CRITICALITY MATRIX				
	SEVERITY CATEGORY			
SOFTWARE CONTROL CATEGORY	Catastrophic (1)	Critical (2)	Marginal (3)	Negligible (4)
1	SwCI 1	SwCI 1	SwCI 3	SwCI 4
2	SwCI 1	SwCI 2	SwCI 3	SwCI 4
3	SwCI 2	SwCI 3	SwCI 4	SwCI 4
4	SwCI 3	SwCI 4	SwCI 4	SwCI 4
5	SwCI 4*	SwCI 5	SwCI 5	SwCI 5

NOTE: Catastrophic (1) / Software Control Category 5 stands corrected to *SwCI 4

Typical Software Safety Risk Index Matrix

MIL-STD-882E TABLE VI. Relationship between SwCI, risk level, LOR tasks, and risk

RELATIONSHIP BETWEEN SwCI, RISK LEVEL, LOR Tasks, AND RISK		
Software Criticality Index (SwCI)	Risk Level	Software LOR Tasks and Risk Assessment/Acceptance
SwCI 1	High	• If SwCI 1 LOR tasks are unspecified or incomplete, the contributions to system risk will be documented as HIGH and provided to the PM for decision. The PM shall document the decision of whether to expend the resources required to implement SwCI 1 LOR tasks or prepare a formal risk assessment for acceptance of a HIGH risk.
SwCI 2	Serious	• If SwCI 2 LOR tasks are unspecified or incomplete, the contributions to system risk will be documented as SERIOUS and provided to the PM for decision. The PM shall document the decision of whether to expend the resources required to implement SwCI 2 LOR tasks or prepare a formal risk assessment for acceptance of a SERIOUS risk.
SwCI 3	Medium	• If SwCI 3 LOR tasks are unspecified or incomplete, the contributions to system risk will be documented as MEDIUM and provided to the PM for decision. The PM shall document the decision of whether to expend the resources required to implement SwCI 3 LOR tasks or prepare a formal risk assessment for acceptance of a MEDIUM risk.
SwCI 4	Low	• If SwCI 4 LOR tasks are unspecified or incomplete, the contributions to system risk will be documented as LOW and provided to the PM for decision. The PM shall document the decision of whether to expend the resources required to implement SwCI 4 LOR tasks or prepare a formal risk assessment for acceptance of a LOW risk.
SwCI 5	Not Safety	• No safety-specific analyses or testing is required.

Hardware & Software Complexities have led to Newer Safety Analysis Techniques

A Systems Safety Analysis Technique

For *COMPLEX & AUTONOMOUS SYSTEMS*

Developed by Dr. Nancy Leveson, Ph.D.

Professor of Aeronautics, Astronautics & Engineering Systems

Massachusetts Institute of Technology

SYSTEMS-THEORETIC ACCIDENT MODEL and PROCESS [STAMP]

&

SYSTEMS-THEORETIC PROCESS ANALYSIS [STPA]

A Brief Overview of STAMP / STPA

- Control processes operate between levels of control.

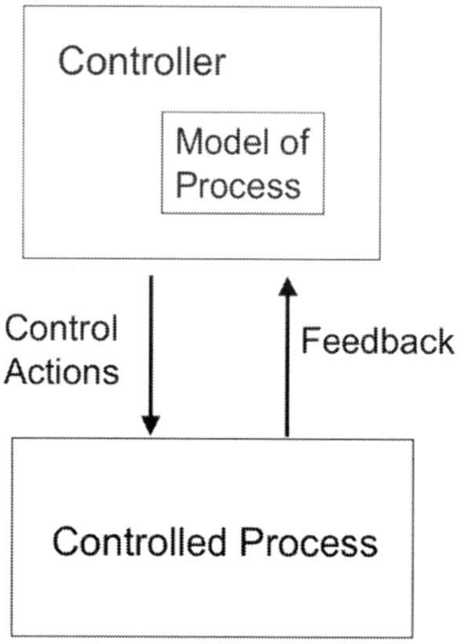

[REALITY BESTS THE MODEL!]
Mishaps occur when <u>model of process</u> is inconsistent with <u>real state of process</u>, and the controller provides inadequate control actions for the <u>real state</u>.

Feedback channels are critical
-- Design
-- Operation

The contents of this document represent the views of the author and not necessarily those of former employers or associated employee personnel.

A Brief Overview of STAMP / STPA

- In it's simplest incarnation, a "system" is a closed loop function. relating inputs, activation, control(s) and corrective feedback as detailed in the following diagram.

A Standard "Classic" System Control Loop With Feedback

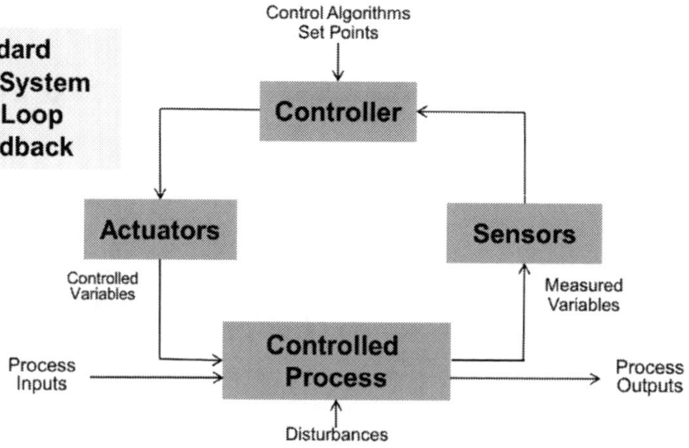

The contents of this document represent the views of the author and not necessarily those of former employers or associated employee personnel.

A Brief Overview of STAMP / STPA

Basic, Fundamental Steps to evaluate the requirements for Controller-Action Response roles or sequences for the system:

1) **Action required but not provided causes hazard**

2) **Unsafe action provided incorrectly causes hazard**

3) **Incorrect Timing / Order**

4) **Stopped too soon or Applied too long**

A Brief Overview of STAMP / STPA

Identification of Potential Control Flaws

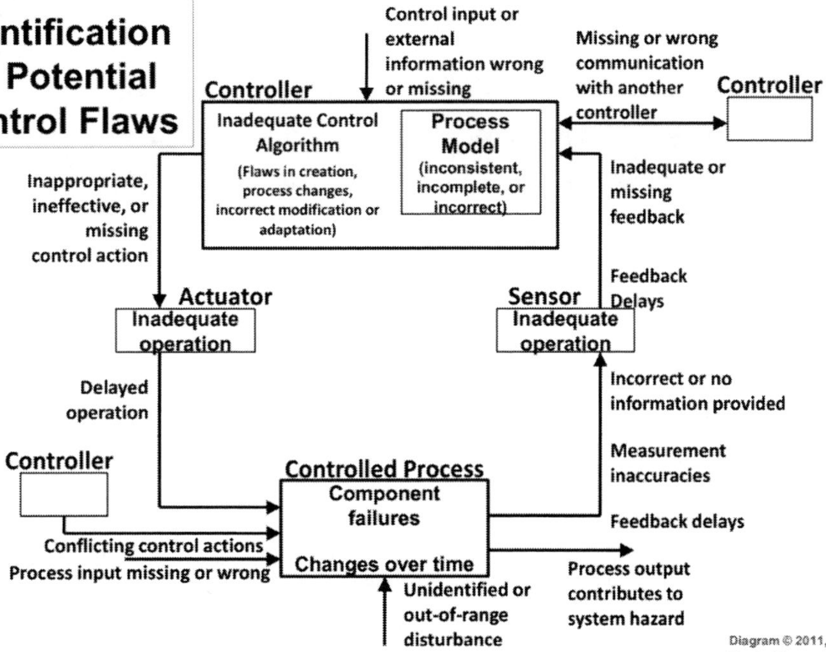

Diagram © 2011, N.Leveson
Used with permission

A Brief Overview of STAMP / STPA

- **SYSTEM REQUIREMENTS must provide comprehensive, "validatable", and verifiable attributes for every step in a system life cycle, including but not limited to:**
  - **Concept**
  - **Design**
  - **Development**
  - **Parts Selection & Procurement**
  - **Manufacture**
  - **Operation**
  - **Operational Environments**
  - **Deployment**
  - **Field Maintenance**
  - **Logistics Support**
  - **Upgrades & Updates**
  - **End-Of-Life and Disposal**

A Brief Overview of STAMP / STPA

- **Development and review of such extensive requirements, covering such "cradle to grave" system performance requires a much more comprehensive assessment methodology for complex systems.**

- **From a *Systems Theory* perspective, a different but effective methodology for a more comprehensive safety hazard analysis assessment emerges.**

A Brief Overview of STAMP / STPA

- "(The) Value of system safety is doing what (design) engineers do not do. (Evaluate a system from) A different viewpoint."

- **For more detailed information, please consult Dr. Leveson's textbook on the topic.**

Engineering a Safer World
Systems Thinking Applied to Safety
© 2011 MIT Press, ISBN 978-0-262-01662-9

A Google Search on "STAMP / STPA" turns up a considerable amount of information, papers, and ongoing annual MIT workshop information.

A Brief Overview of STAMP / STPA

A Google Search for "*STAMP STPA*" turns up papers and various videos and You Tube presentations on the processes for implementing STAMP / STPA. Dr. John Thomas, a Ph.D. graduate of Dr. Leveson's program, has created some online software tools to assist in the process. He, and a number of others, internationally, continue to champion the STAMP / STPA process.

A Brief Overview of STAMP / STPA

- **Dr. Leveson has also alerted folks to the creation of a new *Consortium on Systems Approaches to Safety and Security* (C-SASS).**
- **She is also continuing to hold forums at MIT in Cambridge, Massachusetts and around the globe on STAMP / STPA**
- **For further information on STAMP / STPA and C-SASS, contact Dr. Leveson:**

Prof. Nancy Leveson
Aeronautics and Astronautics and Engineering Systems
MIT, Room 33-334
77 Massachusetts Ave.
Cambridge, MA 02142

Telephone: 617-258-0505
Email: leveson@mit.edu
URL: http://sunnyday.mit.edu

A Brief Overview of STAMP / STPA

- **Note the similarities of STAMP/STPA with the Functional Hazard Assessment (FHA), Task 208, detailed in MIL-STD-882E, *DoD Standard Practice, System Safety:***
- **208.2 Task description**. The contractor shall perform and document a FHA to analyze functions associated with the proposed design. The FHA should be based on the best available data, including mishap data (if obtainable) from similar systems and other lessons learned. This effort will include inputs, outputs, critical interfaces, and the consequence of functional failure.
- 208.2.1 At a minimum, the FHA shall consider the following to identify and evaluate functions within a system:
- a. Decomposition of the system and its related subsystems to the major component level.
- b. A functional description of each subsystem and component identified.
- c. A functional description of interfaces between subsystems and components. Interfaces should be assessed in terms of connectivity and functional inputs and outputs.
- d. Hazards associated with loss of function, degraded function or malfunction, or functioning out of time or out of sequence for the subsystems, components, and interfaces. The list of hazards should consider the next effect in a possible mishap sequence and the final mishap outcome.

A Brief Overview of STAMP / STPA

- 208.2.1 At a minimum, the FHA shall consider the following to identify and evaluate functions within a system [CONTINUED]:

- e. An assessment of the risk associated with each identified failure of a function, subsystem, or component. Estimate severity, probability, and Risk Assessment Code (RAC) using the process described in Section 4 of this Standard. The definitions in Tables I and II, and the RACs in Table III shall be used, unless tailored alternative definitions and/or a tailored matrix are formally approved in accordance with Department of Defense (DoD) Component policy.
- f. An assessment of whether the functions identified are to be implemented in the design hardware, software, or human control interfaces. This assessment should map the functions to their implementing hardware or software components. Functions allocated to software should be mapped to the lowest level of technical design or configuration item prior to coding (e.g., implementing modules or use cases).
- g. An assessment of Software Control Category (SCC) for each Safety-significant Software Function (SSSF). Assign a Software Criticality Index (SwCI) for each SSSF mapped to the software design architecture.
- h. A list of requirements and constraints (to be included in the specifications) that, when successfully implemented, will eliminate the hazard or reduce the risk. These requirements could be in the form of fault tolerance, detection, isolation, annunciation, or recovery.

Why Safety Matters

Safety's goals are to eliminate or mitigate hazard probabilities and severities in the following ***order of precedence***:

1. **Design the hazard out** (eliminate hazards, no probability of occurrence)
2. **Incorporate safety devices** (protect against potential hazards, protects against occurrence)
3. **Provide warning devices** (alert to potential hazards, try to reduce probability of occurrence through human error)
4. **Develop procedures and training** (train personnel to avoid hazards, try to reduce probability of occurrence through human error)

Those hazards that cannot be completely eliminated are known as "*Residual Risk*"

By far the most difficult risk to manage is human error.

- Quality, Quality Control, and Quality Engineering
- Specialty Engineering Definition
- Specialty Engineering Roles and Relationships
- Reliability
- Maintainability
- Supportability
- Human Factors
- Safety
- Information Assurance (IA) / Cyber Security-Safety

BREAK TIME?

ENOUGH OF THE "-ILITIES" FOR NOW?!?

PLEASE BE BACK IN 10 MINUTES

Information Assurance (IA)

Engineers design, procure, implement, build and test security components of systems to prevent espionage, hacking, and ransomware. Such activities can be both international and inter-corporate (to say nothing of the NSA activities, who's hijacked code reputedly led to worldwide "*Wanna Cry*" ransomware!).

The contents of this document represent the views of the author and not necessarily those of former employers or associated employee personnel.

Information Assurance (IA)

- In the Headlines
- What is Information Assurance (IA)?
- Why is Cyber Security - Safety Important?
- Acceptance of Cyber Security - **Safety Requirements**
- Pursuit/Capture Considerations
- Cyber Security Impact on Programs
- Security - Part of the Design

IA, Cyber Security & MSI Pursuit, Capture and Execution

The contents of this document represent the views of the author and not necessarily those of former employers or associated employee personnel.

Information Assurance In the Headlines

The Wall Street Journal – *Computer Spies Breach Fighter-Jet Project* (external attack)
The Los Angeles Times – *Cyber-Attack Hits U.S. Central Command* (malware)
The San Francisco Chronicle – *Sabotage attacks knock out phone service* (physical threat)
WIRED – Hackers Remotely Kill a Jeep on the Highway – With me in it! (external attack)
Agence France-Presse – *Slick Cyber Attack Hits US Security Titan RSA* (external phishing attack)
Associated Press – *Banks, Credit-Card Issuers Warn of e-mail Breach!* (external attack)
National Security Agency – *U.S. Intelligence Analyst Sought for Release of Classified Data* (insider threat)
National Journal – *OPM Announces More Than 21 Million Affected by Second Data Breach* (external attack)
CBS News – *"WannaCry" ransomware attack impacts over 150 countries and losses could reach $4 billion* (internal or external attack)

Cyber attacks take many forms; e.g., digital, physical, phishing!

What is Information Assurance (IA) / Cyber Security-Safety?

Per *National Information Assurance (IA) Glossary*
(CNSS Instruction No. 4009, Revised June 2006)

Basic Services	Basic Functions
Measures that protect and defend information and information systems by ensuring their	These measures include providing for restoration of information systems by incorporating protection, detection, and reaction capabilities

Basic Services

- **Integrity**
- **Confidentiality**
- **Availability**
- **Authentication**
- **Non-repudiation**

Basic Functions

- **Protect**
- **Detect**
- **React**

Why is IA, Cyber Security / Safety Important?

Acting on bad information—whether you're a soldier or system–can lead to deadly and / or major profit loss repercussions to say nothing of company reputations.

This is a military "depiction", but the same holds true for financial institutions, companies, and governments.

It's now often referred to as "*situational awareness*" to understand what is operationally taking place.

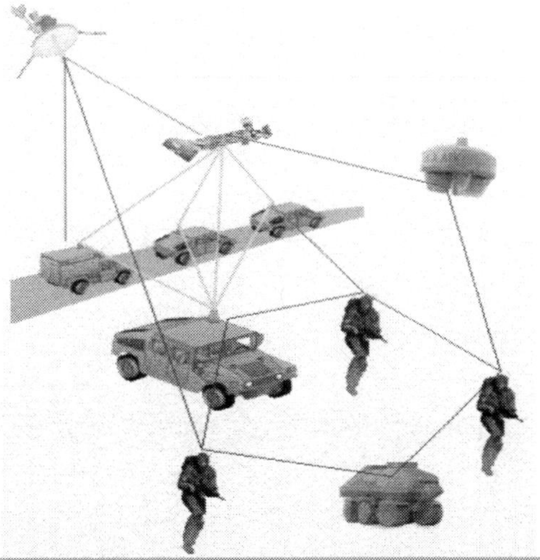

Complexity of today's systems and networks presents significant security challenges for producers and consumers of information

Information Assurance in networks and data!

The contents of this document represent the views of the author and not necessarily those of former employers or associated employee personnel.

Security Information Assurance Life Cycle

Security Life Cycle (NIST SP 800-39)

Missile Systems

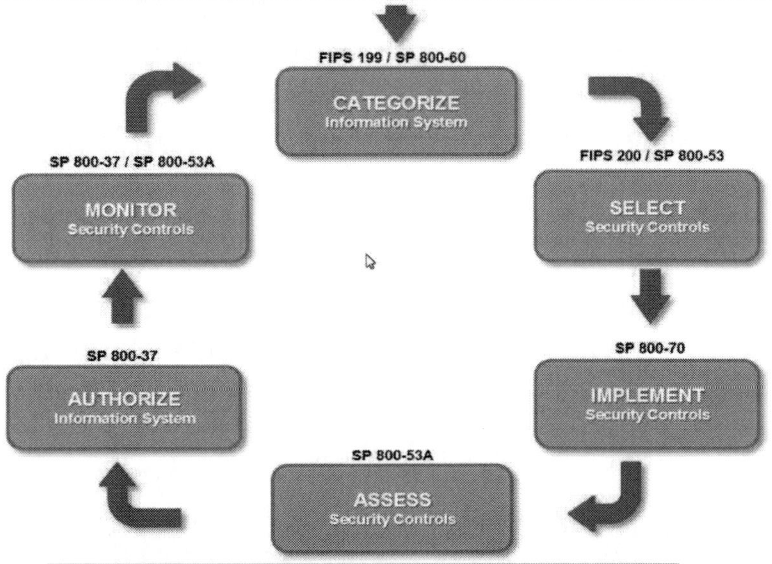

Information Assurance in networks and data!

The contents of this document represent the views of the author and not necessarily those of former employers or associated employee personnel.

Cyber Threat Modeling

Reducing privacy and security risks starts with knowing what the threats really are.

[The following is a condensation of an 8 July 2017 ARS Technica article by Sean Gallagher, "*How I learned to stop worrying (mostly) and love my threat model*"]

The ELECTRONIC FRONTIER FOUNDATION's five-question structure:

1. **What is to be protected?** (The data, communications, and other things that could cause problems for personnel or organizations if misused.)
2. **Protected from whom?** (The people, organizations, and criminal actors who might seek access to that what is to be protected.)
3. **How likely is it that information will need to be protected?** (Level of exposure to those threats.)
4. **How bad are the consequences of failure to secure what is to be protected?**
5. **How much effort is necessary to in order to try to prevent a break-in of protected information?** (The money, time and convenience expended to secure what is to be protected.)

Cyber Threat Modeling

What are the risks and costs to achieve better security? Identify possible threats based on motive, resources, and capabilities.

A sampling of threats individuals and organizations need to concern themselves with in threat modeling:

- At the most basic level, every person who uses the Internet and mobile applications faces a common set of security and privacy threats. Some of these threats are obvious and immediate; others are less intuitive but potentially more damaging in the long term.

Cyber Threat Modeling

- **Criminals** using "crimeware" to steal personal information they can use to empty bank accounts, make fraudulent credit card purchases with, or sell to others for identity theft purposes.
- **Fraudsters** who attempt to fool victims into paying them by disguising their identity, or who extort money from victims by exploiting information they obtained through deception.
- **Ransomware operators** who demand payment to recover access to personal digital assets.
- **Identity thieves** and other criminals who leverage personal information stolen from data collected by a legitimate third party (a bank, a retailer, a government agency).
- **Companies** who collect large quantities of personal data and misuse it or sell it to others who do, or who store it insecurely and inadvertently aid criminals.
- **People** who have a personal motivation to violate other's privacy because they are stalkers, don't like other's tweets or comments, or just because they can.

Cyber Threat Modeling

Other attackers may focus on you as a means to gain access to a bigger target -

- Workers in finance or in the accounting department of nearly any company, might be personally targeted by criminals ultimately aiming for the company's systems.
- Systems administrators might be targeted to gain access to the systems managed.
- A journalist, a non-governmental organization employee, a government employee, or a government contractor, someone may have an intelligence-gathering interest in their work.
- An employer or government may want to keep tabs on personnel activities and opinions for other reasons, too.

Cyber Threat Modeling

- Each of these types of "threat actors" has different levels of skill and available resources. They also have different motives for—and levels of commitment to—getting what is to be protected.
- Typically, attackers motivated by money will not expend more resources than the value of what they're going after. It's unusual for a criminal to spend a year or hundreds of thousands of dollars just for the ability to make a few hundred, and they'll likely not target individuals specifically unless they're a gateway to a big haul.

THERE'S ONE OTHER MAJOR THREAT EVERYONE FACES:

- **Ourselves**. Accidental disclosure or casual information leakage over e-mail, social media, or other channels which can be just as bad as being hacked. Such mistakes can allow others to gain further access to private information by someone who happens across it.

Software Assurance (SwA)

How is cyber security extended to software?

Again, one must assess applicable potential risks, threat sources and events.

An analysis is a good start.

(Brace for Eyecharts!)

Software Assurance (SwA)

Risk Assessment – NIST SP 800-30

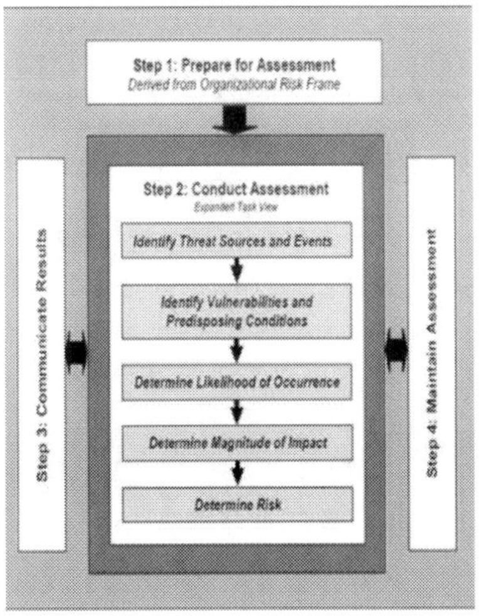

RISK ASSESSMENT PROCESS

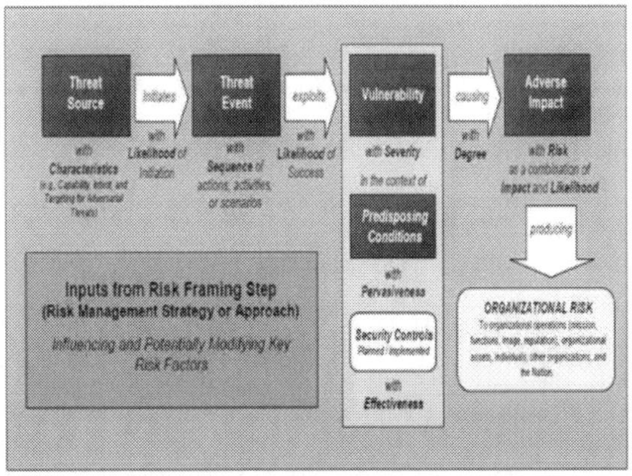

GENERIC RISK MODEL WITH KEY RISK FACTORS

Information Assurance in networks and data!

The contents of this document represent the views of the author and not necessarily those of former employers or associated employee personnel.

Software Assurance (SwA)

SwA Spans The Entire Development Lifecycle

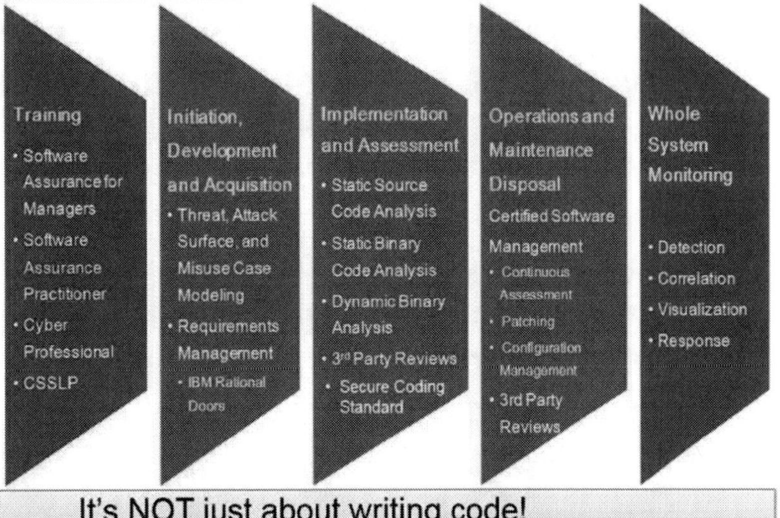

It's NOT just about writing code!

Information Assurance in networks and data!

The contents of this document represent the views of the author and not necessarily those of former employers or associated employee personnel.

Paths for Cyber Security / Safety Activities

Two separate overall paths are generally considered for addressing Cyber Security & Safety Issues –

- **Cyber Security / Cyber Safety by Design –**
  - **When Cyber Security is built into a system design, it enhances both System Security and System Safety (Falls back on REQUIREMENTS!)**
- **Cyber Digital Forensics –**
  - **Post-Breach or Post-Hack Attack analysis after the fact**

 Slide 129 of 156

Cyber Security & Cyber Safety

- **This activity attempts to design-in Cyber Security into a system from the earliest phases of development & requirements.**
- **If a designated "critical system" is involved, attempts may then be initiated by Cyber Subject Matter Experts (SMEs) to "break into" the system to uncover potential "Cyber Attack Vectors" for developing systems and "plugging potential Cyber Security gaps.**

 Slide 130 of 156

Cyber Security & Cyber Safety

- **Attackers focus on systems designed to protect and provide security controls; not to access data, but to overcome the security systems protecting the data**
- **Layered attacks are often necessary to find vulnerabilities via people and processes**
- **<u>CYBER HARDENING TO REDUCE ATTACK VECTORS</u>: Designers are in the best position to understand and deal with system vulnerabilities and capabilities.**

The contents of this document represent the views of the author and not necessarily those of former employers or associated employee personnel.

Cyber Security & Cyber Safety

- **What are "Cyber Attack Vectors"?**
  - **A Cyber Attack Vector is a path or means by which a hacker (or cracker) can gain access to a computer or network server in order to deliver a payload or execute a malicious outcome.**
  - **Cyber Attack Vectors enable hackers to exploit system vulnerabilities, including the human element (e.g. "Phishing Attacks" or "Inadvertently Installed Malware").**

The contents of this document represent the views of the author and not necessarily those of former employers or associated employee personnel.

Cyber Security & Cyber Safety

- Some potential "Cyber Attack Vectors" –
  - System Interfaces: Radio Frequency, Physical Interconnections, Communications & Links
  - Software Weaknesses & Vulnerabilities: Coding Errors, Input Checking & Validation, Fault Isolation, "Dead Code", Corrupted Code, Malware Incorporation Into Code Updates.

The contents of this document represent the views of the author and not necessarily those of former employers or associated employee personnel.

 Slide 133 of 156

Cyber Security & Cyber Safety

- More potential "Cyber Attack Vectors" –
  - Supply Chain or Factory Systems: Factory Online Systems & Test Environments (also extends down to Suppliers and Sub Contractors)
  - Physical: Reverse Engineering, Anti-Tamper Systems, Parts or System Obsolescence, Authentication Activities (including Personnel Insider Threats)

The contents of this document represent the views of the author and not necessarily those of former employers or associated employee personnel.

 Slide 134 of 156

Cyber Security & Cyber Safety

- A thorough assessment of Cyber Security against potential threats can be costly and time consuming.
- It becomes a tradeoff between security requirements, potential threats, potential vulnerabilities, and resources required to "plug the security gaps".

The contents of this document represent the views of the author and not necessarily those of former employers or associated employee personnel.

Cyber Digital Forensics

- **Digital forensics (sometimes known as digital forensic science) is a branch of forensic science encompassing the recovery and investigation of material found in digital devices, often in relation to computer crime.**

The contents of this document represent the views of the author and not necessarily those of former employers or associated employee personnel.

Cyber Digital Forensics

- **Investigative cyber efforts developed <u>after the breach or hack is uncovered</u>**
- **Activities are comparable to similar in efforts to other forensic analyses disciplines (e.g. CSI)**

The contents of this document represent the views of the author and not necessarily those of former employers or associated employee personnel.

Cyber Digital Forensics

- **The following basic questions need to be answered by the digital forensics assessment team to determine the root cause for the breach –**
  - **What happened?**
  - **Whom did it happen to?**
  - **When did it happen?**
  - **Where did it happen?**
  - **How did it happen?**
  - **Why did it happen?**

(*Note similarity to the "5-Why's" technique for Quality Assurance Assessments*)

The contents of this document represent the views of the author and not necessarily those of former employers or associated employee personnel.

Cyber Digital Forensics

- Tracking down the digital trail(s) and "Cyber Attack Vectors" for deployed assets to answer these questions is often a very complicated and intensive process
- Once the root cause for a breach occurrence is determined,
- Follow-on attempts to "close the uncovered security gap" (if possible) may be initiated
- This activity involves a broad based team of Subject Matter Experts (SMEs) including Hardware and Software Designers, Engineers, and Digital Forensics Investigators, AND IS USUALLY COSTLY!!!

Cyber Digital Forensics

- The activity and root cause investigation may ultimately lead to legal action(s) and criminal prosecution(s) against potential personnel, based on the assets or information exposed by the breach
- In other instances, preventive actions taken to preclude future breach or hacking activities may involve political or economic sanctions against other organizations or governments

Cyber Security Pursuit/Capture Considerations

- Customer **Cyber Security Requirements** are getting more specific in Request for Proposals, Statement of Works, Performance Specifications, etc.
- **Staff Requirements** getting more specific as well
- Basis Of Estimate development must capture the **Requirements**
- What happens if Cyber Security is ignored?
  - During the proposal: Unable to bid due to inexperience
  - After submittal: Non-compliant or weak bid
  - After winning contract: Underestimate the task
  - Prior to deployment: Can't gain approval to "turn on"
  - After deployment: Vulnerabilities are exploited

  Thus putting many people and systems at **risk**, compromising system effectiveness and damaging organizational reputations

Bake Cyber Security into the Solution

The contents of this document represent the views of the author and not necessarily those of former employers or associated employee personnel.

Slide 141 of 156

Cyber Security Impact on Programs

- Impact for incorporating Cyber Security into a typical program
  - Cost
    - Plan for it; Budget for it to control costs
    - Avoid Retrofitting later to comply with IA directives
  - Schedule
    - Lots of Documentation
    - Certification and Accreditation
    - Reviews and potential testing
  - Technical
    - **Incorporate and Integrate into System Requirements**
    - Hardware (e.g., TEMPEST, Secure Guards)
    - Software (e.g., access control, authentication)
    - Encryption and Key Management
- **Like all the "-ilities", Cyber Security generally has to be built into the system and not "bolted on" afterward.**
- ***And generally the most compromising factors to Cyber Security are human-based errors where critical access information is inadvertently released.***

Proper Planning Makes Cyber Security More Affordable!

The contents of this document represent the views of the author and not necessarily those of former employers or associated employee personnel.

Slide 142 of 156

Cyber Security and Security Tasks

- Security Policies
- Security Management
- Physical Security
- Cyber Security & Cyber Safety
- Risk Management
- Disaster Recovery
- Incident Response
- Computer Digital Forensics
- Networks and Communications

The contents of this document represent the views of the author and not necessarily those of former employers or associated employee personnel.

 Slide 143 of 156

Cyber Security Design and Evaluation

Security Engineers evaluate **REQUIREMENTS** based on:

- Policy documents such as:
  - National Industrial Security Program Operating Manual (NISPOM, **DoD 5220.22-M**)
- Standards:
  - **ISO-17799/BS-7799** – Information Security Standard
  - Generally Accepted System Security Procedures (GASSP)
    - e.g., **NIST Special Publication 800-14**,
  - DCID
- Best practices
- Risk management concepts and practices

The contents of this document represent the views of the author and not necessarily those of former employers or associated employee personnel.

 Slide 144 of 156

Summary

- ***Think of Specialty Engineering as Part of a Picture Puzzle, there are various "pieces" that fit together to provide "cradle to grave" engineering support for a system:***

- ***ALL are typically Tasks supported through Quality Engineering Concepts.***

The contents of this document represent the views of the author and not necessarily those of former employers or associated employee personnel.

 Slide 145 of 156

Summary (Continued)

- Specialty Engineers:
  - Provide Subject Matter Expert skills in special area(s)
  - Apply specialty expertise at successive levels of the system
  - Support concurrent engineering and account for cross dependencies
  - Assist and Guide Systems Engineers with in-depth knowledge and experience in narrow specialties
  - Avoids the Systems Engineer needing to learn and become familiar in depth with the Specialty Engineering subject matter

- Early integration of Specialty Engineering:
  - Identifies many specialty **risk** areas and structures them into the **system requirements**
  - Reduces overall product life cycle **costs** through Concept, **Requirements**, Design, Development, Manufacture, Delivery, Deployment, Support, and End of Life Disposal

The contents of this document represent the views of the author and not necessarily those of former employers or associated employee personnel.

 Slide 146 of 156

Summary (Continued)

- By integrating all the "-ilities" into a System of Systems (SoS) approach and combining them with all the other major design disciplines, system requirements and subsequent system development become more highly integrated, more productive, with efficiencies reflected in faster schedules, lower costs, and improved hardware and software safety.

- How is this accomplished?

The contents of this document represent the views of the author and not necessarily those of former employers or associated employee personnel.

 Slide 147 of 156

Summary (Continued)

- At a June 2017 Northeast Chapter Safety Society meeting, a presentation detailed how Lockheed-Martin Sikorsky is now moving forward with just such integration that started out life to more clearly define a Software Safety Development Process.

- Sikorsky's project team quickly realized that a defined process should be expanded to overall Systems Safety including both Hardware and Software.
  - (Especially, like the song about "*Love and Marriage*" says, you generally: "*Can't have one without the other*"!)

The contents of this document represent the views of the author and not necessarily those of former employers or associated employee personnel.

 Slide 148 of 156

Summary (Continued)

- The approach establishes a company wide, harmonized and defined, thorough **requirements** definition procedure and process that is traceable through tools such as the *Dynamic Object Oriented Requirements System* (**DOORS**) down to sub- and sub-subsystem ***detail requirement levels*** that can be individually verified and validated during ongoing stages of product development and acceptance.
- This approach can be applied to verify and validate **ALL** system **requirements** if a thorough procedural approach is applied during the requirements development process.
- **Requirements analysis and development should consume at least 30 to 50 percent of the up-front program effort to make the whole project more successful.**

The contents of this document represent the views of the author and not necessarily those of former employers or associated employee personnel.

 Slide 149 of 156

Summary (Continued)

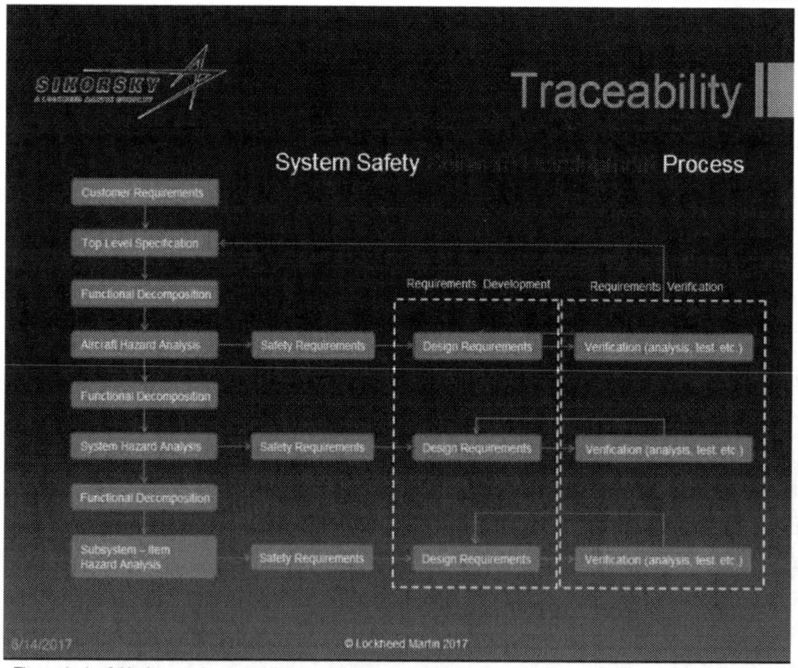

NOTE: The words "Software Development" are fading as this becomes a ***System Safety Process*** initiated through a thorough **Requirements Analysis and Assessment**.

And upon further examination, the process can be easily expanded to an overall ***System Process***

Diagram © 2017, M. Grant, LMCO – Sikorsky
Used with permission

The contents of this document represent the views of the author and not necessarily those of former employers or associated employee personnel.

 Slide 150 of 156

Summary (Continued)

- So, not only are the "-ilities" a crucial part of any project, **their intimate requirements integration**, linkage and ongoing support activities within a project team assist in creating a significant paradigm change in achieving successful systems.

- Identifying many specialty **risk** areas.

- Reducing overall product life cycle **costs** through Concept, **Detailed Requirements**, Design, Development, Manufacture, Delivery, Deployment, Support, and End of Life Disposal.

 Slide 151 of 156

Questions? Comments?

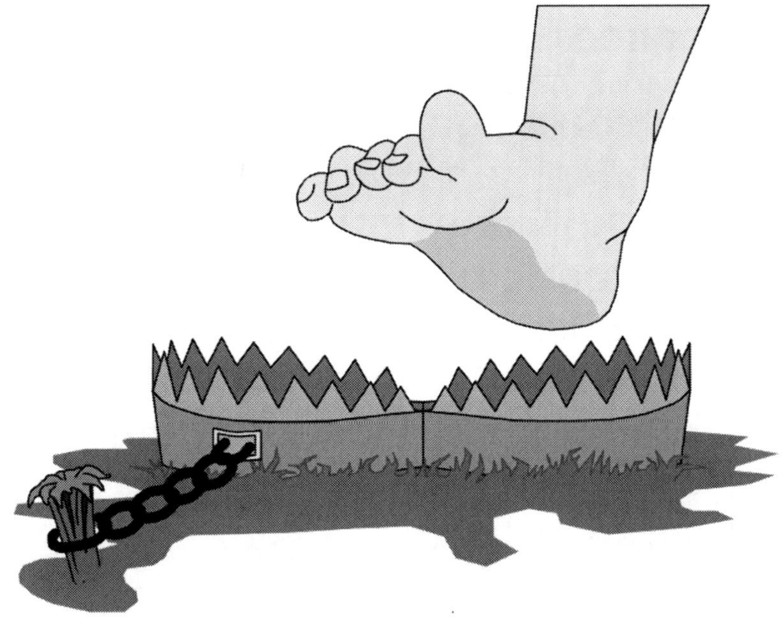

 Slide 152 of 156

Credits

Kudos are due to countless professors, teachers, professionals, managers, business associates, and peers across my career who have provided insights, encouragement, patience, and "golden keys" to understanding products from ideas and concepts, to design, development, manufacture, deployment, use, disposal, and security.

And many, many thanks to the folks at LMCO Sikorsky for providing informative data for this tutorial.

The contents of this document represent the views of the author and not necessarily those of former employers or associated employee personnel.

 Slide 153 of 156

Credits

- And thanks are also due to all in attendance.
- We trust you've gained insights into these "-ilities", and why understanding them and how they integrate into product Quality, Producibility, Reliability, Maintainability, Supportability, Human Factors, Safety, Information Assurance, and Cyber Security - Safety is important in the overall scheme of Systems Engineering, product development, and support!

The contents of this document represent the views of the author and not necessarily those of former employers or associated employee personnel.

 Slide 154 of 156

Additional Reference Sources:

- **American National Standards Institute (ANSI) –**
  - http://www.ansi.org/
- **Military Specifications and Standards (FREE!) –**
  - https://assist.daps.dla.mil/quicksearch/
- **Underwriter's Laboratories**
  - http://www.ul.com/global/eng/pages/
- **Any reputable bookstore (e.g. American Society for Quality, Amazon.com, Barnes & Noble, etc.) –**
  - Juran's Quality Handbook, Sixth Edition
  - Dimitri Kececioglu texts and lectures on Reliability (University of Arizona)
  - Dr. Nancy Leveson papers and textbooks on System Safety, including *Engineering a Safer World, Systems Thinking Applied to Safety, © 2011 MIT Press*
  - Peter Drucker's texts and lectures on business management.

 Slide 155 of 156

Former United Parcel Service (UPS) "That's Logistics" Jingle Lyrics -

- [Intro - Narration]
  Logistics makes the world work better
  [Verse 1 - Nadia Ackerman]
  When it's planes in the sky
  For a chain of supply
  That's logistics
  When the parts for the line
  Come precisely on time
  That's logistics
  A continuous link
  That is always in sync
  That's logistics
  Carbon footprint's reduced
  Bottom line gets a boost
  That's logistics
  With new ways to compete
  There'll be cheers on Wall Street
  That's logistics
  When technology knows
  Right where everything goes
  That's logistics
  Bells will ring, ring-a-ding
  Ring-a-ding ring-a-ding
  That's logistics
  There will be no more stress
  Cause you called UPS
  That's logistics

The contents of this document represent the views of the author and not necessarily those of former employers or associated employee personnel. Copyright © 2018 Alan E. Southwick, All rights reserved. Slide 156 of 156

Verifying Software Control Categories (SCCs) Using Quantitative Fault Tree Analyses (FTAs)

Robert E. Smith, CSP
Booz Allen Hamilton
36th International System Safety Conference
Phoenix, AZ
15 August 2018

Booz | Allen | Hamilton

0

Agenda

- Introduction
- Background / Hypothesis
- Assumptions and Decomposing SCC Definitions
- Fault Tree Examples
- Case Study Verification
- Results
- Conclusion and Recommendations
- References

Booz | Allen | Hamilton

1

Disclaimer

- Any views or opinions presented in this presentation are solely those of the author/presenter and do not represent those of Booz Allen Hamilton nor the U.S. Department of Defense (DoD)

Booz | Allen | Hamilton

2

Introduction

- Proposes an approach to use quantitative Fault Tree Analyses (FTAs) to determine and/or verify the Software Control Category (SCC) assignments in accordance with MIL-STD-882E
- Evaluates and decomposes SCC definitions from MIL-STD-882E
- Uses quantitative FTAs and sets software failures to 1 (always fails) to assess the impact of the top event failure probability to help determine the proper alignment of the SCC assessment to the SCC definitions

Goal – Evaluating the feasibility of using quantitative FTAs to verify SCCs and SwCIs

Booz | Allen | Hamilton

3

Background

- Software Failure Probability
  - Extremely difficult to determine -- <u>*this paper does not attempt to research this topic*</u>
    - MIL-STD-882E - *"Determining the probability of failure of a single software function is difficult at best and cannot be based on historical data. Software is generally application-specific and reliability parameters associated with it cannot be estimated in the same manner as hardware. Therefore, another approach shall be used for the assessment of software's contributions to system risk…"*
    - Joint Software Systems Safety Engineering Handbook (JSSSEH), Section 4.2.1.8.2 – *"Traditionally, and for the purpose of being conservative, software errors in fault trees must be set to a value of one (1) where no supporting analysis or assurance rationale is provided."*
  - For this reason, typically take a conservative approach to assessing software failures in FTAs as "always failure" or failure probability set to 1

Background – Software Control Categories (MIL-STD-882E, Table IV)

- Five SCC Levels:
  1 – Autonomous (AT)
  2 – Semi- Autonomous (SAT)
  3 - Redundant Fault Tolerant (RFT)
  4 – Influential
  5 – No Safety (NSI)

TABLE IV. Software control categories

SOFTWARE CONTROL CATEGORIES		
Level	Name	Description
1	Autonomous (AT)	• Software functionality that exercises autonomous control authority over potentially safety-significant hardware systems, subsystems, or components without the possibility of predetermined safe detection and intervention by a control entity to preclude the occurrence of a mishap or hazard. *(This definition includes complex system/software functionality with multiple subsystems, interacting parallel processors, multiple interfaces, and safety-critical functions that are time critical.)*
2	Semi-Autonomous (SAT)	• Software functionality that exercises control authority over potentially safety-significant hardware systems, subsystems, or components, allowing time for predetermined safe detection and intervention by independent safety mechanisms to mitigate or control the mishap or hazard. *(This definition includes the control of moderately complex system/software functionality, no parallel processing, or few interfaces, but other safety systems/mechanisms can partially mitigate. System and software fault detection and annunciation notifies the control entity of the need for required safety actions.)* • Software item that displays safety-significant information requiring immediate operator entity to execute a predetermined action for mitigation or control over a mishap or hazard. Software exception, failure, fault, or delay will allow, or fail to prevent, mishap occurrence. *(This definition assumes that the safety-critical display information may be time-critical, but the time available does not exceed the time required for adequate control entity response and hazard control.)*
3	Redundant Fault Tolerant (RFT)	• Software functionality that issues commands over safety-significant hardware systems, subsystems, or components requiring a control entity to complete the command function. The system detection and functional reaction includes redundant, independent fault tolerant mechanisms for each defined hazardous condition. *(This definition assumes that there is adequate fault detection, annunciation, tolerance, and system recovery to prevent the hazard occurrence if software fails, malfunctions, or degrades. There are redundant sources of safety-significant information, and mitigating functionality can respond within any time-critical period.)* • Software that generates information of a safety-critical nature used to make critical decisions. The system includes several redundant, independent fault tolerant mechanisms for each hazardous condition, detection and display.
4	Influential	• Software generates information of a safety-related nature used to make decisions by the operator, but does not require operator action to avoid a mishap.
5	No Safety Impact (NSI)	• Software functionality that does not possess command or control authority over safety-significant hardware systems, subsystems, or components and does not provide safety-significant information. Software does not provide safety-significant or time sensitive data or information that requires control entity interaction. Software does not transport or resolve communication of safety-significant or time sensitive data.

Background – SCC and Software Criticality Indices (SwCIs) (MIL-STD-882E, Table V)

- Five SwCIs Levels for performing Level of Rigor (LOR)

  SwCI 1 – Analysis of requirements, architecture, design and code; conduct in-depth safety-specific testing

  SwCI 2 – Analysis of requirements, architecture, design; conduct in-depth safety-specific testing

  SwCI 3 - Analysis of requirements and architecture; conduct in-depth safety-specific testing

  SwCI 4 – Conduct safety-specific testing

  SwCI 5 – Not Safety

TABLE V. Software safety criticality matrix.

SOFTWARE SAFETY CRITICALITY MATRIX				
	SEVERITY CATEGORY			
SOFTWARE CONTROL CATEGORY	Catastrophic (1)	Critical (2)	Marginal (3)	Negligible (4)
1	SwCI 1	SwCI 1	SwCI 3	SwCI 4
2	SwCI 1	SwCI 2	SwCI 3	SwCI 4
3	SwCI 2	SwCI 3	SwCI 4	SwCI 4
4	SwCI 3	SwCI 4	SwCI 4	SwCI 4
5	SwCI 5	SwCI 5	SwCI 5	SwCI 5

SwCI	Level of Rigor Tasks
SwCI 1	Program shall perform analysis of requirements, architecture, design, and code; and conduct in-depth safety-specific testing.
SwCI 2	Program shall perform analysis of requirements, architecture, and design; and conduct in-depth safety-specific testing.
SwCI 3	Program shall perform analysis of requirements and architecture; and conduct in-depth safety-specific testing.
SwCI 4	Program shall conduct safety-specific testing.
SwCI 5	Once assessed by safety engineering as Not Safety, then no safety specific analysis or verification is required.

NOTE: Consult the Joint Software Systems Safety Engineering Handbook and AOP 52 for additional guidance on how to conduct required software analyses.

Hypothesis – With Software Failures set to 1

- If the top event failure probability is 1, this function is likely **SCC 1 - Autonomous (AT)**
- If the top event failure probability is 1e-3 or less, then there are still hardware and/or operator influences on the function, so the SCC is likely **SCC 2 - Semi-Autonomous (SAT)** or lower
- If the top event failure probability is a very small number [less than 1e-6], then the SCC is likely **3 - Redundant Fault Tolerant (RFT); 4 - Influential, or even 5 - No Safety Impact (NSI)**

Overall Assumptions

- Nominal failure probability values
  - Hardware failures = 1e-4
  - Operator errors = 1e-3
- DOES NOT assess or construct safety interlocks in the FTA examples that are considered "software interlocks."
  - JSSSEH states "safety interlocks can be either hardware or software oriented. As an example, a hardware safety interlock would be a key switch that controls a safe/arm switch. Software interlocks generally require the presence of two or more software signals from independent sources to implement a particular function. Examples of software interlocks are checks and flags, firewalls, come-from programming techniques, and bit combinations."
  - Modeling software interlocks in quantitative FTAs would be another excellent paper topic for a future safety conference, but are excluded from this presentation

SCC Assumptions

- Following slides and tables breakdown each SCC definition (SCCs 1-5) by software failure description, hardware failure description, and operator failure description
  - This will form the basis for the Fault Tree model for each SCC level
  - If the column contains "Not Applicable (N/A)" then this failure mode is assumed not present in the SCC definition
  - The last column includes the number of events included in the cut set
  - Text in **BOLD AND UNDERLINED** indicate added descriptors to convert the SCC definitions into failure descriptions to model as failure events in the sample FTAs

FTA Examples – SCC 1

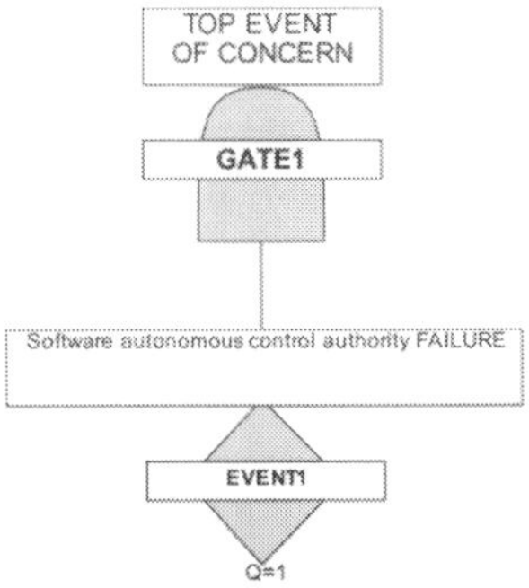

SCC Level	Name	Software Failure Description	Hardware Failure Description	Operator Failure Description	# of Events (in Cut Sets)
1	Autonomous (AT)	Software autonomous control authority **FAILURE**	N/A – no possibility of predetermined safe detection and intervention by a control entity	N/A - no possibility of predetermined safe detection and intervention by a control entity	1

EVENT1 - Software Failure Probability (Q – Unavailability)	GATE1 – Top Event Probability (Q – Unavailability)	SCC Determination Trend	SCC Rationale
1 (always fail)	1 (always fail)	1	Equal failure probability values show Top Event is directly dependent on the Software Functionality
0.10	0.10		
1e-2	1e-2		
1e-3	1e-3		
1e-6	1e-6		
1e-9	1e-9		

FTA Examples – SCC 2 – Two options

	SCC Level	Name	Software Failure Description	Hardware Failure Description	Operator Failure Description	# of Events (in Cut Sets)
Option 1	2	Semi-Autonomous (SAT)	Software control authority **FAILURE**	Time **NOT** allowed for predetermined safe detection and intervention by independent safety mechanisms (Assume at least two (2) independent safety mechanisms **FAIL**)	N/A	3 (or more than 3)
Option 2	2	Semi-Autonomous (SAT)	Software **FAILS** to display safety-significant information	N/A	Immediate operator entity **FAILS** to execute a predetermined action for mitigation or control in the appropriate timeframe.	2

FTA Examples – SCC 2 – Two options (cont)

Option 1

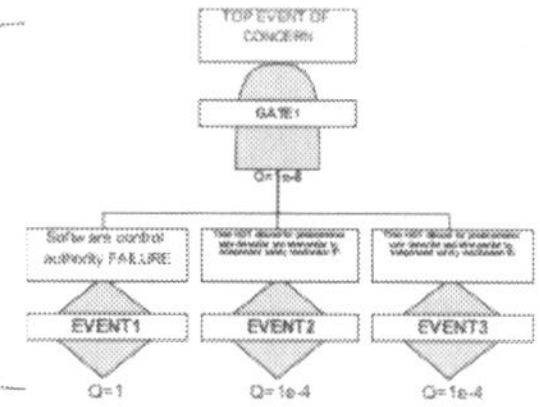

EVENT1 - Software Failure Probability	EVENT2 - Mechanism #1 Failure Probability	EVENT3 - Mechanism #2 Failure Probability	GATE1 - Top Event Probability	SCC Determination Trend	SCC Rationale
1 (always fail)	1e-4	1e-4	1e-8	2	Top event failure probability is the product of the two (2) mechanism failures
0.10	1e-4	1e-4	1e-9		
1e-2	1e-4	1e-4	1e-10		
1e-3	1e-4	1e-4	1e-11		
1e-6	1e-4	1e-4	1e-14		
1e-9	1e-4	1e-4	1e-17		

Option 2

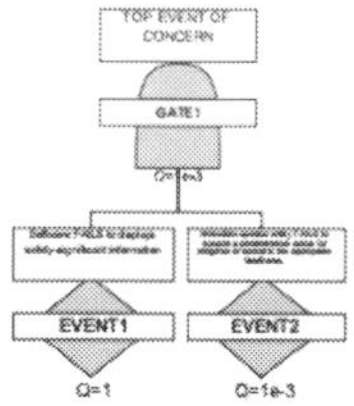

EVENT1 - Software Failure Probability	EVENT2 - Operator Failure Probability	GATE1 - Top Event Probability	SCC Determination Trend	SCC Rationale
1 (always fail)	1e-3	1e-3	2	Top event failure probability is the failure probability of operator failure
0.10	1e-3	1e-4		
1e-2	1e-3	1e-5		
1e-3	1e-3	1e-6		
1e-6	1e-3	1e-9		
1e-9	1e-3	1e-12		

FTA Examples – SCC 3 – Two options

	SCC Level	Name	Software Failure Description	Hardware Failure Description	Operator Failure Description	# of Events (in Cut Sets)
Option 1	3	Redundant Fault Tolerant (RFT)	Software functionality **FAILS** to issue commands over safety-significant hardware systems, subsystems, or components	At least two (2) hardware fault tolerant mechanisms **FAIL**	Control entity **INADVERTENTLY** completes the command function. (Does this count as a failure in the FTA if the software fails to issue appropriate commands?)	3 or more
Option 2	3	Redundant Fault Tolerant (RFT)	Software **FAILS TO** generate information of a safety-critical nature used to make critical decisions	Several (at least three (3)) redundant, independent fault tolerant mechanisms **FAIL** for each hazardous condition, detection and display.		4 or more

FTA Examples – SCC 3 – Two options (cont)

Option 1

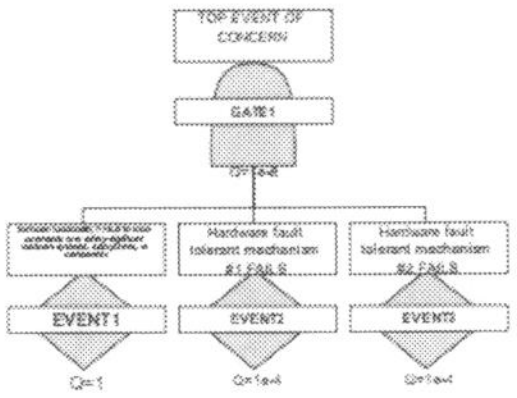

EVENT1 - Software Failure Probability	EVENT2 – Hardware Fault Tolerant Mechanism #1 Failure Probability	EVENT3 - Hardware Fault Tolerant Mechanism #2 Failure Probability	GATE1 - Top Event Probability	SCC Determination Trend	SCC Rationale
1 (always fail)	1e-4	1e-4	1e-8	3	Top event failure probability is the product of the two (2) mechanism failures
0.10	1e-4	1e-4	1e-9		
1e-2	1e-4	1e-4	1e-10		
1e-3	1e-4	1e-4	1e-11		
1e-6	1e-4	1e-4	1e-14		
1e-9	1e-4	1e-4	1e-17		

Option 2

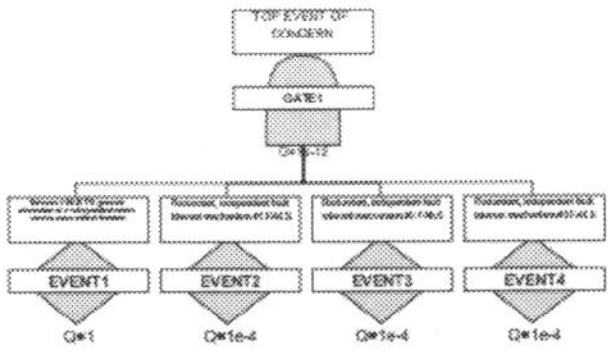

EVENT1 - Software Failure Probability	EVENT2 – Hardware Mechanism #1 Failure Probability	EVENT3 - Hardware Mechanism #2 Failure Probability	EVENT4 - Hardware Mechanism #3 Failure Probability	GATE1 - Top Event Probability	SCC Determination Trend	SCC Rationale
1 (always fail)	1e-4	1e-4	1e-4	1e-12	3	Top event failure probability is the product of the three (3) mechanism failures
0.10	1e-4	1e-4	1e-4	1e-13		
1e-2	1e-4	1e-4	1e-4	1e-14		
1e-3	1e-4	1e-4	1e-4	1e-15		
1e-6	1e-4	1e-4	1e-4	1e-18		
1e-9	1e-4	1e-4	1e-4	1e-21		

FTA Examples – SCC 4

- SCC 4 definition implies:
  - 1) there is no mishap (or FTA top event) if this safety failure occurs and
  - 2) safety-related nature is related to a Marginal / Negligible severity.
- Therefore, there is no need to develop a FTA since there is no mishap / top event if software failure occurs.

SCC Level	Name	Software Failure Description	Hardware Failure Description	Operator Failure Description	# of Events (in Cut Sets)
4	Influential	Software **FAILS** to generate information of a safety-related nature used to make decisions by the operator, but does not require operator action to avoid a mishap.	N/A	N/A	No Mishap / Top Event if software failure occurs

FTA Examples – SCC 5

- Based on the SCC 5 definition:
  - No need to develop a FTA since software functionality is not related to any safety significant function and there is no mishap / top event if software failure occurs

SCC Level	Name	Software Failure Description	Hardware Failure Description	Operator Failure Description	# of Events (in Cut Sets)
5	No Safety Impact (NSI)	N/A	N/A	N/A	Software functionality **NOT** related to any safety significant function. No Mishap / Top Event if software failure occurs

Initial Results

- While the sensitivity analyses did not expose any revelations, they did provide the following range of failure probabilities
- Probability ranges could be used as a "rule of thumb" during SCC assessment when software failure probabilities are set to 1

Software Failure Probability	GATE1 - Top Event Probability Range	SCC Determination Trend
1 (always fail)	1	1 – Autonomous (AT)
1 (always fail)	1e-3 to 1	*(further SCC determination needed to decide if SCC 1 or SCC 2)*
1 (always fail)	1e-3 to 1e-8	2 - Semi-Autonomous (SAT)
1 (always fail)	1e-8 to 1e-12	3 - Redundant Fault Tolerant (RFT)
1 (always fail)	N/A – no mishap/top event	4 – Influential (I)
N/A – no software functionality	N/A – no mishap/top event	5 - No Safety Impact (NSI)

Case Study to Verify Initial FTA Examples

- Using a more realistic model, a sample fault tree of a fictitious launching system with a variety of fault events
- Top event is "Inadvertent Launch"

Case Study to Verify Initial FTA Examples (cont)

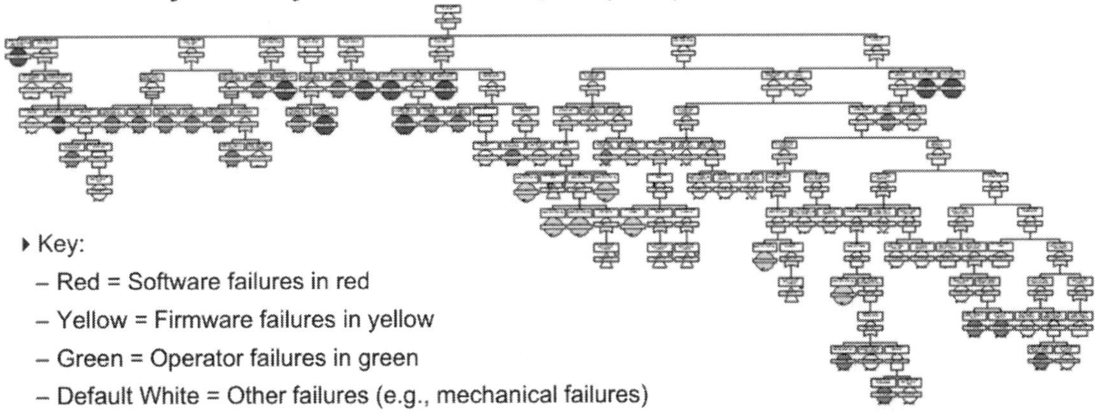

- Key:
  - Red = Software failures in red
  - Yellow = Firmware failures in yellow
  - Green = Operator failures in green
  - Default White = Other failures (e.g., mechanical failures)

Introduction | Background | Assumptions / SCCs | FTA Examples | Case Study | Results | Conclusion | References

Case Study to Verify Initial FTA Examples (cont)

- For this sample fault tree, a Fault Tree application is used including the use of a failure model library to easily and quickly change failure probabilities to perform sensitivity analyses of software failures

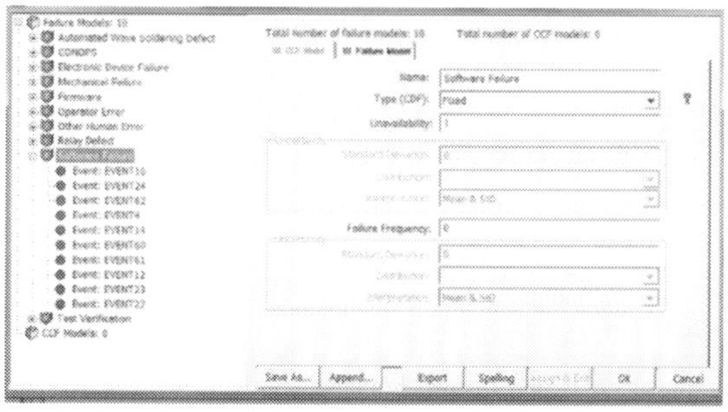

- All other failure probabilities for the various failure models are kept at their assumed failure levels
  - Hardware failures = 1e-4
  - Operator errors = 1e-3

Booz | Allen | Hamilton

20

Introduction | Background | Assumptions / SCCs | FTA Examples | Case Study | Results | Conclusion | References

Case Study Results

Software Failure	Firmware Failure	Top Event Probability – Inadvertent Launch	SCC Determination Trend	SCC Rationale
1 (always fail)	1	1.01e-6	2-SAT	Top Event probability is between 1e-3 to 1e-8 as listed in Table on Slide 17
0.10	1	3.77e-12	3-RFT	Top Event probability is close to 1e-13 as listed in Option 2 Table on Slide 14 when Software Failure is 0.1.
1e-2	1	5.18e-18	3-RFT	Top Event probability is close to 1e-14 as listed in Option 2 Table on Slide 14 when Software Failure is 1e-2.
1e-3	1	4.87e-23	3-RFT	Top Event probability is close to 1e-15 as listed in Option 2 Table on Slide 14 when Software Failure is 1e-3.
1e-6	1	1.22e-29	3-RFT	Top Event probability is close to 1e-18 as listed in Option 2 Table on Slide 14 when Software Failure is 1e-6.
1e-9	1	1.01e-32	3-RFT	Top Event probability is close to 1e-21 as listed in Option 2 Table on Slide 14 when Software Failure is 1e-9.

Cut Set Report (partial)

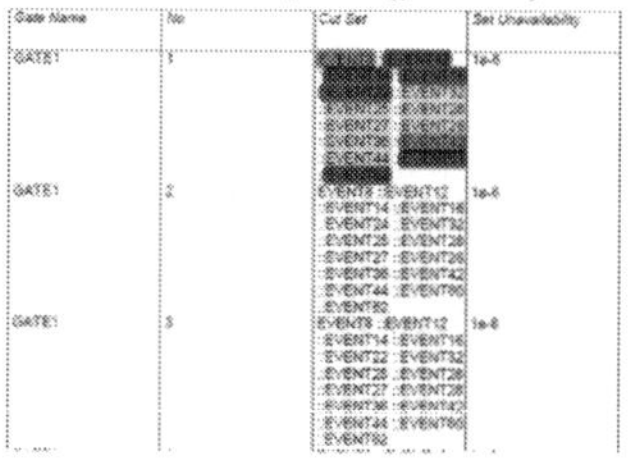

Results – SCC assessed as 2-SAT (conservative assessment); additional verification could be provided by the Cut Set Report, Functional Hazard Analysis (FHA) and System Safety Working Group (SSWG)

Booz | Allen | Hamilton

21

Introduction	Background	Assumptions / SCCs	FTA Examples	Case Study	Results	Conclusion	References

Conclusion

- Quantitative FTAs can be used to verify the SCC level
- Rough approximation of the top event failure probability ranges to determine the SCC when software failure probabilities are set to 1
  - Further refinement may be necessary as additional case studies are performed for more complex and realistic fault tree models
  - Safety interlocks that are software interlocks (e.g., checks and flags, firewalls, bit combinations) are excluded from this paper - Modeling software interlocks could impact the conclusions of this paper
- Cut set reports can also be used to assess the combinations of failures required to cause the top event

Booz | Allen | Hamilton

22

Introduction	Background	Assumptions / SCCs	FTA Examples	Case Study	Results	Conclusion	References

Recommendations

- If it is desired to reduce the SCC, the System Safety Practitioner should closely exam the results of FTAs and cut set reports
- Consider design enhancements that would add additional hardware controls, operator verification, and/or design features into the system functionality to reduce software autonomy
- Lowering the SCC could reduce the SwCI and LOR tasking required, which may save program resources when it comes to performing complex LOR tasks, such as code analysis
  - Understood that in some cases, operational and design requirements will dictate that software functionality for safety critical operations can only be autonomous
  - Inserting additional safety interlocks or operator interventions may not be feasible

Booz | Allen | Hamilton

23

Introduction | Background | Assumptions / SCCs | FTA Examples | Case Study | Results | Conclusion | References

References

- MIL-STD-882E, "Department of Defense Standard Practice System Safety," May 11, 2012.
- Department of Defense (DoD) Joint Software Systems Safety Engineering Handbook (JSSSEH), August 27, 2010.

Booz | Allen | Hamilton

24

Questions?

Robert E. Smith, CSP
Senior Lead Engineer

Booz | Allen | Hamilton

Booz Allen Hamilton
1550 Crystal Dr, Suite 1100
Arlington, VA 22202
Tel (703) 412-7661
smith_bob@bah.com

Booz | Allen | Hamilton

25

Designed-in Logic to Ensure Safety of Integration and Field Engineering of Large Scale CBTC Systems

Fenggang Shi, PhD; Thales Canada Transportation Solutions; Toronto, Canada

Keywords: safety engineering, safety critical system, railway signaling, CBTC system, system integration, system migration safety

Abstract

This paper discusses the necessity and challenges for suppliers of mass transportation signaling systems to design extra safety features on top of modern signaling systems' operational safety properties to support safe integration and migration (i.e. cut-over transition) during field implementation. Suppliers traditionally focus on designing a system to be safe for delivering advanced operation functions and leave the field engineering safety to be managed through procedures. However, with increases of complexity associated with various field integration and migration scenarios as required by customers or enforced by field engineering environments, the stepwise integration and migration of a signaling system itself can raise new hazards, which cannot easily be managed by procedures. There are additional safety challenges in a re-signaling project during migration from the existing legacy system. Thus, this paper suggests that the system's design should have designed-in safety mechanisms to ensure the safety of not only the future operation, but also the field integration and migration. Specifically, it highlights the significance of identifying hazard conditions associated with interactions between the many controllers and devices at each step of system integration and migrations. It then discusses how to manage challenges of designing safety logic to mitigate these field migration hazards.

Introduction

Advanced signaling systems maximally automate train operations to make urban rail transit systems offer high reliability, punctuality, and operational efficiency. In large cities, urban rail transit systems are considered the main approach to resolve traffic difficulties and living environment problems. As the world's population is constantly on the rise, more people are living in cities, which results in:

- Extension of cities in size, requiring constructions of new metro lines and extending tracks of existing ones. This offers green field projects for signaling in new tracks;
- Increase of population density, requiring upgrades of existing lines with advanced signaling systems to improve capacity and efficiency. This situation offers brown field projects to replace or overlay existing signaling systems with more advanced systems.

Almost all signaling projects have very demanding construction schedules and complicated field conditions, which raise significant challenges of how to ensure system integration safety. System integration is a complicated process to compose the system capability by assembling and installing many components and tuning them through testing so that they work together as designed to deliver expected functions and safety features for revenue operation. A more advanced signaling system has more components and functions, thus it needs more time in installation, integration, and commissioning. Also, the railway working environment presents various hazards. Signaling system suppliers and integrators endeavor to find an effective field integration approach on each project to manage schedule and safety risks.

In the signaling domain, Communications-Based Train Control (CBTC) signaling systems are designed based on the most advanced technology from computers and communication networks, which offer not only advanced signaling functions but also the flexibility for incremental implementation and integration. A CBTC system delivers Automatic Train Supervision (ATS) functions for routing trains according to predefined schedules and Automatic Train Operation (ATO) functions for controlling train movement. This can effectively reduce human operation delays and separation distance between trains to improve service capacity. More importantly, comparing against traditional signaling systems, a CBTC system significantly enhances the train operational safety through real-time Automatic Train Protection (ATP) functions, which prevent hazards from human errors, internal failures, or unexpected events resulting in accidents. Because of these mentioned advantages, CBTC systems are very popular in both new mass transit system projects and re-signaling projects.

However, implementing a CBTC system in the real field itself is much more complicated comparing to a traditional interlocking signaling system, leading to great safety challenges. At first, there are many pieces of equipment and devices to be installed in different geographic locations along tracks and each of them must be validated against its specifications fitting in various CBTC functions. Second, the CBTC system itself has a large number of functions delivered by interactions between many controllers, other electronics, and electrical devices. Due to civil construction progress limitations, the field installation, integration, and validation can only be done incrementally when commissioning a system. Third, a re-signaling project has additional complexity from cut-over mechanisms or mixed operation scenarios between the CBTC system and the existing legacy system. Re-signaling projects which upgrade existing service lines raise significant challenges in CBTC integration logic designs. Switching back and forth between legacy systems (for continuing normal operation during service time) and the new CBTC integration (during engineering time for field testing) is naturally prone to hazards.

This paper discusses safety challenges associated with field integration of a CBTC system, and proposes to design safety features in the CBTC system integration logic to ensure field engineering safety. A CBTC system is normally integrated in the manner of track zone by track zone, and thus how to prevent a testing train unintentionally going out of the integration zone needs technical design support. Especially, CBTC field integration and testing on a re-signaling project needs special safety features to ensure safety of cut-over transitions between two systems. This paper proposes an approach to designing safety features into CBTC systems to mitigate their field engineering hazards. These features need systematic efforts to identify and design them as built-in safety logic of the system to support integration safety management. Thus, the approach to developing these safety features should parallel and complement the normal system safety program. The analysis in the proposed approach can enhance traditional system safety engineering programs to achieve designed-in safety logic and safety features to ensure the safety of not only future operation, but also system field integration and migration.

Safety Concerns in CBTC Signaling System Integration and Migration

CBTC system suppliers naturally focus on designing a system to be safe for delivering advanced train operation functions in order to survive as a business in the signaling domain. As enforced by common standards (American Railway Engineering and Maintenance-of-Way Association, 2011; European Committee for Electrotechnical Standardization, 2003; International Electrotechnical Commission, 2002; US Department of Defense, 1993, 2012), a supplier defines and executes a systematic safety engineering program to develop the safety case of a final system to achieve safety certification for service operation. However, there is no standard to obligate suppliers to design safety features in signaling systems to facilitate field integration safety. It is quite common that field engineering safety is managed by procedures. In reality, integration of CBTC systems shows insufficiency of using procedures to mitigate most field hazards due to:

- Increased complexity of CBTC systems, which makes integration steps often have mutual dependency. The partially integrated configuration may show some unexpected behavior against previously defined procedures.
- Various field integration and migration scenarios as enforced by customers, which make procedures very different between projects. Especially, procedures developed for a re-signaling project can be very complicated for managing transitions between the existing legacy system and a configuration of the partially integrated CBTC system. Insufficiency of procedures results in hazards not only in the CBTC integration, but also in the legacy system operation.

Thus, it is necessary to design certain safety features in CBTC systems to facilitate field integration safety management.

Referring to the simplified CBTC system model illustrated in Figure 1, a CBTC system has several kinds of subsystems as follows:

- Automatic Train Supervision (ATS), which consists of a number of controllers located in the control center and interlocking stations. The ATS provides scheduling and automatic routing of trains for continuous operation, and offers user interfaces for operators to command the CBTC system for special operational maneuvers. It commands Zone Controllers to implement trains' routes and control trains' movement authority, as well as to implement operator commands for controlling trackside devices. ATS controllers collect wayside and trackside equipment statuses including train locations to display to operators. The ATS communicates with train onboard controllers to supervise and collect train operation statuses for operators. In a real system, the number of both central and local ATS subsystems often exceeds 10.
- Zone Controller (ZC). The ZC installed for each geographic signaling zone controls and monitors wayside devices, protects each train in the zone, sets up train routes and enforces interlocking, and provides train movement authority for safe train separation from any obstruction. The ZC tracks train locations and status information through communications with train onboard controllers, and detects non-communicating trains based on track block occupancy status. The ZC also monitors trackside devices in a real-time manner, and responds to any failure in these devices by informing trains to react appropriately. In a real system, the number of ZC subsystems exceeds 10.
- Vehicle Onboard Controller (VOBC). The VOBC on a train offers ATO and ATP functions according to the movement authority issued by a ZC. ATP functions in the VOBC ensure the

train to be operated within the current movement authority. The VOBC detects and mitigates failures and unexpected events from train-lines and driver errors. The VOBC determines the train location in real-time based on detected transponders, the internal track map, switch positions from ZC communications, and data from speed sensors and accelerometers. The VOBC reports train position and status to the ATS and the ZC. In a real system, the number of VOBC subsystems can exceed 100.

- Data Communication System (DCS). The DCS is the backbone of the CBTC system to enable all controllers to communicate with each other to deliver the expected CBTC functions. In CBTC designs, the safety and security mechanisms are important built-in properties for safe operations. For reliable communications between CBTC controllers, redundant backbone networks and mobile radio communication networks are used to give the CBTC system flexibility of integration and feasibility of extension in the future.

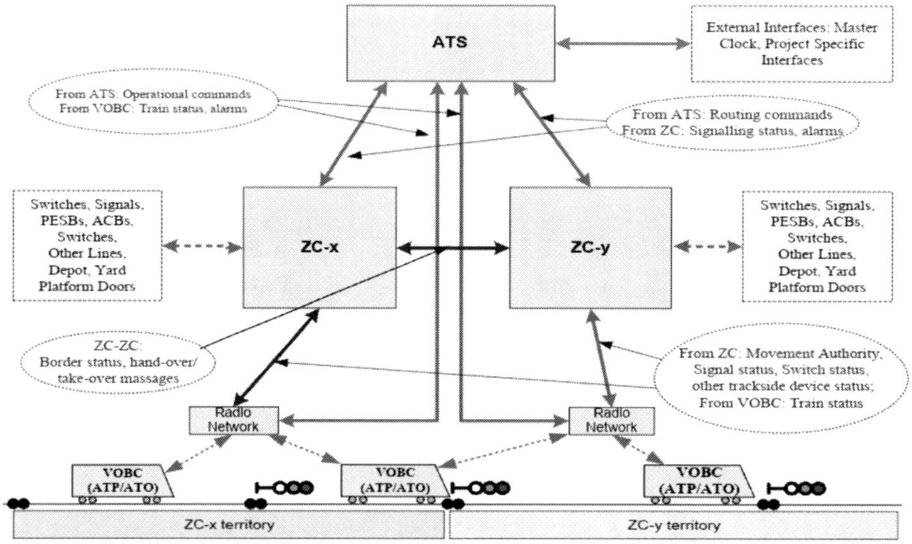

Figure 1 — Abstract CBTC System

Based on our experience of developing CBTC systems on multiple projects (Shi, 2012, 2013), safety of CBTC system integration faces significant challenges to manage the following hazards:

- Hazard 1: High speed train movement intruding into a trackside work zone. During CBTC field integration, people often need to work on the trackside for various reasons, and a train moving into the work area at a high speed is a hazard. It is expected to have some effective technical measures to protect a work zone by enforcing trains be driven manually at low speed in the work zone.
- Hazard 2: Train movement on a moving or unlocked switch. This situation is a hazard resulting in train derailment. During integration, this hazard is raised very often due to using an interlocking route without completing the route validation.
- Hazard 3: Unintended train movement going out of integration testing area. Especially, a train used for the CBTC integration testing may unexpectedly go out of the integration possession area, possibly moving to the installation area where workers are on the track.
- Hazard 4: Unexpected interactions between a certified service zone controller and a zone controller under testing. This situation can raise hazards because the zone controller under

testing may not correctly track train traversal from its territory to the revenue operation zone resulting in train detection and protection errors in the service ZC. The consequences of this hazard can be train collisions.

A re-signaling project not only has the hazards mentioned in the previous paragraph, but also adds hazards from switching back and forth between the existing legacy signaling system and the partially integrated CBTC system. Because the legacy signaling system's service operation must not be interrupted, the CBTC field integration can only be performed at night in a 4 or 5 hour time window. Thus, switching between the existing signaling system and the partially integrated CBTC system is daily routine work, which needs time to power up or down the CBTC devices and also to confirm both systems' working condition on each transition. All these make the CBTC integration time window even smaller, which increase the risk to project schedules. Thus, it is important to design special safety mechanisms that can confidently let CBTC controllers stay in the powered up state (i.e. a shadow mode) during legacy system service operation hours. Because these CBTC controllers have not been validated to be safe, they may intrude on the legacy system. The following conditions are hazards:

- Hazard 5: CBTC controllers under integration intruding into legacy system service operation may result in hazards in the legacy signaling train separation functions leading to collisions.
- Hazard 6: Legacy system intruding into the CBTC integration. Possible hazardous conditions can be created due to conflicting switch lock control resulting in a CBTC test train derailment.

Field integration of a signaling system has many chances to result in the above mentioned hazards during field integration. Hazard 1 and Hazard 2 are noteworthy hazardous conditions for almost all signaling projects. If a project strongly demands early revenue service, the new signaling system often has to be opened incrementally in a track zone by track zone manner. In such a situation, Hazard 3 and Hazard 4 are notable safety concerns. Re-signaling projects are notorious difficulties and have the extra distinguished hazards: Hazard 5 and Hazard 6.

Systematic Approach to Designing Safety Features for Integration and Migration

As discussed in the previous section, the safe integration logic with sufficient safety features for ensuring field integration of a system should be systematically designed into the system. These safety features are expected to simplify field procedures to reduce the risk of hazards associated with system integration. The effectiveness of these features in the integration logic is strongly related to the integration approach on a project. An effective integration approach lays the foundation for defining and designing practical safety features into the system to ensure safety of field integration and to meet the customer's integration requirements. Also, these safety features should be part of the future CBTC system safety properties and must be developed based on reviewing previous projects' integration experience, analyzing the current projects' integration plans, and predicting future CBTC integration scenarios. Thus, these safety features not only facilitate integration hazard management on a project but will also be used in the final system for managing special operation needs and maintenance scenarios.

In essence, the systematic approach for developing these safety features as part of the system integration logic follows the generic safety engineering process:

- Performing hazard analysis, which includes identifying hazards in possible engineering activities in various integration scenarios and environment conditions associated with the system integration and migration approach. The outputs of hazard analyses result in enhancing the integration and migration plan and defining corresponding technical hazard mitigations to be specified as safety requirements;
- Designing safety features to meet these safety requirements and implementing them in hardware and software, as well as defining the necessary instructions for using these features;
- Validating and demonstrating the safety features in both in-house and field testing to ensure their correctness in supporting field system integration and testing.

For identifying all possible contributors in the system integration and testing phase to the hazards mentioned in the previous section, the hazard analyses are performed from the following aspects for identifying practical and effective safety features:

- Hazardous conditions from external factors, which may exist in customer's requirements and field engineering constraints for system integration and commissioning. Mitigations to these conditions are imported inputs for defining safety features.
- Possible incomplete validation of interlocking routes resulting in train traversal to an unlocked switch during integration testing and subsequent derailment. In reality, integration testing often needs trains going through a switch that has not completed validation of its locking logic on all related routes. Thus, identifying all possible contributors to the switch hazards and their corresponding mitigations is very important for field integration testing.
- Unexpected behavior or conditions in controllers' interactions in a partially integrated system configuration. The corresponding analysis needs to cover possible combinations of controllers and devices as a field configuration during system integration and testing. This analysis leads to enhancing existing safety mechanisms or adding new safety features.
- Defects in the integration strategy, which may lead to a hazardous sequence of integration. With consideration of possible errors from intensive human involvement during integration, the analysis leads to consolidating the integration strategy and adding safety features for ensuring the safety of transitions from one step to the next during integration and testing.

Based on the attributes of the CBTC system configuration and previous field integration experience, including lessons learned from previous projects, the effective integration strategy is the incremental integration to be carried out in control zone by control zone as follows:

- Control Zone internal integration: Under the condition that the zone under integration is isolated from its neighboring zones, all devices and controllers in this control zone are integrated against their responsibilities with the exemption of interfaces with the neighboring zones.
- Control Zones' interface integration: When two neighboring zones have their internal integration completed, the interface integration between them can be started and subsequently completed for delivering CBTC train functions.

Thus, the hazard analyses can be divided into two categories: hazards associated with the zone internal integration and hazards associated with zone interfaces for integrating any two zones.

Safety features for supporting CBTC system integration and testing must be effective in design and correct in implementation. They are derived from the hazard mitigations mentioned above with consideration of reusing existing CBTC safety properties. All safety features are designed in software and hardware to meet vitality. On a project, due to customization driven by guideway data and environmental constraints, they must be verified and validated through in-house and field testing to ensure their correctness before use.

Expected Safety Features in CBTC Designs to Prevent Field Integration Hazards

From our practice on multiple CBTC projects and knowledge of possible challenges in integration of future CBTC systems, we expect to design the generic integration logic and safety features in the CBTC product. They can be customized for managing various integration and migration scenarios requested by customers or limited by field environment conditions. By applying the systematic approach as described in the previous section, we have analyzed the current projects' integration plans and our CBTC integration experience on previous projects, as well as possible field engineering scenarios predicted for future projects. This systematic analysis effort leads us to determine the generic integration strategy, the integration logic and safety features as designed-in properties of the CBTC product. The design of these features offers flexibility to customize these safety features on a project for ensuring safety of the system integration and migration. This approach has been demonstrated as effective on the current projects' field integration and migration scenarios.

The safety features are designed at first to facilitate safety management of integrating all devices in a zone (i.e. a zone internal integration) and re-signaling project cut-over migrations within a zone, and then to provide safety mechanisms for integrating any two zones for testing train traversal through the zone boundary. There are different integration and migration scenarios in a zone internal integration, which are chosen by either the customer or the integrator on a project. These safety features offer the flexibility to support these scenarios by defining the integration and migration steps, which satisfy the customer's expectation and make the cost effective tradeoffs for the integrator. Also considering possible human operator errors in enabling and disabling safety features during the system integration and migration, the safety features are designed with diverse logic to overlap each other to mitigate a hazard condition. As a result of our effort, the following safety features are designed in the CBTC product:

- Safety features for a zone internal integration and testing to use:
  - Work Zone protection, which prohibits a train in an automatic mode from entering into the zone and enforces a low speed for a manual train. This feature mitigates Hazard 1.
  - Automatic Train Mode Inhibit Zone, which can require a train travel through the zone in a manual train operation mode other than an automatic mode. This feature can be used to further mitigate Hazard 1.
  - Operator Switch lock, which enables the operator to lock a switch in a specific position to prevent it moving to the other position by a route calling and it also only permits a manual train route to go through it, which enforce a testing train to be driven in manually at a quite low speed. This is designed to mitigate Hazard 2.
  - Operator Switch Blocking, which enables the operator to block any switch movement command and prevent any movement authority to be granted to an approaching train to go to the blocked switch. This is designed to mitigate Hazard 2 and Hazard 3 in the case of the switch being used to limit the testing area.
  - Lock a signal on Red, which locks a signal in Red even if its permissive condition is true. This feature is intended to prevent a manually driven train from moving into a work

zone, and can be used to enforce the ends of the testing area. This is designed to mitigate Hazard 3 for any train regardless its mode to stop before the signal, and also Hazard 4 by locking the boundary entry signal to Red of a service zone to prevent any train entry.

  - Close Tracks, which prevents a CBTC train movement to or within these tracks. This feature can be used for managing emergency situations encountered during integration testing. This feature can also be used further to mitigate Hazard 3 by closing the end tracks of a testing area and Hazard 4 by closing the testing zone boundary tracks.
  - Temporary Speed Restriction (or Go Slow Zone), which can require a CBTC controlled train to travel at the intended low speed in a specific track zone during integration. This feature can be used for mitigating Hazard 1 by setting a lower speed on top of a work zone protection and Hazard 3 by setting zero speed at the end tracks of a testing area.
- Safety features for supporting integration between zones to prevent Hazard 2 and other train operation hazards on a zone boundary, which include:
  - The safety futures mentioned for zone internal integration to manage the border area by setting Temporary Speed and Automatic Train Mode Inhibit Zone.
  - The following are existing CBTC safety logic, which can be validated first and then used further to facilitate the hazard management during integration of two control zones:
    - Crossing border route interlocking: All routes crossing a ZC-ZC border have interlocking logic, and the authorization of each route in the hand-over zone (i.e. departure zone) has the pre-condition that the take-over zone (i.e. destination zone) has already locked and authorized the portion of the route in its territory. This ensures safety of train traversal across the zone boundary.
    - Crossing border route cancellation interlocking: If the operator cancels a crossing border route, the take-over zone can cancel the portion of the route if only if the hand-over zone completes its cancellation. This ensures that the train approaching the route or already on the route has stopped before the route is cancelled.
- Safety features for separating two control zones to prohibit trains' traversal: This is designed as further mitigation of Hazard 4 for the case that one zone is already in service operation while the other zone is still under integration testing. These features are explained as follows:
  - Closing border, which closes a specific border of a control zone with its neighboring zone to prevent any train going to the neighboring zone and also to prohibit a train entry from the neighboring zone into its territory. This feature can be used in the service zone controller with safety confidence.
  - Prohibit collaboration with another zone controller, which can be used to inform a revenue operation zone controller not to make train detection and tracking decisions based on any information from the neighboring zone controller under integration and testing. This prevents any testing zone's error in tracking a train crossing the border from causing failures of detecting a non-communicating train entry in the revenue zone.
- Safety features for migrating Hazard 5 and Hazard 6, which are designed for managing cut-over between the legacy signaling system and the CBTC system under integration:
  - Cut-over box in a control zone, which is a vital hardware mechanism to switch trackside device controls exclusively between the CBTC system and the legacy signaling system. This cut-over box switching status can be used to trigger the CBTC zone controller to go to a shadow mode, in which no outputs from it can reach physical devices, and vice versa for the legacy system. It is also important that the zone controller in shadow mode should not generate a movement authority to be used for any train. To ensure this,

related trains need to know the ZC mode and have cut-over mechanisms as well for safety of the legacy system operation.

  - Cut-over switch for a train, which is a vital switch circuit that can switch the train to be controlled either by the controller of the legacy system or by the VOBC of the CBTC system exclusively. When a train is controlled by the legacy system controller, the VOBC outputs are cut off (i.e. no capability to command the train system). The VOBC will inform the ZC that it is in the cut off state (also known as the shadow mode). If the ZC is in control, the train can only be routed by using the fixed block logic.

The safety features mentioned above are designed in the CBTC product based on a generic CBTC system integration strategy (in the manner of control zone by control zone). On a project, the integration and cut-over plan will be made by following the generic integration strategy to define effective integration steps by using the built-in safety features to satisfy the customer integration requirements and specific environment constraints.

Based on our practice on the integration and migration of several CBTC systems, the designed-in safety features have demonstrated their effectiveness in mitigating hazards associated with the system integration and migration, which significantly reduced the field integration schedule risk on these projects. For a specific project, the CBTC product including these safety features is customized by the specific guideway data (such as tracks, blocks, platforms, and zones) and trackside physical devices (such switches, signals, and platform doors). The system integration as planned is performed in steps for zone internal integration or the integration between zones. These safety features must be validated as early as possible in the first integration zone, and can then be used in subsequent integration activities. For each remaining zone, these safety features only need to test their correspondence with the trackside devices and guideway data in the zone to achieve safety and efficiency of integration and testing in the zone. Internal integration of a control zone consists of the following steps:

1. Pre- and Post- Installation Check Out tests of all devices, which confirm that each device is qualified and connections between these devices are correct as designed.
2. Element functional tests, which verify functionality of each trackside device as specified and qualify trains for the CBTC VOBC to control.
3. Integrating CBTC wayside core safety functions, which verify switch movement and locking logic, route setting and interlocking. Especially, the designed safety features for supporting integration must be validated through field testing.
4. Testing ATP functions with protection provided by the safety features. Testing train interfaces first and then the positioning function. Subsequently, integrate the rest of ATP functions incrementally.
5. Testing ATO functions, which now have protection provided by ATP functions.

The integration of two zones which have their internal integration done is not complicated in our practice because safety features have been tested and can now be used in this integration. The crossing border route interlocking and the crossing border route cancellation interlocking need to be tested first and then train traversal boundary logic can be tested.

For a project with re-signaling or multiple stage opening attributes, the cut-over box in a control zone and the cut-over switch for a train must be tested before other integration testing. This can support the CBTC equipment to stay in a powered on state while trains operate in the legacy signaling system. After validation of the zone separation safety features (closing border and prohibiting collaboration with another zone controller) is done, they can be used to manage safety of the boundary between a revenue zone and a zone under integration.

Conclusion

Integration of a large scale safety critical system such as a CBTC system itself has various hazards that need mitigations from safety features to be designed into the system. This paper presented a systematic approach for developing these expected safety features as an important part of the system integration logic. Based on our experience on a number of CBTC projects, the safety features designed in the CBTC system in this approach have demonstrated their effectiveness to ensure safety of the CBTC systems' integration and testing, as well as safety of switching back and forth between a legacy and CBTC system on a re-signaling project.

The safety features developed in the systematic approach discussed in this paper can be used not only to facilitate safety management during the system integration and testing, but also to offer safety measures for the final system with respect to failure management and corrective maintenance.

References

American Railway Engineering and Maintenance-of-Way Association. (2011). Communications & signals manual of Recommended Practice. *AREMA.*

European Committee for Electrotechnical Standardization. (2003). Railway applications – Communication, signaling, and processing systems – Safety related electronic systems for signalling (CENELEC EN 50129).

International Electrotechnical Commission. (2002). Railway applications – the specification and demonstration of dependability, reliability, availability, maintainability and safety (RAMS) *IEC 62278* (CENELEC EN 50126).

US Department of Defense. (1993). Military Standard MIL-STD-882C. System Safety Program Requirements.

US Department of Defense. (2012). Military Standard MIL-STD-882E. Standard Practice System Safety.

Shi, F. (2012). A safety engineering practice, experience, and confidence on integration of a large scale CBTC system. *Proceedings of the ISSC, 2012.*

Shi, F. (2013). Achieving safety confidence of a large scale system product and its applications. *Proceedings of the ISSC, 2013.*

Materials and Substances Declaration in the Aerospace and Defense Industry

Author: Timothy J. Sheehan, CIH, CSP, PE; Raytheon; Portsmouth, RI USA

Keywords: substance, declaration, IPC-1754, AD-DSL, NAS411, HMTL

Abstract

Managing product-related chemical (materials[1] and substances) regulatory compliance, product safety and supply chain risks is critical and challenging for the Aerospace and Defense (AD) industry as chemical regulatory requirements continue to emerge and evolve. Materials and substances declaration is being used increasingly to obtain information from both the supply chain and in-house manufacturing processes to support product-related compliance and supply risk management efforts. This paper identifies and discusses recent AD industry declaration standardization and support development activities, specifically the recent release of IPC-1754. It is expected that the use of the new standard and related industry-developed support tools will greatly enhance the ability to meet company and customer information needs. As an example, the paper will discuss how standardized declarations are expected to support meeting contracted product reporting and system safety efforts for military acquisition hardware.

Background

In order to address the increasing regulatory and availability pressures on the materials and chemicals required to make and/or maintain hardware products, AD companies must obtain more information from their supply chains regarding the chemical content of parts and components they purchase. As with many other industries, AD companies are turning to materials and substances declaration processes to obtain information from their supply chains in order to obtain such information for their own purposes, as well as to provide information to their customers.

In its common usage, materials and substances declaration is meant to denote the reporting of product-related materials and substances data in a specified format, comprised of defined, standardized data elements. Use of a standardized approach allows suppliers to better anticipate and prepare for inquiries about the chemicals that are contained in the hardware products they deliver to customers. In order to consistently obtain such data, companies may use contract requirements for product declarations from direct suppliers. Requirements to provide information may be "flowed' through the supply chain; through each supplier "tier", information is then provided from supplier to customer. The ability to obtain information from even the most remote portions of the hardware supply chain is critically important, as the chemical composition of finished industry product may be affected at any point in the supply chain due to supplier product manufacturing processes (e.g, from welding, coating application, etc.) at each supply chain tier.

Industry Efforts to Development Declaration Capabilities

The International Aerospace Environmental Group (IAEG®; www.iaeg.com) "…was created to collaborate on and share innovative environmental solutions for the (AD) industry…" (IAEG, 2016). One of the initial projects established by IAEG was to develop a common format for the

[11] The term "material" is used herein to designate a mixture of at least one substance.

use of materials and substances declarations that would provide efficiencies across the industry and supply chain. Members of the AD industry (along with suppliers and consultants) have also been heavily involved in the development of the recently-published materials and substances declaration standard, IPC-1754. The IPC-1754 standard, titled *Materials and Substances Declaration for Aerospace and Defense and Other Industries* is expected to form the basis of industry declaration activities. The standard allows considerable flexibility in the information that can be provided in declarations, including optional data elements, some of which are discussed further below. In its industry support role, IAEG is developing tools and supporting information that are consistent with IPC-1754. These tools can be used to enhance efficiency in developing and providing material and substance declarations within the industry and its supply chain.

Declarable Substance List

Materials and substances subject to declarations are also good targets for standardization. Anticipating that various customers will have widely different requirements related to supplier products, some manufacturers and suppliers are providing complete substance breakdowns of their hardware products, a result commonly known as a "Full Substance (or Material) Declaration" (FSD, or FMD). The ability to obtain and report such information can be logistically challenging for many suppliers since the availability of FSD information is limited, especially for more-complex assemblies such as radios or power units. As a result, IAEG has focused on developing a list of substances subject to global regulatory requirements, where critical information may be needed by industry members. This list is known as the Aerospace and Defence Declarable Substances List, or AD-DSL, and currently contains approximately 1200 priority chemical substances. According to IAEG, the AD-DSL is "a list of industry product-related declarable substances reflecting regulatory impacts within the A&D industry and its supply chain" (IAEG, 2017). Use of the AD-DSL, in conjunction with IPC-1754 declarations is intended to standardize the substances being reported, thus allowing supply chains to better prepare information on a limited number of substances.

IPC-1754 Features

IPC-1754 is designed to be used by any industry which produces hardware articles, and is the latest standard developed under the IPC "175X family" of declaration standards. IPC-1754 is designed to be compatible with information provided by other declaration standards, most notably declarations compliant with IPC-1752A, *Materials Declaration Management* that is currently in use in the electronics industry. The standard is designed to support the exchange of product data between customers and their direct suppliers throughout the supply chain, and can support product substance content comparisons against both materials-based substance compliance requirements, as well as hardware (article) based compliance requirements. The standard identifies standard data elements, some of which are mandatory fields (e.g., supplier identity, product information, etc.). The standard also supports optional data elements features that can be used to address company needs, such as the use of numbered Bill of Materials (BOM) levels used to identify the specific compositions of components in complex hardware. IPC-1754 provides an Extensible Markup Language (XML) declaration template that can be used to support the electronic transfer of data between supplier and customer. The XML data format also supports the use of the declaration data across differing company data management structures and applications. The electronic data transfer capability will become increasingly valuable as use of the standard expands in the supply chain, allowing companies to manage and share declaration data across their activities for risk analysis and data reuse.

IPC-1754 provides several new data elements over other IPC-175X standards, including the grouping of chemically-similar, but physically different products under a common declaration for ease of reporting (e.g., rivets of different dimensions made of the same alloy). IPC-1754 also supports the optional declaration for "process" chemicals that are defined by IPC-1754 as those substances required for product manufacturing, operation, maintenance, repair, refurbishment or overhaul. Although the use of the process substance declarations in IPC-1754 is voluntary, its use will become important to help identify industry supply chain dependencies on substances that are at-risk of constrained availability which might not be evident or contained in product declarations alone. The use of process declarations is fairly new in industry and there may be concerns from suppliers that may not wish to disclose product manufacturing information they deem as proprietary.

The use of optional data fields affords considerable flexibility and customization, supporting various information needs among companies using IPC-1754 as the basis for their declaration processes. For example, the standard allows the substance product concentration thresholds to be set for supplier reporting, allowing focus on those substances where the concentration above the threshold might be deemed as the critical indicator of risk.

In its simplest form, an IPC-1754 declaration can be comprised of statements of product-related information, such as the mere absence of AD-DSL substances in the delivered product, or the presence of certain materials (such as conflict minerals or biocides); this is known as an IPC-1754 "Class E" declaration. Alternatively, declarations can be used to report the substances in the AD-DSL that are contained in delivered hardware products, in a "Class F" declaration. The standard also supports the expansion of the requested substance information beyond AD-DSL substances to additional substances (i.e., those not listed in the AD-DSL), allowing companies to obtain information in an IPC-1754 "Class G" declaration which may extend supplier substance information all the way to an FSD.

Declaration Support for the AD Industry

Although it provides the data elements and rules that govern declaration development, the standard does not provide a data form to develop and provide declaration information. As with other related IPC-175X "family" declaration standards, supporting "solution providers" are expected to provide declaration forms, tools and support for individual company declaration activities. Several key service providers were involved in IPC declaration standard development and are expected to also support IPC-1754 declarations. Anticipating a need by some suppliers who may not have data management systems in place, another tool known has the Aerospace and Defence Substance Reporting Tool (AD-SRT) has been developed by IAEG to provide a basic MS Excel declaration form that complies with the IPC-1754 data elements. That basic form will be soon available for download on the IAEG website.

Uses of Declaration Data

As indicated above, there are many uses of data provided by IPC-1754 declarations. Most prominently, product substance content information provides insight into product composition, supporting product compliance determinations such as those required for Restriction of Hazardous Substances (RoHS) regulations or "Communications" requirements under Article 33 of the European Registration, Evaluation, Authorisation and Restriction of Chemicals (REACH) regulation.

Another use of the declaration information would be to identify business continuity risks that may result from a company's, or its supply chain's dependence on substances constrained by regulatory or market conditions. These risks may arise by regulatory action restricting the manufacturing, sale, import and/or use of substances, or may be due to other impacts such as the non-availability of raw materials, natural disasters or geopolitical actions (e.g. embargos affecting supply). Any of these impacts on a chemical supply may trigger the reformulation of chemical products which may necessitate lengthy processes to qualify replacement formulations. Having information on dependence on specific substances would allow industry companies to identify timely risk management measures, such as seeking alternate sources of supplied products or materials, before impacts are realized.

Another prominent use of declaration data is to anticipate product-related substance risks to human health and/or the environment over the product life cycle. Using declaration information generated internally and from the supply chain, product designers and developers can make informed decisions about lifecycle product compliance and risk in the design phase, when changes can be made most feasibly. Knowing the chemical content of products, and those required for use, maintenance, repair, refurbishment or overhaul supports making proper management decisions over the product lifecycle to minimize risks.

Declarations in the US Defense Industry

For US military systems supplied by the defense industry (such as aircraft, weapons or radars), substance reporting requirements are contained in two separate standards: National Aerospace Standard 411 (NAS411), *Hazardous Material Management Program;* and MIL-STD-882E, *Standard Practice - System Safety*. Both standards require industry reporting to military customers of hazardous substances in supplied system equipment, and those required for operations and support activities. These standards focus on identifying and managing risks to human health and the environment over the system lifecycle, including during the disposal or reuse of system materials. The hazardous substances information is used to assess risks where exposures to chemical hazards by humans and/or the environment are possible, and is combined with exposure characterization and assessment, supporting the development of proper risk management measures to reduce unacceptable product-related risks. Further, declaration information is initially provided in the design phase of the product development cycle, when risk management is most effective and efficient in mitigating risks associated with the use and support of military hardware.

US Defense Requirements

NAS411 and MIL-STD-882E, Task 108 (*Hazardous Material Management Plan*) are commonly used together on defense system acquisition contracts to identify, report and minimize hazardous material risks to human health and the environment. Task 108 identifies reporting and risk management requirements, while NAS411 provides the methodology to assess and select materials and substances in order to minimize product lifecycle risk for "targeted" hazardous materials. NAS411/Task 108 requirements are supported by the use of NAS411-1, *Hazardous Materials Target List* (HMTL), a recently-developed, separate list representing a common source of substances subject to reporting for military system acquisition programs. For increased risk management control, these standards also have an established risk category ("Prohibited"), with requirements that restrict the use of high-risk substances such as hexavalent chromium, mercury or asbestos in system designs, unless prior military customer approvals are obtained. The HMTL focuses on the needs of the military customer by including substances imposing not only applicable regulatory risk (as was the basis for the AD-DSL), but also operational risks associated with system operations, maintenance and repair (e.g. use of flammable liquids) for substances may not be regulated by hardware-related regulatory requirements (e.g., acetone).

Defense Hazardous Substance Reporting

Currently, hazardous substance reporting for military acquisition hardware is typically accomplished by a supplier providing an HMMP Report (HMMPR) to the military customer as a contractually-required document. However, HMMPRs can be provided in a wide variety of non-standard formats, including text and/or tables. A non-standard document format often makes it difficult to centrally store data for access by the end user of the delivered hardware. For a variety of reasons (including increased format compatibility), IPC-1754 could be used to facilitate electronic data exchange to a military customer using NAS411-1, AD-DSL, or other customer selected substance lists. IPC-1754 could also provide a possible basis for electronic data exchange in support of MIL-STD-882E risk assessment requirements. Electronically transferred data through the supply chain could then increase the efficiency, lower costs, and facilitate the availability of the data to military end users across many defense product programs and types.

Putting it All Together for the AD Industry

Because many AD companies manage both commercial and defense product lines, it is expected that IPC-1754 and the AD-DSL will form the basis for obtaining information from the supply chain. AD companies will use internal manufacturing and product support data, along with IPC-1754 and the AD-DSL, in supply chain declarations to support meeting commercial reporting requirements, as well as defense acquisition programs reporting requirements contained in MIL-STD-882E/NAS411/HMTL. Declaration data, along with hazard and product support information, will support the assessment and management of lifecycle risks for military products, including during system reuse or disposal.

Future Directions

With the new IPC standard and support capabilities developed by IAEG, the AD industry must now focus on expanding and supporting both industry, and supply chain capacity to provide quality product material and substance declarations. As this capacity increases over time, industry companies will be able to more effectively focus resources on identifying elevated regulatory and related supply risks. Such data will also support identifying critical needs for the development of specific alternative substances and/or processes that could be addressed through various industry collaborations. The increased availability of product-related data on materials and substances will also promote making informed design decisions to reduce regulatory and supply chain risks. For military system programs, the use of an industry standard format containing data that can be supplied and managed electronically could enable data use for multiple purposes, most notably efficiently conducting risk assessments across many DoD acquisition programs at once, and being able to share and reuse data that has already been provided.

References

Aerospace Industries Association (2013). *National Aerospace Standard 411, Hazardous Material Management Program*. Arlington, VA, USA

Association Connecting Electronics Industries (2018). *IPC-1754, Materials and Substances Declaration for Aerospace and Defense and Other Industries,* Bannockburn, IL, USA

Aerospace Industries Association (2016). *National Aerospace Standard 411-1, Hazardous Materials Target List,* Arlington VA, USA

International Aerospace Environmental Group. (2016) *About Us*, Retrieved June 19, 2018 from: http://www.iaeg.com/about/

International Aerospace Environmental Group. (2017). *Aerospace and Defense Declarable Substances List (AD-DSL), Version 2*. Warrendale, PA, USA

US Department of Defense (2012), *System Safety Standard Practice*

FREQUENTIS
FOR A SAFER WORLD

Hands-On System Safety Basics, Focused on FHA

W. Winkelbauer

August 2018

Content

1. **What is System Safety?**
2. **Basic Definitions / Terminology**
3. **Safety Process and Methodologies**

+ Supporting Case Study

  FREQUENTIS

What Is System Safety?

Questions

1. **What is System Safety all about?**

2. **Why is System Safety necessary?**

3. ***What do we* need for System Safety?**

Question 1

What is System Safety all about?

Objectives

- **Minimize risk of accidents**
- **With reasonable costs**
- **Systematic approach**

Example: ICAO Safety Definition

- The **state** in which the possibility of **harm to persons** or of property damage **is reduced to**, and maintained at or below, an **acceptable level** through a continuing process of hazard identification and safety risk management
- Controlled risk and controlled error are acceptable in an inherently safe system
- No approach like this…

Fly – Crash – Fix - Fly

Benefits

- Saving of lives …

  … and huge amounts of money

(considering lifecycles and not only the next milestone!)

  FREQUENTIS

Question 2

Why is System Safety necessary?

  FREQUENTIS

Motivation to System Safety

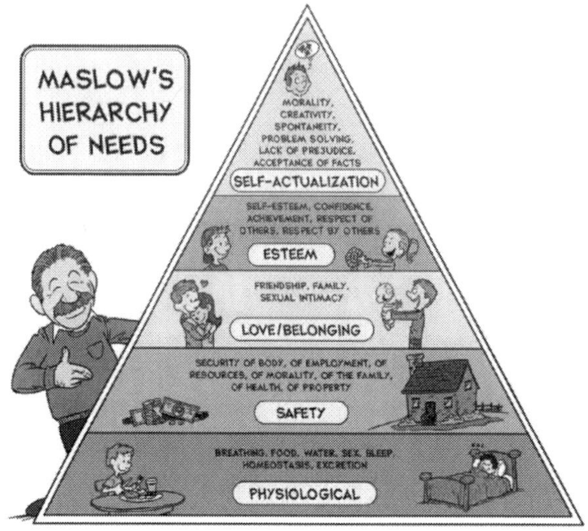

Reasons

- Systems used to be simple ...

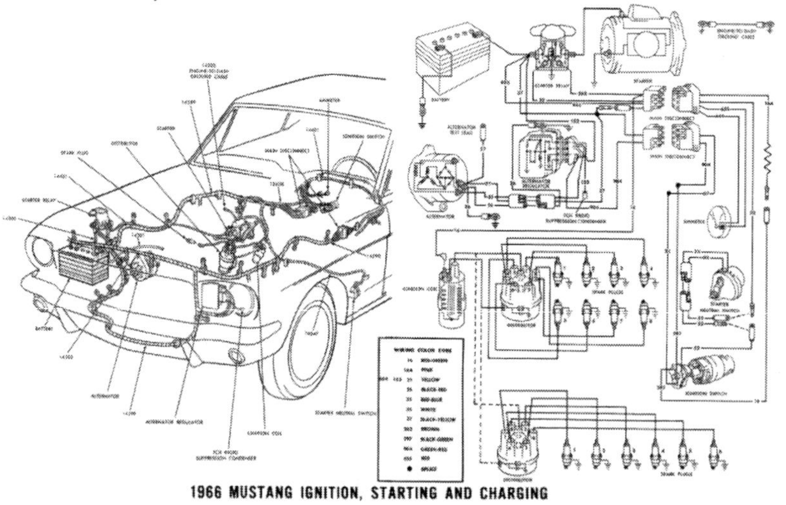

1966 MUSTANG IGNITION, STARTING AND CHARGING

Reasons

- A single person could understand them completely

… but they are not any more!

Reasons

- ~ 100 microprocessor-based electronic control units
- ~ 10.000 controlled signals
- ~ 100 million lines of code

Operational Context

Systems of Systems

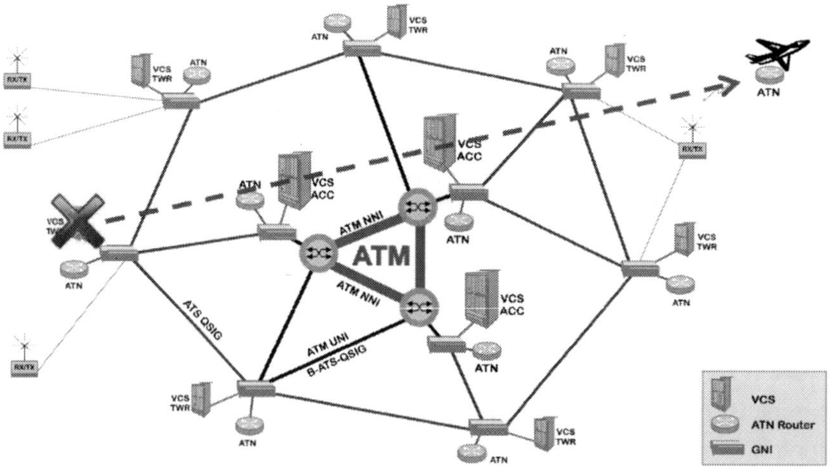

Systematic Approach Necessary

- Increased complexity
- Pace of technology change
- Safety relevant tasks are more and more centralised and automated
- Growing safety awareness of broad public
  - with often less personal sense of responsibility
  - resulting in more stringent product liability laws and standards/regulations

- Therefore a systematic, team-based approach is necessary
  ...to ensure completeness and avoid omissions

FREQUENTIS

Question 3

What do we need for System Safety?

FREQUENTIS

What Do We Need?

- **Safety Policy**: Commitment from top management
  - the importance of safety
  - the responsibility of all employees
- **Safety Culture**
  - awareness of all
- **Safety Management**
  - Organisation
  - Trainings / Communication / Promotion
- **Safety Engineering**
  - Hands on System Safety Work in projects

... this is near-sighted!

"We've saved a lot of money with this safety plan so far."

Undesirable Safety Culture

Mandatory Mindcheck

"Sorry, your mind isn't on safety.
You'll have to go out
and come in again."

Safety has to grow up with care ...

23 | Hands-On System Safety Basics | © 2017 Frequentis AG FREQUENTIS

...that this never happens...

24 | Hands-On System Safety Basics | © 2017 Frequentis AG FREQUENTIS

Basic Definitions

25 | Hands-On System Safety Basics | © 2017 Frequentis AG

FREQUENTIS

What is a Hazard?

- Accidents (= mishaps) arise from hazards
- Hazard
  - "an accident waiting to happen"
  - a condition of the platform that, unless mitigated, can develop into an accident through a sequence of normal events and actions
  - ICAO: A hazard is defined as a condition or an object with the potential to cause injuries to personnel, damage to equipment or structures, loss of material, or reduction of ability to perform a prescribed function.
- Examples:
  - oil spilled on staircase
  - failed train detection system at an automatic railway level crossing
  - loss of thrust control on a jet engine

26 | Hands-On System Safety Basics | © 2017 Frequentis AG

FREQUENTIS

Failure Modes - Hazards - Accidents

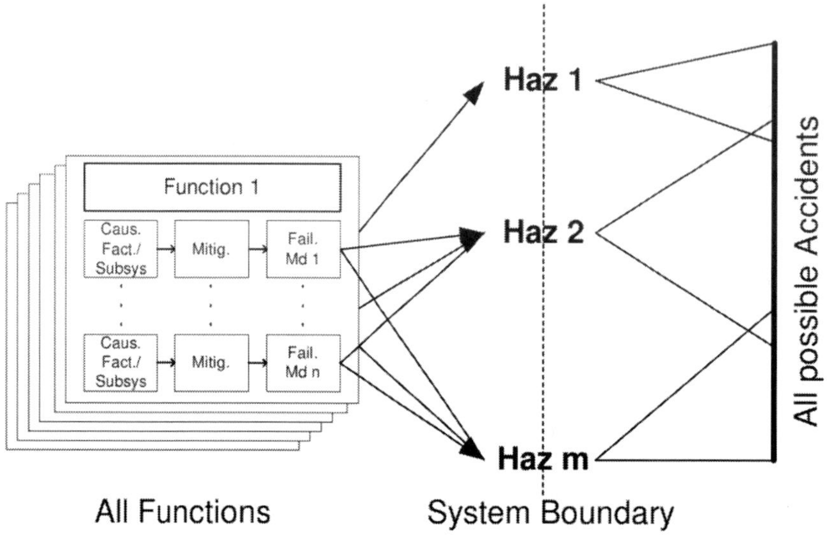

FREQUENTIS

Failure Modes - Hazards - Accidents

- Bow-Tie Diagram

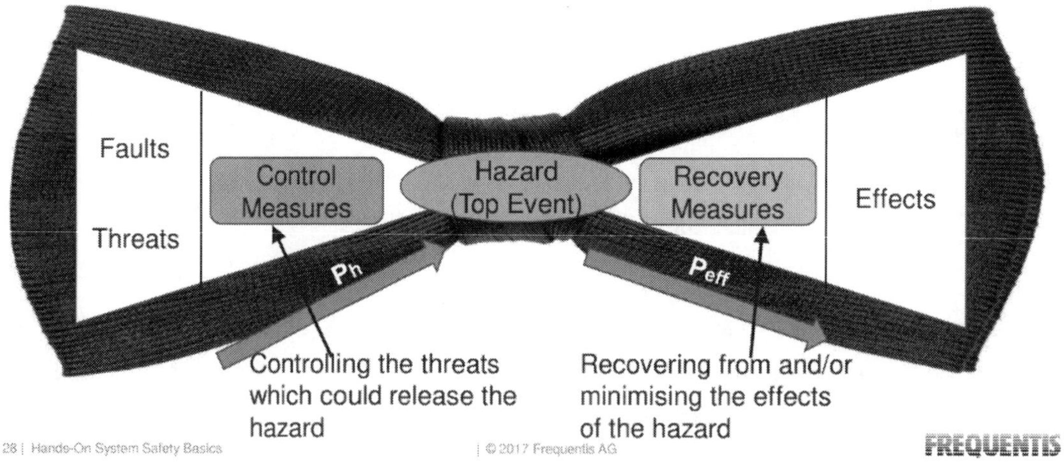

FREQUENTIS

Failure Modes – Hazards – Accidents

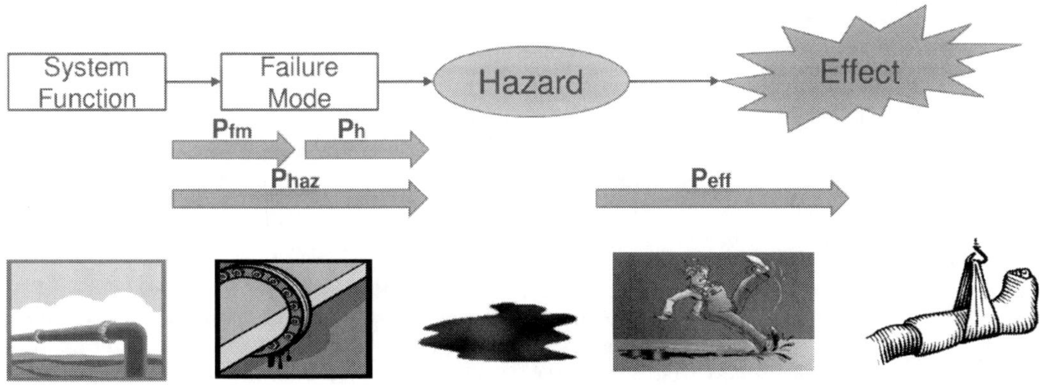

What is Risk?

- Safety Risk associated with a hazard
  - Product of the probability and severity of hazard's consequences (i.e. accidents)

Risk = Probability x Severity

- Probability
  - How probable is the hazard/accident?
    - Per operation hour / during system lifetime / typical operation
- Severity
  - How severe is the accident?
    - Consequences on man (death, injury etc)
    - Environmental consequences (contamination, pollution, etc.)

Hazard Severity

- Hazard Severity Categories permit qualitative description of worst case credible consequences of hazard
- Below is an example definition of categories (from MIL-STD-882D)
  - usually defined either by regulatory context or through agreement with customer

Description	Category	Environmental, Safety, and Health Result Criteria
Catastrophic	I	Could result in death, permanent total disability, loss exceeding $1M, or irreversible severe environmental damage that violates law or regulation.
Critical	II	Could result in permanent partial disability, injuries or occupational illness that may result in hospitalization of at least three personnel, loss exceeding $200K but less than $1M, or reversible environmental damage causing a violation of law or regulation.
Marginal	III	Could result in injury or occupational illness resulting in one or more lost work days(s), loss exceeding $10K but less than $200K, or mitigatible environmental damage without violation of law or regulation where restoration activities can be accomplished.
Negligible	IV	Could result in injury or illness not resulting in a lost work day, loss exceeding $2K but less than $10K, or minimal environmental damage not violating law or regulation.

Hazard Probability

- Use historical results, analysis, and engineering judgement to determine appropriate qualitative probability category
- Again, particular interpretation will typically be defined by standards and / or agreed with customers

Level	Probability per h	Definition
Frequent	$P \geq 10^{-3}$	may occur several times a month or more often
Probable	$10^{-3} > P \geq 10^{-4}$	likely to occur once a year
Occasional	$10^{-4} > P \geq 10^{-5}$	likely to occur once in the life of the system
Remote	$10^{-5} > P \geq 10^{-6}$	unlikely but possible to occur in the life of the system
Improbable	$10^{-6} > P \geq 10^{-7}$	very unlikely to occur
Incredible	$10^{-7} > P$	extremely unlikely, if not inconceivable to occur

Determining Risk

- e.g. via Risk Matrix

	Hazard Severity			
Hazard Probability	CATASTROPHIC	CRITICAL	MARGINAL	NEGLIGIBLE
Frequent	A	A	B	C
Probable	A	B	B	C
Occasional	B	B	C	D
Remote	B	C	D	D
Improbable	C	D	D	D
Incredible	D	D	D	D

Risk Class	Interpretation
A	Intolerable
B	Undesirable and shall only be accepted when risk reduction is impracticable
C	Tolerable with the endorsement of either the Project Manager together with the internal ordering party or the Safety Director
D	Acceptable with the endorsement of the normal project reviews

FREQUENTIS

Risk Tolerability

	Hazard Severity			
Hazard Probability	CATASTROPHIC	HAZARDOUS	MARGINAL	NEGLIGIBLE
Frequent	A	A	B	C
Probable	A	B	B	C
Occasional	B	B	C	D
Remote	B	C	D	D
Improbable	C	D	D	D
Incredible	D	D	D	D

FREQUENTIS

Risk Acceptance

Means, if there is a hazard it must be shown:

- That the risk is so low to be considered at least "tolerable".
- That steps have been taken, so far as is reasonably practicable, to reduce the risk to "acceptable" level.
(As Low As Reasonably Practicable - ALARP)

Risk Acceptance Limits

- Limits of risk acceptability/tolerability depend on
  - Customer
  - User/Operator
  - Regulator/Law/Standards
  - Society
- Decision criteria for risk acceptance / rejection
  - Absolute vs. relative risk (compare with previous, background)
  - Risk-cost trade-offs (e.g. ALARP, GALE)
  - Risk-benefit of technological options

Risk Management

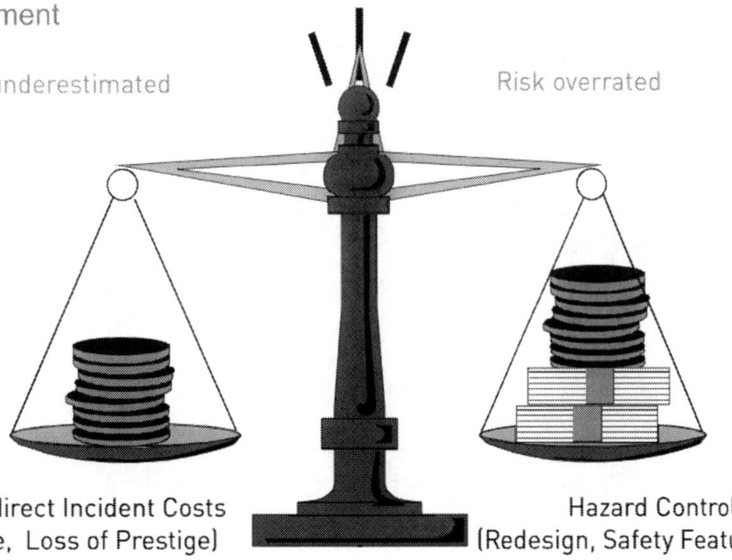

Direct and Indirect Incident Costs
(Maintenance, Loss of Prestige)

Hazard Controls
(Redesign, Safety Features, etc.)

  FREQUENTIS

Risk Reduction

Precedence in Risk Reduction:

1. Redesign to eliminate risk
   - Best where practicable (at a realistic cost)
2. Redesign to reduce hazard risk
   - Reduce hazard likelihood through design selection
     - E.g. duplex architecture rather than simplex
     - E.g. choose higher integrity (lower failure rate) components
   - Reduce hazard severity through design selection
     - E.g. limit size/pressure of chemical storage tanks
3. Incorporate additional mitigations
   - Safety devices
     - Automatic or other protective safety design features or devices
     - E.g. release valve to dissipate excessive pressure in vessel
     - Where applicable, provision should be made for periodic functional checks of safety devices

  FREQUENTIS

Risk Reduction

Precedence in Risk Reduction (cont.):

4. Provide monitoring and alarming devices
   - Used to detect the hazardous condition and to produce an adequate warning signal to alert personnel of the hazard
     - E.g. indicate that landing gear has not fully deployed
     - E.g. warning to evacuate when build up of toxic fumes
5. Develop procedures and training
   - Procedures may include the use of personal protective equipment
   - Can't assume procedures will be followed
     - E.g. evolution of protection on power guillotines
6. Reduce risk by adding warning signs and notices

Risk Reduction

Precedence in Risk Reduction - Example:

"Aircraft retractable landing gear fails to extend for landing, resulting in a gear-up crash landing that causes death/injury of passengers"

Risk Reduction

Precedence in Risk Reduction - Example:

"Aircraft retractable landing gear fails to extend for landing, resulting in a gear-up crash landing that causes death/injury of passengers"

Precedence Order	Method of Resolution
Eliminate Hazard	Use of fixed landing gear.
Reduce Hazard-Probability	Provide redundant extension systems with redundant power and controls.
Safety Device / Feature	Perform a self-test of the system prior to retracting; prohibit retraction if failure is discovered.
Alarming Device	Provide light, horn or voice warning if gear fails to extend and lock.
Procedure	Provide instructions and training for landing gear-up.

Safety Process

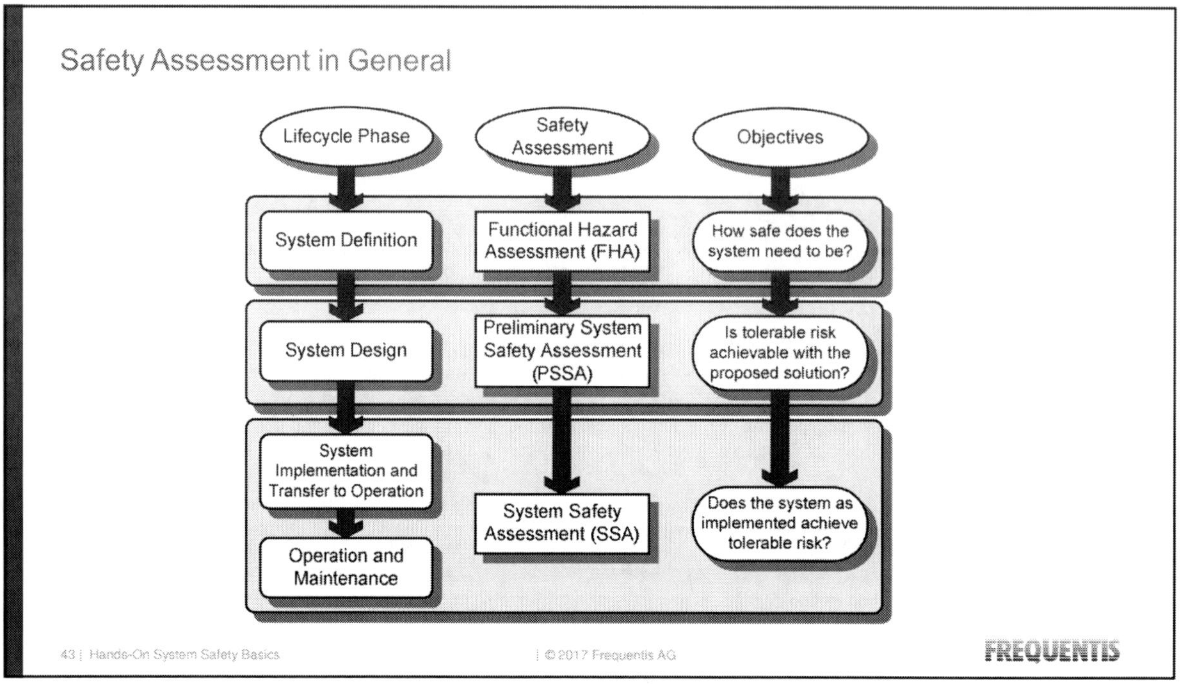

Safety Assessment in General
Lifecycle Phase
Safety Assessment
Objectives
System Definition
Functional Hazard Assessment (FHA)
How safe does the system need to be?
System Design
Preliminary System Safety Assessment (PSSA)
Is tolerable risk achievable with the proposed solution?
System Implementation and Transfer to Operation
System Safety Assessment (SSA)
Does the system as implemented achieve tolerable risk?
Operation and Maintenance
43 | Hands-On System Safety Basics
| © 2017 Frequentis AG
FREQUENTIS

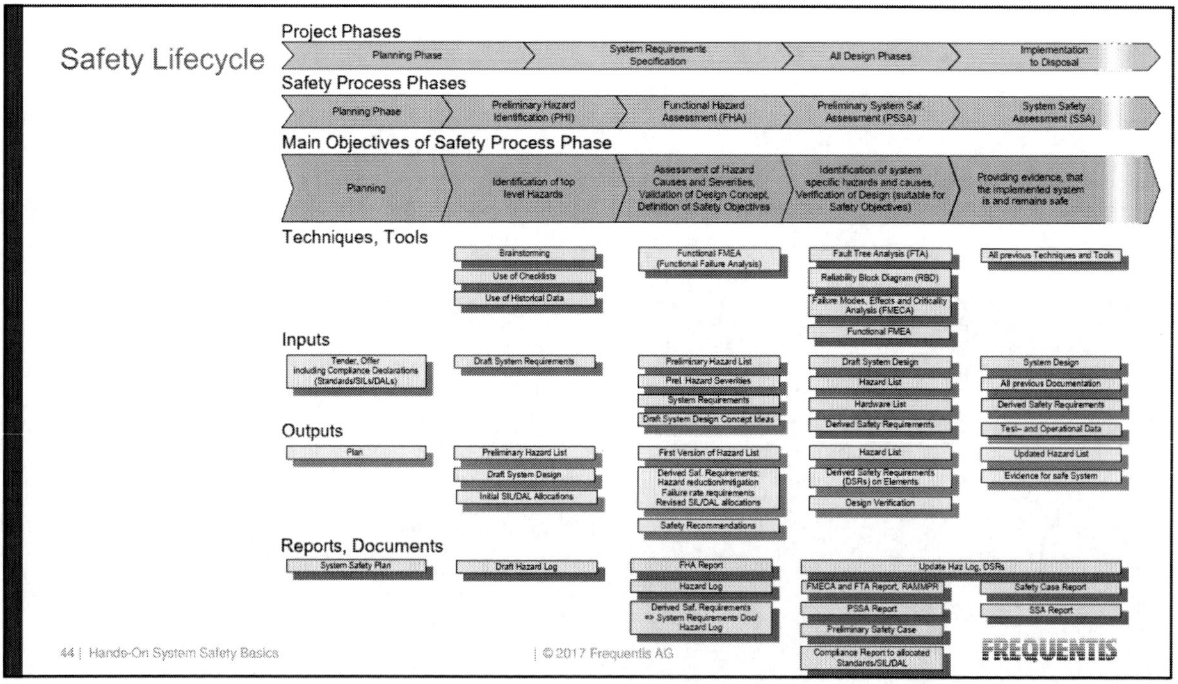

Safety Lifecycle
Project Phases
Planning Phase
System Requirements Specification
All Design Phases
Implementation to Disposal
Safety Process Phases
Planning Phase
Preliminary Hazard Identification (PHI)
Functional Hazard Assessment (FHA)
Preliminary System Saf. Assessment (PSSA)
System Safety Assessment (SSA)
Main Objectives of Safety Process Phase
Planning
Identification of top level Hazards
Assessment of Hazard Causes and Severities, Validation of Design Concept, Definition of Safety Objectives
Identification of system specific hazards and causes, Verification of Design (suitable for Safety Objectives)
Providing evidence, that the implemented system is and remains safe
Techniques, Tools
Brainstorming
Use of Checklists
Use of Historical Data
Functional FMEA (Functional Failure Analysis)
Fault Tree Analysis (FTA)
Reliability Block Diagram (RBD)
Failure Modes, Effects and Criticality Analysis (FMECA)
Functional FMEA
All previous Techniques and Tools
Inputs
Tender, Offer including Compliance Declarations (Standards/SILs/DALs)
Draft System Requirements
Preliminary Hazard List
Prel. Hazard Severities
System Requirements
Draft System Design Concept Ideas
Draft System Design
Hazard List
Hardware List
Derived Safety Requirements
System Design
All previous Documentation
Derived Safety Requirements
Test– and Operational Data
Outputs
Plan
Preliminary Hazard List
Draft System Design
Initial SIL/DAL Allocations
First Version of Hazard List
Derived Saf. Requirements: Hazard reduction/mitigation Failure rate requirements Revised SIL/DAL allocations
Safety Recommendations
Hazard List
Derived Safety Requirements (DSRs) on Elements
Design Verification
Updated Hazard List
Evidence for safe System
Reports, Documents
System Safety Plan
Draft Hazard Log
FHA Report
Hazard Log
Derived Saf. Requirements => System Requirements Doc/ Hazard Log
Update Haz Log, DSRs
FMECA and FTA Report, RAMMPR
PSSA Report
Preliminary Safety Case
Compliance Report to allocated Standards/SIL/DAL
Safety Case Report
SSA Report
44 | Hands-On System Safety Basics
| © 2017 Frequentis AG
FREQUENTIS

Preliminary Hazard Identification

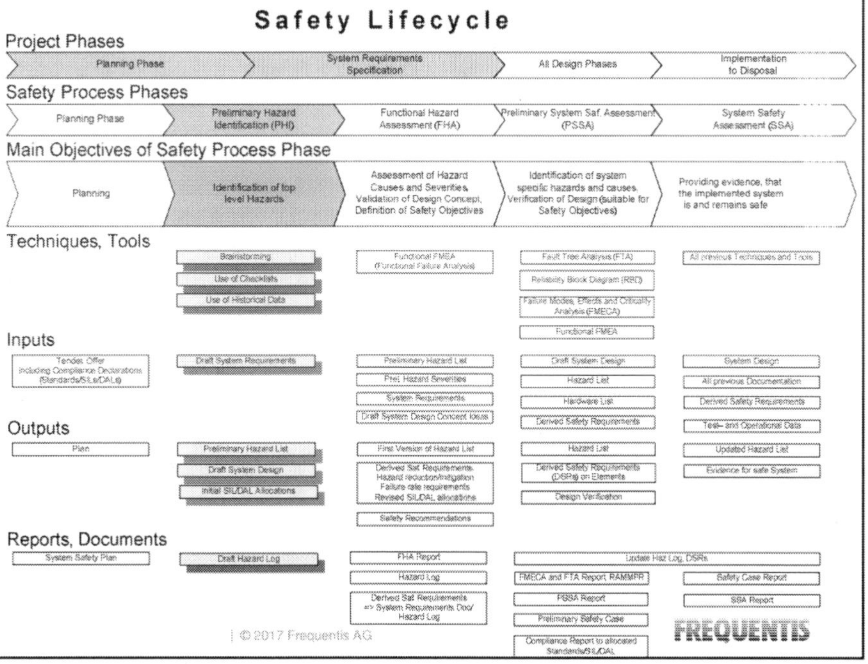

FREQUENTIS

Preliminary Hazard Identification

- Bow-Tie Diagram

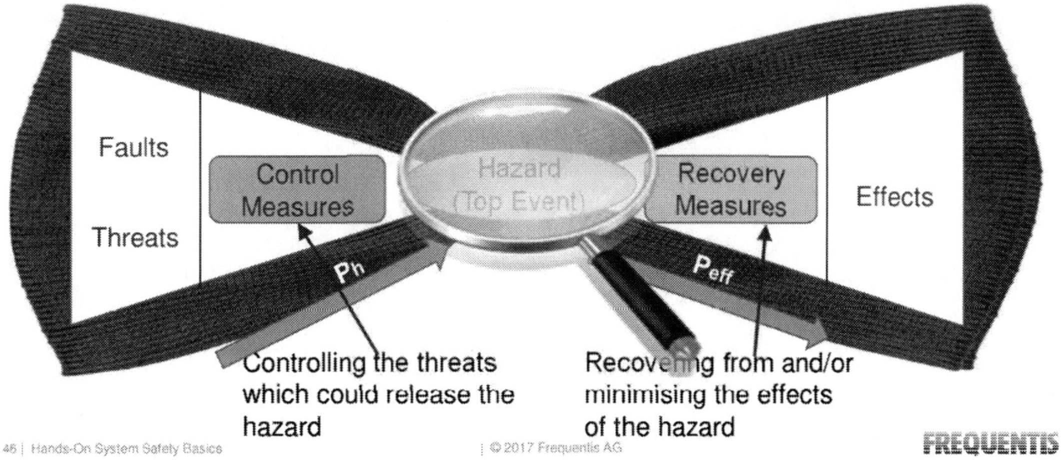

FREQUENTIS

Preliminary Hazard Identification

- Start of safety process with PHI (Preliminary Hazard Identification) and PHA (Preliminary Hazard Assessment)
  - This phase is often included in the FHA phase

- Preliminary hazard list and severities
  - Brainstorming
  - Historical Data
  - Checklists
  - Target rates for hazards (Risk Matrix), Safety Objectives
  - Initial SIL / AL Allocations

FREQUENTIS

Preliminary Hazard Identification

Hazards are identified by a number of means:

- Experience – Hazard Identification is usually a collation / filtering exercise on data from:
  - previous projects (review hazard logs)
  - similar systems / technologies (domain knowledge)
  - accidents / incidents (lessons learned)
  - perhaps variations for new technologies (unstable aircraft?)
- Checklists
  - comprehensive or short prompt lists
  - Note: usually prompt with causes which must be interpreted
- Brainstorming
  - expert knowledge, creative thinking
  - structured techniques such as Energy Trace & Barrier Analysis, Structured What If Technique (SWIFT)

FREQUENTIS

Preliminary Hazard Identification

- Hazardous materials
  - Explosives, fuels, propellants, corrosives, asphyxiants, toxic substances
- Environment
  - Vibration, noise, temperature
- Energy Sources
  - Kinetic and potential mechanical energy, electrical energy, pressure, ionic radiation, RF radiation
- Human interactions / processes
  (ways humans can place system in hazardous state)
  - Assembly, operation, maintenance, testing, training, life support / safety equipment

Assumptions

- Whole safety analysis is based on assumptions on
  - environmental conditions,
  - other systems,
  - procedures
  - other influences which are outside of our control
  - local assumptions about what can be achieved later in design
- Have to be recorded explicitly!
- Have to be evaluated and verified!
  - If invalid, re-assessment of all analyses that are based on this assumption is necessary

Case Study

Go Cart - Preliminary Hazard Identification

FREQUENTIS

Functional Hazard Assessment

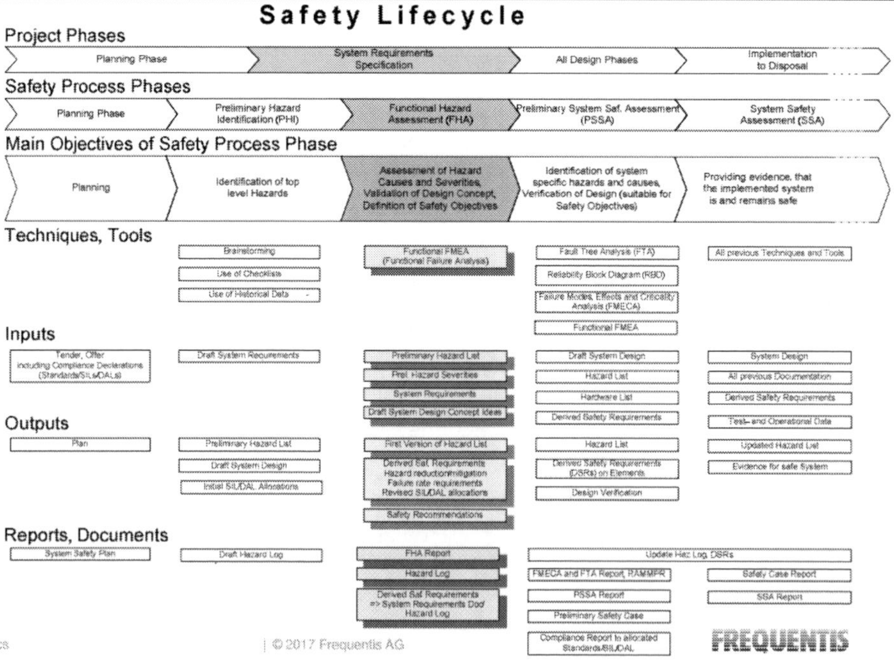

FREQUENTIS

Functional Hazard Assessment

"How safe does the system need to be?"

- Functional Failure Modes and Effects Analysis
  - Guided brainstorming of domain experts (Requirements Engineer, Designer, Developer, IV&V, Safety Engineer, Human Factors Engineer, End User, ...)
  - Basic functions
  - Theoretical failure modes and severities
- Mapping of failure modes to hazards, check for omissions
- Derived Safety Requirements (DSRs) - recorded during the whole assessment - main means for risk reduction by safety process

Functional Hazard Assessment

HAZOP Analysis / Functional Failure Analysis (FFA):

- A Functional Failure Analysis (FFA) is a structured and systematic examination of a planned or existing process or system in order to identify and evaluate problems that may represent risks to personnel, equipment, the environment, or prevent efficient operation.
- The FFA technique was initially developed to analyse chemical process systems, but has later been extended to other types of systems and also to complex operations and to software systems.
- A FFA is a qualitative technique based on guide-words and is carried out by a **multi-disciplinary team** during a set of meetings.
- The FFA should preferably be carried out as early in the design phase as possible – to have influence on the design – and shall be repeated/completed at later stages (add mitigations).

Functional Hazard Assessment

HAZOP Analysis / Functional Failure Analysis – Process:

- Define system/operation to be analyzed
- Define all functions that will be analyzed
- Record assumptions/conditions
- Analyze failure modes for all functions using the **guide-words** (thereby record all mitigations required to reduce the risk of safety related failure modes)
- Map safety related failure modes to identified hazards and define additional hazards if required
- Define safety requirements and safety recommendations for the found mitigations

FREQUENTIS

Functional Hazard Assessment

Guideword	Description
AFTER	The activity occurs too late in the sequence
AS WELL AS	An additional activity occurs
BEFORE	The activity occurs too early in the sequence
EARLY	The activity occurs earlier than expected
LATE	The activity occurs later than expected
LESS	Quantitative decrease in a parameter
MORE	Quantitative increase in a parameter
NO/NOT	Design intent is not achieved
OTHER THAN	Complete substitution – another activity takes place
PART OF	Only some of the design intention is achieved
REVERSE	Logical opposite of the design intention occurs

FREQUENTIS

Functional Hazard Assessment

HAZOP Example:

- Function: Open power operated doors on train once train has stopped at plattform.

Functional Hazard Assessment

Guideword	Deviation	Cause	Effect
NO	Doors fail to open	Defective mechanism	No passenger egress
EARLY	Doors open too early (train moving) or not adjacent to plattform	Operator error	Possible harm to Passengers
LESS	Only one door opens	Defective mechanism	Restricted passenger egress, may lead to injuries
AS WELL	Doors open on both sides of train	Failure in control circuitry	Possible harm to passengers if they exit the wrong door
PART OF	Same as less	-	-
OTHER THAN	Doors open wrong side	Failure in control circuitry	Possible harm to passengers if they exit the wrong door

Case Study

Go Cart – Functional Failure Analysis

FREQUENTIS

Preliminary System Safety Assessment

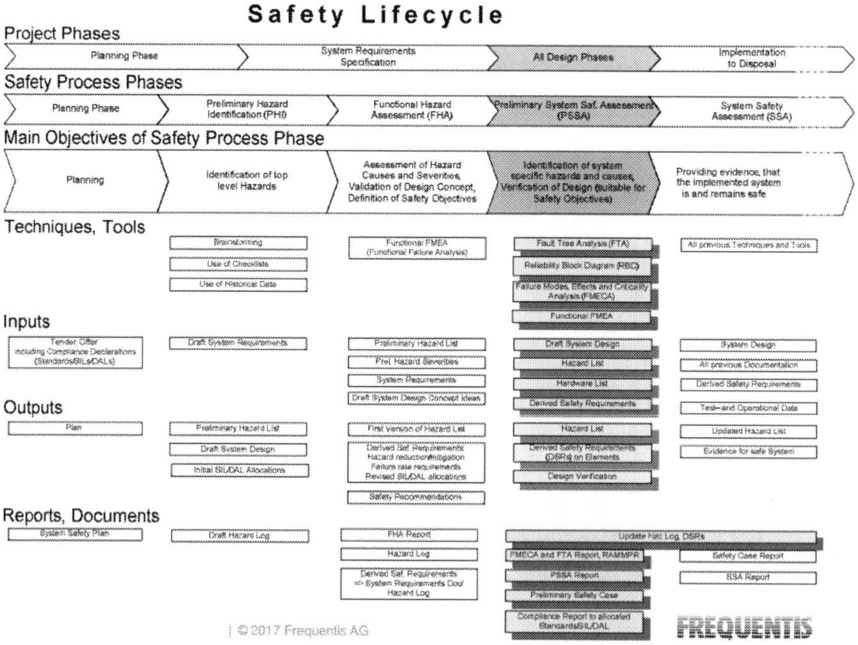

FREQUENTIS

Preliminary System Safety Assessment

"Does the proposed design reach the safety objectives?"

- Breaks down causes of hazards and functional failures
  - e.g. with Fault Tree Analysis (FTA)
- Further analyses of design
  - Reliability Block Diagrams (RBDs)
  - Hardware Failure Modes, Effect and Criticality Analysis (FMECA)
  - Interface Failure Modes and Effect Analysis (IF- FMEA)
  - Software Failure Modes and Effect Analysis (SW-FMEA)
- Can lead to further requirements, e.g. additional redundancy necessary to meet hazard target rates

Preliminary System Safety Assessment

- Bow-Tie Diagram

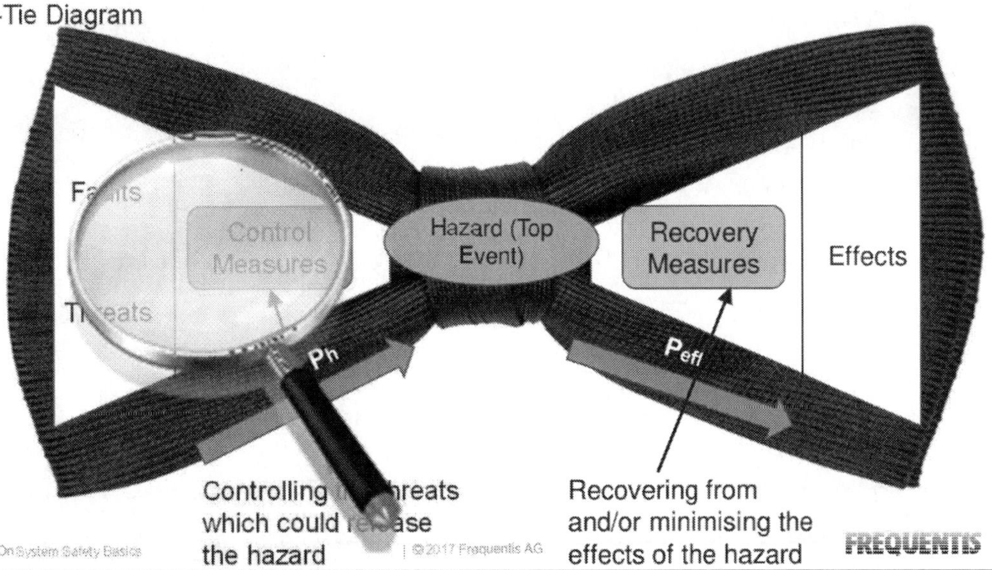

Controlling ... threats which could ... se the hazard

Hardware FMECA

- Analysis of effects of single hardware failures (inductive)
- Used to
  - investigate effects of known component failures within (sub-) systems
  - provide information about sub-system failures for incorporation into system and platform level analyses
  - show that single component failures will not lead to system failure (hazard)
  - complement fault tree
- Results presented in tabular form

Hardware FMECA

- Define System to be analysed
  - Drawings, charts, system descriptions, ...
- Define targets of analysis
  - Eliminate single points of failure
  - Define maintainability actions
- Break system down into convenient and logical elements
  - single pieces/components (e.g. resistor)
  - Line Replaceable Units (LRU) – lowest level at which repair is made by customer
  - Systems/Sub-systems
  - Interfaces

Hardware FMECA

- List of failure modes
  - e.g. Switch – open, partially open, closed, partially closed, chatter
  - Operator – wrong operation to proper item, wrong operation to wrong item, proper operation to wrong item, perform too early, perform too late, fail to perform
- Identification of effects of failure
  - Consequence a failure has on the operation, function or status of component/system
  - Can be hierarchically built up (lower level FMEA effect -> higher level FMEA failure mode)
- Criticality Analysis
  - Rank each potential failure mode according to the combined influence of severity classification and its probability of occurrence based upon the best available data
- Maintainability Information
  - Provide early criteria for maintenance planning analysis, LSA, test planning etc. and identify maintainability design features requiring corrective action

FREQUENTIS

Hardware FMECA

ID/Item	Failure Mode/Faults	Effects of the Failure Mode	Failure Detection Method	Recovery Provisions	Criticality, Rationale
SWITCH 08 JIF-board	one JIF-A: loss or corruption of communications with SDC-A	The communication in switch A to all devices (EPOS, LIF, ERIF, ALIF) connected to this JIF is lost Switch redundancy is reduced no effect to user	SDC-A reports to TMCS: JIF-A fault; all connected devices report via JIF-B: JIF-A fault to TMCS; fault indication on JIF-Board	automatic: connected devices (EPOS, LIF, ERIF, ALIF) use all voice and data information from Switch-B manual: Remove and replace JIF-Board of Switch-A	Severity is none, because Switch-B is used; redundancy is reduced
SWITCH 09 ISO-Board	one ISO-Board-A: loss or corruption of output to associated Highway-A	One Highway-A out of service Highway redundancy is reduced no effect to user	all feeding JIF-A report to TMCS: ISO-A fault;	automatic: connected devices (EPOS, LIF, ERIF, ALIF) use all voice information from Switch-B; manual: Remove and replace ISO-Board-A	Severity is none, because Switch-B is used; redundancy is reduced

ID/Item	Failure Mode/Fault	Failure Rate Lambda / hours	Failure Mode/Item Criticality	Failure Predictability	Maintenance Actions
SWITCH 08 JIF-board	one JIF-A: loss or corruption of communications with SDC-A	1.48311E-05	$C_{[none]}$ = 1.95	Intermittent failure of JIF; intermittent communication alarms from SDC and/or connected devices	Manual: Remove and replace JIF-Board of Switch-A
SWITCH 09 ISO-Board	one ISO-Board-A: loss or corruption of output to associated Highway-A	8.99655E-07	$C_{[none]}$ = 0.12	Intermittent highway alarms from JIF-A	Manual: Remove and replace ISO-Board-A

FREQUENTIS

Reliability Block Diagram

- Define and describe the system
  - physical configuration and functional operation
- Model "what is necessary for success" of defined function
  - Model a component state as "Working" or "Failed"
- Can be used for
  - design decisions – which design/configuration will reach RAM targets
  - verification – does the system reach the RAM targets
  - logistic support calculations (for repairable systems)

MTBF = 50 000h

MTTR = 0,5h

A_s = 99,999%

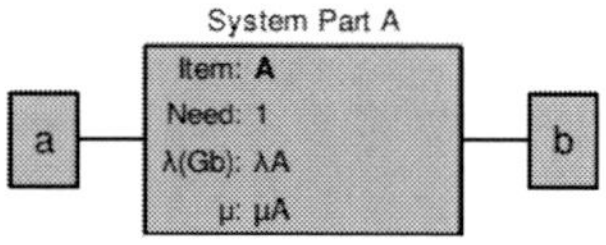

Reliability Block Diagram

Failure Rate λ_s: $$\lambda_S = \lambda_A + \lambda_B = \frac{MTBF_A + MTBF_B}{MTBF_A * MTBF_B}$$

Repair Rate μ_s: $$\mu_S = \frac{MTBF_A + MTBF_B}{MTBF_A * MDT_B + MTBF_B * MDT_A + MDT_A * MDT_B}$$

Availability A_s: $$A_S = A_A * A_B$$

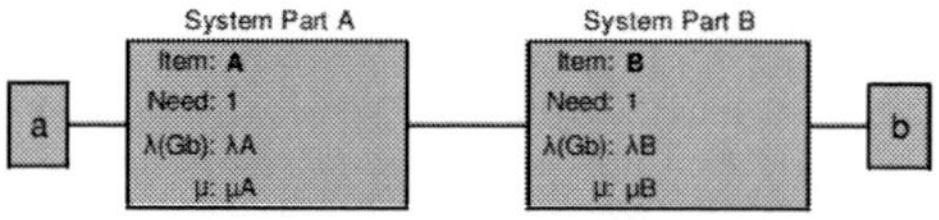

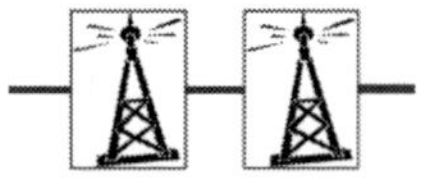

MTBF = 25 000h

MTTR = 0,5h

A_s = 99,998%

Reliability Block Diagram

Failure Rate λ_p: $$\lambda_P = \frac{MDT_A + MDT_B}{MTBF_A * MTBF_B + MTBF_A * MDT_B + MTBF_B * MDT_A}$$

Repair Rate μ_p: $$\mu_P = \mu_A + \mu_B$$

Availability A_p: $$A_P = A_A + A_B - A_A A_B$$

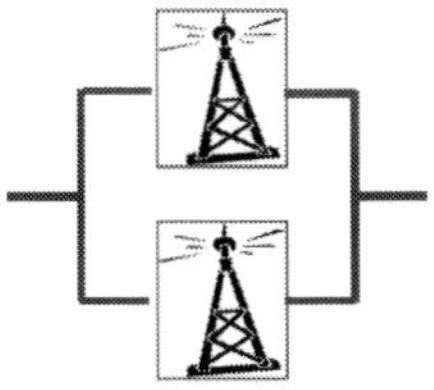

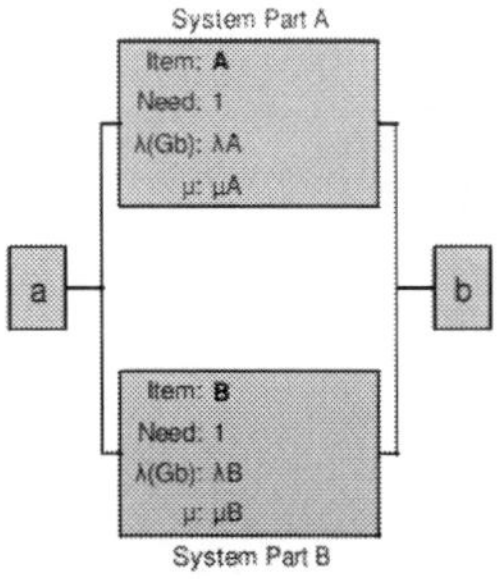

MTBF = 2 500 000 000h
MTTR = 0,25h
A_p = 99,99999999%

Reliability Block Diagram

Failure Rate λ_{red}: $$\lambda_{red} = \frac{\left(1 - \sum_{i=k}^{n} \binom{n}{i} * A_A^{\,i} * UA_A^{\,n-i}\right) * (n - k + 1)}{MDT_A * \sum_{i=k}^{n} \binom{n}{i} * A_A^{\,i} * UA_A^{\,n-i}}$$

Repair Rate μ_{red}: $$\mu_{red} = \mu_A * (n - k + 1)$$

Availability A_{red}: $$A_{red} = \sum_{i=k}^{n} \binom{n}{i} * A_A^{\,i} * UA_A^{\,n-i}$$

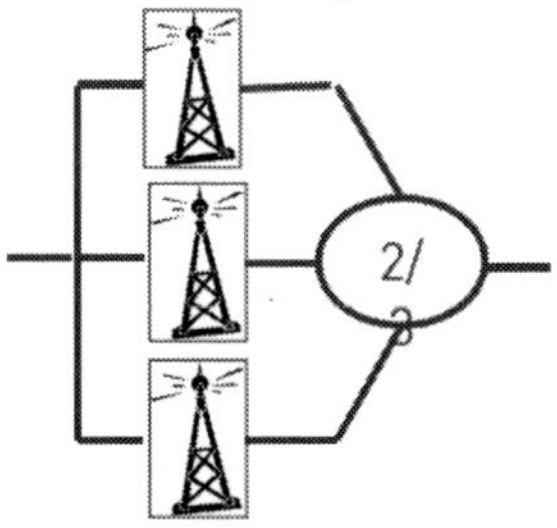

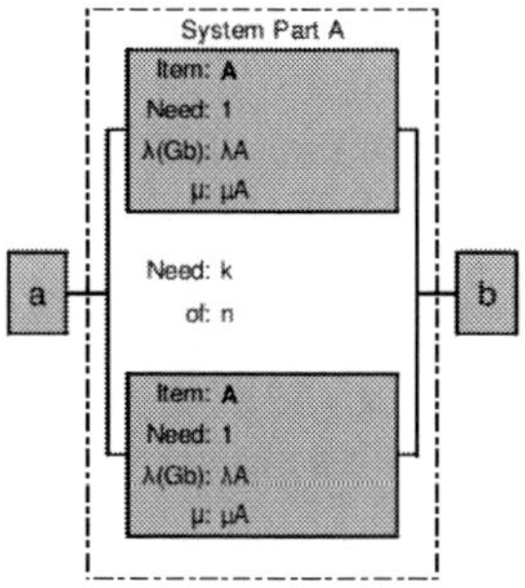

MTBF = 833 333 333h
MTTR = 0,25h
A_{red} = 99,99999997%

Reliability Block Diagram

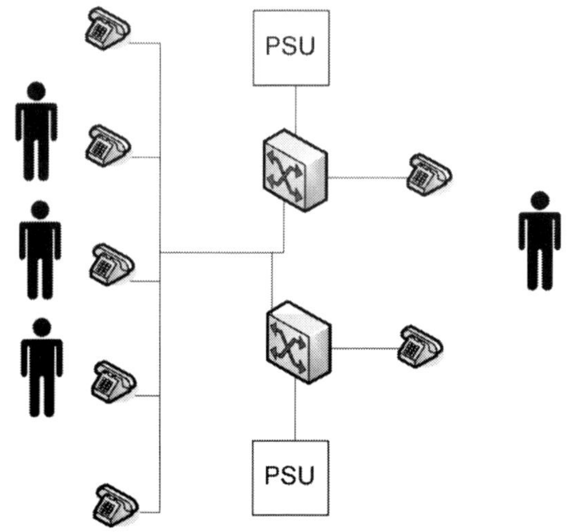

Reliability Block Diagram

- **Operational Availability**

$$A_o = \frac{MTBF}{MTBF + MDT}$$

$$MDT = MLDT + MTT + MTTR$$

- **Inherent Availability**

$$A_i = \frac{MTBF}{MTBF + MTTR}$$

MLDT… Mean Logistic Down Time

MTT… Mean Travel Time

MTTR… Mean Time To Repair

Down-Time / year	Availability
1 day	99,7%
1 hour	99,98%
1 minute	99,9998%
1 second	99,999996%

Reliability Block Diagram

MTBF = 50 000h

MDT = 0.5h   Ao = 99.999%

MDT = 5h   Ao = 99.99%

MDT = 50h   Ao = 99.9%

73 | Hands-On System Safety Basics | © 2017 Frequentis AG FREQUENTIS

Fault Tree Analysis

- Well known and widely used safety tool
- Deductive, top down Approach
- Start with top level hazard and "work your way down"
  - Hazards have to be known in advance
- Can consider hardware, software, humans
- Identifies also multiple points of failure
- Based on Boolean Logic (AND, OR gates)
- Quantitative and qualitative analysis possible
  - Are there any single points of failure?
  - Which factors have to occur simultaneously to cause a failure?
  - What are the probabilities associated with each failure?

74 | Hands-On System Safety Basics | © 2017 Frequentis AG FREQUENTIS

Fault Tree Analysis

Basic Event
An initiating fault requiring no further development

Intermediate Event
An event arising from the combination of other, more basic events

Barriers!

Gate - AND
All input events must occur for the output to occur
P = P(A) * P(B)

Gate - OR
The occurrence of one or more input events will cause the output to occur
P = P(A) + P(B) – P(A) * P(B)

Fault Tree Analysis

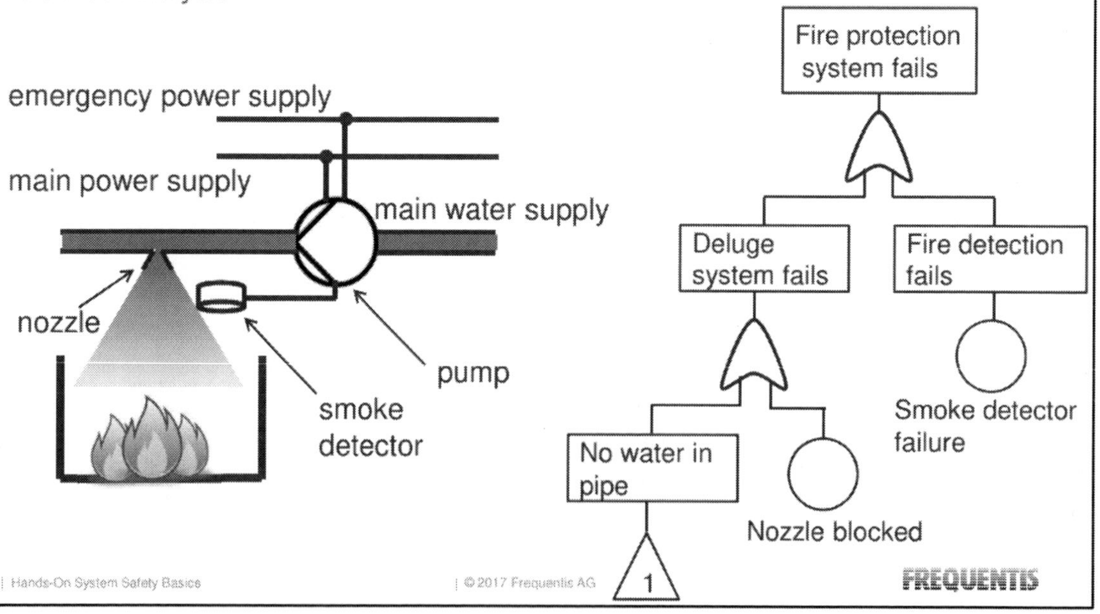

Fault Tree Analysis

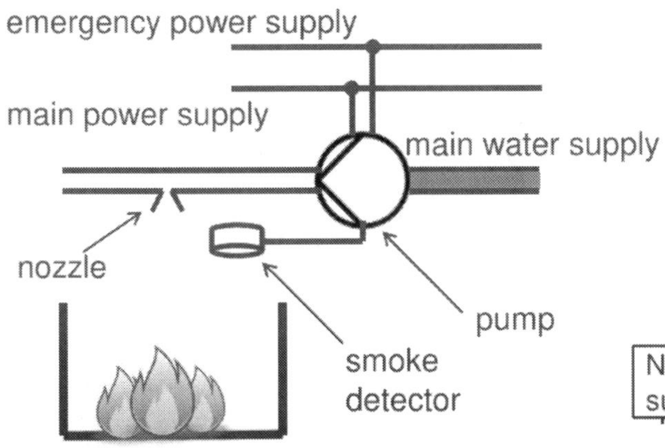

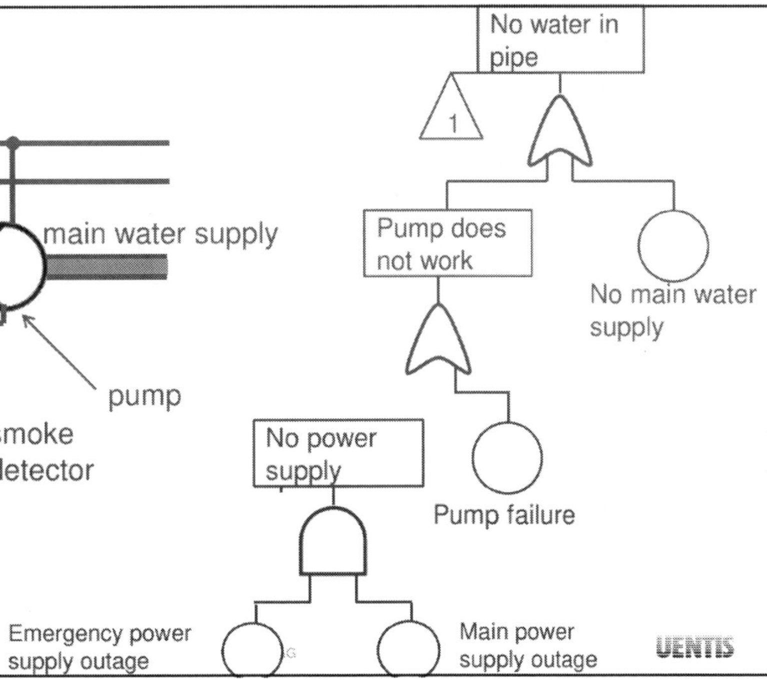

UENTIS

Case Study

Fault Tree Analysis

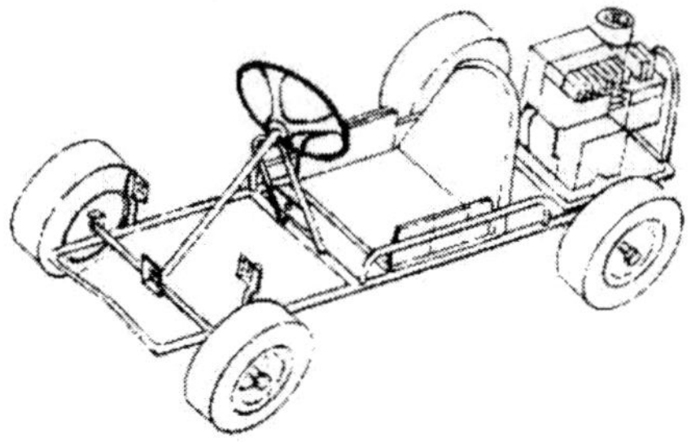

FREQUENTIS

Common Cause Analysis

- Frequent assumption: Failures are independent.
  - May be subverted by systematic errors/interference/coupling i.e. Common Cause Failure
- Definition of Common Cause Failure
  - "A failure of two or more components, systems, or structures due to a single specific event or cause."
  - "Common cause failures are defined as that cutset of dependent failures for which causes are not explicitly included in the logic model as basic events."
- Approaches to Mitigation
  - Diversity, Separation, Checks and Tests,
  - thorough Analysis (FTA, RBD)
  - dedicated Common Cause Analysis

FREQUENTIS

Common Cause Analysis

- Consider a redundant system. Both components of the system must fail before the system does fail.
- If each of the components has a failure rate of 10-4 per hour and the failures are completely independent then the overall system would have a failure rate of 10-8 per hour.
- However if just 1% of the failures are common cause failures then the failure rate rises to 10-6 per hour.

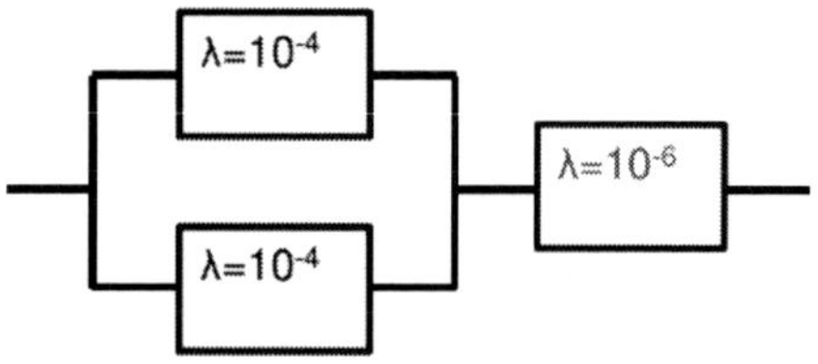

Common cause failure modes tend to dominate highly reliable systems!

FREQUENTIS

Common Cause Analysis

- Environmental Hazards
  - Ambient parameters, extremes
  - Influence from accidents outside system boundary
- Design and Analysis Errors
  - Misunderstandings and -interpretations of requirements and environment
  - Faulty or insufficient analysis (e.g. EMC protection, power consumption)
  - Damage caused by tests
  - Poor maintainability
- Manufacturing & Assembly Errors
- Operation and Maintenance Errors

FREQUENTIS

Common Cause Analysis

- Identification of Common Causes is difficult!
- Analysis techniques: extension of deductive analysis targeted at common causes of items previously considered as independent
- Very detailed system knowledge necessary
- General outline:
  - Identification of groups of critical components
  - Grouping of parts by common features
  - Identification of credible failure modes
  - Consideration of generic failure mechanisms and generic causes
  - Identification of affected system parts/areas
  - Recording of observations and conclusions

FREQUENTIS

Common Cause Analysis - Example

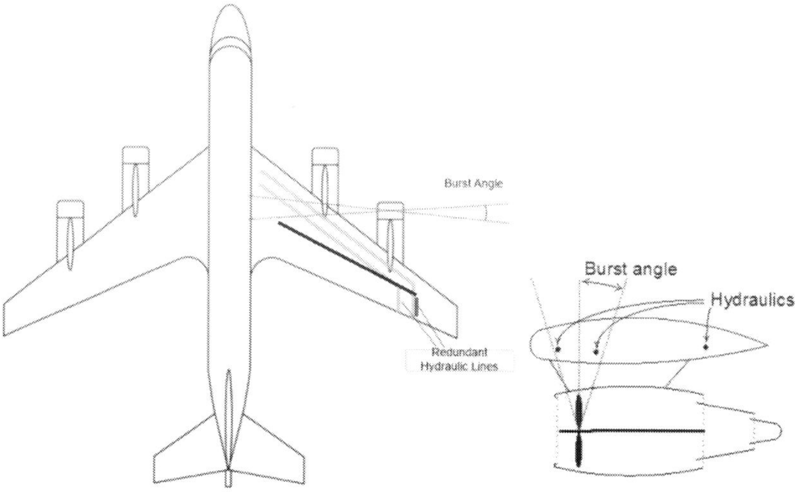

Consequence Analysis

- Bow-Tie Diagram

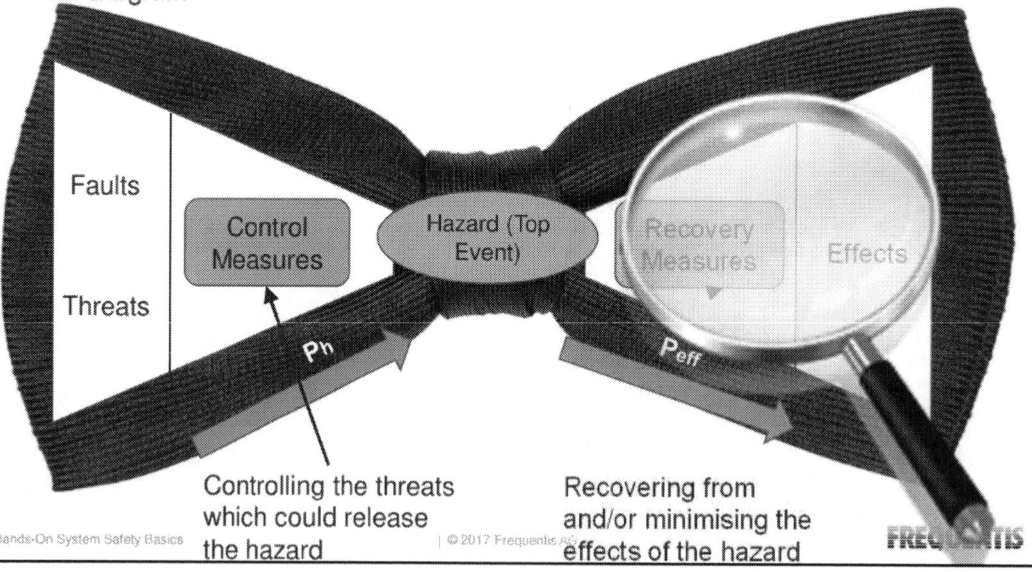

Consequence Analysis

- Purpose
  - To determine the intermediate conditions and final consequences arising from the identified hazards
- Approach
  - Diagrammatic representation
  - Quantitative estimate of probabilities
- Techniques
  - Cause Consequence Diagrams
  - Event Trees

Consequence Analysis

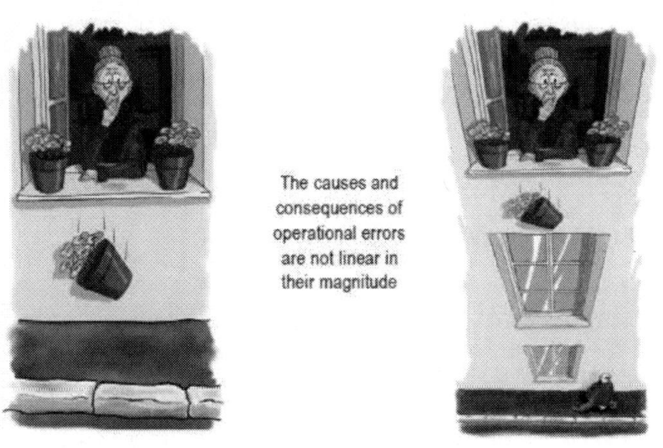

Source: Dedale

Consequence Analysis

Cause Consequence Diagram (CCD):

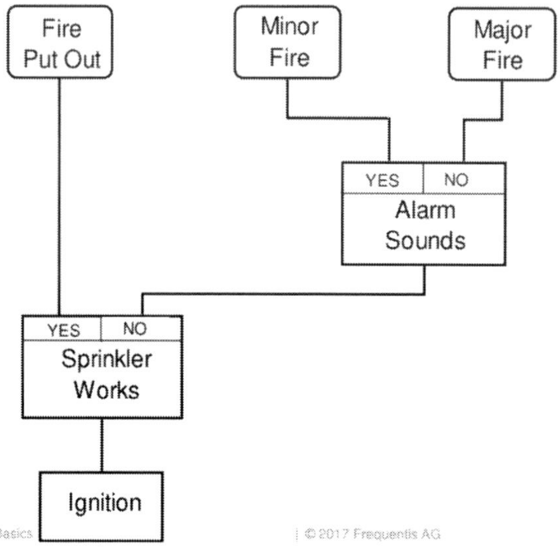

Methods - Limitations

- All techniques have their limitations due to
  - representation → abstraction of real system that is "good-enough" is hard to find
  - data availability and accuracy
  - analysis is based on incomplete model of the system
    E.g. mechanical engineering drawings - they show how a system is constructed, but not what it does
- Important to respect limitations of techniques because
  - inappropriate use of techniques produces inaccurate results
- Analyses can identify sets of potential hazards, failure sequences and accident sequences, but they are only as good as domain knowledge, engineering knowledge, creativity, ... of participants!

System Safety Assessment

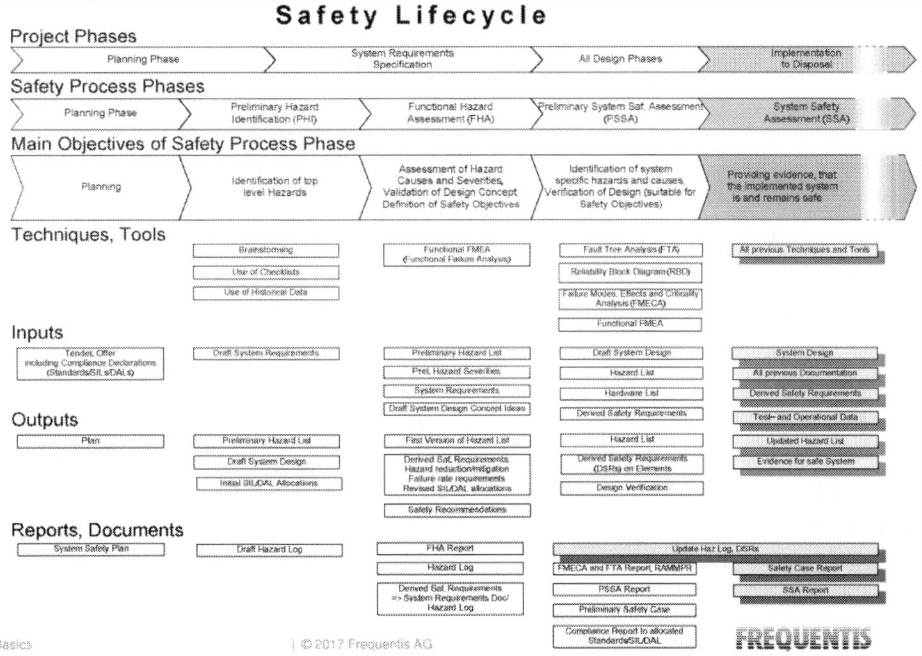

FREQUENTIS

System Safety Assessment (SSA)

"Does the system as implemented achieve tolerable Risk?"

- Update of all previously performed analyses
- Verification, whether assumptions are still valid and all safety targets and safety requirements are met
- Production of a safety case or safety assessment report
- Transition to operation and maintenance
- Maintenance of safety case

FREQUENTIS

What is a Safety Case?

- Similar to a legal case
- Proves, that the system is safe for its intended use
- Provides conclusive argument

Goal Structuring Notation

- Graphical argumentation notation
- Can be used to explicitly document
  - the elements of any argument (claims, evidence and context) and
  - the relationships that exist between them.
- Presents, how goals are supported by sub-goals
  - sub-goals supported by subsequent supporting goals.
- Supporting evidence documented via so called "solution"

Goal Structuring Notation

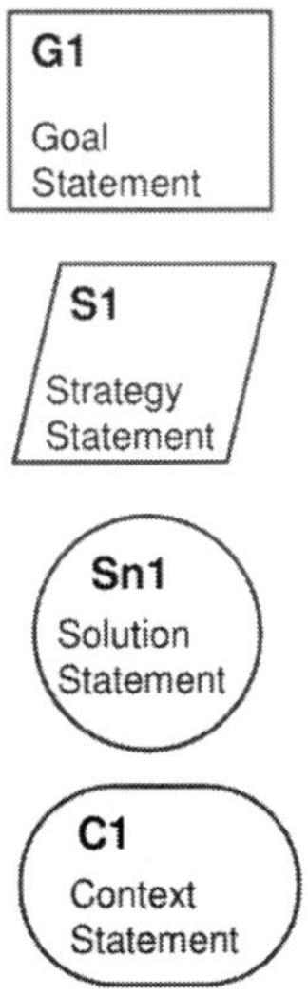

A **goal** presents a claim forming part of the argument.

A **strategy** describes the nature of the inference that exists between one or more goals and another goal.

A **solution** presents a reference to evidence items.

A **context** presents a contextual artefact. This can be a reference to contextual information or statement.

Goal Structuring Notation

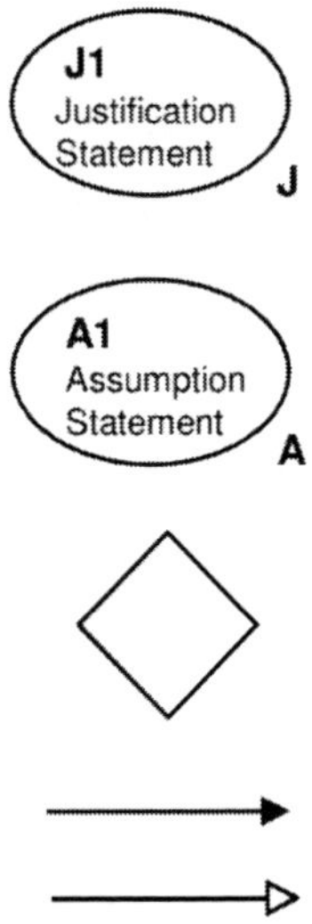

A **justification** presents a statement of rationale.

An **assumption** presents an intentionally unsubstantiated statement.

Undeveloped entity indicates that a line of argument has not been developed. It can apply to goals and strategies.

Supported by declares an inferential or evidential relationship.

In context of declares a contextual relationship.

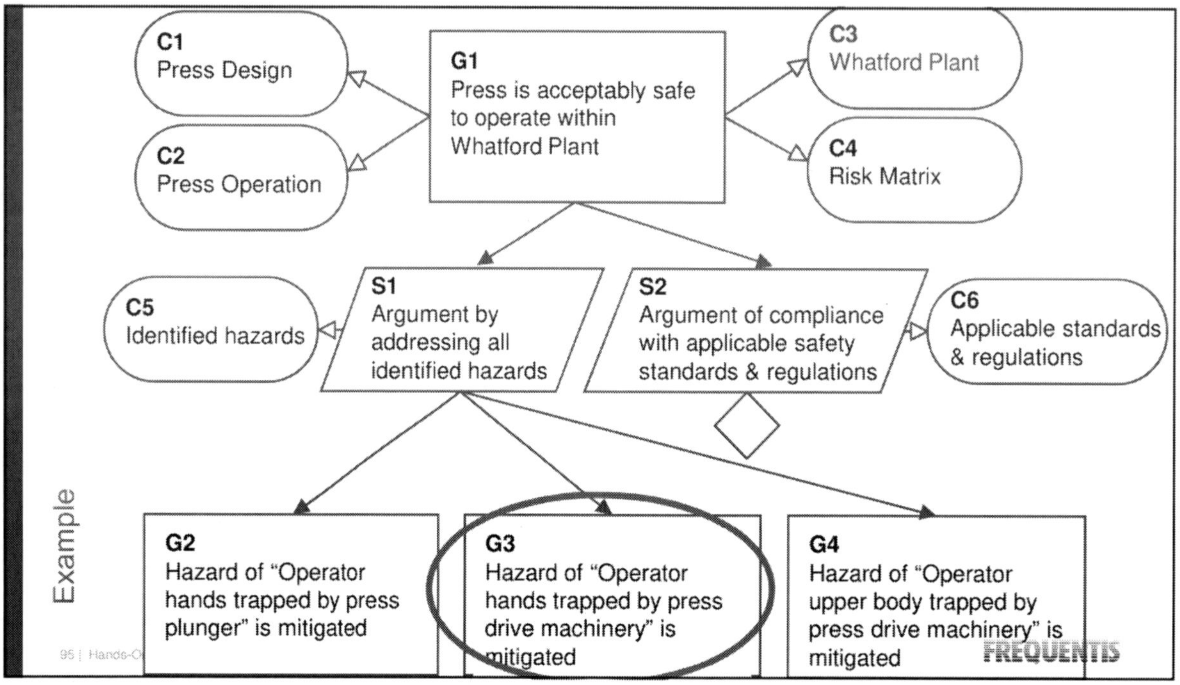
Example
C1
Press Design
C2
Press Operation
G1
Press is acceptably safe to operate within Whatford Plant
C3
Whatford Plant
C4
Risk Matrix
C5
Identified hazards
S1
Argument by addressing all identified hazards
S2
Argument of compliance with applicable safety standards & regulations
C6
Applicable standards & regulations
G2
Hazard of "Operator hands trapped by press plunger" is mitigated
G3
Hazard of "Operator hands trapped by press drive machinery" is mitigated
G4
Hazard of "Operator upper body trapped by press drive machinery" is mitigated
FREQUENTIS

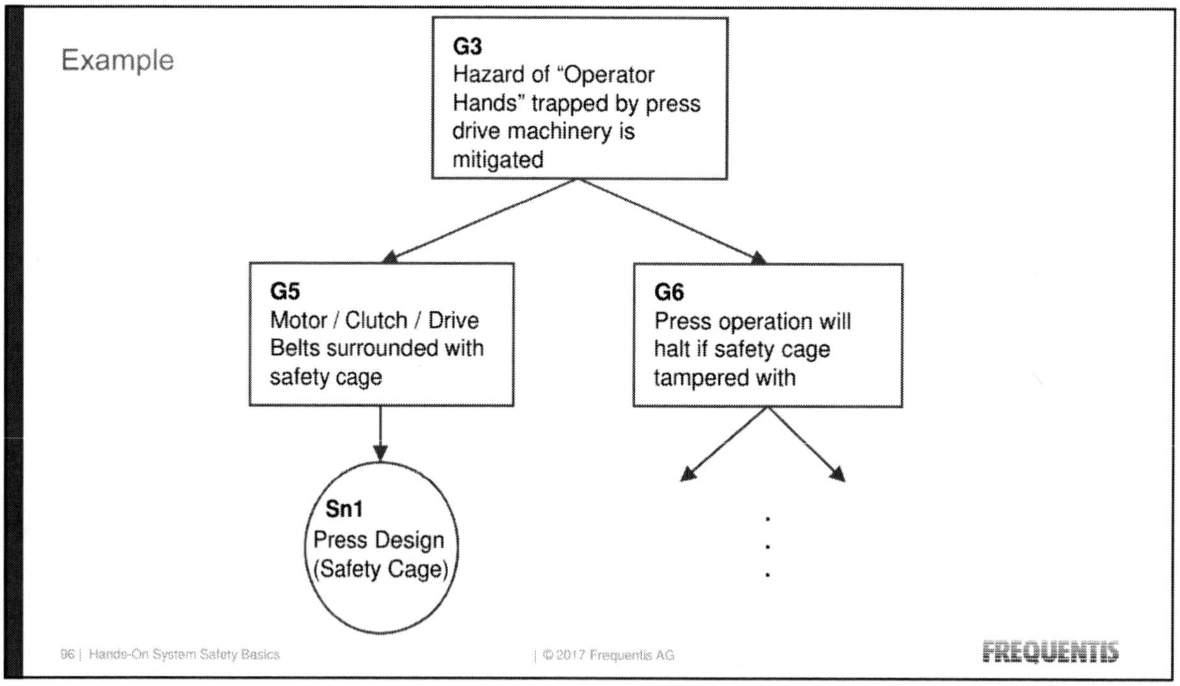
Example
G3
Hazard of "Operator Hands" trapped by press drive machinery is mitigated
G5
Motor / Clutch / Drive Belts surrounded with safety cage
G6
Press operation will halt if safety cage tampered with
Sn1
Press Design (Safety Cage)
96 | Hands-On System Safety Basics
| © 2017 Frequentis AG
FREQUENTIS

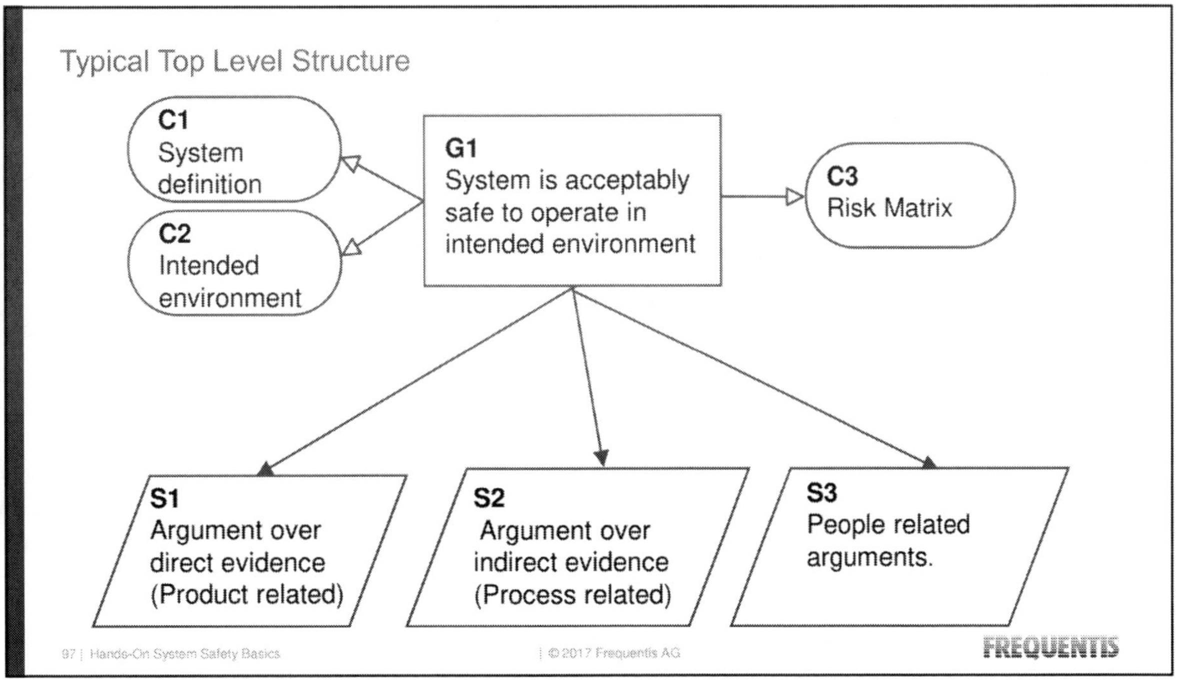
Typical Top Level Structure
C1
System definition
C2
Intended environment
G1
System is acceptably safe to operate in intended environment
C3
Risk Matrix
S1
Argument over direct evidence (Product related)
S2
Argument over indirect evidence (Process related)
S3
People related arguments.
97 | Hands-On System Safety Basics
| © 2017 Frequentis AG
FREQUENTIS

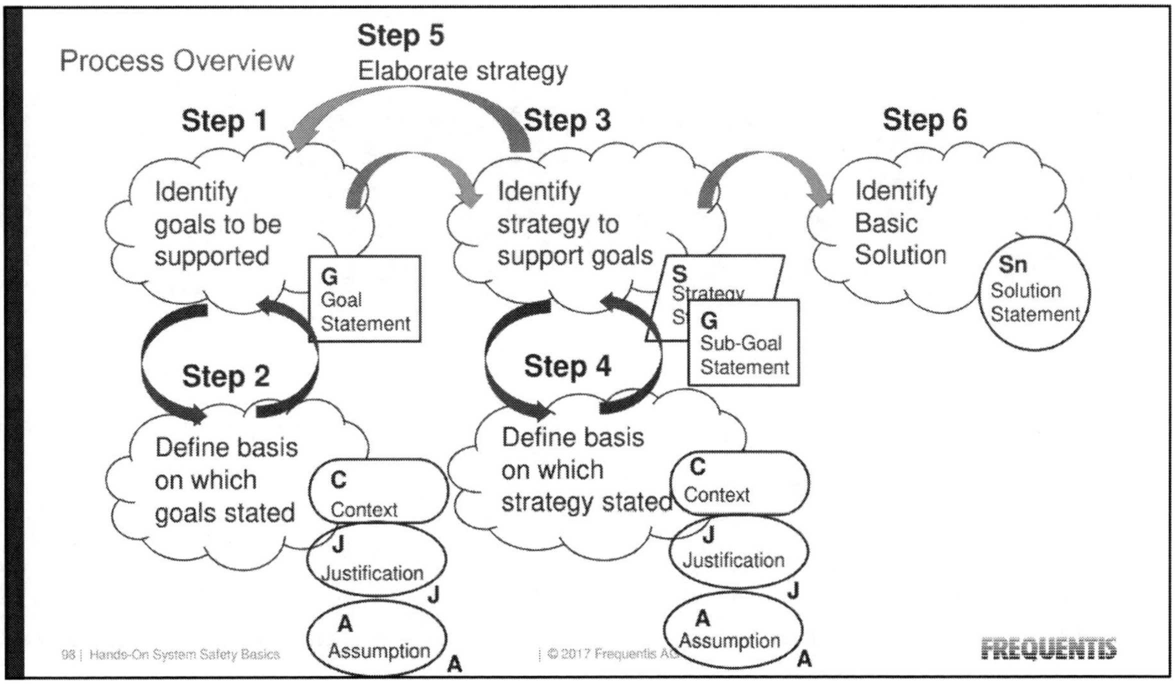
Process Overview
Step 5
Elaborate strategy
Step 1
Identify goals to be supported
G
Goal Statement
Step 2
Define basis on which goals stated
C
Context
J
Justification
J
A
Assumption
A
Step 3
Identify strategy to support goals
S
Strategy
G
Sub-Goal Statement
Step 4
Define basis on which strategy stated
C
Context
J
Justification
J
A
Assumption
A
Step 6
Identify Basic Solution
Sn
Solution Statement
98 | Hands-On System Safety Basics
| © 2017 Frequentis AG
FREQUENTIS

Sources of Evidence

- Organisational issues, safety management, competency
- The development processes
- The design
- Formal analysis
- Testing
- Simulated experience (via reliability testing)
- Prior field experience (proven in use)

FREQUENTIS

Links

FREQUENTIS

Links

- The System Safety Society:
  - http://www.system-safety.org/
- The Aviation Safety Network:
  - http://aviation-safety.net/index.php
- EUROCONTROL:
  - http://www.eurocontrol.int
- Safety Assessment Methodology Level:
  - https://www.eurocontrol.int/articles/safety-assessment-methodology-sam
- UK Defence Standards (registration necessary):
  - http://www.dstan.mod.uk/

Links (2)

- Health and Safety Executive, UK:
  - http://www.hse.gov.uk/
- International Electrotechnical Commission (IEC)
  - http://www.iec.ch/
- IEC 61508
  - http://www.iec.ch/functionalsafety/
- NASA Safety Standards, Info:
  - http://www.hq.nasa.gov/office/codeq/doctree/index.htm
- US Standards:
  - http://standards.gov
- Dependability Information:
  - http://www.dependability.org/

Thank you for your attention!

FREQUENTIS
FOR A SAFER WORLD

System Safety Part 3: Cyber Safety and Security

ISSC 2018, Phoenix, USA

Andreas Gerstinger

Open Brainstorming

If you think about **Security**, what comes into your mind?

Highly reliable communication and information solutions for a safer world

More than 65 years of innovation in safety-critical applications

We set standards

Frequentis group 2015

Global market leader

Headquarters Vienna

95% Export

Solutions partners and regional offices in over 50 countries

228 M EUR turnover 2015

1947 Established

1,309 Employees

80% STEM*

12% R&D

*) Science, Technology, Engineering, Math

Frequentis product portfolio – driven by know-how, experience and synergies
Communication and information solutions for a safer world

ATM Civil	Defence	Public Safety	Public Transport	Maritime
• Voice communication systems • Remote tower • ATM systems • Intelligent networks • Aeronautical information management	• Red/black communications • National air policing • Last minute briefing system • Joint forces command	• Call handler and radio dispatcher • Network components and emergency applications • ECO system	• Fixed terminal systems - GSM-R and bearer independent • Incident management	• Integrated maritime solutions and networks • smartVTS • GMDSS /SAR • Tactical communication

Safety critical solutions

Common products
Voice communication | Information management | Networking

R&D: Leveraging cross-industry heritage in product development

Frequentis – a strong network around the world

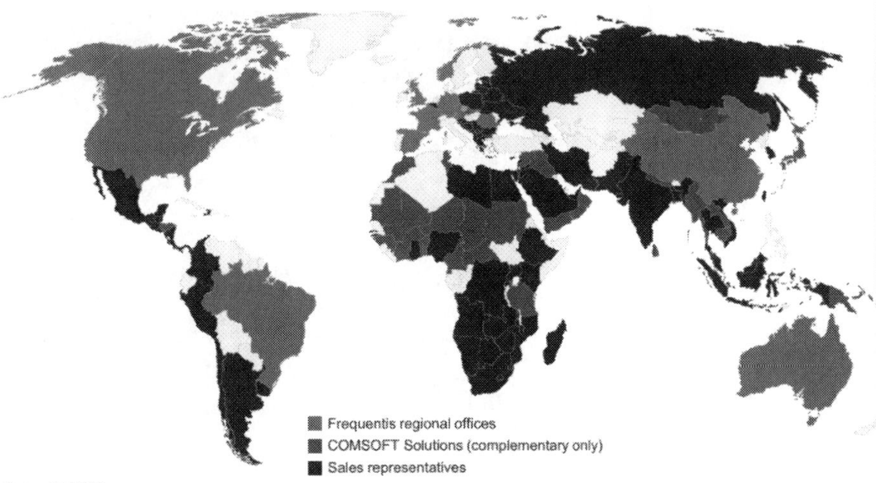

Status: E01/2018

25,000 working positions using Frequentis solutions

more than **300** customers

120+ countries

90% of all passengers worldwide are served by Frequentis customers

33% of the world safer with Frequentis networks

#1 in GSM-R dispatcher terminals

200,000km protecting the largest maritime coastline

Projects in 120 countries around the world

- More than **300** customers
- **#1 VCS ATM** market share
- **Largest** public safety control centre in Europe
- **#1 GSM-R** dispatcher terminal market share
- Largest maritime coastline safer - **200,000km**

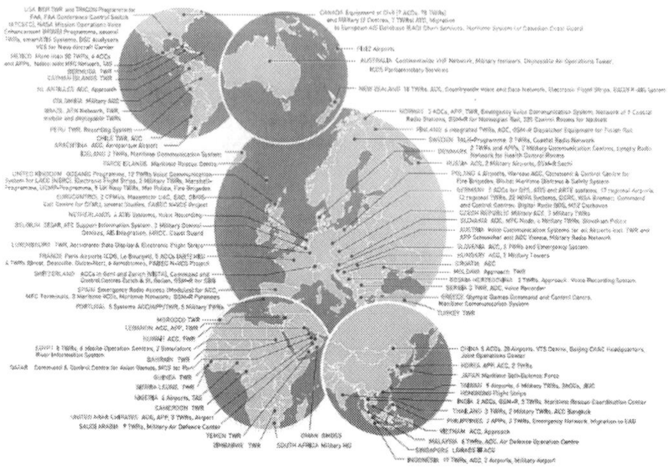

Agenda

- Motivation & Background
- Vulnerabilities & Exploits
- Safety & Security
- What can we do?
- Risk Assessment
- Case Study

What is Security?

- Security is a composite of
  - **C**onfidentiality: Absence of unauthorized disclosure of information
  - **I**ntegrity: Absence of improper system alterations
  - **A**vailability: Readiness for correct service

"CIA"

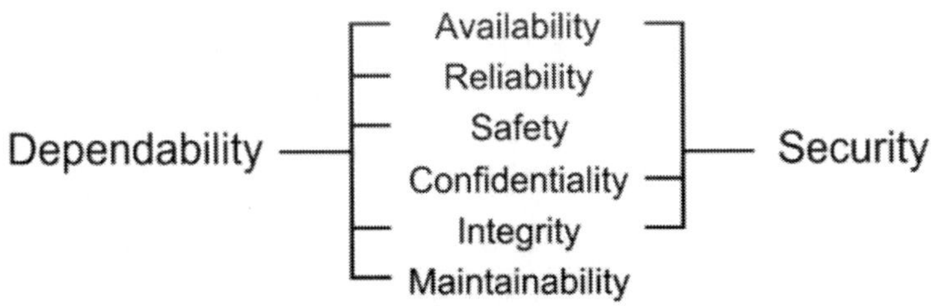

Terminology

Term	Definition
Asset	???
Threat	???
Vulnerability	???
Exploit	???
Zero Day Exploit	???
Security Risk	???

The Window of Exposure – "Zero Days"

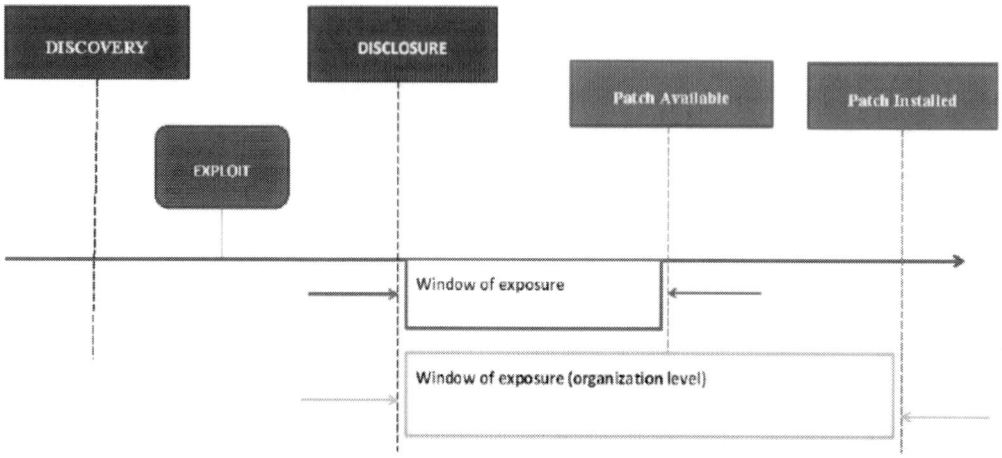

Security Awareness is a Mindset!

- Lack of security awareness might compromise all other dependability attributes
- Take it personal!
  - When have you last changed your passwords?
  - Where do you store your passwords?
  - Are your passwords secure?
  - Do you use different passwords for all services?
  - Do you ever transmit passwords in plain text?
  - Do you ever check e-mail via POP, IMAP, http? (i.e. without SSL/TLS)
  - Do you read the permissions for Smartphone apps?
  - Do you have a virus scanner? On all your computers?
  - How do you weigh usability vs. security?
  - Do you regularly install all critical updates?
  - Do you use Adobe Flash Player, Java Applets,…?
  - Do you use public Wi-Fi Hotspots?
  - What about your camera on your laptop? Microphone?
  - …

Security Mindset? ;-)

Defender's Dilemma

"An attacker only needs to find one weakness while the defender needs to find every one."

Attacker	Defender
Attacker has to find ***only*** one bug	Defender has to remove ***all*** bugs
Attacker only needs ***one*** short time to attack	Defender has to protect the system ***all*** the time
Attacker has to find only ***one*** weak link in the chain	Defender needs to keep ***all*** chain links strong
Attacker can choose ***one*** instant in time which is convenient	Defender has to be ready and active ***all*** the time

Who has an advantage?

Safety Standards

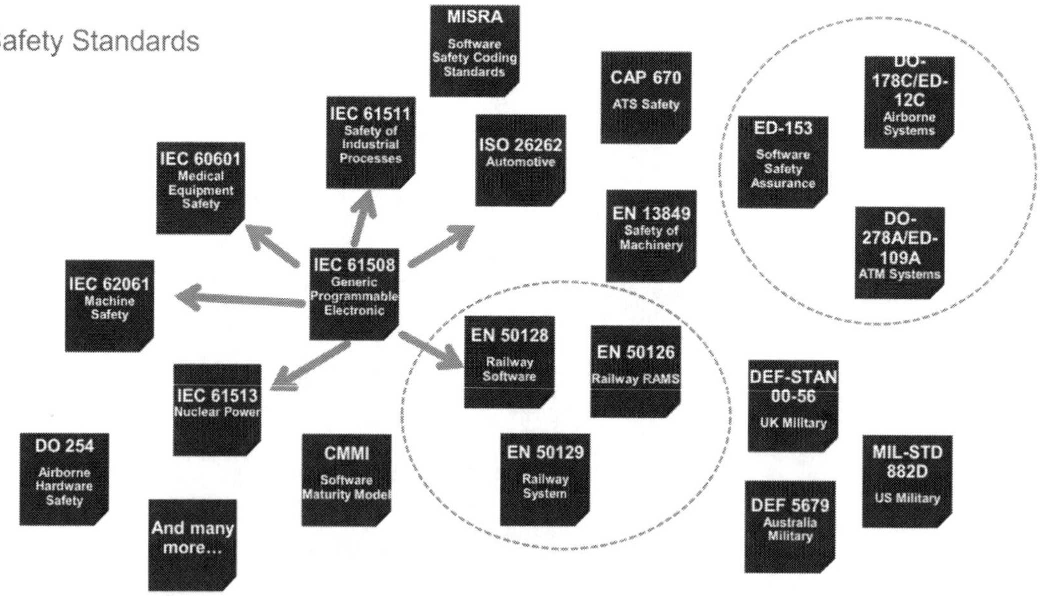

Security Standards

IEC 62443 Industrial Comm Networks Security

PCI Payment Card Industry

NIST 800-64 Security in Development Lifecycle

ISO 21827 System Security Maturity Model

NIST 800-100 Information Security for Managers

ISO 27005 Security Risk Management

ISO 27004 Security Management

NIST 800 Security Series

ISO 28000 Security in Supply Chain

BSIMM Maturity Model

FIPS Federal Information Processing

ISO 27000 Information Security Series

ISO 27001 Security Requirements

NIST 800-30 Risk Management

NIST 800-12 Computer Security

ISO 15408 Common Criteria

SAMM Maturity Model

CERT Secure Coding Guidelines

ISO 27034 IT Application Security

OWASP Guidelines

And many more…

Safety and Security: Is there a Harmonisation in Sight?

not sure…

Motivation & Background

Motivation – Driving Factors

- Reliance on electronic systems
  - Hardware, software, networks, ...
- Cyber-Security has become a global economic and social concern
  - Threats and vulnerabilities harm humanity and society
- Safety critical infrastructures are attractive targets
  - Increasing use of Commercial-Off-The-Shelf (COTS) components
  - Net-centric approach (e.g. SWIM)

COTS ... Commercial Off-The-Shelf
SWIM ... System Wide Information Management

Motivation – Change of Environment

Current systems	Future systems
"Closed" System	Service Oriented Architecture (SOA)
Point-to-Point connections	Net-centric
"Monolithic" system	Interconnected sub-systems, and extended to include airports, pilots and data providers
Proprietary interface definition	Standard protocols with published vulnerabilities
Diversity of suppliers and systems	Fewer suppliers
Lots of redundancy	Efficiency
Existing users have security management systems in place	Some new end-users have little security management (e.g. general aviation)

Motivation – New Vulnerabilities

- Increased inter-connection and propagation vectors
  - Between safety-critical area and others (e.g. remote access)
- Increased level of exposure
  - Change of point-to-point to net-centric communication architecture
- Use of standard components (COTS, TCP/IP, …)
  - Publication of vulnerabilities, e.g. Heartbleed
- Varying levels of cyber-security maturity
  - Maturity levels may vary and create weak links in cyber-security chain
- …

Motivation – Threats to Safety

- Harm of environment
- Disruptive attacks reduce operational capacity
- Financial and reputational damage
- Loss of confidence

Cybercrime

- Service outage
- Malware (Viruses, Ransomware, Trojan Horses, Adware, Spyware,…)
- Website Defacements
- Doxing
- Spam
- …

WannaCry

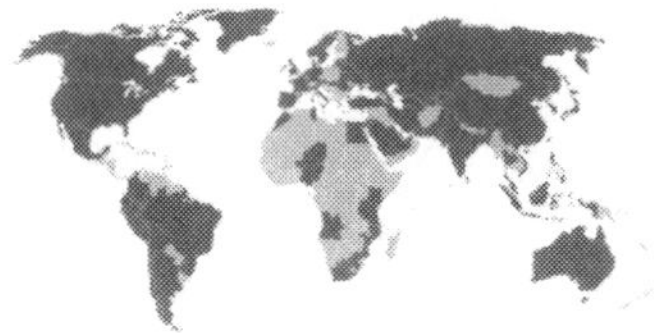

- First Ransomware combined with a Worm/Virus
- Based on vulnerability in MS SMB Protocol
- Vulnerability was supposedly exploited by government agencies for years
- Vulnerability became publicly known before patch was available for all OSs (April 2017)
- Some effects:
  - Renault production halt
  - UK hospitals – lots of delays
  - Deutsche Bahn
  - Telecom operators,…

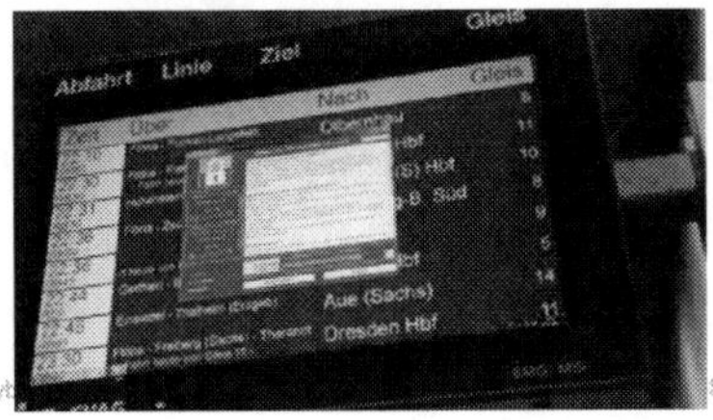

Hacking Techniques and Attacks

- Social Engineering
- Brute-force attacks
- Botnets
- Phishing, Spear Phishing
- (Distributed) Denial of Service (DoS, DDoS)
- Spoofing
- Man-in-the-middle

- or – most effectively – any combination of the above

Cyberterrorism, Cyberattacks, Cyberwar

- Hostile acts against governments, countries, certain groups,…
- E.g. "Sony Hack", attributed to North Korea

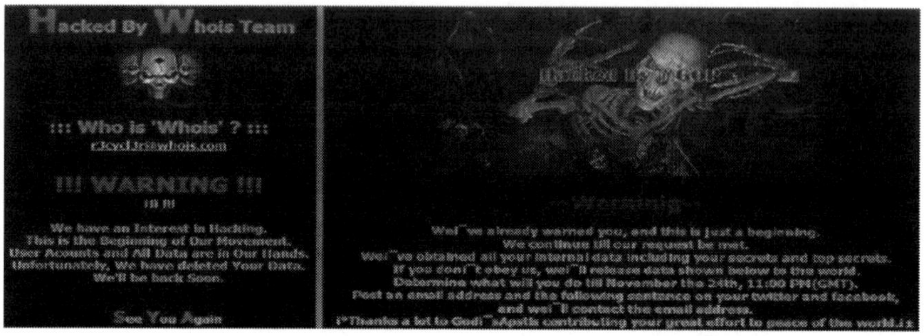

Cybersecurity

- Google search trends for term "cybersecurity" (2006-2017)
  - http://www.google.com/trends/

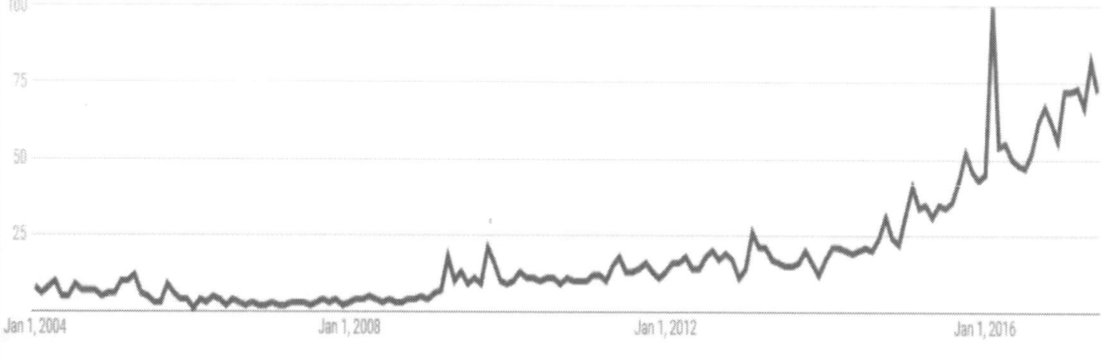

Motivation – Things are happening NOW

See e.g. http://map.norsecorp.com/, http://www.sicherheitstacho.eu, …

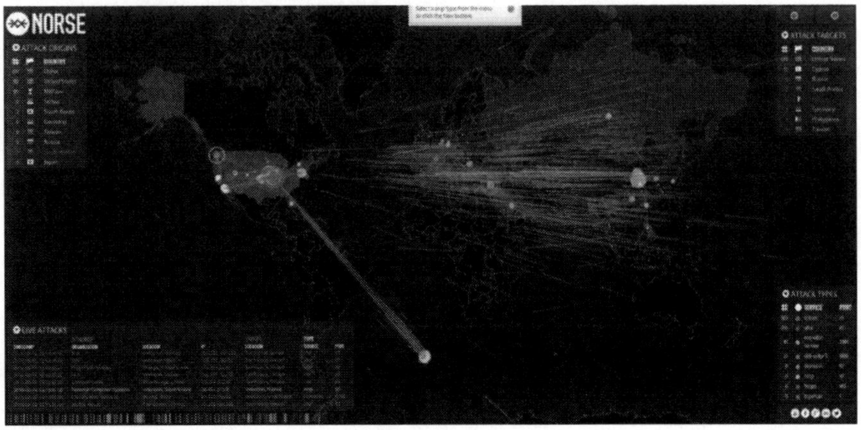

Motivation – Security News-Ticker 2015/16

- 15,435 vulnerabilities across 3,870 applications were recorded in 2014
  - Pasted from <http://www.net-security.org/secworld.php?id=18132>
- European Aviation Safety Agency – Airplane hacking is reality
  - Pasted from http://securityaffairs.co/wordpress/40975/hacking/easa-airplane-hacking.html
- ConnectedDrive: The BMW-Hack in detail
  - Pasted from <http://www.heise.de/newsticker/meldung/ConnectedDrive-Der-BMW-Hack-im-Detail-2540786.html?from-mobi=1>
- Power outage probably caused by hackers in Ukraine
  - Pasted from <http://www.heise.de/security/meldung/Stromausfall-in-der-Ukraine-augenscheinlich-durch-Hacker-ausgeloest-3063343.html>
- BSI Security Report: Successful cyber attack in German Steel Mill
  - Pasted from <http://m.heise.de/newsticker/meldung/BSI-Sicherheitsbericht-Erfolgreiche-Cyber-Attacke-auf-deutsches-Stahlwerk-2498990.html>

Motivation – Cyber Attacks in ATM

- Cyber-attacks against the ATM Cyber Space can be defined as an offensive activity executed against the confidentiality, integrity and availability of the ATM cyber space elements. Cyber-attacks are designed to:
  - Deny
  - Degrade
  - Disrupt
  - Manipulate or Destroy
- A cyber-attack may lead to the malfunction of the ATM/ANS operations, e.g. safety, confidentiality and business degradation/continuity
- The implementation of the new Air-Ground Data links based on IP protocols will increase the risks of a cyber-attack on avionics systems such as Flight Management Systems

Security and Embedded Systems

- Many (legacy) Embedded Systems were designed without security in mind
- Embedded Systems are increasingly interconnected ("Internet of Things")
- SCADA Systems:
  - Supervisory Control and Data Acquisition Systems: control and monitor technical processes
  - → highly vulnerable, consequences may be dramatic (safety-related!)

- Not easy to retrospectively build-in security into embedded systems
- Embedded systems are more vulnerable than larger computer systems
  - because they often do not have the same amount of security measures
  - because they are not updated frequently (or never)
- Embedded systems are less vulnerable
  - because they are often not based on operating systems with known vulnerabilities
  - because tailored attacks would be needed, which are more expensive

Motivation – Easy Targets

- How to find (potentially vulnerable) embedded systems: http://www.shodan.io/ ("Google for hackers")
- Shodan finds computers
  - Webservers, critical-infrastructure, refrigerators, webcams,…
  - Shodan indexes the "banners" the servers return
- Many devices still have their default passwords set…

33 | Cyber Safety and Security   ISSC 2018 | © 2018 Frequentis AG   FREQUENTIS

Motivation – Easy Targets

http://money.cnn.com/gallery/technology/security/2013/05/01/shodan-most-dangerous-internet-searches/index.html

34 | Cyber Safety and Security   ISSC 2018 | © 2018 Frequentis AG   FREQUENTIS

A swimming pool acid pump

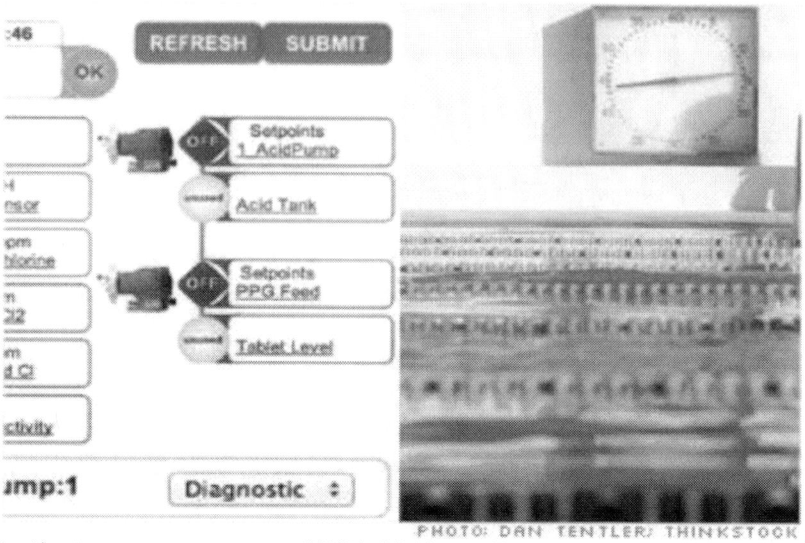

PHOTO: DAN TENTLER/ THINKSTOCK

Jeep Hack (July 2015)

- Wireless controlling Jeep Cherokees over the Internet
  - Radio, ventilation, windshield wipers, wiper fluid, cut transmission, disable brakes,…
- How does it work?
  - Fiat Chrysler cars have a system called Uconnect
  - Each car has an IP adress for convenience functions…
  - From here, malware accesses CAN bus
- Patch can only be applied via USB (not remotely)
  - Many cars will stay vulnerable…

The Reaction

En Español   Media Contacts   RSS

FCA

FIAT CHRYSLER AUTOMOBILES

BRANDS & PRODUCTS   CORPORATE   PHOTOS   VIDEO   AUTO SHOWS & EVENTS

Home

Share   Download   Print

FCA US LLC Releases Software Update to Improve Vehicle Electronic Security and Communications System Enhancements

July 16, 2015 , Auburn Hills, Mich. - The security and confidence of our customers is important. As part of its ongoing software security and quality efforts, FCA has an Embedded System Quality Engineering team dedicated to identifying and implementing software best practices across FCA globally. The team's responsibilities include development and implementation of cybersecurity standards for all vehicle content, including on-board and remote services. A number of best practices, procedures, standards, and policies govern FCA's cybersecurity program. Generally, there are many tools and techniques that are utilized throughout the vehicle lifecycle.

Today, this group at FCA released a Technical Service Bulletin (TSB) for a software update that offers customers improved vehicle electronic security and communications system enhancements.

Similar to a smartphone or tablet, vehicle software can require updates for improved security protection to reduce the potential risk of unauthorized and unlawful access to vehicle systems. Today's software security update, provided at no cost to customers, also includes Uconnect improvements introduced in the 2015 model year designed to enhance customer convenience and enjoyment of their vehicle. Customers can either download and install this particular update themselves or, if preferred, their dealer can complete this one-time update at no cost to customers.

Customers with questions may call Vehicle Care at 1-877-855-8400.

"New features via free software updates – as with every Model S, the 60 and 60D will receive free over-the-air software updates that add functionality and continue to improve the driving experience for years to come."

TESLA

Air Gap

- Air Gap: Physical separation between networks
- Air Gap = Security Protection?

- Good hackers can circumvent an air gap:
  - Removable Media (e.g. USB Sticks)
  - Malware in Hardware (e.g. graphics card)
  - Compiler, Build chain
  - Malicious Updates
  - Social Engineering, use of subcontractors,...

- Best-known example to overcome air gap: Stuxnet

Is there an Air Gap in modern aircraft?

No!

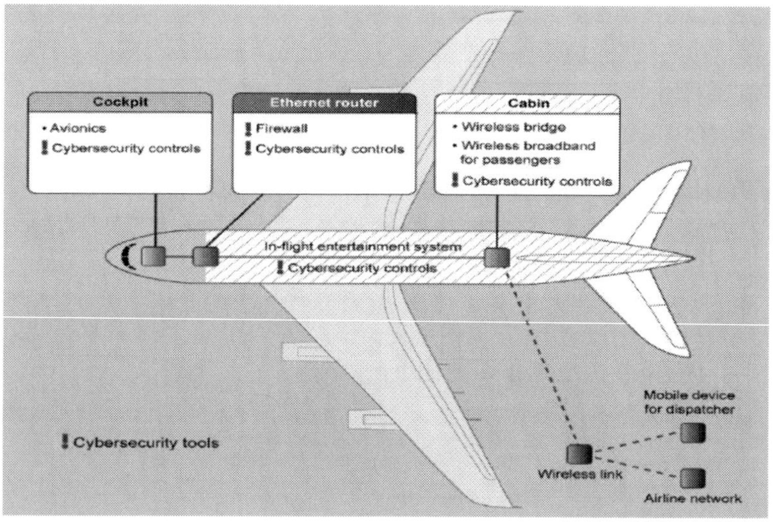

Source: GAO-15-370, FAA Needs a More Comprehensive Approach to Address Cybersecurity, 2015

WannaCry

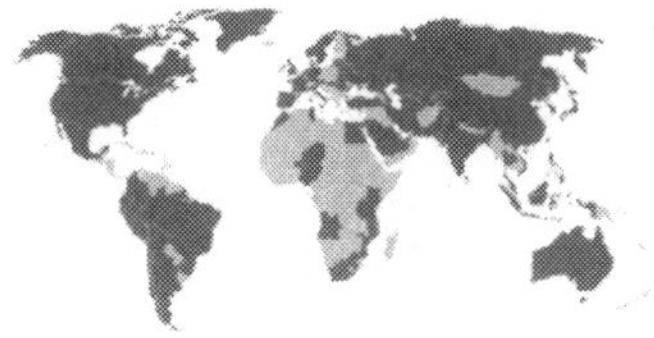

- First Ransomware combined with a Worm/Virus
- Based on vulnerability in MS SMB Protocol
- Vulnerability was supposedly exploited by government agencies for years
- Vulnerability became publicly known before patch was available for all OSs (April 2017)
- Some effects:
  - Renault production halt
  - UK hospitals – lots of delays
  - Deutsche Bahn
  - Telecom operators,...

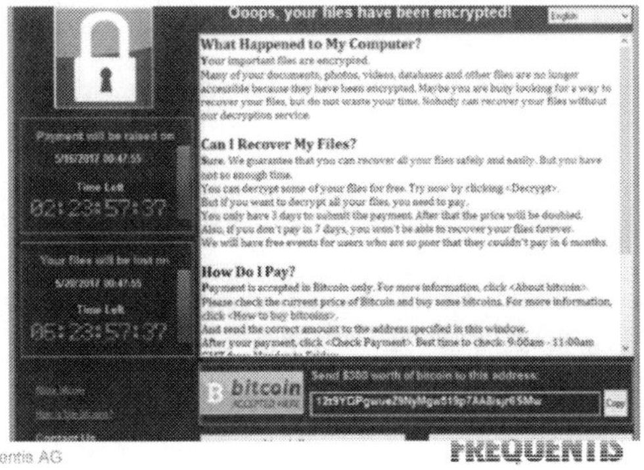

Vulnerabilities & Exploits

CWEs and CVEs

- CWE = Common Weakness Enumeration (https://cwe.mitre.org)
- CVE = Common Vulnerability and Exposure (https://cve.mitre.org)

- A CWE is a generic weakness in a software system that can lead to a CVE
- A CVE is a concrete vulnerability in a specific software version
- E.g. the Heartbleed bug has ID CVE-2014-0160, and is caused by CWE-130, CWE-119 and CWE-201

FREQUENTIS

Top 10 CWEs

ID	Description
CWE-89	Improper Neutralization of Special Elements used in an SQL Command ('SQL Injection')
CWE-78	Improper Neutralization of Special Elements used in an OS Command ('OS Command Injection')
CWE-120	Buffer Copy without Checking Size of Input ('Classic Buffer Overflow')
CWE-79	Improper Neutralization of Input During Web Page Generation ('Cross-site Scripting')
CWE-306	Missing Authentication for Critical Function
CWE-862	Missing Authorization
CWE-798	Use of Hard-coded Credentials
CWE-311	Missing Encryption of Sensitive Data
CWE-434	Unrestricted Upload of File with Dangerous Type
CWE-807	Reliance on Untrusted Inputs in a Security Decision

FREQUENTIS

"Monster" Mitigations

ID	Mitigation
M1	Establish and maintain control over all of your inputs.
M2	Establish and maintain control over all of your outputs.
M3	Lock down your environment.
M4	Assume that external components can be subverted, and your code can be read by anyone.
M5	Use industry-accepted security features instead of inventing your own.
GP1	(general) Use libraries and frameworks that make it easier to avoid introducing weaknesses.
GP2	(general) Integrate security into the entire software development lifecycle.
GP3	(general) Use a broad mix of methods to comprehensively find and prevent weaknesses.
GP4	(general) Allow locked-down clients to interact with your software.

How many CVEs are there?

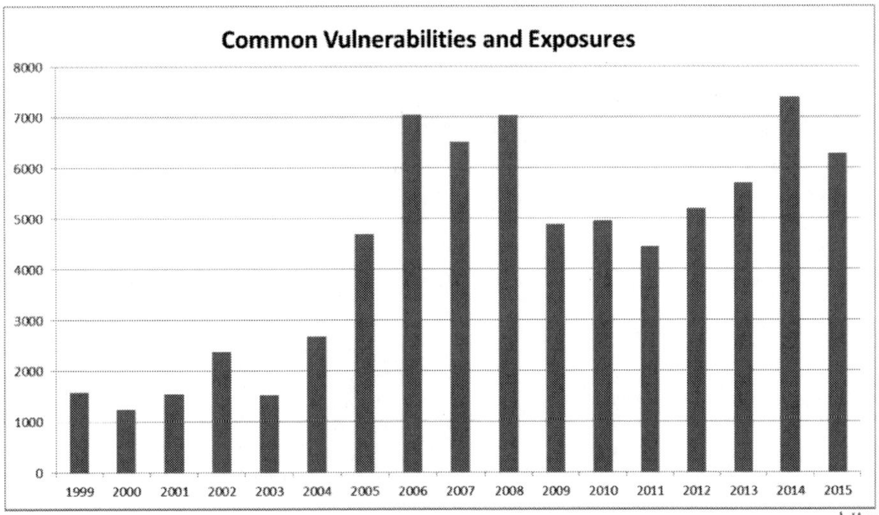

https://cve.mitre.org/

Price-list of a zero-day in black market

ADOBE READER	\$5,000-\$30,000
MAC OSX	\$20,000-\$50,000
ANDROID	\$30,000-\$60,000
FLASH OR JAVA BROWSER PLUG-INS	\$40,000-\$100,000
MICROSOFT WORD	\$50,000-\$100,000
WINDOWS	\$60,000-\$120,000
FIREFOX OR SAFARI	\$60,000-\$150,000
CHROME OR INTERNET EXPLORER	\$80,000-\$200,000
IOS	\$100,000-\$250,000

*) Source: http://www.forbes.com/sites/andygreenberg/2012/03/23/shopping-for-zero-days-an-price-list-for-hackers-secret-software-exploits/

High monetary reward for zero-days attracting more hackers to find them -> organisations need to invest for zero-day discovery and harden their infrastructure.

48 | Cyber Safety and Security ISSC 2018 | © 2018 Frequentis AG FREQUENTIS

Selling bugs and exploits?

- Various companies specialise in dealing with bugs and exploits
- There is a big (partly black, partly official) market for such bugs
- E.g. http://www.vupen.com

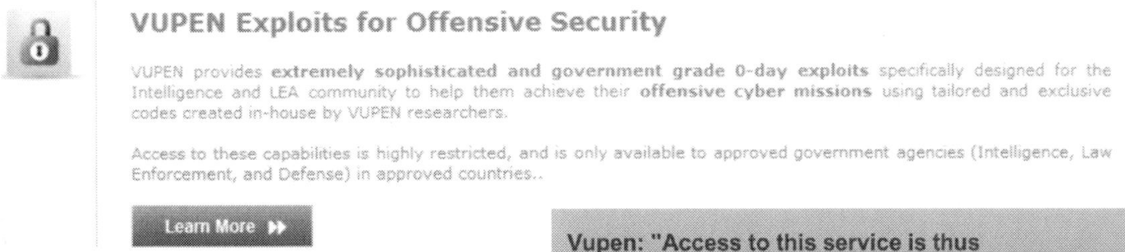

Vupen: "Access to this service is thus highly restricted, and is only available to approved government agencies (Intelligence, Law Enforcement, and Defense) in approved countries."

Selling bugs and exploits?

zerodium

- Sell bugs to the manufacturer or to a broker?

- Quotes from website:
  - "ZERODIUM pays premium bounties and rewards to security researchers to acquire their original and previously unreported zero-day research affecting major operating systems, software, and/or devices."
  - "ZERODIUM customers are major corporations in defense, technology, and finance, in need of advanced zero-day protection, as well as government organizations in need of specific and tailored cybersecurity capabilities. "

Some Quotes

- "Cybercriminals will buy so-called zero-day vulnerabilities in the black market, while government agencies and corporations purchase them from brokers and exploit clearinghouses, such as VUPEN Security, ReVuln, Endgame Systems, Exodus Intelligence, and Netragard. "
- "Endgame sold 25 zero-day exploits a year for $2.5 million."
- "average vulnerability sells from around $35,000 to $160,000."

all from
http://www.pcworld.com/article/2070662/vendor-security-patches-lag-dangerously-study-suggests.html

Safety & Security

Background – Safety & Security

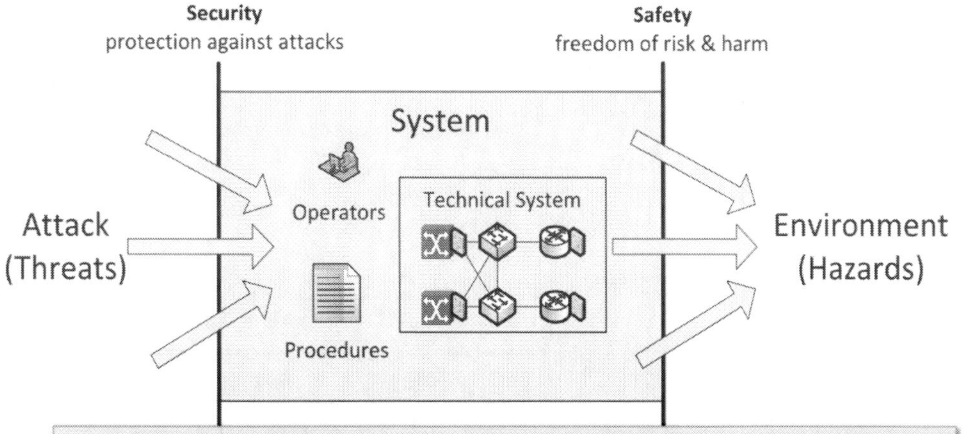

Strong connection of System Safety & System Security regarding the **availability** of functions for **authorized** parties

Background – Safety & Security Example 1

- **Example:** Technical Monitoring and Control System (TMCS)
  - Configuration of radio frequencies and roles
  - Change may be necessary at a specific point in time
  - Depending on daytime and task
  - Rush hours!
- **Safety**
  - **Availability** of the Voice Communication System is **critical**
  - **Sufficient resources** required to operate airspace **safely**
  - Backup system required to clear the sky
- **Security**
  - **Unauthorized** access to TMCS is **critical**
  - Misconfiguration or sabotage could lead to **safety incidents** (e.g. frequency change)

Background – Safety & Security Example 2

- **Example:** Car to Car Communication

Benefits for Safety	*Security Risks*
• Warning messages • Regulated speed and distances • Traffic control to avoid risks	• Fake safety messages could cause safety risk • Vulnerabilities in the software (Threats!) • Driving information (speed, location, daytime)

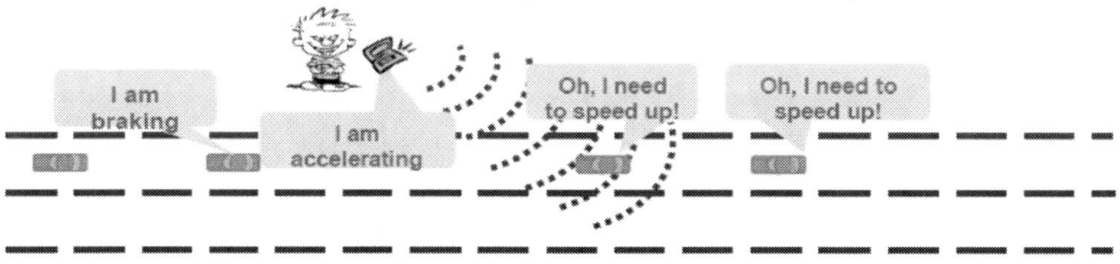

© DaimlerChrysler

Safety and Security – Fundamental Differences

- Accidental ("Murphy's Law")
- Intentional ("Satan's Law")

- Probability calculations often useful
- Random and systematic causes
- Probability calculations not helpful
- Systematic causes only

- Redundancy can help
- Diversity can help
- Redundancy does not help
- Diversity can be helpful and detrimental

- Most problems: high-level (requirements)
- Most problems: low-level (implementation)

- No intelligent adversary
- Approved software unchanged for years
- Intelligent adversary changes and evolves
- Software needs to adapt quickly (to respond to changing attack patterns)

Background – Safety & Security

Commonalities and Overlapping

- Process-oriented and life-cycle approach
  - Must be considered in early design phase, no "add-on"
- Additional expenses (technical and monetary) that pay off
  - Long-term benefits
- Risk assessment based approach
  - Evaluate residual risk
  - Classification and prioritization of risks

Background – Safety & Security

Differences

- No common international Safety & Security standard
  - E.g. IEC61508, ISO27000
- Safety requirements overrule security requirements (?)
  - Conflicting situations, for example:
    - Security requires complex and unique passwords to login
    - Safety requires short term login to avoid critical loss of time in stressful situation

Another difference: Security Risk increases over lifetime

- Important difference between Safety and Security
  - The security risk changes over the lifetime, as the attackers' competence changes
  - The safety risk typically does not change
  - → Security needs to be re-evaluated over the lifetime

e.g. SHA-1 was probably secure 10 years ago. Not any more...
see also https://www.keylength.com/en/compare/

Background – Safety & Security

Remember: No safety without security!

Connection between Safety & Security

- Security affects safety
  - Risks must be considered globally
- Both areas aim to improve the reliability and availability
  - Reduction of "Bugs"
  - Common cutting point is availability
  - Commonalities in hazard and threat management (process based)
- Awareness, culture and training
  - Unlike safety, cyber security needs to become part of daily mindset

Background - Cyberspace

- **Cyberspace**
  - Systems and services connected **directly or indirectly** to the internet or networks
  - Border of cyberspace is hard to describe
  - **Non-physical** events
- **Typical situation for Frequentis Systems**
  - Data is transmitted through **shared IP networks**
  - Trustful and sealed-off environment is hard to archive
  - Air-gap can be bypassed (e.g. by USB thumb drive, weakest link)
    - Maintenance done with devices which had direct access to the internet?
    - Infected hardware, compilers, upgrades,…
- **Cyberspace concerns other safety-related areas**
  - Energy, Defense, Automotive, Public Transport, Health …

USB ... Universal Serial Bus
IP... Internet Protocol

Background – Cyber Safety & Security

- **Non-physical** security events in cyberspace may have **real implications**
  - Denial of Service attack (**non-physical**)
  - Disruption of safety-related ATM procedures **(reality)**

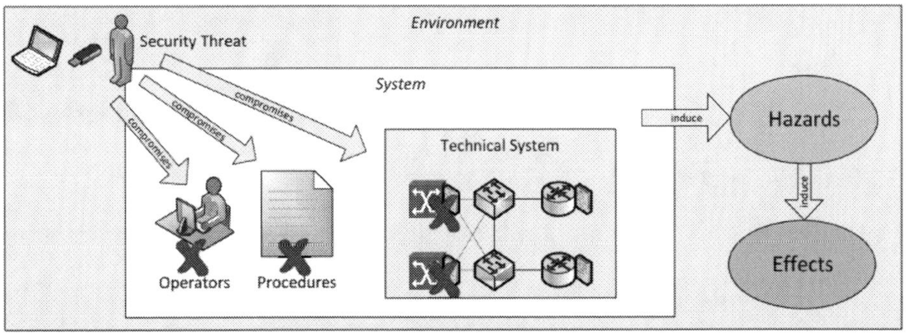

Sara Sadvandi, Nicolas Chapon, Ludovic Piètre-Cambacédès, "Safety and Security Interdependencies in Complex Systems and SoS: Challenges and Perspectives"

What can we do?

63 | Cyber Safety and Security ISSC 2018 | © 2018 Frequentis AG FREQUENTIS

Scenarios - Attackers

- Individual hackers
- (H)activists
- Insiders
- Business competitors
- Terrorists
- Organised crime
- State cyber-forces

➢ Motivation and capabilities of attackers vary, readiness for diverse attacks required

ENISA 2013 Threat Landscape
CANSO 2014 Cyber Security and Risk Assessment Guide

64 | Cyber Safety and Security ISSC 2018 | © 2018 Frequentis AG FREQUENTIS

Mitigation Examples

- Integrate Security into your (Safety) Lifecycle!
- Secure Requirements
- Secure Development
- Security and Penetration Testing
- Security Case
- Keep critical infrastructure physically separated by design
  - If physical separation is not possible, apply Security Zones (perimeters)
- Patch Management
  - Software Safety Assurance Issue!
- Establish a CSIRT

Basic Safety and Basic Security Requirements

- These requirements shall apply "by default" to all systems
  - Applicability is evaluated for each development effort

- Some random examples
  - For password storage, strong protection mechanisms shall be used.
  - The entire login transaction for password transport shall be encrypted (credentials).
  - System security shall be included in the early stages of system development.
  - Perfect Forward Secrecy (PFS) for IPsec connections should be used.
  - Stateful Packet Inspection firewalls shall be the minimum firewalls supported.

Secure Development: Secure Design and Coding Standard

- Design Standard
  - Secure Design Rules
  - Guidelines on Password handling
  - Principle of Least Privilege
  - Complexity limitation rules

- Software Coding Standard
  - CWE/OWASP lists considered
  - Based on secure coding rules
  - Logging of sensitive data
  - Concrete rules to avoid security relevant bugs (undefined behaviour, buffer overflows, SQL Injection, XSS, XSRF,...)

OWASP Top 10

- **A1 – Injection**
- **A2 – Broken Authentication and Session Management**
- **A3 – Cross-Site Scripting (XSS)**
- **A4 – Broken Access Control**
- **A5 – Security Misconfiguration**
- **A6 – Sensitive Data Exposure**
- **A7 – Insufficient Attack Protection**
- **A8 – Cross-Site Request Forgery (CSRF)**
- **A9 – Using Components with Known Vulnerabilities**
- **A10 – Underprotected APIs**

FREQUENTIS

Security and Penetration Tests

- All systems have to go through rigorous security and penetration testing
- All vulnerabilities have to be treated

Security Case

- Extend your Safety Case with a Security Case:
  "The system is acceptably secure for the intended operation within the specified environment"

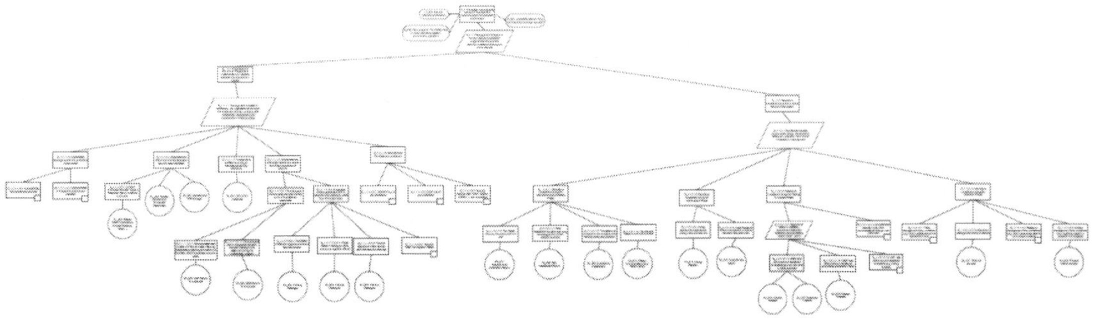

Security Case: Top Level Claim

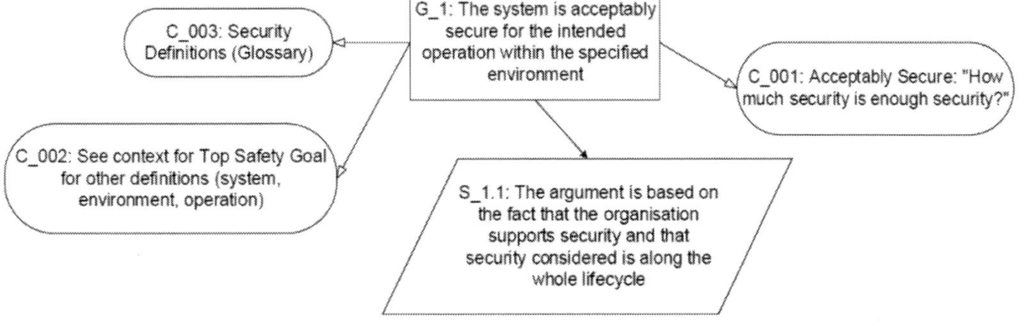

Mitigation – Security Zones 1/2

- Exemplary assessment of a Voice Communication System
  - Voice connections may cross **different parts** of cyberspace

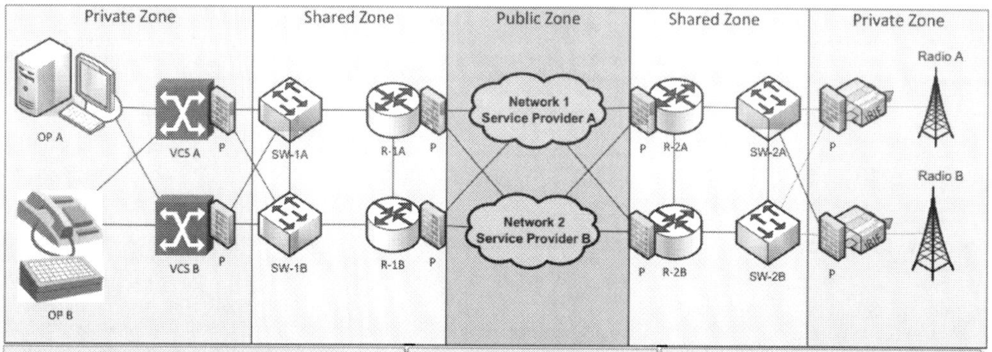

VCS ... Voice Communication System
OP ... Operator Position

SW ... Layer 2 Switch
R ... Layer 3 Router

P ... Perimeter
IRIF ... IP Radio Interface

Mitigation – Security Zones 2/2

- **Security zones** through perimeter functions necessary
  - Classifying network zones is a great instrument in the course of security analysis
  - Physical and logical separation of parts of cyberspace by perimeters
  - Shared and public zone are of **special interest**
  - Private zone is the most protected because of the security measures of other zones

Security Zones	Assumptions	Security Risk
Public	Non-trusted environment (e.g. Service Provider, 3rd party) No control over technology No dedicated resources available (worst case is best effort)	High
Shared	Trusted environment but not under full control Resources are shared with other (e.g. radar devices) Increased risk of insider attacks	Middle
Private	Control over technology Dedicated resources (bandwidth, quality of service) Devices and personnel fully trusted	Low

Patch Management

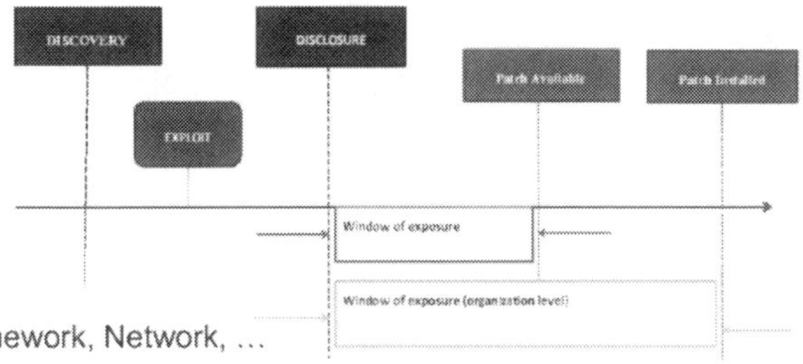

- **Patch Management vs. Software Safety Assurance!**
- Provide patches to equipment
  - Equipment: Operating System, Libraries, Framework, Network, …
- Test in non-operational environment before rolled out to operational machines
- After testing, apply in two phases
  - The first phase will involve half of the intended operational clients for verification of correct functionality over the course of 2-3 days of normal operations
  - The second phase will apply the patch package to all operational clients
- As usual: keep risk of patching in mind!
  - Have a backup!
- Prerequisite: Configuration Management
  - Which versions are running in the operational environment?

ENISA Recommendations for Europe on SCADA patching, Dec 2013

CSIRT - Computer Security Incident Response Team

- Establish a CSRIT Team in your company!
- Proactive distribution of security information
  - Threats, attacks and vulnerabilities
  - Vulnerability & Security Notifications
- Investigations and disclosures
  - Related to the company's deliverables
  - Support for incident handling
- Team
  - Members of all relevant departments involved
  - Specialists for different kinds of safety & security

Mitigation – More ideas

- Redundancy and diversity in (backup) systems
  - Primary system is safe, secondary system is secure (software updates)
- Black / Whitelisting
  - Communication Matrix
- System Hardening & Fault Tolerance
  - Sandboxing, Virtualization, Isolation
- Logging and Monitoring
  - Important for forensic analysis, false positives are a problem
- Reporting of security incidents will become mandatory
  - European General Data Protection Regulation (GDPR)

ISO 27005 Risk Assessment

1. Asset Identification

- Asset = anything that has value to the organization

- Primary Assets
  - Business processes & activities
  - Information
- Supporting Assets
  - Hardware (computers, peripherals, ...)
  - Software (operating system, database, middleware, business applications, administration software, ...)
  - Network (active or passive)

- Assets can be assigned a value
- Supporting assets can be mapped to primary assets
  - e.g. a database contains all customer information

2. Threat Identification

- Threat = a potential cause of an unwanted incident, which may result in harm to a system or organization

- Examples for threats: Eavesdropping, theft of equipment, tampering with hardware, tampering with software, interception, destruction of equipment, abuse of rights, denial of actions, corruption of data, unauthorized use of equipment, software malfunction, disclosure of data,...

- A threat is mapped to an asset
- Threats can be classified according to their likelihood

3. Vulnerability Identification

- Vulnerability = a weakness of an asset or group of assets that can be exploited by one or more threats
- Vulnerabilities enable threats to attack assets
  - a hole in my fence (vulnerability) enables a theft (threat) and my barbecue equipment (asset) is stolen
  - a weak encryption protocol enables eavesdropping, which discloses private communication
- Examples for vulnerabilities: well-known flaws in software, wrong allocation of access rights, susceptibility to weather conditions, unprotected storage, poor password management, insecure network architecture, use of standard passwords, single point of failure, unprotected network traffic, lack of periodic software update, outdated encryption, transport of unencrypted traffic,...
- Vulnerabilities can be classified according to their "ease of exploitation"
  - if the vulnerability is present, how easy is it by the given threat to exploit that vulnerability

4. Risk Analysis

- Risk = a security risk is the loss potential to an organization's asset(s) that will likely occur if a threat is able to exploit a vulnerability
- Each Asset-Threat-Vulnerability combination can be assigned a risk

	Likelihood of occurrence – Threat	Low			Medium			High		
	Ease of Exploitation	L	M	H	L	M	H	L	M	H
Asset Value	0	0	1	2	1	2	3	2	3	4
	1	1	2	3	2	3	4	3	4	5
	2	2	3	4	3	4	5	4	5	6
	3	3	4	5	4	5	6	5	6	7
	4	4	5	6	5	6	7	6	7	8

5. Risk Treatment

- Controls to reduce, retain, avoid, or share the risks should be selected and a risk treatment plan defined

- Four ways for risk treatment:
  - Accept, or tolerate (no action needed)
  - Reduce or treat (through controls)
  - Avoid or terminate (change or stop the activity)
  - Transfer (to another party)

How does all this fit together???

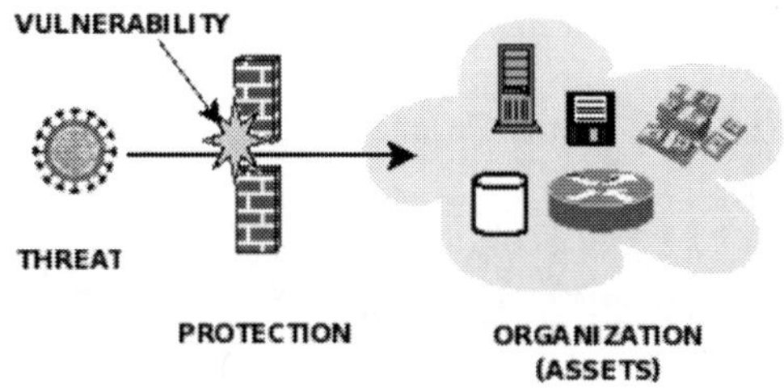

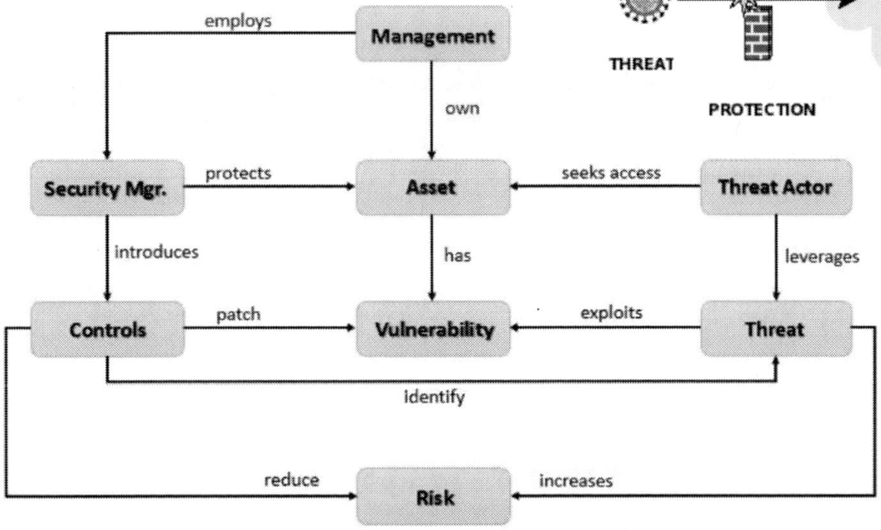

ISSC 2018 | © 2018 Frequentis AG

Microsoft Security Development Lifecycle

Microsoft Security Development Lifecycle

- Security Practices for each stage in the software development lifecycle

1. TRAINING	2. REQUIREMENTS	3. DESIGN	4. IMPLEMENTATION	5. VERIFICATION	6. RELEASE	7. RESPONSE
1. Core Security Training	2. Establish Security Requirements	5. Establish Design Requirements	8. Use Approved Tools	11. Perform Dynamic Analysis	14. Create an Incident Response Plan	Execute Incident Response Plan
	3. Create Quality Gates/Bug Bars	6. Perform Attack Surface Analysis/ Reduction	9. Deprecate Unsafe Functions	12. Perform Fuzz Testing	15. Conduct Final Security Review	
	4. Perform Security and Privacy Risk Assessments	7. Use Threat Modeling	10. Perform Static Analysis	13. Conduct Attack Surface Review	16. Certify Release and Archive	

Threat Analysis with STRIDE and DREAD

1. Model System with Data Flow Diagrams
2. Apply STRIDE – Risk Identification
3. Apply DREAD – Risk Quantification

Model System with Data Flow Diagrams

- Start with person, processes, data flows, data stores
  - Unique shape per item
  - Data flows should be one way each
  - Label them with data, not read/write
- Draw attack surfaces/trust boundaries
- Tell a story to see if your picture is ok

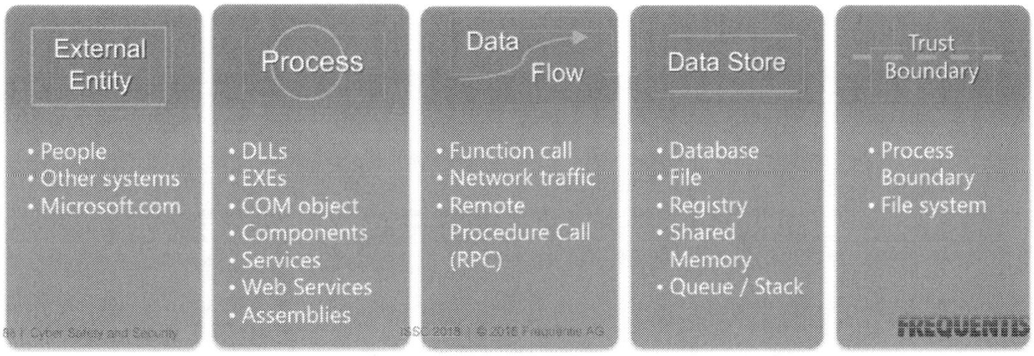

STRIDE

Threat	Property	Definition	Example
Spoofing			
Tampering			
Repudiation			
Information Disclosure			
Denial of Service			
Elevation of Privilege			

DREAD

	High (2)	Medium (2)	Low (1)
D – Damage potential	The attacker can subvert the security system; get full trust authorization; run as administrator; upload content.	Leaking sensitive information	Leaking trivial information
R – Reproducibility	The attack can be reproduced every time and does not require a timing window.	The attack can be reproduced, but only with a timing window and a particular race situation.	The attack is very difficult to reproduce, even with knowledge of the security hole.
E – Exploitability	A novice programmer could make the attack in a short time.	A skilled programmer could make the attack, then repeat the steps.	The attack requires an extremely skilled person and in-depth knowledge every time to exploit.
A – Affected users	All users, default configuration, key customers.	Some users, non-default configuration.	Very small percentage of users, obscure feature; affects anonymous users.
D – Discoverability	Published information explains the attack. The vulnerability is found in the most commonly used feature and is very noticeable.	The vulnerability is in a seldom-used part of the product, and only a few users should come across it. It would take some thinking to see malicious use.	The bug is obscure, and it is unlikely that users will work out damage potential.

Summary
Safety & Security

Summary Safety & Security

- Risk assessments are common for both areas
- Life-cycle processes considered from the very beginning
- Awareness and mindset for both areas are essential

Summary Safety & Security

Some problematic areas remain currently unresolved:

- Software Assurance vs. Security Updates in the field of ATM
  - Comprehensive verification and validation activities mandatory by standards
  - Software related **security updates** would require re-certification by authorities
    - Security updates on a daily basis, but assurance activities last for weeks

- Focus of interest
  - Safety requirements overrule security features **and vice versa**

- Speaking the same language between project members
  - Comprehensive understanding and clear definitions required

Security Facts & Problems

- Software has bugs (vulnerabilities, security holes)
  - Operating Systems, Frameworks, Libraries, Open Source, ... are affected
  - Median number of vulnerabilities per application = 14
  - Heartbleed, Shellshock, BadUSB, Poodle, goto fail, ... just in 2014

- People search for vulnerabilities (or introduce them)
  - Nation States, Government Agencies, Foreign Intelligence Services, Hackers, Insiders, Political Activists, Terrorists, Organized Crime, Investigative Journalists, Industrial Competitors, ...

- Safety-critical systems are open to security threats
  - Long-term in operation, outdated software, no (security) updates allowed
  - More and more inter-connection or access to internet, remote access
  - Safety needs Security Safeguards

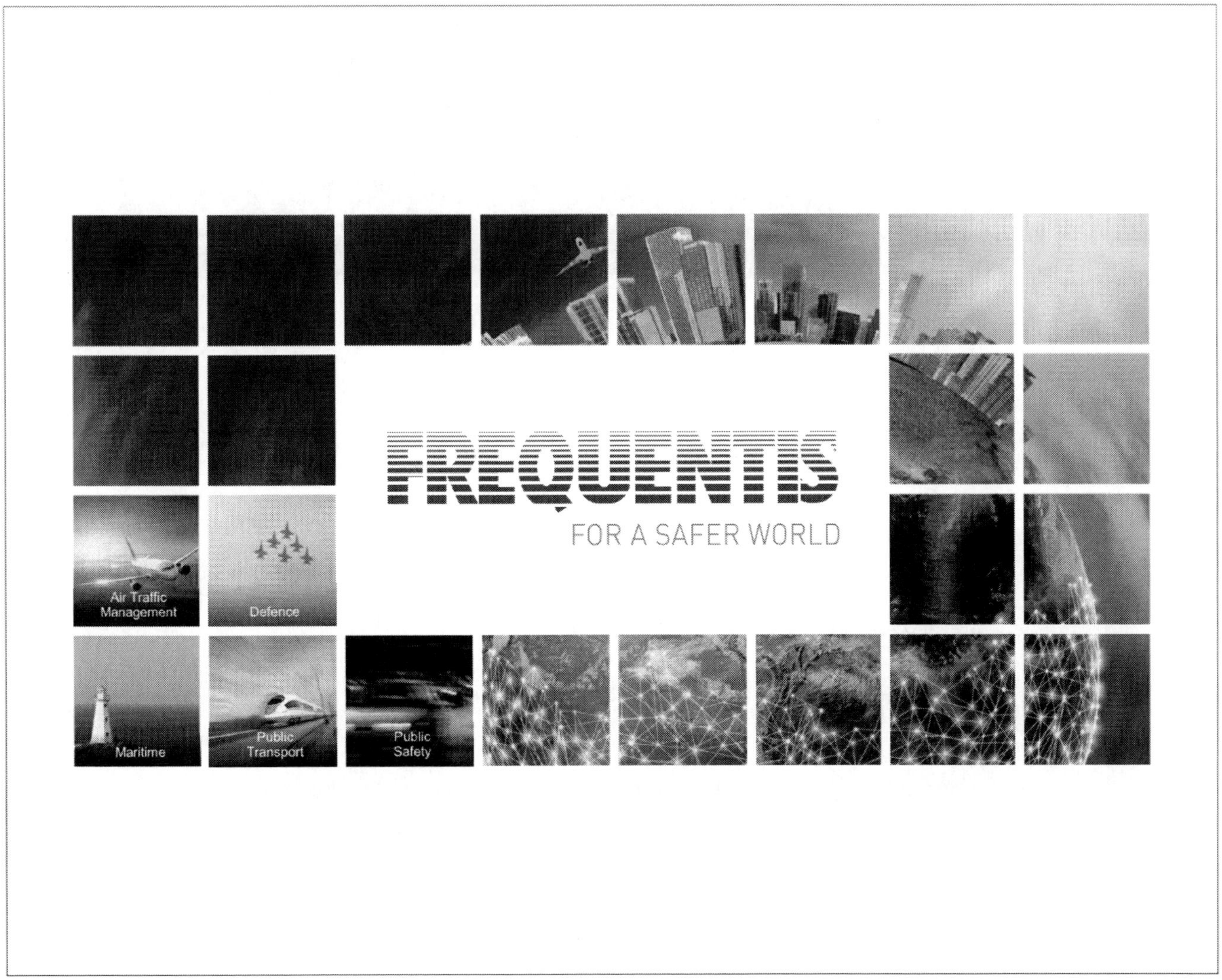
FREQUENTIS
FOR A SAFER WORLD
Air Traffic
Management
Defence
Maritime
Public
Transport
Public
Safety

FREQUENTIS
FOR A SAFER WORLD

System Safety Part 2: Safety Cases with the Help of GSN

ISSC 2018, Phoenix, USA

Andreas Gerstinger

Your competences after the workshop

- Understanding of the concept of safety cases
- Understanding of the benefits and potential pitfalls of safety cases
- Knowledge of the Goal Structuring Notation (GSN)
- Ability to read GSN
- Ability to create simple arguments in GSN

Agenda

- What are Safety Cases?
- The Goal Structuring Notation (GSN)
- Common Errors in GSN arguments
- Case Study
- Concluding Remarks

Acknowledgements

- The original work on GSN is Tim Kelly's doctoral thesis [Kel98]
- The GSN slides in this presentation are heavily based on [Spr12], which we highly recommend as a very readable introduction to safety arguments and GSN
- A useful web resource is http://www.goalstructuringnotation.info

Literature

[Ade98] Adelard Safety Case Development Manual. 1998.

[EUR06] Eurocontrol. Safety Case Development Manual. DAP/SSH/091. 13 Oct 2006.

[Gre&06] William S. Greenwell, John C. Knight, C. Michael Holloway, Jacob J. Pease. A Taxonomy of Fallacies in System Safety Arguments. Proceedings of the 24th International System Safety Conference, 2006.

[Kel98] T. P. Kelly, Arguing Safety – A Systematic Approach to Safety Case Management, DPhil Thesis YCST99-05, Department of Computer Science, University of York, UK, 1998.

[Kel&04] Tim Kelly, Rob Weaver. The Goal Structuring Notation - A Safety Argument Notation. Conference on Dependable Systems and Networks (DSN). Florence, Italy, 2004.

[Ori11] Origin Consulting. GSN Community Standard Version 1. November 2011. http://www.goalstructuringnotation.info/

[Spr12] John Spriggs. GSN - The Goal Structuring Notation: A Structured Approach to Presenting Arguments. Springer, 2012.

3 publicly available Safety Cases:

[EUR01] Eurocontrol. The EUR RVSM Pre-Implementation Safety Case. RVSM 691. 14 Aug 2001.

[Kin01] Steve Kinnersly. Whole Airspace ATM System – Preliminary Study. A report produced for EUROCONTROL by AEA Technology. Report number AEAT LD76008/2. 2001.

[NAG02] NAGRA. Project Opalinus Clay Safety Report. TECHNICAL REPORT 02-05. December 2002.

Introduction to Safety Cases

What is a "Safety Case"?

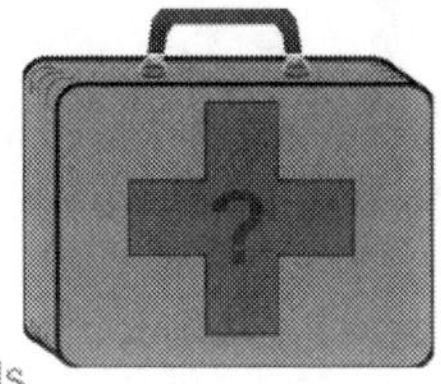

- The "Robens Report" (1972)
  - Balance between "prescriptive" and "goal setting" legislation needed to shift towards the latter
- Piper Alpha Accident (1988)
  - Conclusion that compliance with detailed prescriptive regulations was not sufficient to ensure safety

→ It is necessary to "make a case" for safety!

- "Make a case": to show that what you say is true
- Safety Case: shows that sufficient safety is given
- Term "safety case" has a legal origin

Prescriptive vs. Goal-based Standards

Prescriptive

- Describes what to do (way)
- Process-focus
- Requires the application of specific techniques and methods
- Less freedom, less responsibility
- Based on the assumption: "good process leads to good product"
- (Generally) does not require a safety case

Goal-Based

- Describes what to achieve (goal)
- Product-focus
- Requires certain product characteristics
- More freedom, more responsibility
- Based on the general approach:
  - Determine hazards and safety requirements
  - Design and implement them
  - Demonstrate achievement
- (Generally) requires a safety case

IEC 61508 (2010)

- No safety case required
- Requires processes, documents, verification, validation and functional safety assessment
- Requires detailed techniques and measures based on required safety integrity
- Very prescriptive

9 | Safety Cases with the Help of GSN   ISSC 2018 | © 2018 Frequentis AG   FREQUENTIS

DO-178C (2012)

- No safety case required
- A "software accomplishment summary" is required, which shows compliance to the planned lifecycle
- Detailed documentation and processes required
- Very prescriptive

10 | Safety Cases with the Help of GSN   ISSC 2018 | © 2018 Frequentis AG   FREQUENTIS

Def Stan 00-56, Issue 5 (2014)

- Safety Case required: "A structured argument, supported by a body of evidence that provides a compelling, comprehensible and valid case that a system is safe for a given application in a given operating environment."
- Safety Management Requirements for Defence Systems
- Strongly goal-based
- No specific processes or documentation structure suggested
- Safety Case is a major requirement

CENELEC EN 50129 (2003)

- Safety Case required: "the documented demonstration that the product complies with the specified safety requirements"
- Although detailed processes, documents, techniques and measures are required, a safety case is also required
- But: A very prescriptive description of how a safety case shall be structured, containing even the parts, sections and subsections of the complete safety case
- Practically no freedom how to argue safety

ISO 26262 (2011)

- Safety Case: "argument that the safety goals for an item are complete and satisfied by evidence compiled from work products of the safety activities during development"
- Required for ASILs B, C, D
- No detailed requirements on structure of safety case, but "the safety case shall be sufficiently complete to evaluate the achievement of functional safety of the item."
- Processes, documents, techniques and measures are nevertheless required in detail
- Safety Case is a prerequisite for assessment

Comparison

Standard	Safety Case	Comment
IEC 61508	No	-
DO-178C	No	-
Def Stan 00-56	Yes	• Very high level, very goal based • Safety Case shall demonstrate safety
CENELEC 50129	Yes	• Prescriptive processes and prescritpive safety case generation • Safety case shall show that specified requirements are met
ISO 26262	Yes	• Quite prescriptive processes, lots of freedom for safety case generation • Safety case shall show that safety goals are complete and met

Content of a Safety Case

- Generally, a Safety Case is a document containing a top level claim saying:

"The system is safe BECAUSE..."

... compelling and convincing arguments and evidence follow

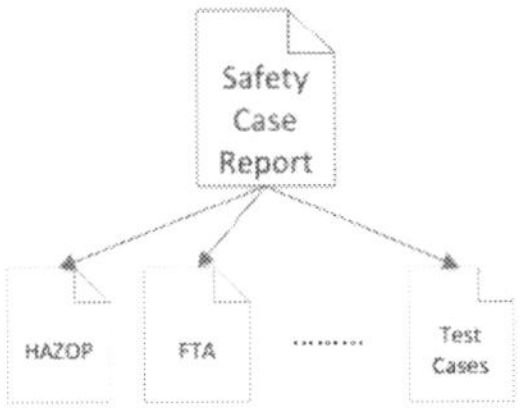

- What "safe" means in the context has to be defined (e.g. ALARP)
- Often other documents and analyses are referenced

General Form of a Safety Case

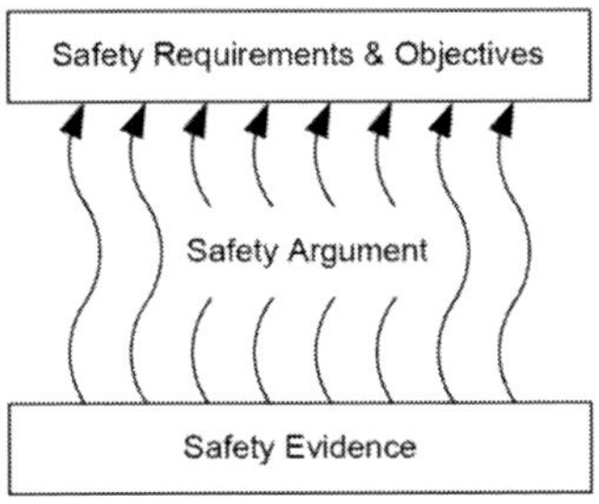

[Kel&04]

The claims, goals, etc. that we want to prove

The valid arguments

The pieces of evidence (documents, test results,...) supporting the arguments

- Form:
  - Can be simply textual
  - But: Difficult to structure, difficult to read

Is a Safety Case a Proof?

- In an ideal world: Yes.
- In the real world: No.

- But it depends on your understanding of the word "proof"...
- A safety case is rarely as strong as a mathematical proof
- But it should be as strong as a proof in law

Law	Safety
Defendant is innocent until proven guilty	System is dangerous until proven safe
In case of the slightest doubts, the defendant is not guilty	In case of the slightest doubts, the system is not safe

- And of course, as all proofs: it can contain flaws...

Arguments vs. Rhetorics

- A Safety Case must be "convincing" (not merely "persuasive")
- It must contain good (valid, compelling, comprehensible) arguments!!!
- Good rhetorics is not necessary (but can help)

If you don't understand a safety case, there is a high chance that it is crap!

Guidelines for a persuasive (not convincing) Safety Case Report (1) ;-)

- Write a **lot of text**, e.g. copy the complete system description and safety plan into the safety case document
- **Don't be too clear** – this allows you to always interpret the statements in your preferred way
- Use many **different terms for the same concept**
- Use the **same term for different concepts** (the context helps to understand the right meaning anyway)
- **Use lots of technical jargon** that has no relevance to the overall safety, but that sounds professional
- **Make the assessor look incompetent** when questions are asked
- **Include some easy to find typos** and other irrelevant errors so that reviewers can comment without understanding the contents
- Use a lot of **marketing phrases** from your products
- **Write that your company is successful** with the product
- Play **bullshit bingo** with your safety case
- Mention **how hard everybody has worked**

Guidelines for a persuasive (not convincing) Safety Case Report (2) ;-)

- Use **lots of references**, so that readers are intimidated to check them
- **References ad infinitum**: always put lots of further references in your referenced documents, so that readers have to hop many times before finding the information they are looking for
- **Circular references**: You can design it that way that after some hops you land at the originating document again
- Preferably **reference books and papers that are out of print/not available** any more
- Always make **conclusions from one to all**
- Always **extrapolate** from some event in the past into the future
- **Repeat invalid conclusions** many times, then they will eventually be believed
- Remember: *"Tell a man that there is wet paint on a bench and he will have to touch it to make sure. Tell a man there are 100 billion stars in the universe and he will believe you."*

Disclaimer and Warning

- Use the above guidelines at your own risk! We strongly advise not to use a single one!
- If you work with people with only the slightest bit of experience with safety cases, these guidelines will *not work at all*!

You should believe in what you say... ☺

The Safety Case is not a document!

- The *Safety Case* is "a structured argument, supported by a body of evidence that provides a compelling, comprehensible and valid case that a system is safe for a given application in a given operating environment." [DS00-56]
- The *Safety Case Report* is the corresponding document, i.e. "a key deliverable that summarises the Safety Case at a particular instant in time" [DS00-56]
- A document-centric approach is not desirable
  - "We need the safety case" is often misunderstood to mean "This annoying document has to be written up by someone now"

"It is possible to possess a document *called* the Safety Case and for there to be no safety case" [Kel&04]

Safety Argument

- "An argument is a connected series of statements intended to establish a proposition" [Spr12, p.2]
- "You use an argument to persuade others of the validity of some claim" [Spr12, p.2]
  - My opinion: "persuade" should be replaced by "convince"

- Properties of a good safety argument presentation
  - It has to be understandable
  - It has to be easy to read
  - Its logic correctness has to be verifiable
  - Logical faults shall be easy to spot
  - The notation shall be well defined and uniquely interpretable
  - It has to be clearly visible if there are unfinished parts
  - It shall be reusable

Textual Arguments

…can be good…

```
The Defence in Depth principle (P65) has
been addressed in this system through
the provision of the following:
•  Multiple physical barriers between
   hazard source and the environment
   (see Section X)
•  A protection system to prevent
   breach of these barriers and to
   mitigate the effects of a barrier
   being breached (see Section Y)
```

```
   For hazards associated with warnings,
the assumptions of [7] Section 3.4
associated with the requirement to
present a warning when no equipment
failure has occurred are carried
forward. In particular, with respect to
hazard 17 in section 5.7 [4] that for
test operation, operating limits will
need to be introduced to protect against
the hazard, whilst further data is
gathered to determine the extent of the
problem.
```

…but are more often horrible!

Tabular Structure

- (+) Clear differentiation between elements of an argumentation:
  - Claims
  - Arguments
  - Evidences
- (-) Not practicable for large safety cases
- (-) Hierarchical Levels not straightforward to represent

Claim	**Argument**	**Evidence / Assumptions**
There is no fault in the software implementation	Formal proof of specified safety properties	The design is simple enough to be amenable to proof
	Formal proof that code implements its specification	Proof tool is correct (or unlikely to make a compensating error)
		Compiler generates correct code (sub-argument might use formal proof, past experience, or compiler certification
		High quality V&V process
		Test results
Software reliability exceeds system requirement	Reliability can be assessed under simulated operational conditions	***Statistical test results***

GSN-
Goal Structuring Notation

GSN – Goal Structuring Notation

- Developed by Tim Kelly et al., University of York
- "Forces" author to develop clear arguments
- Graphical Notation
- Safety cases in GSN easier to read than text
- Reduces fault probability in safety cases
- Tool support available
- Currently being standardized

- Clearly shows
  - Goals (aka "Claims")
  - Arguments (aka "Strategies")
  - Evidence (aka "Solutions")

GSN Symbols Overview (Subset)

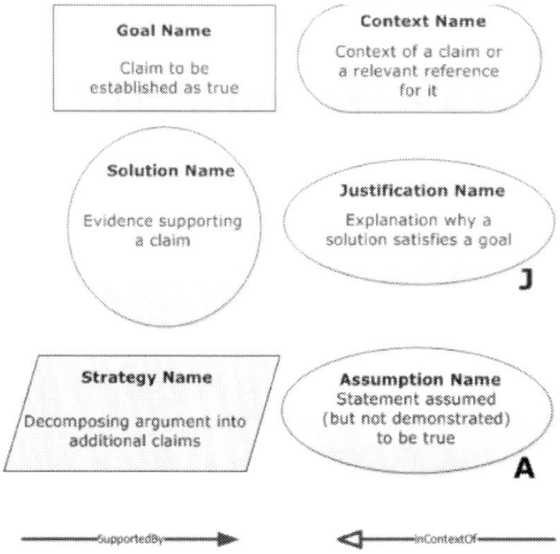

GSN "GOAL"

GSN GOAL

- A Goal is a proposition to be established.
  - Is a statement that can be "TRUE" or "FALSE"
- Represents a claim, the truth of which is to be demonstrated by argument
- The Goal text should be of the form subject-verb(-object)

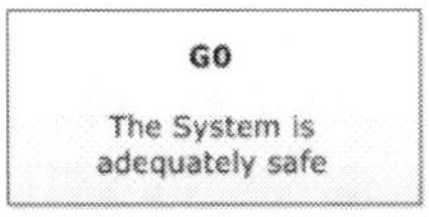

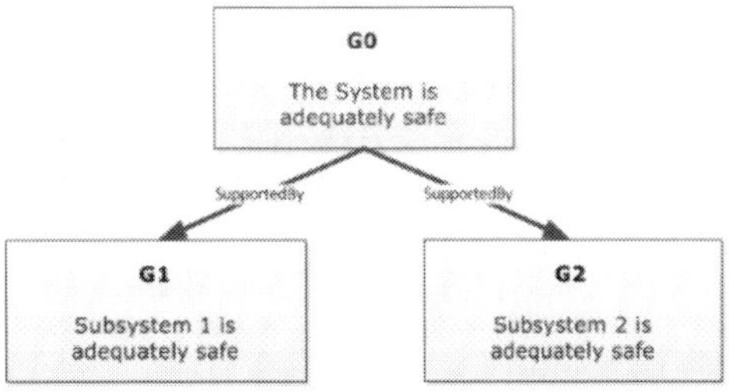

Top Goal – your top level claim

- For a safety case, it is typically something like "The system is acceptably safe for a given application in a given environment"
- The top goal is typically divided into several sub-goals, sub-sub-goals, etc. which are easier to prove
- GSN development typically is a top-down approach – you start with the top level proposition you want to show to be true

"A claim can be purely subjective, for example I could make a claim about wine grape varieties, "Syrah is better than Merlot". I may believe it to be true and make an argument on that basis, but you may believe the opposite and refute my argument. At this point bottles of wine could be opened, and we may lose track of the arguments..." [Spr12]

Excercise: Which of the following claims could be used as a Top Goal?

1. Our Quality Management System is ISO9001:2008 compliant (ISO 2008)
2. My Business Plan is complete and ready for review by the Board
3. This burial site is probably that of Rædwald, King of the East Angles
4. This painting should be attributed to Albrecht Dürer
5. This equipment fulfils the essential requirements of the RTTE Directive
6. Beryllia is a carcinogen
7. Hazard Identification and Risk Assessment
8. Assurance is provided that safety requirements raised on the software are valid
9. The GSN Symbol for a Goal is a rectangle
10. The colour of the sky

GSN "Context"

GSN CONTEXT

- The truth of a claim depends on the context!
- What does a typical top level claim "The system is acceptably safe" actually mean?
  - What does safe mean here?
  - How much/little safety is acceptable?
  - In which environment?
  - For which use or application?

It all depends on context...

The causes and consequences of operational errors are not linear in their magnitude

So, what does "safe" mean?

GSN Context

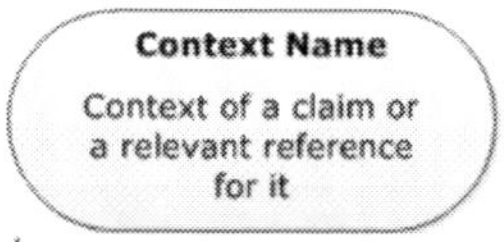

- Context provides, or references out to, definitions and other supporting material
- Always on the end of an open-headed arrow
  - Important: DO NOT hang other contextual information from them
- Environmental Context

- External References

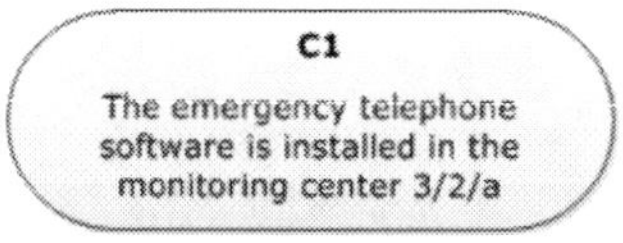

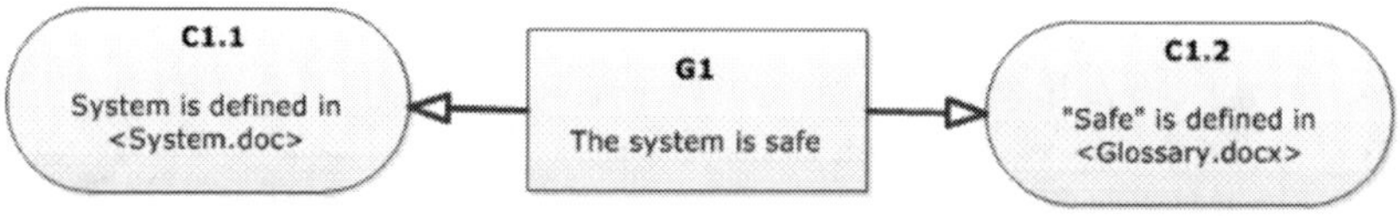

GSN CONTEXT

- Another example

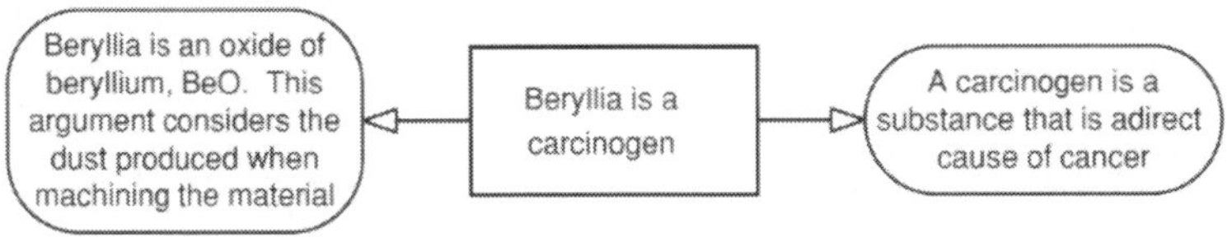

- Too much context probably means your goal uses too many vague terms
- Makes GSN less readable

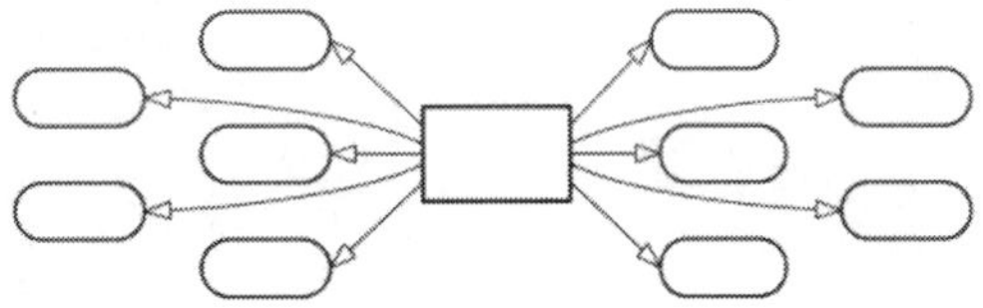

FREQUENTIS

Context Excercise

My factory manager wants to persuade me that one of her preventative maintenance procedures, known as PMP5, is adequate to keep the factory power supply running. She claims, "PMP5 is fit for purpose". We want to document the argument so that in future, if someone wants to change the procedure, they will be able to ensure that they do not "break" it. Using GSN, how could the claim, "PMP5 is fit for purpose", and its Contexts be presented?

FREQUENTIS

GSN "Goals and SubGoals"

GSN Goals and Sub-Goals

- Goals are typically decomposed into sub-goals
- Truth of Sub-Goals is *sufficient* to establish truth of Goal
- GSN is meant to be read in the deductive form
  - "D is true because A, B and C are true"
- Not in the inductive form
  - "Because A, B and C are true, we can conclude that D is true"

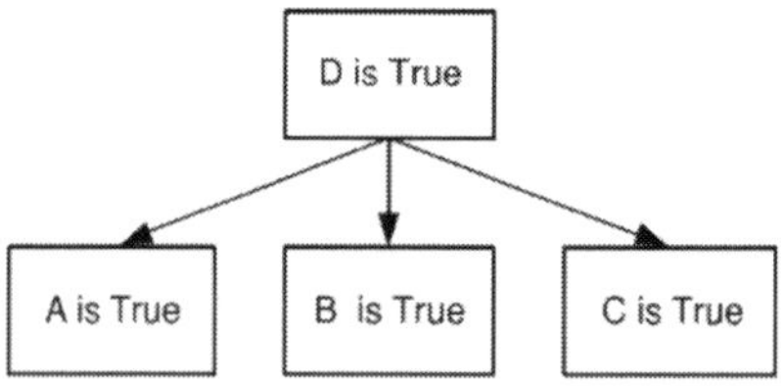

GSN Goals and Sub-Goals

- Similar to a mathematical proof, which is usually in the form: Theorem – Proof

- Sub-Claims which are accepted by the reader without detailed proof can be skipped by the reader

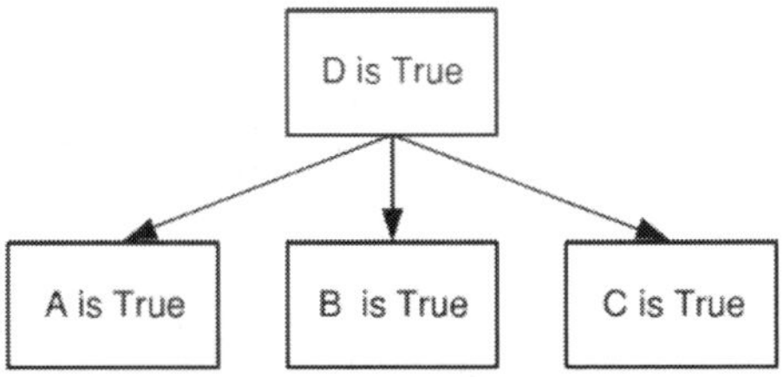

GSN does not preclude fallacies

- The reader must judge if the argument is logically flawed!

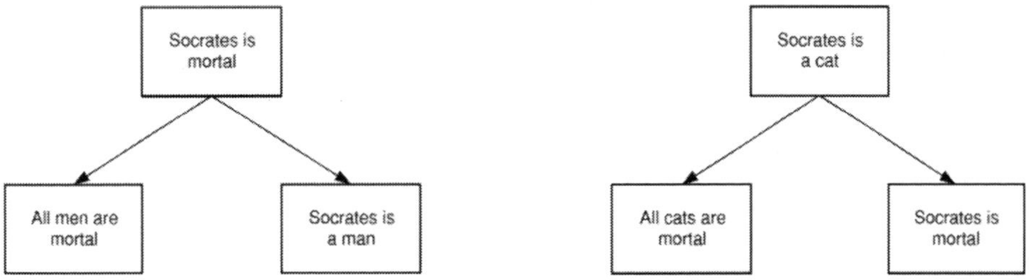

- Of course again, all depends on context (which is missing here)! Who is meant by "Socrates" here?

A more realistic example

- Important to add enough information into goals to make argument understandable

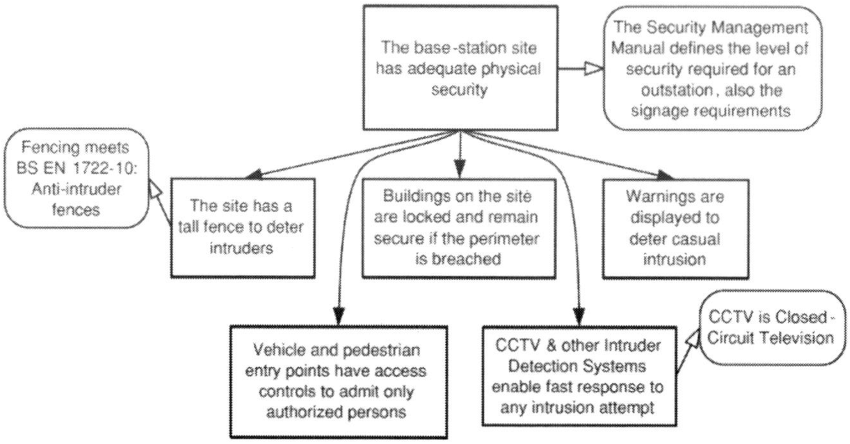

Excercise

Adelle is the daughter of Bertrand and Celine. Celine's parents are Didier and Estelle. Construct a simple argument in GSN claiming that Adelle is Estelle's granddaughter.

Excercise

Adelle is the daughter of Bertrand and Celine. Celine's parents are Didier and Estelle. Estelle's brother Frederic is married to Gabrielle; they have a son, Henri. Construct an argument in GSN that Gabrielle is the great aunt of Adelle by decomposing this Top Goal into two appropriate Sub-Goals, and then decompose your Sub-Goals one level, as necessary.

GSN "Argument Strategy"

GSN STRATEGY

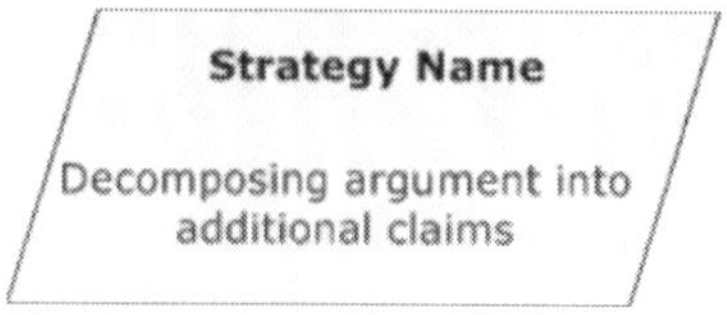

- Part of the argumentation
  - Contain a brief description of the argument approach
- Always links to Goals with a solid-headed arrow
  - Only one incoming arrow from above
  - Many outgoing arrows below
- Contextual information referenced with open-headed arrow

- Note that the symbol is optional, sub-goals can be linked directly to goals
- Describes the rationale why goals are divided into the specific chosen sub-goals
- Massively improves readability and comprehensibility

GSN STRATEGY

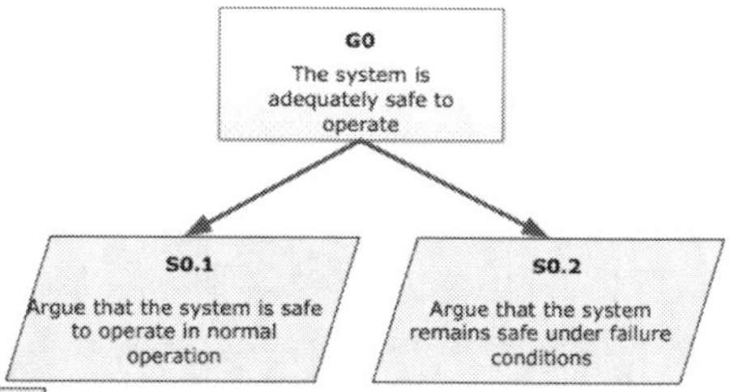

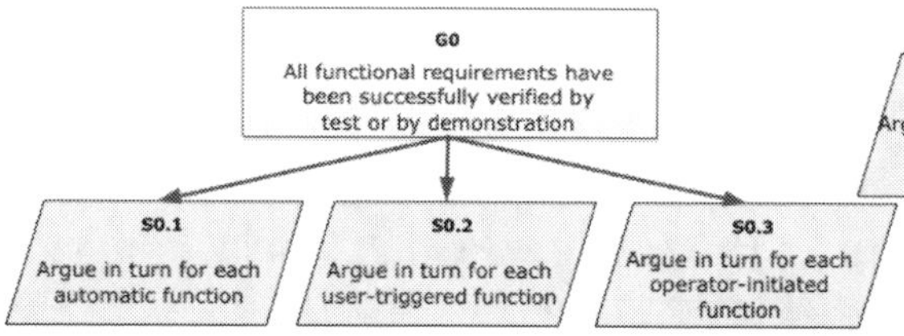

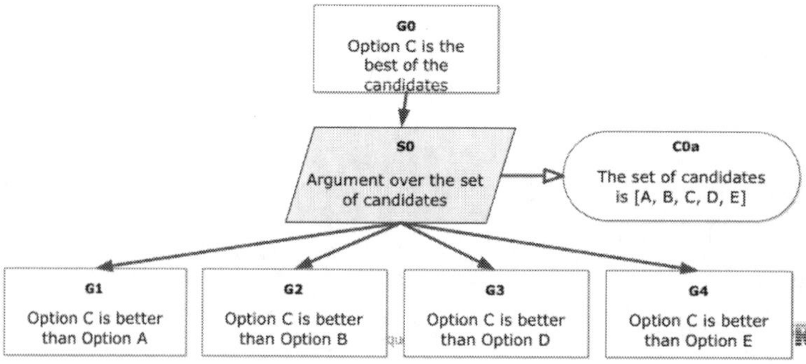

Note: Numbering GSN elements

- It is convenient to give unique IDs to all elements in a GSN
- Makes references and reusing elements possible
- GSN does not specify how elements shall be numbered

- There are several methods, e.g.
  - Unique Names
  - Numerical sequential IDs
  - Hierarchical numbering (preferred way, used here)

Security Example with Strategy

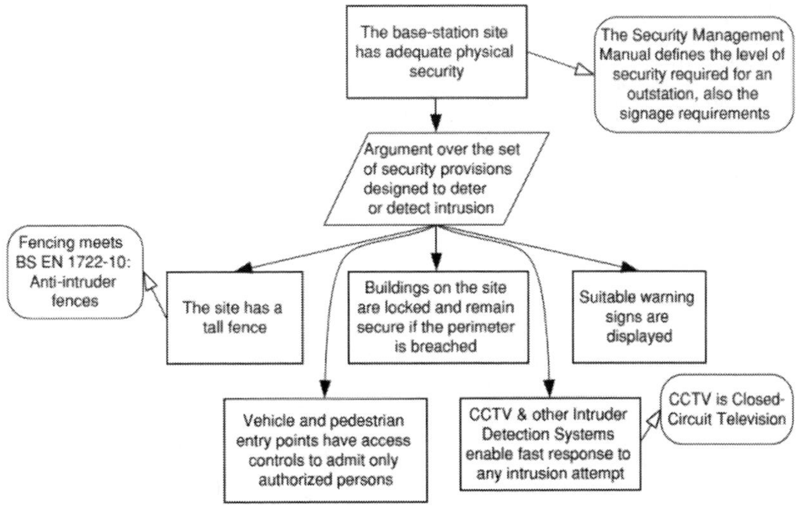

Excercise

- Is there anything missing from the top level of this Goal Structure?
- How would you express this example using Sub-Goals, rather than multiple Strategies?

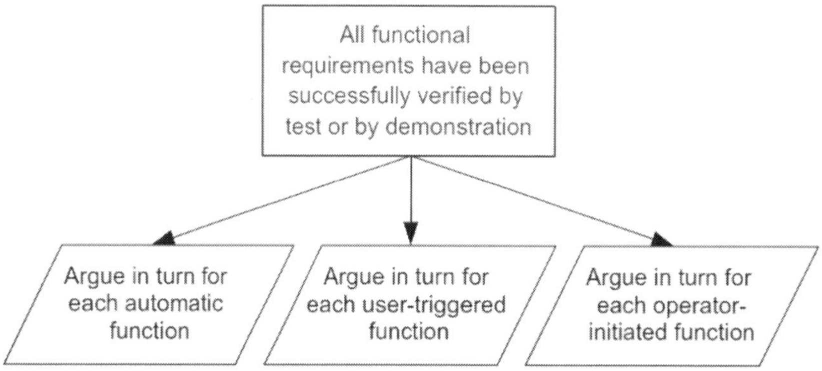

GSN "Justification"

GSN JUSTIFICATION

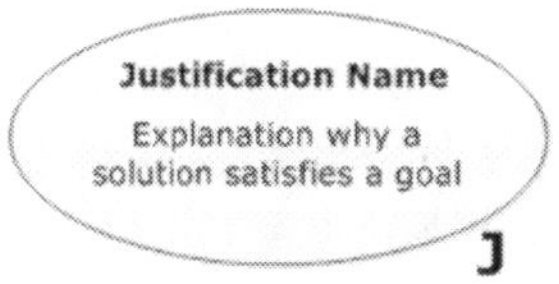

- Provides extra explanation or rationale
  - A reason for what you have done
- Is a contextual information
  - Always associated with the element being justified
- We use it to say...
  - Why the sub-goals have been chosen when others may have been more obvious
  - Alternatively, a Justification may contain a simple "If A then B" argument

GSN JUSTIFICATION

- Refer out to an existing argument

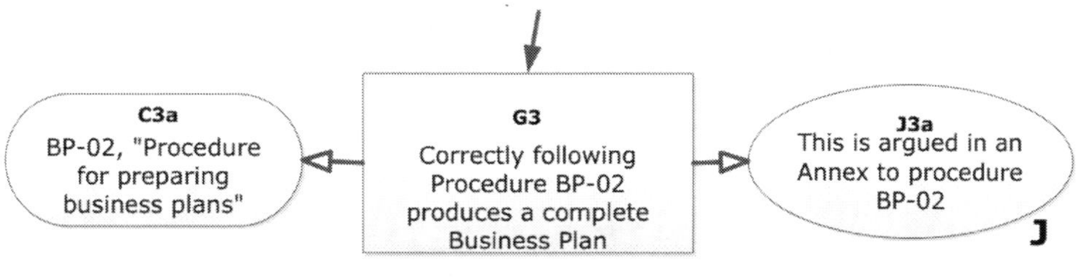

GSN JUSTIFICATION

- Split-up

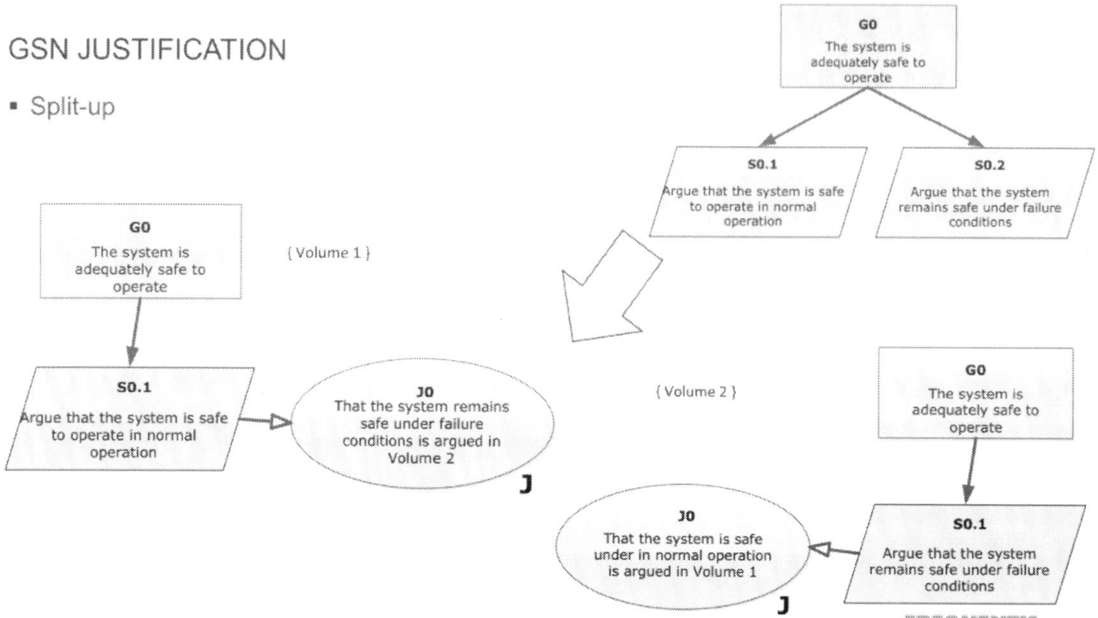

57 | Safety Cases with the Help of GSN   ISSC 2018 | © 2018 Frequentis AG   FREQUENTIS

GSN JUSTIFICATION

- If A than B

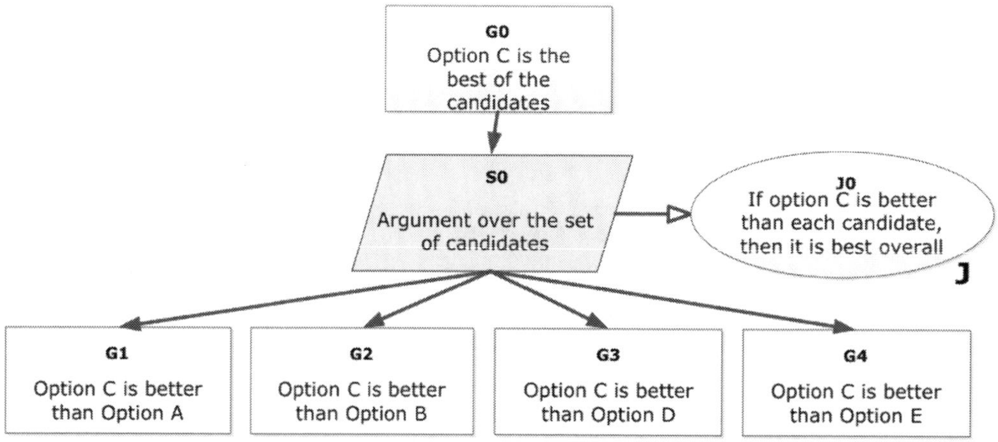

58 | Safety Cases with the Help of GSN   ISSC 2018 | © 2018 Frequentis AG   FREQUENTIS

GSN "Assumption"

GSN ASSUMPTION

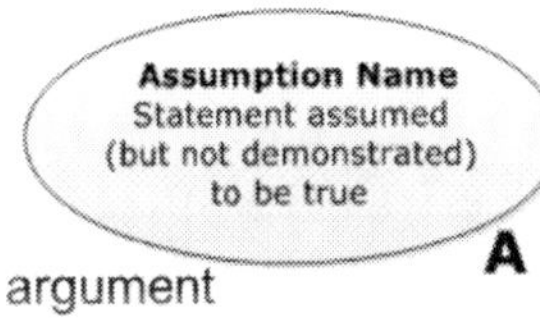

- An assumption is something taken to be true for the purpose of the argument
- Simplify a situation
  - Argument may be invalid in general, but perfectly adequate in the conditions you assume.
  - Argument is valid for specified conditions.
- It is very important to state your assumptions explicitly
- The symbol itself say "I assume that …", so there is no need to repeat it in the text.
- An assumption helps you to say that a statement in a Goal is TRUE

GSN ASSUMPTION

- Fragment of an argument about traffic lights at a road junction with pedestrian crossings
- Exercise: Are the three assumptions appropriate?

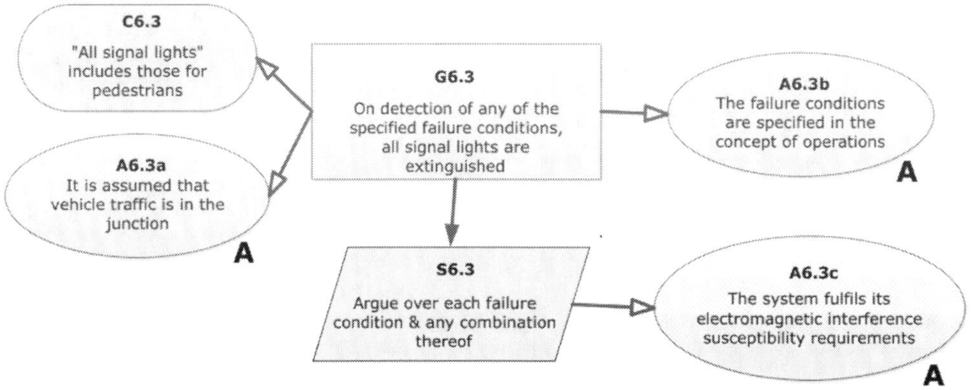

FREQUENTIS

GSN ASSUMPTION

- Revised fragment of an argument about traffic lights at a road junction with pedestrian crossings

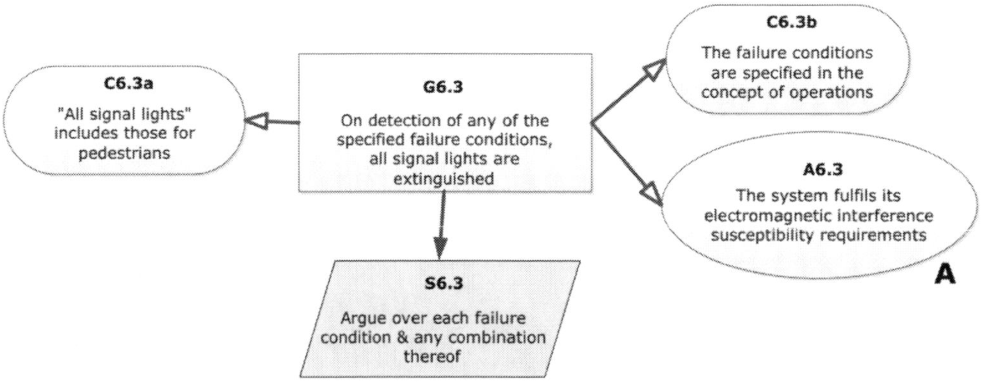

FREQUENTIS

GSN "Solution"

Where is the final proof?

- Well, the argument is correct
- But who says that the premises are true?
  - Are all men mortal?
  - Is Socrates a man?

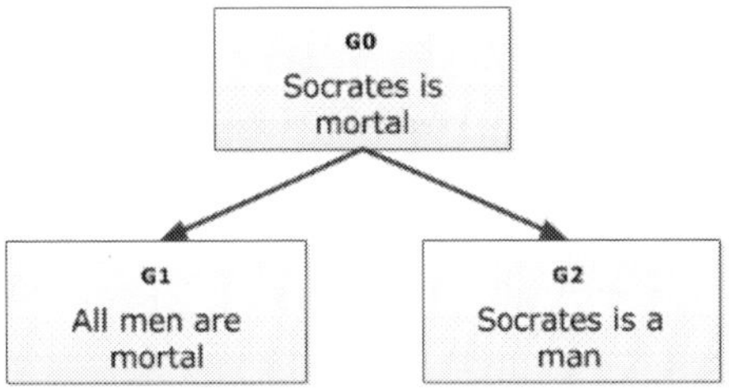

- Solutions provide the evidence that the lowest sub-goals are actually true
- Without this evidence, the argument is not complete!

Solutions (aka Evidence)

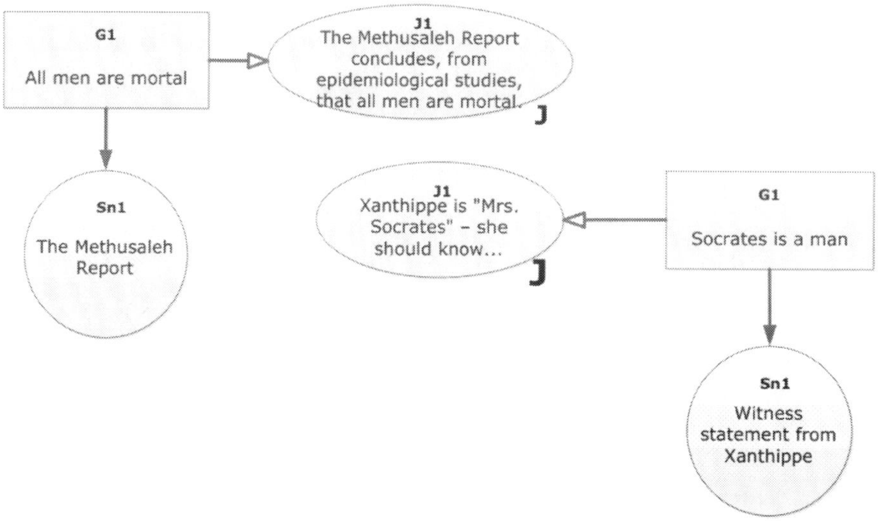

GSN SOLUTION

- A single Goal can have one or more evidences
  - Do not bundle them
  - Use separate Evidence symbol for each
- If an evidence supports more than one Goal
  - Label each evidence item uniquely
  - Use the same Evidence and not update the index
- Solutions or Evidences make no claim
  - Simply references to evidence artefact that provide support for a particular claim

GSN SOLUTION

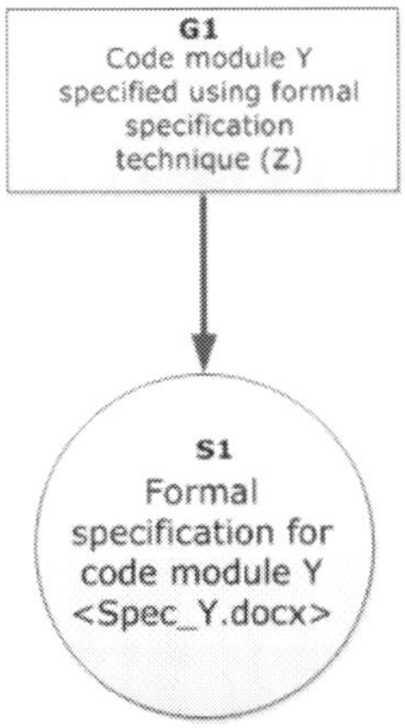

"Both argument and evidence are crucial elements of the safety case that must go hand-in-hand. Argument without supporting evidence is unfounded, and therefore unconvincing. Evidence without argument is unexplained – it can be unclear that (or how) safety objectives have been satisfied." [Kel&04]

Where does Evidence come from?

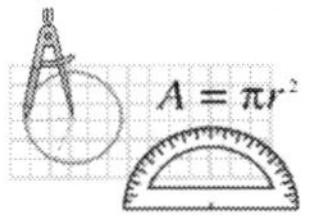

- Direct Evidence
  - tells something about the **product**
  - e.g. product features, test results, static analysis results, formal proofs,...
- Backing (indirect) Evidence
  - tells something about the **process**
  - e.g. well established process according to ISO9000, reviews were conducted properly,...

- Due to the difficulty of providing sufficient direct evidence for software, backing evidence plays a crucial role

GSN RELATIONSHIP INDICATION

- GSN elements are intended to be combined to represent logical structure. GSN provides two types of linkage between elements
  1. SupportedBy ⟶
     - Inferential relationships declare that there is an inference between goals in the argument
     - Evidential relationships declare the link between a goal and the evidence used to substantiate it
     - Goal-to-goal, goal-to-strategy, goal-to-solution, strategy to goal
  2. InContextOf ⟶▷
     - Declares a contextual relationship
     - Goal-to-context, goal-to-assumption, goal-to-justification, strategy-to-context, strategy-to-assumption and strategy-to-justification

COMMON ERRORS

Confirmation Bias

- You look for what you want to find
- Searching for counter-evidence is crucial
- Somebody needs to challenge the safety case

Avoidance of Common Errors in GSN

- The statements made in GSN **goal**, context and solution elements should be stated atomically
  - A single node should contain exactly one claim or reference
  - Goals should only contain claims
  - Solutions should only refer to evidence
  - Strategies should only summarise the argument approach
- The statements made in GSN **goal** elements capture the claims made in the argument
  - The statements should be expressed in the form <noun-phrase><verb-phrase>
- Similarly, **assumptions** should be stated atomically in GSN

Avoidance of Common Errors in GSN

- GSN **strategy** elements record the approach used in structuring the argument
  - It should be possible to remove all of the strategy elements without affecting the logical flow of the claims being made
  - Like "comments" in programming languages, they enhance readability
- **Strategy** elements are intended as a description of the argument approach which has been carried out to relate claims stated at different levels of detail
  - For example, the strategy "Interlocks used" should be phrased "Argument by appeal to the use of interlocks", to focus the reader's attention on the argument process, rather than on the design of the system.

Avoidance of Common Errors in GSN

- **Context** elements should not be used to refer to information which is intended to support the validity of a claim.
- **Context** elements are sometimes used where a GSN assumption or justification may be more appropriate.
- **Context** and **Solution** elements in GSN should provide references to artefacts stored elsewhere
  - A single noun-phrase should be sufficient to identify these artefacts
  - It is not necessary to summarize the content of the artefact in the GSN node

Fallacies in Safety Cases [Gre&06]

- A critical review of three publicly available safety cases showed that fallacies are quite common

Table 1 — Tally of Fallacies Identified in the EUR RVSM Safety Case

Fallacy	*Reviewer A*	*Reviewer B*	*Total*[1]
Using the Wrong Reasons	5	15	16
Drawing the Wrong Conclusion	3		3
Red Herring	1		1
Fallacious Use of Language	2	2	4
Hasty Inductive Generalization	4		4
Omission of Key Evidence		1	1
Total	15	18	29

Table 2 — Tally of Fallacies Identified in the Opalinus Clay Safety Case

Fallacy	*Reviewer A*	*Reviewer B*	*Total*[1]
Arguing from Ignorance	1[2]		0
Omission of Key Evidence	2		2
Total	3	0	2

Table 3 — Tally of Fallacies Identified in the EUR Whole Airspace Safety Case

Fallacy	*Reviewer A*	*Reviewer B*	*Total*[1]
Red Herring	4		4
Fallacious Use of Language	2	6	6
Fallacy of Composition	2	2	2
Omission of Key Evidence	2		2
Total	10	8	14

Safety Argument Fallacy Taxonomy [Gre&06]

- Circular Reasoning
  - Circular Argument, Circular Definition
- Diversionary Arguments
  - Irrelevant Premise, Verbose Argument
- Fallacious Appeals
  - Appeal to Common Practice, Appeal to Improper/Anonymous Authority, Appeal to Money, Appeal to Novelty, Association Fallacy, Genetic Fallacy
- Mathematical Fallacies
  - Faith in Probability, Gambler's Fallacy, Insufficient Sample Size, Pseudo-Precision, Unrepresentative Sample
- Unsupported Assertions
  - Arguing from Ignorance, Unjustified Comparison, Unjustified Distinction
- Anecdotal Arguments
  - Correlation Implies Causation, Damning the Alternatives, Destroying the Exception, Destroying the Rule, False Dichotomy
- Omission of Key Evidence
  - Omission of Key Evidence, Fallacious Composition, Fallacious Division, Ignoring Counter-Evidence, Oversimplification
- Linguistic Fallacies
  - Ambiguity, Equivocation, Suppressed Quantification, Vacuous Explanation, Vagueness

Any fallacies here?

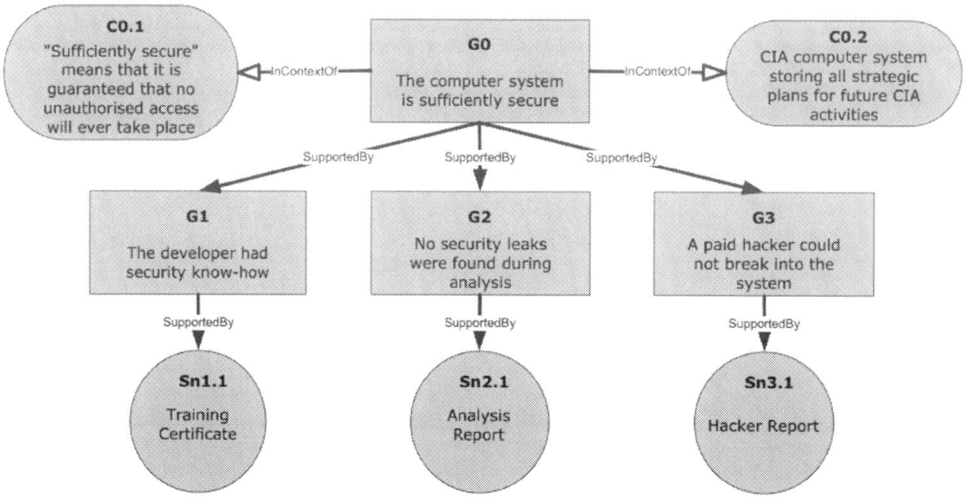

Any fallacies?

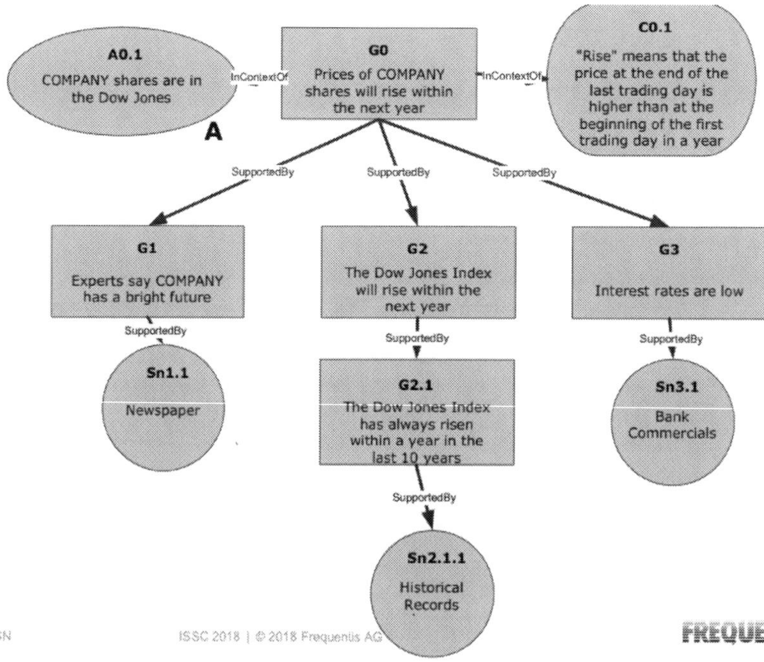

Any fallacies?

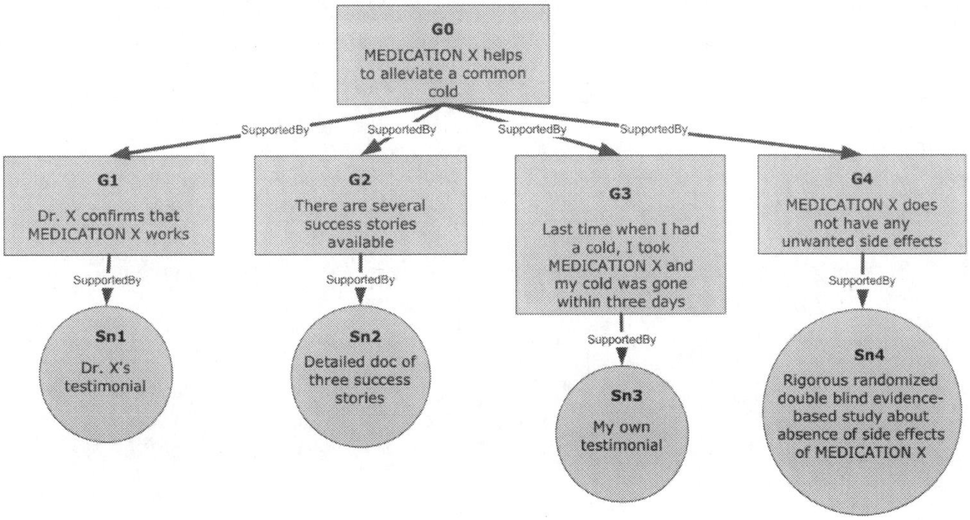

Excerpt of EUR RVSM Safety Case – can you find fallacies?

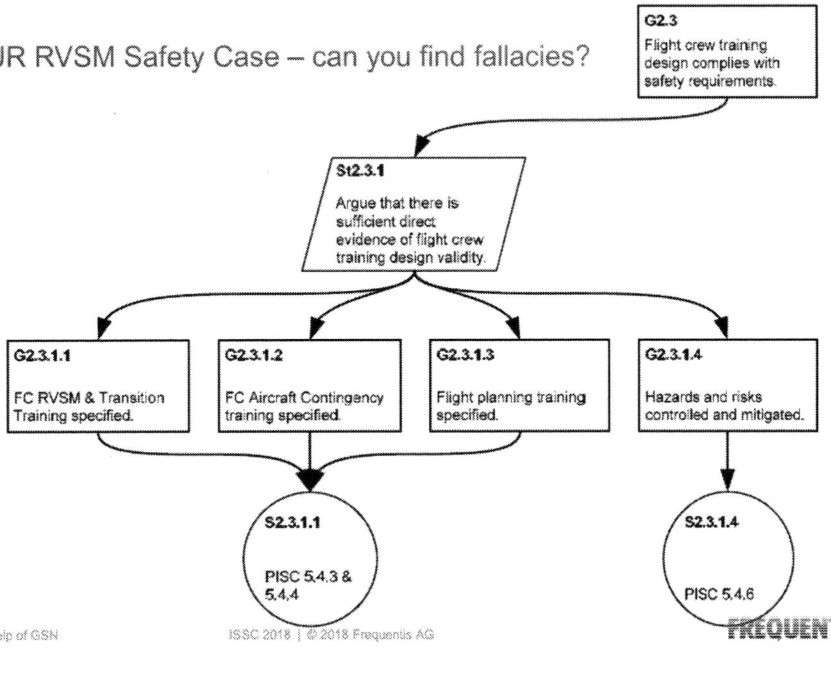

UK DEF-STAN 00-56

- 13.2.1 The Contractor shall ensure that the Safety Case consists of a structured argument, supported by a body of evidence that provides a compelling, comprehensible and valid case that a system is safe for a given application in a given environment.
- 13.2.5 The Contractor shall provide evidence to demonstrate the competence of individuals and organisations responsible for tasks that have a bearing on safety.
- 13.2.6 The Contractor shall develop, maintain and refine the Safety Case as defined in the SMP and in developing the Safety Case the Contractor shall address the full lifecycle (CADMID/T) of the PSS.
- 13.2.7 Where practicable, the Contractor should provide objective evidence.
- 13.2.8 The Contractor should provide diverse evidence, to ensure that that the overall safety argument is not compromised by errors or uncertainties in individual pieces of evidence.
- 13.2.9 The Contractor should demonstrate that the arguments and evidence in Safety Cases are sound, comprehensive and trustworthy.
- 13.2.10 The Contractor should provide evidence to demonstrate the adequacy and suitability of the methods and techniques used for safety and risk analysis and in safety engineering.
- 13.2.11 The Contractor should develop, maintain and refine the Safety Case through the life of the Contract.
- 13.2.12 The Contractor should provide evidence of competency of those whose work could impact safety and confidence in the Safety Case.
- 13.2.13 The Contractor should ensure that any related Safety Cases or information sets already in existence and identified in the scope of analysis are utilised and integrated as necessary.

- The Contractor shall produce Safety Case Reports that incorporate the key elements of the safety argument and references to evidence so that, in principle, it would be possible to access the complete Safety Case, starting from the Report, or counter-evidence where it has been identified.
- Where there are shortfalls in the evidence the Contractor shall ensure that the Safety Case Report provides the rationale for operating the PSS, and the ways of mitigating the residual risk.
- The Contractor should ensure that any related Safety Case Reports or ISSSs already in existence and identified in the scope of analysis are utilised and integrated as necessary.
- The Contractor should deliver the Reports incrementally, as Contracted, to give the MOD visibilit of progress in safety engineering and safety analysis.

Case Study

Case Study

- Read the handout
- Create a GSN for a claim like

"The system is acceptably safe..."

- Please form groups of <=5 people
- Time: 40min for elaboration, 20min for discussion

Some Final Notes

Problems with Traditional Safety Case Development: "Retrospective Safety Case"

Design Lifecycle **Safety Lifecycle** [Kel98], p. 67

- Large amounts of re-design necessary because safety case cannot be constructed
- Less robust safety case – safety engineers have to live with the current design instead of influence the design
- Lost safety rationales – rationales for certain design features might not be recorded and therefore lost

87 | Safety Cases with the Help of GSN ISSC 2018 | © 2018 Frequentis AG FREQUENTIS

Better: Evolutionary Safety Case Development

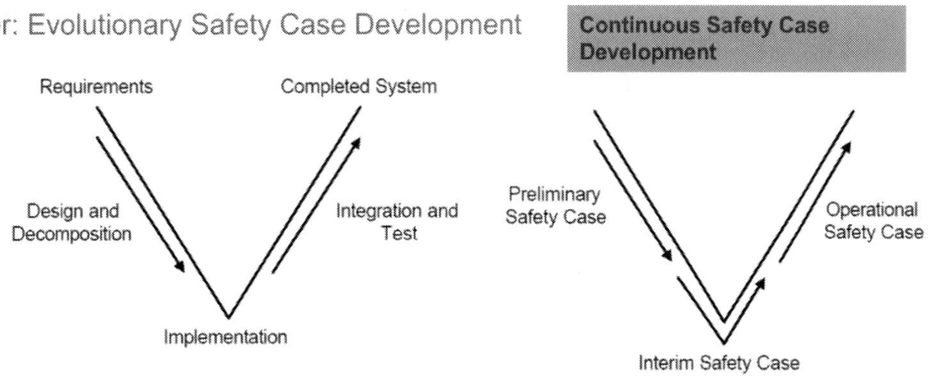

Design Lifecycle **Safety Case Lifecycle**
[Kel98], p. 69

- (Intermediate) Safety Cases are produced at each major milestone in a project
- GSN supports the evolutionary development of safety cases

88 | Safety Cases with the Help of GSN ISSC 2018 | © 2018 Frequentis AG FREQUENTIS

Three publicly available Safety Cases

- Unfortunately, most safety cases are not publicly available
- Should safety cases affecting the public be publicly available? (cf. sessions and decisions in a criminal court)

1. [EUR01] The EUR RVSM Pre-Implementation Safety Case
   Reduced vertical separation safety case
   GSN and text
2. [Kin01] Eurocontrol Whole Airspace ATM System Safety Case
   Common airspace for all Eurocontrol member states
   GSN and text
3. [NAG02] Project Opalinus Clay: Safety Report
   Long-term radioactive waste storage facility
   Text, heavy use of bullet points

Potential problems with Safety Cases

- Confirmation bias: People who have a vital interest that the top level claim is true provide the evidence
- People who build the system also build the safety case, they only see the positive evidence
- Re-inventing the wheel many times instead of using successful processes which are successful over many years
- "The problem is that it is always possible to find or produce evidence that something is safe." [Lev11]
- "Care should be taken when utilizing techniques such as Goal Structured Notation [...] to avoid falling into the trap of assuming the conclusion [...], or looking for supporting evidence for the conclusion instead of carrying out a proper analysis of risk." [Lev11]

[Lev11] Nancy Leveson. The Use of Safety Cases in Certification and Regulation. Journal of System Safety, Vol. 47, No. 6, 2011.

→ Active searching for *counter-evidence* is important! (and *not* finding counter-evidence is *no* guarantee that it does not exist)

Some conclusions with my personal view

- Good processes, techniques and measures are *necessary* but not *sufficient* to assure safety
- The Safety Case is the most important document for assuring safety
- A Safety Case must be easy to follow and understandable
- GSN improves readability of Safety Cases massively
- GSN is an excellent way to document or to support the documentation of Safety Cases

FREQUENTIS

Complex Hyperloop Capsule Safety Requirements and Risk Mitigations

August 21-25, 2018

Mike Overton, BSE, Safety Team Contributor; Hyperloop Transportation Technologies, Culver City, CA, 90230, USA

Michael C. Sarin, PE, BSE, BA; Safety HyperLeader; Hyperloop Transportation Technologies, Culver City, CA, 90230, USA

Keywords: Hyperloop, Capsule safety, Hyperloop passenger, HTT

Abstract

Hyperloop, a 5th mode of transportation, was promoted worldwide in August 2013 by a White Paper released on the internet by Elon Musk (Contributors, 2013). Hyperloop Transportation Technologies (HTT) was the first company to announce it was taking the idea "from concept to funding" (Insider, 2016) (Kudarauskas, 2007) (Wikipedia, 2018) The technologies used in the Hyperloop are not new, but they are combined in a new manner and thus present new safety challenges. Beyond safe operations the most vitally important challenge is passenger safety within the capsule. Due to capsule operation inside of a low pressure tube (~ 1/1000 atmosphere), speeds approaching Mach 1 and life support requirements similar to those of space travel, there are special hazard mitigations which must be developed. This paper describes capsule hazards and mitigations along with specialized evacuation processes appropriate for this new form of specialized transportation.

Introduction and System Overview

Hyperloop™ is a technically advanced transportation system that has the operational structure to be unparalleled in safety. The Hyperloop™ tube creates an enclosure that is immune to weather, disturbance from outside events and concerns about crossing traffic. The lack of "at grade" intersections also allows safe crossing for vehicles, pedestrians, bicycles and wildlife, which is not possible with today's land based systems. Capsules travel only one direction during operation thus there is nil chance of frontal collisions. Digital control and communication allow instantaneous reporting of capsule position, speed and status. These physical and control system advantages are clearly bringing us to the conclusion that this new mode of transportation has the potential to surpass anything the planet has ever seen in terms of safety, reliability, scheduling and comfort. However, there are also obvious challenges associated with this new technology, due to high capsule speeds in a confined space, moving in an operating environment that is at low vacuum, and including a passenger cabin that needs self-contained life support. The Hyperloop Transportation Technologies (HTT) safety team, comprised of doctors, engineers and highly experienced safety experts has developed strategies to mitigate and reduce the risks associated with those unique operating conditions. This paper describes Hyperloop's risks in more detail and proposes mitigating solutions focused primarily on capsule and passenger requirements found in rail and aerospace standards.

The Hyperloop is simply a transportation system which moves passenger capsules at high speeds inside of evacuated tubes. The concept was first proposed by Robert Goddard in 1904 as the Vactrain which has had numerous champions over the years including scientific articles in the 1970's by Robert M. Salter of the Rand Institute (Salter, 1972), and most recently a Swissmetro project in the late 1990's and early 2000's (Blog, 2013). The idea catapulted to worldwide interest after the publishing of a 2013 White Paper by a group of Tesla and Space-X engineers and scientists (Contributors, 2017). There are now many groups around the world working in various ways to bring the idea to reality. Hyperloop Transportation Technologies (HTT), a crowd-based effort with engineers and scientist located around the world, and for whom the authors of this paper are contributors, is constructing two full scale prototypes in Toulouse, France. The Hyperloop system (Figure 1) is a purely electrical propelled mode of transportation which takes advantage of the significant reduction in drag due to the low tube pressure and also benefits from major improvements in solar panel efficiency and linear motor control. The imperative created by an overburdened transportation system, gridlocked cities and the need for improved efficiency and safety has propelled this technology to the edge of commercialization. What is left is to test and optimize the system, integrate the numerous technologies and create a certifiably safe system with tubes connecting cities ideally no more than 1000 km apart. This paper is mainly focused on the safety aspects of capsule operations including life-support, losses of capsule pressure, emergency evacuations and other challenges of operating within a near space environment.

Figure 1: Hyperloop System Components

The following is a description of various capsule operation risks and how they can be overcome or mitigated using solutions taken from high speed rail and aviation standards as well as space vehicle operations. These safety solutions are presented for the general public as well as to inform possible certifying agencies.

Highest System Risk – Capsule Doors

We used FMECA (Figure 2) and calculated risk priority numbers to identify which systems have the highest impact on operational safety. The highest risk area from that analysis is leakage of cabin air due to faulty door operation. This is not surprising: the door system is used frequently, has a major impact on system operation, and most importantly for Hyperloop, presents a major risk during failure in the form of reduced cabin pressure and life support. Metro systems around the world experience high door failure rates (Sarin, 2018) and those experienced in metro line safety point to this as one of the two most failure-prone systems in metro transportation. The Risk Priority Number, which is very subjective for new systems, hit 270 on a three input assessment as shown below.

Category	Potential Causes of Failure	Potential Effect of Failure	Severity	Current design Controls Preventing fault	Occurrence	Current Design Control Detection	Detection	RPN-Risk Priority Number
Door Capsule	Critical system failure - Door failure	Loss of pressure in Capsule, Unable to open at station, injury to passengers	9	Robust door seals that inflate with pressure differential like aircraft. Safety Latch. Routine inspection and maintenance	5	Capsule telemetry (pressure in capsule and door seal)	6	270

Figure 2 - Hyperloop System FMECA and Door RPN

The door of the Hyperloop capsule is complex, much more complex than aircraft, and similar in function to space docking systems but with the advantage of fixed locations for the capsule and station. The primary similarity is the need for a pressure tight seal on both ends of the passage way. The HTT door, and the associated passenger gateway, referred to as a Docklock®, performs several functions which are unique to this form of transportation.

The seals within the capsule door are of utmost importance as any leakage will slowly deplete air within the capsule pressure vessel. The doors and seals need to be robust such that they can operate thousands of times without damage. A capsule has a turnover rate of approximately 3 times per hour. Given a day of 18 working hours, a typical door will perform approximately 108 (54 opens, 54 closes per day) moves per day or 39,420 operations per year. Seals, actuators, sensors, latches, bellows and cleanliness are all items that must be robust and reliable at that success level. The door design is an inside sliding structure and due to a positive pressure differential with the tube aids in pushing it against the fuselage and sealing it against leaks. With wear it can be expected that small leaks around the door seals will be experienced. Small leaks will be countered by adding air from onboard pressurized bottles. The onboard air bottles are currently sized to compensate for larger leaks which will be addressed later. Even for long trips, due to these air reserves, the hazard of a door leak is an exceptionally low risk to passenger safety.

There are two types of doors on the capsule. The passenger loading doors which connect to the station Docklocks, or alternatively to emergency ports along the route, and a second set of emergency exits which are most similar to aircraft evacuation doors. The emergency doors are sized per Code of Federal Regulations (14.1C Part 25D, §25.807: Emergency Exits) and follow the guidelines for size and location based on capsule capacity. The emergency doors can only be used under conditions that the tube has been repressurized to ambient conditions. Those emergency condition evacuations will be described fully under the evacuation section of this paper.

DockLock® Passenger Gateway and Emergency Exits

The Docklock® is the primary seal against tube vacuum for the capsule door while it is open. It is a pressurized gateway style device that moves from the station wall to the capsule where it seals tightly. The gateway is then pressurized and the doors opened. There is indeed a simpler method to transfer passengers which moves the capsule into an area, such as an airlock, that can be repressurized. However, the added time to repressurize and then evacuate such an air lock chamber, combined with added complexity of isolating that chamber makes it an inefficient method and we deem not an economical solution to transferring passengers quickly. The Docklock® allows passengers and cargo to be loaded quickly while leaving the capsule in a vacuum environment

The Docklock is also used along the route to provide a primary capsule evacuation point. During an emergency that requires passengers to evacuate the capsule enroute this passage is available at periodic locations. No slides are required as these exit points are located at pylons to which are mounted platforms for escape. This method is preferred and most common as long as the capsule can move safely to the emergency exit point.

In the event of a tube blockage or disabled capsule the secondary evacuation doors are used and the tube must be backfilled to atmospheric pressure prior to evacuations. The secondary doors meet the requirements of the previously cited federal standard and allow passengers to disembark the disabled capsule and proceed in the air filled tube to secondary tube exit ports. The secondary exit ports are spaced much more frequently per regional train tunnel evacuation requirements and allows passengers to exit onto a platform located at the tube pylon.

Speed (m/s)	Speed (mph)	Braking G force	Pax alert time (s)	Brake ramp time (s)	Brake ramp rate (m/s^3)	Stop Time (s)	Stop distance (m)	Pod separation @ 40s HW (m)	Stopping Clearance to lead Pod (m)
340	760	-1.0	10	4	-2.45 (-0.25G)	46.1	9,533	13,590	4,507
		-0.6	9	4	-1.47 (-0.15G)	68.0	13,240	13,590	350
170	380	-1.0	10	4	-2.45 (-0.25G)	28.8	3,162	6,795	3,633
		-0.6	9	4	-1.47 (-0.15G)	39.4	4,094	6,795	2,701
85	190	-1.0	10	4	-2.45 (-0.25G)	20.2	1,081	3,398	2,317
		-0.6	9	4	-1.47 (-0.15G)	25	1,362	3,398	2,036
45	100	-1.0	10	4	-2.45 (-0.25G)	16	353	1,788	1,435
		-0.6	9	4	-1.47 (-0.15G)	18.1	496	1,788	1,292

Figure 3 - Capsule Braking Distances Vs G Force

Time is of most critical value during any evacuation. From the second that an emergency is state is identified the evacuation time is related to the interaction of capsule speed, braking force, capsule position relative to exit points, and time to extend the Docklock (primary evacuation) or repressurize the tube (secondary evacuation). This chart (Figure 3) shows the interactions between speed, stop times (braking plus alert times), and total stopping distance based on 2 levels of emergency braking forces of -0.6 and -1.0 G. The capsule stopping distance must be less than the separation distance and is shown to be safe under shown conditions. Included is a passenger alert time, plus a ramp in braking forces to create an extended stopping time for passenger comfort. In summary, the emergency brake sequence includes a generous passenger alert time coupled with a smooth 4 second ramp to the full braking force.

Safe Capsule Environment – Cabin Life Support

Maintaining proper balance of oxygen, carbon dioxide, humidity, and removal of trace contaminants is accomplished through typical environmental control systems (ECS) used primarily in aircraft but with added systems required to monitor and adjust the capsule air without the availability of outside make-up air. The Hyperloop will use onboard supplies as the air density in the tube is not sufficient to provide the same make-up air as used in aircraft. The Hyperloop pod, which operates in a vacuum tight tube system, is similar to a space capsule in that it must supply its own oxygen, plus include carbon dioxide and carbon monoxide removal systems. This integrated life support system, operating in a self-contained environment, is responsible for maintaining a safe and comfortable cabin per CFR requirements 25.831 et al. This system controls cabin pressure and also removes noxious gases and insures that the vital factors such as O2, CO2, temperature and humidity are always at safe and comfortable levels (Figure 4). Recirculated air will be HEPA filtered prior to reentering the passenger area. The life critical environmental systems shall be redundant such that the failure of one system does not pose a risk to the passengers.

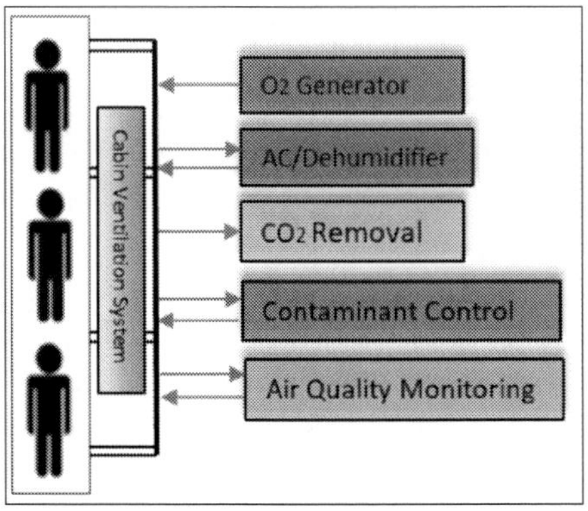

Figure 4 - Onboard ECS

Capsule Breaches and Loss of Pressure

As cited at the beginning of this paper the highest risk identified by FMECA is that of a door seal failure. This life critical seal has a safety redundant feature to minimize the risk. But in the unlikely event of catastrophic seal(s) failure the passenger cabin must maintain survivable cabin pressure and oxygen for as long as possible. Two mitigation methods come into action under this failure scenario. The primary method is to release air into the cabin from the onboard pressurized bottles. The bottles are sized (15,000 liters) to maintain a minimum 60kPa (8.8 psi) cabin pressure for three minutes while encountering a leak equivalent to a hole the size of 51.6 cm^2 (3.14 in^2). We have calculated that three minutes of reserve air allows enough time for the capsule to brake to a stop, attach to an emergency Docklock® along the route, and introduce ambient air prior to evacuating passengers. Our design requirement is that the door seal cannot experience a leak greater than 51.6 cm^2, even under total failure, and thus the evacuation mitigation is always attainable. For smaller leaks, a decision point is required evaluating cabin pressure reduction vs time to destination. Continuing safely to the destination is usually the preferred solution.

A capsule breach is another event that would allow cabin air to leak into the tube vacuum. A breach could occur due to a Foreign Object or Debris (FOD) resting in the tube, likely sitting on the guideway, which could collide with the moving capsule. FOD can originate from items being dislodged from the tube, items potentially separated from a previous capsule or even tools left behind after maintenance. Sloppy or uncontrolled maintenance practices cannot be allowed in this high speed route and special tool procedures are required to prevent any objects left behind that could collide with the capsule. A closed tube provides an environment free from the typical FOD that autos, trains or aircraft are exposed to. Another possibility is that some part of the communications, control or instrumentation gets dislodged and protrudes into the capsule path. The first and best hazard mitigation is always removing the hazard if possible to do so. Instrumentation and controls infrastructure inside the tube must be secured, wire tied or lock nut fastened whenever possible, to insure they cannot move from their location. FOD and tube (tunnel) caused hazards are ones that are most identifiable and preventable with a Hyperloop totally contained travel envelope. There is a high probability that monitoring of the guideway path via video may be required for certification. This two level approach, reducing the likelihood of debris on the track, combined with monitoring the track condition, is the safest way to protect the capsule from debris collisions.

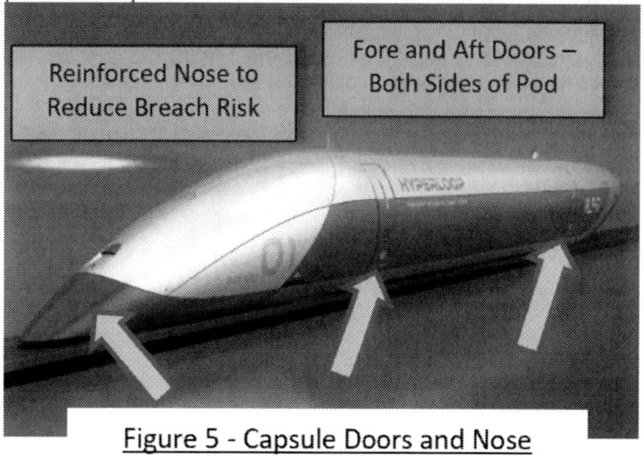

Figure 5 - Capsule Doors and Nose

The nose of the capsule, most vulnerable to forward collisions, is reinforced to resist puncture by debris. (Figure 5) The sloping front geometry will aid in deflecting any object and reduce chances of penetration. Additionally, the entire capsule is constructed as a dual wall containment vessel with nearly 80mm (3.15 in) of separation between walls. An object impacting the outer wall will be slowed, perhaps deflected entirely, and would need to have enough remaining kinetic energy to puncture the second containment wall before entering the inside of the capsule. Small penetrations from FOD and their associated air leaks will be compensated by releasing more air from the onboard pressurized air bottles. The decision to continue to the destination or make an emergency stop will be made by noting the rate of pressure drop as compared to the reserve air supply. Continuing to the destination is in most cases preferred. For events that are more extreme we need to look at the possibility of an evacuation. In the event of a moderate breach requiring evacuation the emergency stopping times, (Figure 3), position/speed of the capsule and location of the next primary exit are used to arrive at optimal evacuation strategy.

The emergency air supply is designed to maintain life support in the capsule in the event of a moderate breach, 51.6 cm^2 (3.14 in^2), through both hulls. In the event that the air tank cannot maintain a safe capsule pressure, the main tube is also fitted with a repressurization system. This system can bring the tube back to atmosphere in minimal time so that the leak rate is diminished and allows air to flow back into the capsule through the breach. Our current design includes 12 repressurization valves per km. A complex interaction between capsule speed/position, next emergency exit in the tube, and location of isolation valves needs to be analyzed before safe repressurization is begun. Once started, full atmospheric repressurization can be achieved in about two minutes. Below is shown Figure 6 depicting the tube pressure rise and times. Note that pressures of 0.5 bar (1/2 atmosphere) can be reached in less than one minute.

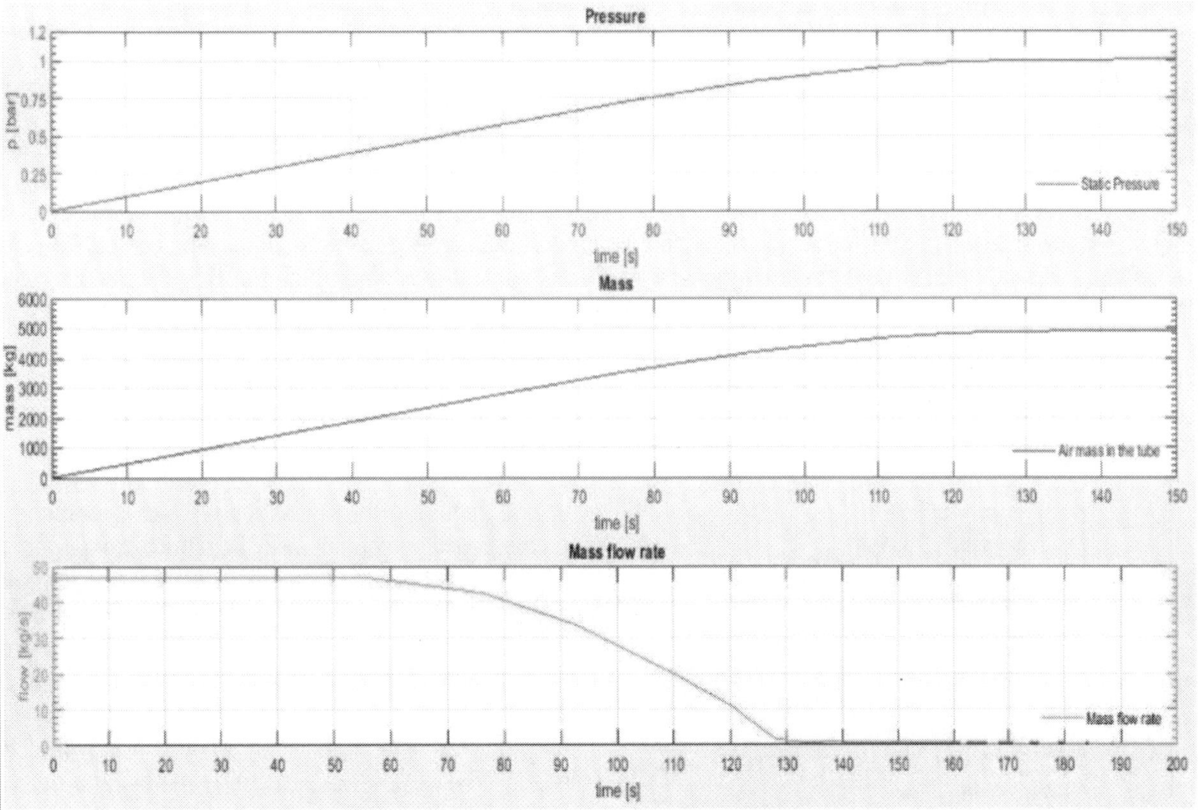

PRESSURE [bar]	AIR MASS INSIDE TUBE [kg]	TIME [s]
0,5	2,44*10^3	52
1	4,86*10^3	127

Figure 6: Tube Repressurization Graphs – 12 Valves/km

Stranded Capsules and Secondary Evacuations

In the event that a capsule is stranded and cannot move to the primary exit point it can stop at any point in the tube. Every 10km section is referred to as an Isolation Zone. On each side of the zone is located a shutoff valve large enough to seal the entire 10km section. Once a capsule is safely within the isolation zone then the isolation valves are closed and tube repressurization can begin. When the tube reaches atmospheric pressure, about two minutes from the simulations seen above, the capsule emergency doors can be opened (similar to aircraft evacuation doors) and passengers exit the capsule into the tube. The standard requirements for identification of exits and paths in commercial aviation are used to guide passengers to frequent situated tube exit ports. Passengers use the tube exit ports, again similar to aviation escape doors, and exit onto platforms located at pylons. The spacing of the tube exit ports will follow regulations currently used in train travel inside of tunnels and allows all passengers to safely leave the stranded capsule.

A stranded capsule presents the added hazard of not allowing capsules behind it to complete their journey. The preferred option is for rearward capsules to reverse direction and move back toward the origination station or any intermediate station on that route. The origination station is provided with a maintenance area suitable to hold the incoming capsules and allow passenger debarking. Less preferred options are for the rearward capsules to move to primary exit points and use emergency Docklocks to exit the system.

Several additional hazards result of passenger evacuations into the tube which must be addressed. First is the difficulty of exiting the capsule which is sitting inside of the tube. Depending on the capsule and tube diameter sizes the room to exit along the capsule will be very limited. The currently geometry for the Hyperloop Transportation Technologies system provides a crescent shaped walkway approximately 24 inches wide (Figure 7) along the capsule. US aviation requirements (CFR 14.1.C.25.D.25-810(b)(1), Type II exits) define a minimum walkway of 24" for emergency exits. Due to the round nature of the tube the exit path around the capsule must be curved. Thus, the Hyperloop capsule walkway does meet the general width requirement as stated in the Federal Regulations, but in this case due to the crescent shape, is perhaps not a direct application. Many such issues will require conversations between Hyperloop and the Authority Having Jurisdiction. In all safety cases, HTT intends to meet or exceed existing codes as may be applied. There are other CFR requirements such as step up and step down limitations, the need to have a clear walkway that can be reached without seeing outside the aircraft, door size and location, etc. Our current capsule is designed to meet or exceed all of these requirements with some adaptations required.

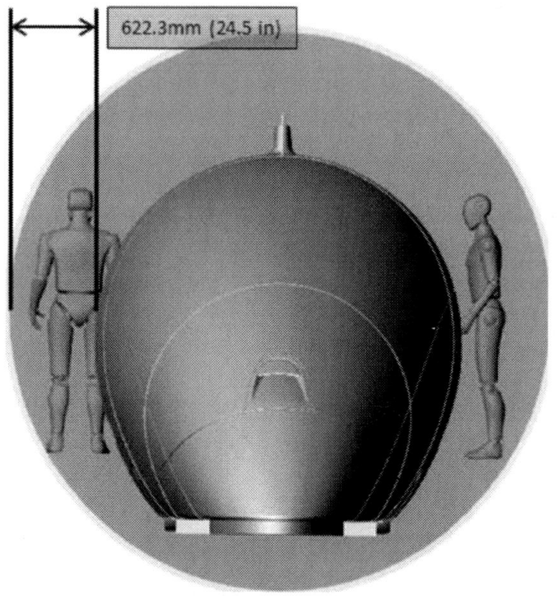

Figure 7 - Passenger Evacuation Aisles at Capsule

A unique hazard to the Hyperloop is keeping passengers (and emergency personnel) away from the extremely strong Halbach magnet arrays located under the capsule. One benefit is that these magnets are aligned in a special way to focus the vast majority of the magnetic field downward. These magnets are located beneath the capsule and for evacuations will be out of reach of the passengers. High magnetic field hazards exist in existing EMS (Electro-Magnetic System) style maglev trains, and typical restrictions and procedures will be incorporated. A final hazard to passenger evacuations inside the tube is the temperature. Due to the thermodynamic work created by the air filling the tube during a repressurization there will be spike in the tube air temperatures. These higher tube temperatures will abate as energy is transferred through the tube walls and back into the ambient atmosphere.

Many variables impact this heat transfer such as local outside temperature, humidity, wind, solar irradiance and shading among those having the strongest effects. Mitigation methods range from localized tube cooling to passenger cooling vests and safety environments. The combination of aviation exit requirements for size and lighting, along with special precautions for high magnetic fields and mitigations for high tube temperatures will be all need to be implemented for safe tube style (secondary) evacuations. It is important to remember that tube evacuations are the fourth choice in case of an emergency. The primary choice is to continue to the destination, the second choice is to shelter in the capsule, followed by evacuation through the Docklock, and as a final option we refill the tube with air and move passengers inside of the tube to an evacuation point.

Braking – Normal and Emergency Situations

Normal braking forces for the Hyperloop capsule are similar to those of other conventional transportation methods and fall within the range of -0.05-0.3 G. The normal braking methods are of two types that are similar to those in use on Maglev trains. Primary braking is accomplished by reversing the linear induction propulsion system and directing the energy back into battery arrays. The concept of regenerative braking has been used successfully in Maglev systems (Stephan, Ferreira, Mattos, & Oliveira, 2013). This regenerative style of braking directs the energy back into to the electrical supply system which may be a utility grid or local energy storage method. Multiple phases on the track stator can be used to provide redundancy. Secondary braking is accomplished through using the magnetic fields of the levitation system (Halbach array magnets) above a non-ferrous track material. The movement of the powerful permanent magnets induces an eddy current in the track which induces an opposing magnetic field. This method is quite strong, especially at lower speeds, and can be controlled by adjusting the distance between the magnets and the reaction plates in the track. The multiple magnetic arrays also provide braking system redundancy. The ability to conserve braking energy, combined with using electrical energy sources such as photovoltaic arrays, gives the Hyperloop braking and operational system a lower net energy footprint than current modes of transportation.

There are additional braking methods available to the Hyperloop system. Just as an airplane experiences parasitic fuselage drag plus an induced aerodynamic drag from its wings, the Hyperloop experiences a parasitic drag from its fuselage and an "induced" drag caused by restricted air flow past the capsule. In most cases the aerodynamic forces on the capsule are much less than with aircraft due to the low density of the air inside of the evacuated tube. But the operation of the capsule within a tube provides new options to increase drag (braking) forces. Aerodynamic drag in normal conditions is a function of the square of velocity. In an enclosed tube there are additional factors due to the restricted flow in the limited bypass area (Kantrowitz limit) so at high Hyperloop speeds it is possible to significantly increase drag even at low pressure. Thus, the Hyperloop style parasitic and "induced" drags, referred to as passive aerodynamic braking, are used to effectively slow the capsule. This combination of multiple aerodynamic drags also provides options to increase the braking levels above the normal operation envelope (Figure 8).

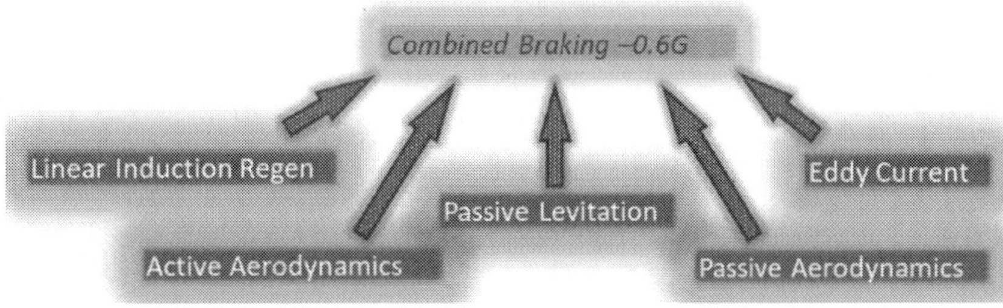

Figure 8 – Combined Emergency Braking

Emergency braking G force requirements are higher so that braking distances can be reduced as necessary for optimum headways. As seen previously in Figure 3, capsule separation can be minimized with higher G force braking, thus allowing more frequent departures. Emergency braking uses a combination of normal and expanded braking systems to achieve that higher level G force. Thus, the normal capsule braking system described above is augmented by additional system(s) to create the stronger emergency forces. One considered option is an eddy current system. Eddy currents, as discussed above, induce separate counter-magnetic fields in non-magnetic materials such as aluminum. There are also several active aerodynamic methods which can be utilized in emergency operations. This combined brake system, depicted in Figure 8, can easily attain emergency stop forces of up to -0.6 G as a result of the integration of normal and expanded braking system described above.

Passenger Safety and Comfort during Braking

The deceleration braking profiles expected for a typical Hyperloop journey are planned to be less than -0.30 G (-2.94 m/s^2). To put that in perspective, a modest car with 0-100 k/hr (0-60mph) times of 9 seconds has the same acceleration of 0.3 G (2.94 $m/^2$). Auto braking forces are usually higher than acceleration forces as all four tires are used to apply brake force equally to the maximum point of slippage. A recent study compared braking G forces for cars equipment with ABS vs non-ABS and found "general" braking forces of ~7.7 m/s^2 (-.78G). (Kudarauskas, 2007)

From the graph of automobile braking, used as a comparison to Hyperloop braking (Figure 9), normal braking G forces (green line with circles) of 7.5 to 7.7 m/s^2 (-0.76 to -0.78 G) which are 27-30% higher than a Hyperloop at emergency braking peak. The "emergency" braking forces for typical ABS equipped cars (red line with diamonds) are 8 to 8.7 m/s² which are 36-48% higher than a Hyperloop emergency stop. One difference should be noted and that is the status of restraints. As opposed to automobile travel which mandates fastened seat belts in the United States, the current plan as proposed by outside safety consultants, recommends passenger restraints while seated during a Hyperloop trip. Seat belts will be available, and recommended for safety while seated, but the freedom to socialize and move during the short trips is deemed to be reasonably safe.

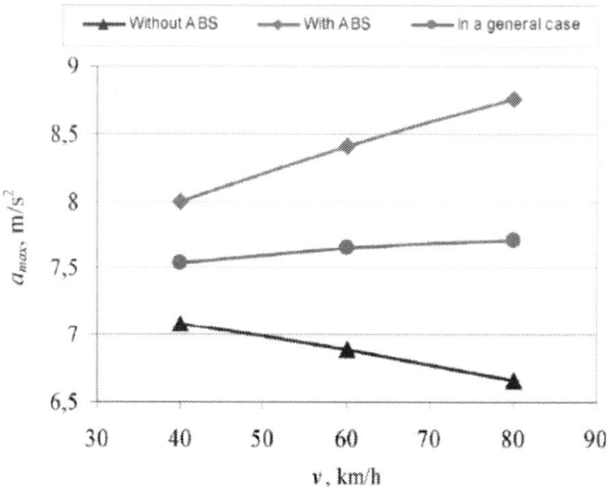

Figure 9 - Sample Automobile Braking G Forces (Kudarauskas, 2007)

Recent passenger testing with respect to unusual environments and forces has been done for certification purposes of consumer space travel vehicles. Companies such as Blue Origin, Virgin Galactic, Space-X, Bigelow and others have plans to launch vehicles into suborbital space with commercial passengers. One published report for Virgin Galactic (Blue, Riccitello, Tizard, Hamilton, & Vanderploeg, 2012) subjected 77 passengers of various ages (22-88 years) and health to simulated flights using the National Aerospace Training and Research (NASTAR) Center centrifuge. Different flight profiles were tried with peak forces of 2.3 to 6.0 G. The results of testing showed, "..... that most individuals with well-controlled medical conditions are capable of withstanding the acceleration forces involved in the launch and landing profiles of commercial spaceflight vehicles...". Note: these tests were performed on a wide range of passengers at levels 5 to 12 times greater than a Hyperloop trip. Thus, with comparisons from auto to space travel the range of passenger decelerations in a Hyperloop journey are all much lower and much more comfortable.

Fire Hazards: Capsule, Li-ion batteries, and Tubes

The level of fire hazard can be measured by identifying the possible sources of combustible material, presence of oxygen and heat source. The capsule fuselage, stiffeners and skin are a fiber reinforced resin that has flame retardant additives which are rated <25 on the ASTM E-84 standard. This level is in the A group of least flammable materials, similar to that currently used in the latest composite aircraft manufacturing. A key advantage to the Hyperloop is that because the propulsion is 100% electric there is no flammable fuel carried. The certification of cabin material will require following CFR limitations on flammability for seats, walls, carpeting and flooring.

The presence of over 500 kg of lithium-ion batteries to power life support, communication, controls, and low speed propulsion is the largest fire source within the entire Hyperloop infrastructure (excluding stations which are not covered herein). For redundancy, there are two of these power systems, one fore and one aft of the passenger cabin. Either system can operate the capsule systems individually for the duration of the trip with reserves—although at reduced speeds. There have been many incidents with lithium batteries, especially aboard aircraft, which have caused crashes. The fires tend to start quickly and burn very hot as the battery heat reaches a stage of thermal runaway. The Hyperloop battery areas will be isolated from the cabin and well monitored. Due to lengthy commercial experience with these batteries, even as late as the Boeing 787 fires and grounding (Wikipedia, 2018), and over a million automobiles using hybrid technology, much is known about how to reduce these risks. A significant safety advantage to Hyperloop travel is that ground level is always nearby and thus for certain hazards, such as cabin fire or smoke, cabin depressurization or passenger danger, the capsule can more quickly stop and evacuate (<3 minutes) than it takes an aircraft to descend, change course to the nearest airport, land, stop and begin evacuation.

The tubes within which the Hyperloop travels provide an envelope of safety which must be protected from fire and smoke. The most likely tube materials are steel, fiber reinforced resins or concrete. Although steel is being currently tested as the primary material it is important to cover possible future materials for comparison. Within the tube is fitted the propulsion and levitation guideway, an analog to the tracks for a railroad system. The guideway will be constructed of non-flammable metallic materials, including induction motor coils which require wire insulation at the stator windings. Flammability requirements for wire insulation are taken from the aircraft industry (CFR 25.851-25.869 including Appendix F) Heat from the propulsion and braking systems must be transferred through the guideway and then dissipated through various temperature sinks into the tube shell. The heat buildup due to emergency braking is included in the thermal calculations to reduce temperatures at the propulsion coils and stay well within the thermal rating of the wire insulation.

Pachen Effect – Arcing in Low Pressure Environments

Among the unique challenges to building a safe Hyperloop system is that the large voltages within the guideway, and to a lesser extent in capsule bogies, coupled with a low pressure environment creates a high arcing potential. This potential is not only a factor of conductor separation, but in the case of operation within a vacuum environment, includes the ambient pressure conditions surrounding the conductors. This hazard has been known since Friedrich Paschen ran voltage tests in the late 1880s comparing arc distances to ambient pressure in the presence of different gases. Space flights have dealt successfully with this hazard to prevent shorting of circuits by using these well-known relationships. The graph below (Figure 10) shows that at typical operating conditions of 100Pa (0.75 mg Hg) and 1000V that a conductor spacing of 9.33 mm is required in air (0.75 mm Hg x 9.33 cm = 7). The relationship between voltage and pressure-distance is not linear and varies significantly by gas type. Luckily, air outperforms most gases as an insulator in typical tube conditions. The science, and prevention, of low pressure arcing is well known and it can be applied to the Hyperloop system.

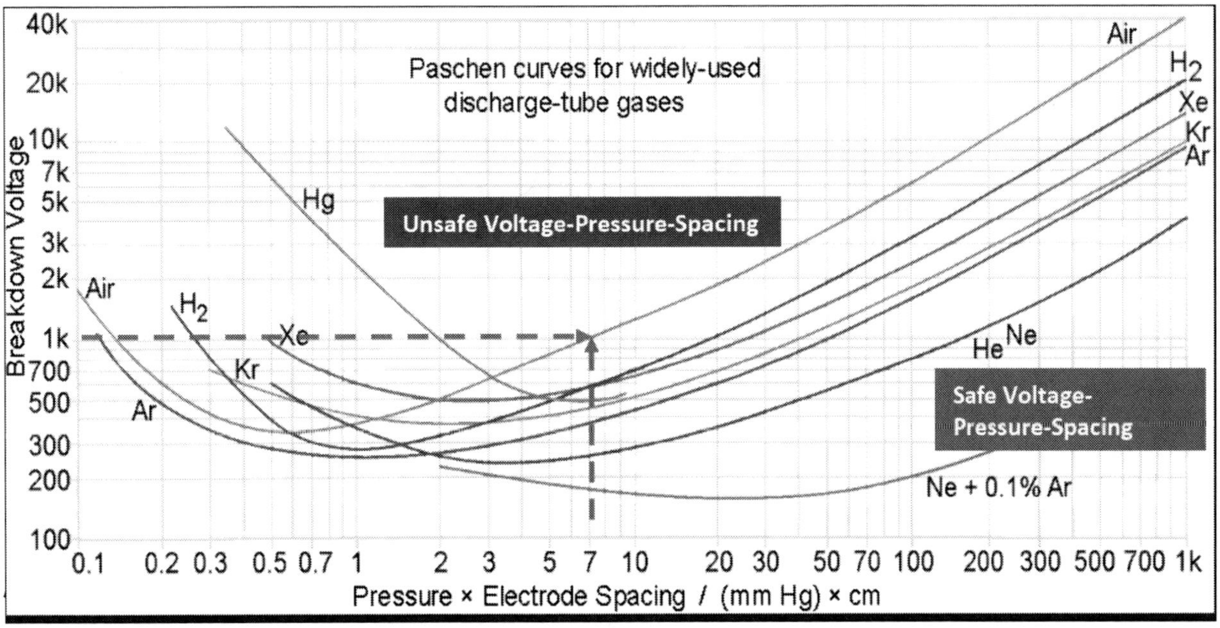

Figure 10 – Pressure-Electrode Spacing Required at 100 Pa (0.75mm Hg) and 1000V in Air

Conclusion

The development of Hyperloop as the 5th mode of travel has the potential to provide a revolutionary transportation alternative in the rapidly evolving modern world. Hyperloop has many inherent safety and performance advantages over existing transportation methods, however like all modes of transportation it has associated risks and hazards. This paper has discussed some of the development efforts at HTT to identify those risks and hazards and mitigate them through careful capsule design and operational procedures. These and other efforts will continue through the design, verification and certification stages of this new transportation technology. This process along with on-going development of new standards and regulatory activities will result in Hyperloop installations that exceed the expectations for modern transportation systems.

References:

Contributors. (2013). *Hyperloop Alpha.* Retrieved July 26, 2017, from www.spacex.com/sites/spacex/files/hyperloop_alpha-20130812.pdf

Insider, Crowdfund. (2016). *JumpstartFunds Hyperloop Project Tops #30 Million in Investment.* Retrieved July 26, 2017, from https://www.crowdfundinsider.com/2016/12/93315-jumpstartfunds-hyperloop-project-tops-30-million-investment/

Salter, R. M. (1972). *The Very High Speed Transit System.* Rand Corperation. Retrieved July 29, 2018, from https://www.rand.org/pubs/papers/P4874.html

Blog. (2013). *All the Hype for the Hyperloop and they forgot the Swissmetro.* Retrieved July 29, 2018, from https://wellpreparedmind.wordpress.com/2013/07/23/all-the-hype-for-hyperloop-but-they-forgot-swissmetro/

Sarin, M. (2018). *Hyperloop Transportation Technologies and TUV-SUD Conference.* Culver City, CA.

Stephan, R., Ferreira, A. C., Mattos, L. S., & Oliveira, R. A. (2013). Regenerative braking of a linear induction motor used for the traction of a MagLev vehicle. *Brazilian Power Electronics Conference proceedings.*

Kudarauskas, N. (2007). Analysis of emergency braking of a vehicle. *Transport, 22*(3), 154-159. Retrieved July 29, 2018, from https://www.tandfonline.com/doi/abs/10.1080/16484142.2007.9638118

Blue, R. S., Riccitello, J. M., Tizard, J., Hamilton, R. J., & Vanderploeg, J. M. (2012). Commercial Spaceflight Participant G-Force Tolerance Diring Centrifuge-Simulated Suborbital Flight. *Aviation Space Environment Medicine, 83*, 929-934.

Wikipedia. (2018). *Boeing 787 Dreamliner battery problems.* Retrieved July 29, 2018, from https://en.wikipedia.org/wiki/Boeing_787_Dreamliner_battery_problems

A General Theory of System Safety

David R. Sadler, MSSE, BSME
Department of the Navy, Naval Ordnance Safety and Security Activity
Indian Head, Maryland, USA

Energy is a Hazard

Some Examples

Heat - 22 known deaths due to hot springs in Yellowstone National Park since 1890

Radiant – 1 known death due to Therac-25 radiation overdose of patients

Nuclear - Sodium Reactor Experiment, 1959, complete loss of reactor

Chemical – 15 deaths at BP Texas City, TX, 2005 isomerization unit explosion

Mechanical – 55 known deaths due to falling into the Grand Canyon, AZ

Electrical – 82 electrocutions reported by USA Department of Labor for 2016

Loss of control of sufficient energy will produce a Catastrophic Mishap

The Theory

Energy is the universal hazard for catastrophic mishaps.

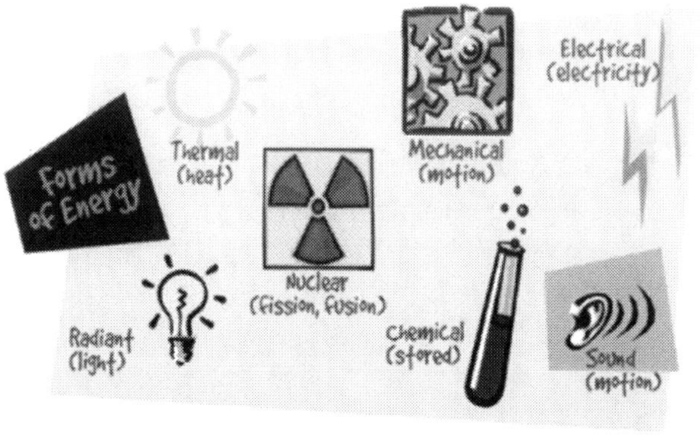

This theory is limited to catastrophic mishaps.

What is a Hazard...It Depends

- **Canada's National Centre for Occupational Health and Safety-CSA Z1002 / Hazard:**

A hazard is any source of potential damage, harm or adverse health effects on something or someone.

- **USA Department of Defense-MIL-STD-882E / Hazard:**

A real or potential condition that could lead to an unplanned event or series of events (i.e. mishap) resulting in death, injury, occupational illness, damage to or loss of equipment or property, or damage to the environment.

- **USA Civilian-ANSI/IASSE Z10-2012 (2017) / Hazard:**

A condition, set of circumstances, or inherent property that can cause injury, illness, or death.

What is Catastrophic...It also Depends

Definition of catastrophic harm depends on history, social customs, politics, and/or a given legal system(s).

So the paper defines it as;

Catastrophic Mishap is any event(s) that produces or results in harm that is beyond the available resources for recovery.

What We Know About Risks

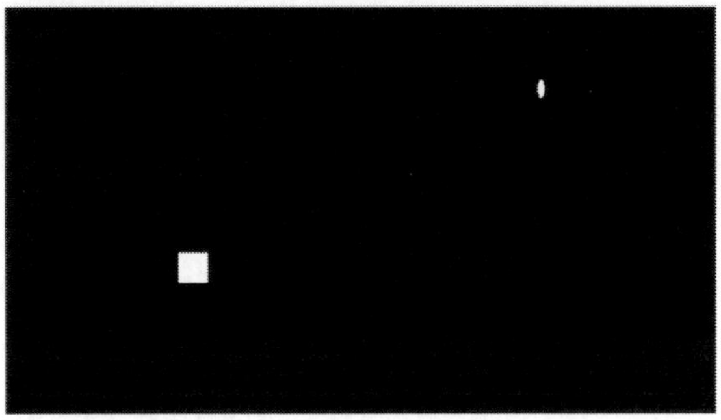

White Oval - Chemicals with a proven link to cancer.
White Square – Chemicals tested for a link to cancer.
Black Space – The set of known chemical substances.

RISK by Dr. John Adams, Routledge, 2001

Dr. Adams is a Professor at University College London and has been considering and writing about risk for decades.

Energy is Conserved but Not Inert

Le Chatelier's principle

- If a system in equilibrium is disturbed, the system will adjust itself to minimize the effect of the disturbance.

Risk Assessments

Typical Risk Assessment Starts by

Collecting Information / Identifying Hazards –

Low frequency hazards are difficult to model because we have limited understanding.

Common hazards produce lots of data.

From data we can learn.

Building codes are an example of this learning process.

Risk Assessments - Learning

Old Code Handrail

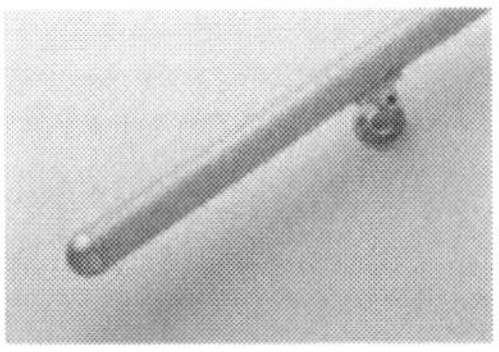

WHY?

Lots of Data
Frequent Events
Forensic Analysis

New Code Handrail

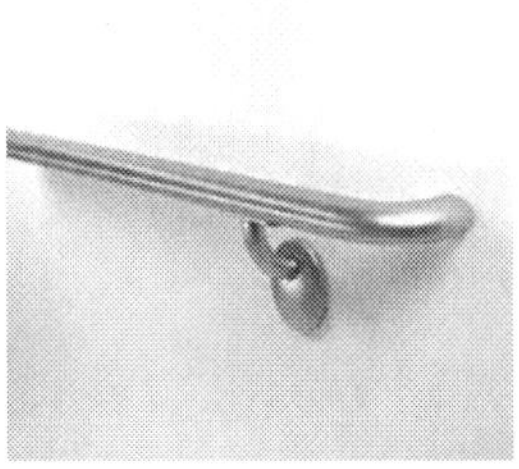

Catastrophic Mishaps

The linkage between the hazard, causal event(s), and catastrophic mishap are obscured;

1] **Risk:**
Difficult to rigorously or universally define harm.

2] **Cognitive Dissonance:**
Difficult to identify and control.

3] **Low Probability:**
Difficult to model and support the predictions.

Why are Catastrophic Hazards Hard?

Energy Trace and Barrier Analysis (Accident Investigation)

- Focus on consequences versus causal factors.
- Not expected to identify;
  - Ignition source, explosive vapors, logical errors, or the effects of multiple component failures.

Failure Modes and Effects Analysis (Reliability Analysis)

- Focus on single point failures
- Not expected to identify multiple point failures.

Dr. William Haddon (Not Predictive)

- All car injuries are the result of energy delivery to the body.
- Forensically driven risk mitigations based on lots of data.

None Were Developed as a Safety Risk Assessment Tool
No gap analysis

Energy
Universal Hazard for Catastrophic Mishaps

Energy as the

universal hazard for catastrophic mishaps

changes the way one identifies risk.

Energy
Universal Hazard for Catastrophic Mishaps

- **Boundary:** Defines what is within the system
- **Environment:** Everything outside the boundary that interacts with the system or is influenced by the system.

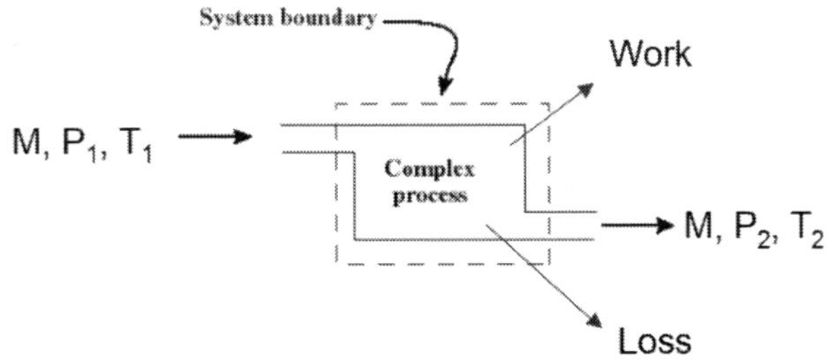

Energy
Universal Hazard for Catastrophic Mishaps

Stepping Through the Risk Assessment

1 Define the System and Boundaries

2 Define the amounts and types of Energy
Within the system boundary
Crossing the system boundary

3 Define energy states and uses

4 Identify all targets that can be catastrophically harmed

5 Identify linkage between energy and catastrophic targets

6 Identify and Assess Risk(s)

Energy
Universal Hazard for Catastrophic Mishaps

1 Define the System and Boundaries

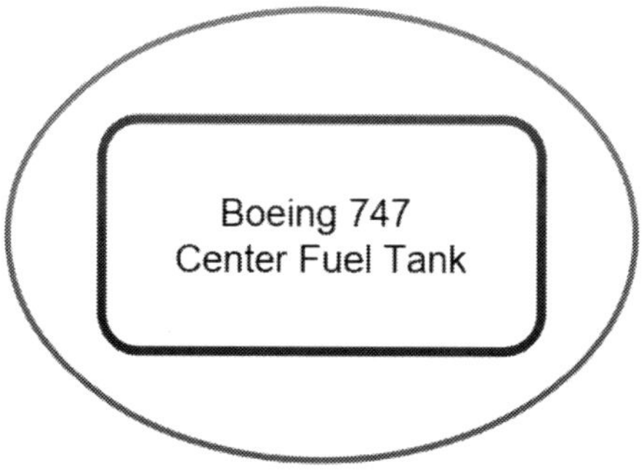

Tank System Boundary

Energy
Universal Hazard for Catastrophic Mishaps

2 Define the amounts and types of Energy

Within the system boundary
Crossing the system boundary

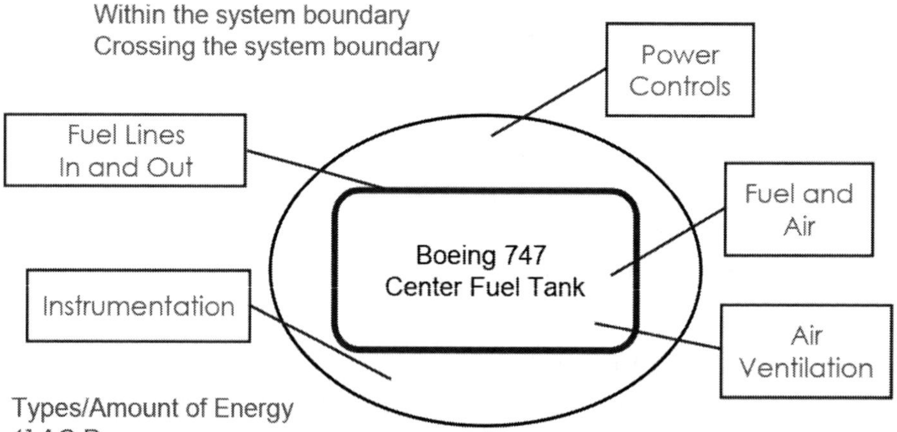

Types/Amount of Energy
1] AC Power
2] DC Power
3] Fuel/Air

Tank System Boundary
(Example does not consider the structure / grounding.)

Energy
Universal Hazard for Catastrophic Mishaps

3 Define energy states and uses

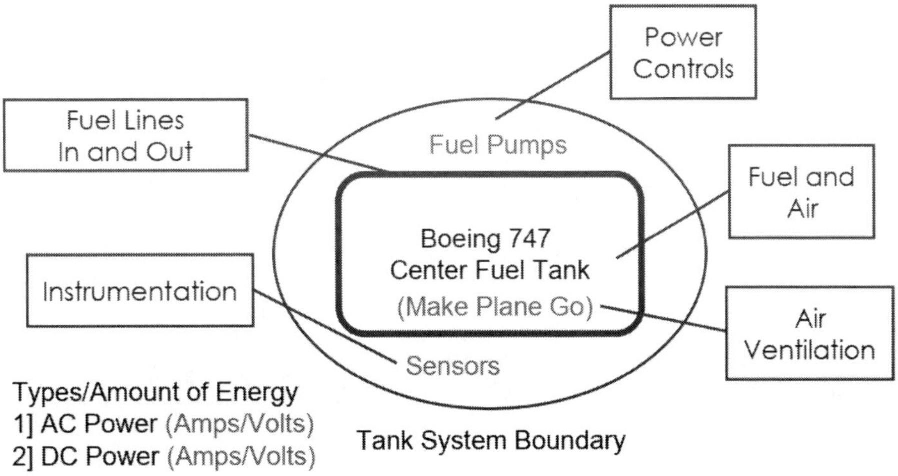

Types/Amount of Energy
1] AC Power (Amps/Volts)
2] DC Power (Amps/Volts)
3] Fuel/Air
Liquid
Vapor Mix

Energy
Universal Hazard for Catastrophic Mishaps

4 Identify all targets that can be catastrophically harmed

Targets:
People

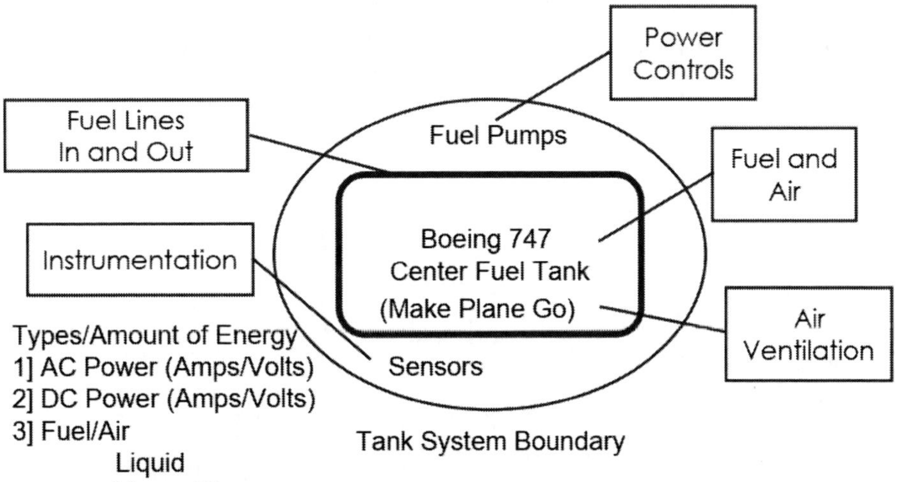

Types/Amount of Energy
1] AC Power (Amps/Volts)
2] DC Power (Amps/Volts)
3] Fuel/Air
Liquid
Vapor Mix

Energy
Universal Hazard for Catastrophic Mishaps

5 Identify linkage between energy and catastrophic targets

Targets:
People

Linkage:
Boeing 747

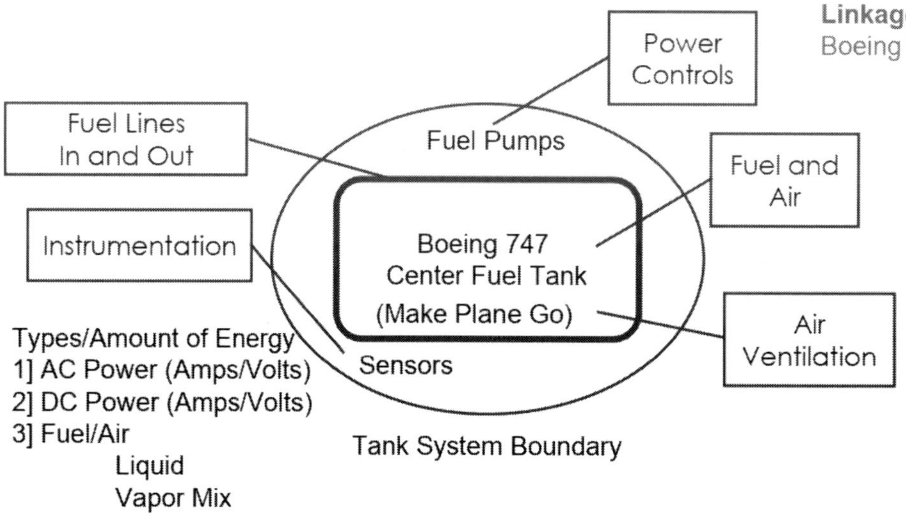

Energy
Universal Hazard for Catastrophic Mishaps

6 Identify and Assess Risk(s)

Catastrophic Risks
Fire
Exposition

Targets:
People

Linkage:
Boeing 747

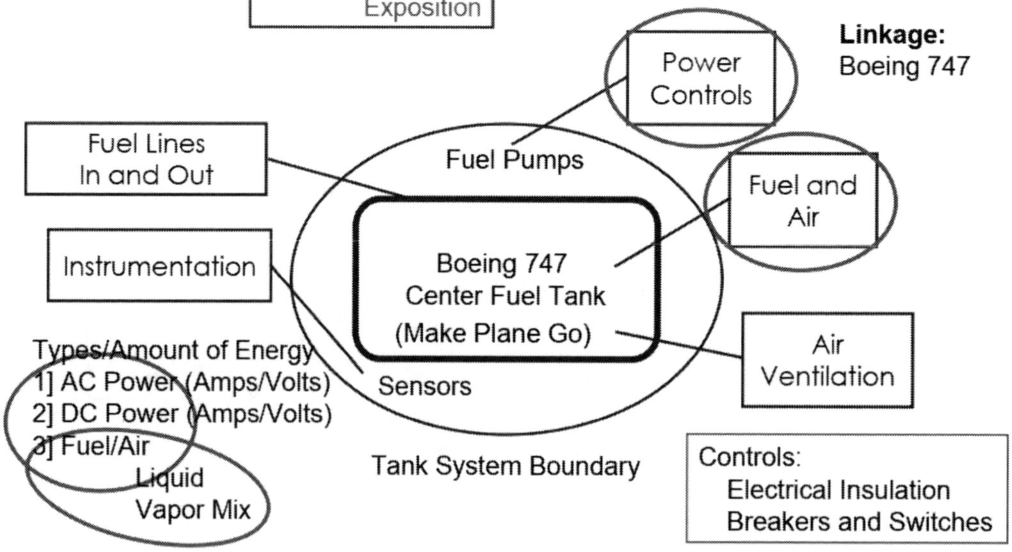

Recap of Catastrophic ID and Assessment

- Searched for energy within and crossing the boundary of a B-747 center fuel tank.
- Documented the amounts, energy states, and uses.
- Identified the targets of energy release.
- Identified link between targets and energy release.
- Assessed Risk
  - Fire or Fuel/Air explosion
  - Low frequency event
  - Loss of life – Catastrophic outcome

Energy
Universal Hazard for Catastrophic Mishaps

TWA Flight 800
New York
17 July 1996

At about 4.5 Km, the plane exploded.
All 230 people died.

Targets:
People

Fuel / Air Event in Center Fuel Tank

Linkage:
Boeing 747

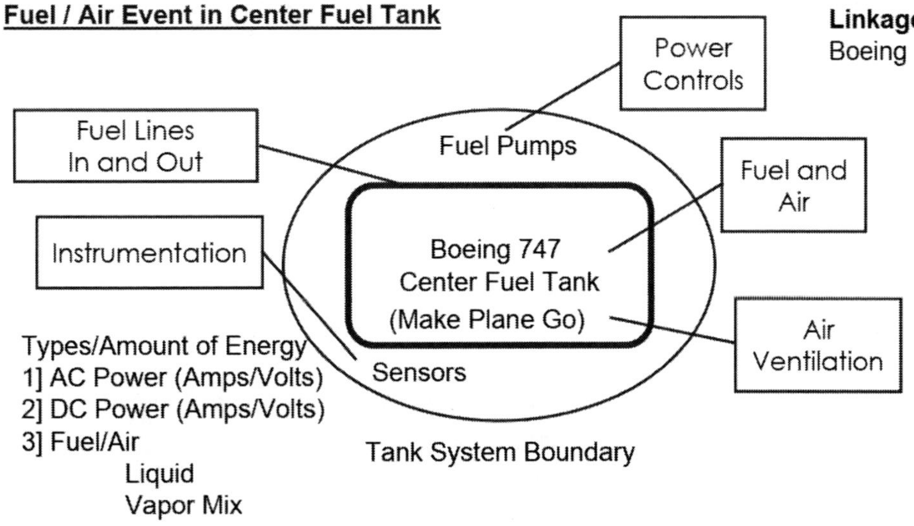

We Tend to Not Repeat the Same Catastrophe Twice...sort of

Problems with the aircraft's [Flight 800] wiring were found, including evidence of arcing in the Fuel Quantity Indication System (FQIS) wiring which enters the tank.

The FQIS on Flight 800 is known to have been malfunctioning; As a result of the investigation, new requirements were developed for aircraft to prevent future fuel tank explosions.

Lowery, Joan (July 16, 2008). "Jet fuel-tank protection ordered". Seattle Post-Intelligencer. The Associated Press. Retrieved April 5, 2011.

Energy Universal Hazard for Catastrophic Mishaps

- It is easy to embrace all the analysis we can do; PHA, SRHA, ETBA, O&SHA, Naked Man, Fault Tree...
  None of them are Catastrophic centric.
- There is software safety, system safety, regulation based safety, and other types of safety professionals.
- Safety professional of all kinds need to have energy as the hazard for catastrophic mishaps as part of their safety perspective.

What theory and method do you use to identify Low Frequency Catastrophic Mishaps?

Energy
Universal Hazard for Catastrophic Mishaps

Pros:

-Not dependent on the sample size for risk assessment

-Hazard is defined by energy amounts and targets

-Frequency of occurrence is assumed as low

Challenges:

- Defining the boundary
- Identifying all sources of energy
- Identifying all energy/target linkage

Energy
Universal Hazard for Catastrophic Mishaps

Questions / Comments

David R. Sadler, System Safety Engineer,
3817 Strauss Ave, Suite 108, Indian Head, MD 20640-5151,

telephone - (301) 744-6073,

email – David.R.Sadler@navy.mil.

David Sadler's Bio

- David Sadler's safety experience includes over 25 years in private industry and the Department of Defense, is a Mechanical Engineer, Electronics Engineer, and has a master's in System Safety Engineering.
- He has received numerous awards recognizing his contributions, including the Secretary of the Navy Safety Excellence Award, Senate Productivity Award, and the Naval Sea Systems Command Star Award, as well as recognition for saving the life of a co-worker.
- His career includes deployment of safety critical software on United States Navy (USN) ships, development and testing of weapon systems aboard USN ships, published works in safety, a safety patent, Principal for Safety, Warfare System Engineer for CVN21, and Weapon System Explosives Safety Review Board member for the Naval Ordnance Safety and Security Activity.
- David is an expert in the identification and analysis of risk, risk management, and near miss

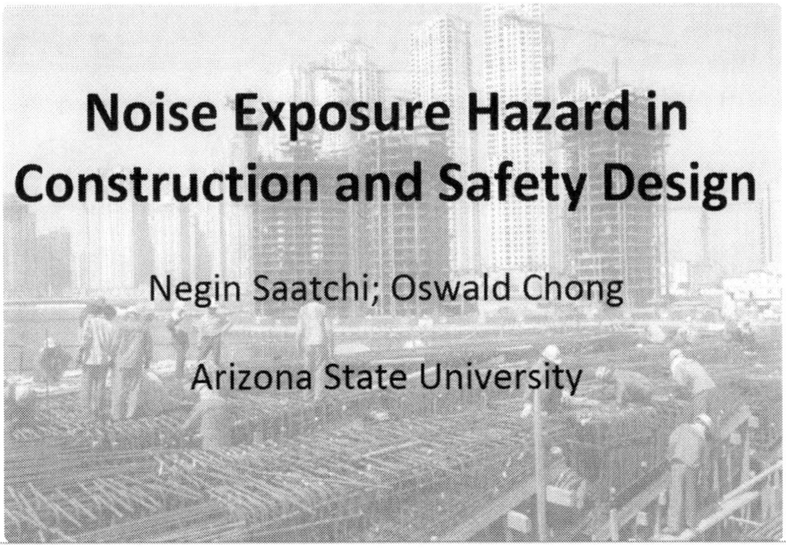

Noise Exposure Hazard in Construction and Safety Design

Negin Saatchi; Oswald Chong

Arizona State University

Goals

- Noise reduction of concrete chipping

- Find the most hazardous task in construction

- Find the current regulations' deficiencies

- Suggest the new safety measures

Introduction

➢ Noise → most irritating aspect of construction

➢ Problems of construction noise hazard (Construction industry noise exposure, 2004)

Hearing impairment

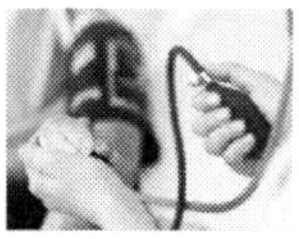

High blood pressure

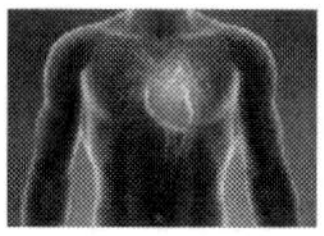

Coronary artery disease

Sleep disorder

Birth defects

➢ 12% of all US construction workers, 30 million, suffer from hearing difficulties (Kerns, 2018)

Construction Regulations Regulations Deficiency

1. Reduce duration of the work →

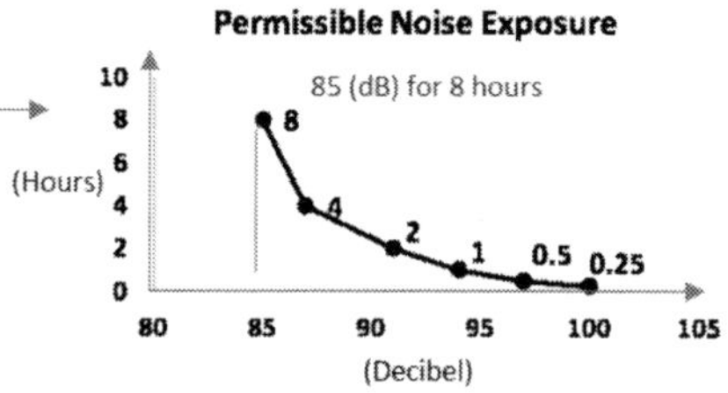

2. Use ear muff & ear plugs → Prevents from hearing other noises of job site

3. Annual health records

4. Train workers

(3, 4) → Not practical

(OSHA; NIOSH)

Hazardous Constriction Task

- **Concrete works** → The trade with highest number of workers exposed to hazardous noise (40%) (Suter, 2002)
- **Cement Mason** → Longest time of being exposed to the hazardous noise in a day. (46% of an eight-hour working shift) (Neitzel, 2005)
- **Concrete chipping & Chipping gun** → Noisiest task and equipment (103 dB) (Edelson, 2009)
- **Concrete workers used HPDs** → Only 19% of concrete workers used hearing protection devices (Suter, 2002)

Current Solution

- Eliminate the cause of the hazard: Not using chipping gun

- Micro blasting
  - Faster
  - Still noise & dust making
- Expansive grout
  - Less noise making
  - Time consuming
- Hydro demolition
  - Cleaner
  - Great amount of water used

(Phillips, 2017)

Prospective Solution

- Active Noise Cancelation System

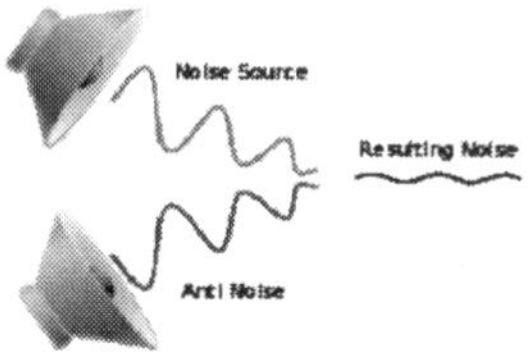

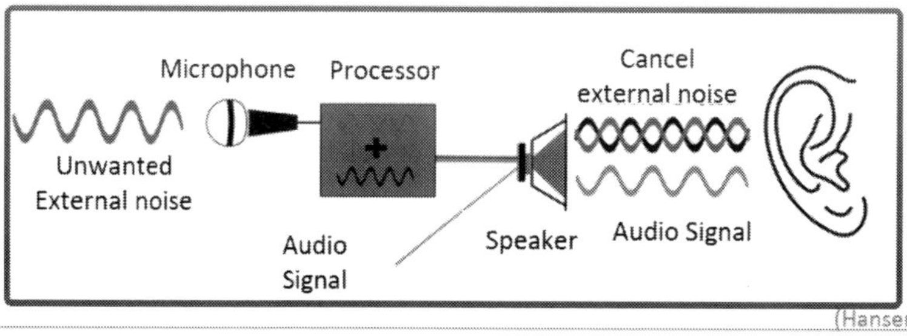

(Hansen, 1999)

6

36th International System Safety Conference, Aug. 13 – 17, 2018

Current ANC Applications

- Cancelling the low-frequency noise

- Reduction the noise

- Reducing low-frequency noise at the ears

- Helicopter cabin noise reduction

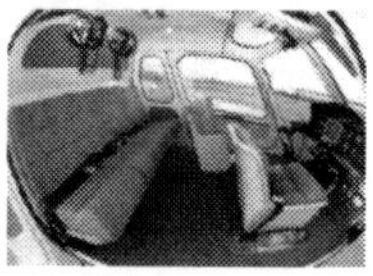

- Diesel engine exhausts on stationary equipment and buses

- Automobile engine vibration isolation

(Hansen, 1999)

7

36th International System Safety Conference, Aug. 13 – 17, 2018

Proposed method

- Factors of active noise canceling for concrete chipping

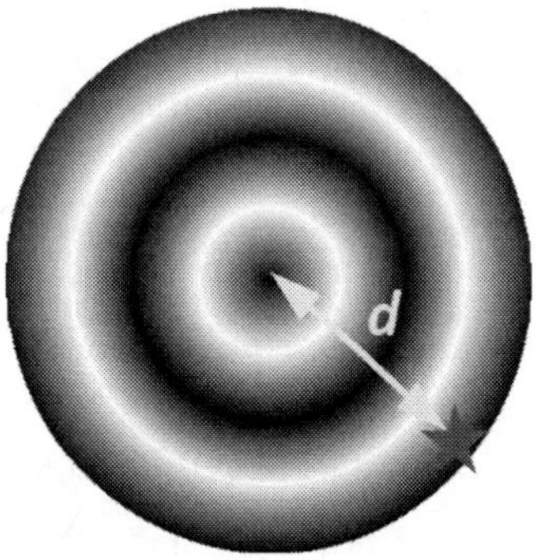

- Frequency range (both high and low frequency)
- $\text{Power}_{\text{Received}} \begin{cases} \propto (\textit{path Loss} \propto \frac{1}{d^2}) \text{ (d= 3 Ft)} \\ \propto \text{Decibel (103 dB)} \end{cases}$

<u>Conclusion</u>

- More effective and reliable
- Better communication
- More safety for construction employees

Future work:

- Improve the ability to damp wider frequency ranges
- Reduce the price of the technology

References

1. Construction industry noise exposure. (2004). Department of environmental and occupational health sciences, 16.
2. Kerns, E., Masterson, E. A., Themann, C. L., & Calvert, G. M. (2018). Cardiovascular conditions, hearing difficulty, and occupational noise exposure within US industries and occupations. American journal of industrial medicine.
3. Rosenstock, L. (1998). Criteria For The Recommended Standard, Occupational Noise Exposure (pp. 98-126): NIOSH.
4. Suter, A. H. (2002). Construction noise: exposure, effects, and the potential for remediation; a review and analysis. AIHA Journal, 63(6), 768-789.
5. Neitzel, R., & Seixas, N. (2005). The effectiveness of hearing protection among construction workers. Journal of occupational and environmental hygiene, 2(4), 227-238.
6. Edelson, J., Neitzel, R., Meischke, H., Daniell, W., Sheppard, L., Stover, B., & Seixas, N. (2009). Predictors of hearing protection use in construction workers. Annals of Occupational Hygiene, 53(6), 605-615. Palmer, B. (2012). Alternative Concrete Demolition Techniques.
7. Phillips, D. (2017). What's the difference between active and passive noise cancellation? Retrieved from http://www.electronicdesign.com/industrial-automation/what-s-difference-between-passive-and-active-noise-cancellation
8. Hansen, C. N. (1999). Understanding active noise cancellation: CRC Press.

Thank you

Questions ?

Email: nsaatchi@asu.edu

Migrating a Department of Defense (DoD) Acquisition Program to an Automated Information System (AIS) using a Model-Based Systems Engineering (MBSE) Approach

Gene Rosenthal, Lockheed Martin Space, Sunnyvale, California, USA

Keywords: Safety Critical Function, Model-Based Systems Engineer, MBSE, Safety, Mitigation, Safety Standard, Department of Defense

Abstract

One of the risks of performing Systems Engineering tasks on a program that uses a document-based approach is manually creating a set of documents such as CONOPS, Requirement Specifications, and Interface Control Documents (ICDs) that quickly become inconsistent and disjointed. One ends up having a set of text documents, spreadsheets, and presentations that must be maintained separately for consistency. Taking a Model-Based Systems Engineering (MBSE) approach eliminates this risk by capturing information such as system design, requirements, and verification information within a digital, object-oriented System Architecture Model (SAM). Digital definition of this information eases configuration management and readily allows reuse, so that engineers can focus more of their time on the technical challenges of system development and less on the tedium of document management. This paper will discuss the journey, challenges, and planned path forward to transition a legacy DoD Acquisition Program related to System Safety from a document-centric approach to model-based Automated Information System (AIS).

Introduction

The Department of Defense (DoD) Acquisition Program, subsequently referred to as DoD Program, has been performing safety assessments using a defined set of safety critical functions whenever proposed architecture changes affect safety critical components. These types of reviews have been performed for decades against legacy systems. Safety critical function assessments utilize a system engineering approach to perform assessments, which involves generating numerous documents, spreadsheets analysis, and PowerPoint presentations that are periodically reviewed at Safety Review Boards (SRBs). With the growing need to accommodate fix-priced contract, be cost affordable, and be faster/agile the safety community determined a need to improve how safety assessments are performed. Defense, Automotive, and the Health Care industries are transitioning more and more systems engineering practices into a Model-Based Systems Engineering (MBSE) approach, which takes a model-centric approach at systems engineering. The safety community that performs these safety reviews for the DoD pulled together a team consisting of subject matter experts from their prime contractors, as well as system modelers, to collaborate on a pilot project to capture safety critical functions into a SAM. Once the model is in place, the capability to perform trade studies on future system architectures can be easily facilitated.

Change can be tough, especially for a project that has been achieving mission success through a document-based system engineering approach for decades. This project went through its own set of challenges and lessons learned. This paper will discuss the journey taken to transition a legacy DoD program into a model-centric program. While substantial progress has been made, the program is still in the initial stages of transition and this safety effort reflects one of many systems engineering practices that will continue to evolve over the coming years.

A Brief Background on Model-Based Systems Engineering (MBSE)

Model-Based Systems Engineering (MBSE) is Systems Engineering but performed in a model. The same Systems Engineering activities are performed (e.g. System Design, Architecture, Requirements Management and Verification, Concept of Operations (CONOPS), etc. are used, but instead of generating a series of documents and spreadsheets, this information is captured within a SAM. The model is the primary artifact and "source of truth" for system definition. Information can be defined once and then referenced in many different views that address different stakeholder needs. In this way, if a characteristic of the system is updated, any views referencing this characteristic automatically reflects those updates. In addition, traditional documents can still be generated using report tools and templates within the modeling tool.

System modelers generally use the Object Management Group (OMG) System Markup Language (SysML®) to capture information in the model (OMG, n.d.). SysML® is a general purpose graphical modeling language. Various Custom Off-The-Shelf (COTS) tools are available to model SysML®, such as No Magic's Cameo System Modeler, IBM's Rhapsody, and Sparx Systems' Enterprise Architect. The modeling team for this DoD program elected to use Cameo System Modeler.

Breaking Down Safety System Critical Functions

The safety team manages critical functions using a text document which describes the set of safety standards the system must meet. Each standard has associated event categories which are used to categorize the safety critical function. Critical functions are defined at the system-level and decomposed into subsystem-level critical functions. Individual contractors are responsible for managing the safety critical subsystem functions that their respective subsystem performs. Table 1 — Subsystem Critical Function Classification Structure describes the subsystem critical functions classification structure.

Table 1 — Subsystem Critical Function Classification Structure

Safety Standard	Applicable safety standard the subsystem critical function satisfies. Satisfying the standard(s) is a requirement on the subsystem to prevent hazardous condition(s).
Event Category	Event categories were also used to classify subsystem critical functions. These event categories are closely related to the safety standards and allows critical functions related to a particular event easily identified.
System Critical Function	System critical functions are used to "bucket" subsystem system critical functions. One or more subsystem critical functions may fall under one system-level function.
Subsystem Critical Function	Name of the Subsystem Critical Function

To migrate to a model-centric environment, the team had to understand the document structure and how subsystem critical functions were captured. The document starts off stating the top-level safety standards that each critical function must adhere to, including how they are categorized. Subsystem critical functions are distributed across various appendices depending on the subsystem. Each subsystem critical function is captured within a table, capturing the definition, potential safety hazards, affected critical components, and related source documentation. Table 2 — Subsystem Critical Function Definition describes the subsystem critical function definition, hazard/rationale, and critical components. In addition, the related event category, system function, and safety standard is also shown.

Table 2 — Subsystem Critical Function Definition

Definition	Definition of the subsystem critical function
Hazard/Rationale	In addition to the definition, each subsystem critical function lists the potential hazards that may result if the function does not meet the intent; related to the safety standards/event categories.
Critical Component(s)	Each subsystem critical functions list the affected component(s) related to the critical function

There are definite challenges to maintaining safety critical function in a document with multiple tables and diagram showing the same information. Information must be manually updated every time the document is updated, which can be a time-consuming process with the potential for errors resulting in discrepancies throughout the document. Also, when safety reviews are conducted, the safety team must pull together presentations that relate safety critical functions to other systems engineering concerns (CONOPs descriptions, interfaced descriptions, etc.) resulting in further duplication of information across artifacts that can quickly become out of sync.

Transitioning to Model-Based Environment

Transitioning to a model-based environment was done using a phased approach. This section will describe the objectives of each phase of the project.

1. Setting up the Model

The first phase was to establish the model. This included setting up a metamodel, profile, and package structure. These are essential SysML® concepts when developing models and considered a best practice. Table 3 — Safety Model SysML® Concepts defines each of these concepts.

Table 3 — Safety Model SysML® Concepts

Metamodel	A metamodel is used by system modelers to depict how modeling elements related to each other.
Profile	A collection of unique element classifiers (called stereotypes) and the diagrams that explain their use (such as the

	metamodel). A profile can be commonly shared across models to enforce consistency.
Package Structure	The folder structure of the model

Figure 1 — System Safety Profile shows the Profile developed for the safety model. This profile allows model elements to be uniquely identified, such as safety standards, consequences, derived functions, critical functions, critical components, etc. Also, if an element was related to the safety document, an additional stereotype was applied with the document number. This allows the reader to easily determine if the model content comes from the safety document or something else. Note: the term 'legacy document' is being used in leu of the actual document number. The document comment stereotype can be applied to comments in the model questioning content from the safety document.

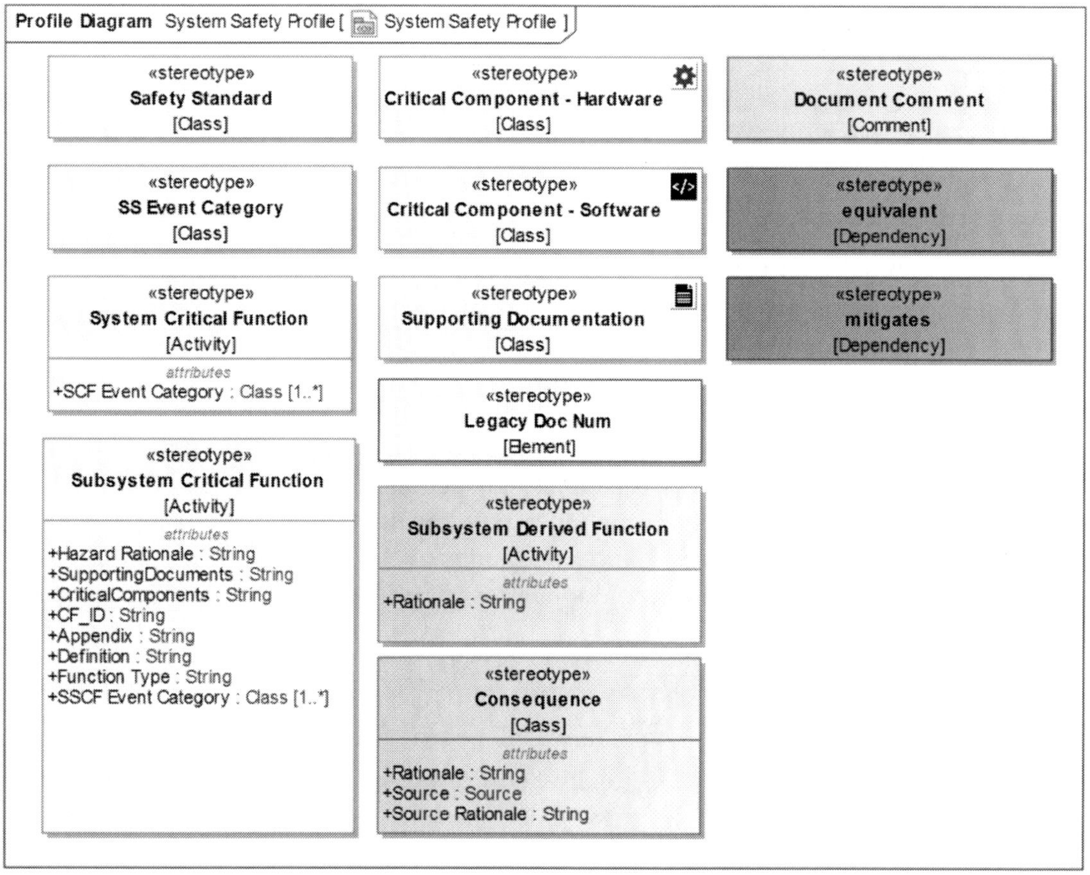

Figure 1 — System Safety Profile

Figure 2— System Safety Metamodel the metamodel that was established. A metamodel includes all element types in the model and shows how they can/should relate.

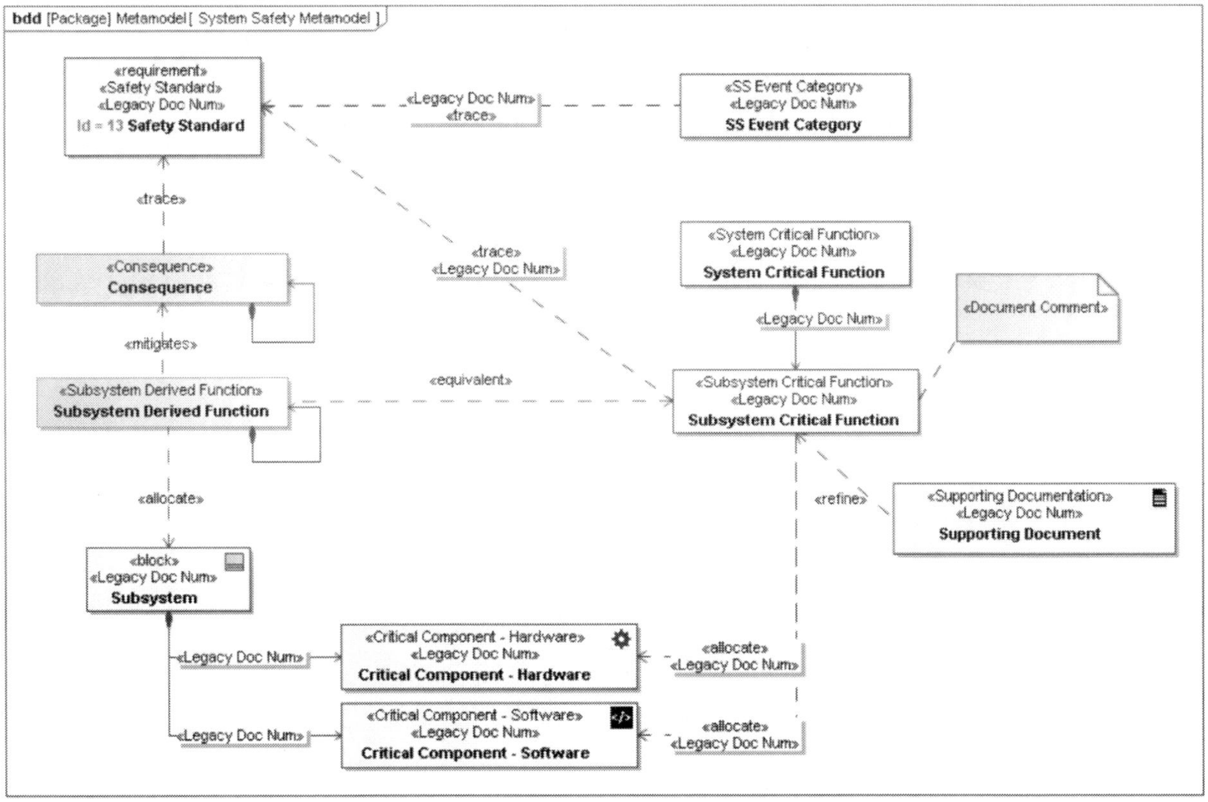

Figure 2— System Safety Metamodel

2. Reproduce document content in the model

After the model was established, the goal was to capture content from the document in model format and ensure that content matched (word for word) within the model; including generating table views that resemble the document's appendices. Due to how the paper version reused classifications and naming conventions, numerous relationship issues were discovered. Modeling in SysML® takes a similar approach to software programming concepts where model "element" (blocks) should not reuse names more than once. This is not a good modeling practice. In other situations, the model had to break classifications into separate elements because compound functions/names were used within the document which is another practice that is a discouraged.

Several of these nuances resulted in discussions with safety subject matter experts to understand the background of the documents structure, the rationale for reusing names, and to determine a path forward. Some of these issues are described in the next sections, where modeling structure and relationships will be discussed in further detail.

3. Capturing design- agnostic functions and rationale

On top of capturing document content (standards, functions, critical components, etc.), the team also took the initiative to capture derived content. There were two levels of derived content: Subsystem Derived Functions (SSDF) and Consequences. SSDFs were derived from critical function definitions, with the top-level derived function being flagged as "equivalent" to the critical function. Consequences were derived from either the Safety Standards, Hazard/Rationale of the Critical Function, or Subject Matter Expert (SME) review. By deriving this type of information from critical function definitions, the team captured the intent of the functions and provided a means of knowledge capture for future workforce that will perform safety assessments.

A visual representation of each subsystem critical function was developed using a SysML® Block Definition Diagram (BDD) or "thread". To enable each contractor to develop threads with a common look and feeling, modeling guidance was provided. Figure 3 — Thread Development Guidance depicts the guidance provided.

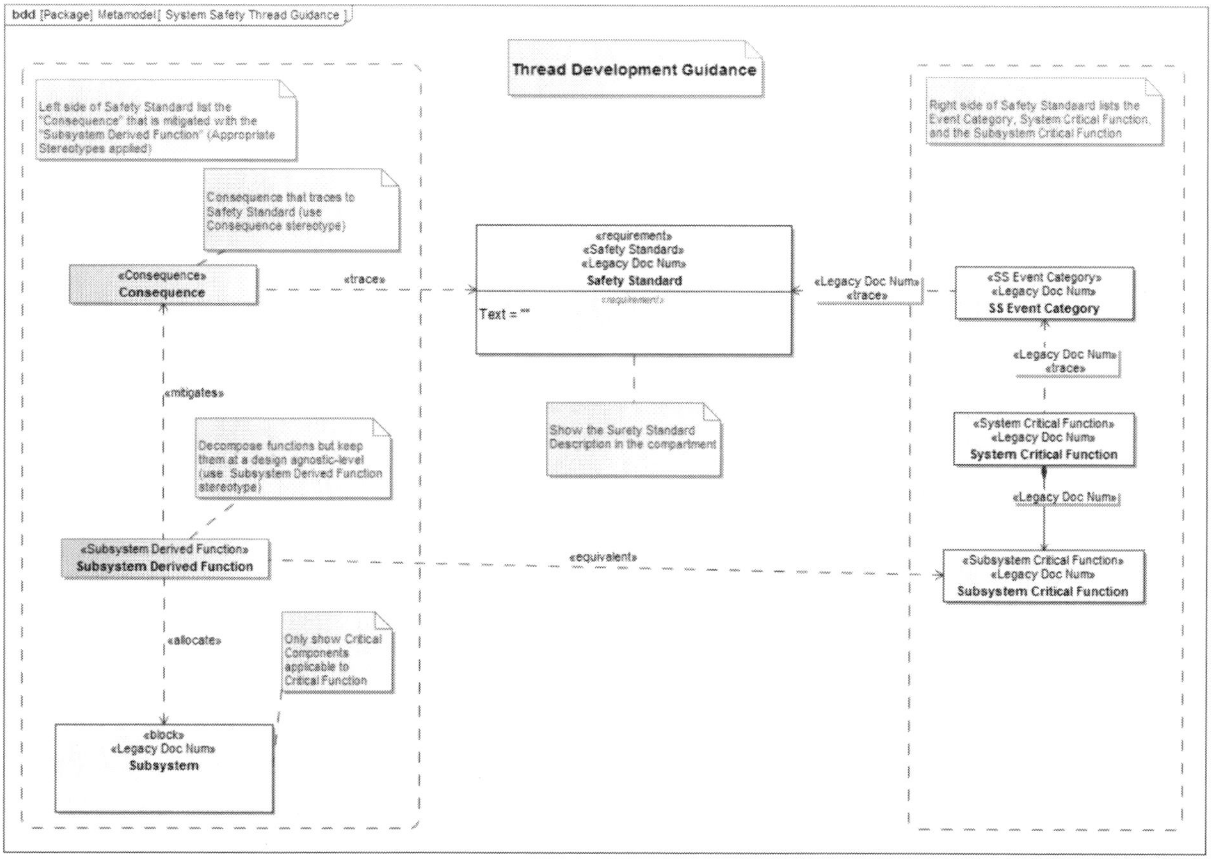

Figure 3 — Thread Development Guidance

In addition to the visual threads, other views were established to aid reviews, such as tables, allocation matrices, dependency matrices, and relationship maps. Being able to generate several views is one of the many benefits of using a model-centric approach. In addition, if an update is needed to a model element (e.g. derived function name), this change would automatically update any views where the element is used. This allows for rapid reviews of model content.

4. *Identify approach and benefits to using the model for safety activities*

Realizing the benefits of a model-centric approach while working with the safety community, use cases were captured in the model to describe how it could support various safety activities in the future. Figure 4 —Safety Model Use Case Diagram below shows the initial set of use cases captured in the model

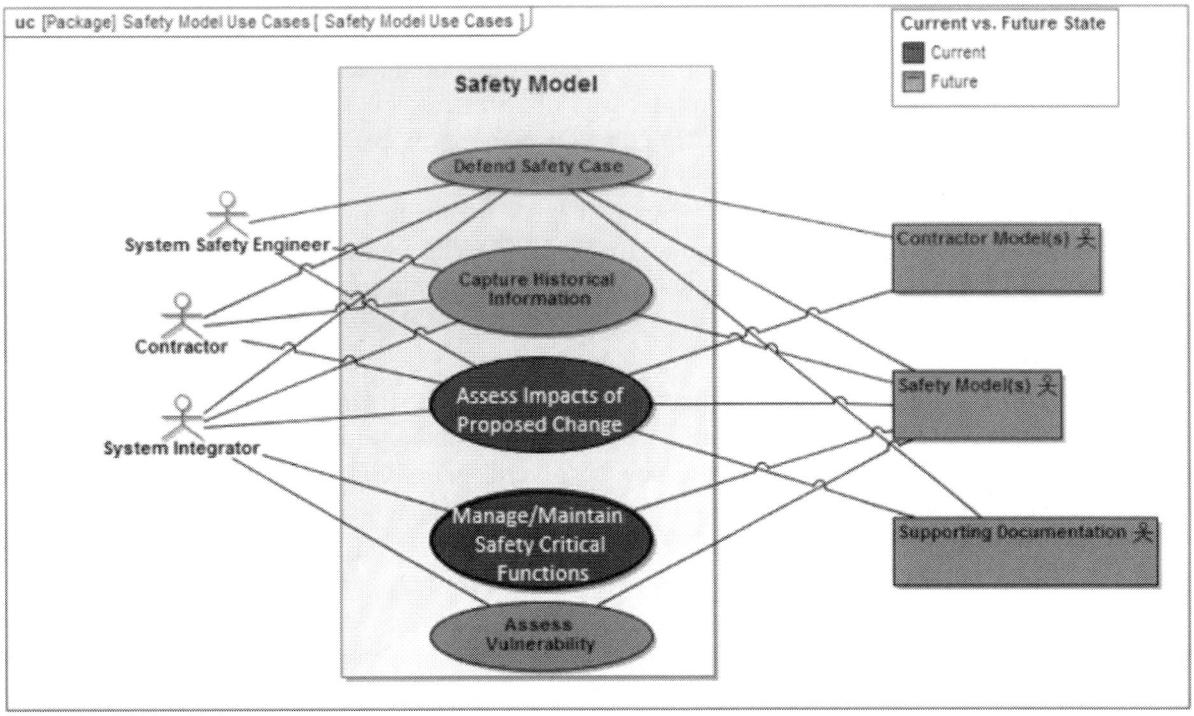

Figure 4 —Safety Model Use Case Diagram

As the model matured, the true power of having safety content in a model was being realized, but there were definite challenges along the way. The next section will discuss some of these challenges in greater detail.

Challenges Faced Along the Way

There were several challenges and lessons learned on this project. This section will describe them in more detail.

1. *The Difficulties of Change*

   In general, change is not easy for most people. This legacy DoD program has been performing safety assessments for decades using this defined set of critical functions to ensure any architecture change has no impact to the safety. Architecture boards do not approve changes if there is any risk of violating a critical function. As the team captured derived functions, the concern was raised that this effort was introducing new requirements against legacy systems, which was met with some resistance. Through discussions, the safety members of the team gained a better understanding of the purpose of the modeling and grew more accepting of the effort, and the modeling members of the team gained a better understanding of the intent of the document and thus revised model content and even the metamodel to better address the intent. The purpose was extremely beneficial and resulted in a more mature and useful model.

2. *Collaboration Challenges*

   Like a software development team having a source control utility to collaborate, system modeler also need a collaborative environment. This was especially true collaborating among multiple contractors. The team was unable to establish a commonly accessible environment across contractors, so they had to work around this issue. After starting with a baseline model with defined stereotypes and metamodel, and kicking off the effort providing guidance, the model was distributed to the team for each contractor to develop their critical function threads. Once a point of maturity was reached, each version of the model was merged together. After some clean up, we established another baseline of the model, and distributed it back to the team. To minimize merging, we coordinated exchanging the model back and forth to make updates. Although this situation was far from ideal, the team worked through these challenges successfully.

3. *SysML® Education*

   Several colleagues on this project were new to MBSE and using SysML®. General concepts on what model elements mean were understood, but the nuances of the modeling language and tool were new to several people. Understanding the differences between relationship types (e.g. associations, dependencies) and the direction of a relationship are key concepts in SysML®. The biggest challenge for the team in learning SysML® modeling was how to deal with redundant elements. For example- if you create a relationship between two elements on one diagram, you didn't need to create it again on another diagram, it already exists in the model. Training the team to look for relationships and elements in the model tree to add to a diagram, rather than creating them anew, was a big learning curve. Also, understanding a functional decomposition captured in a BDD does not mean that you have to place the decomposed functional model elements in order of occurrence. That type of ordering is captured in a behavior diagram (e.g. Activity Diagram). System engineers typically want to place things in order. This is not to say it is discouraged, it was just something that was not required in functional decomposition.

4. *Data Structure Transition from a Document to a Model*

   The visual representation (threads) of the critical functions gave the safety community a way to understand how the document was structured but several inconsistencies were discovered. The document has an implied ontology across multiple diagrams and tables, and once that ontology was formalized into a metamodel and visualized in diagrams, the team realized that it had flaws and didn't fully accomplish the objectives of the safety team. This was not apparent when the data was unstructured in the document, but it was revealed in the process of modeling the data. While this was a challenged to work through, ultimately it was a benefit because the safety team now has a more robust data structure to manage their critical functions

5. *Safety Community Buy-In*

Getting buy-in by the safety community was a key part of the project. As mentioned before, there were concerns by the safety team regarding introducing new requirements. The team did not introduce new requirements, but we had to reach an agreement on our modeling approach since this is the community that will be using the model. Another big concern was the idea of the model becoming the primary artifact and source of truth vs. having a paper version. The paper version can be one of many types of views generated from the model, depending on the stakeholder need. For people who maintain the paper copy, and do not know how to maintain or develop a model, concern over the loss of "ownership" of critical functions would be lost. The team had to explain to the document owners that this is not the case. The different contractors will still retain ownership of their critical functions, but within a collaborative infrastructure.

Model Validation

To ensure that the work the team did developing and maturing the safety model was accurate and useful, a model validation effort was kicked off earlier this year. This validation effort extended to additional members of the safety community. With all the content captured in the model, it made sense to break-up the validation effort into phases to focus on specific content. Table 4 — Model Validation Phased Approach describes each phase in detail.

Table 4 — Model Validation Phased Approach

Phase 1	The focus of Phase 1 was to ensure the model accurately captured all content from the safety document.
Phase 2	The focus of Phase 2 was on the derived functions. Are they design agnostic? Use consistent terminology (e.g. verbs, not compound actions)? Can any functions be reused?
Phase 3	The focus of Phase 3 was on consequences to ensure derived consequences accurately reflect rationale, relationship to derived functions are correct, terminology, and if we can reuse any consequences
Phase 4	The focus of Phase 4 was to look at derived functions again for critical functions that cross subsystems. If one subsystem sends something to another subsystem, the affected critical functions should have the proper send and receive derived functions. We called these derived functions "handshake functions".
Phase 5	The focus here was to validate each subsystem critical function thread based on the previous phases to visually see how all the elements relate to each other.

Each phase required a deep dive into the model, which proved to be very valuable, as issues were uncovered, or general model cleanup was needed. A big issue was uncovered related to our metamodel. Because the goal was to structure the model relationships similar to how the document was structured, ambiguous relationship issue were discovered. It was possible in some cases to trace to the wrong safety standard for a critical function because several critical functions were categorized under a common category (model element). This forced the team to rethink how the metamodel was structured, which resulted in updating relationships and creating additional attributes (tags) to the critical functions stereotype, which led to a better product.

Phase 4 took that most time. To perform this phase, the team used activity diagrams. For example, if critical function A and B were related and affected more than one subsystem, a SysML® Activity Diagram was created for the derived function within A and B. "Swimlanes" were used for each subsystem to show interfaces. This allowed the team to validate how these functions "connected" and determine if functions were missing or needed to be reworded. This was proved to be extremely valuable.

Conclusions and Path Forward

This paper described the work and journey for this model-based transition. Some were resistant to change, and others struggled with concepts, but the team remained resilient and patient working through these challenges. The result of this effort is a valuable mature model, which has the framework to support future trade studies and safety assessments since impacts are easily visible in a model vs. reviewing independent documents. At some point, the paper document will be retired, and the model will serve as the main artifact for these safety critical functions. Documents/views will be produced from the model.

The team continues to work validation efforts, including setting up a collaborative environment for each contractor. In addition, the team is also working with the DoD to identify a program to pilot the use of the safety model. Piloting the usage will prove the value of the model and give more insight to any additional views that need to be generated. Also, as more and more programs begin to transition into a model-based environment, more people are investing time to learn about MBSE, SysML®, and the tools available. As mentioned before, the desire is to be more affordable and utilize common products, when appropriate. MBSE can help satisfy these needs and provide significant cost saving to programs working under fixed-priced contracts. This also helps keep MBSE and the program sold.

References

1. International Business Machine (IBM) Rationale Rhapsody (n.d.) https://www.ibm.com/us-en/marketplace/rational-rhapsody

2. No Magic. Magic Draw (n.d.) https://www.nomagic.com/products/magicdraw

3. Object Management Group (OMG) Systems Markup Language (SysML®) (n.d.) http://www.omgsysml.org/

4. Sparx Systems Enterprise Architecture http://sparxsystems.com/products/ea/index.html

Biography

Gene Rosenthal, Model-Based Systems Engineer Staff, Lockheed Martin Space, Sunnyvale, California; Email gene.rosenthal@lmco.com

Gene Rosenthal has been working at Lockheed Martin Space for almost 15 years as a Systems Engineer. He has worked multiple programs, including the International Space Station (ISS) program, Near Infa-Red Camera (NIRCam) program and various Navy and Missile Defense Agency projects. He has been practicing MBSE for almost 3 years now and is now leading multiple efforts for various customers.

Synergistic Risk Management Strategies

Galen Ressler; General Motors Company; Warren, MI

Keywords: risk assessment, risk management, synergy, MIL-STD-882E, ISO 26262

Abstract

System safety standards and processes exist in a variety of industries to support the development of safety through design. Each is created with the intention that it provides complete risk assessment and management, reflecting the needs, perspectives, uses and techniques specific to its intended application.

MIL-STD-882E, ISO 26262 and Systems-Theoretic Process Analysis (STPA) are three examples. MIL-STD-882E, a well-established standard used in military applications, emphasizes the elimination of hazards and minimizing associated risk when elimination is not possible. ISO 26262, specifically for automotive applications, provides process and design guidance based on risk levels of potential hazards. STPA emphasizes a system perspective for assessing accident causation and is able to identify risks which are not associated with any system failures. Each of these methods include unique approaches for safety which can be used in combination.

In a simple example of a high voltage battery charging system, the application of the unique features of each approach work together to create a final system design which has less risk then if only one were applied. Such a combination of approaches is intuitively applied by many system safety engineers and may provide a foundation for a cross-industry approach to system safety.

Main Body

Introduction

Various system safety standards and processes exist to support the development of safety through design. These approaches each use different risk assessment and management methods, depending on application industry, approach, theoretic foundation and history of development. Each safety standard or process is created with the intention that it provides complete risk assessment and management within its intended context. Further, they each include application-specific techniques and reflect the unique needs, perspectives and uses that guide system safety engineers in their respective industries.

MIL-STD-882E (Department of Defense, 2012), a well-established standard used extensively in military and aerospace applications, emphasizes the elimination of hazards and minimizing associated risk when elimination is not possible. ISO 26262 (International Organization for Standardization (ISO) - 1, 2011) was specifically developed for the automotive industry. Originally released in 2011, with an update due later in 2018, it emphasizes functional safety and provides process and design guidance based on assessed risk levels of potential hazards. Systems-Theoretic Process Analysis (STPA) (Leveson & Thomas, 2018) emphasizes a system perspective to accident causation and, in particular, is able to identify risks which are not associated with any system failures. Each of these methods include valuable approaches for safety and also can be combined so that new insights emerge.

Risk Assessment

A common characteristic of system safety standards and processes is consideration and assessment of risk. Risk can generally be defined as the combination of the severity of an event and the likelihood that the event will occur (Department of Defense, 2012). An event with a very severe outcome and a high likelihood of occurrence would be considered as high risk. Alternatively, an event with a low severity outcome that is unlikely to occur would be considered low risk. Evaluating the relative risk of a high severity but unlikely event compared to a low severity but likely event is where specific risk assessment methods are most useful. While each of the considered methods has a similar concept for risk, the specifics of assessment vary.

MIL-STD-882E Method.

MIL-STD-882E considers severity category and probability level of potential mishaps. Severity category is a 4 level qualitative assessment based on the possible outcome of a risk. Values range from catastrophic to negligible. Probability level is a 6 level scale, from frequent to eliminated, which qualitatively describes the likelihood of occurrence of a mishap. These two values are combined to obtain a risk assessment value, ranging from high to low (Figure 1).

RISK ASSESSMENT MATRIX				
SEVERITY / PROBABILITY	Catastrophic (1)	Critical (2)	Marginal (3)	Negligible (4)
Frequent (A)	High	High	Serious	Medium
Probable (B)	High	High	Serious	Medium
Occasional (C)	High	Serious	Medium	Low
Remote (D)	Serious	Medium	Medium	Low
Improbable (E)	Medium	Medium	Medium	Low
Eliminated (F)	Eliminated			

Figure 1 – MIL-STD-882E Risk Assessment Matrix *(Department of Defense, 2012)*

The risk assessment method in MIL-STD-882E has a couple of unique features. First, severity includes both human injury risk as well as environmental damage and financial loss. This broadens the definition of safety compared to other methods which emphasize human injury risk. Second, the likelihood of occurrence combines effects of circumstances (where risk of mishap varies depending on the situation) with effects from the operation or malfunction of system components and effects due to operator error.

STPA Method.

STPA does not have a formal risk assessment process as part of its approach. In fact, one of the framers of the approach argues that, in particular, likelihood of occurrence is nearly always unknown or unknowable (Leveson, 2011). Instead, its approach focuses, first, on identifying potential accidents and then identifying what can cause them. Explicit assessment of the likelihood of any hazard or accident occurring is not done. It also does not attempt to discriminate severity of an accident.

The unique characteristic of this approach is that the simple presence of the potential for an accident is sufficient to warrant consideration within the process described by STPA. Thus, reduction of risk is not specifically identified. By not assessing either severity or likelihood, the STPA process is intended to help assure that any potential situation is addressed, not simply those which are judged to be most likely or most severe.

ISO 26262 Method.

ISO 26262, which was originally based on IEC61508 (International Electrotechnical Commission, 2010), uses a risk assessment technique which results in an Automotive Safety Integrity Level (ASIL). It uses three factors to develop an ASIL value (International Organization for Standardization (ISO) - 2, 2011). First, potential severity, based on "worst case plausible" outcome, is determined based on a 3 level scale. Next, circumstances where the mishap can occur are considered and "exposure," or "probability class" is determined based on the frequency of occurrence of those circumstances. Exposure is assessed on a 4 level scale where each level is roughly an order of magnitude different, starting from high probability to very low probability. Finally, "controllability" is considered. This is intended to account for the ability of a person potentially at risk to take an action which prevents the mishap or prevents harm from occurring as a result of the mishap. Controllability is also assessed on a 3 level scale from simply controllable to uncontrollable. ISO 26262 emphasizes hazards which are caused by malfunctions. However, the likelihood of occurrence of a particular malfunction is not considered in the risk assessment. Required design actions for a given risk level define what must be done to provide an acceptable likelihood of malfunction occurrence. See Figure 2 for relationship of ASIL to each of the three factors.

ISO 26262 is unique from the other processes considered here because it separates an overall likelihood of occurrence into 3 distinct parts. Those parts are "operational circumstance," "capability of user to prevent accident," and "likelihood of malfunction." "Operational circumstance" is comprehended in the Exposure factor; "capability of user to prevent accident" is the controllability factor; and "likelihood of malfunction" is the outcome of completing the actions required for each ASIL value. Together, these parts are equivalent to the MIL-STD-882E probability level. By separating them, though, it is possible to consider mitigation approaches which may impact each of the various parameters separately.

Severity class	Probability class	Controllability class		
		C1	C2	C3
S1	E1	QM	QM	QM
	E2	QM	QM	QM
	E3	QM	QM	A
	E4	QM	A	B
S2	E1	QM	QM	QM
	E2	QM	QM	A
	E3	QM	A	B
	E4	A	B	C
S3	E1	QM	QM	A
	E2	QM	A	B
	E3	A	B	C
	E4	B	C	D

Figure 2 – ISO 26262 ASIL Determination Table *(International Organization for Standardization (ISO) - 1, 2011)*

Risk Management

System safety engineering is not primarily about risk assessment. Rather, it is about designing and developing products which are safe, or have an acceptable level of risk for their intended usage (International Organization for Standardization (ISO) - 3, 2011). The process by which identified risks are minimized is risk management or, simply, the system safety process.

MIL-STD-882E Method.

MIL-STD-882E describes a process in which identified risks are reduced based on a prioritized list of approaches. That list is:

- Eliminate hazards through design selection.
- Reduce risk through design alteration.
- Incorporate engineered features or devices.
- Provide warning devices.
- Incorporate signage, procedures, training, and PPE. (Department of Defense, 2012)

Using this design order of precedence, the system safety engineer initially identifies possible approaches, selects and implements the best approaches within overall project constraints, validates the effect of the selected approaches and then re-assesses risk using the same risk assessment process as before. At the end of the project, an appropriate decision maker agrees that the remaining risk after all approaches have been implemented is acceptable.

Of the three approaches discussed in this paper, MIL-STD-882E is the only approach which conducts a risk assessment at the end of the project. It also provides a useful preferential list of ways that risk can be reduced, emphasizing approaches which are likely more effective as first priority.

STPA Method.

STPA primarily uses a requirements/constraints based approach to risk management, based on possible system actions which could result in a hazardous situation. Its foundation is to consider the system using a general controls structure model. A generic control structure is shown in Figure 3. The specific system under analysis is modeled at an appropriate level of detail using multiple, interconnected controllers, processes, control actions and feedback elements.

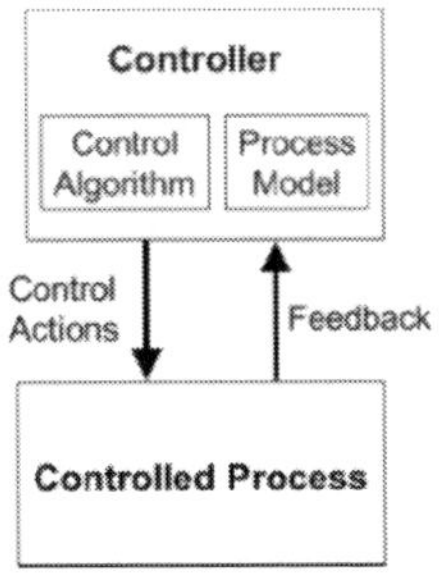

Figure 3 – Generic Control Structure *(Leveson & Thomas, STPA Handbook, 2018)*

The overall risk management method used can be viewed as shown in Figure 4. The unsafe action step is based on application of hazard and operability process (HAZOP) guidewords to each control action and feedback element within the overall system design. Each of these functions is assessed to determine the effect of a) the function not being provided, b) a wrong function being provided, c) wrong timing for the function or d) wrong duration of the function. Possible causes of these unsafe actions are then identified and constraints (or requirements) are placed on the system to prevent the cause, and therefore, the unsafe action. By preventing the unsafe action, the hazard and, therefore the accident, is prevented. The overall risk management approach, illustrated as a progression of analysis steps from accidents to requirements is shown in Figure 4.

Figure 4 – Progressive Analysis Flow for STPA *(Vernacchia, 2016)*

One the unique features of this approach is that it can be applied recursively using this same pattern throughout the complete design process since a control structure can be built at varying abstraction levels within the system, from the very highest conceptual system level to very specific controller component behavior. In addition, for systems involving human interactions, the human can be considered as a controller and user interactions with the system can be analyzed in the same way. This consideration is not well comprehended in other methods and makes STPA particularly useful when evaluating systems with human-machine interactions (HMI).

ISO 26262 Method.

ISO 26262 manages risk by defining product and engineering process requirements which are judged to be sufficient to reduce risk to an acceptable level based on the initial risk assessment value, i.e., ASIL. Product related requirements may, for example, be specific diagnostic functions, acceptable quantitative failure rates, or the number of independent failures which must be present before the hazard can occur. Process related requirements may include requirements on types of testing to be completed, frequency and type of peer reviews held, and analyses which must be conducted. If all required product and process criteria are met, then the remaining risk associated with the hazard is acceptable. Reassessment of the risk is not done.

ISO 26262 uniquely provides very specific information to define what has been judged sufficient mitigation to reduce risk to an acceptable level. Whereas both of the other two approaches leave final risk acceptance to the user, this standard pre-defines it. This is particularly useful for maintaining consistency of safety performance within a larger organization. It is not necessary to have individual decision makers for each project who may have different judgements on acceptable residual risk levels.

A Simple Example

As described above, each of these methods have unique risk assessment and risk management methods which may be able to be combined such that the resulting approach is better than any one approach is alone. To illustrate this point, a simple example can be considered.

The example is a high voltage automotive battery used as the sole propulsion energy source for the vehicle. As the sole energy source, it must be periodically recharged from an external source in order for it to be able to continue to operate (Figure 5). In this process of recharging the battery, safety risks exist. In particular, there is a risk of electrocution of a person during the process of recharging due to exposure to high voltage electrical energy.

Some relevant details of this hypothetical system include:

- High voltage cabling has functional insulation only, using the minimum necessary to allow the system to operate. Material selection, thickness and performance were selected without consideration for any safety or durability criteria.

- On the vehicle connection, there is no latch to hold the connector in position. To inform the user that the vehicle is charging, there is a small indicator light located on the charge stations.

- Electrical energy is allowed to flow through the cable and connectors when the user requests charging through a button control. It continues until it detects a low current level indicating that the battery is "full."

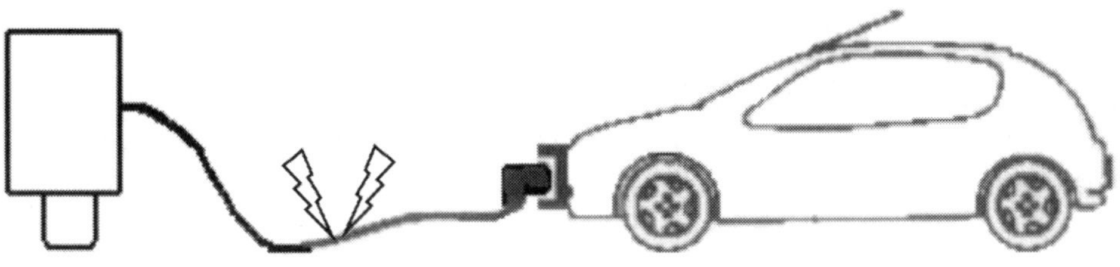

Figure 5 – Diagram of generic high voltage charging system

Risk Assessment.

Risk assessment for this hypothetical situation can be done applying each approach.

For the potential of electrocution due to direct contact with conductors, application of MIL-STD-882E would result in a Risk Assessment Code of "high." Severity is category 1 since death could occur do to the voltage level of a charging system. Probability would be Level B or C since the material can be assumed to degrade over life and not provide adequate protective insulation.

The insulation condition assessed above is considered outside of the scope of ISO 26262. That standard is intended to address only electrical or electronic functional behavior (International Organization for Standardization (ISO) - 1, 2011). Therefore, it would apply to the control of electrical energy going through the cables and connections. One malfunction which could result in risk of electrocution is if electrical energy is present when the connector is not attached to the vehicle. The highest level of severity again applies, S3. Since this is an electric vehicle, a user would be likely to recharge the vehicle regularly, perhaps daily, resulting an exposure level of E4. Although a user cannot observe the presence of electrical energy, the small indicator light may be argued to provide a level of controllability, C2. These assessments result in an ASIL C risk assessment.

In an STPA assessment, the user would be modeled as a controller and the indicator light would be the feedback method. User control action would be inserting the connector in to the vehicle and initiating the charging. If the user initiated charging too soon, before the connection was made to the vehicle, they would be exposed to a potential high voltage risk. In addition, this analysis would show an additional risk associated with removing the connector from the vehicle while electrical energy was still flowing, resulting in another potential hazard of arc flash. These are examples of STPA's use of causal scenarios to highlight situations where no failure of a system element has occurred. Application of the other methods would not necessarily have identified the presence of this additional risk.

Risk Management.

To manage this risk, principles from each of these methods can also be applied.

First, the order of precedence from MIL-STD-882E can be applied. It is not possible to completely eliminate the electrocution hazard as the existence of high voltage is what provides the utility of the system being designed. However, it is possible to reduce the risk through design alteration, specifically revising the insulating material selection. While selection of a durable material for the insulation may seem to be an obvious design change, application of the principles in the standard assures that changes like this are methodically considered and made.

In STPA, one of the user functions would be to connect and disconnect the high voltage source to and from the high voltage battery. The outcome if the user failed to connect the vehicle to the charge station would be an inability to use the vehicle, a loss of utility but not necessarily a safety concern. However, if the user disconnected too soon, while current was still flowing through the connection, an arc flash event and subsequent injury risk to the user could occur. The potential risk of this condition may not be initially obvious until the STPA analysis clearly identified it. This would result in the identification of a requirement that a means of preventing disconnection while current is flowing shall be provided. A latch/switch mechanism can be added to the connection point to prevent disconnection while current is flowing.

Finally, ISO 26262 can provide specific requirements on the latch/switch mechanism that was selected to prevent removing the connection during charging. The latch would prevent removal while current was flowing while the switch, to indicate that a connection has been made, would be used to prevent current flow without a complete connection. ISO 26262 provides specific diagnostic requirements to be applied to the switch to ensure that any malfunction of the switch can be detected and appropriate action (for example, preventing charge current from flowing) can be taken. Additionally, diagnostics on the latch itself could be performed to make sure that the mitigation device was capable of preventing disconnection during charging.

While these are just examples, it is clear that a combined application of principles from each of these processes provides for more complete risk mitigation. Although not illustrated here, there are also areas of overlap among the methods making a full application of each of them unnecessary.

Conclusion

This very simple example illustrates two important points for system safety engineers.

1) Although the techniques may appear to be unique and distinct, they are, in reality closely related. As was obvious in this example, an engineer would likely already have applied principles from each approach without necessarily realizing it. Durable insulation on the conductors would be obvious, for example, yet represents application of the order of precedence for reducing risk. Preventing arc flash risk would likely have been included from the beginning as well. Therefore, engineers and system safety engineers in particular already combine the principles of multiple approaches to system safety, generally without even realizing it.

2) It is only by combining and integrating principles from each of these methods that the "best" design can be accomplished. Individual application of any single one of them could have readily missed some aspect of risk associated with the system or developed a solution which was not as efficient as possible. This is particularly true for the more complex systems which is where system safety engineers bring the greatest value.

With this in mind, a "unified" standard or process for system safety may be a worthwhile endeavor for the industry. This is more complex than simply taking the content of each approach and putting it in to a single document. Areas of overlap should be clearly identified and the unique strengths of each included together. While there are certainly unique needs and characteristics by industry, a combination of approaches provides an enhanced strategy that is more complete than any of the methods individually.

References

Department of Defense. (2012, May 11). Department of Defense Standard Practice - System Safety. MIL-STD-882E. United States Department of Defense.

International Electrotechnical Commission. (2010, April). Functional Safety of electrical / electronic / programmable electronic safety-related systems. IEC 61508. *Second Edition*. International Electrotechnical Commission.

International Organization for Standardization (ISO) - 1. (2011, November 15). International Standard: Road Vehicles - Functional Safety. ISO 26262. *First Edition*. Geneva: International Organization for Standardization.

International Organization for Standardization (ISO) - 2. (2011, November 15). International Standard: Road vehicles — Functional safety — Part 3: Concept Phase. ISO 26262-3. *First Edition*. Geneva: International Organization for Standardization.

International Organization for Standardization (ISO) - 3. (2011, November 15). International Standard: Road vehicles — Functional safety — Part 1: Vocabulary. ISO 26262-1. *First Edition*. Geneva: International Organization for Standardization.

Leveson, N. G. (2011). *Engineering a Safer World.* Cambridge, MA: The MIT Press.

Leveson, N. G., & Thomas, J. P. (2018). *STPA Handbook.* Cambridge, MA: Self-published.

Vernacchia, M. A. (2016). Defining Safety Requirements for Human-Machine Interactions. *34th International System Safety Conference.* International System Safety Society.

36th International System Safety Conference
Phoenix, AZ, August 13-17, 2018

(U) Evaluation Methodology Improvements of the Hazard Severity of Fragments Projected from Deflagrating Warheads

Daniel J. Pudlak, MS; US Army Armament Research, Development and Engineering Center; Picatinny Arsenal, NJ, USA

Kevin T. Miers, MS; US Army Armament Research, Development and Engineering Center; Picatinny Arsenal, NJ, USA

Brian E. Fuchs, Ph.D.; US Army Armament Research, Development and Engineering Center; Picatinny Arsenal, NJ, USA

(U) Abstract

(U) While warhead developers have a fundamental understanding of the damage a detonating munition inflicts from intended warhead fragmentation [2], there appears to be some inconclusive evidence regarding the damage a fragment can inflict from a lower order, accidental deflagrating munition. Both the Safety community and the Insensitive Munition (IM) community attempt to characterize this phenomena, utilizing generic characterization methods such as mass vs. throw distance, mass quantity density statistics, etc. However, it is not clear how much of a physical science basis some of these methods have. A fragment's geometry, along with its exterior / terminal ballistics characteristics, should not be overlooked when evaluating its hazard potential.

(U) The U.S. Army conducted a hazardous fragment study to analyze the methods in which fragments projected from munitions (e.g. warheads) are evaluated and characterized for their projection energy and level of threat they pose to soldiers and their materiel. This study was initiated due to the result of concerns raised by the community, questioning the validity of the current metric (20J) used by the IM community to differentiate between a benign burning reaction and a semi-violent deflagration. The purpose of the study was to determine if the current 20J kinetic energy at 15m requirement is appropriate, if the previous 79J at 15m metric was more appropriate, or perhaps if evidence proves an even more appropriate metric or criterion.

(U) This paper discusses the research conducted to investigate the origins of the current/previous metrics used to categorize a fragment's level of hazard, including blunt injury and skin penetration tests performed as far back as the 1800's. The equations used to develop the original mass-distance curves that were used to evaluate fragment energy were recreated and analyzed by the U.S. Army, are referenced in this paper, and discussed in a 'sister' paper, 'Aeroballistics Calculations for the Insensitive Munitions Hazardous Fragment Criterion, K. Miers, et. al.' [1]. Several errors were discovered in the original ballistics equations of the existing energy-based methodology, such as it improperly being based on launch energy, instead of impact energy. The updated curves are discussed on this paper, and discussed in [1]. Furthermore, the U.S. Army identified an advanced methodology to improve the evaluation of fragment hazard levels. This paper discusses the newly proposed 'energy density' methodology that is currently under evaluation for future use as a standard requirement, as well as the metrics under consideration by the U.S. Army for final implementation.

(U) The criterion of interest indicates the maximum distance a fragment of a given mass could travel before it would be hazardous, presumably to a person standing, at 15m [1,2,6,] This paper discusses the events that led to the review and improved revision of the method and metrics used to evaluate the hazard severity of a munition fragments. This paper sets the stage for its sister paper [1] which discusses in detail the exterior ballistic trajectory code that was written and validated, the equations of motion utilized in the code, coupled with the appropriate modeling assumptions (e.g. shape factors, drag coefficient data, etc.), the trajectories calculated forward or backward in time, the univariate optimization routines utilized to perform the maximum distance calculations, etc. Inherent characteristics and limitations of such curves (e.g. fragment size, geometry) are explained, and the advantages and disadvantages of several suggested criteria and their implementation are reviewed.

(U) The U.S. Army successfully identified the origins of the current/previous metrics used to evaluate the hazard severity of fragments from deflagrating munitions. The original equations used to formulate the curves used for this methodology were recreated, examined, corrected and successfully reformulated. Finally, a new methodology was developed and proposed for review and assessment, and current ballistics, lethality and non-lethality investigations are on-going to determine the appropriate metric suitable for measuring the hazard levels of a fragment projected from a deflagrating munition. This paper will discuss these metrics and how they will be incorporated into the new methodology.

(U) BACKGROUND AND OBJECTIVES

(U) AOP-39 [5] is the NATO document that provides guidance for the development, assessment and testing of Insensitive Munitions (IM). This document has recently been reviewed and revised by the NATO IM Working Group to reflect the latest developments in IM progression, as well as improvements to the methods in which munitions are evaluated for their sensitivity. One of the major updates to this document is the munition Response Descriptors section, which defines the six munition response types (Detonation, Partial Detonation, Explosion, Deflagration, Burning, No Reaction). Each of these responses are defined, using both qualitative and quantitative measures, which assist evaluators in their decision-making process to assign a response level to a particular munition. It is imperative that these measures are relevant, reasonably attainable, scientifically accurate, and based on historical evidence and technical data.

(U) In the fall of 2015, the NATO IM Working Group began the review and revision of the Response Descriptors. One major topic of importance included the relevance of the quantitative metric governing hazardous fragment projection of munitions. Per AOP-39 [5], for a Type IV (Deflagration), 'At least one piece (e.g., casing, packaging or energetic material) travels (or would have been capable of travelling) beyond 15m and with an energy level greater than 20J based on the distance versus mass relationships in figure B-1'; and for a Type V (Burn), 'No piece (e.g., casing, packaging or energetic material) travels (or would have been capable of travelling) beyond 15m and with an energy level greater than 20J based on the distance versus mass relationships in figure B-1. This criterion is being used by the IM community to distinguish between Type IV and Type V responses. After an IM test, fragments are measured for their weight and distance thrown from reaction origin. Based on their mass-distance relationship, if this critical distance is exceeded, the munition is assigned a Type IV. If this distance is not exceeded, the munition is assigned Type V (as long as other criterion are satisfied, such as absence of blast overpressure and witness plate gouging).

(U) During the review of this criterion, the NATO IM Working Group posed several questions, including: Where did the metric '20J' come from? -- Why did we switch from 79J to 20J? – Where did '79J' come from? -- Why is the 15m (50ft) significant? -- Are these the best metrics? -- What methods are we using to measure these metrics? -- Is there a better method to measure these metrics? Unfortunately, at this initial meeting, no member nations were able to answer any of these questions. Only speculations were thrown about by even the most senior participants.

(U) In the spring of 2016, per the Proceedings of the 5th Response Descriptors Working Group Meeting [9], MSIAC, NATO Headquarters, Brussels, Belgium, 11-12 April 2016, 'The third briefing was also related to the fragment projection topic and was given by Mr. Pudlak (US). This was offered in response to Action Item 3 that was assigned to all nations at the prior meeting. Mr. Pudlak provided a considerable amount of background information, basically historical, on the origin of the hazardous/lethal fragment factors and how they relate to the fragment energy levels currently in use for IM and HC. This information was nearly identical to the background research information given by Mr. van der Voort at the beginning of his presentation. Mr. Pudlak highlighted the key issue from his analysis – the comparison of launch vs. impact energy. At this point a more detailed explanation was provided that related to the launch/impact energy and how this relates to the 20 vs. 79J issue.' [9]

(U) Historical Research. The first question(s) in which to investigate were: 'W*here did the 20J metric come from*?', and '*Why did we switch from 79J to 20J*'?

(U) AOP-39 Ed 2 (2009) and MIL-STD-2105C (July 2003) both utilized 79J as the threshold.
(U) AOP-39 Ed 3 (2010) and MIL-STD-2105D (April 2011) both utilized 20J as the threshold.
*MIL-STD-2105 is the US DoD Hazard Assessment Tests for Non-Nuclear Munitions.

(U) In the late 1800's, Colonel Journee (French Infantry Officer) established the 15ft-lb & 58ft-lb criterion. His work considered the upper and lower bounds of what a man could endure from recoil of a rifle.

- 15ft-lb (20J) was set as the maximum recoil suitable for a military rifle.
- 58ft-lb (79J) recoil energy was estimated to provide significant bruising/damage to typical male shoulder.

Weapon System	Muzzle Recoil Energy (ft-lbs)
Lee-Enfield Rifle	12.75 ft-lbs
.45 Cal. Rifle	14.40 ft-lbs
.30 Cal Garand	15.18 ft-lbs
Springfield '03 Rifle	14.98 ft-lbs

Computed Recoil Energy	Limitation
Less than 15 ft-lb (20.3 Joules)	Unlimited Firing
15-30 ft-lb (20.3 - 40.7 Joules)	200 rounds / day / shooter
30-45 ft-lb (40.7 - 61.0 Joules)	100 rounds / day / shooter
45-60 ft-lb (61.0 - 81.4 Joules)	25 rounds / day / shooter
Greater than 60 ft-lbs (81.4 Joules)	No Shoulder Firing

Table 1. TOP 3-2-504 – Daily Firing limit for safety of hand and shoulder weapons

(U) As an example, a typical shotgun produces 25 ft-lb to 35 ft-lb of recoil, and a typical elephant gun produces ~52 ft-lb of recoil. "The recoil energy of the Lee-Enfield rifle is well below the maximum energy of recoil advisable for a military rifle, which should not exceed 15 ft-lbs, --1909 British Textbook of Small Arms.

(U) Historical Literature:

- Burns and Zuckerman, 1941, 3/32" steel ball study
    - 20J is optimum energy to wound a man
- Beyer, "Wound Ballistics", Office of the Surgeon General, 1962
    - Journee - 58 ft-lb rule (79J)
        - Pistol / Rifle calibers: 4.5mm - 21.2mm
        - Projectile weights: 3 grams - 56 grams
        - Unjacketed, full-jacketed (copper German silver, steel), lead core bullets: Lead, zinc, aluminum
- Sperazza, "Handbook for Human Vulnerability Criteria", 1976
    - Journee – Levels required for wounding soft tissue and bone
        - 15 ft-lb to penetrate soft tissue
        - 36 ft-lb to crack bones
        - 115 ft-lb to assure fracture of large bone (e.g. femur)
        - Determined 58ft-bs rule
- USARIEM, "Technical Report T04-05", 2004 Weapon Recoil Health Hazard Study
    - 93% of volunteers experienced significant shoulder bruising when asked to fire 15 rounds of ammo w/ recoil of 59ft-lbs (well within firing rate of limitation of the TOP).

(U) Examples of projectiles and their associated energy:

- Paintball 300ft/s – 12J
- 0.177 cal pellet 900ft/s– 21J
- Football 50mph – 112J
- Baseball 90mph – 120J
- 40mm non-lethal grenade 200ft/s – 150J

(U) It can easily be seen from the data above that 20J may not be an accurate metric for measuring a munitions 'lethality' or 'hazardousness'. Now that we have a better understanding of where the 20J and 79J metrics come from, and how they compare to commonly used objects of similar energy, we need to determine if one of these metrics are more accurate than the other, or if there is a more appropriate number not being considered, or if there is a better method of measurement than currently being utilized.

(U) DISCUSSION

(U) Understanding the Current Methodology. *How did we acquire 20J?* The current AOP-39 Ed 3 utilizes the 20J curve as seen below in Figure 1 (left). This curve is built from data points representing masses of IM-interest, in the range of 50g-500g. This curve is actually a derivation from the plot on the right, which is found in TB 700-2, which is the US DoD Standard for Ammunition & Explosives Hazard Classification Procedures. Notice that both the 20J and 79J curves are superimposed on this chart, as well as a lower threshold, 8J. These three curves are used by the US DoD Safety Community to differentiate the Hazard Classification of munitions. It is evident that both of these curves come from this plot, however, it is not clear why we have switched to 20J, from 79J.

Mass	Projection distance (m)	
(g)	20 J	8 J
25	83.6	46.8
50	58.4	28.7
75	44.4	20.6
100	35.6	16.2
125	29.8	13.3
150	25.6	11.4
175	22.43	10
200	20	8.8
300	13.9	6.3
400	10.9	4.9
500	8.9	4.1

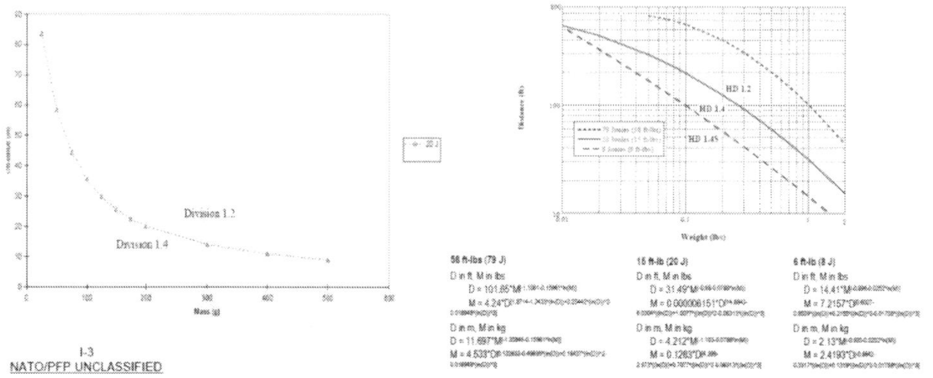

(U) Figure 1. The 20J Curve, as it appears in AOP-39 (left) and TB-700-2 (right)

(U) Understanding how the curves work. In order to evaluate which curve is more relevant for fragments associated with munition sensitivity/hazardousness, it was important to understand how the curves were built, and what inputs/assumptions were utilized. To begin, the guidance (AOP-39, MIL-STD-2105D) states that 'At least one piece (e.g. casing, packaging, or energetic material) travels (or would have been capable of travelling) beyond 15m and with an energy level greater than 20J based on the distance versus mass relationships.' This would indicate that we are to measure the fragment's energy at *impact*. Unfortunately, there was no documentation to review which would explain the creation of the curves. The originators of the curves were contacted for explanation of inputs/assumptions made to create the curves. The 20J curve was then recreated by ARDEC and matched quite well. Unfortunately, the same assumptions were made to create the 79J curve, but they did not exactly match. Nevertheless, after analysis, it was discovered that both the 20J & 79J curves were built with *launch energy basis, not an impact energy basis*. This raised a flag as this is not what is intended in the guidance. The 20J curve, for example, based on launch energy, uses is a curve fit for max projection distance of 20J fragments *at launch* as a function of mass. It works based on calculating the maximum distance a given mass can travel when launched at 20J. Therefore, it does not calculate the fragment's impact energy, but rather it compares its travel distance to the maximum distance its mass could travel with 20J launch energy. If the fragment is less than the maximum distance the fragment could have flown with 20J, then it must have less than 20J at impact (due to factors like air drag). Actual impact energy cannot be determined based on mass and distance without a known trajectory. Only minimum impact energy required to reach the given distance can be calculated accurately.

(U) Creating the Impact Energy-based curves. Point-mass trajectories can be run backwards in time. Thus the line search technique can be used, starting at the origin with a fixed impact velocity, to adjust the impact angle until the maximum distance backward is reached. Figure 2 demonstrates how the impact energy curve calculation is similar to the launch energy curve calculation but backwards.

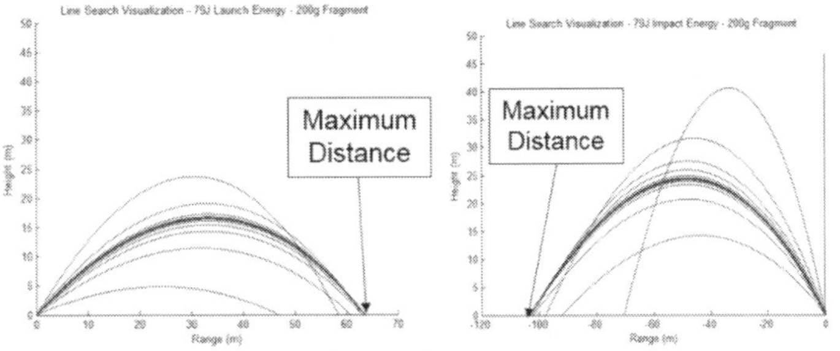

(U) Figure 2. Visualization of a line search algorithm to quickly find the maximum throw distance for a fixed launch energy (left) and for a fixed impact energy (right).

(U) This technique finds the same maximum as the previously described technique (which tries to find a combination of launch angle and velocity that yields the largest range at which a 79J impact can occur). It also runs into the same problem – at a sufficiently low mass, the maximum range at which the impact criterion is satisfied goes off to infinity, or at least outside the range of validity for the drag coefficient data. This is due to terminal velocity coming into play. Figure 3 shows the results of this methodology to generate 20J and 79J impact energy curves.

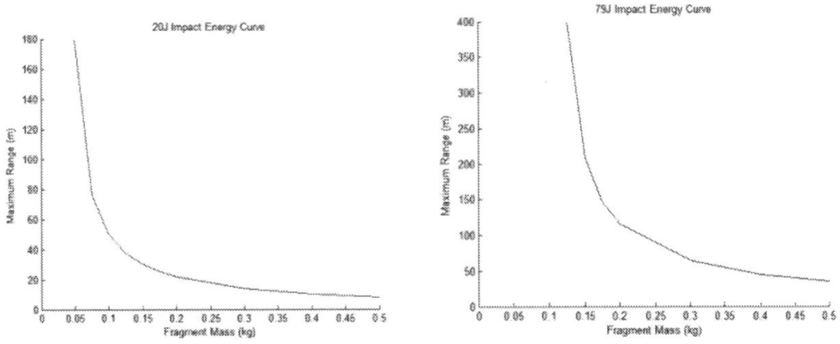

Figure 3. Calculated impact energy curves

(U) It should be noted that the curves appear to go off to infinity for the smaller masses. For IM evaluation purposes, this would appear to be an issue, more so for the 79J curve than the 20J curve. For example, the 20J curve would allow a 0.05g to travel ~160m. However, a fragment of 0.05g travelling 160m would most likely not represent a munition reacting in the Deflagration regime, but rather in an Explosion-Detonation regime. Further analysis of historical data may help draw a 'ceiling', or horizontal line across the left side of the curve, eliminating those fragments from this evaluation.

(U) Further Improved Methodology – 15m (50ft) threshold. As mentioned above, the threshold, per AOP-39, is worded such that energy of the fragments should be measured at 15m. While the section above explains the improvements made to the original curve(s) to address energy at impact, not at launch, the curve still required improvements to address energy at a specific distance (i.e. 15m). Adjustments made to the curve were of substantial improvement for the impact-based curves. By adjusting the curve to only address impact (with no specified distance), the curve(s) appeared to go off to infinity for smaller, faster masses. By adjusting the impact-based curves to include 15m, the curve flattens out and converges, failing the smaller, faster masses; and produced a 'cut-off' for larger, slower masses. Figure 4 illustrates a 20J at 15m for steel fragments.

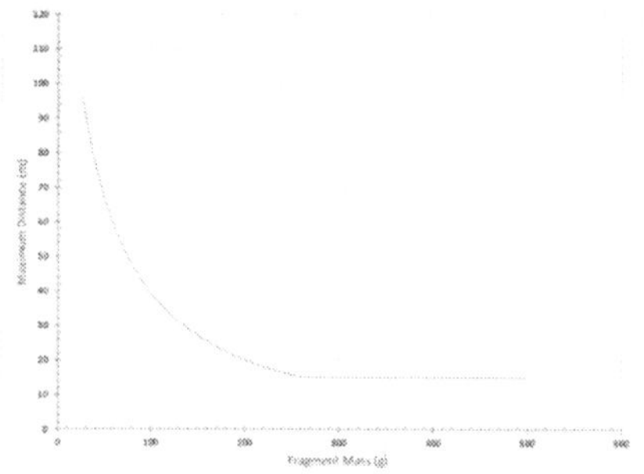

Figure 4. 20J @ 15m curve for steel fragments.

MSIAC presented a 20J at 15m curve using TRAJCAN with similar results [8].

(U) Further Improved Methodology – Energy Density based Curve. While utilizing an Impact Energy based curve is an improvement to the Launch Energy based curve, it should be noted that energy alone is not the best method in which to evaluate impact severity for human hazardousness. As mentioned above, a pellet gun threatens the 20J threshold, and a football/baseball produces ~5X$^+$ that of the 20J threshold. While these sport projectiles would be assigned a Type IV with this energy based criteria, they are no match for acceptable wartime hazards. This is primarily due to the fact that the energy based methodology does not take into account surface area of the mass's impact. To compare actual *applied* energy amongst projectiles, the impacting surface area – mass relationship must be considered. This is why it was proposed to implement an Energy Density Methodology (J/cm^2).

(U) The following curve in Figure 5 is an Impact Energy Density based curve with a threshold of 7.9 J/cm^2. This metric (7.9 J/cm^2) was selected as an example, as it is the Probability of Skin Penetration criterion given AASTP-1. While the method is a better method to utilize, the metric does not meet the regime of IM Burning/Deflagrating munitions. A more suitable metric must be selected for this method to be utilized for IM fragment evaluation.

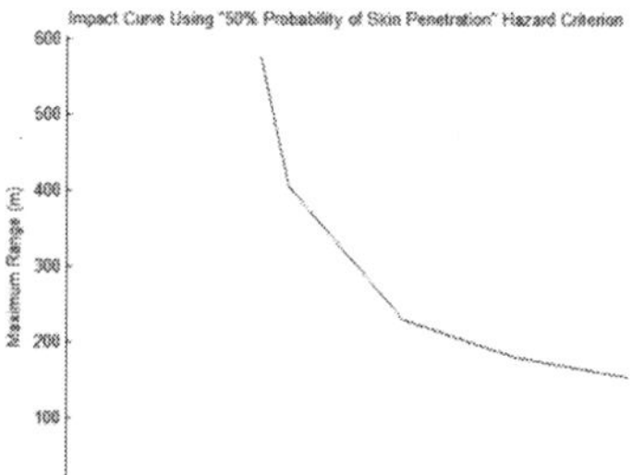

(U) Figure 5. 7.9 J/cm^2 Energy Density Curve

(U) Prior research indicates that a range of 1 J/cm^2 – 6 J/cm^2 may be more appropriate for the IM Type IV/V fragment evaluation. These are metrics that have been identified for similar safety concerns used in other industry and government products/processes. Figure 5 illustrates how the Energy Density curves associated with these metrics plot in comparison to the 20J & 79J Launch Energy based curves. Notice that the Energy Density based curves alleviate some of the larger, slower moving masses, and restrict some of the smaller, faster moving fragments. It should be noted that these curves may coincide with the theory mentioned before that a 'ceiling', or horizontal line, could be drawn across the Impact Energy based curves to eliminate the super small fragments travelling at super high velocities from this evaluation.

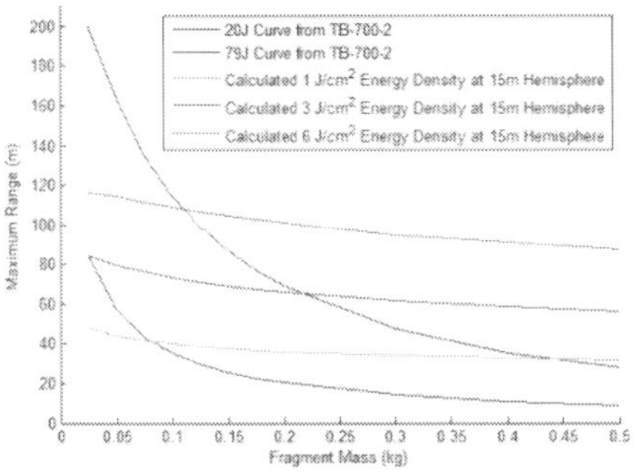

(U) Figure 6. Example Energy Density Curves superimposition

(U) The Energy Density curves must also be adjusted for the 15m threshold. Figure 6 illustrates such for the 1J/cm^2, 3J/cm^2, & 6J/cm^2 curves, and Figure 7 illustrates the 7.9J/cm^2 curves.

(U) Figure 7 includes all of the curves mentioned in this paper, illustrating how each methodology/metric compares to one another. The original 20J & 79J launch-based curves are plotted in black, and it can be seen how they compare with the impact based curves. More importantly, the improvement to the 20J & 79J curves by adjusting them to reflect 15m can been compared. It can be seen how the Energy Density curves are much flatter, taking the fragments mass into account. Notice that the 7.9J/cm^2 skin penetration model does not apply so well for the mass-distance relationships of IM Type IV/V fragments. The lower energy density curves do match quite well, however. Non-lethality research indicates that 1.6J/cm^2 might be an appropriate number for blunt injury, however, further investigation is required to determine a metric that appropriately incorporates both blunt and penetration impacts, perhaps lying somewhere between the 7.9J/cm^2 and 1.6J/cm^2.

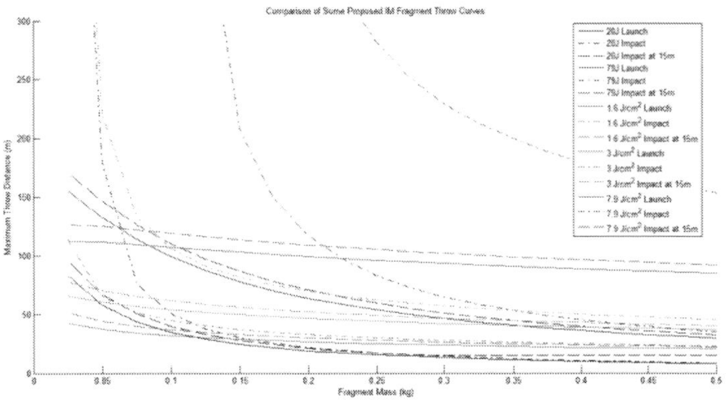

Figure 7. Superimposition of all curves.

(U) Current status of on-going work to improve the IM fragment evaluation methodology. To implement the Energy Density methodology, further lethality/non-lethality work needs to be conducted to determine a technically justifiable metric to utilize for implementation. Additionally, as taking into account the impacting surface area of the fragment/mass is the prevailing reason for the Energy Density methodology being more accurate than an energy only based methodology, it is imperative that the impacting surface area of the fragment is accurately measured/assumed. For uniform/symmetric fragments, this is easily done, however, for asymmetric fragments, this can be a challenge. Several methods of measuring/assuming the surface area have been proposed:

- (U) Automated 3-D optical measurement devices can measure icosahedrons quickly and precisely.
- (U) Generic fractional volume categories (frag-in-a-box) can be assigned. The volume fraction in which a fragment shape occupies inside of a cube it fits in, for example:
    - Cubical fragment – A cube occupies 4/4 of a cube's volume in which it fits inside.
    - Convex fragment - A sphere occupies ~3/4 of the cube's volume
    - Concave fragment – An 'hour glass' occupies ~2/4 of the cube's volume.
    - Length/Diameter – A long, thin rod/strip ~1/4 of the cube's volume.

(U) Penetration and blunt impact characteristics, as well as aerodynamic flight/orientation must be taken into account (e.g. tumble, Frisbee, etc.). For example, research indicates that a long, thin rod/strip may tend to fly in an orientation that causes the least drag resistance. Therefore, the surface area of the point / sharp edge may be appropriate to use for its evaluation.

(U) The current curve is built based on assumptions such as a chunky, tumbling, steel fragment. This, however, is not an accurate method for fragments with different characteristics, such as: density, shape, stability, etc. Therefore there must be several curves in which to reference when evaluating unique fragments. For example, Figure 8 illustrates four 20J at 15m impact based curves, of which each represents fragments of various densities associated with material commonly found on modern-day munitions systems. These four densities represent the majority of fragment material typically evaluated during IM tests, including: tungsten, steel, aluminum, and HDPE. These four curves should be replicated for other factors, such as fragment shape, and flight orientation. While creating several curves for this evaluation would appear to be more complex than utilizing one generic curve, these curves can be superimposed on one plot for the user, and only the curve representing the fragment of interest need be utilized. The upfront work goes into creating the curves. Once created, it will be quite simple for the user.

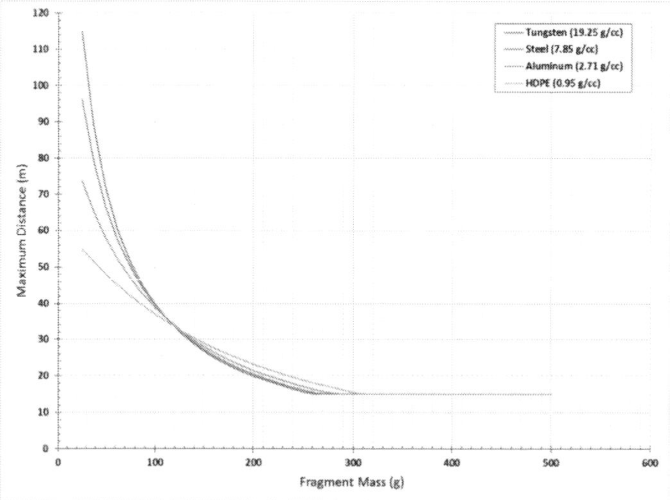

Figure 8. (U) New AOP-39 Mass-Distance curve

(U) The NATO IM Working Group has verbally accepted to implement this methodology, pending an appropriate metric is provided. As for now, the Working Group has voted to implement the 20J Impact Energy based curve as the first improvement.

(U) SUMMARY AND CONCLUSIONS; FUTURE WORK

(U) Summary and Conclusions

(U) During the review and revision of the Response Descriptors within AOP-39 [5], the IM NATO Working Group questioned the validity of the hazardous fragment criterion which is one major factor for differentiating between a Type V Burning response and a Type IV Deflagration response. The initial question was with respect to the 20J energy threshold at the time, and whether the older 79J metric was more appropriate, or if another metric would be more appropriate than both. The US Army DoD took the action to investigate the history of the criterion, and evaluate which maybe more appropriate. After extensive investigation, the US determined that the question itself was invalid. Neither 20J, nor 79J, actually mean much without incorporating the mass's impact force with relation to the impacting surface area. The US developed and presented an Energy Density methodology to the NATO IM Working Group as a potential new criterion to adopt for the IM hazardous fragment evaluation. This methodology was accepted by the group, however, a metric (numerical value) must be technically justified before implementation.

(U) Additionally, the IM NATO Working Group questioned where the 20J and 79J curves came from, and how they were derived. After inspection of the curve, and investigation of its origins, the US found the originators of the curve and discovered that there is no existing documentation for the creation of the curve. So the US back-calculated the curve using the masses-distance relationships associated with the curve, and successfully mimicked the 20J curve. Unfortunately, the same inputs/assumptions used for the 20J curve did not produce an exact match for the 79J curve. Some speculations were made regarding this matter, however no concrete evidence found. Moreover, during evaluation/manipulation of the factors included in the curve, it was discovered that the curves did not represent the criterion called out in AOP-39. The curves were built based on launch energy of 20J, not impact energy of 20J. The US adjusted the curves to reflect such, only to find further issues with the use of such curves (convergence issues). Fortunately, by tying in the 15m factor, the convergence issues were resolved, and furthermore a 'ceiling' has been proposed to omit non-Type IV/V type fragments from the evaluation.

(U) Future Work

(U) The NATO IM Working Group concurred with potential future implementation of the Energy Density Methodology, pending an appropriate metric is provided. Additionally, the surface area measurement/identification methodology must be complete in order to develop the associated curves to support the evaluation procedure. The final deliverable will be approximately 16 curves superimposed on one plot, with a legend for the user to reference the appropriate curve for the fragment of interest. This work is currently on-going at ARDEC and seeking funding to leverage the expertise of lethality/non-lethality SMEs at ARL and ARDEC. Until then, the Working Group voted to implement the 20J at 15m impact energy based curve as the first improvement.

(U) REFERENCES

1. Miers, K., Pudlak, D., Fuchs B., "Aeroballistics Calculations for the Insensitive Munitions Hazardous Fragment Criterion", ISSC, 2018.
2. Swisdak, M. M., Powell, J. G. "Fragmentation Effects: An Overview". In Design Considerations for Toxic Chemical and Explosives Facilities; Scott, Ralph A., et al.; ACS Symposium Series; American Chemical Society: Washington, DC, 1987.
3. Montanaro, P. E. "TRAJ – A Two Dimensional Trajectory Program for Personal Computers". Naval Surface Warfare Center, August 1990.
4. "Department of Defense Ammunition and Explosives Hazard Classification Procedures". Joint Technical Bulletin TB-700-2, 1998.
5. "Guidance on the Assessment and Development of Insensitive Munitions". NATO Allied Ordnance Publication AOP-39 (Edition 3), 2010.
6. "Manual of NATO Safety Principles for the Storage of Military Ammunition and Explosives". NATO Allied Ammunition Storage and Transport Publication AASTP-1 (Edition 1), 2010.
7. Pudlak, D., Miers, K. "Hazardous Fragment Analysis". Insensitive Munitions AOP-39 Response Descriptors. NATO HQ, Brussels, Belgium. 11-13 Apr, 2016.
8. Van der Voort, M., Baker, E., Schultz, E., Sharp, M. "Projection Criteria for Insensitive Munitions and Hazard Classification". 2016 Insensitive Munitions & Energetic Materials Technology Symposium, Nashville, TX.
9. Proceedings of the 5th Response Descriptors Working Group Meeting, MSIAC, NATO Headquarters, Brussels, Belgium, 11-12 April 2016.

A Self-Contained Approach to Human Error in Hazard Management

Željka Požgaj, Dipl.-Ing.; Frequentis AG; Vienna, AUSTRIA

Gabriele Schedl, Dipl.-Ing.; Frequentis AG; Vienna, AUSTRIA

Keywords: human error, human performance, human factors issues, cognitive neuroscience

Abstract

There is extensive cross-disciplinary expertise available encompassing an extraordinary diversity of practical as well as philosophical approaches to human error and its management. However, the majority of safety professionals still struggle to understand how best to prevent, model or lessen human errors due to the absence of a satisfying, coherent approach and response to them.
With the aim of understanding how information processing in the human brain supports day-to-day functioning and how this functioning may be disturbed, the discipline of cognitive neuroscience can be used to reveal some significant new insights about error mechanisms.
This paper uses findings of cognitive neuroscience research as the foundation for better comprehension of the rooted taxonomies of human errors and presents arguments for a shift of emphasis from error probability assessment to emerging strategies of enhanced error recognition and response.
Based on this, it then provides steps that should be taken not only to build in mechanisms for tolerating and coping with the human errors that will inevitably occur but also to draw the line between customer/supplier responsibility for those errors. Finally, it discusses ways in which the new findings can influence how the field approaches risk assessment and how we move forward as a discipline.

Introduction

For the past one hundred years the business world has continuously worked toward improvement of human performance and greater workplace efficiency. What started out as explanatory work studies of industrial workers, their selection, training, work-rest schedules, and task time & motion studies (Taylor, 1911) has grown to encompass assessment of performance in almost any interaction of people with their work environments. Regardless of whether these interactions are social or technical in nature, the recurring insight is that human performance is inseparable from the performance of the whole system in which people are currently operating. (Locke, 2009) Safety-critical organizations, in contrast to other organizations, need to ensure not only economic profitability but, above all, safety of operation as an overarching priority, for adapting effectively in order to cope with and respond to the needs and interests of the society, providing a 24/7 high reliability performance in their operating environments, under huge social and political pressure. High-reliability organizations are committed to rigorous management of the risks inherent in their technical as well as human, organizational complexity. (Saunders, 2015)
The question becomes: how can safety-critical organizations enhance and/or improve work efficiency in their operations? Technological changes, either in response to economic competitive pressures or due to changed legislative context, are often introduced because the state of technology in any organization significantly influences the efficiency of the business. But the effect that technology deployment and lack of understanding how it may fail had in the history of safety-critical organizations on organizational structures was farther reaching than assumed. The complexity in human activities and human-machine interactions had gradually increased followed by more failures in operation with a heavy impact on organizations themselves. The catastrophic accidents in the safety critical fields that have received wide public attention revealed this unknown fragility of organizational complexity, showing an existing gap between presumed safe and reliable operation and actual day-to-day decision-making processes at all organizational levels. The investigation of those accidents led to new research approaches on "human error" after Three Mile Island in 1979 (Oedewald & Reiman 2007, Hollnagel, 2015) and on "safety culture" after Chernobyl in 1986 (Oedewald & Reiman, 2007) which have evolved and prevailed in research until today.
Almost four decades of specialized research offers an abundance of practical as well as philosophical approaches on the issue of human error and indicates that the concept of human error is far more complicated than originally anticipated (Woods et al., 1994) because "people are the ultimate Off-The-Shelf system component, which sets them apart from most engineered system components". (DEFSTAND 00-250 (PTO)/1, 2008, p.45) Different needs and interests in defining human error within the theoretical framework of diverse disciplines, led to confusion regarding the label "human error" being perceived and depicted differently-- as cause, or consequence, as action, event, or process, or as a function of judgment. (Forsythe et al. (2014) A large number of errors classification systems exist, which are generic or developed to the

specific scope of safety-critical industries and their areas of application. For example, there are error types classified based on their dependent origination (e.g.: design, or operation) (Meister, 1989) or on the timing of their appearance in an accident sequence (e.g.: human reliability analysis and probabilistic safety assessment) (ASME, 2002) or on the information processing stage at which they took place (Wickens, 1992). Also, frequently used, and proposed by Swain and Guttman, (1983) is a two-part classification: omission errors and commission errors, SRK (skill, rules, knowledge) model by Rasmussen (1983), which classifies human behavior according to conscious level or cognitive control used, and slips, lapses and mistakes taxonomy by Reason (2008). The large number of taxonomies also led to their classification into three categories: behavioral, contextual, and conceptual (Reason, 1990). All of these models are backed with a great determination, improvements, and efforts but still leave safety professionals with a sense of incompleteness and confusion about the right or best approach.
Human error is also repeatedly cited as a major contributing factor or cause of incidents by percentage contribution approximately from 70% (aviation) to 90% (nuclear industry). Consequently, either: 1) people spontaneously develop new types of errors that previous analyses could not predict (Oedewald & Reiman, 2007) or, 2) new types of errors arise from technology that advances and is changing faster than organizations can understand and/or prescribe how to use. The fact is, that both human error (incorrect performance) and correct human performance "result from the same cognitive and neurophysiological mechanisms". (Forsythe et al. 2014) Considering this, we decided to turn to valuable research of cognitive neuroscience and direct our attention towards understanding error mechanism in the human brain.

Cognitive Neuroscience

Since the 1990s, the field of cognitive neuroscience has been devoted to understanding how the human brain through neural mechanisms, supports human cognition or internal mental processes, including learning, memory, perception, attention, decision making, cognitive control, language, motor control, and social cognition. With the rise of numerous types of structural brain-imaging and functional brain-imaging technologies used in cognitive neuroscience (for example, MRI, fMRI, EEG, PET, CAT, MEG) the interest in understanding the structural and functional relationships in the human brain among scientists and the lay audience has grown tremendously. Cognitive neuroscientists perform behavioral tests on both animals and humans, both inside and outside of the laboratory, and researchers have employed computational modeling, genetic and candidate gene studies, and pharmacologic manipulations to better understand how the brain underlies cognitive processes. Research integrated into the discipline of cognitive neuroscience includes the cross-discipline expertise of neuropsychology and cognitive psychology, neurophysiology, clinical psychology, neurology, pharmacology, and computational neuroscience. The current state of ongoing research toward understanding the information process mechanisms and anatomy of human error is of interest in the study of human factors and safety.

Human Performance

For the purpose of our study, we concentrate on control rooms and operator positions of safety-critical organizations in the fields of air traffic management, defense, public safety, public transport and maritime, where our communication and information systems are deployed. The technology upgrade or change in control rooms of high-reliability organizations represents at any time the collaborative work between customer organisation and technology supplier organisation. The common, created and provided value after this undertaking, we all strive to, is to enhance performance and satisfaction of end users and, above all, assure the safety of operations. The requirement that "the system shall integrate humans in ways which minimize the opportunity for human error" (DEF STAN 00-251 (Part-0), 2016) is, for us, the foundation for discussion of known and unknown challenges and issues, organizations are confronted with when undertaking technical change. Control rooms of safety-critical organizations could be looked at as "extreme environments" which comprise those situations which place a high demand on the physiological, cognitive, and/or social processing resources of the individual. These environments strongly challenge the body and mind of individual, which in turn initiate complex cognitive and affective response strategies. To analyze human performance at work position we lean on depiction of work environment by DEFSTAND 00-250 (PTO)/1, 2008.
The individual is performing tasks at his work position using: 1) work equipment, 2) his/her personal and organizational education, and 3) training he/she has received as well as all information needed for task execution, and is following learned and memorized procedures. (fig. 1) We assume that, these tasks reflect interactions between the human and the inputs received from work equipment and that they are purposeful, controlled actions, intended to result in not just any output but in a certain output that must meet some set of requirements. If this set of requirements is met we call it "desired success". If outputs do not satisfy

requirements or if the desired output has not been achieved, we talk about failures or errors and examine the direct causal factors in safety, which are:

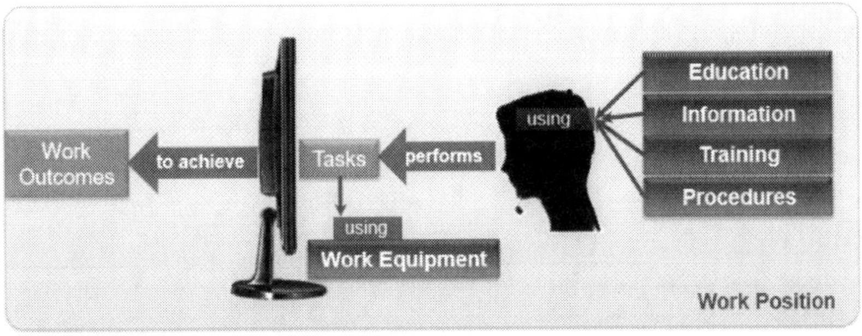

Figure 1— Work position (DEFSTAND 00-250 (PTO)/1, 2008), modified

- The employee performing the task
- The task itself
- Any equipment directly or indirectly used in the task

When we look at the smallest system containing only one individual, one piece of equipment and one task, we notice that even at this level there are other "unknown or unidentified" humans who may have more of an impact on the successful performance of this smallest entity than anticipated. This "invisible" part of the human component of the system represents all people involved in the employee's training and educational development, those involved in task creation and procedures development, and those involved in manufacturing of equipment and development of graphical user interface. Only the fact that their performance output at the moment of completing their tasks had not necessarily met the same set of requirements as the employee's output, reflect the complexity of interactions. Considering their potential impact on end user performance and on the system, we argue that at this simple level would be hard to predict and model all failure modes and would get even more complex with each additional piece of equipment directly or indirectly used in the task. To understand the direct causal factor "The employee is performing a task" we need to understand what happens in the human brain in the meantime (applicable for any individual performance at any organizational level).

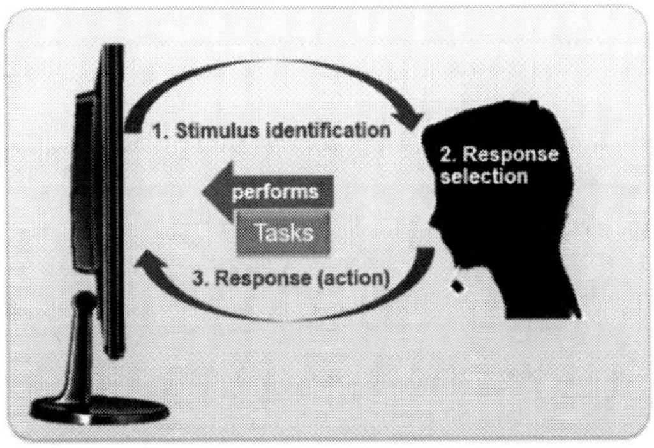

Figure 2— Information-processing model (Schmidt & Wrisberg, 2008) modified

At any time, human performance reflects the integration of: 1.) Stimulus identification- perception of sensory information or incoming stimuli, 2.) Response selection- attention allocation, retrieval from memory, filing of newly learned information (experience update) and final decision-making, and 3.) Response- initiation of a response via the appropriate modality be it speech or motor (action). (fig.2)

In parallel, our brain monitors this performance on a moment-by-moment basis so that when there is a mismatch between information, decision making and action it may be recognized and responded to (self-correction) for this process to run successfully. But, within the performance process there is a wide range for error possibilities.

An explanation, going from stage to stage of this process will be delivered, explaining how the human brain works at each stage, why there is a scope of errors, and the relevance of those errors to safety.

We will also discuss how findings in cognitive neuroscience research teach us the importance of cultivating our errors as a source of essential information which can be incorporated into the learning and training methods, thereby helping individuals improve their internal and situational awareness of how errors occur, and helping them learn to better recognize potential errors and respond to them, particularly when responses must be fast.

1. Stimulus identification (perception)

Perception makes sense of the world around us by using incoming sensory information through sight, hearing, touch, smell and taste. The purpose of perception is to rapidly understand our surroundings and to act upon generated signals from environmental information. The brain makes assumptions about the world to overcome the inherent ambiguity of all sensory data. Once this is done, if the scene is not perceived to have changed, features of the scene should not need to be updated and that change will not be detected, except for objects in the focus of attention. Our brains give us only an approximate view of reality because the way in which we perceive our environment is also greatly dependent upon what we have previously seen (experienced) and learned (knowledge stored in memory). (Wickens 1992, Gazzaniga et al. 2008, Forsythe et al. 2014) Perception then is an active process of constructing a reality, a conversation between the senses and the brain that balances new information from the outside world with predictions from the interior world of memories. Among all of the senses sight (vision) and hearing (audition) are the most well understood.

Vision

"Seeing" is a very complex higher-order brain function, and approximately half of our brain's resources are required for doing nothing else other than construct and understand the world around us based on visual input. Photoreceptors convert the light that enters the eye into nerve signals which are then sent to the brain, where they are analyzed and interpreted into the images that we "see". Our eyes see edges, shapes, and motion and our brains interpret that to attempt to recognize, what sort of thing those edges, shapes and motion might represent, form images based on pattern recognition. Our brains seamlessly cause us to perceive whatever that object might be. (Ward, Grinstein & Keim 2015) At birth, our brains are not able to interpret all of the messages from the sense receptors, but instead develop these abilities with each new experience, and store the knowledge for future use. When the brain is then presented with something unfamiliar, it searches for familiar patterns (objects placed in meaningful categories) from past experiences. (Healey 2012) The world around us is filled with an infinite number of stimuli that we might attend to, but the human brain does not have the resources to pay attention to everything. So, it instead, learns to filter and prioritize stimuli and placing more importance on certain images than on others. (Gazzaniga et al. 2008, Forsythe et al. 2014)

Audition

"Hearing" is another complex higher-order brain function in which sound pressure waveforms that are disseminated through the air, contain references about the environment around us. These impulses are received by the ear and are sent to the brain via the auditory nerve. There are four fundamental functions that the brain carries out to make sense of sound. Using input from both ears, the brain must determine the position or source of the sound, separate the various sound sources, focus on what is important, recognize what each sound is, and make sense of, or interpret the sounds that we "hear." (Gazzaniga et al. 2008) Those images of sound are stored either in short-term or in long-term memory. When competition occur during integration of visual and auditory information, and generate cognitive conflicts, one modality often dominates the other in the resolution of a conflict. The vision dominates audition for processing spatial information, audition often dominates vision for processing temporal information. (Guttmann, Gilroy & Blake, 2006)

Relevance to safety

Our prior experience and knowledge, emotional state, and value system (including prejudices) determine our perception. It is increasingly clear that decision-making is tightly interlinked with learning how to perceive and filter information as well as how to memorize the same information. (Gazzaniga et al. 2008, Forsythe et al. 2014) Responding incorrectly to certain information (visual, audio) in complex environments especially when under the pressure of time, are common. Errors at this level are based on false filtering and prioritization of certain external information followed by the inability to select the relevant dimensions for the task at hand.

Approach

The goal for organisations is to gather all known errors which could be traced to this level and to harness them as a foundation for creating a "perception template" as a learning guide for operators, on how to filter and prioritize incoming external information during visual scanning (Wickens & Hollands,1999) in any particular situation. Also, to use them for creating new scenarios in simulation training with competing visual and audio stimuli (e.g.: blinking, ringing). This template needs to also consider and include any time pressure component. Usually, the beginning trainees need much longer to process the new information and to filter out relevant information from a flood of other, irrelevant ones, and thus react quickly. Training can be optimized through guidance and learning from failures of the past which is a moment we call "shaping of work environment experience." Important input from cognitive neuroscience is that the brain learns and remembers best through pictures and animations. The brain treats text as images and interprets each letter as an image which requires additional brain resources. (Ward, Grinstein & Keim 2015)

2. Response selection (decision)
Attention allocation, retrieval and updating memory, decision making

Attention allocation

Attention is the ability to concentrate on any of the perceived stimuli. Selective attention refers to the processes that allow an individual to select and focus on certain input for further processing while simultaneously suppressing irrelevant or distracting information. This is a very important ability due to the huge amount of information as well as constantly competing information which human beings have to contend with on a daily basis. The competing information can occur both externally, as in visual stimulation in the environment, or internally, as in distracting thoughts or habitual responses. Both get in the way of performing the task at hand. The ability to focus while resisting distractions and staying present is an important driver of excellence. But this ability to stay focused on a particular task is limited, resulting in decreasing performance with increasing time on task. (Langner, & Eickhoff 2013) "The brain operates optimally when it toggles between being focused and being unfocused." (Pillay, 2017) There are two large-scale brain networks that operate in parallel and work in opposing ways – as one increases in activity, the other decreases, and vice versa. (fig. 3) The attention network is a task-focused network involving focused attention and mental effort, as when we work to solve problems, make decisions or pursue goals. This is the brain in gear. The default mode network is a resting, mind wandering network that throws up spontaneous associations and is related to day-dreaming, and personal, introspective thinking and imagining. This is the brain in neutral.
Mind wandering is the term for the thoughts a person has when not performing a specific task that requires attention but is just letting his/her thoughts stray. One is not normally conscious of these thoughts, as this inner conversation goes on in one's mind almost constantly and cannot be switched off whether in or outside of the work environment.

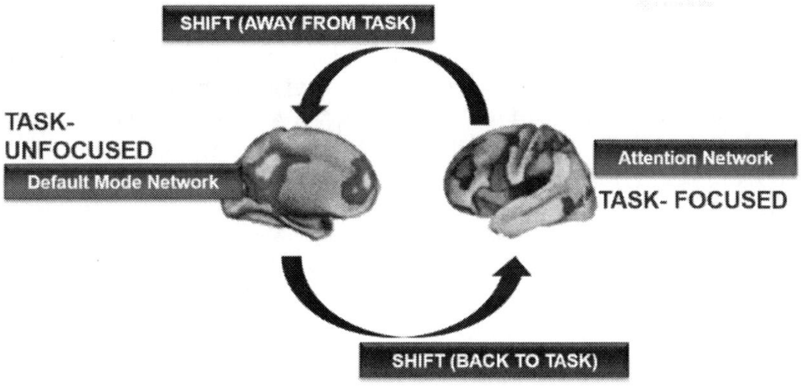

Figure 3—Attention Network- Default Mode Network

People's minds wander frequently, and do so during almost all activities. The shift between those two networks can occur through either external sensory distractions, the things happening around us or emotional distractions, one's inner dialogue, thoughts and concerns about things happening in one's life. (Langner, & Eickhoff 2013, Forsythe et al. 2014)
Attention is the gateway to information processing and memory. It is where we consciously direct memory recall, attending to external information or internal thought processes. Information we selectively "focus on" and "attend to" is where we start to "think" and initiate responses and actions.

Retrieval and updating memory

A task may require the manipulation, or updating of stored information, or may engage simultaneous processing and storage of items. The information is stored simultaneously in different areas of the brain, and connected as a network. The amount of connections a single piece of information has, will affect the ease of retrieval. (Rumelhart and McClelland, 1988, Gazzaniga et al. 2008, Forsythe et al. 2014)

Three types of memory are relevant to general model of information processing: sensory memory, short-term memory and long term-memory:
1) Sensory memory is high capacity information storage, acting as an eye filter, by focusing on what is important, and forgetting what is unnecessary. Large amount of information is processed very fast, is automated and can take between 200-500 milliseconds to complete after the perception of an item. These memories, usually unconscious, last for a very short amount of time, ranging up to three seconds. Sensory information catches our attention, and thus progresses into working memory, only if it is seen as relevant, or is familiar. This knowledge is gained and stored by repeated actions. (Healey 2012, Ward, Grinstein & Keim 2015)
2) Short-term memory/ working memory analyzes incoming information from both sensory registers and long-term storage. It has limited information capacity occurring at a high level of processing. The time span of information retrieval is limited, less than 30 seconds and it represents the beginning of thinking. It can be harnessed by grouping and repetition, by not requiring users to remember too many things, and by organization of information such as chunking and chronology. (Baddeley, 2001, Gazzaniga et al. 2008, Forsythe et al. 2014) The chunks are grouped objects remembered as a unit. The number of units that can be processed at any one time as 7 + 2 (Miller,1956) or as the subsequent studies have indicated that 5 + 2 may apply to most of the items we wish to remember (Ward, Grinstein & Keim 2015).
3) Long-term memory is complex and theoretically limitless. Information storage is redundantly stored, and organized in a complex network structure. The crucial factor of long term memory is how well organized the information is. This is affected by proper elaboration processes in transferring to long term memory (encoding) and scanning memory for the information and transferring into working memory so that it could be used (retrieval processes). Information retrieval is a key problem and access is unreliable and slow. The degree of similarity between the way information was encoded and the way it is being accessed will shape the quality of retrieval processes. It can be harnessed by using association, pictures and animations and chunking. (Ward, Grinstein & Keim 2015)

<u>Decision making</u>

The decision-making is a subset of our information processing capabilities, grounded in basic perceptual, attentional, and memory processes. To make decision one's relies on the sensory inputs, either externally or internally generated drawing upon one's capacity of working memory to process these stimuli and to access long-term memory for prior experience and knowledge, selecting from several choices the final one to initiate and take an action. The fundamental elements of any decision are its potential outcomes, and specifically their values. (Smith & Huettel, 2010, Connors et al., 2013, Boss, 2015)
Decision-making depends heavily on task features (e.g., task complexity, source of information, task novelty and framing of choice options) and is influenced by situational/environmental conditions e.g., time pressure or social context. How humans approach decision-making situations and role the individual differences in decision making play, are a topic of longstanding and ongoing decision- making research. (Smith & Huettel, 2010, Connors et al., 2013, Murty et al., 2016)

Relevance to safety

Frequently used taxonomies, omission errors and commission errors, (Swain and Guttman, 1983) and slips, lapses and mistakes taxonomy by Reason (2008), as well as a large number of other error taxonomies are related to attention allocation, retrieval and updating of the memory and decision making.
Attentional lapses had and can have serious consequences, therefore both external (e.g. distractions, task interruptions, work over-, or underload, fatigue, boredom) and internal (personal life) factors which can affect attention, must be managed carefully.
Operator's situation awareness to build and maintain a mental picture of the current and projected traffic situation and control it, critically depend on their 'working memory', 'long-term memory' and 'prospective memory' (e.g. remembering to issue a planned instruction at some point close in the future).

Approach

The inputs from cognitive neuroscience regarding attention allocation, retrieval and updating memory, decision making, provide the opportunities for organizations to build new conceptual frameworks for improvement of overall organizational performance. They challenge organization's current work design,

current requirements specification for tasks, equipment, rules and procedures, training and documentation as well as the ways of communication, information exchange and learning methods.
The ability to sustain attention for prolonged periods of time without being distracted is vital but unfortunately limited. (L.van den Brink et al., 2016) Slips in attention are challenging for everyone. A new concept in supporting operators to re-focus on the task after a distraction emerges, where external, competing influences on his/her attention can interfere with his/her ability to recognize and respond to errors, is required. The organization should finally recognize the importance of limiting/discouraging all work stressors (e.g. interruptions, distractions) and include those limitations/discouragement in workplace design/ procedures as well as team communication and active supervision.
There are, also the times of work underload, with little traffic/events to manage over long period of time, resulting in boredom and mind wandering. The organizations should think about what would help operator in sustaining attention, how the work can be reorganized or what else would contribute to maintain attention.
"People 'have a life'." (DEFSTAND 00-250 (PTO)/1, 2008, p.46) One's inner dialogue, thoughts and concerns about things happening in one's life can cause mood change and mental fatigue and prolonged mind wandering.
It would be from huge importance for organizations to train people to be "active observers" of all the warning signals of their internal condition and external environment and be able to ask for support when needed.
This is an input for fatigue and stress management as well as input for design of team communication and interaction as well as position handover process.
Excessively detailed instructions/procedures and poorly designed documents/guidelines (most of which are not required), do not support one's memory or decision-making process either in routine, repetitive well-known situations or completely novel, but contribute to user overload and stress and increase the risk of errors and mistakes. Their simplification must be the priority.

3. Response programming (action).

Response programming occurs in the final stage of the information processing model. Once a stimulus has been identified and the proper response has been selected, the response programming stage is responsible for the preparation of initiation of a response via the appropriate modality, be it speech or motor, and execution of the task. (Schmidt & Wrisberg, 2008)

Performance monitoring System

Cognitive neuroscientists studying performance monitoring have been particularly interested in errors occurring in computer-dependent tasks to build a more complete picture of what happens in the brain when one makes an error. (Rabbitt et al., 1977, Coles et al., 2001) There are two components of error processing in the brain: a 'monitoring system' to detect errors which identifies instances of mismatch between what response should have occurred with what response actually occurred, and a 'remedial action system' which may then intervene to correct and/or compensate for the error. (Coles et al., 2001) The monitoring system allows for the detection of errors as they occur, monitoring activity in tasks in order to facilitate optimum allocation of attention resources. It can recruit additional brain areas when there are competing demands on attention, allowing us to pay more attention when a problem is recognized. Current monitoring system capacity may be affected by such factors as mood, stress, and anxiety. And fatigue can greatly decrease this capacity.
The remedial action system reflects the degree to which errors/conflict are consciously perceived by the individual and is associated with remedial and physiological changes. Subjectively perceived errors reflect more conscious post-error processing and the initiation of remedial actions after an error has occurred; this reaction may be: (1) fast, (2) prolonged, and (3) a delayed response to errors. (Neta et al., 2015)
Immediate self-correction of incorrect motor commands initiated by the brain in stimulus-response tasks may be terminated before being carried out, but only within a certain time frame (approximately ~200 ms) of an error occurring. If that time frame has been surpassed it demonstrates that a slower process of self-correction is taking place. (Hogan et al., 2005) Unperceived errors, which decrease the capacity of the monitoring system, which are not detected, because of fatigue or interruption, are of course those 'human errors' involved in incidents and accidents.

Relevance to safety

Self-correction is a human capability correcting or compensating for one's own errors and occurs frequently during all activities. That is why errors are not more common than they are. (Forsythe et al.2014, Hollnagel, 2015)

Approach

There are times of recognized action-density in the workplace when the performance monitoring system might come under challenges. External, competing influences on one's attention at these times can interfere with one's ability to recognize and respond to errors. But the capability of self-correction can be strengthened to incorporate all of those influences (e.g. interruption, distraction, cognitive overload, time pressure etc.) into learning and into the training process of organizations.

Also, our performance monitoring system can be activated simply by watching those around us make an error, confirming that we can monitor the actions of others and our own performance at the same time. (Van Schie et al., 2004, Forsythe et al. 2014) We or those around us can help recognize errors even when not directly involved in the task at hand. This is the moment we call "human redundancy". This ability could also be integrated into the learning process, simultaneously recording potentials in task performers and observers.

Accepting and coping with the human errors

As a foundation for our approach on how to see errors as a source of essential information and crucial learning moments and how to build in mechanisms for tolerating and coping with them, we use several established techniques or methods at different stages of the safety assessment process to support our safety case.

1) Long established hazard & safety issue database: A good reporting system help any organisation to gain information about safety occurrences in operations with related systems. The review of already known incidents is essential. Safety database enables safety professionals to look at many different safety events that influence human and system performance, and look for patterns, and similarities among issues and incident types which usually reveal a comprehensive range of human factors issues. (Wallace & Ross, 2006) Our reporting process and hazard database, helps us to set and specify effective basic safety requirements regarding operator position, which are mandatory, and are assigned to product/project development team in order to eliminate or prevent hazards, or reduce their frequency, thus reducing risk to the required level.

2) Human factors supporting material: After the review of a very large number of scientific literature on human performance and human error, we find the Human Factors Pie (fig.4), a list with a wide spectrum of human factors issues the best support for our hazard identification. It is an extensive structured map/list of known human factors problems which are classified into six broad main categories, (Human in System, Working Environment, Organisation and Staffing, Procedures, Roles and Responsibilities, Teams and Communication, Training and Development), created as support material for the Human Factor Case. The HF Case process has been developed by EUROCONTROL (2007) to support a development process of the ATM complex cooperative systems, where interactions occur between a number of humans and machines.

The elicitation of human factors issues in categories and sub-categories gives us the ability not only for a clear definition of where the collaborative work between customer & supplier is required, but also where are the boundaries of responsibility between them for human factors work and management within the process of technical transition.

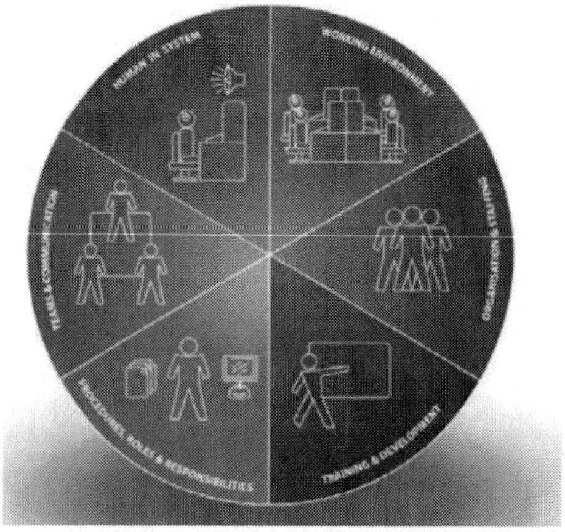

Figure 4—HF Pie (EUROCONTROL, 2007)

3) Task analysis: Task analysis can be defined as the study of what a user is required to do, in terms of actions and/or cognitive processes, to achieve a task objective. The task analysis we use, assists us in providing an outline of all user groups which use the system e.g. operator, maintainer, administrator and is a multifunctional tool, supporting:

- Hazard identification & mitigation
- User interface design development & evaluation
- Training development & evaluation
- User & training documentation

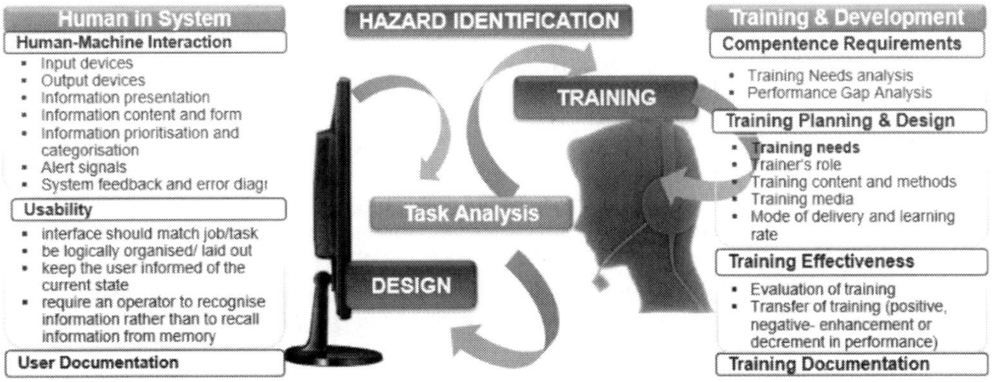

Figure 5—Categories of HF Pie as a support for the hazard identification, modified

Task analysis reflects not only how users may operate products that are being developed but is also the basis for communication and information exchange between user interface developers/designers, human factors and safety professionals, training professionals as well as others project stakeholders involved in the development process e.g. end users or their representatives. (Wickens et al., 2004) By clearly identifying tasks and examining the relationships between them, and leaning on human factors issues list (HF Pie) helps to identify issues at an early stage of user interface design process that can be improved by a designer, or made safer or easier to learn. (fig.5) It can already, at an early stage of development, reveal the lack of understanding, ambiguities or misunderstanding of how the task itself should be properly translated and integrated within the technology and if the task itself is comprehensible. It can, also reveal the necessity for additional requirements regarding equipment, training contents and methods, because of inadequate or ambiguous requirements specification.

4) Performance observation and measurement: The design development of our products evolves through five stages Understand, Design, Visualize, Prove and Deliver of user-centric design process. The first three stages of the process cannot provide the level of accuracy required to make finer judgements regarding human performance, but they can offer significant opportunities for hazard reduction resulting in design change, additional requirements for training needs and improved user satisfaction. The "Prove" stage containing usability tests, reveals the extent of success in creating safe and efficient human performance in user interaction with a new user interface. After accomplishment of usability tests which allow us to see how successful user representatives (three to five of them) with their tasks are, and they usually are, the raising of internal and situational awareness of how brain-centric errors occur, then starts.

To capture the data of simple scenarios the user's activities are video recorded for more precise analysis of these in detail later. Concurrently, depending on performance measurement demands, eye tracking software and keystroke level model (KLM) as well as finger-stroke level model (FLM) for the touch-sensitive user interfaces, can be used.

Having the description of physical, perceptual, and cognitive activities involved with each task, we choose one between several frequent, more complex tasks considering phone/radio/text communication and shorten significantly its time duration requiring users to accomplish it faster. When they start executing the task, shortly after, they are exposed to interruption through second task, usually in form of emergency call (visual and audio signal) which always has priority. The execution of the first task is already occurring when the interruptive task presents itself. So, the users must attend to the interruptive event, which has priority, switch over from the primary to the new task, and finally execute it. After this, the users must switch back to the first task, prepare for its resumption, and continue executing it from an appropriate point in time. At their first attempt and under time pressure of the first task they usually fail to complete the first task. Pushing wrong button or forgetting where they were in the task sequence, when they switched back to the first task, are well known slips and attention lapses. (Reason, 1990) Looking at short videos and discussing those errors and how work stressors (interruptions, time pressure or distraction) can easily cause them as well as what consequences in real-world operation for the person performing the tasks, they can have, is what we try to underpin and make them aware of. The important feedback we generate, is the information around equipment reliability and robustness to human errors as well as how user interface design supports self-correction and overall recovery from error.

If the feedback reflects any residual human factors issue, which result in additional human factors design requirements, appropriate and timely design interventions will follow that increase contribution to maturity and stability of the system as well as the contribution to safer human-machine interaction.

Further direction in our work is to create more sophisticated scenarios for usability testing and training sessions which could harness mechanisms to improve error recognition and response as well as to utilize information processing model for verification and improvement of user interface design, learning and training methods and overall user documentation.

Risk assessments in sociotechnical systems

Identifying the things that may go wrong and the ways in which this may happen is an essential part of risk analysis. Being able to foresee, clarify and evaluate potential risks of different ways in which tasks can fail to achieve their designed objective, and the factors that might influence performance and then to mitigate them with cost effective, timely actions, is the goal organizations strive for, but rarely achieved. (Locke, 2009)

In the past the understanding of how humans can most safely and efficiently be integrated with the technology was not always timely and properly translated into safety-critical projects, equipment design, training, policies, or procedures causing lack of desired enhancement of human performance. (EUROCONTROL & FAA, 2015)

Underestimated risks regarding introduction of conceptual and technological novelty as well as increased technological and organizational complexity, resulted in overall risk of inadequate consideration of the role of humans in relation to technology and how new technology will impact upon existing people-systems. (team, organization). (Hollnagel, 2004, Dekker, 2011) So, technological complexity in current advanced information and communication systems has increased to the point where all the potential interactions among system components cannot be anticipated or identified, and properly protected in design and operations. The current organizational complexity is the same, revealing the same level of interactions ambiguities, dilutes accountabilities, excessive processes, user overload and stress in the human-machine and human-human interaction, thereby increasing the risks of error and accidents. (Dekker, 2014, Hollnagel, 2015) Consequently, after four decades of research on human error, the time has come to define and understand what correct human performance is (Reason, 1990) to be able to minimize the opportunity for human error. By applying the lessons of cognitive neuroscience and leaning on several human performance approaches available for use at different parts of the safety assessment we could finally approach the challenge to rethink and learn from past mistakes. The next steps should be made toward a systematic management of human performance at all organizational levels and to advocate the establishment of human performance management system across safety-critical organizations. (EUROCONTROL & FAA, 2010, 2015, IAEA, 2014, ISO 27500, 2016)

Conclusions

The comprehension of how the information processing in the human brain supports day-to-day functioning and how this functioning may be disturbed, can help us to acknowledge mistakes when they happen. The current findings of ongoing research in cognitive neuroscience teach us the importance of understanding the extent by which error experience, and knowledge can shape the brain and can help individuals improve their internal and situational awareness of how errors occur, how to better recognize them and response to them. This opens many areas of further work in improvement of human performance and workplace efficiency. We strongly believe, that fostering an environment that accepts human error as a part of human nature in response to its environment and not as its deviation, and understands and appreciates, the experience gained in learning from them, should be an integral part of any organization's culture and one of its core strengths.

By applying the lessons of cognitive neuroscience, we could approach the change in design of our organizational systems, that will work with the human mind and not against it. Otherwise we are apt to keep making the same missteps again and again, to the detriment of the safe and efficient integration of humans with the technology.

References

Amso, D. & Scerif, G. (2015). *The attentive brain: insights from developmental cognitive neuroscience.* Retrieved from https://www.ncbi.nlm.nih.gov/pmc/articles/PMC4885514/

ASME, Standard for Probabilistic Risk Assessment for Nuclear Power Plant Applications, 2002.

Baddeley, A. D. (2001). *Is working memory still working?* American Psychologist, 56(11), 851.

Boss, Jeff (2015). *How to Overcome The 'Analysis Paralysis' Of Decision-Making.* Retrieved from https://www.forbes.com/sites/jeffboss/2015/03/20/how-to-overcome-the-analysis-paralysis-of-decision-making/#c0ca44a1be5a

Coles, M.G., Scheffers, M.K., Holroyd, C.B. (2001). *Why is there an ERN/Ne on correct trials? Response representations, stimulus-related components, and the theory of error-processing.* Retrieved from https://www.sciencedirect.com/science/article/pii/S030105110100076X

Connors, B.L., Rende, R., Colton, T.J. (2013). *Predicting individual differences in decision-making process from signature movement styles: an illustrative study of leaders.* Retrieved from https://www.ncbi.nlm.nih.gov/pmc/articles/PMC3781361/

DEFSTAND 00-250 (PTO)/1, (2008), *Human Factors For Designers of Systems – Part 0: Human Factors Integration, NJ, USA: SAI Global*

DEFSTAND 00-251 (PTO)/1, (2016), *Human Factors For Designers of Systems – Part 0: Human Factors Integration, NJ, USA: SAI Global*

Dekker, S. (2011). *Drift into failure: From hunting broken components to understanding complex systems.* Burlington, VT: Ashgate Publishing.

Dekker, S. (2014). *The Field Guide to Understanding 'Human Error' 3rd Edition*- New York: CRC Press, Taylor & Francis Group, LLC

EUROCONTROL & FAA, (2010). *Human Performance in Air Traffic Management Safety*, Action Plan 15 Safety White Paper. Retrieved from https://www.eurocontrol.int/sites/default/files/article/content/documents/nm/safety/hp_white_paper_2010_low.pdf

EUROCONTROL & FAA, (2015). *A Human Performance Standard of Excellence.* Action Plan 15 White Paper. Retrieved from http://skybrary.aero/bookshelf/books/3291.pdf

EUROCONTROL, (2007). *The Human Factors Case: guidance for Human Factors Integration, Edition 2.0.* Retrieved from http://www.eurocontrol.int/sites/default/files/article/content/documents/nm/safety/hf-case-guidance-v2.pdf

EUROCONTROL, (2011). *Support Material for Human Factors Case application*, Edition 3.0. Retrieved from https://www.eurocontrol.int/sites/default/files/article/content/documents/nm/safety/latest-guidance-of-hf-case-application.pdf

Forsythe, C., Liao, H., Trumbo, M. & Cardona-Rivera R. E. (2014) *Cognitive Neuroscience of Human Systems: Work and Everyday Life.* New York: CRC Press, Taylor & Francis Group, LLC.

Gazzaniga, M. S., Ivry R.B. & Mangun G.R. (2008). *Cognitive Neuroscience: The Biology of the Mind.* NYC, USA: W. W. Norton & Company

Goleman, D. (2013). *Focus: The Hidden Driver of Excellence. NY:* HarperCollins

Guttman, S.E., Gilroy, L.A. & Blake, R. (2006). *Hearing What the Eyes See- Auditory Encoding of Visual Temporal Sequences.* Retrieved from https://www.ncbi.nlm.nih.gov/pmc/articles/PMC1431611/

Healey, C.G. (2012). *Perception in Visualization.* Retrieved from https://www.csc2.ncsu.edu/faculty/healey/PP/

Hogan, A.M., Vargha-Khadem, F., Kirkham, F.J., Baldeweg, T. (2005) *Maturation of action monitoring from adolescence to adulthood: an ERP study.* Dev. Sci, vol. 8 (p. 525-534)

Hollnagel, E. (2004). *Barriers and accident prevention.* UK: Ashgate Publishing Limited.

Hollnagel, E. (2015) *The ETTO Principle: Efficiency- Thoroughness Trade-Off"- Why Things That Go Right Sometimes Go Wrong.* England: Ashgate Publishing Limited.

IAEA Nuclear Energy Series No. NG-T-2.7 (2014), *Managing Human Performance to Improve Nuclear Facility Operation,* Retrieved from https://www-pub.iaea.org/MTCD/Publications/…/ Pub1623_web.pdf

ISO 27500, (2016). *The human-centred organization- Rationale and general principles.* Geneva, Switzerland, ISO Store

L. van den Brink , R., Murphy, P.R. & Nieuwenhuis S. (2016). *Pupil Diameter Tracks Lapses of Attention.* Retrieved from https://www.ncbi.nlm.nih.gov/pmc/articles/PMC5074493/

Langner, R., Eickhoff, S. B. (2013) *Sustaining attention to simple tasks: A meta-analytic review of the neural mechanisms of vigilant attention.* Retrieved from https://www.ncbi.nlm.nih.gov/pmc/articles/PMC3627747/

Locke, E.A. (2009). *Handbook of Principles of Organizational Behavior, Second Edition.* UK: John Wiley & Sons.

Meister, D. (1989). *The nature of human error.* Global Telecommunications Conference and Exhibition 'Communications Technology for the 1990s and Beyond' (GLOBECOM), 1989, IEEE. 2, pp. 783-786

Miller, G.A. (1956). *The Magical Number Seven, Plus or Minus Two: Some Limits on Our Capacity for Processing Information.* Retrieved from http://www.musanim.com/miller1956/

Murty, V., FeldmanHall, O., Hunter, L.E., Phelps, E. A., Davachi, L. (2016). *Episodic memories predict adaptive value-based decision-making.* Retrieved from http://www.feldmanhalllab.com/publications/

Neta, M., Miezin, F. M. Nelson, S. M., Dubis, J. W., Dosenbach, N. U.F., Schlaggar, B. L. & Petersen, S. E. (2015). *Spatial and Temporal Characteristics of Error-Related Activity in the Human Brain.* Retrieved from https://www.ncbi.nlm.nih.gov/pmc/articles/PMC4287146/

Oedewald P., Reiman T. (2007). *Special characteristics of safety critical organization: Work psychological perspective.* Retrieved from https://www.vtt.fi/inf/pdf/publications/2007/P633.pdf

Pillay, S. (2017). *Your Brain Can Only Take So Much Focus.* Retrieved from https://hbr.org/2017/05/your-brain-can-only-take-so-much-focus

Poort, J., Khan, A.G., Pachitariu, M., Nemri, A., Orsolic, I., Krupic, J., Bauza, M., Sahani, M., Keller, G.B., Mrsic-Flogel, T.D. & Hofer, S.B. (2015). *Learning Enhances Sensory and Multiple Non-Sensory Representations in Primary Visual Cortex.* Retrieved from https://www.cell.com/neuron/fulltext/S0896-6273(15)00476-6.

Rabbitt P. & Rodgers B. (1977). *What does a man do after he makes an error? An analysis of response programming.* Q J Exp. Psychol, vol. 29 (p. 727-743)

Rasmussen, J. (1983). *Skills, rules, knowledge, signals, signs, symbols, and other distinctions in human performance models.* IEEE Transactions on Systems, Man, and Cybernetics, p. 257-266.

Reason, J. (1990). *Human Error.* UK, Cambridge University Press

Reason, J. (2008). *The human contribution.* Farnham, UK: Ashgate

Rumelhart, D. E., McClelland, J. L., & PDP Research Group. (1988). *Parallel distributed processing* (Vol. 1, pp. 354-362). IEEE.

Saunders, F. C. (2015). *Toward High Reliability Project Organizing in Safety-Critical Projects.* Project Management Journal Volume 46, Issue 3 (June/July), p. 25–35.

Schmidt, R.A. & Wrisberg, C.A. (2008). *Motor Learning and Performance: From Principles to Application.* US, Human Kinetics

Smith D.V., Huettel S.A. (2010). *Decision Neuroscience: Neuroeconomics.* Retrieved from https://www.ncbi.nlm.nih.gov/pmc/articles/PMC3384699/

Swain A. & Guttman, H. (1983). *A Handbook of Human Reliability Analysis with Emphasis on Nuclear Power Plant.* Washington DC: Nuclear Regulatory Commision

Sweeney M., (2018). *What is Human Nature? - Definition, Theories & Examples* Retrieved from http://study.com/academy/lesson/what-is-human-nature-definition-theories-examples.html

Taylor, F.W. (2010). *The Principles of Scientific Management.* New York: Copyright by Cosimo Inc., *the book was originally published in **1911***

Van Schie, H.T., Mars, R.B., Coles, M.G., Bekkering H. (2004) *Modulation of activity in medial frontal and motor cortices during error observation*, Nat Neurosci , vol. 7 (p. 549-554)

Wallace, B. & Ross, A. (2006). *Beyond Human Error: Taxonomies and Safety Science.* New York: CRC Press, Taylor & Francis Group, LLC

Ward M.O., Grinstein G. & Keim D. (2015) *Interactive Data Visualization: Foundations, Techniques, and Applications, Second Edition.* New York: CRC Press, Taylor & Francis Group, LLC

Wickens, C.D. (1992). *Engineering Psychology and Human Performance*, 1st Edition, UK, Good Years Books.

Wickens, C.D. & Hollands, J.G. (1999). *Engineering Psychology and Human Performance*, 3rd Edition, UK, Pearson Education

Wickens, C.D., Lee, J.D., Liu, Y. & Becker, S.E. Gordon (2004). *"An Introduction to Human Factors Engineering", 2nd edition.* Pearson Education

Woods D. D., Leila J. JOHANNESEN, Richard I. COOK & Nadine B. SARTER (1994). Behind human error: cognitive systems, computers, and hindsight. Wright-Patterson Air Force Base: Crew Systems Ergonomics Information Analysis Center (Ohio, USA), 1994.

Speaking Risk with Our PMs

Dustin Nix, M.S., PMP; A-P-T Research, Inc.; Huntsville, AL, USA

John Fellows, M.S., PMP; A-P-T Research, Inc.; Huntsville, AL, USA

John Hall, Ph.D.; A-P-T Research, Inc.; Huntsville, AL, USA

Keywords: risk, risk management, project management, risk mapping

Abstract

Effective communication between the system safety engineer and the Project Manager is an essential characteristic of good risk management in a robust system safety program. However, these two disciplines utilize similar terms with disparate meanings than can lead to sub-optimal technical or programmatic outcomes. MIL-STD-882E defines risk as "A combination of the severity of the mishap and the probability that the mishap will occur." *The Project Management Book of Knowledge (PMBOK) Guide, 6th Edition*, defines individual project risk as "an uncertain event or condition that, if it occurs, has a positive or negative effect on one or more project objectives."[1] It is incumbent upon the system safety professional to clearly communicate safety-related issues, hazards, risks, and concerns using language most likely to be understood by the Project Manager to ensure he or she has the requisite information to make a sound programmatic decision. This paper explores discrepancies between project risk management and safety risk management standard processes that hinder clear communication and can drastically impact program performance. We present methods to consider that will improve understanding between the system safety professional and the Project Manager and two framework approaches for integrating safety and project risks.

Introduction

Ineffective communication has been separating groups and stunting or stopping projects dating back to the Tower of Babel. In today's approach of integrated project management, each contributing discipline employs a unique language. Similar words or phrases are often used across disciplines, though with disparate meanings. Of all the relationships system safety professionals maintain during a project, perhaps none are as important as the relationship with the Project Manager (PM). In most projects, the PM is either the approval authority of each identified safety risk, or the conduit to upper managers for final approval. The PM also controls budgets and schedules associated with risk mitigations, investment, and verification. Meanwhile, the characteristics of safety risks are fundamentally different than the characteristics of risks regularly managed by the PM – the probability scales differ by orders of magnitude, the severity definitions have minimal overlap, and the general PM definition of "risk" includes positive outcomes. Do we understand these differences as system safety professionals? How can we mitigate the effects to improve the success of the system safety program and, by extension, the project? How do we quantify risks to effectively assist the PM with decision-making?

---

[1] Project Management Institute Inc., *PMBOK Guide, 6th Edition, 2017.*

Risk in Project Management

Project Management principles are applied differently across industries, with nuances in approach and terminology. The *PMBOK Guide* serves as a collection of Project Management terms, processes, and best practices independent of specific industries. The *PMBOK Guide* outlines and explains five process groups that make up any project and 14 knowledge areas needed to accomplish a project efficiently. One knowledge area is risk management, which encompasses much of the work of the system safety professional.

The *PMBOK Guide* defines "individual project risk" as "an uncertain event or condition that, if it occurs, has a positive or negative effect on one or more project objectives." This definition includes business risks, manufacturing risks, development risks, and risk related to human resources. The range of consideration goes from negative outcomes to positive outcomes, called "threats" and "opportunities," respectively. Thus, even within the knowledge area of Risk Management, the system safety program is just a portion of the overall risk discussion.

The *PMBOK Guide* is not industry-specific and does not specify risk outcome definitions or associated probability ranges. As an example of how the risk management process is applied, consider the Department of Defense *Risk, Issue, and Opportunity Management Guide for Defense Acquisition Programs* (*DoD Risk Management Guide*), which is similar to risk management guidance across government agencies. In this guide, risk is defined as "potential future events or conditions that may have a negative effect on achieving program objectives for cost, schedule, and performance. Risks are defined by (1) the probability (greater than 0, less than 1) of an undesired event or condition and (2) the consequences, impact, or severity of the undesired event, were it to occur." Therefore, risk is scoped down to negative or undesired events, while the term "opportunities" describes the positive spectrum of uncertain events.

The *DoD Risk Management Guide* provides sample consequences and probability criteria, which are depicted in Table 1 and Table 2, respectively.

The sample consequences criteria define five consequence levels from Minimal Impact to Critical Impact. Impacts associated with cost increases are primarily quantified as percentage ranges of the Acquisition Program Baseline (APB). Schedule and performance impacts typically contain more subjective definitions for the five consequence levels.

Table 1 — DoD Risk Management Guide – Sample Consequence Criteria

Level	Cost	Schedule	Performance
5 Critical Impact	10% or greater increase over APB objective values for RDT&E, PAUC, or APUC Cost increase causes program to exceed affordability caps	Schedule slip will require a major schedule re-baselining Precludes program from meeting its APB schedule threshold dates	Degradation precludes system from meeting a KPP or key technical supportability threshold; will jeopardize program success Unable to meet mission objectives (defined in mission threads, ConOps. OMS/MP)
4 Significant Impact	5% - <10% increase over APB objective values for RDT&E, PAUC, or APUC Costs exceed life cycle ownership cost KSA	Schedule deviations will slip program to within 2 months of approved APB threshold schedule date Schedule slip puts funding at risk Fielding of capability to operational units delayed by more than 6 months	Degradation impairs ability to meet a KSA. Technical design or supportability margin exhausted in key areas Significant performance impact affecting System-of System interdependencies. Work-arounds required to meet mission objectives

Level	Cost	Schedule	Performance
3 Moderate Impact	1% - < 5% increase over APB objective values for RDT&E, PAUC, or APUC Manageable with PEO or Service assistance	Can meet APB objective schedule dates, but other non-APB key events (e.g., SETRs or other Tier 1 Schedule events) may slip Schedule slip impacts synchronization with interdependent programs by greater than 2 months	Unable to meet lower tier attributes, TPMs, or CTPs Design or supportability margins reduced Minor performance impact affecting System-of System interdependencies; Work-arounds required to achieve mission tasks
2 Minor Impact	Costs that drive unit production cost (e.g., APUC) increase of <1% over budget Cost increase, but can be managed internally	Some schedule slip, but can meet APB objective dates and non-APB key event dates	Reduced technical performance or supportability; can be tolerated with little impact on program objectives Design margins reduced, within trade space
1 Minimal Impact	Minimal impact. Costs expected to meet approved funding levels	Minimal schedule impact	Minimal consequences to meeting technical performance or supportability requirements Design margins will be met; margin to planned tripwires
APB: Acquisition Program Baseline; APUC: Average Procurement Unit Cost; ConOps: Concept of Operations; CTP: Critical Technical Parameter; PAUC: Program Acquisition Unit Cost; PEO: Program Executive Officer; KPP: Key Performance Parameter; KSA: Key System Attribute; OMS/MP: Operational Mode Summary/Mission Profile; RDT&E: Research, Development Test & Evaluation; TPM: Technical Performance Measure			

The sample probability criteria define five likelihood levels from 1 (Not Likely) to 5 (Near Certainty). The quantitative ranges encompass approximately equal quintiles. The level 1 (Not Likely) probability of occurrence range is 1-20%. Probabilities below 1% are not addressed in the sample probability criteria.

Table 2 — DoD Risk Management Guide – Sample Probability Criteria

Level	Likelihood	Probability of Occurrence
5	Near Certainty	>80% to ≤ 99%
4	Highly Likely	>60% to ≤ 80%
3	Likely	>40% to ≤ 60%
2	Low Likelihood	> 20% to ≤ 40%
1	Not Likely	> 1% to ≤ 20%

Consequence and likelihood are combined in a risk matrix commonly used on DoD acquisition programs, which is regularly reviewed by the PM as part of risk management, as shown in Figure 1. In this risk matrix, red represents areas of High project risk, yellow represents areas of Medium project risk, and green represents areas of Low project risk.

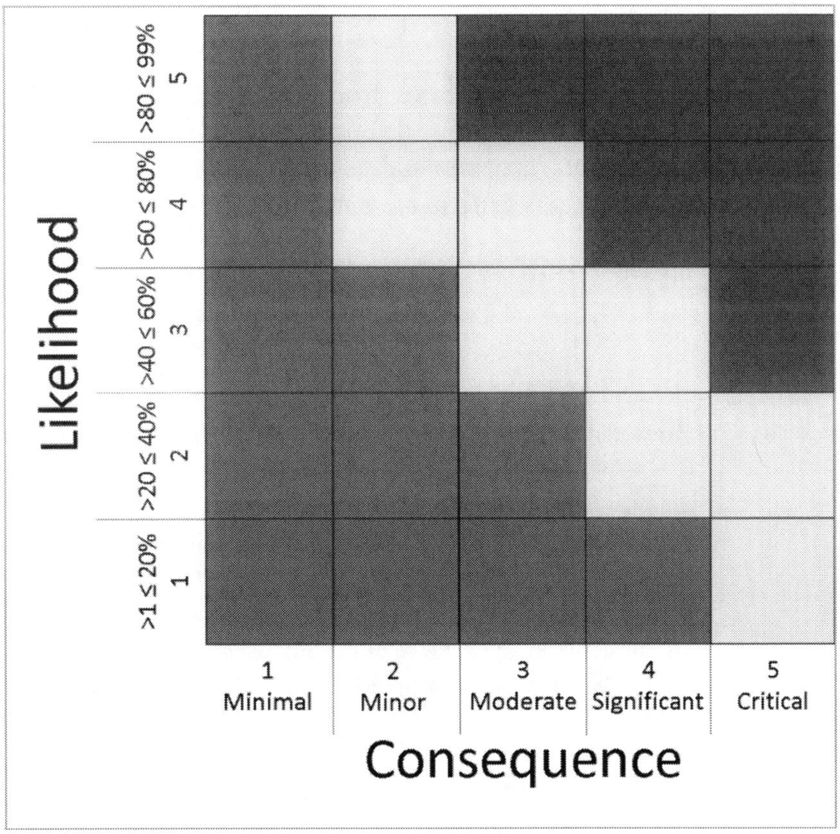

Figure 1 — Sample Risk Matrix

Finally, the *DoD Risk Management Guide* provides this direction related to incorporation of system safety in the risk management paradigm:

> Since safety and system hazard risks typically have cost, schedule, and performance impacts for the program, they should be addressed in the context of overall risk management. As a best practice, programs should include current high system hazard/Environmental Safety and Occupational Health (ESOH) risks together with other program risks on the prioritized risk matrix presented at key program decision points. Programs should use a Service-developed method to map these risks to the risk matrix and register, as appropriate.

The question for both the PM and system safety professional becomes, how to map safety risks to program risks?

Risk in System Safety

The system safety discipline widely accepts MIL-STD-882E as a primary authority on system safety practice. Additionally, since it is a DoD standard, it should adequately serve as the system safety equivalent to the example *DoD Risk Management Guide*. MIL-STD-882E defines risk as "a combination of the severity of the mishap and the probability that the mishap will occur." This definition loosely fits within the definition of the *DoD Risk Management Guide* definition for risk, while encompassing approximately half of the *PMBOK Guide's* definition for risk.

MIL-STD-882E provides severity categories and an example for probability levels, which are depicted in Table 3 and Table 4. Both tables are tailorable IAW MIL-STD-882E section 4.3.3.d.

MIL-STD-882E defines four severity categories from "Negligible" to "Catastrophic." Impacts associated with cost are quantified as a range of dollars, as opposed to percentage of the APB. Schedule and performance impacts are not addressed. Personnel safety impacts are mostly objective, while environmental impacts criteria are subjective.

Table 3 — MIL-STD-882E - Severity Categories

Description	Severity Category	Mishap Result Criteria
Catastrophic	1	Could result in one or more of the following: death, permanent total disability, irreversible significant environmental impact, or monetary loss equal to or exceeding $10M.
Critical	2	Could result in one or more of the following: permanent partial disability, injuries or occupational illness that may result in hospitalization of at least three personnel, reversible significant environmental impact, or monetary loss equal to or exceeding $1M but less than $10M.
Marginal	3	Could result in one or more of the following: injury or occupational illness resulting in one or more lost work day(s), reversible moderate environmental impact, or monetary loss equal to or exceeding $100K but less than $1M.
Negligible	4	Could result in one or more of the following; injury or occupational illness not resulting in a lost work day, minimal environmental impact, or monetary loss less than $100K.

MIL-STD-882E example probability levels include six likelihood levels from F (Eliminated) to A (Frequent). The associated ranges are quantitatively defined by orders of magnitude, with A (Frequent) mishaps having a probability of occurrence >10% and E (Improbable) mishaps having a probability of occurrence <0.0001%. It is of note that only probability levels A (Frequent) and B (Probable) safety risks would fall on the *DoD Risk Management Guide* sample probability criteria scale. Therefore, all level C (Occasional), D (Remote), and E (Improbable) safety risks do not naturally fit within the typical PM risk management paradigm.

Table 4 — MIL-STD-882E Example Probability Levels

Description	Level	Individual Item	Fleet/Inventory	Quantitative
Frequent	A	Likely to occur often in the life of an item	Continuously experienced.	Probability of occurrence greater than or equal to 10^{-1}.
Probable	B	Will occur several times in the life of an item	Will occur frequently	Probability of occurrence less than 10^{-1} but greater than or equal to 10^{-2}.
Occasional	C	Likely to occur sometime in the life of an item	Will occur several times.	Probability of occurrence less than 10^{-2} but greater than or equal to 10^{-3}.
Remote	D	Unlikely, but possible to occur in the life of an item	Unlikely but can reasonably be expected to occur.	Probability of occurrence less than 10^{-3} but greater than or equal to 10^{-5}.

Description	Level	Individual Item	Fleet/Inventory	Quantitative
Improbable	E	So unlikely, it can be assumed occurrence may not be experienced in the life of an item	Unlikely to occur, but possible.	Probability of occurrence less than 10^{-6}
Eliminated	F	Incapable of occurrence within the life of an item. This category is used when potential hazards are identified and later eliminated.		

The system safety professional typically combines the severity and probability levels in a safety risk matrix, as shown in Figure 2.

SEVERITY / PROBABILITY	Catastrophic (1)	Critical (2)	Marginal (3)	Negligible (4)
Frequent (A) > 10%	HIGH	HIGH	SERIOUS	MEDIUM
Probable (B) >1<10%	HIGH	HIGH	SERIOUS	MEDIUM
Occasional (C) ≥0.1<1%	HIGH	SERIOUS	MEDIUM	LOW
Remote (D) ≥0.0001<0.1%	SERIOUS	MEDIUM	MEDIUM	LOW
Improbable (E) <0.0001	MEDIUM	MEDIUM	MEDIUM	LOW
Eliminated (F)	Eliminated			

Figure 2 — Safety Risk Matrix

Summary of Communication Disconnects

While the *DoD Risk Management Guide* directs programs to map high safety risks to program risks and include them on the prioritized risk matrix, there is no direction on how to do this task. In fact, it is unclear if "high" indicates those safety risks with a HIGH safety rating on the safety risk matrix, or subjectively high safety risks (both HIGH and SERIOUS safety risks). Additionally, almost every characteristic of the two risk paradigms differs, as summarized in Table 5.

Table 5 — Communication Disconnect Summary

Characteristic	PM	System Safety Professional	Assessment
Risk definition – clear and consistent?	May include uncertain positive outcomes	Only addresses uncertain negative outcomes	Clear; Not consistent
Consequence/ severity – objective and equivalent?	Addresses cost, schedule, and performance – cost objectively	Addresses safety, environmental impact, and cost – cost and safety objectively	Partially objective; Not equivalent

Characteristic	PM	System Safety Professional	Assessment
Likelihood/ probability – ranges overlap?	Five equally divided percentage ranges between 1-99%	Five percentage ranges with order of magnitude difference between 0.0001–99%	Minimal overlap
Risk matrices – equivalent?	Five by Five; Lowest risk in bottom left, highest risk in top right	Four by Six; lowest risk in bottom right, highest risk in top left	Not equivalent
Risk levels – equivalent in number and required action?	Three risk levels – High, Medium, and Low; Action to burn-down High, Medium, and some Low risks. No required action to elevate risks.	Four risk levels – HIGH, SERIOUS, MEDIUM, & LOW; Action to reduce risk to the extent practical. HIGH and SERIOUS risks require elevation for risk acceptance.	Not equivalent in number or required action.
Finding: Safety risks cannot be directly mapped to program risks without modifications in severity, probability, and risk levels.			

If it is assumed only HIGH safety risks should be mapped, the nearest graphical depiction (as shown in Figure 3) would show "Catastrophic" safety risks with probability ratings of A, B, and C on the far right edge of the Critical program risk column, and "Critical" safety risks with probability ratings of A and B centered in the Critical program risk column. In almost all cases, safety risks are relegated to the bottom-right blocks of the program risk matrix, and are unlikely to be considered above a Medium program risk, no matter the severity of the uncertain event. This approach to safety risk mapping does not adequately capture the potential risk to the program. For example, let's assume the first manned-flight of an experimental aircraft has a 10% risk of two fatalities (represented as "R1" in Figure 3). Should such a risk be assessed as Medium on the programmatic risk scale?

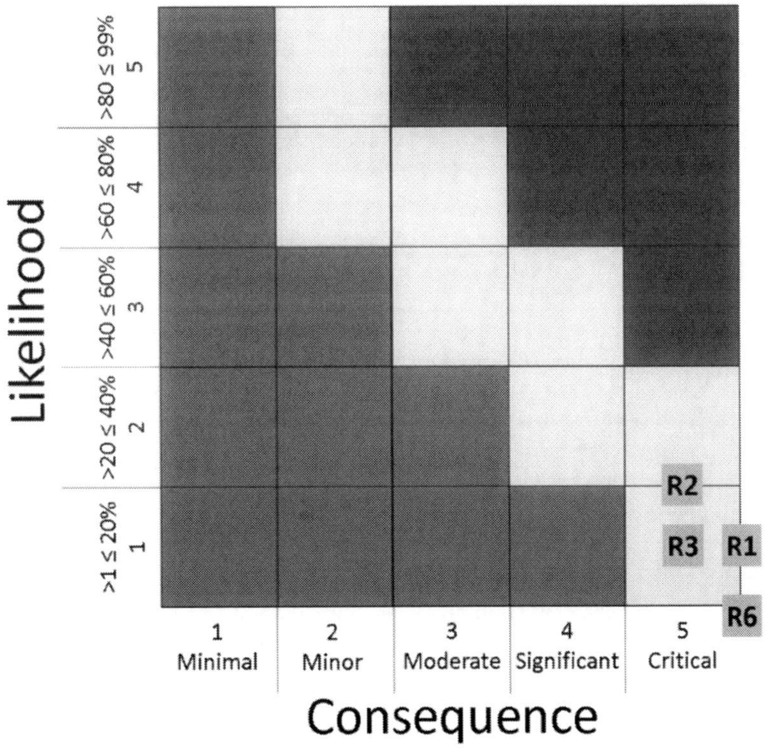

Figure 3 — HIGH Safety Risks Mapped

Solution 1: Risk Program Tailoring

As most system safety and risk management programs are tailorable, early recognition of the differences in risk definitions, consequence/severity equivalence, likelihood/probability range overlap, and risk matrix overlap could be documented and leveraged to tailor these two programs for a specific project/program. Tailored system safety and risk management programs would improve communication throughout the project/program. For example, the system safety program could implement the cost consequence definitions from the risk management program as opposed to standard system safety severity cost definitions, and map the system safety mishap result criteria to the Minor through Critical severity categories while adding a Catastrophic category to include death, as shown in Table 6 — Modified, Summarized Risk Management Guide – Example Consequence Criteria.

Table 6 — Modified, Summarized Risk Management Guide – Example Consequence Criteria

Level	Cost	Schedule	Performance	Safety
6 Catastrophic Impact	15% or greater increase over APB objective values	N/A	Degradation precludes system from meeting multiple key technical supportability thresholds; will jeopardize program success	Results in one or more fatalities
5 Critical Impact	10%- <15% increase over APB objective values	Schedule slip will require a major schedule re-baselining Precludes program from meeting its APB schedule threshold dates	Degradation precludes system from meeting a key technical supportability threshold; will jeopardize program success Unable to meet mission objectives	Results in one or more of the following: permanent total disability, irreversible significant environmental impact

Level	Cost	Schedule	Performance	Safety
4 Significant Impact	5% - <10% increase over APB objective values	Schedule deviations will slip program to within 2 months of approved APB threshold schedule date Schedule slip puts funding at risk	Technical design or supportability margin exhausted in key areas Significant performance impact affecting System-of System interdependencies. Work-arounds required to meet mission objectives	Results in one or more of the following: permanent partial disability, injuries or occupational illness that may result in hospitalization of at least three personnel, reversible significant environmental impact.
3 Moderate Impact	1% - < 5% increase over APB objective values	Can meet APB objective schedule dates, but other non-APB key events may slip	Unable to meet lower tier attributes. Design or supportability margins reduced Minor performance impact affecting System-of System interdependencies. Work-arounds required to achieve mission tasks	Results in one or more of the following: injury or occupational illness resulting in one or more lost work day(s), reversible moderate environmental impact.
2 Minor Impact	Costs that drive unit production cost increase of <1% over budget	Some schedule slip, but can meet APB objective dates and non-APB key event dates	Reduced technical performance or supportability; can be tolerated with little impact on program objectives Design margins reduced, within trade space	Results in one or more of the following; injury or occupational illness not resulting in a lost work day, minimal environmental impact.
1 Minimal Impact	Minimal impact. Costs, expected to meet approved funding levels	Minimal schedule impact	Minimal consequences to meeting technical performance or supportability requirements Design margins will be met	N/A

APB: Acquisition Program Baseline

Additionally, a sixth likelihood definition category could be added to encompass the bottom three non-zero system safety probability categories, as demonstrated in Table 7.

Table 7— Modified Risk Management Guide – Example Probability Criteria

Level	Likelihood	Probability of Occurrence
5	Near Certainty	>80% to ≤ 99%
4	Highly Likely	>60% to ≤ 80%
3	Likely	>40% to ≤ 60%
2	Low Likelihood	> 20% to ≤ 40%
1	Not Likely	> 1% to ≤ 20%
0	Remote	≤ 1%

These modifications would allow for direct mapping of HIGH and SERIOUS safety risks to the project/program risk matrix as well as a numerical count of MEDIUM and LOW safety risks into the project/program risk categories. This ensures safety risks of concern receive regular PM-level visibility. Leveraging the previous example of the first manned-flight of an experimental aircraft, with a 10% chance of two fatalities, a more accurate risk posture emerges on the hypothetical programmatic risk matrix. Namely, "R1" is depicted as a High program risk. An example of this and other modifications is depicted in Figure 4.

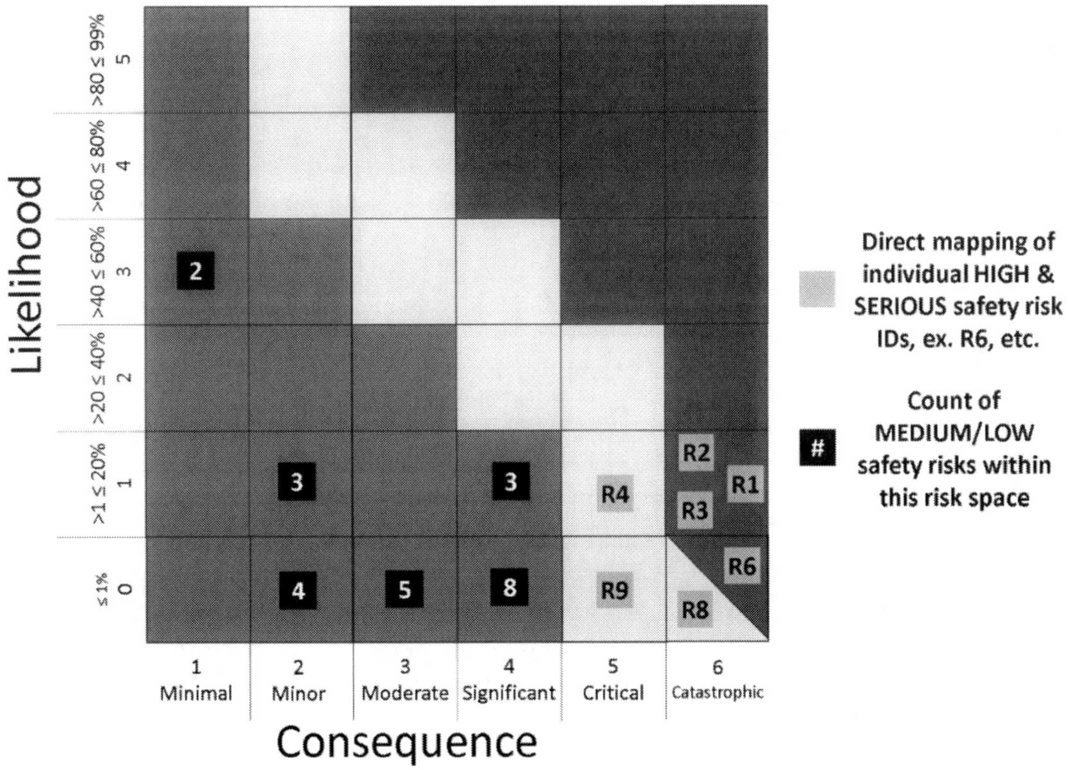

Figure 4 — Program Risk Matrix - Expanded

Solution 2: Quantifying Safety Impacts of Project Execution

Not all projects are in a phase to accommodate risk program tailoring. While MIL-STD-882E allows for risk acceptance of SERIOUS and HIGH safety risks, the existence of those risks present cost, schedule, and performance risks to the project/program. Sometimes they present themselves as risks to key milestones due to a low risk appetite among upper management. Other times, a low risk appetite among external stakeholders may impact cost, schedule, and performance negatively.

As a hypothetical example, a missile system under development suffers a late failure in environmental testing for a pressure vessel containing hazardous material. The system is scheduled for transport via military ship to a test range in two months to conduct a missile test in support of a fielding decision. The responsible agency assesses the safety risk as 1D (Catastrophic/Remote) – SERIOUS – and the acceptance authority accepts the risk. However, the test range or military ship commander declines the risk. This results in a Critical Impact to the schedule and cost baselines, while the system undergoes redesign and/or retesting.

Any safety risk that may impact external stakeholders and has not been driven to the MEDIUM or LOW safety risk areas and closed with verifications, has potential program/project implications. To address this type of scenario, the program/project should include each SERIOUS and HIGH safety risk in the program/project risk matrix. The risk consequence becomes "Residual risk (risk description) may be unacceptable to (external stakeholder)." The severity of that outcome should be assessed based on the complexity and interrelationship of the system and the impact to cost or schedule baselines should the external stakeholder decline the risk. The risk probability is assessed based on the number of planned mitigations, mitigation contingencies, verification schedules relative to decision dates, and estimated risk appetite of external stakeholders who must also accept the risk.

An example of this approach is demonstrated in Table 8, with mapping to the program/project risk matrix depicted in Figure 5.

Table 8 - DoD Risk Management Guide – Example Risk Register Excerpt

Risk Number	821	822
Linked WBS/IMS ID#	3.1.2	3.1.2
Owner	Nix	Nix
Type of Risk	Technical - Safety	Technical - Safety
Status	Open	Open
Risk Event	Residual SERIOUS risk "Support arm failure due to corrosion" may be unacceptable to test range	Residual HIGH risk "Haz Mat Release during transit" may be unacceptable to ship commander
Likelihood, Consequence Rating	**L=3, C=4**	**L=3, C=5**
Risk Mitigation Strategy	Control – Prioritize completion of verifications on subject risk; Include range rep in safety verification planning	Control – Prioritize completion of verifications on subject risk; Include ship rep in safety verification planning; Coordinate alternate transport
Risk Identified Date	8/20/2015	8/20/2015
Risk Approval Date	2/10/2016	2/10/2016
Planned Closure Date	7/15/2016	7/15/2016
Target Risk Rating	**L=1, C=4**	**L=1, C=4**
Plan Status	On Schedule	On Schedule

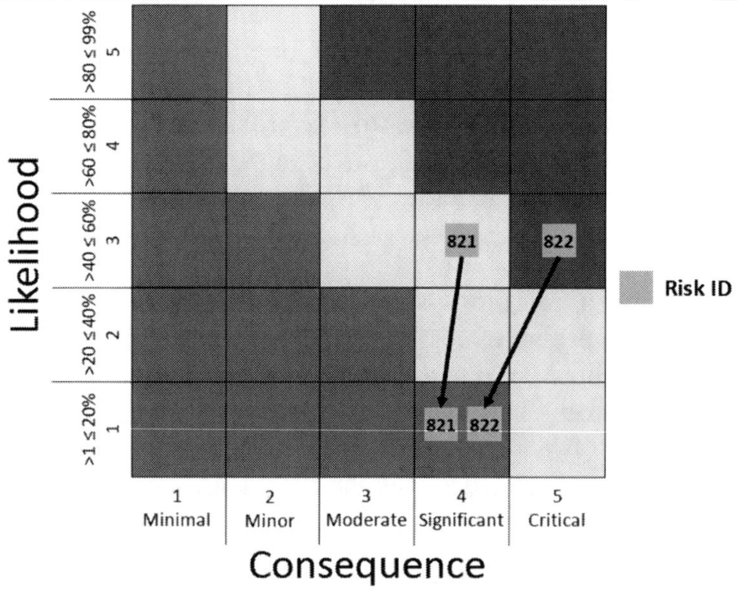

Figure 5 — Program Risk Matrix – Safety Impact Mapped

Simple Recommendation for Clarity

In all cases, the system safety professional should orient the PM to the system safety risk matrix by correlating it to the project/program risk matrix when seeking safety risk acceptance. Use the top-right, highest-risk formatting for the briefing, as demonstrated in Figure 6. Explain the differences in risk, severity, and probability definitions early in the discussion. Be prepared to discuss potential program impacts associated with HIGH and SERIOUS safety risks, or safety risks lacking robust closure verifications.

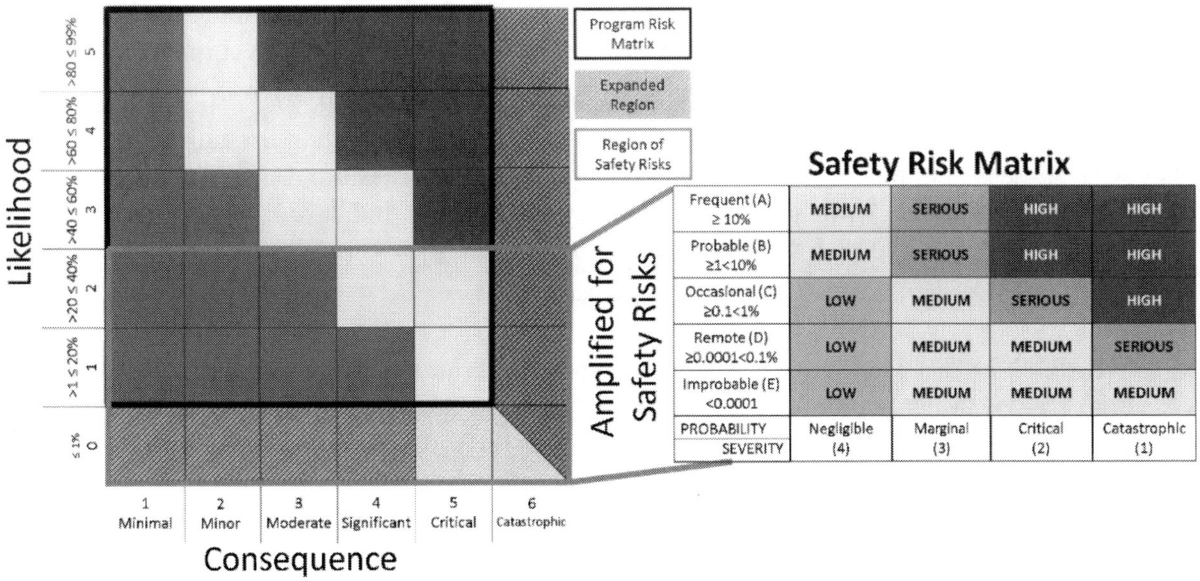

Figure 6 — System Safety Risk Matrix – Oriented

Conclusions

Effective communication with the PM may be the most important interdisciplinary trait for the system safety professional to acquire and apply. An essential safety responsibility is to ensure a PM considers and integrates safety-related risks with other program/project risks as each has a measure of statistical probability of occurrence and could, therefore, positively or negatively impact the eventual outcome. The honest exchange and early notification of concerns are key to productive stakeholder interactions. By cultivating a better understanding of how the PM nominally approaches risk, the system safety professional can most appropriately influence and map safety risks to program/project risks. This "tailoring" of program/project and safety risks is essential for the PM to optimize his/her limited resources associated with risk mitigation actions. By participating in the program/project risk development discussion, the system safety professional can effectively minimize safety-related impacts and ensure program/project success.

Biography

Mr. Nix is a Systems Safety Engineer and Project Manager with APT Research, Inc. in Huntsville, AL. He has been responsible for various areas of safety-related work in APT's business base, including project management and serving as an instructor for APT's System Safety and Software Safety professional development courses. His primary role is system safety support to the Missile Defense Agency (MDA). Mr. Nix holds a M.S. in Missile Systems from the University of Alabama in Huntsville and recently acquired a Project Management Professional (PMP) Certification.

Colonel (Retired) Fellows is the Chief Executive Officer of APT Research, Inc. in Huntsville, AL. He has over 32 years U.S. Army and industry experience in Research & Development, Defense Acquisition, Program Management and Operational Risk & Safety. Prior to joining APT in 2015, he was the Vice President for Programs, DoD Agencies & Commands for Science Applications International Corporation (SAIC). He also managed multiple ACAT 1D weapons and radar systems for the Army and Missile Defense Agency during his military career. He holds a B.S. in Business Management from Brigham Young University, an M.S. in Management from Florida Institute of Technology, and an M.S. in National Resource Strategy from the Industrial College of the Armed Forces. He is Defense Acquisition, level 3 certified and a PMP.

Dr. Hall is the Technical Director of APT Research, Inc. in Huntsville, AL. He has over 33 years of military, technical, and executive experience with 15 years providing executive-level technical and management support within the Safety, Quality, and Mission Assurance disciplines. He holds a B.S. from the U.S. Military Academy, an M.S. in Industrial Engineering (IE) from California Polytechnic State University, and a Ph.D. from Mississippi State University in IE.

References

1. MIL-STD-882E, "Department of Defense Standard Practice, System Safety," 11 May 2012. https://www.system-safety.org/Documents/MIL-STD-882E.pdf
2. *Project Management Book of Knowledge Guide*, 6th Edition, 2017.
3. Merriam-Webster Online Dict. https://www.merriam-webster.com/dictionary/communication
4. *DoD Risk, Issue, and Opportunity Management Guide for Defense Acquisition Programs*, January 2017.

Integrating STAMP-Based Hazard Analysis with MIL-STD-882E Functional Hazard Analysis

A consistent and coordinated process approach to MIL-STD-882E Functional Hazard Analysis

Nicolas H. Malloy
nmalloy@uab.edu
Advanced Safety Engineering and Management Master of Engineering
University of Alabama at Birmingham School of Engineering

Table of Contents

Table of Tables

Table of Figures

Abstract

This research demonstrates the integration of STAMP-Based Hazard Analysis with MIL-STD-882E Functional Hazard Analysis (FHA) and the advantages of using an iterative analysis approach that continually shapes the safety mechanisms of a system throughout the design process. To do this, a mapping exercise was performed which first broke the MIL-STD-882E FHA tasks into their respective elements followed by an allocation of the STAMP processes and STPA steps. As this was being performed rationale was documented that further reinforced the allocations. This information can be used as guidance for performing STAMP-Based Hazard Analysis on an actual system.

There are many benefits to be realized from taking a model-based approach to system design. This is particularly evident in system safety engineering and more specifically hazard analysis. Model based hazard analysis allows for rapid hazard identification and mitigation development through safety requirements and constraints in a real-time environment. Such an approach enables safety practitioners to assess their systems through hypothetical conditions and then observe their potentially adverse behavioral responses. The systems theory derived tops down approach is a new way to perform hazard analysis that can compensate for the inadequacies associated with using dated approaches like Fault and Event Tree Analysis to assess today's complex systems.

1 Introduction

MIL-STD-882E effectively provides high-level descriptions of tasks required to achieve standard compliance but certain tasks would greatly benefit from consistent instructions to support analysis execution. An example of this is the Functional Hazard Analysis (FHA). The FHA provides a point directed list of eight tasking elements that are to be performed to demonstrate that the analysis has been satisfied. Some of these sub-tasks are straight forward while others are not.

For instance, system decomposition must be performed at the beginning of the analysis. Because decomposition is commonly a part of the systems engineering process this task (for the most part) is an easily satisfied objective. In other words, safety practitioners should not be banging their heads against a wall to figure it out. Similarly, the next two elements are intuitive and build upon the information gained during the decomposition. This is achieved by documenting detailed descriptions for each of the functional components and defining their associated interfaces. Despite its straight forwardness, decomposition can go south quickly. This is in fact the basis of argument for providing safety practitioners with a recommended approach like the one proposed in this paper.

The remaining analysis becomes less simplistic with a set of steps in the process that are increasing prone to subjective interpretation. The safety practitioner proceeds with identifying hazards by analyzing the functional components and their associated interfaces. Determining permutations of adverse behavior that introduce hazards will allow the safety practitioner to capture unsafe conditions. But there is no guidance describing how this should be achieved.

An experienced safety practitioner will note that this activity resembles a technique known as, What-if-Analysis. What-If-Analysis focuses on the inter-relational communications that occur between functional components. What-If-Analysis can be a powerful technique, in that it varies the timing (sequencing) of disturbances applied to functional components through targeted sensitivity testing which allows the safety practitioner to better understand the systems response to adverse conditions. What-If-Analysis is not as effective if the practitioner has performed an inadequate decomposition.

Example illustrations of recommended approaches would be helpful to validate the efforts leading up to this point. Unfortunately, What-If-Analysis is not listed as part of the task instruction so applying this approach is based purely upon assumption. This facilitates the struggle, confusion, and over reaching on behalf of the safety practitioner to meet the task description. If the decomposition is in fact flawed the effectiveness and quality of hazard identification and mitigation controls becomes susceptible to serious degradation. A decreasingly safe system ensues.

The MIL-STD-882E FHA activities can be broken into three parts. The first is hazard identification which begins with the before mentioned system decomposition and interface analysis. Next, management of the hazards identified must occur to ensure that they are being handled accordingly. This activity starts with the establishment of a Hazard Tracking Database (HTD). Lastly, in parallel the safety practitioners establish hazard mitigations which are characterized by controls and reflected in safety requirements and constraints that decrease the calculated risk. Their instantiation will reflect the systems safe performance.

Because the FHA tasking element descriptions lack specific instruction safety practitioners may unknowingly perform inadequate safety analyses. Indeterminate guidance allows them to approach system safety analysis in an inconsistent fashion. This means that if individual safety practitioners were each handed the same system design and instructed to perform a MIL-STD-882E FHA they would all likely take different approaches. This of course begs the question, "which approach is correct?"

2 Purpose

This paper intends to demonstrate an approach for integrating a new hazard analysis process and approach with MIL-STD-882E FHA. System-Theoretic Accident Model and Processes (STAMP)-Based Hazard Analysis can be used to improve upon traditional hazard analysis techniques. This new way of thinking was developed to account for the complexity of today's socio-technical systems. STAMP and Systems-Theoretic Process Analysis (STPA) are consistent approaches that utilize stepwise methodology which can be used to analyze the safety significance of any system. They are particularly effective for developing system models, performing safety analysis, and implementing safety through design. All of this is linked directly to STAMP and STPAs collective effectiveness in identifying and understanding system hazards.

The MIL-STD-882E FHA is a foundational analysis that sets the stage for its safety programs instantiation of the standard. It is the cornerstone in a safety programs ability to identify, manage, and control its systems hazards. As such, its correctness proves to determine its completeness throughout the life cycle of the design process. STAMP-Based Hazard Analysis can be used to generate an improved MIL-STD-882E compliant FHA.

3 Method

A new consistent approach in hazard identification adapted for complex systems is needed. To achieve standardization in the process and approach of generating a MIL-STD-882E FHA it is necessary to explore alternative techniques. STAMP-Based Hazard Analysis provides the needed conceptual rigidity and contextual flexibility to perform accurate and complete hazard analysis consistently. It is comprised of the STAMP process and STPA approach and has shown to be successful in performing hazard analysis on systems in a variety of fields. Examples of a few of these are nuclear power, healthcare, automobiles, spacecraft, defense systems, and aviation. Nancy Leveson conducted a research study relevant to this paper where she discusses STAMP and STPAs compliance with MIL-STD-882E which includes FHA. Integrating STAMP-Based Hazard Analysis with MIL-STD-882E FHA is achieved through a simple mapping exercise as illustrated by Figure 1. This exercise traces the processes and approaches of STAMP and STPA to the eight tasking elements.

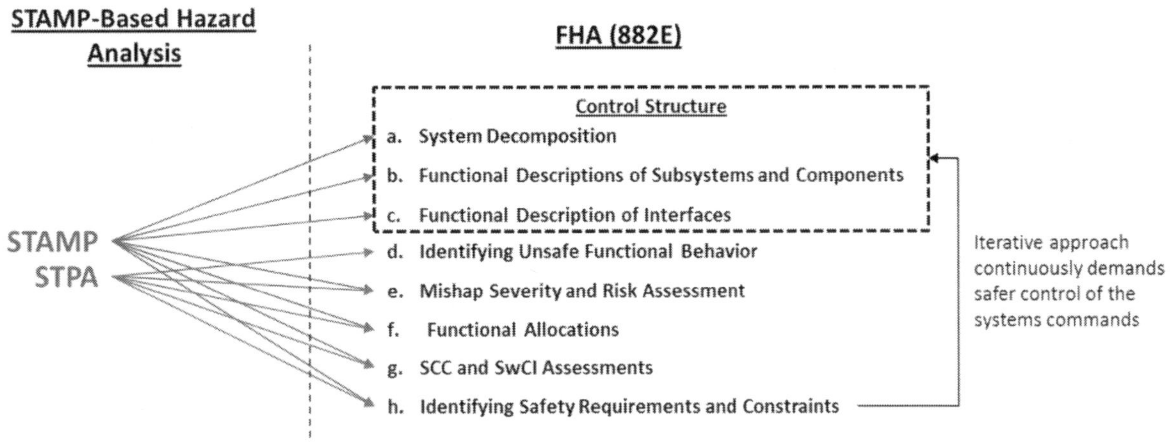

Figure 1 Mapping STAMP-Based Hazard Analysis to MIL-STD-882E FHA

3.1 What is STAMP and STPA?

STAMP changes the emphasis in system safety from preventing failures to enforcing behavioral safety constraints. Component failure accidents are still included, but the conception of causality is extended to include component interaction accidents. Safety is reformulated as a control problem rather than a reliability problem. This change leads to much more powerful and effective ways to engineer safer systems, including the complex sociotechnical systems of most concern today. The three main concepts in this model are safety constraints, hierarchical control structures and process models.[2]

STPA depends upon the establishment of these concepts prior to its own execution and can be used at any stage of the system life cycle. It has the same general goals as any hazard analysis technique: accumulating information about how the behavioral safety constraints, which are derived from the system hazards, can be violated. Depending on when it is used, it provides the information and documentation necessary to ensure the safety constraints are enforced in the system design, development, manufacturing, and operations, including the natural changes in these processes that will occur over time.

STPA uses a functional control diagram and safety requirements, system hazards, and the safety constraints and safety requirements for the component. When STPA is applied to an existing design, this information is available when the analysis process begins. When STPA is used for safety-guided design, only the system-level requirements and constraints may be available at the beginning of the process. In the latter case, these requirements and constraints are refined and traced to individual system components as the iterative design and analysis process proceeds.

Figure 2 depicts a control structure for a generic man/machine system that consists of a Human Operator and two subsystems/components. Their associated interfaces are identified, and further information is provided to indicate some of the commands passing through them.

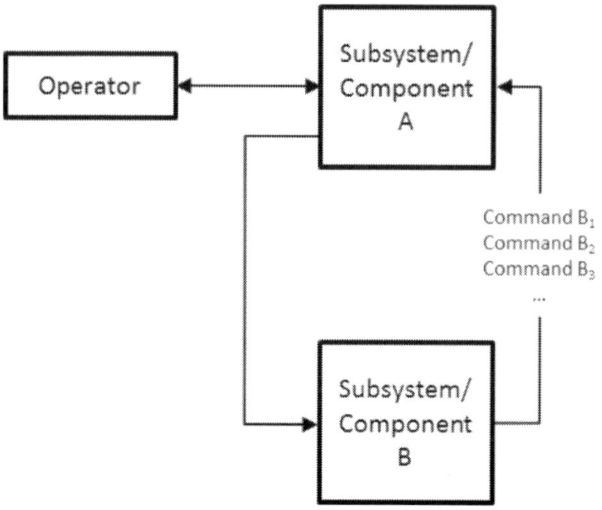

Figure 2 Control Structure for a Generic Man/Machine System

STPA has two main steps:

1. *Identify the potential for inadequate control of the system that could lead to a hazardous state. Hazardous states result from inadequate control or enforcement of the safety constraints, which can occur because:*
    a. *A control action required for safety is not provided or not followed.*
    b. *An unsafe control action is provided.*
    c. *A potentially safe control action is provided too early or too late, that is, at the wrong time or in the wrong sequence.*
    d. *A control action required for safety is stopped too soon or applied too long.*
2. *Determine how each potentially hazardous control action identified in step 1 could occur.*
    a. *For each unsafe control action, examine the parts of the control loop to see if they could cause it. Design controls and mitigation measures if they do not already exist or evaluate existing measures if the analysis is being performed on an existing design. For multiple controllers of the same component or safety constraint, identify conflicts and potential coordination problems.*
    b. *Consider how the designed controls could degrade over time and build in protection, including*
        i. *Management of change procedures to ensure safety constraints are enforced in planned changes.*
        ii. *Performance audits where assumptions underlying the hazards analysis are the preconditions for the operational audits and controls so that unplanned changes that violate the safety constraints can be detected.*
        iii. *Accident and incident analysis to trace anomalies to the hazards and to the system design.*

While the analysis can be performed in one step, dividing the process into discrete steps reduces the analytical burden on the safety engineers and provides a structured process for hazard analysis. The information from the first step (identifying the unsafe control actions) is required to perform the second step (identifying the causes of the unsafe control actions).[2]

3.2 Improving MIL-STD-882E FHA through the Integration of STAMP and STPA

The primary purpose FHA serves is identification and classification of system functions and safety consequences of a functional failure or malfunction. In other words, what are the inherent hazards in the design? This is what STAMP and STPA were designed for. By analyzing the control structure inadequate control actions and their associated hazards are revealed. This allows the safety practitioner to draw correlations between areas of safety significance and non-safety-significance within the system. In doing so further focus can be applied to identifying the consequences of the hazards. Furthermore, in practice as a system begins to take shape the design team can generate safety requirements and constraints to improve its overall safety.

Table 1 captures the analysis results of the mapping exercise depicted by Figure 1. The intention is to show how STAMP and STPA can be integrated to support and in fact improve the FHA tasking elements framework provided in MIL-STD-882E. Note that there are certain aspects of FHA that call out Probabilistic Risk Assessment (PRA) and various software specific assessments that are based on software implementation unique to MIL-STD-882E. Instructions regarding these are contained in Section 4 of the standard and should be referenced to meet their full intent. Details are provided in the table acknowledging the uniqueness's which are accompanied by explanations to support the integration of STAMP and STPA.

Table 1 Terminology

Tasking Element – The alpha designator corresponds to the alpha designator provided in MIL-STD-882E.
MIL-STD-882E FHA Tasking Element Description – The description corresponds to the alpha designator tasking description provided in MIL-STD-882E.
Allocation – The allocation corresponds with the corresponding MIL-STD-882E FHA Tasking Element Description ability to be accomplished by STAMP or STPA.
Rationale – The rationale provides justification pertaining to the corresponding MIL-STD-882E FHA Tasking Element Description and Allocation.

Table 1 Mapping STAMP and STPA to MIL-STD-882E

Tasking Element	**MIL-STD-882E FHA Tasking Element Description**	**Allocation**	**Rationale**
a.	*Decomposition of the system and its related subsystems to the major component level.*[4]	STAMP	Decomposing the system and its related subsystems to the major component level feeds directly into STAMP with the construction of the Control Structure. Also includes early safety Requirements and Constraints development and preliminary identification Hazards and Mishaps.

Tasking Element	MIL-STD-882E FHA Tasking Element Description	Allocation	Rationale
b.	*A functional description of each subsystem and component identified.*[4]	STAMP	Documenting the behavioral characteristics of the system using functional descriptions contributes to STAMP with the continued construction of the Control Structure. Also includes early safety Requirements and Constraints development and preliminary identification of Hazards and Mishaps continue to occur.
c.	*A functional description of interfaces between subsystems and components. Interfaces should be assessed in terms of connectivity and functional inputs and outputs.*[4]	STAMP	Documenting the behavioral characteristics of system interfaces contributes to STAMP and the continued construction of the Control Structure. Also includes early safety Requirements and Constraints development and preliminary identification of Hazards and Mishaps continue to occur.
d.	*Hazards associated with loss of function, degraded function, or malfunction, or functioning out of time or out of sequence for the subsystems, components, and interfaces. The list of hazards should consider the next effect in a possible mishap sequence and the final mishap outcome.*[4]	STPA	STPA step 1 identifies the potential for inadequate control of the system leading to a hazardous state. STPA step 2 considers multiple controllers of the same components and seeks to identify conflicts and potential coordination problems. This aids in identifying next effects and top-level events.
e.	*An assessment of the risk associated with each identified failure of a function, subsystem, or component. Estimate severity, probability, and Risk Assessment Code (RAC) using the process described in Section 4 of 882E.*[4]	STAMP STPA	*STAMP together with STPA identifies the system-level Hazards associated with each function (and unsafe control action) so the classification as to severity comes from the classification of the system level hazards and their associated mishaps.*[1] *STPA can be used to make risk acceptance decisions and to plan mitigations for open safety risks that need to be changed before a system is deployed and field tested.*[2]

Tasking Element	MIL-STD-882E FHA Tasking Element Description	Allocation	Rationale
f.	*An assessment of whether the functions identified are to be implemented in the design hardware, software, or human control interfaces. This assessment should map the functions to MIL-STD-882E their implementing hardware or software components. Functions allocated to software should be mapped to the lowest level of technical design or configuration item prior to coding (e.g., implementing modules or use cases).*[4]	STAMP STPA	Determining how system functionality and components are to be implemented is based on the safety Requirements and Constraints that are developed while the safety practitioner works through STAMP and STPA steps 1 and 2 iteratively. "Like" Commands can also be Functionally Grouped. This can be used to establish traceability between the Functions, Commands, Hazards, Safety Requirements, and Constraints. Example: RTM
g.	*An assessment of Software Control Category (SCC) for each Safety-significant Software Function (SSSF). Assign a Software Criticality Index (SwCI) for each SSSF mapped to the software design architecture.*[4]	STAMP STPA	SCC and SwCI are unique to MIL-STD-882E but the determination for how software functionality is to be implemented is in part based upon the technology needed to support the safety Requirements and Constraints that are developed while the safety practitioner works through STAMP and STPA steps 1 and 2 iteratively.
h.	*A list of requirements and constraints (to be included in the specifications) that, when successfully implemented, will eliminate the hazard, or reduce the risk. These requirements could be in the form of fault tolerance, detection, isolation, annunciation, or recovery.*[4]	STAMP STPA	STAMP begins with the preliminary identification of safety requirements and constraints. Analysis of the system and component hazards identified during STPA steps 1 and 2 aids in the iterative development of the safety Requirements and Constraints necessary to address the unsafe controls leading to hazards.

3.2.1 System Decomposition

STAMP is used as a mechanism by the safety practitioner to understand the decomposition of the system and its related subsystems to the major component level. This lays the framework for the creation of the control structure to be used for STPA. The system must be analyzed functionally from the perspective of both "what the system is documented to do functionally", and "what you think the system can do functionally". The former is an assessment of documented functionality from the functional specifications and the latter is assessed by analyzing the functionality of the physical components of the system. The analysis of the physical attributes of the system is likely to provide insight to "hidden" or undocumented functionality. This is especially true for systems heavily using COTS components.

To ensure that a system is adequately understood safety practitioners should perform three separate yet related decompositions:

- Hardware Level Decomposition
- System Level Decomposition
- Software Level Decomposition (if needed)

In the context of developing an FHA the physical system can viewed as any system consisting of hardware components which in some way interface with the total system. One must consider from a physical design perspective whilst analyzing system functionally that the system itself is likely comprised of multiple subsystems. Figure 3, depicts a generic decomposition system architecture diagram.

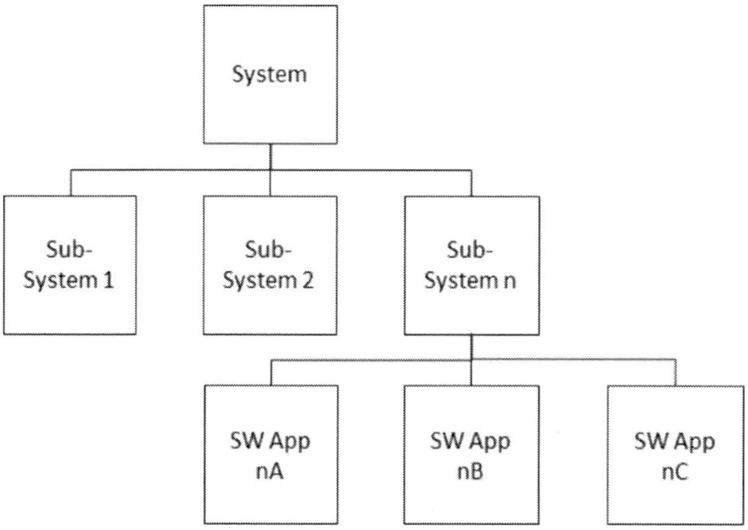

Figure 3 Generic Decomposition Diagram

Establishing physical aspects (physical boundaries) will allow for increased granularity of the system architecture at the functional level. This is the beginning of establishing the delineation between separate physical components and the systems expected behavior (discrete events over time). Software applications are to be grouped and/or categorized so that they correspond with their related upper level physical components. Such lower level detail can be captured once all the physical boundaries of the upper level components have been determined.

Organization of the system architecture involves an approach through which the system design is decomposed and grouped by behavioral functions. These functions (which are conceptualized by the system architecture) represent the structure of the hardware and its software (if present) accompanied by its expected behavior. Categorizing the system by behavioral characteristics allows its basic functionality to be understood more intuitively. Furthermore, if any of the sub-groupings of functions are overly complex on their own continued decomposition can be considered.

Be aware that this is a first step towards the development of control structures. Later, as the FHA progresses an examination of different hazards will occur. Only certain subsets (functional groupings or elements) of the overall structure may be relevant. Therefore, only these will require detailed consideration. When building the structure of a basic control loop it should be noted that the function serves the role of the Controlled Process which receives Controlled Variables, Process Inputs, and experiences Disturbances. These will represent inadequate control actions exercised during the first part of the STPA. Likewise, the Controlled Process will generate and transmit Measured Variables and Process Outputs. These will later become the unsafe conditions which have been created because of the inadequate control actions having been applied.

If software exists in a system, it should also be decomposed. Commonly software functions are referred to as Computer System Configuration Items (CSCI) and are viewed as single entities comprised of a group of software. Software grouped in a manner such that it is defined as a CSCI consists of two or more Computer Software Components (CSCs). CSCs may be further decomposed into other CSCs and Computer Software Units (CSUs). A CSU is an element specified in the design of a CSC. Figure 4 depicts the three levels of decomposition that can be applied to a software function.

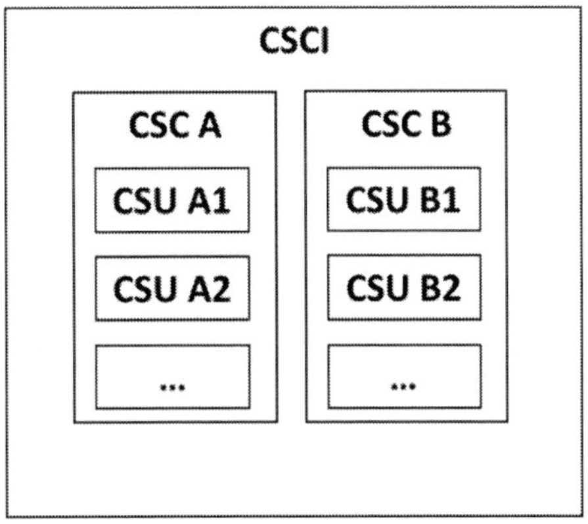

Figure 4 CSCI, CSC, and CSU Decomposition

A software-level functional decomposition is generated in a hierarchical manner that takes into consideration the nesting characteristics of Figure 4. A different perspective in understanding the interactive relationship between CSCs (SW App) and CSUs can be established by developing diagrams like the one depicted in Figure 3.

Such a diagram aids in showing the hierarchical relationship through associated interfaces. These interfaces can provide further insight into the flow of messaging information that is being passed to and from applications throughout the systems software architecture.

Once all necessary information regarding the systems makeup has been determined the construction of the STAMP control structure can begin. Figure 5 depicts a control structure for a generic man/machine system with pronounced green boarders that are intended to place emphasis on its functional components.

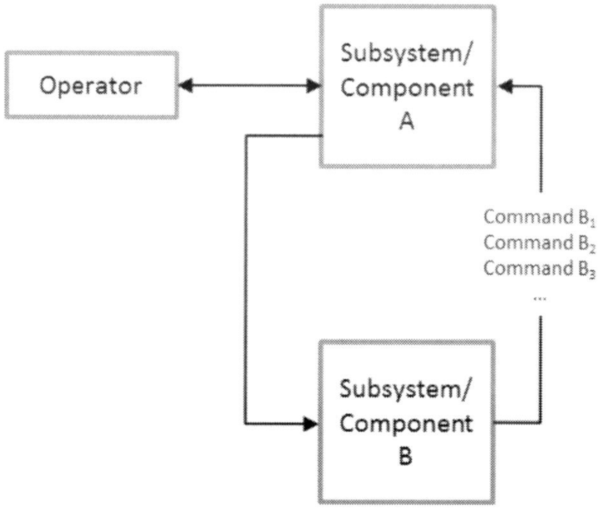

Figure 5 Control Structure for a Generic Man/Machine System (System Decomposition)

3.2.2 Functional Descriptions of Subsystems and Components

The safety practitioner uses the STAMP based processes as a mechanism for determining the functional description of each subsystem and component identified. The functional design description should be completed in parallel with the functional decomposition of the system. It makes sense to do it this way because if the functions are to be defined correctly a proper descriptive understanding of their behavior must be first well documented.

As suggested by the Joint Services - Software Safety Authorities (JS-SSA) Implementation Guide when capturing functional descriptions, there are three things that should be considered:

- *First, the identification of what the element can or should do functionally. Creating a detailed list can be helpful in developing incorrect process models at a later point.*
- *Second, a comparison of the functionality identified with the documented functionality of the functional specification followed by a reconciliation of the two lists.*
- *Last, identification of any functionality that is identified in hardware literature or the performance specification to determine if there are "hidden" or unintended functions residing in the system.*

As the practitioner works through this exercise a table can be used to capture the physical boundaries, functional decomposition (behavior), associated software decomposition, and corresponding functional descriptions. Figure 6 depicts a control structure for a generic man/machine system with pronounced green shading that is intended to place emphasis on its functional description of the system components.

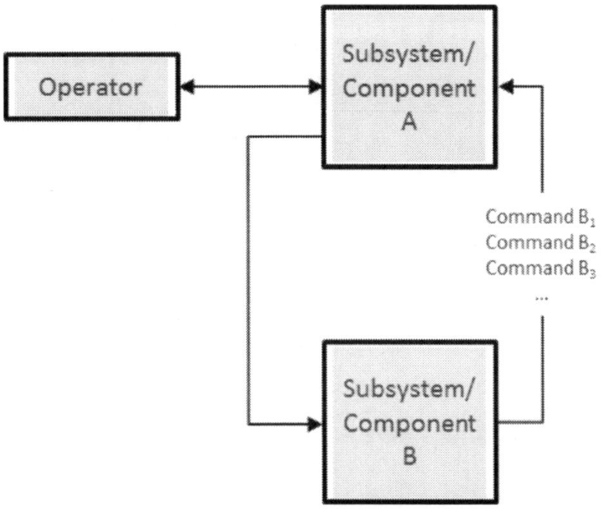

Figure 6 Control Structure for a Generic Man/Machine System (Functional Descriptions of Subsystems and Components)

This is a convenient artifact that can be used for other applications in the future which serve in meeting the expected outputs of various Level of Rigor (LoR) tasking. One such example of reuse is as contribution to the development of a Requirements Traceability Matrix (RTM). Additional details regarding the contents and guidance for creating an RTM can be found in the Joint Software System Safety Engineering Handbook (JSSSEH).

3.2.3 Functional Descriptions of Interfaces

The STAMP based processes can be used as a mechanism for documenting the functional description of interfaces between subsystems and components. Interfaces should be assessed in terms of connectivity and functional inputs and outputs. Interfaces amount to be the medium through which subsystems and components communicate. In some cases, these lines of communication are one directional while under different circumstances they may be bi directional. Identifying the interfaces that exist within the control structure is the final step required to prepare it for STPA step 1.

Figure 7 depicts a control structure for a generic man/machine system with pronounced green shading that is intended to place emphasis on its functional description of the system interfaces.

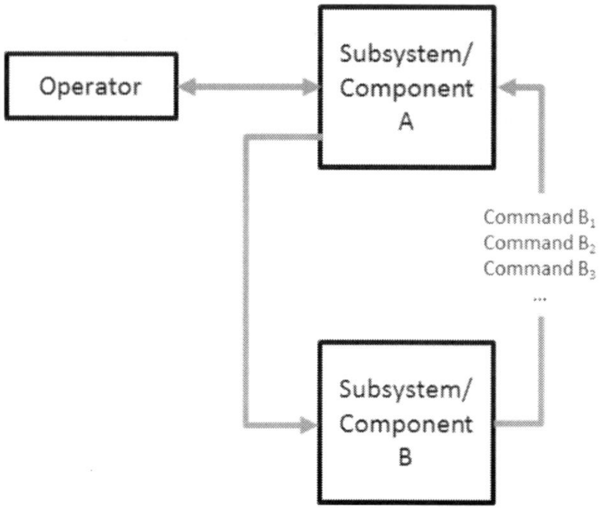

Figure 7 Control Structure for a Generic Man/Machine System (Functional Descriptions of Interfaces)

3.2.4 Identifying Unsafe Functional Behavior

STPA step 1 is used by the safety practitioner to determine hazards associated with loss of function, degraded function, or malfunction, or functioning out of time or out of sequence for the subsystems, components, and interfaces. The list of hazards should consider the next effect in a possible mishap sequence and the final mishap outcome. Performing interface analysis aids the safety practitioner in understanding the consequences associated with the presence of adverse control actions. This is achieved through the application of What-if-Analysis which is a technique that varies the sequence of signal initiation. In the same way that unsafe control actions can be determined unsecure control actions can be determined as well.

Unsafe control actions can also be associated with security implications. Modifying the context of the analysis to consider unsafe control actions linked to security vulnerabilities provides the practitioner with an opportunity to apply hypothetical point directed system penetrations. This reveals the systems theoretical response and allows mitigations to be developed in the form of security features. Security requirements and constraints characterize these features. While safety and security are contextually different conceptually they can equally contribute to mishaps or in general terms loss.

Table 2 shows the four categories of unsafe control actions that can be applied to a control process. The green shading is intended to place emphasis on the types of unsafe control actions that can occur for any given system.

Table 2 Identifying Unsafe Control Actions

Action	Not Providing Causes Hazard	Providing Causes Hazard	Incorrect Timing / Order	Stopped Too Soon / Applied too long

3.2.5 Mishap Severity and Risk Assessment

MIL-STD-882E instructs the safety practitioner to perform an assessment of the risk associated with each identified failure of a function, subsystem, or component. Additionally, it requires that the safety practitioner estimate severity, probability, and Risk Assessment Code (RAC) using the process it describes in its own Section 4. These activities are clearly not identified as being a part of either STAMP or STPA but Figure 8 attempts to demonstrate a potential approach to using information obtained through STAMP-Based Hazard Analysis to determine the probability and severity assessments required to develop a risk assessment.

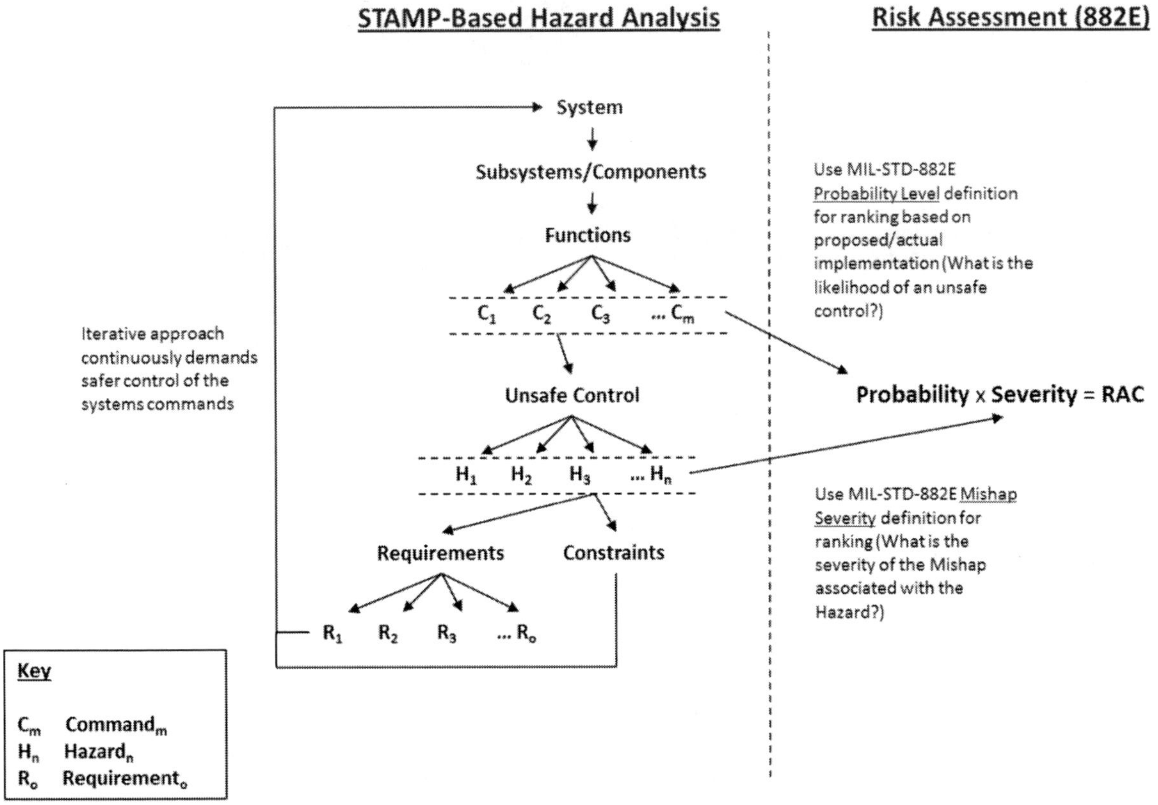

Figure 8 STAMP-Based Risk Assessment

STPA and STAMP can be used to make risk acceptance decisions and to plan mitigations for open safety risks that need to be changed before a system is deployed and field tested. Additionally, it should be acknowledged that Hazards are not just the result of functional failure or malfunction. STPA identifies the system-level hazards associated with each function (and unsafe control action) so the classification as to severity comes from the classification of the system level hazards and their associated mishaps.[2]

As the safety practitioner goes through the iterative STAMP and STPA process they can begin assigning mishap severities and probabilities of occurrence (qualitative or quantitative) to the hazards identified. As the safety requirements and constraints are developed educated design decisions can be made to alter the control structure which will in theory improve the safety of the system. It should also be mentioned that the safety requirements and constraints are intended to reduce the likelihood of occurrence through their implementation. For the readers' clarity Figure 9 depicts the Risk Assessment Matrix found in Section 4 of MIL-STD-882E. Through the identification of a hazards probability of occurrence and mishap severity a ranked risk can be calculated and used as a method for describing the magnitude of risk.

RISK ASSESSMENT MATRIX				
SEVERITY / PROBABILITY	Catastrophic (1)	Critical (2)	Marginal (3)	Negligible (4)
Frequent (A)	High	High	Serious	Medium
Probable (B)	High	High	Serious	Medium
Occasional (C)	High	Serious	Medium	Low
Remote (D)	Serious	Medium	Medium	Low
Improbable (E)	Medium	Medium	Medium	Low
Eliminated (F)	Eliminated			

Figure 9 Risk Assessment Matrix [4]

PRA as it pertains to complex systems is inherently flawed but in order to maintain compliance with MIL-STD-882E it is necessary to complete the risk assessment tasking element. The information collected while performing STAMP-Based Hazard Analysis can be combined with risk assessment specific data and managed using a traceability matrix like the one provided in Table 3.

Table 3 Risk Assessment Traceability Matrix

Probability x Severity = RAC

Subsystem/ Component	Function	Command	Unsafe Control	Hazard	Severity	Probability	RAC
• *Electromechanical,* • *Digital,* • *Human, or* • *Social*[2]	A well order set of unique commands	A specific order issued by a Subsystem/ Component	A specific order issued by a Subsystem/Component that contributes/leads to a hazard	A real or potential condition that could lead to a mishap	An event or series of events that result in a loss	A quantitative or qualitative assessment used to express the likelihood of an events occurrence	An assessment comprised of mishap probability and severity

3.2.6 Function Allocations

STAMP and STPA are used by the safety practitioner to perform an assessment of whether the functions identified are to be implemented in the design hardware, software, or human control interfaces. This assessment should map the functions to MIL-STD-882E their implementing hardware or software components. Functions allocated to software should be mapped to the lowest level of technical design or configuration item prior to coding (e.g., implementing modules or use cases). Figure 10 illustrates a proposed approach for depicting the functional decomposition of a system subsystem/component down to the command level.

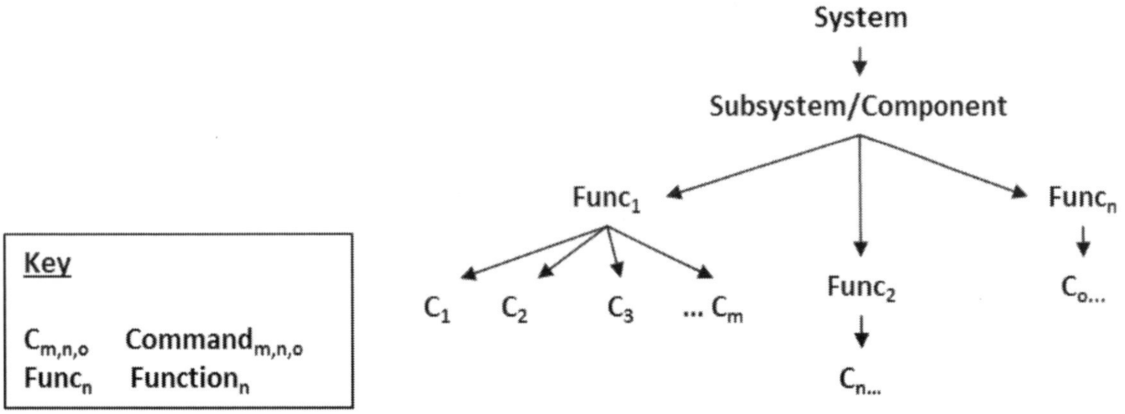

Figure 10 Functional Decomposition

When embarking down the path of FHA the practitioner can easily become lost in the breakdown of the eight tasking elements. What must be done to satisfy them? Is there an order of operations that works best? And lastly, how do they relate to each other? In other words – are their shared dependencies between tasking elements and does that drive a sequence that which they need to occur? Advance knowledge of this can aid in the efficiency of the exercise. Case and point – certain steps can be performed in parallel which can help the safety practitioner manage the process more efficiently. To be successful in the analysis these questions must be understood.

Depending on the complexity of the system there can be several factors driving its composition. Today's systems reflect *both complex technical and social processes*[2]. The relationship between man, machine, and software has led to the development of socio-technical systems that represent a mixture of people, technology, and their environment.

The first three elements of FHA instruct the practitioner to perform detailed system decomposition. The goal of this exercise is to develop a control structure that captures the systems characteristics. A common mistake that safety practitioners fall prey to is misrepresenting their functions. Often it is easy to assume that individual system inputs and outputs (signals) are functions. This is not the case. Signals represent a single result that is dependent upon specific system processing but not a function per say. A simplified way of conceptualizing this is by taking a mathematical approach. In mathematics, a set is a well-defined collection of distinct objects. The objects within the set are referred to as elements. Thus, to complete the comparison – a system function can be characterized as a well-defined collection of distinct signals.

The development of functions begins first by defining the characteristics of the systems control structure. The controls are to be identified by drawing a control structure that identifies each of the subsystems that make up the greater system. If the system depends on operator of environmental inputs these should be represented as separate subsystems. The subsystems are the controls within the control structure. Such an approach is simple, straight forward and conveniently enables others who are less familiar with the system to gain a high-level perception of its composition. The practitioner must define the interfaces between the controls to complete the control structure. These interfaces carry control actions that are representative of the stimulus outputted by the controls. Figure 11 depicts a generic control structure.

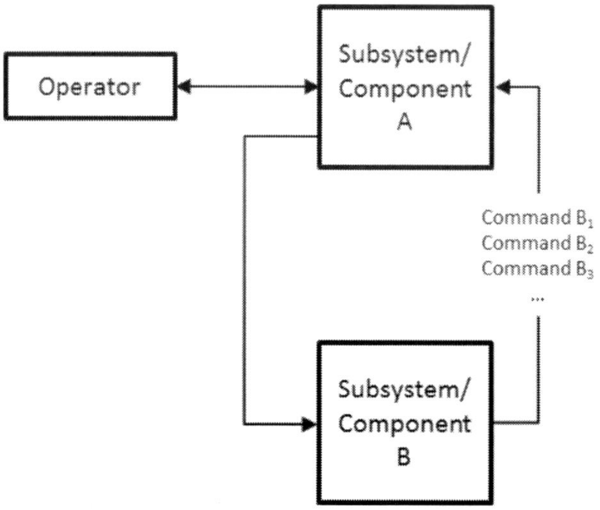

Figure 11 Generic Control Structure

Once the control structure has been created the safety practitioner can begin establishing functional categories by grouping control actions together based on their shared intent. The functional categories will ultimately become the system functions. This is necessary for establishing traceability to the hazards identified during the first step of STPA. Figure 12 depicts a generic functional hazard traceability exercise.

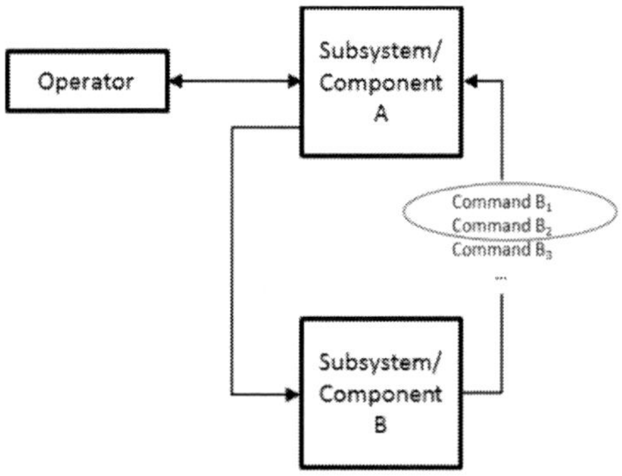

Function	Command	Control Interface Implementation	Software Only		
			CSCI	CSC	CSU
$Func_1$	Command B_1	• Hardware, • Software, or • Human			
	Command B_2				
$Func_2$	Command B_3				
	Command B_4				
	Command B_5				
	Command B_6				
$Func_n$	Command B_7				

Key

$Func_n$	**$Function_n$**
CSCI	**Computer Software Configuration Item**
CSC	**Computer Software Component**
CSU	**Computer Software Unit**

Figure 12 Functional Hazard Traceability Matrix

Greater granularity can be established by taking the traceability and integrating additional layers of detail that pertain specifically to how the functions are to be implemented. Will the function be hardware? Is the function intended to be a combination of hardware and software? Perhaps the functional will be reflective of a human characteristic? Further detail into the relationship between system functions and their implementation will allow the practitioner to specify safety-significant hardware, software, and operator controls through the already established hazards. Careful consideration can be applied to detailed implementation with such an approach.

3.2.7 Software Control Category and Software Criticality Index Assessments

STPA step 1 is used to determine an assessment of Software Control Category (SCC) for each Safety-significant Software Function (SSSF). Assign a Software Criticality Index (SwCI) for each SSSF mapped to the software design architecture. Every step of the way STPA lays the framework necessary to perform an FHA. Its order of operations allows for straight forward execution. Additionally, the simplicity of its format makes it easy for safety practitioners to use the process on new and legacy systems alike.

Table 4 depicts the Software Safety Criticality Matrix and Level of Rigor (LoR) Tasking provided in Section 4 of MIL-STD-882E.

Table 4 Software Safety Criticality Matrix [4]

SOFTWARE SAFETY CRITICALITY MATRIX				
	SEVERITY CATEGORY			
SOFTWARE CONTROL CATEGORY	Catastrophic (1)	Critical (2)	Marginal (3)	Negligible (4)
1	SwCI 1	SwCI 1	SwCI 3	SwCI 4
2	SwCI 1	SwCI 2	SwCI 3	SwCI 4
3	SwCI 2	SwCI 3	SwCI 4	SwCI 4
4	SwCI 3	SwCI 4	SwCI 4	SwCI 4
5	SwCI 5	SwCI 5	SwCI 5	SwCI 5

SwCI	Level of Rigor Tasks
SwCI 1	Program shall perform analysis of requirements, architecture, design, and code; and conduct in-depth safety-specific testing.
SwCI 2	Program shall perform analysis of requirements, architecture, and design; and conduct in-depth safety-specific testing.
SwCI 3	Program shall perform analysis of requirements and architecture; and conduct in-depth safety-specific testing.
SwCI 4	Program shall conduct safety-specific testing.
SwCI 5	Once assessed by safety engineering as Not Safety, then no safety specific analysis or verification is required.

For systems in which software is present STPA aids in identifying where safety-significant functionality resides. This information when combined with the appropriate SCC and Mishap Severity can be used to determine the SwCI and associated LoR tasking that is required per MIL-STD-882E. This provides the safety practitioner with an opportunity to apply code, architecture, and requirements analysis and safety specific testing if deemed necessary by the LoR tasking instructions. The JSSSEH describes these tasks in detail. Additionally, it defines software process, standards, and guidance in the form of requirements. These are to be interpreted as recommended best practices and are tailorable to meet the needs of any given system. The information collected while performing STAMP-Based Hazard Analysis can be combined with SwCI assessment specific data and managed using a traceability matrix like the one provided in Table 5.

Table 5 SwCI Assessment Traceability Matrix

SCC x Severity = SwCI → LoR

Subsystem/ Component	**Function**	**Command**	SCC	**Unsafe Control**	**Hazard**	Severity	SwCI	LoR
• *Electromechanical,* • *Digital,* • *Human, or* • *Social*[2]	A well order set of unique commands	A specific order issued by a Subsystem/ Component	The degree of software control (Autonomous, Semi-Autonomous, Redundant Fault Tolerant, Influential, or Not Involved)	A specific order issued by a Subsystem/ Component that contributes/ leads to a hazard	A real or potential condition that could lead to a mishap	An event or series of events that result in a loss	An event or series of events that result in a loss	*Depth and breadth of software analysis and verification activities necessary to provide a sufficient level of confidence*[3]

SCC and SwCI are unique to MIL-STD-882E but its calculation can be treated as a function of the STPA outputs. Figure 13 attempts to demonstrate a potential approach to using information obtained through STAMP-Based Hazard Analysis to determine the SCC and severity assessments required to develop a SwCI assessment.

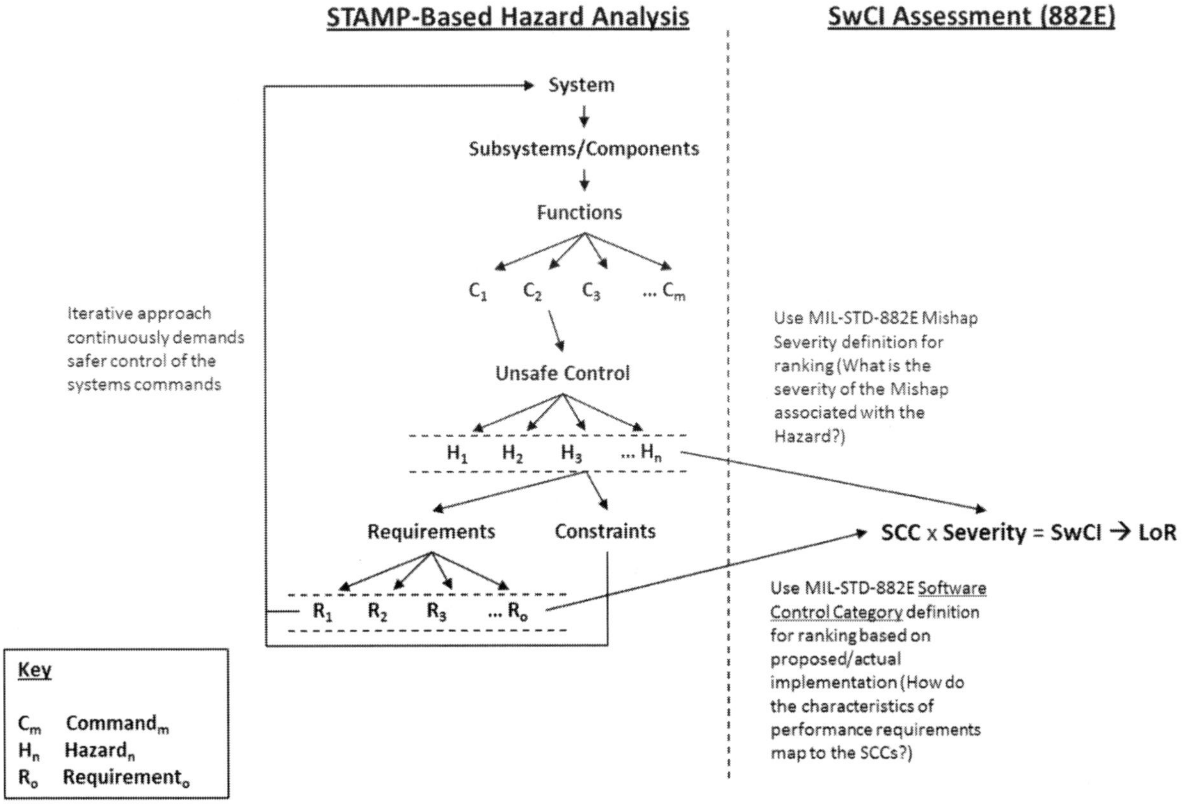

Figure 13 STAMP-Based SwCI Assessment

Mishaps are determined throughout the execution of STPA step 1 to aid in the determination of unsafe control actions and their associated hazards. Assessments of the documented mishaps in accordance with MIL-STD-882E guidance are required. Combining the SCCA and Mishap Severity assessment provides the safety practitioner with the data needed to calculate the SwCI and determine the associated LoR tasking required for standard compliance.

3.2.8 Identifying Safety Requirements and Constraints

STPA step 2 is used to develop a list of requirements and constraints (to be included in the specifications) that, when successfully implemented, will eliminate the hazard, or reduce the risk. These requirements could be in the form of fault tolerance, detection, isolation, annunciation, or recovery. The list of potential hazards threatening the safety of a system is the driving force behind the development and implementation of safety requirements and design constraints.

Once the hazards have been identified and documented the practitioner can begin to determine how they will be prevented. This is accomplished through the hierarchy of controls in traditional system safety theory. The hierarchy of controls is an engineering approach used to manage risk at a level that is reasonably practicable. This is accomplished through the utilization of a series of six controls which are elaborated upon in *Table 6.*

Table 6 Hierarchy of Controls[6]

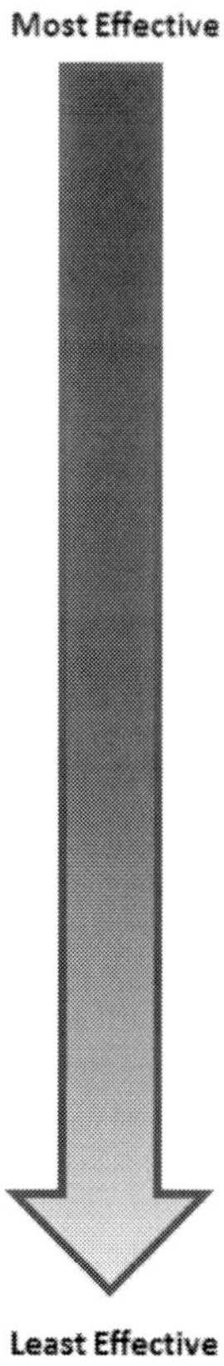

Controls	Examples
Elimination	Design to eliminate Hazards, such as falls, hazardous materials, noise, confined spaces, and manual material handling
Substitution	Substitute for less hazardous material Reduce energy. For example: Lower speed, force, amperage, pressure, temperature, and noise.
Engineering Controls	Ventilation systems Machine guarding Sound enclosures Circuit breakers Platforms and guard railing Interlocks Lift tables, conveyors, and balancers
Warnings	Signs Backup alarms Beepers Horns Labels
Administrative Controls	*Procedures* Safe job procedures Rotation of workers Safety equipment inspections Changing work schedule *Training* Hazard Communication Training Confined space entry
Personal Protective Equipment	Safety glasses Hearing protection Face shields Safety harnesses and lanyards Gloves Respirators

The examples provided in *Table 6* are intended to create a sense for what safety design constraints are seeking to achieve. A constraint is a statement of restriction that modifies a requirement or set of requirements by limiting the range of acceptable solutions. In a socio-technical system it should not be surprising that design constraints associated to system performance, operability and personal protection are present. When considering the implementation of the controls it is evident that the preferred approach is hazard elimination. This can drive cost increases, so it may be decided that less effective approaches will be exercised to reduce the associated risk to an acceptable level.

Maintaining the documented risks through a traceability matrix is an effective approach to keeping track of the hazards present in a systems design and the safety design constraints that have been developed to address them. The information collected throughout the iterative execution of STAMP-Based Hazard Analysis can be managed using a traceability matrix like the one provided in Table 7.

Table 7 Safety Requirements and Constraints Traceability Matrix

Subsystem/ Component	Function	Command	Unsafe Control	Hazard	Mishap	Safety Requirement	Constraint	Requirement Type
• *Electromechanical,* • *Digital,* • *Human, or* • *Social*[2]	A well order set of unique commands	A specific order issued by a Subsystem/ Component	A specific order issued by a Subsystem/Component that contributes/leads to a hazard	A real or potential condition that could lead to a mishap	An event or series of events that result in a loss	*Derived from the mission or reason for the systems existence*[2]	*Represents acceptable ways the system can achieve mission goals*[2]	• *Fault tolerance,* • *Detection,* • *Isolation,* • *Annunciation, or recovery.*[3]

System-level constraints are refined and allocated to each component during the systems engineering decomposition process.[2] it's possible that as the design process progresses constraints may conflict with each other. There is great value in this because *identifying these types of conflicts early in the design process will lead to better solutions. Choices may be more limited later when it may not be possible or practical to change the early decisions*[2]. Ideally, as a system is developed and then further refined through more targeted design decisions the safety requirements and constraints will mature with the obvious result being a safer system.

4 Conclusion

STAMP-Based Hazard Analysis provides the needed conceptual rigidity and contextual flexibility to perform accurate and complete FHA consistently. It is especially useful for the safety practitioner to have at their disposal an approach to hazard analysis that is constructed upon iterative steps. These steps and their repetition add consistency and repeatability. It also enables safety practitioners to easily delegate work to associated team members without the burden of excessive tutelage being required.

The mapping Exercise works. Using a table to break down the eight MIL-STD-882E FHA tasking elements allows for easy traceability from the appropriate STAMP-Based Hazard Analysis process to an associated tasking element. There are certain tasking elements which call out PRA and various software (functional control) specific assessments that are based on software implementation and unique to MIL-STD-882E. Although, this is not a problem considering that these assessments can be influenced by the information captured from the STAMP-Based Hazard Analysis approach.

This mapping exercise should be used as the basis for generating a document that serves to instantiate STAMP-Based Hazard Analysis to perform MIL-STD-882E FHA. In doing so safety practitioners would be provided with the continued flexibility that MIL-STD-882E is intended to offer along with the strength of a consistent hazard analysis approach. Recognizing a consistent approach for the FHA in MIL-STD-882E would ensure that all safety practitioners can begin their safety programs on the right foot.

5 References

1. DoD. (2012). *Department of Defense Standard Practice: System Safety.* Washinton DC.: Department of Defense (DoD).

2. Kotter, J. P. (2012). *Leading Change.* Boston, Massachusetts: Harvard Business Review Press.

3. Leveson, N. (2011). *Engineering a Safer World: Systems Thinking Applied to Safety.* Cambridge, Massachusetts: The MIT Press.

4. Leveson, N. (2016). *STPA Compliance with Army Safety Standards and Comparison with SAE ARP 4761.* Cambridge, Massachusetts: The MIT Press.

5. Young, W., & Leveson, N. (2014). Inside Risks: An Integrated Approach to Safety and Security Based on Systems Theory. *Communications of the ACM,* 1-5.

6. Bidez, M. W. (n.d.). Module 1a: Fundemental Concepts ASEM 610. Birmingham, Alabama, United States.

Using Formal Notations to Augment a Hazard Analysis Method

Fryad M. Rashid, MSc; Clemson University/School of Computing; Clemson, SC, USA

John D. McGregor, PhD; Clemson University/School of Computing; Clemson, SC, USA

Keywords: Error ontology, Hazard Analysis, Safety-Critical Systems

Abstract

Safety-critical systems are those systems whose failure could result in loss of life. For that reason, it needs specific development activities in the software development life cycle to ensure that the system will operate safely. The overall objective of this research is to develop a theoretical framework that identifies unsafe functional behavior for each component in the system. Current safety analysis methods do not use formal methods to find hazardous conditions in a design. We provide guidance concerning mathematical notations to formalize an error ontology used in the architecture descriptions of systems represented in AADL (Architecture Analysis and Design Language) and to improve the rigor of STPA (Systems-Theoretic Process Analysis), a hazard analysis method. In this study, we investigated how a formalized error ontology could assist in identifying unsafe behavior. The ontology can aid in identifying mathematical expressions for each error flow in the canonical feedback control loop architecture. The results of our studies have shown that providing a formal notation for the feedback control loop and providing formal specification for the error ontology lead to finding hazards in the operational system context that other methods miss. By augmenting STPA with an error ontology described in a formal notation, we are able to find more hazards.

Introduction

Development of safety-critical systems requires an explicit design to manage variations, component failures and emergent behavior between system components resulting in hazards. Process control architectures are the core of safety-critical systems used for defining process control variables and computing their change. Based on those variations, the systems can be classified into two types: open-loop and closed-loop. The open-loop system performs a function on the input variable to determine how to control the process. For example, for a lamp, the output of the system is light and the switch is the controller of the lamp. Any change in light has no effect on the on-off position of the switch or its controlling action. But, the closed-loop system measures changes in the output variable and feeds it back as an input variable into the system. Home heating systems and cruise control systems are examples of closed-loop systems (Bergen, 2004).

This paper describes an approach to providing a description for each open-loop component in the canonical feedback control loop architecture based on a functional notation and evaluation theory. Also, we describe an error ontology in the form of algebraic notations to describe a relationship among the component functions and different types of errors. This will allow us to augment the current accepted standard, STPA (System-Theoretic Process Analysis) (Leveson, 2011), with a theoretical framework which consists of component functions and error event conditions described in a formal notation to identify hazards in the feedback control loop that other methods miss.

The main reason for doing this research is to augment the hazard analysis processes of STPA making the process more comprehensive to uncover additional hazards and to reduce the reliance on human expertise. STPA identifies hazardous control actions based on the values of the process model variables which are used to create safety constraints for the controller. To identify hazards, each relevant value will be examined to determine the context of the control action. This context will be used by the controller to decide which command to send. If one of the existing values in the process model is not compatible or reliable within the control action context, that action can be considered an unsafe action. From an architecture perspective, what will happen if the value/variable is not defined or missed in that context? Does it lead to missing safety constraints for the system? How does STPA solve this problem? For modeling the system, we need to know the specific information about each component in the feedback control loop such as functions, inputs, outputs, variables, and values. In addition, we need to know specifically how the process model in the controller makes a decision based on the existing variables and their values.

Specifically, operation of the safety-critical system can be expressed as a function relating system inputs to outputs. There is a relationship among inputs and outputs where each output value will be related to one or more input values. The system consists of components whose interaction achieves the function of the component. When the system is working correctly, it means that the system satisfies all functional requirements. This, however, does not mean the system is safe. The system should be analyzed regarding the safety aspects and verified according to its safety requirements.

The overall objective of this research is to identify execution flows that produce erroneous values that can lead to the component failing to satisfy its functional requirements. This allows us to identify unsafe functional behavior for each component in the system. We need to identify safety constraints for unsafe functions because any unsafe behavior in the function of the component should be mitigated by safety requirements to ensure that the system is safe.

The primary contribution of this work is a method to augment STPA with an error ontology described using formal notations and expressions. This will allow us to identify the unsafe behavior of a component based on certain criteria for existing application examples, build expressions to specify input / output / functionality for each component in the feedback control loop, identify unsafe functional behavior finding more hazardous possibilities using the error ontology and identify mathematical expressions for each error flow. The augmented method is used to help stakeholders or safety analysts during the hazard analysis process. Formal notations and expressions are created in the canonical feedback control loop architecture and are used to find additional unsafe possibilities in the operational system context. Finding hazardous possibilities before development of the system improves confidence that the system will behave correctly when it faces hazardous conditions.

Background

In this section, we give background on current hazard analysis approaches and error ontologies that provide information about error types.

Systems-Theoretic Process Analysis (STPA): STPA is a top-down hazard analysis approach built on the Systems-Theoretic Accident Model and Process (STAMP). The major idea behind this approach is to investigate an accident before it occurs. The main goal is to identify potential causes of accidents, that is, scenarios that may lead to losses, so they can be controlled or eliminated in the system design or operations before damage happens. In a nutshell, it provides scenarios to control and mitigate the hazards in the system design. The method consists of four steps to provide scenarios (Abdulkhaleq and Wagner, 2013):

(1) The stakeholder establishes fundamental analyses to identify accidents and the hazards associated with those accidents.
(2) The stakeholder designs a feedback control loop for the system to identify major components such as sensors, controllers, actuators, and the controlled process.
(3) The stakeholder identifies unsafe control actions that could lead to hazardous states. The stakeholder can use the control table to identify unsafe control actions and can translate it to corresponding safety constraints.
(4) The stakeholder identifies causal factors for the unsafe control actions. The safety analyst determines how each hazardous control action could occur by identifying the process model variables for the controller in the feedback control loop and analyze each path to find out how each hazard could occur.

Error Ontology: The error ontology, defined in the Error Annex for AADL, represents error types in a hierarchical structure to support hazard analysis. It provides the concept of error type to characterize the types of errors to be propagated. It presents an error event for an activated fault type and presents an error behavior state for each failure mode type. The error type can be described as a categorical label to characterize the type of error declarations in error propagations, error events, error behavior states, error flows, and error containment. Also, the label is used to characterize condition declarations for state transitions, detections, and outgoing error propagations. The stakeholders can use error types to describe how the components could fail and to associate with error events. For instance, the effect of a sensor failure might be that it dispatches an incorrect reading (value error), it misses a reading (item omission), or it does not provide any readings (service omission). These effects can be caused by different factors like overheating, radiation, and low power. The error ontology classifies errors into six major error types (Feiler and et-al, 2016):

(1) *Service Errors:* Represent errors which are related to delivering service for items. Service errors can be categorized as omission errors, which represent no service delivered for the items (such as loss of a message or command), and commission errors, which represent unexpected service provided for the items (such as unintended incoming data).
(2) *Value Errors:* Represent errors which are related to value domain of a service. Value errors can be categorized as value errors for individual service items like out of range sensor reading, value errors for sequences of service items like bounded value change, and value errors related to the service as a whole like out of calibration.
(3) *Timing Errors:* Represent errors which are related to the time domain of a service. Timing errors can be categorized as individual service items like early/late item delivery, timing errors for sequence of service items like rate errors, and timing errors related to the service as a whole like early/delayed services.

(4) *Replication Errors:* Represent errors which are related to delivery of replicated services. For example, replicated service items delivered for one recipient or to multiple recipients.
(5) *Concurrency Errors:* Represent errors which are related to behavior of concurrent systems like executing tasks concurrently to access shared resources. Errors are distinguished between race condition errors and mutual exclusion errors.
(6) *Access Control Errors:* Represent errors which are related to operation of access control services like authentication and authorization errors.

Architecture Discussion

The heart of safety-critical systems is a feedback control loop architecture used to analyze the safety of the system. We wish to improve the safety of such systems by introducing a more thorough safety analysis for system development. Figure 1 shows the feedback control loop annotated with expressions written in the formal notation. The figure consists of four component types: sensors, controllers, actuators, and controlled processes. These components have incoming and outgoing variables used to send and receive information. For example, measured variables (*Vme*) are used to send information from the sensor to the controller in the form of measured values of the attributes, control actions (*CA*) are the output of the controller and can be considered a command to the actuator, manipulated variables (*Vma*) are the output of the actuator and are used to control the behavior of the controlled process, controlled variables (*Vc*) are the output of the controlled process and are used to monitor the actual behavior of the controlled process and update the information read by the sensor.

In addition, the components have functions to provide a relationship among input and output variables: **First**, sensor functions ($Fs(Vc)=Vme$) can provide a relationship among controlled and measured variables, reading values of the attributes and updating the values. **Second**, controller functions ($Fc(Vme, F_{PM}(Var, Val, Cond)) = CA$) describe the relationship among measured variables (*Vme*) as an input to the controller and control actions (*CA*) as an output of the controller. The controller functions can be used to take input from the sensor, process it, and make a decision to give a command to the actuator. The controller has a mental model function, also known as the process model function (F_{PM}), which can be used to determine what control action is needed based on receiving the content of the measured variables. The mental model function ($F_{PM}(Var, Val, Cond)$) has three important elements: (*Var*) is the set of variables which are used by the process model, (*Val*) is the set of values that can be used by the variables and (*Cond*) is the set of conditions that can be used by the process model to make a decision. The conditions are the values expected for the measured variables by the process model function. The output of the controller (i.e *CA*) depends on the process model decision, or the condition, where: $\{\forall CA: CA \rightarrow True \text{ iff } Cond \rightarrow True\}$ means the control action is safe if and only if the condition is true. Otherwise, the control action is inadequate and can become an unsafe action. Also, in the controller we have some relationship among variables such as: $\{Vme \in Var\}$ means measured variables of the sensor are one of the elements defined by the process model variables, $\{\{Var, Val\} \in Cond\}$ means the process model make a decision based on the defined variables and their values, and $\{F_{PM} \subseteq Fc\}$ means the process model function is a part of the controller function. The controller has a duration condition $\{\forall CA: TCA=\{MinT_{CA}, MaxT_{CA}\}\}$ which can be described as the minimum and maximum time for each duration of control action (T_{CA}). **Third**, the actuator function ($FA(CA)=Vma$) can build a relationship among the control actions and manipulated variables to follow controller instructions and execute the commands. **Fourth**, the controlled process function ($F_{CP}(Vma)=Vc$) can make a relationship among manipulated variables and controlled variables to implement the controller's decision and update the information of the sensor through the controlled variables. **Fifth**, we have a faulty component identifier (*INTF*) to show that the component will deliver incorrect information to the next component and the faulty component will become a source of error propagation, where $\{INTF \in DC\}$ means (*INTF*) is in the set of detection conditions (*DC*). Also, the result of the faulty component is an error (*Err*). The error has an effect on the component's behavior. If the error propagates to the other components, it may or may not lead to unsafe interaction among components, and it may or may not cause hazards. $\{Err \in EO\}$ means (*EO*) is in the AADL error ontology.

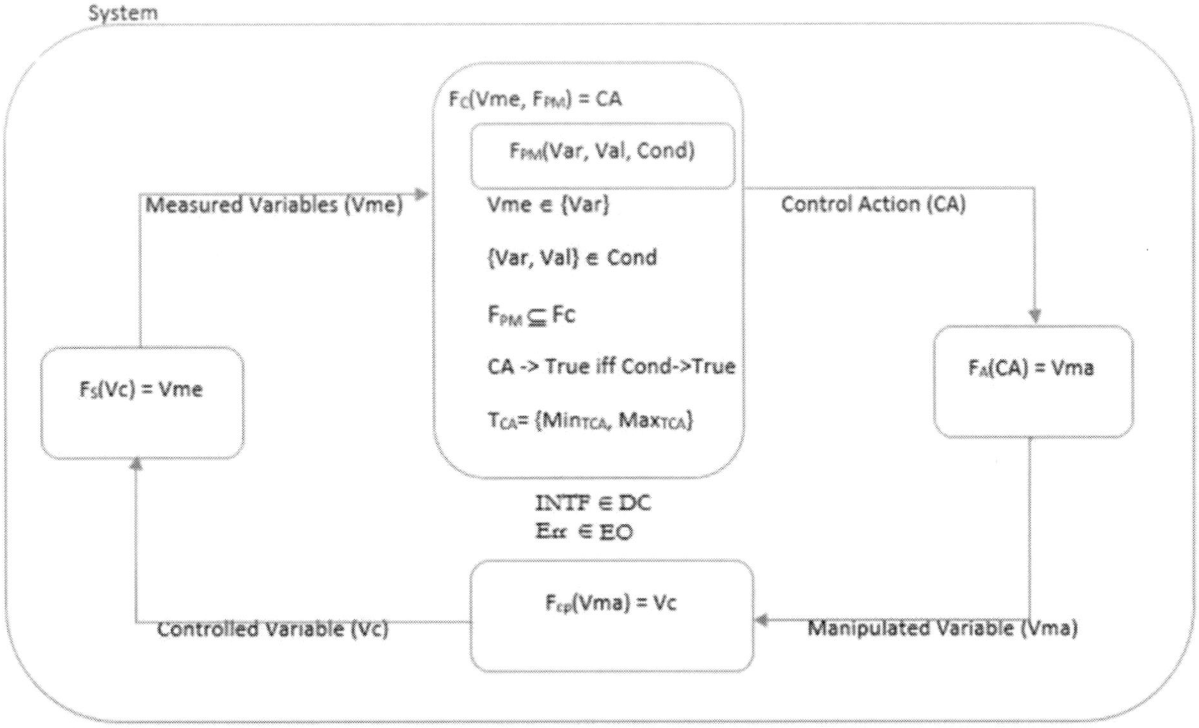

Figure 1— Feedback control loop augmented with mathematical notations and expressions

Method Discussion

We extend each step in STPA with the error ontology described in a formal notation. The steps are:

1. **Specify criteria to identify the unsafe behavior of a component:** This step involves specifying an identifier to represent a faulty component in the feedback control loop that propagates an error to the next component. In this step, we have *INTF* as a faulty component identifier and *Err* as a result of the fault.
2. **Build notation to specify input/output as well as functions for each component:** The purpose of this step is the construction of the feedback control loop with mathematical notation and expression for describing the functional behavior of each component as shown in Figure 1. In this step, we have input and output variables for each component such as *Vc, Vme, CA,* and *Vma*. Also, we provide a specific function for each component to build a relationship among input and output variables such as F_S, F_C, F_{PM}, F_A, and F_{CP}.

3. **Identify unsafe functional behavior and find more hazardous possibilities using the error ontology:** This step helps to identify unsafe functional behavior of a component that violates safety requirements for the associated overall system. For example, the internal failure of a component can give incorrect results to the component leading to the function of that component potentially becoming an unsafe function. In addition, we use the error ontology described in a formal notation to find the possibilities of unsafe functional behavior which leads to the system behaving incorrectly. Then, we identify the corresponding safety constraints which are needed to mitigate the effect(s) of the unsafe functional behavior.
4. **Identify mathematical notation for each error flow:** This step assists in identifying a formal expression for each error flow in the feedback control loop architecture. Based on our previous work (M. Rashid and McGregor, 2017), we know the propagated error cuts across three components based on a three-way interaction format. For that reason, each error flow should contain three functions. In this case, the proposed safety constraints should cover three components to mitigate the effect of the error flow.

Example: We take the automated train door controller system, as described in (Thomas and Leveson, 2011), as an example. We have the following steps to find more hazardous possibilities:

1) Train doors are locked. The train driver is unable to open the door because the sensor provides incorrect readings to the controller. This leads to the passengers being stuck inside the train when the train is stopped at the station platform.

$$F_S(Vc) = \begin{cases} Vme \quad if\ Measured\ Values \in Vme & (1) \\ Err \quad if\ Measured\ Values \notin Vme,\ where\ F_S(INTF) \rightarrow Err,\ Err \in EO & (2) \end{cases}$$

   In (eqn. 1), we express the behavior of the sensor when it sends the correct measured values to the controller via measured variables. The controller is able to recognize the values that were previously defined in the variables. But, in (eqn. 2), we express a faulty sensor; it will send different values to the controller. The controller, then, is not able to understand those values leading to the stuck door.

2) The following identified functions are used to express the response of the controller for the faulty sensor expression.

Table 1 — Unsafe Functional Behavior

Function	Sensor Function	Controller Function
Open Door	$F_S(Vc, INTF)=Err$, $if\ Err \in ErrValues$	$F_C(F_{PM}(Var, Val, Cond)) \neq CA$, $if\ ErrValues \notin Val,\ Then\ Cond \rightarrow False$

   As shown in Table 1, the function of the sensor shows the internal failure of the component and provides incorrect information to the controller (i.e. the output of the sensor is an error (*Err*) which can be considered as one of the errors in the AADL error ontology [such as Error Values]). The function of the controller shows that the incoming error value is not an element in the defined values of the process model function. For that reason, the decision of the process model is going to be incorrect. This affects the output of the controller because the condition of the decision is false. Thus, the output of the controller is not correct and could lead to a hazard.

Table 2 — Finding unsafe possibilities

Possibilities	Description	Is this possibility hazardous?
If ErrValue > MaxVal	The controller does not open the door when it gets above of the range values.	Yes
If ErrValue < MinVal	The controller does not open the door when it gets below of the range values.	Yes
If ErrValue $\notin$ *Val*	The controller does not open the door when it gets none of the defined values.	Yes
If ErrValue = "Null Value"	The controller does not open the door when it gets omitted error value.	Yes
If ErrValue= "Stuck Value"	The controller does not open the door when it gets the same repeated value.	Yes

In Table 2, we show the possibilities of error values from the faulty sensor function to the controller function. We show an expression for each possibility and have a description for it. These possibilities are hazardous because the controller does not send the command to open the door due to receiving different values from the sensor function.

3) How the faulty sensor can impact the door actuator function?

Table 3 — Error flow expression and safety constraint notation

Application Example	Flow Expression	Safety Constraint
Train Automated Door Control System	$F_S(Vc, INTF) \rightarrow F_C \rightarrow F_A(Vma, Err)$	*SC(S, C, A, Err)*

As shown in Table 3, the flow expression demonstrates the internal failure of the sensor which effects the output (i.e., manipulated variables) of the actuator. The sensor propagates an error to the actuator through the incorrect action of the controller. For example, when the door controller receives abnormal values from the sensor, the controller will do incorrect computations and sends incorrect commands to the actuator. This will lead to the actuator executing incorrect actions; it can be seen then as an error in the output of the actuator. To solve this problem, we need to provide a safety constraint to mitigate the effect of the error on the actuator which comes from the sensor. In this case, we need to build a specific safety constraint based on the three-way interaction format to cover the flow. For that purpose, we build *SC(S, C, A, Err)* which means the controller *(C)* is required to provide a control action for the actuator *(A)* with respect to the error *(Err)* context for the message that comes from the sensor *(S)*.

Method Implementation

In this section, we implement the method described in previous section, Architecture Safety Analysis Method (ASAM). It is used for developing safety-critical systems, that will allow system stakeholders or safety analysts to mitigate the effects of the errors through safety constraints. Generally, in the method, we focus on finding safety constraints and satisfy them within the system model. Specifically, we inject the AADL error ontology into the architecture model to identify the unsafe control actions and causal factors of the unsafe control actions. We satisfy the safety constraints that we have found within the system model to ensure the hazardous situations do not occur. For that purpose, we focus on introducing compositional reasoning in our method to ensure that the unsafe control action will not happen.

From a technical perspective, ASAM is a new software safety analysis tool which works with AADL models annotated with an annex (i.e. asam annex) and supported by the Open Source Architectural Tool Environment (OSATE). It is used to analyze and generate a report based on information attached to each component in the feedback control architecture model. In fact, ASAM provides several statements to feed the method's steps into the system's architecture model such as error statements, error propagation statements, internal failure statements, safety constraint statement that either handle or prevent hazards. The goal of the statements is to not let errors propagate from one component to another. If it is propagated, ASAM can handle incoming errors and prevent outgoing errors via the implementations of the safety constraints. ASAM lets the safety analyst record the severity level of the hazard for the specific error type based on the probability of occurrence for that type of error. Also, ASAM satisfies the safety constraint statements to ensure that the error effect or unsafe action has been mitigated.

Example: What will happen if the sensors in an adaptive cruise control (ACC) report incorrect values for speed and distance of the car in front of its car during driving because of an internal failure?

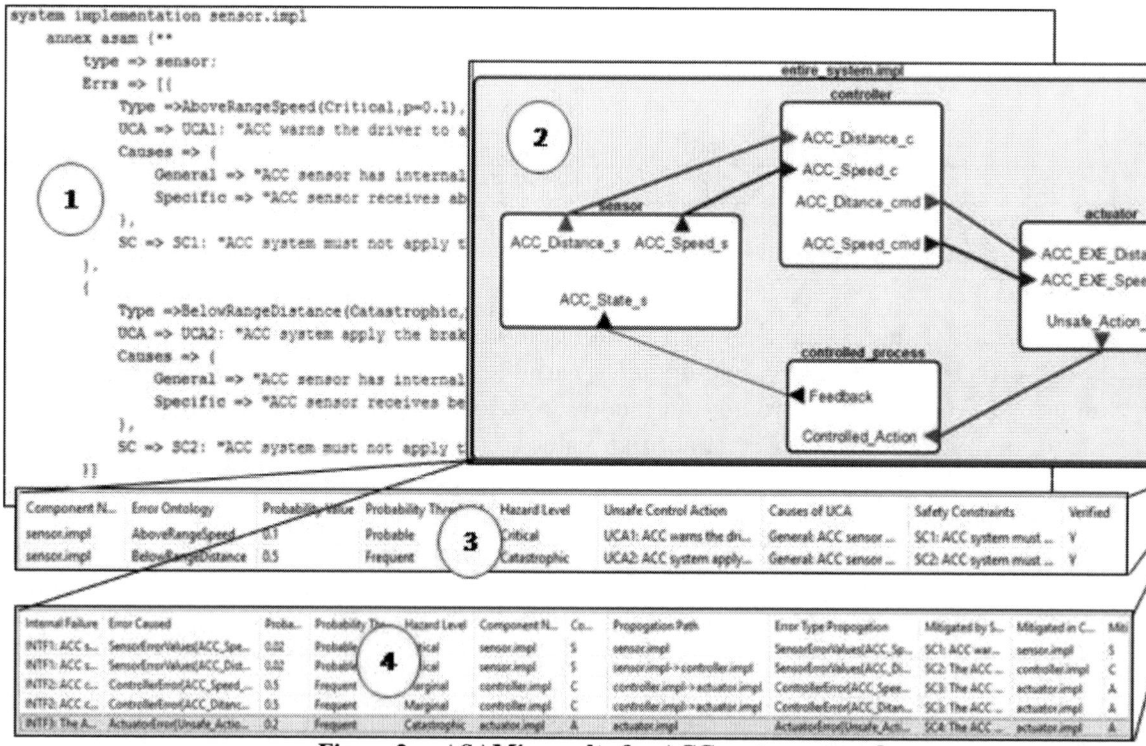

Figure 2— ASAM's results for ACC system example

We divide Figure 2 into four steps. The numbers in Figure 2 correspond to the steps shown below:

(1) The ASAM annex allows stakeholders to record the specific information in the implementation part of each component in the ACC architecture model. For example, we have recorded the following information: error types for the sensor's internal failure (above range of speed and below range of distance), unsafe control action for each error type, general or specific causes for each unsafe control action, probability of occurrence for each error type, severity level of hazards for each error type, and safety constraints to mitigate the effects of the error types. Also, ASAM allows the safety analysts to record the particular information in the specification part of each component to verify the information have been recorded in the implementation part. For example, in the ACC model, we need to ensure the system does not apply the brake when it has incorrect values of speed or distance.

(2) A feedback control loop has been built for the ACC system. Figure 2 shows error flow for each error type based on the three-way interaction format. Figure 2 shows two error flow: one for distance error and the other for speed error. The first error flow (i.e., red line) shows the error propagation from sensor to actuator. The error in measuring of distance propagates to the controller through the output data port. The error distance value in the sensor can be prevented from being communicated through a safety constraint statement. But, if it is not prevented, it propagates to the controller. The controller also can handle the incoming error distance value through in data port according to the safety constraint. If the controller is not able to handle that, it sends an inadequate command to the actuator. Then, the actuator will execute an inadequate action. The effect of that error on the manipulated variable which is the output of the actuator. The second error flow (i.e. blue line) has the same description.

(3) The analysis report shows the source of faults in the ACC model, which is the sensor. Each fault in the sensor produces errors. Each error has a chance to harm people based on the probability of occurrence for that error. ASAM compares the recorded probability value with probability of occurrence thresholds to find the probability of which hazard could occur. For example, an "above range of speed" error results in a critical level and a "below range of distance" error results in a catastrophic level. Each error in the sensor gives an unsafe control action to the controller which results in sending an inadequate command to the actuator. For example, the ACC controller warns the driver to apply the brake. If the driver does not do that action, the system will automatically do it. Also, general and specific causes for each unsafe control action have been identified. Finally, ASAM satisfies the safety constraints that have been recorded to mitigate the effect of the errors. For example, the ACC system verifies that should not apply the brake when it has incorrect values of distance and speed.

(4) The report shows three internal failures in the ACC model. We have a description for each one: First, the sensor has an internal failure, it gives two errors to the sensor. The sensor has a safety constraint to mitigate the effect of the first error (i.e., above range of speed error). But, the second error (i.e., below range distance error) propagates to the controller because the sensor does not have a safety constraint for it. For that reason, the controller mitigates the effect of the sensor's error. Second, the controller itself has an internal failure, it gives two errors (above range of speed and below range of distance) on the output data port. Those two errors are propagated to the actuator because the controller has a safety constraint to handle incoming errors only. But, the actuator is able to handle both

controller's errors. Third, the actuator has an internal failure, it gives an error to the actuator, but the actuator is able to prevent it being propagated out to the controlled process.

Conclusion and Discussion

It can be concluded that ASAM is different than STPA because it provides mathematical notation/expression and error ontology for the feedback control loop architecture to find more safety constraints during hazard analysis. This allows stakeholders to use formal methods to find more hazardous possibilities and mitigate them using safety constraints.

ASAM is different than STPA in finding more hazards using the three-way communication format as opposed to using the two-way format. This allows the identification of potential internal failures of the major components in the feedback control loop architecture. The result of each internal failure is an error. The error propagates and cuts across components based on the three-way interaction format. This allows stakeholders to identify a new unsafe control action and allows the reduction of the potential effects of residual hazards in the operational system context.

ASAM is different than STPA in using verification procedures to verify that each hazardous condition cannot occur. ASAM verify the safety constraints against the system model with injected errors. The output of the automatic model checking identifies the behavior of the system. This allows us to determine that either unsafe behaviors occur (which means the error leads to the hazardous condition in the system) or verify that the error does not lead to unsafe behavior of the system.

All in all, ASAM allows system stakeholders to find new hazards and new safety constraints that STPA does not find. This does not mean that our method is a replacement for STPA; however, it supports more effective and rigorous analyses of the elements of safety-critical systems.

References

Bergen, P. v. (2004). *Garfixia Software Architectures*. Retrieved from Architectural Patterns: http://www.dossier-andreas.net/software_architecture/index.html

Leveson, N. (2011). *Engineering a Safer World: Systems Thinking Applied to Safety*. Boston: MIT Press.

M. Rashid, F. and McGregor, J. (2017). Augmenting a Hazard Analysis Method with Error Propagation Information for Safety-Critical Systems. *The 35th International System Safety Conference (ISSC)*. Albuquerque, New Mexico, USA: System Safety Society Publications.

Thomas, J. and Leveson N. (2011). Performing Hazard Analysis on Complex, Software-and Human-Intensive Systems. *The 29th International System Safety Conference (ISSC)*. Las Vegas, Nevada, USA: System Safety Society Publications.

Abdulkhaleq A. and Wagner S. (2013). Integrating State Machine Analysis with System-Theoretic Process Analysis. *LNI Processing of Software Engineering Workshop Band* (pp. 501-514). Kollen, Germany: Kollen Druck and Verleg GmbH.

Feiler P. and et-al. (2016). *Architecture Fault Modeling and Analysis with the Error Model Annex, Version 2*. Pittsburgh: CMU/SEI-2016-TR-009, Carnegie Mellon University/Software Engineering Institute.

KMS Solutions, LLC

Lessons Learned from a Functional Hazard Analysis (FHA)

Michael Levesque

August 14, 2018

KMS Solutions, LLC

BLUF & Outline

BLUF

- High level overview
- Share some lessons learned from our experience
- Create a healthy group dynamic that encourages sharing of experiences, both positive and negative

Outline

- Intro, Perspective & Background
- How an FHA Adds Value
- Importance of a Well Designed Worksheet
- Challenges We Faced
- A Few Lessons Learned, Programmatic Advice
- Simple Error-Proofing Opportunities

2

KMS Solutions, LLC

Hazards are Ubiquitous

- Almost Anyone can identify the RIDICUOUSLY OBVIOUS Safety issues (yet they still exist…)
- An FHA is a tool that enables a professional to identify the non-obvious hazards

Issues are Not Always Visible

3

KMS Solutions, LLC

Perspective

- Total Ownership Cost includes Development cost, Procurement cost, and the Over-The-Horizon Costs
- Affordability encourages us to understand the impact of today's decisions on tomorrow's obligations, and to use that knowledge to influence the system design

4

KMS Solutions, LLC

Affordability & Safety Best Started Early

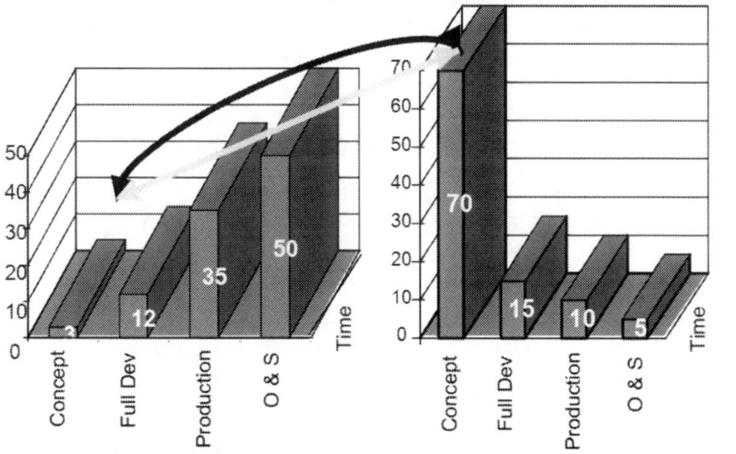

Total Ownership Cost <u>Spent</u> (Percent)

<u>Impact</u> On Total Ownership (Percent)

Affordability's greatest impact is Earliest in the Program Life Cycle
*** Safety is one of the Key Early Influencers ***

5

KMS Solutions, LLC

FHA Background

- **Charter:**
  - **Introduced in 2012 via MIL-STD-882E**
  - **Expected for most new DoD systems**
- **When:**
  - **After the system concept is developed**
  - **<u>Before</u> design is established**
- **What:**
  - **Implementation-Agnostic Functional Decomposition**
  - **Risk Assessment**
  - **Complex analysis spreadsheet w/ multiple interconnected worksheets**

6

KMS Solutions, LLC

Where it Fits

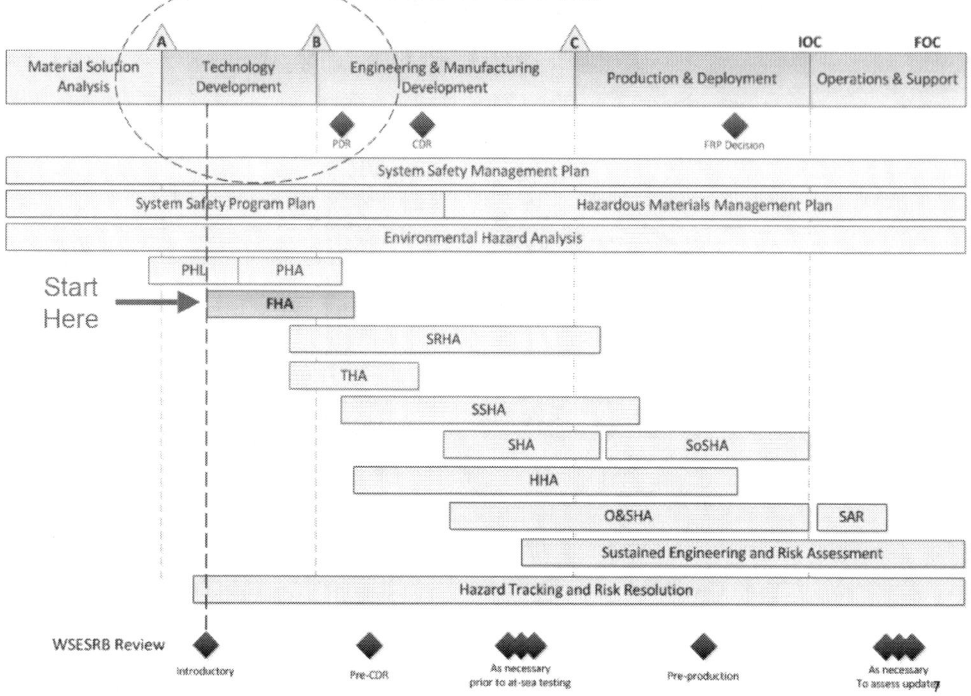

7

KMS Solutions, LLC

How an FHA Adds Value

- Uncovers potential Safety issues that other analysis techniques sometimes miss
- When done early in design stage it can better influence the design, making the system safer
- When done early, as it should be, it is MUCH more cost effective
- Can influence design while it is still inexpensive to do so

8

Value of a Well Designed Worksheet

KMS Solutions, LLC

- The analysis will flow as the Worksheet is populated
- The analysis should illuminate
  - System functions
  - Hazards
  - Software Criticality Index (SwCI)
- This will identify
  - Safety Critical Items
  - Required Level of Rigor for Software Modules
- The FHA Worksheet will provide valuable input to the FHA Report

9

Challenges We Experienced

KMS Solutions, LLC

- Defining the scope – What is In / Out
  - Functional point of view
  - Program Life-Cycle point of view
- Functional decomposition
  - Thinking functionally, at a System Level
  - Not a requirements driven approach
  - Completely implementation-agnostic
- Severity Determination
  - MIL-STD-882E for determining SwCI
  - NAVSEA 5100.12-M for RAC in Hazard Definition
- Worksheet layout was not intuitive
- Commenting on my own work, candidly

10

Functional Decomposition

KMS Solutions, LLC

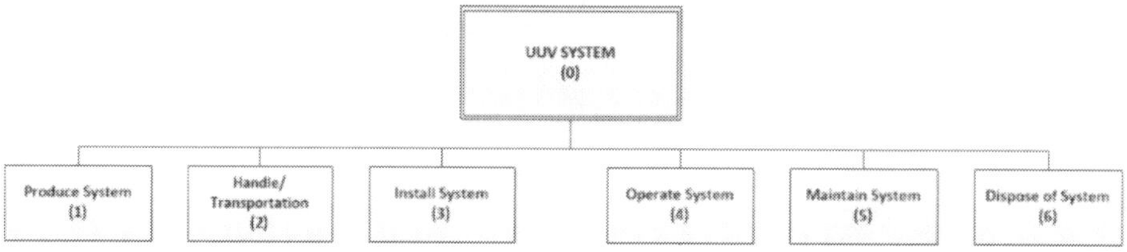

11

Overlooked Failure Modes

KMS Solutions, LLC

Functional Decomposition		In Scope	
Index	System Function	Life Cycle	New / Modified
1	Produce System	N	N/A
2	Handle/Transport System	N	N/A
3	Install System	N	N/A
4	Operate System	Y	Y
4.1	Launch Vehicle	Y	Y
4.1.1	Connect to Launch Controller	Y	Y
4.1.2	Power-Up Vehicle	Y	Y
4.1.3	Perform Checks	Y	Y
4.1.4	Provide Launch Commands	Y	Y
4.2	Swim	Y	Y
4.2.1	Provide Power	Y	Y
4.2.2	Create Propulsion	Y	Y
4.2.3	Guide Vehicle	Y	Y
4.2.3.1	Maintain Safety	Y	Y
4.2.3.2	Control Vehicle	Y	Y
4.2.3.2.1	Control Motor	Y	Y
4.2.3.2.2	Control Fins	Y	Y
4.3	Record Data	Y	N
5	Maintain System	N	N/A
6	Dispose of System	N	N/A

12

KMS Solutions, LLC

Example Workshee‌t

Division Newport CPI Office

13

KMS Solutions, LLC

Lessons Learned

- Defining the scope / boundaries of the analysis
  - System
  - Functions
  - Life-cycle phases
- Running list of Assumptions
- Do not overlook the importance of a truly implementation-agnostic functional decomposition, it is the foundation, the "F" in FHA. Take your time to get it right (How does it do that...?)
- Create a template that is comprehensive, intuitive, flexible, and tailorable
- Document your process, and your progress

14

Lessons Learned, cont.

KMS Solutions, LLC

- Ambiguity is the enemy of efficiency, so Make the Time to add Candid Comments (to yourself)
- Performing an FHA Early in the project allows you to identify the Software Criticality Index (SwCI), which correlates to the required Level of Rigor for software. This will result in a more efficient architecture of software modules.
- If you need approval of a review board, share the Worksheet and the comments
- Often overlooked failure modes (other than, "Fails to Operate" and "Malfunction") may identify hazards / risks not previously identified
- Timing…

15

Lessons Learned, cont.

KMS Solutions, LLC

- FHA review process
  - Functional Decomposition is the foundation of the analysis, get feedback from Systems Engineering
    - Do NOT ask if it is OK…
    - Do ask what is missing
    - Functional Decomposition describes the Capability of the system, Not the Implementation of it
  - Effects (Local and System) should be reviewed with other Safety Engineers
  - Have I mentioned Comments…? Potential comments could be:
    - Is this possible?
    - Could be any number of things, including but not limited to: malfunction in X1, faulty X2, faulty X3, bad X4, faulty X5, etc.

16

Simple Error-Proofing Opportunities

KMS Solutions, LLC

- No magic, simply reducing the opportunities to make human errors
- Conditional formatting – colors & font styles to draw attention to summary rows / cells, and to differentiate between different rows
- Take advantage of simple formulas for automation
  - =MIN(X17:X22)
  - =IF(MIN(AB17:AB22)=0,"",MIN(AB17:AB22))
  - {=IF(CHAR(SMALL(CODE(AC31:AC36),1))="N","",CHAR(SMALL(CODE(AC31:AC36),1)))}
  - =CONCATENATE(AB30,AC30)
- Protect the cells with formulas

17

Programmatic Advice

KMS Solutions, LLC

- **The Earlier you perform this analysis, the more Effective *and* Affordable it is**
  - Some Program Managers do not get Safety involved in a program at the point when a FHA should be done.
  - Rule of 10 - What needs to be changed, what does it cost?

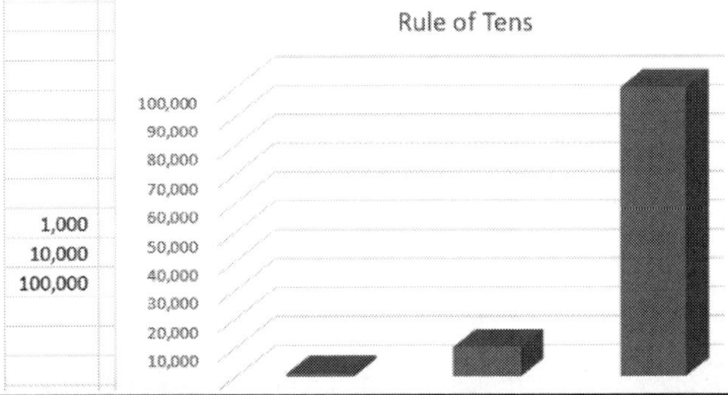

Safety, and the FHA - "Proxies for Affordability"

18

Pay Me Now, or Pay Me Later

KMS Solutions, LLC

We did the math…

Later is <u>ALWAYS</u> More

19

KMS Solutions, LLC

Questions?

20

Hazard Considerations for Atlas V and Delta IV Integrated Space Vehicle and Launch Vehicle Operations

Shawn M. Laabs; System Safety Lead; United Launch Alliance; Centennial, Colorado, USA

Dae Kim; System Safety Engineer; United Launch Alliance; Centennial, Colorado, USA

Stephen A. Seidl; System Safety Engineer; United Launch Alliance; Centennial, Colorado, USA

Keywords: Safety, Hazard, Space Vehicle, Launch Vehicle, Atlas, Delta, Mission Integration

Abstract

Personnel safety is a major concern throughout integrated space vehicle and launch vehicle operations and testing. The safety concern exists for the personnel that handle the launch vehicle and space vehicle. The hazard risks associated with integrated space vehicle and launch vehicle operations increases as the two vehicles are integrated together. These risks must be controlled to acceptable levels prior to the start of integrated operations. This paper will explore controls for cranes and hoists, sling assemblies, hydrasets and loadcells, handling structures, flight hardware lift points, work platforms, RF emitters, ionizing radiation sources, hazardous materials, flight hardware pressure systems, ordnance systems, electrical and electronic systems, and seismic designs. This paper will also explore operational controls that must be in place after the designs have been finalized. Range Safety requirements will be the catalyst of discussion for this paper as most launch operations occur on a military installation.

Introduction

"Formed in December 2006, United Launch Alliance (ULA) is a 50-50 joint venture owned by Lockheed Martin and The Boeing Company. ULA brings together two of the launch industry's most experienced and successful teams – Atlas and Delta – to provide reliable, cost-efficient space launch services for the U.S. government. U.S. government launch customers include the Department of Defense, NASA, the National Reconnaissance Office and other organizations (ref. 1)." ULA is currently developing the Vulcan Centaur Launch Vehicle. "In step one, with a planned initial launch capability in 2020, Vulcan Centaur will exceed the capability of Atlas V, serving the vast majority of our customers' mission needs. Step one consists of single booster stage, the high-energy Centaur second stage and a 5-meter-diameter payload fairing. Up to six solid rocket boosters (SRBs) can be used to augment the lift off power. In step two, the Centaur second stage will be replaced by the more powerful Advanced Cryogenic Evolved Stage (ACES) in 2023. With the addition of ACES, Vulcan Centaur will achieve the current capability of the Delta IV Heavy, which carries the largest payloads for our most critical customers (ref. 2)."

Space launch can present significant hazards to ground personnel and the public. The ULA System Safety process covers both ground personnel and public safety from concept design through the end of mission. For this reason, it is important to establish and involve a System Safety program in the early stages of concept design. Early engagement ensures that all hazards and operations are assessed to ensure ground and public safety risks are controlled to acceptable levels. This paper will focus on the integration between a Launch Vehicle (LV) and a Space Vehicle (SV), which can also present significant hazards to ground personnel during integrated (SV-LV) operations. Hazard considerations will be explored for these integrated operations using applicable Air Force requirements as a guide. The Atlas V and Delta IV System Safety Programs have been designed to be compliant with Air Force (MIL-STD-882E) and Range Safety (EWR 127-1 and RCC 324) requirements. To properly scope this paper, it is important to note the following points:

- This paper will not discuss Federal safety requirements (e.g. OSHA, FAA)
- This paper will not discuss MIL-STD-882 requirements.
- This paper will not discuss the SS-LV process.
- This paper will not discuss flight or public safety.
- This paper will not discuss product safety.
- This paper will not discuss human spaceflight.
- This paper will not discuss facility safety.

System Safety Mission Integration Scope

For the purpose of this paper, the term ground personnel refers to "the technicians and engineers who come in contact with the launch vehicle during manufacture and test" (ref. 3 & ref. 4). The System Safety Mission Integration (SS-MI) process is primarily concerned with ground personnel safety during integrated operations at the Payload Processing Facility (PPF) and the Launch Complex. Integrated operations include (but is not limited to) SV mate to LV adapter, payload fairing encapsulation, transportation from the PPF to the Launch Complex, encapsulated payload mate to the LV, integrated systems testing, and PLF closeout. Once the launch pad area is cleared of essential personnel, the SS-MI process is considered to be complete. In the event of a launch delay (e.g. weather constraints), ground personnel may be required to access the launch vehicle to perform operations to prepare the LV for another launch attempt. Hazards associated with potential launch delays and subsequent launch attempts will not be addressed in this paper, although there is a point where the standard SS-MI process will be followed for these additional launch attempts. Figure 1 depicts a notional timeline to illustrate the SS-MI scope for this paper.

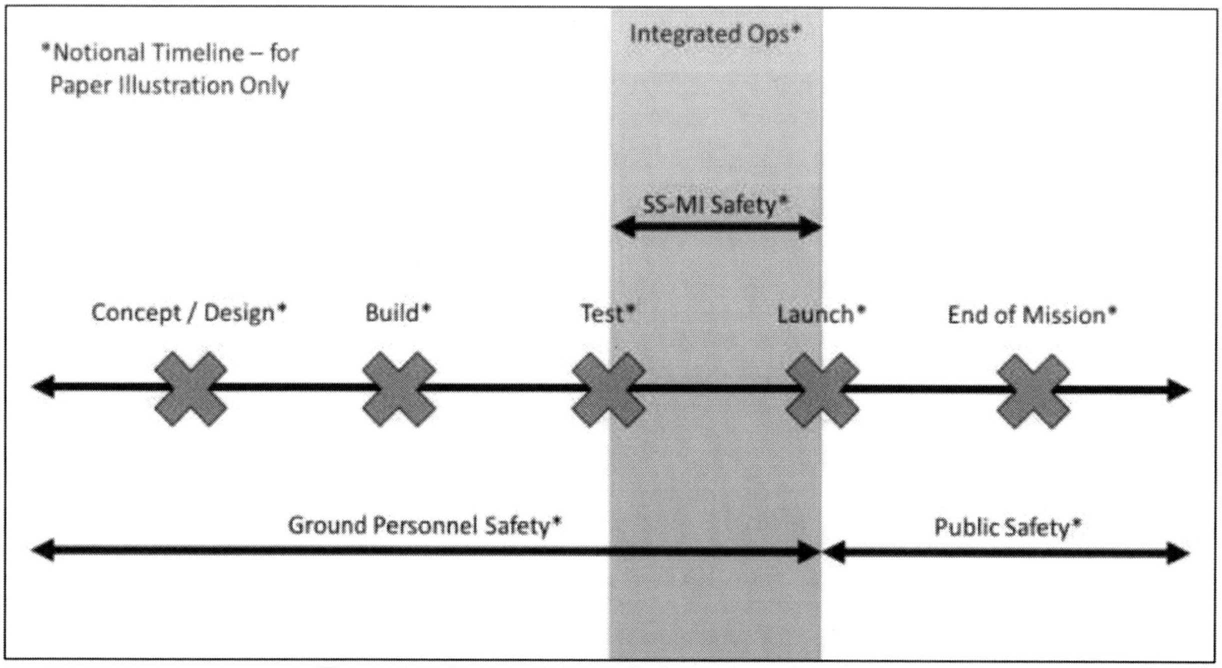

Figure 1 — System Safety Mission Integration Scope

<u>Range Safety Requirements Summary</u>

The Atlas V and Delta IV System Safety Programs have been designed to be compliant with Range Safety (EWR 127-1 and RCC 324) requirements. Table 1 provides a summary of the Range Safety requirements documents. For completeness all Range Safety requirements are included, but only those applicable to the scope of this paper (i.e. sections relating to hazardous systems and hazardous operations during the SS-MI process) will be discussed further. The requirement sections that will be discussed in this paper are colored in blue.

Table 1 — Range Safety Requirements Summary (ref. 5)

Requirement Document / Section	Requirement Scope
EWR 127-1 Chapter 1 (ref. 5)	Range Safety Policies and Processes
EWR 127-1 Chapter 2 (ref. 5)	Flight Analysis Requirements
EWR 127-1 Chapter 3 (ref. 5)	Launch Vehicle, Payload, and Ground Support Equipment Documentation, Design, and Test Requirements
EWR 127-1 Chapter 4 (ref. 5)	Airborne Range Safety System Documentation, Design, and Test Requirements
EWR 127-1 Chapter 5 (ref. 5)	Facilities and Structures Documentation, Design, Construction, Test, and Inspection Requirements
EWR 127-1 Chapter 6 (ref. 5)	Ground Personnel, Equipment, Systems, and Materials Operations Safety Requirements
EWR 127-1 Chapter 7 (ref. 5)	Flight Control Documentation, Systems, and Procedural Requirements
RCC 324 (ref. 6)	Global Positioning and Inertial Measurements Range Safety Tracking Systems

Hazard Considerations from EWR Chapter 3 Requirements

EWR 127-1 Section 3.6 Material Handling Equipment: The SS-MI process starts with integrated operations at the PPF. Operations for SV mate to the LV adapter, PLF encapsulation, and PLF encapsulated assembly mate to the LV require various hardware lifts to occur. Lifting hardware can be either SV or LV provided, depending on the operation. Lift hardware can include cranes, hoists, slings, hydrasets, load cells, handling structures, flight hardware lift points, and work platforms. These lift operations present significant hazards to ground personnel in the event the lifting hardware fails and there is an uncontrolled release of the load. This chapter also addresses work platforms that are used to access the LV and SV. These access operations present significant hazards to ground personnel in the event the work platform fails and there is a fall from the tower or someone is struck by a falling object. Table 2 documents required controls to mitigate personnel hazards to acceptable levels.

Table 2 — Material Handling Equipment Controls (ref. 5)

Requirement Document / Section	Required Controls
Cranes and Hoists	• Minimization / Elimination of Single Failure Points (SFPs) • Design Factors of Safety • Elimination of Brittle Materials • Positive Latching Mechanisms • Reeving • Limit Switches • Dead Man Type Movement Controls • Load Visibility • Bonding, Grounding, and Electrical Insulation • Emergency Brakes • Initial and Periodic Load Tests • Initial and Periodic Non-Destructive Evaluation
Sling Assemblies	• Minimization / Elimination of Single Failure Points (SFPs) • Design Factors of Safety • Initial and Recurring Proof Load Tests • Initial and Periodic Non-Destructive Evaluation
Hydrasets and Loadcells	• Design Factors of Safety • Initial and Recurring Proof Load Tests • Initial and Periodic Non-Destructive Evaluation
Handling Structures	• Minimization / Elimination of Single Failure Points (SFPs) • Design Factors of Safety

	• Initial and Recurring Proof Load Tests • Initial and Periodic Non-Destructive Evaluation
Flight Hardware Lift Points	• Design Factors of Safety • Initial and Recurring Proof Load Tests • Initial and Periodic Non-Destructive Evaluation
Removable, Extendible, and Hinged Work Platforms	• Design Factors of Safety • Initial and Recurring Proof Load Tests • Initial and Periodic Non-Destructive Evaluation • Fall Protection

EWR 127-1 Section 3.8 Non-Ionizing Radiation Sources: SVs typically have one or more radio frequency emitter, depending on their telemetry and mission requirements. These SV radio frequency emitters may need to be tested during integrated operations or be turned on prior to launch to provide telemetry data to the ground. These non-ionizing radiation operations present significant hazards to ground personnel if the power levels are above the safe limit, avionics fails causing uncontrolled release of energy, or ordnance inadvertently functions. Planned radiation on the Ranges must be coordinated with the Range Safety Radiation Protection Officer to ensure personnel safety and prevent Range interference issues. Table 3 documents required controls to mitigate personnel hazards to acceptable levels.

Table 3 — Non-Ionizing Radiation Sources Controls (ref. 5)

Requirement Document / Section	Required Controls
Radio Frequency Emitters	• Fault Tolerance to Preclude Inadvertent Radiation • RF Hats During Ground Operations • Personnel Exposure Below 10 mW/cm2 • Personnel Clear Zones During Radiation • Electromagnetic Interference Safety Margin for Ordnance and Avionics

EWR 127-1 Section 3.9 Ionizing Radiation Sources: Some SVs have ionizing radiation sources, depending on their mission requirements. These ionizing radiation sources need to be installed into the SV, typically later in the integrated operations timeline. These ionizing radiation operations present significant hazards to ground personnel if personnel are exposed to radiation levels that are above the safe limit. The use of ionizing radiation sources on the Ranges must be coordinated with the Range Safety Radiation Protection Officer to ensure personnel safety and environmental safety. Table 4 documents required controls to mitigate personnel hazards to acceptable levels.

Table 4 — Ionizing Radiation Sources Controls (ref. 5)

Requirement Document / Section	Required Controls
Ionizing Radiation Sources	• Design to Prevent Release • Shielding • Compatibility with Ordnance, Propellants, Pressure Systems, and Structures • Late Installation • Interlocks • Leak Tests • Warning Signs and Labels • RF Hats During Ground Operations • Personnel Clear Zones During Radiation • Electromagnetic Interference Safety Margin for Ordnance and Avionics • Personnel Protective Equipment

EWR 127-1 Section 3.10 Hazardous Materials: SVs and LVs often contain hazardous materials in order to perform their intended functions or to adequately protect them from harsh environments. Operations using, or in proximity to, hazardous materials present significant hazards to ground personnel if personnel are exposed to hazardous material concentrations that are above the safe limit, if hazardous materials catch on fire, or if material incompatibilities cause uncontrolled release of energy. Table 5 documents required controls to mitigate personnel hazards to acceptable levels.

Table 5 — Hazardous Materials Controls (ref. 5)

Requirement Document / Section	Required Controls
Hazardous Materials	• Elimination of Hazardous Materials • Substitution to Less Toxic Materials • Substitution to the Least Flammable Materials • Material Compatibility • Electrostatic Discharge • Personnel Protective Equipment

EWR 127-1 Section 3.12 Flight Hardware Pressure Systems: SVs and LVs contain pressure systems for a variety of functions, from containing fuels, to providing pneumatic and hydraulic pressure, and providing power (i.e. batteries). Operations using, or in proximity to, pressure systems present significant hazards to ground personnel if personnel are exposed to an uncontrolled release of energy or the potentially hazardous commodities within the pressure systems (i.e. chemicals, fuels, oxidizers, and asphyxiants). Table 6 documents required controls to mitigate personnel hazards to acceptable levels.

Table 6 — Flight Hardware Pressure Systems Controls (ref. 5)

Requirement Document / Section	Required Controls
Flight Hardware Pressure Systems	• Fault Tolerance to Preclude Inadvertent Release / Leakage (Solenoids, Pyrovalves, etc.) • Design Factors of Safety • Regulators / Relief Devices / Vents • Initial and Recurring Proof Load Tests • Initial and Periodic Non-Destructive Evaluation • Approved Connections (Tubes / Fittings) • Leak Tests • Functional Tests • Reduced Operating Pressure while Personnel are Exposed • Pressure Indicating Devices • Restraints (Flex Hoses) • Service Life / Safe Life • Material Compatibility • Bonding / Grounding • Personnel Clear Zones During Cryogenic Loading / Operations • Flare Stacks (Hydrogen) • Low Point Drains

EWR 127-1 Section 3.13 Ordnance Systems: SVs and LVs contain ordnance systems for a variety of functions, from separation, to flight termination, and deployment (e.g. solar arrays). Operations performed in the proximity to ordnance systems present significant hazards to ground personnel if personnel are exposed to an uncontrolled release of energy (i.e. inadvertent ordnance function). Table 7 documents required controls to mitigate personnel hazards to acceptable levels.

Table 7 — Ordnance Systems Controls (ref. 5)

Requirement Document / Section	Required Controls
Ordnance Systems	• DOT Compliance (Transportation) • Ordnance Classification (Cat A, Cat B, Non-Explosive Initiators, etc.) • Explosive / Pyrotechnic Mix Integrity • Fault Tolerance to Preclude Inadvertent Initiation (Switches, Relays, SAFE & ARM Devices, Interrupters) • Redundant Circuits • Separate Power Circuits for Initiating Systems • Component Qualification • Lot Acceptance Testing • Wiring (Twisted Shielded Pairs) • Isolation from Energy (Shielded, Filtered, Grounded, etc.) • Electromagnetic Safety Margin • Proper Connections • Bonding / Grounding • End Tip Caps (Pre-Installation) • Late Installation to Reduce Personnel Exposure • ARM / SAFE Status Monitoring

EWR 127-1 Section 3.14 Electrical and Electronic Systems: SVs and LVs contain electrical and electronic systems to control a variety of functions for telemetry systems, pressure systems, ordnance systems, instrumentation systems, and software systems. Operations using, or in proximity to, electrical and electronic systems present significant hazards to ground personnel if personnel are exposed to an uncontrolled release of energy or unintended propagation of hazards due to a power surge or unintended activation of the electronic system (i.e. propellant exposure, ordnance initiation, and RF emission). Table 8 documents required controls to mitigate personnel hazards to acceptable levels.

Table 8 — Electrical and Electronic Systems Controls (ref. 5)

Requirement Document / Section	Required Controls
Electrical and Electronic Systems	• Electrical Power OFF Prior to Installation, Repair, and Replacement • Protection from Power Transients • Fuses / Circuit Breakers • Power Cut Off Switches • Power Indicator Lights • Electromagnetic Safety Margin • Keyed, Color Coded, or Design Limited (Mismating Impossible) Connectors • Locking Connectors • Wire Isolation • Bonding / Grounding /Shielding • Material Compatibility • Bent Pin Analysis

EWR 127-1 Section 3.17 Western Range Seismic Design: SVs and LVs that are processed on the Western Range perform operations in a seismic zone 4, which is the most severe category for seismic activity. Operations within this seismic zone present significant hazards to ground personnel if a seismic event were to occur. Table 9 documents required controls to mitigate personnel hazards to acceptable levels.

Table 9 — Seismic Controls (ref. 5)

Requirement Document / Section	Required Controls
Seismic Design	• Eliminate or Minimize Designs / Configurations that would Tip Over During a Seismic Event • Seismic Restraints

Hazard Considerations from EWR Chapter 6 Requirements

Not only do SVs and LVs contain hazardous systems, the processes to ready and operate the systems may also present hazards. These processes may include, but are not limited to, transportation, integration, mechanical and electrical connections, test, and launch operations. These operations, if not performed correctly, present significant hazards to ground personnel if personnel are exposed to an uncontrolled release of energy or the potentially hazardous commodities that may be present (i.e. chemicals, fuels, oxidizers, and asphyxiants). In the event a hazard still exists after the design process, procedural controls and personnel protective equipment must be considered. Although the operational requirements in EWR 127-1 Chapter 6 are broken down into sections similar to those in Chapter 3, only one table of required controls will be presented. Table 10 documents required controls to mitigate personnel hazards to acceptable levels during operations.

Table 10 — Operational Controls (ref. 5)

Requirement Document / Section	Required Controls
Ground Support Personnel, Equipment, Systems, and Material Operations	• OSHA Compliance • Periodic Inspections / Audits • Operations Safety Plans • In-Service, Operating, Maintenance, and Inspection Plans • De-conflicting Hazardous Operations • Environmental Restrictions on Operations (e.g. Lightning) • Remote Operations • Warning Lights • Training and Certification • Procedural Controls (Warnings, Cautions, and Notes) • Essential Personnel Only / Clear Non-Essential Personnel • Pre-Task Safety Briefing • Personnel Work Hour Restrictions • Road Blocks • Use of Spotters • PPE (e.g. SCAPE Suits, ESD Wrist-Stats, Fall Protection) • Pathfinder Operations with Less Hazardous Systems • Stop of Operations Command (performable by anyone) • Hot-Work Permits • Lockout/Tagout Program • Grounding / Bonding • Alternate Space Confined Entry Program • Suspended Load Exposure Elimination / Mitigation • Drop Mitigation Program • Drug and Alcohol Free Workplace • Contingency Plans / Emergency Plans • Support Personnel Availability (e.g. Fire, Medical) • Incident Response • Safety Working Group Meetings

References

1. "Company Overview." About ULA. United Launch Alliance: 2016. Web. 3 March 2017. www.unitedlaunchalliance.com.

2. "Vulcan Centaur and Vulcan ACES." Launch Vehicles. United Launch Alliance: 2016. Web. 3 March 2017. www.unitedlaunchalliance.com.

3. Iyengar, Srinath. "Personnel and Public Safety Hazards and Controls for Evolved Expendable Space Launch Vehicles" United Launch Alliance: Web. 1 Feb 2018. www.unitedlaunchalliance.com.

4. Becker, E., Laabs, S., Russell, C., Vaid, A. "Hazard Considerations for Vulcan Launch Vehicle Major Development" United Launch Alliance: 2017. Web. 1 Feb 2018. www.unitedlaunchalliance.com.

5. US Air Force. "Eastern and Western Range 127-1 Range Safety Requirements as Tailored for the Atlas V and Delta IV Programs" United Launch Alliance. Internal document.

6. Range Safety Group. "*Global Positioning and Inertial Measurements Range Safety Tracking Systems' Commonality Standard as Tailored for the Atlas V and Delta IV Programs*" United Launch Alliance. Internal document. United Launch Alliance. Internal document.

Biographies

Shawn M. Laabs, United Launch Alliance System Safety, Enterprise Safety Lead, 9501 E. Panorama Circle, Centennial, CO 80112, USA, telephone – (303) 391-4616, e-mail – Shawn.M.Laabs@ULALaunch.com

Mr. Laabs is currently involved and actively participating in research, projects, and activities that serve in maturing and promoting the United Launch Alliance (ULA) Safety Program for Atlas, Delta, and Vulcan Centaur rocket production and launch operations. Mr. Laabs graduated from the University of Colorado in 2009 with a Bachelor's Degree of Science in Mechanical Engineering, specializing in Aerospace Engineering and Mathematics. Mr. Laabs is currently pursuing his MSE in Interdisciplinary Engineering at Purdue University. Mr. Laabs began his professional career at ULA in January 2010. Mr. Laabs is currently the Enterprise Safety Lead for the Atlas, Delta, and Vulcan Centaur rockets ensuring that all identified hazards are adequately assessed and have risks mitigated to acceptable levels by internal and external customers. Mr. Laabs is a proud father of twin girls, and a new baby girl, who make him thankful each day for his professional safety experience and its applicability to the home environment.

Dae Kim, United Launch Alliance System Safety Engineer, 9501 E. Panorama Circle, Centennial, CO 80112, USA, telephone – (303) 391-4987, e-mail – Dae.Kim@ulalaunch.com

Mr. Kim is currently responsible for systems safety aspects of the New Graphite Epoxy Motors for Atlas and for Vulcan Centaur rockets, ensuring that all identified hazards are adequately assessed and have risk mitigated to acceptable levels by internal and external customers. Mr. Kim is also actively working on the Vulcan Centaur Flight Termination System (FTS) and Separation System to identify hazards and adequately assessing the risks to verify they are being mitigated to an acceptable level by our internal and external customers. Mr. Kim graduated from The University of Texas at Austin with a Bachelor's Degree of Science in Mechanical Engineering in 2002. Mr. Kim also obtained a Systems Engineering Certificate from California Institute of Technology in 2006. Mr. Kim started his professional career at United Launch Alliance in 2006. Mr. Kim actively worked and designed the Separation System for the Interim Cryogenic Propulsion Stage (ICPS) on NASA's SLS vehicle. Mr. Kim also actively worked in supporting the Atlas and Delta rockets by providing qualified separation and flight termination hardware.

Stephen A. Seidl, United Launch Alliance System Safety, System Safety Engineer, 9501 E. Panorama Circle, Centennial, CO 80112, USA, Telephone – (303) 391-4559, Email – Stephen.A.Seidl@ulalaunch.com

Mr. Seidl is currently participating in projects and activities that promote the United Launch Alliance (ULA) Safety Program and safety in Mission Integration. Mr. Seidl graduated from University of Central Florida in 2015 with a Bachelor's Degree of Science in Mechanical Engineering. Beginning his professional career at ULA in April of 2016, Mr. Seidl is currently a System Safety Engineer for the Atlas, Delta, and Vulcan Centaur Programs ensuring proper identification of hazards and application of mitigations to those hazards in current and developing programs.

Chasing the Black Swan

Malcolm Jones, B.Sc., Ph.D., F. Inst. P., C. Phys., C Eng; AWE; Aldermaston, Berks., UK, RG7 4PR.

Keywords: The Black Swan, High Consequence, Uncertainty.

Abstract

The term Black Swan is a familiar concept in the context of high consequence operations. There is the continual concern that there may be an 'as yet' undiscovered flaw or lack of understanding in the design of a product, process or facility that could lead to a catastrophic event. Concern lies in the potential incompleteness of understanding of any design concept, implementation and associated assessment. Given that 'absolute confidence' may never be possible, the question arises as to how best to continue to search for such a possible flaw with a view to subsequent removal or mitigation. This at first sight appears to be a process without end but the level of commitment must be balanced against the detrimental consequence that could ensue given that a Black Swan might exist. But when is 'enough-enough'? This subject is covered in the context of the ownership of nuclear warheads where the Black Swan can indeed be catastrophic should it exist. The paper is framed somewhat in terms of what can be learned from the general literature associated with Black Swan thinking.

Introduction

The contents of this document represent the views of the author and not necessarily those of AWE plc.
Aspects of this subject have been covered in previous papers (refs 1, 2) which have taken different perspectives of an independent strength in depth approach to safety and its assessment. The first paper concentrated on organisational structures in relation to the necessary organisational levels, each having independent responsibilities for safety ensurance and assurance, coupled with final decision making responsibilities and of course each having the appropriate level of technical capability and experience. The overall organisational responsibility is that of ensuring a safe product, process or facility with appropriate technical and evidential support, with the level of scrutiny proportional to the potential consequence of getting it wrong. The first organisational layer is responsible for ensurance through making the safety case with a supporting evidence base. The second independent structure scrutinises and challenges this case for appropriate depth and completeness, including assuring that the appropriate level of expertise has been applied and that the evidence and analysis offered is complete and not flawed.

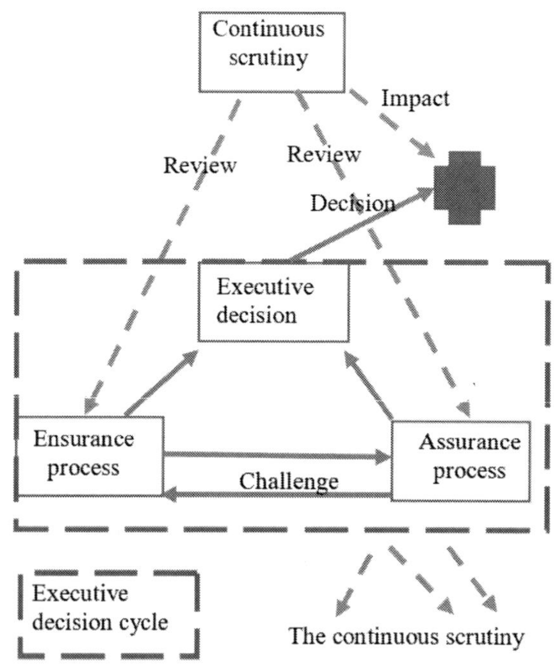

Figure 1 _ The continuous assessment process

The third independent organisational layer is responsible for final decision making, having taken into account and scrutinising the ensurance and assurance evidence provided by the first two layers and in turn, adding its own independent assessment based on a complementary fund of knowledge and experience. This third layer will also manage and resolve any disagreement arising from the views arising from the first two layers. Some of the fundamental competences needed for correct operation of this structure were identified in that paper together with some of the remaining difficulties.

However this overall approach alone may not be sufficient for ensuring the absence of a Black Swan for a product such as a nuclear warhead. For this reason a fourth layer, figure1, is introduced. That is a somewhat undefined layer which continues to probe into the product, process or facility with the intention of taking a 'what if' and 'expecting the unexpected' mind-set. This layer's job in essence is never finished and sets its target in the broadest sense. More is said later.

The second paper covered two independent technical strategies for safety ensurance and assessment. The first was based on an independent strength in depth technical analogue of the organisational structure. This is based on a deterministic approach founded on fundamental and independent levels of technical defence which is intended to include a hedge against uncertainty. The second approach complements this with a realistic, but conservative, evidential based numerical risk assessment looking for compliance with risk standards. Of course any risk assessment will contain an element of foundational judgment for supporting such an analysis. In principle this judgement could be in error and for this reason an acceptable level of conservatism has to be included in order to cater for any remnant uncertainty. Of course this risk assessment relates directly to a particular (or set of) design solution as opposed to the deterministic approach which is based simply on 'how to design for safety'. The latter risk approach aims more for a demonstration of meeting acceptable risk standards given the design solution. The two approaches have elements of fundamental difference but in concert compensate for individual potential limitations and statutory requirements. From a philosophical point of view the deterministic approach does offer the better of the two approaches for protection against the potential of a Black Swan because of its greater potential for protecting against any limits in our 'complete knowledge'. The risk assessment is necessary because of the societal demand to understand 'what the level of risk is' and whether it is acceptable. However, the risk assessment inevitably bases its approach on an 'accepted level' of understanding with some conservatism included to cover any potential deficiency in knowledge.

There is some value in the argument that, given a history of a product or process performing satisfactorily over a given period, this adds further to the confidence that the Black Swan may well not exist. However, the value of such evidence must be set against the level of potential detrimental consequence. For example if the requirement is that a major consequence should not have a frequency of greater than a 1 in 100 years, then a 10 year successful history only gives additional confidence that all seems well. In fact if the frequency requirement for a catastrophic event is far more demanding, then typical design history perspectives may be somewhat less comforting. History also shows us that past success does not always support future success.

Historical Experience

History shows us that many if not most catastrophic events occur though an 'unfortunate' sequence of linked events rather than from a single technical cause. Such previously undiscovered sequences are often related to an incomplete knowledge of the range of possible states leading to the propagation of the failure sequence or perhaps more correctly the level of dependency between such states in such a sequence. For example, an initial technical failure will not propagate if all states potentially influenced by such a failure have been fully identified, characterised and configured through independence to terminate such a sequence. The problem arises when there is incomplete knowledge about the range of states that may be mutually or dependently influenced. So incomplete information is the enemy of safety assurance of termination of a mishap occurrence. This is often pictorially displayed in the Swiss Cheese model. In the general case the states involved may take on a wide range of types. For example in a simple technical product an initial analysis may appear relatively simple i.e. that of tracking the well-known and fully defined influenced states together with their known mitigating/independent resilience. However, the response of these states may in turn be influenced by external actors, for example environments at the time of the initial flaw and without this information the response robustness of the argument for terminating the sequence prior to the mishap will be questionable. Of course nuclear warheads need to remain safe given a wide range of potentially severe environments. To treat any real case it is necessary to establish, as far as possible, a complete definition of the 'system' of all states and influences. This is perhaps analogous to the goal of fundamental physics of seeking a complete understanding of all of nature's subatomic particles and forces and their potential interactions. As the 'system and influences grow' so does the difficulty of being able to fully identify and characterise the response of such states given any initiating event. In essence complexity can become the enemy of safety and enhances the difficulty of identifying a Black Swan should it indeed exist. This complexity is perhaps best illustrated in simple form by a fictitious but not improbable example given in the form of a somewhat dated cinema film *(Fate is the Hunter)* shown during the 2017 ISSC by John Rankin who used this by way of example. It is para-phrased as follows: Following an aircraft take-off one of the engines was struck by a bird which was rarely found in that part of the world – an unlikely initiator. The plane suffered a jolt due to the loss of that engine and as a result a cup of coffee, just supplied to the Captain, spilled onto an equipment box. Because the box was unsealed coffee leaked onto the underlying equipment. The coffee was somewhat conducting in nature and as a result this interfered with underlying critical circuits, which led to the loss of the other engine. Because of aircraft congestion at the airfield at that time, the Captain took the reasonable option of landing on a nearby suitable beach. It so happened, unknown to the captain, that a pier on that beach, which had been scheduled for removal the previous week, was still in place, because of a decision by the contractor that there was no real need to hurry. Hence the fateful collision.

Although the initial verdict was judged to be human failure careful analysis showed this not to be the case. The sequence is fictitious but it does exemplify the need to fully understand what the 'system and the influences' really consists of and hence all of the potential interacting events given a somewhat unexpected fault initiator. Who would initially have identified the potential presence of a cup of coffee, the importance of an unsealed equipment box, congested airport conditions at the time and the continued existence of the pier that should have been absent? Simplicity in the 'bounding of the system' is an important goal for minimising the opportunity for failing to fully characterise it. This in fact represents an important element in the safety approach to nuclear warheads: bounding the system (in the safety sense) as far as possible and aiming for simplicity, independence and clarity in the safety argument. Some of these aspects are covered in more detail later in this paper. The additional lesson learned from this fictitious example is that the sequence initiator was an abnormal environment, i.e. is an 'insult' to the technical system rather than a design flaw, although one could argue that design flaws helped the sequence to propagate. In fact history shows that many sequences which have led to mishaps come from initial 'insult' initiators. This lesson is not lost on the strategy for minimising the opportunity of a Black Swan manifesting itself in nuclear warheads. The strategy is based on both the effort expended in both preventing such insults and the safety resilience given such an insult.

Human failure is often cited as the main cause leading to catastrophic failure and for this reason design safety has to be resilient to human failure, in addition to minimising the potential for such human failures.

General Background to the Black Swan Term

Origin of the Phrase 'Black Swan': A rare event, based on the belief widely held in England in the 1600s that swans could only be white. All swans in England were white. The phrase "a Black Swan" was a metaphor for "that which could not exist". In the late 1600s in Australia, black swans were discovered.

Current Understanding of the Phrase: An event judged through best established inductive/inferred logic to be assessed as rare – but this process does not remove the possibility of occurrence.

- **a.** *That the knowledge that we base our inductive assessment on is not quantitatively or logically correct*. **Its impact on risk assessment.**
- **b.** *Or more importantly that the scope of our inductive process is not complete i.e. there are some possibilities we have not yet visualised.* **Its impact on both risk assessment and defence in depth.**

The bottom line is, given the application of our best knowledge, a quantitative assessment may be broadly realistic but does not discount the possibility of an occurrence. In most cases this quantitative assessment is sufficient and the whole subject areas of 'cost benefit and insurance risks' work on this principle. However, this approach may be inappropriate if the Black Swan event has a major or catastrophic consequence. In this case there are two emerging issues:

- *a. The incompleteness in the quantification of the probability of mishap occurrence may be small but this delta does matter.*
- *b. That the true nature and impact of the mishap may itself not be understood and underestimated. Although there may be a reasonable description of the mishap, the real follow on consequences are usually less well understood and often turn out to be of a far greater nature than first anticipated.*

Hence, the context of the Black Swan is that it applies to an unwanted mishap which is assessed to be somewhat improbable but cannot be discounted and that its outcome can be severe or catastrophic and not fully understood. In fact in a general sense it might be unclear as to what the mishap itself may be and this is typified by the lessons from economic/financial traumas.

Some Terms and Definitions:

a. **Unexpected**
The 'best analysis' suggests that the event has a low probability of occurrence. Such analysis cannot claim to be absolutely free of incompleteness and as such cannot assure us it can't happen. There is often a quantitative definition of what is meant by unexpected.

b. **Inconceivable**
That there is some fundamental reason why it cannot happen or that one cannot imagine how it can possibly happen. This in principle (particularly the latter) is a human construct and does not completely remove the possibility of a high consequence event.

c. **Consequence**
This relates to the range of impacts (detrimental in this case) given the event and in the case of safety this will take many forms:

Death or harm/ Environmental damage/ Loss of asset/Financial loss/Reputational loss/Political harm/Etc.

Black Swans are generically spoken of in the context of a major detriment and for nuclear warheads (NW) can be associated with a major issue in relation to performance or safety. In the latter case this can be directly related to the occurrence of the worst case catastrophic event itself, or to realisation that there may be a major flaw in the safety argument which requires urgent mitigating action. Of course this is a key issue in the continued ownership and safety scrutiny of a stockpile of nuclear warheads.

Some Differing Categories of Black Swan and AWE's Culture

a) Known - but not to the degree necessary
Knowledge about such a possibility is available but is not sufficient for correct judgement on probability and/or consequence. Of course there is always the judgmental problem of when 'enough is enough' in relation to the depth of scrutiny which is necessary for elimination of the Black Swan's possibility.
With regards to detrimental event occurrence: The warhead programme has strived to avoid falling into this category. It has taken a very much 'what if' and 'expecting the unexpected' approach. All known possibilities are subject to in depth scrutiny. If there is any reason why an issue has not been completely closed out it is subject to continued scrutiny and of course this may give rise to a necessary change of design. We continue to strive to establish a more comprehensive understanding of the underlying characteristic of the known issues, whether they be of technical, human factors, implementation or governance nature. We retain a culture of assuming that we may not have reached the end of the road towards this goal and there is always more to be done – a culture of continued in depth assessment.

b) Unknowns – but knowable unknowns that could have been looked for or known by others.
The problem here is that such unknowns may have been regarded (erroneously) as being of no consequence e.g. for safety.
With regards to detrimental event occurrence: The relevance to warhead activity follows from the comments under the last heading in the sense that there should be no assumption, without sufficient evidence, that the knowable unknowns can be discounted. If the unknowns are knowable then this gives us a direction in which to focus further effort and scrutiny with the goal of reaching a position where such unknowns are converted into 'fully characterized' and their impact determined. Included in this is the need to be aware of what's happening elsewhere in the world where similar technologies may be exercised and where there are technology enhancements taking place which can have an advantage in enhancing our safety. Of course in this respect one covers the whole associated subject area included in SETM (Science, Engineering, Technology and Mathematics) where it is necessary to keep a close eye on worldwide developments in both industry and academia, which can be incorporated to our advantage. Our close collaboration with our US colleagues plays a major mutual role in this. In addition, one needs to keep abreast of 'state of the art' developments in the range of methodologies for safety assessment and assurance, much of which are bound up in the general subject area of System Safety and as such where we need to be expert practitioners. On course this again is a constantly moving and evolving activity with an acknowledgement that there will be no perfection. Any 'judgement' that we have reached a position of having identified and characterized such known unknowns is subject to constant challenge. Again the 'what if' attitude and 'expecting the unexpected' culture at AWE does provide a strong defense

against this form of failure. Of course the primary element of protection relating to 'known by others' comes through collaboration with our US colleagues and other work, particularly in the nuclear industry at large. The aim here is to establish confidence that no potential influencing subject area is left untouched.

c) Unknown – but unknowable unknowns

*No absolute basis for being able to make any assured prediction for occurrence expectation or consequence – **a true Black Swan!** Nevertheless even here 'confident' predictions may well be made but of course with the potential for failure due to ignorance.*

With regards to detrimental event occurrence: This presents the most difficult aspect with regard to warhead safety assurance in that if such flaws exist in our knowledge we have little or no guidance of where to look further. The best practical protection against this uncertainty comes from the independent strength in depth approach to design, ownership and assessment both in terms of the technical and organisational aspects. The best overall solution we are able to come up with in this respect, given no clear guidance of where further to look, is a continued commitment to ensure that we have a cadre of high calibre staff working at the cutting edge of all of the relevant technologies, processes and assessment methodologies and giving them sufficient freedom and encouragement 'to probe' into 'looking for the unexpected'. This activity is not solely restricted to 'in house' activity but also includes keeping a close look at developments of interest in the external world and how best to take advantage of such developments. Such unknowns are not likely to be uncovered through standard process and routine. From a business perspective, this may appear to be an untargeted, unproductive and non-cost effective overhead – but we fail here at our peril. This **continuous scrutiny** process is identified in figure1. **AWE's culture strongly supports and encourages this approach.**

Lessons from the Open Literature

Nassim Nicholas Taleb: Taleb is well known for his work in this area and describes a Black Swan in terms of:

a. *Is unpredictable and as such cannot be truly sentenced as low probability.*

b. *Causes an extreme or catastrophic impact, and*

c. *Is retrospectively predictable – with the warning that there can be a tendency to simplify (and possibly erroneously) the post event analysis of the cause.* **There may be a telling lesson here for us in relation to the Review Learn and Improve (RLIs) we undertake – we need to be clear that we really do have the correct post event analysis – otherwise it can happen again.**

Taleb's (Ref 3) interest in unpredictability comes from his association with economics and the financial industries where prediction has been shown on many occasions to be unwarranted with major detrimental consequences. There may be some success in predicting the near future but this gives no assured guidance for the longer term and the longer term may not be too extensive in this context. This aspect is somewhat like weather prediction where longer term prediction is also fraught with uncertainty. This can manifest itself via so called chaos theory. In both cases predicting the future is bedevilled by the vast number of interacting contributors of not always perfectly defined knowledge, and starting conditions. In the case of the economic and financial industries the situation is further complicated by the emotional response of people, whereas weather prediction is primarily governed by the laws of physics. **It is salutary to note that a nuclear weapon (or even a warhead) design, including its processing and ownership, is itself a somewhat complex subject area with inherent complicated relationships. However, a key lesson from Taleb experience is that we should strive to limit complexity (in respect to its relationship to safety) because of its impact on the ability to predict with confidence. As a result we continue to strive to limit complexity and to gain as complete an understanding as possible of what we have – with the mind set of 'what if' – is it complete?**

There have been many attempts to model economic and financial futures, some based on a statistical basis, for example on the normal distribution for occurrence probability and range of consequence. In the context of financial industries the 'well known' distribution peaks can be associated with the 'currently understood' in the relatively short term and the tails, with all their uncertainties, can be represented by the longer term 'judgements'. Because of the complex nature of the financial industries these 'tails' often turn out to be completely misleading. Distributed approaches are sometimes applied to warhead safety assessments. Such distributions usually have far more evidential support near the peaks and less in the tails, where the low probability high consequence predictions are made and where prediction can be in significant error. This is where the Black Swans, if they exist, may lie. **The safety of warheads depends on the evidential confidence in the application of such distributions, where such distributions need to be applied.**

Taleb's View in Combatting Uncertainty: His view was that because of the complexity associated with the financial industry, effort expended in trying to prevent catastrophic occurrence was not well spent. He felt that catastrophes were inevitable and most effort should be best directed towards robustness in coping with Black Swan events when they occur rather than on predicting or preventing their occurrence. His experience was associated with economic and financial subject areas where his assumption (based on substantial historical evidence) was that these events **will occur** and one should have plans in place on how to deal with them and mitigate the consequences. Given the assumption that the event will occur Taleb's approach appears correct. **However, the priority for nuclear warheads lies firmly in the direction of preventing the occurrence and particularly in relation to the 'worst case' occurrence of Inadvertent Nuclear Yield (INY), rather than prioritising on the mitigation actions following such an event, if indeed this was realistically possible. For this reason we concentrate on limiting complexity, particularly in the context of the principal safety arguments, in order to enhance transparency and confidence in the evidence to support an assessment of a very low occurrence probability.**

Perrow is well known for his work in accident theory (e.g. ref 4): As such he provides another guide to how Black Swans can arise and what approaches should be put in place to avoid their occurrence. He has spent a great deal of his career in the field of historical accident assessment and the reasoning behind their occurrence. These have covered a wide range of subject areas but their applicability are generally pertinent to nuclear warhead safety. The principles that clearly emerge from his work are again simplicity, clarity and independence. These are evidenced by his observations and recommendations noted below.

a. *Complex, interconnected, and highly-coupled systems should be expected to fail.*

Response in warhead design. Warheads by their very nature have to be interconnected but this is different in the sense of being highly coupled in the context of safety. For example interconnectivity in the sense of arming safety requires a unique set of authorizing actions/conditions for 'fault progression' and their absence prevents unintended fault progression. This principle also applies to other aspects of the warhead. As such in the safety sense there is limited inadvertent connectivity. The same is true for the AWE safety organizational structure in that although there are interconnections they are designed to be independent in the safety ensurance and assurance sense. Design also aims to minimize complexity and this helps towards unintended (undetected) safety interconnectivity. For example safety systems strive to minimize component counts (and particularly those that are safety related). In addition, principal safety arguments are based on a demanding requirement to demonstrate mutual independence between safety systems including the fundamentals of principles and implementation. Coupled with this is a strategy aimed at making the principal safety argument transparent and simple as opposed to being complex in nature. The more complex the safety argument the more challenges that can be realistically raised and the greater the difficulty in providing the appropriate level of assurance. Both simplicity and independence minimize the opportunity for failure through unintended coupled and undetected paths. In turn simplicity and independence ease the burden of providing safety assurance given that one is always tasked to continue to look for all the 'possibilities' leading to mishap. It is certainly not a stance of taking more and more comfort from what we have achieved so far. A strong continuous probing, analysis, testing and surveillance culture is key in relation to early detection of any flaws that might exist or may be developing over time and is supported with a commitment to maintaining a strong cadre of experts probing in the relevant technology areas.

b. *Focus on those aspects with catastrophic consequences*

Response in warhead design. Although we focus on safety across the board we nevertheless concentrate particularly on the worst case events of Inadvertent Nuclear Yield (INY) and major radioactive material (RAM) release, and as such go to great lengths to prevent their occurrence both by way of design, associated processes and independent organizational assessment activity. Again the prevention of INY and RAM release is based on a number of foundational safety principles which are in turn scrutinized with respect to the probity of their underlying scientific, technical, engineering, implementation and evidential basis. This includes assurance that their implementation fully meets these principles both for normal and abnormal (accident) environments. Of course the ownership approach also aims to minimize the occurrence of abnormal environments and the impact of human error.

c. *Strive for systems that are simple, easily understood, disconnected, and decoupled*

Response in warhead design. This is essentially a re-statement of (a) above. We adopt this strategy for NW design safety focusing on; clarity, simplicity and strong independent arguments in the defense in depth approach. Safety is based on a limited number of very strong and independent principles, arguments and technical implementations. These together with the clarity of their safety intent and quality of implementation enables a clear and comprehensive challenging process to be undertaken in order to fully test and analyze for overall safety completeness and compliance. The principal arguments supporting the safety case should be simple and clear and should not arise as a result of a complex set of contributing arguments.

The strategy is based on the application of **a limited number** of clear strong and independent safety arguments and implemented safety systems based upon: Ensuring maximum resilience against the undermining of safety that can occur through added complexity as the number of safety systems increases. Increasing the number inevitably leads to increasing complexity and increasing concerns about maintaining true independence between the implemented safety systems. Added complexity generally increases the difficulty of ensuring confidence of overall safety because of the multiplicity of potential sneak paths or fault sequences that can give rise to failure. In addition, a warhead is confronted by constraints on available volume and mass and the need for the complementary requirement that these safety systems can be reliably removed when fully 'authorised' to do so and such authorisation is based on a principle of uniqueness which effectively decouples it from the safety argument.

Some Additional Factors

A Lesson from History - Predicting the Future based on the Past: *"But in all my experience, I have never been in any accident.....of any sort worth speaking about. I have seen but one vessel in distress in all my years at sea. I never saw a wreck and have never been wrecked nor was I ever in any predicament that threatened to end in disaster of any sort." E. J. Smith, 1907. Captain of RMS Titanic, quoted five years before he went down with his ship.*

The clear lesson here is that past history (or perceived past history), although it may be a guide to the future nevertheless it is only a guide and as such gives no assurance about the future. Confidence (false) was also based on the safety built into the Titanic, where all potential threats were deemed to have been considered and catered for. The ship was judged 'unsinkable' but in fact suffered a catastrophe on its maiden voyage. This resulted from a combination of failure to prevent the collision and an overestimate of the ship's capability to withstand such a collision. **This was an example of a known but not to the degree necessary.** Similar arguments can be applied to the Columbia and Challenger tragedies where confidence was again based on 'past successes and inadequate technical assessment of known threats'.
Warnings from the past come in the form of failures and 'near misses' and if acted upon can improve the situation. However, near misses are not always recognized for what they are and as such there is no guarantee they are fully understood with regards to the future. AWE however scrutinizes issues of this nature to ensure that the fundamental reasons for their cause are fully understood and removed. We 'may' take some comfort from the past history of UK's nuclear weapons ownership where there have been no major safety events but one cannot take this as assurance in respect to the future. Certainly the number of successful weapon lifetimes in our history comes nowhere near to proving compliance with the exacting safety standards that we strive to comply with. We certainly take heed of any issues that have arisen and have acted upon them with high priority.

Human Factors and Independence: Humans are not exempt from failure. Assumptions of true independence in human actions – which is often used as a major redundancy element in preventing a failure, has a long history of being undermined, note the US Minot incident. This type of failure has been noted in dual 'independent' checking processes where enhanced confidence is based on an assumption that true independence is assured in the process. Humans are seldom truly independent in this context. For this reason the safety of nuclear warheads is based principally on scientific, technical and engineering principle foundations. Nevertheless 'independent' checking and dual control, together with human error assessment, do have an important place in nuclear warhead safety in preventing and quantifying inadvertent actions. Of course in the limit even safeguards based on technical principles are not absolutely free from human influence. For example, engineering based safeguards need human actions for design manufacture, inspection and maintenance for ensuring and maintaining design intent compliance.

Conservatism, Worst Case and Probability Function: The approach to nuclear warhead safety design and assessment is conservatively based. This conservatism is applied to combat any possible remnant uncertainty in occurrence probability and consequence and usually takes the form of a somewhat 'worst-case' rather than best estimate approach to risk assessment. This less onerous (in application) approach is well understood and provides a sensible hedge against uncertainty but will not always be usable. In some cases 'worst-case' assumptions can be too conservative and lead to difficulty in meeting exacting risk safety standards. As such somewhat less conservative but still supportable statistical approaches, figure 2, are deemed more appropriate. This tends towards a more onerous approach (in application) and can carry with it a smaller conservative margin in protecting against uncertainty. As noted previously distributions often have greater evidential support near their peaks and far less in the tails, which typically characterise the low probability associated with potentially catastrophic events – Black Swans. The safety assessment of nuclear warheads sometimes puts us in these regions where we need to apply such tails of distributions with suitable caution and with a sound evidential base founded on substantial supporting technical and historical arguments. Such distributions are only accepted if detailed scrutiny provides the evidence noted above and that in turn this evidence stands up to independent challenge. This typically applies to assessment of explosive response to environmental challenge.

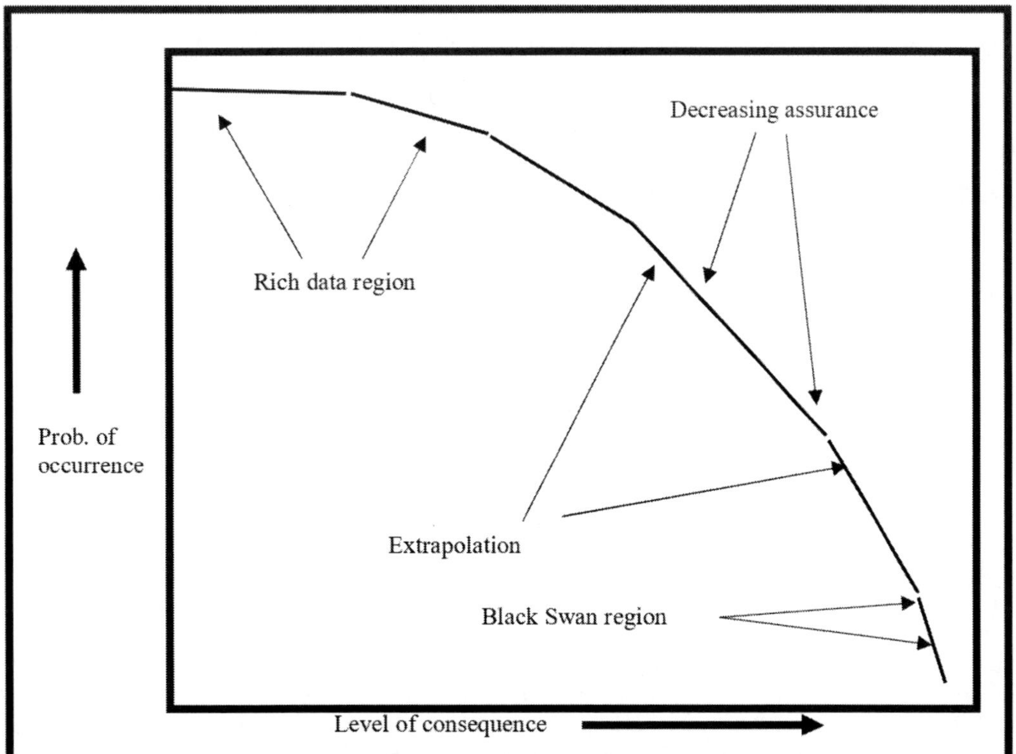

Figure 2 _ Distribution approach to safety assessment

The Importance of and Achieving Independence

The occurrence of mishaps and even Black Swans are often the result of an initiator setting off a related sequence which is not truncated. Protection against this occurrence will rely heavily on:

(a) A full understanding of the inventory of possible hazardous sequences leading on from any given initiator and culminating in a mishap.
(b) Ensuring a suitable level of independence between such events in the sequence so that the sequence is truncated before reaching the mishap stage. Some of these aspects were covered in reference 2 in terms of the identification of the strength in depth of barriers or Lines of Defence (LOD) in relation to their number and strength in preventing such a mishap. In particular, the importance of independence between such LOD. The choice of LOD are based on the widest range of categories possible in order to meet the independence requirement. For example

(1) Fundamental physics or chemical properties based on the laws of nature which directly support the LOD resilience

(2) Uniqueness of response. In the sense that defeat of the LOD can only occur as a result of unique circumstances.
(3) That microelectronics/firmware/software elements are clearly decoupled from the primary safety arguments.
(4) Best practices engineered implementation of a concept to the extent that failure is unlikely even under challenging circumstances – e.g. accident conditions.
(5) Procedure based. This relies on humans doing the correct thing at the correct time and not doing the incorrect things at the wrong time. Examples are fully trained staff and application of the two-man checking principle.

These can be broadly categorised as having the resilience properties of; **Isolation, Incompatibility, Inoperability, Independence**. Of course, although correct procedure can have a significant influence in safety, it takes the lowest place in the hierarchy of attributes in the strength in depth argument.
The ability to deterministically make an LOD resilience case and to support the principle of LOD independence will follow this hierarchy. A structured sequence protection argument based strongly on correct LOD based procedures alone will not be acceptable. Although human LOD are least favourable in the overall choice, all LOD have some element of human involvement because of human relationship to judgement, inspection, testing, maintenance etc.
In addition to the choice of LOD category the overall strength in depth arguments for LOD in any particular fault sequence is enhanced by applying the following hierarchy of application for independence in as far as technical implementation allows:

1. Fundamentally different concepts
2. Fundamentally different applications of the same concept
3. Different engineering implementations of the same concept
4. Application of different and different sourced materials in the same concepts or engineering implementation.

All of these LOD attributes form the major basis of preventing sequences propagating to the mishap conditions.

The Influence of Environmental Factors on Black Swan Assurance

An initiator can take the form of a design flaw (failure) or an 'insult'. The latter represents an abnormal environment (accident) and this environment could in turn be applied simultaneously to all LOD in the strength in depth strategy. As such it is important to avoid common mode failure in the application of the LOD. General historical evidence shows that many major mishaps have indeed arisen from common cause environmental based failures of this manner. The potential for abnormal environments presents the greatest challenge in ensuring that all of the sequence paths are identified for any warhead design. In turn one must show that there is sufficient resilience to ensure that such sequences, through design and testing, are truncated under these circumstances and that there is no common mode failure. Prevention of abnormal environment occurrence is of course also a major objective in the overall safety theme and every effort possible is made to prevent/limit the potential for such insults/accidents and in turn the prevention of such environmental propagating to the warhead. Nevertheless such events cannot be totally discounted and as such the safety characteristics of a warhead design must show appropriate resilience against such threats.

Conclusions

Hunting for the Black Swan in the context of safety can represent a somewhat uncertain activity in the sense that one may be looking for something that does not exist. One cannot prove a negative. However, there is a compelling history of disasters which evidence the existence of such Black Swans which were not identified in advance. The level of scrutiny applied to the search for Black Swans must be related to the potential consequence of failure. Of course for nuclear warheads we are well aware of the worst case catastrophe represented by inadvertent nuclear yield (INY) and as a result have established a sound culture aimed at minimising the potential for such an occurrence. In addition, we need to provide a compelling level of evidence/assurance that the probability of such an (man-made) occurrence will be less than natural catastrophes of a similar magnitude. We do this based on an independent strength in depth approach coupled with state of the art application of science, engineering and technology with all of the associated requirements set by established best practice. Such designs are then subjected to an independent conservative numerical risk assessment based on a foundation of supporting evidence to demonstrate compliance with demanding national risk standards. Both fundamental design aspects and the risk assessment are in turn subject to organisational independent assurance challenge. The latter covers the fidelity and completeness of the: logic, evidence, implementation and a search for any aspects which might have been missed or not covered in sufficient depth. Both contributions are then considered at the organisational executive decision making level where a further level of knowledge and experience is applied. These activities go a long way to eradicating the presence of Black Swans but of course this does not guarantee that one is not present. The final layer in the defence comes from the strong organisational support to a continuing probing culture which applies a 'what if' and 'expecting the unexpected' mind-set. As such the campaign for assuring safety never ends. This latter contribution is based on a strong and continuing organisational commitment to engaging the best brains, which continue to probe into the various science, technology and design areas with the goal of achieving even greater depths of understanding in the cause of Black Swan identification and early eradication before such can manifest itself. This is exercised both through direct in-house activity and through what can be gleaned from the external world. One cannot claim that this last layer leads to perfection and at times may appear to be somewhat 'undirected' in its approach. However, it is still the best way me know of with regard to tackling the demanding challenge of **Unknown Unknowns**. The overall strategy is hence based on: (1) A sound approach for developing a safe product and process - ensurance. (2) A sound independent scrutinising/challenging element - independent assurance. (3) A knowledgeable and experienced executive decision making element – final accountability. (4) An organisational commitment to applying the best brains to a continuing probing approach into all of the technology and procedural areas – the last possible hiding place of the Black Swan – safety is never finished.

References

Reference 1: Jones, M., 'Organisational Problems – Potential Causes – Unintentional Consequences' 34th International System Safety Conference, Orlando, Florida, USA, August 2016. System Safety Society, PO Box 70, Unionville, Virginia 22567-0070.

Reference 2: Jones, M., 'Strength in Depth and Quantitative Risk Assessment in the Context of Low Frequency High Consequence Systems', 35th International System Safety Conference, Albuquerque, New Mexico, August 2017. System Safety Society, PO Box 70, Unionville, Virginia 22567-0070.

Reference 3: Taleb, N. N., 'The Black Swan: The Impact of the Highly Improbable', Penguin.

Reference 4 Perrow, C, 'The Next Catastrophe Reducing our Vulnerabilities to Natural, Industrial and Terrorist Disasters, Princeton University Press.

Reference 5: Perrow, C – see Jones, M., 'High Consequence Accident/Failure Theories', 19th International System Safety Conference, Huntsville, Alabama, USA, September 2001. System Safety Society, PO Box 70, Unionville, Virginia 22567-0070.

Reference 6: Perrow, C, 'Complex Organisations: A critical Essay', 1972, ISBN 0-07-554799-6.

Biography

Malcolm Jones, Atomic Weapons Establishment, Reading, Berkshire, United Kingdom,
Postal code RG7 4PR, Fax UK 01189827589, Phone UK 01189855495, e-mail Malcolm.Jones@awe.co.uk.

Malcolm has previously led the Distinguished Scientists group at AWE and currently holds the position of Scientific Adviser to AWE's Chief Scientist and directly supports AWE's Chief of Product Assurance. His career at AWE has taken him through a wide range of scientific and engineering topics, but he has maintained a continuous association with nuclear weapon design and process safety and top level nuclear safety standards. His interests extend to corporate safety cultures and the root cause reasons for failures. He is a Fellow of the International System Safety Society and is an adviser to a number of senior UK Ministry of Defence and AWE safety bodies. He has been awarded an MBE in the Queen's Birthday Honours List for contributions to the UK defence industry and is a recipient of the John Challens' Medal, which is AWE's highest award for lifetime contributions to Science, Engineering and Technology. He has also been honoured by VNIIA in the RF for his work in fostering nuclear weapon safety collaboration between the UK and the RF.

Safety is from Mars, Security is from Venus: *Exploring the Practical and Socio-technical Challenges of Safety-Security Co-assurance*

Nikita Johnson
Supervisor: Prof. Tim Kelly

High Integrity Systems Engineering Depar tment of Computer Science, University of Y ork

and BAE Systems

15th August 2018

Agenda

- critically survey the current state-of-the-art techniques and standards
- socio-technical challenges
- candidate solution and future work

Review: Safety-Security Approaches

Safety-Security Approaches

1. Hazard Analysis
   - Security-Aware STPA: STPA-Sec and STPA-SafeSec
   - Security-Aware HAZOP: SAHARA for Automotive Security
2. Mitigations and Control
   - Security-Integrated Fault Trees: Attack-Defence Trees
3. Architectural and System Analysis
   - Architecture Tradeoff Analysis Method
   - Dependibility Deviation Analysis
4. Assurance Arguments and Standards
   - Security Cases
   - Standards

Combined Analysis

Each better than those that precede i t ...

- Still missing
  - fundamental philosophy
  - unifying language
  - standard set of practices
  - safety-informed security?
- Major differences remain
  - Differences in proportionality
  - Uncertainty of Security
  - Intent of Attacker
  - Language and ontologies

Socio-Technical Challenges

Trade-off

Conceptual and Philosophical Trade-off

- safety has been around for longer
- safety has mature conceptual framework: definition of "harm"
- differing values: *e.g.*
  - safety openness and transparency vs. security through obscurity
  - safety build and analyse once vs. security update to protect
- security poses unique challenge to safety: undercuts argume nts

Trade-off

Organisational Trade-off

- experts in each domain rarely appreciate the concerns from the other domain
- domain specific specialisms
- sovereignty? other drivers *e.g.* business objectives, autono my
- communities usually physically separate
- lack of Suitably Qualified and Experienced People

Trade-off

Trade-off Considerations for Individuals

- understand complex models and interactions
- practitioners are not omniscient
- biases: confirmation bias and Dunning-Kruger

Adversarial Nature of Security

- safety
  - domain openness,
  - collaboration,
  - top-down system analyses and
  - assumes benevolent operators making mistakes
- security: space of adversarial competition - attacker with potentially infinite attack vectors
  - information hiding
  - bottom-up vulnerability mitigations (checklists)
  - fast-evolving threats by intelligent attackers
- In many cases adversarial nature causes security to be in versely proportional to safety *e.g.* transparency encouraged by standards provides attack blueprint

Communicatio
n

- safety-security challenge compounded by
  - lack of shared language between teams
  - lack of synchronised development techniques during lifecycle
- models diverge and the link becomes obscured
- research has been done (mainly with one attribute)
  - combining processes, argumentation approaches, controlled vo cabularies
- No widely adopted systematic way of information sharin g.

Risk Challenge

Evolving Threat

- increased cyber-security threat from activist, criminal and state-sponsored groups
- highly organised, many resources, sophisticated
- "What would Mitnick do?"
- motive, not means is missing

Risk Measure

- Researchers have attempted to use probability as a meas ure
- uncertainty precludes single, meaningful *quantitative* risk measure
- alternative *qualitative* measures for risk widely used such as
  - Common Criteria evaluation assurance levels for security
  - development assurance levels for safety
- no widely adopted integrated measure
- criticism for methods that bluntly combine safety and secu rity

Representation

- lack of constrained or standardised language leads to misunderstandings, lost information and asynchronous duplicate processes
- models: it is unclear what constitutes a joint model or r epresentation of risk
- proliferation of causal models without much justification
- when creating models, what is left out is important: risk at boundary conditions
- both domains over-reliant on expertise and knowledge
- difference between information representation and inte rpretation

Timin

- g synchronisation problem during PDLC, mismatch with s oftware and systems methodologies *e.g.* unclear integra tion with agile
- sustainability of security components
- incorporating new risk information in a timely fashion
- response to new legislation

Example

Auror

- a 2014 Scott Ainslie received an unexpected response fro m the Department of Homeland Security
- DHS Control Systems Security Program, that operation was focused on hacking into a 27-ton generator
- opening its circuit breakers long enough for the machine to slip out of sync.
- caused the generator to experience “tremendous over-tor que stresses”
- system explosion

The Future (.. at least for this PhD)

Open Question

- Do we need new techniques for safety/security analysis ?
- Yes: more effective ways to find safety/security interacti ons
- No: already a proliferation of techniques dealing with th ese attributes
- So we borrow concepts from model driven engineering and argumentation

Independent Co-Assurance as a Solution?

1. "independent co-assurance" (as opposed to unifie d co-assurance)
2. potentially greater confidence as more deficits ca n be discovered and mitigated

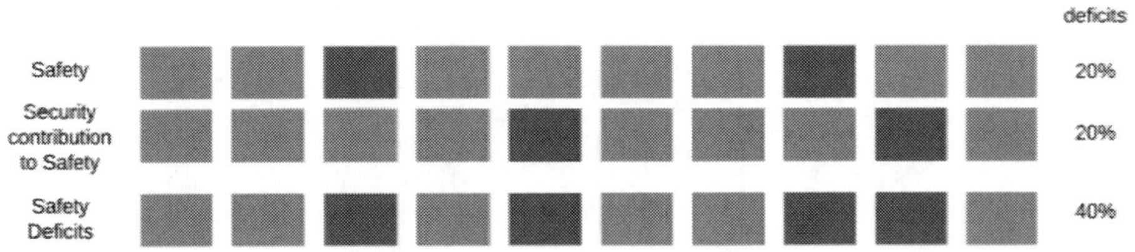

Proposed Solution Framework

- First Task: How will safety and security know w hat information to share and when to share it?
- Candidates:
  - specific techniques
  - standards
  - points in the V development

Possible Solution Framework

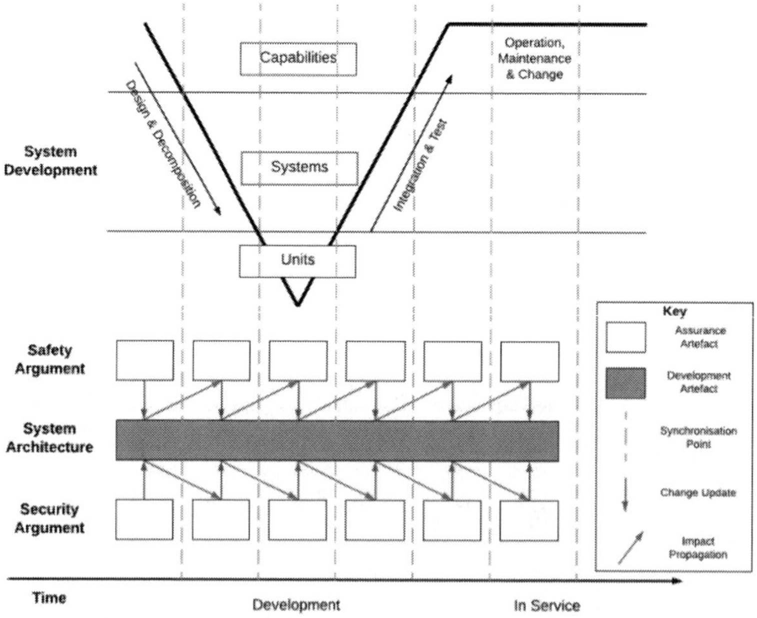

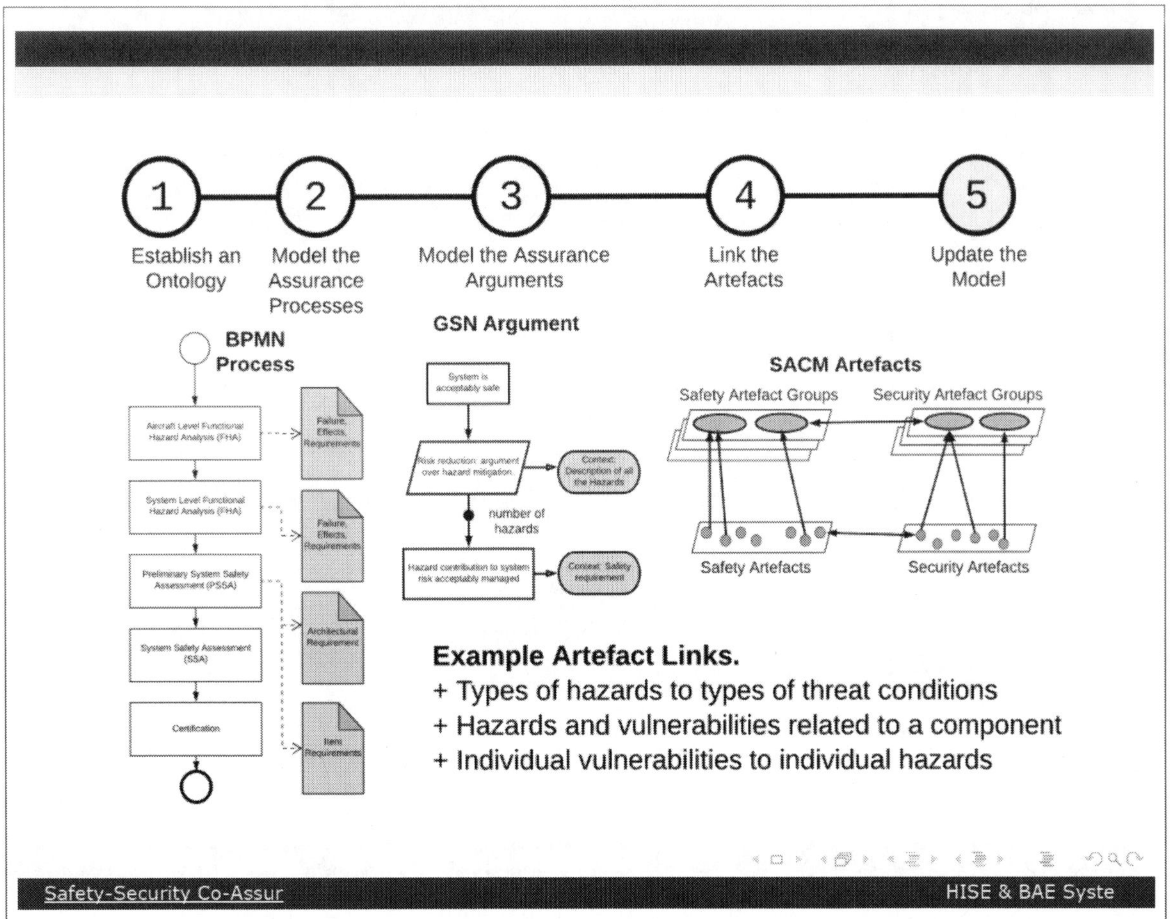

1
2
3
4
5
Establish an Ontology
Model the Assurance Processes
Model the Assurance Arguments
Link the Artefacts
Update the Model
BPMN Process
GSN Argument
SACM Artefacts
Safety Artefact Groups
Security Artefact Groups
Safety Artefacts
Security Artefacts
number of hazards
Example Artefact Links.
+ Types of hazards to types of threat conditions
+ Hazards and vulnerabilities related to a component
+ Individual vulnerabilities to individual hazards
Safety-Security Co-Assur
HISE & BAE Syste

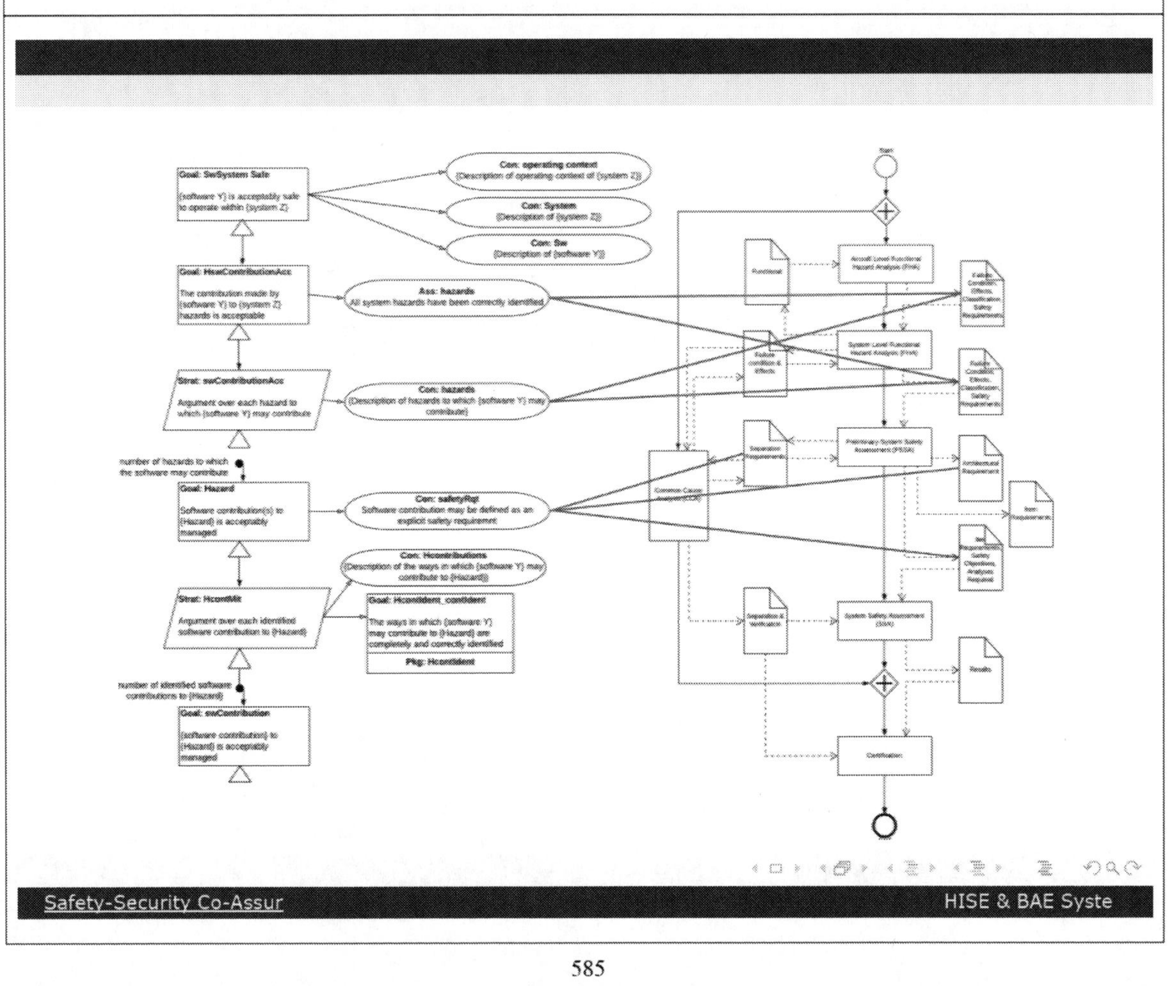

Safety-Security Co-Assur
HISE & BAE Syste

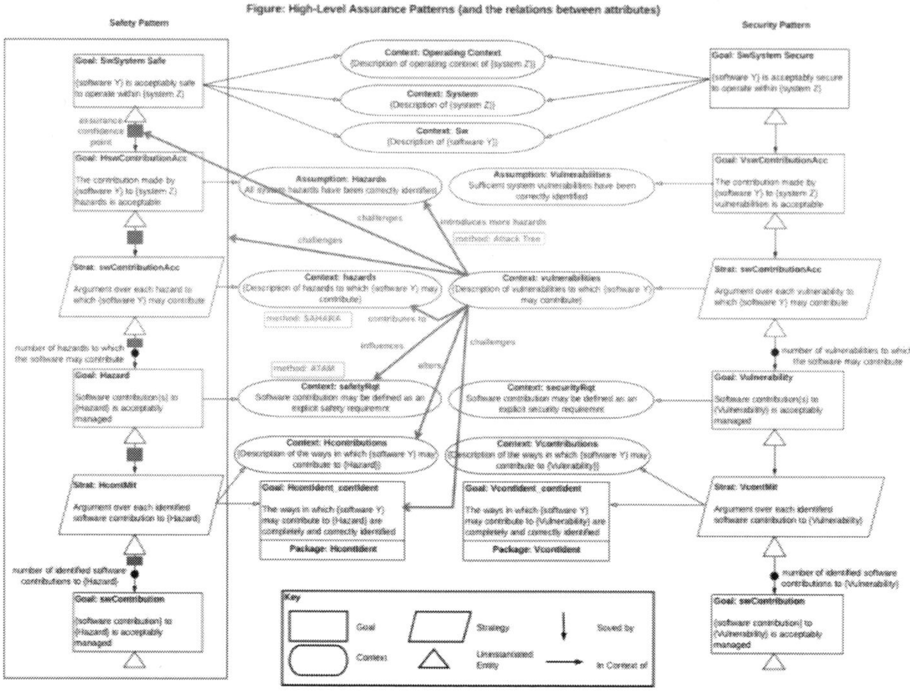

Figure: High-Level Assurance Patterns (and the relations between attributes)
Safety Pattern
Security Pattern
Goal: SwSystem Safe
{software Y} is acceptably safe to operate within {system Z}
assurance confidence point
Goal: HswContributionAcc
The contribution made by {software Y} to {system Z} hazards is acceptable
Strat: swContributionAcc
Argument over each hazard to which {software Y} may contribute
number of hazards to which the software may contribute
Goal: Hazard
Software contribution(s) to {Hazard} is acceptably managed
Strat: HcontMit
Argument over each identified software contribution to {Hazard}
number of identified software contributions to {Hazard}
Goal: swContribution
{software contribution} to {Hazard} is acceptably managed
Context: Operating Context
{Description of operating context of {system Z}}
Context: System
{Description of {system Z}}
Context: Sw
{Description of {software Y}}
Assumption: Hazards
All system hazards have been correctly identified
Assumption: Vulnerabilities
Sufficient system vulnerabilities have been correctly identified
challenges
introduces more hazards
method: Attack Tree
challenges
Context: hazards
{Description of hazards to which {software Y} may contribute}
Context: vulnerabilities
{Description of vulnerabilities to which {software Y} may contribute}
method: SAHARA
contributes to
influences
challenges
method: ATAM
alters
Context: safetyRqt
Software contribution may be defined as an explicit safety requirement
Context: securityRqt
Software contribution may be defined as an explicit security requirement
Context: Hcontributions
{Description of the ways in which {software Y} may contribute to {Hazard}}
Context: Vcontributions
{Description of the ways in which {software Y} may contribute to {Vulnerability}}
Goal: HcontIdent_confident
The ways in which {software Y} may contribute to {Hazard} are completely and correctly identified
Package: HcontIdent
Goal: VcontIdent_confident
The ways in which {software Y} may contribute to {Vulnerability} are completely and correctly identified
Package: VcontIdent
Goal: SwSystem Secure
{software Y} is acceptably secure to operate within {system Z}
Goal: VswContributionAcc
The contribution made by {software Y} to {system Z} vulnerabilities is acceptable
Strat: swContributionAcc
Argument over each vulnerability to which {software Y} may contribute
number of vulnerabilities to which the software may contribute
Goal: Vulnerability
Software contribution(s) to {Vulnerability} is acceptably managed
Strat: VcontMit
Argument over each identified software contribution to {Vulnerability}
number of identified software contributions to {Vulnerability}
Goal: swContribution
{software contribution} to {Vulnerability} is acceptably managed
Key
Goal
Strategy
Solved by
Context
Uninstantiated Entity
In Context of

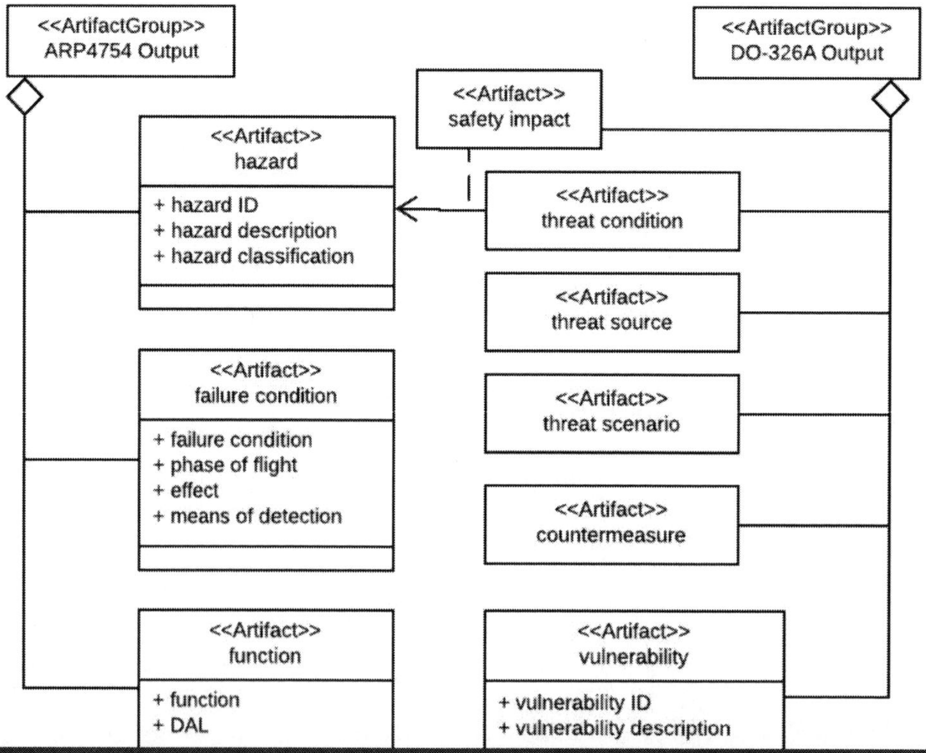

<<ArtifactGroup>>
ARP4754 Output
<<ArtifactGroup>>
DO-326A Output
<<Artifact>>
safety impact
<<Artifact>>
hazard
+ hazard ID
+ hazard description
+ hazard classification
<<Artifact>>
threat condition
<<Artifact>>
threat source
<<Artifact>>
failure condition
+ failure condition
+ phase of flight
+ effect
+ means of detection
<<Artifact>>
threat scenario
<<Artifact>>
countermeasure
<<Artifact>>
function
+ function
+ DAL
<<Artifact>>
vulnerability
+ vulnerability ID
+ vulnerability description

- Process
  - Steps to develop an integrated assurance confidence argument.
  - Points of communication during system development.
  - Method for confidence propagation and management.
  - Steps to configure or restrict information sharing.
- Models
  - Meta-model for safety and security assurance artefacts, and causal models
  - Common argument patterns for safety, security and confidence.
- Language
  - Method for standardising language and terminology used during assurance.
  - Mechanism for linking the system development dictionary with the standardised assurance language.

Implications

- make explicit the assurance arguments
- it does not matter which analyses, methods or information as long as it is justified and delivered in a timely manner
- we can start to form patterns for interactions with safety
- the meta-data collected is valuable
- parts of this framework could be automated, leaving more time for creativity

Conclusion

- socio-technical issues are not incidental, they *are* the prob lem
- managing complexity and uncertainty should be a primary goal
- what is needed is clarity of thought and reasoning, and onl y tools that support that

Thank You! & Questions

This project is funded by the UK's Engineering and Physical Scienc es Research Council through an Industrial Cooperative Award in S cience & Technology (EPSRC iCASE) studentship, in partnership with BAE Systems and the University of York.

A Safety-Centric Change Management Framework by Tailoring Agile and V-Model Processes

Abdallah M. Salameh, Ph.D. Candidate; University of Salford, Manchester, UK*

Omar T. Jaradat, Ph.D. Candidate; Mälardalen University; Västerås, Sweden*

Keywords: safety case, contracts, impact analysis, change management, agile software development, agile tailoring, V-model, XP, Kanban

Abstract

Safety critical systems are evolutionary and subject to preventive, perfective, corrective or adaptive changes during their lifecycle. Changes to any part of those systems can undermine the confidence in safety since changes can refute articulated claims about safety or challenge the supporting evidence on which this confidence relies. Changes to the software components are no exception. In order to maintain the confidence in the safety performance, developers must update their system and its safety case. Agile methodologies are known to embrace changes to software where agilists strive to manage changes, not to prevent them. In this paper, we introduce a novel framework in which we tailor a hybrid process of agile software development and the traditional V-model. The tailored process aims to facilitate the accommodation of non-structural changes to the software parts of safety critical systems. We illustrate our framework in the context of ISO 26262 safety standard.

Introduction

Many safety critical systems are subject to compulsory or advisory certification process which often necessitates building the systems in compliance with domain-specific safety standards (Jaradat & Bate, 2017). Safety standards are becoming the main guide of the development and maintenance of hardware and software parts of safety critical systems. Safety standards, also, form the basis for the approval and certification of those systems (Denney et al., 2015). Software systems, in general, are subject to different types of changes (e.g., preventive, perfective, corrective or adaptive) during the different stages in their life-cycle. In order to maintain the confidence in safety after accommodating a change, developers are required to update the safety case, which in turn requires identifying, re-analysing, and re-checking the impacted parts of the system and generate a new valid set of evidence (Jaradat & Bate, 2017). Despite the obvious recommendations to adequately maintain and review the systems and their safety cases by different safety standards, the latter offer little or no advice on how such operations can be carried out (T. Kelly & J. McDermid, 1999). There is an increasing need for globally-accepted methods and techniques to enable easier change accommodation in safety critical systems without incurring disproportionate cost compared to the size of the change. However, since broader re-verification and re-validation require more effort and time, it is important for any proposal aims to facilitate system changes to delimit the impact of changes.

---

*The author's names are listed in alphabetical order

Safety standards in many safety critical system domains adopt the traditional V-model as a development process for building the systems. Despite the effectiveness of validation and verification that the V-model provides, in addition to other advantages (e.g., easy to estimate costs, create timeliness, and stick to deadlines), the model has a well-known drawback when it comes to handling system changes. This is particularly true when it comes to changes to software systems and their requirements. Following the V-model implies that changes to software components requires re-visiting the system requirements and all later stages to perform a broad and costly impact analysis process. Hence, accepting software changes while using a V-model based process is not a trivial task.

Unlike the series of isolated phases in the V-model, agile methods depend on iterative and incremental development of software to enable reduction in cost, acceleration of time to market in addition to the focus of providing more maintainable code (Salameh, 2011; Tarwani & Chug, 2016). Software developers who follow agile methods breakdown their project into manageable fragments which enables a rapid responsive ways to handle software changes. The Agile way of working minimises the shortcomings of traditional sequential methods and improves the software development process in a more cost-efficient way (Tarwani & Chug, 2016). The alignment of the development process with a dynamic environment is a critical motivation for adopting Agile Software Development (ASD) (Cao et al., 2010). Test Driven Development (TDD) is an important agile process that brings many benefits such as reducing the potential consequences of software defects. TDD protects the system from future failures proactively, which leads to an acceleration of the maintenance process (Knippers, 2011).

The work in this paper does not seek to conduct a comparative study between agile methods and the V-model. The main contribution of this paper, however, is to propose XP-Kan-Safe as a novel maintenance framework to facilitate the accommodation process of software non-structural changes in safety critical systems by utilising the strengths of agile methods and the V-model. More clearly, we reconcile the known effective validation & verification process of the V-model to the known effective practices and the TDD process of agile methods. We exploit the usage of safety contracts (Bate et al., 2003) as: 1) stitches that connect the V-model, Extreme Programming (XP) and Kanban into our tailored process, and 2) means to enable a tri-directional impact analysis process. The hypothesis we make is that ASD can resolve some observed maintenance challenges in the V-model while maintaining software parts of systems.

Background and Motivation

Safety Cases and Safety Arguments

A safety case (also known as assurance or safety assurance case) is: "*A structured argument, supported by a body of evidence that provides a compelling, comprehensible and valid case that a system is safe for a given application in a given operating environment*" (00-56 Standard, 2015). A safety case shall comprise both safety evidence (e.g., safety analyses, software inspections, or functional tests) and a safety argument explaining that evidence (Jaradat et al., 2014). Safety cases might contain an implicit safety argument but some safety standards require an explicit argument that is usually expressed in terms of a defined hierarchy of safety claims and sub-claims that are supported by a body of evidence (00-56 Standard, 2015). There are several ways to represent safety arguments (e.g., textual, tabular, graphical, etc.). In this paper, we use the Goal Structuring Notation (GSN) (GSN Standard, 2011), which provides a graphical means of communicating (1) safety argument elements, claims (goals), argument logic (strategies), assumptions, context, evidence (solutions), and (2) the relationships between these elements (Jaradat et al., 2015a). Figure 1 shows the main notations of the GSN.

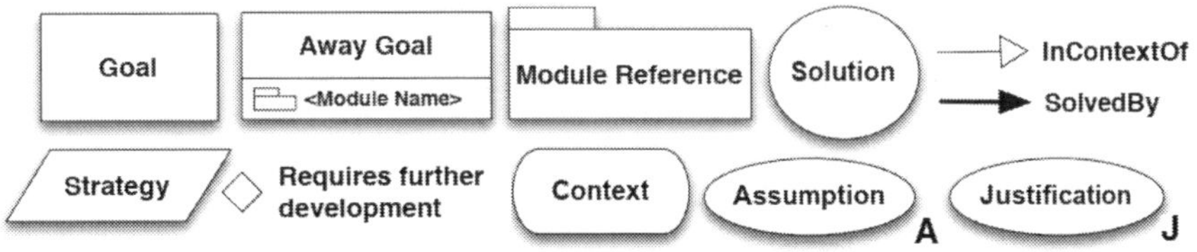

Figure 1— Notation Keys of the GSN

Maintenance of Safety Critical Systems and Their Safety Cases

Change requests should be assessed before decision makers decide whether or not to accept them. The assessment should reveal if the change can cause unreasonable risks, and the required cost to implement the change. Hence, system developers should understand the change and the potential risks that it might carry before they identify the impacted parts. Misunderstanding the change might lead to skip those parts of the system which are dependent on that assumptions. Also, the developers need to understand the dependencies between the system parts to identify the affected parts correctly. For example, the effect of a change can propagate to other parts of the system — creating a ripple effect — and cause unforeseen violations of the acceptable safety limits. If the impact of change is not clear, developers might be conservative and do wider analyses and verification (i.e., check more elements than strictly necessary), and this will exacerbate the cost problem of safety cases. It is also necessary for the developers to describe how the change affects the system parts in order to correctly estimate the cost of the response to that change. Otherwise, the response to a change might generate unplanned further changes to which the system must again respond, and this requires more cost than originally estimated.

ISO 26262 Safety Standard

ISO 26262 (ISO 26262:2011, 2011) regulates the automotive domain and it is intended to be applied to safety-related systems that include one or more electrical and/or electronic systems. The following parts are summarised descriptions of the safety requirements decomposition directly from ISO 26262 guidelines:

1. After identifying hazards, the standard recommends to formulate Safety Goals (SGs) to eliminate or mitigate hazards. The standard defines a safety goal as a top-level safety requirement resultant of the hazard analysis and risk assessment. Safety goals are not expressed in terms of technological solutions, but in terms of functional objectives.

2. Identification of SGs leads to the functional safety concept. The objective of the functional

safety concept is to derive the Functional Safety Requirements (FSRs) from the SGs, and to allocate them to the preliminary architectural elements. At least one FSR shall be specified for each SG. Derivation of FSRs can be supported by safety analyses (e.g., Failure modes and effects analysis (FMEA), Fault Tree Analysis, Hazard and Operability Study (HAZOP)) in order to develop a complete set of effective functional safety requirements.

3. The functional concept leads to the technical safety concept. The first objective of the latter is to specify the Technical Safety Requirements (TSRs) and their allocation to system elements. The second objective is to verify that the TSRs comply with the functional safety requirements. TSRs are used to derive Software Safety Requirements (SSRs).

Safety Contracts

Contract-based design (Benvenuti et al., 2008) is defined as an approach in which the design process is seen as a successive assembly of components where a component behaviour is represented in terms of assumptions about its environment and guarantees about its behaviour. Hence, contracts are intended to describe functional and behavioural properties for each design component in form of assumptions and guarantees. A contract is said to be a safety contract if it guarantees a property that is traceable to a hazard. Using contracts in development of safety critical systems is not a novel idea since there are many works utilise contracts for building, reusing or maintaining safety critical systems (e.g., (Bate et al., 2003; Jaradat et al., 2015a; Jaradat et al., 2015b)). The cost of maintaining, reusing and changing software components is lessened while using contracts as developers may rework software components with knowledge of the constraints placed upon them (Bates et al., 2003). In this paper, we use contracts to support the maintainability of safety critical systems. We also suggest to include additional information into safety contracts in order to enable effective traceability.

Agile Software Development (ASD)

Compared to traditional software engineering approaches, ASD targets complex systems and product development with dynamic, non-deterministic and non-linear characteristics. ASD methods (e.g., XP, Kanban, Scrum) evolve through collaboration between self-organising and cross-functional teams by sharing the same philosophy and utilising the appropriate practices for their contexts.

Each agile method has its own set of features (e.g., practices, terminologies, and tactics) and those features should reflect ASD values and principles. However, agile methods vary when it comes to the strategies they adopt to reflect those values and principles. For example, Kanban is known to have a rapid response to software requirement changes since it allows the team to instantly postpone some change requests to start with other emergent requests. Scrum might do the same but not after the completion of a sprint planning meeting and team commitment. XP teams are amenable to change within their iterations as long as a team has not started work on a particular feature that needs to be exchanged with the new feature. There is no standard recommendation as to how an agile method should implement its features (Campanelli &

Parreiras, 2015).

Organisations, typically, adapt software development methodologies to be in line with their needs and contexts, which covering the full spectrum of the software development life-cycle (Heeager & Rose, 2015; Salameh, 2011). In fact, there is no single agile method that can be adopted for any arbitrary context or to efficiently cover all phases in the development life-cycle. Hence, organisations might not adopt an entire agile method, but rather they combine different processes from different agile methods based on their needs and contexts.

Agile Tailoring

The process in which an agile method is adapted for a specific project situation in a responsive way to accommodate the encountered challenges and to cover the indented interplay between contexts in a dynamic way, is called Agile Tailoring. There are two main approaches to tailor agile methods: the contingency factors and the method engineering theory (Campanelli & Parreiras, 2015). The first approach, handles the tailoring by choosing multiple methods to be on standby in an organisation (i.e., Crystal family (Abrahamsson et al., 2003)). The selection of any standby method is based on project size and criticality, as well as the development context, such as uncertainty level, impact and structure. The second approach is based on meta-method processes and proposes the creation of a new method to be applied on specific contexts based on existing method fragments (a fragment represents a set of practices) (Campanelli & Parreiras, 2015). Despite the flexibility of this approach, it introduces challenges such as how to control the fragments or how to assemble the method for a context specific situation by bringing the appropriate fragments and integrating them into one framework (Campanelli & Parreiras, 2015). In this paper, we tailor our framework using the method engineering approach.

The Kanban Method

Kanban is based on lean principles: it tries to remove the waste of the production process by embracing rules to limit Work In Progress (WIP) and measures the time to finish the tasks (Campanelli & Parreiras, 2015). Kanban does not prescribe a specific set of roles or process steps, but rather it encourages its users to start from the existing context by understanding and emphasising the customers' needs (Ahmad et al., 2013). Kanban is deemed as an approach to process change for organisations by providing sufficient visibility and understanding of the workflow and its progress. Kanban is all about visual signs (aka Kanban Cards) which represent individual work items accompanied with their critical information. Those cards move across a board (aka Kanban board). The latter is partitioned by vertical lanes which are titled, typically, according to the names of the development life-cycle phases (e.g., Analysis, Development, testing). These lanes can be partitioned further to specify the current state of each phase (To Do, Doing and Done). The location of a card on the board indicates the progress of the work and its current state. Kanban shows the assigned work for each team member, communicates priorities and highlights bottlenecks via cycle or lead time and the cumulative flow diagram (Ahmad et al., 2013; Campanelli & Parreiras, 2015).

The XP Method

The XP method intends to improve software quality and responsiveness to the changing customer requirements. XP is considered a lightweight agile method that focuses on cost savings, unit tests before and along code activities, frequent full system integration and frequent releases (Campanelli & Parreiras, 2015). XP comprises five phases: exploration, planning, iterations to release, productionising, maintenance and death (Salameh, 2011). The exploration, planning and iterations to release are the only phases involved in our tailored framework.

During the exploration phase, the customers describe the features they wish to have in the first release of their system by writing each of them into a story card (Abrahamsson et al., 2017). Our tailored framework is designed to deal with changes to a system that has been already built by the V-model. Hence, the features are considered as changes to the software system in our case. More clearly, safety engineers (who represent the customers) write change requests into story cards and discuss them with the team manager. During the planning phase, the story cards should be prioritised, an agreement on the first small release should be made and the time span required to implement the story cards should be estimated (Abrahamsson et al., 2017). In the iteration and release planning phase, each release should be incremented by exactly one iteration. The development team should break down requested features (i.e., requested changes in our case) into several small releases. The customer selects the stories that should be implemented in a specific iteration. XP Planning Game is a close interaction between the customer and the development team. The latter should estimate the effort needed to implement the stories.

A Maintenance Framework to Facilitate Change Management

In this section, we build upon the background section to propose a new framework which aims to streamline the change management process of non-structural software changes in safety critical systems. The framework is referred to as XP-Kan-Safe and it comprises two main processes: The Preliminary Process and The Change Management process.

Figure 2 provides a conceptual model of the framework. The conceptual model encompasses three phases: 1) Analysis phase to cover the derivation of safety contracts, 2) Planning phase to cover the game planning, and 3) Implementation phase to cover the TDD and other XP practices. The grey background of the model represents the Kanban board.

After completing the safety analysis on the system level, safety contracts should be derived to guarantee the resultant SGs. A safety contract that guarantees a SG is referred to as "SG contract". The assumptions of a SG contract should capture the FSRs that fulfil the guaranteed SG. Furthermore, a contract should be derived to guarantee every assumed FSR in SG contracts after completing the safety analysis on the safety function level. A safety contract that guarantees a FSR is referred to as *"FSR contract"*. The assumptions of a FSR contract should capture the TSRs that implement the guaranteed FSR. Finally, a contract should be derived to guarantee every assumed TSR in FSR contracts; such contracts are referred to as *"TSR contracts"*. The assumptions of a TSR contract should capture the SSRs that implement the guaranteed TSR after completing the safety analysis on the software components level.

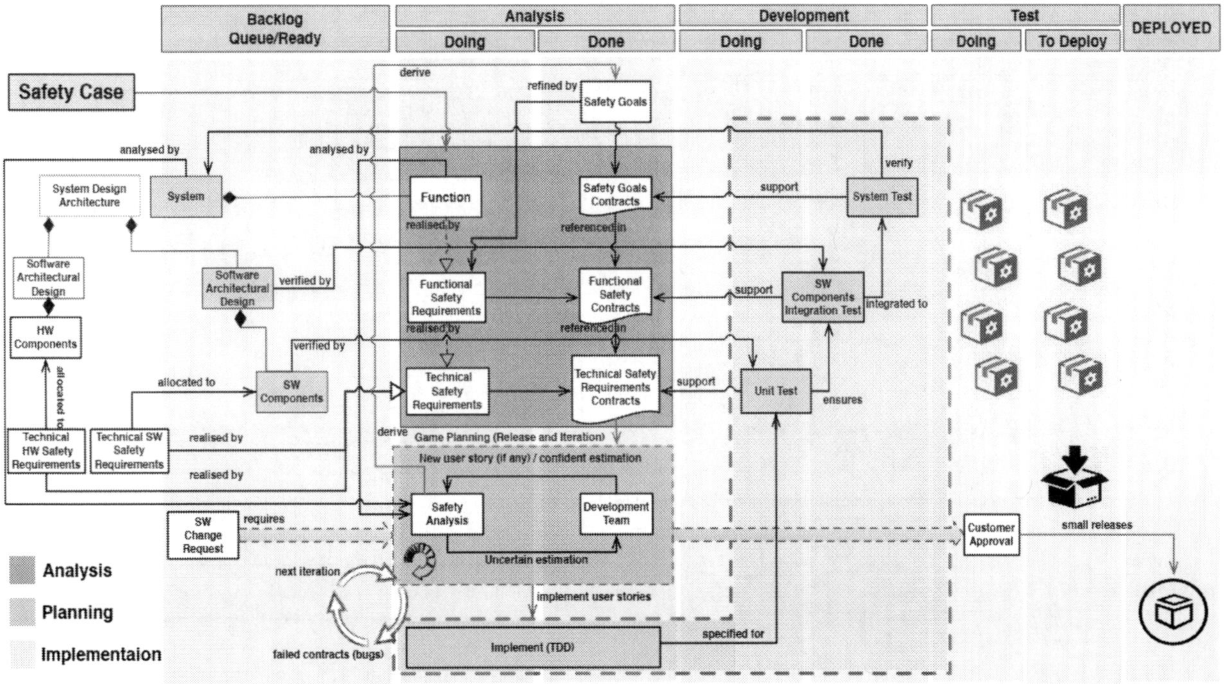

Figure 2— A conceptual model of XP-Kan-Safe framework

Failure modes and effects analysis (FMEA) is recommended by many safety standards (including ISO 26262) as a safety analysis tool to identify potential failures modes. We enable the derivation of safety contracts from FMEAs by adding an extra column to the FMEA table so that safety analysts, together with requirement engineers, should cite their derived contracts in it. FMEA might have a deficiency when it comes to a multiple failures investigation. Hence, safety analysts might use different tools, such as Fault Tree Analysis (FTA) to search for the effects of multiple failures. Our preliminary process takes this into account and manages the derivation of safety contracts from FMEAs and FTAs. Figure 3 shows the connection between FTA and FMEA in addition to an example of a derived safety contract.

A guarantee in a contract and its related assumptions are the main elements of the contracts and they help to understand the relationships and the dependencies among the safety requirements. However, they might not be enough for analysts to identify the impacted artefacts and the elements in the GSN safety argument due to changes because they do not provide information as how the different parts are related to each other. For instance, identifying an impacted TSR will not directly lead to the impacted test cases and the items of evidence which need to be replaced. In order to enhance the traceability between the requirements (i.e., guarantees) and other related artefacts as well as GSN elements, safety contracts should be enriched with additional information. To this end, system developers should include additional information into the derived contracts as follows:

1. Elements in the system architecture: all derived safety requirements should be allocated to elements of the system architecture. However, since the changes we are after in this work are non-structural, we assume that the changes have no effect on the system architecture.

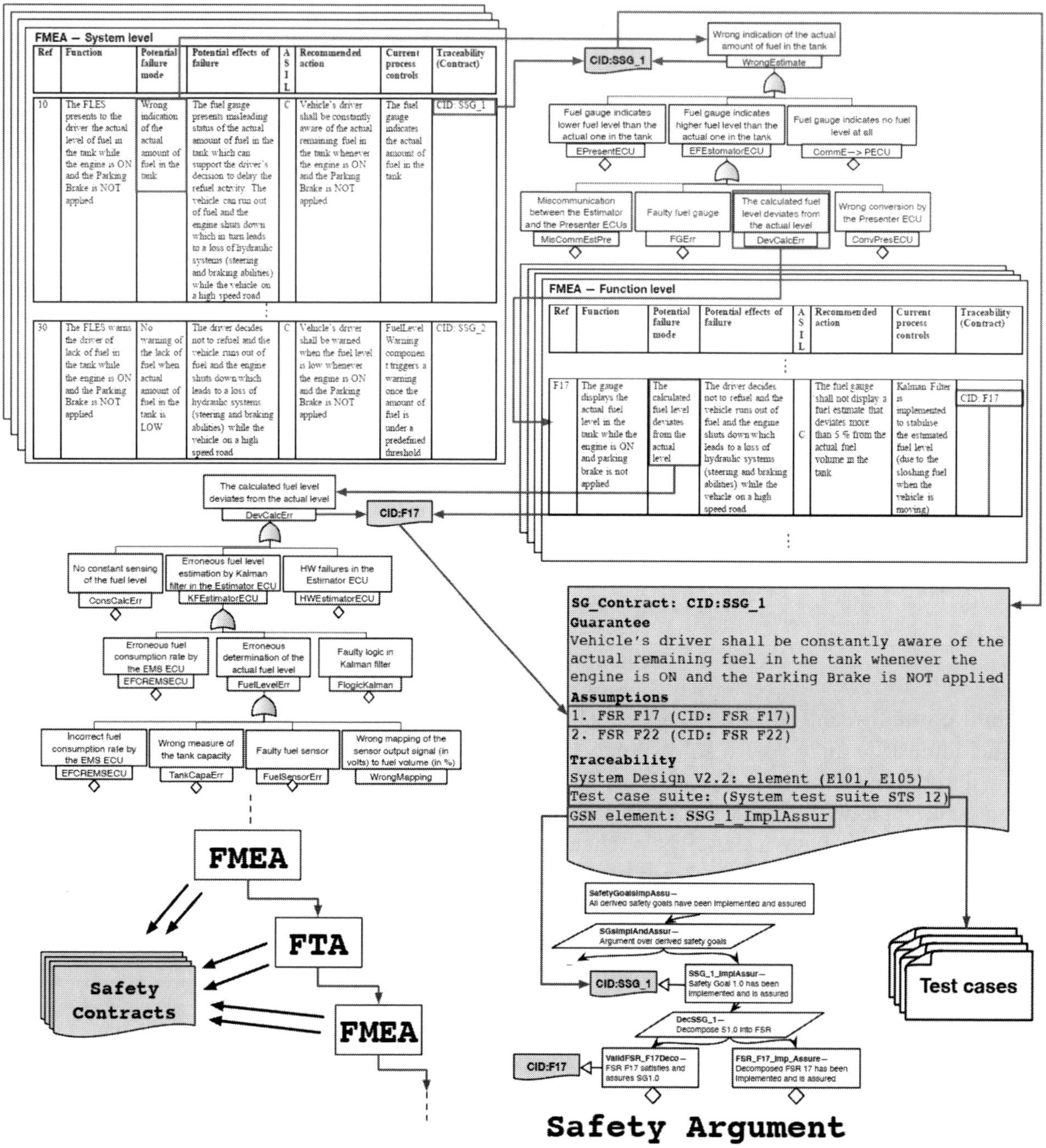

Figure 3— An illustration of a contract derivation by the Preliminary Process

2. Test cases: potential failure modes for which a safety requirement is derived should be considered as testing criteria during the verification phase to ensure the prevention of those failures. Including a reference to test cases in safety contracts enables direct traceability between safety analyses (i.e., FMEA and FTA), safety requirements (i.e., guarantees) and test cases. This traceability enables a top-down change impact analysis from the safety analysis down to the test cases. This top-down analysis represents the **first** direction of the tri-directional impact analysis process in our maintenance framework. While documenting the safety contracts, the reference of test cases might not be available as the test cases

themselves might not be built yet. System developers are required to revisit each contract and add the corresponding test case references whenever they are made available. Furthermore, given that the test cases are available and complete, system developers can annotate them with the contracts' references. The annotations in the source code of the test cases are important to establish a traceability that enables a bottom-up impact analysis from the test cases up to the safety analysis. This bottom-up analysis represents the **second** direction of the tri-directional impact analysis process in our maintenance framework.

3. Elements of safety arguments: each safety contract should contain a reference to the related goals, contexts or items of evidence from safety arguments. Whenever GSN references are made available, system developers are required to revisit each contract and add the corresponding GSN reference to it. Including a reference to GSN elements in safety contracts enables direct traceability between a system and its safety case. This traceability enables a bi-directional impact analysis from the system to its safety case and vice versa. More clearly, an affected guarantee can lead to an affected GSN element. Since the safety case presents the logic of how different artefacts are related, impact analysts might use it to highlight the change impact in the related system. The bi-directional change impact analysis represents the **third** direction of the tri-directional impact analysis process in our framework.

Figure 3 highlights the suggested traceability information and connects them to specimen artefacts and a GSN element.

The Change Management Process

In this section, we describe the second process of XP-Kan-Safe. This process and its activities represent the result of tailoring ASD and the V-model. The main objective of this tailored process is to guide whoever involved in the change management activities from the arrival of a change until the generation of a new test results report. Figure 4 presents the flow of these activities. The Change Management Process activities are described as follows:

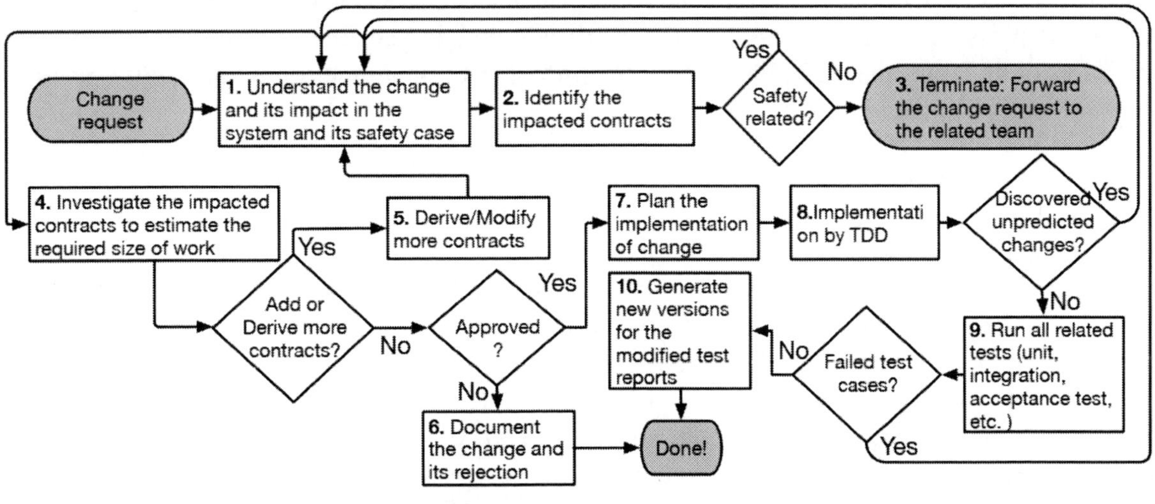

Figure 4— The change management process of XP-Kan-Safe framework

Activity 1: Understand the change and its impact in the system and its safety case. Once a change request is placed, *Activity 1* should be followed in which the safety engineers should understand the nature of the change and determine its potential effects in the system and its safety case. In order to initiate the Kanban management process, safety engineers should create a card that describes the change request in more technical specifications and visualise it as a WIP in the analysis phase. The outcome of this activity should provide plausible data about the impacted parts of the system and its safety case.

Activity 2: Identify the impacted contracts. In this activity, all related safety contracts to the change should be identified. The benefit of applying the first process of XP-Kan-Safe (i.e., preliminary) will be more realised in this activity since using safety contracts should help to provide a systematic impact analysis through the utilisation of the tri-directional impact analysis. The identified contracts should be listed in the Kanban card.

Activity 3: Terminate: Forward the change request to the related team. If there is no safety contract identified as suspect in *Activity 2*, this implies that the change request has nothing to do with the functional safety in the system (no safety requirements are affected). In this specific case, the change request should be forwarded to the relevant team and no further continuation of the change management process is needed.

Activity 4: Investigate the impacted contracts to estimate the required size of work. There is no perfect impact analysis that can determine the effects of a change in the system and its artefacts at the first glance. That is, it is unlikely that the team will find out what might, precisely, get impacted merely by looking at the documented requirement and without iterating the impact analysis process. Hence, further investigation should be conducted to gain sufficient confidence in the perceived impact of a change. To this end, this activity should be followed to make further investigation of the impacted contracts. During this activity, a preliminary meeting should be carried out in which safety engineers, who represent the on-site customer with respect to XP, together with the development team, should determine the possibility of identifying more impacted contracts. Any additional identification of safety contracts should be added to the Kanban card. Safety contracts should support the collaboration between safety engineers and the development team to delimit the impacted parts of a system through the tri-directional impact analysis process. It is worth mentioning that any need to modify an existing contract or derive a new one will necessitate the application of this activity.

Activity 5: Derive new contracts or modify existing contracts. Since changes might introduce other changes, this might lead to modifying or deriving other contracts (i.e., requirements) that were not thought of earlier in *Activity 2*. In this activity, safety engineers and system developers derive new contracts or modify the existing ones to capture the newly introduced requirements or to update the already captured requirements, respectively. An initial cost of the change accommodation and its timeframe are two among several other factors upon which the approval decision is made. The involvement of the development team in the Activities 4 and 5 should cover the estimation of the initial amount of work and the time needed to complete it. Safety engineers and system developers should agree on: 1) what should be changed or added (i.e., size of the work) and 2) the acceptance of the accompanied potential risk on safety functions. Subsequently, they should submit their agreement to the management where the latter can either decline or accept the change request. Submission of the agreement concludes the Analysis Phase, and this means that the Kanban card should move on the board from (Analysis → Doing) to (Analysis → Done).

Activity 6: Document the change and its rejection. If the change request receives a rejection by the management, the change request, the performed investigation and the management decision should be documented (ISO 26262:2011, 2011). The rejection implies that the Kanban card should be closed.

Activity 7: Plan the implementation of change. If the change request receives an approval by the management, the Kanban card should be available for development. The adopted planning method, in our change management process, complies with XP. This implies that the implementation of the change request is initiated by the planning game. The input of the planning game is the estimated work and the impacted safety contracts. The output are more fine-grained estimated tasks than the earlier estimated tasks in *Activity 4*.

Activity 8: Implementation by TDD. In this activity, the implementation of the change is carried out using TDD. For those contracts that are subject to modification, system developers should find the related test cases (using the parameters that refer to them in the contracts) and modify them accordingly. Since modifying a contract might require creating new test cases, system developers should cite the newly added test cases in the corresponding contracts and vice versa. This is particularly important to support bi-directional traceability between the test cases and the contracts while is deemed as a preparation for future changes. Citing the newly added test cases in the contracts applies to the derived contracts during the impact analysis process — after the preliminary process — as well *Activity 5*. Moreover, after implementing required production code to satisfy the derived test cases, other already existing test cases might get impacted by newly added code. If the solution is to modify or add new requirements, system developers should inform the safety engineers about the suggested changes to the requirements. In this case, the suggested changes by system developers should be declared as unexpected changes. Afterwards, safety engineers and system developers should arrange an on-the-fly meeting to investigate the discovered unexpected changes *Activity 4*. The meeting should reveal 1) whether or not the suggested changes might introduce unreasonable risks (i.e., criticality level) and 2) the size of work required to cope with the suggested changes. The size of work is defined, in this context, based on its influence on the earlier gaming plan *Activity 7* so that big work means a modification of the release planning is required. If the suggested changes are non-critical, system developers should implement them or forward them to the relevant team. If the suggested changes are critical, one of two possible actions should be performed:

1. If the size of work is small, developers should do the fixes on-the-fly and cite the related test cases in the contracts and vice versa.

2. If the size of work is big and critical, developers should either follow the exchange strategy by XP to re-prioritise the tasks within the current iteration of the planned release or plan the tasks for the next release.

Activity 9: Run all related tests. In this activity, system developers should utilise the continuous integration as a first step, according to XP, to avoid delays caused by integration problems. Subsequently, a continuous testing process should be initiated to obtain immediate feedback on the possibility of violating safety countermeasures to prevent unreasonable risks associated with a software release. The scope of testing should be extended from a bottom-up assessment (from test cases to safety requirements) to validate safety goals. In case of any violation of safety requirements after running the continuous testing, system developers should follow *Activity 8*.

Activity 10: Generate new versions for the modified test reports. This activity should be followed once the continuous testing is completed successfully. New reports of the test results should be generated to replace the out-of-date reports in the safety case. It is significant to update the references of these reports in the safety contracts of the system and its safety case.

Discussion and Conclusion

Maintaining safety critical systems due to changes is a challenging process because of: 1) the lack of awareness of the change's effects and the ripple of these effects on the system, 2) the lack of documentation of dependencies among the generated artefacts during the development process, and 3) the lack of traceability between a system and its safety case. Following the V-model to accommodate system changes might be very strict, which might be justifiable for structural system changes since many parts get impacted and there is no precise clue about the size of work needed to maintain the system. For software non-structural changes, this might not be justifiable. ASD can provide promising methods to maintain software changes. For example, XP puts great emphasis on the technical aspects (e.g., TDD, continuous integration and code refactoring). Also, Kanban brings the visibility of the workflow and improves the communication and collaboration among the stakeholders. Using ASD for maintaining safety critical systems can be promising but it still needs to comply with the current safety standards. In this paper, we introduced XP-Kan-Safe as a novel framework in which we tailor a hybrid process of ASD and the traditional V-model. The tailored process exploits safety contracts to connect ASD and the V-model, and enable a tri-directional impact analysis process. Future work will focus on creating a more in-depth case study to validate both the feasibility and efficacy of the process as well as to fully automate its application.

Acknowledgment

This work has been partially supported by the Swedish Foundation for Strategic Research (SSF) (through SYNOPSIS and FiC Projects) and the EU-ECSEL (through SafeCOP project). Both authors contributed equally to the paper and their names are listed in alphabetical order.

References

Abrahamsson, P., Salo, O., Ronkainen, J., & Warsta, J. (2017). Agile software development methods: Review and analysis. *CoRR, abs/1709.08439*.

Abrahamsson, P., Warsta, J., Siponen, M. T., & Ronkainen, J. (2003). New directions on agile methods: A comparative analysis. In *Proceedings of the 25th International Conference on Software Engineering (ICSE)*. Washington, DC, USA.

Ahmad, M., Markkula, J., & Oivo, M. (2013). Kanban in software development: A systematic literature review. In *Proceedings of the 39th EUROMICRO Conference on Software Engineering and Advanced Applications (SEAA)*.

Bate, I., Hawkins, R., & McDermid, J. (2003). A contract-based approach to designing safe systems. In *Proceedings of the 8th Australian workshop on safety critical systems and software - volume 33* (pp. 25–36). Darlinghurst, Australia. Australian Computer Society, Inc.

Benvenuti, L., Ferrari, A., Mazzi, E., & Vincentelli, A. L. (2008). Contract-based design for computation and verification of a closed-loop hybrid system. In *Proceedings of the 11th international workshop on hybrid systems: Computation and control* (pp. 58–71). Berlin, Heidelberg: Springer-Verlag.

Campanelli, A. S., & Parreiras, F. S. (2015). Agile methods tailoring – a systematic literature review. *The Journal of Systems & Software, 110*, 85–100.

Cao, L., Ramesh, B., & Abdel-Hamid, T. (2010). Modeling dynamics in agile software development. *ACM Trans. Manage. Inf. Syst., 1* (1), 5:1–5:26.

Denney, E., Pai, G., & Habli, I. (2015). Dynamic safety cases for through-life safety assurance. In *Proceedings of the 37th IEEE international conference on software engineering (ICSE).*

GSN Standard (2011). *Goal Structuring Notation working group.*

Heeager, L., & Rose, J. (2015, December). Optimising agile development practices for the maintenance operation: nine heuristics. *Empirical Software Engineering, 20*(6), 1762–1784.

ISO 26262:2011 (2011). Road Vehicles — Functional Safety, Part 1-9. International Organization for Standardization.

Knippers, D. (2011). Agile software development and maintainability. In *Proceedings of the 15th Twente Student conference.*

Jaradat, O., Bate, I. (2017). Using safety contracts to guide the maintenance of systems and safety cases. In *Proceedings of the 13rd European Dependable Computing Conference (EDCC).*

Jaradat, O., Bate, I. & Punnekkat, S. (2015a). Facilitating the maintenance of safety cases. In *Proceedings of the 3rd International Conference On Reliability, Safety and Hazard - Advances In Reliability, Maintenance and Safety (ICRESH-ARMS).* Luleå, Sweden.

Jaradat, O., Bate, I. & Punnekkat, S. (2015b). Using sensitivity analysis to facilitate the maintenance of safety cases. In *Proceedings of the 20th International Conference on Reliable Software Technologies (Ada-Europe).*

Jaradat, O., Graydon, P. & Bate, I. (2014). An approach to maintaining safety case evidence after a system change. In *Proceedings of the 10th European Dependable Computing Conference (EDCC)*. Newcastle, UK.

Bates, S., Bate, I., Hawkins, R., Kelly, T., McDermid, J., & Fletcher, R. (2003). Safety case architectures to complement a contract-based approach to designing safe systems. In *Proceedings of the 21st International System Safety Conference (ISSC)*.

Salameh, A. (2011). *On Process Tailoring - An Agile Example.* Master Thesis. Chalmers University.

Kelly, T., & McDermid, J. (1999). A systematic approach to safety case maintenance. In *Proceedings of the Computer Safety, Reliability and Security (SAFECOMP)* (Vol. 1698, p. 13-26). Springer Berlin Heidelberg.

Tarwani, S., & Chug, A. (2016). Agile Methodologies in Software Maintenance: A Systematic Review. *Informatica*, 40(4), 415.

00-56 Standard (2015). Defence Standard — Issue 6. Safety Management Requirements for Defence Systems — Part 1: Requirements and Guidance. U.K. Ministry of Defence.

Biographies

Abdallah M. Salameh, Ph.D. candidate, School of Computing, Science & Engineering, University of Salford, Manchester, UK, Tel: +46 721844015, e-mail – a.salameh@edu.salford.ac.uk.

Abdallah Salameh is a senior developer at Bambora Group AB - Sweden and a Ph.D. candidate in the School of Computing, Science and Engineering at the University of Salford, U.K. His research interests include agile software development, where the main focus is on tailoring the processes in large-scale software intensive organisations.

Omar T. Jaradat, Ph.D. candiate, School of Innovation, Design and Engineering, Mälardalen University, Högskoleplan 1, SE-72123, Västerås, Sweden, Tel: +46 21101369, Fax: +46 21101460 e-mail – omar.jaradat@mdh.se.

Omar Jaradat is a Ph.D. candidate in the Innovation, Design and Engineering department at Mälardalen University. His research interests include safety argumentation for safety critical systems, where the main focus is on maintenance of safety-critical systems and safety cases.

36th International System Safety Conference Paper
August 13th – 17th, 2018

Research Study of Scaffolding Accidents in Construction

Kelsey Dawn Henry, BA;
"Arizona State University Construction Management Graduate Student"
Tempe, AZ, USA

Abstract

The purpose of this research paper is to investigate the current programs directed toward increasing the safety for scaffolding which ultimately mitigates the risk of fall accidents. In the construction industry, fall accidents is one of the leading cause of serious injury or fatality. The paper will examine numerous programs around the world that are being implemented on jobsites to ensure the safety of workers who are using scaffolding. In the industry, there will always be a number of accidents but with the right prevention programs in place companies and organizations will have the ability to control the outcome of the number of accidents that occur. Along with analyzing prevention programs, the paper will discuss current regulations for scaffolding, required PPE for jobsites, and calculate the annual number of fall accidents according to OSHA.

Introduction

Scaffolding is well-known element in construction. According to Merrian-Webster Dictionary scaffolding is defines as "a temporary or movable platform for workers (such as bricklayers, painters, or miners) to stand or sit on when working at the height above the floor or ground" (Webster, 2018). The definition is limited to the number of trades that use scaffolding as a tool for construction. According to OSHA, the top standard violations includes; Fall Protection, Construction; Scaffolding, General Requirements, Construction; and Fall Protection-Training Requirements (OSHA, 2018). On the OSHA website, 29 CFR 1926.451, Scaffolding General Requirements, Construction; which state the requirements for expected load/weight on equipment, material that will be on the equipment, person who will be on the equipment, how equipment should be installed depending on type, specific distance from certain equipment, how they should be braced or tied, security and support, fall protection, PPE, etc (OSHA, United States Department of Labor, 2018). The OSHA general requirements clearly state all aspects when using equipment on jobsite.

OSHA standard, 29 CFR 1926.501, Fall Protection in Construction, which indicates when fall protection is required depending on current state of equipment, what way the scaffold is set up, height of the equipment, descriptive way on how to install fall protection depending on what field you are in the construction industry, etc (OSHA, United States Department of Labor, 2018). OSHA standard, 29 CFR 1926.503, Fall Protection-Training Requirements, state training programs for employees how have the risk of being exposed to potential fall accidents, how to inspect fall protection before using, fall protection plans, nature of the fall hazards, equipment state, after training employees will receive a certification (OSHA, United States Department of Labor, 2018).

Throughout the construction industry, PPE is a requirement which is an essential key to safety. PPE includes gloves, safety glasses, boots, earplugs, hard hats, vests, and more when required.

Scaffolding safety has the potential to increase if the workforce is properly trained on equipment along with fall protection and simply be compliant with OSHA standards. If the construction industry could implement the culture of the importance of safety on jobsite, they will benefit by decreasing the rate of potential fall accidents from scaffolding. In the literature review, there are a number of case studies that are attempting to implement different prevention programs that would tackle to current problem of injuries cased from falling on scaffolding equipment.

Research Questions

1. What fall prevention programs are being implemented into the construction industry decrease the risk of serious injury or fatality accidents?

→ (In this question, I am investigating what current prevention programs are being used in the industry to decrease the fatality and serious injury rate from scaffolding. Examples; of educating the workforce, implementing incentive program, spreading awareness, thoroughly evaluating equipment, etc.)

2. What is the current fatality rate from scaffolding in the construction industry? (Year of 2017)

→ (In this question, I am investigating the current results in terms of fatalities from scaffolding according to OSHA.)

3. When a worker is injured from a falling accident, are they wearing the proper PPE?

→ (In this question, I am investigating when an accident occurs are the employees wearing the mandatory PPE; such as hardhat, harness, boots, etc.)

4. Which fall prevention program is the best?

→ (In this question, I am wanting to prove which fall prevention program is the best based on results such as; serious injury & fatality statistics, workforce response, and current research.)

Research Hypothesis

In the construction industry, the correlation between current average rate of fall accidents and past rates is decreasing due to the involvement of companies and organizations who value the importance of worker safety on the jobsite.

Research Method

For this paper, the research method is to thoroughly review scholarly case studies along with articles and include statistics from the previous years on fall accidents in the construction industry. The scholarly case studies will discuss in-depth research gathered around the world in hopes to improve the scaffolding safety which will ultimately decrease the risk of fall accidents. The scholarly articles will mention the final results of the research or practice that was implemented onto a jobsite to mitigate the risk of fall accidents. The results will vary from success or a start with multiple limitations which needs to be slightly adjusted to reach maximum opportunities to potentially decrease the high rate of fatalities or serious injuries from fall accidents specifically from scaffolding. Lastly, statistics will be mentioned in the research paper to help readers view one of the highest risk in construction industry. The end result will be proven by the results of prevention programs, statistics, and current regulations set on scaffolding safety.

Literature Review

A) Characteristic Analysis of Occupational Accidents at Small Construction Enterprises;

The scholarly article was written on the Taiwan Construction Industry. Researchers decided that the best approach to analyze the Construction Industry in Taiwan was to use methodology of descriptive statistics and ANOVA which is best known as the correlation coefficient analysis. For this research, the data used for the study was collected from Council of Labor Affairs of Taiwan Central Government which consisted of 1546 occupational accident reported in the construction industry from year 2000 to 2007. Of the 1546 accidents reported, 800 accidents were associated with small construction companies who employed an average of 10 workers or less. According to the research paper, "Taiwan Labor Safety and Health Act, a major occupational accident is defined as an accident that causes injuries to three or more persons or causes the death of at least one person at the time it occurs" (Cheng, Leu, Lin, & Fan, 2010). Cheng, Leu, Lin and Fan (2010) concluded that "causes of most occupational accidents in the construction industry are largely attributable to management negligence or inadequate worker safety awareness" (Cheng, Leu, Lin, & Fan, 2010). Management is an important factor to the way workforce is operating in the industry. They are the start point of spreading awareness to any field in the industry. If management, decides to lead with showing no importance to safety then it will negatively affect the labor force. A major conclusion for this research, small construction companies are a higher accident rate than large companies due to the following reasons; management is not qualified, safety awareness is low, tend to be non-compliant with safety regulations/laws, insufficient safety protection, protocol, and facilities. An important regulation Taiwan Labor Safety and Health Act attempts to advocate to the construction industry is to provide training for a minimum of 6 hours along with mandatory health and safety test which must be passed.

Before determining what characteristics are associated with occupational accidents among small construction enterprises, researchers created a two-way contingency table. The table gave researchers the ability to "calculate the potential factors affecting the occurrence of occupational accidents in order to explore the relationship between safety management and occupational accidents for small construction enterprises" (Cheng, Leu, Lin, & Fan, 2010). Researchers we able to create a mathematical function that would show the relationship between management and the occupational accident rate. After analyzing 800 occupational accidents, the factors included the following; health and safety management work, project jurisdiction, condition of victim, gender, project contract amount, interval between worker arrival at jobsite and accident, unsafe condition, unsafe act, worker type, worker age, and project type. At the end of the study, Cheng, Leu, Lin and Fan (2010) the major "problems included not to value the importance of safety measures implemented on the workplaces, not to practice sufficient safety education for new workers, not to hire well-trained safety and health personnel to implement safety measures" (Cheng, Leu, Lin, & Fan, 2010). Currently, occupational accident rate is associated with problems like; proper training for workforce on safety, not expressing the importance of individual safety/health along with entire site and hiring non-compliant workforce which shows they have no prior experience in the industry. The suggested prevention program for small construction enterprises is to promote excellent health and safety management which benefit companies in the long run with their current accident rate.

B) Accident Patterns and Prevention Measures for Fatal Occupational Falls in the Construction Industry;

The scholarly article research data is based on 621 occupational fatal falls which identifies factors such as victim's individual factors, accident site, company size, and the cause of the accident. The individual factors associated with victims are age, gender, construction experience, and the proper use of PPE, personal protection equipment. Scaffolding accidents are associated with a lack of complying scaffolds and bodily action. In the research, two prevention programs (primary and secondary) are being implemented to prevent future falls or mitigate the risk of falling which is easily adaptable to each type of accidents. The primary prevention measures handrails, guardrails, surface opening protections, crawl boards and planks, and strong roofing materials. The secondary prevention measures safety belt, safety harness, and safety nets. According to the article, "the construction industry has been identified as one of the most hazardous industries in many parts of the world and falls from height are a leading cause of fatalities in construction operations" (Chi, Chang, & Ting, 2005). Construction is known to be one of the most dangerous occupation due to the multiple reasons; operation of heavy machinery, equipment being used, materials being used, process of how to complete the project, etc.

The MLID, Manitoba Labor and Immigration Division, Fall Protection Guidelines, state six categories of fall protection measures. The six categories include; (1) surface protection, (2) fixed barriers, (3) surface opening protections, (4) travel restraint systems, (5) fall arrest systems, and (6) fall containment systems (Chi, Chang, & Ting, 2005). The following categories measure all aspects of scaffolding equipment when being used which has the capability of preventing fall accidents. The prevention program measures will help the industry prevent a number of future fall accidents just by simply analyzing the equipment.

C) Using BIM for Smarter and Safer Scaffolding and Framework Construction: A Preliminary Methodology;

The scholarly article was written on the Queensland and Australia Construction Industry. Chi, Hampson, Biggs (2012) "goal of this research project is to develop specific BIM objects for temporary construction activities which are fully integrated with object design, construction efficiency, and safety parameters" and "the project will deliver modularized electronic scaffolding and formwork objects that will allow designers to easily incorporate them into BIM models to facilitate smarter and safer infrastructure and building construction". Researchers aim to create temporary BIM objects which will be available for use by a number of groups during the entire construction process of any given project. The two countries believe in "harmonization." According to Cambridge Dictionary, harmonization is defined as "the act of making systems or laws the same or similar in different companies, countries, etc. so that they can work together more easily" (Dictionary, 2018). When countries practice "harmonization" they create the ability of knowing the process because they share the same systems and laws for a given industry. So, countries are able to adapt to any given location because they use the same laws & systems to operate. The research was based on a strategic three-phase research and industry development methodology. First step, is a preliminary review on industrial scaffolding and formwork practices and BIM implementation. Second step, BIM object development with specifics to safety and productivity functions. Lastly, is the workshop which includes training and product dissemination. In the year of 2007 to 2008, there were a total of 14,760 worker comp claims which 3%, 410 claims, were considered to be scaffolding and formwork related. An equation they calculated the total cost of the number of claims that given year (Chi, Hampson, & Biggs, 2012). The equation calculates the total cost of claims by multiplying the # of claims that given year by the median payment for claims that year. The research team aims to decrease the potential risk of fall accidents on the jobsite along with improving their productivity simply by implementing BIM technology to create objects for temporary work.

The main goal to consider in the research is construction safety. Construction safety and BIM can create opportunity for design for safety, safety integrated models, structural safety analysis, on-site inspection and monitoring, safety planning, safety training, and facilitate management and emergency responses. The proposed prevention program for safer scaffolding and framework construction will benefit the construction industry by the following; "(1) enable design in accordance with safety requirements , (2) incorporate design codes, (3) design for constructability in 4D and 3D with schedule, (4) provide visualization of the installation procedure, design, and installation options and give working condition analyses, such as limited clearance with the surrounding environment, (5) enable structural safety analysis, (6) highlight opportunities for design innovation and (7) provide BIM checklists for routine on-site inspections that would benefit practical safety assessment on construction sites" (Chi, Hampson, & Biggs, 2012). Every aspect of incorporating technology with scaffolding safety is benefited. In conclusion, the future research outcome is to completely created various BIM object which is scaffolding and formwork that designers and constructors can access to use for a number of projects. The end goal is giving the ability to designers and constructors to implement a BIM object which is benefit by creating safe and efficient construction process.

D) Fall Related Deaths in the Construction Industry;

The scholarly article is based on the data retrieved from OSHA fatality inspection records. The data was used to determine the potential causes for a number of occupational falls which resulted into a fatality. According to the article, "fatal work-related falls continue to remain one of the leading causes of death in the workplace" and "fatal-work related falls continue to be a leading cause of death in the construction industry" (Janicak, 1998). As said before, the Construction Industry is a dangerous occupation which also has the highest fatality rate among all other industries. The fatality inspection records from OSHA were analyzed from 1992 to 1995. The inspection information included industry, nature of injury, accident abstract, location of fall, height, cause of fall. After the first set of information is documented, the fatality is categorized by the following; structural collapse, no fall protection presented, fall protection not attached, damaged fall protection, improper work surface, erecting/dismantling scaffolding, fall from ladder, other, and unknown. The number of fatal-work related fall in the construction industry that was examined a total of 566. In conclusion, the four prevention areas that need to be enforced employee training, the use of fall protection systems, inspection, and testing of the fall protection systems in use.

E) An Evaluation of Scaffold Safety at Construction Sites

The scholarly article was written on 113 scaffolds which were in nine areas of the eastern part of the United States. The areas included; Baltimore, MD; Birmingham, AL; Central Connecticut; Jacksonville, FL; New Orleans, LA; Philadelphia, PA; Providence, RI; South Florida; and Washington, DC. Before designing a solution that can be used to address the uprising problem which specific to scaffolding accidents resulted into serious injury or fatality. The research approach was to design a checklist to evaluate supported scaffolding which was labeled as acceptable or unacceptable. Acceptable rating must have no hazards or any sort. The scaffold may have numerous errors but not have any major hazards that might but workers at the risk of fatal fall. Unacceptable rating indicates that the current equipment has serious hazards and/or imminent hazards. Some example of imminent hazards is the following; "are workers on a single plant where a slip could result in a fall, workers on scaffolds without railing or fall arrest systems, and severely overloaded or scaffolds without ties" and "an example of a serious but not imminent hazard, would be missing railings, on the same platform as the workers, but more than 10 feet away from them" (Halperin & McCann, 2004). The following stated above are some of the potential accidents that may occur due to the negligence of practicing proper safety. After using the checklist on the 113 scaffolds, 77 of them received a rating or acceptable and 36 of them received the rating of unacceptable.

According to the article, "scaffold injury incidents occur in two ways- falls from scaffolds or scaffold collapses" (Halperin & McCann, 2004). Scaffolding accidents occur on a yearly basis which result from an individual fall due to a number of risks to pick from and a collapse of equipment which results from failure of material. The scaffolding checklist consists of information based on the following; general background on job, use of scaffold, determine if there is a competent person on the scaffold, scaffold information, platforms, access, PPE, and other important information. In the general section of the checklist, questions are asked about the

GC, number of workers, trades observed, site, city, etc. In the use of scaffold section, information asked is about what trades are using the scaffold, contractor responsible for scaffold, work being performed, items seen on the equipment, and number of workers using the equipment. Competent person section of the checklist indicates if there is an employee who received scaffolding training from OSHA, scaffolding license or certification, years of experience, title of employee, if they are present, and etc. The scaffolding information section indicates the length, weight, height, width, material, and information on how the equipment is set up on the jobsite. Platform section gathers information on the total number of platforms, height, width, length, if they are being used properly, etc. Access section ask questions regarding the type of access points, if they are tied properly, what frames are being used, etc. An important section is PPE, which indicates if workers are wearing the correct PPE for jobsite and scaffolding and if they are being used correctly. Last section is the other which gathers information on hardhat count, eye protection count, general safety of equipment, and rating of equipment which is based on all the information gathered for the survey.

In conclusion, by implementing this particular survey for an all project basis that is utilizing scaffolding equipment has the potential to benefit companies but most importantly ensure the safety of workers. If they use the survey, jobsite will be able to indicate whether the equipment is rated as acceptable or unacceptable. By rating an essential equipment to construction, the industry has the ability to mitigate the risk of potential accidents involving scaffolding. The article states, "with the lack of such injury records, it is still better to implement these scaffold safety recommendations than not to, because a scaffold that cannot collapse and one that the workers cannot fall off should prevent future injuries" (Halperin & McCann, 2004). Even though specific data related to serious injury or fatality rate are unavailable, its beneficial to implement all scaffolding safety recommendations because at the end of the day everyone wants to go home and see their families. To ensure these particular results, a number of recommendations must be implemented to decrease the risk of a potential accident occurring in the future.

Analysis

There are a number of different prevention programs that are being used to increase scaffolding safety. According to OSHA, Commonly Used Statistics, the construction industry has a term referred to as the "Fatal Four." The "Fatal Four" are the following; falls, struck by object, electrocutions, and caught in or between equipment which results into a worker fatality (OSHA, United States Department of Labor, 2018). The following stated above are the common cases that cause fatalities in the construction industry. OSHA indicates that by eliminating the "Fatal Four" it would save 631 workers; lives in America every year (OSHA, United States Department of Labor, 2018). After thoroughly review of scholarly articles, the most common prevention program is proper training for employees and advocating the importance of wearing the required PPE. Employees who are able to be properly educated on scaffolding safety, scaffolding information, and overall safety on an individual basis and group basis shows the best results in the construction industry. When wearing the correct PPE for scaffolding, workers ensure their safety when working in the construction zone.

As said before, the prevention programs that are being implemented into scaffolding safety are; proper employee training, implementation of technology to creating BIM objects which can be used for temporary activities on the jobsite, strict compliance policy on regulations and laws for scaffolding, implementing a scaffolding survey to determine if equipment is acceptable to use or unacceptable, must use equipment such as guardrails, handrails, opening protection, and lastly management skills. Prevention programs have the ability to adapt to the industries workforce culture. Simply implementing a program for the workforce will have the potential to increase the safety which has the capability to decrease the risk of future accidents. As said before, there are a number of programs being tested today, but also show some limitations to implementing these programs. Proper training for employee's limitation would be finding the time to train the workforce and ensuring if the workforce will retain the information. Implementing technology limitations would be an expensive tactic which usually gets the industry tuned off because the goal is to save money but ensure quality. Being compliant with regulations and laws comes from management, if the management shows excellent leadership skills then companies will be complaint but there is also management who don't show this trait. Lastly, taking a survey to rate the current equipment acceptable or unacceptable would simply take too much time to complete. The current survey is very lengthy and very detailed questions.

Although, these prevention programs each have their limitation when attempting to implement into the industry, the workforce must remember that there is no price on ensuring the safety of everyone. I once heard a Superintendent state "The goal is to get everyone home safely to their families each day" which I agree with completely. When working construction, everyone wants to be as safe as they can be but also work with speed, efficiency, and effectiveness. After in-depth review of programs, the best prevention program is to provide training to the workforce and provide the proper PPE for scaffolding. Simply holding safety training for specific equipment would help educate the workforce on what they will be working with, how to avoid potential risk of accidents, know when equipment is safe and unsafe, etc. Also, in the near future implementing technology as a prevention program will begin to take over the industry but for now the best program will be to educate the industry.

Conclusion

According to OSHA, Fatality Inspection Data, 2017, 20 fatalities were reported which was out of 769 fatalities (OSHA, United States Department of Labor, 2018). 20 fatalities account for 38.45% which is the fatality rate for scaffolding accidents in 2017. In conclusion, this research was to search for current prevention programs that are specific to the current problem of scaffolding accidents. Scaffolding accidents in the construction industry typically lead into serious injury or a fatality of a worker. The construction industry is now attempting to implement more programs that have the potential of decreasing the risk of future accidents on the jobsite. After thorough review of programs, the prevention programs that receives more of a positive response is training which educates the workforce on scaffolding equipment. Many of the literature review, mentions to require training for the workforce especially when operating or working on dangerous equipment. Required training also should be followed with required protection from falls. From the results of this research paper, it is found that education is the best prevention program because it is widely accepted from the workforce and shown to show positive results.

Works Cited

Cheng, Leu, Lin, & Fan. (2010). Characteristic analysis of occupational accidents at small construction enterprises. *Safety Science 48(6)*, 698-707.

Chi, Chang, & Ting. (2005). Accident patterns and prevention measures for fatal occupational falls in the construction industry. *Applied Ergonomics 36(4)*, 391-400.

Chi, S., Hampson, K., & Biggs, H. (2012). Using BIM for smarter and safer scaffolding and formwork construction: a preliminary methodology. *Modelling and building health and safety*.

Dictionary, E. (2018, 29 March). Retrieved from English Dictionary: https://dictionary.cambridge.org/us/dictionary/english/harmonization

Halperin, & McCann. (2004). An evaluation of scaffold safety at construction sites. *Journel of Safety Research 35(2)*, 141 - 150.

Janicak, C. (1998). Fall-Related Deaths in the Construction Industry. *Journel of Safety Research 29(1)*, 35-42.

OSHA. (2018, March 30). Retrieved from United States Department of Labor: https://www.osha.gov/oshastats/commonstats.html.

OSHA. (2018, April 30). Retrieved from United States Department of Labor: https://www.osha.gov/pls/oshaweb/owadisp.show_document?p_table=STANDARDS&p_id=10752

OSHA. (2018, April 2). Retrieved from United States Department of Labor: https://www.osha.gov/pls/oshaweb/owadisp.show_document?p_table=STANDARDS&p_id=10757

OSHA. (2018, April 2). Retrieved from United States Department of Labor: https://www.osha.gov/pls/oshaweb/owadisp.show_document?p_table=standards&p_id=10759

OSHA. (2018, April 5). Retrieved from United States Department of Labor: https://www.osha.gov/dep/fatcat/dep_fatcat.html

Webster, M. (2018, March 29). Retrieved from Merriam Webster Dictionary: www.merriamwebster.com/dictionary/scaffold.

Establishing a Standard List of Hazards for Automatic Driving

Robert C. Hammett; Draper; Cambridge, MA, USA

Keywords: Automatic Driving, Autonomous Vehicles, Safety Assessment, Hazards

Abstract

Fully automatic (self-driving) automobiles (SAE level 5 - steering wheel optional) safety assessment begins with an analysis to identify potential hazards. Examples of hazards include failure to sense an obstacle in the vehicles path, incorrect determination of an obstacles location or boundary box, incorrect prediction of a moving obstacles future location, etc. These types of hazards are not unique to one system developer and establishing a standardized list would be useful for developers, safety professionals, system buyers and for legal use. The paper presents a proposed list of standard hazards and some discussion of their consequences, risks levels and mitigation's. The author believes there is value in maintaining and evolving a list of standard hazards to be used in all phases of automatic driving system design, development and verification.

Introduction

Self-driving or Autonomous Vehicles (AV) are attracting a lot of interest. Virtually all car manufactures, major technology companies and transportation companies such as GM (Hawkins, 2018), Ford, Google, Apple and Uber are making large investments towards their development. The argument is being made that that AV's will reduce the large US fatal accident rate (40,000/year) associated with highway travel by eliminating human driver error. There are many economic benefits from driverless taxi and trucking services, improved use of commuting time, and perhaps reduced traffic congestion. The convenience of self-parking cars and cars that respond to a summons for pickup are appealing.

Can the goal of exceeding the safety levels of human drivers be exceeded? Can they be as safe as human driver? In a self-driving AV, even with an experience driver onboard with access to controls, it is unrealistic to assume that he/she can take over control should the automation fail. And since the goal is to provide robotic taxi services, self-parking cars, and to transport non-drivers, this is not even an option in those cases. The AV can't rely upon a human back-up for safety. It must also be assumed that self-driving vehicles must share the road with human driven vehicles and with all of the usual difficulties such as weather conditions, road construction, human errors, pedestrians, and mechanical failures remain unchanged.

Designing these vehicles is very challenging. They are made possible by recent advances in electronics for high-speed computing and sensing. Success would be an extraordinary accomplishment in mobile robotics and artificial intelligence. Our proudest human accomplishments in aerospace control systems have not had to operate in chaotic environment of our streets and highways.

Summary

Operating motor vehicles on public roadways is an inherently risky activity. The potential for collisions that can cause injury and death are always present. Mil-Std-882 (Mil-Std-882E, 2012) states *The objective of system safety is to achieve acceptable mishap risk through a systematic approach of hazard analysis, risk assessment, and risk management.*

Developers of AVs are understandably concerned about the potential for accidents and their underlying causes. The prevention of accidents is the goal and this is accomplished by reducing exposure to hazardous operating conditions. It is easy to get lost in the details and conditions that may lead to accidents and the underlying causes can be confused with the hazards they create. The objective of this work was to identify and document a proposed list of standard hazards that can be applied to the design and safety evaluation of AV's. The magnitude and difficulty of this task was underestimated and the goal was only partially reached. But it is believed the progress made is worth presenting and the process used of interest. The author would like to continue the effort, perhaps with collaboration from others. The effort would be informed by a detailed study of traffic laws (AAA, Digest of Motor Laws, 2018), traffic control devices (MUTCD, 2009), and established practices for student driver training (AAA, How to Drive Guide, 2013).

The original premise for the work remains unchanged. The bedrock of safety engineering such as is outlined in Mil-Std-882E (Mil-Std-882E, 2012) is identification of system hazards and, at least in public literature, it does not appear that a complete and organized list of AV hazards has been published.

In this work, a *standard hazard* is defined as one that is generic and not specific to a particular AV design. In fact, these hazards are generally applicable to vehicles with human drivers. Identification of standard hazards can serve to guide the process of identifying the lower level causes of these hazards with the goal of providing mitigations. Although road vehicles potentially have many types of hazards such flammable gasoline or lithium batteries, the focus here is upon AV hazards that lead to a collision mishap (accident). Collisions include impacts with other vehicles, with stationary objects including terrain, and with other moving objects such as bicycles or pedestrians. Note that a hazard does not always result in a mishap, but increases the likelihood of a mishap occurrence. For example, driving off of the road surface will only result in a collision if a roadside obstacle is in its path. Figure 1 illustrates how the identification of standard hazards, and causes for them can be used to generate a hierarchy (tree) of lower level causes, ultimately down to the root cause(s) of the hazard.

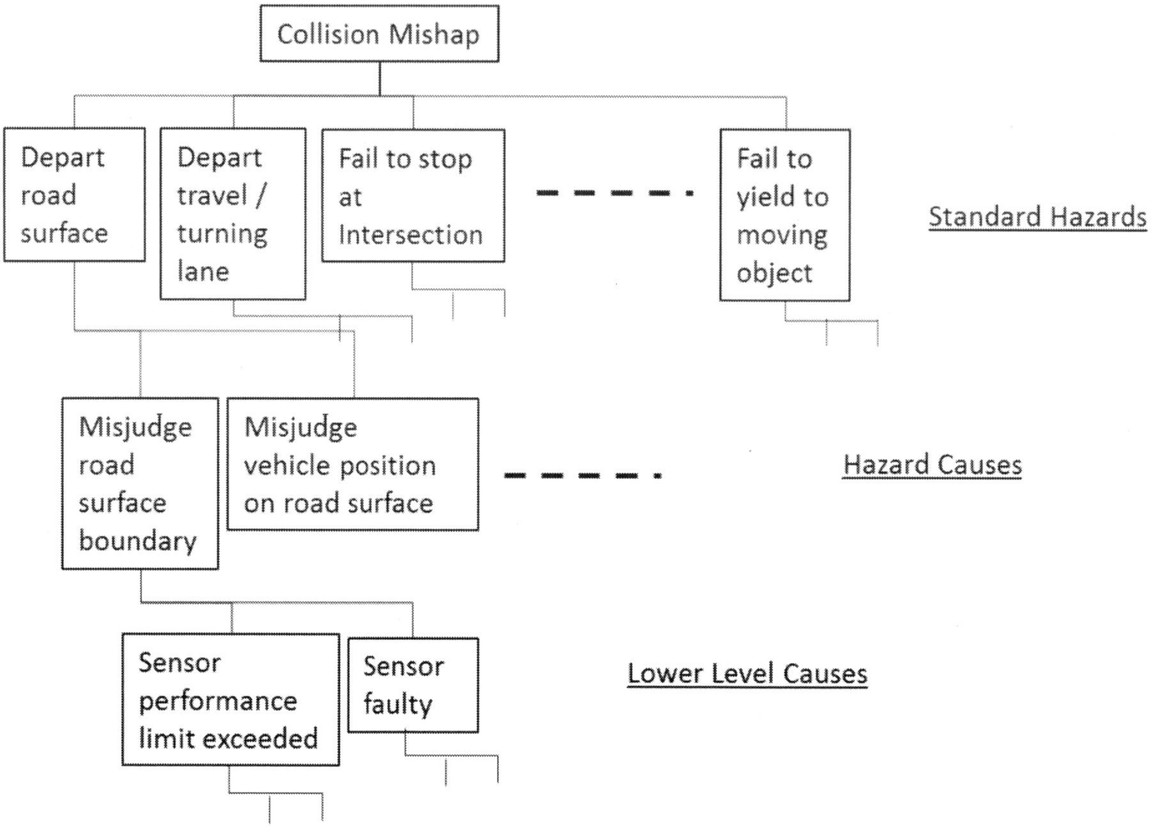

Figure 1— Hazard Hierarchy for Collision Mishaps

This work did not attempt to assign risk levels to the identified AV hazards. This would require assessing the probability of the cause(s) of the hazard condition and the likelihood that the hazard will lead to a mishap and the severity of the consequences. And these probabilities are influenced by external variables such as weather conditions that result in a loss of traction leading to a loss of control. The likelihood that a hazard such as a loss of control leading to a mishap depends upon the presence of obstacles that might be impacted. The severity of the consequences depend upon the speeds involved and obstacle being impacted. Loss of control could result in minor consequences or a major collision.

Developing a complete hazard hierarchy for an AV design is a challenging task. Driving is a complex task that requires years for a human driver to master. The human driver learns much about the hazards, understands their causes and is able to weigh the relative risks associated with different hazards.

Approach to Generic Hazard Identification

There are many possible collision hazards associated with AVs and a systematic approach is needed to identify them. The systematic approach selected for this effort was a series of use cases based upon the analogy of a student driver being introduced to new and progressively more challenging driving situations. The analogy begins with the student driver beginning his training by driving on simple and uncongested roads in clear daytime weather with only simple traffic laws and signals to obey. As the training progresses, he/she are introduced to progressively more difficult driving situations of increased traffic and more complex roadways, more elaborate traffic laws and signals, pedestrians, bicycles, construction, nighttime, poor weather and mechanical malfunctions.

Although the student driver analogy is a useful approach, there are many specialized use cases involved in mastering the task of driving. There are many scenarios such safe driving with obstructed views, traffic rotaries, construction, urban conditions, tunnels, bridges, one-way streets, and many others that must be included for complete hazard identification.

Use case 1 - Operate on back roads without other traffic (empty back road)

To identify potential hazards, the starting use case is analogous to that of a student driver, leaning to negotiate hazards in the least hazardous of driving conditions, operating on empty back roads in clear weather, ideally with no other moving objects present. In this scenario, the student driver takes the wheel on the side of a quiet back road with simple signs, signals, pavement markings, and driving laws and assuming no other vehicles, pedestrians, bicycles or animals. There is some potential for stationary obstacles (parked vehicles, debris) in the roadway. The route is selected to avoid complex intersections and with clear lines of sight. The vehicle being driven is assumed to remain in good operating condition. The task is to maintain the posted speed, remain within the lane boundaries (usually centered), avoid any stationary objects, stop at intersections with stop signs and make turns at intersections. Intersection hazards and associated traffic law observance only become safety concerns when other traffic is introduced, but should become habit for the student driver. Similarly, turning lane pathes through intersections only become important when other vehicles are making turns in the same intersection but the student should develop good habits. Regardless of posted speeds, the vehicle must be operated at speeds safe for making turns and without loss of traction that could lead to a loss of control. Assuming no other traffic, the proposed standard hazards are: *departure from road surface, departure from travel/turning lane, fail to avoid stationary objects in roadway, fail to obey traffic signs, fail to observe intersection traffic laws, exceeding vehicle performance limits (traction, stopping distance, cornering), not become a slow/stopped road obstacle.*

And although task at hand is hazard identification, it is noted that perhaps the most severe hazard consequence in this situation might be *departure from travel/turning lane* where the roadway centerline is crossed with the potential for a head on collision with other vehicles. Yet to avoid the hazard *fail to avoid stationary objects in roadway,* it may become necessary to temporarily cross the roadway centerline to avoid another vehicle stopped and partially blocking the travel lane. So in some cases, it may become necessary to increase exposure to one hazard to avoid another.

Once the student becomes proficient on the back roads, more complex roads (again without other traffic) can be attempted. More complex roads introduce more complex intersections with traffic lights, multiple lanes and multiple lane markings. The additional standard hazards include *fail to obey traffic signals* and *fail to obey lane markings*. Table 1 summarizes the hazards that were identified from the first student driver use case.

Table 1 — Empty Back Road Hazards

	Departure from road surface
	Departure from travel/turning lane
	Fail to avoid stationary objects in roadway
	Fail to obey traffic signs

	Fail to observe intersection traffic laws
	Exceeding vehicle performance limits
	Do not become a slow/stopped road obstacle
	Fail to obey traffic signals
	Fail to obey lane markings

Use case 2 - Include other vehicles on back roads in clear weather (back road with other traffic)

As the student driver becomes more adept at the basic tasks of lane keeping, speed control and responding to intersection markings, the difficulty level (hazard potential) can be increased by including other vehicles being operated by (hopefully) responsible drivers driving in a safe and predictable manor.

The added tasks of operating on back roads with other vehicles include maintaining a safe following distance, stopping behind stopped vehicles (at intersections or other reasons), maintaining a safe distance from vehicles entering or exiting the roadway, negotiating with other vehicles at intersections (includes signaling intent) and overtaking slow moving vehicles. An added task is to recognize and negotiate unmarked intersections (no stop sign or signal). These added tasks generate additional proposed standard hazards: *failure to maintain safe separation distance from other vehicles, failure to stop for other vehicles, failure to yield to other vehicles, improper passing, fail to signal for turns, fail to follow intersection rules of the road.*

Table 2 — Back road with other traffic

	Failure to maintain safe separation distance from other vehicles
	Failure to stop for other vehicles
	Failure to yield to other vehicles
	Improper passing
	Fail to signal for turn
	Fail to follow intersection rules of the road

Each of these standard hazards has a rich set of casual conditions. The identification of the hazard provides the framework for the task of elaborating these.

Use case 3 - Include pedestrians, bicycles and animals on back roads in clear weather

The inclusion of Pedestrians, Bicycles and Animals (PBA) adds new hazards to the back road scenario. Other vehicles such as cars and motorcycles are subject to motor vehicle laws and in general will behave in predictable manor. Pedestrians, bicycles and animals may not be as predictable and it is the task of the student driver to learn how to safely interact. In some cases, such as pedestrians crossing the road in a crosswalk, the driver is required to stop and wait for pedestrians to cross. In other settings not involving a crosswalk or pedestrians, it may still be safest to stop and wait for the object to move safely away. But this is often impractical and introduces new hazards if the vehicle becoming a stationary obstacle hazard to other vehicles. An appropriate action can become a very nuanced task that requires understanding the potential motions of these non-vehicle moving objects and predicting the intended motion. Potential motions can include consideration of age (old people or children), disabilities (a white cane) and animal behavior (turkeys take their time, squirrels dart about randomly). Consequences vary. Hitting a squirrel is sad. Hitting a person is may be manslaughter crime. Once the motion is predicted, a plan to maximize the safe separation distance must be developed and executed. During execution of this plan, actual motion of the object is observed and if necessary a new prediction and plan developed and executed. The hazards become: *failure to properly predict motion of pedestrians, bicycles and animals, failure to maintain safe separation from pedestrians, bicycles and animals.*

Operate in darkness or adverse weather

The introduction of darkness or adverse weather impact visibility. Adverse weather can also impact vehicle performance by reducing road surface friction. Darkness and adverse weather will also impact the behavior and performance of other nearby vehicles. Although these elements elevate the risk associate with previously identified hazards, they do not generate new hazards. Arguably, the risk associated with operating too fast for the vehicle to safely stop is covered under a standard hazard such as *failure to stop for other vehicles* and is introduced in the casual factors for the standard hazard.

Operate on hazardous roadways

The design of the roadway can increase the risk of the previously established standard hazards, can contribute the causal factors for these hazards and can introduce unique standard hazards. For example, a roadway without a safe roadside buffer region will increase the severity of a *depart road surface* incident. The lack of clearly painted road edge lane marking can be a casual factor in a *depart road surface* incident. The addition of one-way streets introduces a new standard hazard *wrong direction of travel.* Road design features such as obstructed views, traffic rotaries, tunnels, bridges, and ferry boats all will introduce. Inadequate or confusing road signs and signals will also introduce new hazards.

Future Work

The limited number of use cases examined by this work and presented in this paper are inadequate to produce a comprehensive list of standard hazards. The author acknowledges that there is much more work to be done. A detailed investigation of driver training approaches, traffic laws, highway design standards and traffic control devices would all help inform developing a comprehensive list of hazards. It is also apparent that once a comprehensive list of hazards is developed, there is also a large effort to identify potential causes for these hazard to exist. Some of these causes will be generic to all AV's while others will be specific to an AV's design. It is at this level of detail that the design can include hazard mitigations to reduce the probability of occurrence. For example, if fog or dust obscuring the view of a visual sensor results in various hazards associated with not seeing, localizing or identifying objects, perhaps an additional RADAR sensor can mitigate the hazard(s).

Finally, determine if the risks have been adequately mitigated, the risk levels must be at least approximately quantified. The overall goal is to develop systems that once placed in service will result in a decrease in annual highway fatalities and other accidence statistics.

References

Hawkins, A. J. (2018, January 12). *www.theverge.com*. Retrieved from The Verge: https://www.theverge.com/2018/1/12/16880978/gm-autonomous-car-2019-detroit-auto-show-2018
References
Mil-Std-882E. (2012). *Mil-Std-882E DEPARTMENT OF DEFENSE STANDARD PRACTICE SYSTEM SAFETY*. DOD.
AAA. (2018). *Digest of Motor Laws*. Retrieved from http://drivinglaws.aaa.com/about-the-digest-of-motor-laws/.
MUTCD, D. (2009). *The Manual on Uniform Traffic Control Devices (MUTCD)*. US DOT Federal Highway Administrator.
AAA. (2013). *HOW TO DRIVE INSTRUCTOR GUIDE.*

An Analysis of the Role of Safety Nets in the National Airspace System

Steven Geuther; NASA Langley Research Center; Hampton, VA, USA

Ersin Ancel, Ph.D.; NASA Langley Research Center; Hampton, VA, USA

Keywords: Aircraft Incident, Event Sequence Diagram, Safety Net, Aviation Safety

Abstract

Safe operations of aircraft in the National Airspace System (NAS) may be attributed to many factors, including the application of a variety of safety nets (SNs) as a last line of defense. In preparation for the Next Generation Air Transportation System (NextGen), a review of Aviation Safety Reporting System (ASRS) reports for incidents with positive outcomes was conducted to investigate the importance of current safety nets. The examination of positive outcomes not only shows what went wrong, but also what went right to prevent accidents and "save the day." More than 400 incident reports for 2015 from the voluntary ASRS reporting database were studied in detail to create event sequence diagrams (ESDs), illustrating the role of SNs. The developed ESDs are considered top-level, representative models and are limited with respect to being reliably quantitative because they are based on only reports from a single year. The ESDs could offer insights into human systems integration research, such as strategically using technologies as SNs without human interface or alleviating human workload with new technologies to provide resilient recovery from off-nominal conditions ensuring flight safety.

Introduction

With years of persistent efforts analyzing accidents and incidents and taking safety measures, the U.S. National Airspace System (NAS) has remained one of the safest in the world, especially for commercial aviation (Dorr, 2017). Safety net (SN) technologies and techniques, combined with other lines of defense such as safety procedural rules, regulations, and redundancies in design, are largely responsible for the historical safety record of the NAS. In the aviation domain, these lines of defense are built into the processes to prevent individual failures. Consequently, a complete failure would only happen if individual breakdowns in all available lines of defense occur, which is analogous to Reason's Swiss Cheese Model (Reason, 1997).

Safety nets are typically the last line of defense for a failure prior to producing an accident. However, in order to maintain or improve the current level of safety, NASA's Aeronautics Research Mission Directorate (ARMD) intends to approach aviation safety concerns more proactively instead of reactively, especially considering the new generation of aircraft fleets in the Next Generation Air Transportation System (NextGen). This approach, which includes examining successful mitigations, will further promote the accident preventative technology development, including safety nets.

With a decrease in the number of accidents over the years, there is an increasing desire to investigate incidents, which are still frequent. The NTSB defines accidents as occurrences where any person suffers death or serious injury or the aircraft receives substantial damage whereas an incident is defined as an occurrence, other than an accident, that could affect the safety of the operation of an aircraft. Examples of incidents include damage to property, other than the aircraft, that exceeds $25,000 for repairs, in-flight fire, flight control system failure, complete loss of information, etc. (National Transportation Safety Board, 2010) The investigation of incidents provides insights on the causal relationships in order to develop next-generation safety technologies to ensure flight safety. Given that incidents and accidents share many of the same causal factors, incidents can be considered as precursors to potential accidents. The Aviation Safety Reporting System (ASRS) database of voluntary, confidential reports from various sources, including maintenance workers, air traffic controllers, and flight crews, is employed for the collection of the incident reports. In order to utilize these reports to influence safety, one must collect the data and project them in a more meaningful way. Many Event Sequence Diagrams (ESDs) were developed to show the progression of events that occur leading to an outcome. ESDs can be used to show the benefit of safety nets in the NAS that appear in the reports from the ASRS. In addition, the ESDs may assist in identifying safety gaps that currently exist in the NAS for the development of future SNs.

Overview

Positive Taxonomy

In order to aid the use of aviation accident and incident reporting systems, common aviation terminologies and definitions have been established by the Commercial Aviation Safety Team (CAST)/International Civil Aviation Organization (ICAO) Common Taxonomy Team (CICTT), which is composed of several entities ranging from manufacturers to pilots (CAST/ICAO, 2017). The resulting series of common taxonomies help create consistency among reports, allow keyword queries for easier data collection, and improve the quality of information and communication.

In 2011, the CICTT developed a positive taxonomy document that classifies both technical and human factors safety nets (CAST/ICAO, 2013). The positive taxonomy document includes definitions and categories for decisions, external interventions, and soft safety nets that help in avoiding an accident or contribute to limiting the consequences. For instance, a safety net or external intervention will generally lead to a maneuver, from the decision category, in order to return to nominal flight conditions. A safety net is a technology or human/operator action that supports safe operations within the aviation domain by being the last line of defense prior to a failure. Safety nets can be separated into two categories, hard and soft. A hard safety net is equipment-based technology, typically an airborne or ground-based warning system that can detect a problem and potentially suggest a solution to the situation. A hard safety net can be further classified into commercial, military, and general aviation categories. In contrast, soft safety nets represent human-based attributes such as the accurate usage of documentation, communications, or logical problem solving skills.

For this study, commercial aviation hard safety nets were the main focus in conjunction with the soft safety nets and decisions from the CAST/ICAO document (CAST/ICAO, 2013). The development of the positive taxonomy provides a way for the safety nets to be searched in the accident and incident reports in order to show the role of safety nets in the NAS. The positive taxonomy can also support the classification of incidents, which can aid in finding new accident precursors by placing more emphasis on causal factors instead of just the consequences (Stephens, 2008). In an incident report review, the positive taxonomy can assist in discovering successful safety net intervention, allowing the data collection to not only include the undesirable sequence of events but also the actions to prevent a serious incident or accident. This technique of research offers a proactive prevention of accidents and incidents instead of reactive.

Aviation Safety Reporting System

Figure 1 shows the total and fatal domestic accidents for flights operating under Part 121 and Part 135 for the years of 1986 to 2014 (Evans, 2014)[1]. The reduction in number of accidents over the years suggests that the aviation safety community should focus more on incident reports (Stephens, 2008).

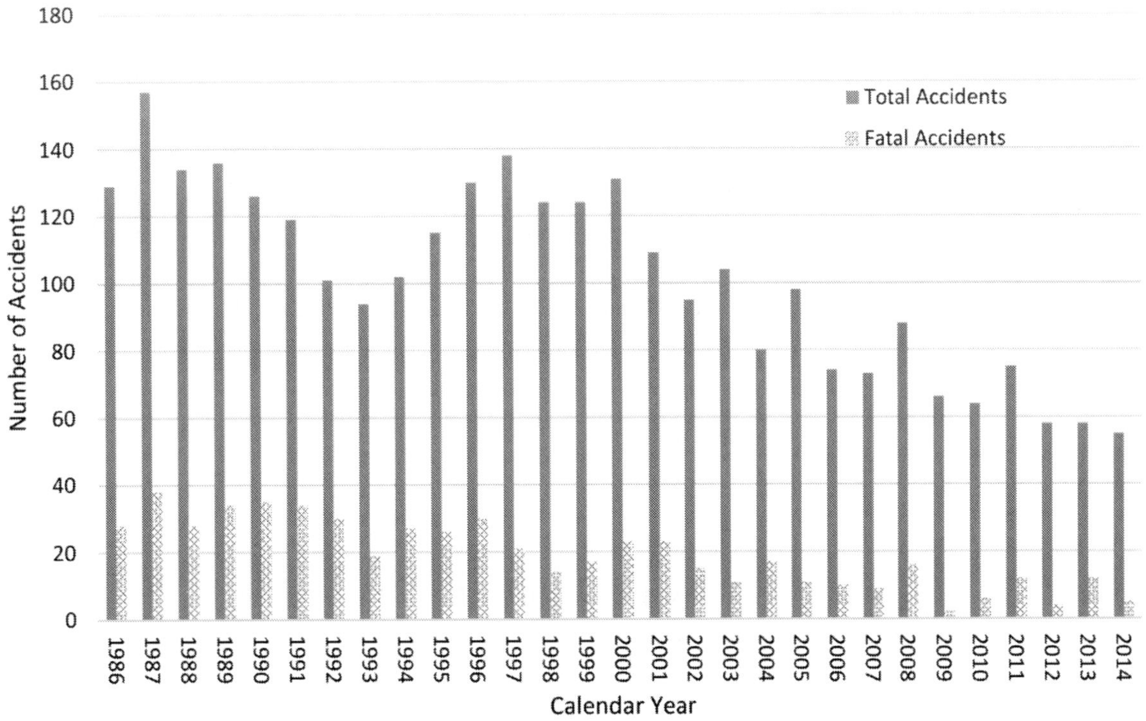

Figure 1 — Part 121 and Part 135 Domestic Accidents, 1986-2014

Given the decrease in total aviation accidents over time, this study relies on a larger sample size of incident reports from the ASRS in order to identify the safety nets encompassed in the NAS. The ASRS is a voluntary reporting system developed by NASA that is accessible by any party involved in an incident, including pilots, passengers, maintenance workers, and air traffic control (ATC), etc., to describe aviation incidents in detail. In this study, general aviation (GA) flights and all flights without a declared Federal Aviation Regulations part in the ASRS report were included in the incident report search since these flights may have been involved in incidents with aircraft flying under Part 121 or Part 135. By the National Transportation Safety Board (NTSB) definition, compared to accidents, the outcomes of incidents are often more desirable partly due to the proper operation of safety nets (Hadley, 2016). The ASRS reports provide information on the role and usage of safety nets in real world operations. For this study, only positive outcome incidents from

[1] The data was updated by Evans to include dates prior to 2001 and after 2010 for use in this paper.

the ASRS database were investigated to highlight the role of safety nets that avert accidents rather than reviewing accident reports, which identify failures and causal factors that caused accidents.

Although the ASRS reports are written mostly by professionals, the reliability and details of these reports are only as good as the knowledge and recall of the person reporting the information. During an incident, ATC and pilots typically have many tasks. Therefore, they may not be able to recall all information from the event accurately. The reporting system also has multiple points of view, which when collected provide a more comprehensive description of the incident. This description can encompass the events prior to the incident and the resolution that prevented an accident. Typically, accident reports have more details than incident reports since they cover the entire timeline including the crew members' life a few days prior to the flight, the previous trips taken by the aircraft, and a maintenance history. Reporting of incidents is voluntary and it is unlikely that the reporting system captures all the annual incidents in the NAS. However, there are still a significant number of incident reports each year as shown in Figure 2 (Aviation Safety Reporting System, 2016-2017). The frequency of incident reports in a single year allows for a variety of causal factors to be reviewed, compared to the few accidents over many years contributing limited causal factors. More conclusions can be drawn from several instances of what works in the NAS architecture and what does not from the numerous incident reports. For instance, given the very limited occurrence rate of mid-air collision accidents, the investigation of numerous loss-of-separation incidents can potentially shed more light on underlying issues and solutions.

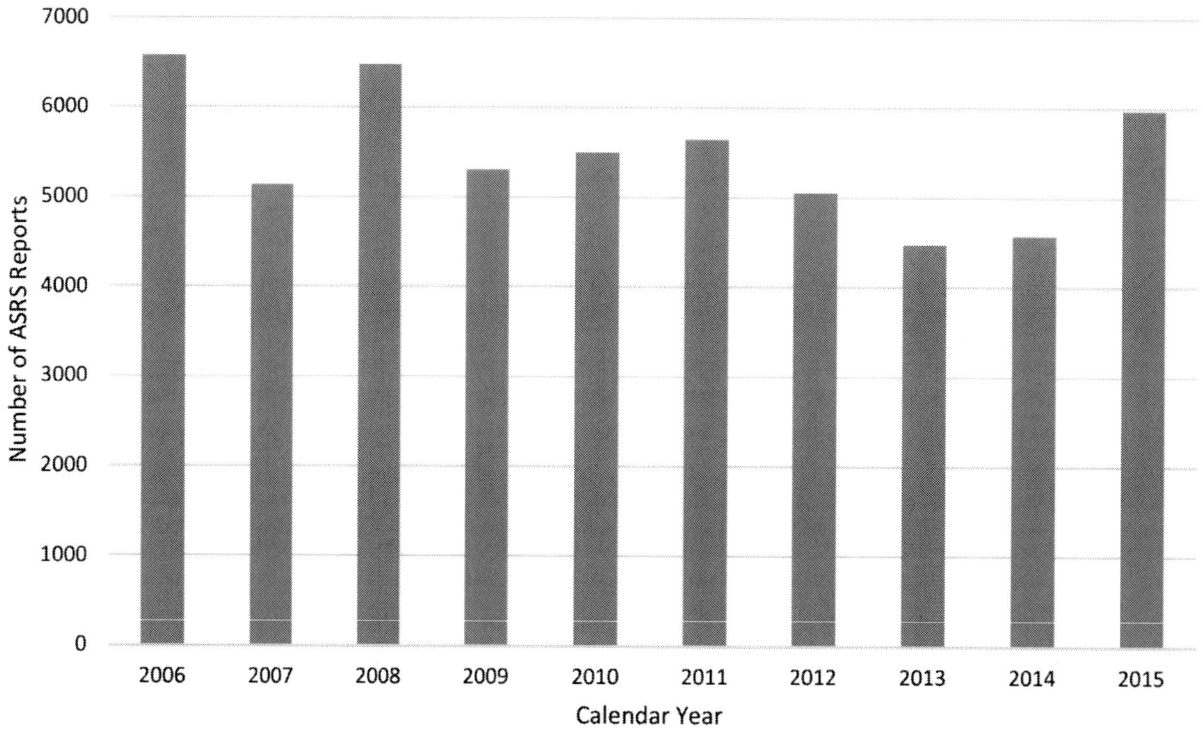

Figure 2 — Number of Incident Reports from the ASRS, 2006-2015

The ASRS reporting system allows the inclusion of search criteria, which helps navigation through the available reports. In this study, the CAST/ICAO's Positive Taxonomy was used to isolate the reports that contained these positive outcomes along with technologies that were used as safety nets. Commercial aviation safety nets were added to the search criteria to further condense the available reports. In order to make sure all reports were captured, both the full name and the acronym of the technology were used in the search criteria. Some of the safety nets that were searched included: Enhanced Ground Proximity Warning System (EGPWS), Automatic Dependent Surveillance – Broadcast (ADS-B), Traffic Collision Avoidance System (TCAS), Airbus Electronic Centralized Aircraft Monitoring (ECAM), and Boeing Engine Indication and Crew Alerting System (EICAS) (Smith, 2017). The search criteria produced reports that included the safety nets and positive taxonomy and captured a substantial number of the incidents of interest, with the caveat that not all reports follow the taxonomy published by CAST/ICAO. In an effort to reduce the number of incidents to analyze from the vast number available, the search criteria was set to only include reports from the year 2015. This was the most recent available calendar year at the time of study. Because only reports from 2015 were analyzed, the identified SNs within this paper may not be representative of SNs from other years or in the future.

Safety Nets and ESD Representation

To illustrate the role of SN technologies, the narratives in the ASRS reports were clustered based on technology purpose to create generalized Event Sequence Diagrams (ESDs). ESDs are used to graphically demonstrate the order of events that take place in an incident. Figure 3 depicts a generic ESD. Typically, ESDs are formed using initiating events, key events, and end states. Based on the presence or absence of the key and initiating events, multiple scenarios with various paths and end states can be represented (Roelen, 2008). In this study, incident reports were searched for only positive taxonomy words or phrases; therefore, key events included the use of safety nets and the different end states were all positive outcomes.

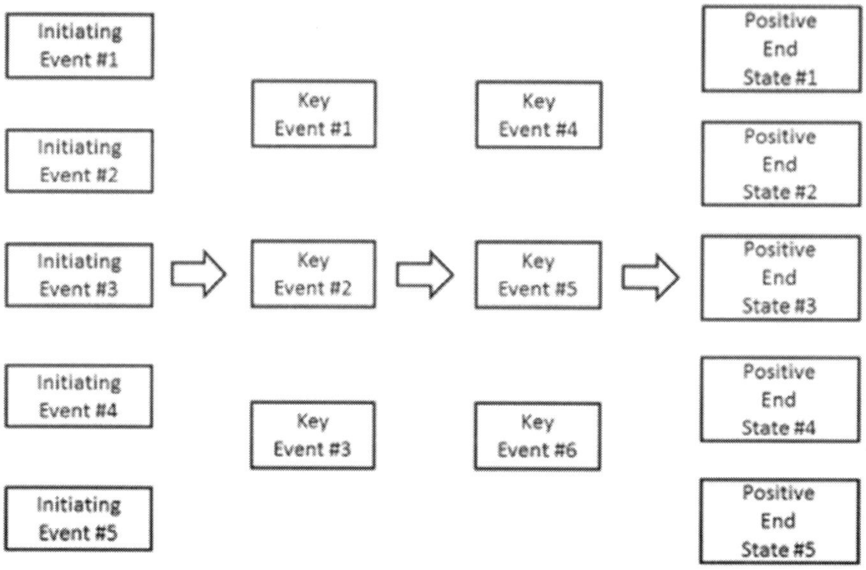

Figure 3 — Generic ESD

The level of detail in the ESDs can vary depending on how descriptive the incident reports are. The number of key events leading to the positive end state can be changed based upon the detail in the reports. The beginning state of each instance, prior to an initiating event, is assumed to be nominal operations. Similarly, the positive end states represent potentially altered, but still desirable, nominal operations. The graphical use of ESDs facilitates the demonstration of all available paths and scenarios that can occur after an initiating event.

ESDs are often used in the investigation of aviation accidents. Following an official accident investigation, a comprehensive report is published by the NTSB. The report tracks all of the events associated with the accident, leading back to the possible initiating event and the hazards that preceded the accident (Ale, 2009). Although this retrospective investigation process has already been conducted to construct ESDs for major accidents categories (Roelen, 2005), this process has been overlooked for incidents due to the nature of voluntary reporting systems. In addition, the large number of the reports, each report being written by a different entity, and the potential inconsistencies between reports make ESD construction for incidents much more difficult.

Results

The hard safety nets that prevented an accident and led to a positive outcome can be grouped into two categories based upon the initiating events. The first category is Airspace Operations Centric and the second category is Aircraft Operations Centric. The Airspace Operations Centric ESD shown in Figure 4 provides a chronological structure, starting on the left with initiating events or causal factors that lead to undesirable events/conflicts. Next, the anomaly is acknowledged and a solution is provided by the stakeholders (ATC, flight crew, and/or SN), which results in an action that clears the conflict. The Airspace Operations Centric ESD combines all the individual ESDs from safety nets that mitigate operational events including loss of separation, loss of control, runway incursion, etc. Approximately 80% of the reports were related to airspace operational events. The Aircraft Operations Centric ESD, shown in Figure 5, provides causal factors that are recognized by either warning systems or the flight crew. The Quick Reference Handbook (QRH), which contains procedures to resolve abnormal and emergency conditions (*Quick Reference Handbook (QRH)*, 2017), is then referenced. Based on the outcomes of the QRH mandated tasks, the aircraft can either continue to its destination or perform one of the maneuvers listed in red in Figure 5. Although less desirable, alternative maneuvers such as rejecting takeoff or performing an unscheduled landing are still considered positive outcomes since an accident is avoided.

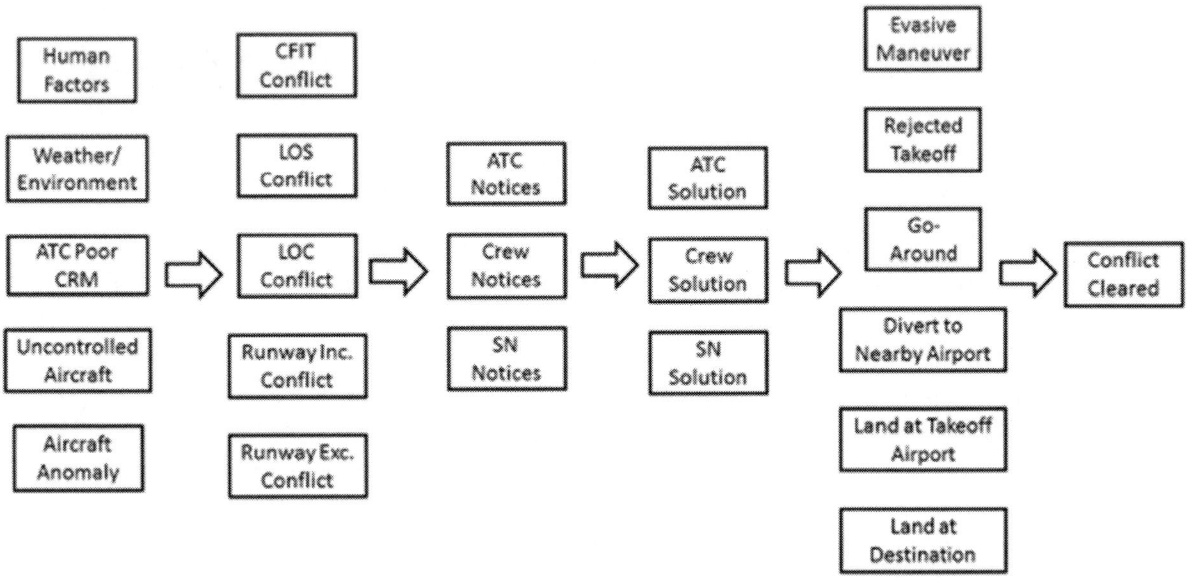

Figure 4 — Airspace Operations Centric ESD

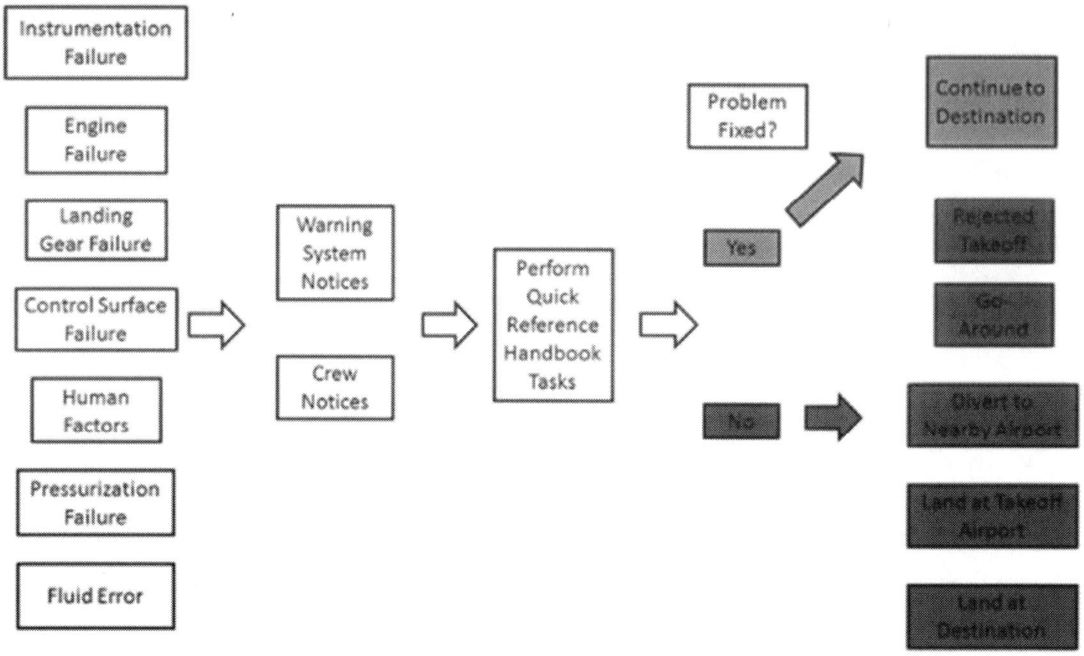

Figure 5 — Aircraft Operations Centric ESD

The ESDs shown in Figure 4 and Figure 5 were developed using data excerpted from a single year query (Aviation Safety Reporting System, 2016-2017). Using the specified safety nets and positive taxonomy restrictions, the number of reports was reduced from the 5971 reports available for 2015 to 445. Due to the limited sample size, the ESDs are high-level, qualitative representations of the real-world operations. It should also be noted that the majority of the reports are associated with technologies and safety nets that are used on commercial airliners. Among the reviewed reports, there were one general aviation specific technology report, no military reports, 24 reports solely on soft safety nets, and 3 reports that explicitly stated both a hard and soft safety net were employed for the resolution.

Compared to the extensive list of existing SNs (Smith, 2017), it should be noted that only 12 different hard safety nets were found as a last line of defense in the 2015 reported incidents investigated in this study. Those 12 SNs were: TCAS, EGPWS, Airport Surface Detection Equipment Model X (ASDE-X), ADS-B, ECAM, Predictive Wind Shear (PWS), Final Monitor Aid (FMA), EICAS, Minimum Safe Altitude Warning System (MSAW), Terrain Avoidance and Warning System (TAWS), Takeoff Configuration Alerting (TOCA), and Passive Collision Avoidance Systems (PCAS). The 12 hard SNs captured in this review were predominantly used as the last line of defense prior to Mid-Air Collision (MAC), Controlled Flight into Terrain (CFIT), or flight with a System Component Failure (SCF). Two soft SNs, crew resource management (CRM) and ATC ground support, were identified as the last line of defense in 14 of the 24 soft safety net related reports.

In addition to the generalized ESDs, two specific ESDs were developed and are illustrated in Figure 6 and Figure 7. Figure 6 shows the details of the Enhanced Ground Proximity Warning

System (EGPWS) ESD, which can be considered as a representative Airspace Operations Centric ESD. The EGPWS ESD lists the causal factors that can lead to a CFIT conflict (e.g., adverse weather, procedural, aircraft anomaly, etc.). The numbers within the arrows in Figure 6 indicate the total number of instances that each causal factor, stakeholder, remedial action, or outcome occurred/contributed for a CFIT conflict-resolution as mentioned in the reviewed reports. However, the sum of the numbers in each column of arrows should not be interpreted as the number of reports associated with the specific technology or action. Not all of the reports explicitly indicate a specific initiating event and/or positive end result. It is also important to note that causal factors or the entities that notice or apply the remedial actions are not mutually exclusive, i.e., more than one causal factor or individual/system can play a role in each CFIT conflict, causing the sums in each column to differ. The EGPWS ESD provides the numerical breakdown of all remedial actions (rejected takeoff, go-around, and evasive maneuver) that are considered to be the positive outcome. Based on the incident reports demonstrating the use of EGPWS, the most significant initiating event prior to a CFIT conflict is Human Factors.

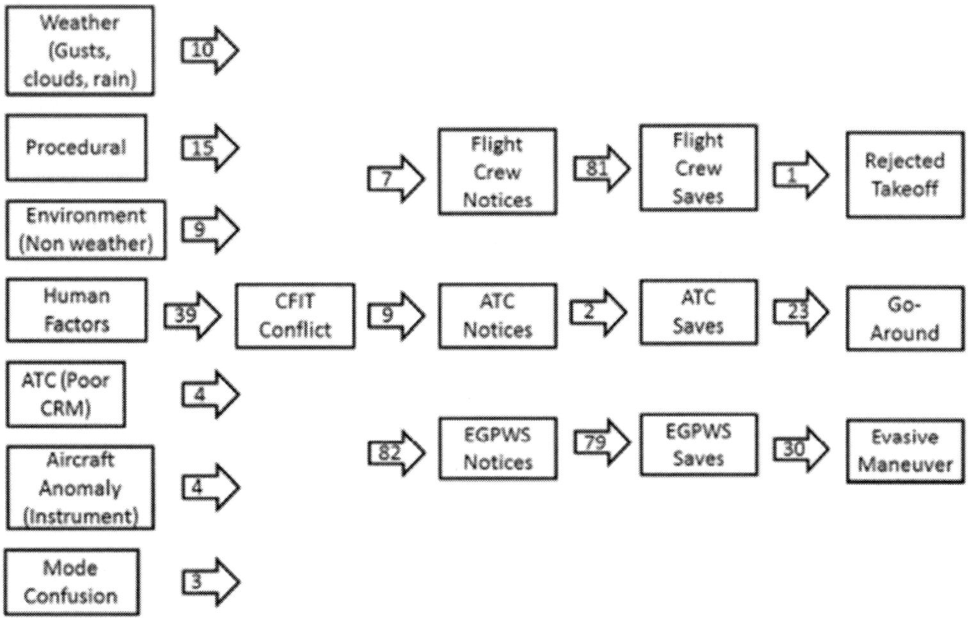

Figure 6 — EGPWS ESD

The same level of detail can be applied to the Aircraft Operations Centric ESD safety nets. One example ESD for ECAM is given in Figure 7. The ESD for ECAM includes color-coded final paths to indicate whether the aircraft is healthy and can continue flight (green) or needs to end flight safely (red). An important observation from this ESD for ECAM is that the flight crew did not notice the component failure in any incident report, indicating the significance of SNs in aircraft operations. It is also important to note that the majority of the flights did not have a successful fix of the SCF from following the QRH in order to continue to the destination with a healthy aircraft.

An ESD can also be developed for soft safety nets in a similar manner. A soft SN ESD may have many different causal factors leading up to a dangerous situation. Soft safety nets such as CRM, ATC support, and training may be utilized in order to prevent an incident and/or accident. However, significantly fewer of the 445 reviewed reports for 2015 give credit to soft SNs for accident/incident prevention. A proper construction of soft safety net ESDs may require a review and study of ASRS reports across multiple years, which is beyond the current study scope.

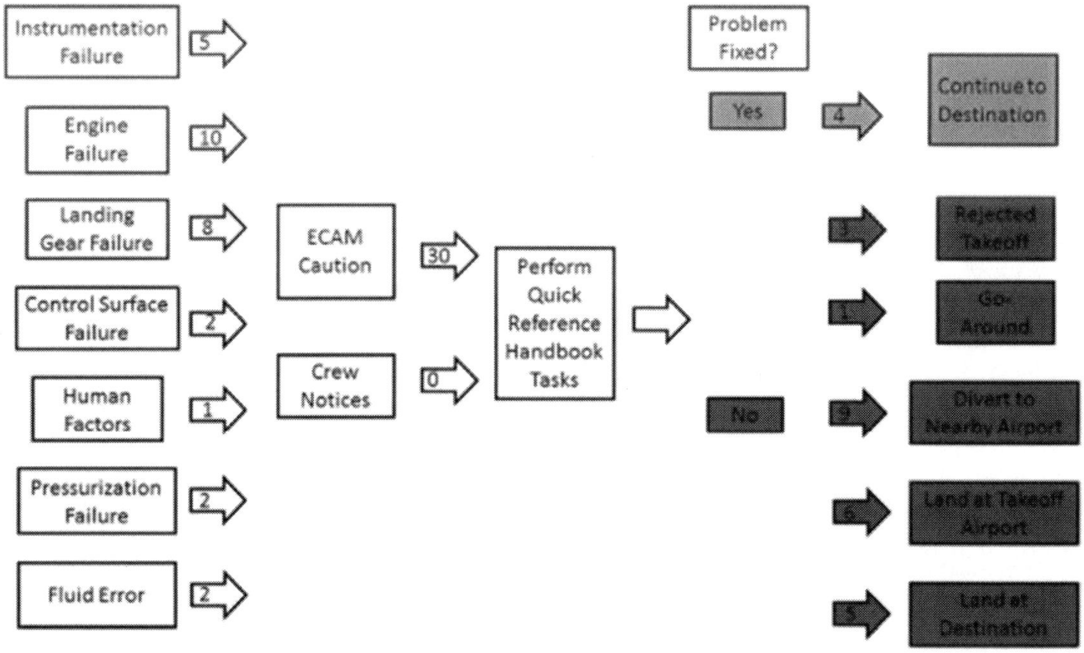

Figure 7 — ECAM ESD

Conclusions

Today in the U.S., commercial aviation enjoys an unprecedented safety record, primarily due to reactive safety measures that were put in place in response to past accidents. However, with the decrease in both fatal and total accidents over the years, NASA has been focused on investigating incidents in order to maintain or further improve commercial aviation safety while developing next-generation safety technologies. As part of this effort, more than 400 incidents that took place in 2015 were examined to identify and classify safety nets that prevented accidents. Although restricting the search to a single year may have resulted in a limited scope in identifying the safety net role, the study revealed a large number of causal factors and their interactions with safety nets. Additionally, the positive outcomes in all of the reports researched in this study might indicate that hard safety nets are critically employed in overcoming the adverse conditions in flight. Finally, despite the effective use of safety nets, the ESDs indicated breakdowns for human factors as well as aircraft and airspace operations that could have potentially led to an accident. The ESDs that were developed within this study could further be used to identify potential areas of improvement within the NAS.

References

Ale, B., Bellamy, L. J., Cooke, R., Duyvis, M., Kurowicka, D., Lin, P., ... Spouge, J. (2009, March 2). *Causal Model for Air Transport Safety* [Final Report]. Retrieved from Netherlands Ministry of Transport

Aviation Safety Reporting System (ASRS). (n.d.). Retrieved November 2016 – March 2017, from NASA Ames Research Center website: https://asrs.arc.nasa.gov/

CAST/ICAO Common Taxonomy Team, (2013, April). *Positive Taxonomy, Definition and Usage Notes* [Version 1.2]

CAST/ICAO Common Taxonomy Team. (2017, December). *Aviation Occurrence Categories Definitions and Usage Notes*. [Version .4.7]

Dorr, L. (2017, December 29). *Fact Sheet - Commercial Aviation Safety Team*. Retrieved April 20, 2018, from Federal Aviation Administration website: https://www.faa.gov/news/fact_sheets/news_story.cfm?newsId=22455

Evans, J. K. (2014). Frequency of Specific Categories of Aviation Accidents and Incidents During 2001-2010. *NASA/CR - 2014-218184*

Hadley, E. (2016, May 4). *What's the Difference Between an Accident and an Incident?* Retrieved 2018, from Aircraft Owners and Pilots Association website: https://pilot-protection-services.aopa.org/news/2016/may/04/did-i-just-have-an-accident-or-an-incident

National Transportation Safety Board, 49 C.F.R. pt. B8 § 830.2, 2010.

Reason, J. T. (1997). *Managing the Risks of Organizational Accident*. Hampshire, UK: Ashgate.

Roelen, A. L., & Wever, R. (2005, November). *Accident scenarios for an integrated aviation safety model* (NLR-CR-2005-560). Retrieved from National Aerospace Laboratory NLR website: http://www.nlr-atsi.nl/fast/downloads/CATS/App%203%20NLR%201%20-%202005-560-cr.pdf

Roelen, A. L.C., van Doorn, B. A., Smeltink, J. W., Verbeek, M. J., & Wever, R. (2008, October). *Quantification of Event Sequence Diagrams for a causal risk model of commercial air transport* (NLR-CR-2008-646). Retrieved from National Aerospace Laboratory NLR website: http://www.nlr-atsi.nl/fast/downloads/CATS/App%204a%20NLR%2013%20-%202008-646.pdf

Quick Reference Handbook (QRH). (2017). Retrieved 2018, from SKYbrary website: https://www.skybrary.aero/index.php/Quick_Reference_Handbook_(QRH)

Smith, B. E., Evans, C. (2017). Current Safety Nets within the U.S. National Airspace System. *NASA/TN - 2017-49109*,

Stephens, C., Ferrante, O., Olsen, K., & Sood, K. (2008). Standardizing International Taxonomies. *ISASI Forum January - March 2008*, 8-13.

Reliability Enhancement Test Evaluation Based on Accelerated Growth Model

Yuankai Gao, MS; Beihang University; Beijing, Beijing, China

Xiaogang Li; Ph.D.; Beihang University; Beijing, Beijing, China

Keywords: quantitative assessment, RET, variable acceleration model

Abstract

Reliability enhancement test has been widely used as a practical technology to improve product reliability. Because the purpose of the RET is to make the product more robust in a short time, it can only qualitatively evaluate the product reliability and cannot quantitatively obtain the product reliability index. Therefore, in order to improve product robustness in a short period of time, it is also possible to quantitatively calculate the reliability level of the product , this paper introduces an evaluation method for accelerating the reliability growth test. First of all, the acceleration model (Arrhenius model) in the accelerated life test is used to convert the test time at each stage of high temperature step stress into the corresponding life time under normal stress. In the process of reliability enhancement test, continuous improvement of the product is accompanied by an increase in the inherent reliability of the product. Therefore, we analyze the data under normal stress through the reliability growth model (Duane model). Then calculate the life of the product at the end of the test to achieve a quantitative assessment of the reliability enhancement test. On this basis, a variable acceleration model with time varying acceleration is also derived. Finally, the rationality and availability of the evaluation method are further verified by enumerating concrete calculation examples.

Introduction

The development of reliability test technology has formed two major types of methods, stimulation test and simulation test, since its birth . The simulation test is to simulate the actual use conditions of the mission profile as much as possible, plus the design margin to ensure the reliability of the product. A typical representative is the reliability growth test. However, such tests for high reliability and long-life products are not suitable, because this will not only lead to a longer development cycle, but will also greatly increase the cost of the test. Therefore, the stimulation test has emerged. The stimulation test does not simulate the real conditions of the equipment mission profile. Instead, the method of artificially applying accelerated stress accelerates the stimulating of potential defects , and improves the product reliability through analysis and improvement to achieve product robustness. Typical representative is reliability enhancement test. However, the reliability enhancement test cannot be used to quantitatively evaluate the reliability index of the product at the end of the test as the reliability growth test, but can only qualitatively evaluate the product reliability. Therefore, how to quantitatively evaluate the reliability of the tested product by the failure data of RET becomes a hot topic in the field of reliability testing technology. Firstly, the accelerated time model in the accelerated life test (Arrhenius model) was used to extrapolate the test time under the high temperature step stress to the corresponding normal stress life time. Secondly, considering the continuous improvement of the product in RET, the inherent reliability of the product is increasing continuously, so the extrapolated data is analyzed by the reliability growth model (Duane model). As a result, a quantitative assessment of reliability enhancement testing is achieved. On this basis, a variable acceleration model with time varying acceleration is also derived. Finally, the specific examples were used to further verify the usability and correctness of the method.

1 Basic Theory

1.1 Accelerated Model

Accelerated models can be divided into three categories according to their proposed methods: physical acceleration model, empirical acceleration model, and statistical acceleration model. Several phenomena often occur during reliability enhancement testing, including mechanical fatigue damage, wear, electron migration, and chemical reactions. These have established different mathematical models and respond differently to different incentives or actions. Arrhenius model is mainly used to describe the failure mechanism of non-mechanical, chemical reaction, corrosion, material diffusion or migration process. For products whose life is subject to an exponential distribution. According to the Arrhenius model, the expression of a product's life-time characteristics with temperature stress can be obtained, ie:

$$L = A \times e^{\frac{E_a}{kT}} \tag{1}$$

Where A is a constant, E_a is activation energy, k is Boltzmann's constant, and T is absolute temperature.

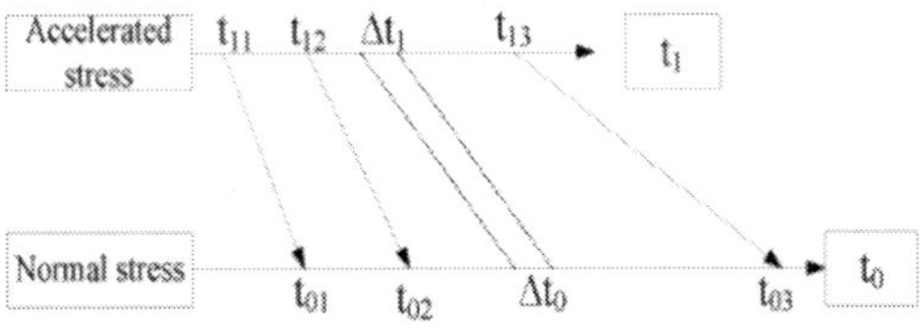

Figure 1— Data Extrapolation Process

Obviously, the acceleration factor converted from different temperature stress failure data can be obtained from equation 1:

$$A_F = \frac{L_N}{L_A} = \frac{A \times e^{\frac{E_a}{kT_N}}}{A \times e^{\frac{E_a}{kT_A}}} = e^{\frac{E_a}{k}(\frac{1}{T_N} - \frac{1}{T_A})} \tag{2}$$

In the formula, L_A is the life characteristics of the product under accelerated stress levels; L_N is the product life characteristics under normal stress levels; T_N is the normal level of temperature stress; T_A is the temperature stress at the acceleration level. Further deductions are:

$$L_N = L_A \times A_F = L_A \times e^{\frac{E_a}{k}(\frac{1}{T_N}-\frac{1}{T_A})} \quad (3)$$

1.2 Reliability Growth Model

Reliability growth tests must have a growth model. The reliability growth model can track the current reliability level of the product in the test process based on the number of failures or failure time series provided during the reliability growth test, and quantitatively evaluate the reliability level that the product ultimately achieves after the test is completed. The reliability growth model is a mathematical expression that describes the law and general trend of product reliability growth during the reliability growth test. Reliability model is divided into continuous type and discrete type. The commonly used models are Duane model, AMSAA model and so on. The Duane model is first introduced. The method used in this article is the Duane model, so only the Duane model is introduced here. The Duane model expression represented by the instantaneous MTBF is:

$$MTBF(\mathrm{t}) = \frac{t^m}{a(1-\mathrm{m})} \quad (4)$$

The Duane model expression expressed as cumulative MTBF is:

$$MTBF(\mathrm{t}) = \frac{t^m}{a} \quad (5)$$

Where, m is the growth rate and a is a constant.

2 Quantitative Assessment of RET

2.1 Data Extrapolation Methods

Accelerated model analysis and processing of accelerated test data and extrapolation of accelerated test data to failure data under normal stress conditions are the core issues in the study of reliability assessment methods for high acceleration tests. During the test, as the test stress level continues to increase, product failures continue to be revealed, it is necessary to analyze the failure mechanism of the product and then improve the product to achieve an increase in the inherent reliability of the product. This process makes the activation energy needed to activate the fault increase as the inherent reliability of the product increases. From the perspective of activation energy, the inherent reliability of the product will increase stepwise with each improvement of the product, and the activation energy will also increase stepwise (as shown in Figure 1), at each stress level. The failures have different activation energy and different acceleration factors.

Obviously, the activation energy in the time zone $(t_{1i}, t_{1(i+1)})$ of the i-th failure to the (i+1)-th failure in the RET test is equal to the activation energy in the time interval $(t_{0i}, t_{0(i+1)})$ extrapolated to the normal stress level. We need to record the product's continuous (failure) time at different stress levels. The failure time of the test unit at each stress level (in terms of cycle times or time) must be converted in stages to the corresponding normal stress. This can be achieved by experimenting with "deceleration" (ie: extrapolation of data) and converting the number of trials to actual duration. We denote the activation energy at the i-th failure at the j-th acceleration stress level as $E_a(\mathrm{ij})$, and the acceleration factor is recorded as:

$$A_{F_{ij}} = e^{\frac{E_a(\mathrm{ij})}{k}(\frac{1}{T_N}-\frac{1}{T_{A_i}})} \quad (6)$$

For ease of understanding, the high-temperature step stress test was used as an example to illustrate, so the Arrhenius model was selected. When the failure data of the product at the accelerated stress level is recorded (only one failure occurs at each stress level), the acceleration factor can be extrapolated to the i-th failure data of the product at the normal stress level. Therefore equation 6 and equation 3 can be used to further derive:

$$L_{N_i} = L_{A_{ij}} \times A_{F_{ij}} = L_{A_i} \times e^{\frac{E_a(\mathrm{ij})}{k}(\frac{1}{T_N}-\frac{1}{T_{A_i}})} \quad (7)$$

In the formula, $L_{A_{ij}} = t_{ij} - t_{i(j-1)}$ is the time from the (j-1)-th failure to the j-th failure at the i-th stress level; $L_{N_i} = t_{0j} - t_{0(j-1)}$ is the time from the j-1-th failure to the j-th failure at extrapolation to the normal stress level.

In the above case, for ease of understanding we assume that only one failure occurs in each stage of the product, and the feasibility of data extrapolation is studied from the perspective of activation energy. However, the number of failures in each phase of the actual test process is often more than one, so the following describes how the data is extrapolated when the number of failures in each phase is not less than one . The specific process is as follows:

It is assumed that the product undergoes reliability enhancement tests at different levels of environmental stress in time interval （0, T]. The number of stress levels experienced in the test was m (m $\geq$ 2), the number of failures occurred was r (r $\geq$ n-1>1), and the number of improvement was n-1. This is an n-stage strengthening test under different levels of environmental stress, from the beginning of the test to the first improvement to the first phase, with the adjacent two improvements being a phase, and the n-1th improvement to the end of the test as n stage. If we consider from the perspective of failure rate, the failure rate of the i-th stage product under the reference stress is λ_i (i=1,...,n). Generally, each improvement reduces the failure rate, ie, $\lambda_1 > \lambda_2 > ... > \lambda_n$. The details of the test are as follows:

The product started the test from time $t_{1,0} = 0$. In the first stage, the stress level applied on time interval $(t_{1,j-1}, t_{1,j}]$ is $f_{1,j}$ （ $j = 1,...,k_1$ ） , and r_1 ($r_1 \geq 1$) failures occur in total. The stress at the time of the l-th failure was recorded as $f^*_{1,l}$ （ l=1, ..., l ） . The first $r_1 - 1$ failures are only repaired, and the r_1-th failure occurs at the t_{1,k_1} , after which improvements are made. The corresponding baseline test time for the first phase is:

$$T_1(\mathrm{A})=\sum_{j=1}^{k_1}(t_{1,j}-t_{1,j-1})\mathrm{e}^{(\frac{A}{f_0}-\frac{A}{f_{1,j}})} \quad (8)$$

According to the above idea, in the i-th (i=1, 2, ..., n-1) stage, the stress level applied by the equipment at time interval $(t_{1,j-1},t_{1,j}]$ is $f_{1,j}$ ($j=1,...,k_1$). A total of r_1 ($r_1 \geq 1$) failures occurred during the $(t_{i,0},t_{i,k_i}]$ period, and stress $f^*_{i,l}$ (l=1, …, r_1) at the time of the l-th failure. The previous failures were only repaired, and the th failure occurred at the , after which improvements are made. The corresponding baseline test time for the i-th phase is:

$$T_i(\mathrm{A})=\sum_{j=1}^{k_i}(t_{i,j}-t_{i,j-1})\mathrm{e}^{(\frac{A}{f_0}-\frac{A}{f_{i,j}})} \quad (9)$$

In the n-th stage, the stress level applied by the device during the $(t_{n,j-1},t_{n,j}]$ is $f_{n,j}$ ($j=1,...,k_n$) , and $r_n(r_n \geq 1)$ failures occur in $(t_{n,0},t_{n,k_n}]$. Failures were only repaired. The stress at the moment of l-th failure $f^*_{n,l}$ (l =1, …, r_n) . The test ended at time $t_{n,k_n}=T$. Therefore, the corresponding baseline test time is:

$$T_n(\mathrm{A})=\sum_{j=1}^{k_n}(t_{n,j}-t_{n,j-1})\mathrm{e}^{(\frac{A}{f_0}-\frac{A}{f_{n,j}})} \quad (10)$$

From the above, the corresponding likelihood functions for failure probability density function are:

$$L(\mathrm{A};\lambda_1,...,\lambda_n)=\prod_{i=1}^{n}[\prod_{l=1}^{r_i}\lambda_i\,\mathrm{e}^{(\frac{A}{f_0}-\frac{A}{f^*_{i,l}})}]\mathrm{e}^{-\lambda_i T_i(\mathrm{A})} \quad (11)$$

The log likelihood function is further derived as:

$$l(\mathrm{A};\lambda_1,...,\lambda_n)=\sum_{i=1}^{n}[r_i\ln\lambda_i+\sum_{l=1}^{r_i}(\frac{A}{f_0}-\frac{A}{f^*_{i,l}})-\lambda_i T_i(\mathrm{A})] \quad (12)$$

Likelihood equations are:

$$\frac{\partial l}{\partial \lambda_i}=\frac{r_i}{\lambda_i}-T_i(\mathrm{A}), i=1,...,\mathrm{n}, \quad (13)$$

$$\frac{\partial l}{\partial A}=\sum_{i=1}^{n}[\sum_{l=1}^{r_i}(\frac{1}{f_0}-\frac{1}{f^*_{i,l}})-\lambda_i\sum_{j=1}^{k_i}(t_{i,j}-t_{i,j-1})\exp\{\frac{A}{f_0}-\frac{A}{f_{i,j}}\}(\frac{1}{f_0}-\frac{1}{f_{i,j}})] \quad (14)$$

If equation 13 is equal to zero then there are:

$$\lambda_i = \frac{r_i}{T_i(\mathrm{A})}, i = 1,..,n, \tag{15}$$

Bringing equation 15 into equation 14 has:

$$h(\mathrm{A}) = \frac{\partial l}{\partial A} = \sum_{i=1}^{n}\{\sum_{l=1}^{r_i}(\frac{1}{f_0} - \frac{1}{f^*_{i,l}}) - \frac{r_i[\sum_{j=1}^{k_i}(t_{i,j} - t_{i,j-1})\exp\{\frac{A}{f_0} - \frac{A}{f_{i,j}}\}(\frac{1}{f_0} - \frac{1}{f_{i,j}})]}{\sum_{j=1}^{k_i}(t_{i,j} - t_{i,j-1})e^{(\frac{A}{f_0} - \frac{A}{f_{i,j}})}}\} \tag{16}$$

Because $h^{'}(\mathrm{A}) < 0$, $h(\mathrm{A})$ are strictly monotonic decreasing, the unique solution of $h(\mathrm{A}) = 0$ exists, and is the maximum point of the log-likelihood function. (Proved to skip) When $\mathrm{A} \to 0^+$,

$$\lim_{\mathrm{A}\to 0^+} h(\mathrm{A}) = \sum_{i=1}^{n}\{\sum_{l=1}^{r_i}(-\frac{1}{f^*_{i,l}}) - r_i[\sum_{j=1}^{k_i}(t_{i,j} - t_{i,j-1})(-\frac{1}{f^*_{i,l}})]/\sum_{j=1}^{k_i}(t_{i,j} - t_{i,j-1})]\} > 0 \tag{17}$$

When $\mathrm{A} \to \infty$,

$$\lim_{\mathrm{A}\to\infty} h(\mathrm{A}) = \sum_{i=1}^{n}\{\sum_{l=1}^{r_i}(-\frac{1}{f^*_{i,l}}) - r_i(-\frac{1}{\max\limits_{1\le j\le k_i} f_{i,j}})\} \le 0 \tag{18}$$

Therefore, the necessary and sufficient condition for the existence and unique solution of the solution of the likelihood equation is:

$$\sum_{i=1}^{n}\{\sum_{l=1}^{r_i}(-\frac{1}{f^*_{i,l}}) - r_i(-\frac{1}{\max\limits_{1\le j\le k_i} f_{i,j}})\} < 0 \tag{19}$$

And,

$$h(0) = \frac{\partial l}{\partial A} = \sum_{i=1}^{n}\{\sum_{l=1}^{r_i}(-\frac{1}{f^*_{i,l}}) - r_i[\sum_{j=1}^{k_i}(t_{i,j} - t_{i,j-1})(-\frac{1}{f^*_{i,l}})]/\sum_{j=1}^{k_i}(t_{i,j} - t_{i,j-1})]\} > 0 \tag{20}$$

Note that $f^*_{i,l}$ is the stress applied at the l-th failure in the i-th stage, and $\max\limits_{1\le j\le k_i} f_{i,j}$ is the maximum stress applied at the i-th stage. The right end of equation 19 should be less than or equal to 0. Therefore, as long as not all failures occur at the highest stress level of their stage, equation 19 must be true. If A's maximum likelihood estimate $\hat{A}$ exists, $T_i(\hat{A}) = \sum_{j=1}^{k_i}(t_{i,j} - t_{i,j-1})e^{(\frac{\hat{A}}{f_0} - \frac{\hat{A}}{f_{i,j}})}$ can be used instead of $T_i(\mathrm{A})$. Therefore, the reliability growth process under the above-mentioned different levels of high accelerating environmental stress can be transformed into the reliability growth problem under the same environment, so that data analysis methods can be used for analysis.

In summary, considering that there are few samples of accelerated test products at the engineering development stage, the above method is aimed at the accelerated test of single products. In fact, in the search for the stress model parameter A, as much as possible, the test information of all exponential products with the same working environment and similar test conditions should be used. Because in such cases, these products should have the same environmental factors, and the obtained parameter values are more accurate.

2.2 Extrapolation Data Processing

In the process of implementing reliability enhancement tests, the weak points of the product are continuously exposed as the test stress level increases. This is actually a test-improvement-retest process. Therefore, as the stress level increases, it is necessary to continuously improve the products for the design defects exposed in the tests so as to achieve a rapid increase in the inherent reliability of the products. This is actually a test-improvement-retest process. Traditional reliability growth tests must also be tested-improved-retested until they meet the requirements. From the above, it can be seen that the growth process of the reliability growth test has something in common with the growth process of the reliability enhancement test. For example, product reliability growth is usually only related to reducing the impact of systemic weaknesses; The failure of systemic weak points was revealed and failure analysis was carried out, improvement measures were taken, and the effectiveness of the improvement measures was verified; the reliability of the product was continuously improved during the test. The traditional reliability growth test after the end of the test, according to the failure data of each growth phase to select the appropriate growth model, and then the product can be quantitatively evaluated at the end of the test reliability. Therefore, we can consider the extrapolated accelerated test data as a set of reliability growth test data to quantitatively evaluate the reliability of the product at the end of the accelerated test through the reliability growth test evaluation method.

The indispensable information in the data analysis of the reliability growth test is the failure time. When calculating the failure time under normal stress by the failure data in the accelerated test, extrapolation of the test data is required through the data extrapolation method in the 2.1, and the extrapolated data obtained are arranged in ascending order and analyzed in accordance with the reliability growth model. Due to the fact that the number of products under test and the type of stress during the test are different, the types and characteristics of the extrapolated data are different. When selecting a reliability growth model, the selection of the most appropriate growth model needs to be selected based on the type and characteristics of the extrapolated data. The reliability growth model is not only an important tool to describe the product reliability changes regularly with the test time, but also an effective method to evaluate the reliability status of the product at any moment of change.

2.3 Duane Model Evaluation Method

According to the results recorded during the experiment, the growth model was selected for evaluation. The commonly used models were the Duane model and the AMSAA model. The AMSAA/Crow model is usually preferred, and the Duane model is recommended only if a few experiments fail. Since the product is in the development stage during the accelerated testing phase, the number of samples is small, and the failure data after the RET test is less, so the growth model selected for the convenience analysis is the Duane model.

As a time function model, Duane model can dynamically evaluate the reliability of products and can perform reliability prediction. When the Duane model is used to estimate the product lifetime, the estimation of parameters in the model is mainly used, and the commonly used parameter estimation methods are divided into map estimation and least squares estimation.

2.3.1 graph estimation

To perform the graph estimation of the Duane model, follow the following steps to plot the growth curve based on the Duane model.

① As the test progresses, continuously record the cumulative number of failures N(t) of the product under test and the corresponding cumulative test time t; ② Calculate the corresponding t/N(t) for each selected time t value. If t is too large, transform the ratio d to it. ③ Mark each point (t, t/N(t)) on double logarithmic paper; ④ If the plotted points can form a straight line, then the Duane model can be used. On the plotted Duane curve, the following method is used to calculate the estimated value of each parameter.

1) The parameter m is given directly by the slope of the line;

2) The parameter a can be determined according to the ordinate value of the intersection point of the Duane curve and the vertical axis 1/N(1), ie:

$$a=\begin{cases}(1/N(1))^{-1}, \text{No transformation}\\(1/N(1))^{-1}d^{m-1}, \text{Transformation}\end{cases} \tag{21}$$

3) MTBF value is $\hat{\theta}(t)=\frac{t^m}{a(1-m)}$, and $\hat{R}=\exp(-\frac{t}{\hat{\theta}(t)})$.

2.3.2 least squares estimation

The accuracy of the least-squares estimation is higher than that of the map, and it can be used for both complete data analysis and packet data analysis. It can be used for both the failure-closure analysis and time-closure analysis. However, for incomplete data, it is required to have a certain amount of cumulative failures.

The Duane model uses double logarithmic coordinates and can be expressed as

$$\ln\theta_c(t)=-\ln a+m\ln t \tag{22}$$

Accumulated MTBF is obtained from the cumulative test time $t_1<t_2<...<t_n$ and the corresponding cumulative failure times $N(t_1),N(t_2),...,N(t_n)$.

$$\theta_c(t_j)=\frac{t_j}{N(t_j)}(j=1,2,...,n) \tag{23}$$

According to the Duane model there are

$$\ln\theta_c(t_j) = -\ln a + m\ln t_j + \varepsilon_j (j = 1, 2, ..., n) \tag{24}$$

Therefore, the least squares estimate for m and a is

$$\hat{m} = \frac{n\sum_{j=1}^{n}\ln\theta_c(t_j)\ln t_j - (\sum_{j=1}^{n}\ln\theta_c(t_j)) \times (\sum_{j=1}^{n}\ln t_j)}{n\sum_{j=1}^{n}(\ln t_j)^2 - (\sum_{j=1}^{n}\ln t_j)^2} \tag{25}$$

$$\hat{a} = \exp\{\frac{1}{n}(\hat{m}\sum_{j=1}^{n}\ln t_j) - \sum_{j=1}^{n}\ln\theta_c(t_j)\} \tag{26}$$

So, the least square estimate of instantaneous failure rate $\lambda(t)$ is

$$\hat{\lambda}(t) = \hat{a}(1-\hat{m})t^{-\hat{m}} (0 < t \le t_n) \tag{27}$$

Since the repairable product does not improve or correct after time t_n , it can reasonably be assumed that after the product is shaped, its failure time obeys an exponential distribution, ie, the least square estimate of MTBF at time t_n is

$$\hat{\theta}(t) = \frac{t_n^{\hat{m}}}{\hat{a}(1-\hat{m})} \tag{28}$$

After further shaping, if the task time of the product in use is t, the least square estimate of its reliability is:

$$\hat{R} = \exp(-\frac{t}{\hat{\theta}(t)}) \tag{29}$$

After the parameter estimation, the Duane model needs to be tested for goodness of fit to further verify the closeness of the test data to the fitted line. This article will not be described again.

2.4 The Establishment of Variable Acceleration Model

As shown in Figure 1 of the 2.1, as the reliability of the product improves constantly, the activation energy needed to stimulate the potential defects of the product will also increase with the increase of the inherent reliability of the product. In accordance with the idea of using the Duane model to extrapolate data in the 2.2, we can further extend the stepwise growth relationship that can change with time to a continuous growth relationship. The activation energy in the time zone $(t_{1i}, t_{1(i+1)})$ in the RET from the i-th failure to the $i+1$-th failure is equal to the activation energy in the time interval $(t_{0i}, t_{0(i+1)})$ pushed to the normal stress level. For an exponential life-time product, the MTTF and MTBF of the product are the same. We can reasonably assume that the current MTBF of the product is equal to the current MTTF of the product. Therefore, the following relationship can be obtained from (1) and (4):

$$\hat{MTBF} = \frac{t_0^{\,m}}{a(1-m)} = \hat{MTTF} = A \times e^{\frac{E_a(t)}{kT_0}} \tag{30}$$

Where, t_0 is the cumulative test time of the product in the normal stress environment, $\hat{MTBF}$ is the instantaneous $MTBF$ of the product at time t_0, and $\hat{MTTF}$ is the mean time to failure of the product at the time t_0. Further derivation,

$$E_a(t_0) = kT_0 \times \ln \frac{t_0^{\,m}}{Aa(1-m)} \tag{31}$$

From equation 31, we can regard the stepwise growth process of activation energy E_a as a continuous growth with cumulative test time under normal environmental stress. Therefore, at any moment t_1 under the accelerated stress environment, the product has the same activation energy as the moment t_0 in the normal stress environment. From the calculus point of view, the small intervals $\Delta t_1 \to 0$ and $\Delta t_0 \to 0$ are taken respectively after the t_1 and t_0 moments, and the activation energy of the product can be considered to be constant in the small interval. If the value is $E_a(t_0)$, then Δt_1 and Δt_0 satisfy equation 7, which is

$$\Delta t_0 = \Delta t_1 \times e^{\frac{E_a(t_0)}{K}\left(\frac{1}{T_0}-\frac{1}{T_1}\right)} \tag{32}$$

By equation 32 we can get the integration relationship between t_1 and t_0 is

$$t_1 = \int_0^{t_0} e^{\frac{E_a(t_0)}{K}\left(\frac{1}{T_0}-\frac{1}{T_1}\right)} dt_0 \tag{33}$$

According to equation 31 and equation 33, the relationship between cumulative test time t_0 under normal stress level and cumulative test time t_1 under accelerated stress environment can be obtained as

$$t_0 = \left\{ t_1 \left[\left(\frac{1}{T_1} - \frac{1}{T_0} \right) T_0 m + 1 \right] \times \left[Aa(1-\mathrm{m}) \right]^{\left(\frac{1}{T_1}-\frac{1}{T_0}\right)T_0} \right\}^{\frac{1}{\left(\frac{1}{T_1}-\frac{1}{T_0}\right)T_0 m+1}} \tag{34}$$

Substituting equation 34 into equation 31, the expression of the activation energy E_a with the cumulative test time for the reliability enhancement test can be expressed as

$$E_a(t_1) = kT_0 \times \ln \frac{\left\{ t_1 \left[\left(\frac{1}{T_1} - \frac{1}{T_0} \right) T_0 m + 1 \right] \times \left[Aa(1-\mathrm{m}) \right]^{\left(\frac{1}{T_1}-\frac{1}{T_0}\right)T_0} \right\}^{\frac{m}{\left(\frac{1}{T_1}-\frac{1}{T_0}\right)T_0 m+1}}}{Aa(1-m)} \tag{35}$$

When the expression of the activation energy E_a is determined, the expression of the Arrhenius acceleration model that changes with the RET time is

$$L = Ae^{\frac{E_a(t_1)}{kT}} \tag{36}$$

Thus, the expression that the acceleration factor varies with the time of the reliability enhancement test is

$$A_{F_i} = \frac{L_{0i}}{L_{1i}} = e^{\frac{E_a(t_1)}{k}(\frac{1}{T_0}-\frac{1}{T_1})} \tag{37}$$

The conditions for establishing the variable acceleration model mentioned above must meet the following three conditions:

(1) At each stress level, the life of the product is subject to the exponential distribution, and after the product is improved, the distribution type of the product life is not changed and only the parameters of the distribution are changed.

(2) The relationship between the product's characteristic lifetime and the accelerated stress level satisfies the Arrhenius acceleration model, and the data extrapolated to the normal stress level satisfies the Duane growth model.

(3) The remaining life of the product is only related to the accumulated failure part and the current stress level, but has nothing to do with the accumulation mode.

The above assumptions for the product at the prototype stage can be satisfied. First of all, the distribution of life of most electronic and electromechanical products obeys the exponential distribution. Secondly, the improvement of product design defects is usually carried out locally, and will not change the basic properties of the product, that is, electromechanical products will still be electromechanical products. Therefore, the first condition is satisfied. The application of the Arrhenius accelerated model in accelerated life test assessment has validated its effectiveness. In the case where failures caused by tests conducted in different stress environments take the same degree of corrective measures, it can be assumed that the growth rates calculated from the extrapolated test data are equal. So, the second condition can also be satisfied. The third condition is that Nelson proposed based on failure physics, which is mainly for the problem of extrapolation of step-by-step test plan data. It can also be satisfied. Therefore, the variable acceleration model proposed in this paper can express the relationship between acceleration factors over time.

3 Case Study

In order to verify the correctness and feasibility of the method, this paper illustrates the reliability enhancement test of a certain avionics. The sensitive stress of the electronic product is temperature, so only the reliability enhancement test under temperature step stress is considered. After failure analysis, the failure mechanism at each stage is unchanged. In the 2.1, the data extrapolation method (9) represents that each test phase is divided according to the number of improvements to the product, and in each phase, according to the stress level of the product, it is divided into several sub-stages ,where each fault only repair does not improve(repair time is very short),and only taking improvement actions at the last failure of each phase. The information after the test is shown in the following Table 1.

Table 1 — Test Data

Experimental phase-i	Number of failures	Sub-phases-j	The last failure time of phase-i	Failure time under normal stress
1	4	2	1.3	128.05
2	3	2	2.6	390.75
3	3	2	4.3	665.43
4	2	2	5.8	1149.56
5	2	2	8.1	1833.03

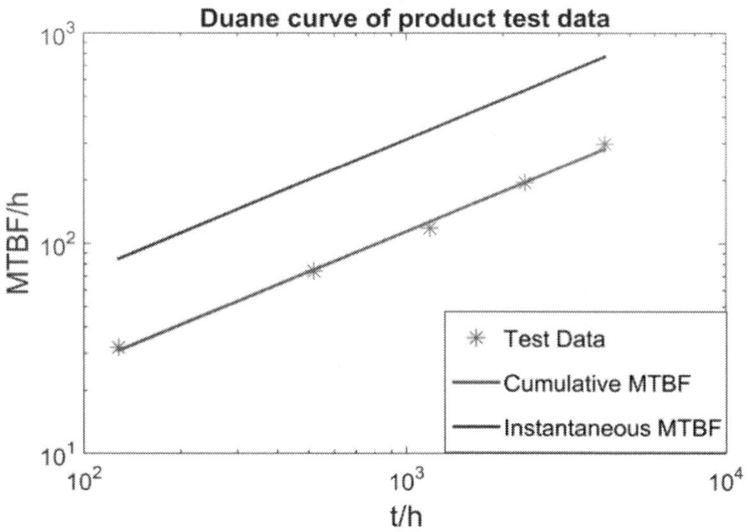

Figure 2— Duane curve of product test data

The Duane curve of the reliability enhancement test can be obtained after the parameters of Table 1 are estimated by the least-square method.

Therefore, according to the estimation method in 2.2.2, the growth rate, the MTBF at the end of the test, and the reliability at time t can be calculated. The specific results are as follows:

①Growth rate m = 0.6638, a = 0.7035; MTBF at the end of the test = 619.8h

②Product specified life time 100 h, so reliability at t = 100 h: R(t) = 0.85.

4 Conclusion

In this paper, by using the method of life assessment in accelerating reliability growth test, we propose a method for quantitatively evaluating product life based on the comprehensive use of accelerated test data (Arrhenius model) and reliability growth model (Duane model). The extrapolation formulae for the experimental data under accelerated stress and the test data under normal stress were deduced, and the growth process of extrapolated test data was further evaluated quantitatively according to the reliability growth test evaluation method. It not only realizes quantitative evaluation based on RET test data, but also derives a variable acceleration model with acceleration factor varying with time. Finally, the feasibility and effectiveness of the application of the method in engineering are preliminarily verified by combining specific examples, which provides a new idea for product reliability evaluation research based on reliability enhancement test data.

References

Hobbs, G. K. (2000). *Accelerated reliability engineering : HALT and HASS. Wiley.*

Liu, K., Lv, C., Dang, W., Li, L., Zou, T., & Li, P. (2016). Research on reliability assessment of space electronic products based on integration of highly accelerated life test and accelerated degradation test. *IEEE International Conference on Industrial Engineering and Engineering Management* (pp.1651-1654). IEEE.

Liu, L., Li, X. Y., & Jiang, T. M. (2017). Integration method for reliability assessment with multi-source incomplete accelerated degradation testing data. *Quality Engineering, 29*(3), 366-376.

Li, W., & Feng, R. C. (2006). Highly Accelerated Life Test for the Reliability Assessment of the Lead-Free SMT Mainboard. *Microsystems, Packaging, Assembly Conference Taiwan, 2006. IMPACT 2006. International* (pp.1-4). IEEE.

Calixto, E. (2013). *Accelerated Test and Reliability Growth Analysis Models. Gas and Oil Reliability Engineering*. Elsevier Inc.

Nelson, W. (2009). Accelerated life testing - step-stress models and data analyses. *IEEE Transactions on Reliability, R-29*(2), 103-108.

Y. Zhou and C. Weng. (1992).Reliability growth. *Beijing: Science Press.*

Duane, J. T. (1964). Learning curve approach to reliability monitoring. *IEEE Transactions on Aerospace, 2*(2), 563-566.

Shi, S. J., & Zhao, W. (2009). Research on Pre-HALT analysis and the application of test data in MTBF evaluation. *International Conference on Reliability, Maintainability and Safety* (pp.1197-1199). IEEE.

Zhang, H., Chen, Y., & Kang, R. (2010). Optimal design of step stress accelerated degradation test and reliability assessment for quartz flexible accelerometers. *Reliability and Maintainability Symposium* (pp.1-6). IEEE.

Introduction To Fault Tree Analysis

Clifton A. Ericson II
Design Safety Solutions LLC
cliftonericson@cs.com

FTA Outline

1. FTA Introduction
2. FTA Process
3. FT Terms/Definitions
4. FT Construction
5. FT Construction Rules
6. FT of Design Models
7. FT Mathematics
8. FT Evaluation
9. FT Validation
10. FT Pitfalls
11. FT Auditing
12. FTA Application Examples
13. FTA of Example Systems
14. FT Codes

2

--- FTA Introduction ---

Fault Tree Handbook with Aerospace Applications (updated NUREG-0492), 2002

NASA has been a leader in most technologies it has employed in its programs over the years. One of the important NASA objectives is now to add Probabilistic Risk Assessment (PRA) to its repertoire of expertise in proven methods to reduce technological and programmatic risk.

Fault Tree Analysis (FTA) is one of the most important logic and probabilistic techniques used in PRA and system reliability assessment today.

Methods to perform risk and reliability assessment in the early 1960s originated in US aerospace and missile programs. Fault tree analysis is such an example that was quite popular in the mid sixties. Early in the Apollo project the question was asked about the probability of successfully sending astronauts to the moon and returning them safely to Earth. A risk, or reliability, calculation of some sort was performed and the result was a mission success probability that was unacceptably low. This result discouraged NASA from further quantitative risk or reliability analysis until after the Challenger accident in 1986. Instead, NASA decided to rely on the use of failure modes and effects analysis (FMEA) and other qualitative methods for system safety assessments. After the Challenger accident, the importance of PRA and FTA in systems risk and reliability analysis was realized and its use at NASA has begun to grow.

Credibility

3

FTA – System Analysis Tool

- Evaluates complex systems (small to large)
- Identifies causal factors that can result in an Undesired Event
- Visual Model - displays complex cause-consequence combinations
- Combines failures, errors, normal events, time, HW, SW, HE
- Deductive (general to the specific)
- Provides risk assessment (Quantitative / Qualitative)
- Defined, structured and rigorous
- Easy to learn, perform and follow
- Utilizes Boolean Algebra, probability theory, reliability theory, logic
- Proven over time

4

Example FT

System

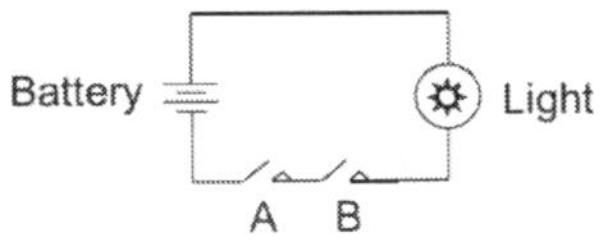

System Undesired Event: *Light Fails Off*

FT Model

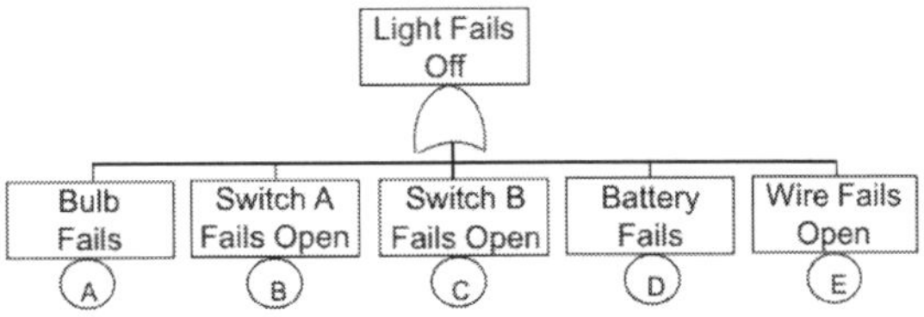

Cut Sets

Event combinations that can cause Top Undesired Event to occur

CS	Probability
A	$P_A=1.0x10^{-6}$
B	$P_B=1.0x10^{-7}$
C	$P_C=1.0x10^{-7}$
D	$P_D=1.0x10^{-6}$
E	$P_E=1.0x10^{-9}$

5

FT Building Blocks

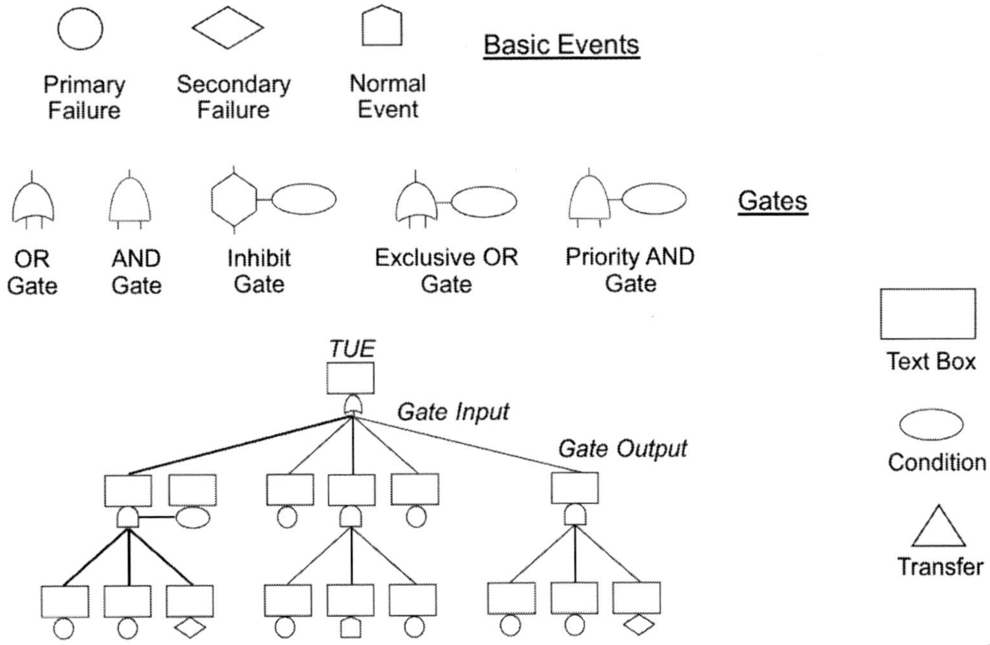

6

FTA – Deductive Approach

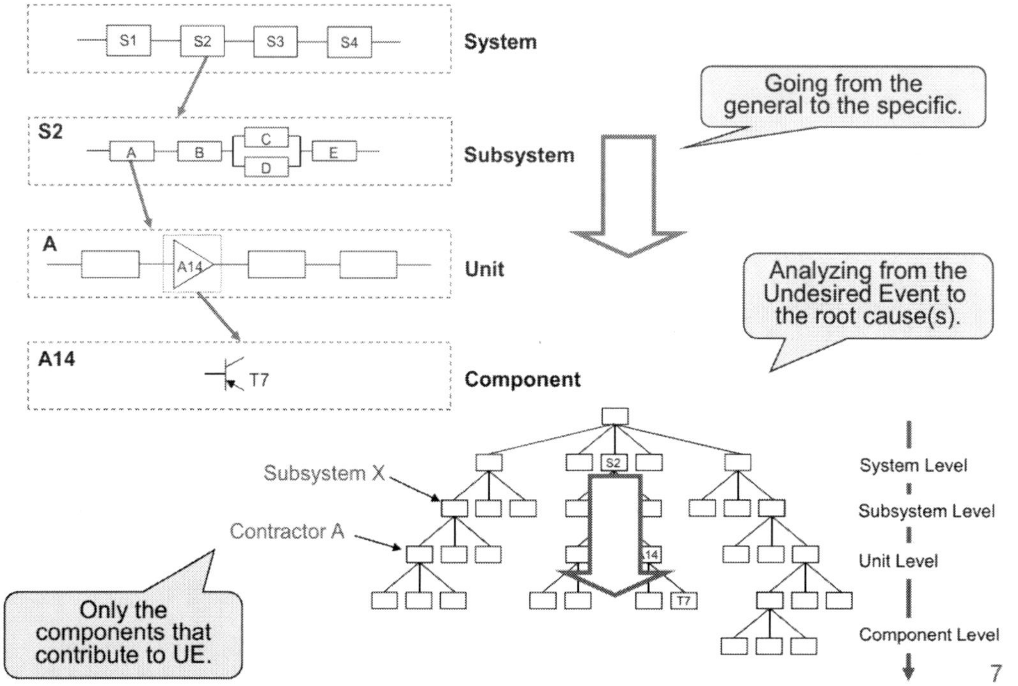

7

Two Types of FTA

- Proactive FTA
  - FTA during system design development
  - Improve design by mitigating weak links in the design
  - Prevent undesired events and mishaps
- Reactive FTA
  - FTA during system operation
  - Find root causes of a mishap/accident
    - Modify the design to prevent future similar accidents

8

FTA Coverage

- Hardware
  - System level
  - Subsystem level
  - Component level
  - Environmental effects
- Software
  - System level control
  - Hardware/software interface
- Human Interaction
  - Human error
  - Human performance
  - Organizational structures
- Procedures
  - Operation, maintenance, assembly
- System Events
  - Failures Events
  - Normal Events
  - Environmental Events

9

FT Strengths

- Visual model -- cause/effect relationships
- Easy to learn, do and follow
- Models complex system relationships in an understandable manner
  - Follows paths across system boundaries
  - Combines hardware, software, environment and human interaction
  - Interface analysis - contractors, subsystems
- Probability model
- Scientifically sound
  - Boolean Algebra, Logic, Probability, Reliability
  - Physics, Chemistry and Engineering
- Commercial software is available
- FT's can provide value despite incomplete information
- Proven Technique

10

Why Do A FTA?

- Root Cause Analysis
  - Identify all relevant events and conditions leading to Undesired Event
  - Determine parallel and sequential event combinations
  - Model diverse/complex event interrelationships involved
- Risk Assessment
  - Calculate the probability of an Undesired Event (level of risk)
  - Identify safety critical components/functions/phases
  - Measure effect of design changes
- Design Safety Assessment
  - Demonstrate compliance with requirements
  - Shows where safety requirements are needed
  - Identify and evaluate potential design defects/weak links
  - Determine Common Mode failures

11

Example FTA Applications

- Evaluate inadvertent arming and release of a weapon
- Calculate the probability of a nuclear power plant accident
- Evaluate an industrial robot going astray
- Calculate the probability of a nuclear power plant safety device being unavailable when needed
- Evaluate inadvertent deployment of jet engine thrust reverser
- Evaluate the accidental operation and crash of a railroad car
- Evaluate spacecraft failure
- Calculate the probability of a torpedo striking target vessel
- Evaluate a chemical process and determine where to monitor the process and establish safety controls

12

FTA Misconceptions

- FTA is a Hazard Analysis
  - Not true
  - Sort of meets definition of hazard analysis (HA), but not a true HA
  - Normally used for root cause analysis of a hazard
  - FTA is a secondary HA technique
- FTA is Like an FMEA
  - Not true
  - FMEA is bottom up single thread analysis of all item failure modes
  - FTA is a top down analysis
  - FTA only includes those failures pertinent to the top Undesired Event

13

FTA Criticisms

- It's too difficult for an outside reviewer to know if a FT is complete
- The correctness of a tree cannot be verified (subjective)
- FTA cannot handle timing and sequencing
- FTA failure data makes results questionable
- FTs become too large, unwieldy and time consuming
- Different analysts sometimes produce different FTs of the same system – so one must be wrong

Most are not true

14

Two Equivalent FTs

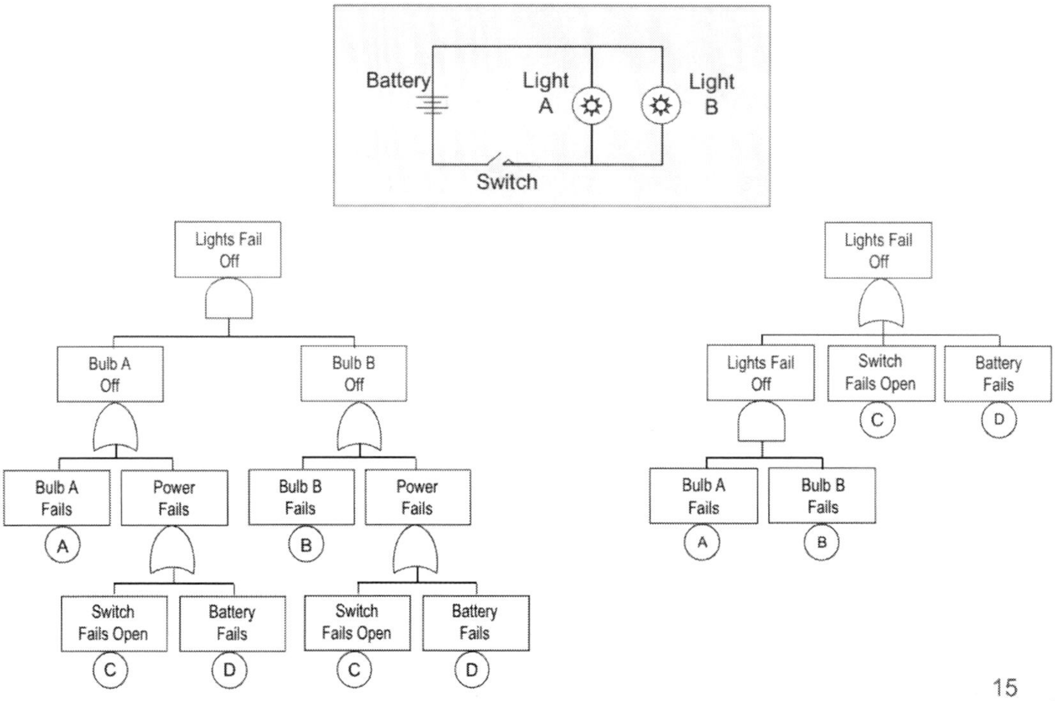

15

FTA Historical Stages

- H. Watson of Bell Labs, along with A. Mearns, developed the technique for the Air Force for evaluation of the Minuteman Launch Control System, circa 1961
- Recognized by Dave Haasl of Boeing as a significant system safety analysis tool (1963)
- First major use when applied by Boeing on the entire Minuteman system for safety evaluation (1964 – 1967, 1968-1999)
- The first technical papers on FTA were presented at the first System Safety Conference, held in Seattle, June 1965
- Boeing began using FTA on the design and evaluation of commercial aircraft, circa 1966
- Boeing developed a 12-phase fault tree simulation program, and a fault tree plotting program on a Calcomp roll plotter
- Adopted by the Aerospace industry and Nuclear Power Industry
- High quality FTA commercial codes developed that operates on PCs

16

Reference Books

- Reliability and Fault Tree Analysis, Conference On Reliability And Fault Tree Analysis; UC Berkeley; SIAM Pub, R. E. Barlow & J. B. Fussell & N. D. Singpurwalla, 1975.
- NUREG-0492, Fault Tree Handbook, N. H. Roberts, W. E. Vesely, D. F. Haasl & F. F. Goldberg, 1981.
- IEC 1025, Fault Tree Analysis, International Electrotechnical Commission, 1990.
- Reliability and Risk Assessment, Longman Scientific & Technical, 1993, J. D. Andrews & T. R. Moss, 1993.
- Probabilistic Risk Assessment and Management for Engineers and Scientists, E. J. Henley & H. Kumamoto, IEEE Press (2nd edition), 1996.
- NASA (no number), Fault Tree Handbook with Aerospace Applications, August 2002.
- NASA (no number), Probabilistic Risk Assessment Procedures Guide for NASA Managers and Practitioners, August 2002.
- Hazard Analysis Techniques for System Safety, C. A. Ericson, John Wiley & Sons, 2005, Chapter 11.
- Fault Tree Analysis Primer, C.A. Ericson, CreateSpace, 2012

17

Example of the Power of FTA

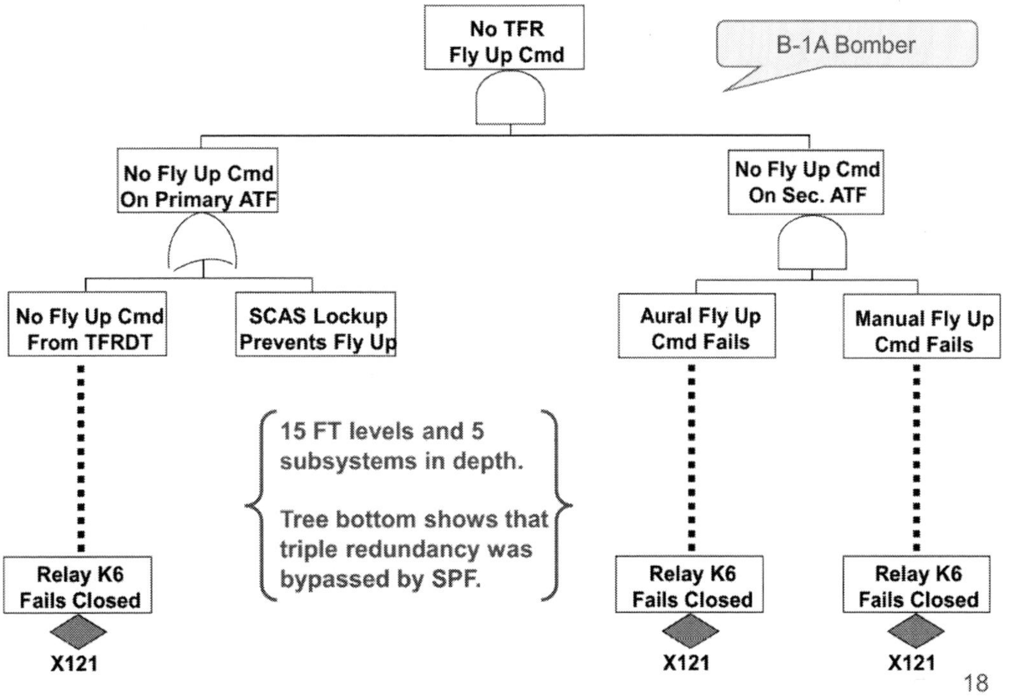

18

--- FTA Process ---

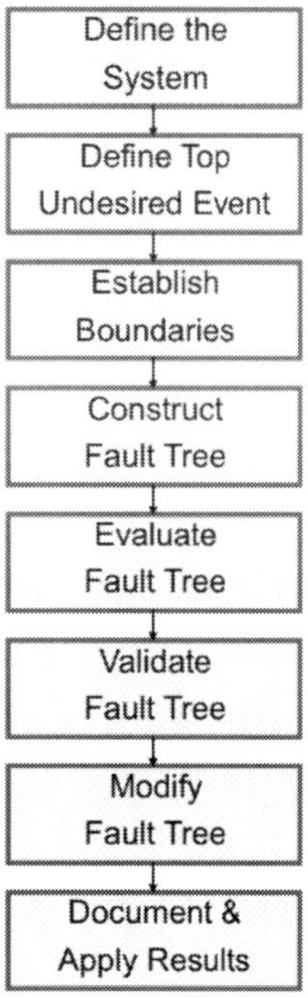

1 - Acquire data, understand system operation.

2 - Descriptively define the problem.

3 - Define analysis ground rules and boundaries.

4 - Follow FT construction process and rules.

5 - Generate FT cut sets and probabilities.

6 - Check FT for correctness.

7 - Modify FT as found necessary.

8 - Document and apply the results.

19

Step 1 – Define The System

- Obtain system design information
  - Drawings, schematics, procedures, timelines
  - Failure data, exposure times
  - Logic diagrams, block diagrams, IELs
- Know and understand
  - System operation
  - System components and interfaces
  - Software design and operation
  - Hardware/software interaction
  - Maintenance operation
  - Test procedures

Guideline -- If you are unable to build block diagram of the system, your understanding may be limited.

20

Step 2– Define The Top Undesired Event

- Purpose
  - The analysis starts here, shapes entire analysis
  - Very important, must be done correctly
- Start with basic concern
  - Hazard, requirement, safety problem, accident/incident
- Define the UE in a long narrative format
- Describe UE in short sentence
- Test the defined UE
- Determine if UE is achievable and correct
- Obtain concurrence on defined UE

21

Example Top UE's

- Inadvertent Weapon Unlock
- Inadvertent Weapon Release
- Incorrect Weapon Status Signals
- Failure of the MPRT Vehicle Collision Avoidance System
- Loss of All Aircraft Communication Systems
- Inadvertent Deployment of Aircraft Engine Thrust Reverser
- Offshore Oil Platform Overturns During Towing
- Loss of Auto Steer-by-wire Function

22

Step 3 – Establish Boundaries

- Define the analysis ground rules
- Define assumptions
- Bound the overall problem
- Obtain concurrence
- Document the ground rules, assumptions and boundaries

Boundary Factors

- System performance – areas of impact
- Size – depth and detail of analysis
- Scope of analysis – what subsystems and components to include
- System modes of operation – startup, shutdown, steady state
- System phase(s)
- Available resources (i.e., time, dollars, people)
- Resolution limit (how deep to dig)
- Establish level of analysis detail and comprehensiveness

23

Step 4 – Construct Fault Tree

- Follow rules and definitions of FTA
- Iterative process
- Continually check against system design
- Continually check ground rules
- Tree is developed in layers, levels and branches

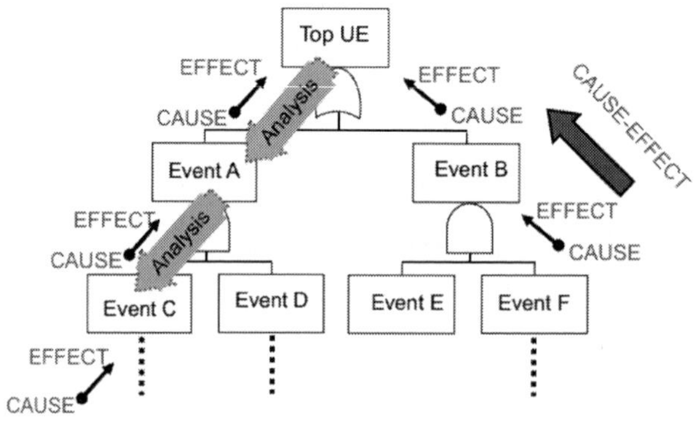

24

Step 5 – Evaluate Fault Tree

- Qualitative Analysis
  - Generate cut sets
  - Verify correctness of cut sets
  - Evaluate cut sets for design impact
- Quantitative Analysis
  - Apply failure data to tree events
  - Compute tree probability
  - Compute importance measures
  - Evaluate probability for design impact

Generate FT results and interpret the findings

25

Basic Evaluation Methods

- Manual
  - possible for small/medium noncomplex trees
- Computer
  - Required for large complex trees
  - Two approaches
    - Analytical
    - Simulation
- Methods
  - Cut Set computation
    - Boolean reduction
    - Algorithms (eg, MOCUS, MICSUP)
    - Binary Decision Diagram (BDD)
  - Probability computation
    - Boolean reduction
    - Approximations

26

Step 6 – Validate Fault Tree

- Verify the FT is correct and accurate (Objective)
  - Check FT for errors
  - Ensure correctness
  - Best method is to check validity of every generated cut set

27

Step 7 – Modify Fault Tree

- Modify FT when design changes are proposed/incorporated
- Make changes in FT structure as found necessary from validation
  - Validation results
  - Risk analysis results
  - Better system knowledge
- Features that can be modified
  - Tree logic
  - Tree events
  - Event failure rates

28

Step 8 – Document & Apply Results

- Document the study
  - Customer product (in-house or external)
  - Historical record
  - May need to update FTA some day for system upgrades
  - May need to reference the FTA study for other projects
  - Adds credibility

- Apply FTA Results
  - Interpret results
  - Present the results (using the document)
  - Make design recommendations
  - Follow-up on recommendations

29

Summary – FTA Process

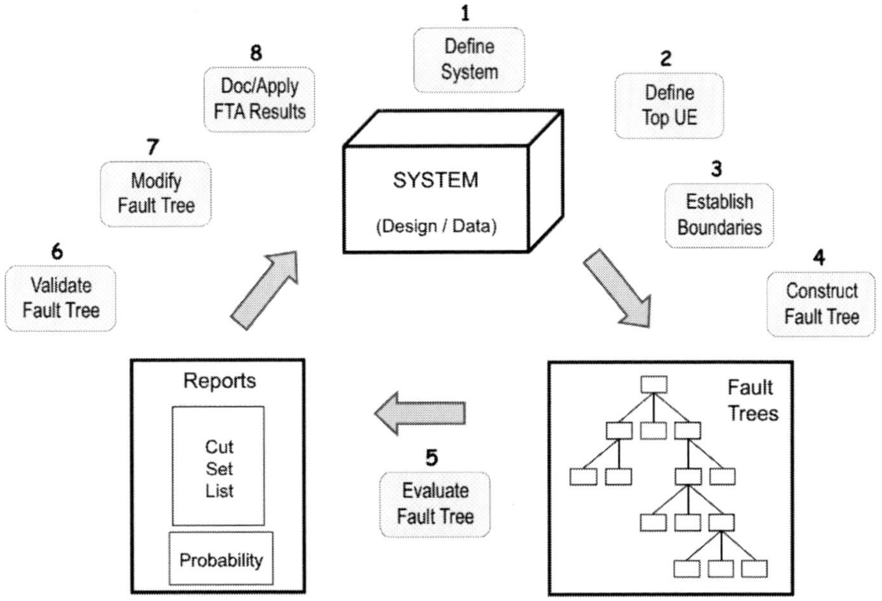

30

--- FTA Terms / Definitions ---

- FT Event
  - A basic failure event on the FT
  - A normally occurring event on the FT
- FT Node
  - Any gate or event on the FT
- FT Undesired Event
  - The hazard or problem of concern for which the root cause analysis is necessary
  - The top node or event on the FT
  - The starting point for the FT analysis

31

Basic Fault Tree Symbols

Symbol	Action	Description
	Text Box	Contains the text for a tree node

Tree Node

Symbol	Action	Description
	Primary Failure	Basic primary component failure mode
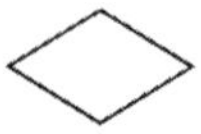	Secondary Failure	a) Secondary component failure mode b) Event that could be further expanded
	Normal Event	An event that is normally expected to occur

Basic Events

32

Basic Events (BEs)

- Failure Event
  - Primary Failure - basic component failure (circle)
  - Secondary Failure - failure caused by external force (diamond)
- Normal Event
  - An event that describes a normally expected system state
  - An operation or function that occurs as intended or designed, such as "Power Applied At Time T1"
  - The Normal event is usually either On or Off, having a probability of either 1 or 0
  - House symbol

The BE's are where the failure rates and probabilities enter the FT

33

Event Symbol Examples

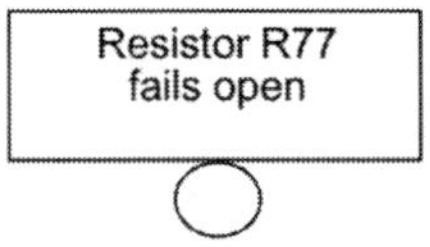

Circle
Primary Failure — Basic inherent component failure

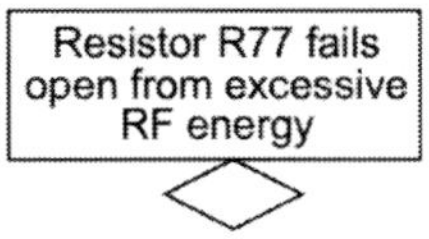

Diamond
Secondary Failure — A) Failure caused by external force

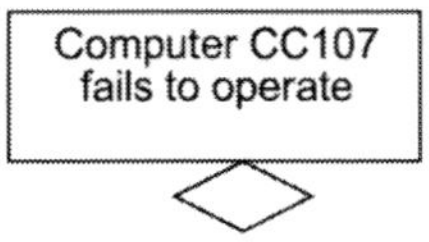

Diamond
High Level Failure — B) Failure that could be further developed

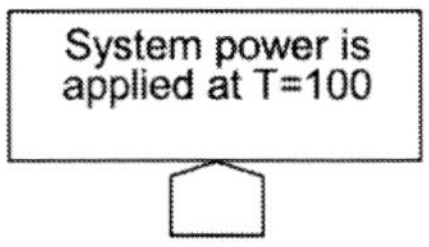

House
Normal Event — An event that would occur under normal Operation (without failure)

34

Gate Events (GEs)

- A logic operator combining input nodes
- Five basic logic operator types
  - AND, OR, Inhibit, Priority AND and Exclusive OR
  - Additional types do exist, but usually not necessary
- Represents a fault state that can be further expanded

Gate Symbols

Symbol	Action	Description
	OR Gate	The output occurs only if at least one of the inputs occur
	AND Gate	The output occurs only if all of the inputs occur together
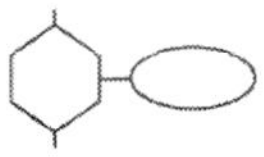	Inhibit Gate	The output occurs only if the input event occurs and the attached condition is satisfied
	Exclusive OR Gate	The output occurs only if at least one of the inputs occurs, but not both
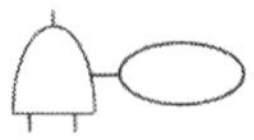	Priority AND Gate	The output occurs only if all of the inputs occur together, but in a specified sequence (input 1 must occur before 2)

Condition Events (CEs)

- A condition attached to a gate event
- It establishes a condition that is required to be satisfies in order for the gate event to occur

Symbol	Action	Description
	Condition Event	A conditional restriction or an event probability

Transfer Event (TE)

- Indicates a specific tree branch (subtree)
- A pointer to a tree branch
- A Transfer only occurs at the Gate Event level
- Represented by a Triangle
- The Transfer is for several different purposes:
  - Starts a new page (for FT prints)
  - It indicates where a branch is used numerous places in the same tree, but is not repeatedly drawn (Internal Transfer)
  - It indicates an input module from a separate analysis (External Transfer)

OR Gate

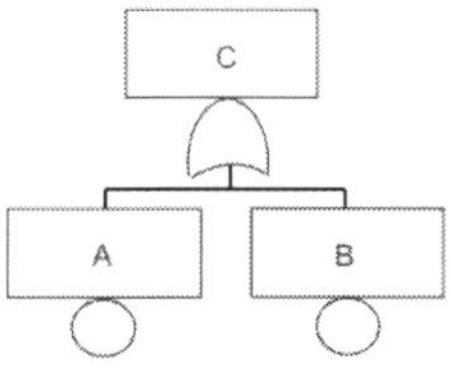

Fault Tree

A	B	C
0	0	0
1	0	1
0	1	1
1	1	1

Truth Table

- Either A or B is necessary and sufficient to cause C
- Both A and B can occur together to cause C
- Example: Light is off because light bulb fails OR power fails

39

OR Gate

- Causality passes through an OR gate
  - Inputs are identical to the output, only more specifically defined (refined) as to cause
  - The input faults are never the cause of the output fault
    - Passes the cause through
    - Not a cause-effect relationship

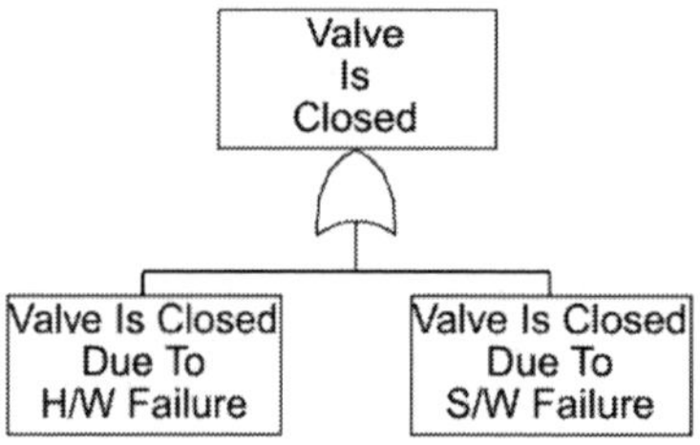

40

AND Gate

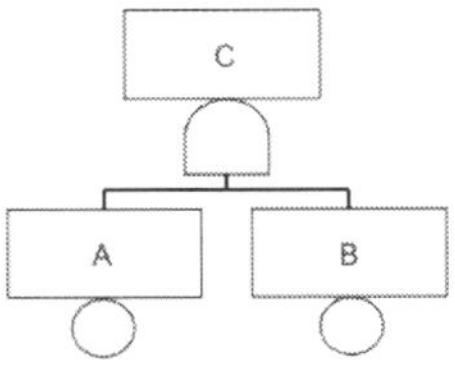

Fault Tree

A	B	C
0	0	0
1	0	0
0	1	0
1	1	1

Truth Table

- Both A and B are necessary to cause C
- A and B must occur simultaneously
- Example: No power available because Primary power fails AND Secondary power fails

41

AND Gate

- Specifies a <u>causal</u> relationship between the inputs and the output
  - Causality is created at the AND gate
  - The input faults collectively represent the cause of the output fault
  - Implies nothing about the antecedents of the input faults

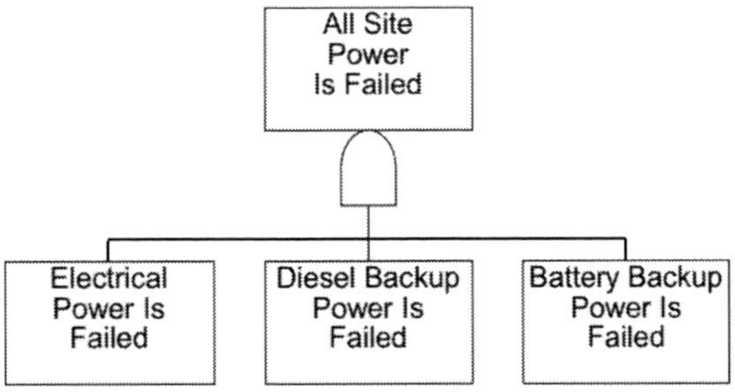

42

Exclusive OR Gate

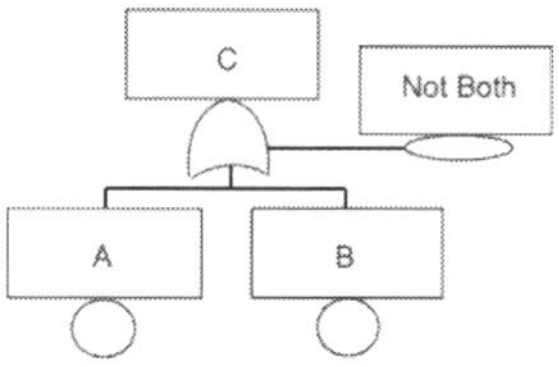

Fault Tree

A	B	C
0	0	0
1	0	1
0	1	1
1	1	0

Truth Table

- Either A or B is necessary and sufficient to cause C
- But, both A and B cannot occur together (at same time)
- Only allow two inputs (cascade down for more ExOR inputs)
- Example: Relay is energized OR Relay is de-energized, but not both

43

Priority AND Gate

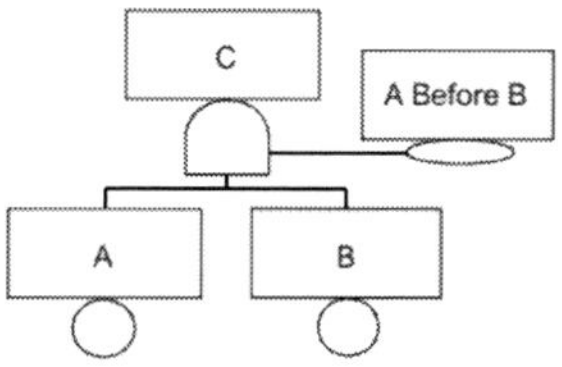

Fault Tree

A	B	C
0	0	0
1	0	0
0	1	0
1	1	1

Truth Table

- Both A and B are necessary to cause C
- But, A must occur before B
- Show priority order with inputs from left to right
- Example: Fault is not detect because Monitor fails before Computer fails

44

Inhibit Gate

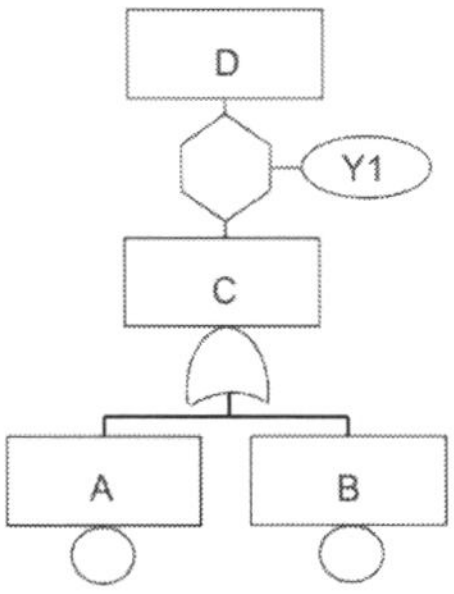

Effectively an AND gate

- Both C and Y1 are necessary to cause D
- Y1 is a condition or a probability
- Pass through if condition is satisfied
- Example: Ignition temperature is present, given faults cause overtemp AND probability that 700 degrees is reached

Transfer Symbols

Symbol	Action	Description
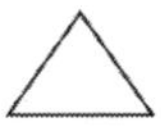	Internal Transfer	Indicates the start of a subtree branch, internal to present FT
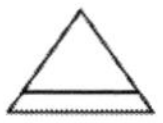	External Transfer	Indicates the start of a subtree branch, external to present FT
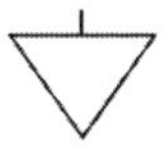	Similar Transfer	Indicates the start of a subtree branch that is similar to another one, but with different hardware

- The transfer is a Pointer to a tree branch.
- Helps to partition trees when they become large and unwieldy.

Transfer Example

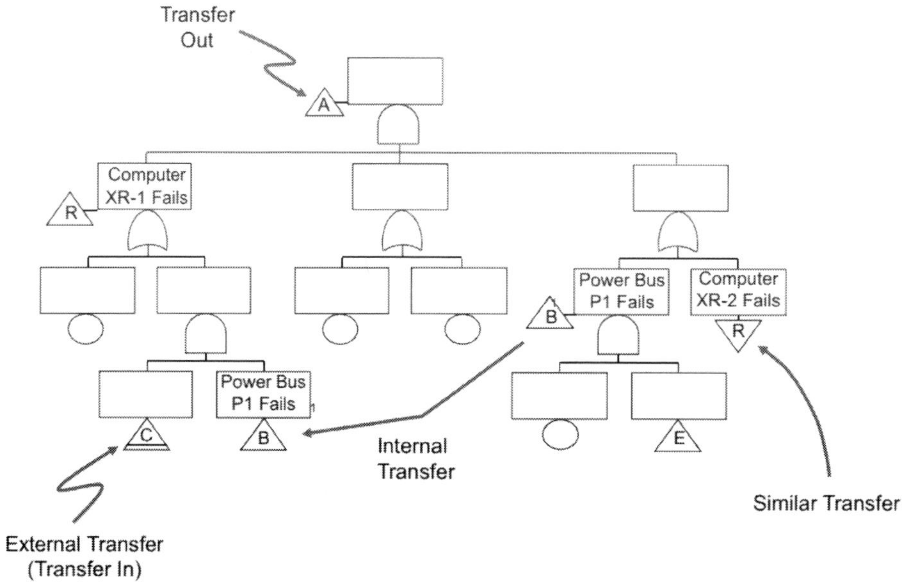

47

FT Diagramming (3 Ways)

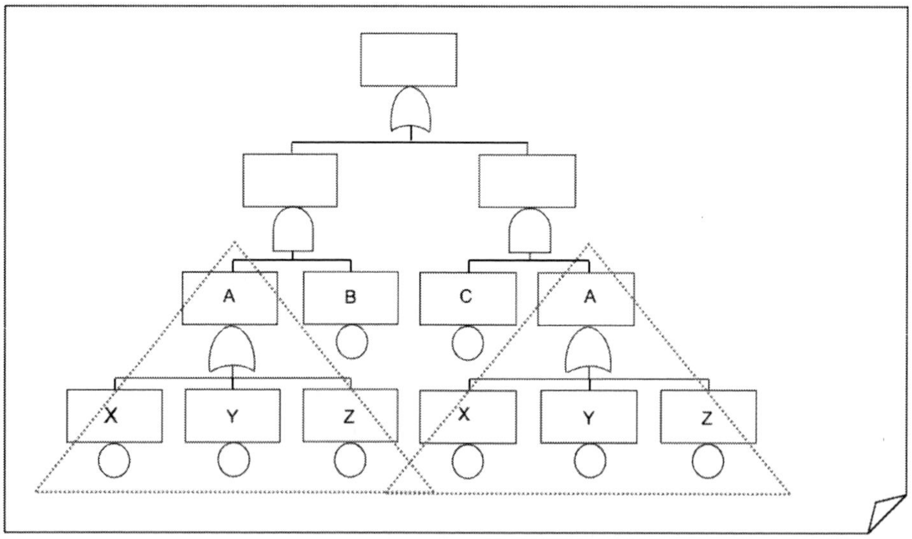

Method 1 – No Internal Transfer, MOBs on same page

48

Internal Transfer - Equivalent FT

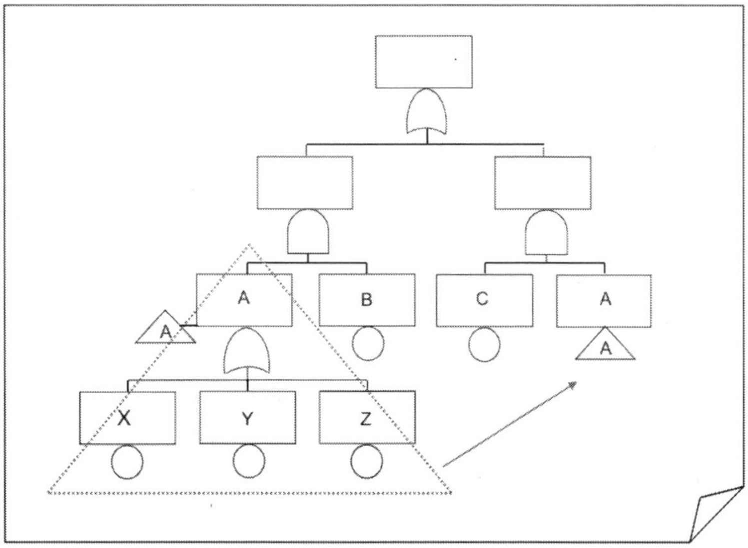

Method 2 – Internal Transfer, MOB on same page

49

Internal Transfer - Equivalent FT

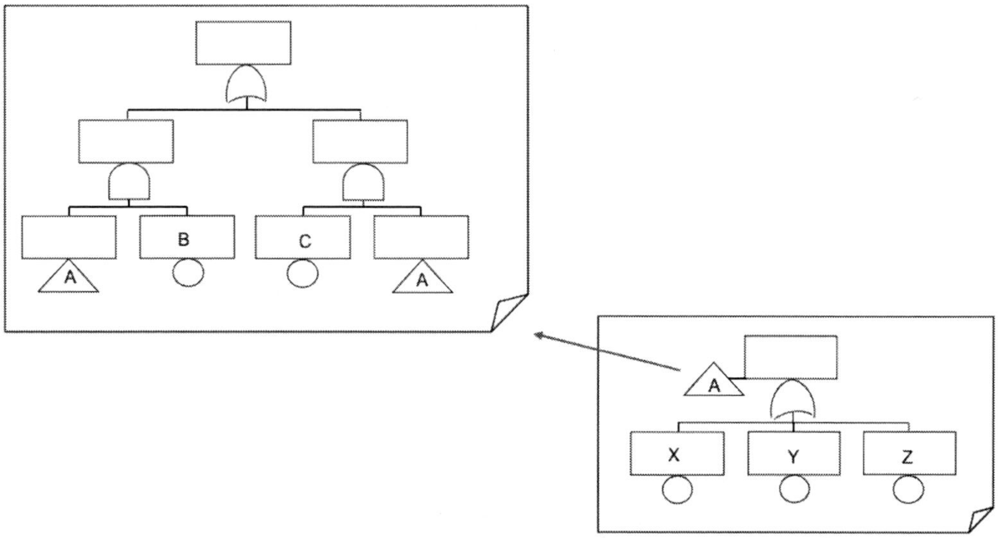

Method 3 – Internal Transfer, MOB on different page

50

Internal Transfer - Paging

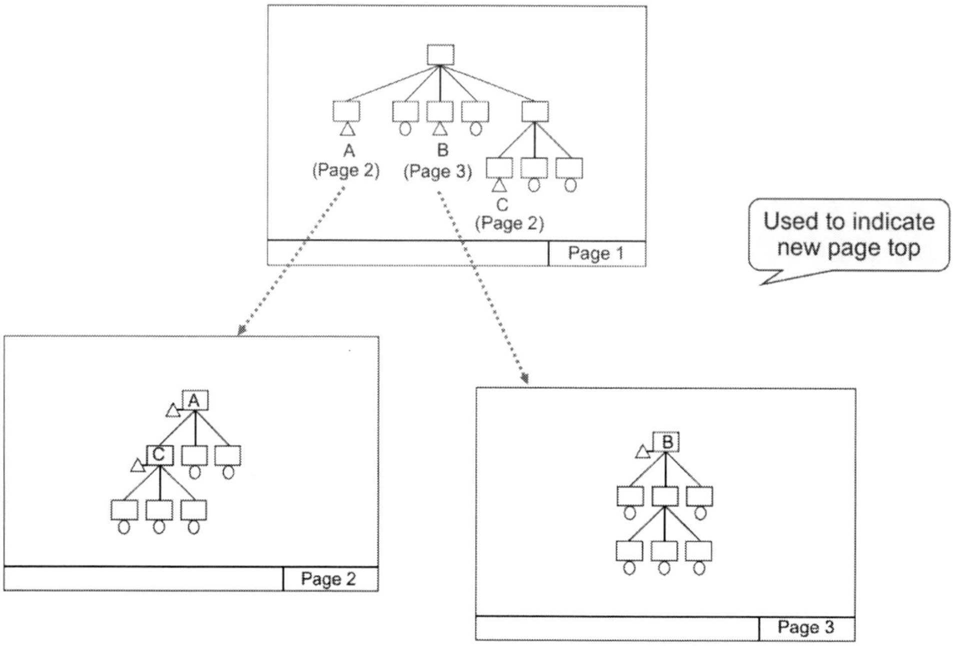

51

External Transfer

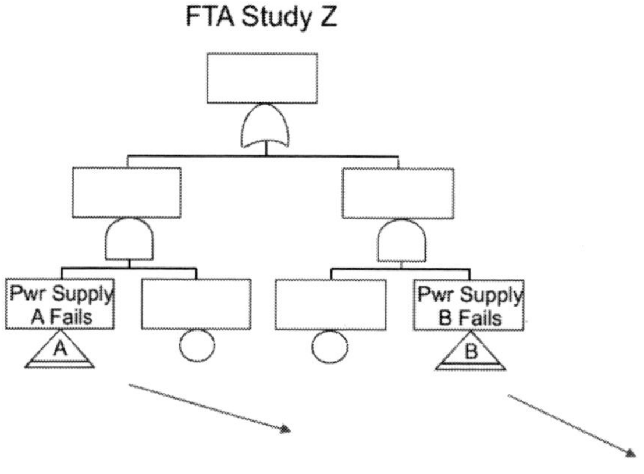

- Branches A and B are not within this FT
- They are documented in FTA Study A
- Use branch top probability from Study A
- Must import if CSs are desired

52

Failure / Fault

- Failure
  - The occurrence of a *basic component failure.*
  - The result of an internal inherent failure mechanism, thereby requiring no further breakdown.
  - Example - *Resistor R77 Fails in the Open Circuit Mode.*
- Fault
  - The occurrence or existence of an *undesired state* for a component, subsystem or system.
  - The result of a failure or chain of faults/failures; can be further broken down.
  - The component operates correctly, except at the wrong time, because it was commanded to do so.
  - Example – The light is failed off because the switch failed open, thereby removing power.

53

Failure / Fault Example

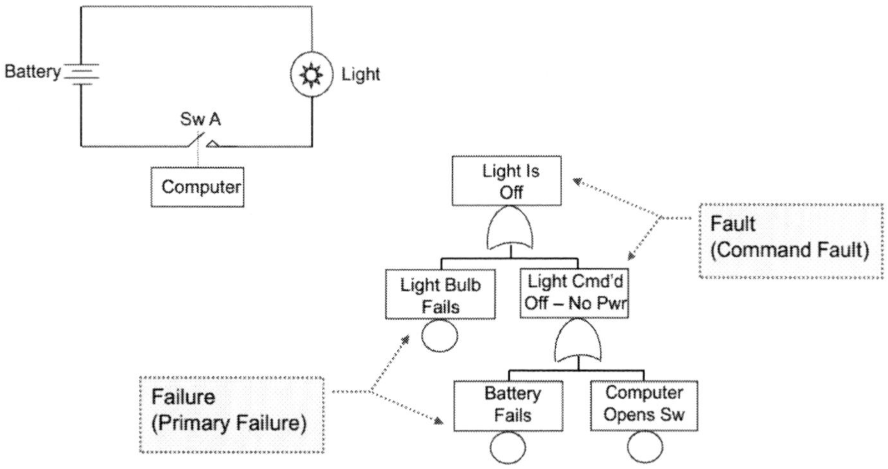

All failures are faults, but not all faults are failures

54

Independent / Dependent Failure

- Independent Failure
  - Failure is not caused or contributed to by another event or component
- Dependent Failure
  - Failure is caused or contributed to by another event or component
  - A component that is caused to fail by the failure of another component
  - The two failure are directly related, and the second failure depends on the first failure occurring
  - Example - An IC fails shorted, drawing high current, resulting in resistor R77 failing open

Dependency complicates the FT mathematics

55

Primary Failure

- An inherent component failure mode
- Basic FT event
- A component failure that cannot be further defined at a lower level
- Example – diode inside a computer fails due to materiel flaw
- Symbolized by a Circle
- Has a failure rate (λ) or probability of failure

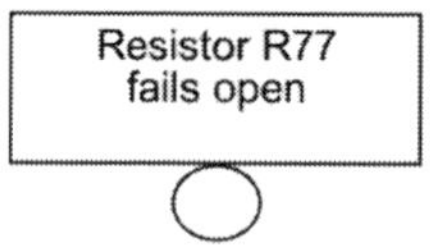

56

Secondary Failure

- A component failure that is caused by an external force to the system
- Basic FT event
- Example – Integrated circuit fails due to external RF energy
- Important factor in Common Cause Analysis
- Symbolized by a Diamond
- Has a failure rate (λ) or probability of failure

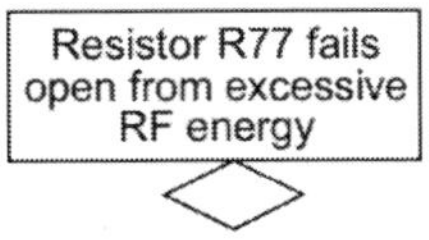

57

Undeveloped Failure

- A component failure that can be further defined at a lower level of detail, but is not for various reasons
  - Ground rules
  - Save analysis time and money
  - May not be a critical part of FTA
- Example – computer fails (don't care about detail of why)
- Basic FT event
- Symbolized by a Diamond
- Has a failure rate (λ) or probability of failure

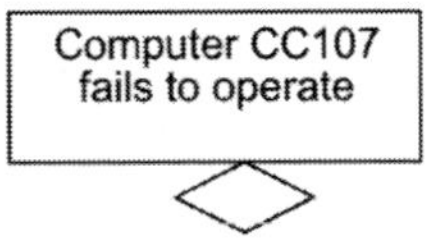

58

Command Failure

- A fault state that is commanded by an upstream fault / failure
- Normal operation of a component, except in an inadvertent or untimely manner. The normal, but, undesired state of a component at a particular point in time
- The component operates correctly, except at the wrong time, because it was commanded to do so by upstream faults
- Example – a bridge opens (at an undesired time) because someone accidentally pushed the Bridge Open button
- Symbolized by a gate event requiring further development

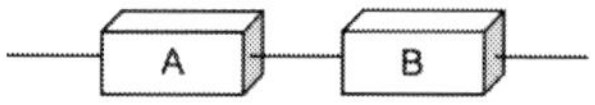

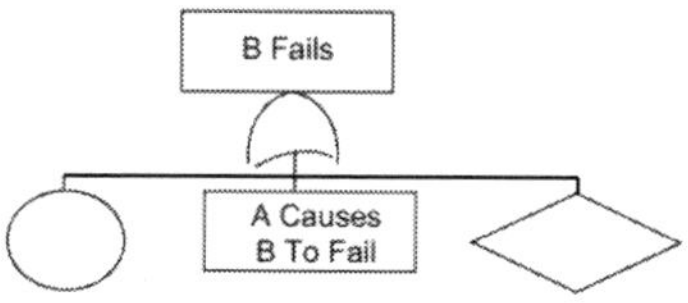

59

FT Time Parameters

- Mission Time
  - The length of time the system is in operation to complete the mission
  - Most equipment is in operation during this period of time
- Exposure Time
  - The length of time a component is effectively exposed to failure during system operation ($P=1.0 - e^{-\lambda T}$)
  - The time assigned to equipment in FT probability calculations
  - Exposure time can be controlled by design, repair, circumvention, testing and monitoring
- Fault Duration Time
  - The length of time a component is effectively in the failed state
  - This state is ended by repair of the component or by system failure

Time

$$P = 1.0 - e^{-\lambda T}$$

60

System Complexity Terms

- MOE
  - A Multiple Occurring Event or failure mode that occurs more than one place in the FT
  - Also known as a redundant or repeated event
- MOB
  - A multiple occurring branch (i.e., a repeated branch)
  - A tree branch that is used in more than one place in the FT
  - All of the Basic Events within the branch would actually be MOE's
- Branch
  - A subsection of the tree (subtree), similar to a limb on a real tree
- Module
  - A subtree or branch
  - An independent subtree that contains no outside MOE's or MOB's, and is not a MOB

61

MOE/MOB Example

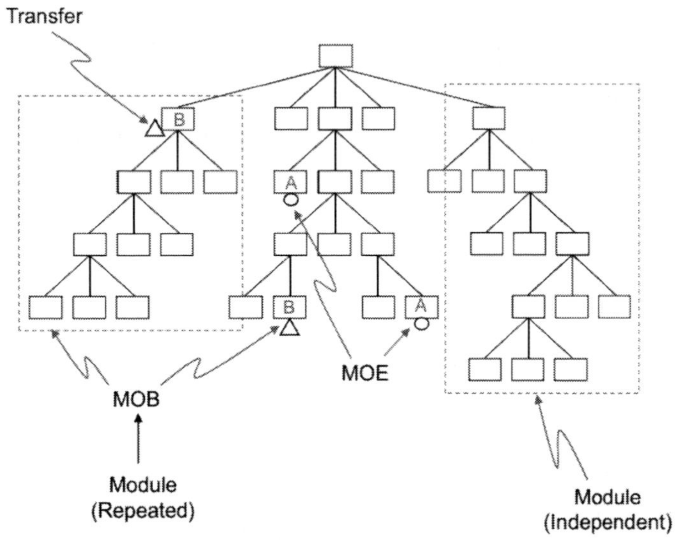

- MOE is an repeated event
- MOB is a repeated branch
- All events within an MOB are effectively MOEs

62

Cut Set Terms

- Cut Set
  - A set of events that together cause the tree Top UE event to occur
- Min CS (MCS)
  - A CS with the minimum number of events that can still cause the top event
- Super Set
  - A CS that contains a MCS plus additional events to cause the top UE
- Critical Path
  - The highest probability CS that drives the top UE probability
- Cut Set Order
  - The number of elements in a cut set
- Cut Set Truncation
  - Removing cut sets from consideration during the FT evaluation process
  - CS's are truncated when they exceed a specified order and/or probability

63

Cut Set

- A unique set of events that together cause the Top UE event to occur
- One unique root cause of the Top UE (of possibly many)
- A CS can consist of one event or multiple simultaneous events or elements

Note:
A CS element can be a:
- Failure
- Human error
- Software anomaly
- Environment condition
- Normal action

64

The Value of Cut Sets

- CSs identify which unique event combinations can cause the UE
- CSs provide the mechanism for probability calculations
- CSs reveal the critical and weak links in a system design
  - High probability
  - Bypass of intended safety or redundancy features

Note:
Always check all CS's against the system design to make sure they are valid and correct.

65

Cut Sets

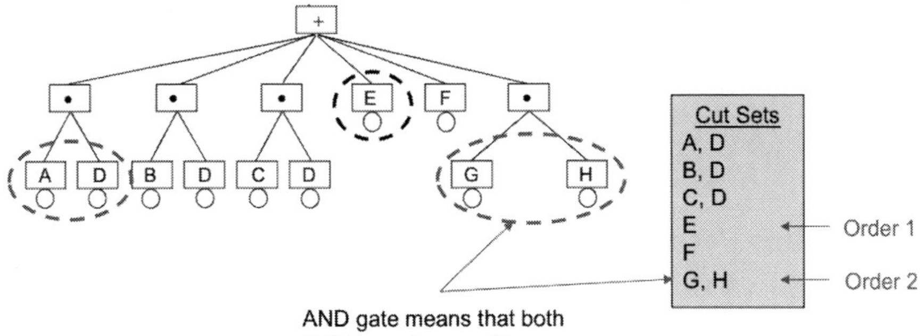

AND gate means that both G & H must occur. Since they go directly to top, they comprise a CS, denoted by {G, H}.

Cut Set (CS)
A unique set of events that cause the Top UE to occur.

66

Min CS

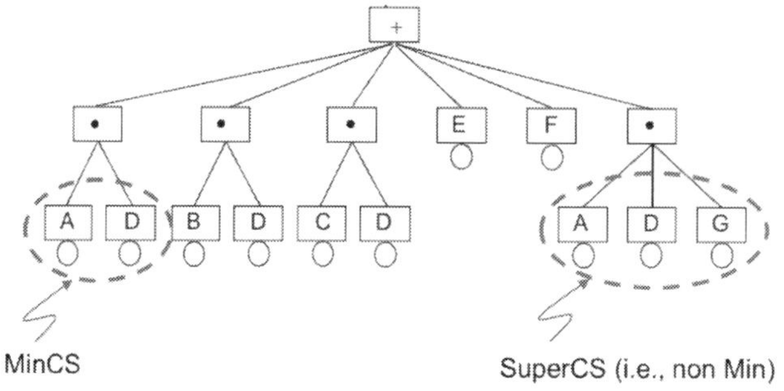

<u>Min CS</u>
A set of events that contain the minimum number of *necessary* events to cause the Top UE; it cannot be further reduced.

<u>Super CS</u>
A set of events that contain a number of events *sufficient* to cause the Top UE (ie, more than necessary as a minimum).

67

Min CS Example

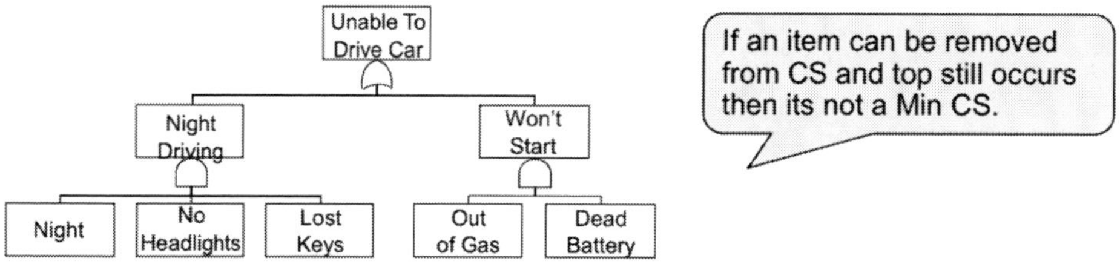

CS1 - Night **&** No Headlights **&** Lost Keys
CS2 - Out of Gas **&** Dead Battery

← Invalid FT
(Not Min CS's)

Should be:
- Night **&** No Headlights
- Lost Keys
- Out of Gas
- Dead Battery

68

Min CS

- A CS with the minimum number of events that can still cause the top event
- The true list of CS's contributing to the Top
- The final CS list after removing all SCS and DupCS
- Additional CS's are often generated, beyond the MinCS's
  - Super Cut Sets (SCS) – result from MOE's
  - Duplicate Cut Sets (DupCS) - result from MOE's or AND/OR combinations
- Why eliminate SCS and DupCS?
  - Laws of Boolean algebra
  - Would make the overall tree probability slightly larger (erroneous but conservative)

69

Min CS

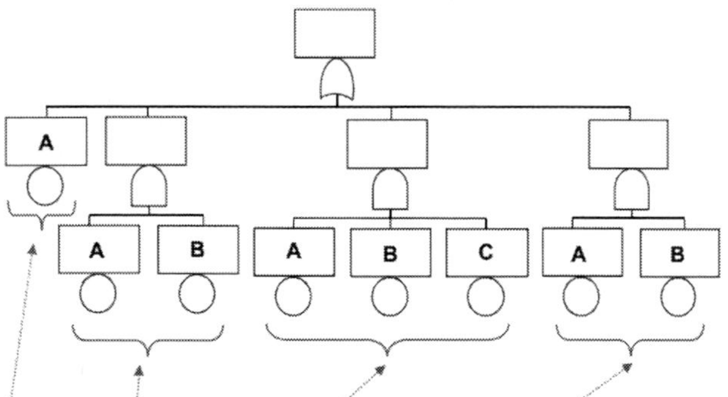

Cut Sets:
A
A,B ← **SCS**
A,B,C ← **SCS**
A,B ← **DupCS, SCS**

⇨ Min Cut Sets:
A

70

Alternate Gate Symbols

Symbol	Action	Description	Alternate Symbol
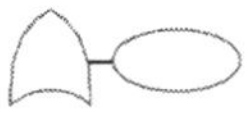	Exclusive OR Gate	Only one of the inputs can occur, not both. Disjoint events.	
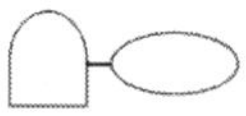	Priority AND Gate	All inputs must occur, but in given order, from left to right.	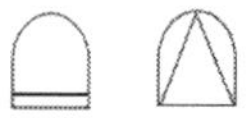
	M of N Gate	M of N combinations of inputs causes output to occur.	 Voting Gate

71

M/N Gate Example

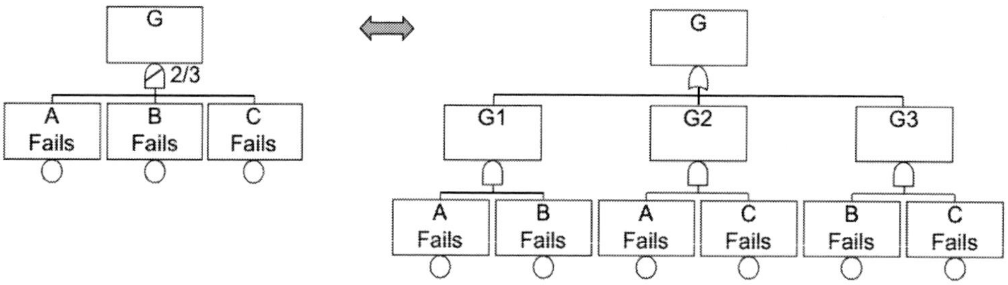

- M of N gate
- Also known As Voting gate

72

--- FT Construction Process ---

- Tree is developed in:
  - Layers
  - Levels
  - Branches
- Tree Levels:
  - Top Level
    - Defines the top in terms of discrete system functions that can cause the top UE
    - Shapes the overall structure of the tree
  - Intermediate Level
    - Defines the logical relationships between system functions and component behavior
    - Function – systems – subsystems – modules - components
  - Bottom Level
    - Consists of the Basic Events or component failure modes

73

FT Construction

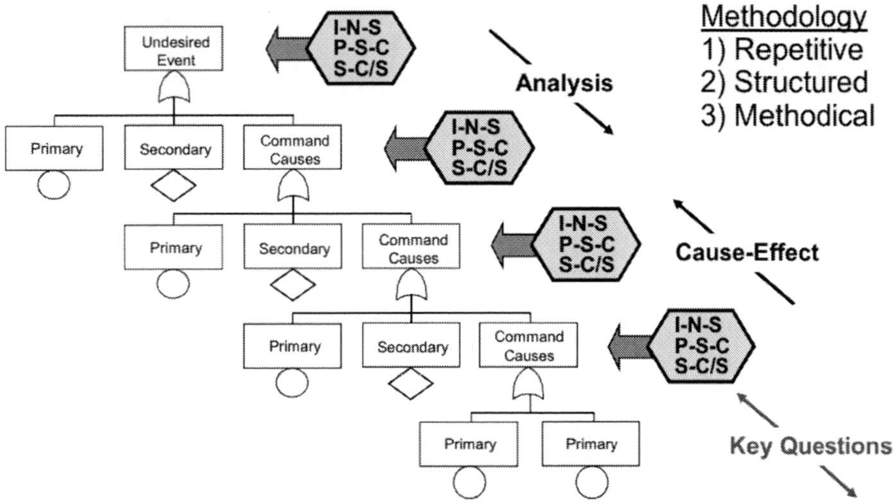

I-N-S=Immediate, Necessary, Sufficient
P-S-C=Primary, Secondary, Command
S-C/S=State of the Component or System

74

The 4 Basic FTA Approaches

- Component
  - Immediately focuses on components
  - "Shopping list" approach
  - Can overlook detailed causes
- Subsystem
  - Immediately emphasizes subsystems
  - Can overlook detailed causes
  - Can use Functional flow method after subsystem breakdown
- Scenario
  - Breaks down UE into fault scenarios before detailed design analysis
  - Sometimes necessary at FT top level for complex systems
- Functional Flow
  - Follows system functions (command path)
  - More structured
  - Less likely to miss detail causes

Component Approach

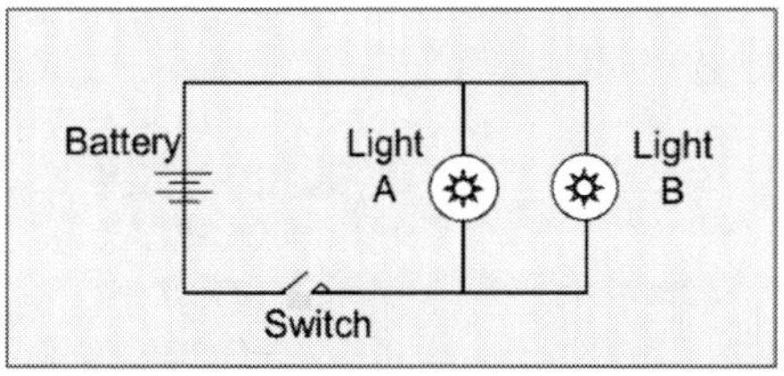

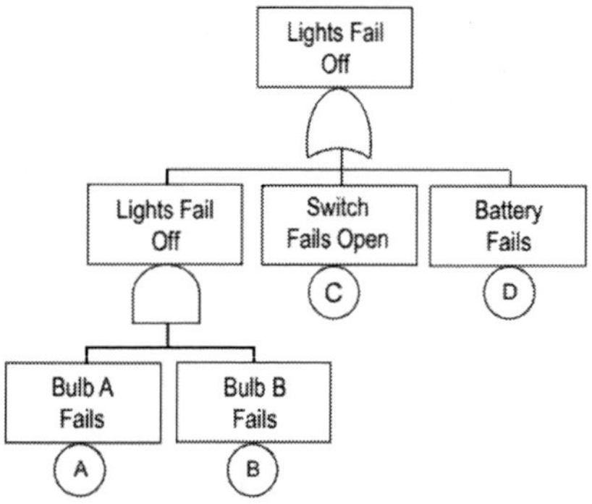

- Immediate breakdown by component
- Ignores immediate cause-effect relationships
- Tends to logically overlook things for large systems

Subsystem Approach

- Breakdown by subsystem
- Ignores immediate cause-effect relationships
- There can be hazard overlap between subsystems
- Tends to logically overlook things
- Eventually switch back to Functional approach

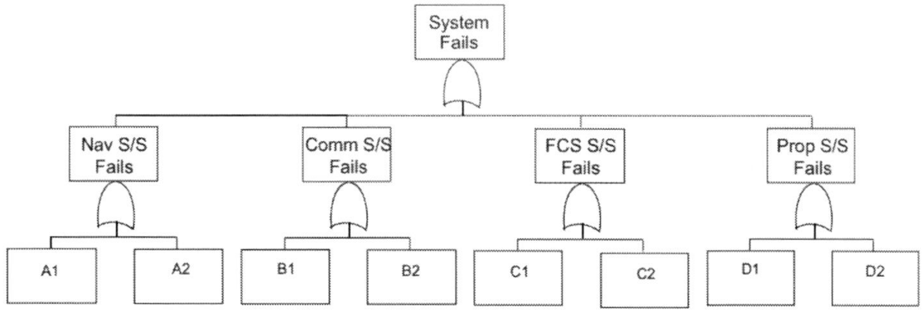

77

Scenario Approach

- Breakdown by Scenario
- Sometimes necessary to start large FTs
- Ignores immediate cause-effect relationship
- Eventually switch back to Functional approach
- Could be some overlap between subsystems

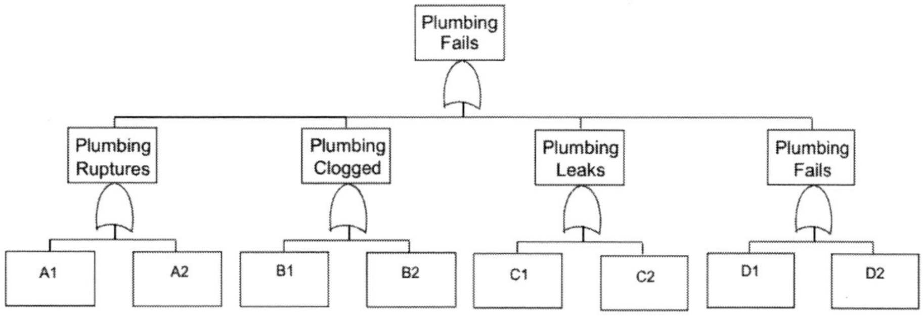

78

Functional Approach

- Breakdown by system function
- FTA follows system function
- Follows logical cause-effect relationship
- Has more levels and is narrower
- Less prone to miss events
- More structured and complete analysis
- Use for about 90% of applications
- FTA follows functional command path
- Structured approach

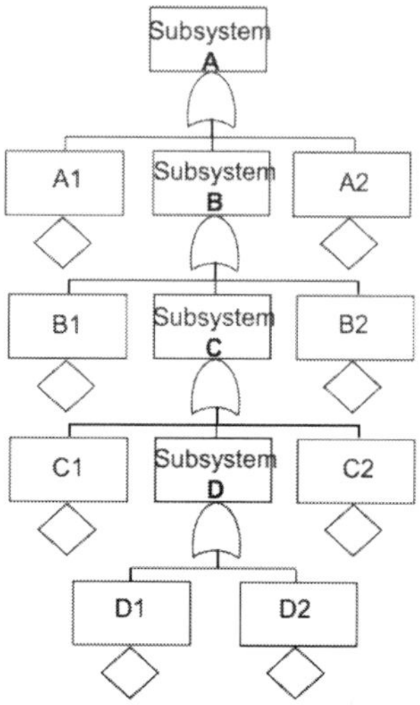

Recommended approach

79

Functional Approach

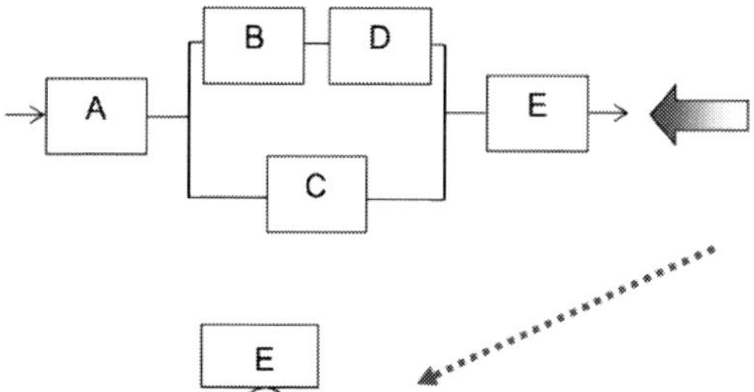

Follow the functional path

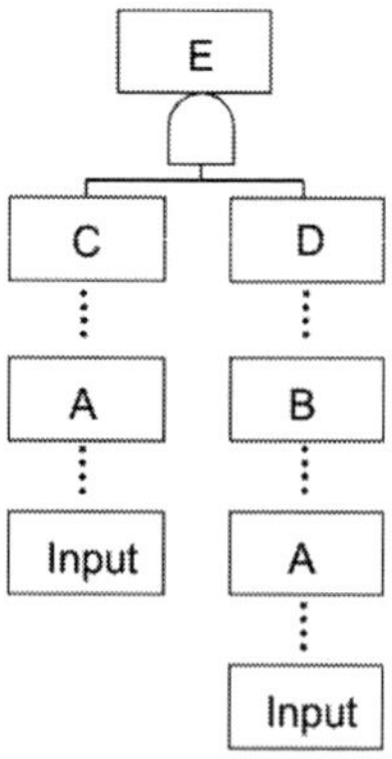

- Start at UE location (E in this example)
- Follow signal flow backwards
- Take each component one at a time

80

Series Example

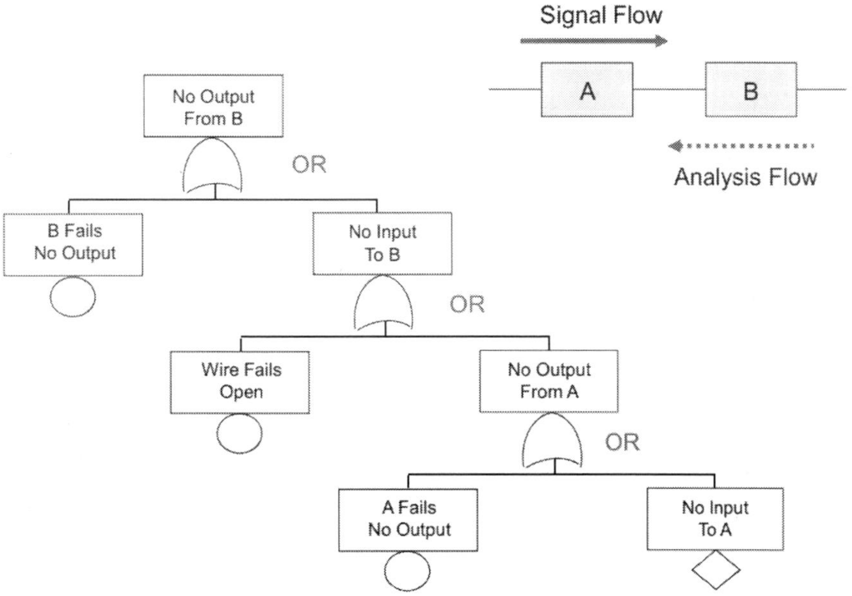

81

Series-Parallel Example

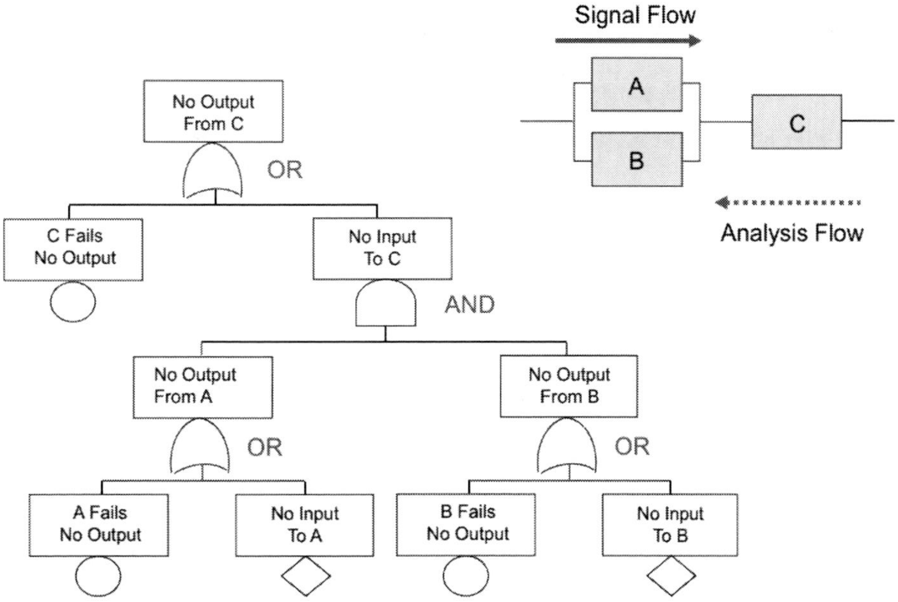

82

FT Construction Methodology

- Construction at each gate involves a 3 step question process:
  - Step 1 – Immediate, Necessary and Sufficient (I-N-S) ?
  - Step 2 – Primary, Secondary and Command (P-S-C) ?
  - Step 3 – State of the Component or System (S-C/S) ?

These are the 3 key questions in FTA construction

83

Step 1

- Step 1 – *What is* Immediate, Necessary and Sufficient (I-N-S) ?
  - Read the gate event wording
  - Identify all ***Immediate***, ***Necessary*** and ***Sufficient*** events to cause the Gate event
    - Immediate – do not skip past events
    - Necessary – include only what is actually necessary
    - Sufficient – do not include more than the minimum necessary
  - Structure the I-N-S casual events with appropriate logic
  - Mentally test the events and logic until satisfied

84

Step 1

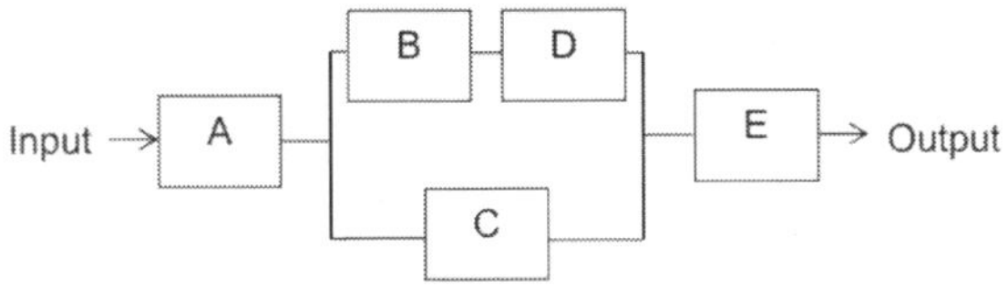

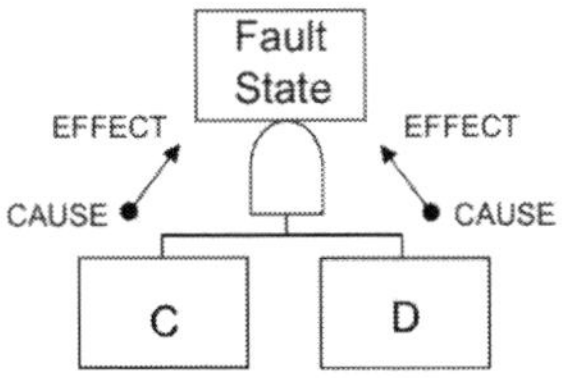

C and D are *Immediate*
C and D are *Necessary*
C and D are Sufficient.

} To cause Fault of E

85

Step 2

- Step 2 – *What is* Primary, Secondary and Command (P-S-C) ?
  - Read the gate event wording
  - Review I-N-S events from Step 1
  - Identify all ***Primary***, ***Secondary*** and ***Command*** events causing the Gate event
    - Primary Fault – basic inherent component failure
    - Secondary Fault – failure caused by an external force
    - Command Fault – A fault state that is commanded by an upstream fault or failure
  - Structure the P-S-C casual events with appropriate logic

If there are P-S-C inputs, then it's an OR gate

86

Step 2

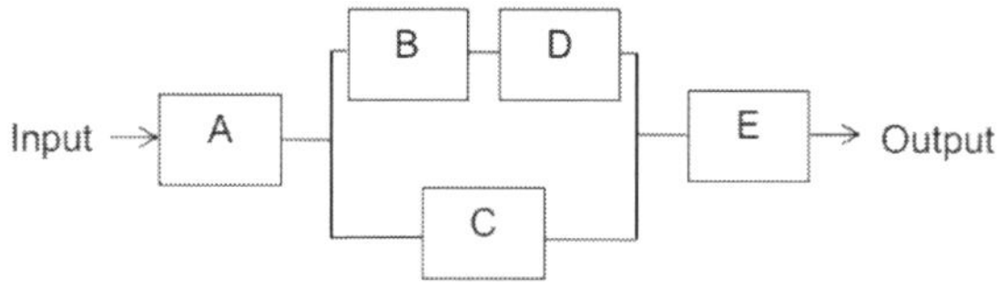

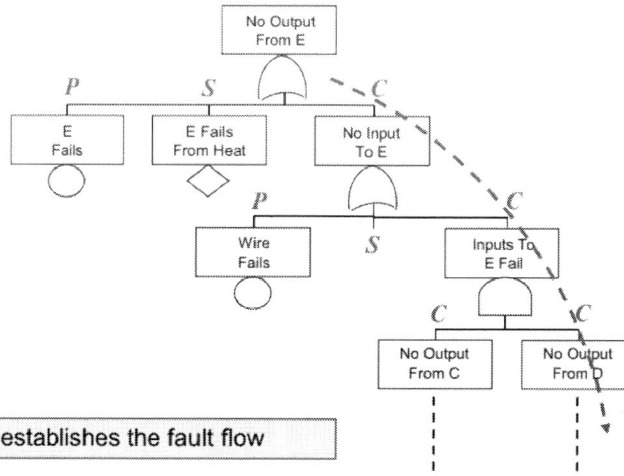

P = Primary Failure
S = Secondary Failure
C = Command Failure

The Command path establishes the fault flow

87

Step 3

- Step 3 – *Is it a* State of the Component or System (S-C/S) *fault* ?
  - Read the gate event wording
  - Identify if the Gate involves
    - a *State of the Component* fault
      - ☞ **Being directly at the component level**
      - ☞ **Evaluating the causes of a component failure**
    - a *State of the System* fault
      - ☞ **Being a system level event**
      - ☞ **If it's not a state of the component fault**
  - Structure the casual events with appropriate logic

88

Step 3 (continued)

- If State of the Component, then:
  - Ask "what are the P-S-C causes"
  - Generally this results in an OR gate
  - If a Command event is not involved, then this branch path is complete

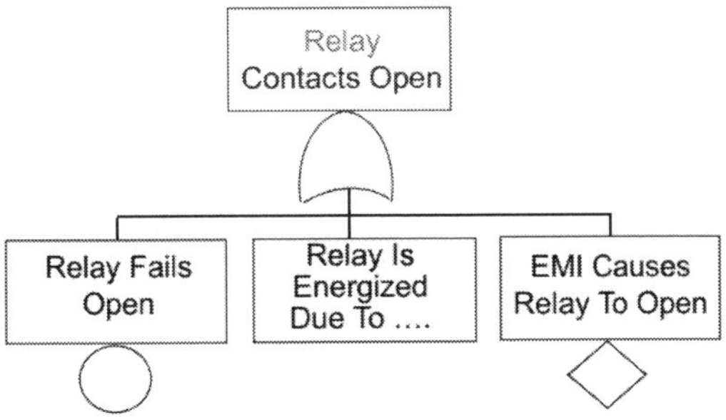

89

Step 3 (continued)

- If State of the System, then:
  - Ask "what is I-N-S" to cause event
  - Compose the input events and logic (functional relationships)
  - This gate can be any type of gate, depending on system design
  - The input events are generally gate events

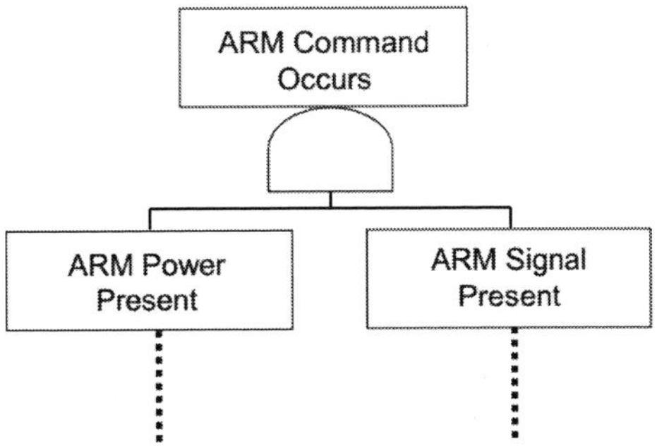

90

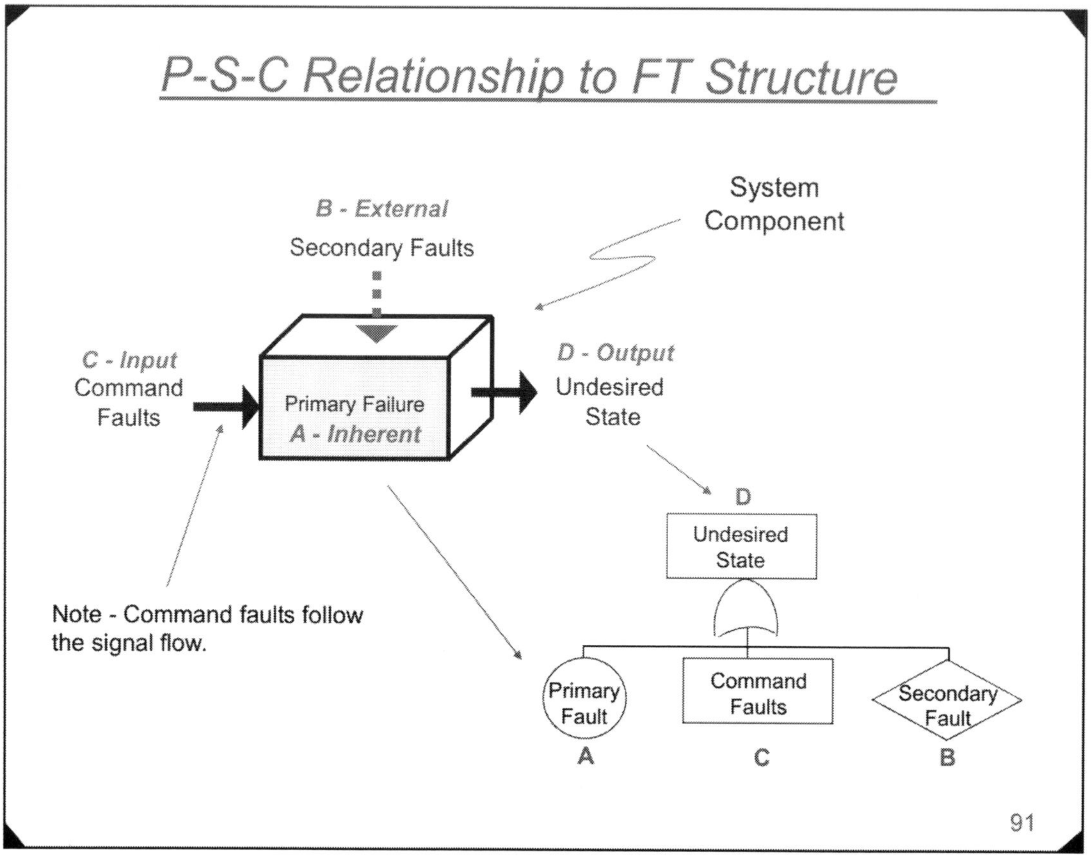
P-S-C Relationship to FT Structure
System
Component
B - External
Secondary Faults
C - Input
Command
Faults
Primary Failure
A - Inherent
D - Output
Undesired
State
Note - Command faults follow
the signal flow.
D
Undesired
State
Primary
Fault
A
Command
Faults
C
Secondary
Fault
B
91

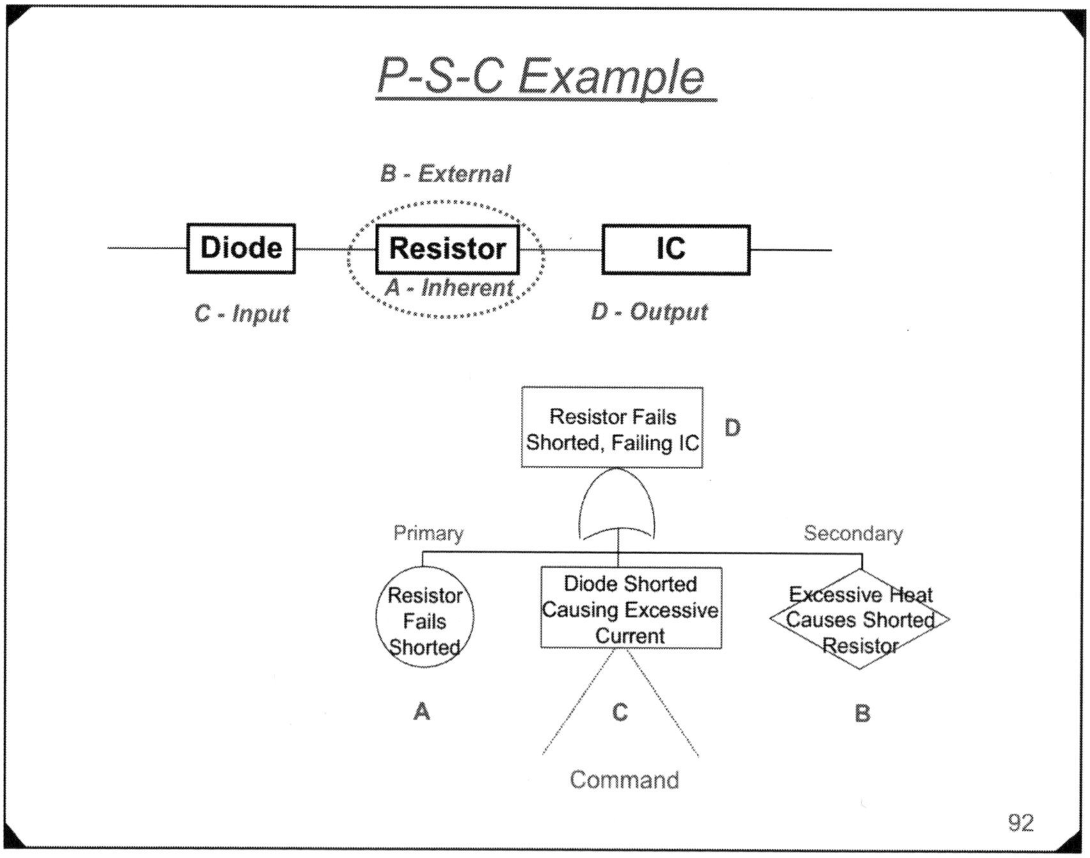
P-S-C Example
B - External
Diode
Resistor
A - Inherent
IC
C - Input
D - Output
Resistor Fails
Shorted, Failing IC
D
Primary
Secondary
Resistor
Fails
Shorted
Diode Shorted
Causing Excessive
Current
Excessive Heat
Causes Shorted
Resistor
A
C
B
Command
92

Isolate and Analyze

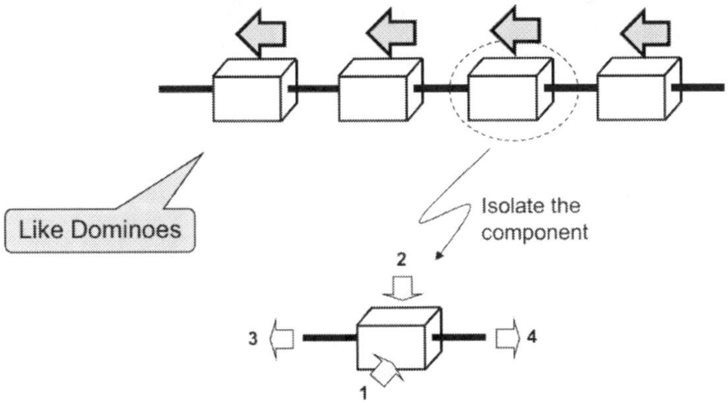

Analysis Views:

1) Primary - look inward
2) Secondary - look outward for incoming environmental concerns
3) Command - look backward at incoming signals
4) Output - look forward at possible undesired states that can be output

93

Example of Command Path

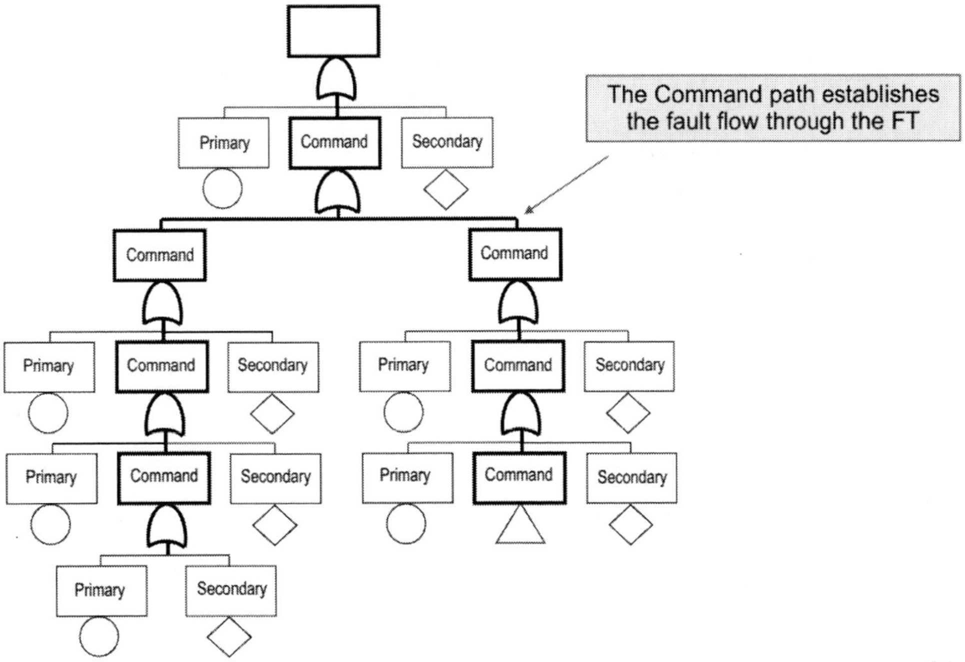

94

Example

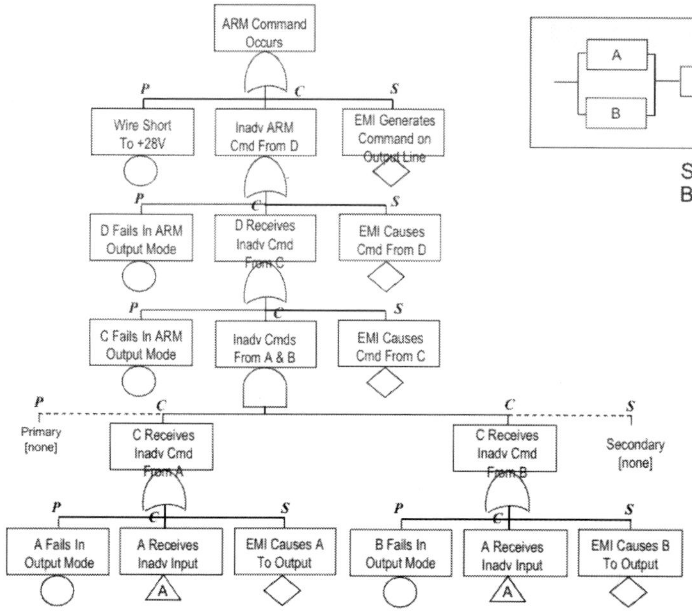

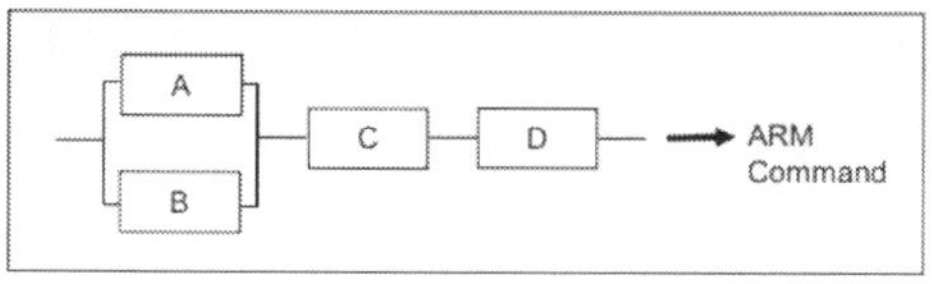

System design -- both A and B are necessary to cause C.

95

Example Fault Tree

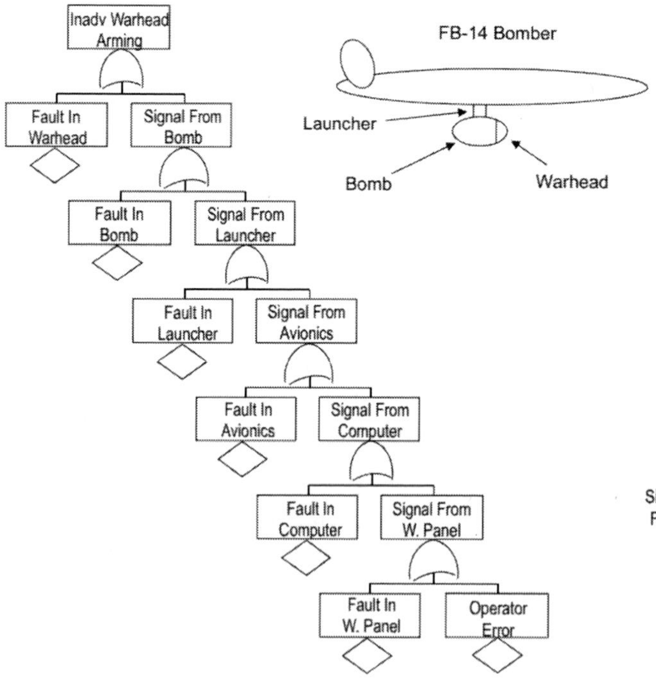

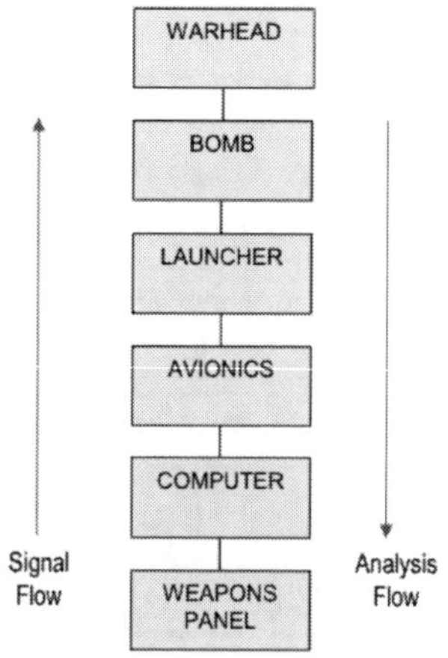

96

Construction Example

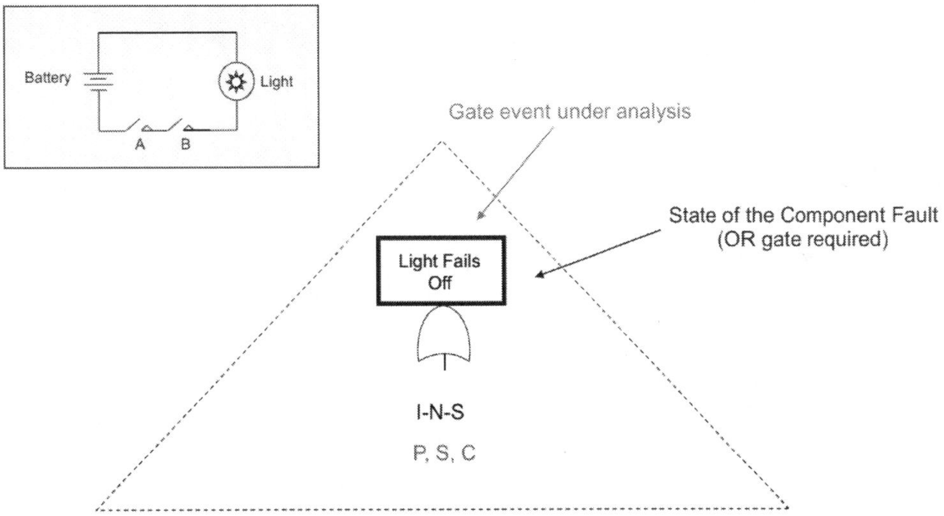

P – primary failure
S – secondary failure
C – command fault

97

Construction Example

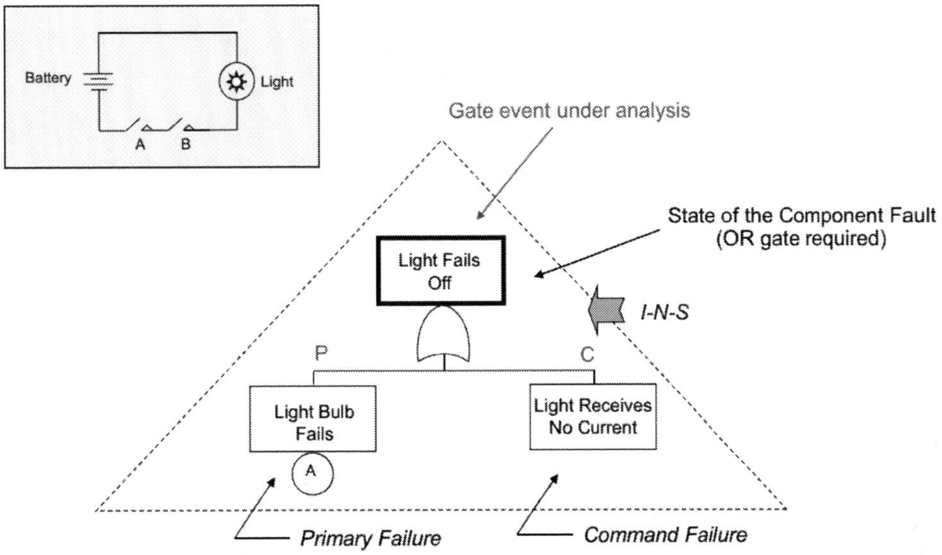

Note – This uses P-S-C, I-N-S and S-C/S

98

Construction Example (continued)

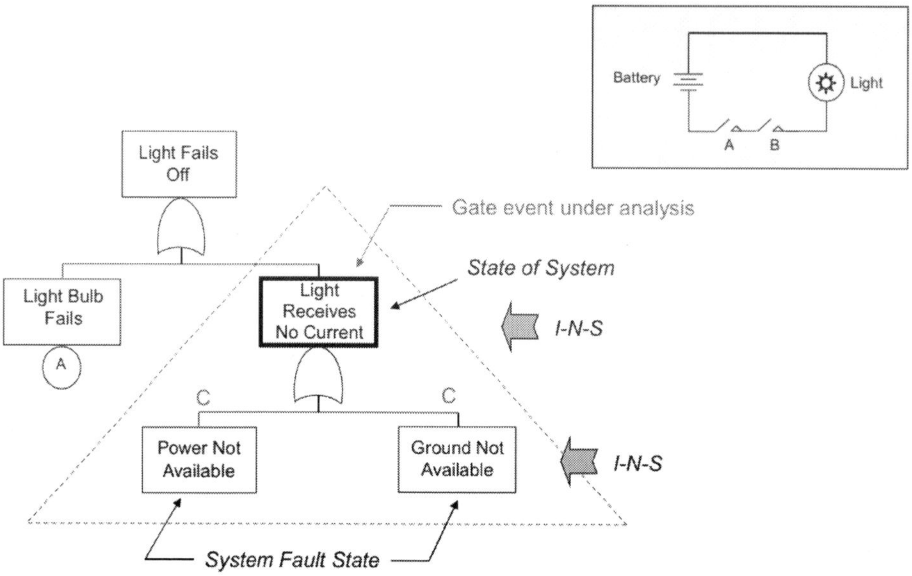

C – command fault

99

Construction Example (continued)

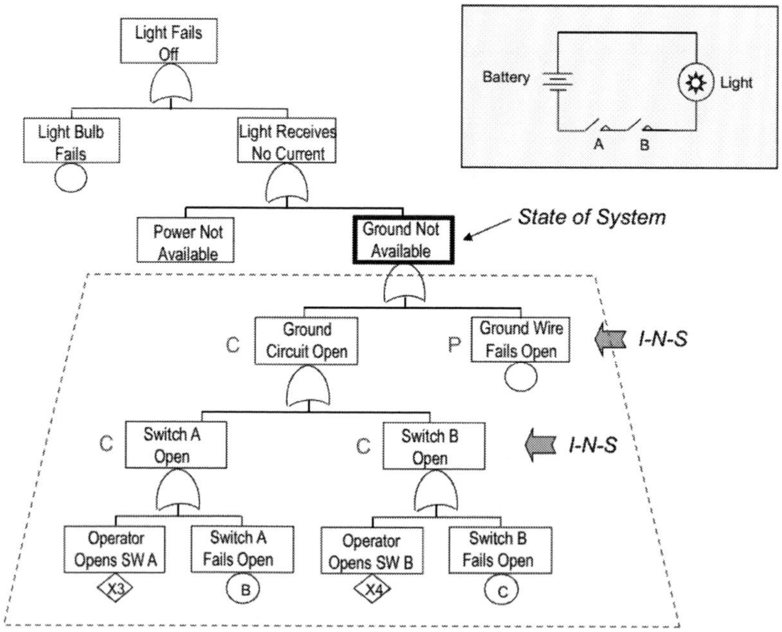

100

Construction Example (continued)

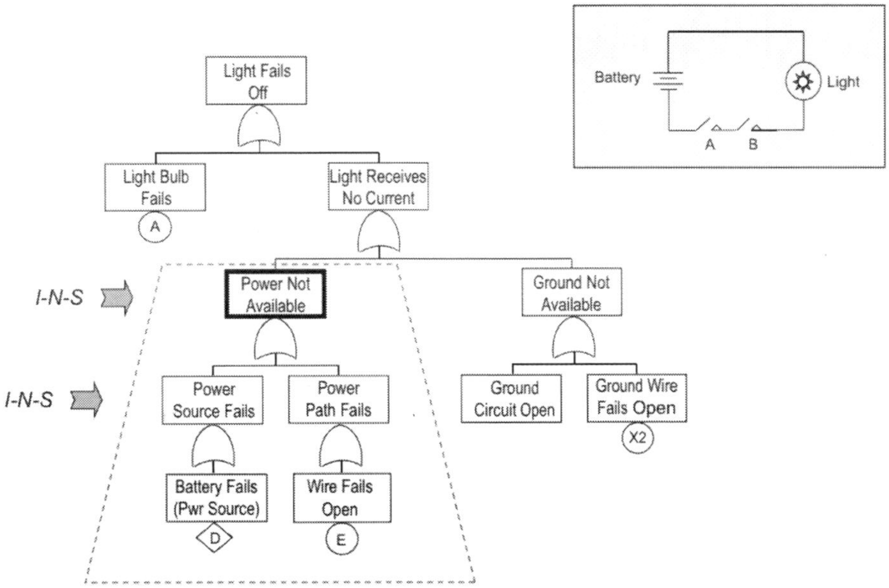

101

FT Process – Functional Flow

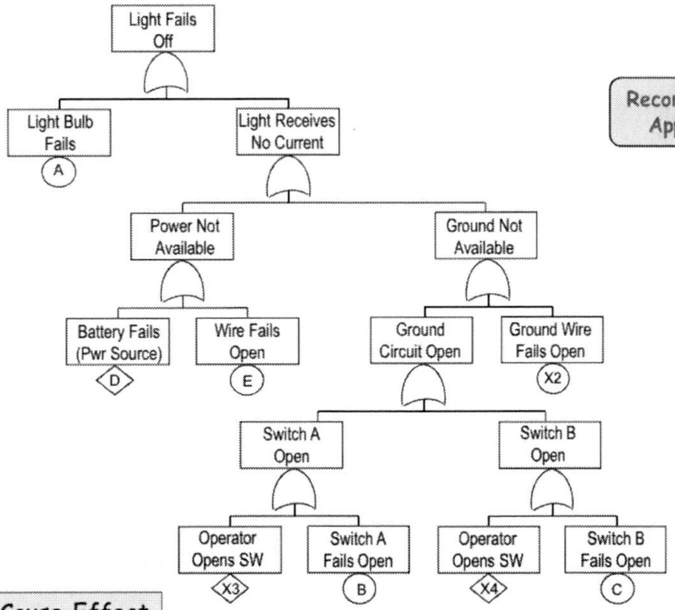

Recommended Approach

Note that logical Cause-Effect relationships are visible

102

FT Process – Unstructured

- The unstructured approach jumps ahead
  - Misses some important items, such as the total number of wires involved, human interaction, etc.
  - Does not depict system fault logic

Shopping List Approach

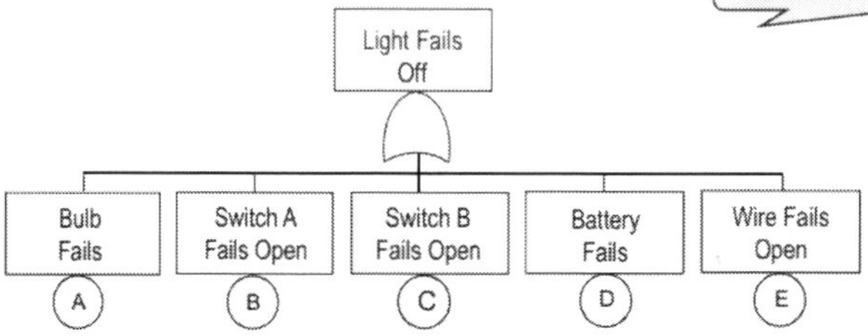

Note that Cause-Effect relationship is **not** visible

103

--- FT Construction Rules ---

1 - Know Your System

- It is imperative to know and understand the system design and operation thoroughly
- Utilize all sources of design information
  - Drawings, procedures, block diagrams, flow diagrams, FMEAs
  - Stress analyses, failure reports, maintenance procedures
  - System interface documents
  - CONOPS
- Drawings and data must be current for current results
- Draw a Functional Diagram of the system

Rule of thumb - if you can't construct a block diagram of system you may not understand it well enough to FT

104

2 - Understand The Purpose Of Your FTA

- It's important to know why the FTA is being performed
  - To ensure adequate resources are applied
  - To ensure proper scope of analysis
  - To ensure the appropriate results are obtained

- Remember, FTA is a tool for
  - Root cause analysis
  - Identifies events contributing to an Undesired Event
  - Computes the probability of an Undesired Event
  - Measures the relative impact of a design fix
  - Logic diagrams for presentation

105

3 - Understand Your FT Size

- FT size impacts the entire FTA process
- As FTs grow in size many factors are affected
  - Cost (e.g., manpower)
  - Time
  - Complexity
  - Understanding
  - Traceability
  - Computation
- System factors that cause FT growth
  - System size
  - Safety criticality of system
  - System complexity
- FT factors that cause FT growth
  - MOEs and MOBs (e.g., redundancy)
  - Certain AND / OR combinations

FT size is important and has many implications

106

4 - Intentionally Design Your Fault Tree

- As a FT grows in size it is important develop an architecture and a set of rules
- The architecture lays out the overall FT design
  - Subsystem branches (for analysts and subcontractors)
  - Analyst responsibilities
- The rules provide consistent development guidelines
  - Ground rules for inclusion/exclusion (e.g., Human factors, CCFs)
  - Ground rules for depth of analysis (subsystem, LRU, component)
  - Ground rules for naming conventions (component types, MOEs)
  - Ground rules for component database

Foresight helps avoid future problems

107

Don't Do This! -- Plan Ahead

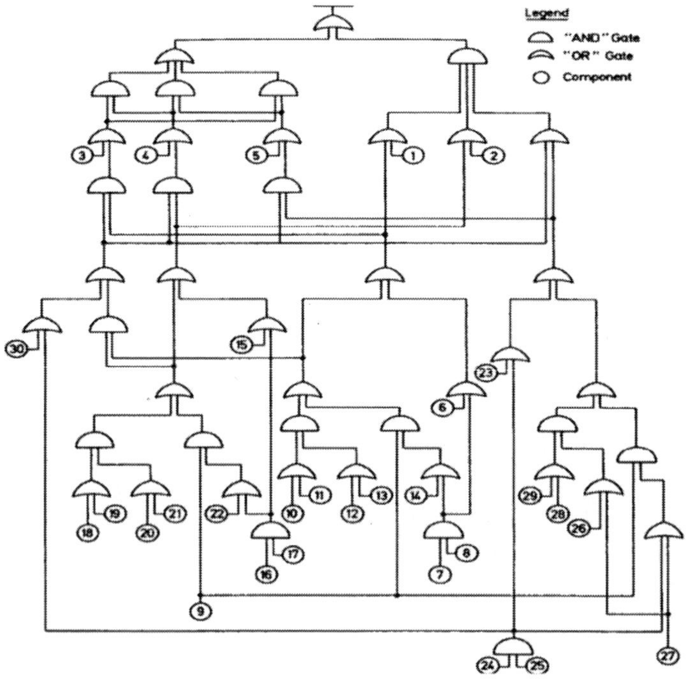

108

5 - Ensure the FT is Correct and Complete

- FT completeness is critical
  - Anything left out of the FTA skews the answer
  - The final result will only reflect what was included in the FT
  - The FTA is not complete until all root causes have been identified
- FT correctness is critical
  - If the FT is not correct the results will not be accurate
- Conduct FT peer review to ensure completeness/correctness
  - Involve other FT experts
  - Involve system designers
- Items often overlooked in FTA
  - Human error
  - Common cause failures
  - Software factors (design may have dependencies)
  - Components or subsystems considered not applicable

FT results are skewed if the FT is not complete and correct

109

6 - Know Your Fault Tree Tools

- Know basic FT tool capabilities
  - Construction, editing, plotting, reports, cut set evaluation
- Know FT tool user friendliness
  - Intuitive operation
  - Easy to use and remember
  - Changes are easy to implement
- Single vs. multi-phase FT
- Qualitative vs. quantitative evaluation
- Simulation vs. analytical evaluation (considerations include size, accuracy, phasing)

110

Tools (continued)

- Know FT tool limitations
  - Tree size (i.e., max number of events)
  - Cut set size
  - Plot size
- Understand approximations and cutoff methods, some can cause errors
- Gate probabilities could be incorrect when MOEs are involved
- Test the tool; don't assume answers are always correct

Don't place complete trust in a FT program

111

7 - Understand Your FTA Results

- Verify that the FTA goals were achieved
  - Was the analysis objective achieved
  - Are the results meaningful
  - Was FTA the right tool
  - Are adjustments necessary
- Make reasonableness tests to verify the results
  - Are the results correct
  - Look for analysis errors (logic, data, model, computer results)
  - Are CSs credible and relevant (if not revise tree)
  - Take nothing for granted from the computer
  - Test your results via manual calculations

112

8 - Document Your FTA

- Formally document the entire FTA
  - May need to provide to customer (product)
  - May need to defend at a later date
  - May need to modify at a later date
  - May perform a similar analysis at a later date
  - May need records for an accident/incident investigation
- Even a small analysis should be documented for posterity
- May support future questions or analyses

Documentation is essential

113

Documentation (continued)

- Provide complete documentation
  - Problem statement
  - Definitions
  - Ground rules
  - References
  - Comprehensive system description
  - Data and sources (drawings, failure rates, etc.)
  - FT diagrams
  - FT tree metrics
  - FT computer tool description
  - Results
  - Conclusions

Document the number of hours to perform the FTA for future estimates

114

9 - Think in Terms of Failure Space

- Remember, it's a "fault" tree, not a "success" tree
  - Analysis of failures, faults, errors and bad designs
- No magic
  - Do not draw the fault tree assuming the system can be saved by a miraculous failure
  - This is normally referred to as the "No Magic Rule"
- No operator *saves*
  - When constructing FT logic do not assume that operator action will save the system from fault conditions
  - Only built-in safety features can be considered
  - Operator errors can be considered in the FT, but not operator saves
  - The system design is under investigation, not the operator performing miracles

115

10 - Correct Node Wording Is Important

- Be clear and precise
- Express fault event in terms of
  - Device transition
  - Input or output state
- Be very descriptive in writing event text
  - "Power supply fails" vs. "Power supply does not provide +5 VDC"
  - "Valve fails in closed position" vs. "Valve fails"
- Do not
  - Use the terms Primary, Secondary or Command
    - Thought process
    - Symbols already show it
  - Use terms Failure or Fault (if possible) – not enough information

Good node wording guides the analysis process

116

Wording Example

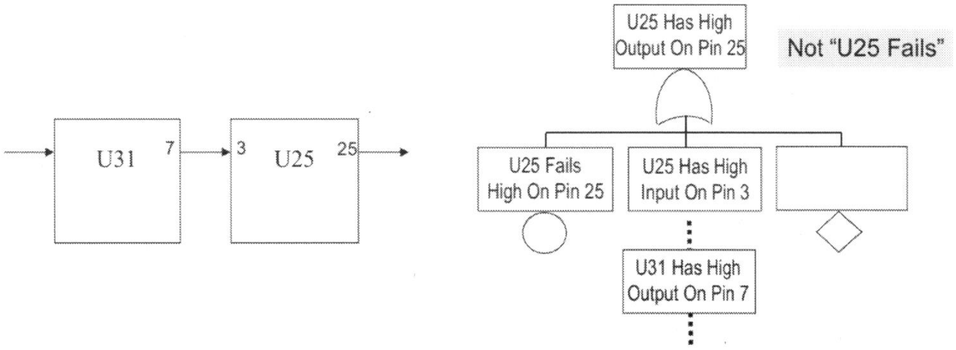

Proper wording enhances the logic process

117

11 - Follow Standard Construction Rules

- No gate-to-gate diagrams
  - Do not draw a gate without a gate node box and associated descriptive text and rectangle
- Use only one output from a node
  - Do not connect the output of a node to more than one input nodes.
  - Some analysts attempt to show redundancy this way, but it becomes cluttered and confusing.
  - Most computer codes cannot handle this situation anyway.

118

Construction Errors

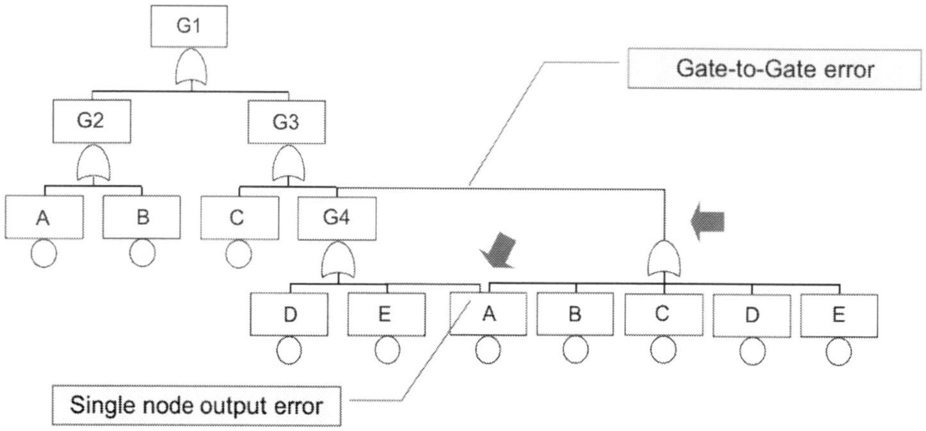

Usually not possible with computer FT programs

119

FT Construction Rules (cont'd)

- Construct the FT to most accurately reflect the system design and logic
  - Do not try to modify the tree structure to resolve an MOE.
  - Let the FT computer software handle all MOE resolutions.
- Keep single input OR gates to a minimum
  - When the words in a Node box exceed the box limit, you can create another input with a Node box directly below just to continue the words
  - Use the Notes if additional words are needed. Its okay to do but prudence is also necessary
- Use House events carefully
  - A House (Normal event) never goes into an OR gate, except in special cases, such as a multi-phase simulation FT

120

FT Construction Rules (cont'd)

- Do not label fault events on the tree as *Primary*, *Secondary* and *Command* failures
  - Go into detail and be descriptive. These terms are more for the thought process than the labeling process.
- When possible add traceability detail
  - Put drawing numbers and part numbers in the fault event or in the notes.
  - This provides better traceability when the tree is being reviewed or checked, or when the tree is being modified after a lengthy time period.

121

FT Construction Rules (cont'd)

- Operator error should be included in the analysis where appropriate
  - It is up to the analyst and the purpose/objective of the FTA as to whether the event should be included in quantitative evaluations
  - The decision needs to be documented in the analysis ground rules
- Take a second look at all tree logic structure
  - Sometimes what appears to be a simple and correct tree logic structure might actually be flawed for various reasons
    - Example -- mutually exclusive events, logic loops, etc.
  - Make sure there are no leaps or gaps in logic
  - The tree structure may need revising in these cases

122

12 - Provide Necessary Node Data

- Node name
- Node text
- Node type
- Basic event probability (for quantification only)

Four items are essential

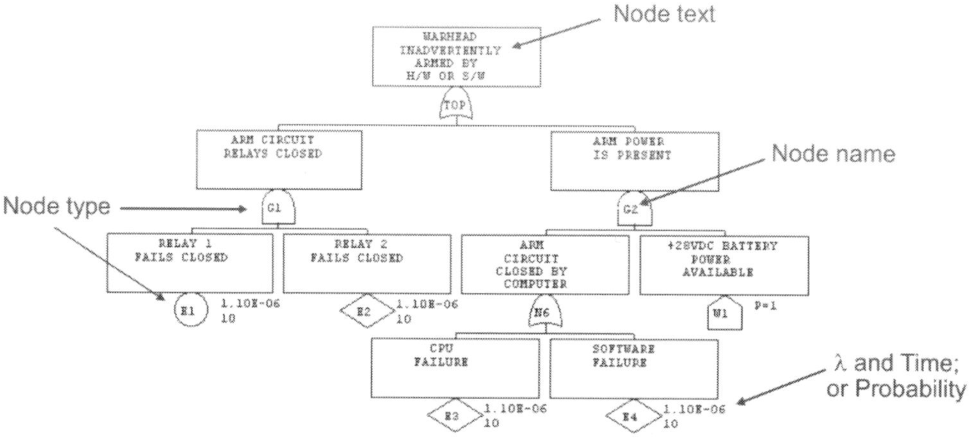

123

13 - Apply FT Aesthetics

- When the FT structure looks good it will be better accepted
- A level FT structure looks best
  - No zig-zags
- Balance page breaks & FT structure
  - Avoid too little info on a page (i.e., 2 or 3 events)
- Always use standard FT symbols (defined in NUREG book)
- Computerized construction tools provides better graphics than manual methods

A level and balanced FT structure is easier to read

124

Poor Aesthetics Example

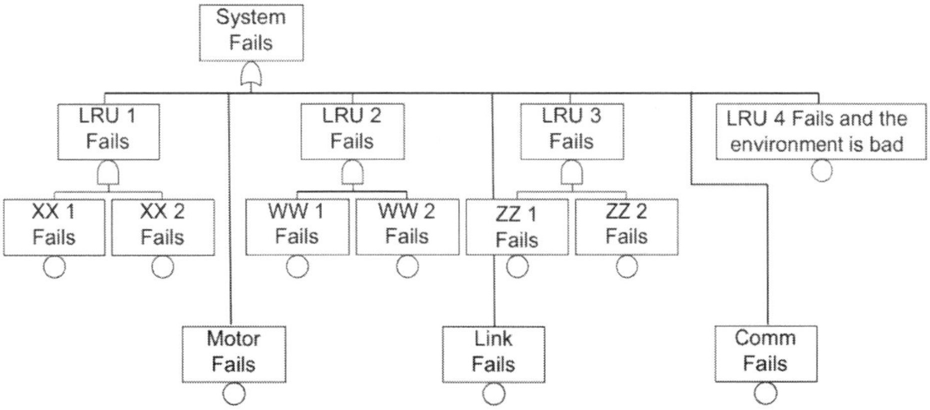

125

14 - Computerized Evaluation Is Essential

- FT quantification is easy when the FT is small and simple
  - Manual calculations are easy
- FT quantification is difficult when the FT is large and complex
  - Manual quantification becomes too difficult without errors
- Hand drawn FTs typically have more errors

126

15 - Validate all CSs

- CSs are very important
  - They show where to fix system (weak design points)
  - They show the importance of specific components
  - They are necessary for most numerical calculations
- Always verify that all CSs are valid
  - If they are not right the FT is incorrect

127

16 - Perform a Numerical Reality Check

- Never completely trust the results of a computer program
  - Some algorithms may have errors
  - Proprietary approximations may not always work
- Perform a rough calculation manually to check on the computer results
- A large deviation could indicate a problem

128

17 - Verify All MOEs and MOBs

- Review MOEs very carefully
  - Their effect can be important - common cause, zonal analysis
  - They can cause large numerical error (or none at all)
  - They can hide or emphasize redundancy
- An MOE or MOB can be inadvertently created by erroneously using the same event name twice

129

18 - FTs Are Only Models

- Remember that FT's are models
  - Perception or model of reality
  - Not 100% fidelity to exact truth
- Remember that models are approximations (generally)
  - Not necessarily 100% exact
  - Still a valuable predictor
  - Newton's law of gravity is an approximation
- Do not represent FTA results as an exact answer
  - Use engineering judgment
  - Small number are relative (2.0×10^{-8} is as good as 1.742135×10^{-8})
  - Anything overlooked by the FTA skews the answer
    - Minor things left out can make results conservative (understate results)
    - Major things left out can be significant (overstate results)

130

19 - Understand Your Failure Data

- Failure data must be obtainable for quantitative evaluation
- Must understand failure modes, failure mechanisms and failure rates
- Data accuracy and trustworthiness must be known (confidence)
- Proven data is best
- Don't be afraid of raw data
  - Data estimates can be used
  - Useful for rough estimate
  - Results must be understood

Even raw data provides useful results

131

20 – Always Provide Data Sources

- MIL-HDBK-217 Electronic Parts Predictions
- Maintenance records
- Vendor data
- Testing
- Historical databases

132

21 – The Human Is A System Element

- The human is often a key element in the system lifecycle
  - Manufacturing, assembly, installation, operation, decommissioning
- The human might be the most complex system element
- Human error includes
  - Fails to perform function (error of omission)
  - Performs incorrectly
  - Performs inadvertently (error of commission)
  - Performs wrong function
- Human error can
  - Initiate a system failure or accident
  - Fail to correctly mitigate the effects of a failure (e.g., ignored warning lights)
  - Exacerbate the effects of a system failure

133

Include Human Error in FTs

- Human error should be considered in FT model when appropriate
  - When the probability could make a difference
  - When the design needs to be modified
- Key rule – anything left out of the FT causes the results to be understated
- A poor HSI design can force the operator to commit errors
  - Mode confusion (e.g., Predator mishap)
  - Display confusion
  - Too many screens, modes and/or functions
  - GUI Widget confusion
  - Designing the system to complement the human operator

134

Human Reliability is Complex

- Finding human error failure data is difficult
- Rates could theoretically vary based on many factors
  - System type
  - Design
  - Human skills
  - Repetitiveness
- In general, studies show:
  - $P = 10^{-3}$ for general error
  - $P = 10^{-4}$ to 10^{-6} if special designs and checks are performed

135

22 - Node Name Length

- Short node names tend to be better than long names
  - Long names become burdensome & time consuming
- A 5 char name is easier to work with than a 24 char name
  - Typing original
  - Typing in a search
  - Storing in a database
- Random node names generated from node text tends to be more difficult to follow than shorted coded names

136

Node Naming Convention

- FT naming conventions (or coding) can be very useful
- Must maintain explicit configuration control of Event, Transfer and Gate names
  - Incorrect Event names will cause inadvertent MOE's or none when intended
  - Incorrect Transfers names will cause use of wrong modules
  - Incorrect Gate names will cause inadvertent MOB's or none when intended
- Most important for very large trees, not as critical for small trees
- Example: two analysts may use same diode, but each give it a different FT name
- A FT name coding scheme should be developed for the FT project
  - before the FT construction begins, planned, consistent

137

Sample Coding Scheme

- Use only 5 characters for a node name
- Specific characters are used to quickly identify event types
- Establish a pattern for *tree families*

1st Char	Symbol Type
G	Gate
X	Circle (primary failure)
Z	Diamond (secondary failure)
W	House (normal event)
Y	Oval (condition event)

Chars	Family	Represents
A	Top level family	Computer System
B	Top level family	Navigation System
AA	Member of A	
BB	Member of B	
ABC	Member of AB	

138

Coding Example

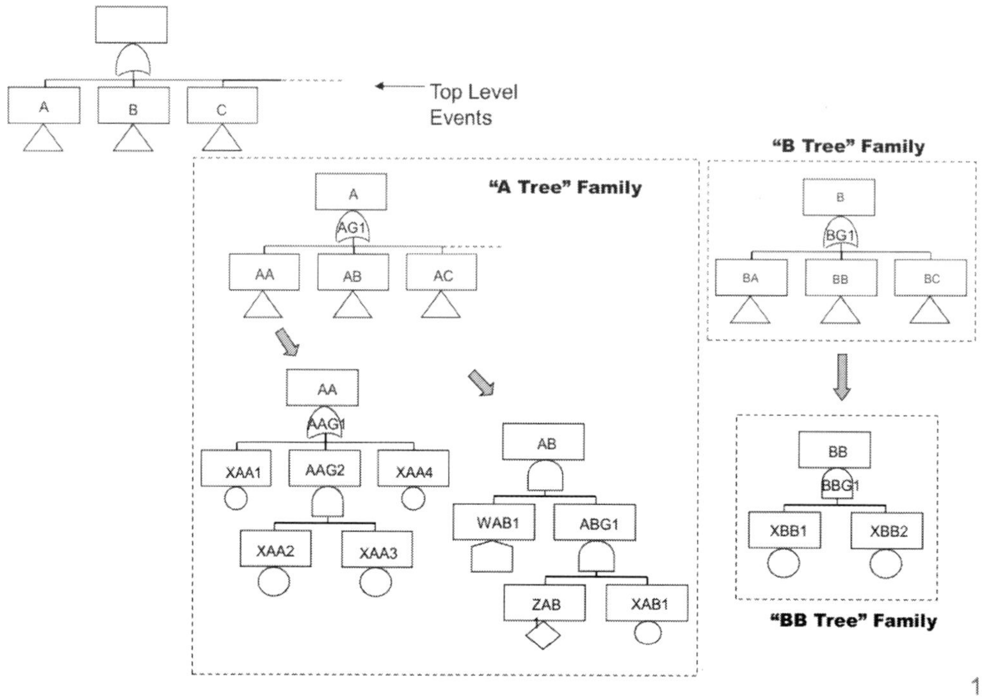

139

23 - FT Accounting

- Large FT's necessitate FT accounting
- This is a form of data control
- Used in conjunction with the input roadmap
- Keep accurate track of basic events:
  - Name
  - Text
  - Failure rate
  - Exposure time
  - Source of data for event failure rate
  - Trees where the event is used
  - If it is an MOE
- Generally requires a database

140

24 – Tools and Simplicity Help

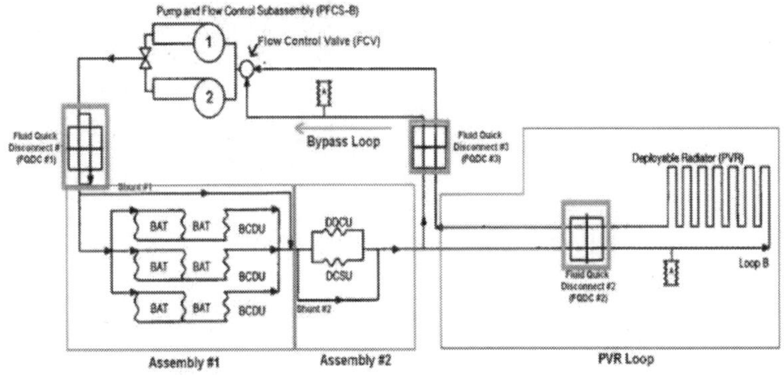

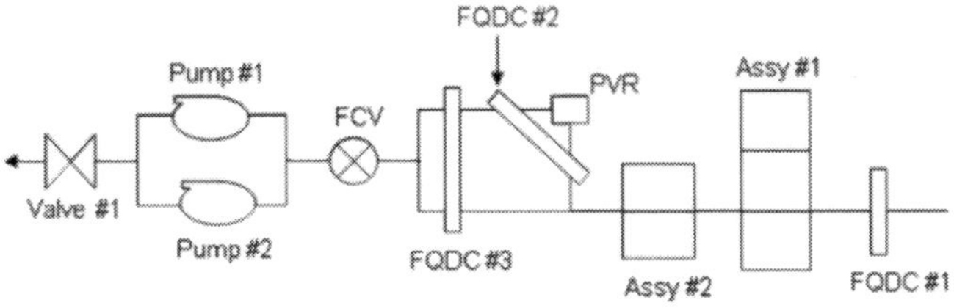

141

--- Example FTs of System Designs ---

System Scenario

System Design:

A system is comprised of fuel, oxidizer and an ignition source. When properly applied they run an engine.

Fire scenario requires 4 things:
1) Fuel
2) Oxidizer
3) Ignition source
4) Correct flammable mixture

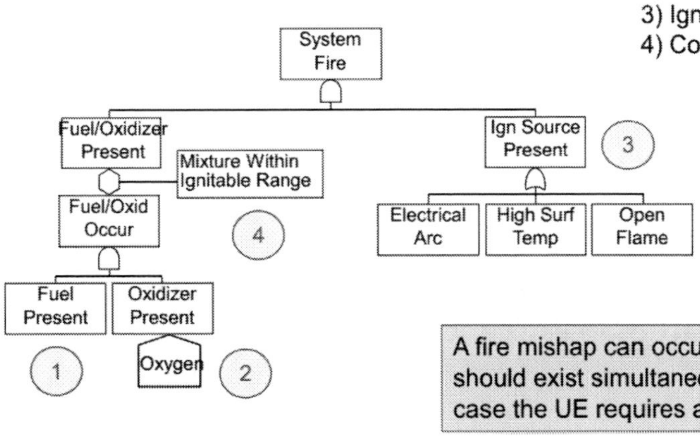

A fire mishap can occur if these elements should exist simultaneously due to faults. In this case the UE requires an AND gate.

142

Series System

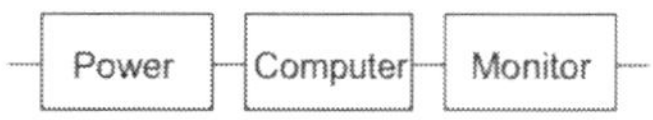

- System success requires all 3 components operational.
- System failure occurs when any one component fails.
- Therefore, requires an <u>OR</u> gate.

A ST is often the inverse of a FT

System Success

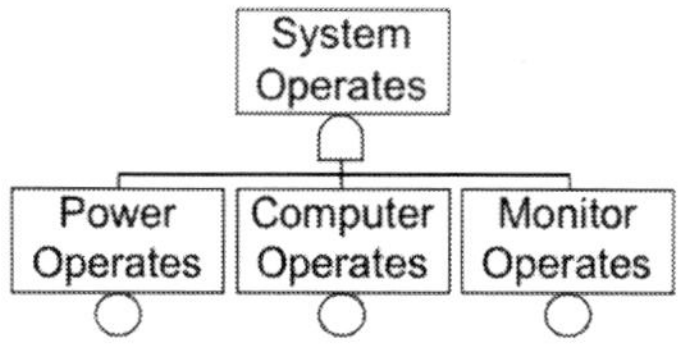

Success Tree (ST)

System Failure

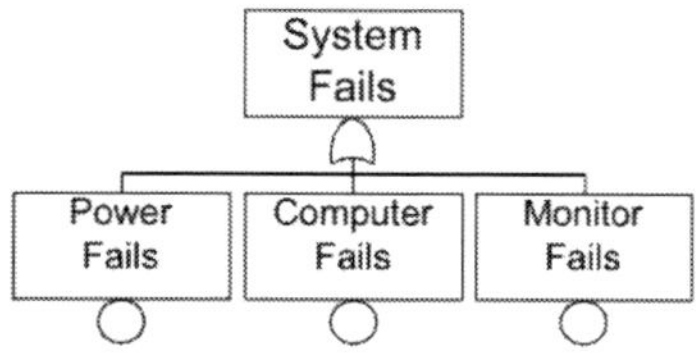

143

Parallel System

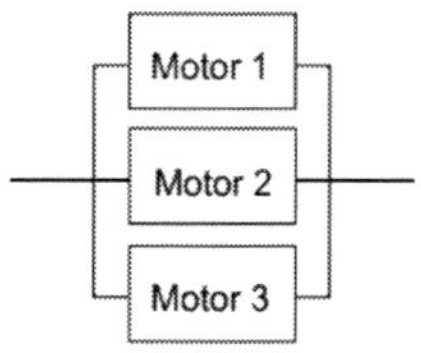

<u>Case 1</u>
- System success requires all 3 Motors operational.
- System failure occurs when any one Motors fails.
- Therefore, requires an <u>OR</u> gate.

System Success

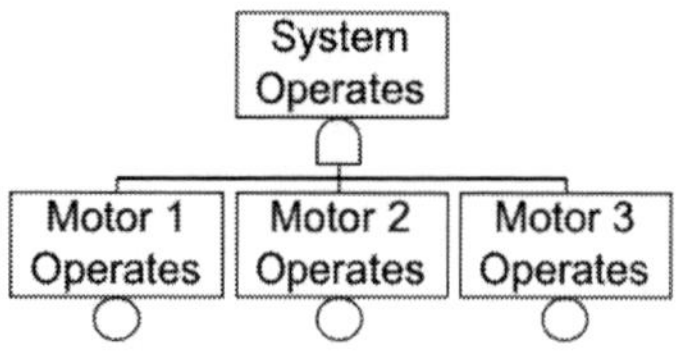

System Failure

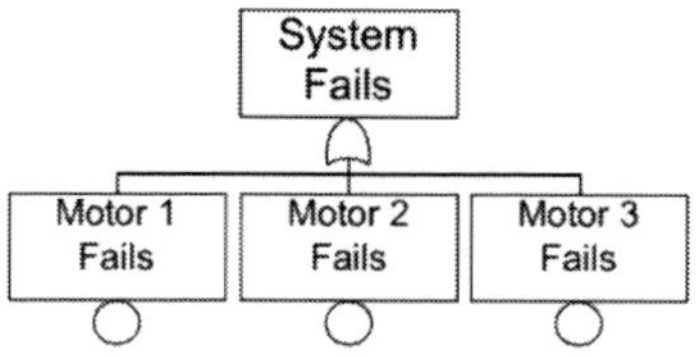

144

Parallel System

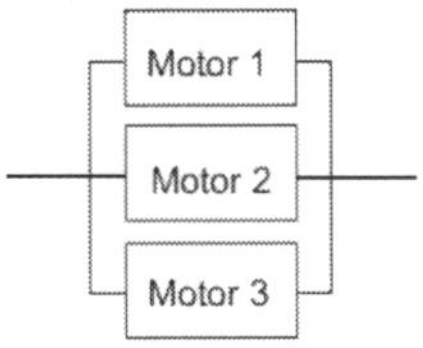

Case 2
- System success requires only 1 Motor operational.
- System failure occurs only when all three Motors fail.
- Therefore, requires an AND gate.

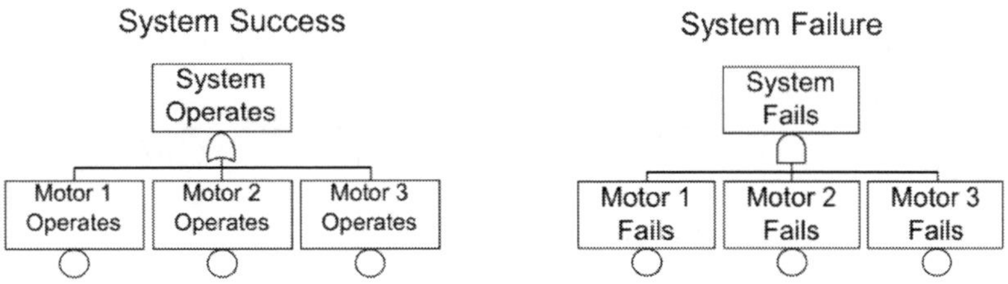

145

Parallel System

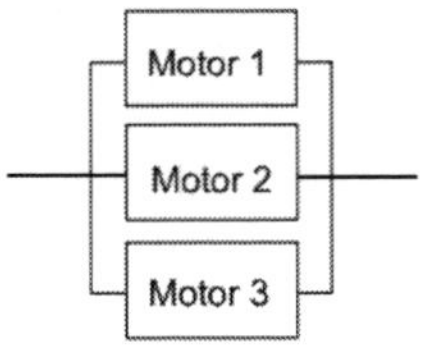

Case 3
- System success requires any 2 of 3 Motors operational.
- System failure occurs when any 2 Motors fail.
- Therefore, requires combination logic.
- Note how the MOE arises in this case.

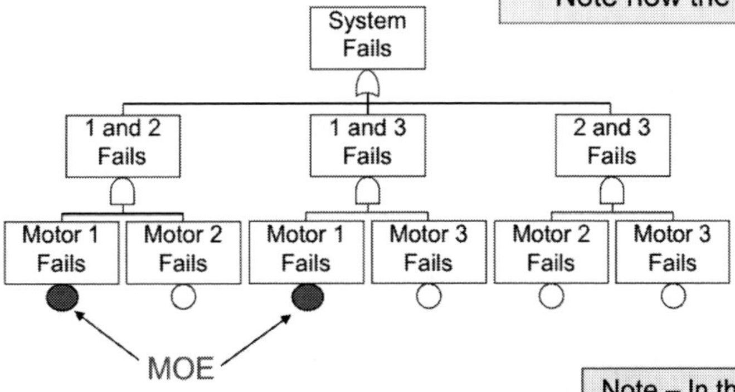

Note – In this case, If the FT is an inverted ST, the FT looks incorrect, but does work mathematically.

146

Series-Parallel System

System Design:

A system is comprised of multiple components in series and parallel.

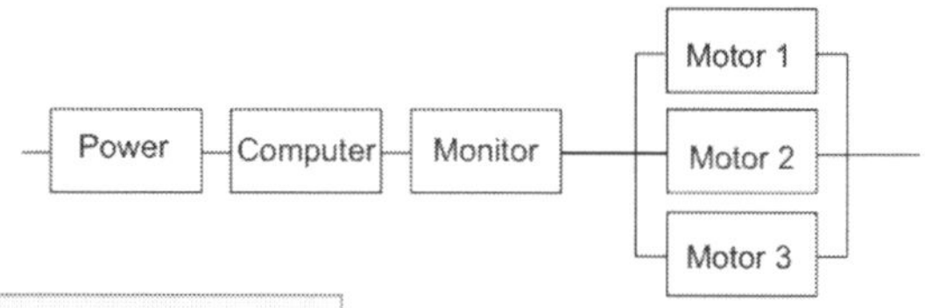

Therefore:

- System success requires that all series components must operate and at least one parallel component must operate successfully
- system failure occurs if one or more series components fail, or all parallel components fail

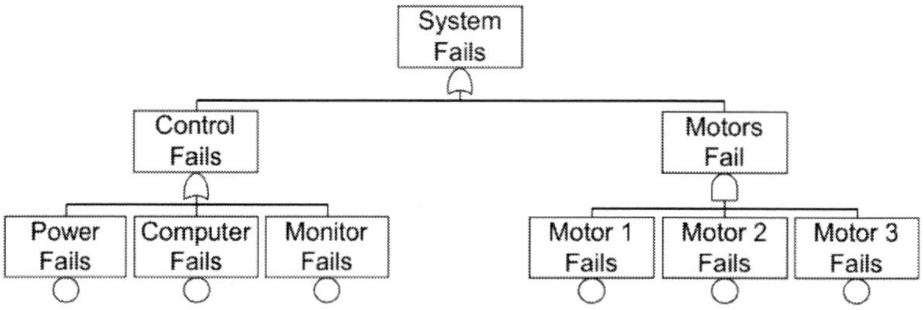

147

Sequence Parallel System

System Design:

A system is comprised of two components A and B. System success requires that both must operate successfully at the same time. System failure occurs if both fail, but <u>only if A fails before B</u>.

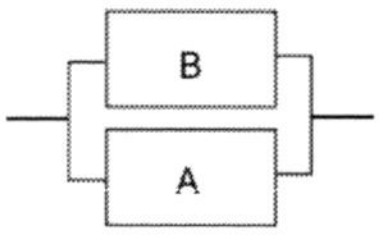

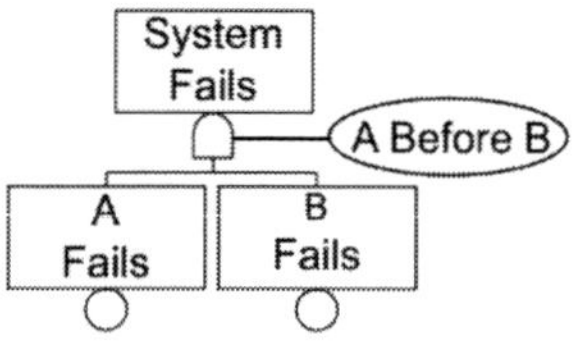

Therefore:

- Both must fail
- Sequential problem (A before B)
- The fault state logic requires a <u>Priority AND</u> gate.

148

Monitor System

System Design:

A system is comprised of two components, Monitor A and component B. Monitor A monitors the operation of B. If it detects any failure in B it takes corrective action. System success requires that B must operate successfully. System failure occurs if component B fails, which can only happen if Monitor A fails to detect a problem with B, and B subsequently fails. If A works it always corrects any failure in B or provides a warning.

This design has 2 different cases:

1. Full Monitor (full coverage)
2. Partial Monitor (partial coverage)

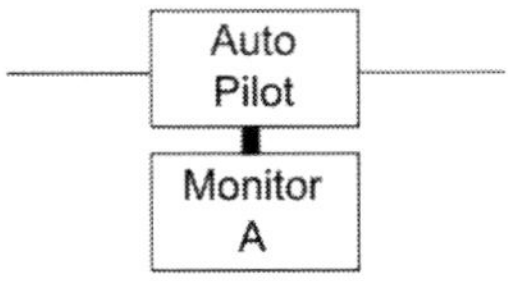

Coverage refers to part of subsystem that is tested. Full coverage means 100%.

149

Monitor System

Case 1 – Full Monitor

Monitor A monitors the operation of B, and it is designed to monitor 100% of B. In this example B is the Auto Pilot (A/P).

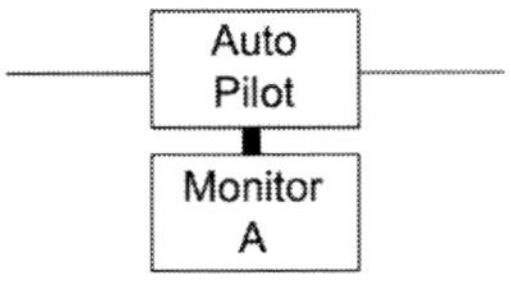

Therefore:

- Both must fail
- Sequential problem (A before B)
- The fault state logic requires a Priority AND gate

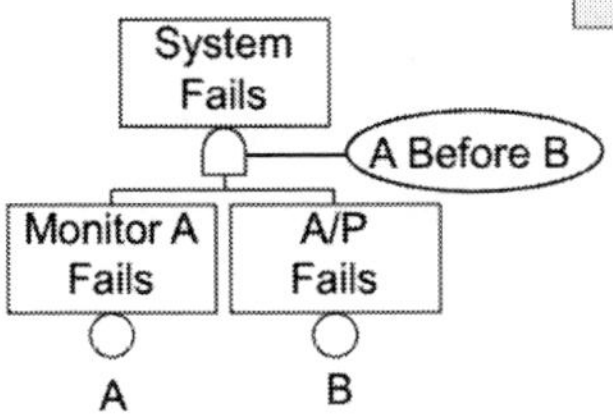

150

Monitor System

Case 2 – Partial Monitor

Monitor A monitors the operation of B, however, it is only designed to monitor 80% of B (A/P in this case).

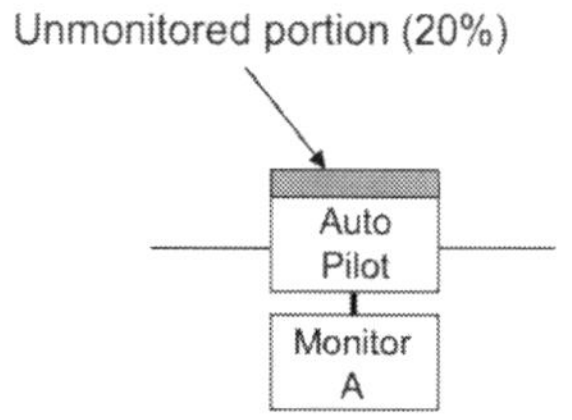

Therefore:

- Two problems, covered and uncovered segments, thus an OR gate
- Covered segment is sequential problem (A before B), thus the fault state logic requires a Priority AND gate

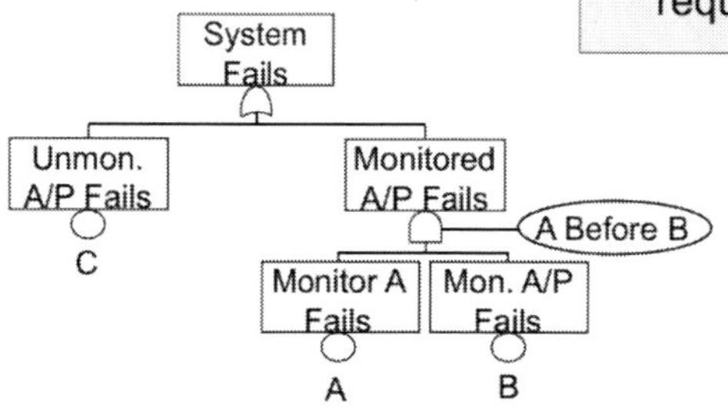

151

Standby System

System Design:

A system is comprised of two main components A and B, and a monitor M. System operation starts with component A in operation and B on standby. If A fails, then B is switched on-line and it takes over. System success requires that either A or B operate successfully. System failure occurs if both components A and B fail. Note that B can be failed if switching fails to occur.

There are three classes of Standby systems:

1. Hot Standby - powered during standby (uses operational λ_O)
2. Warm Standby - partially powered during standby ($\lambda_W<\lambda_O$)
3. Cold Standby - un-powered during standby ($\lambda_C=0$)

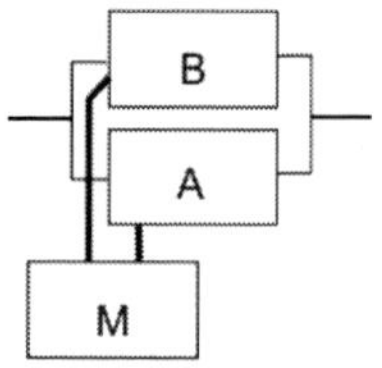

The major difference between each of these modes is that the failure rate is different in the standby mode.

152

Standby System

Case 1 – No Assumptions
Recognizes that the Monitor is fallible, and therefore does not assume the Monitor is perfectly reliable.

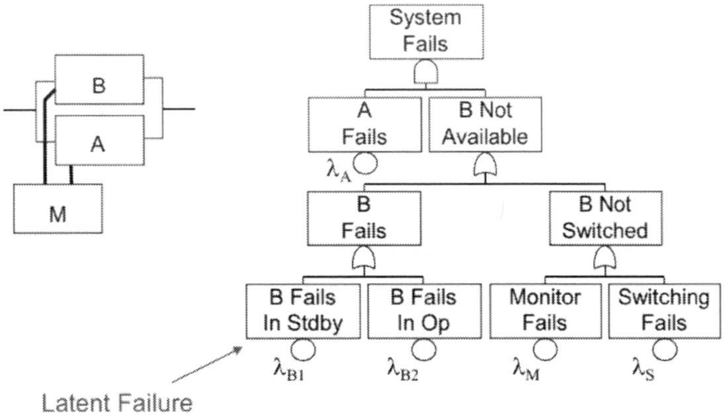

153

Standby System

Case 2 – Reliable Monitor Assumption
Assume that the Monitor is perfectly reliable.

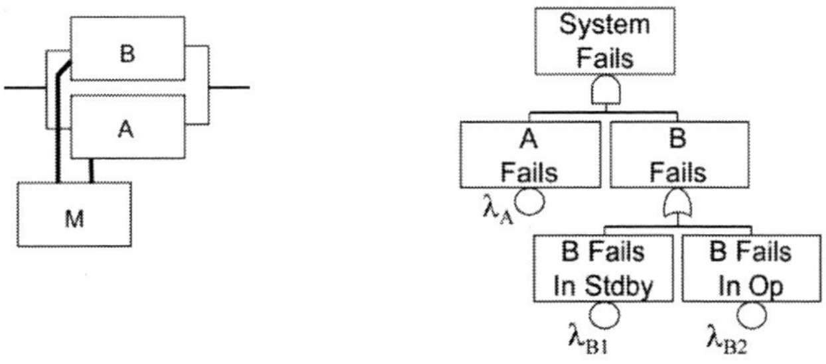

Often modeled this way to compare with Markov analysis results, and when Case 1 is too difficult for Markov.

154

Basic Reliability Equations

- $R = e^{-\lambda T}$
- $R + Q = 1$
- $Q = 1 - R = 1 - e^{-\lambda T}$ ← Main equation of FTA
  - $Q \approx \lambda T$ when $\lambda T < 0.001$ (approximation)

- Where:
  - R = Reliability or Probability of Success
  - Q = Unreliability or Probability of Failure
  - λ = component failure rate = 1 / MTBF
  - MTBF = mean time between failure
  - T = time interval (mission time or exposure time)

155

Effects of Failure Rate & Time

- The longer the mission (or exposure time) the higher the probability of failure
- The smaller the failure rate the lower the probability of failure

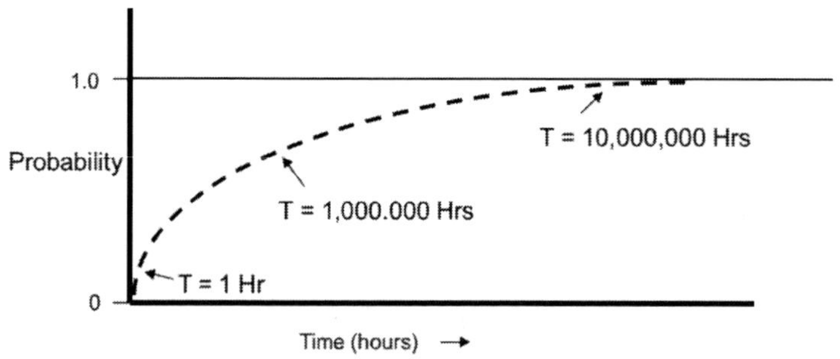

$\lambda = 1.0 \times 10^{-6}$

$P = 1 - e^{-\lambda T}$

The Effect of Exposure Time on Probability is Significant

156

Probability

Union (OR Gate)
For two events A and B, the union is the event {A or B} that contains all the outcomes in A, in B, or in both A and B.

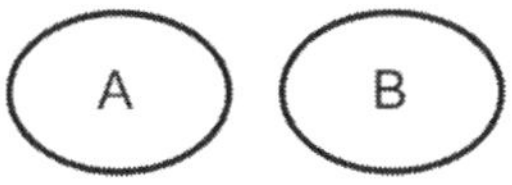

Case 1 - Disjoint Events
$P=P(A) + P(B)$

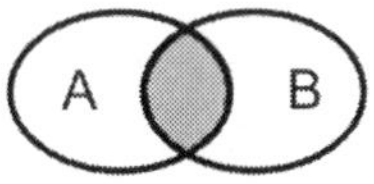

Case 2 - Non Disjoint Events
$P=P(A) + P(B) - P(A)P(B)$

Case 3 - Mutually Exclusive Events
$P=P(A) + P(B) - 2P(A)P(B)$

Note - Exclusive OR is not the same as Disjoint.

157

Probability

Intersection (AND Gate)
For two events A and B, the intersection is the event {A and B} that contains the occurrence of both A and B.

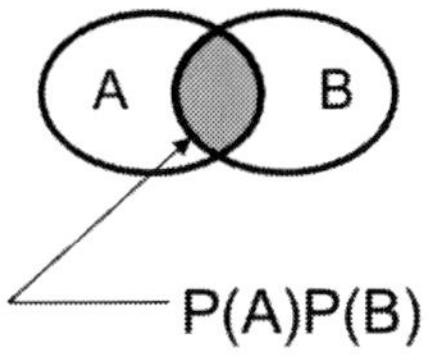

Case 1 - Independent Events
$P=P(A)P(B)$

Case 2 - Dependent Events
$P=P(A)P(B/A)$

158

CS Expansion Formula

$$P = \Sigma(\text{singles}) - \Sigma(\text{pairs}) + \Sigma(\text{triples}) - \Sigma(\text{fours}) + \Sigma(\text{fives}) - \Sigma(\text{sixes}) + \bullet\bullet\bullet$$

CS {A; B; C; D}

$$\begin{aligned} P = \; & (P_A + P_B + P_C + P_D) \\ & - (P_{AB} + P_{AC} + P_{AD} + P_{BC} + P_{BD} + P_{CD}) \\ & + (P_{ABC} + P_{ABD} + P_{ACD} + P_{BCD}) \\ & - (P_{ABCD}) \end{aligned}$$

$$P = P_A + P_B + P_C + P_D - (P_{AB} + P_{AC} + P_{AD} + P_{BC} + P_{BD} + P_{CD}) + (P_{ABC} + P_{ABD} + P_{ACD} + P_{BCD}) - (P_{ABCD})$$

Size and complexity of the formula depends on the total number of cut sets and MOE's.

159

Inclusion-Exclusion Approximation

CS {A; B; C; D}

$$P = \underbrace{P_A + P_B + P_C + P_D}_{\text{1st Term (all singles)}} - \underbrace{(P_{AB} + P_{AC} + P_{AD} + P_{BC} + P_{BD} + P_{CD})}_{\text{2nd Term (all doubles)}} + \underbrace{(P_{ABC} + P_{ABD} + P_{ACD} + P_{BCD})}_{\text{3rd Term (all triples)}} - \underbrace{(P_{ABCD})}_{\text{4th Term}} \bullet\bullet\bullet$$

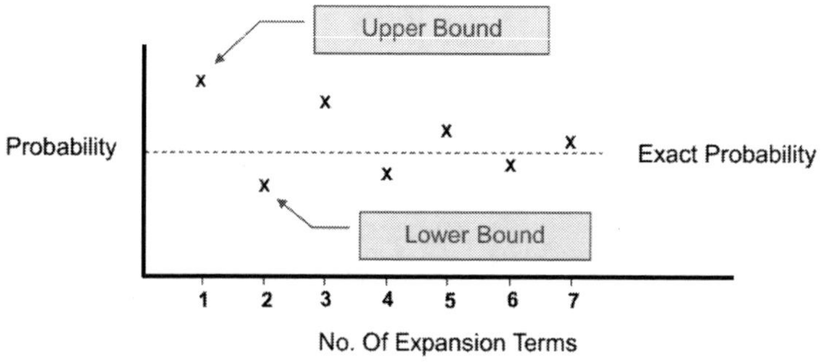

160

Min Cut Set Upper Bound Approximation

$$P = 1 - [(1 - P_{CS1})(1 - P_{CS2})(1 - P_{CS3}).....(1 - P_{CSN})]$$

CS{A; B}

$$\begin{aligned} P &= 1 - [(1 - P_A)(1 - P_B)] \\ &= 1 - [1 - P_B - P_A + P_A P_B] \\ &= 1 - 1 + P_B + P_A - P_A P_B \\ &= P_A + P_B - P_A P_B \end{aligned}$$

Equivalent to standard expansion

161

FT Quantification

Note: AND gate reduces probability

$P = P_A \bullet P_B \bullet P_C \bullet P_D$

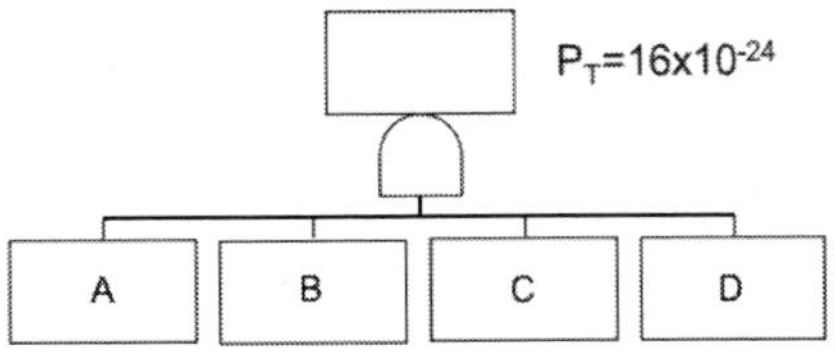

$P_A=2x10^{-6}$ $P_B=2x10^{-6}$ $P_C=2x10^{-6}$ $P_D=2x10^{-6}$

$P = P_A + P_B + P_C + P_D - (P_{AB} + P_{AC} + P_{AD} + P_{BC} + P_{BD} + P_{CD}) + (P_{ABC} + P_{ABD} + P_{ACD} + P_{BCD}) - (P_{ABCD})$

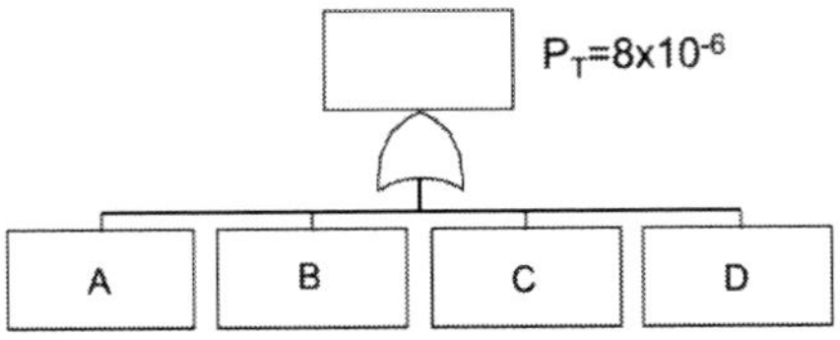

$P_A=2x10^{-6}$ $P_B=2x10^{-6}$ $P_C=2x10^{-6}$ $P_D=2x10^{-6}$

Note: OR gate increases probability and math complexity

162

FT Quantification

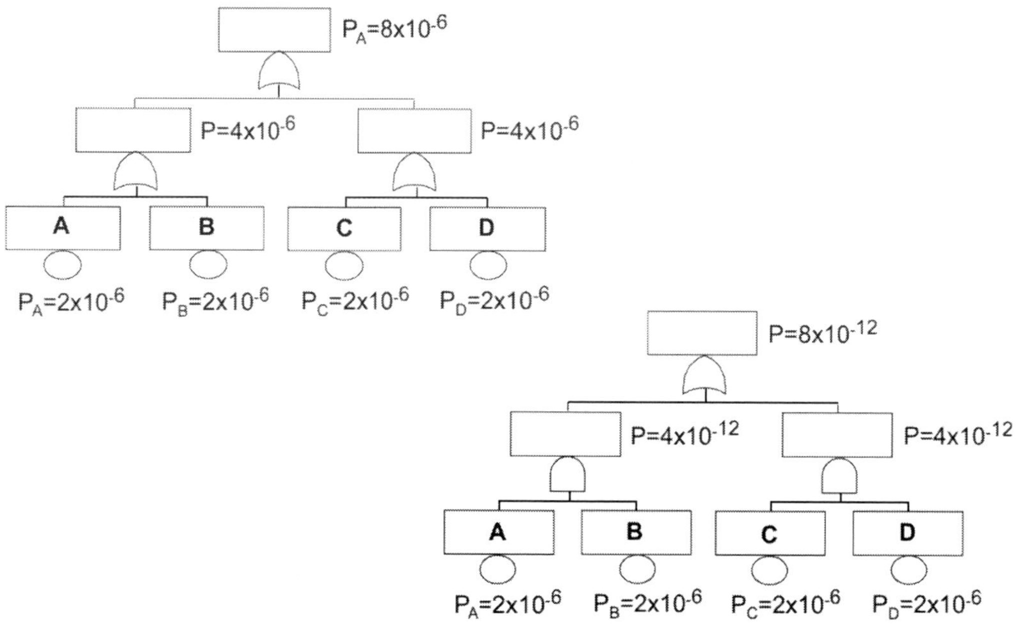

163

Axioms of Boolean Algebra

[A1]	$ab = ba$	Commutative Law
[A2]	$a + b = b + a$	
[A3]	$(a + b) + c = a + (b + c) = a + b + c$	Associative Law
[A4]	$(ab)c = a(bc) = abc$	
[A5]	$a(b+c) = ab + ac$	Distributive Law

164

Theorems of Boolean Algebra

[T1] $a + 0 = a$

[T2] $a + 1 = 1$

[T3] $a \bullet 0 = 0$

[T4] $a \bullet 1 = a$

[T5] $a \bullet a = a$ ✓

[T6] $a + a = a$ ✓ } Idempotent Law

[T7] $a \bullet \bar{a} = 0$

[T8] $a + \bar{a} = 1$

[T9] $a + ab = a$ ✓

[T10] $a(a + b) = a$ ✓ } Law of Absorption

[T11] $a + \bar{a}b = a + b$

where $\bar{a}$ = not a

165

Example

[T5] $a \bullet a = a$ ✓

[T6] $a + a = a$ ✓ } Idempotent Law

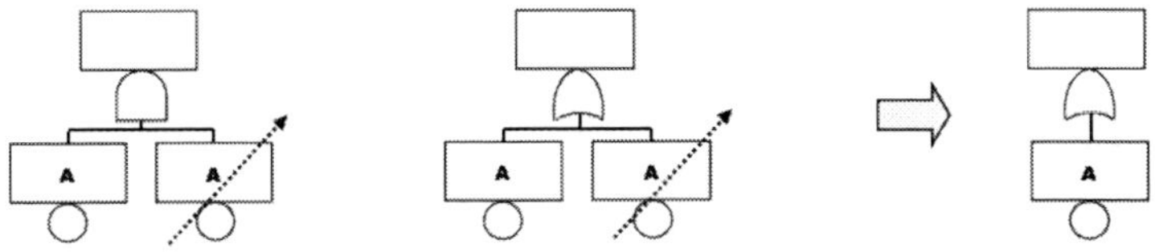

166

Example

[T9] a + ab = a ✓
[T10] a(a + b) = a ✓
} Law of Absorption

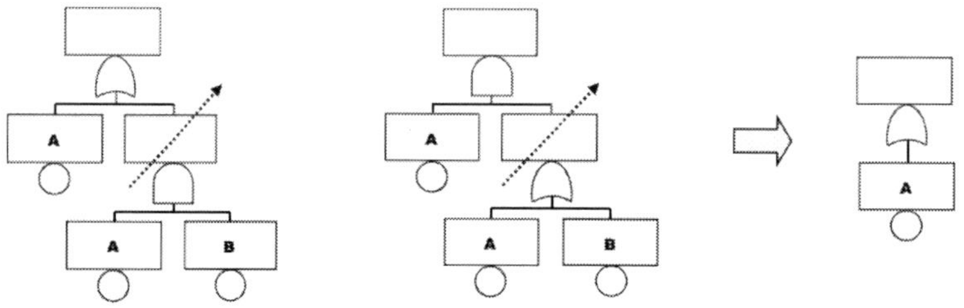

167

MOE Error Example 1

Incorrect

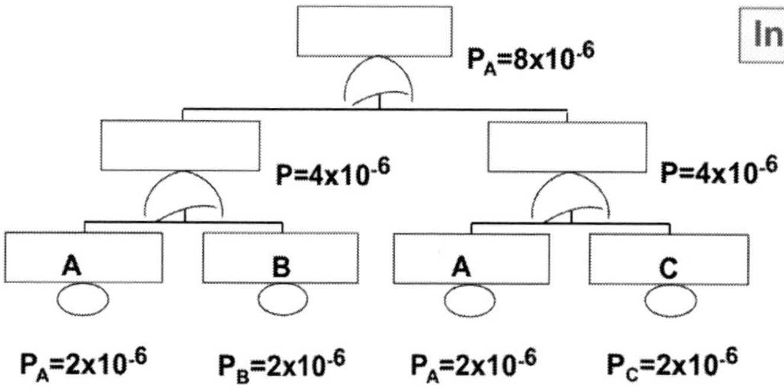

Correct

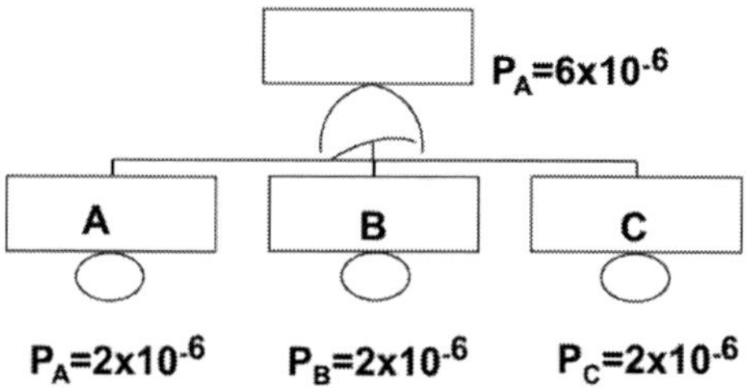

Cut Sets = A ; B ; C

P= $P_A + P_B + P_C$
= (2x10^{-6}) + (2x10^{-6}) + (2x10^{-6})
= 6x10-6 [upper bound]

168

MOE Error Example 2

Incorrect

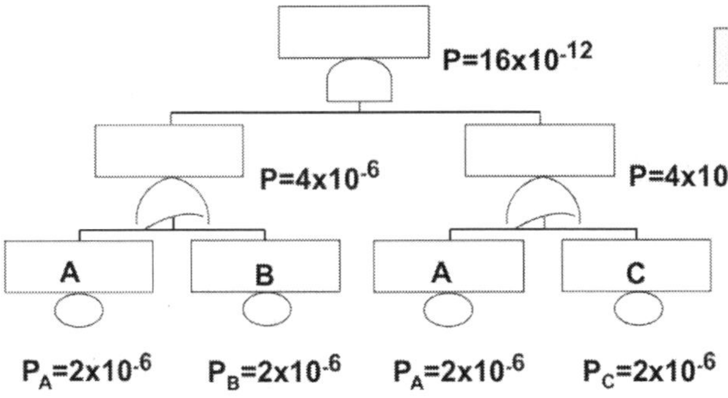

Correct

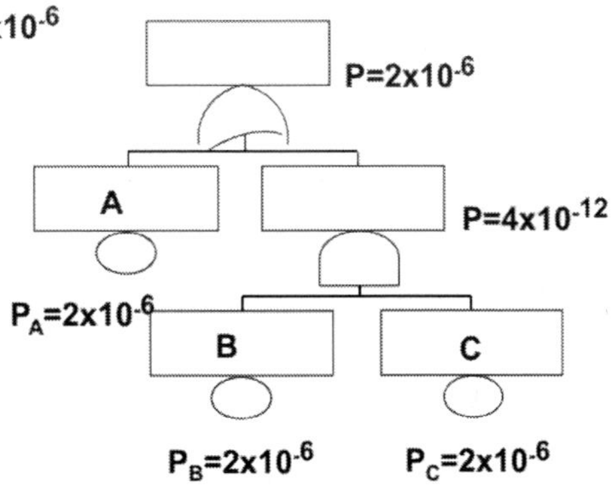

Cut Sets = A ; B,C

$P = P_A + P_B P_C$
$= (2x10^{-6}) + (2x10^{-6})(2x10^{-6})$
$= 2x10^{-6} + 4x10^{-12}$
= 2x10-6 [upper bound]

169

MOE Error Example 3

Incorrect but accidentally Correct

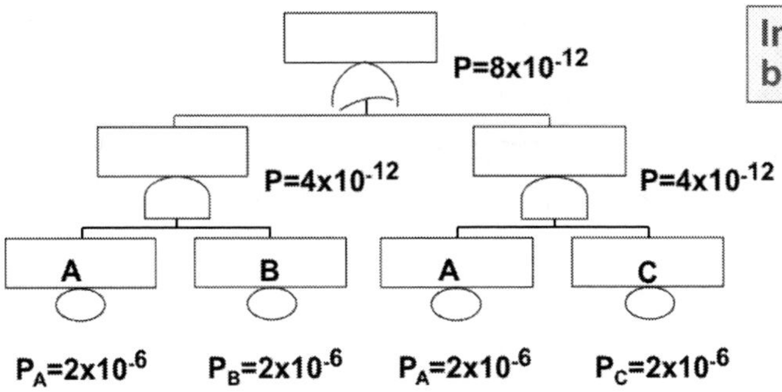

Correct

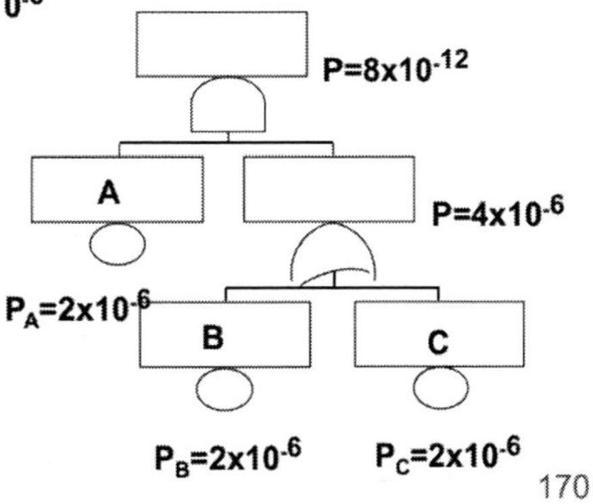

Cut Sets = A,B ; A,C

$P = P_A P_B + P_A P_C$
$= (2x10^{-6})(2x10^{-6}) + (2x10^{-6})(2x10^{-6})$
$= 4x10^{-12} + 4x10^{-12}$
= 8x10-12 [upper bound]

170

--- FT Evaluation ---

Purpose

- Obtaining the results and conclusions from the FT
- Using the FT for its intended purpose
  - Identify root causes of UE
  - Identify critical components and paths
  - Evaluate probabilistic risk
- Using the FT to impact design
  - Identify weak links
  - Evaluate impact of changes
  - Decision making

Evaluation Types

- Qualitative
  - Cut Sets
- Quantitative
  - Cut Sets
  - Probability
  - Importance Measures

171

Methods For Finding Min CS

- Boolean reduction
- Bottom up reduction algorithms
  - MICSUP (Minimal Cut Sets Upward) algorithm
- Top down reduction algorithms
  - MOCUS (Method of Obtaining Cut Sets) algorithm
- Binary Decision Diagram (BDD)
- Min Terms method (Shannon decomposition)
- Modularization methods
- Genetic algorithms

172

Evaluation Trouble Makers

- Tree size
- Tree Complexity
  - Redundancy (MOEs and MOBs)
  - Large quantity of AND/OR combinations
- Exotic gates and Not logic gates
- Computer limitations
  - Speed
  - Memory size
  - Software language
- Combination of any of the above

Solutions: 1) Prune FT, 2) Truncate FT or 3) FT Simulation

173

CS Truncation

- Reduces number of CS's when tree is too large or complex
- Order Truncation
  - Throw away all CS's having more elements than order N_{CO}
  - Example – if N_{CO} is 3, then CS{A, B, C, D} would be dropped
- Probability Truncation
  - Throw away all CS's having probability smaller than P_{CP}
  - Example – if P_{CP} is 1.0×10^{-6}, then CS(1.0×10^{-7}) would be dropped

174

Potential CS Truncation Errors

- With Probability truncation
  - Could discard a SPF event if the probability is below the CO
- With Order Truncation
  - Could discard a significant MinCS if all the elements have a high probability
  - If algorithm used does not completely resolve CS before discarding, could miss a MOE reduction
- With either Truncation method
  - Discarded CS's are not included in the final probability
  - Must make sure the error is insignificant; accuracy is sacrificed
  - Circumvents any Common Cause analysis of AND gates

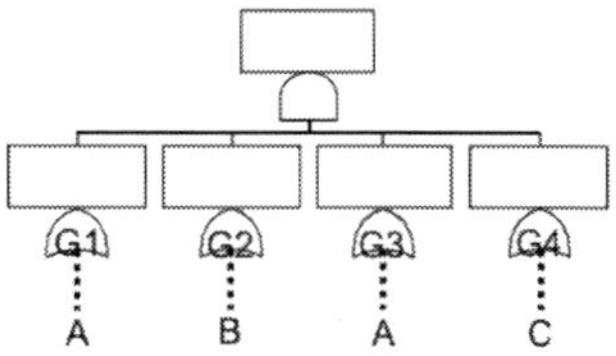

Do not truncate at gate level

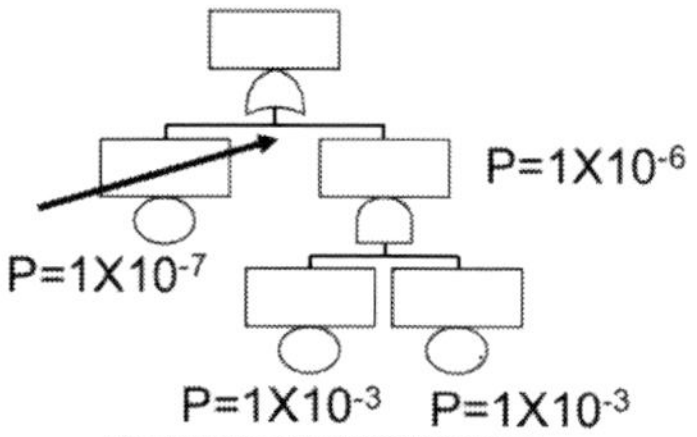

Watch for SPFs

175

Min CS

- A CS with the minimum number of events that can still cause the top event
- The true list of CS's contributing to the Top
- The final CS list after removing all SCS and DupCS
- Additional CS's are often generated, beyond the MinCS's
  - Super Cut Sets (SCS) – result from MOE's
  - Duplicate Cut Sets (DupCS) - result from MOE's or AND/OR combinations
- Why eliminate SCS and DupCS?
  - Laws of Boolean algebra
  - Would make the overall tree probability slightly larger (erroneous but conservative)

176

Min CS

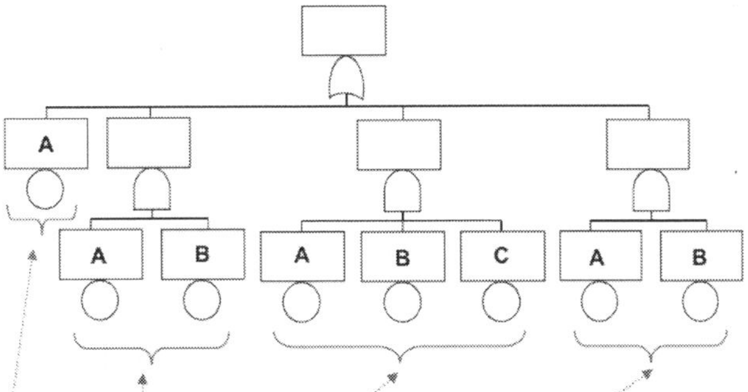

Cut Sets:
A
A,B ← **SCS**
A,B,C ← **SCS**
A,B ← **DupCS, SCS**

⇨ Min Cut Sets:
A

177

MOCUS Algorithm

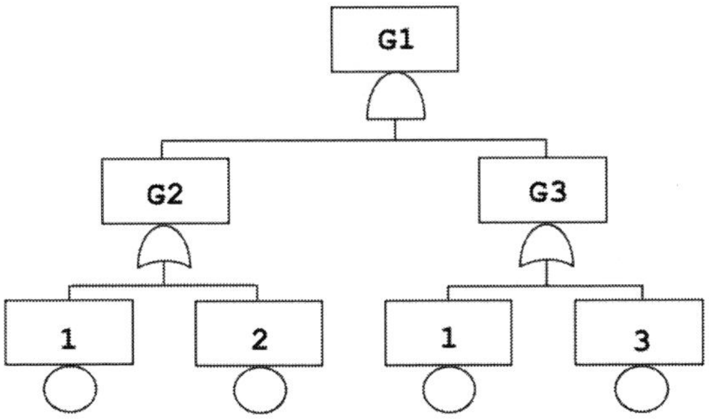

1	2	3	4	5	6
G1	G2,G3	1, G3	1, 1	1	1
			1, 3	1, 3	
		2, G3	2, 1	1, 2	
			2, 3	2, 3	2, 3

1	2	3	4	5	6
~~G1~~	~~G2~~,G3	1, ~~G3~~	1, ~~1~~	1	1
			1, 3	~~1, 3~~	
		2, ~~G3~~	2, 1	~~1, 2~~	
			2, 3	2, 3	2, 3

SuperCS   MinCS

MOCUS - Method of Obtaining Cut Sets

178

Are these two FTs equal?

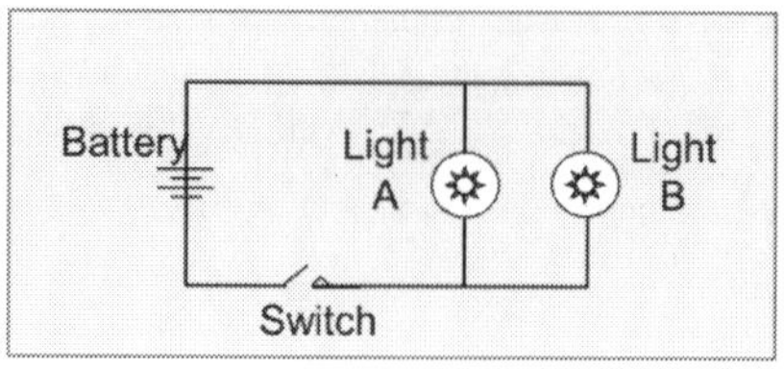

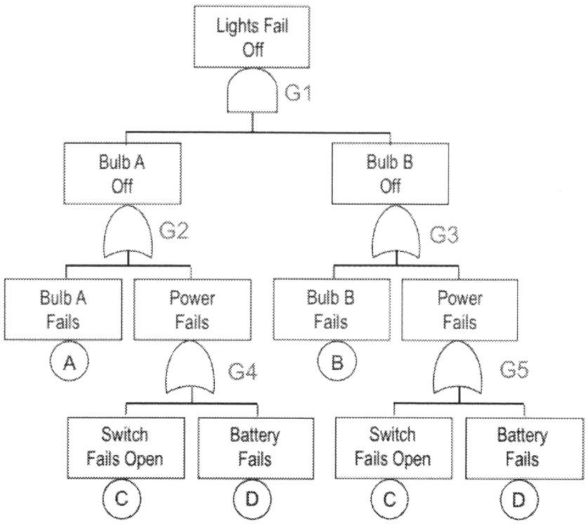

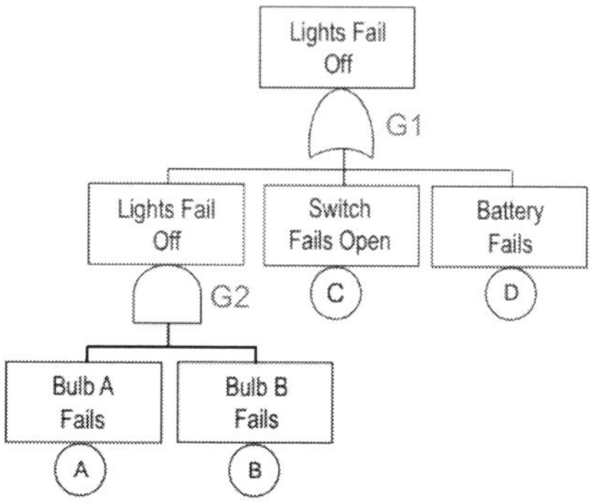

G1=G2 • G3
G1=(A+G4) • G3
G1=(A+C+D) • G3
G1=(A+C+D) • (B+G5) = (A+C+D) • (B+C+D)
G1=AB+AC+AD+CB+CC+CD+DB+DC+DD
G1=AB+AC+AD+CB+C+CD+DB+DC+D
G1=AB+C+D

G1=G2 + C + D
G1=AB+C+D

179

Evaluation Example

Top Down Approach (MOCUS)

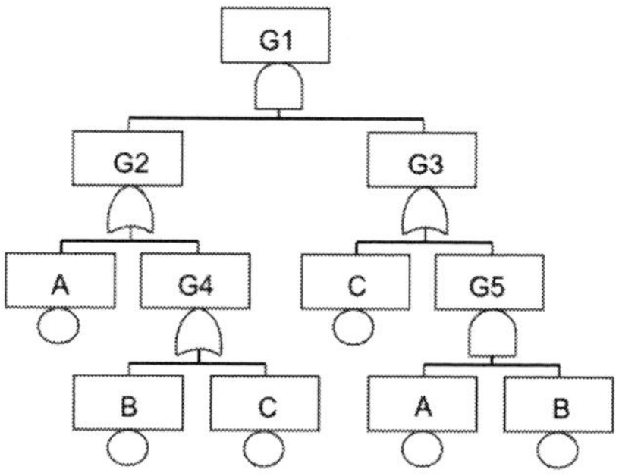

G1=G2 • G3 → C, G5 → AB; C+AB

A • G3
G4 • G3

B • G3
C • G3

G1=AB+AC

A • (C+AB) = AC +AAB = AC + AB
B • (C+AB) = BC +BAB = BC + AB
C • (C+AB) = CC +CAB = C + ABC

√ √ √ √
AC+AB + BC + AB + C + ABC

C + AB

180

Evaluation Example

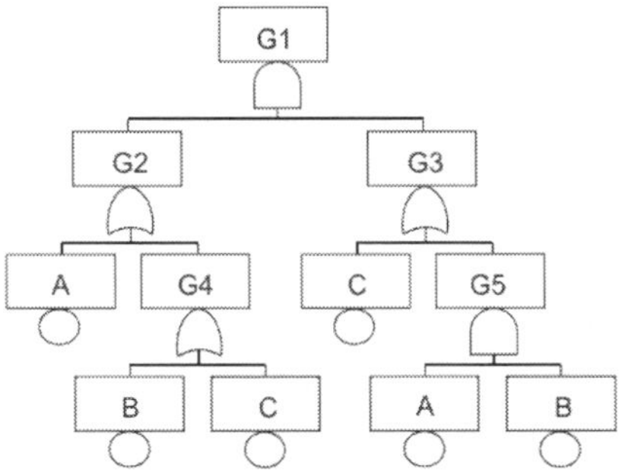

Bottom Up Approach

$G5 = A,B$

$G3 = C + G5 = C + A,B$

$G4 = B + C$

$G2 = A + G4 = A + B + C$

$G1 = G2 \bullet G3$

$= (A + B + C)\ (C + A,B)$

$= A,C + A,A,B + B,C + B,A,B + C,C + C,A,B$

$= A,C + A,B + B,C + A,B + C + A,B,C$

$= C + A,C + B,C + A,B + A,B,C$

$= \mathbf{C + A,B}$

181

Boolean Reductions

$a \bullet a = a$

$a + a = a$

Idempotent Law

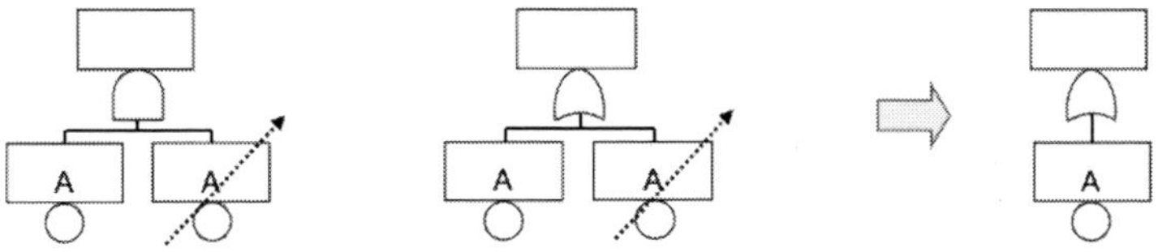

$a + ab = a$

$a(a + b) = a$

Law of Absorption

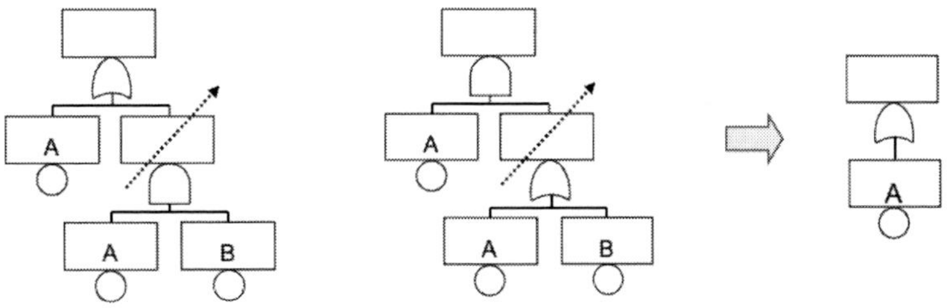

182

MOE Reduction

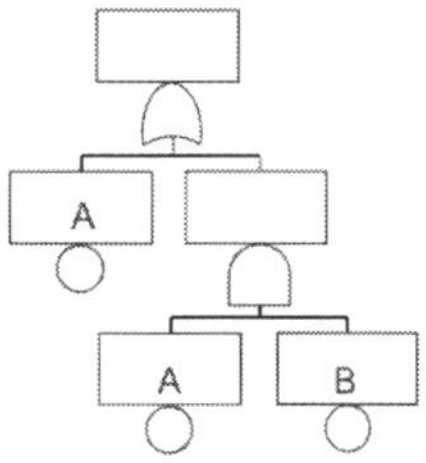

[1] A
[2] A,B

[1] A

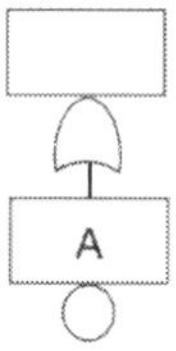

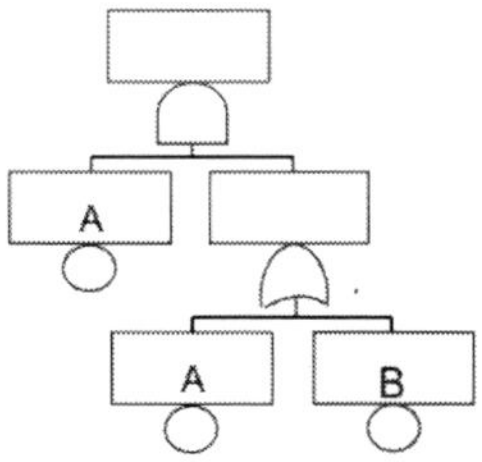

[1] A,A
[2] A,B

[1] A

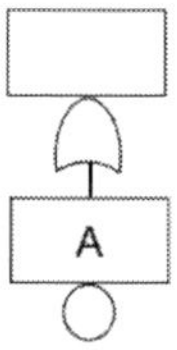

183

MOE Reduction

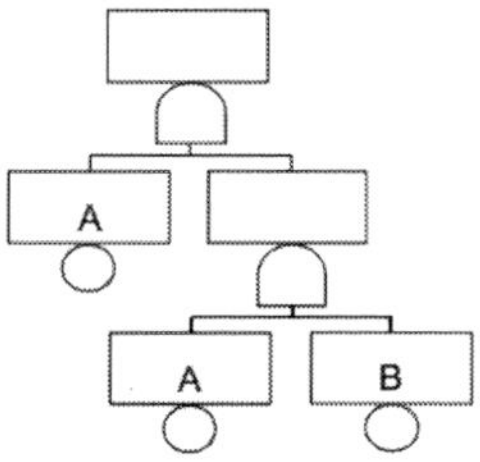

[1] A,A,B

[1] A,B

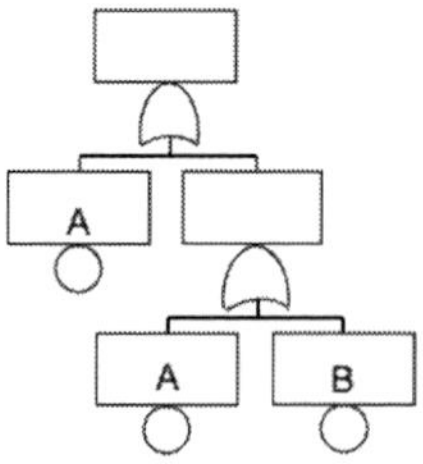

[1] A
[2] A
[3] B

[1] A
[2] B

184

FT Approximations vs. Markov

- MA
  - Small models only
  - Good numerical accuracy
  - Model is difficult to follow
- FTA
  - Defined, structured and rigorous methodology
  - Easy to learn, perform and follow
  - Provides root causes
  - Displays cause-consequence relationships
  - Sufficient accuracy when approximations are used

FTA is often criticized as not being accurate enough.

185

Series System

Description
A system is comprised of two components A and B in series. System success requires that both must operate successfully at the same time. System failure occurs if either one or both fail.

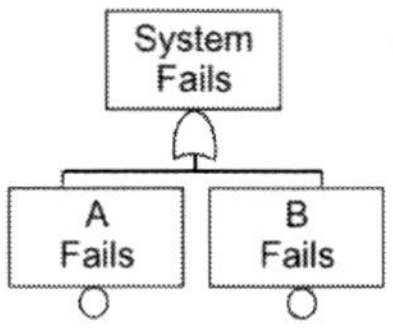

$$P = (1 - e^{-\lambda AT}) + (1 - e^{-\lambda BT}) - (1 - e^{-\lambda AT})(1 - e^{-\lambda BT})$$
$$= 1 - e^{-(\lambda A + -\lambda B)T}$$

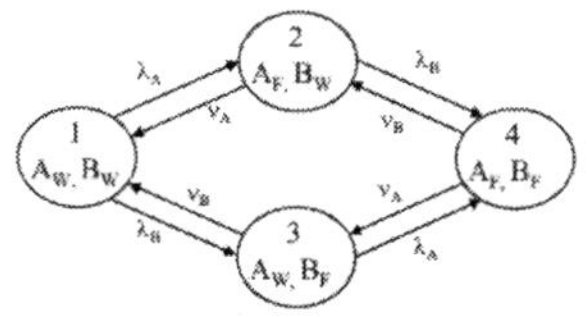

$$dP_1 / dt = -(\lambda_A + \lambda_B)P_1 + \nu_A P_2 + \nu_B P_3$$
$$dP_2 / dt = \lambda_A P_1 - (\lambda_A + \nu_A)P_2 + \nu_B P_4$$
$$dP_3 / dt = \lambda_B P_1 - (\lambda_A + \nu_A)P_3 + \nu_A P_4$$
$$dP_4 / dt = \lambda_B P_2 + \lambda_A P_3 - (\nu_A + \nu_B)P_4$$
$$P = P_2 + P_3 + P_4$$
$$P = (1 - e^{-\lambda AT}) + (1 - e^{-\lambda BT}) - (1 - e^{-\lambda AT})(1 - e^{-\lambda BT})$$
$$= 1 - e^{-(\lambda A + -\lambda B)T}$$

Conclusion
Both methods produce the same results (for non-repair case).

186

Parallel System

Description

A system is comprised of two components A and B in parallel. System success requires that either one (or both) must operate successfully. System failure occurs only if both are failed at the same time.

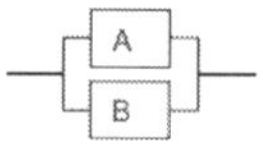

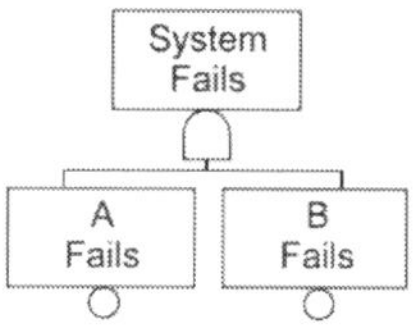

$$P = (1 - e^{-\lambda AT})(1 - e^{-\lambda BT})$$

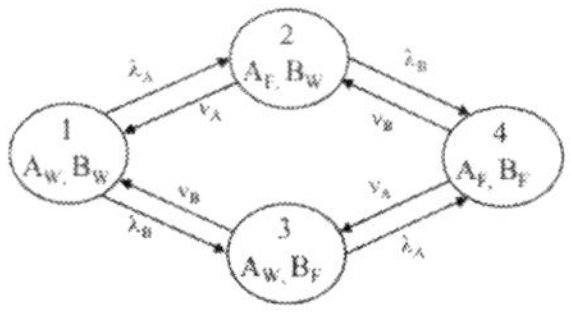

$$dP_1 / dt = - (\lambda_A + \lambda_B)P_1 + \nu_A P_2 + \nu_B P_3$$
$$dP_2 / dt = \lambda_A P_1 - (\lambda_A + \nu_A)P_2 + \nu_B P_4$$
$$dP_3 / dt = \lambda_B P_1 - (\lambda_A + \nu_A)P_3 + \nu_A P_4$$
$$dP_4 / dt = \lambda_B P_2 + \lambda_A P_3 - (\nu_A + \nu_B)P_4$$
$$P = P_4$$
$$P = (1 - e^{-\lambda AT})(1 - e^{-\lambda BT})$$

Conclusion
Both methods produce the same results (for non-repair case).

187

Sequence Parallel System

Description

A system is comprised of two components A and B in parallel. System success requires that either one (or both) must operate successfully. System failure occurs if both fail, but only if A fails before B.

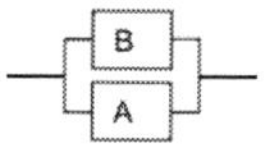

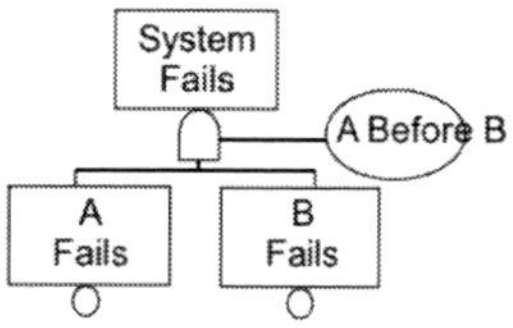

$$P = (P_A \bullet P_B) / N!$$
$$P = (P_A \bullet P_B) / 2$$
$$= ((1 - e^{-\lambda AT})(1 - e^{-\lambda BT})) / 2$$

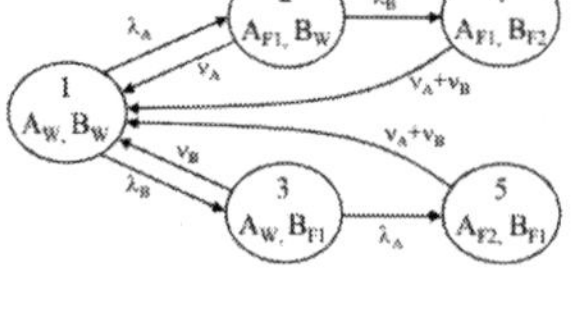

$$P = \frac{\lambda_A(1 - e^{-\lambda BT}) - \lambda_B(e^{-\lambda BT} - e^{-(\lambda A + \lambda B)T})}{\lambda_A + \lambda_B}$$

Conclusion
Each method produces a different equation, but results are comparable.

188

Sequence Parallel System

Comparison of Results for Sequence Parallel System
Where $\lambda_A=1.0\text{x}10^{-6}$ and $\lambda_B=1.0\text{x}10^{-7}$

Time (Hrs)	FTA	MA
1	5.00000E-14	5.00000E-14
10	4.99947E-12	4.99998E-12
100	4.99973E-10	4.99980E-10
1,000	4.99725E-8	4.99800E-8
10,000	4.97260E-6	4.98006E-6
100,000	4.73442E-4	4.80542E-4
1,000,000	3.00771E-2	3.45145E-2

Conclusion
Both methods produce different equations. However, for small numbers, the FTA result is a very close approximation.

189

--- FT Validation ---

Purpose

- Checking the FT for errors
- Verifying the FT is correct and accurate
- Checks to convince yourself that the tree is correct

Why

- Very easy to introduce errors into the FT
- FT misuse and abuse is very easy
- Helps to ensure the results are correct
- Helps to reassure the customer
- Helps to reassure management

Validation is probably one of most ignored steps in the FTA process

190

How Errors Are Introduced

- Analyst does not understand system
- Analyst does not fully understand FTA
- FTs can become very complex
  - Modeling a complex system design
  - FT understanding can decrease as FT size increases
- Communication errors between several FT analysts
- Errors in tree structure logic sometime occur (wrong gate selected)
- A MOE component is given the wrong name (it's not really a MOE)
- Computer evaluation codes are erroneous
- Computer evaluation codes are used incorrectly
- Incorrect (or out of date) system data is used
  - Failure rates, drawings, design data

191

Methods For Validating The FT

- **CS reality check**
- Probability reasonableness test
- Success tree inversion
- Gate check
- Review of failure data
- Peer review
- MOE check
- Intuition check
- Logic Loop check

192

--- FTA Audit ---

- Purpose – To verify and validate a contractual FTA product
- To evaluate an existing FT for:
  - Correctness
  - Completeness
  - Thoroughness
- To determine if the results from a FTA are valid
  - Determine if the FTA contains defects
  - Avoid making decisions on incorrect analysis results

193

Audit vs. Validation

- A FTA audit is similar to FT validation, but not the same
- FT Audit
  - Typically performed by independent reviewer after FTA is complete
  - Auditor may not have all detailed design information or knowledge
- FT Validation
  - Typically performed by the product developer
  - Analyst has detailed design information
- Validation items that can be used for audit
  - CS reality check
  - Probability reasonableness test
  - Gate check
  - Review of failure data
  - MOE check

194

Audit Guidelines

- Need a basic understanding of system design (optimally)
- Evaluate FT for each potential defect category
- Question everything
  - Check with SME if possible
- If something looks funny, it probably is
- Documents audit data and results

A FT auditor:
- Must understand FT construction thoroughly
- Must be a highly experienced FT analyst

195

Defect Categories

- Math
- Fault logic
- Failure data
- Evaluation methods
- Completeness
  - Anything omitted
- Analysis ground rules
  - Are rules established and followed?
  - Rules on SW, HSI, CCF, exposure time, depth of analysis
- Diagramming
  - Symbol use
  - Aesthetics

196

FTA Error/Defect Levels

Error	Consequence
■ High	Erroneous top probability
■ Medium	Insufficient Info; not sure if results are incorrect
■ Low	Poor FT diagram, however, results are likely correct

197

High Consequence Errors

- Gate logic error
  - AND vs. OR, logic does not correctly model system design, etc.
  - House event into an OR gate
- Omitting necessary design detail
  - Subsystems
  - Human error, SW, HSI interface design
- Cut set errors
  - Incorrect, missing, contradicting
- Mathematical errors
  - MOE resolution error, calculation error, normalizing error
- Input data errors
  - Incorrect failure rate or time
- Common FT pitfall type errors
  - Extrapolation, dependency, truncation, mutual exclusion, latency, CCF

198

Medium Consequence Errors

- Inadequate information errors
  - Missing text description (e.g., "Resistor fails" – open, short, tolerance?)
  - Vague text description (e.g., "Spring way too strong")
- Missing information
  - Blank text boxes
  - Missing text boxes
- Jumping ahead in system fault path
  - Skipping fault logic steps
- Manipulations used to obtain favorable probability results
- Failure data
  - No reference sources
  - Failure rates are questionable (reasonable?)

199

Low Consequence Errors

- Violation of common FT rules
  - Gate to gate
  - Multiple outputs (double connects)
  - No text in boxes
  - Inputs/outputs on side of box (vice top/bottom)
  - Incorrect symbol usage
- FT Sloppiness
  - Messy diagram
  - Unreadable text (hand drawn)
  - Too small to read

200

Audit Checklist

- Do CSs make sense and do they cause UE
- Are all of the CSs minimal
- Are any CSs mutually exclusive
- Is the Probability reasonable (based on data and experience)
- Do Gates appear correct
- Is failure data reasonable
- Are MOEs and MOBs correct
- Does FT diagram follow basic rules
- Do all nodes have text boxes with words
- Does wording in text boxes make sense
- Does the overall fault logic seem reasonable
- Is the math correct
- Has latency been considered
- Has common cause been considered
- Has human error been considered
- Are the component exposure times correct

201

Audit Example #1

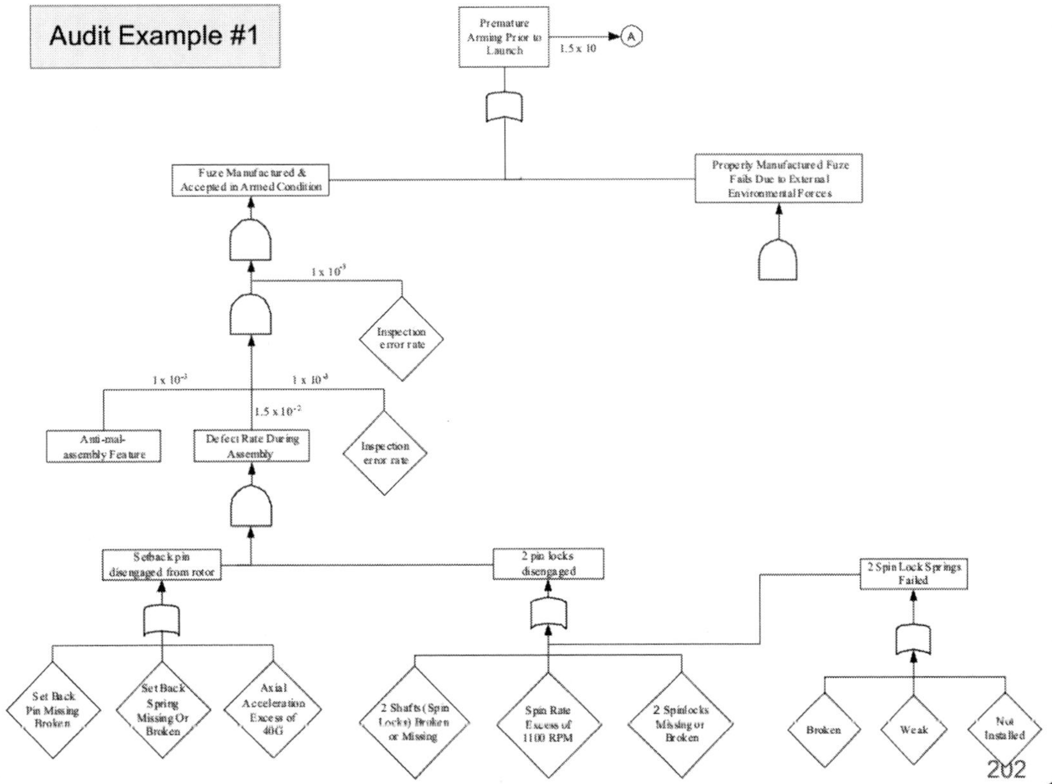

202

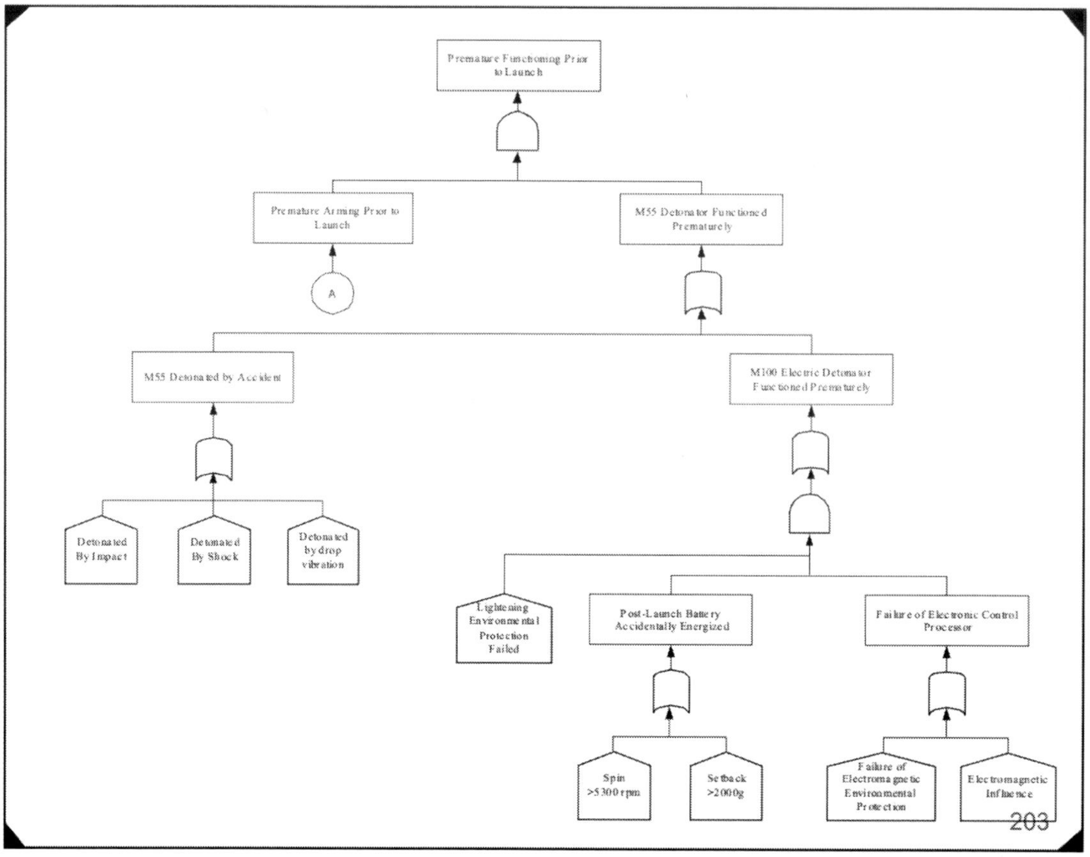
Premature Functioning Prior to Launch
Premature Arming Prior to Launch
M55 Detonator Functioned Prematurely
A
M55 Detonated by Accident
M100 Electric Detonator Functioned Prematurely
Detonated By Impact
Detonated By Shock
Detonated by drop vibration
Lightening Environmental Protection Failed
Post-Launch Battery Accidentally Energized
Failure of Electronic Control Processor
Spin >5300 rpm
Setback >2000g
Failure of Electromagnetic Environmental Protection
Electromagnetic Influence
203

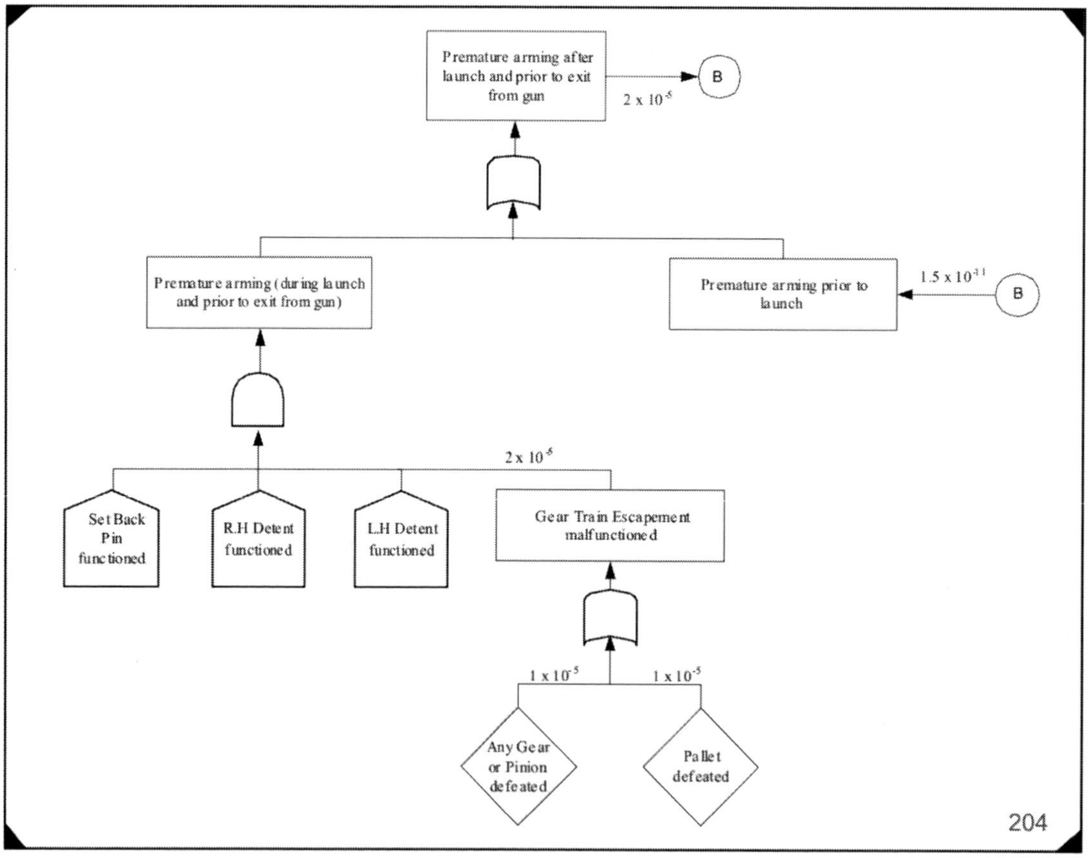
Premature arming after launch and prior to exit from gun
2 x 10-5
B
Premature arming (during launch and prior to exit from gun)
Premature arming prior to launch
1.5 x 10-11
B
2 x 10-5
Set Back Pin functioned
R.H Detent functioned
L.H Detent functioned
Gear Train Escapement malfunctioned
1 x 10-5
1 x 10-5
Any Gear or Pinion defeated
Pallet defeated
204

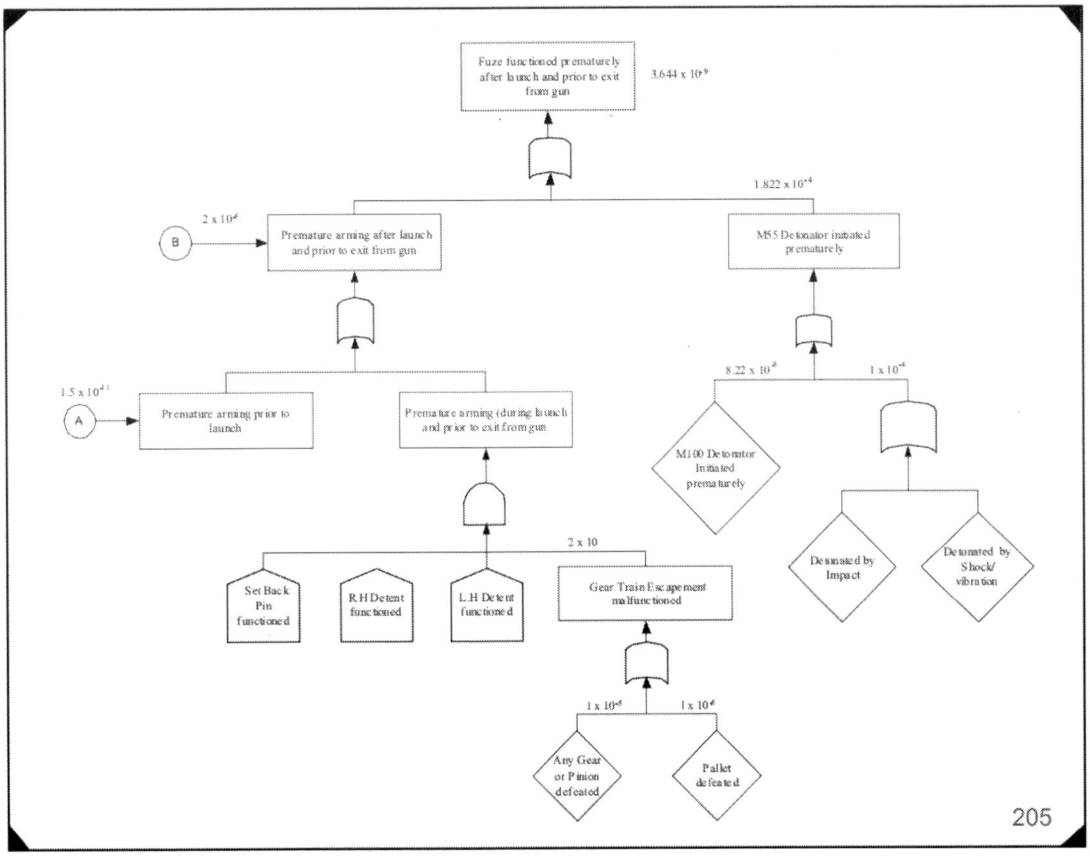
Fuze functioned prematurely after launch and prior to exit from gun
3.644×10^{-9}
1.822×10^{-4}
2×10^{-6}
B
Premature arming after launch and prior to exit from gun
M55 Detonator initiated prematurely
1.5×10^{-11}
A
Premature arming prior to launch
Premature arming (during launch and prior to exit from gun
8.22×10^{-5}
1×10^{-4}
M100 Detonator Initiated prematurely
2 x 10
Set Back Pin functioned
R.H Detent functioned
L.H Detent functioned
Gear Train Escapement malfunctioned
Detonated by Impact
Detonated by Shock/ vibration
1×10^{-5}
1×10^{-6}
Any Gear or Pinion defeated
Pallet defeated
205

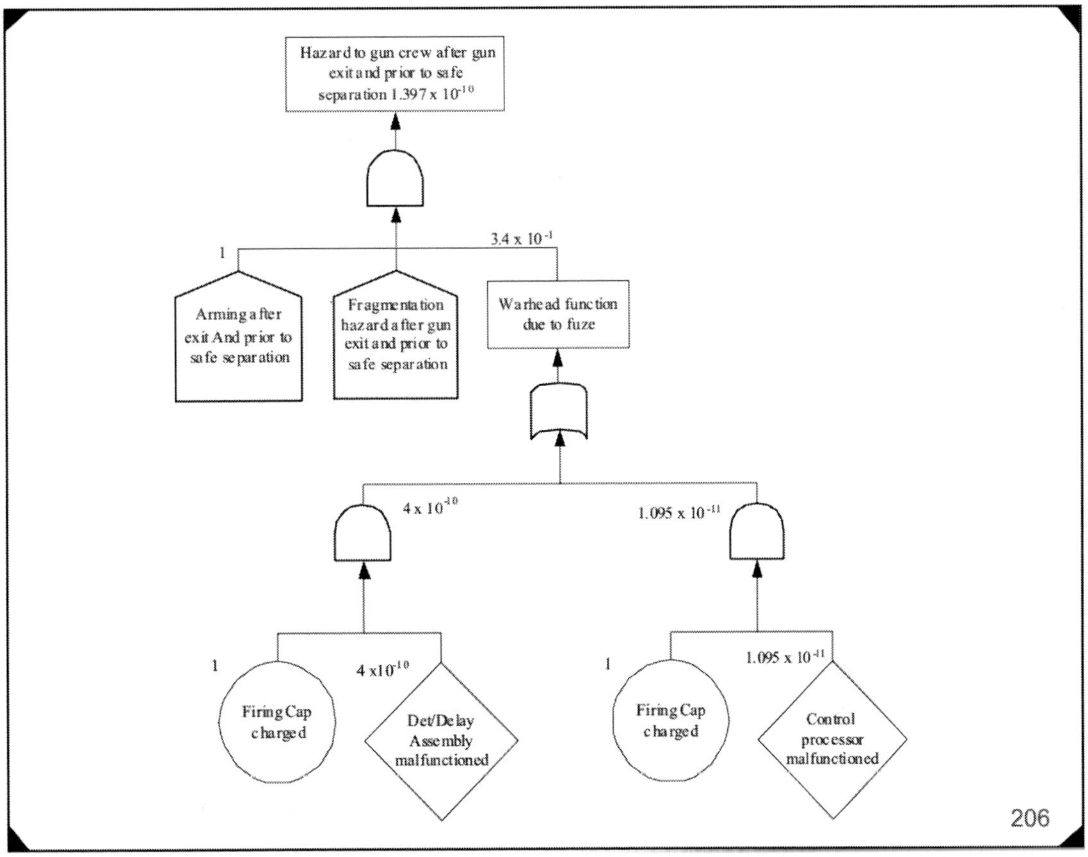
Hazard to gun crew after gun exit and prior to safe separation 1.397×10^{-10}
1
3.4×10^{-1}
Arming after exit And prior to safe separation
Fragmentation hazard after gun exit and prior to safe separation
Warhead function due to fuze
4×10^{-10}
1.095×10^{-11}
1
4×10^{-10}
Firing Cap charged
Det/Delay Assembly malfunctioned
1
1.095×10^{-11}
Firing Cap charged
Control processor malfunctioned
206

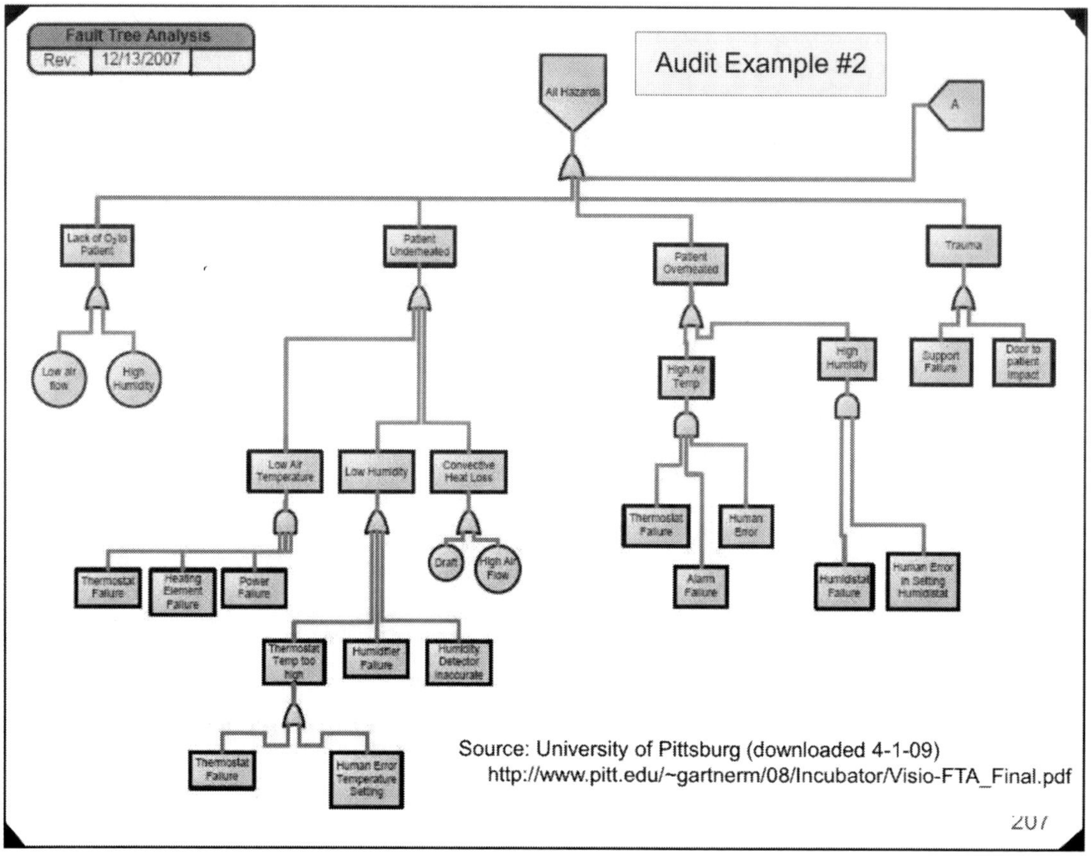
Fault Tree Analysis
Rev: 12/13/2007
Audit Example #2
All Hazards
A
Lack of O2 to Patient
Low air flow
High Humidity
Patient Underheated
Low Air Temperature
Thermostat Failure
Heating Element Failure
Power Failure
Low Humidity
Thermostat Temp too high
Thermostat Failure
Human Error Temperature Setting
Humidifier Failure
Humidity Detector Inaccurate
Convective Heat Loss
Draft
High Air Flow
Patient Overheated
High Air Temp
Thermostat Failure
Alarm Failure
Human Error
High Humidity
Humidistat Failure
Human Error in Setting Humidistat
Trauma
Support Failure
Door to patient impact
Source: University of Pittsburg (downloaded 4-1-09)
http://www.pitt.edu/~gartnerm/08/Incubator/Visio-FTA_Final.pdf
207

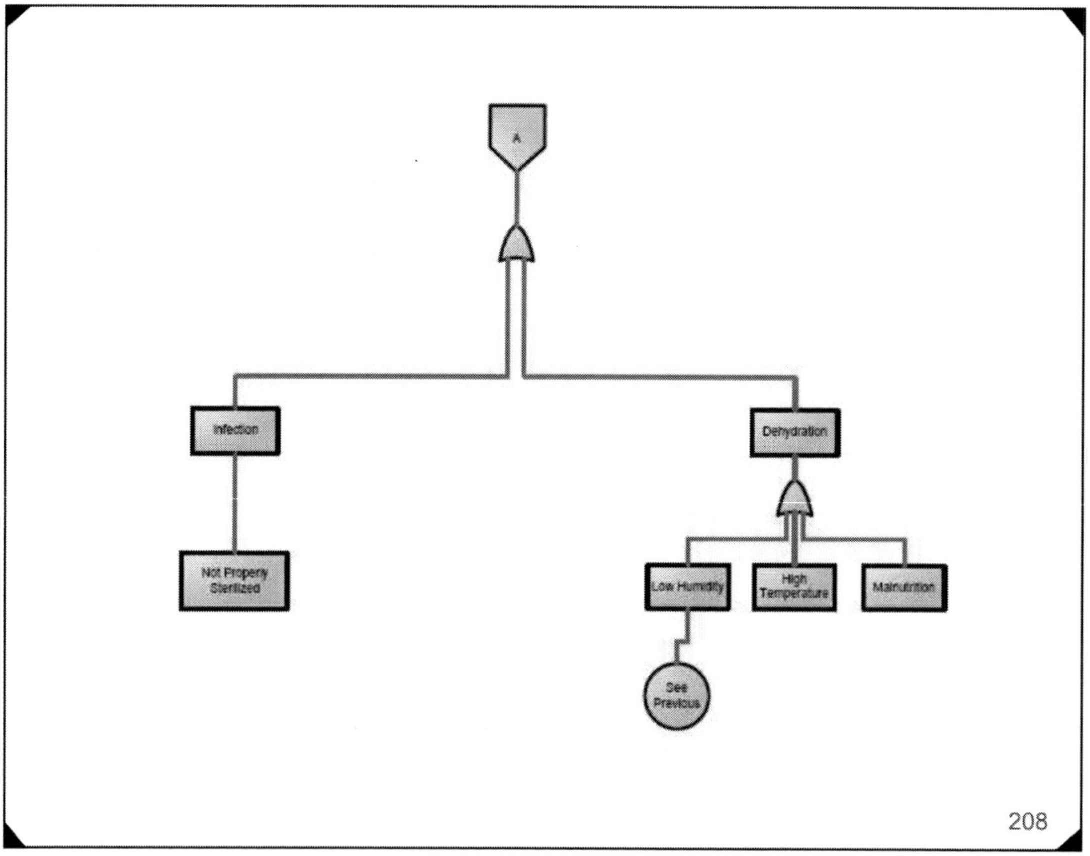
A
Infection
Not Properly Sterilized
Dehydration
Low Humidity
See Previous
High Temperature
Malnutrition
208

Audit Example #3

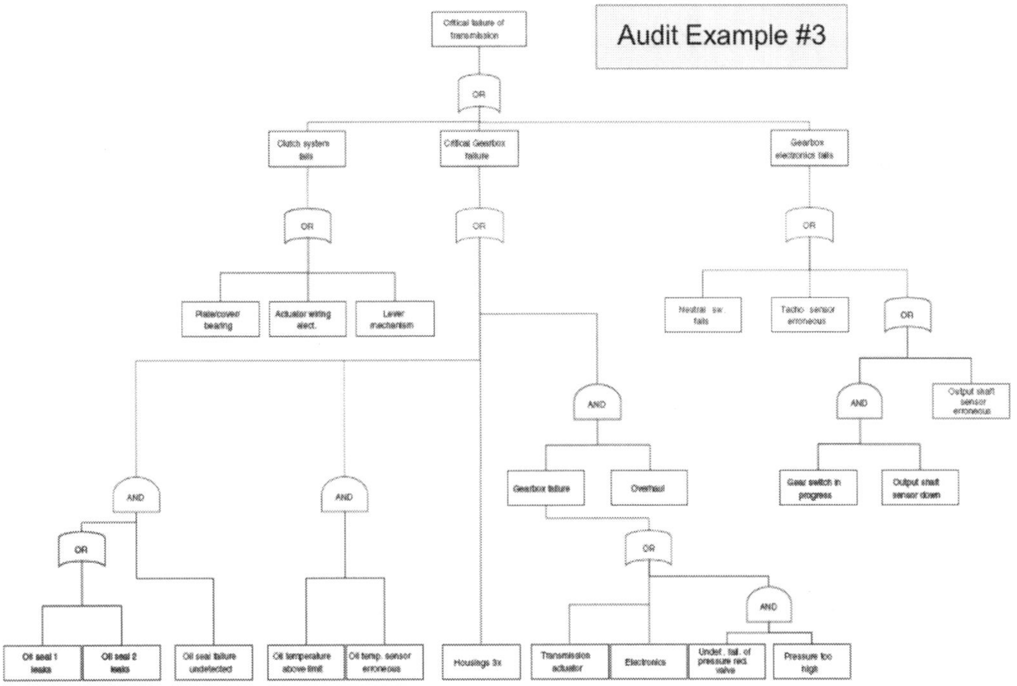

Fig. 2 Early design stage fault tree of an automatic transmission

Sources: Modelling Uncertainty In Fault Tree Analyses Using Evidence Theory, Proc. IMechE Vol. 222 Part O: Journal Risk and Reliability, 2008.

209

Audit Guidance

- If you have received a FTA from a contractor or supplier, it's important to obtain an independent audit of the analysis
  - Ensure the probabilities you are basing decisions on are correct
  - Require a written audit report
- Check for three defect categories
  - High, Medium and Low
- Any defects in the High category mean the FT is incorrect

210

--- Misc FTA Aspects ---

Latency

- Latency refers to a latent component failure, which is a component could be failed for some time without knowledge.
- A Latent component is a component that is not checked for operability before the start of a mission. Thus, it could already be failed at the start of the mission.
- This effectively increases the component exposure time. The latent time period is the time between checks (ie, Maintenance), which can often be significantly greater than the mission time. This large exposure time can make a large impact on the probability.

211

Latency

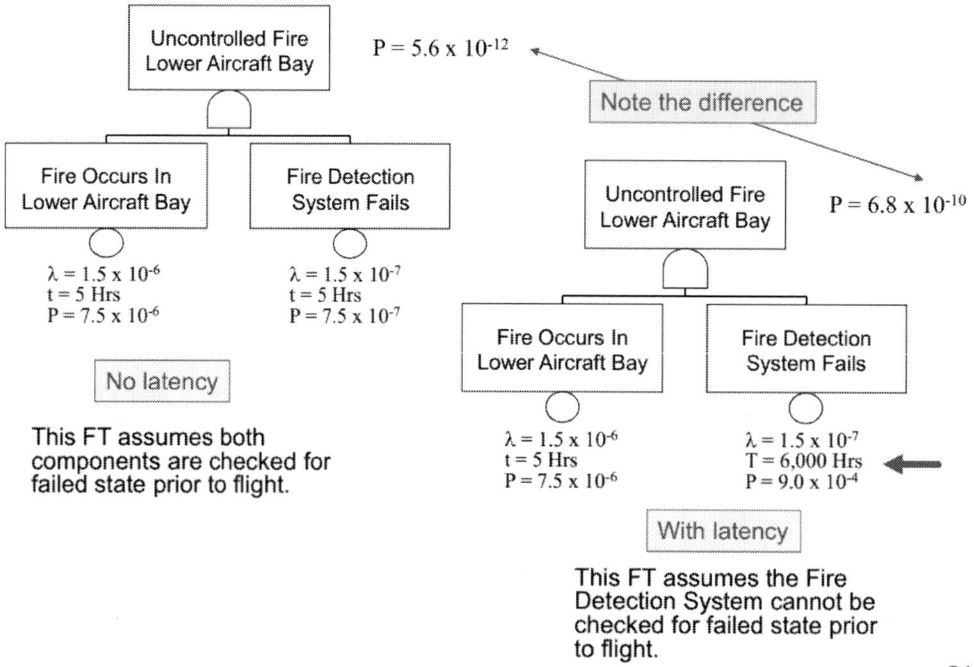

212

CCF

- A Common Cause Failure (CCF) is a single point failure (SPF) that negates independent redundant designs
- Typical CCF sources
  - Common weakness in design redundancy
    - Example – close proximity of hydraulic lines
  - The use of identical components in multiple subsystems
  - Common software design
  - Common manufacturing errors
  - Common requirements errors
  - Common production process errors
  - Common maintenance errors
  - Common installation errors
  - Common environmental factor vulnerabilities

213

CCF

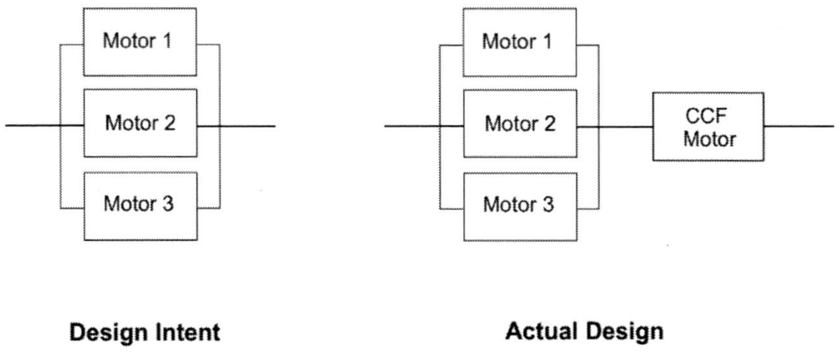

214

CCF Examples

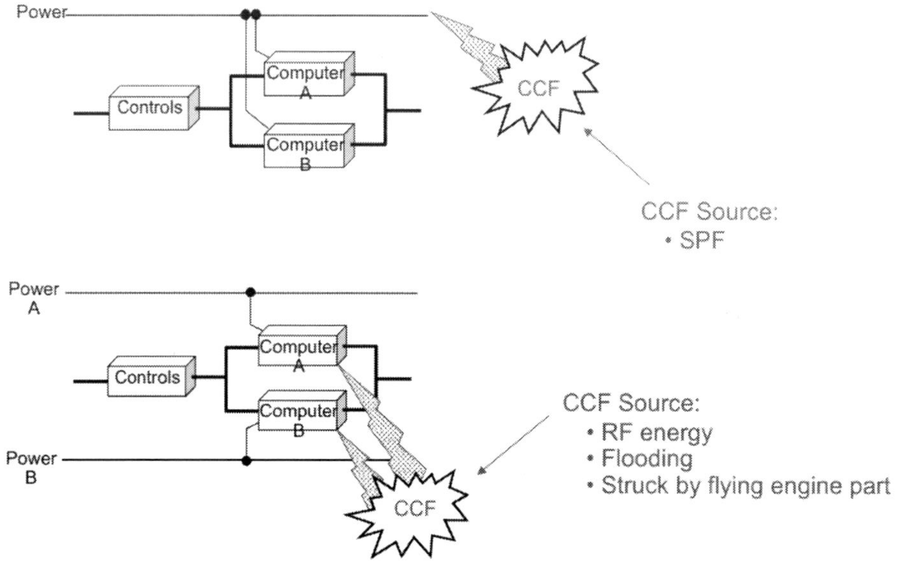

215

Example CCF FTA

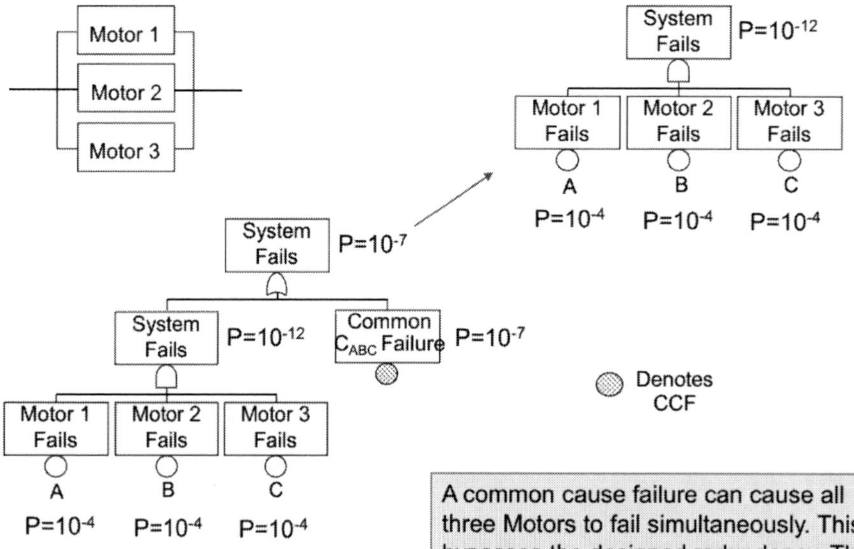

A common cause failure can cause all three Motors to fail simultaneously. This bypasses the designed redundancy. The probability of P_{ABC} is the critical factor.

216

Example CCF FTA

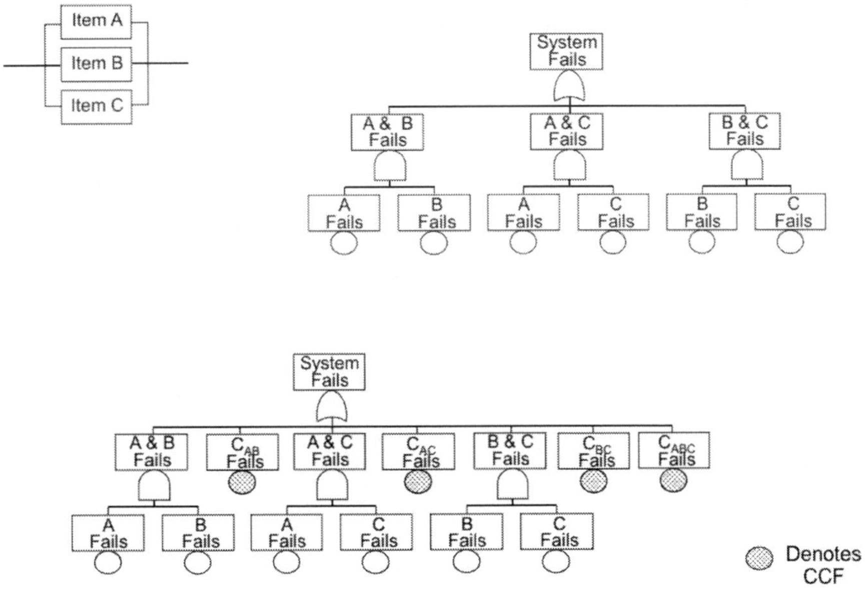

217

Interlocks

- An interlock is usually designed into a system for one of two purposes:
  - To help prevent the inadvertent operation of a critical function
  - To stop the operation of a hazardous operation or function before a mishap occurs
- A safety interlock is a single device that is part of a larger system function; only necessary for safety, not functionality
- Its purpose is to prevent the overall system function from being performed until a specified set of safety parameters are satisfied.
- An interlock can be implemented in either hardware or software

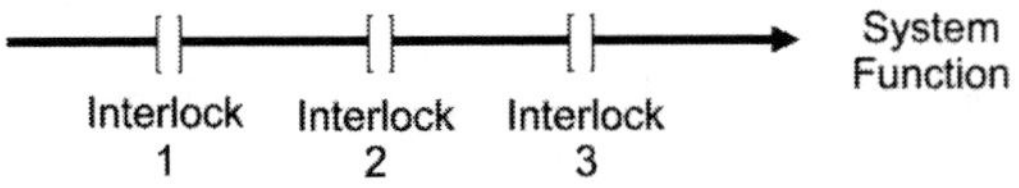

218

Interlock Example

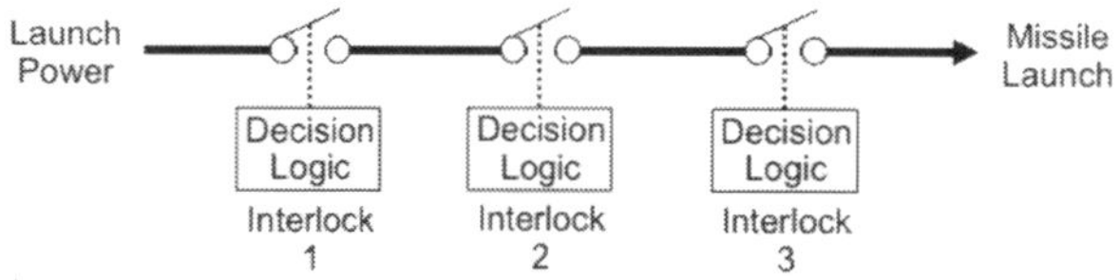

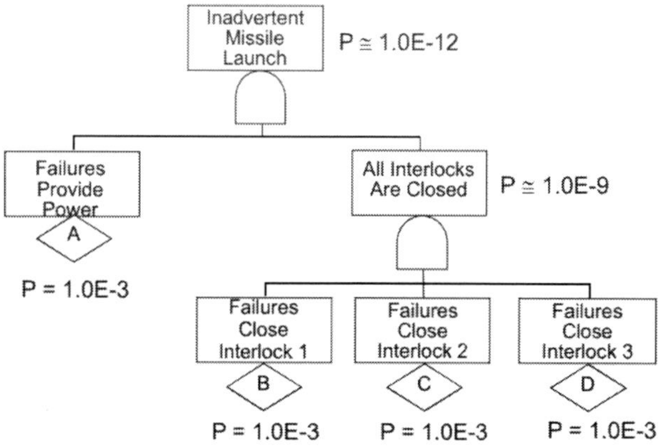

Number of Interlocks	Top Probability
0	P ≅ 1E-3
1	P ≅ 1E-6
2	P ≅ 1E-9
3	P ≅ 1E-12

219

Dependency

- An Independent event is an event that <u>is not</u> influenced or caused by another event
- A Dependent event is an event that <u>is</u> influenced or caused by another event
- Dependencies complicate FT math considerably
  - Conditional probability
  - Requires Markov analysis for accuracy
  - However, FT approximations are quite accurate
- Sometimes dependencies are difficult to identify
  - A Secondary failure may or may not be the cause of a dependent failure
  - If A causes B, then in this case Prob(B/A) should be more likely than independent Prob(B)
  - Secondary RF energy may cause a transistor to fail, but they are "typically" considered independent (the approximation is accurate enough)

220

Dependency vs. Independency

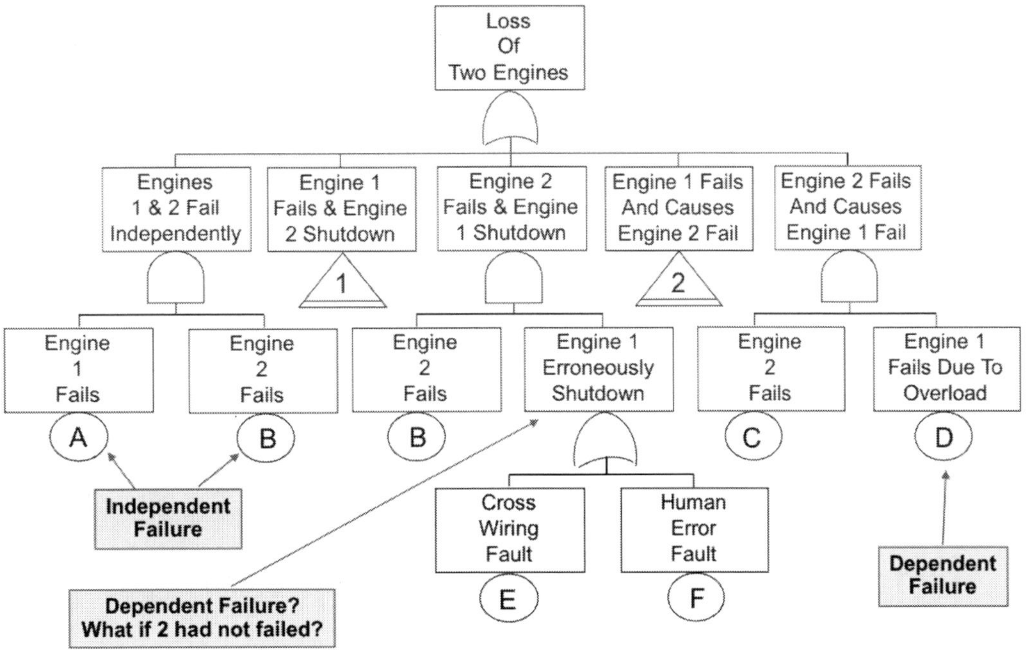

221

RTCA DO-178B

- Software level is based upon the contribution of software to potential failure conditions as determined by the system safety assessment process (SSAP).
- The software level implies that the level of effort required to show compliance with certification requirements varies with the failure condition category.

Level	Definition
A	Software whose anomalous behavior, as shown by the SSAP, would cause or contribute to a failure of system function resulting in a catastrophic failure condition for the aircraft
B	Software whose anomalous behavior, as shown by the SSAP, would cause or contribute to a failure of system function resulting in a hazardous/severe-major failure condition of the aircraft
C	Software whose anomalous behavior, as shown by the SSAP, would cause or contribute to a failure of system function resulting in a major failure condition for the aircraft
D	Software whose anomalous behavior, as shown by the SSAP, would cause or contribute to a failure of system function resulting in a minor failure condition for the aircraft
E	Software whose anomalous behavior, as shown by the SSAP, would cause or contribute to a failure of function with no effect on aircraft operational capability or pilot workload

222

FT for SIL Level

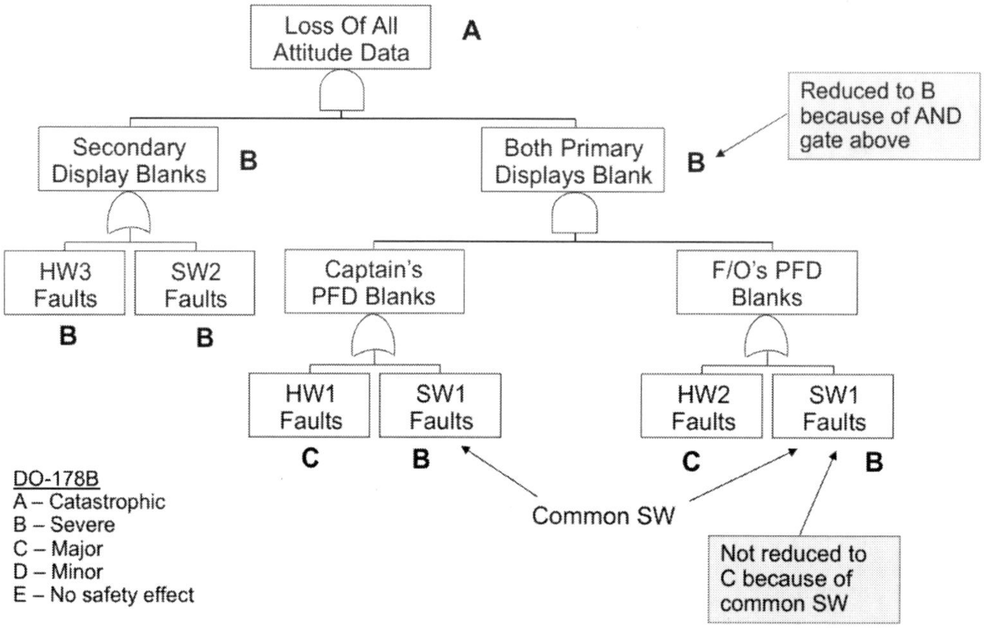

PFD=Primary Flight Display

223

--- FTA Software ---

Basic Tasks of FTA Software

- Construction
  - creating FT
  - editing FT
- Evaluation
  - cut sets
  - probability
  - importance measures
- Plotting / Printing
  - plotter
  - printer
- Reports
  - data
  - results

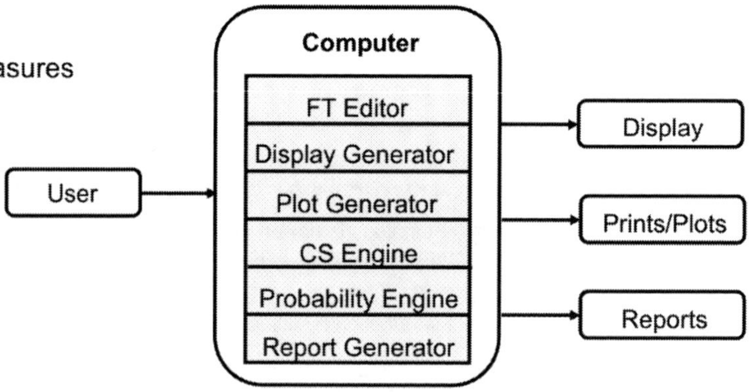

224

Properties of FT Software

	Required	Desired
• Construction (create, edit, copy, past)	X	
• Generate Min CS	X	
• Generate probabilities (top, gates)	X	
• Employ CS cutoff methods (order, probability)		X
• Numerical accuracy	X	
• Generate reports	X	
• Detect tree logic loops		X
• Data export capability (tree structure, failure data)		X
• Graphic export capability (BMP, JPG)		X
• Tree Pagination for prints	X	
• User select print size		X
• Program fit on a floppy disk		X
• Notes on FT print/plot		X
• Find feature		X
• Undo feature		X

225

Properties (continued)

	Required	Desired
• Employ MOEs / MOBs	X	
• Correctly resolve MOEs / MOBs	X	
• Global data change (failure rates, exposure time)		X
• Print/plot selected pages or all pages	X	
• Unrestricted FT tree size	X	
• Automatic naming of gates and events when created	X	
• Capability to resolve large complex FTs	X	
• User friendly (intuitive commands)	X	
• Print/plot results visually aesthetic		X
• Verification of mathematical methods and accuracy	X	
• Open data file structure	X	

226

Commercial FT Software

CAFTA	CAFTA sales 650-384-5693 (part of EPRI)
Fault Tree+	www.Isograph.com
Item	www.itemsoft.com
Relex	www.relexsoftware.com
FaulTrEase	http://www.chempute.com/faultrea.htm
Risk Spectrum FT	http://www.relcon.com
Shade Tree	http://www.qrainc.com
Tree-Master	http://www.mgtsciences.com
FTA Pro	http://www.dyadem.com
OpenFTA (free source)	http://www.openfta.com
Logan	http://www.arevarmc.com/logan-faulttreeanalysis.php
RAM Commander	http://www.aldservice.com
Saphire (free?)	https://saphire.inl.gov/faq.cfm

227

Purchase Considerations

- Many commercial FT codes are available -- some good and some ?
- Know FT tool limits and capabilities
  - Tree size, Cut set size, Print size, numerical accuracy
  - Easy to use (without tech support)
  - Single phase, multi-phase
- Understand algorithms
  - Some codes have errors in approximations and cutoff methods
  - Gate probability calculations must resolve MOEs correctly
- Test the tool; don't assume answers are always correct
- Consider
  - Price
  - Lease vs. Ownership
  - User flexibility – networks, stations, individuals
  - Maintenance
  - Lease / Buy
  - User friendliness
  - Training

228

Mission Calculation Errors

Example 1

- *Shortcut error (calculate for 1 hr, then multiple by 100 hrs for trade study)*

P≠(Prob of 1 Hr Mission) x (100 Hrs)

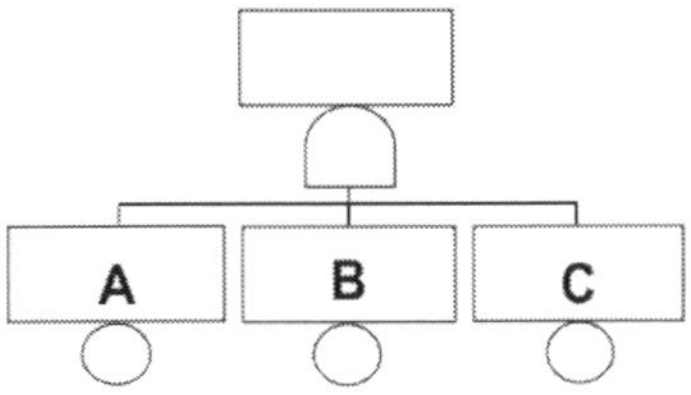

Incorrect

1 Hr Mission

$$P_{TOP} = P_A \bullet P_B \bullet P_C = \lambda_A T \bullet \lambda_B T \bullet \lambda_C T = (1x10^{-6})(1) \bullet (1x10^{-6})(1) \bullet (1x10^{-6})(1) = 1x10^{-18}$$

Adjusted for 100 Hr Mission

$$P_{TOP} = P_{TOP} \text{ x100 Hrs} = (1x10^{-18})(100) = 1x10^{-16}$$

Correct

100 Hr Mission

$$P_{TOP} = P_A \bullet P_B \bullet P_C = \lambda_A T \bullet \lambda_B T \bullet \lambda_C T = (1x10^{-6})(100) \bullet (1x10^{-6})(100) \bullet (1x10^{-6})(100) = 1x10^{-12}$$

229

Mission Calculation Errors (cont'd)

Example 2

- *Shortcut error (multiply λ's)*

P≠(λ_{TOTAL}) x (Mission Time)

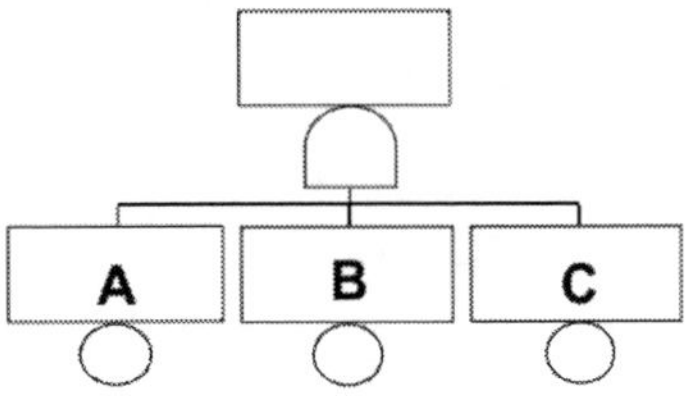

Incorrect

100 Hr Mission

$$P_{TOP} = \lambda_{TOP} \bullet T = (\lambda_A \bullet \lambda_B \bullet \lambda_C) \bullet (T) = (1x10^{-6}) \bullet (1x10^{-6}) \bullet (1x10^{-6})(T) = 1x10^{-18}(T) = 1x10^{-18}(100) = 1x10^{-16}$$

Correct

100 Hr Mission

$$P_{TOP} = \lambda_A T \bullet \lambda_B T \bullet \lambda_C T = (\lambda_A \bullet \lambda_B \bullet \lambda_C) \bullet (T^3) = (1x10^{-6})(1x10^{-6})(1x10^{-6})(10^6) = 1x10^{-12}$$

230

Ignoring Critical Items

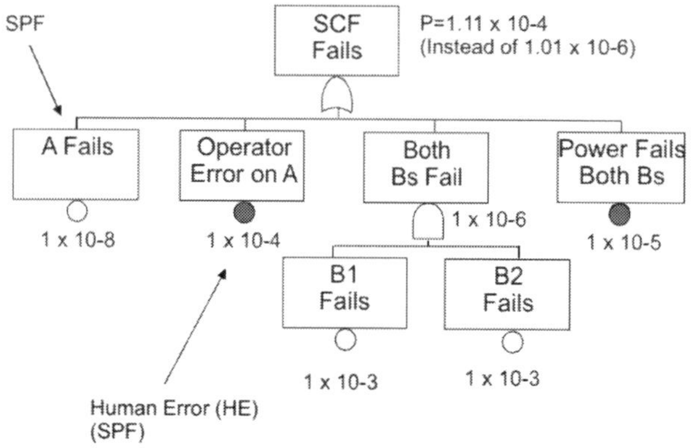

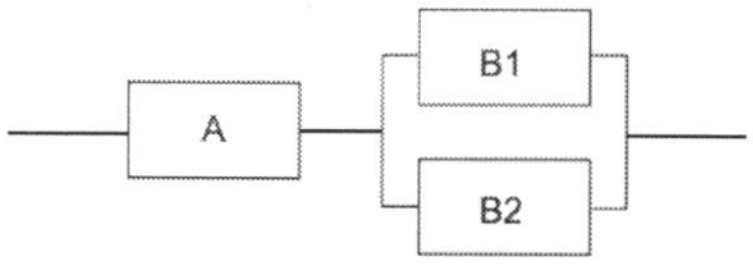

Safety Critical Function (SCF)

Some important items are often ignored or overlooked

- Latency
- Human error
- CCFs

HE & CCF can have significant impact

231

Summary

- There are good FTs, mediocre FTs and bad FTs
- Strive to construct good FTs
- Understanding FT rules and intentionally designing a FT helps to make a quality product
- Don't just spit out a mediocre FT in order to meet a deadline or CDRL
- It's easy to visually inspect the quality of a FT
  - A good FT analyst can tell how much effort and <u>credibility</u> someone put into their FT just through a visual inspection
- In order to perform a quality FTA the analyst must thoroughly understand the system and the unique process of FTA

232

NAVSEA WARFARE CENTERS DAHLGREN

Risk Reduction Distributions Relating to the Benefits of Safety Efforts

Robert W. L. Thomas, Ph.D.; AECOM; Annapolis Junction, Maryland, USA

Marilyn J. Eichelberger, BA; Department of the Navy, Naval Surface Warfare Center Dahlgren Division Dam Neck Activity, Dahlgren, Virginia, USA

Missey Lee, MS; Department of the Navy, Naval Surface Warfare Center Dahlgren Division Dam Neck Activity, Dahlgren, Virginia, USA

Keywords: Balancing Safety Effort Cost and Benefit, Probability and Consequence, Lognormal Approximation Validity, Quantitative Risk Analysis

Abstract

The benefit of including safety in new efforts has historically been described qualitatively. The objective of this paper is to update our recently defined equations showing value added from a safety activity and establish a method for the future quantification of a safety benefit. This paper approximates the distributions of mishap risk and compares the likely differences of mishap risk distributions before and after a safety effort. The result is a measure of safety improvement to a given effort. With this new approach, we show that, in many cases, the distribution can be approximated as lognormal with a small offset term.

Introduction

This paper computes mathematically modeled risk, i.e., severity multiplied by probability, for general mishaps before and after a system safety program is implemented. Such an attempt may be difficult for all such programs (ref. 1) given the complexity of risk and its elements as defined in MIL-STD 882E (ref. 2). In our earlier work (refs. 3-6), the distribution of mishap probability was characterized given a combination of practical experience, simulation based testing and incorporating expert opinion. Here, mishap probability and consequence data before and after the safety program is used to compute the initial risk distribution and estimate the financial risk reduction distribution that might be generated by a safety program.

In our paper at this conference last year (ref. 6), we showed that any viable safety program would not only reduce the risk, but also the relative uncertainty in that risk. This is due to the variability of the forces in the plane of mishap probability and consequence. In order to illustrate this effect, we approximated the distributions of both the probability and consequence, resulting in a risk, which is the product of the probability and the consequence. In order to model the savings created by a safety program, we expanded our definition of the lognormal distribution to allow an offset. This is still an approximation, but we were able to describe the cumulative distribution for the difference. We discuss the validity of the parameters as derived from the raw mishap distributions and demonstrate that the mean and variance can be derived by simple formulae. Limitations of the formulae are reviewed, and applicability conditions are discussed.

Analysis

First, we consider the risk characterization with a lognormal approximation and derive the associated parameters from our earlier models (refs. 3-6). The distribution is then generalized to include an offset, which is the minimum risk difference allowed. Positive results indicate a risk reduction, but it is also remotely possible, but unlikely, to increase the risk. Since both risk distributions are defined from zero to infinity, the risk difference is defined from $-\infty$ to $+\infty$, however, in practice, the risk difference density is often very small for differences less than small negative numbers.

Figure 1 shows the computed probability distributions for risk obtained from simulated data in last year's study (ref. 6). The abscissa gives the risk expressed in dollars per 1000 miles driven. The distributions before and after the (hypothetical) safety program are drawn in blue and red, respectively. These risk distribution curves formed the basis for the calculation of the risk reduction probability distribution. The first intersection is the result of the functional characterization that was used for the risk. The second intersection is very important as it points out where the benefit of the safety program presents itself through a reduced probability of high risk. Note the higher probability of low risk and lower probability of high risk will always be the case for any rational safety program.

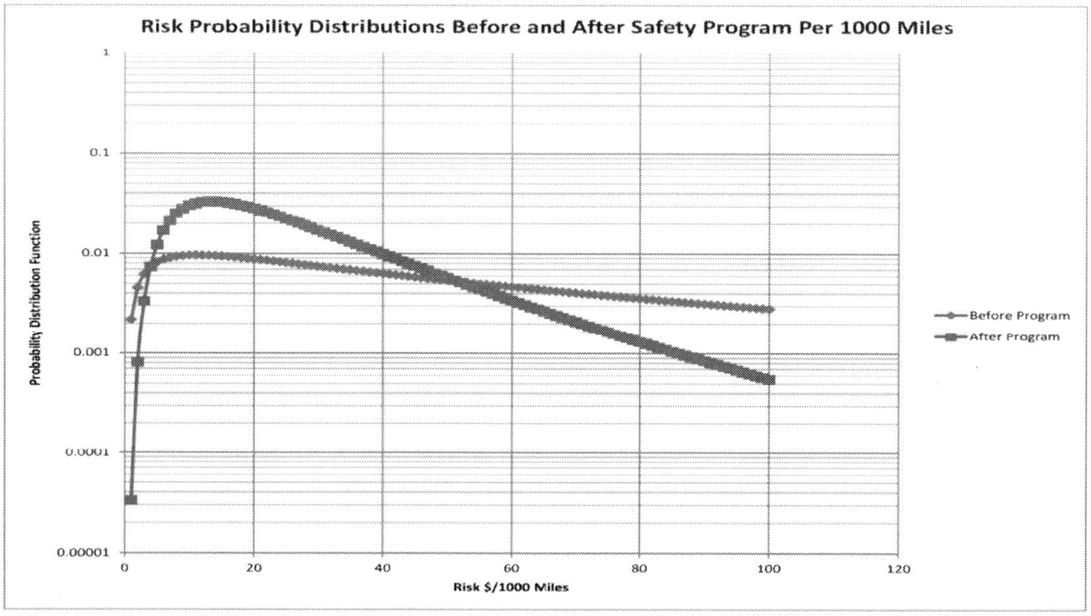

Figure 1 - Probability Distribution Approximations for Risk Before and After Safety Program

A general parameter, X, with a lognormal distribution can be written as

$$X = \delta + \exp(\mu + \sigma Z) \quad (1),$$

where Z is a standard Normally distributed parameter,
δ is an offset parameter (usually negative, in our case),
μ is the median parameter (median = $\delta + \exp(\mu)$), and
σ is the shape parameter (standard deviation of $\ln(X - \delta)$).

In last year's paper (ref. 6), we assumed that δ was zero as this is usually valid for risk characterization. However, for describing risk reduction, a small negative value for this parameter is often required. Hence, we have expanded the lognormal definition to include a non-zero offset. We do not usually solve for δ in a formal sense, as we might have to compute the logarithms of negative numbers, which, of course, are complex numbers. Therefore, we generally select a small value that gives a superior fit for the higher percentile data.

The mean, m, and variance, V, of X in terms of μ, σ and δ are:

$$m = \delta + \exp(\mu + \sigma^2/2) \quad (2), \text{ and}$$
$$V = [\exp(\sigma^2) - 1]\exp(2\mu + \sigma^2) \quad (3).$$

For any general distribution with a minimum abscissa of δ, mean value, m, and variance, V, we can obtain a corresponding lognormal distribution approximation by solving equations (2) and (3) for μ and σ^2 as follows:

$$\mu = \ln[(m-\delta)/\sqrt{\{1+V/(m-\delta)^2\}}] \quad (4) \text{ and}$$
$$\sigma^2 = \ln(1+V/(m-\delta)^2) \quad (5).$$

We assume that the mean and variance of the risk can be estimated before and after the safety program, and then compute parameters for the savings generated from the parameters before and after the safety program as given in the following table:

Table 1 - Computation of Savings Statistics

	Before	After	Savings
Mean	m_B	m_A	$m_S = m_B - m_A$
Variance	V_B	V_A	$V_S = V_B + V_A$
Offset parameter	0	0	Small negative number obtained by trial and error

Figure 2 illustrates the numerical process we used for computing the risk reduction distribution. The savings amounts for the before and after cases were estimated from the lognormal parameters for all integer cumulative percentiles as well as 0.5 percent and 99.5 percentiles. This created two lists, each containing 101 percentiles (one through 99 in additions to 0.5 and 99.5). We then computed the difference between every member of the list before the safety program and every member on the list after the program. This yielded a total of 10,201 differences, whose statistics were computed. The savings distribution parameters were modeled as a lognormal population with a negative offset parameter.

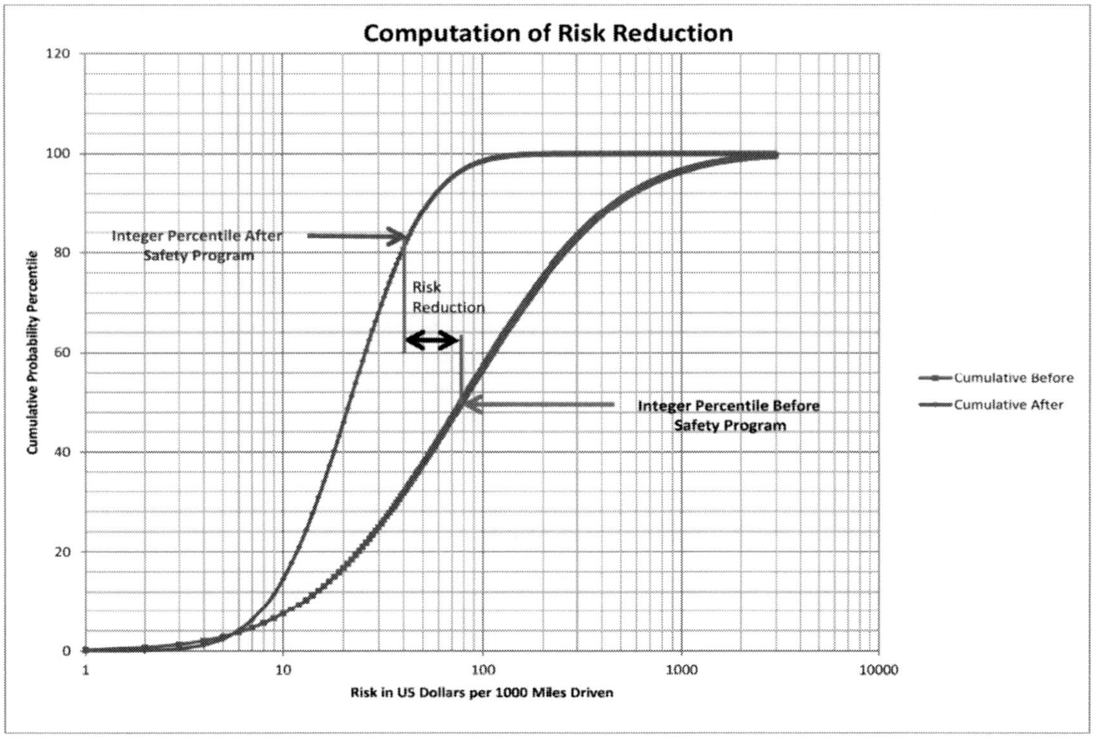

Figure 2 - Illustration of Procedure Used to Compute the Risk Reduction Distribution.

Discussion of Results

With our new approach this year, we used the distributions shown in Figure 1 where, we simulated 50 random realizations for each case. The computed parameters before and after the safety program are specified in Table 2 together with those from the savings. Note that while the mean and variance of the savings can be estimated from the formulae given in Table 1, the median and shape parameters must be obtained in a more complicated fashion. Equations (2) and (3) were used to calculate the mean and variance for the before and after cases, while Equations (4) and (5) were used to compute μ and σ for the savings.

Table - 2 Results for Accident Repair Cost Parameters

	Before	After	Savings
Mean ($ per 1000 miles)	210.5	28.1	182.4
Variance ($ per 1000 miles)^2	270242	500	270742
Offset ($ per 1000 miles)	0	0	-50
Median parameter, μ	4.369	3.091	4.100
Shape parameter, σ	1.4	0.7	1.487
Median ($ per 1000 miles)	79	22	45

The cumulative savings distribution is given in Figure 3, together with the computed lognormal fit. The value of the offset was -$50 per 1000 miles driven, and the parameters we obtained from Equations (4) and (5) are specified on the graph. Note that the savings can be negative, but in practice, the probability of any value below δ (-$50 per 1000 miles driven) is very small.

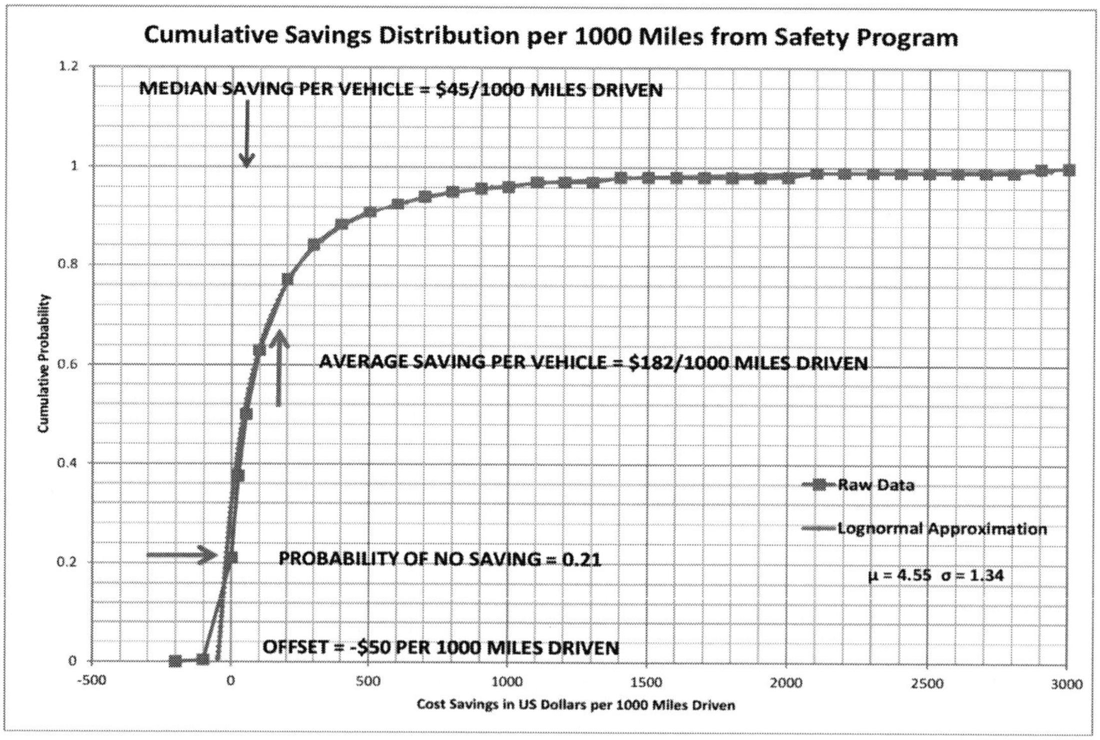

Figure 3 - Cumulative Distribution of Savings Resulting from Safety Program

NAVSEA WARFARE CENTERS DAHLGREN

Now it is possible to judge the value of the expenditures on risk reduction activity and generate percentile confidence that the safety program will be justified. Even a very high risk reduction program cost could easily provide a significant return on investment. In this case there is data that could reasonably be expected to be collected for every accident, so that a fitting process worked well. In practice, the parameters might be more difficult to obtain, but the lognormal approximation is very often a good starting point. It should be noted that all of the equations used in this approach are also applicable to the performance improvement domain with the simple expediency of interpreting the risk as that of system performance failure.

The lognormal assumption for risk is an approximation whose validity can be assessed for real-world situations. The mishap probability has a Beta distribution while the mishap consequence distribution is highly variable. Nevertheless, our approximation here appears to be conservative (ref. 6), and can be used with reasonable consequence for many cases.

Conclusions

This result allows management to estimate the percentile probability of returns on investment for any planned safety program. The lognormal assumption is an approximation that must be checked, but is generally very helpful. The conclusions for the safety risk also apply to performance risk because the safety and performance risk planes have identical characterizations.

References

1 Kady, R.A., Ranasinghe, A., Zemore, M.G. and Eller, R.A., "The Challenges of a Quantitative Approach to Risk Assessment", 32nd ISSC, St Louis MO, August 4-8, 2014.

2 Military Standard 882E, "System Safety." May 11, 2012, http://www.system-safety.org/Documents/MIL-STD-882E.pdf, retrieved March 24, 2016.

3 Thomas, R.W.L., Eichelberger, M., Lee, M. and Haan, J, "An Innovative Approach to Hypothesis Testing for System Safety Assessment", 33rd ISSC, San Diego, August 21-24, 2015.

4 Thomas, R.W.L., Eichelberger, M., Lee, M. and Haan, J, "An Innovative Approach to Hypothesis Testing for System Safety Assessment", International Systems Safety Journal, Fall 2015, Pages 18-23.

5 Thomas, R.W.L., Eichelberger, M., Lee, M., "Setting Testing Requirements for Simulation Based System Safety Assessments", 34th ISSC, Orlando, August 8-12, 2016.

6 Thomas, R.W.L., Eichelberger, M., Lee, M., "The Theory of Risk Uncertainty Reduction", 35th ISSC, Albuquerque, August 21-25, 2017.

Biographies

Robert W. L. Thomas, Ph.D., AECOM, 430 National Business Highway, Suite 400, Annapolis Junction MD 20701, USA, telephone — (443) 737-1287, facsimile — (443) 737-9010, e-mail — robert.w.thomas@aecom.com.

Dr. Thomas is a scientist at AECOM working on safety issues pertaining to electromagnetic environments near to high power emitters. He also has experience with the verification and validation of combat systems software with a particular emphasis on critical-timing issues. Additionally, he has developed models used by the National Aeronautics and Space Administration (NASA) to scope the independent verification and validation of satellite and spacecraft borne software and has designed optical instrumentation for space measurements to characterize planetary atmospheres.

Marilyn J. Eichelberger, BA, Naval Surface Warfare Center Dahlgren Division Dam Neck Activity, Combat Systems Safety Branch, 5375 Marple Road, Suite 153, Dahlgren, VA 22448-5155, USA, telephone — (540) 653-4967, facsimile — (540) 653-5155, e-mail — marilyn.eichelberger@navy.mil.

Ms. Eichelberger is currently a member of the Combat Systems Safety Branch at the Naval Surface Warfare Center Dahlgren Division Dam Neck Activity. She has 21 years of experience supporting U.S. Navy, U.S. Marine Corps, and Foreign Military Programs, of which 9 years have been in the role of Principal for Safety.

Missey Lee, MS, Naval Surface Warfare Center, Dahlgren Division Dam Neck Activity, Combat Systems Safety Branch, 5375 Marple Road, Suite 153, Dahlgren, VA 22448-5155, USA, telephone — (540) 653-7900, facsimile — (540) 653-5155, e-mail — missey.lee@navy.mil.

Ms. Lee is currently a member of the Combat Systems Safety Branch at the Naval Surface Warfare Center Dahlgren Division Dam Neck Activity. She has over 11 years of experience practicing System Safety Engineering for the U.S. Navy. Prior to this, she worked developing and implementing code for Weapon Systems of the U.S. Navy.

Safety Considerations with Kalman Filters

Anthony S. Cantone; Naval Air Warfare Center Weapons Division (NAWCWD); China Lake, California, US

Kenneth R. Chirkis; NAWCWD, China Lake, California, US

Keywords: Kalman, Filter, Propagation, Update, Estimation, Safety

Abstract

Navigation systems typically contain a Kalman filter, whose function is to develop a current optimal estimate of the state of a system based on the previous state, a system model, and measurements, while incorporating measurement noise statistics and instrumentation error characteristics. A description of the processes typical of generic linear Kalman filters is presented along with hazards in the event of a Kalman filter malfunction. Hazards are considered from the viewpoint of an air vehicle application, although this analysis can also be applied to arguably less hazardous applications such as an autonomous automobile. A list of hazards to consider is presented for use by the safety engineer.

Introduction

A typical hazard associated with a failed Kalman filter is the inability to furnish navigation aids. For an air vehicle, this could result in the inconvenience of having to navigate visually, having to navigate using noisy sensors, or losing the ability to perform critical maneuvers such as landing or navigating through heavy air traffic.

The purpose of this paper is to give the safety engineer a means to understand the structure of a typical Kalman filter found in the navigation system so that s/he can associate aberrant behavior in the operation of an air vehicle with defects in the Kalman filter.

After a short chapter "What is Filtering?" in which filtering is defined, this paper discusses Kalman filter design in the chapter "Design of a Typical Linear Kalman Filter." A chapter with the title "Kalman Filter Structure" presents the notation used to represent the parts of the filter, along with a description. "Kalman Filter Processes" describes the two main processes that Kalman filters typically exhibit. There are several possible Kalman filter errors that are described in the chapter "Kalman Filter Errors." This is the heart of the paper and is designed to give the safety engineer the knowledge s/he needs to judge what the hazards associated with a particular design might be. The chapter "Aberrant Behavior" describes some of the behaviors that a defective Kalman filter can exhibit. The "What Are the Hazards?" chapter describes the observable hazardous behavior that is possible if the filter design is faulty in the way described in the "Kalman Filter Errors" chapter. A mitigation is a feature that helps to alleviate the bad effects of a hazard. The chapter "What Are Some of the Mitigations?" is included to indicate possible mitigations. A list of behaviors and their associated causes appears in the "Behavior – Causes

Relationship" chapter. Finally, examples of a single state filter with defects discussed in this paper are displayed in the chapter "Some Examples of Aberrant Behavior Related to Filter Defects."

What is Filtering?

Filtering is a process of estimating the state of a system at the current time based on past history and measurements. Since measurements are usually noisy, a means for estimating the effect on the state of the system due to the measurement noise is appropriate. A navigation system typically has as sources of errors process noise (due to inaccuracies in the accelerometers and gyroscopes), instrument misalignment (due to assembly errors), measurement noise and biases, and other error sources. A Kalman filter has in it a mechanism for deciding how much the measurements should influence the estimate of the state of a system, given the previous estimate, a model, the covariance of the state errors and noisy measurements.

Filtering should not be confused with smoothing or predicting. While filtering estimates the system state at the time of the last measurements, smoothing estimates the system state given measurements both in the past and in the future of the time of the estimate, while predicting uses past history to estimate the system state past the end of the measurements available.

Filtering has another meaning that of extracting a signal from noise. This should not be confused with the usage of the word filtering, which is a process of estimating as used in this paper.

Every Kalman filter is designed to be recursive. This means that all the past history is incorporated in the latest state and covariance estimates. Therefore, in a recursive filter, it is unnecessary to store the past states or measurements.

Design of a Typical Linear Kalman Filter

A Kalman filter that is linear in both the state propagation and measurement update can be described typically as two processes working in parallel: a propagation or extrapolation process and an update process. For Kalman filters found in navigation systems, the propagation process is based on a model that predicts navigation quantities such as position and velocity at the current time by using previous position, velocity, gyro, and acceleration information. The update process corrects this prediction using measurement data. Instrumentation and measurement errors are estimated and considered in the propagation and update process.

The filter assumes Gaussian noise in the accelerometer, gyro, and measurement sensors.

Kalman Filter Structure

- X Error State Vector: Contains variables being estimated or their errors.
- F System Dynamics Matrix: Dynamics of the system.
- Φ State Transition Matrix: $\Phi = e^{F\Delta t}$.
- H Measurements Matrix: Transformation between state space and measurement space.
- R Measurements Noise Matrix: Sensor noise characteristics. If measurements are independent, then off-diagonal terms are 0.
- Z Observations Vector: Vector of measurements.
- r Measurements Residual Vector: $r = Z - HX^-$ (X^- is the *a priori* state vector).
- P System Covariance Matrix: Contains variances of the errors of each of the states on the main diagonal and covariance between the states at the off-diagonal positions.
- K Kalman Gain Matrix: Answers the question of how much of the measurements to incorporate into the updated state estimate.
- Q Process Noise Covariance Matrix: Contains accelerometer, gyro errors, round-off, computational errors in the states. Often, this matrix can be used to ***tune*** the filter.
- C_E^L DCM from earth-centered inertial (ECI) frame of reference to local level frame of reference.
- C_B^L DCM from body frame of reference to local level frame of reference.
- χ^2 Statistic associated with the measurement residual.

Kalman Filter Processes

This chapter discusses propagation and update of both the error state vector and the system covariance matrix, and calculation of the Kalman gain matrix during the update process.

State Transition Matrix

The state transition matrix $\Phi(t_2, t_1)$ transforms a state vector solution $X(t_1)$ at time t_1 to the state vector solution $X(t_2)$ at time t_2. The state transition matrix is derived from the model as it appears in the system dynamics matrix F.

Propagation of the Error State Vector and the System Covariance Matrix

In a Kalman filter, the values of the error state vector X and system covariance matrix P are extrapolated, or propagated, in time by use of the state transition matrix Φ. If there is no measurement update, the state vector X and the system covariance matrix P are still propagated in time.

The equations of propagation are as follows:

$$\text{Propagation of error state vector: } X_n^- = \Phi_{n-1}^n X_{n-1}^+$$

$$\text{Propagation of system covariance matrix: } P_n^- = \Phi_{n-1}^n P_{n-1}^+ (\Phi_{n-1}^n)^T + Q_n \quad (T = \text{transpose})$$

where the subscript n-1 corresponds to time t_{n-1} before state update; the subscript n corresponds to time t_n after state update.

The system covariance matrix P reflects the opinion of the filter about the accuracy of the state variables. The initialization of this matrix is the estimated variances along the main diagonal. If an initialization error of this matrix is made, the values in this matrix should adjust quickly to more accurate values as each measurement is made. If the initial values of some state vector elements are unknown, the variances of the unknown state vector elements should be set to large values.

The process noise covariance matrix Q reflects the confidence of the designer that the model is accurate (the transition equations are correct and there are no missing states). Smaller values along the diagonal in this matrix reflect a higher confidence.

Update of the Error State Vector and System Covariance Matrix

The update process begins with the reception of measurements. These measurements are collected in measurement space, a coordinate system that may be different from state space, the coordinate system in which the state vector is defined. For example, the time delay in the message from a Global Positioning System (GPS) satellite eventually will be translated into position and velocity of the vehicle by the software in the navigation hardware. The H matrix furnishes the translation between state space and measurement space.

A comparison between the measurements and the estimate of the current state (translated into measurement space) is performed. The result is an estimate of the reasonableness of the measurements. This guards against incorporation of spurious measurements due to instrument failure but may also neglect to incorporate measurements associated with high dynamics maneuvers. See the chapter "Reasonableness Tests May Be Too Stringent or Too Lenient" for details on how this is done. If the decision is that the measurements are not reasonable, they are ignored, and the update cycle is skipped. If the measurements are reasonable, the Kalman gain is then calculated.

The Kalman gain is a matrix that computes the weight which is applied to the measurements, transformed into state space. Equation 1 shows computation of the Kalman gain matrix:

$$K_n = P_n^- H_n^T (H_n P_n^- H_n^T + R)^{-1} \tag{1}$$

Once the Kalman gain matrix has been computed, the decision having been made that the measurements are to be incorporated, the system covariance matrix and error state vector are updated. That is, the states and covariance are updated using information provided by the measurements. The measurement incorporation is weighted by the Kalman gain matrix. If only low weight is given to the measurements, this reflects the filter's belief that the measurements are not very reliable, and the filter tends to trust its propagation more than the measurements. High weight given to the measurements reflects the filter trusting the measurements as much as or more than the propagation.

In the state and covariance measurement update, the superscript "–" is used before a measurement update takes place, and "+" is used after the measurement update.

The update of the error state vector is done as in equation 2:

$$X_n^+ = X_n^- + K_n[Z_n - H_n X_n^-] \quad (2)$$

where X_n^- is the error state vector after the last propagation cycle, H_n transforms the state space to measurement space, and the quantity in the brackets is the difference between the last propagation and the corresponding measurements, called the measurement residual vector.

In an analogous way, the update of system covariance matrix is performed as in equation 3, where I is a unit matrix:

$$P_n^+ = (I - K_n H_n)P_n^- \quad (3)$$

If the elements of the Kalman gain matrix are effectively 0, the system covariance will not be changed. The larger the elements of the Kalman gain matrix, the more change will be incorporated into the covariance.

Kalman Filter Errors

Ill-Conditioning

One of the symptoms of an ill-conditioned problem is the behavior of the solution with respect to variations of the input data. In an ill-conditioned problem, wild and chaotic behavior of the solution is possible with small changes in the input data. Such changes can occur from random variations, such as noisy data. Ill-conditioning is not only a result of noisy data but also of faulty algorithms. For example, there are ways that the computation of the Kalman gain can be affected by modeling errors in the Φ, Q, H, and R matrix parameters, large ranges of values of these matrix parameters, ill-conditioning of intermediate results, computer round-off errors, and large number of states (M. S. Grewal and A. P. Andrews).

Ill-conditioning can play a part in determining observability of a dynamic system. One of the characteristics of an unobservable system is the inability to invert the observability matrix because it is singular. However, arbitrarily small changes in the elements of a singular matrix can make it nonsingular. These small changes can occur because of round-off or truncation errors. Then what one has is a dynamic system that is "almost observable." Various schemes, such as the reciprocal of the condition number of the Gramian matrix, can serve as a quantitative measure of unobservability (M. S. Grewal and A. P. Andrews).

Initialization of the System Covariance Matrix

The effect of initialization errors is not a crucial factor in the performance of the filter. The initial value of the variances along the main diagonal of the System Covariance Matrix (P) reflects the knowledge (or lack thereof) of the initial values in the state vector. For example, if wind buffeting of a vehicle is estimated to cause a variation of 1 degree (1σ) in the tilt errors of the instrument platform, the variance of the tilt error state should be set to 1. After a few filter cycles, the system covariance matrix should converge to more reasonable values.

Initialization of the Process Noise Covariance Matrix

The initialization of the process noise covariance (Q) matrix is crucial for a satisfactory behavior of the filter. If the accelerometers and gyroscopes are used in a self-alignment process, statistics from the data sheets of these instruments can be included on the main diagonal. Otherwise, the values in the Q matrix reflect the noise associated with round-off or truncation errors that appear in the state estimates.

Adjusting these values may help the filter behave in a way to facilitate the estimation process. In other words, the Q matrix can be used to *tune* the filter so that its performance shows the appropriate confidence in the model. If too much confidence (small Q) is shown in the model, the resulting Kalman gain will allow too little a percentage of the measurements and too much of the propagated states to influence the next state vector values. Too little confidence (large Q) will on the other hand weigh on the side of incorporating too low a percentage of the propagated states and too high a percentage of the measurements in the next state vector values. This occurs because the values in the Q matrix add directly to the system covariance matrix.

However, be aware that although a low value in the Q matrix can result in the filter diverging from reality by ignoring the measurements in favor of a possibly faulty model, larger values in the Q matrix can result in the filter overly relying on the measurements and ignoring the model propagation.

Asymmetry of the System Covariance Matrix

If the Kalman filter is implemented using the entire system covariance matrix rather than an upper triangular mechanization, computer round-off and/or truncation error can cause asymmetry in the system covariance matrix. Over a long period of time, this asymmetry can result in zero or negative variances along the main diagonal of the system covariance matrix. Since the variances are theoretically positive definite, this will eventually cause significant errors in the calculation of the states. In order to forestall this possibility, it is recommended that the system covariance matrix be symmetrized after each propagation. The simplest symmetrization is accomplished by copying the upper triangular to the lower triangular portion of the matrix. Another possibility is to average each term with its image across the main diagonal.

Reasonableness Tests May Be Too Stringent or Too Lenient

The χ^2statistic associated with the measurement residual r, shown in equation 4:

$$r = Z - HX^{-}, \tag{4}$$

where X^{-} is the *a priori* state vector, can be used to protect the filter from spurious measurements. It can be designed to protect against large deviations from the expected measurements, for example, on the order of 5 or more times standard deviation. This will ensure that spurious measurements, due to instrument failure or noise spikes, which are most likely to appear as extremely large deviations from the expected measurements, will be rejected, while fairly unlikely measurements will still be accepted. The risk is that measurements during times of large maneuvers may be rejected.

The measurement residual (equation 4) is assumed to be normally distributed with mean zero. If r is the measurement residual vector with dimension d (number of measurements), and S is its covariance matrix

$$S = HP^{-}H^{T} + R \tag{5}$$

then the quadratic form in equation 6

$$\chi^{2} = r^{T}S^{-1}r \tag{6}$$

is known to be χ^2 distributed with d degrees of freedom (DOF) (F. A. Graybill; en.wikipedia.org/wiki/Chi-squared_distribution.). This scalar can be compared to a critical chi-squared value that corresponds to a preselected significance level for the number of DOF, i.e., the dimension of the measurement residual vector.

The usual approach is to choose a significance level and form the null hypothesis "The current measurement is valid."

For example, assume a filter with two independent measurements and that all measurements generating a residual farther than 3σ from the expected measurements are to be rejected. Since 99.73% of the area under a Gaussian distribution lies in the 3σ range, 99.73% is the confidence level; the significance level 0.27% is the percent of measurements rejected.

From a chi-squared table, it is seen that this corresponds to a χ^2 statistic of approximately 12 for 2 DOF, so the χ^2 statistic is established at 12. If the computed χ^2 statistic exceeds the established limit, the null hypothesis is rejected, and no update is performed. In Table 1, the probability level of 0.0027 has an associated χ^2 statistic somewhere around 12 for 2 DOF (see ● in Table 1).

Table 1 — χ^2 Table (Stattrak.com), 3 σ, 2 DOF

DOF	Significance Level					
	0.5	**0.10**	**0.05**	**0.02**	**0.01**	**0.001**
1	0.455	2.706	3.841	5.412	6.635	10.827
2	1.386	4.605	5.991	7.824	9.210	● 13.815
3	2.366	6.251	7.815	9.837	11.345	16.268

If the significance level is too small, the rejection rate will be too low. The result is that the Kalman filter will tend to accept all measurements, and the filter will be exposed to spurious measurements if a sensor fails. If the significance level is too large, the rejection rate will be too high. The result is that the filter will tend to reject all measurements as though it has become smart and has more confidence in its extrapolations than in the measurements, and it will continue uncorrected.

Loss of Orthonormalization

Coordinate transformations use Direction Cosine Matrices (DCMs). The accelerometers and gyroscopes give outputs relative to an inertial frame of reference. In order for the dynamics equations to be solved, a transformation from the inertial frame to the earth-centered earth-fixed (ECEF) frame is needed, followed by a transformation from the ECEF to the local level frame in a tangent plane at the location of the aircraft. Finally, a transformation from the local level to the body frame of the aircraft is needed. The inertial measurement unit (IMU) is fixed to the body frame, but there may be alignment errors, called tilts, which can be modeled as error quantities in the error state vector.

The body frame to local level frame DCM should be an orthonormal matrix. This DCM can be determined from the vehicle Euler angles by considering the yaw, roll, and pitch angles of the vehicle. Round-off errors contribute to a deviation from the orthonormal condition during propagation and update. Therefore, it would be prudent to install a method to preserve the orthonormalization of this matrix. A normal matrix is a square matrix that can be diagonalized with real eigenvalues on the diagonal. Orthogonal matrices have the useful property that their inverses are identical with their transposes. This makes it possible to calculate the inverse of an orthogonal matrix without risking the numerical chaos that ill-conditioning would bring.

Suppose C is a 3x3 DCM. A formal analysis (Paul G. Savage) shows that post-multiplication by $(C^T C)^{-\frac{1}{2}}$ will orthogonalize the matrix C. A useful modification can be developed as follows:

Assuming that C is almost orthonormal, $C^T C$ can be written $C^T C = I + \Delta C$ where I is the 3x3 identity matrix, and ΔC is a 3x3 matrix whose terms are small when compared to C. Then, if M is the modified (i.e., orthonormal) C matrix, equation 7 gives its value:

$$M = C(I + \Delta C)^{-\frac{1}{2}} \tag{7}$$

which becomes, to a first order approximation, in equation 8,

$$M = \frac{1}{2} C(3I - C^T C) \tag{8}$$

The body to local level DCM should be orthogonalized periodically. The period is a tunable parameter. Note that orthogonal matrices are normal.

Incomplete Model

Unknown and unmodeled forces will cause the behavior of the system to diverge from the expected model behavior. This will eventually result in the rejection of the measurements because the measurement residual r will become very large, and the solution will not be corrected. An example is the failure to model drag on an earth satellite due to ballooning of the atmosphere because of uneven heating of the earth's surface.

Inadequate Alignment
The reason for the alignment process is to determine where level is and the direction of north. Level and north are stored in a DCM that determines the relationship between the IMU and the body axes of the vehicle. The longer the alignment process lasts, the more accurate the level and north will be. Navigation with an inaccurate north direction accumulates error the farther one travels in the north-south direction.

Inappropriate Sampling Rate
Accelerometer and gyroscope integration are used during alignment and in some models to form the transition matrix. Integration of accelerometer and gyro outputs generally is noisy, resulting in a potential for poor propagation. The problem is worsened when the readings are either held constant or averaged in the interval between samples.

It is reasonable to assume that the integration interval of the accelerometer and gyro outputs should be small to facilitate accurate integration. Trapezoidal integration or the use of Simpson's Rule for integration of the accelerometer and gyro outputs also helps towards accurate integration when data thruput limits the size of the integration interval. Otherwise, integration errors may result in erroneous propagations.

Absence of In-Air Restart of the Kalman Filter
If the Kalman filter ceases working, a possible mitigation is to restart the filter while the vehicle is in the air. The process is actually an in-air realignment of the navigation system. In-air alignment has the advantage (over on-ground alignment) of being able to use the last known heading and leveling information if attempted soon enough after the Kalman filter ceases working.

Aberrant Behavior

The Kalman filter can suffer a fatal exception and cease working (i.e., crash). If this occurs, look for loss of symmetry in the system covariance matrix caused perhaps by round-off or truncation error, particularly in single precision applications. Fatal exceptions are typically caused by a lack of exception handling for errors such as square roots of negative numbers, stack overflow, null pointers, and other errors associated with risky constructs in various high-level computer languages.

The Kalman filter can reject all measurements and continue to propagate. If this occurs, look for a significance level that is too large, or the process noise covariance matrix values are too small.

The Kalman filter can accept all measurements and operate as a recursive least squares estimator. If this occurs, look for a significance level that is too small, or the process noise covariance matrix values are too large.

The Kalman filter can operate smoothly but diverge from the real solution. If this occurs, look for a missing state, i.e., a force or bias that is not modeled, inadequate alignment, or faulty accelerometer/gyroscope integration.

If the navigation system accumulates error in its solution rapidly, look for inadequate alignment. The accumulation of error may actually take place slowly if the alignment is only moderately faulty, for example, as caused by not enough time in the alignment mode.

If the solution deviates from reality during periods of high maneuvering, one can expect to find that the significance level used in the reasonable test is too large, resulting in too many measurements being rejected.

The values in the process noise covariance matrix can reflect confidence, or lack thereof, in the accuracy of the model. Generally, large values in the Q matrix reflect a lack of confidence in the model, as evidenced by the solution tending to follow the measurement at the expense of the extrapolation via the model. The opposite is true for Q values being too small.

If there is an error in the recursive design resulting in the old measurements not being discarded, that could result in memory overflows.

Ill-conditioning problems can result in wild variations of the state vector.

If DCM orthonormalization is lost, this may be evidenced by chaotic orientation of body axes. This is not a direct result of a Kalman filter fault, but can occur in connection with navigation operation and can be difficult to diagnose.

Some navigation systems do not have the capability for in-air alignment in the event that the navigation system ceases operation. Then, once GPS aiding is lost, it cannot be restored while in flight.

What Are the Hazards?

- Position, time, and velocity references supplied by the navigation system are missing. (Navigator ground and inflight routing not needed with GPS.)
- The position and timing accuracy reverts to thousands of feet instead of the centimeter accuracy sent from the navigation hardware and software to the mission computers.
- Time accuracy synchronization is only to the second instead of to the millionth of a second.
- Landing capability lost in areas where no landing systems exist, and there is limited visibility because of weather conditions and darkness.
- Flights to any point in the Continental United States (CONUS) would become very much more difficult. Routing is longer, necessitating waypoint planning, using excessive fuel and time.
- In military applications, target error increases without GPS.
- In some unmanned applications, loss of GPS can result in the inability to locate landing strips, and so result in damage to or destruction of the vehicle if this hazard is not mitigated.

What Are Some of the Mitigations?

- In-air restart of the Kalman filter (=in-air alignment)
- Instrument landing system (ILS)
- Pilot visuals
- On top position fixes
- Lengthening filter alignments
- Simpson's rule during samplings

Behavior – Causes Relationship

Aberrant behavior of a navigation system is most likely found in the testing environment. However, if the behavior is not detected during tests because of inadequate testing, a hazard may exist that without mitigation could put personnel and/or an expensive piece of equipment at risk. Table 2 ties observed aberrant behavior to possible flaws in the design of the Kalman filter. This will give the safety engineer a tool that s/he can use to identify possible causes of the aberrant behavior.

Table 2 — Observed Aberrant Behavior and Their Possible Causes

Observed Behavior	Possible Causes
Fatal exception	Loss of symmetry in the system covariance eventually results in negative variances
All measurements rejected	Too large a significance level in the reasonableness test Q values too small
All measurements accepted	Too small a significance level Q values too large
Smooth operation but diverges from the real solution	Missing state (faulty model) Inadequate alignment Faulty accelerometer/gyroscope integration
The navigation system accumulates error in its solution rapidly	Inadequate alignment
Solution deviates from reality during periods of high maneuvering	Too many measurements rejected due to too large significance level in reasonableness test
Solution tends to follow measurements, ignoring the extrapolation	Lack of confidence in the model, indicated by Q being too large
Solution tends to follow the extrapolation at the expense of the measurements	Q values too small
Stack/heap overflow	Old measurements not discarded; recursive design has an error
Wild variations of state vector	Ill-Conditioning
Chaotic orientation of body axes	DCM orthonormalization lost
Inability to restore GPS	Absence of in-air realignment

Some Examples of Aberrant Behavior Related to Filter Defects

Some of the following experiments are a modification of examples found in http://www.academia.edu/7547346/. There are others that were formulated by the authors.

The experiments are described as follows:

Experiment 1 – Stationary Vehicle, Measurements With Gaussian Noise
An estimate of the location of a vehicle believed to be stationary is desired. A Kalman filter with a single state (position) is used to derive this estimate. Noisy sensor measurements of this position are used to attempt to establish the location of the vehicle. The issues are as follows:

1. The position is completely unknown. Relative to a local coordinate system, the location is assumed at 0.0. To reflect the lack of confidence in this assumption, the variance (P^{-}) of the position is set at 1000 ft^2. There is an external measurement every 1 second.

DISTRIBUTION STATEMENT A.

2. One of the critical assumptions of a Kalman filter is that the noise characteristics of the measurements are Gaussian. Considering that the number of sample points is small, a normal probability plot can be used to verify this assumption, using the Normal Probability Plot Maker (mathcracker). The measurements (Table 3) are normalized N(0,1).

Table 3 — Measurements File for Experiment 1

t (sec)	Z (ft)
1	0.9
2	0.8
3	1.1
4	1.0
5	0.95
6	1.05
7	1.2
8	0.9
9	0.85
10	1.15

If Figure 1 even remotely resembles a straight line, it can reasonably be concluded that the measurements are a sample from a data set with Gaussian noise.

The filter is not expected to perform correctly if the measurement noise does not reflect the measurement statistics. The initial measurement variance (R) is set at 0.1 ft^2.

Another approach at this analysis is to compute the variance of the measurements, but remember that these measurements are merely a sample of a universe of measurements with the stated variance, so the variance of the actual measurement set may vary. This is one of the penalties of working with such a small sample, that the variance of the sample may be so different from that of the universe from which the sample is derived. For those interested in sample theory, consult the Central Limit Theorem in any reference on statistics.

3. A model for the propagation of the state and system covariance is created. Confidence in the correctness of this model is high. To reflect this high confidence, the process noise covariance (Q) is set to a very small value 0.0001. The filter will not perform satisfactorily if the process noise covariance does not reflect the expected error model. Q can be used to tune the filter. Q is a constant scalar in this application.

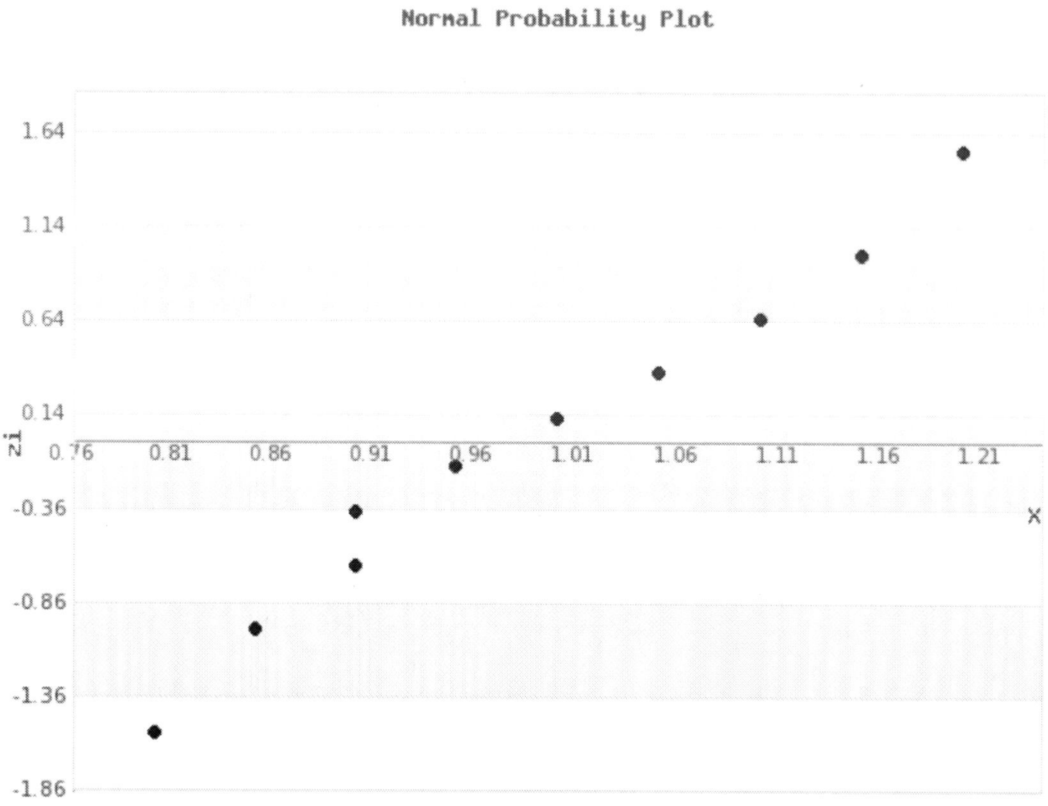

Figure 1 — Experiment 1

Analysis: Even with a terrible original position estimate and noisy measurements, one can see in Figure 2 that the estimate converges quickly to the truth. Note that one of the characteristics of a good Kalman filter is that the estimate noise is much less than the measurement noise.

DISTRIBUTION STATEMENT A.

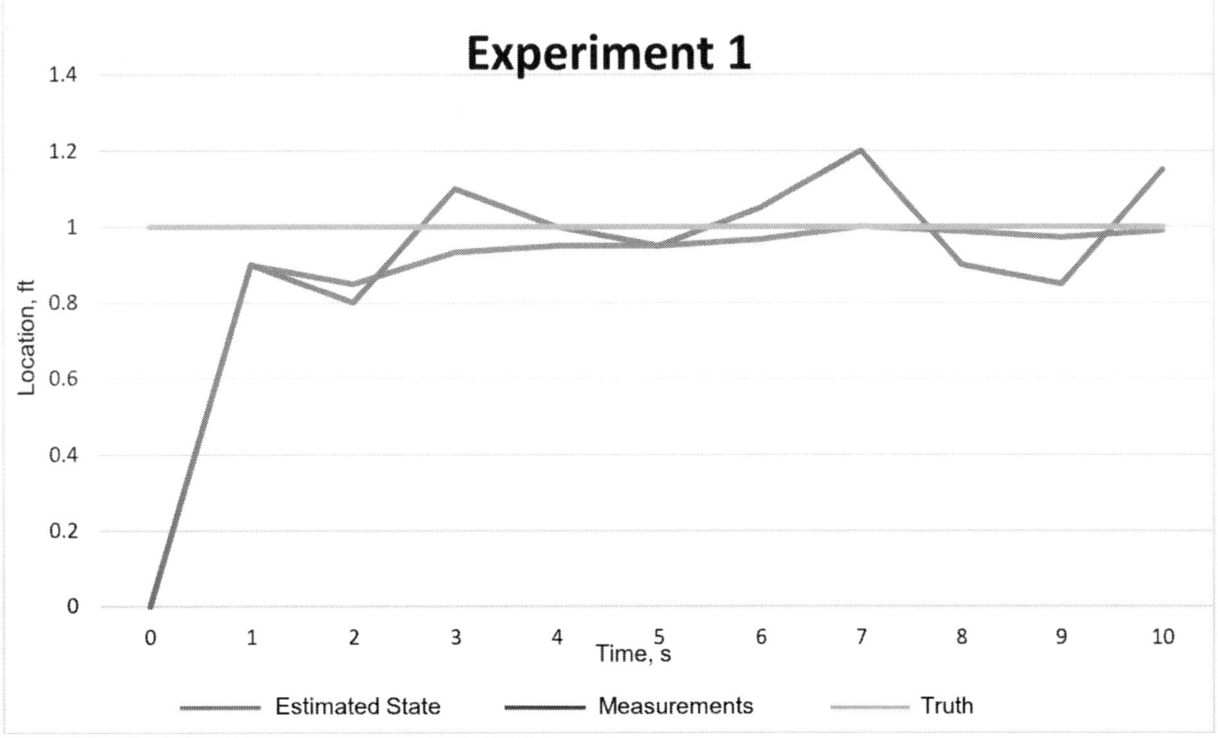

Figure 2 — Result of Experiment 1

Experiment 2 – Erroneous Model With High Confidence

In this navigation experiment, the vehicle is moving. We are trying to establish the position using noisy measurements (Table 4). This navigation system is subject to the following two major error sources:

1. Initial position error. The initial values of the system covariance reflect the confidence in the accuracy of the initial values of the position. The system covariance also reflects round-off error and other process errors. As in Experiment 1, the initial position is unknown, estimated at 0, and the variance of the position is set at a large value, 1000 ft^2.

2. Model error. The model of Experiment 1 is retained. Since the filter is attempting to track a moving vehicle, the underlying model, which assumes a stationary vehicle, is erroneous. The process noise covariance reflects the confidence in the accuracy of the model. The filter will not perform correctly if the process noise covariance does not reflect the expected error model. Q can be used to tune the filter. It is constant with a small value in this application (0.001). This reflects a moderate confidence in the erroneous model.

DISTRIBUTION STATEMENT A.

Table 4 — Measurements File for Experiment 2

t (sec)	Z (ft)
1	0.11
2	0.29
3	0.32
4	0.50
5	0.58
6	0.54
7	0.75
8	0.79
9	0.90
10	1.09
11	0.98
12	1.35
13	1.42
14	1.58
15	1.45
16	1.50
17	1.59
18	1.83
19	1.84
20	2.15

Analysis: The solution is seen to proceed smoothly, except that it bears no resemblance to the truth. The solution drifts slowly away from the truth.

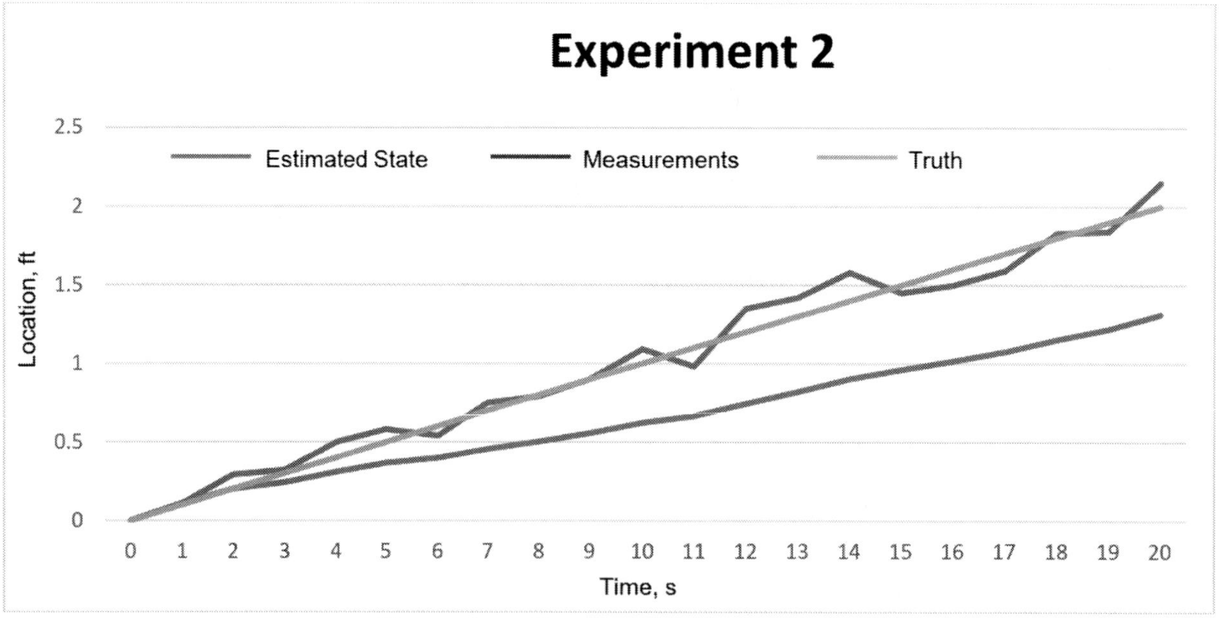

Figure 3 — Result of Experiment 2

DISTRIBUTION STATEMENT A.

Experiment 3 – Erroneous Mode With Some Lack of Confidence
If we're not sure what the correct model is, we can enlarge the value of the process noise covariance, which will reflect some lack of confidence in the accuracy of the model. Let's try 0.01, keeping everything else the same (Figure 4).

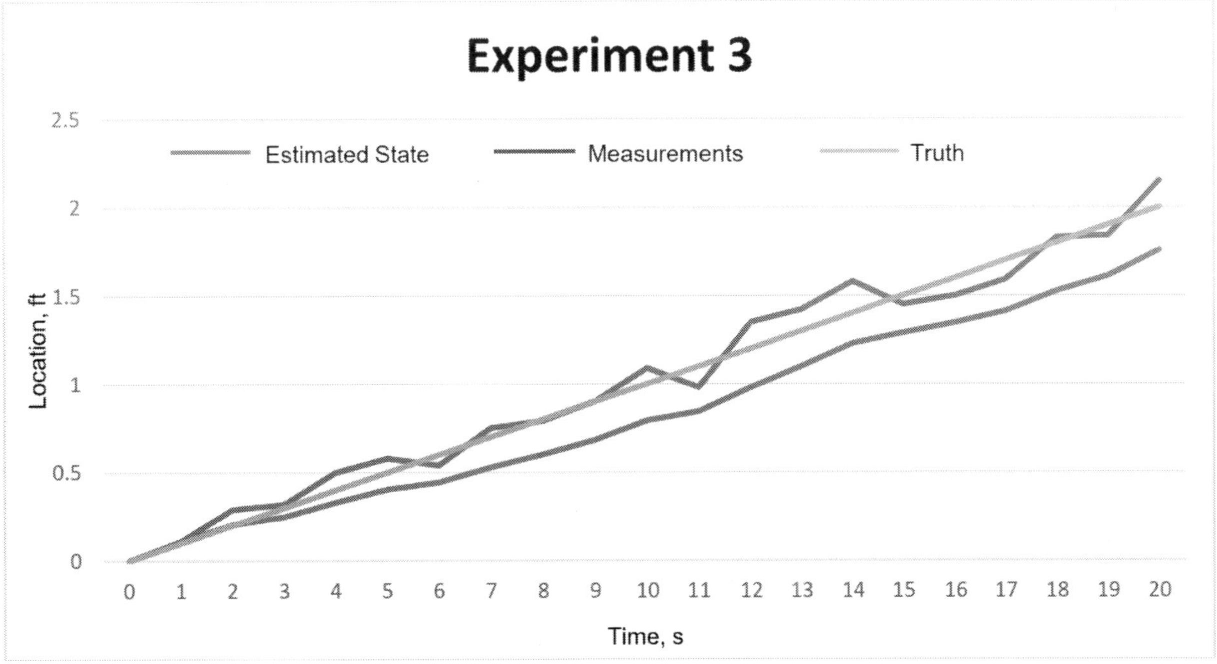

Figure 4 — Result of Experiment 3

Analysis: Now the solution follows the truth better, except that the noise of the estimated position is still larger than the measurement noise. Not good.

Experiment 4 – Erroneous Model With Serious Lack of Confidence
So let's enlarge the value of the process noise covariance by another factor of 10, to 0.1, and see what happens. We are telling the filter that we have a serious lack of confidence in the design of the model (Figure 5).

DISTRIBUTION STATEMENT A.

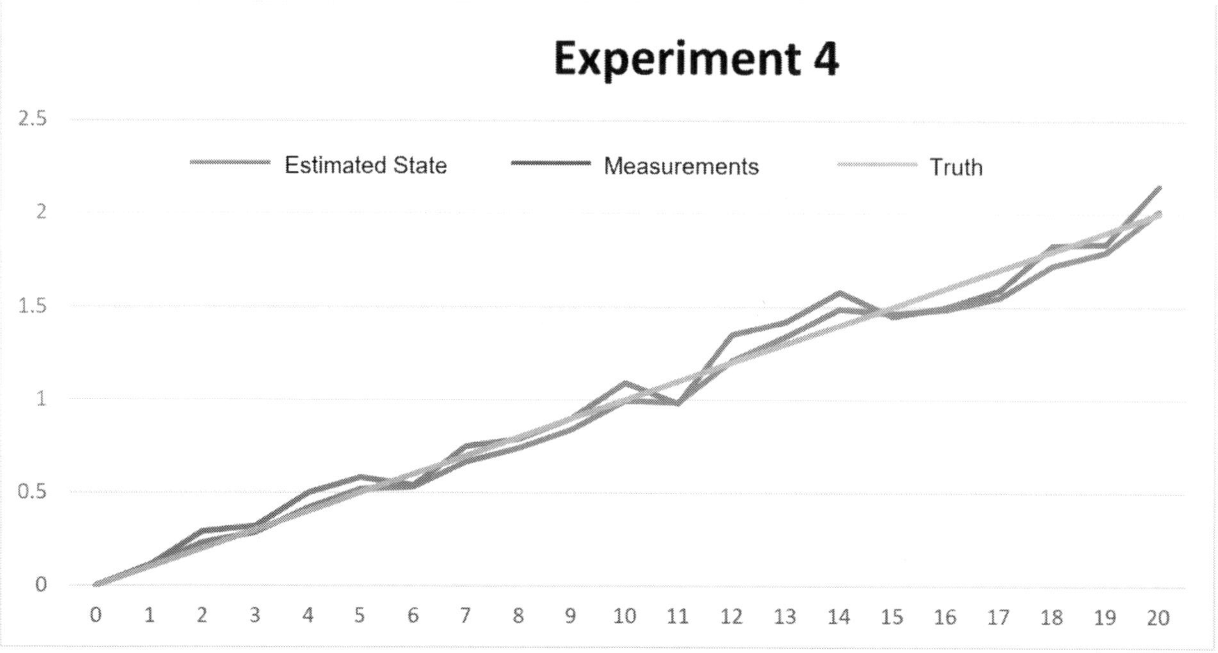

Figure 5 — Result of Experiment 4

Analysis: The estimated solution seems to follow the data, not putting much trust in the propagation at all. Now the noise in the estimated solution is actually less than the measurement noise. Are we getting somewhere?

Experiment 5 – Erroneous Model With No Confidence in Model

In one last try, we enlarge the value of the process noise covariance to 1, announcing that we just don't trust the model. And sure enough, the estimated solution follows the data almost exactly, ignoring the propagation from the model altogether (Figure 6). So, why have a filter? Just trust the measurements!

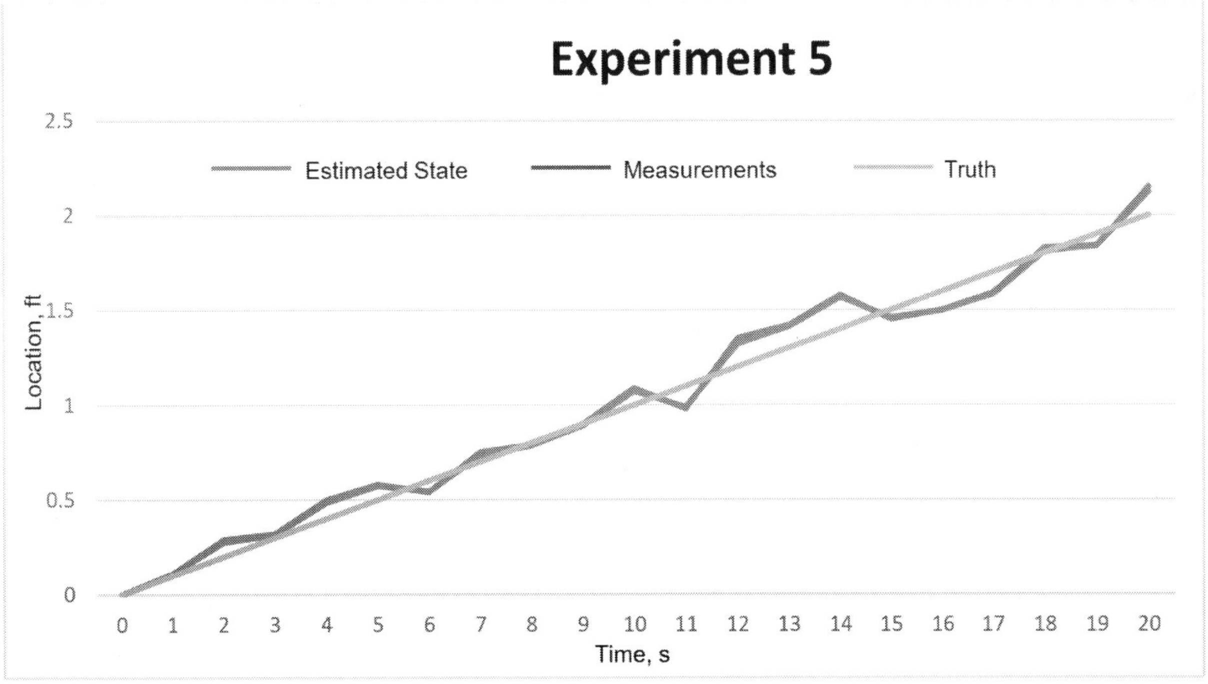

Figure 6 — Result of Experiment 5

Analysis: If your mode is not correct, you will not get a good estimate. However, if you suspect this, you can increase Q, which feeds into the system covariance matrix and influences the Kalman gain, which in turn determines how much of the model state vs. the measurements to include in the updated value of the state. The risk is that the filter will tend to disregard the model propagation and believe the noisy measurements. You can see this when the estimate of the state begins to resemble the measurements.

Experiment 6 – Measurements With Non-Gaussian Noise

What if the measurement noise is not Gaussian? Let's consider the following measurements (Table 5).

Table 5 — Measurements File for Experiment 6

t (sec)	Z (ft)
1	1.20
2	0.75
3	1.25
4	0.25
5	0.23
6	0.85
7	0.25
8	0.76
9	1.45
10	1.50
11	10.0

The model assumes a stationary vehicle at 1.0 ft. A normal probability plot of the measurements reveals that a straight line is hardly indicated by the standardized measurements. See Figure 7.

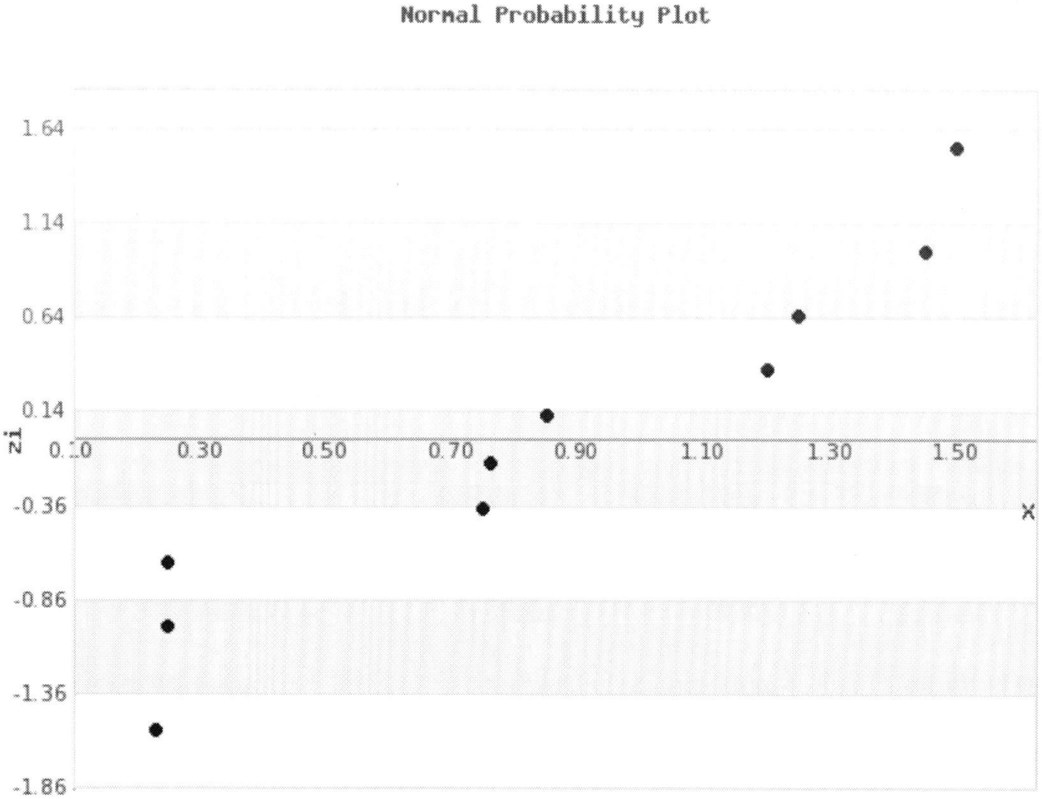

Figure 7 — Experiment 6

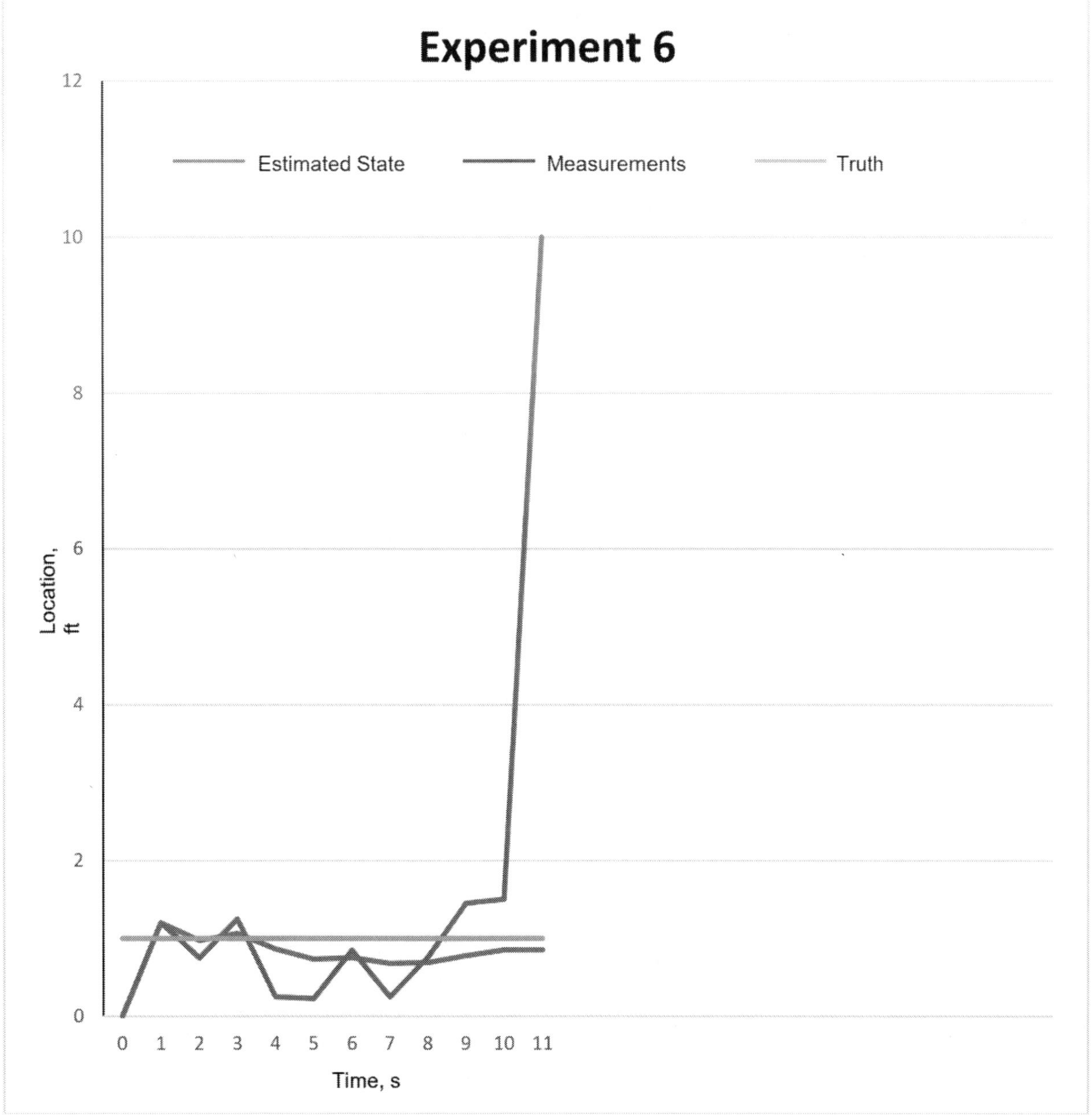

Figure 8 — Result of Experiment 6

Analysis: It is not clear that the estimated solution (blue line) will ever converge to the truth, but if the measurements continue mainly to be biased to one side of the truth, there will probably be no convergence.

The last measurement reflects a sensor gone bad. That measurement was rejected. One can see that the estimated solution is not affected by the spurious measurements. The rejection of measurements criterion is set up so that all measurements beyond 3σ are to be rejected, but except for the last measurement, all measurements were accepted. This is called the data confidence level, not to be confused with the confidence in the model.

DISTRIBUTION STATEMENT A.

Experiment 7 – Rejection of Measurements
The model assumes that the vehicle at 1.0, stationary, and that the measurements are very noisy. The measurement noise distribution is not Gaussian, similar to Experiment 6 (except no spurious measurement at t=11).

Q is small (Q=0.0001), reflecting confidence in the model.

Initial position is completely unknown, 0 assumed with large variance (P=1000). All measurements beyond 2σ are to be rejected. Table 6 shows how to establish the χ^2 limit for 1 DOF at 2σ. The data confidence level is set at 95% while the significance level is at 5% (100% - data confidence level). The χ^2 limit is set therefore at 3.841.

Table 6 — χ^2 Table, 2σ, 1 DOF

DOF	Significance Level					
	0.5	**0.10**	**0.05**	**0.02**	**0.01**	**0.001**
1	0.455	2.706	●3.841	5.412	6.635	10.827
2	1.386	4.605	5.991	7.824	9.210	13.815
3	2.366	6.251	7.815	9.837	11.345	16.268

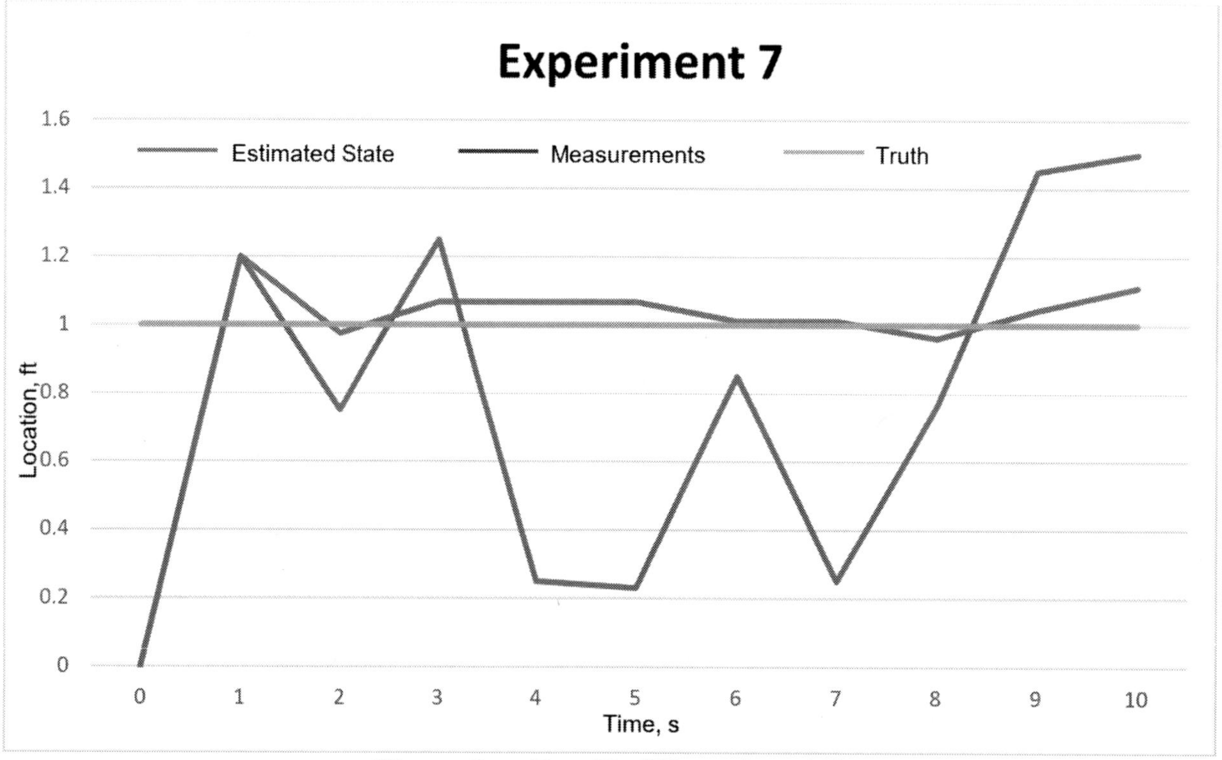

Figure 9 — Result of Experiment 7

Analysis: Measurements at t=4, 5, and 7 seconds were rejected. The estimated solution appears much more reasonable relative to the truth. But what if these were valid measurements during maneuvers? 2σ may cause a rejection of too many valid measurements. This can be detected by observing that the solution deviates from reality during periods of high maneuvering.

DISTRIBUTION STATEMENT A.

Experiment 8 – Rejection of Noisy Measurements Due to Low Significance Level

The model assumes that the vehicle at 1.0, stationary, and that the measurements are very noisy. See Table 7.

Table 7 — Measurements File for Experiment 8

t (sec)	Z (ft)
1	0.60
2	0.20
3	1.40
4	1.00
5	0.80
6	1.20
7	1.80
8	0.60
9	0.40
10	1.60

The measurement noise distribution is Gaussian.

Q is small (Q=0.0001), reflecting confidence in the model.

Initial position is completely unknown, 0 assumed with large variance (P=1000). All measurements beyond 1 σ are to be rejected. Table 8 shows how to establish the χ^2 limit for 1 DOF at 1 σ. The confidence level is set at 68.27% which reflects the significance level of 31.73%. The χ^2 limit is set therefore at 1.0095.

Table 8 — χ^2 Table, 1 σ With 1 DOF

DOF		Significance Level					
	0.5	**0.3173**	**0.10**	**0.05**	**0.02**	**0.01**	**0.001**
1	0.455	●1.0095	2.706	3.841	5.412	6.635	10.827
2	1.386	2.28	4.605	5.991	7.824	9.210	13.815
3	2.366	3.51	6.251	7.815	9.837	11.345	16.268

Analysis: The only measurements accepted are at times 1, 2, 8, and 9 seconds. However, the Kalman gain is fairly high at times 1 and 2, but low at 8 and 9 seconds, so the estimated state tends to follow the measurement at times 1 and 2, and the extrapolation (i.e., the model) in the remainder of the problem (Figure 10). Clearly the confidence level is set at much too low a level.

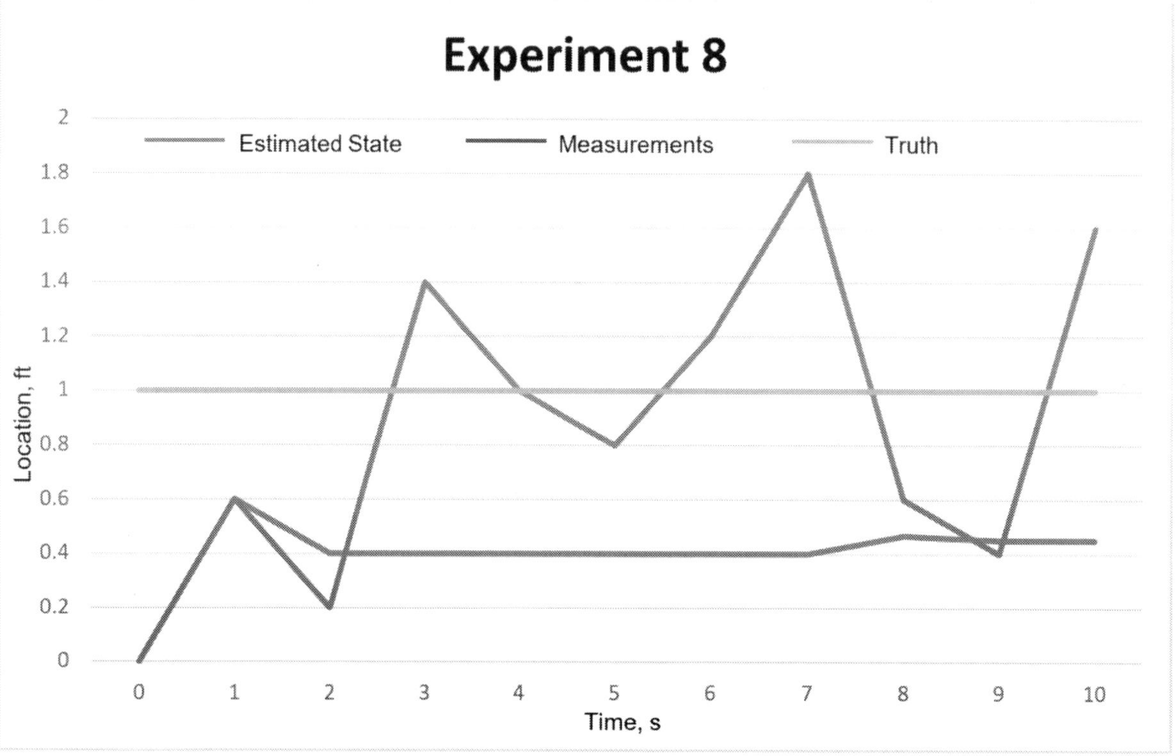

Figure 10 — Result of Experiment 8

Summary

Kalman filtering has been used in a wide variety of aided inertial navigation systems. This paper provides the system safety engineer a means to understand the structure of a typical Kalman filter found in the navigation system so that s/he can associate aberrant behavior in the operation of an air vehicle with defects in the Kalman filter. Kalman filtering and its overall role in the integrated system is still not well understood by many in the navigation safety community. This paper is largely directed toward defining a tool for the safety engineer who is presented with the problem of including Kalman filtering into the design of a navigation system. This perspective is particularly useful in helping the engineer understand potential observed aberrant behaviors and their possible causal factors.

DISTRIBUTION STATEMENT A.

Acronyms

Acronym	Definition
CONUS	Continental United States
DCM	Direction Cosine Matrix
DOF	Degrees of Freedom
ECEF	Earth-Centered Earth-Fixed
ECI	Earth-Centered Inertial
GPS	Global Positioning System
ILS	Instrument Landing System
IMU	Inertial Measurement Unit
NAWCWD	Naval Air Warfare Center Weapons Division

Acknowledgments

Reviewers: Michael Murphree, John Mumford, Shelley Snider.
Editing: Amy Wyatt.

References

Analytic Sciences Corporation Technical Staff, edited by A. Gelb, *Applied Optimal Estimation*, The M.I.T. Press, Cambridge, MA and London, England, Eighth printing, 1984.

M. S. Grewal and A. P. Andrews, *Kalman Filtering, Theory and Practice,* Prentice Hall, Englewood Cliffs, NJ, 1993.

https://mathcracker.com/normal-probability-plot-maker.php#results.

http://www.academia.edu/7547346/.

Paul G. Savage. *Strapdown Inertial Navigation Lecture Notes, Feb. 1, 1990.* Strapdown Associates, Inc., Plymouth, MN.

http://Stattrek.com/online-calculator/chi-square.aspx.

https://en.wikipedia.org/wiki/Chi-squared_distribution.

F. A. Graybill, Theory and Application of the Linear Model, Duxbury Press, Duxbury, MA, 1976.

Biography

Anthony S. Cantone, BS Aeronautical Engineering, PhD Mathematics, ISSS Member, System Safety Analyst at NAWCWD China Lake. Phone: 760-939-1820(W), 805-717-3631(M); email: anthony.cantone@navy.mil

Kenneth R. Chirkis, BS Aeronautical Engineering, MS Aeronautical Science, Doctoral Certification of Advanced Graduate Studies in Business Administration, ISSS Senior Member, AIAA Senior Member. Head System Safety Engineering Branch at NAWCWD China Lake. Phone: 760-939-0600(W), 760-382-7505(M); email: kenneth.chirkis@navy.mil

Overview of the 2nd Edition of ISO 26262: Functional Safety – Road Vehicles

Rami Debouk, General Motors Company, Warren, MI, USA

ABSTRACT

Functional safety is of utmost importance in the development of safety-critical automotive systems, especially with the introduction of driver assist and automated driving systems. ISO 26262, Functional Safety – Road Vehicles, has been the de facto standard for functional safety in the automotive electronics domain since the release of its first edition in 2011. It is currently available as a second edition final draft international standard and is expected to be published as an ISO international standard later in the year.

In this report, we present an overview of the standard that applies to all activities during the safety lifecycle of system development. At the concept phase of ISO 26262, the hazard and risk assessment process focuses on identifying possible hazards caused by malfunctioning behavior of Electrical/Electronic safety-related systems and mitigating them through the identification of safety goals. The design phase includes system, hardware, and software development with requirements developed from the safety goals. ISO 26262 also prescribes the functional safety management activities to be performed during the safety lifecycle and provides requirements on the supporting processes.

In addition to presenting an overview of the standard, this report points to some major changes introduced in the second edition such as the extension of the standard's scope to include all road vehicles, the objective-oriented confirmation reviews approach, and references to Cybersecurity at the Concept and System Level development to name a few.

1 - INTRODUCTION

Safety-critical systems are systems that have the ability to create potentially hazardous issues in case they do not operate properly or as designed [1,2]. These systems are in general analyzed using rigorous and systematic safety processes [3] that define all safety activities during the lifecycle development of the system. In the automotive domain, ISO 26262 [4], Functional Safety – Road Vehicles, emerged in 2011 as the go to standard for functional safety: It was launched as the adaptation of IEC 61508 [5] to comply with needs specific to the application sector of Electrical/Electronic (E/E) systems within road vehicles.

ISO 26262 applies to all activities during the safety lifecycle of system development. At the concept phase, the hazard and risk assessment process focuses on identifying possible hazards caused by malfunctioning behavior of E/E safety-related systems and mitigating them through the identification of safety goals. The design phase includes system, hardware, and software development with requirements derived from the safety goals. ISO 26262 also prescribes the functional safety management activities to be performed during the safety lifecycle and provides requirements on the supporting processes.

As is the case with the introduction of any new process, lessons have been learned from the application of the first edition of ISO 26262 and such learnings necessitated the early release of the second edition which is currently at the final draft international standard stage [6] and expected to be published later this year. The scope of applicability has been extended to include additional-road vehicles as part of the improvement to the standard. In addition, channels of communication between functional safety and cybersecurity have been identified at both the functional safety management level and product development at the system level. Requirements on trucks, buses, trailers and semi-trailers as well as their supporting processes have been introduced in the second edition. A new part defining motorcycles specific requirements in the safety lifecycle has been added. Guidance on semiconductor development has been described in a new informative part of the standard. Finally, improvement on many of the existing definitions and requirements and some restructuring to enhance readability have been introduced.

This report is organized as follows. Section 2 describes the basic definitions used in the standard as well as its scope of applicability. Section 3 introduces the functional safety management while Section 4 discusses the approach for hazard analysis and risk assessment. Section 5 introduces requirements of product development at the system, hardware and software levels, in addition to a brief summary discussing requirements for production, operation, service and decommissioning. Section 6 summarizes required supporting processes and provides a discussion on some safety analyses. Sections 7 and 8 introduce motorcycles specific and trucks and buses specific requirements, respectively. Section 9 provides guidance on semiconductor development. Finally, Section 10 provides a general summary.

2 – SCOPE OF APPLICABILITY AND DEFINITIONS

ISO 26262 is the adaptation of IEC 61508 [5] to comply with needs specific to the application sector of E/E systems within road vehicles. It applies to all activities during the safety lifecycle of system development and its scope includes all series production road vehicles. The latter is a modification of the scope of the first edition which limited the applicability to vehicles with 4 wheels (carrying passengers or goods) with a maximum vehicle gross mass of up to 3500 Kg.

ISO 26262 defines functional safety as the absence of unreasonable risk due to any potential source of harm caused by malfunctioning behavior of electrical and or electronic systems. A malfunctioning behavior is not limited to failures but also includes unintended behavior (with respect to design intent).

Figure 1 below describes how safety is defined in ISO 26262 as the absence of risk judged to be acceptable given valid societal and moral concepts. *Risk* itself is computed using three factors: severity, exposure (as measured by a probability) and controllability. It is worth emphasizing here that the concept of *harm* is defined in the context of injury or damage to humans.

Figure 2 below provides a classification of ISO 26262 specific terminologies starting with the item which is a system or combination of systems to which the standard applies. The item itself implements a given function at the vehicle level. The *system* is a set of components that relates at least a sensor, a controller and an actuator. *Components* are comprised of hardware parts and software units. The concept of an *element* is introduced to refer to a system, component, a hardware part and a software unit.

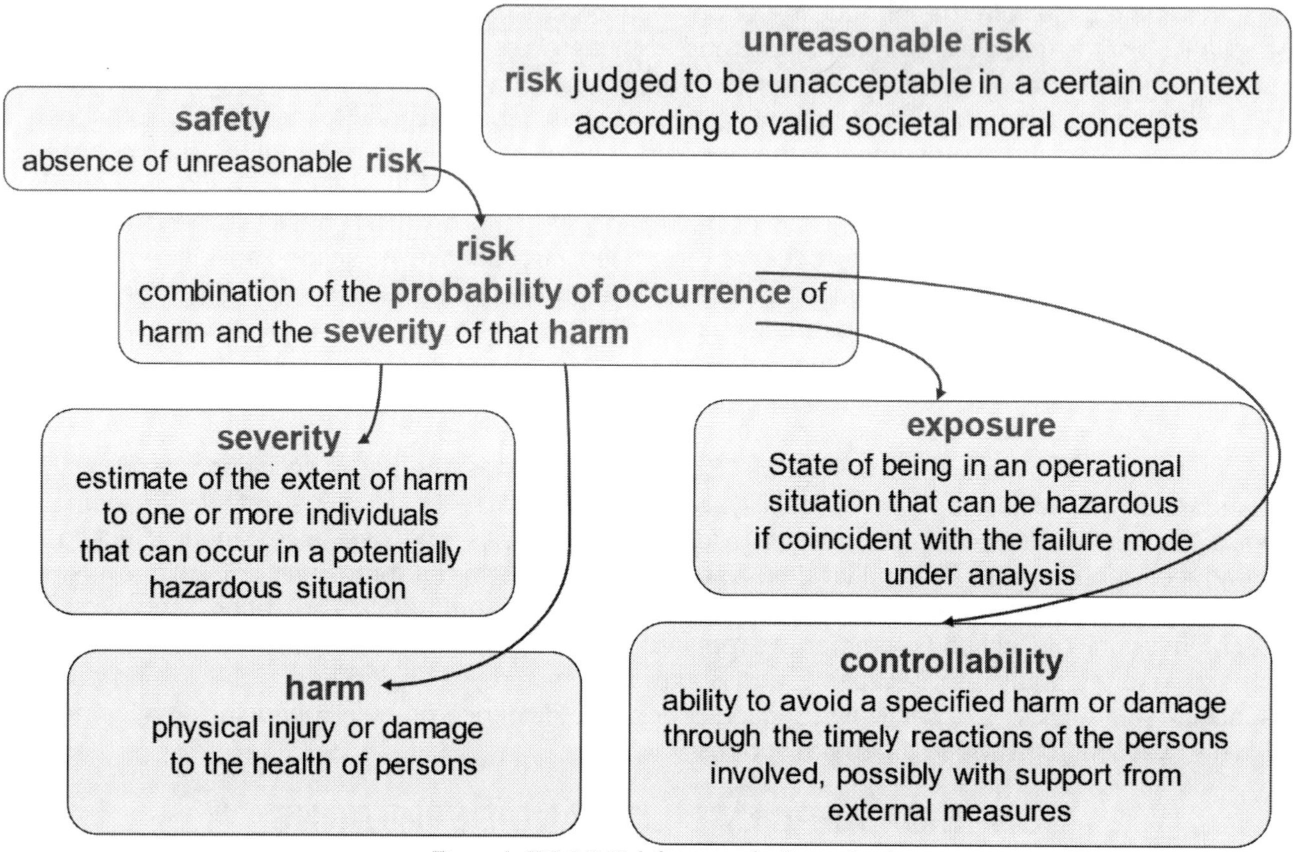

Figure 1: ISO 26262 definitions of safety and risk

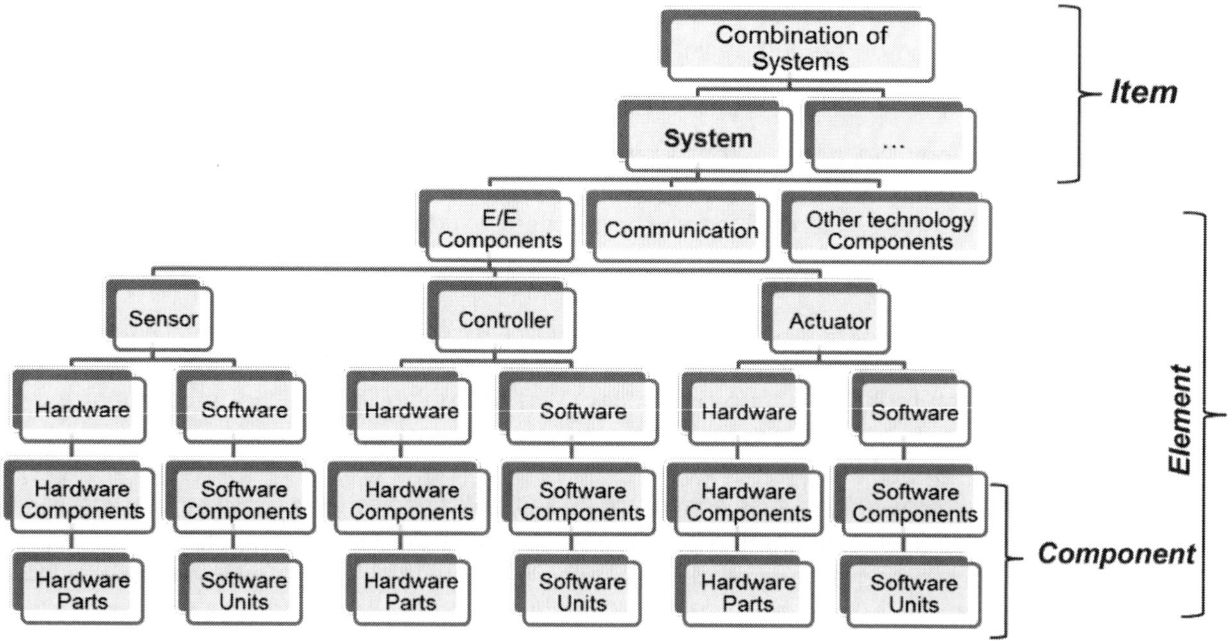

Figure 2: ISO 26262 Terminologies

Finally, the following are definitions of a few concepts introduced or emphasized by ISO 26262.

- Safety goal: top level safety requirement resulting from the hazard analysis and risk assessment as described in Section 4 below.
- Safe state: the mode of operation, without an unreasonable level of risk, of the item, following the occurrence of a failure
- Safety mechanism: technical solution to detect and mitigate (through avoidance or control) faults/failures in order to maintain intended functionality or achieve or maintain a safe state
- Work product: documentation that results from an ISO 26262 requirement(s)
- Confirmation review: confirmation that a work product provides sufficient and convincing evidence to the achievement of functional safety
- Safety case: documentation to communicate a clear, comprehensive and defensible argument (supported by evidence compiled in work products) that a system is acceptably safe to operate in a particular context

3 – FUNCTIONAL SAFETY MANAGEMENT

The functional safety management involves planning, coordinating and documenting all activities related to functional safety. In general, it involves the following as pictured in Figure 3:

- establishing an internal functional safety process for the company,
- establishing a safety organization that oversees the institutionalization of a safety culture within the company and the definition of roles and responsibilities within that organization
- training and qualifying employees to perform safety activities
- institutionalizing the functional safety confirmation measures including reviews, audits and assessments
- managing all the corresponding documentation aspects

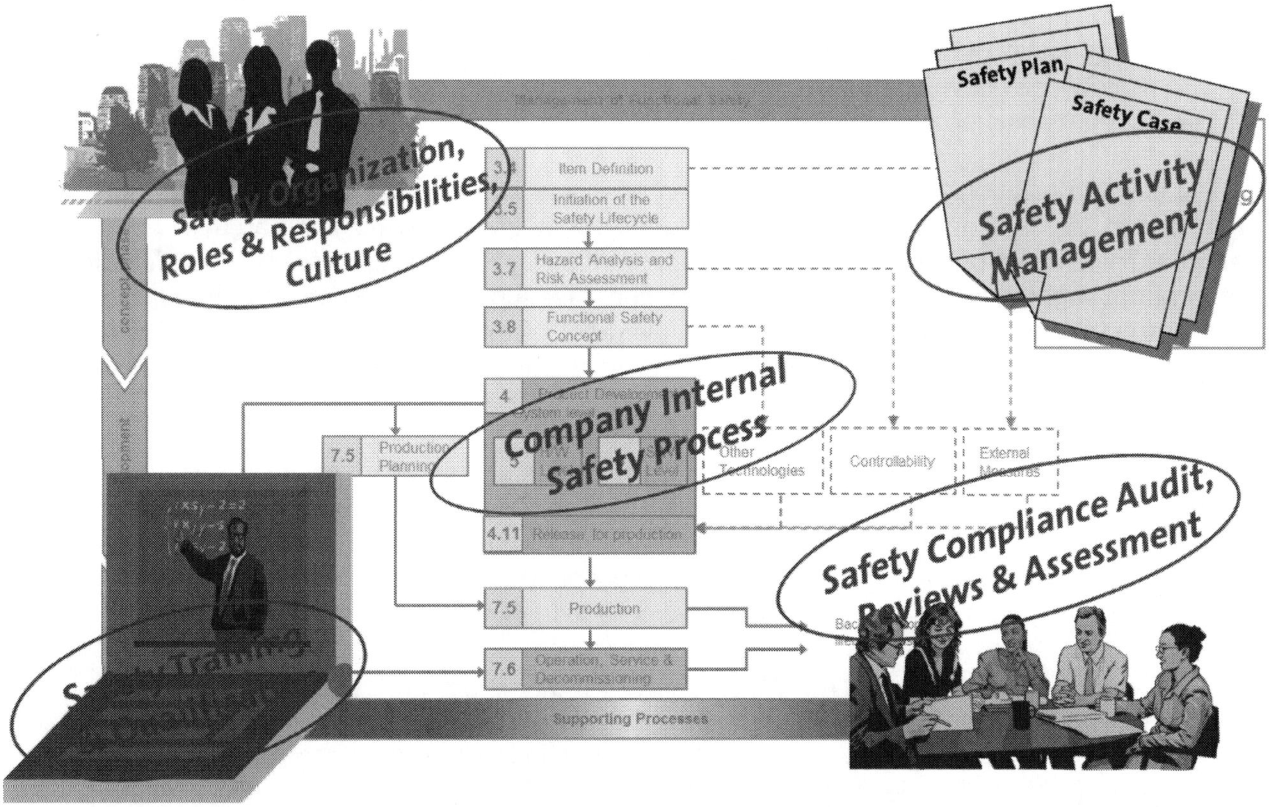

Figure 3: Management of functional safety

Part 2 of ISO 26262 discusses implementing a management plan for all phases of the safety lifecycle, including:

- the overall safety management
- the project dependent safety management
- the safety management for production, operation, service and decommissioning

Overall safety management: involves defining requirements for organizations that are responsible for or perform safety activities in the safety lifecycle. A management plan is put forward to incorporate:

- institutionalization of the safety culture
- effective communication channels between functional safety and cybersecurity (new topic introduced in the 2nd Edition of ISO 26262)
- organization-specific rules and processes
- processes to resolve safety anomalies
- competence management
- quality management
- project-independent tailoring of the safety lifecycle

Project-dependent safety management: involves defining requirements for the safety management during the concept and development phases of a project including roles and responsibilities, as well as performing an impact analysis at the item level in case of a modified/re-used item. A management plan is put forward to incorporate:

- roles and responsibilities in safety management
- impact analyses and tailoring of the safety activities
- planning and coordinating of the safety activities
- progression of the safety lifecycle
- safety case development
- confirmation measures

It is worth mentioning here that the impact analyses and tailoring of the safety activities have been added to the functional safety management of a given project compared to them being performed at different phases of development as required by the 1st Edition of ISO 26262. Moreover, the confirmation reviews (part of the confirmation measures) have been re-defined to provide sufficient and convincing evidence to the achievement of functional safety, an objective oriented approach compared to the prescriptive definition in the 1st Edition of ISO 26262 to meet requirements.

Safety Management for production, operation, service and decommissioning: involves defining responsibilities of persons and organizations in charge for achieving and maintaining functional safety regarding production, operation, service and decommissioning. For instance, requirements are established to appoint persons to execute processes to achieve and maintain the functional safety of the item regarding field monitoring and collection of data.

4 – HAZARD ANALYSIS AND RISK ASSESSMENT

In Part 3 of ISO 26262, potential hazards are identified following an analysis of the operational situations of the item. The item may be a vehicle, a vehicle system, or a vehicle function. The identified potential hazards are then categorized based on the following factors: severity, probability of exposure and controllability. Following the categorization results, an *Automotive Safety Integrity Level or ASIL* is determined for the potential hazard. The ASIL is also assigned to the safety goal(s) formulated to prevent or mitigate the potential hazard, in order to avoid unreasonable risk. Risk reduction (safety) requirements or safety requirements are then derived from these safety goals and inherit the corresponding ASIL. The following provides a brief overview of these activities and the reader is referred to [7] for a detailed account.

Situation analysis and hazard identification: The potential hazards are determined given the operating modes of the item in which a malfunctioning behavior may trigger them. The hazards are described and evaluated and their consequences are identified and documented.

Hazard Classification: The identified potential hazards are classified based on the estimation of severity, probability of exposure, and controllability as defined in Section 2 above. Severity or S has 4 classes ranging from S0 or no injuries to S3 or fatal injuries. Exposure or E ranges from an E0 or extremely unusual situation to E4 or a highly likely situation. Finally, controllability C ranges from C0 or simply controllable to uncontrollable or C3.

ASIL Determination: An ASIL is to be determined for each hazardous event using the parameters S, E and C as shown in Table 1 below. Four ASILs are defined, where ASIL A is the lowest safety integrity level and ASIL D the highest one. In addition to these four ASILs, the class QM (Quality Management) denotes no requirement in accordance with ISO 26262, however any other requirements such as Quality, Reliability, and Durability need to be accounted for.

Table 1: ASIL Determination (Source ISO 26262 2nd Ed. FDIS – Draft)

		C1	C2	C3
S1	E1	QM	QM	QM
	E2	QM	QM	QM
	E3	QM	QM	A
	E4	QM	A	B
S2	E1	QM	QM	QM
	E2	QM	QM	A
	E3	QM	A	B
	E4	A	B	C
S3	E1	QM	QM	A
	E2	QM	A	B
	E3	A	B	C
	E4	B	C	D

Safety goal formulation: A safety goal is to be determined for each hazardous event evaluated in the hazard analysis. Functional safety requirements needed to avoid an unreasonable risk for each potential hazard are derived from these safety goals which are not expressed in terms of technological solutions, rather in terms of functional objectives. Functional safety requirements inherit the ASIL of the safety goal from which they are derived.

The ASIL determined for the hazardous event is assigned to the corresponding safety goal. A potential hazard may have more than one safety goal, and if similar safety goals are determined, they can be combined into one safety goal that will be assigned the highest ASIL of the similar goals.

5 – PRODUCT REQUIREMENTS AT SYSTEM, HARDWARE AND SOFTWARE LEVELS

The product development at the system level starts with developing the technical safety concept. The technical safety concept specifies the technical safety requirements and their allocation to system elements (hardware and software). The technical safety concept defines the system architectural design as well. The development of the technical safety concept is then detailed at both the hardware and software levels. Once the hardware and software development is complete, all elements are integrated and tested. Finally, safety validation is completed at the vehicle level, that is evidence is provided that safety goals have been met. This is graphically represented in Figure 4 and detailed in the following.

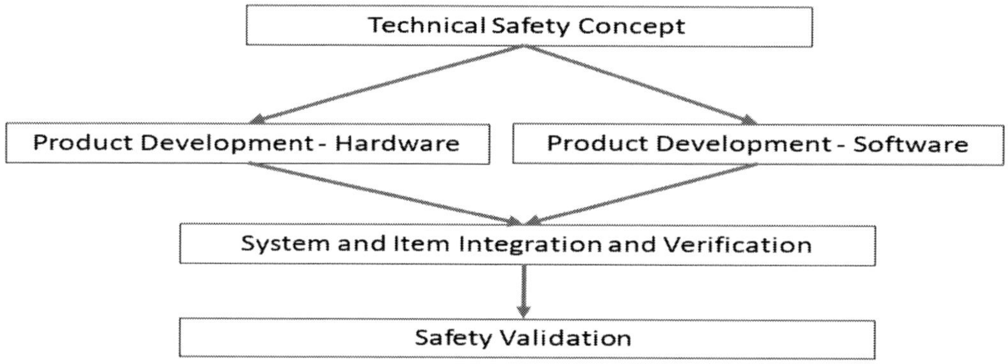

Figure 4: Product development at the system level

Technical safety concept: the technical safety concept comprises all technical safety requirements. These requirements are the technical refinement of their corresponding functional safety requirements: they specify safety mechanisms to detect faults and mitigate or control failures that may lead to the violation of these functional safety requirements and hence the safety goals. These technical safety requirements inherit the ASIL of the functional safety requirements they refine. In addition, a system architectural design that implements the technical safety requirements is defined as part of the technical safety concept and is supposed to be suitable to satisfy the safety requirements according to their respective ASIL.

In defining technical safety requirements, some of these requirements may come from a cybersecurity concept as a result of the established channels of communication between functional safety and cybersecurity discussed in the functional safety management summary above. Moreover, some technical safety requirements are derived to address safety issues during production, operation, service and decommissioning.

Product development at the hardware level: at this level a hardware implementation of the technical safety concept is specified and safety analyses are performed to identify potential faults and their effects on the violation of safety requirements. In addition, any required coordination with development at the software level is identified.

The hardware implementation of the technical safety concept involves identification of hardware requirements or in other words assignment from technical safety requirements to hardware elements given the system architectural design. The hardware design itself is supposed to be consistent with the system architectural design specification and fulfils the hardware safety requirements while protecting for safety concerns considering the performed safety analyses. The suitability of the hardware architectural design (to detect and control random hardware failures) is assessed using two metrics, single fault metric and latent fault metric. Both metrics have target values depending on the ASIL of the requirements being implemented. An alternative approach to assess the suitability of the hardware architectural design (to detect and control random hardware failures) is to evaluate the probability of safety goals violation. The latter can be completed using a global probabilistic approach or by analyzing individual cut sets. In both cases the assessment is also dependent on the ASIL of the safety goal.

Finally, once all hardware elements are integrated, a verification of the compliance of the hardware design with the hardware safety requirements (given their respective ASILs) is expected.

Product development at the software level: at this level of development software safety requirements are derived from technical safety requirements and a software architecture that satisfies all software requirements is developed. In addition, any required coordination with development at the software level is identified and/or refined.

Similar to hardware requirements, software safety requirements are derived from the technical safety concept and the system architectural design specification. These requirements inherit the ASIL of their respective technical safety requirements, in general. The software architectural design is required to be suitable to satisfy the software safety requirements with their respective ASILs and support the implementation and verification of the software being developed. The latter includes the software unit design, implementation and verification; the software integration and verification; and the testing of the resulting embedded software.

System and item integration and verification: the integration steps are defined for all levels of integration including integration of hardware and software of an element, integration of elements resulting in an item, and integration of the item with other systems at the vehicle level. Evidence that the integrated system elements fulfil their safety requirements is also provided. Finally, the proper implementation of safety mechanisms is verified.

Safety validation: this final step as part of the system product development provides evidence that the safety goals are achieved at the vehicle level and that the developed safety concepts are appropriate for the functional safety of the item. Validation of safety goals is applied to the item integrated at the vehicle level and the validation plan includes test procedures for each safety goal with a pass/fail criterion.

As discussed earlier, some technical safety requirements address safety concerns related to production, operation, service and decommissioning. The objective of these requirements is to ensure that functional safety is achieved throughout the whole lifecycle of the vehicle.

As part of planning for production, operation, service and decommissioning, it is required to develop:

- a production process for safety-related system(s) to be installed in road vehicles
- all necessary information and documentation regarding operation, maintenance and repair, and decommissioning to be used by whomever is interfacing with the safety-related system(s)

In addition to the planning, the production process needs to be analyzed to uncover any process failures and their effects on achieving functional safety and implement and verify the effectiveness of measures to mitigate or control these process failures. Related to the information and documentation for operation, maintenance and repair, and decommissioning, a field monitoring process needs to be established to address potential safety-related incidents related to the system(s) with the objective of collecting field data that can be analyzed to detect the presence of functional safety issues and initiate corrective actions for these issues.

6 – SUPPORTING PROCESSES AND SAFETY ANALYSES

Supporting processes are usually labelled as "secondary processes" that come along with the core processes and contribute indirectly in delivering a product. For functional safety, ISO 26262 identified a dozen of these processes each containing a set of consolidated common requirements. The following briefly discusses a few of those supporting processes and the reader is referred to Part 8 of ISO 26262 for a detailed discussion of all the supporting processes.

<u>Interfaces within distributed developments:</u> define the interactions and dependencies between integrators and suppliers for development activities and describe corresponding allocation responsibilities. In addition, it provides a means to evaluate the supplier's capability to develop and produce items of comparable complexity and ASIL according to ISO 26262. The Distributed Interface Agreement (DIA) includes requirements on:

- Safety managers at the integrator's and supplier's
- Joint tailoring of the safety lifecycle, with identification of activities and processes to be performed by the customer and by the supplier;
- The information required; work products to be exchanged; persons responsible
- ...

<u>Specification and management of safety requirements:</u> ensures correct specification of safety requirements with respect to attributes and characteristics and support consistent management of safety requirements throughout the safety lifecycle. These are achieved by defining requirements on the notations used for the specification of safety requirements; attributes, characteristics and properties of safety requirements; and how the safety requirements are managed.

<u>Confidence in the use of software tools:</u> provides criteria to determine the required level of confidence in a software tool and means for the qualification of that software tool. A tool confidence level (TCL) is determined based on analysis, the tool impact and the tool error detection. Given the TCL, ISO 26262 describes methods to be applied to qualify the software tool given the ASIL of the safety goal(s).

<u>Qualification of software components:</u> provides evidence for the suitability of the software components for re-use in items developed per the ISO 26262 standard. ISO 26262 requires information to treat a software component as qualified (specification of the software component,

evidence that the software component complies with its requirements and is suitable for its intended use, and evidence of an appropriate software development process) and prescribes requirements on the verification of the qualification of the software component.

Evaluation of hardware elements: ensures that the element functional behavior is adequate to meet its allocated safety requirement(s). This type of evaluation is used for COTS parts not developed per ISO 26262 or considered safety-related once integrated into an item. In addition, it can be used as an alternative means of compliance with the product development requirements at the hardware level. Different classes are considered depending on the difficulty of the verification of the safety-related functionality and the role of the hardware element within the safety concept. The evaluation is carried through either testing, testing and analysis, or testing, analysis and argumentation.

Part 9 of ISO 26262 provides an overview of some types of safety analyses. The following briefly describes an ISO 26262 specific method for decomposing requirements.

Requirements decomposition with respect to ASIL tailoring: shortly known as ASIL Decomposition, is a method to decompose safety requirements into redundant safety requirements (not necessarily identical) to allow ASIL tailoring at the next level of detail. The redundant requirements are allocated to sufficiently independent design elements. It is worth noting here that even though the development of the design elements to which the redundant requirements are allocated is performed at the decomposed ASIL level, the evaluation of the hardware metrics and the safety goal violations targets due to random hardware failures remains unchanged by ASIL decomposition. Table 2 below provides the rules for ASIL decomposition. These rules can be applied iteratively as long as traceability is maintained.

Table 2: ASIL Decomposition rules

ASIL A	ASIL B	ASIL C	ASIL D
ASIL A(A) + QM(A)	ASIL B(B)+ QM(B)	ASIL C(C)+ QM(C)	ASIL D(D)+ QM(D)
	ASIL A(B)+ ASIL A(B)	ASIL B(C)+ ASIL A(C)	ASIL C(D)+ ASIL A(D)
			ASIL B(D)+ ASIL B(D)

7 – MOTORCYCLES

Part 12 is a new addition to ISO 26262 2nd Edition to give an overview of the adaptation of the standard to motorcycles that were out of scope in the 1st Edition. All requirements of Parts 2 through 9 in ISO 26262 apply to motorcycles, however some tailoring is required. Therefore, requirements in Part 12 supersede the corresponding requirements in all other parts.

The major adaptation of requirements in the case of motorcycles applies to the development of the hazard analysis and risk assessment and the determination of the S, E, and C parameters. A motorcycle specific hazard analysis is performed and accounts for

- The dynamic behavior of motorcycles which differs greatly from other vehicles
- Motorcycle rider dependence to achieve controllability
- Motorcycle specific operational situations and hazard identification

As part of the hazard analysis and risk assessment, a Motorcycle Safety Integrity Level (MSIL) is determined for each hazard from the combination of a motorcycle specific S, E and C of the hazardous event. The MSIL is later mapped to the ASIL as depicted in below and safety goals are assigned to the mapped ASIL and from there onwards confirmation reviews, vehicle integration and testing, and safety validation are performed given the ASIL.

8 – TRUCKS, BUSES, TRAILERS, AND SEMI-TRAILERS

Truck, Buses, Trailers and Semi-trailers (T&B for short) have been added to the scope of the standard in its 2nd Edition version. Similar to motorcycles, requirements of Parts 2 through 9 apply to T&B and any specific modification or new requirements for T&B are listed within the parts of the standard wherever they apply. Additional requirements are listed under:

- Functional safety management – supporting processes
- Hazard analysis and risk assessment
- System level validation environment
- Production, operation, service and decommissioning

Table 3: MSIL to ASIL mapping

MSIL	ASIL
QM	QM
A	QM
B	A
C	B
D	C

Before discussing T&B specific requirements, it is worth noting here that in the context of T&B a body builder is an organization that adds its own equipment to a base vehicle such as a machine, body, or cargo carrier. Consequently, the body builder becomes the integrator in the case of a T&B while the role of the original equipment manufacturer of the base vehicle is relegated to that of a supplier.

As part of the functional safety management in the case of T&B, a tailoring of safety activities is required when a:

- T&B related application that is out of Scope of ISO 26262 is being interfaced with a base vehicle that has been developed in accordance with ISO 26262, or a
- T&B related system not developed according to ISO 26262 is to satisfy the required

level of functional safety needed for the integration into an item developed in accordance with ISO 26262.

In these specific situations, some manufacturer-supplier or DIA requirements do not apply.

Interfacing an application that is out of scope of ISO 26262: an application out of scope of ISO 26262 is supposed not to violate the safety goals of the base vehicle that has been developed in accordance with ISO 26262. In that specific situation, It is required that the integrator is made aware of the modified systems and the permitted safety limits / requirements of the modifications by the manufacturer/supplier. The manufacturer/supplier is in fact responsible to communicate safety measures required to be applied by the integrator so that functional safety is maintained.

Integration of safety-related systems not developed according to ISO 26262: a development not according to ISO 26262 satisfies the required level of functional safety needed to be integrated into an item developed according to ISO 26262. In that specific situation, the integrator is required to define the criteria to argue that the safety-related system that has been developed to another safety standard meets the required level of functional safety. Consequently, the integrator and the supplier are required to agree on the relevant set of measures to verify that the criteria are met.

Hazard analysis and risk assessment: in the context of T&B, variances of T&B vehicle operation are defined as the use of a T&B vehicle with different dynamic characteristics influenced by cargo or towing during the service life of the vehicle. As a consequence, while performing the hazard analysis and risk assessment, the following variances are to be considered:

- type of base vehicle;
- the T&B vehicle configuration; and
- the T&B vehicle operation.

This will impact the operational situations, hazardous events and the S, E, and C classification.

System level validation environment: since the safety goals are validated for the item in a representative context at the vehicle level, then different base vehicle types in the case of T&B could be the subject of a safety validation.

Operation, service and decommissioning: the operation, service and decommissioning of the item is required to be conducted and documented in accordance with the service plan, instructions for service, and instructions for decommissioning. Such a requirement is important for T&B since elements of T&B can be remanufactured and corresponding plans and instructions can be modified. Therefore, it is required that all the right plans and instructions are maintained and documented.

9 – GUIDANCE ON SEMICONDUCTOR DEVELOPMENT

With the introduction of the 1st Edition of ISO 26262, semiconductor manufacturers were not well versed in the area of automotive functional safety. That resulted in some confusion in early application of the standard to semiconductor components. A project was launched within the working group developing ISO 26262 to assess and understand the impact of applying the standard to semiconductors. Two publicly available specifications were developed to address these issues [8,9] and these became the origins of Part 11 in ISO 26262 2nd Edition.

Part 11 of ISO 26262 2nd Edition is an informative part and a necessary extension of the 1st Edition of ISO 26262 to provide guidelines for semiconductors used in automotive application. It provides guidelines on semiconductor components and semiconductor technologies. A semiconductor component can be developed as:

- part of the item – in that case the safety analysis performed per the product development at the hardware level applies, or
- as a Safety Element out of Context (SEooC) – in that case the development is assumed to meet a given ASIL independent of an item and its safety goals and is based on assumptions to be verified at integration. If these assumptions are indeed verified then the SEooC can be integrated into an item without further safety analyses.

10 – SUMMARY

ISO 26262 in its second edition is expected to be released later this year. In this report, we summarized the content of the standard including its scope of applicability, definitions, and requirements per its core and supporting processes as well as some guidelines provided for semiconductor development. While presenting the summary, a few major modifications and additions were discussed. This summary is intended to be informative and is not intended to be a substitute to read the standard in order to apply it.

REFERENCES

1. C. A. Ericson II, Hazard Analysis Techniques for System Safety, John Wiley & Sons, New Jersey, 2005.

2. N.G. Leveson, Safeware: System Safety and Computers, Addison Wesley, 2001.

3. N.J. Bahr, System Safety Engineering and Risk Assessment: A Practical Approach, Taylor and Francis, 1997.

4. ISO 26262 1st Ed., TC 22/SC3/WG16, Road Vehicles – Functional Safety Parts 1-9", Nov 2011.

5. IEC 61508, Functional Safety of Electrical/Electronic/Programmable Electronic Safety Related Systems Parts 1-7, International Electrotechnical Commission, Switzerland, 1998.

6. ISO/FDIS 26262 2nd Ed., TC 22/SC32/WG08, Road Vehicles – Functional Safety Parts 1-12", Mar 2018.

7. R. Debouk and J. Joyce, ISO 26262 Hazard and Risk Assessment Methodology, Proceedings of the 28th International System Safety Conference, August 2010.

8. ISO/PAS 19451-1: Application of ISO 26262:2011-2012 to semiconductors — Part 1: Application of concepts, 2016

9. ISO/PAS 19451-2: Application of ISO 26262:2011-2012 to semiconductors — Part 2: Application of hardware qualification, 2016

Challenges and Benefits of Implementing Hazard Traceability in an Application Lifecycle Management (ALM) Tool

CHIANG Hai Hwee; ST Electronics (Info-Software Systems) Pte Ltd; Singapore

MOK Boon Eang; ST Electronics (Info-Software Systems) Pte Ltd; Singapore

NG Suk Yen; ST Electronics (Info-Software Systems) Pte Ltd; Singapore

Keywords: Requirements Management, Safety Analyses, Requirements Traceability, Hazard Traceability, Tool

Abstract

Traceability of identified hazards to system requirements, design, interfaces and data is required by various system safety engineering standards and certifications such as MIL-STD-882E and RTCA DO-178C. To achieve the traceability requirement, provision for a tracing system is necessary. The tracing system can be a simple spreadsheet or a complicated automatic tracing tool. In this paper, we describe our organization's common practice of performing requirements traceability and hazard traceability using two different tracing systems – by adopting an application lifecycle management (ALM) tool as a *de facto* for requirements traceability; and maintaining hazard traceability within hazard records in a textual document coupled with a hazard traceability matrix in a spreadsheet. We present the motivation and efforts to integrate hazard traceability in the ALM tool by leveraging on its existing requirements management features. In particular, we share the challenges of developing and deploying the hazard traceability feature, with an evaluation of its use after the implementation.

Main Body

Introduction

In the various system safety engineering standards and certifications, traceability of identified hazards to system requirements, design, interfaces and data is essential. For example, in the process tasks of system/subsystem/system-of-systems (SoS) hazard analysis, the Military Standard MIL-STD-882E requires that design requirements to preclude hazards are flowed down from top-level specifications to detailed design specifications and test procedures, and that identified SoS hazards are traceable to architecture locations, interfaces and data (US Department of Defense, 2012). RTCA DO-178C, the standard for airborne systems, specifies that trace data should be provided for the bi-directional associations between lifecycle data items contents (such as system requirements, high-level requirements, low-level requirements and test cases) (RTCA, 2011). The Joint Software Systems Safety Engineering Handbook (JSSSEH), which consolidates the best practices for Software System Safety, sums up the software safety requirements traceability as a flow-down from hazards to Software Requirements Specifications (SRS), and from SRS to design, code and test (Joint Software Systems Safety Engineering Workgroup, 2010).

To achieve the traceability requirement, provision for a tracing system is necessary. A tracing system enables the bi-directional traceability of a requirement from its first level inception to its implementation in a product and the documentation associated with the product. It can be a simple spreadsheet, textual document or a complicated automatic tracing tool (National Aeronautics and Space Administration, 2004).

Through the governance of safety-significant projects within our organization, we observed the common practice of project teams adopting an application lifecycle management (ALM) tool to trace safety requirements through design, test and acceptance; and using a different tracing means such as textual documents to trace safety requirements to its source (that is, hazards and hazard causes). This practice separates traceability into two main paths: (1) the tracing between safety requirements and hazards (to which, for the purpose of discussion in this paper, we will refer as "hazard traceability"); and (2) the flow down of safety requirements to design, implementation, and test (for which we use the term "requirements traceability").

To understand the reason for such division, we looked into the requirements traceability and hazard traceability in the software development and safety lifecycle processes.

Traceability Requirements in the Lifecycle Processes

requirements traceability. Requirements traceability is fundamental to good requirements management in software development. The Capability Maturity Model Integration (CMMI), one of the leading process models for software development, includes requirements traceability as one of the specific practices in its requirements management process area (CMMI Product Team, 2010). Besides being "an established tenet in the software engineering community", requirements traceability is also "essential for assuring that software is safe for use" (Mäder, Jones, Zhang, & Cleland-Huang, 2013).

In order to define requirements traceability in the general software development, we adopt the V-model as a reference process model for the different phases of the development lifecycle. The V-model offers a framework that shows "a transition of requirements down the left-hand side of the V, and `a testing relationship going across the V" (Ratcliffe, 2011). It is thus apt to adapt this framework to define the trace path of artefacts at each phase of the Software Development Lifecycle (SDLC), as shown in Figure 1. For the purpose of illustration, the model is simplified with the solid lines showing the requirements traceability of a typical software development project. It may be extended to include hardware development. For example, we can establish traceability of each requirement from customer requirements to system requirements, flowing down to high-level design, low-level requirements and design, and to source code, and vice versa; and between the respective test descriptions and the elements on the left-side of the V-model. The dashed lines are alternative trace links which specific projects may include. The strategy and the granularity of the trace is dependent on the degree of conformance required of the project.

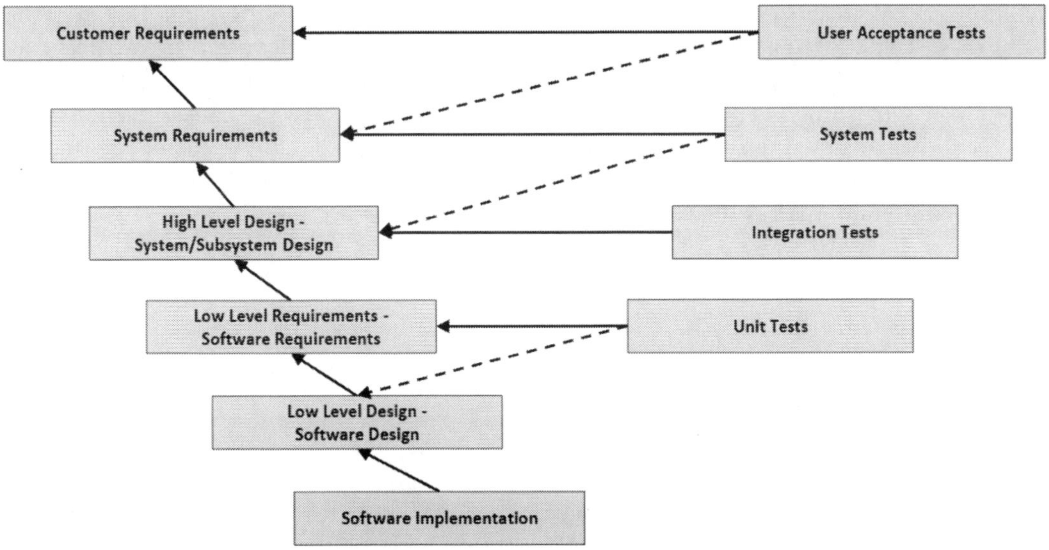

Figure 1 — Adapted SDLC V-Model for Requirements Traceability

In the domain of system safety engineering, requirements traceability is extended to involve "identifying safety-critical requirments/functions and then tracing them through design, test, acceptance, changes and upgrades, and through retirement" (National Aeronautics and Space Administration, 2004). In the context of system development, safety-critical requirements, also known as safety requirements, are requirements identified from safety analyses to mitigate or resolve any hazards. Hence, safety requirements are part of the requirements in the generic SDLC V-model. In our organization's practice, requirements designated as safety requirements are each tagged with a "safety-significant" attribute and are, otherwise, managed no differently from other requirements. On this ground of commonality, our project teams familiar with the tracing system for requirements traceability in non-safety-significant projects employ the same system for safety-significant projects.

PTC Integrity, a product which provides a set of application lifecycle management capabilities, is commonly adopted by our project teams. Many other ALM tools such as Rational DOORS are offered by vendors. The ALM tool provides a full suite of features built for requirements management in the system development lifecycle. Artefacts, such as system requirements specifications, software requirements specifications and design specifications, can be easily entered or imported as itemized requirements into the tool using its built-in templates. The benefits of using an ALM tool to perform requirements traceability are evident from the discussions in various papers, for example, in the "Strategic Traceability for Safety-Critical Projects" article written by Patrick Mäder and his co-authors (Mäder, Jones, Zhang, & Cleland-Huang, 2013); and the "Requirements Traceability and the Effect on the System Development Lifecyle (SDLC)" paper by Glenn A. Stout (Stout, 2001).

hazard traceability. While it is crucial to maintain traceability between software safety requirements, design requirements, and the actual implementation, hazard traceability is of equal importance (Caffery, et al., 2012). Hazard traceability concerns the traceability between hazards, hazard causes and safety requirements. Safety requirements are derived from the safety analyses, including the Preliminary Hazard Analyses (PHA) and System/Subsystem Hazard Analyses (SSHA). The safety requirements either mitigate hazards where software is a potential cause, or enable software to be used as a hazard control (National Aeronautics and Space Administration, 2004). Software safety is particularly concerned with the software causal factors linked to individual hazards and ensuring that the mitigation of each causal factor is traced from requirements to design, code, and test (Joint Software Systems Safety Engineering Workgroup, 2010). Figure 2 summarises the trace path required of the hazard traceability.

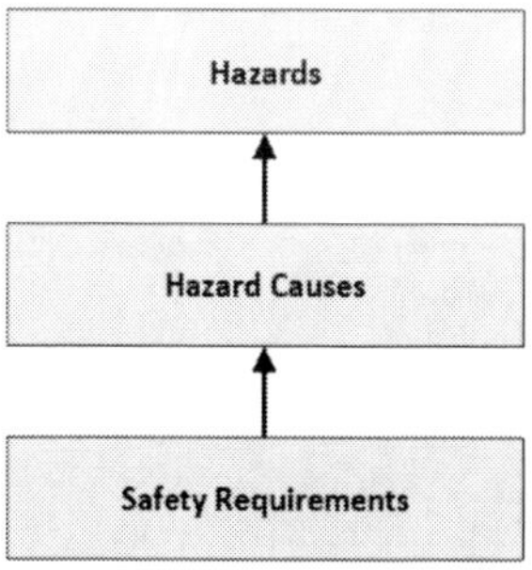

Figure 2 — Trace Path of Hazard Traceability

In conjuction with the safety analyses, residual safety risks must be communicated in detail to stakeholders. This can be in the form of hazard records documented in the hazard database record (Joint Software Systems Safety Engineering Workgroup, 2010). An example of the information to be documented in a hazard record is shown in Figure 3, which is adapted and modified from the JSSSEH. Information related to the identified hazards are derived progressively through the stages of the safety analyses. For example, the hazard description, causes and safety requirements are identified during PHA and hazard control design requirements are defined during SSHA.

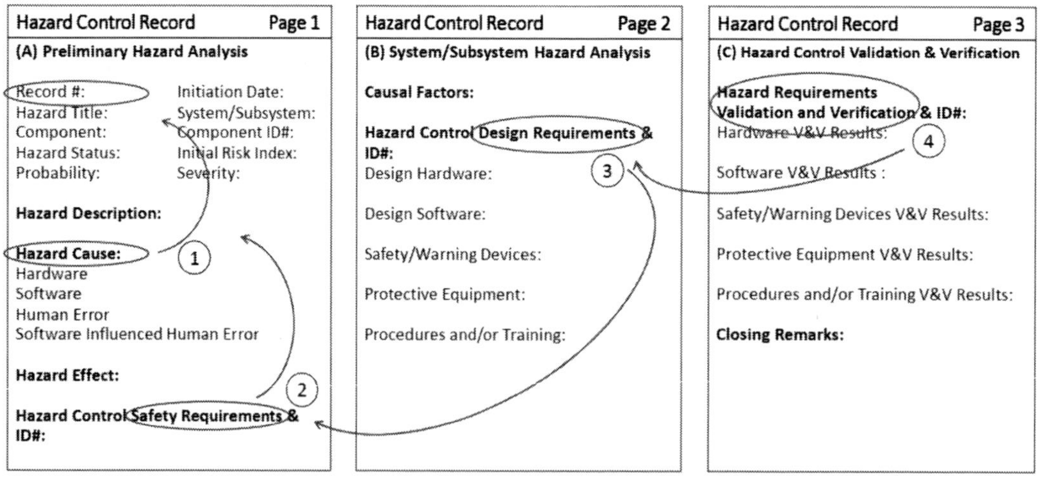

Figure 3 — Example of Hazard Record Document

In our organization, project teams record each hazard record in a textual document and refer to the record as Hazard Control Record (HCR). As depicted by the enclosing numbers in Figure 3, the

HCR provides a means to record and trace causal factors to individual hazards ①, and to ensure that mitigation of each causal factor is traced from requirements ② to design ③ and test ④. Multiple HCRs are consolidated in a spreadsheet to produce a Safety Requirements Traceability Matrix, a compilation of respective trace references from hazard record ID, to requirements, design, code and test (Figure 4), and often a contractual deliverable for safety-significant projects.

Safety Requirements Traceability Matrix

Item #	Hazard Record #	Customer Requirement ID#	System / Software Requirement ID#	Design Requirement ID#	Code Component	Test References	User Manual References
1	H001	Cont #35	SRS #42	SDD #55	\GT\App\Estn\ CheckExpiry	Unit Test #20 System Test #2	n/a
2	H001	Cont #35	SRS #43	SDD #56	\GT\App\Estn\ CheckDate	Unit Test #23 System Test #2	n/a
3	H003	Cont #42	SRS #50	SDD #58	n/a	n/a	User Material Paragraph 3.1
...	...	...	...	...	...	...	...

Figure 4 — Example of Safety Requirements Traceability Matrix

Subsequently, safety and design requirements arising from the safety analyses are either added to or updated in the overall system, software and design requirements. This ensures that safety requirements are incorporated, implemented and traced in the overall system in concern. That, in turn, creates the bridge between requirements traceability and hazard traceability.

Motivation for an Integrated Tracing System

integrating hazard traceability in the v-model. At this juncture, we present a modified V-model in Figure 5 to demonstrate the integration between requirements traceability and hazard traceability. The safety requirements in the hazard branch are traced to the low level requirements of the overall system requirements, as represented by the solid line. This establishes the trace from safety requirements to design, code and test inherent in the existing V-model. As with the other dashed lines in the V-model, the dashed line between system requirements and safety requirements is an alternative trace link that specific projects may include. The modified V-model serves to communicate the otherwise loosely defined integration of traceability between the safety lifecycle and the overall development lifecycle processes.

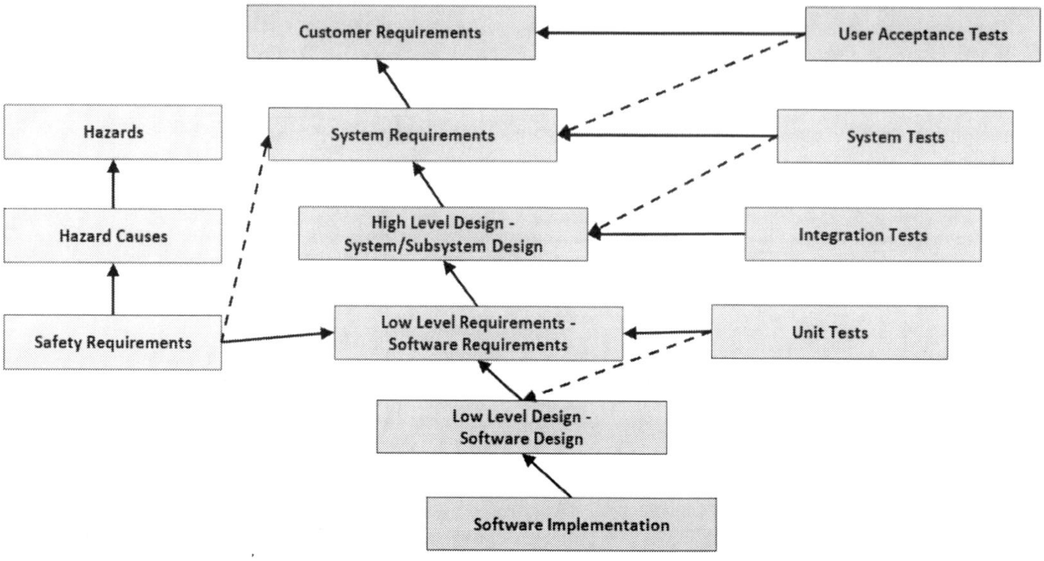

Figure 5 — Modified V-Model with Integration of Hazard Traceability

motivation for an integrated approach. While our project teams use the ALM tool to achieve requirements traceability compliance, they perform hazard traceability separately, usually as a "by-product" of keeping record of hazard-related information. The latter is attributed to the role and evidences required of safety engineers in the safety lifecycle. In most instances, safety engineers will perform the hazard analysis process in conjunction with the software development, software test, and Independent Verification and Validation (IV&V) team(s) (US Department of Defense, 2012). At each stage of the hazard analysis process, the safety engineers are responsible for maintaining evidence (in the HCR, for our case) that hazards, causes and mitigations have been identified, implemented, and verified. Very often, unlike the artefacts involved in requirements traceability, the hazard-related information and required evidences are not easily captured by the plain vanilla ALM tool without much customization.

Despite that, it is possible to trace safety requirements to their associated hazards and hazard causes, and between safety requirements, design, code and test using different tracing systems. This task is often tedious and prone to inconsistencies and errors. Within the requirements traceability, although requirements designated as safety requirements are tagged as "safety-significant", there is the lack of a mechanism to ensure that all safety requirements identified from the hazard analyses are added to, and eventually, tagged and traced in the overall requirements. Conversely, it is labourious to track requirements marked as safety-significant to their respective hazards and hazard causes kept in a separate system. Yet, this tracking is necessary to understand the impact on the system of changing requirements or software elements.

The flaws that entail the fragmented tracing approach can be overcome by leveraging on the features of the ALM tool, which "provides features for establishing, maintaining, and navigating trace links and has the ability to display trace information in formats such as matrices or trace slices" (Mäder, Jones, Zhang, & Cleland-Huang, 2013). We thus embarked on a project to integrate hazard traceability in the tool.

team composition. A working team comprising three safety practitioners from the organization's system/software safety office and one administrator for the ALM tool was formed to work on the project on a part-time basis. The safety practitioners have been involved in governing and providing consultancy, in the aspects of safety processes, to project teams developing safety-significant systems. The administrator of the ALM tool supports the organization's projects in the set-up of the tool environment. The role of the safety practitioners in the working team included specification of the requirements and design, testing, and coordinating with development project teams for pilot runs. The administrator of the ALM tool played the key role of implementing the design in the tool.

requirements and design. The modified V-model with integration of hazard traceability and the HCR textual document were used to facilitate communication of requirements within the working team. The information on the HCR was re-organized into logical segments of hazard, hazard causes and safety requirements. A data dictionary was created for each of the logical segments, snapshots of which are shown in Figure 6. Most fields in the data dictionary were transferred from the HCR template. Various definitions were specified for the fields, including the field types (such as date or short text), allowable list of values (such as I to IV for the initial severity field), and derived values (such as the mishap risk index field which is derived from mishap severity and probability), et al. During the design phase, prototypes of screens were created for the working team to visualize the data entry and the flow between screens.

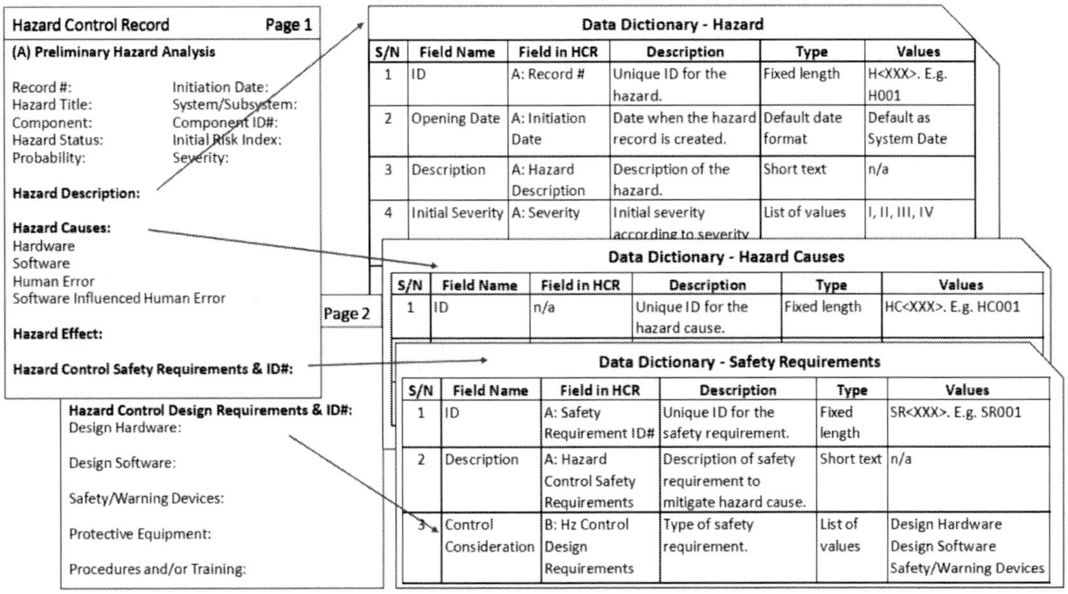

Data Dictionary - Hazard

S/N	Field Name	Field in HCR	Description	Type	Values
1	ID	A: Record #	Unique ID for the hazard.	Fixed length	H<XXX>. E.g. H001
2	Opening Date	A: Initiation Date	Date when the hazard record is created.	Default date format	Default as System Date
3	Description	A: Hazard Description	Description of the hazard.	Short text	n/a
4	Initial Severity	A: Severity	Initial severity according to severity	List of values	I, II, III, IV

Data Dictionary - Hazard Causes

S/N	Field Name	Field in HCR	Description	Type	Values
1	ID	n/a	Unique ID for the hazard cause.	Fixed length	HC<XXX>. E.g. HC001

Data Dictionary - Safety Requirements

S/N	Field Name	Field in HCR	Description	Type	Values
1	ID	A: Safety Requirement ID#	Unique ID for the safety requirement.	Fixed length	SR<XXX>. E.g. SR001
2	Description	A: Hazard Control Safety Requirements	Description of safety requirement to mitigate hazard cause.	Short text	n/a
3	Control Consideration	B: Hz Control Design Requirements	Type of safety requirement.	List of values	Design Hardware Design Software Safety/Warning Devices

Figure 6 — Snapshots of Data Dictionaries Created from HCR

development and implementation. Following the design phase, the prototyped screens were further developed and report templates created. Customized requirement types and trace relationships for hazards, hazard causes and safety requirements were defined. A trace relationship was also configured between safety requirements in the hazard branch and the requirements in the existing model of the overall system, thus completing the integration of hazard traceability in the tool.

An important consideration for the design, and hence implementation, was to simplify the steps for the end user. One such example is the automatic creation of traced links between hazard causes and the associated safety requirements. Figure 7 shows the data-entry screen of a hazard cause. The tool is programmed to construct trace links automatically as safety requirements are added for the hazard cause. At the same time, it allows the end user to establish traceability between the safey requirements and associated requirements in the overall system.

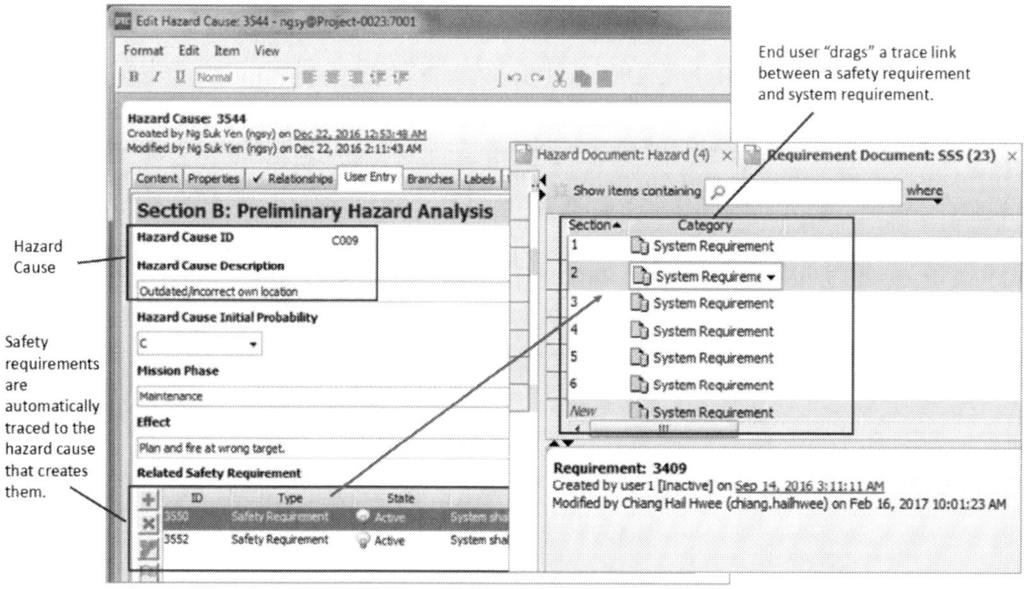

Figure 7 — Establishing Trace Links between Hazard Cause, Safety and System Requirements

pilot and parallel runs. One project was selected for the pilot run and another for the parallel run. The first project was in the testing phase and had a different tracing system from the ALM tool. The second project was in the development phase with an existing database of requirements and traceabilities created in the ALM tool. Hence, separate deployments of the new features were performed for: (1) a fresh set-up of the tool with no previous data in the tool's database, and (2) the tool that was "in-use" with records in the database. Both the pilot and parallel runs provided a platform for the administrator of the ALM tool to perform deployment for each database scenario and a feedback loop to improve the implementation.

Evaluation of the Implementation

benefits. Integrating hazard traceability in the ALM tool enables hazards to be managed centrally with the overall system requirements repository where every member who has access to the repository is able to search, in a consistent manner as other requirements, and see the on-going safety analyses that he/she may be concerned with.

The benefits inherent in the requirements traceability feature of the tool apply to hazard traceability as well. For example, built-in tracing in the tool provides a mechanism to assign a unique identity to each hazard traceability item like the rest of the requirements traceability items. New traceability items can be added, or existing items deleted, without affecting the unique identity of other items. There is also the built-in capability of trace queries for completeness checks, such as flagging hazards without mitigating requirements, or safety requirements not traced to any requirement specifications. Conversely, when the end user establishes a trace link between a safety requirement and software requirement that has been traced to design, code and test, the hierarchy of the full traced path can be retrieved.

As a result, efficiency is improved in the management of hazards and their traceability, through a seamless flow between data entry screens and trace creation for hazards, hazard causes and safety requirements; and in the generation of queries and reports in various formats and dimensions.

challenges. During the implementation, we were met with two main challenges. One emerged from the working team's limited technical knowledge of the tool, the second being the deployment to a project using a different tool version from the standard baselined version.

Firstly, the working team aimed to deliver the hazard traceability with minimal "tweaking" of the ALM tool's built-in features so that projects benefit from the suite of supporting features, such as navigating the trace links and generating queries, with little technical and maintenance support. The working team, however, did not have a good knowledge of the internal workings and technicalities of the tool. This resulted in substantial "trials and errors" and re-work, and in some cases, foregoing of some requirements and design. One such occasion was the desire to reproduce the exact layout of the manual textual HCR with its traceability references using the tool's integrated MS Word document templates, only for the working team to discover later in the development process that much workaround and scripting had to be done. It was after seeking consultation with the tool's manufacturer's support team that the working team replaced the use of the MS Word document templates with the built-in report generator in HTML format, which was less ideal in its presentation but required little scripting effort.

Secondly, the project chosen for the parallel run had its database established with requirements and traceability data, and had used a different tool version from the standard baselined version. As a result, the configuration scripts were tailored specifically for the version that the project used. To avoid the unforeseen effects of running the scripts directly on the project's production server, the working team made an exact duplicate of the original server on a spare server of similar capacity. The production server was then frozen from further updates until the configured environment on the spare server was verified correct and copied back to the live server. Much effort was expended to test that specific version of configuration, under the limited timeframe for the live project to delay updates on its server.

recommendations. From this deployment experience, we recommend the integration of hazard traceability to projects at the stage in which a fresh database can be set up on the standard baselined version of the ALM tool. The configuration scripts, once completed and tested, are standard for projects of similar nature.

For on-going projects in which databases have been loaded with existing data, and particularly, which use a different version of a tool from the standard baselined version, careful planning for deployment is necessary. The extensive deployment effort calls for consideration to integrate hazard traceabilty for such projects. Factors to consider include the current phase of the project and the number of hazards and safety requirements involved. If the project is in its later phases of activity, or the number of hazards and safety requirements involved is small, the value gained from the integration may not be significant.

As for projects that are required, possibility by contract, to use a different ALM tool such as Rational DOORS, the implementation team is able to save the effort of specifying requirements and design, and commence from the prototyping of screens to final deployment. The decision to implement hazard traceability on a different tool very much depends on the implementation team's technical and functional knowledge of the tool, and the subsequent number of projects expected to adopt the tool.

Conclusions

Integrating hazard traceability in the same ALM tool as requirements traceability enables hazards and their traceability to be managed centrally and more efficiently in the overall requirements repository. Various factors contribute to the successful implementation of the integrated traceability, including the working team's technical knowledge of the tool and the allocation of projects' resources for a collaborative deployment exercise.

The working team recognizes that there are areas with potential for improvement. One such area is to extend the hazard traceability branch to include procedures and training adopted as mitigation measures but which do not fit in the current V-model of traceable artefacts. Further research of the tool's capability is also essential to enhance the solution, such as to produce more professional-looking reports without much programming tweaks. Given more time and research, deployment effort should be reduced to encourage more projects to adopt the integrated features.

Despite having all these in place, tracing hazards and requirements in an integrated tracing system can only prove effective if all project members exercise due diligence in keeping the repository of requirements and traceability data up-to-date.

References

Caffery, M. F., Casey, V., Sivakumar, M. S., Coleman, G., Donnelly, P., & Burton, J. (2012). Medical Device Software Traceability. In *Software and Systems Traceability* (pp. 321-339). Springer-Verlag London Limited. Retrieved Mar 16, 2018, from https://ulir.ul.ie/bitstream/handle/10344/2083/2012_MCCAFFERY%2cFV.pdf?sequence=2

CMMI Product Team. (2010, November). CMMI-DEV, V1.3. *CMMI® for Development, Version 1.3.* Software Engineering Institute. Retrieved Mar 16, 2018, from https://resources.sei.cmu.edu/asset_files/TechnicalReport/2010_005_001_15287.pdf

Joint Software Systems Safety Engineering Workgroup. (2010, August 27). Joint Software Systems Safety Engineering Handbook, Version 1.0. US Department of Defense. Retrieved Mar 16, 2018, from http://www.system-safety.org/Documents/SOFTWARE_SYSTEM_SAFETY_HDBK_2010.pdf

Mäder, P., Jones, P. L., Zhang, Y., & Cleland-Huang, J. (2013, May/June). Strategic Traceability for Safety-Critical Projects. IEEE Computer Society. Retrieved Mar 16, 2018, from https://www.computer.org/csdl/mags/so/2013/03/mso2013030058.pdf

National Aeronautics and Space Administration. (2004, July 8). NASA-STD-8719.13B w/Change 1. *Software Safety Standard, NASA Technical Standard.*

Ratcliffe, A. (2011). SAS Software Development with the V-Model. U.K. Retrieved Mar 16, 2018, from http://support.sas.com/resources/papers/proceedings11/124-2011.pdf

RTCA. (2011). RTCA DO-178C. *Software Considerations in Airborne Systems and Equipment Certification.*

Stout, G. A. (2001). Requirements Traceability and the Effect on the System Development Lifecycle (SDLC). Retrieved Mar 16, 2018, from http://cm.techwell.com/sites/default/files/articles/XDD3051filelistfilename1_0.pdf

US Department of Defense. (2012, May 11). MIL-STD-882E. *Department of Defense Standard Practice, System Safety.*

Biography

CHIANG Hai Hwee, Senior System Specialist, 3 Ang Mo Kio Electronics Park Road, #06-01, Singapore 567714, telephone – +65 6679-8959, email – chiang.haihwee@stengg.com.

Hai Hwee obtained her B.Sc (Computer and Information Systems) from the National University of Singapore. She has over 25 years of IT experience as a system analyst and software developer. She joined the System Safety Office of ST Electronics (Info-Software Systems) in May 2015. Prior to this, she has implemented large-scale systems in the defense and enterprise solutions industry. She is currently working on projects in the defense domain as a safety manager and software safety engineer.

MOK Boon Eang, Senior Manager, 3 Ang Mo Kio Electronics Park Road, #06-01, Singapore 567714, telephone – +65 6679-8957, email – mokbe@stengg.com.

Boon Eang received her B.Sc and M.Sc (Management of Technology) from the National University of Singapore. She has more than 30 years of experience in software engineering and management in many large scale systems such as Air Command and Control Systems, Air Traffic Control System, Port Automated Guided Vehicle Pilot System, and Fire Services Location and Management of Emergency System. She started practicing system software safety since 2004 and has pioneered the establishment of the System Safety Management framework and processes for her company. She leads the System Software Safety governance and process improvements in her company. In addition, she drives the system software safety capability buildup for her company through various projects' involvement, training programs, sharing sessions and the Singapore Chapter's activities.

Boon Eang also helps promote system safety through supporting as the System Safety Lead for ST Engineering Electronics group of companies, supporting as an executive committee member of the International System Safety Society Singapore Chapter, supporting as an organizing committee member for the 2008 International System Safety Regional Conference, contributing software safety materials for the Institution of Engineers Singapore (IES) SE manual, training and certification in 2009, and co-authoring a paper and presented it at the 29th International System Safety Conference in 2011.

NG Suk Yen, System Consultant, 3 Ang Mo Kio Electronics Park Road, #06-01, Singapore 567714, telephone – +65 6679-8958, email – ngsy@stengg.com.

Suk Yen obtained her B.Eng (Mech Engineering) from the National University of Singapore and M.Technology (Knowledge Engineering) from the Institute of System Science in Singapore. She has started as Operations Research Officer before transferring to the IT Division during the Y2K downsizing exercise. Since then she has accumulated more than 10 years of software engineering experience, which ranged from supporting 24X7 operational systems, to delivering customized solutions for overseas customers and to managing an independent test team for a large-scale mainframe migration project. At ST

Electronics (Info-Software Systems) Pte. Ltd., she implemented the software safety processes and strives to promote the safety culture by organizing and conducting regular safety training programs.

AUTHOR INDEX